DESTINATION ITALY

No less an observer of life than Goethe once exhaled into the now-famous diaries he kept of his 18th-century journey through Italy, "I can honestly say I've never been as happy in my life as now." The great German poet was neither the first nor the last visitor to fall blissfully under the spell of this justifiably fabled land, with its stunning landscapes, stupendous contributions to Western civilization, and unabashed enthusiasm for life's pleasures. Be prepared to be swept away. It may be while witnessing the conspiracy of dreamlike light and seductive sea from the Belvedere of Infinity at the Villa Cimbrone in Ravello or, for that matter, while encountering any of the many other uniquely Italian scenes—but sooner or later on your own Italian journey, you're bound to succumb to Italy's charms.

Rome—antique, Renaissance, Baroque, always papal—is a veritable Grand Canyon of culture, built of stratified layers of ancient, medieval, and modern. It's the mixture of old and new that gives Rome its vibrancy, with Vespas and compact cars buzzing past

ROME

Ⓐ 47

the famous sights and subtle details that tell the stories of the city. Walk through Old Rome, taking in the Baroque splendor. Continue along the Via Portico d'Ottavia of the Jewish Ghetto, past the Ⓑ**Bocca della Verità,** set into the vestibule of a 12th-century church, and cross the Tiber River to the cobblestone alleys of Trastevere. Stop for a Campari break at a café in the timeless 17th-century Piazza Navona, take pleasure in an hour stolen alongside Bernini's splashing Ⓓ**Fontana dei Quattro Fiumi,** or wander through the colorful Ⓔ**Campo dei Fiori market** to savor the aromas of fresh produce blessed by the

Ⓑ 66

Ⓒ 46

D 55

balm of the Roman sun. Few places are as visited as the Vatican and its collection of buildings—an estimated 14,000 rooms, chapels, and galleries. Decorated in uniforms designed by Michelangelo using the colors of the Medici popes, the Ⓐ**Swiss Guards,** entrusted with protecting the pope, stand guard as you make your way to the impressive Piazza San Pietro. Enter Ⓒ**St. Peter's Basilica** and let the sheer size of the world's most famous Catholic church engulf you. Climb the narrow, winding staircase to the top of the dome for a view of the terra-cotta hues of the city below—a glorious reward.

E 51

Ⓐ 124

FLORENCE

Ⓑ 135

Florence, the "Athens of Italy" and the key to the Renaissance, hugs the banks of the Arno River. Folded among the emerald cypress-studded hills of north-central Tuscany, the city is anchored by the Ⓓ**Duomo,** with its Brunelleschi dome, an engineering tour de force. Elegant and somewhat aloof, as if set apart by its past greatness, Florence shares with Rome the honor of first place among Italian cities for the magnitude of its artistic works. Among them is the Renaissance masterpiece started by Masaccio and Masolino and finished by Lippi, the Ⓑ**Santa Maria del Carmine fresco cycle** in the Cappella Brancacci. Through its innovative style, their creation changed the course of art forever. In the Galleria dell'Accademia, you will find one of the most-visited and powerful works of art in the world, Michelangelo's *David.* You can wander among the great works here or visit the reproduction in the Ⓒ**Piazzale Michelangelo** and enjoy it among the throngs of Florentines sipping aperitifs at one of the outdoor

Ⓒ 137

Ⓓ 120

cafés. Down every *via* (street) and *vicolo* (alley) and in every piazza you'll make new discoveries of Romanesque, Gothic, or Renaissance architecture. Sheltered within the churches, cloisters, and towers are the masterful paintings and sculptures of the Quattrocento and Cinquecento periods. These marvels retain their potency even in the Florence of the Ⓐ**Ponte Vecchio,** with its goldsmiths and jewelry shops and its fine view downriver to the Ponte Santa Trinità, which Florentines call the most beautiful bridge in the world. Pause a moment and judge for yourself.

Without a doubt, Mother Nature outdid herself in Tuscany, the region on the Ligurian and Tyrrhenian seas that radiates from Florence. Punctuated by thickly wooded hills, snow-capped peaks, sun-drenched vineyards, olive groves, and dramatic hill towns, Tuscany's

TUSCANY

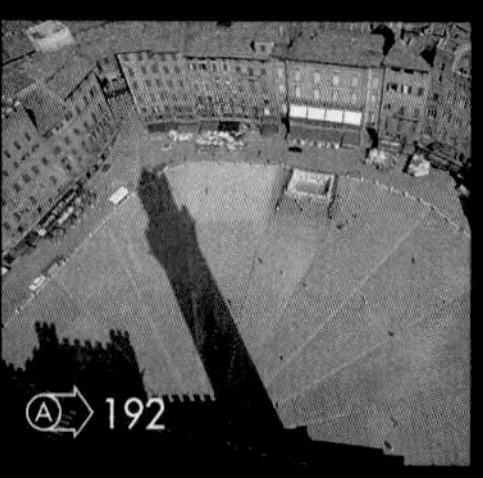
Ⓐ 192

milk-and-honey vistas have changed little since Renaissance artists first beheld them. Not surprisingly, you'll find some of Italy's greatest art treasures here, including the 12th-century Leaning Tower of Pisa and Piero della Francesca's fresco cycle in Arezzo. Travelers are also entranced by medieval Siena, "the Pompeii of the Middle Ages," as it was called by the philosopher Taine. With its shell-shaped Ⓐ**Piazza del Campo** delimited by the austere Palazzo Pubblico, Siena symbolizes the grace and power of a proud city, and its age-old rivalry with Florence still fires its citizenry's tongues and souls. During the Ⓒ**Palio,** the square explodes in a frenzy of pageantry and passion and a

Ⓑ 184

Ⓒ 195

dizzying horse race amid colorful flags. Sunny vineyards and olive groves embrace and characterize Tuscany's bucolic landscape. In Ⓑ**San Gimignano,** the quintessential Tuscan town, linger over a glass of Vernaccia di San Gimignano, then stand on the steps of the Collegiata church at sunset as the swallows, twittering softly in the air, swoop in and out of the famous medieval towers. Or travel farther afield to the Ⓓ**Abbazia di San Galgano** and look up to the sky through the missing rooftop, a haunting suggestion of time past.

Ⓓ 202

VENICE

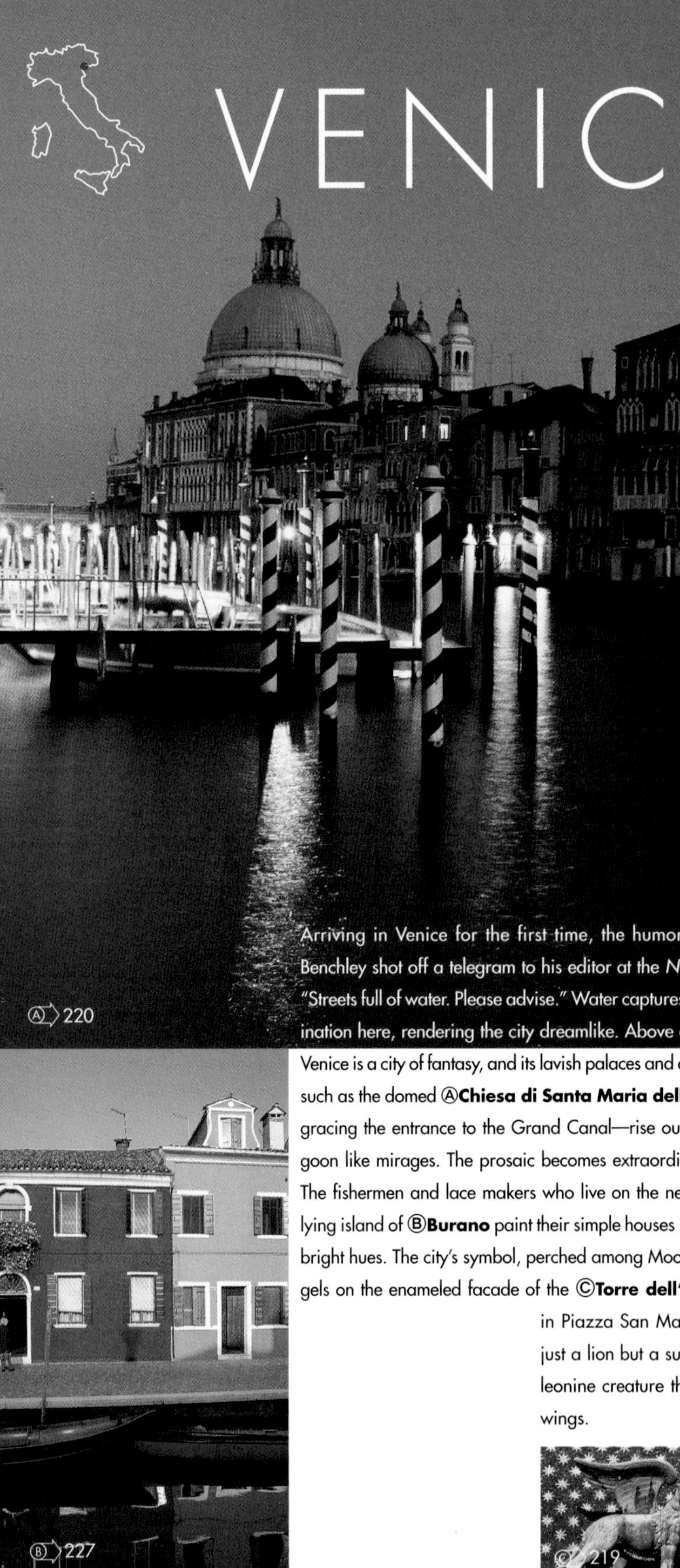

Ⓐ 220

Arriving in Venice for the first time, the humorist Robert Benchley shot off a telegram to his editor at the *New Yorker*, "Streets full of water. Please advise." Water captures the imagination here, rendering the city dreamlike. Above all, watery Venice is a city of fantasy, and its lavish palaces and churches—such as the domed Ⓐ**Chiesa di Santa Maria della Salute,** gracing the entrance to the Grand Canal—rise out of the lagoon like mirages. The prosaic becomes extraordinary here. The fishermen and lace makers who live on the nearby, low-lying island of Ⓑ**Burano** paint their simple houses in playfully bright hues. The city's symbol, perched among Moors and angels on the enameled facade of the Ⓒ**Torre dell'Orologio** in Piazza San Marco, is not just a lion but a supernatural leonine creature that sprouts wings.

Ⓑ 227

Ⓒ 219

Ⓐ 254

VENETIAN ARC

Ⓑ 257

When the sad moment comes to leave Venice, console yourself by seeking out the masterworks of the art-rich cities that spread in an arc to the north and the west. In Padua's Ⓐ**Cappella degli Scrovegni,** the great 13th-century master Giotto introduced a graphic dose of reality to his fresco cycle, including the first blue skies to appear in Western painting. But it was Palladio, the greatest architect of the Renaissance, who endowed the region with its most-visited treasures. In Vicenza his Ⓑ**Villa La Rotonda** and Ⓒ**Palazzo della Ragione,** known simply as the Basilica, bear the telltale and much-imitated hallmarks of Palladian style—serenity, symmetry, order, and harmony.

Ⓒ 254

ITALIAN RIVIERA

Not nearly as worldly as its counterpart across the French border, the "other" Riviera more than compensates by being a little balmier, a lot less discovered, a little sweeter, and, well, more enticingly Italian. The charm of this region, officially known as Liguria and forming an arc around the helter-skelter port city of Genoa, can be as subtle as the soft ocher-color facade of a palazzo in the faded, genteel resort of Ⓐ**Rapallo.** For more drama you need only travel to the easternmost edge of the region, where the Riviera attains a picturesque crescendo. Here, Ⓑ**Riomaggiore** and its four sibling villages cling to seaside cliffs and give a name to one of Europe's most breathtaking coastlines—and most popular walking terrain—the Cinque Terre, or Five Lands.

Ⓐ 300

Ⓑ 307

Ⓐ 331

PIEDMONT VALLE D'AOSTA

"Foot of the mountains" is what Piedmont means, and rare is the patch of earth in this bountiful northern region that doesn't afford at least a glimpse of the Alps. To the south, on the plains of the Po River, well-tended vineyards that surround fortified hill towns produce sparkling Spumanti and hearty Barolos, a formidable match for the region's white truffles. In the center of it all is Turin, where the Savoy legacy is palpable in the Rococo Palazzo Reale, and the legendary Holy Shroud draws pilgrims and scientific controversy. To the north, the highest Alps soar skyward and hem in the Valle d'Aosta. Castles right out of storybooks, like the one at Ⓑ**Fénis,** guard the passes, and renowned resorts, among them Ⓐ**Breuil-Cervinia,** afford the chance to ski on the slopes of the mightiest Alp of them all, the Matterhorn. In the shadow of the pistes are Aosta, a Roman outpost of 1st-century BC fame, and the Parco Nazionale del Gran Paradiso, where ibex, chamois, and a flurry of May blossoms flourish.

Ⓑ 333

MILAN, LOMBARDY & THE LAKES

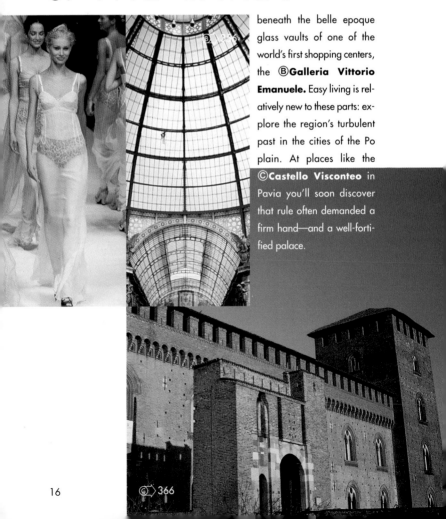

Poets, royals, Roman emperors, and mere mortals have long swooned over the Italian lakes, where deep blue waters and verdant hillsides clad with voluptuous gardens offer respite for the world-weary at Europe's toniest resorts, including the Ⓐ**Villa d'Este** on Lake Como. Other sophisticated pleasures are less than an hour away in Milan. The fashions you see on the runway here can be had (for a price, of course) in the city's chic shops, including those beneath the belle epoque glass vaults of one of the world's first shopping centers, the Ⓑ**Galleria Vittorio Emanuele.** Easy living is relatively new to these parts: explore the region's turbulent past in the cities of the Po plain. At places like the Ⓒ**Castello Visconteo** in Pavia you'll soon discover that rule often demanded a firm hand—and a well-fortified palace.

Ⓑ 356

Ⓒ 366

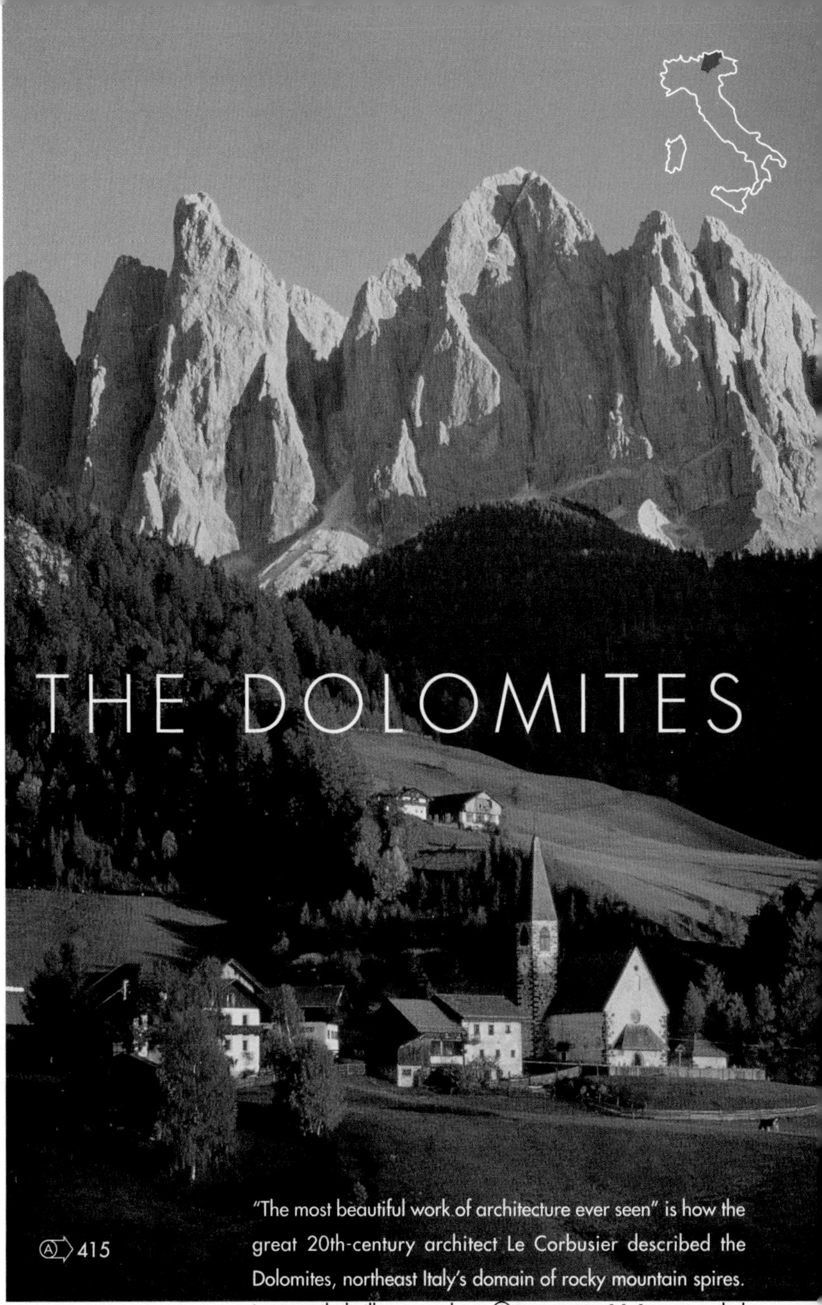

THE DOLOMITES

Ⓐ 415

"The most beautiful work of architecture ever seen" is how the great 20th-century architect Le Corbusier described the Dolomites, northeast Italy's domain of rocky mountain spires. In unspoiled villages, such as Ⓐ**Santa Maddalena,** nestled beneath the raw, craggy peaks and tucked into verdant Alpine valleys, the architecture is of the quaint, centuries-old South Tyrolean variety, at once Italian and Austrian. Whatever the culture, the common asset is snow, on literally hundreds of miles of ski runs at such world-famous resorts as Ⓑ**Madonna di Campiglio.**

Ⓑ 406

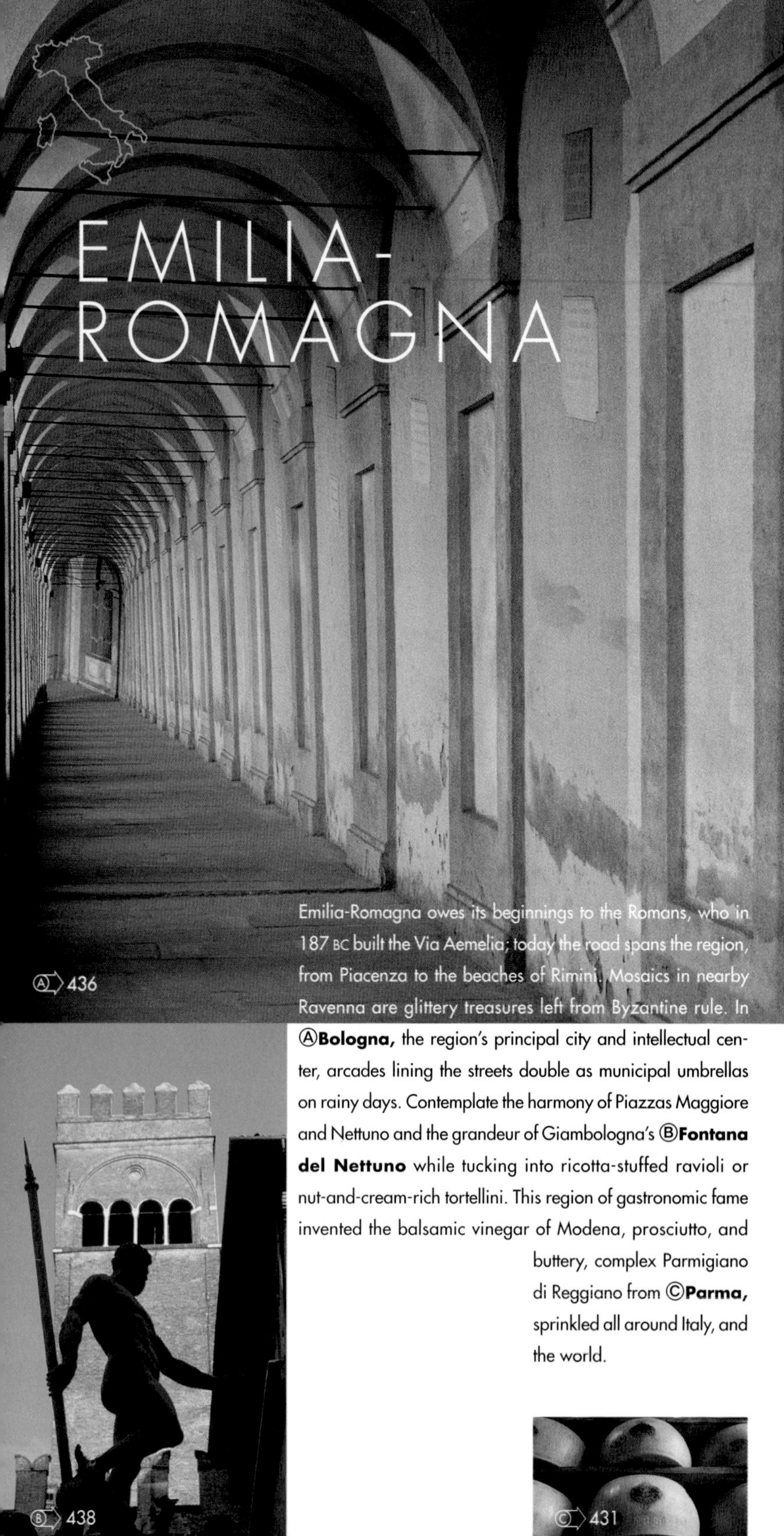

EMILIA-ROMAGNA

Ⓐ 436

Emilia-Romagna owes its beginnings to the Romans, who in 187 BC built the Via Aemelia; today the road spans the region, from Piacenza to the beaches of Rimini. Mosaics in nearby Ravenna are glittery treasures left from Byzantine rule. In Ⓐ**Bologna,** the region's principal city and intellectual center, arcades lining the streets double as municipal umbrellas on rainy days. Contemplate the harmony of Piazzas Maggiore and Nettuno and the grandeur of Giambologna's Ⓑ**Fontana del Nettuno** while tucking into ricotta-stuffed ravioli or nut-and-cream-rich tortellini. This region of gastronomic fame invented the balsamic vinegar of Modena, prosciutto, and buttery, complex Parmigiano di Reggiano from Ⓒ**Parma,** sprinkled all around Italy, and the world.

Ⓑ 438

Ⓒ 431

UMBRIA & THE MARCHES

Ⓐ 477

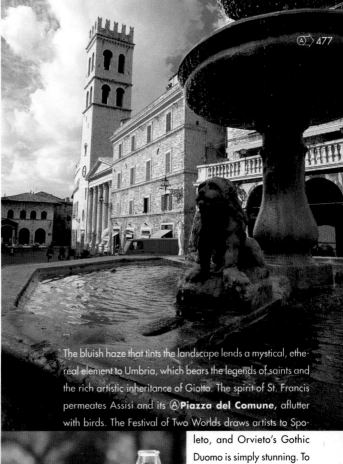

The bluish haze that tints the landscape lends a mystical, ethereal element to Umbria, which bears the legends of saints and the rich artistic inheritance of Giotto. The spirit of St. Francis permeates Assisi and its Ⓐ**Piazza del Comune,** aflutter with birds. The Festival of Two Worlds draws artists to Spoleto, and Orvieto's Gothic Duomo is simply stunning. To the east the turreted castles of the Marches hulk among the Apennines, and the Renaissance Ⓑ**Palazzo Ducale** guards majestic Urbino. Rugged Abruzzo to the south holds remnants of the Roman empire as well as the gifts of nature in its national park. Drive among Umbria's hill towns, stopping for dishes perfumed with black truffles and sun-kissed olive oil.

Ⓑ 469

CAMPANIA

Mount Vesuvius may grumble, the earth around Naples may shoot steaming gases, the dark waters of Lago d'Averno may lend credence to the ancients' belief that this was the entrance to the underworld, the port cities of Pompeii and Herculaneum may be frozen in time forever by a catastrophic volcanic eruption. But blessed by gentle light and washed by warm seas, Campania defies these omens. A vast treasury of Baroque architecture, classical antiquities, and Renaissance masterpieces, it is above all appreciated for its beauty and easygoing ways: It's not a coincidence that the frescoes in Pompeii's Ⓑ**Villa dei Misteri**—perhaps our most astonishing paintings from the ancient world—depict a young woman's initiation into the cult of Dionysus, the god of wine. The very names here—Capri, Positano, Amalfi, and even Naples, the operatic city at center stage—evoke sybaritic pleasures and hedonism, fragrant lemon groves and turquoise seas. Campania delivers on these promises in spades. "The sun, the moon, the stars and Amalfi," it is said, and who could think of anything else, given the atmospheric village's romantic perch on Europe's most beautiful coast, and with such a Ⓐ**Duomo**—a mind-bending blend of Moorish, Romanesque, and Baroque elements—in its midst?

Ⓐ 526

Ⓑ 512

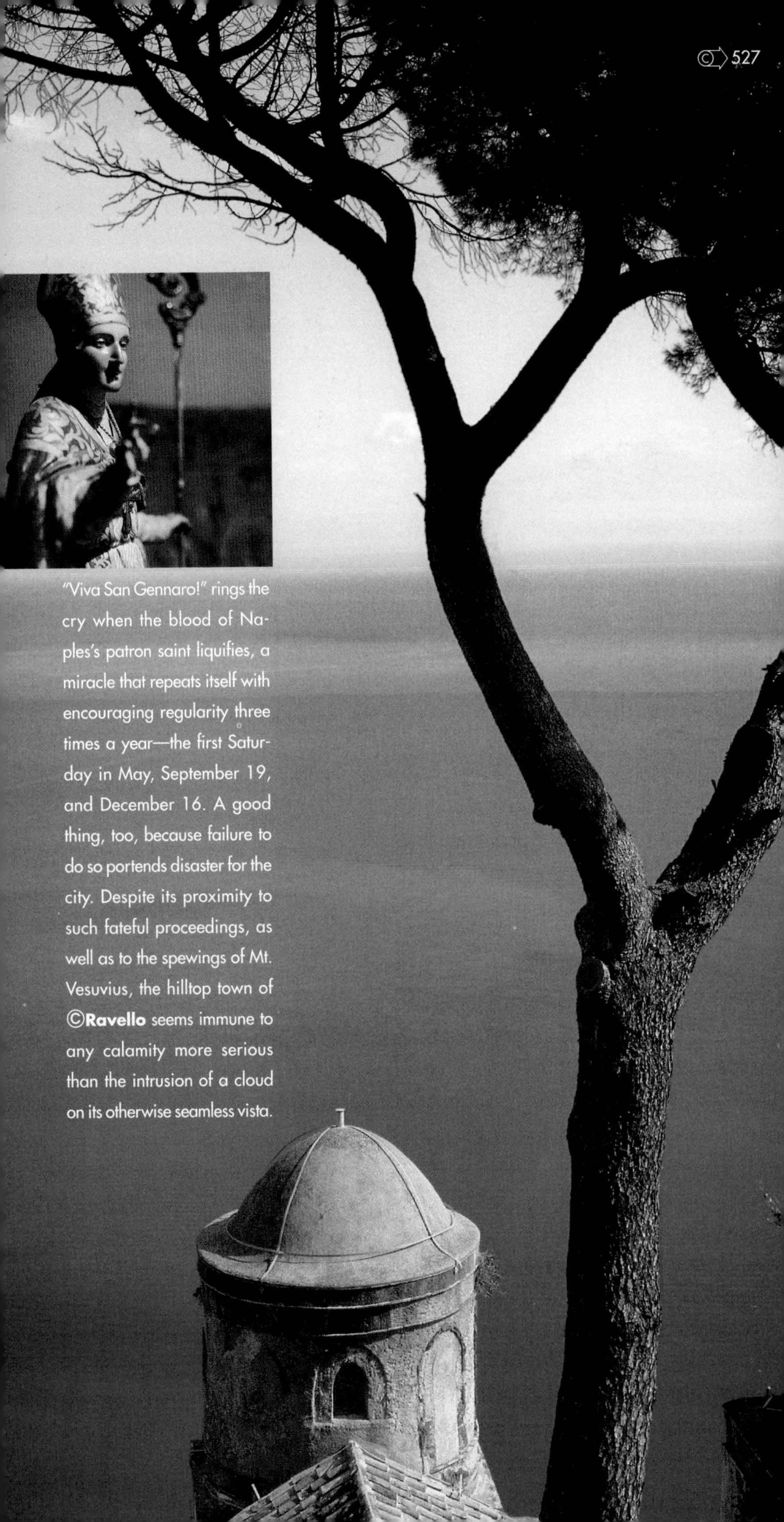

"Viva San Gennaro!" rings the cry when the blood of Naples's patron saint liquifies, a miracle that repeats itself with encouraging regularity three times a year—the first Saturday in May, September 19, and December 16. A good thing, too, because failure to do so portends disaster for the city. Despite its proximity to such fateful proceedings, as well as to the spewings of Mt. Vesuvius, the hilltop town of ©**Ravello** seems immune to any calamity more serious than the intrusion of a cloud on its otherwise seamless vista.

Ⓐ 551

APULIA

En route to Brindisi and Greece-bound ferries, many travelers speed heedlessly through the 250 miles (402½ km) of coast that comprises Italy's heel. (Passing through is something of a tradition here; the crusaders did it on their way to and from the Holy Land.) Linger awhile, though, and you'll discover that the sun-baked landscape yields more than olives and grapes. Greeks, Romans, Holy Roman Emperors, and numerous other conquerors have stayed long enough to leave their mark on little-known places like the Baroque Ⓐ**Duomo** in Ⓒ**Gallipoli,** a coastal city whose whitewashed, Casbah-like fishing port evokes northern Africa. Even more exotic are the eye-catching *trulli,* conical roofed dwellings built efficiently in the shape of igloos, without mortar, from blocks of local limestone. Lore has it that this construction allowed the trulli to be disassembled in a hurry when the royal tax collector came around. However they came into being, more than 1,000 of these eccentric structures add a quirky charm to the inland town of Alberobello. One of the greatest appeals of the region is what isn't here—large-scale development along the seductive coastline, at its most alluring along the cove-studded Ⓑ**Gargano Promontory.**

Ⓑ 541

Ⓒ 551

BASILICATA & CALABRIA

The southernmost regions of the peninsula, the toe of the boot, are known informally as the *mezzogiorno*—literally "midday," for the blazing sun that casts the white villages, shimmering seas, and barren landscapes in a harsh light that will render your impressions all the more vivid. The pleasure of traveling through this untrodden terrain is stumbling upon largely undiscovered places far off the beaten path—the simple *sassi,* dwellings partially hewn from caves, in the Basilicata village of Ⓐ**Matera,** perhaps, or the Ⓒ**Chiesa di Santa Maria della Isola,** atop its rocky promontory in Tropea, on the Calabrian coast. In fact some of the major treasures of the mezzogiorno are only now being unearthed. Dredged from the sea in 1972, the 5th-century BC Ⓑ**Riace Bronzes,** some of the finest examples of Greek art, command pride of place in the dazzling collection of antiquities in the Museo Nazionale della Magna Grecia in Reggio di Calabria.

Ⓐ 560

Ⓑ 566

Ⓒ 564

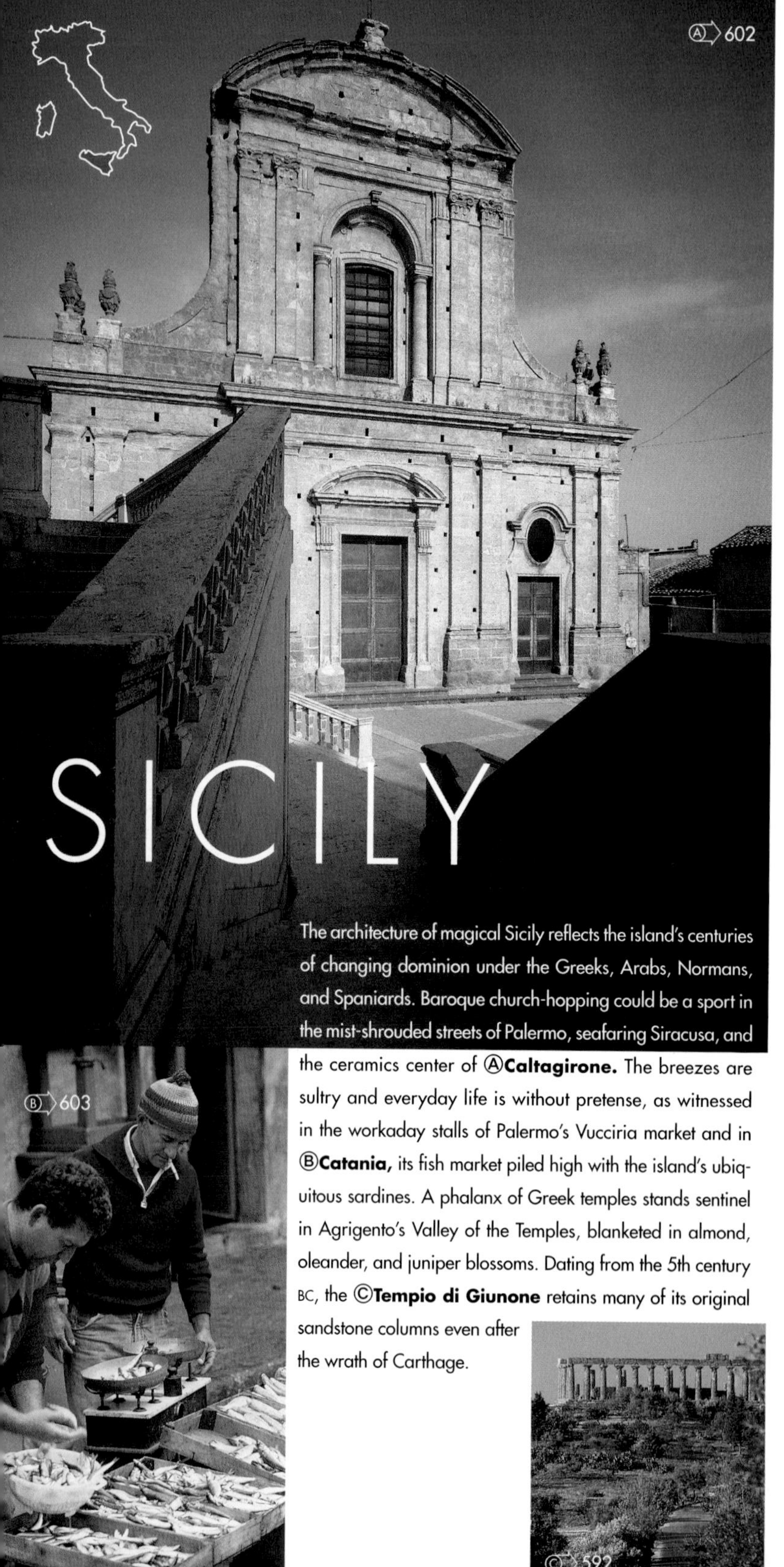

Ⓐ 602

SICILY

The architecture of magical Sicily reflects the island's centuries of changing dominion under the Greeks, Arabs, Normans, and Spaniards. Baroque church-hopping could be a sport in the mist-shrouded streets of Palermo, seafaring Siracusa, and the ceramics center of Ⓐ**Caltagirone.** The breezes are sultry and everyday life is without pretense, as witnessed in the workaday stalls of Palermo's Vucciria market and in Ⓑ**Catania,** its fish market piled high with the island's ubiquitous sardines. A phalanx of Greek temples stands sentinel in Agrigento's Valley of the Temples, blanketed in almond, oleander, and juniper blossoms. Dating from the 5th century BC, the Ⓒ**Tempio di Giunone** retains many of its original sandstone columns even after the wrath of Carthage.

Ⓑ 603

Ⓒ 592

Savagely beautiful landscapes of dense and mountainous bush, rock-strewn beaches, and weathered coves with wind-sculpted granite formations intensify Sardinia's aura of isolation. This Mediterranean island west of mainland Italy is far enough from imperial and

SARDINIA

papal Rome to have its own enigmatic character, which has been shaped by an amalgam of peoples and architectural styles: Phoenician, Spanish, Moorish, Turkish, Genoan, and Pisan. If here in midsummer, you've been cast in the role of an Italian movie star, so grab your yacht and wraparounds and tack to the

Ⓐ 633

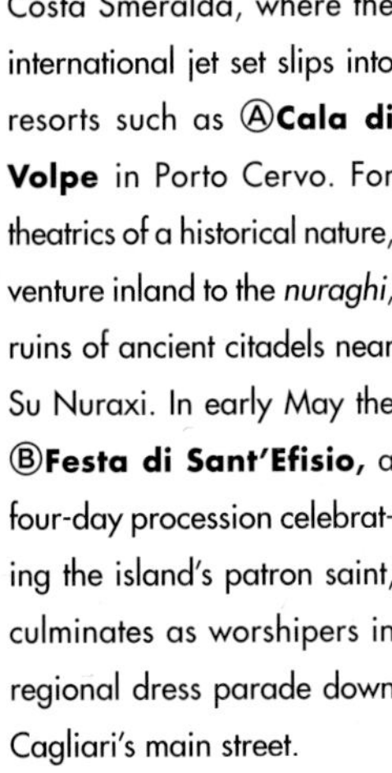

Costa Smeralda, where the international jet set slips into resorts such as Ⓐ**Cala di Volpe** in Porto Cervo. For theatrics of a historical nature, venture inland to the *nuraghi*, ruins of ancient citadels near Su Nuraxi. In early May the Ⓑ**Festa di Sant'Efisio,** a four-day procession celebrating the island's patron saint, culminates as worshipers in regional dress parade down Cagliari's main street.

Ⓑ 623

GREAT ITINERARIES

Italian Gardens

7 to 9 days

Using the living materials and elements of nature to achieve studied aesthetic effects, Italians are masters at creating gardens, and have been from the Renaissance and Baroque ages until well into the 19th century. Usually framing country villas or grand city palaces, the most spectacular gardens are laid out with an artist's eye for perspective and color; many are studded with statuary and fanciful fountains. A tour of some of Italy's most beautiful gardens begins in Milan, gateway to the Lake District—ideally in spring, when azaleas and rhododendrons are in glorious bloom. Note that some gardens are not open in winter or in inclement weather; always call ahead.

STRESA

3 days. Spend the better part of one day on an excursion from the stately Lake Maggiore resort town of Stresa, exploring the Borromean Islands, from the decorative Baroque palace and terraced gardens on Isola Bella to the Renaissance-style villa on Isola Madre, surrounded by a lush park where peacocks strut amid banks of azaleas, rhododendrons, and camellias. To plant the elaborately tiered gardens of Isola Bella and Isola Madre, a 16th-century count had laborers haul soil to the islands in boats. The next day hop on a ferry to Verbania and get off at the embarcadero of the Villa Taranto. Adorned with terraces, cascades, and fountains, its vast garden was laid out in the 20th century and remains one of Europe's finest. Some 20,000 plant species—many rare and exotic—grow here. ☞ *Chapter 8, Lake Maggiore and Lake Orta.*

BELLAGIO

2 or 3 days. Settle into this beauty spot on Ⓐ Lake Como surrounded by romantic vistas. At Villa Melzi, which some regard as the most serendipitous site in the entire Lake District, a fabulous staircase blooms with azaleas in spring and is topped by a neoclassic palace. Just across the lake in Tremezzo, one stop away on the ferry, is Villa Carlotta, a wedding present to Charlotte of Russia in 1843. The luxuriant gardens and park are known for their spectacular rhododendrons and azaleas. From Tremezzo, take the ferry to Sala Comacina, where, during visiting hours, there is regular ferry service to Villa Balbaniello, one of the most romantic sites of all. Check opening times with the Bellagio or Tremezzo tourist offices. Afterward, if you have time, take the leisurely ferry trip around the Maggiore or Como lakes to get glimpses of many more villa gardens from the boat. ☞ *Chapter 8, Lake Como.*

FLORENCE

2 or 3 days. Make Florence your base for a series of visits to the gardens of the Medici villas on the city's outskirts. These gardens feel somewhat austere, their beauty lying in the artful arrangements of evergreens. Roam through the Giardini Boboli, behind Palazzo Pitti, laid out for Eleanor of Toledo, wife of Medici Grand Duke Cosimo I, noting how the plan was ingeniously adapted to a very irregular site. Then, together with some city sightseeing to help you focus on the Medici influence in Florence, continue your villa touring in half-day excursions. Villa Gamberaia, a legacy of the wealthy Capponi family, is an elegant Italian garden set in olive groves in the hills of Settignano. North of Florence, toward Sesto Fiorentino, the vast Medici gardens of Villa di Castello are festooned with more than 500 lemon trees. At the Medici Villa La Petraia, sculptures by Renaissance masters adorn the 16th-century Italian garden and a park is landscaped in 19th-century style. ☞ *Chapter 2, Side Trips from Florence.*

By Public Transportation

Trains make frequent runs between Milan and Stresa (about 60 minutes), Como (30 minutes), and Lecco (30 minutes). The good lake ferry service makes it easy to explore villages on the Maggiore and Como lakes (ferry trips are no more than 30 minutes). Travel by bus from Como to Bellagio and between Lecco and Bellagio (both trips about 75 minutes, depending on traffic). By train it takes about 3½ hours to travel between Milan and Florence. To reach Villa Gamberaia from Florence, take Bus 10, marked Settignano. To reach Villa La Petraia take Bus 28; Villa di Castello is within walking distance.

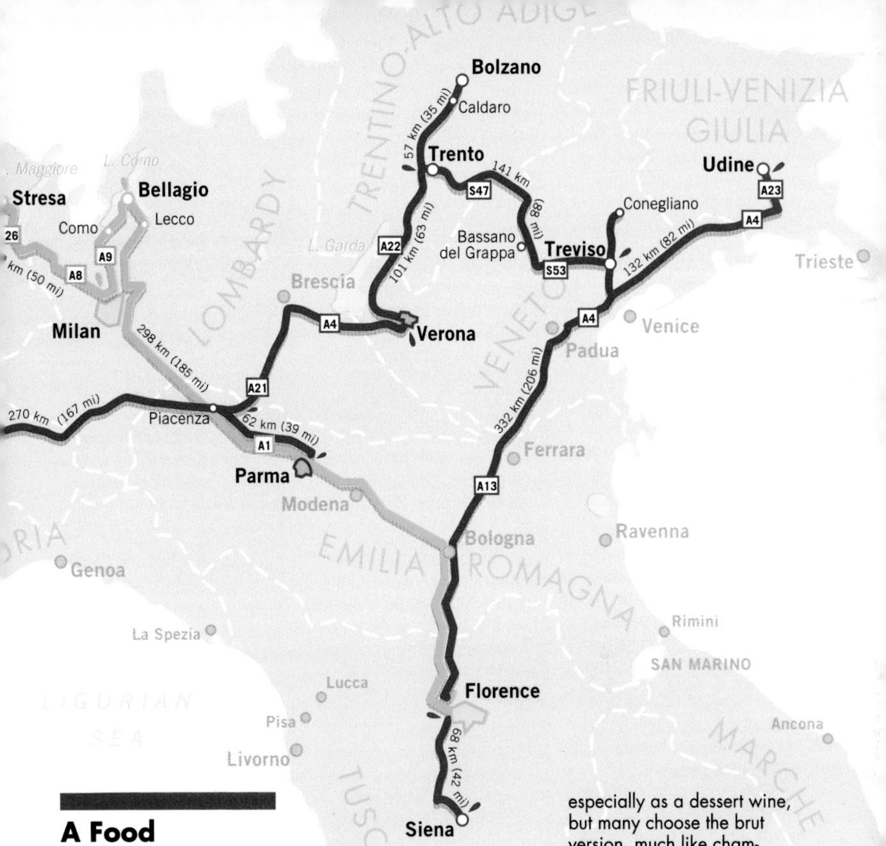

TRENTINO-ALTO ADIGE
FRIULI-VENEZIA GIULIA
Bolzano
Caldaro
57 km (35 mi)
Trento
141 km (88 mi)
S47
Udine
A23
Maggiore
L. Como
Stresa
Bellagio
Lecco
Como
A9
A8
26
km (50 mi)
LOMBARDY
L. Garda
A22
101 km (63 mi)
Bassano del Grappa
Conegliano
Treviso
S53
132 km (82 mi)
A4
Trieste
Brescia
A4
Verona
VENETO
A4
Venice
Padua
Milan
298 km (185 mi)
A21
332 km (206 mi)
270 km (167 mi)
Piacenza
62 km (39 mi)
A1
Parma
Ferrara
A13
Modena
Bologna
Ravenna
EMILIA ROMAGNA
Genoa
La Spezia
Rimini
SAN MARINO
Lucca
Florence
LIGURIAN SEA
Pisa
Ancona
MARCHE
Livorno
68 km (42 mi)
TUSCANY
Siena

A Food Lover's Tour

10 to 14 days

Sampling Italy's best food and wines in the very places they are produced will enrich your understanding of the country and its people. On this itinerary through a country where good eating and drinking is the rule, you'll take in the birthplace of some wonderful wines, a gracious city renowned for exquisite chocolates and its grand fin-de-siècle cafés, truffle country, and, last but not least, Emilia-Romagna's Parma, which is as rich in history and art as in its culinary delights. In northern Italy, near the Dolomites, you'll see how irresistible cooking mixes Italian and Austrian accents.

TURIN

1 or 2 days. Dine on as many as 30 antipasti followed by a creamy risotto, and top off your meal with a delectable dessert. Then head for one of the city's historic cafés to savor the wonderful pastries along with your espresso. And don't forget to pick up some of the city's celebrated hazelnut chocolates, called *gianduiotti*. Southeast of Turin in the Monferrato and Langhe districts, rolling hills are blanketed with the vineyards that produce Barolo, "king of the wines and wine of kings," in addition to Barbaresco and others.

☞ *Chapter 7, Turin* and *Fortified Cities of the Po Plain.*

ASTI AND ALBA

2 days. Spend a day exploring the wineries in the area. Asti has lent its name to Spumante, a sparkling white that brings bubbles of gaiety to every kind of celebration in Italy. Some like it sweet, especially as a dessert wine, but many choose the brut version, much like champagne and made by the same method. Spend another day in Alba, stopping at the Castello di Barolo to sample the wine and visit the wine museum. While in the area, let the aroma of white truffles tickle your senses, and treat your taste buds to a range of culinary specialties that exalt this regal tuber. Alba is the capital of the Langhe wine country; its October wine and truffle fair features a rousing medieval-style tournament. En route to Verona, make a detour to ⒷParma for a quintessential Italian meal.

☞ *Chapter 7, Fortified Cities of the Po Plain* and *Chapter 10, On the Road to Parma and Modena.*

VERONA

1 or 2 days. This could be your base for an excursion north to Trento, where some of Italy's best Spumanti are produced. Verona's ancient Roman Arena, medieval buildings, and characteristic restaurants deserve some attention, too.

☞ *Chapter 5, Padua, Verona, Vicenza* and *Chapter 9, Western Trentino.*

BOLZANO
1 or 2 days. If you spend the night here, you'll have time to enjoy the area's distinctive Austrian-Italian cuisine and to follow the Strada del Vino (Wine Road) that starts at Caldaro, 9 miles (15 km) south of Bolzano.
☞ *Chapter 9, Alto Adige and Cortina* and *Heart of the Dolomites.*

TREVISO
2 days. Medieval buildings, canals, mill wheels, and an abundance of inns where you can savor local dishes and wines make this a good base for exploring the area. Spend a day on an excursion to Udine, or follow the Strada del Vino Rosso (Red Wine Road) through cabernet and merlot country along the Piave River from Conegliano, where sparkling, fruity Prosecco is made. A plate of *pasta e fagioli,* the hearty bean-and-pasta soup, a specialty of the Veneto region, will sustain you.
☞ *Chapter 5, Villa Barbaro, Treviso, and the Hillside Towns* and *Udine and Trieste.*

UDINE
1 day. Another optional overnight stop, this attractive city was ruled by Venice and shows it, with stone Venetian lions rampant on graceful buildings and columns in pretty piazzas. The Collio wine district nearby is known for its amazing and utterly distinctive local cheeses.
☞ *Chapter 5, Udine and Trieste.*

CHIANTI
2 or 3 days. Spend at least two days roaming through the Chianti district between Florence and Siena, where you can delve into the subtle differences in vintages and perhaps swerve out of the district's official confines into the realm of Brunello di Montalcino. Here, it seems that even the tiniest village harbors a precious artwork or two by Tuscan masters. Many wineries offer guided tours of their cellars, often part of historic estates belonging to families that can trace their origins back to the Middle Ages or the Renaissance.
☞ *Chapter 3, Chianti* and *Southern Tuscany.*

By Public Transportation
Local trains and buses make the 45-minute run from Turin to Asti and Alba. Parma is on the Milan line; switch at Piacenza (30 minutes). Return to Turin to get a train on the main east–west line to Verona (3 hours from Turin). In Verona you'll find frequent service on another main line to Trento (1 hour) and Bolzano (a 2-hour trip). Return to Verona for a train to Padua, 60 minutes away. Treviso can be reached by train (60 minutes) or bus (70 minutes) from Padua. Udine is on a main line that passes through Padua; journey time is 2½ hours. There is fast service on the same line to Florence (2¾ hours from Venice), where you can get a local train or bus to make the 90-minute trip to Siena. Local buses serve the Chianti district.

Classical Highlights
8 to 12 days

Well colonized by the ancient Greeks, then epicenter of the Roman Empire, Italy has a wealth of classical sites, many of them in an excellent state of preservation. Rome was, of course, the capital of the Roman Empire, and a number of ancient sites remain here today, seemingly plunked down in the middle of the modern metropolis. Campania, too, is full of important classical landmarks, from both the Roman

and the Greek eras, and Pompeii is not the only vestige of the eruption of nearby Mt. Vesuvius. If you have more time and a more intense interest in ancient history, you'll want to travel all the way to Sicily, the large island just off the toe of Italy's boot. Settled by the Greeks, it was a center of trade and culture in the Hellenic world, and it still is richly endowed with remarkable sites.

ROME
2 or 3 days. Spend at least a day exploring Ancient Rome—the Capitoline Hill, the Roman Forum, the Circus Maximus, the ©Colosseum, the Pantheon—and on subsequent days, venture out to the Via Appia and the Catacombs, or study classical sculptures in the Vatican Museums and antiquities in the Museo Nazionale Romano in Palazzo Altemps. It is quite an experience to turn a corner and see a famous building, such as the Colosseum, across the street, with traffic whizzing blithely past its crumbling arches.
☞ *Chapter 1, Exploring Rome.*

NAPLES AND CAMPANIA
2 or 3 days. After arriving in Naples from Rome, spend the afternoon at the Museo Archeologico Nazionale. Herculaneum and Pompeii can be visited in one day from Naples, but it would be a very full day, and it is best to break it into two separate excursions. The relics being unearthed from the lava at Herculaneum are even better preserved than the once-buried ruins at Pompeii. On another day, enjoy an excursion down the Amalfi Coast or take the A3 to Paestum, with its still-intact Greek temples. Take an optional day to tour the area just west of Naples—the Roman

amphitheater at Pozzuoli, spooky Lake Avernus, the Roman resort town at Baia, with its excavated baths, and the Sibyl's Cave at Cumae, perhaps the oldest Greek colony in Italy.
☞ *Chapter 12, Naples; The Phlegrean Fields; Herculaneum, Vesuvius, Pompeii;* and *The Amalfi Coast.*

PALERMO, SICILY
1 day. Visit the Museo Archeologico Regionale and nearby Segesta, with its fine Doric Greek temple.
☞ *Chapter 15, Palermo* and *Western Coast to Agrigento.*

AGRIGENTO
1 or 2 days. Explore the Valley of the Temples, an extensive Greek site, and if you have time, make your way up the coast to see the spectacular Greek temple complex at ⒹSelinunte.
☞ *Chapter 15, Western Coast to Agrigento.*

SIRACUSA
1 or 2 days. Visit the Parco Archeologico in town, the splendid Museo Archeologico, and, if there's time, take an excursion to see the mosaics at the Imperial Roman Villa at Casale, just north of Piazza Armerina.
☞ *Chapter 15, Siracusa* and *Eastern Sicily.*

TAORMINA
1 day. Get a fine view of Mt. Etna and see the town's Greek theater, its backdrop the shimmering Mediterranean; the theater is still used for a summer arts festival.
☞ *Chapter 15, Eastern Sicily.*

By Public Transportation
Train service between Rome and Naples is fast and frequent, taking less than two hours on express trains. The Circumvesuviana train line can take you conveniently from Naples to Pompeii (a 35-minute trip) and Herculaneum (about 20 minutes' travel time). There is a train station right in Paestum (1½ hours from Naples). A ferry operates from Naples to Palermo, Sicily (it's a 9-hour trip), and a main train line makes the five-hour run between Palermo and Siracusa, which is also reached from Messina (a 3-hour trip) and Catania (1½ hours). Taormina is a one-hour train ride from Messina. Other sites on Sicily—such as Agrigento (2 hours from Palermo)—are better reached by bus than by the unreliable local train service.

Ⓓ 588

FODOR'S
CHOICE
A
B
C
D
E
F
G
H
I
J

QUINTESSENTIAL ITALY

Even with so many special places in Italy, Fodor's writers and editors have their favorites. Here are a few that stand out.

Bellagio, Lake Como. Once called "Italy's prettiest town," Como still seems to be more of an operetta set than a resort. Surrounded by sumptuous villas and gardens, the town has long played host to honeymooners, kings, and other celebrated visitors. ☞ p. 382

Ⓒ **Lecce, Apulia.** Extravagant Baroque churches, a flowering of golden stone, are the showpieces of this city in Italy's deep south, stomping ground of the ancient Greeks, the crusaders, and a 17th-century landed aristocracy. All left their marks. ☞ p. 550

Ⓗ **Piazza del Campo, Siena.** This shell-shaped piazza dominated by the austere Palazzo Pubblico symbolizes the grace and power of the proud medieval city whose prominence in the banking and wool trades spurred a bitter rivalry with Florence. ☞ p. 192

Vucciria outdoor market, Palermo. Experience the in-your-face exuberance of Palermo's daily market. Its packed stalls, pungent aromas, and boisterous hawking constitute a Sicilian opera. ☞ p. 581

SPECIAL MEMORIES

Festa di San Efisio, Cagliari. Tradition isn't just a cliché in Sardinia's lexicon, and none of the island's other time-honored festivals has the passion of Cagliari's annual May binge, when a processional round-trip from Cagliari to Pula and back takes four days. ☞ p. 623

***Passeggiata*, Taormina.** For perfect people-watching in a dazzling seaside setting, head for Corso Umberto at dusk. All turn out for the promenade, pausing for gelato or a *caffè* and casting a vigilant eye toward magnificent Mt. Etna. ☞ p. 605

Ⓘ **Sunset gondola ride, Grand Canal, Venice.** For a truly magic moment, travel this surrealistic waterway, lined with fairy-tale palazzi veiled in silvery mists. ☞ p. 219

Ⓐ **Twilight, Positano.** The utter tranquillity of Positano at sunset is a balm to the soul. Whitewashed houses tumble down to the azure sea, shimmering under a blood-orange sky. Reserve an alfresco table at a café and let it all soak in. ☞ p. 524

WHERE ART COMES FIRST

Galleria degli Uffizi, Florence. A repository of unparalleled Italian masterpieces—including Botticelli's *Birth of Venus* and Leonardo da Vinci's *Adoration of the Magi*—stands steps from the Arno in the offices Vasari designed for the Medici Grand Duke Cosimo I. ☞ p. 121

Giotto fresco cycle, Cappella degli Scrovegni, Padua. The realism of these frescoes, executed between 1303 and 1305, was revolutionary. ☞ p. 254

I Frari, Venice. In this great Venetian Gothic church, you'll find two of Titian's most spectacular altarpieces; their blazing colors and luminosity cast 20th-century electricity into shadow. ☞ p. 225

Ⓓ **La Rotonda, Vicenza.** Italy's most famous Palladian villa inspired Thomas Jefferson's Monticello. If you run into the delightfully friendly owner, Count Ludovico di Valmarana, he'll direct you to the peerless Tiepolo frescoes at his family's Villa of the Dwarfs down the road. ☞ p. 257

Palazzo Ducale, Urbino. In ideal form, the Renaissance was a celebration of the nobility of man and his works, of the light and purity of the soul. This palace illustrates that focus with a clarity seen in no others in Italy. ☞ p. 469

Valley of the Temples, Agrigento, Sicily. More than 20 centuries of silence and solitude greet you at this archaeological site, where evocative temples built before the year AD 1 still rise out of the crests of a valley that undulates down to the blue sea. ☞ p. 592

FLAVORS

Ⓕ **Gualtiero Marchesi, Erbusco, Lago d'Iseo.** Spectacular flights of fancy are handled with classic Lombardian finesse by Italy's first proponent of *la cucina nuova*. Creativity has no limits here; accents range from the whimsy of origami to caviar garnishes. *$$$$* ☞ p. 379

Ⓙ **Buca di Sant'Antonio, Lucca.** A meal to match the divinity of a Puccini aria can be had at this Lucca mainstay, for two centuries relying on the simplicity of the Tuscan hearth with its fresh pastas and roast meats. *$$* ☞ p. 177

Ⓑ **Osteria Du Madon, Bologna.** Gracious chef Lorenzo Boni is quietly turning out traditional Bolognese dishes "of his fantasies" in the country's culinary capital. Sumptuous inventions such as fillet of beef wrapped in prosciutto with a balsamic vinegar sauce take center stage in the unadorned university-quarter space. *$$* ☞ p. 441

Ⓔ **Tazza d'Oro, Rome.** Those who claim that the national coffee habit is the key to the Italian disposition find conclusive proof here in Italy's best cup of coffee. Do as the Romans do: order a glass of water as a chaser. *$* ☞ p. 78

COMFORTS

Certosa di Maggiano, Siena. A 14th-century monastery with a chapel and bucolic garden are now an exquisite country hotel. Rooms are a study in understated luxury and comfort, with fine woods, leathers, and traditional prints. *$$$$* ☞ p. 193

Ⓖ **Accademia, Venice.** Just beyond the hotel's iron gate, a secret garden awaits, complete with a diminutive Palladian-style villa, a canal parterre, and verdant trees. It's enchanting and cheery, although, alas, no secret. *$$–$$$* ☞ p. 239

Teatro di Pompeo, Rome. You truly feel transported back to Old Rome in this refined little hotel with a brick-vaulted breakfast room dating from ancient Roman times and guest rooms with sturdy, stylish beamed ceilings. *$$* ☞ p. 81

1 ROME

In the Eternal City Nero fiddled, Mark Anthony praised Caesar, and Charlemagne was crowned. Today you can marvel at the venerated Renaissance and Baroque treasures in their footsteps while sipping a *caffè*, exploring swank boutiques, and dodging speeding Vespas. In no other city will you find such a heady mix of elegance, earthiness, and energy.

Updated by Carla Lionello and Jon Eldan

HOWEVER YOU ARRIVE in Rome, by autostrada, or train or plane, you can tell by the traffic that you are entering a grand nexus: all paths lead to Rome. As you enter the city proper, edifices, icons, and images to match your expectations take shape: a bridge with heroic statues along its parapets; a towering cake of ornate marble decorated with allegorical figures in extravagant poses; a piazza and an obelisk under an umbrella of pine trees; a massive marble arena, even bigger than you imagined, that you realize with awe is the fabled Colosseum.

More than Florence, more than Venice, Rome is Italy's treasure trove, packed as it is with masterpieces from more than two millennia of artistic achievement—for this is where Republican Rome once bustled around the buildings of the Roman Forum, centuries later Michelangelo Buonarroti painted the ceiling in the Sistine Chapel, and in modern times, Federico Fellini filmed *La Dolce Vita* and *8½* at Cinecittà Studios.

Rome is like a big layer cake, and your job, as a visitor, is to pry it open and get a feel for each of the layers. You'll find pieces of Ancient Rome casually strewn about, topped by Medieval and Renaissance Rome, topped by Fascist Rome, and, finally, slathered on top is today's Rome, where decades of political apathy are giving way to a revitalized city. Ancient Romans, Vandals, Popes and the Borgias, Michelangelo and Gianlorenzo Bernini, Napoléon, and Mussolini all left their physical and spiritual marks on the city. Today Rome's formidable legacy is upheld by its people, their history knit into the fabric of their everyday life. Students walk dogs in the park that was once the mausoleum of the family of the Emperor Augustus; Raphaelesque madonnas line up for buses on busy corners; a priest in flowing robes walks through a medieval piazza talking on a cell phone. Modern Rome has one foot in the past, one in the present—a delightful stance that allows you to have an espresso in a square designed by Bernini, then take the Metro back to your hotel room in a renovated Renaissance palace. "When you first come here you assume that you must burrow about in ruins and prowl in museums to get back to the days of Numa Pompilius or Mark Anthony," Maud Howe observes in her book, *Roma Beata.* "It is not necessary; you only have to live, and the common happenings of daily life—yes, even the trolley car and your bicycle—carry you back in turn to the Dark Ages, to the early Christians, even to prehistoric Rome."

Pleasures and Pastimes

Dining

Rome is a city distinguished more by its good attitude toward eating out than by a multitude of outstanding restaurants. Don't look for star chefs here, nor the latest trends—with a few notable exceptions, the city's food scene is a bit like its historical sights, well worn but still standing. But food lovers nonetheless have much to look forward to. Romans have been known since ancient times for great feasts and banquets, and though the days of the triclinium and the saturnalia are long past, dining out is still all the nightlife most Romans need. In fact, a lingering meal alfresco is one of Rome's great pleasures. Lunch is served from noon to 3, and dinner from 8 until about 10:30 or 11, but some restaurants stay open later, especially in summer, when patrons linger at sidewalk tables to enjoy the *ponentino* (evening breeze).

Jubilee 2000

Rome marks the beginning of the millennium with **Jubilee 2000** (Giubileo 2000), which is projected to bring 30 million tourists and religious pilgrims to the Eternal City. During 1999, Rome sprinted to the finish with large-scale public works and infrastructure projects, including the cleaning of the facade of St. Peter's Basilica. Among the Vatican facilities being constructed to handle the masses is an entirely new entrance to the Vatican Museums, which will be near the former one on Viale Vaticano. On the edge of the Vatican, a huge underground garage has been constructed for tour buses within a bastion of the Vatican walls. The port of Civitavecchia has been completely transformed in anticipation of 30% more traffic than it has ever handled.

Rome will issue 12 million high-tech "Pilgrim ID" cards, with special microchips to facilitate access to public transportation and religious sights and events. Obviously, you will need to plan early and thoroughly if you travel to the capital during the year 2000, especially in August, when Rome expects to bring in 2 million people for **World Youth Day.** (The entire province of Lazio has only 200,000 beds for tourists.) A highly touted multilingual Web site (www.Jubil2000.org) can provide further details (also ☞ Close-Up: Jubilee 2000, *below*). Other cities, including Venice, Florence, Milan, and Turin, have also planned elaborate festivities for the millennial year. For further information pick up Fodor's ***Holy Rome: a Millennium Guide to the Christian Sights,*** a Jubilee handbook with full-color photographs, thematic itineraries, the official Jubilee Calendar, and coverage of more than 300 major Christian sights.

Lodging

Rome has the range of accommodations you would expect of any great city, from the squalid little hotels and *pensione* (pensions) around the railway station to the grand monuments to luxury and elegance on Via Veneto. Appearances can be misleading here: crumbling stucco facades may promise little from the outside, but they often hide interiors of considerable elegance.

EXPLORING ROME

Rome presents a particular challenge for you: just as you begin to feel hopelessly smitten by the spell of the city, you realize you don't have the time to see more than a fraction of its treasures. You may take refuge in the age-old adage, Rome wasn't built in a day. The Italian author Silvio Negro said it best: "*Roma, non basta una vita*" (Rome, a lifetime is not enough). It's wise to start out knowing this, and to have a focused but flexible itinerary. A ramble through a picturesque quarter of Old Rome can be just as enlightening as seeking a chapel redolent of spicy incense or a trek through marbled miles of museum corridors.

Though large, Rome invites walking, and taxis are rarely far off for the weary. Plan your day to take into account the varying opening hours of the sights you plan to visit, which usually means mixing the ancient, classical, and Baroque, museums and parks, the center and the environs. Most churches are usually open from 8 or 9 until noon or 12:30, and from 3 or 4 until about 6:30 or 7.

Numbers in the text correspond to numbers in the margin and on the Rome and Old Rome maps.

Great Itineraries

IF YOU HAVE 3 DAYS

Begin your first day at Piazza Venezia and survey Rome from atop the Capitoline Hill. Next, explore the Roman Forum and see the Palatine

Hill and the Colosseum. In the afternoon, combine sightseeing with shopping and make your way through the neighborhood around the Spanish Steps and the Trevi Fountain. The following morning, visit St. Peter's and the Sistine Chapel. After lunch, walk through Baroque Rome, exploring its splendor. Take it easy on your third morning: explore a museum or sight of interest and then relax at a café and watch the passing parade. Spend your final afternoon and evening exploring the picturesque Ghetto and Trastevere neighborhoods.

IF YOU HAVE 5 DAYS

On the morning of the fourth day wander through Villa Borghese and see the Canova and Bernini sculptures in the Galleria Borghese (make reservations ahead of time). On the fifth day, make an excursion either along Via Appia Antica or to Ostia Antica (☞ Side Trips, *below*), an ancient city comparable to Pompeii for interest and atmosphere. After a sustaining lunch, see some of Rome's most historic churches, with Michelangelo's *Moses* in San Pietro in Vincoli a highlight.

IF YOU HAVE 7 DAYS

Devote more time to the museums and galleries that interest you most. Explore a neighborhood you have not seen yet, or return to one you liked best, allowing plenty of time for poking into odd corners and courtyards and churches, and for café-sitting. Make a couple of excursions outside Rome, to Tivoli or perhaps to Tarquinia and Cerveteri.

Ancient Rome: Glories of the Caesars

A walk through the very core of Roman antiquity, through what was once the epicenter of the known world—the Romun Forum—gives you a look at how Michelangelo transformed the Capitoline Hill, the seat of ancient Rome's government, into a Renaissance showcase. The rubblescape of marble fragments scattered over the area of the Forum makes all but students of archaeology ask: is this the grandeur that was Rome? Just consider that much of the history fed to students the world over happened right here. This square—occasionally an enormous banquet hall where imperial Rome could be simultaneously entertained (as our times have observed thanks to such Hollywood epics as *Quo Vadis, Ben-Hur,* and *Cleopatra*)—was the birthplace of much of Western civilization. Roman law and powerful armies were created here, banishing the barbarian world for a millennium. Here, all Rome shouted as one, "Caesar has been murdered," and crowded to hear Mark Anthony's eulogy for the fallen leader. Legend has it that St. Paul traversed the Forum en route to his audience with Nero. After a more-than-27-centuries-long parade of pageantry, it is not surprising that Shelley and Gibbon reflected on the sense of *sic transit gloria mundi* (so passes away the glory of the world) on these same grounds.

Numbers in the text correspond to numbers in the margin and on the Rome map.

A Good Walk

Begin your walk on the **Capitoline Hill** ①—the site of Michelangelo's spectacular piazza and Rome's city hall, Palazzo Senatorio, which was built over the Tabularium, the ancient hall of records. Flanking the palazzo are both halves of Rome's most noteworthy museum complex, the **Musei Capitolini** ②, made up of the Museo Capitolino and the Palazzo dei Conservatori, which contain works of art gathered by Pope Sixtus IV, one of the earliest papal patrons of the arts. Off to the side of the Capitoline Hill, at the head of its formidable flight of steep steps, stands the ancient redbrick church of **Santa Maria d'Aracoeli** ③. Walk down the road to the left of Palazzo Senatorio and gaze out onto the remains of the Roman Forum. From there, steps descend to the gloomy **Carcere Mamertino** ④, the Mamertine Prison. The road leads out past the Forum of Caesar to Via dei Fori Imperiali. Across the street is the Forum of Trajan and the **Column of Trajan** ⑤. Continue along the Via dei Fori Imperiali, passing the Fora built by Augustus and Nerva, and cross back over the road to the entrance of the **Roman Forum** ⑥. At the end of the ancient Via Sacra is the entrance to the **Palatine Hill** ⑦, site of Rome's earliest settlement. Take the ramp that leads from the Forum–Palatine Hill area to the **Arch of Constantine** ⑧ and, beyond it, the **Colosseum** ⑨, one of antiquity's most famous monuments. Don't forget to check out the view from the park laid out over the ruins of Nero's **Domus Aurea** ⑩, his sumptuous palace, behind the Colosseum.

TIMING

It takes about 45 minutes to walk the route, plus one hour to visit the Musei Capitolini, from two to three hours to explore the Roman Forum and Palatine Hill, and a half hour to see the Colosseum.

Sights to See

❽ **Arch of Constantine** (Arco di Costantino). This imposing arch was erected in AD 315 to celebrate Constantine's (280–337) victory over Maxentius (died 312). The best preserved of Rome's triumphal arches, it is also the largest (69 ft high, 85 ft wide, and 23 ft deep) and one of the last great monuments of ancient Rome.

OFF THE BEATEN PATH

CIMITERO PROTESTANTO – Behind the *Piramide,* a stone pyramid built in 12 BC at the order of the Roman *praetor* (senior magistrate) who was buried there, is a cemetery reminiscent of a country churchyard that was for non-Catholics. You'll find Keats's tomb and the place where Shelley's heart was buried. It's about a 20-minute walk south from the Arch of Constantine along Via San Gregorio and Viale Aventino. ✉ *Via Caio Cestio 6,* ☎ *06/5741141 (ring bell for custodian).* 💴 *Offering of 500 lire–1,000 lire.* ⏲ *Tues.–Sun. 8–5:30.*

★ ❶ **Capitoline Hill** (Campidoglio). Though most of the buildings on Michelangelo's piazza date from the Renaissance, the hill was once the epicenter of the Roman Empire, the place where the city's first and holiest temples stood, including its most sacred, the Tempio di Giove (Temple of Jupiter). The city's archives were kept in the Tabularium (hall of records), the tall, gray-stone structure that forms the foundation of today's city hall, the **Palazzo Senatorio.** By the Middle Ages, the Campidoglio (the Capitol Hill), as the hill was already called then, had fallen into ruin. In 1537, Pope Paul III (1468–1549) decided to restore its grandeur for the triumphal entry into the city of Charles V (1500–58), the Holy Roman Emperor, and called upon Michelangelo to create the staircase ramp; the buildings and facades on three sides of the Campidoglio; the slightly convex pavement and its decoration; and the pedestal for the bronze equestrian statue of Marcus Aurelius. A work from the 2nd century AD, the statue stood here from the 16th century until 1981. The statue—the most celebrated equestrian bronze to survive from classical antiquity—was mistakenly believed to represent the Christian Emperor Constantine rather than the pagan Marcus Aurelius, hence its survival through the centuries. A legend foretells that some day the statue's original gold patina will return, heralding the end of the world. To forestall destiny, the city fathers had it restored and placed in the courtyard of the Museo Capitolino (☞ *below*), saving not only what was left of the gold, but also the statue's bronze, once seriously menaced by air pollution. A copy was placed on the original pedestal in 1997. As Michelangelo's preeminent urban set piece, the piazza sums up all the majesty of High Renaissance Rome.

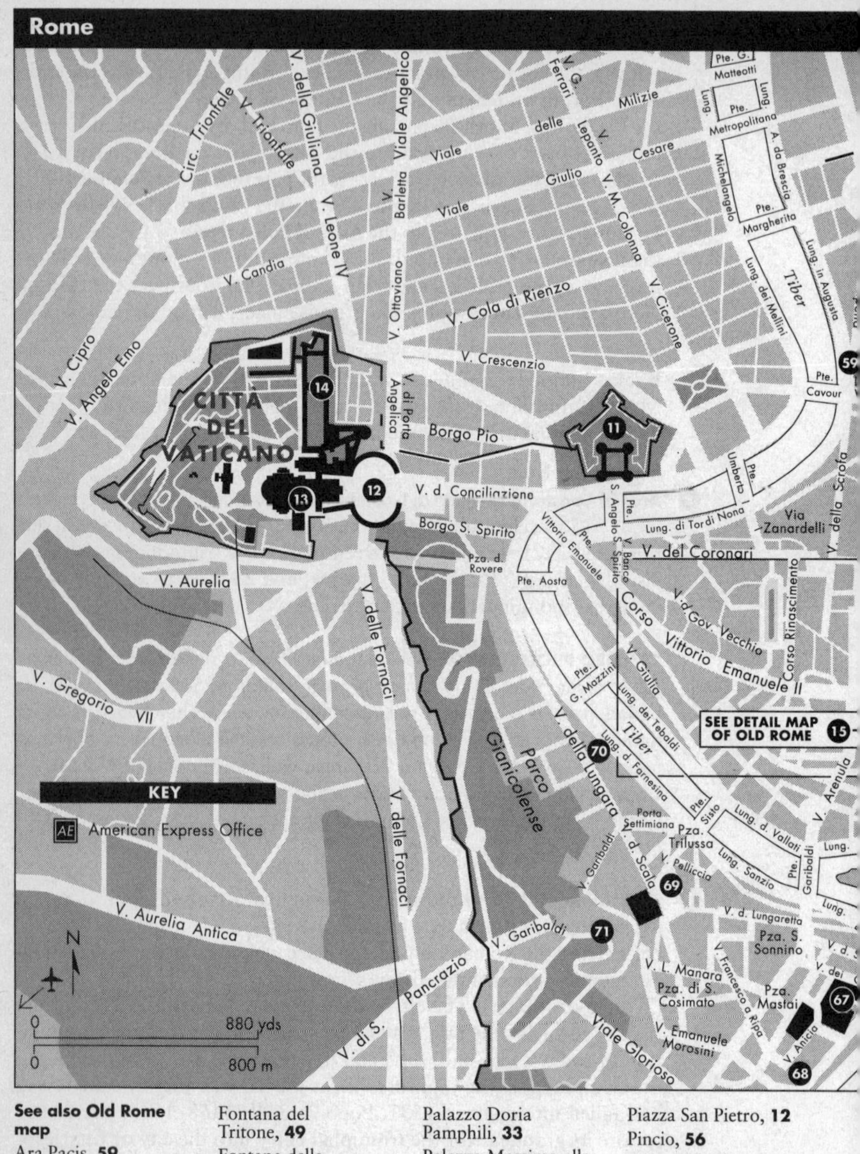

See also Old Rome map

Ara Pacis, **59**

Arch of Constantine, **8**

Capitoline Hill, **1**

Carcere Mamertino, **4**

Castel Sant'Angelo, **11**

Colosseum, **9**

Column of Marcus Aurelius, **35**

Column of Trajan, **5**

Domus Aurea, **10**

Fontana del Tritone, **49**

Fontana delle Tartarughe, **60**

Isola Tiberina, **66**

Keats-Shelley Memorial House, **37**

Monument to Vittorio Emanuele II, **30**

Musei Capitolini, **2**

Museo e Galleria Borghese, **55**

Palantine Hill, **7**

Palazzo Barberini, **48**

Palazzo Colonna, **32**

Palazzo Doria Pamphili, **33**

Palazzo Massimo alle Terme, **53**

Palazzo Pallavicini-Rospigliosi, **45**

Palazzo Venezia, **31**

Palazzo Zuccari, **38**

Piazza Bocca della Verità, **65**

Piazza del Popolo, **57**

Piazza della Repubblica, **52**

Piazza di Santa Maria in Trastevere, **69**

Piazza San Pietro, **12**

Pincio, **56**

Porta Pinciana, **54**

Quirinal Hill, **44**

Roman Forum, **6**

San Carlino alle Quattro Fontane, **47**

San Francesco a Ripa, **68**

San Giovanni in Laterano, **42**

San Pietro in Montorio, **71**

San Pietro in Vincoli, **40**

Santa Cecilia in Trastevere, **67**
Santa Maria d'Aracoeli, **3**
Santa Maria del Popolo, **58**
Santa Maria della Concezione, **50**
Santa Maria della Vittoria, **51**
Santa Maria Maggiore, **41**
Sant'Andrea, **46**
Sant'Ignazio, **34**
Scala Santa, **43**
Sinagoga, **61**
Spanish Steps, **36**
St. Peter's Basilica, **13**
Teatro di Marcello, **62**
Tempio della Fortuna Virilis, **63**
Tempio di Vesta, **64**
Trevi Fountain, **39**
Vatican Museums, **14**
Via Appia Antica, **72**
Villa Farnesina, **70**

4 **Carcere Mamertino** (Mamertine Prison). This series of gloomy, subterranean cells under a 17th-century church is where Rome's vanquished enemies were finished off. Some historians believe that St. Peter was held prisoner here, and legend has it that he miraculously brought forth a spring of water to baptize his jailers. ✉ *Via San Pietro in Carcere.* 🎫 *Donation requested.* ⏲ *Daily 9–12 and 2:30–6.*

Circus Maximus (Circo Massimo). In the giant arena laid out between Palatine and Aventine hills, more than 300,000 spectators watched chariot races while the emperor surveyed the scene from his palace on the Palatine Hill.

★ 9 **Colosseum** (Colosseo). Massive and majestic, ancient Rome's most famous monument was begun by the Flavian Emperor Vespasian (AD 7–79) in AD 72, and inaugurated eight years later with a program of games and shows lasting 100 days. More than 50,000 spectators could sit within the arena's 573-yard circumference, which was faced with marble, accented with hundreds of statues, and had a velarium—an ingenious system of sail-like awnings rigged on ropes manned by imperial sailors—to protect the audience from the sun and rain. Before the imperial box, gladiators would salute the emperor and cry, *"Ave, imperator, morituri te salutant"* (Hail, emperor, men soon to die salute thee); it is said that when one day they heard the Emperor Claudius respond, "or maybe not," they became so offended that they called a strike.

Originally known as the Flavian Amphitheater, it was called the Colosseum, as reported by the Venerable Bede in 730, after a truly colossal gilded bronze statue of Nero that stood in the vicinity until the end of the 6th century. The arena later served as a quarry from which materials were filched to build Renaissance-era churches and palaces. Finally, it was declared sacred by the Vatican in memory of the many Christians believed martyred there (scholars now maintain that no Christians met their death in the Colosseum, but rather in Rome's imperial circuses). During the 19th century, romantic poets lauded the glories of the amphitheater when viewed by moonlight. Now its arches glow at night with mellow golden spotlights—less romantic, perhaps, but still impressive. Portions of the arena will be closed during ongoing restoration. ✉ *Piazza del Colosseum,* ☎ *06/7004261.* 🎫 *10,000 lire.* ⏲ *Mon.–Sat. 9–2 hrs before sunset, Sun. 9–1.*

5 **Column of Trajan** (Colonna di Traiano). Trajan's ashes were buried inside the base of this column, built to commemorate the emperor and his military campaigns in Dacia (Romania). It stands in what was once the **Forum of Trajan** (Foro di Traiano), with its huge semicircular market building, adjacent to the ruins of the **Forum of Augustus** (Foro di Augusto). ✉ *Via dei Fori Imperiali and Via IV Novembre 6,* ☎ *06/67102802.* 🎫 *3,750 lire.* ⏲ *Tues.–Sun. 9–2 hrs before sunset.*

10 **Domus Aurea** (Golden House). On the Colle Oppio (Oppian Hill), a ridge of the Monte Esquilino (Esquiline Hill), are faint traces of Nero's grandiose palace—later buried under Terme di Traiano (Baths of Trajan)—which was built after the great fire of AD 64 destroyed much of the city. (Incidentally, historians now believe Nero to be blameless in this event.) It was a structure so huge it evoked the complaint, "All Rome has become a villa." ✉ *Colle Oppio,* ☎ *06/4815576 tickets.* 🎫 *About 5,000 lire.* ⏲ *Daily 9–8.*

Forum of Caesar (Foro di Cesare). Caesar built this forum, including a temple dedicated to himself and the goddess Minerva, to expand the then crowded original Roman Forum, which had been built up over the preceding five hundred years. In doing so, Caesar set a trend that several emperors followed, building what are now called the Imperial Fora.

2 **Musei Capitolini** (Capitoline Museums). The collections in the twin Museo Capitolino and Palazzo dei Conservatori were assembled in the 15th century by Pope Sixtus IV (1414–84), one of the earliest of the great papal patrons of the arts. Although parts of the collection may excite only archaeologists and art historians, others contain some of the most famous pieces of classical sculpture, such as the poignant *Dying Gaul,* the regal *Capitoline Venus* (recently identified as another Mediterranean beauty, Cleopatra herself), and the delicate *Marble Faun* that inspired 19th-century novelist Nathaniel Hawthorne's novel of the same name. Remember that many of the works here and in Rome's other museums were copied from Greek originals. For hundreds of years, craftsmen of ancient Rome prospered by producing copies of Greek statues using a process called "pointing," by which exact replicas could be created to order.

Portraiture, however, was one area in which the Romans outstripped the Greeks. The hundreds of Roman portrait busts of emperors in the Sala degli Imperatori and of philosophers in the Sala dei Filosofi of the **Museo Capitolino** constitute a "Who's Who" of the ancient world. Within these serried ranks are 48 Roman emperors, ranging from Augustus to Theodosius (346–395). Many of them were eminently forgettable, but some were men of genius; a few added nothing to the Roman way of life except new ways of dying. On one console, you'll see the handsomely austere Augustus, who "found Rome a city of brick and left it one of marble." On another rests Claudius "the stutterer," an indefatigable builder brought vividly to life in Robert Graves's (1895–1985) *I, Claudius.* In this company is also Nero, most notorious of the emperors—though by no means the worst—who built for himself the fabled Domus Aurea (☞ *above*). And, of course, the baddies: cruel Caligula (AD 12–41) and Caracalla (a.k.a. Marcus Aurelius), and the dissolute, eerily modern boy-emperor, Heliogabalus.

Unlike the Greeks, whose portraits are idealized and usually beautiful, the Romans belonged to the "warts and all" school of representation. Many of the busts that have come down to us, seen clearly in that of Commodus (AD 161–192), the emperor-gladiator (found in a gallery on the upper level of the museum), are nearly savage in the relentlessness of their portrayals. As you leave the museum, be sure to stop in the courtyard. To the right is the original equestrian statue of Marcus Aurelius, restored and safely kept behind glass. At the center of the courtyard is the gigantic, reclining figure of Oceanus, found in the Roman Forum and later dubbed Marforio, one of Rome's famous "talking statues" to which citizens from the 1500s up to the 20th century affixed anonymous notes of political protest and satirical verses.

The **Palazzo dei Conservatori** is a trove of ancient and Baroque treasures. Lining the courtyard are the colossal fragments of a head, leg, foot, and hand—all that remains of the famous statue of the Emperor Constantine the Great, who believed that Rome's future lay with Christianity. These immense effigies were much in vogue in the later days of the Roman Empire. The resplendent Salone dei Orazi e Curiazi (Salon of Horatii and Curatii) on the first floor is a ceremonial hall with a magnificent gilt ceiling, carved wooden doors, and 16th-century frescoes. At either end of the hall reign statues of the Baroque Age's most charismatic popes, Bernini's (1598–1680) marble effigy of Urban VIII (1568–1644) and his rival Algardi's (1595–1654) bronze statue of Innocent X (1574–1655). The world-renowned symbol of Rome, the *Capitoline Wolf,* a 6th-century-BC Etruscan bronze, holds a place of honor in the museum; the suckling twins were added during the Renaissance to adapt the statue to the legend of Romulus and Remus (☞

Palatine Hill, *below*). ✉ *Piazza del Campidoglio,* ☎ *06/67102071.* 🎫 *10,000 lire, free last Sun. of month.* ⏲ *Tues.–Sun. 9–7.*

7 **Palatine Hill.** A lane known as the Clivus Palatinus, whose worn paving stones were once trod by emperors and their slaves, climbs from the Forum area to a site that historians identify with Rome's earliest settlement. About a century ago, illustrious archaeologist Rodolfo Lanciani excavated a site on the Palatine Hill and found evidence testifying to Romulus's historical presence, thereby contradicting early critics who deemed Romulus to be a myth. The story goes that the twins Romulus and Remus were abandoned as infants but were nursed by a she wolf on the banks of the Tiber and adopted by a shepherd. Encouraged by the gods to build a city, the twins chose a site in 735 BC, fortifying it with a wall that Lanciani identified by digging on the Palatine Hill. During the building of the city, the brothers quarreled, and in a fit of anger Romulus killed Remus.

Despite its location overlooking the Forum with its traffic, congestion, and attendant noise, the Palatine Hill was the most coveted address for ancient Rome's rich and famous. More than a few of the 12 Caesars called the Palatine Hill home—including Caligula, who met his premature end in the Cryptoporticus tunnel, which today still stands and remains unnerving. The palace of Tiberius was the first to be built here; others followed, most notably the gigantic extravaganza constructed for Emperor Domitian. Views from the ruins of the Imperial palaces extend over the Circus Maximus (☞ *above*). Today the Palatine is one of the most tranquil places in town, its Renaissance gardens a welcome respite, especially on a hot day. The recently restored Palatine Antiquarium holds relics found during excavations on the hill. ✉ *Entrance at the Arch of Titus in the Roman Forum,* ☎ *06/6990110.* 🎫 *12,000 lire.* ⏲ *Mon.–Sat. 9–2 hrs before sunset, Sun 9–1.*

6 **Roman Forum** (Foro Romano). In what was once a marshy valley between the Capitoline and Palatine hills, this was the civic heart of Republican Rome, the austere enclave that preceded the hedonistic society that grew up under the emperors in the 1st to the 4th century AD. Today it seems no more than a baffling series of ruins, marble fragments, isolated columns, a few worn arches, and occasional paving stones. Yet it once was filled with stately and magnificent buildings—temples, palaces, shops—and crowded with people from all corners of the world. What you see today are the ruins not of one period, but of almost 900 years, from about 500 BC to AD 400. Making sense of these scarred and pitted stones is not easy; you may want just to wander along, letting your imagination dwell on Cicero (106–43 BC), Julius Caesar (100–44 BC), and Mark Anthony (circa 81–30 BC), who delivered the funeral address in Caesar's honor from the rostrum just left of the **Arco di Settimio Severo** (Arch of Septimius Severus).

One of the grandest of all antiquity, this arch was built in AD 203 to celebrate victory of the Emperor Severus (AD 146–211) over the Parthians, and was topped by a bronze equestrian statuary group with six horses. Most visitors also explore the reconstruction of the large brick senate hall, the **Curia**; the three Corinthian columns (a favorite of 19th-century poets), all that remains of the **Tempio di Vespasiano** (Temple of Vespasian); the circular **Tempio di Vesta** (Temple of Vesta), where the highly privileged vestal virgins kept the sacred flame alive; and the **Arco di Tito** (Arch of Titus), which stands in a slightly elevated position on a spur of Palatine Hill. The view of the Colosseum from the arch is superb and reminds us that it was the Emperor Titus (AD 39–81) who helped finish the vast amphitheater, begun earlier by his father, Vespasian. Now cleaned and restored, the arch was erected in

AD 81 to celebrate the sack of Jerusalem 10 years earlier, after the great Jewish revolt. A famous relief shows the captured contents of Herod's Temple—including its huge seven-branched menorah—being carried in triumph down Rome's Via Sacra. Audio guides are available at bookshop-ticket office at Via dei Fori Imperiali entrance. ✉ *Entrances at Via dei Fori Imperiali and Piazza del Colosseum,* ☎ *06/6990110.* *Free.* ⏲ *Mon.–Sat. 9–2 hrs before sunset, Sun. 9–1.*

3 **Santa Maria d'Aracoeli.** This stark, redbrick church is one of the first Christian churches in Rome. Legend recounts that it was on this spot that the Sybil predicted to Augustus the coming of a Redeemer. The emperor responded by erecting the Ara Coeli, the Altar of Heaven. The Aracoeli is best known for Pinturicchio's (1454–1513) 15th-century frescoes in the first chapel on the right. ✉ *Piazza d'Aracoeli.* ⏲ *Oct.–May, daily 7–noon and 4–6; June–Sept., daily 7–noon and 4–6:30.*

The Vatican: Rome of the Popes

You might go to the Vatican to behold a work of art—Michelangelo's frescoes, rare archaeological marbles, or Bernini's statues. Others make the pilgrimage to find their souls in the most overwhelming architectural achievement of the Renaissance, St. Peter's Basilica. In between these two extremes lies a sight for every taste and inclination. Museum rooms decorated by Raphael, antique sculptures like the *Apollo Belvedere* and the *Laocoön,* walls daubed by Fra Angelico, paintings by Giotto and Leonardo, and chief among revered *non plus ultras,* the ceiling of the Sistine Chapel: for the lover of beauty, few places are as historically important as this epitome of faith and grandeur. What gave all this impetus was a new force that emerged as the emperors of ancient Rome presided over their declining empire: Christianity came to Rome. Note that dress rules must be adhered to in St. Peter's (☞ St. Peter's Basilica, *below*).

A Good Walk

Start your walk at the **Castel Sant'Angelo** ⑪, the fortress that once served as the pope's refuge, and take in the beauty of the Ponte Sant'Angelo before turning right onto Via della Conciliazione (or taking the more picturesque route west along Borgo Pio) to the Vatican. Once inside **Piazza San Pietro** ⑫, rich architectural detail awaits at **St. Peter's Basilica** ⑬, the largest church of Christendom. Below the church, visit the Vatican Grottoes, the last repose of many of the popes, and, if you have time, arrange a tour of the excavations below the church and the Vatican Gardens.

TIMING

Allow an hour for a visit to Castel Sant'Angelo. You'll need an hour to see St. Peter's, plus 30 minutes for the Museo Storico, 15 minutes for the Vatican Grottoes, and an hour to climb to the top of the dome. Note that free one-hour English-language tours of the basilica are offered Monday–Saturday at 10 and 3, Sunday at 2:30 (sign up at the little desk under the portico).

Sights to See

11 **Castel Sant'Angelo** (Castle of the Holy Angel). For hundreds of years this fortress guarded the Vatican, to which it is linked by the Passetto, an arcaded passageway. According to legend, Castel Sant'Angelo got its name during the plague of 590, when Pope Gregory the Great (circa 540–604), passing by in a religious procession, had a vision of an angel sheathing its sword atop the stone ramparts. Though it may look like a stronghold, Castel Sant'Angelo was in fact built as a tomb for the Emperor Hadrian (76–138) in AD 135. By the 6th century, it

Close-Up

JUBILEE 2000

THE GRANDE GIUBILEO DELL'ANNO 2000 (Great Jubilee of the Year 2000) will bring an estimated 35 million pilgrims to Rome to visit the major basilicas, see the pope, and pay homage to the tomb of St. Peter. Both the city of Rome and the Vatican—which, you must remember, are two separate entities—are working together to see that these record crowds can be welcomed, housed, fed, and moved about more or less efficiently.

While the Vatican has been quietly going ahead with its plans, cleaning up the front of St. Peter's, installing a new entrance-exit system for the Vatican Museums, and organizing the practical aspects of the Holy Year program, Rome's administrators have had to cope with glitches. A projected underpass that would have sped traffic past a perennial bottleneck at Castel Sant'Angelo and a new Metro line in the city center are among the public works that have been scrapped (archaeological risk and delays the main culprits). On the bright side, part of the funds for these projects will instead be spent on improving tourist services for getting hotels and information. More welcome fallout are the extended hours at several major city museums and promises to revamp public transportation lines.

The city has pledged to do what it calls a "restyling" of the areas around the basilicas and will enlarge the Termini Metro station. Even before 1998, city sprucing-up projects saw many monuments and churches shrouded for restoration and several museums undergoing refurbishment. On the eastern outskirts of Rome at Tor Tre Teste, where many nonpilgrims will not venture, an important new church is being built as a symbol of the Jubilee. Designed by Richard Meier, it, too, was started behind schedule, so heavenly intervention may be required to get it finished on time.

Opening ceremonies begin before midnight on December 24, 1999, when the pope strikes the Holy Door with a silver hammer, symbolically opening it. The door will remain open for 54 weeks. Special prayer vigils will be held in the basilica on December 31, 1999 and December 31, 2000; on both occasions, the bells of the world's Roman Catholic churches will be rung at midnight. The Holy Doors at the other patriarchal churches will also be opened: San Giovanni in Laterano and Santa Maria Maggiore on December 25, 1999, and San Paolo fuori le Mura January 18, 2000. St. Peter's feast day on June 29 is sure to be a major celebration, with up to 250,000 people packed into Piazza San Pietro for a papal mass. August 19–20, the culmination of the weeklong Youth Jubilee, will draw some 2 million young people for a mega-prayer meeting at a site on the city's outskirts. The Holy Year will end with the closing of the Holy Door by the pope on January 6, 2001, in St. Peter's. Closing ceremonies at the three other major basilicas in Rome will be held the preceding day, January 5.

THE POPE SHOULD BE IN ROME most of the year, with the exception of his much-heralded visit to the Holy Land. Every evening throughout the Holy Year, the pope will appear at a window of the Palazzo Vaticano to pray with and bless pilgrims in the square. For up-to-date Jubilee information, contact the **Vatican Information Office** (✉ Piazza San Pietro, ☎ 06/69884466), open Monday–Saturday 8:30–7, and pick up Fodor's ***Holy Rome: A Millennium Guide to the Christian Sights,*** a Jubilee handbook that carries the imprimatur of Italy's Official Agency for the Preparation for the Jubilee (also ☞ Jubilee 2000 *in* Pleasures and Pastimes, *above*).

had been transformed into a fortress, and it remained a refuge for the popes for almost 1,000 years. It has dungeons, battlements, cannons and cannonballs, and a collection of antique weaponry and armor.

The upper terrace, below the massive bronze angel commemorating Gregory's vision, evokes memories of Tosca, Puccini's poignant heroine in the opera of the same name, who threw herself off these ramparts with the cry, "*Scarpia, avanti a Dio!*" ("Scarpia, we meet before God!"). One of Rome's most beautiful bridges, **Ponte Sant'Angelo** spans the Tiber in front of the fortress and is studded with graceful angels designed by Bernini.

The lower levels formed the base of Hadrian's mausoleum; ancient ramps and narrow staircases climb through the castle's core to courtyards and frescoed halls and rooms holding a collection of antique arms and armor. Off the loggia is a café. ✉ *Lungotevere Castello 50,* ☎ *06/6819111.* 🎫 *8,000 lire.* ⊙ *Tues.–Sun. 9–7.*

Papal Audience. Pope John Paul II holds mass audiences on Wednesday mornings at 10 in a large modern audience hall or in St. Peter's Square in summer. You must apply for tickets in advance; there are several sources (☞ *below*), but if you are pressed for time, it may be easier to arrange for them through a travel agency. You can avoid the formalities by seeing the pope when he makes his weekly appearance at the window of the Palazzo Vaticano, every Sunday at noon when he is in Rome, to bless the crowd. On summer Sundays he may give the blessing at his summer residence at Castel Gandolfo. For audience tickets, apply in writing well in advance to the **Papal Prefecture** (Prefettura della Casa Pontificia, ✉ 00120 Vatican City, ☎ 06/69883017, FAX 06/69885863), indicating the date you prefer, the language you speak, and the hotel where you will be staying. Or go to the prefecture, through the Porta di Bronzo, the bronze door at the end of the colonnade on the right side of the piazza; the office is open Monday–Saturday 9–1, and last-minute tickets may be available. You can also arrange to pick up free tickets on Tuesday afternoon at **Santa Susanna American Church** (✉ Piazza San Bernardo, ☎ 06/4882748). For a fee, travel agencies make arrangements that include transportation (☞ Guided Tours *in* Rome A to Z, *below*).

12 **Piazza San Pietro** (St. Peter's Square). As you enter the square you are entering Vatican territory. This square (actually an oval) is one of Bernini's most spectacular masterpieces. Completed in 1667, after 11 years' work—a relatively short time in those days, considering the vastness of the task—the square can hold 400,000 people. It is surrounded by a curving pair of quadruple colonnades, which are topped by a balustrade and statues of 140 saints. Look for the two stone disks set into the pavement on either side of the obelisk. If you stand on one disk, a trick of perspective makes the colonnades seem to consist of a single row of columns. Bernini had an even grander visual effect in mind when he designed the square. By opening up this immense, airy, and luminous space in a neighborhood of narrow, shadowy streets, he created a contrast that would surprise and impress anyone who emerged from the darkness into the light, in a characteristically Baroque metaphor. But in the 1930s, Mussolini ruined it all. To celebrate the "conciliation" between the Vatican and the Italian government under the Lateran Pact of 1929, he conceived of Via della Conciliazione, the broad, rather soulless avenue that now forms the main approach to St. Peter's and gives the eye time to adjust to the enormous dimensions of the square and church, nullifying Bernini's grand Baroque effect.

★ 13 **St. Peter's Basilica** (Basilica di San Pietro). The physical statistics of Rome's sublime sanctuary are staggering: it covers about 18,100 square yards, extends 212 yards in length, and carries a dome that rises 435 ft and measures 138 ft across its base. Its history is equally impressive: no fewer than five of Italy's greatest artists—Donato Bramante (1444–1514), Raphael (1483–1520), Peruzzi (1481–1536), Antonio Sangallo the Younger (1483–1546), and Michelangelo (1475–1564)—died during the course of construction of this new St. Peter's. The history of the original St. Peter's goes back to the year AD 319, when the emperor Constantine built a basilica over the site of the tomb of St. Peter (died AD 64). This early church stood for more than 1,000 years, undergoing a number of restorations, until it was on the verge of collapse. Reconstruction began in 1452, but was abandoned due to a lack of funds. In 1506 Pope Julius II (1443–1513) instructed the architect Bramante to raze the existing structure and build a new and greater basilica. In 1546 Pope Paul III persuaded the aging Michelangelo to take on the job of completing the building. Returning to Bramante's ground plan, Michelangelo designed the dome to cover the crossing, but his plans, too, were modified after his death. The cupola, one of the most beautiful in the world, was completed by Giacomo della Porta (circa 1537–1602) and Fontana. The new church wasn't completed and dedicated until 1626—by that time the design had shifted from a Greek cross plan to a Latin cross plan, creating a larger nave but obscuring the view of the dome from the piazza. Under the portico, Filarete's 15th-century bronze doors, salvaged from the old basilica, are in the central portal. Off the entry portico, Bernini's famous *Scala Regia,* the ceremonial entryway to the Vatican Palace and one of the most magnificent staircases in the world, is graced with Bernini's dramatic statue of Constantine the Great.

The cherubs over the holy-water fonts will give you an idea of just how huge St. Peter's is: the sole of the cherub's foot is as long as the distance from your fingers to your elbow. It is because the proportions of this giant building are in such perfect harmony that its vastness may escape you at first. But in its megascale—inspired by the spatial volumes of ancient Roman ruins—it reflects Roman *grandiosità* in all its majesty.

The scale of the aisles and decoration and the vast sweep of the dome over the ceremonial entrance to the crypt, which is surrounded by votive lamps, bring home the point that St. Peter's is much more than a church; it was intended to function as the glorious setting for all the pomp and panoply of ecclesiastical ceremony. Indeed, only when it serves as the brightly lit background for a great gathering do its vast dimensions find their full expression.

Over an altar in a side chapel is Michelangelo's **Pietà.** It is difficult to determine whether this moving work, sculpted when he was only 22, owes more to the man's art than to his faith. As we contemplate this masterpiece we are able to understand a little better that art and faith sometimes partake of the same impulse.

Four massive piers support the dome at the crossing, where the mighty Bernini **baldacchino** (canopy) rises high above the papal altar. "What the barbarians didn't do, the Barberini did," 17th-century wags quipped when Barberini Pope Urban VIII had the bronze stripped from the Pantheon's portico and melted down to make the baldacchino (using what was left over for cannonballs). The pope celebrates mass here, over the grottoes holding the tombs of many of his predecessors. Deep in the excavations under the foundations of the original basilica is what is believed to be the tomb of St. Peter. The bronze throne above the main altar in the apse, the Cathedra Petri (Chair of St. Peter), is Bernini's work (1656) and it covers a wooden and ivory chair that St. Peter himself is said to have used. However, scholars tell us that this throne probably dates only from the Middle Ages. See how the adoration of a million lips has completely worn down the bronze on the right foot of the statue of St. Peter in front of the near right pillar in the transept. *Note: ushers at the entrance of St. Peter's Church and the Vatican Museums will not allow entry to persons with inappropriate clothing (no bare knees or shoulders).* ⏲ *Apr.–Sept., daily 7–7; Oct.–Mar., daily 7–6. Closed during ceremonies in the piazza.*

The entrance to the **Vatican Grottoes** (Grotte Vaticane), which hold the tombs of many popes, is at the crossing. The only exit from the grottoes leads outside St. Peter's, to the courtyard that holds the entrance to the roof and dome. ⏲ *Apr.–Sept., daily 7–6; Oct.–Mar., daily 7–5.*

A small but rich collection of Vatican treasures is housed in the **Museo Storico** (Historical Museum) in the Sacristy, among them precious antique chalices and the massive 15th-century sculptured bronze tomb of Pope Sixtus V (1520–90) by Antonio del Pollaiuolo (1431–98). 🎟 *8,000 lire.* ⏲ *Apr.–Sept., daily 9–6; Oct.–Mar., daily 9–5.*

The roof of the church, reached by elevator or stairs, is a landscape of domes and towers. A short interior staircase leads to the base of the dome for a dove's-eye view of the interior of St. Peter's. Then, only if you are stout of heart and sound of lung should you attempt the very taxing and claustrophobic climb up the narrow stairs—there's no turning back!—to the balcony of the lantern, where the view embraces the Vatican Gardens and all of Rome. 🎟 *Elevator 6,000 lire, stairs 5,000 lire.* ⏲ *Apr.–Sept., daily 8–6; Oct.–Mar., daily 8–5.*

OFF THE BEATEN PATH

VATICAN NECROPOLIS – Visit St. Peter's Tombs and the Pre-Constantine Necropolis under St. Peter's for a fascinating glimpse of the underpinnings of the great basilica, which was built over the cemetery where archaeologists say they have found St. Peter's tomb. Apply in advance by sending a fax with the name of each visitor, possible days for the visit, and a local phone number. They will confirm reservations a few days in advance. Tickets are sometimes available for same-day tours; apply in person at the Ufficio Scavi (Excavations Office), which is on the right beyond the Arco delle Campane (Arch of the Bells) entrance to the Vatican, which is left of the basilica. Tell the Swiss guard you want the Ufficio Scavi, and he will let you by. ☎ *06/69885318,* FAX *06/69885518.* 🎟 *15,000 lire.* ⏲ *Ufficio Scavi: Mon.–Sat. 9–5.*

Vatican Gardens (Giardini Vaticani). A tour offers a two-hour jaunt through the pope's backyard, half by bus and half on foot, with a guide. Tickets are available at the **Vatican Information Office** (✉ Piazza San Pietro, ☎ 06/69884466), open Monday–Saturday 8:30–7. Make reservations two or three days in advance. 🎟 *18,000 lire.* ⏲ *Apr.–Oct., Mon., Tues., Thurs.–Sat. at 10; Nov.–Mar., Sat. at 10, weekdays on request for groups.*

Vatican Museums: Beyond the Sistine Ceiling

The Vatican Palace has been the papal residence since 1377. Actually, it represents a collection of buildings that cover more than 13 acres, containing an estimated (no one has bothered to count them) 1,400 rooms, chapels, and galleries. Other than the pope and his papal court, the occupants are some of the most famous art masterpieces in the world. The main entrance to the museums, on Viale Vaticano, is a long walk from Piazza San Pietro. Some city buses stop near the museums' main entrance on Viale Vaticano: Bus 49 from Piazza Cavour stops right in front; Bus 80 and Tram 19 stop at Piazza Risorgimento, halfway between St. Peter's and the museums. The Ottaviano–S. Pietro stop on Metro A also is in the vicinity.

A Good Tour

Beyond the Sistine Chapel, many sections of the **Vatican Museums** ⑭ are not to be overlooked: the Museo Egiziano; the Chiaramonti and Museo Pio Clementino, which are given over to classical sculptures (among them some of the best-known statues in the world—the *Laocoön,* the *Belvedere Torso,* and the *Apollo Belvedere*—works that, with their vibrant humanism, had a tremendous impact on Renaissance art); and the Museo Etrusco. Finally, you should make sure to visit the Stanze di Raffaello, and see Raphael's paintings in the Pinacoteca.

TIMING

As you are no longer required to follow itineraries (though this is subject to change), it's now possible to walk everywhere in absolute freedom, although guardians will close the shortcut to the Sistine Chapel if the museums get goo crowded. Plan on about an hour if you just want to see highlights, and an in-depth visit will take at least a full morning. To minimize time spent in line, it is usually a good idea to get there just before opening time.

Sights to See

★ ⑭ **Vatican Museums** (Musei Vaticani). The immense collections housed here are so rich that unless you are an art history buff, you will probably just be able to skim the surface, concentrating on pieces that strike your fancy. The Sistine Chapel is a must, of course, and that's why you may have to wait in line to see it; after all, every tourist in Rome has the same idea. Pick up a leaflet at the main entrance to the museums to see the overall layout. The Sistine Chapel is at the far end of the complex, and the leaflet charts two abbreviated itineraries through other collections to reach it. You can rent a taped commentary (6,000 lire, about 90 minutes) in English for the Sistine Chapel, the Stanze di Raffaello, and the main attractions.

The **Galleria delle Carte Geografiche** (Gallery of Maps) is intriguing; the **Appartamento di S. Pio V** (Apartment of Pope Pius V) a little less so. The **Stanze di Raffaello** (Raphael Rooms) are second only to the Sistine Chapel in artistic interest. In 1508, Pope Julius II employed Raphael, on the recommendation of Bramante, to decorate the rooms with biblical scenes. The result was a Renaissance tour de force. Of the four rooms, the second and third were decorated mainly by Raphael. The others were decorated by Giulio Romano (circa 1499–1546) and other assistants of Raphael; the first room is known as the Stanza dell'Incendio, with frescoes of the fire (*incendio*) in the Borgo by Romano.

It's hard to overstate the importance of the **Stanza della Segnatura** (Room of the Signature) where papal bulls were signed. When people talk about the High Renaissance—thought by many to be the pinnacle of Western art—these frescoes often come up. The theme of the room—which may broadly be said to be "enlightenment"—reflects the fact that this was Julius's private library. Theology triumphs in the fresco known as the *Disputa,* or *Debate on the Holy Sacrament.* The *School of Athens* glorifies some of philosophy's greatest exponents, including Plato and Aristotle at the fresco's center. The pensive figure on the stairs is sometimes thought to be modeled on Michelangelo, who was painting the Sistine Ceiling at the same time Raphael was working here. All the revolutionary characteristics of High Renaissance paintings are here: naturalism (Raphael's figures lack the awkwardness that pictures painted only a few years earlier still contained); humanism (the idea that man is the most noble and admirable of God's creatures); and a profound interest in the ancient world, the result of the 15th-century rediscovery of archaeology and classical antiquity. There's a tendency to go into something of a stupor when confronted with "great art" of this kind. The fact remains that the frescoes in this room virtually dared its occupants to aspire to the highest ideas of law and learning—an amazing feat for an artist not yet 30.

The tiny **Cappella di Nicholas V** (Chapel of Nicholas V) is aglow with frescoes by Fra Angelico (1387–1455), the Florentine monk whose sensitive paintings were guiding lights for the Renaissance. The **Appartamento Borgia** (Borgia Apartment) is worth seeing for the elaborately painted ceilings, designed and partially executed by Pinturicchio, but the rooms have been given over to the Vatican's large, but not particularly impressive, collection of modern religious art.

In 1508, while Raphael was put to work on his series of rooms, the redoubtable Pope Julius II commissioned Michelangelo to fresco the more than 10,000 square ft of the **Sistine Chapel** (Cappella Sistina) ceiling singlehandedly. The task took four years of mental and physical anguish. It's said that for years afterward Michelangelo couldn't read anything without holding it up over his head. The result, however, was the masterpiece that you can now see, its colors cool and brilliant after restoration. Bring a pair of binoculars to get a better look at this incredible work (unfortunately, you're not allowed to lie down on the floor to study the frescoes above, the viewing position of choice in decades past; by the time you leave the chapel, your neck may feel like Michelangelo's, so you may also want to study it—to take a cue from 19th-century visitors—with the aid of a pocket mirror).

The ceiling is literally a painted Bible: Michelangelo's subject was the story of humanity before the coming of Christ, seen through Augustinian tenets of faith popular in early 16th-century theological circles. While some of the frescoed panels are veritable stews of figures, others—especially the depiction of God's outstretched hand giving Adam the spark of life in the *Creation of Adam*—are forcefully simple, revealing how much Michelangelo imparted on the school of painting from the discipline of sculpture. In 1541, some 30 years after completing the ceiling, Michelangelo was commissioned to paint the *Last Judgment* on the wall over the altar. If the artist's ceiling may be taken as an expression of the optimism of the High Renaissance, the *Last Judgment,* by contrast, is a virtual guided tour through Hell. This is not surprising, since in the intervening years Rome had been sacked and pillaged by the French (who had used the Sistine Chapel to stable their horses).

In the interim, the grim Counter-Reformation movement had been adopted by the Church, and the papal court was now so offended by the nakedness of Michelangelo's *Last Judgment* figures that they hired artist Daniele da Volterra (1509–1566)—forever after known as *il braghettone* (the breeches-maker)—to paint loincloths over the offending parts. The aged and embittered artist painted his own face on the wrinkled human skin in the hand of St. Bartholomew, below and to the right of the figure of Christ, which he clearly modeled on the *Apollo Belvedere* (now on exhibit in the Vatican galleries). Like the ceiling, the *Last Judgment* has been cleaned, surprising viewers with its clarity and color after restorers unveiled their work in April 1994. Was Michelangelo a master of vibrant color? Or is the "new" Sistine a travesty of Michelangelo's intentions? Opinions remain divided, but most art historians believe the restoration is true to Michelangelo's original vision.

The exhibition halls of the **Biblioteca Vaticana** (Vatican Library) are bright with frescoes and contain a sampling of the library's rich collections of precious manuscripts. Room X, Room of the Aldobrandini Marriage, holds a beautiful Roman fresco of a nuptial rite. More classical statues are on view in the new wing. At the Quattro Cancelli, a cafeteria offers a well-earned break. The **Pinacoteca** (Picture Gallery) displays mainly religious paintings by such artists as Giotto (circa 1266–1337), Fra Angelico, and Filippo Lippi (circa 1406–69), and Raphael's exceptional *Transfiguration, Coronation,* and *Foligno Madonna.*

In the **Museo Profano** (Pagan Antiquities Museum), modern display techniques enhance another collection of Greek and Roman sculptures. The **Museo Pio Cristiano** (Christian Antiquities Museum) has early Christian and medieval art (its most famous piece is the 3rd-century AD statue, the *Good Shepherd*). The **Museo Missionario-Etnologico** (Ethnological Museum) exhibits art and artifacts from exotic places throughout the world; it's open Wednesday and Saturday only. The complete itinerary ends with the **Museo della Storia** (Historical Museum), whose collection of carriages, uniforms, and arms can be opened by a custodian on request. In all, the Vatican Museums offer a staggering foray into the realms of art and history; it's foolhardy to try to see all the collections in one day. ⊠ *Viale Vaticano,* ☎ *06/69883041.* *15,000 lire; free last Sun. of month.* ⏲ *Easter wk and mid-Mar.–Oct., weekdays 8:45–3:45, Sat. 8:45–12:45; Nov.–mid-Mar. (except Easter), Mon.–Sat. 8:45–12:45; last Sun. of every month 8:45–12:45. Closed religious holidays (Jan. 1 and 6, Feb. 11, Mar. 19, Easter Sun. and Mon., May 1, Ascension Thurs., Corpus Christi, June 29, Aug. 15 and 16, Nov. 1, Dec. 8, Dec. 25 and 26) and Sun., excepting last Sun. of month. Note: Ushers at the entrance of St. Peter's Church and the Vatican Museums will not allow entry to persons with inappropriate clothing (no bare knees or shoulders).*

NEED A BREAK? Neighborhood trattorias that are far better and far less popular with tourists than those opposite the Vatican Museums entrance include **Hostaria Dino e Toni** (⊠ Via Leone IV 60), where you can dine on typical Roman fare at moderate, even inexpensive prices. **La Caravella** (⊠ Via degli Scipioni 32 at Via Vespasiano, off Piazza Risorgimento) serves Roman specialties, including pizza during lunch, every day but Thursday, when it's closed.

Old Rome: Gold and Grandeur

The neighborhood between the Corso and the Tiber bend is one of Rome's most beautiful districts, thick with narrow streets with curious names, airy Baroque piazzas, and picturesque courtyards. It has been an integral part of the city since ancient times, and its position between the Vatican and the Lateran palaces, both seats of papal rule, puts it in the mainstream of Rome's development from the Middle Ages onward. It includes such world-famous sights as the Pantheon, but it is mainly an excursion into the 16th and 17th centuries, when Baroque art triumphed. Some of Rome's most coveted residential addresses are here.

The most important clue to the Romans is their Baroque art—not its artistic technicalities, but its spirit. When you understand that, you will no longer be a stranger in Rome. Flagrantly emotional, heavily expressive, and sensuously visual, the 17th-century artistic movement known as the Baroque was born in Rome, the creation of three geniuses, the sculptor and architect Gianlorenzo Bernini and the painters Annibale Carracci (1560–1609) and Caravaggio (1573–1610). From the austere drama found in Caravaggio's paintings to the jewel-laden, gold-on-gold detail of 17th-century Roman palaces, Baroque style was intended to both shock and delight by upsetting the placid, "correct" rules of the Renaissance. By appealing to the emotions, it became a powerful weapon in the hands of the Counter-Reformation.

Numbers in the text correspond to numbers in the margin and on the Old Rome map.

A Good Walk

Start on Via del Plebiscito, near Piazza Venezia, at the huge church of **Il Gesù** ⑮, the grandmother of all Baroque churches. Walk north to Piazza della Minerva, where in the church of **Santa Maria sopra Minerva** ⑯ you will find the tomb of Fra Angelico. Turn down Via della Minerva to reach the **Pantheon** ⑰. From Piazza della Rotonda in front of the Pantheon, take Via Giustiniani onto Via della Dogana Vecchia to the church of **San Luigi dei Francesi** ⑱, a pilgrimage spot for art lovers everywhere. Just north is the church of **Sant'Agostino** ⑲, in the piazza of the same name. Check out historic **Palazzo Altemps** ⑳, off Piazza Sant'Apollinare, before arriving at **Piazza Navona** ㉑, one of Rome's showpiece piazzas, home to Bernini's Fontana dei Quattro Fiumi and the church of Sant'Agnese in Agone, the quintessence of Baroque architecture. Take Via Tor Millina west to Via della Pace and follow it north to Piazza della Pace, where a semicircular portico stands in front of the 15th-century church of **Santa Maria della Pace** ㉒. Explore the byways on the north side of Corso Vittorio Emanuele II before crossing over one of Rome's great thoroughfares and take a side street south to aristocratic **Via Giulia** and continue south to **Palazzo Falconieri** ㉓ and **Palazzo Farnese** ㉔, perhaps the most beautiful Renaissance palace in Rome. On your way back to Corso Vittorio Emanuele II along Via Farnese, go through **Campo dei Fiori** ㉕ before coming to the **Museo Baracco** ㉖. Across the way, note one of the outstanding architectural monuments of Renaissance Rome, **Palazzo Massimo alle Colonne** ㉗, and, two blocks east along the bustling street, the huge, 17th-century church of **Sant'Andrea della Valle** ㉘. Finally, head down Corso del Rinascimento to No. 40, the church of **Sant'Ivo alla Sapienza** ㉙, with a golden lantern atop the dome in the shape of a spiral.

TIMING

Allow about three hours for this walk.

Sights to See

25 **Campo dei Fiori.** The best time to visit this square is in the morning, when the bustling outdoor food market is in full swing. It was once the scene of public executions, including that of philosopher-monk Giordano Bruno (1548–1600), his statue brooding in the square center. ⏲ *Market: Mon.–Sat. 8–1.*

NEED A BREAK? Some of Rome's best pizza comes out of the ovens of the **Antico Forno** (☎ 06/68806662) on Campo dei Fiori. Choose between pizza *bianca* (topped with olive oil) or pizza *rossa* (with tomato sauce), or any of a half dozen baked goodies on hand. The benches at the foot of Palazzo Farnese in the adjacent piazza make a good place to sit down and enjoy your snack.

15 **Il Gesù.** Grandmother of all Baroque churches, this huge structure was designed by Giacomo da Vignola (1507–73) to be the tangible symbol of Jesuits, a major force in the Counter-Reformation in Europe. It

Old Rome

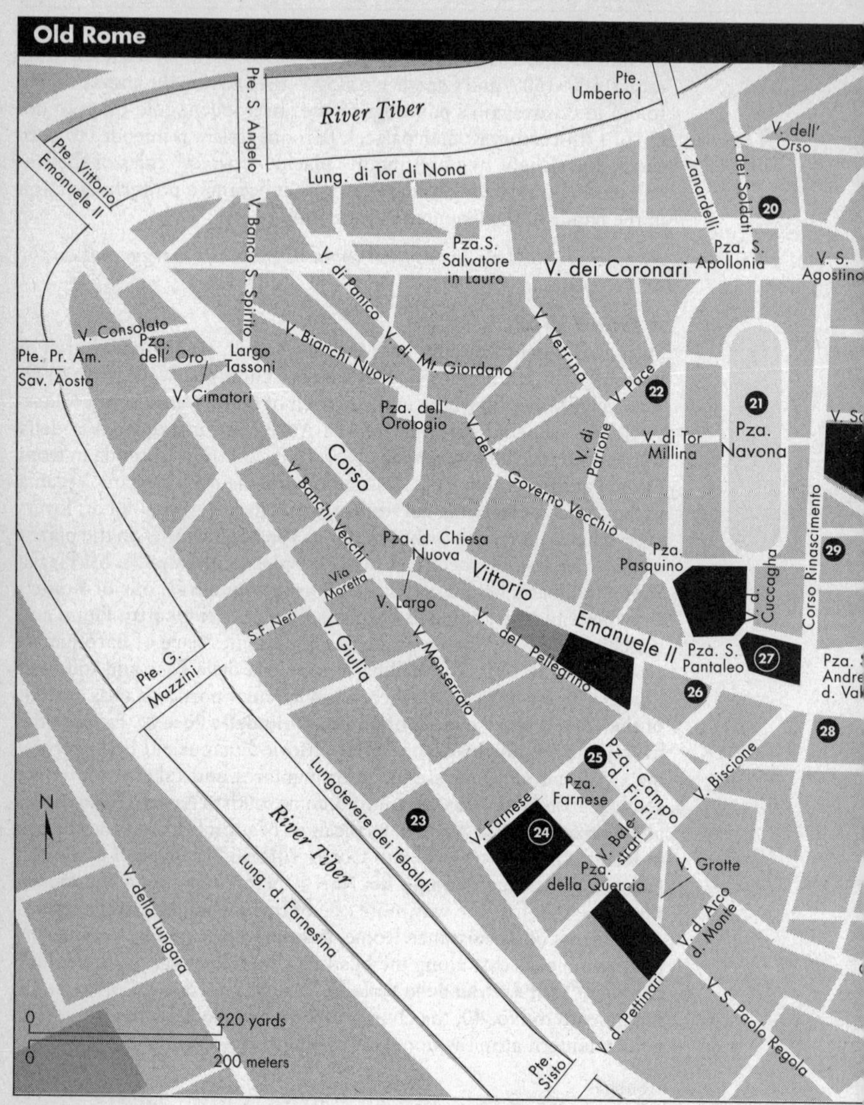

Campo dei Fiori, **25**
Il Gesù, **15**
Museo Baracco, **26**
Palazzo Altemps, **20**
Palazzo Falconieri, **23**
Palazzo Farnese, **24**
Palazzo Massimo alle Colonne, **27**
Pantheon, **17**
Piazza Navona, **21**
San Luigi dei Francesi, **18**
Sant'Agostino, **19**
Sant'Andrea della Valle, **28**
Sant'Ivo alla Sapienza, **29**
Santa Maria della Pace, **22**
Sant Maria sopra Minerva, **16**

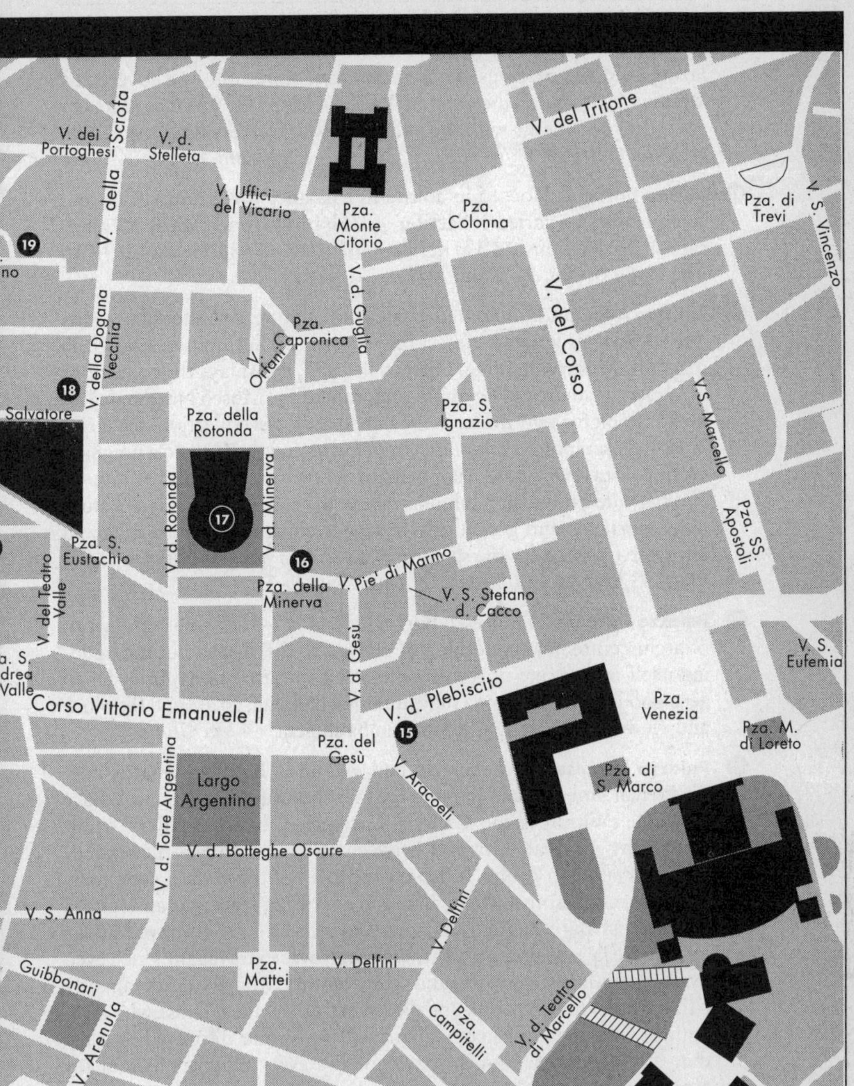
V. dei Portoghesi
V. della Scrofa
V. d. Stelleta
V. Uffici del Vicario
Pza. Monte Citorio
Pza. Colonna
V. del Tritone
Pza. di Trevi
V. S. Vincenzo
V. d. Guglia
Pza. Capronica
V. Orfani
V. della Dogana Vecchia
Salvatore
Pza. della Rotonda
Pza. S. Ignazio
V. del Corso
V.S. Marcello
Pza. SS. Apostoli
V. d. Rotonda
V. d. Minerva
Pza. S. Eustachio
V. del Teatro Valle
Pza. della Minerva
V. Pie' di Marmo
V. S. Stefano d. Cacco
V. d. Gesù
V. S. Eufemia
Corso Vittorio Emanuele II
V. d. Plebiscito
Pza. Venezia
Pza. M. di Loreto
Pza. del Gesù
V. Aracoeli
Pza. di S. Marco
Largo Argentina
V. d. Torre Argentina
V. d. Botteghe Oscure
V. S. Anna
V. Delfini
Pza. Mattei
Guibbonari
V. Arenula
Pza. Campitelli
V. d. Teatro di Marcello

remained undecorated for about 100 years, but when it finally was decorated, no expense was spared. Its interior drips with gold and lapis lazuli, gold and precious marbles, gold and more gold—all covered by a fantastically painted ceiling by Baciccia (1639–1709) that seems to swirl down to merge with the painted stucco figures at its base. ✉ *Piazza del Gesù,* ☎ *06/697001.* ⏲ *Daily 7–12:30 and 4–7.*

26 **Museo Baracco.** Housed in a little Renaissance town house, this museum features a varied collection of sculptures from ancient Mediterranean civilizations. ✉ *Via dei Baullari 1,* ☎ *06/68806848.* 🎟 *3,750 lire.* ⏲ *Tues.–Sat. 9–7, Sun. 9–1.*

20 **Palazzo Altemps.** If interested in ancient sculpture, you should not miss one of Rome's greatest collections of classical antiquities, housed in this 16th-century building. Opened in 1997, it displays the collections of ancient Roman and Egyptian sculpture of the **Museo Nazionale Romano.** Look for two works in the famed Ludovisi collection: the large, intricately sculptured *Ludovisi Sarcophagus* and the *Galata,* a poignant work portraying a barbarian warrior who chooses death for himself and his wife rather than humiliation by the enemy. The palace's stunning courtyard and gorgeously frescoed ceilings and loggia make an impressive setting for the sculptures. ✉ *Piazza Sant'Apollinare 46,* ☎ *06/6833759.* 🎟 *12,000 lire.* ⏲ *Tues.–Sun. 9–7.*

23 **Palazzo Falconieri.** Francesco Borromini's (1599–1667) masterful work of architecture houses nothing of interest to the visitor, but the building itself makes one of Rome's most elegant attractions. In order to get a good look at this gracefully imposing building, go around the block and view it from along the Tiber embankment. ✉ *Via Giulia 1.*

24 **Palazzo Farnese.** Michelangelo had a hand in building what is now the French Embassy and perhaps the most beautiful Renaissance palace in Rome. Within is the **Galleria Carracci** (Carracci Gallery) vault painted by Annibale Carracci between 1597 and 1604—the second-greatest ceiling in Rome. It depicts the loves of the gods, a supremely pagan theme that the artist painted in a swirling style that announced the birth of Baroque. It's said that Carracci was so dismayed at the miserly fee he received—the Farnese family was extravagantly rich even by the standards of 15th- and 16th-century Rome's extravagantly rich—that he took to drink and died shortly thereafter. Those who sympathize with the poor man's plight will be further dismayed to learn that the French government pays one lira every 99 years as rent for their sumptuous embassy. For special permission to view it, write in advance to the embassy, specifying how many people, when you wish to visit, and a local phone number for confirmation a few days before the visit. ✉ *Servizio Culturale, French Embassy,* ✉ *Piazza Farnese 67, 00186 Rome,* ☎ *06/686011.* 🎟 *Free.* ⏲ *By appointment only.*

27 **Palazzo Massimo alle Colonne.** A graceful columned portico marks this inconspicuous but seminal architectural monument of Renaissance Rome, built by Baldassare Peruzzi in 1527. Via del Paradiso, across Corso Vittorio Emanuele II, affords a better view. ✉ *Corso Vittorio Emanuele II 141.*

17 **Pantheon.** Paradoxically, this is one of Rome's most perfect, well-preserved, and perhaps least-appreciated ancient monuments. The Emperor Hadrian designed the Pantheon himself in around AD 120, and had it built on the site of an earlier temple that had been destroyed by fire. The most striking thing about the Pantheon is not its size, immense though it is (until 1960 the dome was the largest ever built); rather, it is the remarkable unity of the building. You don't have to look far to find the reason for this harmony: the diameter of the dome is exactly

equal to the height of the walls. The hole in the ceiling is intentional: the oculus at the apex of the dome signifies the "all-seeing eye of heaven." Note the original bronze doors, which have survived more than 1,800 years, centuries more than the interior's rich gold ornamentation, long since plundered by popes and emperors. ✉ *Piazza della Rotonda,* ☎ *06/68300230.* ⏲ *Mon.–Sat. 9–6:30, Sun. 9–1.*

★ 👍 21 **Piazza Navona.** This famed 17th-century piazza, built over the site and following the form of the 1st-century Stadium of Domitian, is one of Rome's showpiece attractions. It still has the carefree air of the days when it was the scene of Roman circus games, medieval jousts, and 17th-century carnivals. Today, this renowned spot often attracts fashion photographers and Romans out for their evening *passeggiata* (promenade). The Christmas fair held in the piazza from early December through January 6 is lively and fun for children, with games and nativity scenes, and the Befana—the ugly but good witch who brings candy and toys to Italian children on the Epiphany. Bernini's splashing **Fontana dei Quattro Fiumi** (Fountain of the Four Rivers), with an enormous rock squared off by statues representing the four corners of the world, makes a fitting centerpiece. Behind the fountain stands the church of **Sant'Agnese in Agone,** the absolute epitome of Baroque architecture, built by the Pamphili Pope Innocent X and still owned by his descendants, the Doria Pamphili. The facade—a wonderfully rich mélange of bell towers, concave spaces, and dovetailed stone and marble—is by Carlo Rainaldi (1611–91) and Francesco Borromini (1599–1667), a contemporary and sometime rival of Bernini. One story has it that the Bernini statue nearest the church, which represents the River Plate, has its hand up before his eye because it can't bear to look upon the "inferior" Borromini facade. But the facade wasn't built until after the fountain was installed.

NEED A BREAK? **Tre Scalini** café (✉ Piazza Navona 30), closed Wednesday, actually invented the *tartufo,* a luscious chocolate-covered ice-cream specialty.

18 **San Luigi dei Francesi.** In the last chapel on the left are three stunningly dramatic works by Caravaggio, the master of the heightened approach to light and dark. The inevitable coin machine will light up his *Calling of St. Matthew, Matthew and the Angel,* and *Matthew's Martyrdom,* seen from left to right, and Caravaggio's mastery of light takes it from there. Time has fully vindicated the artist's patron, Cardinal Francesco del Monte, who commissioned these works and stoutly defended their worth from the consternation of the clergy of San Luigi, who didn't appreciate the artist's roistering and unruly lifestyle. ✉ *Piazza San Luigi dei Francesi,* ☎ *06/688271.* ⏲ *Fri.–Wed. 7:30–12:30 and 3:30–7, Thurs. 7:30–12:30.*

19 **Sant'Agostino.** Caravaggio's celebrated *Madonna of the Pilgrims*—which scandalized all Rome because it pictured pilgrims with dirt on the soles of their feet—can be found in this small church, over the first altar on the left. ✉ *Piazza di Sant'Agostino,* ☎ *06/68801962.* ⏲ *Mon.–Sat. 7:45–noon and 4–7:30, Sun. 4–6.*

28 **Sant'Andrea della Valle.** This huge, 17th-century church looms mightily over a busy intersection. Aficionados of Puccini, who set the first act of his opera *Tosca* here, have been known to hire a horse-drawn carriage at night for an evocative journey that traces the course of the opera (from Sant'Andrea up Via Giulia to Palazzo Farnese—Scarpia's headquarters—to the locale of the opera's climax, Castel Sant'Angelo). ✉ *Piazza Vidoni 6.* ⏲ *Daily 7–12 and 4–7:30.*

29 **Sant'Ivo alla Sapienza.** Borromini's inspirational church has what must surely be the most fascinating dome in all Rome—topped by a

golden spiral said to have been inspired by a bee's stinger. ✉ *Corso Rinascimento 40.* ⏲ *Sun. 10–12.*

22 **Santa Maria della Pace.** Hidden away in a corner of Old Rome, gracing Piazza Santa Maria della Pace, are a semicircular portico and 15th-century church. In 1656, Pietro da Cortona (1596–1669) was commissioned by Pope Alexander VII (1599–1667) to enlarge its tiny piazza (to accommodate the carriages of the church's wealthy parishioners), and the result was one of Rome's most delightful little architectural stage sets, complete with bijou-size palaces. Within the church are two Renaissance treasures: Raphael's frescoes of the Sibyls (above the first altar on the right near the front door) and the cloister designed by Bramante, the very first expression of High Renaissance style in Rome. It's rarely open, except for guided visits, but the cloister is used in the summer for concerts. ✉ *Piazza Santa Maria della Pace.*

16 **Santa Maria sopra Minerva.** Practically the only Gothic-style church in Rome, the attractions are Michelangelo's *Risen Christ* and the tomb of the gentle 15th-century artist Fra Angelico. Have some coins handy to light up the the **Carafa Chapel** in the right transept, where exquisite 15th-century frescoes by Filippino Lippi (circa 1457–1504) are well worth the small investment (Lippi's most famous student was Botticelli). In front of the church, Bernini's charming elephant bearing an Egyptian obelisk has an inscription on the base stating something to the effect that it takes a strong mind to sustain solid wisdom. ✉ *Piazza della Minerva,* ☎ *06/6793926.*

Via Giulia. Named after Pope Julius II and having functioned for more than four centuries as the "salon of Rome," this street is the address of choice for Roman aristocrats. It is lined with elegant palaces, including Palazzo Falconieri (☞ *above*), and old churches (one, San Eligio, reputedly designed by Raphael himself). The area around Via Giulia is a wonderful section to wander through and get the feel of daily life as carried on in a centuries-old setting; this experience is enhanced by the dozens of antiques shops in the neighborhood.

Vistas and Views: From the Spanish Steps to the Trevi Fountain

Though it has a bustling commercial air, this part of the city also holds some great visual allure, such as the elaborate marble confection that is the monument to Vittorio Emanuele II. Among the things to look for are stately palaces, Baroque ballrooms, and the greatest example of portraiture in Rome, Velázquez's incomparable *Innocent X.* Those with a taste for the sumptuous theatricality of Roman ecclesiastical architecture—heroic illusionistic ceiling painting in particular—will find this a rewarding area. The highlights are the Trevi Fountain and the Spanish Steps, 18th-century Rome's most famous example of city planning.

Numbers in the text correspond to numbers in the margin and on the Rome map.

A Good Walk

Start at the flamboyant **Monument to Vittorio Emanuele II** ㉚ in Piazza Venezia, a mass of marble studded with statuary. As you look up Via del Corso, to your left is **Palazzo Venezia** ㉛, an art-filled Renaissance palace where Mussolini once addressed the crowds. On Saturday, you can visit the picture gallery known as Galleria Colonna, in the **Palazzo Colonna** ㉜, east of Piazza Venezia. From Piazza Venezia head north on Via del Corso, one of the city's busiest shopping streets, to the **Palazzo Doria Pamphili** ㉝, home to an important picture gallery. A quick detour west will bring you to the sumptuous 17th-century church of **Sant'**

Ignazio ㉞. If you continue north on Via del Corso you will reach Piazza Colonna and the ancient **Column of Marcus Aurelius** ㉟. Continue north on Via del Corso and take a right onto chic Via Condotti, which gives you a head-on view of the **Spanish Steps** ㊱ and Piazza di Spagna; to the right of the steps, at No. 26, is the **Keats-Shelley Memorial House** ㊲, where the English Romantic poet Keats lived. A great view across Rome's skyline awaits at the top of the Spanish Steps, from where you can detour to Via Gregoriano to see the **Palazzo Zuccari** ㊳. From the narrow (southern) end of Piazza di Spagna, take Via Propaganda Fide to Sant'Andrea delle Fratte, and take a left onto Via del Nazareno, then cross busy Via del Tritone to Via della Stamperia. This street leads to the **Trevi Fountain** ㊴, one of Rome's most famous landmarks.

TIMING

The walk takes approximately two to three hours.

Sights to See

㉟ **Column of Marcus Aurelius.** This ancient column—like the one Trajan erected (☞ *above*)—is an extraordinary stone history book. Its detailed reliefs spiraling up to the top illustrate the Emperor Marcus Aurelius's (AD 188–217) victorious campaigns against the barbarians. ✉ *Piazza Colonna.*

㊲ **Keats-Shelley Memorial House.** English Romantic poet John Keats (1795–1821) lived in what is now a museum dedicated to him and his great contemporary and friend, Percy Bysshe Shelley (1792–1822). You can visit his tiny rooms, preserved as they were when he died here in 1821. ✉ *Piazza di Spagna 26, next to the Spanish Steps,* ☎ *06/6784235.* 🎫 *5,000 lire.* ⏲ *June–Sept., weekdays 9–1 and 3–6; Oct.–May, weekdays 9–1 and 2:30–5:30.*

㉚ **Monument to Vittorio Emanuele II.** The huge bronze sculpture group atop this vast marble monument is visible from many parts of the city, making this modern Rome's most flamboyant landmark. It was erected in the late 19th century to honor Italy's first king, Vittorio Emanuele II (1820–78), and the unification of Italy. Sometimes said to resemble a typewriter in the Victorian style, it also houses the **Tomb of the Unknown Soldier** with its eternal flame. Although the monument has been closed to the public for many years, plans are in the works to reopen it. The views from the top of the steps are among Rome's best. Opposite the monument, note the enclosed wooden veranda fronting the palace on the corner of Via del Plebiscito and Via Corso. For the many years that she lived in Rome, Napoléon's mother had a fine view from here of the local goings-on. ✉ *Piazza Venezia.*

㉜ **Palazzo Colonna.** Rome's patrician family opens up its fabulous home to the public once a week. The entrance to the picture gallery, **Galleria Colonna,** is a secondary one, behind a plain, obscure-seeming door. The old masters are lackluster, but the gallery should be on your must-do list because the **Sala Grande** is truly the grandest 17th-century room in Rome. More than 300 ft long, and a bedazzlement of chandeliers, colored marble, and enormous paintings, it is best known today as the site where Audrey Hepburn met the press in *Roman Holiday.* ✉ *Via della Pilotta 17,* ☎ *06/6794362.* 🎫 *10,000 lire.* ⏲ *Sept.–July, Sat. 9–1.*

㉝ **Palazzo Doria Pamphili.** The 18th-century facade of this palazzo on Via del Corso is only a small part of a bona-fide patrician palace, still the residence of a princely family, who rent out many of the palazzo's 1,000 rooms. A few of those rooms are remarkably well preserved as the **Galleria Doria Pamphili,** a picture gallery that give you a sense of the sumptuous surroundings of a Roman noble family and how art was once put on display: numbered paintings (the museum catalog, available from the book shop, comes in handy) are packed onto every available wall space. Pride of place is given to the famous (and pitiless) 17th-century Diego Velázquez (1599–1660) portrait of the Pamphili Pope *Innocent X,* but don't overlook Caravaggio's poignant *Rest on the Flight to Egypt*—and, time permitting, catch the guided tour of the state apartments, which gives a discreet glimpse of an aristocratic lifestyle. Pundits say most Roman palazzi consist of one bathroom, two bedrooms, and 40 ballrooms, and after this tour, you can understand why. ✉ *Piazza del Collegio Romano 2,* ☎ *06/6797323.* 🎫 *Galleria Doria Pamphili 12,000 lire, private-apartments tours 5,000 lire.* ⏲ *Fri.–Wed. 10–5.*

31 **Palazzo Venezia.** A blend of medieval solidity and genuine Renaissance grace, this building houses a good collection of mostly early Renaissance paintings, sculptures, and objets d'art in its grand salons, some of which Mussolini (1883–1945) used as his offices. Notice the balcony over the main portal, from which Il Duce addressed huge crowds in **Piazza Venezia** below. Nowadays, the square's most imposing figure is the policeman directing traffic from his little podium in the middle, whose almost comical display of orchestration is a constant source of amusement to passersby. ✉ *Via del Plebiscito 118,* ☎ *06/69994243.* 🎫 *8,000 lire.* ⏲ *Tues.–Sat. 9–2, Sun. 9–1.*

38 **Palazzo Zuccari.** Near the top of the Spanish Steps stands what many consider the most amusing house in all of Italy, with a fanciful facade. It was designed in 1591 by the Mannerist painter Federico Zuccari (1540–1609), whose home this was. Zuccari sank all his money into this bizarre creation, dying in debt before his curious memorial, as it turned out to be, was completed. It is now the property of the **Biblioteca Hertziana,** Rome's prestigious fine art history library. ✉ *Via Gregoriana 30.*

34 **Sant'Ignazio.** The false interior dome in this sumptuous 17th-century church is a trompe l'oeil oddity among the lavishly frescoed domes of the Eternal City. To get the full effect of the illusionistic ceiling painted by Andrea del Pozzo (1642–1709), stand on the small disk set into the floor of the nave to view his *Glory of St. Ignatius Loyola.* The church contains some of Rome's most splendorous, jewel-encrusted altars. If you're lucky, you might be able to catch an evening concert performed here. The church is the focus of Filippo Raguzzini's 18th-century Rococo piazza, where the buildings are arranged almost as in a stage set, reminding us that theatricality was a key element of almost all the best Baroque and Rococo art. ✉ *Piazza Sant'Ignazio,* ☎ *06/6794406.* ⏲ *7:30–12:30 and 4–7:30.*

NEED A BREAK? The **Antico Caffè Greco** (✉ Via Condotti 86, ☎ 06/6791700), a 200-year-old institution, ever a haunt of artists and literati, has tiny, marble-top tables and velour settees. Goethe, Byron, and Liszt were habitués; Buffalo Bill stopped in when his Wild West road show hit Rome. It's closed Sunday.

★ 36 **Spanish Steps** (Scalinata della Trinità del Monte). Both the steps and **Piazza di Spagna** get their names from the Spanish Embassy to the Vatican on the piazza, opposite the American Express office, though the staircase was built with French funds in 1723. In an allusion to the Church of Trinità dei Monti at the top of the hill, the staircase is divided by three landings (beautifully banked with blooming azaleas from mid-April to mid-May). For centuries, the Scalinata (as natives refer to the steps) has been the place to see and be seen. This area has always welcomed tourists: 18th-century dukes and duchesses on their Grand Tour, 19th-century artists and writers in search of inspiration—among them, Stendhal, Balzac, Thackeray, and Byron—and today's enthusiastic hordes. The **Fontana della Barcaccia** (Fountain of the Old Boat) at the base of the steps is by Pietro Bernini, father of the famous Gian Lorenzo. ✉ *Piazza di Spagna.*

★ ㊴ **Trevi Fountain** (Fontana di Trevi). Tucked away on a small piazza off Via del Tritone, the fountain, designed by Nicola Salvi (1697–1751), is a spectacular fantasy of mythical sea creatures amidst cascades of splashing waters. It was featured in the 1954 film *Three Coins in the Fountain* and, of course, was the scene of Anita Ekberg's aquatic frolic in Fellini's *La Dolce Vita.* The fountain is the world's most spectacular wishing well: legend has it that you can ensure your return to Rome by tossing a coin into the fountain. At night, the spotlit piazza takes on the festive air of a crowded outdoor party. ✉ *Piazza Fontana di Trevi.*

OFF THE BEATEN PATH

MUSEO NAZIONALE DI PASTE ALIMENTARI – For a food-history interlude, try the National Museum of Pasta, a showcase of Italy's most famous culinary item. Small galleries named "The Wheat Room" and "The Ligurian Room" unfold the compelling saga of pasta and its present-day production. ✉ *Piazza Scanderbeg 114,* ☎ *06/6991120.* 💳 *12,000 lire.* ⏲ *Daily 9:30–5:30.*

Historic Churches: Heavenly Monuments of Faith

It is hard not to be impressed by the historic and architectural grandeur of Rome's major churches. The churches that highlight this walk date to the early centuries of Christianity, and in their decorations show evidence of the many art movements that have held sway in Rome.

A Good Walk

Not far from the Colosseum and the Roman Forum is the church of **San Pietro in Vincoli** ㊵, off Via Cavour. Look for Via San Francesco da Paola, a street staircase that passes under the old Borgia palace and leads to the church. Return to Via Cavour, which veers northeast to **Santa Maria Maggiore** ㊶, and from there go south on Via Merulana, which leads straight to **San Giovanni in Laterano** ㊷. The adjoining Palazzo Laterano houses the Vatican Historical Museum; across the street, a small building houses the **Scala Santa** ㊸, or Holy Stairs, supposedly from Pilate's Jerusalem palace. Circle Palazzo Laterano to see the 4th-century octagonal Battistero di San Giovanni, forerunner of many such buildings throughout Italy.

TIMING

The walk alone takes approximately 90 minutes, plus 15 to 20 minutes in the churches. Allow at least an hour to explore San Clemente. A visit to the Vatican Historical Museum will take you about 30 minutes.

Sights to See

㊷ **San Giovanni in Laterano.** Many are surprised when they discover that the cathedral of Rome is not St. Peter's but this church. Dominating the piazza whose name it shares, this immense building is where the present pope still officiates in his capacity as Rome's bishop. The towering facade and Borromini's cool Baroque interior emphasize the majesty of its proportions. The **cloister** is one of the city's best, with beautifully carved columns surrounding a peaceful garden.

The adjoining **Palazzo Laterano** (Lateran Palace) was the official papal residence until the 13th century and is still technically part of the Vatican. It houses the offices of the Rome Diocese and the rather bland **Vatican Historical Museum** (Museo Storico Vaticano). Behind the palace is the 6th-century octagonal **Battistero di San Giovanni** (St. John's Baptistery), forerunner of many similar buildings throughout Italy, and Rome's oldest and tallest obelisk, brought from Thebes and dating from the 15th century BC. ✉ *Piazza San Giovanni in Laterano,* ☎ *06/77207991.* 🎟 *Cloister: 4,000 lire; museum: 6,000 lire.* ⏲ *Church: Apr.–Sept., daily 7–7, Oct.–Mar., daily 7–6; cloister: 9–30 mins before church closing; museum: Sat. and 1st Sun. of each month 8:45–1; baptistery: daily 9–1 and 5–1 hr before sunset.*

OFF THE BEATEN PATH

SAN CLEMENTE – The remains of ancient Roman dwellings and a 4th-century church below the upper church of San Clemente are among Rome's most intriguing subterranean sights. ✉ *Via San Giovanni in Laterano,* ☎ *06/70451018.* 🎟 *3,000 lire.* ⏲ *Daily 9–noon and 3:30–6.*

SANTI QUATTRO CORONATI – The 12th-century Four Crowned Saints church, part of a fortified abbey that provided refuge to early popes and emperors, is in one of the most unusual corners of Rome, a quiet island that has resisted the tide of time and traffic flowing beneath its ramparts. Few places in Rome are as reminiscent of the Middle Ages. Don't miss the cloister with its well-tended gardens and 12th-century fountain. The entrance is the door in the left nave; ring if it's not open. You can also ring at the adjacent convent for the key to the Oratorio di San Silvestro (Oratory of St. Sylvester), with 13th-century frescoes. ✉ *Largo Santi Quattro Coronati,* ☎ *06/70475427.* ⏲ *Easter–Christmas, daily 9:30–12:30 and 3:30–6; Christmas–Easter, daily 9:30–12:30.*

40 **San Pietro in Vincoli.** The church takes its name from the chains that once held St. Peter (in the case under the altar), but the throngs of tourists come to see Michelangelo's *Moses,* a powerful statue almost as famed as his frescoes in the Sistine Chapel. The *Moses* was destined for the tomb of Julius II, designed to be the largest in St. Peter's Basilica. But Julius' successors had Michelangelo work on other projects, and the tomb was never finished. ✉ *Piazza San Pietro in Vincoli off Via Cavour,* ☎ *06/4882865.* ⏲ *Daily 7–12:30 and 3:30–6:30.*

41 **Santa Maria Maggiore.** One of the oldest and most spacious churches in Rome, it was built on the spot where a 3rd-century pope witnessed a miraculous midsummer snowfall. The gleaming mosaics on the arch in front of the main altar date from the 5th century. The apse mosaic dates from the 13th century—an opulently carved wood ceiling believed to have been gilded with the first gold brought from the New World. ✉ *Piazza Santa Maria Maggiore off Via Cavour,* ☎ *06/483195.* ⏲ *Daily 7–1 hr before sunset.*

43 **Scala Santa** (Sacred Stairs). A small building opposite the Lateran Palace (☞ *above*) houses what is claimed to be the staircase from Pilate's palace in Jerusalem. The faithful climb the staircase on their knees. ✉ *Piazza San Giovanni in Laterano.* ⏲ *Daily 6:15–12:15 and 3:30–6:30.*

From the Quirinal Hill to Piazza della Repubblica: Princely Palaces and Romantic Fountains

You'll see ancient Roman sculptures and early Christian churches but concentrate on the 16th and 17th centuries, when Baroque art—and Bernini—triumphed in Rome.

A Good Walk

Begin on **Quirinal Hill** 44, the highest of Rome's seven hills. Here you'll find the Palazzo del Quirinale, official residence of the president of Italy.

Also of note is **Palazzo Pallavicini-Rospigliosi** (45), a 17th-century palace. Along Via del Quirinale (which becomes Via XX Settembre) is the church of **Sant'Andrea** (46), considered by many to be Bernini's finest work, and, at the Quattro Fontane (Four Fountains) crossroads, the church of **San Carlino alle Quattro Fontane** (47), designed by Bernini's rival Borromini. Take a left on Via delle Quattro Fontane to reach the imposing **Palazzo Barberini** (48), where the Galleria Nazionale d'Arte Antica is home to splendid masterpieces by Raphael and Caravaggio. Down the hill is Piazza Barberini and the **Fontana del Tritone** (49), another Bernini design. Cross the piazza and begin your gradual climb up Via Vittorio Veneto, which bends past **Santa Maria della Concezione** (50) and the U.S. Embassy and turning off onto Via Bissolati. On the corner of Piazza San Bernardo is the church of **Santa Maria della Vittoria** (51), known for Bernini's Baroque decoration. It's not far down Via Orlando to **Piazza della Repubblica** (52). On one side of the square is an ancient Roman brick facade that marks the church of Santa Maria degli Angeli. Beyond, on the near corner of Piazza del Cinquecento, the vast square in front of Stazione Termini, is the last stop, **Palazzo Massimo alle Terme** (53), which houses part of the Museo Nazionale Romano's collections, highlighting examples of the fine mosaics and masterful paintings that decorated ancient Rome's villas and palaces.

TIMING

The walk takes approximately 90 minutes, plus 10 to 15 minutes for each church visited, and 1½ hours each for visits to the Galleria Nazionale in Palazzo Barberini and Palazzo Massimo alle Terme.

Sights to See

49 **Fontana del Tritone** (Triton Fountain). Centerpiece of Piazza Barberini is Bernini's graceful fountain, designed in 1637 for the sculptor's munificent patron, Pope Urban VIII, whose Barberini coat of arms, featuring bees, is at the base of the large shell. ✉ *Piazza Barberini.*

48 **Palazzo Barberini.** Along with architect Carlo Maderno (1556–1629), Borromini helped make the splendid 17th-century Palazzo Barberini a residence worthy of Rome's leading art patron, Pope Urban VIII, who began this palazzo for his family in 1625. Inside, the **Galleria Nazionale d'Arte Antica** offers some fine works by Raphael (the *Fornarina*) and Caravaggio. Rome's biggest ballroom is here; its ceiling, painted by Pietro da Cortona (1596–1669), depicts Immortality bestowing a crown upon Divine Providence escorted by—"a bomber squadron," to quote Sir Michael Levey—of mutant bees (bees featured prominently in the heraldic device of the Barberini). ✉ *Via delle Quattro Fontane 13,* ☎ *06/4814591.* 🎫 *8,000 lire.* ⏲ *Tues.–Sun. 9–7.*

53 **Palazzo Massimo alle Terme.** This 19th-century palace in early Baroque style holds part of the collections of antiquities belonging to the Museo Nazionale Romano (also exhibited in the Palazzo Altemps, ☞ *above*). Here you can see extraordinary examples of the fine mosaics and masterful paintings that decorated ancient Rome's palaces and villas. Don't miss the fresco—depicting a lush garden in bloom—that came from the villa that Livia, wife of Emperor Augustus, owned outside Rome. ✉ *Largo Villa Peretti 2,* ☎ *06/48903501.* 🎫 *12,000 lire (includes Museo delle Terme di Diocleziano,* ☞ *Piazza della Repubblica, below).* ⏲ *Tues.–Sun. 9–7.*

45 **Palazzo Pallavicini-Rospigliosi.** This palace, built for Cardinal Scipione Borghese, is open the first day of each month, when you can get a look at Guido Reni's *Aurora* fresco, a Baroque landmark. ✉ *Via XXIV Maggio 43, off Piazza del Quirinale,* ☎ *06/4827224.* ⏲ *1st day of month, 10–noon and 3–5.*

52 **Piazza della Repubblica.** This piazza has a typical 19th-century layout, but the curving porticoes echo the immense ancient **Terme di Diocleziano** (Baths of Diocletian), which once stood here. Built in the 4th century AD, they were the largest and most impressive of the baths of ancient Rome, and their vast halls, pools, and gardens could accommodate 3,000 people at a time. Also part of the great baths was an **Aula Ottagonale** (Octagonal Hall) that now holds a sampling of ancient sculptures found there, including two beautiful bronzes. ✉ *Via Romita 8,* ☎ *06/4870690.* ⏲ *Mon.–Sat. 9–2, Sun. 9–1.*

The racy **Fontana delle Naiadi** (Fountain of the Naiads), an 1870 addition to the piazza, delights with voluptuous bronze ladies wrestling happily with marine monsters. The curving ancient Roman brick facade on one side of the piazza marks the church of **Santa Maria degli Angeli,** adapted by Michelangelo from the vast central chamber of the colossal baths. The scale of the church's interior gives you an idea of the grandeur of the ancient building.

44 **Quirinal Hill.** The highest of ancient Rome's seven hills, this is where ancient Romans and, later, the popes built their residences in order to escape the deadly miasmas and the malaria of the low-lying area around the Forum. Every day at 4 PM the ceremony of the changing of the guard at the portal includes a miniparade, complete with band. The fountain in the square boasts ancient statues of Castor and Pollux reining in their unruly steeds and a basin salvaged from the Roman Forum. **Palazzo del Quirinale** passed from the popes to Italy's kings in the 19th century; it's now the official residence of the nation's president.

47 **San Carlino alle Quattro Fontane.** Borromini's church at the Four Fountains crossroads is an architectural gem. In a space no larger than the base of one of the piers of St. Peter's, Borromini attained geometric perfection. Characteristically, the architect chose a subdued white stucco for the interior decoration, so as not to distract from the form. The exterior of the church is Borromini at his bizarre best, all curves and rippling movement. Outside, four charming fountains frame views in four directions. ✉ *Via del Quirinale 23,* ☎ *06/4883261.* ⏲ *Closed for restoration until 2000.*

50 **Santa Maria della Concezione.** One of the most bizarre sights in Rome is the crypt of this Capuchin church, where you can see—if you like this sort of thing—the skeletons and assorted bones of 4,000 dead monks artistically arranged in four macabre chapels. ✉ *Via Veneto 27,* ☎ *06/4871185* 💳 *Donation requested.* ⏲ *Fri.–Wed. 9–12 and 3–6.*

51 **Santa Maria della Vittoria.** This church is known for Bernini's Baroque decoration of the **Cappella Cornaro,** an exceptional fusion of architecture, painting, and sculpture, in which the *Ecstasy of St. Teresa* is the focal point. Bernini's audacious conceit was to model the chapel as a theater: members of the Cornaro family—sculpted in white marble—watch from theater boxes as, center stage, St. Teresa, in the throes of mystical rapture, is pierced by a gilded arrow held by an angel. To quote one 18th-century observer, President de Brosses: "If that is divine love, I know what it is." ✉ *Via XX Settembre,* ☎ *06/4826190.* ⏲ *Sept.–July, daily 7–12 and 4–7:30.*

46 **Sant'Andrea.** This small but imposing Baroque church was designed and decorated by Bernini, who considered it one of his finest works. ✉ *Via del Quirinale,* ☎ *06/48903187.* ⏲ *Mon. and Wed.–Sat. 8–noon and 4–6, Sun. 4–6.*

Amid Sylvan Glades: From the Villa Borghese to the Ara Pacis

Beautiful masterpieces are as common as bricks on this walk, which offers more visual excitement than most cities possess in their entire environs. Along the way, Villa Borghese, Rome's largest park, can alleviate gallery gout by offering an oasis in which to enjoy a picnic under the ilex trees. Just be sure to pick up your foodstuffs in advance, whether ready-to-go from the snack bars or do-it-yourself from *alimentari* (food shops), as you'll find only fast-food carts within the park itself.

A Good Walk

Start at **Porta Pinciana** ⑭, one of the entrances to Villa Borghese. Follow Viale del Museo Borghese to the **Museo e Galleria Borghese** ㊺ and its fabulous art collection in an extraordinary setting. Head to the southwest corner of the park to enjoy the view of Rome from the **Pincio** ㊻ belvedere before descending the ramps to **Piazza del Popolo** ㊼. At the north end of the piazza, next to the 400-year-old city gate, the Porta del Popolo, is the church of **Santa Maria del Popolo** ㊽, with one of the richest art collections of any church in the city. Stroll south along Via di Ripetta to the **Augusteum,** built by Caesar Augustus; next to it is the **Ara Pacis** ㊾, built in 13 BC.

TIMING

The walk takes approximately two hours; allow an additional 1½ hours for the Galleria Borghese, and another 45 minutes for the stroll past the Augusteum and to see the Ara Pacis.

Sights to See

59 **Ara Pacis** (Altar of Augustan Peace). This altar, sheltered in an unattractive modern edifice on the northwest corner of Piazza Augusto Imperatore, was erected in 13 BC to celebrate the era of peace ushered in by Augustus's military victories. The reliefs showing the procession of the Roman imperial family are magnificent and moving. Notice the poignant presence of several forlorn children; historians now believe they attest to the ambition of Augustus's wife, the Empress Livia, who succeeded in having her son Tiberius ascend to the throne by dispatching his family rivals with poison. Next to it is the imposing bulk of the marble-clad **Mausoleo di Augusto** (Mausoleum of Augustus) Augustus built for himself and his family (closed to the public). ✉ *Via Ripetta,* ☎ *06/68806848.* 🎫 *3,750 lire.* ⏲ *Tues.–Sat. 9–7, Sun. 9–1.*

★ 55 **Museo e Galleria Borghese** (Borghese Museum and Gallery). Cardinal Scipione Borghese's (1576–1633) 1613 palace—a place to flaunt his fabulous antiquities collection and elegant fetes—is today a monument to 18th-century Roman interior decoration at its most luxurious, dripping with porphyry and alabaster. Throughout the grand salons are ancient Roman mosaic pavements and statues of various deities, including one officially known as *Venus Vincitrix,* but there has never been any doubt as to its real subject: Pauline Bonaparte, Napoléon's sister, who married Prince Camillo Borghese in one of the storied matches of the 19th century. Sculpted by Canova (1757–1822), the princess reclines on a chaise lounge, bare-bosomed, her hips swathed in classical drapery, the very model of haughty detachment and sly come-hither. Pauline is known to have been shocked that her husband took pleasure in showing off the work to his guests. This coyness seems all the more curious given the reply she is supposed to have made to a lady who asked her how she could have posed for the work: "Oh, but the studio was heated." But then it was exactly the combination of aristocratic disdain and naïveté that is said to have made her irresistible in the first place. Other rooms hold important sculptures by Bernini, including the *David* and *Apollo and Daphne*. The renowned picture collection has splendid works by Titian, Caravaggio, and Raphael, among others. ✉ *Piazza Scipione Borghese, off Via Pinciana,* ☎ *06/8548577 for information, 06/0632810 for reservations.* 🎫 *12,000 lire.* ⏲ *Tues.–Sun. 9–7; reservations are essential.*

57 **Piazza del Popolo.** Designed by neoclassic architect Giuseppe Valadier (1762–1839) in the early 1800s, this square is one of the largest in Rome, and it has a 3,000-year-old obelisk in the middle. The bookend Baroque **Santa Maria dei Miracoli** and **Santa Maria in Montesanto** at the southern end of the piazza are not, first appearances to the contrary, twins. At one end of the square is the 400-year-old **Porta del Popolo,** Rome's northern city gate.

NEED A BREAK? **Rosati** (Piazza del Popolo 5, ☎ 06/3225859) café, with a tearoom and upstairs dining room, has never gone out of style, forever a rendezvous of literati, artists, and actors.

56 **Pincio.** At the southwestern corner of **Villa Borghese,** the Pincio belvedere and gardens were laid out by Valadier as part of his overall plan for Piazza del Popolo. Back then, counts and countesses liked to take their evening passeggiata here in the hopes of meeting Pius IX (1792–1878), the last pope to go about Rome on foot. Nowadays you're more likely to see runners and in-line skaters, as well as a throng of Romans out for a passeggiata.

54 **Porta Pinciana** (Pincian Gate). One of the historic city gates in the Aurelian Walls surrounding Rome, it was built in the 6th century AD, about three centuries after the walls were built to keep out the barbarians. These days it is one of the entrances to Villa Borghese.

58 **Santa Maria del Popolo.** This church next to the Porta del Popolo goes almost unnoticed, but it has one of the richest collections of art of any church in Rome. Here you'll find Raphael's High Renaissance masterpiece, the **Chigi Chapel,** as well as two stunning Caravaggios in the **Cerasi Chapel,** which definitively prove just how modern 17th-century art can be. Elsewhere in the church, the great names—Bramante, Bernini, Pinturicchio, Sansovino (1486–1570), Carracci—resound in the silence. ✉ *Piazza del Popolo,* ☎ *06/3610836.* ⏲ *Mon.–Sat. 7–noon, Sun. 8–2.*

Across the Tiber: The Ghetto, Tiberina Island, and Trastevere

This walk takes you through separate communities, each staunchly resisting the tides of change, including the old Jewish Ghetto. In picturesque Trastevere you will find a resident colony of foreigners coexisting with "the Romans of Rome"—blunt, uninhibited, sharp-eyed, friendly, sincere, often beautiful, and seldom varnished. Despite rampant gentrification, Trastevere remains about the most tightly knit community in Rome, its inhabitants proudly proclaiming their descent—whether real or imagined—from the ancient Romans.

A Good Walk

Begin at Largo Argentina and take Via Paganica to Piazza Mattei, where one of Rome's loveliest fountains, the 16th-century **Fontana delle Tartarughe** ⑥⓪, is tucked away. Take Via della Reginella into Via Portico d'Ottavia, heart of the Jewish Ghetto. On the Tiber is the **Sinagoga** ⑥①. The **Teatro di Marcello** ⑥②, behind the Portico d'Ottavia, was originally a theater designed to hold 20,000 people. Follow Via di Teatro di Marcello south, passing the ruins of two small temples: the **Tempio della Fortuna Virilis** ⑥③ and the circular **Tempio di Vesta** ⑥④. Across **Piazza Bocca**

della Verità (65) is the 12th-century church of Santa Maria in Cosmedin, with the marble Bocca della Verità. Retracing your steps, walk upstream along the Tiber, cross Ponte Fabricio over **Isola Tiberina** (66), and then head into Trastevere.

Begin your exploration of Trastevere at Piazza in Piscinula (you will need a good street map to make your way around this intricate maze of winding side streets), take Via dell'Arco dei Tolomei, cross Via dei Salumi, and turn left onto Via dei Genovesi and then right to the piazza in front of **Santa Cecilia in Trastevere** (67). Baroque enthusiasts will want to walk several blocks southwest down Via Anicia to **San Francesco a Ripa** (68) to see a famous Bernini sculpture. Follow Via San Francesco a Ripa to the very heart of Trastevere, to **Piazza di Santa Maria in Trastevere** (69), site of the lovely 12th-century church of Santa Maria in Trastevere. With a detailed map, find your way through the narrow byways to Piazza Sant'Egidio and Via della Scala, continuing on to Via della Lungara and **Villa Farnesina** (70), where you can see frescoes by Raphael. From Trastevere, climb Via Garibaldi to the Janiculum Hill, which offers views spanning the whole city, and where you'll find the church of **San Pietro in Montorio** (71), built in 1481.

TIMING

The walk takes approximately three hours, plus 10 to 15 minutes for each church visited, and about 30 minutes for a visit to Villa Farnesina.

Sights to See

60 **Fontana della Tartarughe.** The 16th-century Fountain of the Turtles in Piazza Mattei is one of Rome's loveliest. Designed by Giacomo della Porta (1539–1602) in 1581 and sculpted by Taddeo Landini (1550–1596), the piece revolves around four bronze boys, each clutching a dolphin that jets water into marble shells. Several bronze tortoises, thought to have been added by Bernini, are held in each of the boys' hands and drink from the fountain's upper basin. The piazza is named for the Mattei family, which built **Palazzo Mattei** on Via Caetani, worth a peek for its sculpture-rich courtyard and staircase.

66 **Isola Tiberina.** Ancient Ponte Fabricio links the old Jewish Ghetto and neighborhood of Trastevere to this island, where a city hospital stands on a site that has been dedicated to healing ever since a temple to Aesculapius was erected here in 291 BC. If you have time, and if the river's not too high, walk down the stairs for a different perspective on the island and the Tiber.

Jewish Ghetto. Jews have lived in Rome continuously since the 1st century BC, and their living conditions have always followed the vicissitudes of whoever ruled Rome. One of the worst periods began in 1555, when Pope Paul II established a "ghetto" in Rome, the area delineated by the Portico d'Ottavia, the Tiber, and Via Arenula. The word comes from the Venetian name for the walled neighborhood in which Jews were forced to live and abide by restrictive laws. The area quickly became Rome's most squalid and densely populated. At one point, Jews were limited only to the sale of used clothing as a trade. Dismantled around the time of the Risorgimento, not much remains of the Ghetto as it was, but some of Rome's 15,000 Jews still live in the area, and a few old Jewish families still run clothing shops on the Via di Portico d'Ottavia. German troops occupied Rome during World War II, and on October 16, 1943, many of Rome's Jews were rounded up and deported to Nazi concentration camps. In 1986 Pope John Paul II paid a visit to Rabbi Elio Toaff, becoming the first pope ever to pray in a Jewish synagogue; the same synagogue (☞ *below*) had been bombed in 1982 by anti-Semitic Romans.

Palazzo Corsini. This elegant palace holds a collection of large, dark, and dull paintings, but stop in to climb the extraordinary 17th-century stone staircase, itself a drama of architectural shadows and sculptural voids. ⊠ *Via della Lungara 10.*

65 **Piazza Bocca della Verità.** On the site of the Forum Boarium, ancient Rome's cattle market, this square was later used for public executions. Its name is derived from the marble **Bocca della Verità** (Mouth of Truth) set into the entry portico of the 12th-century church of **Santa Maria in Cosmedin.** In the Middle Ages, legend had it that any liar who placed his hand into the mouth of this ancient drain hole cover would have it chomped off.

OFF THE BEATEN PATH

AVENTINE HILL – One of the seven hills of ancient Rome, Aventine Hill is now a quiet residential neighborhood that most tourists don't see. It has several of the city's oldest and least-visited churches, and some surprises: the view from the keyhole in the gate to the garden of the Knights of Malta (Piazza Cavalieri di Malta) and another, unusual view of Rome from the walled park next to the church of Santa Sabina, off Via Santa Sabina.

TERME DI CARACALLA – The scale of the towering ruins of ancient Rome's most beautiful and luxurious public baths, the Baths of Caracalla, hints at their past splendor. Inaugurated by Caracalla in 217, the baths were used until the 6th century. An ancient version of a swank athletic club, the baths were open to all, though men and women used them separately; citizens could bathe, socialize, and exercise in huge pools and richly decorated halls. ⊠ *Via delle Terme di Caracalla.* 🎫 *8,000 lire.* ⊙ *Apr.–Sept., Tues.–Sat. 9–6, Sun.–Mon. 9–1; Oct.–Mar., Tues.–Sat. 9–3, Sun.–Mon. 9–1.*

69 **Piazza di Santa Maria in Trastevere.** The showpiece of this piazza is the 12th-century church of **Santa Maria in Trastevere.** The 13th-century mosaics on the church's facade—which add light and color to the piazza, especially at night when they are spotlit—are believed to represent the Wise and Foolish Virgins. The interior often produces involuntary gasps from unsuspecting viewers: an enormous nave bathed in a mellow glow from medieval mosaics and overhead gilding, the whole framed by a processional of two rows of gigantic columns. There are larger naves in Rome, but none quite so majestic. ⊠ ☎ *06/5819443.* ⊙ *Daily 8–noon and 4–6.*

68 **San Francesco a Ripa.** This church in Piazza San Francesco d'Assisi is a must for fans of the Baroque. It holds one of Bernini's most hallucinatory sculptures, a dramatically lighted statue of the Blessed Ludovica Albertoni, ecstatic at the prospect of entering heaven as she expires on her deathbed. ⊠ *Piazza San Francesco d'Assisi,* ☎ *06/5819020.* ⊙ *Mon.–Sat. 8–noon and 4–6, Sun. 4–6.*

71 **San Pietro in Montorio.** One of the key Renaissance buildings stands in the cloister of this church, built by order of Ferdinand and Isabella of Spain in 1481 over the spot where St. Peter was thought to have been crucified. Bramante's **Tempietto** is an architectural gem and was one of the earliest and most successful attempts to produce an entirely classical building. ⊠ *Via Garibaldi, Gianicolo,* ☎ *06/5813940.* ⊙ *Daily 9–noon and 4–6.*

67 **Santa Cecilia in Trastevere.** Mothers and children love to dally in the delightful little garden in front of this church in Piazza Santa Cecilia. Duck inside for a look at the very grand 18th-century interior and the languid statue of St. Cecilia under the altar. Fragments of a *Last Judge-*

ment fresco cycle by Cavallini, dating from the late 13th century, remain one of his most important works. Though the Byzantine-influenced fragments are obscured by the structure, what's left reveals a rich luminosity in the seated apostles' drapery and a remarkable depth in their expressions. ✉ *Piazza Santa Cecilia,* ☎ *06/5899289.* 🎫 *Frescoes 3,000 lire.* ⏲ *Daily 8–5:30; frescoes Tues. and Thurs. 10–11:30 only.*

61 **Sinagoga** (Synagogue). The large, bronze-roofed synagogue on the Tiber is a Roman landmark. The **Museo Ebraico** (Museum of the Jewish Community) documents the history of the Jewish community in Rome. Most of the decorative crowns, prayer books, holy chairs, and tapestries, dating from the 17th century, were donated by prominent Jewish families whose ancestors once lived in the Ghetto. The collection offers a refreshing change from the religious art found elsewhere in Rome. ✉ *Lungotevere Cenci,* ☎ *06/6840061.* 🎫 *8,000 lire.* ⏲ *Mon.–Thurs. 9–5, Fri. 9–2, Sun. 9:30–12:30.*

62 **Teatro di Marcello.** The Teatro, hardly recognizable as a theater today, was originally designed to hold 20,000 spectators. It was begun by Julius Caesar; today, the apartments carved out in its remains have become one of Rome's most prestigious residential addresses. ✉ *Via del Teatro di Marcello.* ⏲ *Open during concerts only.*

63 **Tempio della Fortuna Virilis** (Temple of Manly Fortune). This rectangular temple dates from the 2nd century BC and is built in the Greek style, as was the norm in the early years of Rome. For its age, it is remarkably well preserved, in part due to its subsequent consecration as a Christian church. ✉ *Piazza Bocca della Verità.*

64 **Tempio di Vesta.** All but one of the 20 original Corinthian columns in Rome's most evocative small ruin remain intact. Like the Temple of Manly Fortune (☞ *above*), it was built in the 2nd century BC, considerably earlier than the ruins in the Roman Forum. ✉ *Piazza Bocca dell Verità.*

Trastevere. This area consists of a maze of narrow streets that is still, despite evident gentrification, one of the city's most authentically Roman neighborhoods. Literally translated, Trastevere means "across the Tiber," and indeed the Trasteverini, a breed apart, have always been proud and combative, chagrined at the reputation their quarter has acquired for purse snatching (but it does happen; don't carry a purse and keep your camera out of sight). Among self-consciously picturesque trattorias and trendy tearooms, you also find old shops and dusty artisans' workshops in alleys festooned with laundry hung out to dry. One of the most unaffected parts of Trastevere lies around **Piazza in Piscinula,** where the tiny **San Benedetto,** the smallest medieval church in the city, is opposite the restored medieval Casa dei Mattei. Take a stroll along Via dell'Arco dei Tolomei and Via dei Salumi, shadowy streets showing the patina of the ages.

Via del Portico d'Ottavia. Along this street in the heart of the Jewish Ghetto are buildings where medieval inscriptions, ancient friezes, and half-buried classical monuments attest to the venerable history of this neighborhood. The old **Chiesa di Sant'Angelo in Pescheria** was built right into the ruins of the Portico d'Ottavia, which was a monumental area enclosing a temple, library, and other buildings within colonnaded porticoes.

70 **Villa Farnesina.** Money was no object to extravagant host Agostino Chigi, a Siena banker who financed many a papal project. His munificence is evident in his elegant villa, built about 1511. When Raphael could steal some precious time from his work on the Vatican Stanze

and from his wooing of the Fornarina, he executed some of the frescoes, notably a luminous *Galatea.* Chigi delighted in impressing guests by having his servants clear the table by casting precious dinnerware into the Tiber. Naturally, the guests did not know of the nets he had stretched under the waterline to catch everything. ✉ *Via della Lungara 230,* ☎ *06/6540565.* 🎫 *6,000 lire.* ⏲ *Mon.–Sat. 9–1.*

Quo Vadis? The Catacombs and the Via Appia Antica

An exploration of the beginnings of Christianity in Rome on this tour offers a respite from museums, but requires a long time on your feet. Do it on a sunny day and take along a picnic or have lunch at one of the pleasant restaurants near the catacombs. The Rome EPT office offers a free, informative pamphlet on this itinerary.

A Good Tour

Resist any temptation to undertake the 1½-km (1-mi) walk between Porta San Sebastiano and the catacombs; it is a dull and tiring hike on a heavily trafficked (unless it's Sunday, when the road is closed to traffic all the way back to Piazza Venezia), cobblestone road, with stone walls the only scenery. Instead, hop on Bus 660 from the Colli Albani Metro stop on Line A to the **Via Appia Antica** ⑫. (Bus 218 from San Giovanni in Laterano also passes near the catacombs, but you have to walk about ½ km/¼ mi east from Via Ardeatina to Via Appia Antica.)

TIMING

Allow one hour for this tour, plus one hour for the catacombs.

Sights to See

72 **Via Appia Antica.** The "Queen of Roads," completed in 312 BC by Appius Claudius, who also built Rome's first aqueduct, connected Rome with Brindisi on the Adriatic coast. **San Callisto** is one of the best preserved of the underground catacombs. A friar will guide you through its crypts and galleries. ✉ *Via Appia Antica 110,* ☎ *06/5136725.* 🎫 *8,000 lire.* ⏲ *Dec.–Oct., Mon.–Sat. 8:30–noon and 2:30–5:30.*

The 4th-century **San Sebastiano** catacomb was named for the saint who was buried here. It burrows underground on four levels. The only one of the catacombs to remain accessible during the Middle Ages, it is the origin of the term "catacomb," for it was in a spot where the road dips into a hollow, a place the Romans called *catacumbas* (near the hollow). Eventually, the Christian cemetery that had existed here since the 2nd century came to be known by the same name, which was applied to all underground cemeteries discovered in Rome in later centuries. *Via Appia Antica 136,* ☎ *06/7887035.* 🎫 *8,000 lire.* ⏲ *Mar.–Jan., Fri.–Wed. 8:30–noon and 2:30–5:30.*

On the east side of Via Appia Antica are the ruins of the **Circo di Massenzio** (Circus of Maxentius), where the obelisk now in Piazza Navona once stood. ⏲ *Tues.–Sun. 9–1 hr before sunset.*

The circular **Tomba di Cecilia Metella** (Tomb of Cecilia Metella), mausoleum of a Roman noblewoman who lived at the time of Julius Caesar, was transformed into a fortress in the 14th century. It marks the beginning of the most evocative stretch of Via Appia Antica, lined with tombs and fragments of statuary. Cypresses and umbrella pines stand guard over the ruined sepulchers, and the occasional tracts of ancient paving stones are the same ones trod by triumphant Roman legions. ✉ *Via Appia Antica.* 🎫 *Free.* ⏲ *Tues.–Sat. 9–1 hr before sunset, Sun.–Mon. 9–1.*

DINING

Roman cooking is simple. Dishes rarely have more than a few ingredients. Meat and fish are most often roasted, baked, or grilled. Although many traditional recipes are based on innards, you won't find much of that on the menu in restaurants in the city center, with the exception of *trippa alla romana* (tripe stewed in tomatoes with wild mint).

The typical Roman fresh pasta is fettuccine, golden egg noodles that are at their classic best when laced with *ragù,* a thick, rich tomato and meat sauce. Spaghetti *alla carbonara* is spaghetti tossed with a sauce of egg yolk, chunks of rendered *guanciale* (cured pork cheek) or pancetta (salt-cured bacon), pecorino romano cheese, and lots of freshly ground black pepper. *Pasta all'amatriciana* has a sauce of tomato, guanciale, and onion. Potato gnocchi, served with a tomato sauce and a dusting of Parmesan or pecorino, are a Roman favorite for Thursday dinner. The best meat on the menu is often *abbacchio,* milk-fed lamb. Legs of lamb are usually roasted with rosemary and potatoes, and the chops are grilled *alla scottadito* (literally "burn your finger" for small chops eaten with your fingers hot off the grill). Most Mediterranean fish are light yet flavorful, among them *spigola* (sea bass), *orata* (bream), and *rombo* (turbot or flounder).

Local cheeses are made from sheep's milk; the most well known is the aged, sharp pecorino romano. Fresh ricotta is a treat all on its own, and finds its way into a number of dishes and desserts. Many restaurants make a specialty of the *fritto misto* (literally "mixed fry") with whatever vegetables are in season. Rome is famous for *carciofi* (artichokes)—the season runs from November to April—traditionally prepared *alla romana* (stuffed with garlic and mint and braised in oil), or *alla giudia* (fried whole, making each petal crisp). A special springtime treat is *vignarola,* a mixture of tender peas, fava beans, and artichokes, cooked with bits of guanciale.

Typical wines of Rome are those of the Castelli Romani, the towns in the hills to the southeast: Frascati, Colli Albani, Marino, and Velletri. Though the water in Rome is good to drink, restaurants will usually have you choose between bottled *gassata* (sparkling) or *liscia* (not sparkling) water.

Old Rome

$$$$ ✕ **El Toulà.** Rome's prestigious El Toulà has the warm, welcoming comforts of a 19th-century country house, with white walls, antique furniture in dark wood, heavy silver serving dishes, and spectacular fruit and flower arrangements. There's a cozy bar off the entrance, where you can sip a Prosecco, a Venetian aperitif best paired with the chef's Venetian specialties that are always on offer, along with contemporary interpretations of Italian classics. ✉ *Via della Lupa 29/b,* ☏ *06/6873750. Reservations essential. Jacket and tie. AE, DC, MC, V. Closed Sun. and in Aug. No lunch Sat.*

$$$$ ✕ **Il Convivio.** It's easy to walk right by this small restaurant, hidden behind an unassuming facade on the corner of a narrow street just north of Piazza Navona, with anything-but-anonymous dishes that combine seasonal Italian cooking and innovation. Chef Angelo Troiani's inventions may have long names, but they are tasty and well presented: *rollé di agnello farcito con frittatine alle erbe* (lamb roll stuffed with herb fritters) and *soufflé di crema di mandorle e prugne, profumato di arancia* (almond and prune soufflé, perfumed with orange). Massimo and Giuseppe, Angelo's brothers, manage the dining room and pour wine, chosen from one of the finest cellars in town. ✉ *Via dell'*

Al Ceppo, **35**
Antico Arco, **24**
Baffetto, **17**
Cecilia Metella, **29**
Checchino dal 1887, **26**
Colline Emiliane, **34**
Da Checco er Carettiere, **21**
Dal Bolognese, **5**
Dal Toscano, **2**
Dar Poeta, **22**
El Toulà, **8**
Enoteca Corsi, **33**
Grappolo d'Oro, **20**
Il Cardinale, **18**
Il Convivio, **10**
Il Leoncino, **9**
Il Simposio di Constantini, **3**
L'Archeologia, **28**
La Bottega del Vino di Anacleto Bleve, **31**
La Pergola, **1**
La Rosetta, **15**
La Soffitta, **38**
La Terrazza dell'Eden, **7**
L'Eau Vive, **16**
Le Sans Souci, **36**
L'Osteria dell'Ingegno, **14**
Myosotis, **13**
Orso 80, **11**
Otello alla Concordia, **6**
Papá Baccus, **37**
Paris, **23**
Perilli, **27**
Pierluigi, **19**
Piperno, **30**
Pommidoro, **40**
Sangallo, **12**
Sora Lella, **25**
Tre Pupazzi, **4**
Trimani Il Winebar, **39**
Vecchia Roma, **32**

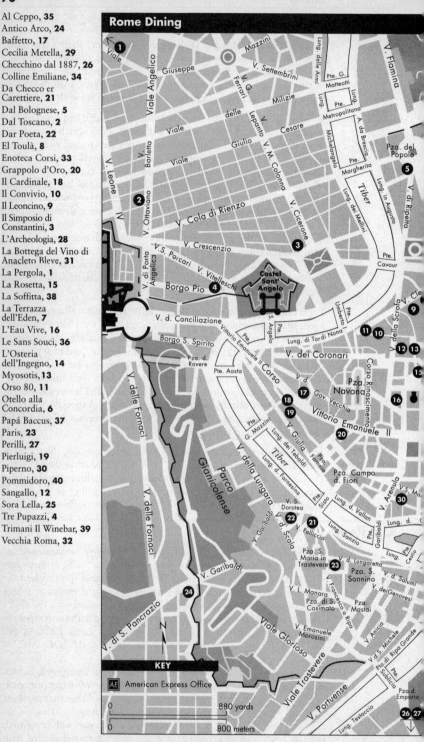

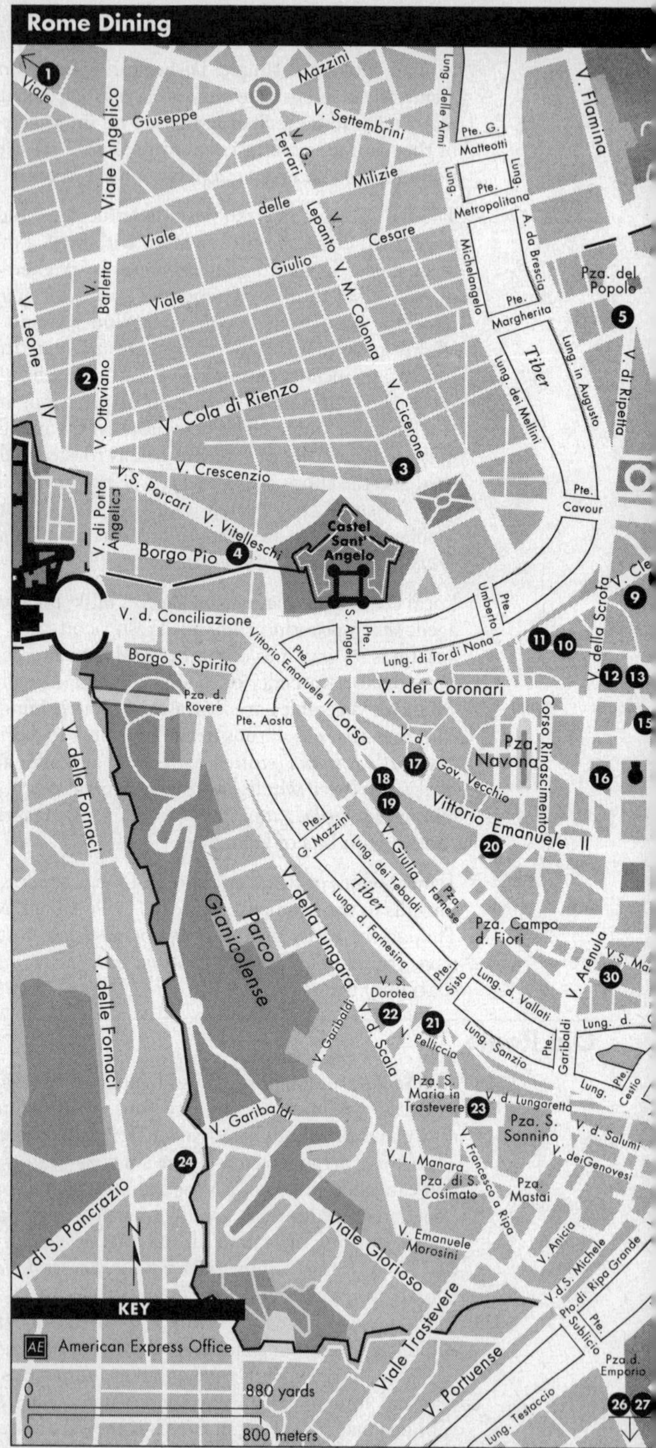

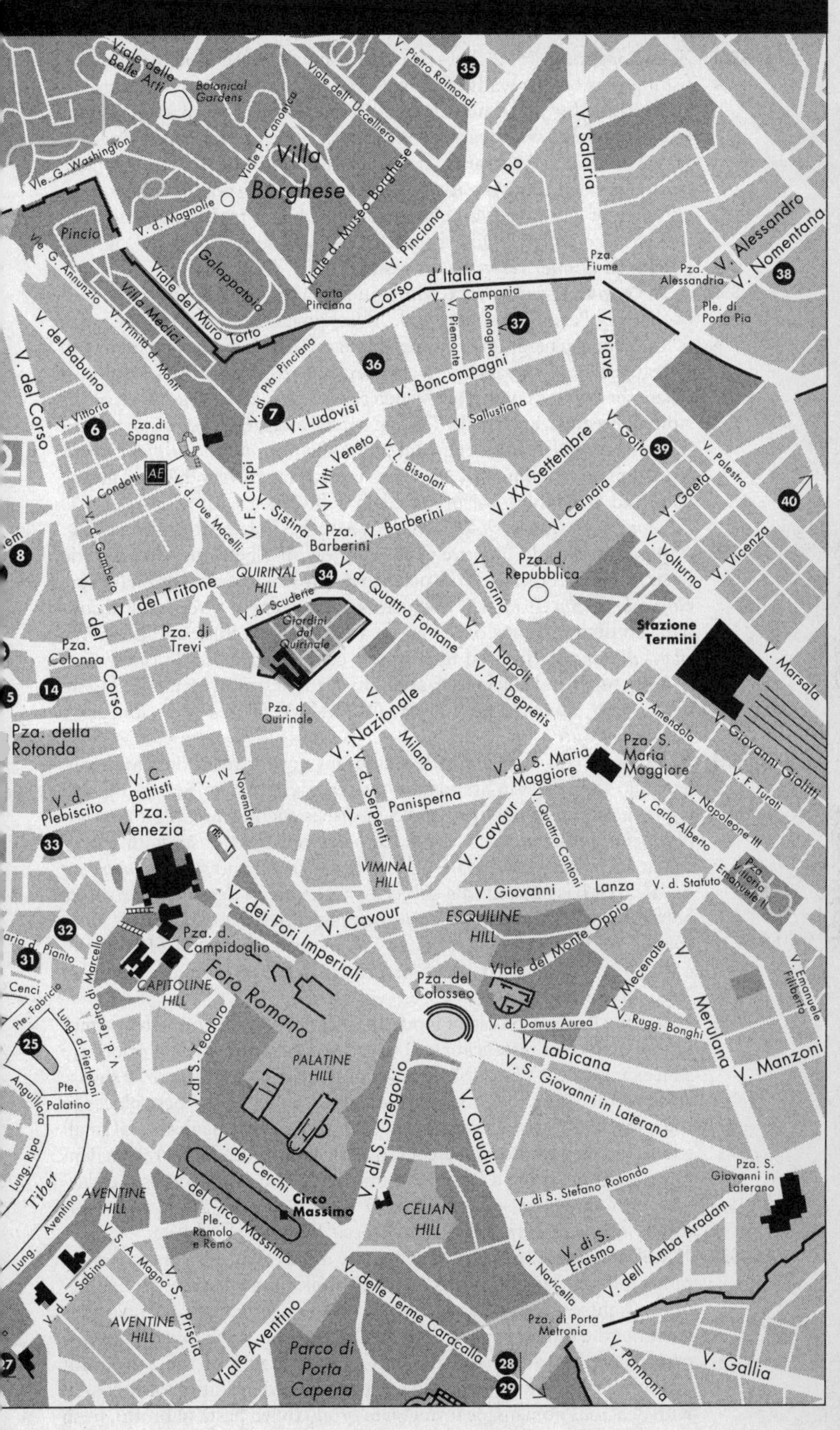

Villa Borghese
Viale delle Belle Arti
Botanical Gardens
Viale P. Canonica
Viale dell' Uccelliera
Viale d. Museo Borghese
V. Pietro Raimondi
Vle. G. Washington
V. d. Magnolie
Pincio
Galoppatoio
Viale del Muro Torto
Villa Medici
Vle. G. Annunzio
V. Trinità d. Monti
Porta Pinciana
V. Pinciana
V. Po
V. Salaria
Corso d'Italia
V. Campania
V. Piemonte
V. Romagna
Pza. Fiume
Pza. Alessandria
V. Alessandro
V. Nomentana
Ple. di Porta Pia
V. Piave
V. del Babuino
V. del Corso
V. Vittoria
Pza.di Spagna
V. Condotti
V. d. Due Macelli
V. di Pta. Pinciana
V. Ludovisi
V. Boncompagni
V. Sallustiana
V. L. Bissolati
V. Vitt. Veneto
V. F. Crispi
V. Sistina
Pza. Barberini
V. Barberini
V. XX Settembre
V. Goito
V. Cernaia
V. Palestro
V. Gaeta
V. Volturno
V. Vicenza
V. d. Gambero
V. del Tritone
QUIRINAL HILL
V. d. Scuderie
V. d. Quattro Fontane
V. Torino
Pza. d. Repubblica
Stazione Termini
V. Marsala
Pza. di Trevi
Giardini del Quirinale
Pza. Colonna
V. del Corso
V. Napoli
V. A. Depretis
V. G. Amendola
V. Giovanni Giolitti
Pza. d. Quirinale
V. Nazionale
V. Milano
Pza. della Rotonda
V. d. Serpenti
V. IV Novembre
V. C. Battisti
V. d. Plebiscito
Pza. Venezia
V. Panisperna
V. d. S. Maria Maggiore
Pza. S. Maria Maggiore
V. F. Turati
V. Napoleone III
V. Carlo Alberto
V. Quattro Cantoni
V. Cavour
VIMINAL HILL
V. Giovanni Lanza
V. d. Statuto
Pza. Vittorio Emanuele II
V. dei Fori Imperiali
V. Cavour
ESQUILINE HILL
Pza. d. Campidoglio
Viale del Monte Oppio
V. Mecenate
V. Merulana
V. Emanuele Filiberto
V. d. Pianto
Cenci
Pte. Fabricio
CAPITOLINE HILL
Foro Romano
Pza. del Colosseo
V. d. Domus Aurea
V. Rugg. Bonghi
V. Labicana
V. Manzoni
Lung. d. Pierleoni
V. d. Teatro di Marcello
V. di S. Teodoro
PALATINE HILL
V. di S. Gregorio
V. Claudia
V. S. Giovanni in Laterano
Pte. Palatino
Anguillara
Lung. Ripa
Tiber
V. dei Cerchi
Circo Massimo
CELIAN HILL
V. di S. Stefano Rotondo
Pza. S. Giovanni in Laterano
AVENTINE HILL
Lung. Aventino
V. del Circo Massimo
Ple. Romolo e Remo
V. S. A. Magno
V. d. S. Sabina
V. S. Priscia
AVENTINE HILL
Viale Aventino
Parco di Porta Capena
V. delle Terme Caracalla
V. d. Navicella
V. di S. Erasmo
V. dell' Amba Aradam
Pza. di Porta Metronia
V. Pannonia
V. Gallia

Orso 44, ☎ 06/6869432. Reservations essential. AE, DC, MC, V. Closed Sun.

$$$$ ★ ✕ **La Rosetta.** In 1992 chef-owner Massimo Riccioli took the nets and fishing gear off the walls of his parents' trattoria to create the place to go in Rome for first-rate fish, artfully presented. The space is elegant in its simplicity, with warm woods, fresh flowers, and a stunning display of fish at the entrance. Particularly good dishes are the *vongole veraci* (sautéed clams), *tonnarelli ai frutti di mare* (poached fish on artichokes or potatoes), and sea bass with black truffles. Homemade desserts are worth saving room for. ✉ *Via della Rosetta 9, ☎ 06/6861002. Dinner reservations essential. AE, DC, MC, V.*

$$$ ✕ **Al Ceppo.** A warm space with antiques and oil paintings in the out-of-the-way Parioli neighborhood, Al Ceppo has been the Sunday lunch favorite for a generation of Roman families. Classic dishes prepared with a creative flair always include a few specialties from the Marche region—where the owners come from—such as *olive ascolane* (large green olives stuffed, breaded, and fried). Trademark starters are *polpettine di melanzane al vapore* (steamed eggplant balls) and *fiori di zucca ripieni e fritti* (fried stuffed zucchini flowers). Pasta is made fresh every day, and meats, fish, and vegetables are prepared in a fireplace with a grill. ✉ *Via Panama 2, ☎ 06/8419696. AE, DC, MC, V. Closed Mon. and in Aug.*

$$$ ✕ **Piperno.** An old favorite in the old Jewish Ghetto next to historic Palazzo Cenci, Piperno is *the* place to go for Rome's extraordinary *carciofi alla giudia* (fried whole artichokes). You eat in three small wood-paneled dining rooms or at one of a handful of tables outdoors. Try *filetti di baccalà* (braised fillet of salt cod), *pasta e ceci* (a thick soup of pasta tubes and chickpeas), and fiori di zucca ripieni e fritti. ✉ *Monte dei Cenci 9, ☎ 06/6542772. AE, DC, MC, V. Closed Mon. and Aug. No dinner Sun.*

$$$ ✕ **Sangallo.** An intimate little restaurant not far from the Pantheon, Sangallo specializes in first-quality fish that is light in presentation, well cooked, and invitingly presented in dishes such as *tagliolini con pomodorini, mazzancolle, e scaglie di pecorino* (fresh pasta with cherry tomatoes, shrimp, and scales of pecorino cheese) and *spigola in crosta di sale* (sea bass baked in a salt crust). The *menu degustazione* offers better value than the à la carte offerings. Service can be less than speedy, so plan on a long meal. ✉ *Vicolo della Vaccarella 11/a, ☎ 06/6865549. AE, DC, MC, V. Closed Sun., 1 wk in Jan., and 2 wks in Aug. No lunch Mon.*

$$$ ✕ **Vecchia Roma.** Consistent food, sure-handed service, and a great atmosphere make this restaurant still worthy of attention, even if prices are a bit exaggerated. With tables outside on a relatively quiet, narrow square close to the Campidoglio, Vecchia Roma is one of the best places in town to eat alfresco. The tasteful interior proceeds through several small rooms, some with floral frescoes, others with stucco panel reliefs. Unlike a great many "old Roman restaurants," the menu covers the classics without being stale. ✉ *Piazza Campitelli 18, ☎ 06/6864604. Reservations essential. AE, DC. Closed Wed. and mid-Aug.*

$$–$$$ ✕ **Dal Bolognese.** Long a haunt of the art crowd, this classic restaurant on Piazza del Popolo is a trendy choice for a leisurely lunch between sightseeing and shopping. An array of contemporary paintings decorate the dining room but the real attraction is the lovely piazza—prime people-watching real estate. As the name of the restaurant promises, the cooking here adheres to the hearty tradition of Bologna, with delicious homemade tortellini *in brodo* (filled pasta in broth), fresh pastas in creamy sauces, and steaming trays of boiled meats. Among the desserts, try the *dolce della mamma* (a concoction of gelato, zabaglione, and chocolate sauce) and the fruit-shape gelato. ✉ *Piazza del Popolo 1, ☎ 06/3611426. AE, MC, V. Closed Mon. and in Aug.*

$$ ✕ **Il Cardinale.** In this small, serene restaurant, fanciful, lightened-up versions of traditional Roman fare are beautifully presented on king-size plates. Oil paintings and enlarged old photos of Roman landmarks hang against golden damask wall coverings; chairs and couches are covered in a pretty floral print. The menu—a selection of composed salads, vegetable soups, and pastas—always has a few suggestions from the chef. Try the *vermicelli cacio e pepe* (pasta with pecorino cheese and black pepper) or ravioli *di borragine* (filled with borage leaves), and various vegetable *sformati* (flans). ✉ *Via delle Carceri 6,* ☎ *06/6869336. AE, DC, MC, V. Closed Sun.*

$$ ★ ✕ **Myosotis.** It may look brand new, but the Myosotis is the sequel to a restaurant on the outskirts of town run by the Marsili family. Central location, extensive menu, and great value make Myosotis a place you might want to return to. The menu rides that delicate line between tradition and innovation, focusing more on the freshness and quality of the ingredients than on elaborate presentation. Fresh pasta gets special attention: it's rolled out by hand to order for the *stracci alla delizia di mare* (pasta with seafood). There's a wide choice of fish, meat, and seasonal veggies to choose from. The wine list is ample, the prices honest. ✉ *Via della Vaccarella 3/5,* ☎ *06/2053943. AE, DC, MC, V. Closed Mon. and 2 wks in Aug.*

$$ ✕ **Otello alla Concordia.** The clientele in this popular spot—it's off a shopping street near Piazza di Spagna—is about evenly divided between tourists and businesspeople. The former like to sit outdoors in the courtyard in any weather; the latter have their regular tables in one of the inside dining rooms. The menu offers classic Roman and Italian dishes, and service is friendly and efficient. Since the regulars won't relinquish their niches, you may have to wait for a table; go early. ✉ *Via della Croce 81,* ☎ *06/6781454. Reservations not accepted. AE, DC. Closed Sun.*

$$ ✕ **Sora Lella.** What was once a simple trattoria ensconced on the Tiberina Island (great view from the bathroom) is now a monument to the late founder herself, a beloved example of true Roman warmth and personality. Inside, two small dining rooms are lined with wood paneling and bottles of wine. Although prices are much higher than when Sora Lella presided over the cash desk, the cooking is still 100% Roman. Daily specials as well as menu standards are written on the chalkboard, but you'll usually find rigatoni all'amatriciana and *maialino all'antica roma* (suckling pig with prunes and baby onions). Leave room for the quintessential Roman ricotta cake. ✉ *Via Ponte Quattro Capi 16,* ☎ *06/6861601. AE, DC, MC. Closed Sun. and Aug.*

$ ✕ **Grappolo d'Oro.** This central trattoria off Campo dei Fiori has been a favorite for decades with locals and foreign residents, one of whom wrote it up in the *New Yorker* some years ago. This measure of notoriety has not induced the graying, courteous owners to change their two half-paneled dining rooms or menu, which features pasta all'amatriciana and scallopini any way you want them. ✉ *Piazza della Cancelleria 80,* ☎ *06/6897080. AE, DC, MC, V. Closed Sun. and Aug.*

$ ✕ **L'Eau Vive.** You're in for a unique Roman dining experience, even if the food isn't Italian. For the last 28 years this restaurant with (very good) classic French food has been run by a society of French missionary nuns. The atmosphere throughout is serene and soothing, though rather plain (of course). Soft devotional music plays as the smiling sisters speedily bring plate after plate. They take a brief pause before dessert to sing "Ave Maria"—you are welcome to join in. The upstairs rooms, reserved for nonsmokers, have beautiful frescoes. ✉ *Via Monterone 85,* ☎ *06/68801095. AE, DC, MC, V. Closed Sun. and Aug.*

$ ✕ **Orso 80.** The good kind of tourist restaurant, this bright and bustling trattoria near Piazza Navona is well known for its fabulous antipasto table. Try the homemade egg pasta or the *bucatini* (thick, hollow spaghetti) all'amatriciana; there's plenty of seafood on the menu, too. For dessert, the ricotta cake, a genuine Roman specialty, is always good. ✉ *Via dell'Orso 33,* ☎ *06/6864904. AE, DC, MC, V. Closed Mon. and Aug.*

$ ✕ **Pierluigi.** This is a longtime favorite with foreign residents of Rome and Italians in the entertainment field. On busy evenings it's almost impossible to get a table. Seafood dominates (if you're in the mood to splurge, try the lobster), but traditional Roman dishes are offered, too, including fried zucchini blossoms and simple spaghetti. Eat in the pretty piazza in summer. ✉ *Piazza dei Ricci 144,* ☎ *06/6868717. Reservations essential. AE, V. Closed Mon. and 2 wks in Aug.*

Veneto

$$$$ ✕ **Le Sans Souci.** All the glitz and glamour of the 1950s dolce vita days lives on in this overdecorated but superb subterranean sanctuary of French and Italian gourmet delights. Impeccably dressed waiters slide over the carpeted floor with unparalleled grace, their gait reminiscent of Swiss walking lessons. An elaborate coffered ceiling, mirrors, and painted ceramics from Perugia decorate the main room. Carved wooden busts of Roman emperors gaze over tables, set in the French fashion, where couples share a couch rather than sit opposite one another (so much easier to see the show). Among the delectable dishes are truffled terrine of foie gras and various sweet and savory soufflés. ✉ *Via Sicilia 20,* ☎ *06/4821814. Reservations essential. Jacket and tie. AE, DC, MC, V. Closed Mon. and in Aug. No lunch.*

$$ ✕ **Colline Emiliane.** Expect a reliable neighborhood trattoria, not far from Piazza Barberini. Behind an opaque glass facade are a couple of plain dining rooms, where you are served light homemade pastas, *tortelli di zucca* (squash-filled ravioli), and meats from *bollito misto* (boiled beef) to *cotoletta alla Bolognese* (fried veal cutlet with cheese and prosciutto). Family run, it's quiet and soothing—a good place to rest after a sightseeing stint. Service is cordial and discreet. ✉ *Via San Nicolò da Tolentino 26,* ☎ *06/4818564. Reservations essential. AE, DC, MC, V. Closed Sun. and Aug.*

$$ ✕ **Papá Baccus.** Italo Cipriani takes his meat as seriously as any Tuscan. He uses real Chianina beef, the prized breed traditionally used for the *bistecca alla fiorentina,* a thick, bone-in steak, grilled but rare in the middle, a house specialty. In this, Rome's best Tuscan restaurant, you can depend on the genuineness of the rest of the dishes, too. Cipriani brings many ingredients from his home town in northern Tuscany. Try the sweet and delicate prosciutto from Pratomagno. The welcome is warm, the service excellent. ✉ *Via Toscana 36,* ☎ *06/42742808. AE, DC, MC, V. Closed Sun., 2 wks in Aug., and over Christmas. No lunch Sat.*

Near Termini

$ ✕ **Pommidoro.** Mamma's in the kitchen and the rest of the family greets, serves, and keeps you happy and well fed at this popular trattoria near Rome's main university, a short cab ride east of Stazione Termini. The menu—not so well translated—offers especially good grilled meats and game birds, and classic home-style *cucina* (cooking). You can dine outside in warm weather. ✉ *Via Marmorata 39,* ☎ *06/5742415. No credit cards. Closed Wed.*

Vatican

$$$$ ★ ✕ **La Pergola.** High atop Monte Mario, the Cavalieri Hilton's rooftop La Pergola restaurant offers a commanding view onto the city below.

The dining room is warmly elegant with trompe l'oeil ceilings, handsome wood paneling, and large windows. Amply spaced tables and low lighting create an intimate atmosphere not matched by other restaurants in town. Celebrated wunder-chef Heinz Beck is a skilled technician, and brings Rome its finest example of Mediterranean *alta cucina* (haute cuisine); dishes are balanced and light, and presentation is striking. The wine list and the cheese cart offer ample and interesting choices from Italy and France. ✉ *Cavalieri Hilton, Via Cadlolo 101,* ☎ *06/3509221. Reservations essential. Jacket and tie. AE, DC, MC, V. Closed Sun.–Mon. No lunch.*

$$$$ ✕ **La Terrazza dell'Eden.** The Hotel Eden's La Terrazza restaurant unfurls an unparalleled view of Rome's seven hills before your eyes, unfairly distracting you from some of the best food in the city. Modern yet simple Italian cuisine—high on flavor and herbs and low on butter and cream—is the vision of chef Enrico Derflingher. Always on the prowl for superior fresh ingredients, he has taken the search to a new level: how many other restaurants have their own fishing boat, which reserves the best of the day's catch for the chef? The restaurant is also open for breakfast (7–10 AM). A piano bar (with jazz from 8:00 PM to 1 AM) with a small outdoor terrace shares the view. ✉ *Hotel Eden, Via Ludovisi 49,* ☎ *06/47812552. Dinner reservations essential. Jacket and tie. AE, DC, MC, V.*

$ ★ ✕ **Dal Toscano.** An open wood-fired grill and classic dishes like *ribollita* (a thick bread and vegetable soup) and *pici* (fresh thick pasta, served with a wild hare sauce) are the draw at this great family-run Tuscan trattoria near the Vatican. The refrigerator opposite the entrance tells you right away that the house special is the prized bistecca alla fiorentina. Wash it all down with a strong Chianti, or a half liter of the Tuscan house wine. Desserts such as pastry cream tarts, apple strudel, and *castagnaccio* (a tasty chestnut and pine nut treat) in wintertime are all homemade. Service is friendly and speedy. ✉ *Via Germanico 58,* ☎ *06/39725717. DC, MC, V. Closed Mon. and Aug. and 2 wks in Dec.*

$ ✕ **Tre Pupazzi.** The "three puppets," after which the trattoria is named, are the worn stone figures on a fragment of an ancient sarcophagus that embellishes a building on this byway near the Vatican. The tavern, founded in 1625, wears its centuries lightly, upholding a tradition of good food, courteous service, and reasonable prices. The menu offers classic Roman and Abruzzese trattoria fare, including fettuccine and abbacchio, plus pizzas at lunchtime (a rarity in Rome) and well past midnight. ✉ *Via dei Tre Pupazzi at Borgo Pio,* ☎ *06/6868371. AE, MC, V. Closed Sun.*

Trastevere/Testaccio

$$$ ✕ **Checchino dal 1887.** Literally carved out of a hillside made of potsherds from Roman times, Checchino turns out the most traditional Roman cuisine served without fanfare in a clean, austere space. Though the slaughterhouses of Rome's Testaccio quarter—a short cab ride from the city center—are long gone, you can still try the variety meats that make up the soul of Roman cooking: *trippa* (tripe), *testina* (head), *pajata* (intestine), *zampa* (trotter), and *coratella* (sweetbreads). There's also plenty to choose from if you're uninterested in innards: house specialties include *coda alla vaccinara* (stewed oxtail), a popular Roman dish the owners claim was invented here, and abbacchio *alla cacciatora* (braised in tomato sauce). Desserts are very good. ✉ *Via di Monte Testaccio 30,* ☎ *06/5746318. AE, DC, MC, V. Closed Mon., Aug., and over Christmas. No dinner Sun.*

$$$ ✕ **Da Checco er Carettiere.** Maybe this is what all Italian restaurants once looked like: an aging doorman, garlic braids hanging from the ceiling, black and white photos in small frames lining the wood-paneled walls. Family-run for three generations, Checco is a great place to soak up genuine Trastevere color and hospitality. All the Roman standards, solidly prepared with first-rate ingredients, plus plenty of local vegetables and an unusually good selection of fish, are true to tradition. You can eat outdoors in summer. ✉ *Via Benedetta 10,* ☎ *06/5817018. AE, DC, MC, V. Closed Mon. No dinner Sun.*

$$–$$$ ✕ **Paris.** On a small square just off Piazza Santa Maria in Trastevere, Paris (named after a former owner) has a reassuring, understated ambience, without the hokey flamboyance of so many eateries in this neighborhood. The menu features the best of classic Roman cuisine: homemade fettuccine, delicate fritto misto, and, of course, baccalà. You can also choose from a good wine list. In fair weather opt for tables on the piazza. ✉ *Piazza San Callisto 7/a,* ☎ *06/5815378. AE, DC, MC, V. Closed Mon. and 3 wks in Aug. No dinner Sun.*

$–$$ ★ ✕ **Antico Arco.** Run by three friends with a passion for wine and fine food, the Antico Arco, at the top of the Janiculum Hill, has quickly won the hearts of Roman foodies with innovative dishes and moderate prices. There are always 30 wines to choose from by the glass, plus an excellent list of Italian and French labels. Particularly good are starters like *sformato di finocchi in salsa d'arancia* (fennel flan with orange sauce) and second courses like *petto d'anatra con salsa di lamponi* (duck breast with raspberry sauce). Don't miss dessert. At press time a plan was in the works to open daily for lunch as well. ✉ *Piazzale Aurelio 7,* ☎ *06/5815274. AE, DC, MC, V. Closed Mon. No lunch Mon.–Sat.*

$ ✕ **Perilli.** A bastion of authentic Roman cooking since 1911 (the decor has changed very little), this trattoria is the place to go to try rigatoni *con pajata* (with baby veal's intestines)—if you're into this sort of thing. Otherwise the all'amatriciana and carbonara sauces are classics. The house wine is a golden nectar from the Castelli Romani. ✉ *Via Marmorata 39,* ☎ *06/5742415. No credit cards. Closed Wed.*

Along Via Appia Antica

$$ ✕ **Cecilia Metella.** From the entrance on Via Appia Antica, practically opposite the catacombs, you walk uphill to a low-lying but sprawling construction designed for wedding feasts and banquets. There's a large terrace shaded by vines for outdoor dining. Although obviously geared to larger groups, Cecilia Metella also gives couples and small groups full attention, good service, and traditional Roman cuisine. The specialties are the searing-hot *crespelle* (crepes), served in individual casseroles, and pollo *al Nerone* (chicken à la Nero, flambéed, of course). ✉ *Via Appia Antica 125,* ☎ *06/5136743. AE, MC, V. Closed Mon. and last 2 wks in Aug.*

$$ ✕ **L'Archeologia.** In this farmhouse just beyond the catacombs, you dine indoors beside the fireplace in cool weather or in the garden under age-old vines in the summer. The atmosphere is friendly and intimate. Specialties include homemade pastas, abbacchio add alla scottadito, seafood, and some Greek dishes. ✉ *Via Appia Antica 139,* ☎ *06/7880494. AE, MC, V. Closed Thurs.*

Pizzerias

It may have been invented somewhere else (☞ Up-Close: Disciplined Pizzas *in* Chapter 12), but in Rome it's hard to walk a block without passing pizza in one form or another. Pizza from a bakery is usually made without cheese—*pizza bianca* (just olive oil and salt) or *pizza rossa* (with tomato sauce). Many small shops specialize in pizza *a taglio* (by the cut), priced by the *etto* (100 grams, about a ¼ pound), according to the kind of topping. Both of these make a great snack any time of day. Here are a few good places to find the real McCoy on the go: **Il Forno di Campo dei Fiori** (✉ Campo dei Fiori), closed Sunday, makes excellent pizza bianca and rossa all day. Just around the corner is **Pizza alla Pala** (✉ Via del Pellegrino), closed Sunday. **Zi Fenizia** (✉ Via Santa Maria del Pianto 64) makes kosher pizza in the old Jewish Ghetto; it's closed sundown Friday, Saturday, and Jewish holidays.

But don't leave Rome without sitting down to a Roman pizza in a pizzeria. Most are open only for dinner, usually from 8 PM to midnight. Look for a place with a *forno a legna* (wood-burning oven), a must for a good thin crust on your plate-size Roman pizza. Standard models are the *margherita* (tomato, mozzarella, and basil) and the *capricciosa* (a little bit of everything, depending upon the "caprices" of the pizza chef: tomato, mozzarella, sausage, olives, artichoke hearts, and prosciutto, even egg), but most pizzerias have a long list of additional options, including tasty mozzarella *di bufala* (buffalo-milk).

$$ ✕ **Baffetto.** Down a cobblestone street not far from Piazza Navona, this is Rome's best-known pizzeria and a summer favorite for outside dining. The plainly decorated interior is mostly given over to the ovens, but there's another room with more paper-covered tables. Turnover is fast; this is not the place to linger. ✉ *Via del Governo Vecchio 114, Centro Storico,* ☎ *06/6861617. Reservations not accepted. No credit cards. Closed Sun. and Aug. No lunch.*

$ ✕ **Dar Poeta.** Romans drive across town for great pizza, a bit cheaper than average, from this neighborhood joint on a small street in Trastevere. Maybe it's the dough—made from a secret blend of flours reputed to be easier to digest than the competition. For dessert, an unusual calzone is baked with Nutella (a chocolate and hazelnut spread) and ricotta. ✉ *Vicolo del Bologna 45, Trastevere,* ☎ *06/5880516. Reservations not accepted. AE, MC, V. Closed Mon. No lunch.*

$ ✕ **Il Leoncino.** Lines out the door on weekends attest to the popularity of the fluorescent-lit pizzeria in the otherwise big-ticket neighborhood around Piazza di Spagna. This is one of the few pizzerias open for lunch as well as dinner. ✉ *Via Via del Lioncino 28, near the Corso, Centro Storico,* ☎ *06/6876306. Reservations not accepted. No credit cards. Closed Sun. and Aug.*

$ ✕ **La Soffitta.** You pay more, but hey, it's imported. This is Rome's hottest spot for classic Neapolitan pizza (thick, though crusty on the bottom, rather than paper thin and crispy like the Roman kind), and the only pizzeria in town that has been certified by the True Neapolitan Pizza Association. Desserts are brought in daily from Naples. ✉ *Via dei Villini 1/e, near Stazione Termini,* ☎ *06/4404642. Reservations not accepted. No credit cards. Closed Sun. and Aug. No lunch.*

Enoteche

It was not so long ago that wine in Rome (and other towns) was strictly local; you didn't have to walk far to find an *osteria,* a tavern-like establishment where you could buy wine straight from the barrel or sit down to drink and nibble a bit, chat, or play cards. The tradition continues today, as many Roman wine shops are also open as *enoteche* (wine bars). The folding chairs and rickety tables have given way to designer interiors and chic ambience. Shelves are lined with hundreds of bottles from all over the country, representing the best in Italian wine making, many available by the glass. Behind the bar you'll find a serious wine enthusiast, maybe even a sommelier. There's usually carefully selected cheeses and cured meats, and a short menu of simple dishes and desserts.

$ ✕ **Enoteca Corsi.** Very convenient to the historic center for lunch (no dinner) or an afternoon break, this little wine bar looks like it missed the revolution; prices and decor are *come una volta* (like once upon a time) when the shop sold—as the sign says—wine (red or white) and oil. The genuinely dated feel of the place has its charm: you can still get wine here by the liter, or choose from a good variety of fairly priced bottles. There are nicely prepared pastas and kind service. ✉ *Via del Gesù 88, Centro Storico,* ☎ *06/6790821. AE, MC, V. Closed Sun. No dinner.*

$ ✕ **Il Simposio di Costantini.** At the classiest wine bar in town, done out in wrought-iron vines, wood paneling, and velvet, you can choose from about 30 wines. Food is appropriately fancy: marinated and smoked fish, composed salads, top-quality salami and cured meats (classical and wild), terrines and pâtés, and several gussied-up hot vegetable and meat dishes. It has 80 assorted cheeses, grouped according to origin or type (French, Italian, goat, hard, herb crusted). ✉ *Via Appia Antica 139, near the Vatican,* ☎ *06/7880494. AE, MC, V. Closed Thurs.*

$ ✕ **La Bottega del Vino di Anacleto Bleve.** This cozy wine shop in the Jewish Ghetto sets out tables and opens up for lunch. Owner Anacleto Bleve and his sons make the rounds, proposing the latest cheese they have procured from the farthest reaches of Italy. Instead of a menu, there's mama at the counter, chatting up a good selection of mixed salads, smoked fish and sliced meats, as well as a few soups and sformati. You point and she plates it up. There are always wines to drink by the glass, or you can choose from the several hundred bottles on the shelves that surround you. ✉ *Via Santa Maria del Pianto, Centro Storico,* ☎ *06/7880494. AE, D, MC, V. Closed Thurs.*

$ ✕ **L'Osteria dell'Ingegno.** A perfect stop for a quick lunch or dinner after sightseeing or shopping, with hip modern decor and happening feel, this trendy wine bar seems almost out of place among the ruins of the old town. The short menu changes weekly, with simple dishes that emphasize fine ingredients. Service is fast. ✉ *Piazza di Pietra 45, Centro Storico,* ☎ *06/6780662. Reservations not accepted. AE, D, MC, V. Closed Sun.*

$ ✕ **Trimani Il Winebar.** This is a handy address for diners in a town where most restaurants don't unlock the door before 8 PM. Trimani opens up at 6 PM for snacks and cold plates, at 7:30 for hot food, and stays open until 11:30. The feel is modern and casually reserved. There's always a choice of a soup and a few pasta plates, as well as second courses and *torte salate* (savory tarts). Around the corner is a wine shop, one of the oldest in Rome, of the same name. Call about wine tastings and short courses (in Italian). ✉ *Via Cernaia 37/b, near Stazione Termini,* ☎ *06/4469630. AE, D, MC, V. Closed Sun. and 2 wks in Aug. No lunch Sat.*

Caffè

As elsewhere in Italy, there is a *caffè* (café-bar) on nearly every corner in Rome where you can get coffee drinks, fruit juices, pastries, sandwiches, liquor, and beer. Locals usually stop in for a quickie at the bar, which is also much less expensive than the same drink taken at table. Pricey **Antico Caffè Greco** (✉ Via dei Condotti 86, ☎ 06/6791700) is a national landmark; its red-velvet chairs and marble tables have hosted the likes of Byron, Shelley, Keats, Goethe, and Casanova. **Caffè Sant'Eustachio** (✉ P. Sant'Eustachio 82, ☎ 06/861309), traditionally frequented by Rome's literati, vies with **Tazza d'Oro** (✉ Via degli Orfani, near the Pantheon, ☎ 06/5835869) for the city's best coffee. If you want your *caffè* (espresso) without sugar, ask for it *amaro*. Other great caffè where you can sit yourself down and watch the world go by are **Rosati** (✉ Piazza del Popolo 5, ☎ 06/3225859), **Antico Caffè della Pace** (✉ Via della Pace 3, ☎ 06/6861216) near Piazza Navona, and **Caffè Teichner** (✉ Piazza Santa Maria in Lucina 17, ☎ 06/6871449) just off the Corso.

Gelaterie and Pasticcerie

Gelato is more a snack for Italians than a serious dessert. **Il Gelato di San Crispino** (✉ Via della Panetteria 42, near the Trevi Fountain, ☎ 06/6793924), closed Tuesday, is perhaps the most celebrated gelato in all of Italy, made without artificial colors or flavors. It's worth crossing town for—nobody else makes flavors this balanced, ice cream this real. Other worthwhile addresses for gelato are **Fiocco di Neve** (✉ Via del Pantheon 51, ☎ no phone), closed Sunday, and **Fonte della Salute** (✉ Via Cardinal Marmagi 2, ☎ 06/5897471), closed Tuesday in winter. The historical **San Filippo** (✉ Via di Villa S. Filippo 8, ☎ 06/8079314), closed Monday, is renowned for flavors like chestnut and clementine in winter, watermelon and peach in summer. Romans consider **Giolitti** (✉ Via Uffizi del Vicario 40, ☎ 06/6991243), near the Pantheon, superlative.

Romans are not known for their sweet tooths, and there are few *pasticcerie* (pastry shops) in town that distinguish themselves with particularly good examples of the few regional desserts. One exception is the **Forno del Ghetto** (✉ Via del Portico d'Ottavia 20/b, ☎ 06/6878637), closed Friday after sundown, Saturday, and Jewish holidays. This hole-in-the-wall—no sign, no tables, just a take-away counter—is an institution, preserving a tradition of Italian-Jewish sweets that cannot be found anywhere else. The ricotta cake (with sour cherry jam or chocolate) is unforgettable. Just down the street is **Dolceroma** (✉ Via del Portico d'Ottavia 20/b, ☎ 06/6892196), where the specialties, alas, are not Roman: American pies and Austrian pastries. It's closed Sunday afternoon and Monday and 4 weeks in July–August.

Salumerie

There are several hundred *salumerie* (gourmet food shops) in town, but a few stand out for a particularly ample selection and items of rare, superior quality. Foodies should head straight for **Franchi** (✉ Via Cola di Rienzo 200, ☎ 06/6864576), closed Sunday, which will vacuum-pack meats and cheeses if you aren't ready to eat them just then. They also have Rome's best deli-style takeout. Right next door is **Castroni** (✉ Via Cola di Rienzo 196, ☎ 06/6864383), closed Sunday, a fine general food shop with lots of imported items. **Volpetti** (✉ Via Marmorata 47, ☎ 06/5742352), closed Thursday afternoon and Sunday, also keeps the highest-quality meats and specializes in aged cheeses from small producers. The **Antico Forno** (✉ Via delle Muratte 8, ☎ 06/6792866), at the Trevi Fountain, is not nearly at the same level, but it is open on Sunday (but closed Thursday afternoon in winter, Saturday afternoon in summer).

LODGING

Palatial surroundings, luxurious comfort, and high standards of service are certainly more likely to be found at the city's pricier establishments, but standards vary considerably; quality and good value should not be taken for granted in any category. Note that the stars allotted to hotels are based on facilities and services offered, but have no bearing on quality. Many hotels in town have upgraded their facilities in expectation of big business during the Holy Year celebrations. Most of the lower priced hotels are actually old-fashioned *pensione* set on one or several floors of a large building. One disadvantage of staying in the center is noise; ask for an inside room if you are a light sleeper, but don't be disappointed if it faces a dark courtyard.

Because Rome's religious importance makes it a year-round tourist destination, there is never a period when hotels are predictably empty, so you should always try to make reservations, even if only a few days in advance, by phone or fax. Always inquire about special low rates, often available in both winter and summer if occupancy is low. If you do arrive without reservations, try **Hotel Reservation Service** (☎ 06/6991000), with an English-speaking operator available daily 7 AM–10 PM, and with desks at Aeroporto Fiumicino and Stazione Termini. A list of all the hotels in Rome, with prices and facilities, is available from the main **EPT** information office (☞ Visitor Information *in* Rome A to Z, *below*).

Old Rome

$$$$ **Albergo del Sole al Pantheon.** This small hotel has been in its central location opposite the Pantheon since the 15th century. It has been tastefully decorated with a blend of modern and antique furnishings. Ceilings are high, floors are tiled in terra-cotta, and there is a charming courtyard for alfresco breakfast in good weather. ✉ *Piazza della Rotonda 63, 00186,* ☎ *06/6780441,* FAX *06/69940689. 25 rooms. Bar. AE, DC, MC, V.*

$$$$ **Holiday Inn Crowne Plaza Minerva.** This hotel is the very stylish reincarnation of the hostelry that occupied this 17th-century palazzo for centuries, hosting literati from Stendhal to Sartre and de Beauvoir. Entirely redone, with a stunning stained-glass lobby ceiling designed by renowned architect Paolo Portoghesi, the Minerva has everything a guest could want in the way of comfort, all in an absolutely central location. And from the roof terrace, open for summer dining in fair weather, you can almost touch the immense, flattened dome of Hadrian's Pantheon. ✉ *Piazza della Minerva 69, 00186,* ☎ *06/69941888,* FAX *06/6794165. 118 rooms, 16 suites. Restaurant, bar. AE, DC, MC, V. EP.*

$$$–$$$$ **Dei Borgognoni.** This quietly chic hotel near Piazza Colonna is as central as you could want, yet the winding byway stage set gives you a sense of being off the beaten track. The centuries-old building provides spacious lounges, a glassed-in garden, and rooms well arranged to create an illusion of space, though they are actually compact. The hotel has a garage (fee), a rarity in such a central location. ✉ *Via del Bufalo 126, 00187,* ☎ *06/69941505,* FAX *06/69941501. 50 rooms. Parking (fee). AE, DC, MC, V. EP.*

$$ **Campo dei Fiori.** Frescoes, exposed brickwork, and picturesque effects throughout this little hotel in Old Rome could well be the work of a set designer. There's an aura of fantasy and romanticism in the decoration, with the layout cleverly designed to make the most of limited space. A few rooms are so compact they're almost claustrophobic; other rooms are larger, and all have an unusual decorative feature of some kind to remind you that you are in the heart of Rome. The hotel has no elevator, but the climb to the roof terrace rewards you with a marvelous view. Rates for the best rooms exceed parameters in this price category. ✉ *Via del Biscione 6, 00186,* ☎ *06/68806865,* FAX *06/6876003. 27 rooms, 13 without bath. MC, V. EP.*

$$ ★ **Cardinal.** Staying at this hotel is like stepping inside a Renaissance painting—it was built by Bramante and is set on magnificent Via Giulia, whose immutable vistas have scarcely changed since the 15th cen-

tury. Cardinals would feel right at home: the lobby is a riot of red, while the rooms upstairs are almost ascetic. Serene, severe, and subdued, many of the rooms feature antique engravings and Olympian-high ceilings. Of course, the interiors don't matter much when Via Giulia—lined with beautiful palazzi and opulent antiques stores—is right outside your doorstep. ✉ *Via Giulia 62, 00186,* ☎ *06/68802719,* FAX *06/6786376. 73 rooms. Bar. AE, DC, MC, V. EP.*

$$ **Portoghesi.** In the heart of Old Rome, the Portoghesi is a small hotel with big atmosphere. From a tiny lobby, an equally tiny elevator takes you to the quiet bedrooms, all decorated with floral prints and reproduction antique furniture. It has a charming roof garden with a view of the city's domes and rooftops. ✉ *Via dei Portoghesi 1, 00186,* ☎ *06/6864231,* FAX *06/6876976. 22 rooms, 6 suites. MC, V.*

$$ ★ **Teatro di Pompeo.** Where else can you breakfast under the ancient stone vaults of Pompey's Theater, historic site of Julius Caesar's assassination? At this intimate and refined little hotel in the heart of Old Rome you are part of that history; at night, you sleep under restored beamed ceilings that date from the days of Michelangelo. The tastefully furnished rooms offer comfort as well as charm. Book well in advance. ✉ *Largo del Pallaro 8, 00186,* ☎ *06/68300170,* FAX *06/68805531. 13 rooms. AE, DC, MC, V.*

$–$$ **Arenula.** This hotel—with a luminous and cheerful all-white interior—is one of Rome's best values. Rooms have pale wood furnishings and gleaming bathrooms, as well as double-glazed windows and air-conditioning (summer only; no help on warm spring or fall days). Two rooms accommodate four beds. The catch at the four-story Arenula is that the graceful oval staircase of white marble and wrought iron is the only way up—there is no elevator. The hotel is on an ageworn byway off central Via Arenula, on the edge of the Ghetto. ✉ *Via Santa Maria dei Calderari 47 (Via Arenula), 00186,* ☎ *06/6879454,* FAX *06/6896188. 50 rooms. DC, MC, V.*

Spanish Steps

$$$$ **De La Ville Inter-Continental.** For the well-heeled, this is a finely honed option just a stone's throw from the top of the Spanish Steps. Guests often ask for the rooms their great-grandparents favored; regulars are treated like family here—one reason the place is usually booked solid. Other lures include a lobby replete with marble and gilt furnishings; tastefully subdued guest rooms; and a staff high on initiative. Don't miss the morning meal or Sunday brunch served in La Piazzetta restaurant—adorned with twinkling chandeliers and taffeta-draped French doors, it has to be the prettiest breakfast in Rome. ✉ *Via Sistina 69, 00187,* ☎ *06/67331,* FAX *06/6784213. 192 rooms, 23 suites. Restaurant, bar, parking (fee). AE, DC, MC, V.*

$$$$ ★ **D'Inghilterra.** Legendary names like Lizst, Mendelssohn, Hans Christian Andersen, Mark Twain, and Hemingway litter the guest book here. With a marvelous residential feel and a staff that is as warm as the surroundings are velvety, this hotel near the Spanish Steps has nearly everything. Even a pedigree: before 1845, it had been the guest house of the fabulously rich Prince Torlonia. The outside still looks suitably vintage, and inside 19th-century elegance has been transposed to the 20th. Just beyond the tiny lobby is the Lounge, a favored luncheon spot whose decor of framed prints and Biedermeier-style furniture is a connoisseur's joy. Upstairs, guest rooms are so full of stylishly arranged carpets, gilt-framed mirrors, and cozy bergères you'll hardly notice the snug dimensions. ✉ *Via Bocca di Leone 14, 00187,* ☎ *06/69981,* FAX *06/69922243. 90 rooms, 12 suites. 2 restaurants, bar. AE, DC, MC, V.*

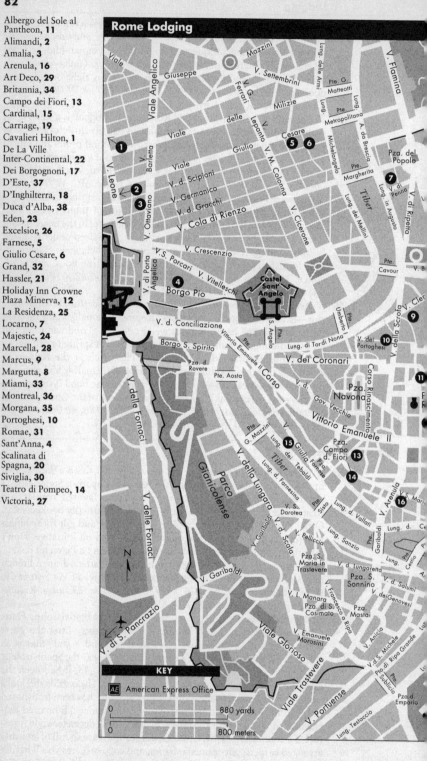

Rome Lodging
Viale Giuseppe Mazzini
V. Settembrini
Viale Angelico
V. G. Ferrari
Viale delle Milizie
V. Lepanto
Viale Giulio Cesare
V. Barletta
V. Leone IV
V. d. Scipioni
V. Germanico
V. d. Gracchi
V. Cola di Rienzo
V. Ottaviano
V. M. Colonna
V. Cicerone
Lung. delle Armi
Pte. G. Matteotti
Pte. Metropolitana
Lung. Michelangelo
A. da Brescia
Pte. Margherita
Lung. dei Mellini
Tiber
Pza. del Popolo
V. Flaminia
V. di Penna
Lung. in Augusta
V. di Ripetta
V. Crescenzio
V.S. Porcari
V. Vitelleschi
V. di Porta Angelica
Borgo Pio
Castel Sant' Angelo
Pte. Cavour
V. d. Conciliazione
Borgo S. Spirito
Pza. d. Rovere
Pte. Aosta
Pte. Vittorio Emanuele II
Corso
Pte. S. Angelo
Pte. Umberto I
Lung. di Tordi Nona
V. dei Portoghesi
V. della Scrofa
V. dei Coronari
V. d. Gov. Vecchio
Pza. Navona
Corso Rinascimento
Vittorio Emanuele II
V. delle Fornaci
Pte. G. Mazzini
Lung. dei Tebaldi
V. Giulia
Pza. Farnese
Pza. Campo d. Fiori
Parco Gianicolense
V. della Lungara
Tiber
Lung. d. Farnesina
V. S. Dorotea
Pte. Sisto
Lung. d. Vallati
V. Arenula
V. Garibaldi
V. d. Scala
V. Pelliccia
Lung. Sanzio
Pte. Garibaldi
Lung. Cestio
Pza. S. Maria in Trastevere
V. d. Lungaretta
Pza. S. Sonnino
V. d. Salumi
V. dei Genovesi
V. Garibaldi
V. L. Manara
Pza. di S. Cosimato
V. Francesco a Ripa
Pza. Mastai
V. di S. Pancrazio
Viale Glorioso
V. Emanuele Morosini
V. Anicia
V.d.S. Michele
V. di Ripa Grande
Pte. Sublicio
Viale Trastevere
V. Portuense
Pza. d. Emporio
Lung. Testaccio
KEY
American Express Office
880 yards
800 meters

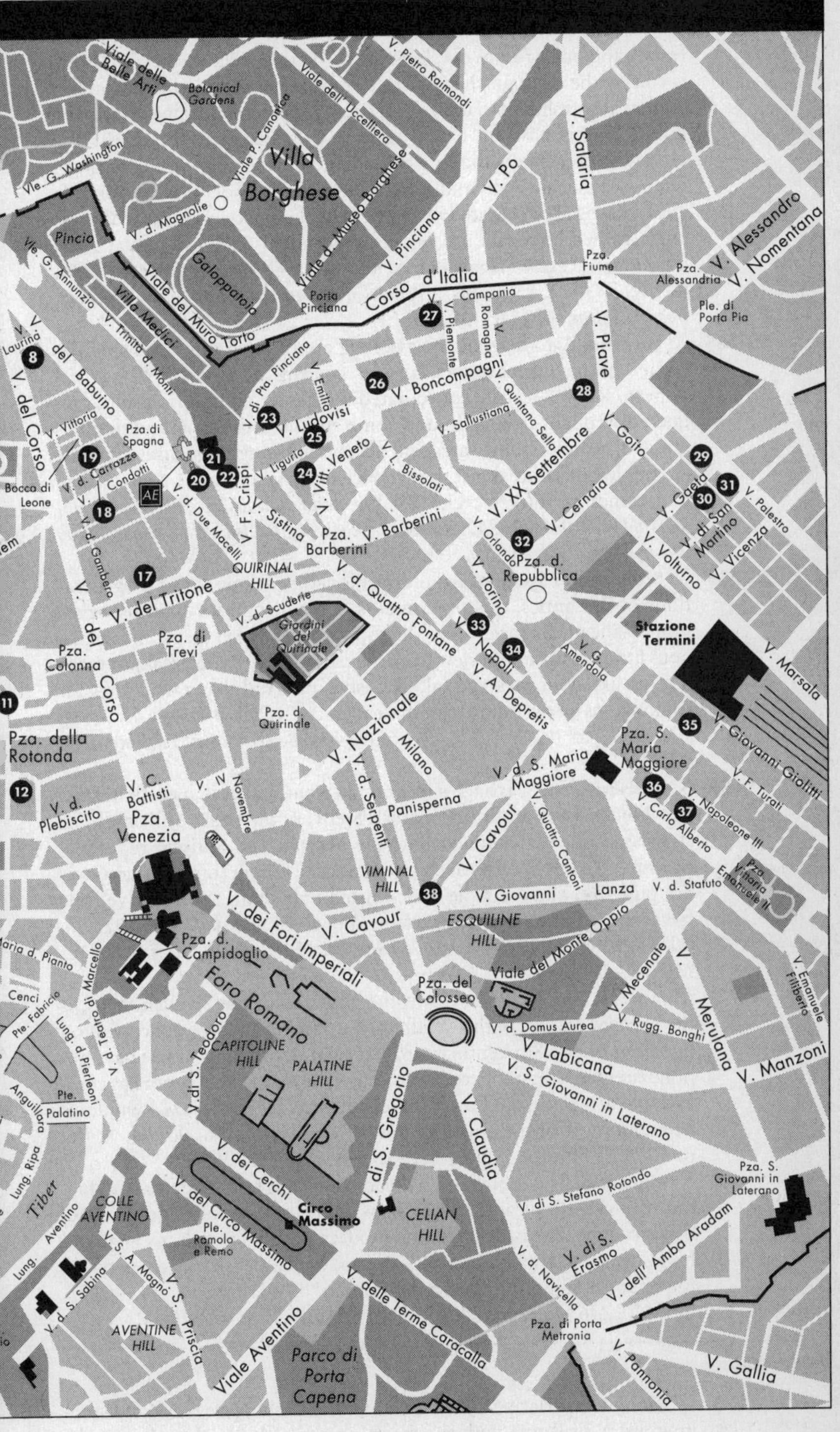
Villa Borghese
Botanical Gardens
Pincio
Villa Medici
Galoppatoio
Porta Pinciana
Corso d'Italia
V. Salaria
V. Po
V. Pinciana
Pza. Fiume
Pza. Alessandria
V. Alessandro
V. Nomentana
Ple. di Porta Pia
V. Piave
V. Boncompagni
V. Ludovisi
V. Vitt. Veneto
V. XX Settembre
V. del Corso
V. del Babuino
Pza. di Spagna
V. d. Condotti
Bocca di Leone
V. Sistina
Pza. Barberini
V. Barberini
V. del Tritone
QUIRINAL HILL
Giardini del Quirinale
Pza. d. Repubblica
V. d. Quattro Fontane
Stazione Termini
V. Marsala
V. Nazionale
Pza. di Trevi
Pza. Colonna
Pza. della Rotonda
Pza. d. Quirinale
V. Giovanni Giolitti
Pza. S. Maria Maggiore
V. d. S. Maria Maggiore
V. Panisperna
V. Cavour
Pza. Venezia
V. d. Plebiscito
V. C. Battisti
V. IV Novembre
VIMINAL HILL
V. Giovanni Lanza
ESQUILINE HILL
V. dei Fori Imperiali
Pza. d. Campidoglio
Foro Romano
Pza. del Colosseo
CAPITOLINE HILL
PALATINE HILL
V. Labicana
V. S. Giovanni in Laterano
V. Merulana
V. Manzoni
V. di S. Gregorio
V. Claudia
Circo Massimo
CELIAN HILL
Tiber
COLLE AVENTINO
AVENTINE HILL
Viale Aventino
Parco di Porta Capena
V. delle Terme Caracalla
V. dell' Amba Aradam
Pza. S. Giovanni in Laterano
Pza. di Porta Metronia
V. Gallia

$$$$ ★ **Hassler.** Positioned at the top of the Spanish Steps, the Hassler boasts sweeping views of Rome from its front rooms and rooftop restaurant; other rooms overlook the gardens of Villa Medici. The hotel is run by the distinguished Wirth family of hoteliers, which assures a cordial atmosphere and imperial service from the well-trained staff. The public rooms have an extravagant 1950s elegance—especially the clubby winter bar, summer garden bar, and the glass-roofed lounge, with gold marble walls and a hand-painted tile floor. The comfortable guest rooms are decorated in a variety of classic styles, some with frescoed walls. The penthouse suite is resplendent with antiques and has a huge terrace. ✉ *Piazza Trinità dei Monti 6, 00187,* ☎ *06/699340,* FAX *06/6789991. 85 rooms, 15 suites. Restaurant, 2 bars, lobby lounge, beauty salon. AE, DC, MC, V. EP.*

$$–$$$ **Locarno.** Art aficionados have long appreciated this hotel's fin-de-siècle charm, intimate feel, and its central location off Piazza del Popolo. Rooms feature coordinated wallpaper and fabric prints, lacquered wrought-iron beds, and some antiques juxtaposed with modern gadgets (electronic safes and air-conditioning). Amenities include an ample buffet breakfast, bar service on the panoramic roof garden, and complimentary bicycles. ✉ *Via della Penna 22, 00186,* ☎ *06/3610841,* FAX *06/3215249. 46 rooms, 2 suites. Bar, breakfast room, lobby lounge. AE, DC, MC, V.*

$$–$$$ **Scalinata di Spagna.** An old-fashioned pensione loved by generations of romantics, this tiny hotel is booked solid for months—even years—ahead. Its location at the top of the Spanish Steps, inconspicuous little entrance, and view from the terrace where you breakfast make it seem like your own special, exclusive inn. And that's why rates for some rooms go over the top of this category. ✉ *Piazza Trinità dei Monti 17, 00187,* ☎ *06/6793006,* FAX *06/69940598. 16 rooms. Parking (fee). AE, MC, V.*

$$ **Carriage.** The Carriage's location is what makes it special: it's just two blocks away from the Spanish Steps, in the heart of Rome. The stylish decor uses subdued Baroque accents and antique reproductions to give the hotel a touch of elegance. Though some of the rooms are pint-size, and a couple open onto an air shaft, several have little terraces; a roof garden adds to the appeal. ✉ *Via delle Carrozze 36, 00187,* ☎ *06/6990124,* FAX *06/6788279. 25 rooms, 2 suites. AE, DC, MC, V.*

$ **Marcus.** The location, down the street from the Spanish Steps, is the premier feature of this small hotel occupying a large apartment on one floor of an 18th-century cardinal's palazzo. Many rooms have antique fireplaces but modern bathrooms. The main living room has comfortable armchairs and a crystal chandelier. Double-glazed windows keep out most of the noise. ✉ *Via del Clementino 16, 00184,* ☎ *06/68300320,* FAX *06/68300312. 15 rooms. AE, MC, V. EP.*

$ ★ **Margutta.** The lobby and halls in this small hotel are unassuming, but rooms are a pleasant surprise, with a clean and airy look, attractive wrought-iron bedsteads, and modern baths. Though it's in an old building, there is an elevator. It's central on a quiet side street between the Spanish Steps and Piazza del Popolo. ✉ *Via Laurina 34, 00187,* ☎ *06/3223674,* FAX *06/3200395. 21 rooms. AE, DC, MC, V.*

Veneto

$$$$ ★ **Eden.** A superlative hotel that combines dashing elegance and stunning vistas of Rome with the warm charm of Italian hospitality, the Eden was once the preferred haunt of Hemingway, Ingrid Bergman, and Fellini, and of many celebrities before them. Precious antiques, sumptuous Italian fabrics, linen sheets, and marble baths exude understated

elegance. The views from the rooftop bar and terrace will take your breath away, and the hotel's top-floor restaurant, La Terrazza dell'Eden (☞ Dining, *above*), merits raves, too. ✉ *Via Ludovisi 49, 00187,* ☎ *06/478121,* FAX *06/4821584. 101 rooms, 12 suites. Restaurant, bar, exercise room, free parking. AE, DC, MC, V. EP.*

$$$$ **Excelsior.** To Romans and many others, the white Victorian cupola of the Excelsior is a symbol of Rome at its most cosmopolitan. The hotel's porte cochere has long sheltered Europe's aristocrats and Hollywood's royalty as they alighted from their Rollses and Ferraris. They entered the polished doors that still open onto a world of luxury lavished with mirrors, carved moldings, Oriental rugs, crystal chandeliers, and huge, baroque floral arrangements. The theme of gracious living prevails throughout the hotel in splendidly appointed rooms and marble baths. ✉ *Via Veneto 125, 00187,* ☎ *06/47081,* FAX *06/4826205. 282 rooms, 45 suites. Restaurant, bar, barbershop, beauty salon, free parking. AE, DC, MC, V. EP.*

$$$$ **Majestic.** In the 19th-century tradition of grand hotels, this establishment on Via Veneto offers sumptuous furnishings and spacious rooms, with up-to-date accessories such as CNN, minibars, strongboxes, and white marble bathrooms. There are authentic antiques in the public rooms, and the excellent restaurant looks like a Victorian conservatory. The Ninfa grill-café on street level is an intimate venue for light meals and drinks. Many suites have whirlpool baths. ✉ *Via Veneto 50, 00187,* ☎ *06/486841,* FAX *06/4880984. 87 rooms, 8 suites. Restaurant, bar, parking (fee). AE, DC, MC, V.*

$$$ **Victoria.** A 1950s luxury in the public rooms, solid comfort throughout at reasonable rates, and impeccable management are the main features of this hotel near Via Veneto. Oriental rugs, oil paintings, welcoming armchairs, and fresh flowers add charm to the public spaces, and the rooms are well furnished with armchairs and other amenities ignored by many modern decorators. American businesspeople, who prize the hotel's personalized service and restful atmosphere, are frequent guests. Some upper rooms and the roof terrace overlook the majestic pines of Villa Borghese. ✉ *Via Campania 41, 00187,* ☎ *06/473931,* FAX *06/4871890. 108 rooms. Restaurant, bar. AE, DC, MC, V. FAP, MAP.*

$$ ★ **La Residenza.** Mainly Americans frequent this hotel in a converted town house near Via Veneto, with first-class comfort and a great atmosphere. The canopied entrance, spacious well-furnished lounges, and the bar and terrace are of the type you would expect to find in a deluxe lodging. Rooms, done out in aquamarine and beige with bentwood furniture, have large closets, color TVs, refrigerator-bars, air-conditioning, and heated towel racks. Rates include a generous American-style buffet breakfast. ✉ *Via Emilia 22, 00187,* ☎ *06/4880789,* FAX *06/485721. 21 rooms, 7 suites. Bar. AE, MC, V.*

$$ ★ **Marcella.** Known to connoisseurs as one of Rome's best midsize hotels, with the feel of a smaller, more intimate establishment, this is 10 minutes from Via Veneto or Stazione Termini. Here you can do your sightseeing from the roof terrace, taking in the view while you breakfast. Rooms are furnished with flair, showing a tasteful use of color, floral prints, and mirrored walls, echoing the elegant winter-garden decor of the lounges and bar. The spacious and flexible suites are ideal for families. ✉ *Via Flavia 106, 00187,* ☎ *06/4746451,* FAX *06/4815832. 73 rooms, 2 suites. Bar. AE, DC, MC, V.*

Near Termini

$$$–$$$$ **Grand.** A 100-year-old establishment of class and style, this hotel caters to an elite international clientele. It's only a few minutes from Via Veneto. Off the richly decorated, split-level main salon—where afternoon tea is served every day—is an intimate bar, a chic rendezvous. The spacious bedrooms are decorated in gracious Empire style, with smooth fabrics and thick carpets in tones of blue and pale gold. Crystal chandeliers and marble baths add a luxurious note. The Grand also offers one of Italy's most beautiful dining rooms, called simply Le Restaurant. ✉ *Via Vittorio Emanuele Orlando 3, 00185,* ☎ *06/47091,* FAX *06/4747307. 134 rooms, 36 suites. Restaurant, bar, free parking. AE, DC, MC, V. EP.*

$$$ **Art Deco.** This hotel's name tells all about its glamorous decor, attuned to the elegance and fancy of the 1920s, with whimsical accents in Deco paintings and antiques. Underlying the style is reassuring technology: a fail-safe electrical system, air-conditioning, and whirlpool baths. The hotel is in a residential neighborhood 10 minutes from Stazione Termini and handy to public transport. Book through Best Western or directly for the best rates. ✉ *Via Palestro 19, 00185,* ☎ *06/4457588,* FAX *06/4441483. 49 rooms. Restaurant, bar, hot tub. AE, DC, MC, V. EP.*

$$$ ★ **Britannia.** This fine small hotel, with frescoed halls and breakfast room, is a very special place, offering superior quality at moderate rates. Its quiet but central location is one attraction; a caring management is another. You are coddled with such service as English-language dailies and local weather reports delivered to your room each morning, with sybaritic marble bathrooms (some with whirlpool baths) and well-furnished rooms, two with roof terraces. ✉ *Via Napoli 64, 00184,* ☎ *06/4883153,* FAX *06/4882343. 32 rooms, 1 suite. Breakfast room, free parking. AE, DC, MC, V.*

$$ **Duca d'Alba.** This elegant hotel has made a stylish contribution to the ongoing gentrification of the Suburra neighborhood, near the Colosseum and the Roman Forum. The tasteful neoclassic decor is in character with ancient Roman motifs with custom-designed furnishings and marble bathrooms. All rooms are entirely soundproofed; a few have tiny terraces. The four-bed suite with kitchenette is a bargain for a family or a group of friends. This well-run establishment offers exceptionally good value: rates are at the lowest rung in the category. The attentive staff is another plus. ✉ *Via Leonina 14, 00184,* ☎ *06/484471,* FAX *06/4884840. 27 rooms, 1 suite. AE, DC, MC, V.*

$–$$ **D'Este.** The fresh-looking decor in this distinguished 19th-century hotel evokes belle-epoque comfort, with brass bedsteads and lamps and dark wood period furniture. Rooms are quiet, light, and spacious; many can accommodate family groups. The attentive owner-manager likes to have fresh flowers in the halls and sees that everything works. He encourages inquiries about special rates, particularly during the slack summer months. It's within hailing distance of Santa Maria Maggiore and close to Stazione Termini (you can arrange to be picked up there by the hotel car). ✉ *Via Carlo Alberto 4/b, 00185,* ☎ *06/4465607,* FAX *06/4465601. 37 rooms. Bar. AE, DC, MC, V.*

$–$$ **Miami.** Its location in a dignified 19th-century building on Rome's important Via Nazionale puts this hotel in a strategic spot for sightseeing, shopping, and getting around in general; it is on main bus lines and near Stazione Termini and the Metro. Rates are moderate for the category. The marble floors, chrome trim, and dark colors are brightened by the friendly family-style management. Rooms on the courtyard are quieter. ✉ *Via Nazionale 230, 00184,* ☎ *06/4817180,* FAX *06/484562. 32 rooms, 2 suites. AE, DC, MC, V.*

$–$$ **Montreal.** This is a compact hotel on a central avenue across the square from Santa Maria Maggiore, only three blocks from Stazione Termini, with bus and subway lines close by. On three floors of an older building, it has been totally renovated and offers fresh-looking rooms. The owner-managers are pleasant and helpful, and the neighborhood has plenty of reasonably priced eateries. ✉ *Via Carlo Alberto 4, 00185,* ☎ *06/4457797,* FAX *06/4465522. 20 rooms. Parking (fee). AE, DC, MC, V.*

$–$$ ★ **Morgana.** After enjoying the richly marbled lobby, the antique accents in fully carpeted halls, and soundproofed rooms decorated with fine fabrics, you'll agree this is an elegantly conceived hotel. The Morgana offers excellent value and shows the management's attention to comfort and detail. The atmosphere is cordial and the rates are low in this category. It's also convenient to Stazione Termini. ✉ *Via Filippo Turati 33, 00185,* ☎ *06/4467230,* FAX *06/4469142. 100 rooms, 2 suites. Bar, airport shuttle, parking (fee). AE, DC, MC, V.*

$–$$ **Siviglia.** You are transported back to a more opulent era in this 19th-century mansion in the quieter residential fringe of the Stazione Termini area. Like the several embassies in the neighborhood, it, too, has bright flags flying at the entrance. Inside, Venetian glass chandeliers and antique reproduction furniture give the lounges considerable character; rooms are simpler, with a light, airy touch. ✉ *Via Gaeta 12, 00185,* ☎ *06/4441197,* FAX *06/4441195. 42 rooms. Bar. AE, MC, V.*

$ **Romae.** In the better part of the Stazione Termini neighborhood, the Romae has the advantages of a strategic location, a very friendly and helpful management, and good-size rooms that are clean and airy. The pictures of Rome in the small lobby and breakfast room, the luminous white walls and light wood furniture in the rooms, and the bright little baths all have a fresh look. Amenities such as satellite TV, safe, and hair dryer in every room make this hotel a very good value. Families benefit from special rates and services. ✉ *Via Palestro 49, 00185,* ☎ *06/4463554,* FAX *06/4463914. 38 rooms. Breakfast room. AE, MC, V.*

Vatican

$$$$ **Cavalieri Hilton.** Though the Cavalieri is outside the imaginary confines of the city's center, distance has its advantages, one of them being the magnificent view from the hotel's hilltop position (ask for a room facing the city). This hotel is a stylish oasis of quiet and comfort, with good taste and a distinctive Italian flair. If you can tear yourself away from your balcony, the terraces, gardens, and swimming pool, you will find a courtesy shuttle bus leaving for the center of Rome every hour. Don't miss the deservedly acclaimed rooftop restaurant, La Pergola (☞ Dining, *above*). ✉ *Via Cadlolo 101, 00136,* ☎ *06/35091,* FAX *06/35092241. 358 rooms, 18 suites. 2 restaurants, bar, indoor pool, outdoor pool, beauty salon, spa. AE, DC, MC, V.*

$$$ ★ **Farnese.** A late-19th century mansion, the Farnese is near the Metro and within walking distance of St. Peter's. Furnished with great attention to detail in art deco style, it has an intimate atmosphere, dazzling modern baths, charming fresco decorations, and a roof garden. ✉ *Via Alessandro Farnese 30, 00192,* ☎ *06/3212553,* FAX *06/3215129. 24 rooms. Bar, free parking. AE, DC, MC, V. EP.*

$$–$$$ **Giulio Cesare.** An aristocratic town house with a garden in the residential, but central, Prati district, the Giulio Cesare is a 10-minute walk across the Tiber from Piazza del Popolo. It's beautifully run, with a friendly staff and a quietly luxurious air. The rooms are elegantly furnished, with chandeliers, thick rugs, floor-length drapes, and rich damasks in soft colors. Public rooms have Oriental carpets, old prints and paintings, marble fireplaces, and a grand piano. The buffet breakfast is a veritable banquet. ✉ *Via degli Scipioni 287, 00192,* ☎ *06/3210751,* FAX *06/3211736. 90 rooms. Bar. AE, DC, MC, V.*

$$ **Amalia.** Handy to St. Peter's, the Vatican, and the Cola di Rienzo shopping district, this small hotel is owned and operated by the Consoli family—Amalia and her brothers. On several floors of a 19th-century building, it has large rooms with functional furnishings, TV sets, minibars, pictures of angels on the walls, and gleaming marble bathrooms (hair dryers included). The Ottaviano stop of Metro A is a block away. ✉ *Via Germanico 66, 00192,* ☎ *06/39723356,* FAX *06/39723365. 30 rooms, 7 without bath. Minibars, parking (fee). AE, MC, V.*

$$ **Sant'Anna.** An example of the gentrification of the picturesque old Borgo neighborhood in the shadow of St. Peter's, this fashionable small hotel has ample, air-conditioned bedrooms in art deco style. The frescoes in the breakfast room and fountain in the courtyard are typical Roman touches. The spacious attic rooms have tiny terraces. ✉ *Borgo Pio 134, 00193,* ☎ *06/68801602,* FAX *06/68308717. 20 rooms. Breakfast room, parking (fee). AE, DC, MC, V.*

$ ★ **Alimandi.** On a side street a block from the Vatican Museums, this family-operated hotel offers excellent value in a neighborhood with moderately priced shops and restaurants. A spiffy lobby and ample lounges, a tavern for night owls, terraces, and roof gardens are some of the perks. Rooms are spacious, airy, and well furnished; many can accommodate extra beds. Handy public transportation gets you downtown in 10 minutes or so. ✉ *Via Tunisi 8, 00192,* ☎ *06/39723948,* FAX *06/39723943. 35 rooms. Bar, parking (fee). AE, DC, MC, V. EP.*

NIGHTLIFE AND THE ARTS

The Arts

Rome has a varied and vibrant cultural life, with music, dance, theater, film, and socializing opportunities for every taste. Trends and offerings change constantly, so the best way to take stock of the leisure activities at hand is to avail yourself of one of the many local publications devoted entirely to free time. You'll find listings in English in the back of the weekly *Roma c'è* booklet, along with handy bus and metro information. A new issue is on sale at newsstands every Thursday. The weekly *Time Out Roma* gives comprehensive event schedules as well as editor's picks; listings are in Italian but easy to decipher. Schedules of events are also published in daily newspapers: pick up *Trovaroma,* the weekly entertainment guide published in Italian every Thursday as a supplement to the daily newspaper *La Repubblica*; the *Guest in Rome* booklet is distributed free at hotels; flyers are available at EPT and city tourist information offices. An English-language biweekly, *Wanted in Rome,* is available at central newsstands and has good listings of events.

Dance

The **Rome Opera Ballet** performs regularly at the Teatro dell'Opera (☞ Opera, *below*), often with leading international guest stars. Rome is regularly visited by classical and modern ballet companies from Russia, the United States, and Europe; performances are at the Teatro dell'Opera, Teatro Olimpico (☞ Music, *below*), or at one of the open-air venues in summer. Small dance companies from Italy and abroad perform in various places; check concert listings for details.

Film

Rome has dozens of movie houses, but the only one to show exclusively English-language films, in English, is the **Pasquino** (✉ Piazza Sant' Egidio, near Piazza Santa Maria in Trastevere, ☎ 06/5803622). The **Quirinetta** (✉ Via M. Minghetti 4, off Via del Corso, ☎ 06/6790012) shows films in their original language every day, usually English but occasionally Spanish, French, and others. A few other theaters in the center reserve one night a week for original-language movies: try **Nuovo Sacher** (Largo Ascianghi 1, ☎ 065818116) on Monday and Tuesday, **Alcazar** (Via Merry del Val 14, ☎ 06/5880099) on Monday, and

Quirinetta (✉ Via Minghetti 4, ☎ 06/6790012) on weekdays. Also check listings in *Roma c'è*. Tickets are usually 12,000 lire, 8,000 lire for matinees and all day Wednesday.

Music

CLASSICAL

Despite the long-standing criticism that Rome doesn't have a central concert hall (a new one is currently under construction), the city hosts a wide variety of classical music concerts at various small venues throughout the city. This can make for memorable performances in smaller halls and churches whose ambience make up for the less grand spaces, particularly at Christmastime, an especially busy concert season in Rome. Of the larger companies, one principal concert series is organized year-round by the **Accademia di Santa Cecilia** (concert hall and box office: ✉ Via della Conciliazione 4, ☎ 06/68801044 or 06/3611064). The **Accademia Filarmonica Romana** (✉ Piazza Gentile da Fabriano 17, ☎ 06/3234890 or 06/3234936) concerts are performed at the Teatro Olimpico. Other reputable companies performing here include **Istituzione Universitaria dei Concerti** (✉ Aula Magna, Piazzale Aldo Moro 5, ☎ 06/3610051), **Gonfalone** (✉ Via del Gonfalone 32, ☎ 06/6875952), and **Concerti all'Orologio** (☎ 06/68308735).

Il Tempietto (☎ 06/4814800) organizes music festivals and concerts throughout the year. Depending on the venue, tickets run from about 15,000 to 50,000 lire. In addition to the formal concert companies, there are also many small concert groups who perform in cultural centers and churches. Many concerts are free, including all those performed in churches. Look for posters outside churches announcing free concerts, particularly at the spectacularly frescoed church of **Sant'Ignazio** (✉ Piazza Sant'Ignazio, near the Pantheon, ☎ 06/6794406).

ROCK, POP, AND JAZZ

Rock, pop, and jazz concerts are frequent, especially in summer, although even performances by big-name stars may not be well advertised. Most of the bigger-name acts perform outside the center, so it's worth asking about transportation *before* you buy your tickets. Tickets for these performances are usually handled by **Orbis** (✉ Piazza Esquilino 37, ☎ 06/4744776). **Ricordi** music store (✉ Via del Corso 506, ☎ 06/3612331; ✉ Viale Giulio Cesare 88, ☎ 06/3720216) also sells tickets. For smaller venues, ☞ Music Clubs, *below*.

Opera

Rome's opera season runs from November or December to May, and performances are staged in the **Teatro dell'Opera** (✉ Piazza B. Gigli, ☎ 06/48160255 or 06/481601). Prices range from about 30,000 to 220,000 lire for regular performances; they can go much higher for an opening night or an appearance by an internationally acclaimed guest singer. Standards may not always measure up to those set by Milan's fabled La Scala, but, despite strikes and shortages of funds, most performances are respectable. The summer opera season was evicted from the ruins of the ancient **Terme di Caracalla** (☞ Across the Tiber *in* Exploring Rome, *above*), and temporary venues have been created in **Villa Borghese** and most recently at one end of the **Stadio Olimpico**, Rome's soccer stadium.

Nightlife

La Dolce Vita notwithstanding, Rome's nightlife is not among the world's most exciting, but locals say it is improving, with the proliferation of discos, live-music spots, and quiet late-night bars in recent years. In keeping with the changing times, the "flavor of the month" factor works here, too, and many places fade into oblivion after their five minutes of fame. The best sources for an up-to-date list of late-night spots are the "Night Scene" section of *Roma c'è.*

Bars

The last few years have brought an inexplicable inundation of English and Irish-style pubs to Rome, and judging from their tremendous popularity among young Italians and foreigners, it looks like Guinness is here to stay. One of the first of the British invasion, **Flann O'Brien** (✉ Via Napoli 29, ☎ 06/4480418) has the look and atmosphere of a good Irish pub but also serves decent cappuccino. **Trinity College** (✉ Via del Collegio Romano 6, near Piazza Venezia, ☎ 06/6786472) has two floors of university-style pub trappings (and Italian snacks all day), with an old-school look and convivial music and drinks until 2 AM. The granddaddy of Rome's authentic Hibernian-style pubs, **Fiddler's Elbow** (✉ Via dell'Olmata 43, ☎ 06/4872110) encourages singing and good *craic* (lively chat). **Four Green Fields** (✉ Via Costantino Morin 42, off Via della Giuliana, ☎ 06/3595091) features live music and is open until 2 AM.

So where do you go for a cocktail? Jacket and tie are in order at **Le Bar** of the Grand Hotel (✉ Via Vittorio Emanuele Orlando 3, ☎ 06/482931). **Bar della Pace** (✉ Piazza della Pace, ☎ 06/6861216) is still the people-watching cocktail bar of choice in stylish Piazza Navona. **Bar del Fico** (✉ Piazza del Fico 26, ☎ 06/6865205), around the corner, is a down-to-earth, authentically Roman alternative, but expect huge crowds on weekend and summer nights. **Taverna del Campo** (✉ Piazza Campo dei Fiori 16, ☎ 06/6874402), at Campo dei Fiori, is the spot of the moment for wine and elegant hors d'oeuvres.

Music Clubs

Jazz, folk, pop, and Latin music clubs are flourishing in Rome, particularly in Trastevere and Testaccio. Jazz clubs are especially popular, and talented local groups may be joined by visiting musicians from other countries. As admission, many clubs require that you buy a membership card for 10,000 to 20,000 lire. For popular shows or weekend nights, it's a good idea to reserve a table in advance no matter where you're going.

In the Trionfale district near the Vatican, **Alexanderplatz** (✉ Via Ostia 9, ☎ 06/39742171), Rome's most famous jazz club, has both a bar and a restaurant and features live jazz and blues played nightly by both local and internationally known musicians; it's closed Sunday. **Big Mama** (✉ Vicolo San Francesco a Ripa 18, Trastevere, ☎ 06/5812551) offers live blues, R&B, African, jazz, and rock. Latin rhythms are the specialty at **Berimbau** (✉ Via dei Fienaroli 30/b, Trastevere, ☎ 06/5813249), closed Monday and Tuesday, a live music club with a Brazilian accent and disco dancing after the show.

In trendy Testaccio, **Four XXXX Pub** (✉ Via Galvani 29, ☎ 06/5725091) is a combination restaurant–beer hall–jazz club, with live jazz groups and no-smoking sections downstairs. **Il Locale** (✉ Vicolo del Fico 3, near Piazza Navona, ☎ 06/6879075), closed Monday, pulls in a lively crowd for new rock sounds from both sides of the Atlantic. The **Jazz Club** (✉ Via Zanardelli 12, ☎ 06/6861990), near Piazza Navona, is a classic watering hole with seating at the bar or in leather-upholstered booths. Light meals are available, and there's live music a few nights a week. Live performances of jazz, soul, funk, and dance music get people moving at **Jam Session** (formerly St. Louis Music City, ✉ Via del Cardello 13/a, ☎ 06/4745076), closed Monday and Tuesday. There is also a restaurant.

Nightclubs

Most clubs open about 10:30 PM and charge an entrance fee of around 30,000 to 35,000 lire, which may include the first drink; subsequent drinks cost about 10,000 to 15,000 lire. Most clubs are closed Monday. **Jackie O'** (✉ Via Boncompagni 11, ☎ 06/4885754) is an upscale favorite with the rich and famous for dinner and disco dancing. At **Gilda** (✉ Via Mario de' Fiori 97, near Piazza di Spagna, ☎ 06/6784838) you may spot Italian actors and politicians and American celebrities. This sophisticated nightspot has a piano bar, as well as a restaurant, dance floors, and live music. Jackets are required. Newer but just as exclusive is **Bella Blu** (✉ Via Luciani 21, ☎ 06/3230490), a Parioli club that caters to Rome's thirtysomething elite.

One of Rome's first discos, **Piper** (✉ Via Tagliamento 9, ☎ 06/8414459) is still hot and a magnet for young movers and shakers. It has disco music, live groups, and pop videos, and Latin nights once a week. Occasionally, there's ballroom dancing for an older crowd, and Sunday afternoons it's open for teenagers. Testaccio's **The Saint** (✉ Via Galvani 46, ☎ 06/5747945) is a three-level complex with two discos that play everything from house to New Age music and rooms designated "Paradiso" and "Inferno" (Heaven and Hell). The under-25 crowd lets loose to indie rock and weekend live shows at post-industrial **Black Out** (✉ Via Saturnia 18, ☎ 06/70496791). **Follia** (✉ Via Ovidio 17, ☎ 06/68308435), a favorite for film parties, lures celebrities and a tony young crowd with disco music and a piano bar.

Rome's Latin dance fad is still going fast and furious, and new Latin-theme clubs seem to open every day. **Caruso** (✉ Via di Monte Testaccio 36, ☎ 06/5745019) is one that has proven its staying power; this Testaccio disco offers a Latin alternative to the many rock clubs that line this strip. **M.A.I.S.** (✉ Via Cesare Beccaria 22, ☎ 06/36251780) is the latest reinvention of one of Rome's storied nightclub venues, mainly a disco with some nights dedicated to Latin music and even cabaret. The **Open Gate** (✉ Via San Nicola da Tolentino 4, ☎ 06/42000848), open every night, is near Via Veneto and swings to a Latin beat, with disco and live music in a splashy tropical setting complemented by Cuban, Brazilian, and Mexican food.

OUTDOOR ACTIVITIES AND SPORTS

Participant Sports

Biking

You can rent a bike at **Collalti** (✉ Via del Pellegrino 82, ☎ 06/68801084), closed Monday, which is also a reliable bike repair shop. Also try **St. Peter's Motor Rent** (✉ Via di Porta Castello 43, ☎ 06/6875714).

Golf

Nonmembers are welcome in these clubs, all with 18 holes, but must show the membership cards of their home golf or country clubs. The oldest and most prestigious golf club here is the **Circolo del Golf Roma** (✉ Via Appia Nuova 716/a, ☎ 06/7803407), closed Saturday–Monday. Among the newest is **Golf Club Parco de' Medici** (✉ Viale Parco de' Medici 22, ☎ 06/6553477), closed Tuesday. You can also get into the swing at **Country Club Castel Gandolfo** (✉ Via Santo Spirito 13, Castel Gandolfo, ☎ 06/9312301). The **Golf Club Fioranello** (✉ Via della Falcognana 61, ☎ 06/7138080), closed Wednesday, is at Santa Maria delle Mole, off Via Appia Antica. Also try **Olgiata Golf Club** (✉ Largo Olgiata 15, Via Cassia, ☎ 06/30889141), closed Monday.

Health Clubs

The **Cavalieri Hilton** (✉ Via Cadlolo 101, ☎ 06/35091) has a running path on its grounds as well as outdoor and indoor pools, two clay tennis courts, and a luxurious spa, fitness, and beauty center, all open to nonguests. The **Sheraton Roma** (✉ Viale del Pattinaggio, ☎ 06/5453) has a heated outdoor pool, tennis court, two squash courts, and a sauna, but no gym. The **Sheraton Golf** (✉ Viale Parco de' Medici 22, ☎ 06/659788) has a fitness center and 18-hole golf course. Two tennis courts and a 25-m pool are at the **St. Peter's Holiday Inn** (✉ Via Aurelia Antica 415, ☎ 06/6642). The **Roman Sport Center** (✉ Via del Galoppatoio 33, ☎ 06/3201667) is a vast, full-fledged health club next to the underground parking lot in Villa Borghese; it has two swimming, a gym, aerobic workout areas, squash courts, and saunas. A day pass costs 50,000 lire. It is affiliated with the **American Health Club** (✉ Largo Somalia 60, ☎ 06/86212411).

Horseback Riding

There are several riding clubs in Rome. The most central is the **Centro Ippico Villa Borghese** (✉ Via del Galoppatoio 23, ☎ 06/3226797). Try the **Società Ippica Romana** (✉ Via Monti della Farnesina 18, ☎ 06/3240592) and the **Circolo Ippico Olgiata** (✉ Largo Olgiata 15, ☎ 06/30888043), closed Monday, outside the city on Via Cassia.

Running

The best bet for running in the inner city is the **Villa Borghese,** with an approximate ⅔-km (½-mi) circuit of the Pincio, among the marble statuary. A longer run in the park itself might include a loop around **Piazza di Siena,** a grass horse track. Although most traffic is barred from Villa Borghese, government and police cars sometimes speed through. Be careful to stick to the sides of the roads. For a long run away from all traffic, try **Villa Ada** and **Villa Doria Pamphili** on the Janiculum. On the other hand, if you really love history, run at the old **Circus Maximus,** or along **Via delle Terme di Caracalla,** flanked by a park.

Swimming

The outdoor pools of the **Cavalieri Hilton** (✉ Via Cadlolo 101, ☎ 06/35091) and the **Hotel Aldovrandi** (✉ Via Ulisse Aldovrandi 15, ☎ 06/3223993) are lush summer oases open to nonguests. The **Roman Sport Center** (✉ Via del Galoppatoio 33, ☎ 06/3201667) has two swimming pools, and there's another one at the **American Health Club** (✉ Largo Somalia 60, ☎ 06/86212411).

Spectator Sports

Basketball

Games are played, usually on Sunday, at the **Palazzo dello Sport** in the EUR district (✉ Piazzale dello Sport, ☎ 06/5925107).

Horseback Riding

The **International Riding Show,** held in May, draws a stylish crowd to the amphitheater of Piazza di Siena in Villa Borghese. The competition is stiff, and the program features a cavalry charge staged by the dashing mounted corps of the *carabinieri* (military police). Check with the tourist office (☞ Visitor Information *in* Rome A to Z, *below*) for information.

Soccer

Italy's favorite spectator sport stirs passionate enthusiasm among partisans. Games are usually held on weekend afternoons throughout the fall to spring season. Two teams—Roma and Lazio—play their home games in the Olympic Stadium at the extensive **Foro Italico** sports complex (✉ Via dei Gladiatori, ☎ 06/3336316), built by Mussolini on the banks of the Tiber. There is a chance of tickets being on sale at the box office before the games, but it's a better idea to buy them in advance from **Lazio Point** (Via Farini 34, ☎ 06/4826688) to see the Lazio team play, or go to **Orbis** (☞ Nightlife and the Arts, *above*) if you want to see the Roma team.

SHOPPING

Shopping is a must in Italy, no matter what your budget. Don't expect to get bargains on Italian designers that are exported to the United States; prices are about the same on both sides of the Atlantic. Shops are open from 9 or 9:30 to 1 and from 3:30 or 4 to 7 or 7:30. There's a tendency in Rome for shops in central districts to stay open all day, and hours are generally becoming more flexible throughout the city. Remember that most stores are closed Sunday, though this is changing, too. Generally, with the exception of food and technical-supply stores, most stores also close on Monday mornings from September to mid-June and Saturday afternoons from mid-June through August.

Bargains

You can often find good buys in knitwear and silk scarves at stands on the fringes of outdoor food markets. Bargaining is still an art at **Porta Portese** flea market (☞ Markets, *below*) and is routine when purchasing anything from a street vendor. On **Via Cola di Rienzo** there is usually a stand with a range of blown-glass items. The market at **Via Sannio** (San Giovanni in Laterano) features job lots of designer shoes and ranks of stalls selling new and used clothing at bargain prices. It is open weekdays 10–1, Saturday 10–6. The morning market in **Piazza Testaccio,** in the heart of the neighborhood of the same name, is known for stands selling designer shoes. Bargain hunters will also love **Vesti a Stock** (✉ Via Germanico 170).

Department Stores and Malls

Rinascente (✉ Near Piazza Colonna, ☎ 06/6797691) sells clothing and accessories only. Another Rinascente (✉ Piazza Fiume, ☎ 06/8841231) has the same stock, plus furniture and housewares. Both stores are open daily 9–9. **Coin** (✉ Piazzale Appio, near San Giovanni in Laterano, ☎ 06/7080020; ✉ Cinecittà Due, ☎ 06/7220931) carries housewares, as well as fashions for men and women. The **UPIM** and **Standa** chains offer low- to moderately priced goods ranging from bathing suits to first-aid supplies to while-you-wait shoe-repair service counters. The mall **Cinecittà Due** (✉ Piazza di Cinecittà, Viale Palmiro Togliatti, ☎ 06/7220902) was the first of several megamalls, with 100 stores; take Metro A to the Subaugusta stop.

Markets

All outdoor food markets are open Monday–Saturday from early morning to about 1 PM (a bit later on Saturday), but get there in the early part of the day for the best selection. Beware of pickpockets and don't go if you can't stand crowds. Downtown Rome's most colorful outdoor food market is at **Campo dei Fiori** (✉ South of Piazza Navona). Equally big and bustling is the so-called **Trionfale market** (✉ Via Andrea Doria), officially called the Mercato di Via Andrea Doria, about a five-minute walk north of the entrance to the Vatican Museums. Smaller markets can be found throughout the city. There's room for bargaining at the Sunday-morning flea market at **Porta Portese** (✉ Take Via

Rome Shopping

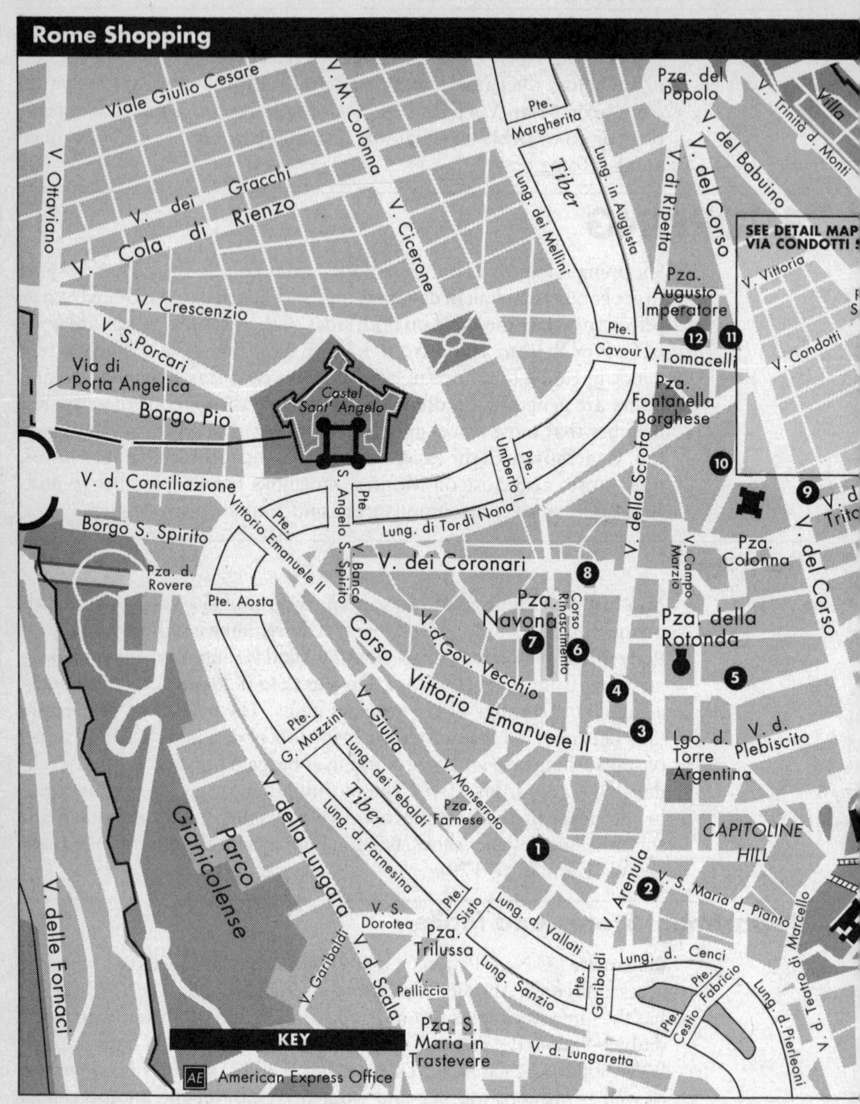

Ai Monasteri, **8**
Aston, **15**
Bruno Magli, **14**
Cinecittà Due, **19**
Coin, **20**
Di Cori, **18**
Fratelli Bassetti, **3**
Frugoni, **2**
Furla, **11**
Lavori Artigianali Femminili, **13**
Le Tartarughe, **5**
Myricae, **10**
Nardecchia, **7**
Nickol, **16**
Officina Farmaceutica di Santa Maria Novella, **6**
Rinascente, **9**
Sac Joli, **12**
Tanca, **4**
Volterra, **17**
Wazoo, **1**

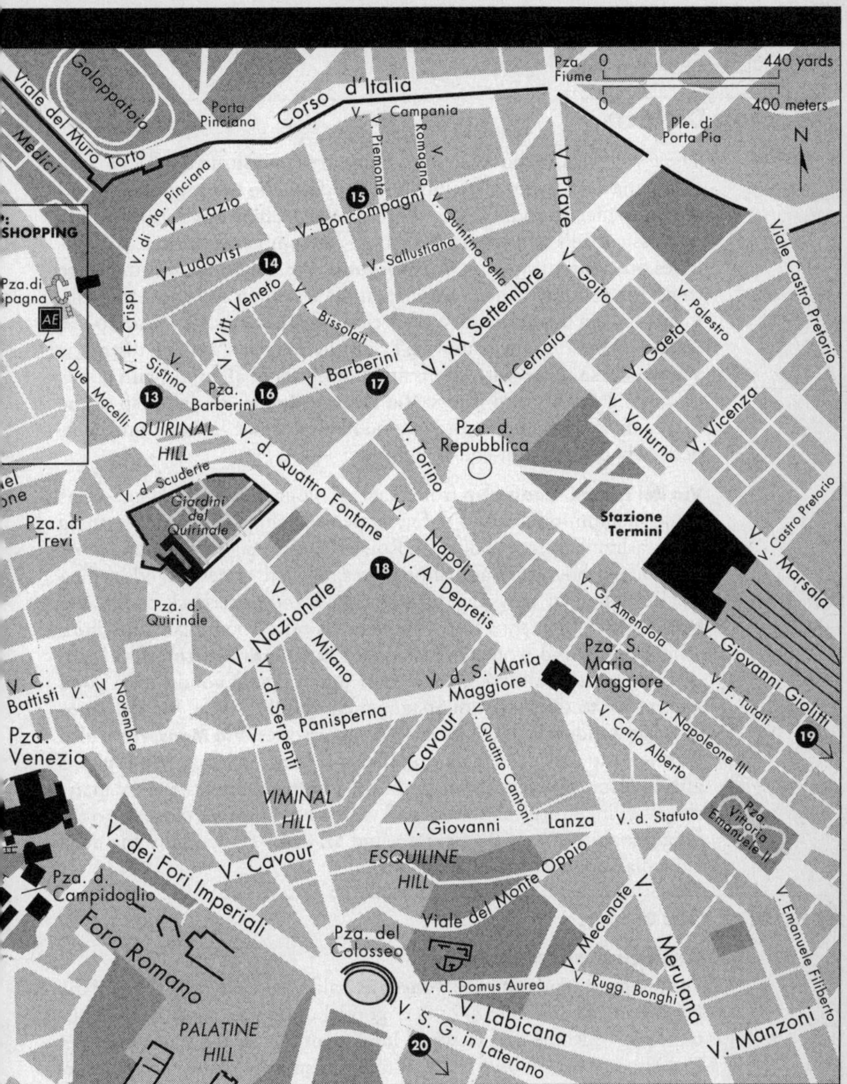
Galoppatoio
Viale del Muro Torto
Medici
Porta Pinciana
Corso d'Italia
V. Campania
V. Piemonte
V. Romagna
Pza. Fiume
0 440 yards
0 400 meters
Ple. di Porta Pia
N
V. Piave
Viale Castro Pretorio
V. di Pta. Pinciana
V. Lazio
V. Boncompagni
V. Quintino Sella
V. Sallustiana
V. Ludovisi
SHOPPING
Pza.di Spagna
AE
V. F. Crispi
V. Vitt. Veneto
V. L. Bissolati
V. XX Settembre
V. Goito
V. Palestro
V. Gaeta
V. Cernaia
V. Barberini
V. Sistina
V. d. Due Macelli
Pza. Barberini
QUIRINAL HILL
V. Volturno
V. Vicenza
V. Torino
Pza. d. Repubblica
V. d. Quattro Fontane
V. d. Scuderie
Giardini del Quirinale
Pza. di Trevi
Stazione Termini
V. Castro Pretorio
V. Marsala
V. Napoli
V. A. Depretis
V. G. Amendola
Pza. d. Quirinale
V. Nazionale
V. Milano
Pza. S. Maria Maggiore
V. Giovanni Giolitti
V. d. S. Maria Maggiore
V. F. Turati
V. C. Battisti
V. IV Novembre
V. d. Serpenti
V. Panisperna
V. Cavour
V. Quattro Cantoni
V. Carlo Alberto
V. Napoleone III
Pza. Venezia
VIMINAL HILL
V. Giovanni Lanza
V. d. Statuto
Pza Vittoria Emanuele II
V. dei Fori Imperiali
V. Cavour
ESQUILINE HILL
Viale del Monte Oppio
V. Mecenate
Pza. d. Campidoglio
Foro Romano
Pza. del Colosseo
Merulana
V. Emanuele Filiberto
V. d. Domus Aurea
V. Rugg. Bonghi
V. Labicana
V. S. G. in Laterano
V. Manzoni
PALATINE HILL
13
14
15
16
17
18
19
20

Ippolito Nievo, off Viale Trastevere); it now offers mainly new or secondhand clothing, but there are still a few dealers in old furniture and intriguing junk.

Shopping Districts

The most elegant and expensive shops are concentrated in the Piazza di Spagna area, especially along **Via Condotti. Via Borgognona** is lined with designer boutiques. The shops on **Via Frattina** have either trendy or classic men's and women's fashions at competitive prices. Art galleries are concentrated on **Via Margutta. Via del Babuino** is the place to go for antiques. There are several high-fashion designer establishments on **Via Gregoriana.** Well-heeled clotheshorses also head to **Via Sistina.** Bordering the top-price Piazza di Spagna shopping district is **Via del Corso,** lined with shops and boutiques of all kinds with goods of varying quality and prices. **Via Campo Marzio,** on the cusp of the Piazza di Spagna area, is also a good bet for classic fashions and competitively priced, high-end boutiques.

Via del Tritone, leading up from Piazza Colonna off Via del Corso, has some medium-priced and a few expensive shops selling everything from fashion fabrics to books on Rome. On **Via Veneto** you'll find more high-priced boutiques and shoe stores, as well as newsstands selling English-language newspapers, magazines, and paperback books. **Via Nazionale** features shoe stores, moderately priced boutiques, and shops selling men's and women's fashions. **Via Cola di Rienzo** offers high-quality wares of all types; for variety and range of goods, it's a good alternative to the Piazza di Spagna area. In Old Rome, **Via dei Coronari** has antiques and designer home accessories. **Via Monserrato** also features antiques dealers galore, plus a few art galleries. **Via Giulia** is also a decorative arts bonanza. In the **Pantheon** area there are many shops selling liturgical objects and vestments. Another place to go for religious souvenirs is the area around **St. Peter's,** especially Via della Conciliazione and Via di Porta Angelica.

Specialty Stores

Antiques and Prints

For old prints and antiques, **Tanca** (✉ Salita dei Crescenzi 12, near the Pantheon, ☎ 06/6875272) is a good hunting ground. Early photographs of Rome and views of Italy from the archives at **Alinari** (✉ Via Alibert 16/a, ☎ 06/6792923) make memorable souvenirs. **Nardecchia** (✉ Piazza Navona 25, ☎ 06/6869318) is reliable for prints. Stands in **Piazza della Fontanella Borghese** sell prints and old books.

Clothing

All the big names in Italian fashion have emporiums in the Piazza di Spagna area. **Sorelle Fontane** (✉ Salita San Sebastianello 6, ☎ 06/6798652), one of the first houses to put Italy on the fashion map, has a large boutique with an extensive line of ready-to-wear clothing and accessories. **Dolce & Gabbana** (✉ Piazza di Spagna 82, ☎ 06/6792294), a spin-off of the top-of-the-line D&G store on Via Borgognona, shows the trendiest designer fashions in casual wear and accessories for men and women. Miucca's trademark sleek and vaguely futuristic **Prada** (✉ Via Condotti 92, ☎ 06/6790897) designs demonstrate that a good bag is just the beginning. **Giorgio Armani** (✉ Via Condotti 77, ☎ 06/6991460) installs his quietly elegant designs in this Via Condotti fashion repository. Donatella continues to dazzle with the Versace satellite line **Versus** (✉ Via Borgognona 33, ☎ 06/6783977).

Alinari, **2**
Amadei, **20**
Bozart, **27**
Brioni, **24**
Bruno Magli, **35**
Buccellati, **29**
Bulgari, **13**
Campanile, **28**
Charles, **31**
C.u.c.i.n.a., **1**
Di Cori, **11**
Dolce & Gabbana, **7**
Ermenegildo Zegna, **14**
Ferragamo Donna, **18**
Ferragamo Uomo, **23**
Fornari, **30**
Frette, **5**
Furla, **6**
Galassia, **15**
Gianni Versace Donna, **25**
Gianni Versace Uomo, **26**
Giorgio Armani, **16**
Gucci, **12**
Il Portone, **3**
J.P. Tod's, **33**
Marisa Padovan, **22**
Mariella Burani, **21**
Mariselaine, **17**
Merola, **32**
Prada, **8**
Roland's, **9**
Sermoneta, **10**
Sorella Fontana, **4**
Venier Colombo, **34**
Versus, **19**

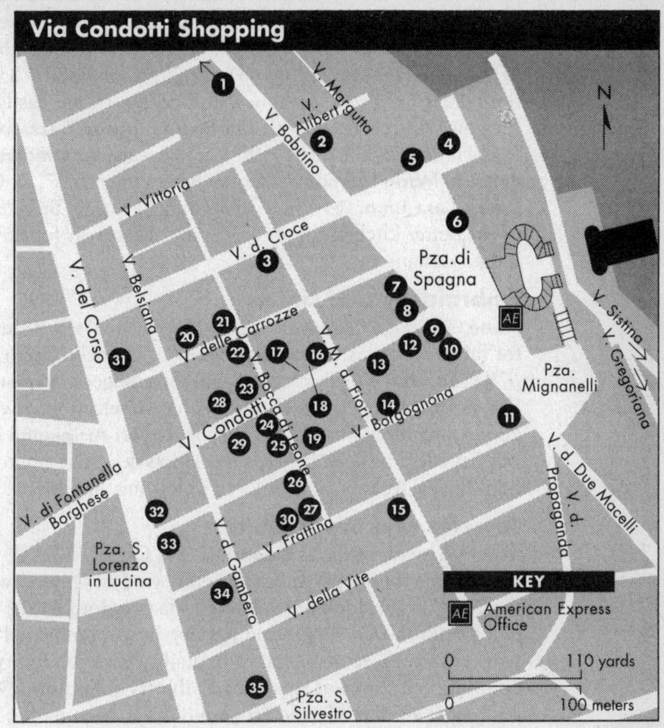

MEN'S CLOTHING

Ermenegildo Zegna (✉ Via Borgognona 7/e, ☎ 06/6789143) has the finest in elegant men's styles and accessories. **Gianni Versace Uomo** (✉ Via Borgognona 24, ☎ 06/6795037) offers the classic Mediterranean-in-a-blender prints and the mod, elegant suits that earned the Calabrian boy his name. **Il Portone** (✉ Via della Carrozze 71, ☎ 06/6793355) embodies a tradition in custom shirtmaking. For decades a man was a fashion flop without Portone's classic cuts and signature stripes in his closet. **Brioni** (✉ Via Barberini 79, ☎ 06/484517) has a well-deserved reputation as one of Italy's top tailors. In addition to impeccable custom-made apparel, you can suit up in ready-to-wear garments.

WOMEN'S CLOTHING

Galassia (✉ Via Frattina 21, ☎ 06/6791351) has expensive, extreme, and extravagant women's styles by Gaultier, Westwood, and Yamamoto—this is the place for feather boas and hats with ostrich plumes. **Mariselaine** (✉ Via Condotti 70, ☎ 06/6795817) is a top-quality women's fashion boutique. **Le Tartarughe** (✉ Via del Piè di Marmo 17, ☎ 06/6792240) has understated and versatile garments for women, including packable knits and jerseys. **Mariella Burani** (✉ Via Bocca di Leone 28, ☎ 06/6790630) mixes classy chic with judicious high-fashion overtones. **Wazoo** (✉ Via dei Giubbonari 28, ☎ 06/6869362) is one of Rome's trendiest boutiques for designer pieces, funky shoes, and special dresses. After a spree at **Versace Donna** (✉ Via Bocca di Leone 26, ☎ 06/6780521), the runway will seem a mere cakewalk.

Crafts and Gifts

For fine pottery, handwoven textiles, and other handicrafts, **Myricae** (✉ Piazza del Parlamento 38, ☎ 06/6873643) has a good selection. A bottle of liqueur, jar of marmalade, or bar of chocolate handmade by Cistercian monks in several monasteries in Italy makes an unusual, tasty gift to take home; pick from among these and other goodies at **Ai Monasteri** (✉ Piazza Cinque Lune 66, ☎ 06/68802783). Herbal and floral soaps, lotions, perfumes, and potpourri are easily carried gifts for yourself or a friend and can be found near Piazza Navona in the Rome branch of Florence's historic apothecary, the **Officina Farmaceutica di Santa Maria Novella** (✉ Corso Rinascimento 47, ☎ 06/6872446). Pricey **C.u.c.i.n.a.** (✉ Via del Babuino 118/a, ☎ 06/6791275) is one of the better kitchen supply stores in town, great for those handsome Italian designs.

Embroidery and Linens

Frette (✉ Piazza di Spagna 11, ☎ 06/6790673) is a Roman institution for fabulous linens. **Marisa Padovan** (✉ Via delle Carrozze 81, ☎ 06/6793946) shows exclusive and expensive lingerie. **Venier Colombo** (✉ Via Frattina 42, ☎ 06/6792979) has a selection of exquisite lace goods, including lingerie and linens. **Lavori Artigianali Femminili** (✉ Via Capo le Case 6, ☎ 06/6781100) offers delicately embroidered household linens, infants' and children's clothing, and blouses.

Jewelry and Silver Objects

What Cartier is to Paris, **Bulgari** (✉ Via Condotti 10, ☎ 06/6793876) is to Rome; the shop's elegant display windows hint at what's beyond the guard at the door. **Buccellati** (✉ Via Condotti 31, ☎ 06/6790329) is a tradition-rich Florentine jewelry house renowned for its silver work; it ranks with Bulgari for quality and reliability. You'll find tempting selections of small silver objects at **Fornari** (✉ Via Frattina 133, ☎ 06/6780105) and **Frugoni** (✉ Via Arenula 83, 2nd floor, ☎ 06/68806732). **Bozart** (✉ Via Bocca di Leone 4, ☎ 06/6781026) features dazzling costume jewelry in keeping with the latest fashions.

Shoes and Leather Accessories

The most revered of Rome's leather shops is **Gucci** (✉ Via Condotti 8, ☎ 06/6789340). It has a full assortment of accessories on the first floor, a fashion boutique for men and women and a scarf department on the second floor, and many Japanese customers, who line up to get in on busy days. **Roland's** (✉ Piazza di Spagna 74, ☎ 06/6790391) has an extensive stock of good-quality leather fashions and accessories, as well as stylish casual wear in wool and silk. For the latest styles in handbags and a selection of scarves and costume jewelry at reasonable prices, go to **Furla** (✉ Piazza di Spagna 22, ☎ 06/6878230), which has several stores in downtown Rome. **Sac Joli** (✉ Via Tomacelli 154, ☎ 06/6878431), despite its French name, displays a large collection of fine Italian-made handbags in up-to-the-minute styles. Offbeat and trendy, one-of-a-kind handbags in leather and/or fabrics are made and sold by **Amadei** (✉ Via delle Carrozze 20, ☎ 06/67833452). **Volterra** (✉ Via Barberini 102, ☎ 06/4819315) is well stocked and offers a wide selection of handbags at moderate prices. For gloves as pretty as Holly Golightly's, head to **Sermoneta** (✉ Piazza di Spagna 61, ☎ 06/6791960). **Di Cori** (✉ Piazza di Spagna 53, ☎ 06/6784439) has a spectrum of gloves in every color imaginable. **Merola** (✉ Via del Corso 143, ☎ 06/6791961) carries a line of expensive top-quality gloves and scarves.

For timeless elegance in splendid silk scarves and ties, leather accessories, and fine shoes, **Ferragamo** (Donna: ✉ Via Condotti 72, ☎ 06/6791565; Uomo: ✉ Via Condotti 64, ☎ 06/6781130) is one of Rome's best; you pay for quality here, but you can get great buys during the periodic sales. **Nickol** (✉ Via Barberini 21, ☎ 06/4741648) is in the moderate price range and is one of the few stores in Rome that stocks shoes in American widths. **Charles** (✉ Via del Corso 109, ☎ 06/

6792345) has a broad range of shoes, handbags, leather clothing and accessories, and a bilingual sales staff. **Bruno Magli** (✉ Via del Gambero 1, ☎ 06/6793802; ✉ Via Veneto 70, ☎ 06/4884355) is known for well-made shoes and matching handbags at high to moderate prices. **Campanile** (✉ Via Condotti 58, ☎ 06/6790731) has four floors of shoes in the latest—as well as classic—styles and other leather goods. **J.P. Tod's** (✉ Via Borgognona 45, ☎ 06/6786828) might sound British, but the signature button-soled moccasins are strictly Italian made. This exclusive Tod's carries every model and style as well as its line of handmade bags often spotted on the arms of celebrities.

Silks and Fabrics

Fratelli Bassetti (✉ Corso Vittorio Emanuele II 73, ☎ 06/6892326) has a vast selection of world-famous Italian silks and fashion fabrics in a rambling palazzo. **Aston** (✉ Via Buoncompagni 27, ☎ 06/42871227) stocks couture-level fabrics for men and women. You can find some real bargains when *scampoli* (remnants) are on sale.

SIDE TRIPS FROM ROME

Ostia Antica; Cerveteri and Tarquinia; Tivoli, Palestrina, and Subiaco

One of the easiest excursions from the capital takes you west to the sea, where tall pines stand among the well-preserved ruins of Ostia Antica, the main port of ancient Rome. The rolling landscape along the coast northwest of Rome was once Etruscan territory, and at Cerveteri and Tarquinia it holds some intriguing reminders of a people who taught the ancient Romans a thing or two about religion, art, and a pleasurable way of life. East of Rome lie some of the region's star sights, which could be combined along a route that loops through the hills where ancient Romans built their summer resorts. The biggest attraction is Tivoli. Here, Villa Adriana shows you the scale of individual imperial Roman egos, and Villa d'Este demonstrates that Renaissance egos were no smaller. Eastward at Palestrina lies a vast sanctuary famous in ancient times. The monastery where St. Benedict founded the hermitage that gave rise to Western monasticism is farther east in Subiaco.

Ostia Antica

Founded around the 4th century BC Ostia served as Rome's port city for several centuries until the Tiber changed course, leaving the town high and dry. What has been excavated here is a remarkably intact Roman town in a pretty, parklike setting. Fair weather and good walking shoes are requisites. On hot days, be here when the gates open or go late in the afternoon. A visit to the excavations takes two to three hours, including 20 minutes for the museum.

Numbers in the margin correspond to numbers on the Side Trips from Rome map.

1 **Ostia Antica** was inhabited by a cosmopolitan mix of rich businessmen, wily merchants, sailors, and slaves. The great *horrea* (warehouses) were built in the 2nd century AD to handle huge shipments of grain from Africa; the *insulae* (forerunners of the modern apartment building) provided housing for the growing population. Under the combined assaults of the barbarians and the *anopheles* mosquito, and after the Tiber changed course, the port was eventually abandoned. Tidal mud and windblown sand covered the city, which lay buried until the

Side Trips from Rome

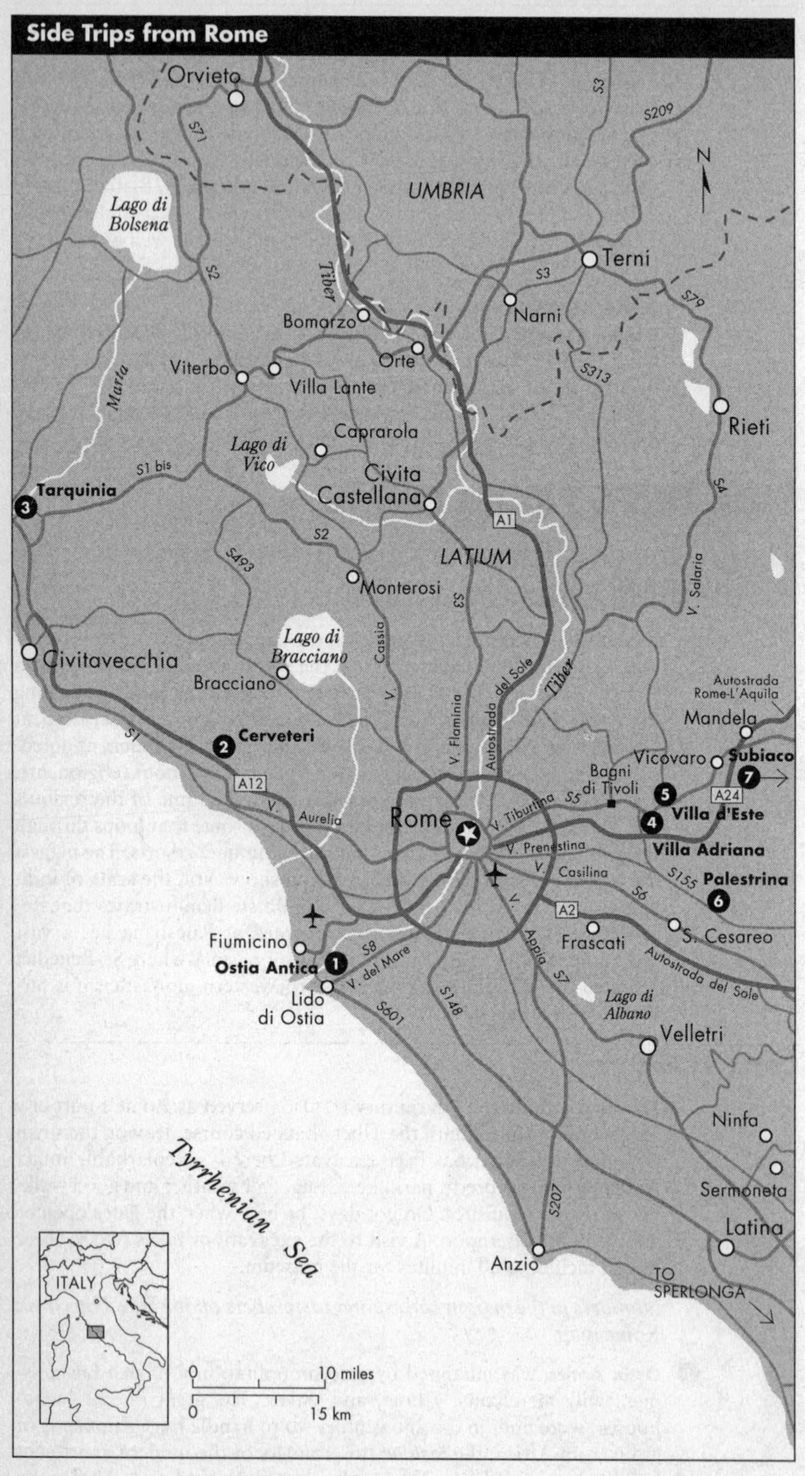

beginning of this century. Now it has been extensively excavated and is well maintained. **Porta Romana,** one of the city's three gates, opens onto the **Decumanus Maximus,** the main thoroughfare crossing the city from end to end. Black-and-white mosaic pavements representing Neptune and Amphitrite decorate the **Terme di Nettuno** (Baths of Neptune). Directly behind the baths is the barracks of the fire department, which played an important role in a town with warehouses full of valuable goods and foodstuffs.

On one side of the Decumanus Maximus is the beautiful **theater,** built by Agrippa and completely restored by Septimius Severus in the 2nd century AD. In the vast Piazzale delle Corporazioni, where trade organizations similar to guilds had their offices (notice the floor mosaics, which correspond to the various trades), is the **Tempio di Cerere** (Temple of Ceres): this is appropriate for a town dealing in grain imports, since Ceres, who gave her name to cereal, was the goddess of agriculture. You can visit the **Casa di Apuleio** (House of Apuleius) built in Pompeiian style—containing fewer windows then, and built lower than those in Ostia. Next to it is the **Mithraeum,** with balconies and a hall decorated with symbols of the cult of Mithras. This men-only religion, imported from Persia, was especially popular with legionnaires.

On Via dei Molini you can see a **mill,** where grain for the warehouses next door was ground with the stones that are still there. Along Via di Diana you come upon a *thermopolium* (bar) with a marble counter and a fresco depicting the fruit and food that were sold here. At the end of Via dei Dipinti is the **Museo Ostiense,** which displays some of the ancient sculptures and mosaics found among the ruins. The **Forum** holds the monumental remains of the city's most important temple, dedicated to Jupiter, Juno, and Minerva; other ruins of baths; a basilica (in Roman times a basilica served as a secular hall of justice); and smaller temples. **Via Epagathiana** leads toward the Tiber, where there are large warehouses, erected in the 2nd century AD, to deal with the enormous amounts of grain imported into Rome during the height of the Empire.

The **Casa di Cupido e Psiche** (House of Cupid and Psyche), a residential house, was named for a statue found there (now on display in the museum); you can see what remains of a large pool in an enclosed garden decorated with marble and mosaic motifs. Even in ancient times a premium was placed on water views: the house faces the shore, which would have been only about ⅓ km (¼ mi) away. On Via della Foce are the **Casa del Serapide** (House of Serapis), a 2nd-century multilevel dwelling, and the **Terme dei Sette Sapienti** (Baths of the Seven Wise Men), named for a fresco found here. There is another apartment building on Cardo degli Aurighi.

The **Porta Marina** leads to what used to be the seashore. In the vicinity are the ruins of the **Jewish Synagogue,** one of the oldest in the Western world. On Via Semita dei Cippi you can see the **Casa di Fortuna Annonaria,** the richly decorated house of a wealthy Ostian. This is another place to marvel at the skill of the mosaic artists and, at the same time, to realize that this really was someone's home. One of the rooms opens onto a secluded garden. The **Museo Ostiense** is also on the grounds. ✉ *Ostia Antica,* ☎ *06/5650022.* 💰 *8,000 lire includes excavations and Museo Ostiense.* ⏲ *Excavations: daily 9 AM–1 hr before sunset. Museum: daily 9–1:30.*

Ostia Antica A to Z

ARRIVING AND DEPARTING

By Car. From Porta San Paolo (Piramide), Via Ostiense leads southwest and becomes **Via del Mare,** which leads directly from to Ostia (a

30- to 40-minute trip). Signs indicate the turnoff for Ostia Antica, which comes before the modern town of Ostia.

By Train. There is regular train service to the Ostia Antica station from Ostiense train station, near Porta San Paolo; the ride takes about 30 minutes. Call ☎ 1478/88088 for toll-free train information. Another way to go is to take Metro Line B to the Magliana station and switch to the Ostia line (trains every half hour).

Cerveteri and Tarquinia

An excursion northwest of Rome takes you to Etruscan sites on hills near the sea. The Etruscans were an apparently peaceable and pleasure-loving people who held sway over what is now Central and Southern Tuscany and Northern Lazio, before the rise of the Roman Republic. They loved life and they were sure that they would enjoy the afterlife, too. The Etruscan necropolis, or "city of the dead," was a cemetery faithfully reproducing the homes and lifestyles of the living. Both of the sites you visit are necropolises.

Beyond Rome's city limits, the countryside is green with pastures and endless fields of artichokes, a premium crop in these parts. You catch glimpses of the sea to the west, where the coast is dotted with suburban developments. Because the beaches in this area are popular with Romans, highways and public transportation can be uncomfortably crowded on weekends from spring to fall. Exploring the Etruscan sites requires some agility in climbing up and down uneven stairs, and you need shoes suitable for walking on rough dirt paths.

Cerveteri is the principal Etruscan site closest to Rome and features the Necropoli della Banditaccia, a sylvan setting among mossy stones and variously shaped monuments that are memorials to revered ancestors. Tarquinia is farther north, but offers even better tombs, as well as an excellent museum full of objects recovered from tombs throughout the region. On the way, you'll pass Civitavecchia, Rome's principal port. From the highway or train you can see the port installations, which include a fort designed by Michelangelo. The low mountains to the east are the Tolfa range, where the Etruscans mined metals for export to ancient Mediterranean markets.

Cerveteri

2 The nucleus of the town, in the shadow of a medieval castle, stands on a spur of tufa rock that was the site of the Etruscan city of Caere, a thriving commercial center in the 6th century BC. The necropolis is about 2 km (1 mi) on foot or a taxi ride from Cerveteri's main piazza.

In the **Necropoli della Banditaccia** (Banditaccia Necropolis), the Etruscan residents of Caere left a heritage of great historical significance. In this monumental complex of tombs set in parklike grounds, they laid their relatives to rest, some in simple graves, others in burial chambers that are replicas of Etruscan dwellings. In the round tumulus tombs you can recognize the prototypes of Rome's tombs of Augustus and Hadrian (in the Mausoleo di Augusto and Castel Sant'Angelo) and the Tomb of Cecilia Metella on the Via Appia. Look for the **Tomba dei Capitelli,** with carved capitals; the **Tomba dei Rilievi,** its walls carved with reliefs of household objects; and the similar **Tombe degli Scudi e delle Sedie.** The **Tomba Moretti** has a little vestibule with columns. Some tombs have several chambers. ✉ *Necropoli della Banditaccia.* 🎫 *8,000 lire.* ⏲ *May–Sept., Tues.–Sun. 9–7; Oct.–Apr., Tues.–Sun. 9–4.*

In Cerveteri's medieval castle, the **Museo Nazionale Cerite** is a small archaeological museum with some of the finds, mostly pottery, from the various Etruscan cemeteries that have been located in the area. ⊠ *Piazza Santa Maria,* ☎ *06/9941354.* 🎟 *Free.* ⊙ *Tues.–Sun. 9–7.*

Tarquinia

3 Tarquinia sprawls on a hill overlooking the sea. Once a powerful Etruscan city, its medieval core shows that it was a major center in the Middle Ages, too. Though it lacks the harmony of better-preserved medieval towns, Tarquinia offers unexpected visual pleasures, among them views of narrow medieval streets opening onto quaint squares dominated by palaces and churches, and the sight of the majestic, solitary church of Santa Maria di Castello, encircled by medieval walls and towers. To focus on Tarquinia's Etruscan heritage, visit the museum in Palazzo Vitelleschi, and then see the frescoed underground tombs, in the fields east of the city. You can walk to the necropolis from town. From Piazza Matteotti, the town's main square, take Via Porta Tarquinia south past the church of San Francesco; go through the Porta Tarquinia, also known as Porta Clementina, and continue south on Via Ripagrotta. At the intersection with Via delle Croci, head east on the main road to reach the necropolis. There is very sketchy bus service from Piazza Cavour to the necropolis, with only a couple of morning and afternoon departures.

The **Museo Nazionale Tarquiniense** (National Museum of Tarquinia), is housed in Palazzo Vitelleschi, a splendid 15th-century building that contains a wealth of Etruscan treasures. Even if pottery vases and endless ranks of stone sarcophagi leave you cold, what makes a visit here memorable are the horses. A pair of marvelous golden terra-cotta winged horses gleam warmly against the gray stone wall on which they have been mounted in the main hall. They are from a frieze that once decorated an Etruscan temple, and they are strikingly vibrant proof of the degree of artistry attained by the Etruscans in the 4th century BC. The museum and its stately courtyard are crammed with sarcophagi from the underground tombs found under the meadows surrounding the town. The figures of the deceased recline casually on their stone couches, mouths curved in enigmatic smiles. Upstairs are vases and other Etruscan artifacts, together with some of the more precious frescoes from the tombs. The frescoes were removed to keep them from deteriorating. ⊠ *Piazza Cavour,* ☎ *076/6856036.* 🎟 *8,000 lire.* ⊙ *Tues.–Sun. 9–7.*

The entrance to the **Necropoli** (Necropolis), the Etruscan city of the dead, is about 800 m (½ mi) outside the town walls. Frequent, regularly scheduled guided tours leave from the ticket office, visiting about 10 of the 100 most interesting tombs, on a rotating basis. The tombs date from the 7th to the 2nd century BC, and they were painted with lively scenes of Etruscan life. The colors are amazingly fresh in some tombs, and the scenes show the vitality and highly civilized lifestyle of this ancient people. Of the thousands of tombs that exist throughout the territory of Etruria (there are 40,000 in the vicinity of Tarquinia alone), only a small percentage have been excavated scientifically. Many more have been found and plundered by "experts" called *tombaroli,* who dig illegally, usually at night. The tombs in the Tarquinia necropolis are bare; the only evidence of their original function are the stone platforms on which the sarcophagi rested. But the wall paintings are intriguing, and in many cases quite beautiful. The visit takes about 90 minutes, and good explanations in English are posted outside each tomb. ⊠ *Monterozzi, on the Strada Provinciale 1/b (Tarquinia–Viterbo).* 🎟 *8,000 lire.* ⊙ *Tues.–Sun. 9–1 hr before sunset.*

Cerveteri and Tarquinia A to Z

ARRIVING AND DEPARTING

By Bus. COTRAL buses leave every 30 minutes from the Lepanto stop of Metro A for Cerveteri (about 80 minutes) and for Tarquinia (about two hours, sometimes a bus change is necessary in Civitavecchia).

By Car. For Cerveteri, take either the A12 Rome–Civitavecchia toll highway to the Cerveteri-Ladispoli exit, or take the Via Aurelia. The trip takes about 40 minutes. To get to Tarquinia, take the A12 Rome–Civitavecchia highway all the way to the end, where you continue on the Via Aurelia to Tarquinia. The trip takes about 60 minutes.

By Train. Hourly trains from Termini, Ostiense, and Trastevere stations take you to the Cerveteri–Ladispoli station (50 minutes) and Tarquinia (70 minutes). Both stations are a short bus ride out of their respective towns.

VISITOR INFORMATION

Cerveteri (✉ Piazza Risorgimento 19, ☎ 06/99551971). **Tarquinia** (✉ Piazza Cavour 1, ☎ 0766/856384), open Monday–Saturday 8–2.

Tivoli, Palestrina, and Subiaco

East of Rome are two of Lazio's most attractive sights—Villa Adriana and the Villa d'Este in Tivoli—and two less conspicuous attractions, in the mountains farther east. The road from Rome to Tivoli passes through some uninspiring industrial areas and burgeoning suburbs that used to be lush countryside. You'll know you're close to Tivoli when you see vast quarries of travertine marble and smell the sulfurous vapors of the little spa, Bagni di Tivoli. Both sites in Tivoli are outdoors and entail walking.

With a car, you can continue your loop through the mountains east of Rome, taking in two very different sights that are both focused on religion: the ancient pagan sanctuary at Palestrina is set on the slopes of Mt. Ginestro, from which it commands a sweeping view of the green plain and distant mountains. Subiaco, the cradle of Western monasticism, is tucked away in the mountains above Tivoli and Palestrina. Unless you start out very early and have lots of energy, plan an overnight stop along the way if you want to take in all three.

Tivoli

4 **Villa Adriana** (Hadrian's Villa), 3 km (2 mi) south of Tivoli, should be visited first, especially in summer, to take advantage of cool mornings. Hadrian's Villa was an emperor's theme park, a retreat where the marvels of the classical world were reproduced for a ruler's pleasure. Hadrian, who succeeded Trajan as emperor in AD 117, was a man of genius and intellectual curiosity. Fascinated by the accomplishments of the Hellenistic world, he decided to re-create it for his own enjoyment by building this villa over a vast tract of land below the ancient settlement of Tibur. From AD 118 to 130, architects, laborers, and artists worked on the villa, periodically spurred on by the emperor himself, as he returned from another voyage full of ideas for even more daring constructions. After his death in AD 138, the fortunes of his villa declined. It was sacked by barbarians and Romans alike; many of his statues and decorations had ended up in the Vatican Museums, but the expansive ruins are nonetheless compelling. A visit here should take about two hours, more if you like to savor antiquity slowly. ✉ *Villa Adriana,* ☎ *0774/530203.* 🎫 *8,000 lire.* ⏲ *Daily 9 AM–90 mins before sunset.*

5 **Villa d'Este.** Ippolito d'Este (1509–72), an active figure in the political intrigues of mid-16th-century Italy, was also a cardinal, thanks to

his grandfather, Alexander VI (1430–1503), the infamous Borgia pope. To console himself at a time when he saw his political star in decline, Ippolito tore down part of a Franciscan monastery that occupied the hillside site he had chosen for his villa. Then the determined prelate diverted the Aniene River into a channel to run under the town and provide water for the Villa d'Este's fountains. Big, small, noisy, quiet, rushing, and running, the fountains create a late-Renaissance playground. Though time has taken its toll, and the fountains and gardens aren't as well kept as in the cardinal's day, it is easy to see why many travelers of the past considered Villa d'Este one of the most beautiful spots in Italy. Villa d'Este requires a lot of stair climbing and takes about an hour. ✉ *Villa d'Este.* 🎫 *8,000 lire.* ⏲ *Tues.–Sun. 9 AM–90 mins before sunset.*

Palestrina

6 Giovanni Pierluigi da Palestrina, born in Palestrina in 1525, was the renowned composer of 105 masses, as well as madrigals, magnificats, and motets. But the town was celebrated long before the composer's lifetime. Ancient Praeneste, modern Palestrina, was founded much earlier than Rome. It was the site of the Temple of Fortuna Primigenia, which dates from the beginning of the 2nd century BC. This was one of the biggest, richest, and most frequented temple complexes in all antiquity. People came from far and wide to consult its famous oracle, yet in modern times no one had any idea of the extent of the complex until World War II bombings exposed ancient foundations that stretched way out into the plain below the town. It has since become clear that the temple area was larger than the town of Palestrina is today. Now you can make out the four superimposed terraces that formed the main part of the temple; they were built up on great arches and were linked by broad flights of stairs. The whole town sits on top of what was once the main part of the temple.

Large arches and terraces scale the hillside up to the **Palazzo Barberini,** built in the 17th century along the semicircular lines of the original temple. It's now a museum containing material found on the site, some dating back to the 4th century BC. The collection of splendid engraved bronze urns, plundered by thieves in 1991 and later recovered, takes second place to the chief attraction, a 1st-century BC mosaic representing the Nile in flood. This delightful work—a large-scale composition in which form, color, and innumerable details captivate the eye—is alone worth the trip to Palestrina. But there's more: a model of the temple as it was in ancient times, helps you appreciate the immensity of the original construction. ✉ *Museo Nazionale Archeologico, Palazzo Barberini,* ☎ *06/9538100.* 🎫 *4,000 lire.* ⏲ *Mid-Sept.–mid-Nov. and mid-Mar.–May, daily 9–6; June–mid-Sept., daily 9–7:30; mid-Nov.–mid-Mar., daily 9–4.*

Subiaco

7 Between the town and St. Benedict's hermitage on the mountainside is the **Convento di Santa Scolastica,** the only one of the hermitages founded by St. Benedict to have survived the Lombard invasion of Italy in the 9th century. It has three cloisters; the oldest dates from the 13th century. The library was the site of the first print shop in Italy, set up in 1474. ⏲ *Daily 9–12:30 and 4–7.*

The 6th-century **Monastero di San Benedetto** (Monastery of St. Benedict), a landmark of Western monasticism, was built over the grotto where the saint lived and meditated. Clinging to the cliff on nine great arches, it has resisted the assaults of humans for almost 800 years. Over the little wooden veranda at the entrance, a Latin inscription augurs PEACE TO THOSE WHO ENTER. Every inch of the upper church is covered with frescoes by Umbrian and Sienese artists of the 14th century. In front of the main altar, a stairway leads down to the lower church, carved out of the rock, with yet another stairway down to the grotto where Benedict lived as a hermit for three years. The frescoes here are even earlier than those above; look for the portrait of St. Francis of Assisi, painted from life in 1210, in the Cappella di San Gregorio, and for the oldest fresco in the monastery, in the Shepherd's Grotto. ⏲ *Daily 9–12:30 and 3–6.*

Tivoli, Palestrina, and Subiaco A to Z

ARRIVING AND DEPARTING

By Bus. COTRAL buses (☏ 167/431784 toll-free) leave for Tivoli every 15 minutes from the terminal at the Rebbibia stop on Metro B, but not all take the route that passes near Hadrian's Villa. Inquire which bus passes closest to Villa Adriana and tell the driver to let you off there. The ride takes about 60 minutes. From Rome to Palestrina, take the COTRAL bus from the Anagnina stop on Metro A. From Rome to Subiaco, take the COTRAL bus from the Rebbibia stop on Metro B; buses leave every 40 minutes; the circuitous trip takes one hour and 45 minutes.

By Car. For Tivoli, take Via Tiburtina or the Rome–L'Aquila autostrada (A24). To get to Palestrina directly from Rome, take either Via Prenestina or Via Casilina or take the Autostrada del Sole (A2) to the San Cesareo exit and follow signs for Palestrina; this trip takes about one hour. It's best to drive from Rome to Subiaco. Take S155 east for about 40 km (25 mi) before turning left onto S411 for the remaining 25 km (15 mi) to Subiaco; the trip takes about 70 minutes.

By Train. FS trains connect Rome's Termini and Tiburtina stations with Tivoli in about 30 minutes; Villa d'Este is about a 20-minute walk from the station in Tivoli. The FS train from Stazione Termini to Palestrina takes about 40 minutes; you can then board a bus from the train station to the center of town.

GETTING AROUND

By Bus. There is local bus service between Tivoli and Palestrina, but check schedules locally.

By Car. From Tivoli to Palestrina, follow signs for Via Prenestina and Palestrina. To get to Subiaco from either Tivoli or Palestrina, take the autostrada for L'Aquila (A24) to the Vicovaro–Mandela exit, then follow the local road to Subiaco.

GUIDED TOURS

CIT (☏ 06/47941) has half-day excursions to Villa d'Este in Tivoli. **American Express** (☏ 06/67641), **Appian Line** (☏ 06/4884151), and **Carrani Tours** (☏ 06/4880510) have tours that include Hadrian's Villa.

VISITOR INFORMATION

Palestrina (✉ Piazza Santa Maria degli Angeli, ☏ 06/9573176). **Tivoli** (✉ Largo Garibaldi, ☏ 0774/334522). **Subiaco** (✉ Via Cadorna 59, ☏ 0774/822013).

ROME A TO Z

Arriving and Departing

By Bus

There is no central bus terminal in Rome. **COTRAL** (☏ 167/431784 toll-free) is the suburban bus company that connects Rome with outlying areas and other cities in the Lazio region. Long-distance and suburban buses terminate either near Tiburtina Station or near outlying Metro stops such as Rebbibia and Anagnina. The COTRAL terminal at the Lepanto Metro station, for buses to Civitavecchia and towns along the coast northwest of Rome, will be relocated after the late 1999 or early 2000 opening of the new extension of Metro A to Circonvallazione Cornelia. For COTRAL bus information, call weekdays 8 AM–8 PM.

By Car

The main access routes from the north are A1 (Autostrada del Sole) from Milan and Florence or the A12/E80 highway from Genoa. The principal route to or from points south, including Naples, is the A2. All highways connect with the Grande Raccordo Anulare (GRA), which channels traffic into the center. Markings on the GRA are confusing: take time to study the route you need.

By Plane

Most international flights and all domestic flights arrive at **Aeroporto Leonardo da Vinci** (✉ 30 km/19 mi southwest of Rome, ☎ 06/65953640), also known as **Fiumicino**. Some international and charter flights land at **Ciampino** (✉ Via Appia Nuova, 15 km/9 mi southeast of Rome, ☎ 06/794941), a civil and military airport.

BETWEEN THE AIRPORT AND DOWNTOWN

By Car. Follow the signs for Rome on the expressway from the airport, which links with the GRA, the beltway around Rome. The direction you take on the GRA depends on where your hotel is, so get directions from the car-rental people at the airport.

By Taxi. A taxi from Fiumicino to the center of town costs about 70,000 to 80,000 lire, including supplements for airport service and luggage, and the ride takes 30 to 40 minutes, depending on traffic. Private limousines can be hired at booths in the arrivals hall; they charge a little more than taxis but can take more passengers. Ignore gypsy drivers who approach you inside the terminal; stick to the licensed cabs, yellow or white, that wait by the curb. A booth inside the arrivals hall provides taxi information.

By Train. To get to downtown Rome from Fiumicino Airport, you have a choice of two trains. Inquire at the airport (at EPT or train information counters) as to which takes you closest to your hotel. The nonstop **Airport-Termini express** (marked FS and run by the state railway) takes you directly to Track 22 at Stazione Termini, Rome's main train station, which is well served by taxis and is the hub of Metro and bus lines. The ride to Termini takes 30 minutes; departures are hourly, beginning at 7:50 AM from the airport, with a final departure at 10:05 PM. Tickets cost 13,000 lire. **FM1,** the other airport train, runs from the airport to Rome and beyond, with its terminal in Monterotondo, a suburban town to the east. The main stops in Rome are at Trastevere, Ostiense, and Tiburtina stations; at each you can find taxis and bus and/or Metro connections to other parts of Rome. This train runs from Fiumicino from 6:35 AM to 12:15 AM, with departures every 20 minutes, a little less frequent in off-hours. The ride to Tiburtina takes 40 minutes. Tickets cost 7,000 lire. For either train buy your ticket at automatic vending machines (you need Italian currency). There are ticket counters at some stations (at Termini/Track 22, Trastevere, Tiburtina). Date-stamp the ticket at the gate before you board.

By Train

Stazione Termini is Rome's main train terminal; the Tiburtina and Ostiense stations serve some long-distance trains, many commuter trains, and the FM1 line to Fiumicino Airport. Some trains for Pisa and Genoa leave Rome from, or pass through, the Trastevere Station. For **train information,** call ☎ 1478/88088, 7 AM–9 PM. You can find

English-speaking staff at the information office at Stazione Termini, or ask for information at travel agencies. You can purchase tickets up to two months in advance either at the main stations or at travel agencies bearing the FS (Ferrovie dello Stato) emblem. Lines at station ticket windows may be very long, and electronic ticket machines are complex, though they have instructions in English; you can save time by buying your ticket at a travel agency. Remember that you can reserve a seat up to one day in advance at a travel agency, or up to three hours in advance at a train station. Tickets for train rides within a radius of 100 km (62 mi) of Rome can be purchased at tobacco shops and at some newsstands, as well as at ticket machines on the main concourse. Like all train tickets, they must be date-stamped before you board, at the machine near the track, or you will be fined.

Getting Around

Although most of Rome's sights are in a relatively circumscribed area, the city is too large to be seen solely on foot. Take the Metro (subway), a bus, or a taxi to the area you plan to visit, and expect to do a lot of walking once you're there. Wear a pair of comfortable, sturdy shoes to cushion the impact of the *sampietrini* (cobblestones). Heed our advice on security. Get away from the noise and polluted air of heavily trafficked streets by taking parallel streets whenever possible. You can get free city and transportation-route maps at municipal information booths; the transportation maps are probably more up-to-date than those you can buy at newsstands.

Rome's integrated Metrebus transportation system includes buses and trams (ATAC), Metro and suburban trains and buses (COTRAL), and some other suburban trains (FS) run by the state railways. A ticket valid for 75 minutes on any combination of buses and trams and one entrance to the Metro costs 1,500 lire. You are supposed to date-stamp your ticket when you board the first vehicle, stamping it again when boarding for the last time within 75 minutes (the important thing is to stamp it the first time). Tickets are sold at tobacconists, newsstands, some coffee bars, automatic ticket machines positioned in Metro stations and some bus stops, and at ATAC and COTRAL ticket booths (in some Metro stations, on the lower concourse at Stazione Termini, and at a few main bus terminals). A BIG tourist ticket, valid for one day on all public transport, costs 6,000 lire. A weekly ticket (Settimanale, also known as CIS) costs 24,000 lire and can be purchased only at ATAC booths. Try to avoid the rush hours (8–9, 1–2:30, 7–8), and beware of pickpockets, especially when boarding and getting off vehicles, particularly on the Metro and on Buses 64 (Termini–Vatican) and 218 and 660 (Catacombs). When purchasing tickets for excursions outside Rome on COTRAL buses or trains, buy a return ticket, too, to save time at the other end.

By Bicycle

Pedaling through Villa Borghese, along the Tiber, and through the center of the city when traffic is light is a pleasant way to see the sights, but remember: Rome is hilly. (For information on bicycle rentals, ☞ Outdoor Activities and Sports, *above*). **Scala Reale** (✉ Via Varese 52, 00185 Rome, ☎ 06/44700898) and **Secret Walks** (✉ Viale Medaglie d'Oro 127, 00136 Rome, ☎ 06/39728728) organize all-day bike tours of Rome for small groups covering major sights and some hidden ones. The same tours are available by moped.

By Bus

ATAC (☎ 167/431784 information) city buses and tram lines run from about 6 AM to about midnight, with night buses (indicated N) on some lines. *Remember to board at the back and exit at the middle.* The com-

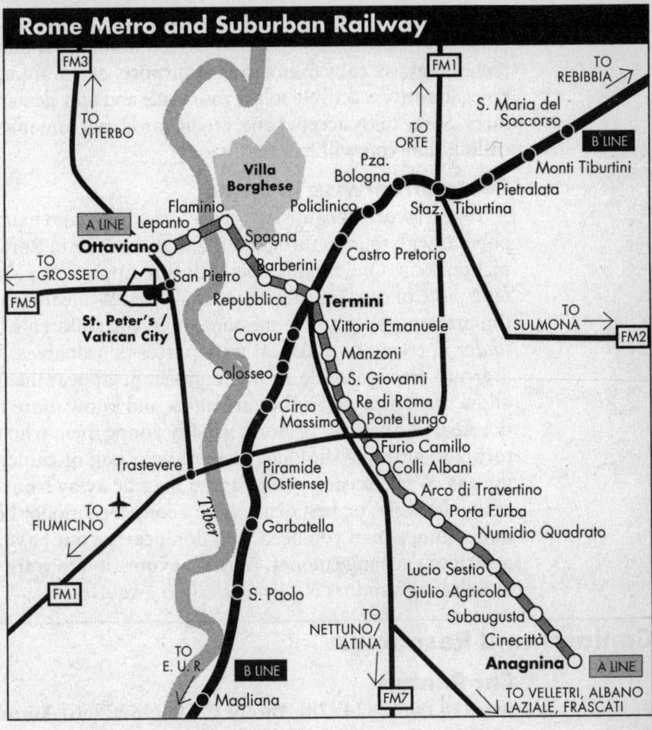

pact electric buses of Lines 117 and 119 take handy routes through the center of Rome that can save lots of steps.

By Horse-Drawn Carriage

A ride in a horse-drawn carriage can be fun when traffic is light, especially on a Sunday or holiday or during the summer. Come to terms with the driver before starting out. City-regulated rates are about 50,000 lire for a 30-minute ride, and about 85,000 for an hour. Refuse to pay more. You can find carriages at Piazza di Spagna, Piazza Venezia, and on Via del Corso near the Hotel Plaza.

By Metro

This is the easiest and fastest way to get around and there are stops near most of the main tourist attractions. The Metro opens at 5:30 AM, and the last trains leave the farthest station at 11:30 PM (on Saturday night trains run until 12:30 AM). There are two lines—A and B—which intersect at Stazione Termini.

By Moped

You can rent a moped or scooter and mandatory helmet at **Scoot-a-Long** (✉ Via Cavour 302, ☎ 06/6780206). Also try **St. Peter's Motor Rent** (✉ Via di Porta Castello 43, ☎ 06/6875714) and **Happy Rent** (✉ Piazza Esquilino 8/h, ☎ 06/4818185) rents scooters, too.

By Taxi

Taxis in Rome do not cruise, but if empty they will stop if you flag them down. Taxis wait at stands and can also be called by phone (☎ 5551, 3570, 4994, or 88177), in which case you're charged a small supplement. The meter starts at 4,500 lire; there are supplements for night service (5,000 lire extra from 10 PM to 7 AM) and on Sunday and holidays, as well as for each piece of baggage. Use only licensed, metered yellow or white cabs, identified by a numbered shield on the side, an illuminated taxi sign on the roof, and a plaque next to the license plate reading SERVIZIO PUBBLICO. Avoid unmarked, unauthorized, unmetered gypsy cabs (numerous at airports and train stations), whose renegade drivers actively solicit your trade and may demand astronomical fares. Some taxis accept some credit cards, but you must specify when calling that you will pay that way.

Being Streetwise in Rome

A (repeat) word of caution: "gypsy" children, who hang around sights popular with tourists throughout Europe, are rife in Rome and are adept pickpockets. One modus operandi is to approach a tourist and proffer a piece of cardboard with writing on it. While the unsuspecting victim attempts to read the message *on* it, the children's hands are busy *under* it, trying to make off with purses or valuables. If you see such a group (recognizable by their unkempt appearance), do not even allow them near you—they are quick and know more tricks than you do. Also be aware of persons, usually young men, who ride by on motorbikes, grab the shoulder strap of your bag or camera, and step on the gas. Wear or carry your bag on the side away from the street edge of the sidewalk, or, best of all, wear a concealed money belt. Don't carry more money than you need, and don't carry your passport unless you need it to exchange money. A useful expression to ward off pesky panhandlers or vendors is *"Vai via!"* (Go away!).

Contacts and Resources

Car Rentals

Avis (☎ 06/42824728). **Thrifty** (☎ 06/4820966). **Eurodollar** (☎ 167/018668). **Hertz** (☎ 167/808016). **Maggiore** (☎ 147/867067).

Consulates

U.S. Consulate (✉ Via Veneto 121, ☎ 06/46741). **Canadian Consulate** (✉ Via Zara 30, ☎ 06/445981). **U.K. Consulate** (✉ Via Venti Settembre 80/a, ☎ 06/4825441).

Emergencies

Police (☎ 113). **Ambulance** (☎ 118). **Red Cross** (☎ 06/5510).

English-Language Bookstores

Economy Book and Video Center (✉ Via Torino 136, ☎ 06/4746877). **Anglo-American Bookstore** (✉ Via della Vite 102, ☎ 06/6795222). **Lion Bookshop** (✉ Via dei Greci 33/36, ☎ 06/32654007). **Open Door** (✉ Via della Lungaretta 25, Trastevere, ☎ 06/5896478). **Corner Bookstore** (✉ Via del Moro 48, Trastevere, ☎ 06/5836942).

English-Speaking Doctors

Salvator Mundi International Hospital (Viale delle Mura Gianicolensi 66, ☎ 06/588961). **Rome American Hospital** (Via Emilio Longoni 69, about 30 minutes by cab from the center of town, ☎ 06/22551).

Guided Tours

BUS TOURS

American Express (✉ Piazza di Spagna 38, ☎ 06/67641). **Appian Line** (☎ 06/4884151). **ATAC** (☎ Call the tourist office for information). **CIT** (✉ Piazza della Repubblica 64, ☎ 06/47941).

ORIENTATION TOURS

American Express (☞ *above*). **CIT** (☞ *above*).

WALKING TOURS

Scala Reale (✉ Via Varese 52, 00185 Rome, ☎ 06/44700898, 800/732–2863 ext. 4052 in U.S.). **Secret Walks** (✉ Viale Medaglie d'Oro 127, 00136 Rome, ☎ 06/39728728).

Late-Night Pharmacies

The following pharmacies have some English-speaking staff. **Farmacia Internazionale Capranica** (⊠ Piazza Capranica 96, ☎ 06/6794680). **Farmacia Internazionale Barberini** (⊠ Piazza Barberini 49, ☎ 06/4825456). **Farmacia Cola di Rienzo** (⊠ Via Cola di Rienzo 213, ☎ 06/3243130). Most are open 8:30–1 and 4–8; some are open all night. A schedule posted outside each pharmacy indicates the nearest pharmacy open during off hours (afternoons, through the night and Sunday).

Travel Agencies

American Express (☞ *above*). **Appian Line** (☞ *above*). **Carrani Tours** (⊠ Via Vittorio Emanuele Orlando 95, ☎ 06/4880510). **CIT** (☞ *above*).

Villa Rentals

For stays of a week or more, especially for families or groups of friends, an apartment or villa rental may be more convenient than a hotel. Always insist on photos, a map with indication of location, and detailed description of the property. **Property International** (⊠ Viale Aventino 79, 00153, ☎ 06/5743170, FAX 06/5743182) handles monthly and weekly rentals in Rome and Tuscany. **Homes International** (⊠ Via San Basilio 41, 00187, ☎ 064881800, FAX 06/4881808) offers short- and long-term accommodations in Rome.

Visitor Information

Tourist office (Ente Provinciale de Turismo, EPT ⊠ Via Parigi 5, ☎ 06/48899255), open Monday–Friday 8:15–7:15 and Saturday 8:15–1:30; ⊠ Stazione Termini, near Track 4, ☎ 06/4871270), open daily 8:15–7:15; ⊠ Aeroporto Leonardo da Vinci, ☎ 06/65956074), open daily 8:15–7:15.

2 FLORENCE

Birthplace of the Renaissance, Florence has been a mecca for travelers since the 19th century, when English ladies flocked here to stay in charming pensiones and paint watercolors. They were captivated by a wistful Botticelli smile, impressed by the graceful dignity of Donatello's bronze *David,* and moved by Michelangelo's provocative *Slaves* twisting restlessly in their marble prisons.

Updated by Patricia Rucidlo

FLORENCE IS ONE OF THE PREEMINENT TREASURES of Europe, and it is a time-honored mecca for visitors from all over the world. But as a city, Florence (Firenze in Italian) can be surprisingly forbidding—at first glance. Its historic center has 15th-century *palazzi* lining its narrow streets. The plain and unprepossessing facades often give way to delightful courtyards. With the exception of a very few buildings, the classical dignity of the High Renaissance and the exuberant invention of the Baroque are not to be found here. The typical Florentine exterior gives nothing away, as if obsessively guarding secret treasures within.

The treasures, of course, are very real. And far from being a secret, they are famous the world over. The city is a veritable museum of unique and incomparable proportions. A single historical fact explains the phenomenon: Florence gave birth to the Renaissance. In the early 15th century the study of antiquity—of the glory that was Greece and the grandeur that was Rome—became a Florentine passion, and with it came a new respect for learning and a new creativity in art and architecture. In Florence, that remarkable creativity is everywhere in evidence.

Though there had been a town here since Roman times, it wasn't until the 11th and 12th centuries that Florence started to make its mark. At this time Florentine cloth began to do particularly well in foreign markets, the various trades organized themselves in powerful guilds (or *arti*), and the Florentines took over as the most important bankers in Europe, thanks to their florin-based currency. They were perpetually at loggerheads with other Tuscan towns, such as Pisa and Siena, and this is why Florence has such a defensive air, and why its cathedral—the town's symbol—is so huge: it had to be bigger and more splendid than anyone else's. They kept expanding, despite periodic devastating plagues, and equally destructive civil strife. (One of the victims of the internal rift was the great poet Dante, author of the *Divine Comedy,* who happened to be on the losing side; he died in exile, cursing his native town.)

Meanwhile the banking families became more and more powerful, and in the early 15th century one of them, the Medici, began to outstrip all others. The most famous of them, Lorenzo de' Medici (1449–92), was not only an astute politician, he was also a highly educated man and a great patron of the arts. "Il Magnifico," or The Magnificent, gathered around him, in the late 15th century, a court of poets, artists, philosophers, architects, and musicians, and organized all kinds of cultural events, festivals, and tournaments. It was Florence's golden period of creativity, when art made great leaps toward a new naturalism through the study of perspective and anatomy, when architects forged a new style based on the techniques used by the ancient Romans. The Renaissance man was born, a man who, like Leonardo da Vinci (1452–1519), could design a canal, paint a fresco, or solve a mathematical problem with equal ease.

Things changed with Lorenzo's death in 1492. First, his son and successor, Piero (1471–1503), handed over most of Florence's key territories to the invading French king, Charles VIII (1470–98), and then the city was sacked by the French army. A "republic" was set up, and one of its most vocal citizens was a charismatic, hellfire-preaching Dominican monk, Girolamo Savonarola (1452–98), who activated a moral cleanup operation to which the Florentines took with fanatical enthusiasm. He himself was accused of heresy and hanged (his corpse was burned on a pyre in Piazza della Signoria). After a decade or so of internal unrest, the republic fell and the Medici were recalled to power.

But even with the return of the Medici, Florence never regained its former prestige. By the 1530s all the major artistic talent had left the city—Michelangelo, for one, had settled in Rome. The now ineffectual Medici, having been given the title of grand dukes, remained nominally in power until the line died out in 1737, and thereafter Florence passed from the Austrians to the French and back again, until the unification of Italy (1865–70), when it briefly became the capital under King Vittorio Emanuele II (1820–78).

Florence was "discovered" by those intrepid souls making their grand tours in the 18th century. It became a mecca for travelers, particularly the Romantics, including John Keats (1795–1821) and Percy Shelley (1792–1822), who were inspired by the elegance of its palazzi and its artistic wealth. Today, millions of modern visitors follow in their footsteps. As the sun sets over the Arno and, as Mark Twain described it, "overwhelms Florence with tides of color that make all the sharp lines dim and faint and turn the solid city to a city of dreams," it's hard not to fall under the city's magic spell.

Pleasures and Pastimes

Dining

Florentines are justifiably proud of their robust food, claiming that it became the basis for French cuisine when Catherine de' Medici took a battery of Florentine chefs with her when she reluctantly relocated to become Queen of France in the 16th century. You can sample such specialties as creamy *fegatini,* a chicken liver spread, and *ribollita* (minestrone thickened with bread and swirled with extra virgin olive oil) in bustling, convivial *trattorie* where you share long wooden tables set with paper place mats. Like the Florentines, take a break at an *enoteca* (wineshop and/or wine bar) during the day and discover some little-known but excellent types of Chianti.

Lodging

No stranger to visitors, Florence is equipped with hotels for all budgets, and they are interspersed throughout the city; for instance, you can find both budget and luxury hotels in the *centro storico* (historic center) and along the Arno. Whether you are in a five-star hotel or a more modest establishment, you may have one of the greatest pleasures of all: a room with a view. Florence has so many famous landmarks that it's not hard to find lodgings with a vista to remember. And the equivalent of the genteel pensiones of yesteryear still exist, though they are now officially classified as hotels. Usually small and intimate, they often have a quaint appeal that fortunately does not preclude modern plumbing. Make reservations well in advance for the 2000 Jubilee year.

Shopping

Since the days of the medieval guilds, Florence has been synonymous with fine craftsmanship and good business. Such time-honored Florentine specialties as antiques (and reproductions), bookbinding, jewelry, lace, leather goods, silk, and straw attest to that. More recently, the Pitti fashion shows and the burgeoning textile industry in nearby Prato have added fine clothing to the long list of merchandise available in the shops of Florence. Another medieval feature is the distinct feel of the different shopping areas, a throwback to the days when each district supplied a different product.

EXPLORING FLORENCE

Sightseeing in Florence is space intensive. Everything that you probably want to see is concentrated in the relatively small historic core of the city. But there is so much packed into the area that you may find yourself slogging from one mind-boggling sight to another and feeling overwhelmed. If you are not an inveterate museum enthusiast, take it easy. Don't try to absorb every painting or fresco that comes into view. There is second-rate art even in the Galleria degli Uffizi and the Palazzo Pitti (*especially* the Pitti), so find some favorites and enjoy them at your leisure.

Walking through the streets and alleyways in Florence is a discovery in itself, but to save time and energy (especially on your third or so day in the city), make use of the efficient bus system. Buses also provide the least-fatiguing way to reach Piazzale Michelangelo, San Miniato, and the Forte di Belvedere. It is easy to make excursions to, say, Fiesole or the Medici villas by city bus. Most churches are usually open from 8 or 9 until noon or 12:30, and from 3 or 4 until about 6. Usually the Duomo in larger towns and cities is open all day throughout the year.

In between your blitzes into the Renaissance and beyond, stop to breathe in the city, the marvelous synergy between history and modern Florentine life. Firenze is a living, bustling metropolis that has managed to preserve its predominantly medieval street plan and mostly Renaissance infrastructure while successfully adapting to the insistent demands of 20th-century life. During the Guelph-Ghibelline conflict of the 13th and 14th centuries, Florence was a forest of towers—more than 200 of them, if the smaller three- and four-story towers are included. Today only a handful survive, but if you look closely you'll find them as you explore the city's core.

Numbers in the text correspond to numbers in the margin and on the Florence map.

Great Itineraries

You can see most of Florence's outstanding sights in three days. Plan your day around the opening hours of museums and churches; to gain a length on the tour groups in high season, go very early in the morning or around closing time. If you can, allow a day to explore each neighborhood.

IF YOU HAVE 3 DAYS

Spend day one exploring the historic core of Florence, which will give you an eyeful of such masterpieces as Ghiberti's renowned bronze doors at the Battistero, Giotto's Campanile, Brunelleschi's cupola hovering atop the Duomo, and Botticelli's mystical *Primavera* and *Birth of Venus* at the Galleria degli Uffizi. On day two, wander north of the Duomo and take in the superb treasury of works ranging from Michelangelo's *David* at the Galleria dell'Accademia to the lavish frescoes at the Cappella dei Magi and the Museo di San Marco (don't miss San Lorenzo, and Michelangelo's Biblioteca Medicea Laurenziana, and the Cappelle Medicee). On this afternoon (or on the afternoon of day three) head southeast to Santa Croce or west to Santa Maria Novella. On the third day, cross the Ponte Vecchio to the Arno's southern bank and explore the Oltrarno, being sure not to miss the Brunelleschi-designed church of Santo Spirito, Masaccio's frescoes in the church of Santa Maria del Carmine, and the effusion of local color.

IF YOU HAVE 5 DAYS

Break down the tours in the above itinerary into shorter ones, adding a few sights such as Piazzale Michelangelo, halfway up a hill on the Arno's southern bank, and San Miniato—both with expansive views of the city that are yours to savor. Climb Giotto's Campanile (bell tower), which rewards with sweeping views of the city and hills beyond. Take

Bus 7 from the station or Piazza del Duomo to enchanting Fiesole. Spend more time in the Galleria degli Uffizi and Bargello or one of the smaller museums such as the Museo dell'Opificio delle Pietre Dure, around the corner from the Galleria dell'Accademia, or the excellent Arno-side Museo di Storia della Scienza, and the Museo di Santa Maria Novella.

IF YOU HAVE 8 DAYS

Add an all-day excursion to Siena or a couple of half-day trips to the Medici villas around Florence (☞ Side Trips from Florence, *below*). Visit more of Florence's interesting smaller churches, including Santa Maria Maddalena dei Pazzi and the Oltrarno's Santa Felicita to see masterpieces by Perugino and Pontormo. On the trail of additional and lesser-known artistic gems, see Andrea del Castagno's fresco of the *Last Supper* in the former refectory at Sant'Apollonia, northwest of the Museo di San Marco. There are other treasures in the Chiostro dello Scalzo, just north of the Museo di San Marco, and the church of Santo Spirito, west of Piazza Pitti.

Centro Storico: From the Duomo to the Ponte Vecchio

To say that Florence's centro storico, stretching from the Piazza del Duomo south to the Arno is beautiful could be misconstrued as an understatement. Indeed, this relatively small area is home to some of the most important artistic treasures in the world. This smorgasbord of churches, medieval towers, Renaissance palaces, and world-class museums and galleries is not a static testimony to the artistic and architectural genius of the past millennium, but a shrine to some of the most outstanding aesthetic achievements of Western history.

A Good Walk

Start at the **Duomo** ① and **Battistero** ②, climbing the **Campanile** ③ if you wish, then visit the **Museo dell'Opera del Duomo** ④, behind the Duomo. You can go directly south from in front of the Duomo to the Piazza della Signoria by way of Via dei Calzaiuoli (from here you can take a quick detour west on Via degli Speziali to **Piazza della Repubblica** ⑤ and take Via Orsanmichele to **Orsanmichele** ⑥), or go instead directly south from the Museo dell'Opera del Duomo along Via del Proconsolo to the **Bargello** ⑦, opposite the ancient **Badia Fiorentina** ⑧, built in 1285. Head west on Via della Condotta to Via Calzauioli, then south to discover the architectural splendors of the **Piazza della Signoria** ⑨, including the Loggia dei Lanzi and the **Palazzo Vecchio** ⑩. The **Galleria degli Uffizi** ⑪, perhaps Italy's most important art gallery, is off the south side of the piazza. Leave from the piazza's southwest corner along Via Vacchereccia. To the left, at the corner with Via Por Santa Maria, lined with stores, is the **Mercato Nuovo** ⑫. Follow Via Por Santa Maria to the river; walk east along the north side of the Arno to Piazza dei Giudici to see the **Museo di Storia della Scienza** ⑬. Backtrack west along the Arno to the **Ponte Vecchio** ⑭.

TIMING

Before much of the centro storico (historic center) of Florence was closed to traffic, you had to keep dodging passing cars and mopeds as you walked the narrow streets. Now you have to elbow your way through moving masses of fellow tourists, especially in the neighborhood delimited by the Duomo, Piazza Signoria, Galleria degli Uffizi, and Ponte Vecchio. It takes about 40 minutes to walk the route, with 45 minutes to one hour each for the Museo dell'Opera del Duomo and for Palazzo della Signoria; one to one and a half hours for the Bargello, and a minimum of two hours for the Uffizi (reserve tickets in advance to avoid long lines).

A special museum ticket valid for six months at seven city museums, including the Palazzo Vecchio, the Museo di Firenze com'era (Museum of Florentine History), and the Museo di Santa Maria Novella, costs 15,000 lire and is a good buy. Inquire at any city museum.

Sights to See

8 **Badia Fiorentina.** This ancient church was rebuilt in 1285; its graceful bell tower, best seen from the interior courtyard, is beautiful for its unusual construction—a hexagonal bell tower built on a quadrangular base. The interior of the church proper was halfheartedly remodeled in the Baroque style during the 17th century; its best-known work of art is Filippino Lippi's (1448/57–1504) delicate *Vision of St. Bernard,* on the left as you enter. The painting—one of Lippi's finest—is in superb condition; take a look at the Virgin Mary's hands, perhaps the most beautiful in the city. ✉ *Via del Proconsolo,* ☎ *055/2344545.* 🎫 *Free.* ⏲ *Mon.–Sat. 4:30–6:30, Sun. 10:30–11:30.*

★ 7 **Bargello.** During the Renaissance this building served as the headquarters for the *podestà,* or the chief magistrate in the city. It was also used as a prison, and the exterior served as a "most wanted" billboard: effigies of notorious criminals and Medici enemies were painted on its walls. Today, it houses the **Museo Nazionale,** home to what is probably the finest collection of Renaissance sculpture in Italy. The concentration of masterworks by Michelangelo (1475–1564), Donatello (circa 1386–1466), and Benvenuto Cellini (1500–71) is remarkable, though the works stand among an eclectic array of arms, ceramics, and enamels. For Renaissance art lovers, the Bargello is to sculpture what the Uffizi is to painting.

One particular display, easily overlooked, should not be missed. In 1401 Filippo Brunelleschi (1377–1446) and Lorenzo Ghiberti (circa 1378–1455) competed to earn the most prestigious commission of the day: the decoration of the north doors of the baptistery in Piazza del Duomo. For the competition, each designed a bronze bas-relief panel on the theme of the Sacrifice of Isaac; both panels are on display, side by side, in the room devoted to the sculpture of Donatello on the upper floor. The judges chose Ghiberti for the commission; you can decide for yourself whether or not they were right. ✉ *Via del Proconsolo 4,* ☎ *055/2388606.* 🎫 *8,000 lire.* ⏲ *Mon., Wed., Fri 8:30–1:50, Tues. and Sat. 2–5. Closed 1st, 3rd, 5th Sun. and 2nd, 4th Mon. of month.*

★ 2 **Battistero** (Baptistery). The octagonal baptistery is one of the supreme monuments of the Italian Romanesque and one of Florence's oldest structures. Local legend has that it was once a Roman temple of Mars; modern excavations, however, suggest its foundations date from the 4th to 5th and the 8th to 9th centuries AD, well after the collapse of the Roman Empire. The round-arched Romanesque decoration on the exterior probably dates from the 11th century. The interior dome mosaics from the beginning of the 14th century are justly famous, but—glitteringly beautiful as they are—they could never outshine the building's most renowned feature: its bronze Renaissance doors decorated with panels crafted by Lorenzo Ghiberti. The doors—or at least copies—on which Ghiberti spent most of his adult life (1403–52) are on the north and east sides of the baptistery, and the Gothic panels on the south door were designed by Andrea Pisano (active circa 1290–1348) in 1330. The original Ghiberti doors were removed to protect them from the effects of pollution and acid rain and have been beautifully restored; some of the panels are now on display in the Museo dell'Opera del Duomo (☞ *below*).

Badia Fiorentina, **8**
Bargello (Museo Nazionale), **7**
Battistero, **2**
Biblioteca Medicea Laurenziana, **16**
Campanile, **3**
Cappelle Medicee, **17**
Casa Buonarroti, **38**
Duomo, **1**
Forte di Belvedere, **33**
Galleria degli Uffizi, **11**
Galleria dell'Accademia, **20**
Giardini Boboli, **32**
Mercato Nuovo, **12**
Museo Archeologico, **23**
Museo dell'Opera del Duomo, **4**
Museo di San Marco, **19**
Museo di Storia della Scienza, **13**
Museo Marino Marini, **28**
Orsanmichele, **6**
Ospedale degli Innocenti, **21**
Palazzo Medici-Riccardi, **18**
Palazzo Pitti, **31**
Palazzo Rucellai, **29**
Palazzo Strozzi, **27**
Palazzo Vecchio, **10**
Piazza della Repubblica, **5**
Piazza della Signoria, **9**
Piazzale Michelangelo, **39**
Ponte Vecchio, **14**
San Lorenzo, **15**
San Miniato al Monte, **40**
Santa Croce, **37**
Santa Felicita, **34**
Santa Maria del Carmine, **36**
Santa Maria Maddalena dei Pazzi, **24**
Santa Maria Novella, **26**
Santa Trinità, **30**
Santissima Annunziata, **22**
Santo Spirito, **35**
Sinagoga, **25**

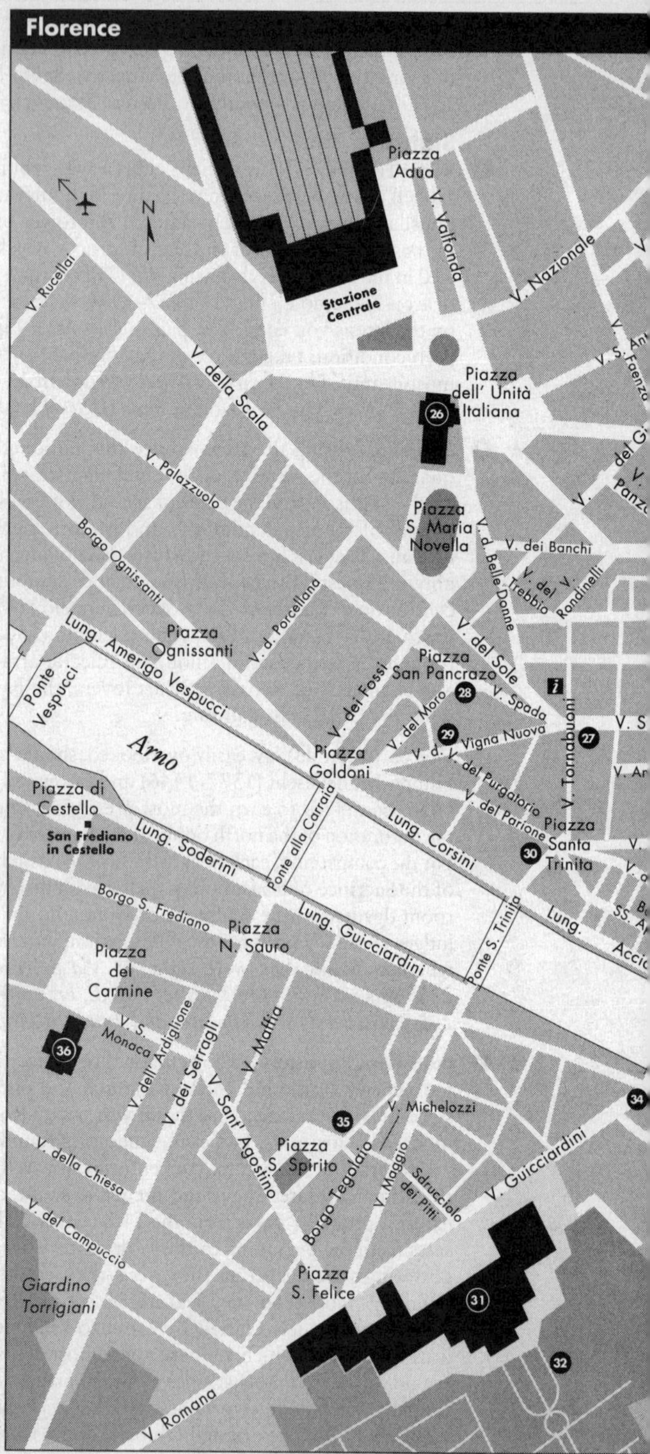

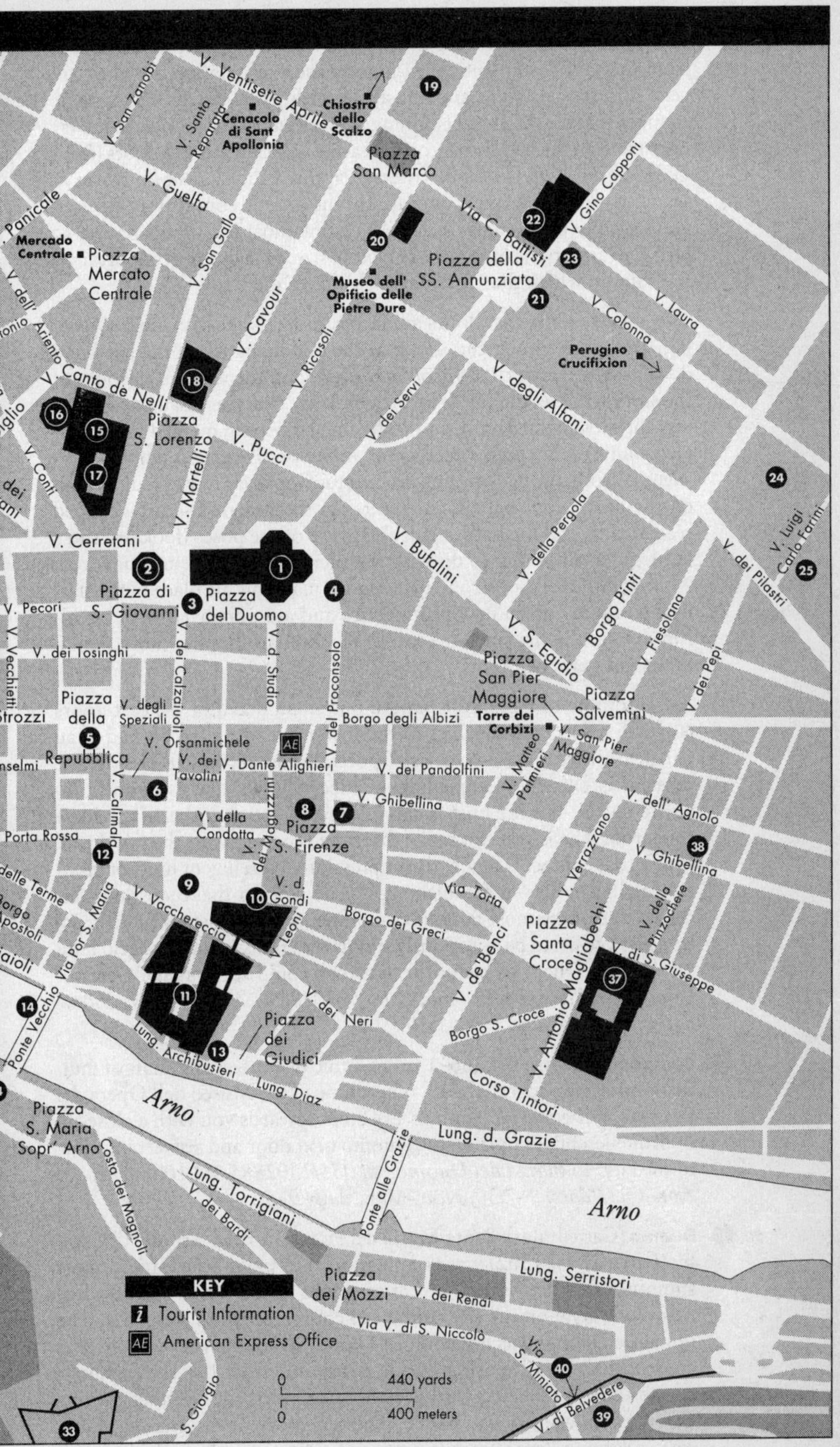
V. Ventisette Aprile
Chiostro dello Scalzo
Cenacolo di Sant Apollonia
V. Santa Reparata
V. San Zanobi
Piazza San Marco
V. Guelfa
Via C. Battisti
V. Gino Capponi
Panicale
Mercado Centrale
Piazza Mercato Centrale
V. San Gallo
Museo dell' Opificio delle Pietre Dure
Piazza della SS. Annunziata
V. Cavour
V. Colonna
V. Laura
V. dell' Ariento
V. Ricasoli
Perugino Crucifixion
V. Canto de Nelli
V. degli Alfani
V. dei Servi
Piazza S. Lorenzo
V. Pucci
V. Conti
V. Martelli
V. della Pergola
V. Bufalini
V. Cerretani
V. Luigi Carlo Farini
V. dei Pilastri
Piazza di S. Giovanni
Piazza del Duomo
Borgo Pinti
V. Pecori
V. S. Egidio
V. Fiesolana
V. dei Tosinghi
V. d. Studio
V. del Proconsolo
Piazza San Pier Maggiore
V. dei Pepi
V. Vecchietti
V. dei Calzaiuoli
Piazza della Repubblica
V. degli Speziali
Strozzi
Borgo degli Albizi
Torre dei Corbizi
Piazza Salvemini
V. Orsanmichele
V. San Pier Maggiore
V. dei Tavolini
V. Dante Alighieri
V. Matteo Palmieri
V. dei Pandolfini
V. Calimala
V. Ghibellina
V. dell' Agnolo
V. della Condotta
Piazza S. Firenze
V. dei Magazzini
Porta Rossa
V. Verrazzano
V. Ghibellina
V. d. Gondi
delle Terme
Via Torta
V. della Pinzochere
V. Vaccherecia
Borgo dei Greci
Via Por S. Maria
V. Leoni
Piazza Santa Croce
V. de' Benci
V. Antonio Magliabechi
V. di S. Giuseppe
Borgo Apostoli
Ponte Vecchio
V. dei Neri
Piazza dei Giudici
Borgo S. Croce
Lung. Archibusieri
Lung. Diaz
Corso Tintori
Arno
Piazza S. Maria Sopr' Arno
Lung. d. Grazie
Ponte alle Grazie
Costa dei Magnoli
Lung. Torrigiani
V. dei Bardi
Arno
Piazza dei Mozzi
Lung. Serristori
V. dei Renai
Via V. di S. Niccolò
Via S. Miniato
V. di Belvedere
S. Giorgio
KEY
Tourist Information
American Express Office
0 440 yards
0 400 meters

Ghiberti's north doors depict scenes from the *Life of Christ*; his later east doors (dating 1425–52), facing the Duomo facade, render scenes from the Old Testament. They merit close examination, for they are very different in style and illustrate with great clarity the artistic changes that marked the beginning of the Renaissance. Look at the far right panel of the middle row on the earlier (1403–24) north doors (*Jesus Calming the Waters*). Ghiberti here captured the chaos of a storm at sea with great skill and economy, but the artistic conventions he used are basically pre-Renaissance: Jesus is the most important figure, so he is the largest; the disciples are next in size, being next in importance; the ship on which they founder looks like a mere toy.

The panels on the east doors are larger, more expansive, more sweeping, and more convincing. Look at the middle panel on the left-hand door. It tells the story of *Jacob and Esau,* and the various episodes of the story—the selling of the birthright, Isaac ordering Esau to go hunting, the blessing of Jacob, and so forth—have been merged into a single beautifully realized street scene. A perspective grid is employed to suggest depth, the background architecture looks far more credible than on the north door panels, the figures in the foreground are grouped realistically, and the naturalism and grace of the poses (look at Esau's left leg) have nothing to do with the sacred message being conveyed. Although the religious content remains, man and his place in the natural world are given new prominence and are portrayed with a realism not seen in art since the fall of the Roman Empire, more than a thousand years before.

As a footnote to Ghiberti's panels, one small detail of the east doors is worth a special look. Just to the lower left of the Jacob and Esau panel, Ghiberti placed a tiny self-portrait bust. From either side, the portrait is extremely appealing—Ghiberti looks like everyone's favorite uncle—but the bust is carefully placed so that there is a single spot from which you can make direct eye contact with the tiny head. When that contact is made, the impression of intelligent life—of *modern* intelligent life—is astonishing. It is no wonder that these doors received one of the most famous compliments in the history of art from an artist known to be notoriously stingy with praise: Michelangelo himself declared them so beautiful that they could serve as the Gates of Paradise. ✉ *Piazza del Duomo,* ☎ *055/2302885.* 🎫 *5,000 lire.* ⏲ *Mon.–Sat. 1:30–6:30, Sun. 8:30–1:30.*

❸ **Campanile.** Giotto's (1266–1337) Gothic bell tower is a shaft of multicolor marble decorated with reliefs now in the Museo dell'Opera del Duomo (☞ *below*). A climb of 414 steps rewards you with a close-up of Brunelleschi's cupola on the Duomo next door and a sweeping view of the city. ✉ *Piazza del Duomo,* ☎ *055/2302885.* 🎫 *10,000 lire.* ⏲ *Apr.–Oct., daily 9–7:30; Nov.–Mar., daily 9–5.*

★ ❶ **Duomo** (Cattedrale di Santa Maria del Fiore). In 1296 Arnolfo di Cambio (circa 1245–1302) was commissioned to build "the loftiest, most sumptuous edifice human invention could devise" in the newest Romanesque style on the site of the old church of Santa Reparata. The immense Duomo was not completed until 1436, the year when it was consecrated. The imposing facade dates only from the 19th century; it was added in the neo-Gothic style to complement Giotto's genuine Gothic 14th-century campanile. The real glory of the Duomo, however, is Filippo Brunelleschi's dome, presiding over the cathedral with a dignity and grace that few domes, even to this day, can match.

Brunelleschi's **cupola** was an ingenious engineering feat. The space to be enclosed by the dome was so large and so high above the ground that traditional methods of dome construction—wooden centering and scaffolding—were of no use whatever. So Brunelleschi developed entirely new building methods, which he implemented with equipment of his own devising (including the modern crane). Beginning work in 1420, he built not one dome but two, one inside the other, and connected them with common ribbing that stretched across the intervening empty space, thereby considerably lessening the crushing weight of the structure. He also employed a new method of bricklaying, based on an ancient Roman herringbone pattern, interlocking each new course of bricks with the course below in a way that made the growing structure self-supporting. The result was one of the great engineering breakthroughs of all time: most of Europe's great domes, including St. Peter's in Rome, were built employing Brunelleschi's methods, and today the Duomo has come to symbolize Florence in the same way that the Eiffel Tower symbolizes Paris. The Florentines are justly proud, and to this day the Florentine phrase for "homesick" is *nostalgia del cupolone* (homesick for the dome).

The interior is a fine example of Florentine Gothic. Much of the cathedral's best-known art has been moved to the nearby Museo dell'Opera del Duomo (☞ *below*). Notable among the works that remain, however, are two equestrian frescoes honoring famous soldiers: Andrea del Castagno's (circa 1419–57) *Niccolò da Tolentino,* painted in 1456, and Paolo Uccello's (1397–1475) *Sir John Hawkwood,* painted 20 years earlier; both are on the left-hand wall of the nave. *Niccolò da Tolentino* is particularly impressive: he rides his fine horse with military pride and wears his even finer hat—surely the best in town—with panache. Restorers worked from 1983 to 1995 to repair the structure of Brunelleschi's dome and clean the vast and crowded fresco of the *Last Judgment*—painted by Vasari and Zuccaro—on its interior. Originally, Brunelleschi wanted mosaics to cover the interior of the great ribbed cupola, but by the time the Florentines got around to commissioning the decoration, 150 years later, tastes had changed.

You can explore the upper and lower reaches of the cathedral. Ancient remains have been excavated beneath the nave; the stairway down is near the first pier on the right. The climb to the top of the dome (463 steps) is not for the faint of heart, but the view is superb. ✉ *Piazza del Duomo,* ☎ *055/2302885.* ⏲ *Weekdays 10–5, Sat. 8:30–5 (1st Sat. of month 8:30–3:20). Excavation: Mon.–Sat. 10–5. Dome: Weekdays 9:30–7 and Sat. 8:30–5 (1st Sat. of month 8:30–3:20).* 🎫 *Excavation: 5,000 lire. Dome: 10,000 lire.*

★ ⓫ **Galleria degli Uffizi.** The venerable Uffizi Gallery occupies the top floor of the U-shape **Palazzo degli Uffizi** (Uffizi Palace) fronting on the Arno, designed by Giorgio Vasari (1511–74) in 1560 to hold the administrative offices—*uffizi* means offices in Italian—of the Medici Grand Duke Cosimo I (1519–74). Later Medici installed their art collections, creating what was Europe's first modern museum, open to the public (at first only by request, of course) since 1591. If you're a hard-core museum aficionado, you might want to pick up a complete guide to the collections, sold in bookshops and on newsstands.

The collection's highlights include Paolo Uccello's *Battle of San Romano* (its brutal chaos of lances is one of the finest visualmetaphors for warfare ever committed to paint); Fra Filippo Lippi's (1406–69) *Madonna and Child with Two Angels* (the foreground angel's bold, impudent eye contact would have been unthinkable prior to the Renaissance); Sandro Botticelli's (1445–1510) ethereal interpretation of the *Birth of Venus* (Venus seems to be floating on air rather than anchored in her scallop shell as two young zephyrs provide the ballast to bring her to shore—note that he depicted Venus as even longer and taller than a 20th-century supermodel) and the *Primavera* (its nonrealistic fairy-tale charm exhibits the painter's idiosyncratic genius at its zenith); Leonardo da Vinci's *Adoration of the Magi* (unfinished and perhaps the best opportunity in Europe to investigate the methods of a great artist at work); Raphael's (1483–1520) *Madonna of the Goldfinch* (darkened by time, but the tenderness with which the figures in the painting touch each other is undimmed); Michelangelo's *Doni Tondo* (one of the very few works in tempera on panel he ever painted, clearly reflecting his stated belief that draftsmanship is a necessary ingredient of great painting); Rembrandt's (1606–69) *Self-Portrait as an Old Man*; Titian's (circa 1485–1576) *Venus of Urbino*; and Caravaggio's (circa 1571/72–1610) *Bacchus* (two very great paintings whose attitudes toward myth and sexuality are—to put it mildly—diametrically opposed). If panic sets in at the prospect of absorbing all this art at one go, bear in mind that the Uffizi is, except on Sunday, open late and isn't usually crowded in the late afternoon. The coffee bar inside the Uffizi has a terrace with a fine close-up view of Palazzo Vecchio. Advance tickets can now be purchased from Consorzio ITA. ✉ *Piazzale degli Uffizi 6,* ☎ *055/23885. Advance tickets:* ✉ *Consorzio ITA, Viale Gramsca 9/a, 50121,* ☎ *055/2347941.* 🎫 *12,000 lire.* ⏲ *Tues.–Sat. 8:30–10, Sun. 8:30–6.*

⓬ **Mercato Nuovo** (New Market). This open-air loggia was new in 1551. Beyond the slew of souvenir stands, its main attraction is a copy of Pietro Tacca's bronze *Porcellino* (Little Pig) fountain on the south side, dating from around 1612 and copied from an earlier Roman work now in the Uffizi. Touching the pig is said to bring good luck. ✉ *Corner of Via Por San Maria and Via Porta Rossa.* ⏲ *Market: Tues.–Sat. 8–7, Mon. 1–7.*

★ ❹ **Museo dell'Opera del Duomo** (Cathedral Museum). Ghiberti's original Baptistery door panels and the *cantorie* (choir loft) reliefs by Donatello and Luca della Robbia (1400–82) are in good company with Donatello's *Mary Magdalen* and Michelangelo's *Pietà* (not to be confused with his more famous *Pietà* in St. Peter's, ☞ Chapter 1). Renaissance sculpture is in part defined by its revolutionary realism, but for its palpable suffering, Donatello's *Magdalen* goes beyond realism. Michelangelo's heart-wrenching *Pietà* was unfinished at his death; the female figure supporting the body of Christ on the left was added by one Tiberio Calcagni (1532–65), and never has the difference between competence and genius been manifested so clearly. ✉ *Piazza del Duomo 9,* ☎ *055/2302885.* 🎫 *10,000 lire.* ⏲ *Mar.–Oct., Mon.–Sat. 9–7:30; Nov.–Feb., Mon.–Sat. 9–7.*

⓭ **Museo di Storia della Scienza** (Museum of the History of Science). Though it tends to be obscured by the glamour of the neighboring Uffizi, this science museum has a wealth of interest: Galileo's own instruments, a collection of antique armillary spheres, some of them real works of art, and a host of other reminders that the Renaissance made not only artistic but also scientific history. ✉ *Piazza dei Giudici 1,* ☎ *055/2398876.* 🎫 *10,000 lire.* ⏲ *Tues., Thurs., Sat. 9:30–1; Mon., Wed., Fri. 9:30–1 and 2–5.*

❻ **Orsanmichele.** This multipurpose building began as an 8th-century oratory, and then was turned in 1290 into an open-air loggia selling grain. Destroyed by fire in 1304, it was rebuilt as a loggia-market. Between 1367 and 1380 the arcades were closed and two additional stories added; finally, at century's end it was turned into a church. Inside is a beautifully detailed 14th-century Gothic tabernacle by Andrea Orcagna (1308–68). The exterior contains niches furnished with sculptures dating from the early 1400s and spanning the century by Donatello and Verrocchio (1435–88), among others, which were paid for by the guilds. Though it is a copy, Verrocchio's *Doubting Thomas* (circa 1470)—is particularly deserving of attention. Here you see Christ, like the building's other figures, entirely framed within the niche, and St. Thomas standing on its bottom ledge, with his right foot outside the niche frame. This one detail, the positioning of a single foot, brought the whole composition to life. Appropriately, this is the only niche to be topped with a Renaissance pediment. ✉ *Via dei Calzaiuoli,* ☎ *055/284944.* ⏲ *Daily 9–noon and 4–6. Closed 1st and last Mon. of month.*

10 **Palazzo Vecchio** (Old Palace). Looming over Piazza della Signoria is Florence's forbidding, fortresslike city hall. The palazzo was begun in 1299 and designed (probably) by Arnolfo di Cambio, and its massive bulk and towering campanile dominate the piazza. It was built as a meeting place for the heads of the seven major guilds that governed the city at the time; over the centuries it has served lesser purposes, but today it is once again the City Hall of Florence. The interior courtyard is a good deal less severe, having been remodeled by Michelozzo (1396–1472) in 1453; the copy of Verrocchio's bronze *puttino* (little putto), topping the central fountain, softens the effect considerably.

The main attraction is on the second floor: two adjoining rooms that supply one of the most startling contrasts in Florence. The first is the vast **Sala dei Cinquecento** (Room of the Five Hundred), named for the 500-member Great Council, the people's assembly established by Savonarola, that met here. The Sala was decorated by Giorgio Vasari, around 1563–65, with huge—almost grotesquely huge—frescoes celebrating Florentine history; depictions of battles with nearby cities predominate. Continuing the martial theme, the Sala also contains Michelangelo's *Victory* group, intended for the never-completed tomb of Pope Julius II (1443–1513), plus other sculptures of decidedly lesser quality.

The second room is the little **Studiolo,** to the right of the Sala's entrance. The study of Cosimo de' Medici's son, the melancholy Francesco I (1541–87), it was designed by Vasari and decorated by Vasari and Il Bronzino (1503–72). It is intimate, civilized, and filled with complex, questioning, allegorical art. It makes the vainglorious proclamations next door ring more than a little hollow. ✉ *Piazza della Signoria,* ☎ *055/2768465.* 🎫 *10,000 lire.* ⏲ *Mon.–Wed. and Fri.–Sat. 9–7, Sun. 8–1.*

5 **Piazza della Repubblica.** This square marks the site of the ancient forum that was the core of the original Roman settlement. The street plan in the area around the piazza still reflects the carefully plotted orthogonal grid of the Roman military encampment. The Mercato Vecchio (Old Market), located here since the Middle Ages, was demolished and the current piazza was constructed between 1885 and 1895 as a neoclassic showpiece. Nominally the center of town, it has yet to earn the love of most Florentines.

★ 9 **Piazza della Signoria.** This is by far the most striking square in Florence. It was here, in 1497, that the famous "bonfire of the vanities" took place, when the fanatical monk Savonarola induced his followers to hurl their worldly goods into the flames; it was also here, a year later, that he was hanged as a heretic and, ironically, burned. A bronze plaque in the piazza pavement marks the exact spot of his execution.

The statues in the square and in the 14th-century **Loggia dei Lanzi** on the south side vary in quality. Cellini's famous bronze *Perseus Holding the Head of Medusa* is his masterpiece; even the pedestal is superbly executed. Other works in the loggia include *The Rape of the Sabine*

Women and *Hercules and the Centaur,* both late 16th-century works by Giambologna (1529–1608), and, in the back, a row of sober matrons that date from Roman times.

In the square, Bartolomeo Ammannati's (1511–92) Neptune Fountain, dating from between 1550 and 1575, takes something of a booby prize. Even Ammannati himself considered it a failure, and the Florentines call it *Il Biancone,* which may be translated as "the big white man" or "the big white lump." Giambologna's equestrian statue, to the left of the fountain, pays tribute to the Medici Grand Duke Cosimo I. Occupying the steps of the Palazzo Vecchio are a copy of Donatello's proud heraldic lion of Florence, known as the *Marzocco* (the original is now in the Bargello); a copy of Donatello's *Judith and Holofernes* (the original is inside the Palazzo Vecchio); a copy of Michelangelo's *David* (the original is now in the Galleria dell'Accademia, ☞ Michelangelo Country, *below*); and Baccio Bandinelli's *Hercules* (1534).

★ ⓮ **Ponte Vecchio** (Old Bridge). This charmingly simple bridge is to Florence what Tower Bridge is to London. It was built in 1345 to replace an earlier bridge that was swept away by flood, and its shops housed first butchers, then grocers, blacksmiths, and other merchants. But in 1593 the Medici Grand Duke Ferdinand I (1549–1609), whose private corridor linking the Medici palace (Palazzo Pitti) with the Medici offices (the Uffizi) crossed the bridge atop the shops, decided that all this plebeian commerce under his feet was unseemly. So he threw out all the butchers and blacksmiths and installed 41 goldsmiths and eight jewelers. The bridge has been devoted solely to these two trades ever since.

Take a moment to study the **Ponte Santa Trinità,** the next bridge downriver. It was designed by Bartolomeo Ammannati in 1567 (possibly from sketches by Michelangelo), blown up by the retreating Germans during World War II, and painstakingly reconstructed after the war ended. By virtue of its graceful arc and subtle curves, Florentines like to claim it is the most beautiful bridge in the world. Given its simplicity, this could be idle Tuscan boasting.

Michelangelo Country: From San Lorenzo to the Accademia

Poet, painter, sculptor, and architect, Michelangelo was a consummate genius. His prodigious energy and virtuoso technique overcame the political and artistic vicissitudes of almost a century to produce some of the greatest sculpture of his—or any—age. The Biblioteca Medicea Laurenziana is perhaps his most intuitive work of architecture. The key to understanding Michelangelo's genius is in the magnificent Cappelle Medicee sculptures. The towering and beautiful *David,* his most recognized work, resides in the Galleria dell'Accademia.

A Good Walk

Start at the church of **San Lorenzo** ⑮, visiting the **Biblioteca Medicea Laurenziana** ⑯ and its famous anteroom, before circling the church to the northwest and making your way through the San Lorenzo outdoor market on Via del Canto de' Nelli to the entrance of the **Cappelle Medicee** ⑰. Retrace your steps through the market and take Via dei Gori east to Via Cavour and the **Palazzo Medici-Riccardi** ⑱, home to Florence's most important family throughout the Renaissance. Follow Via Cavour two blocks north to Piazza San Marco and the church of the same name, attached to which is the **Museo di San Marco** ⑲, which houses marvelous works by the pious and exceptionally talented painter-monk, Fra Angelico. If you have time, go northwest from Piazza San Marco to see Castagno's *Last Supper* at Sant'Apollonia and then north to the Chiostro dello Scalzo. From Piazza San Marco, walk a half block south down Via Ricasoli (which runs back toward the Duomo) to the **Galleria dell'Accademia** ⑳. Return to the east side of Piazza San Marco and take Via Cesare Battisti east into Piazza della Santissima Annunziata, one of Florence's prettiest squares, site of the **Ospedale degli Innocenti** ㉑ and, at the north end of the square, the church of **Santissima Annunziata** ㉒. One block southeast of the entrance to Santissima Annunziata, through the arch and on the left side of Via della Colonne, is the **Museo Archeologico** ㉓. Continue down Via della Colonna to **Santa Maria Maddalena dei Pazzi** ㉔, harboring a superb fresco by Perugino. Return to Via della Colonna and take a right on Via Luigi Carlo Farini, where you'll find the **Sinagoga** ㉕ and its Museo Ebraico. Conclude your tour with a Mediterranean-kosher lunch at Ruth or at a trattoria.

TIMING

The walk alone takes about one hour, plus 45 minutes for the Cappelle Medicee, 20 minutes for the Palazzo Medici-Riccardi, 40 minutes for the Museo di San Marco, 30 minutes for the Galleria dell'Accademia (*David*), and 40 minutes for the Museo Archeologico. Note that the Cappelle Medicee and the Museo di San Marco close at 1:50. After visiting San Lorenzo, resist the temptation to explore the market that surrounds the church before going to the Palazzo Medici-Riccardi; you can always come back later, when the churches and museums have closed; the market is open until 7 PM.

Sights to See

16 **Biblioteca Medicea Laurenziana** (Laurentian Library). Michelangelo the architect was every bit as original as Michelangelo the sculptor. Unlike Brunelleschi (the architect of San Lorenzo), however, he was not bent on proportion and perfect geometry. He was interested in experimentation and invention and in expressing a personal vision at times highly idiosyncratic.

It was never more idiosyncratic than in the Laurentian Library, begun in 1524 and finished in 1568, and its famous **vestibolo** (anteroom). This strangely shaped anteroom has had scholars scratching their heads for centuries. In a space more than two stories high, why did Michelangelo limit his use of columns and pilasters to the upper two-thirds of the wall? Why didn't he rest them on strong pedestals instead of on huge, decorative curlicue scrolls, which rob them of all visual support? Why did he recess them into the wall, which makes them look weaker still? The architectural elements here do not stand firm and strong and tall, as inside the church next door; instead, they seem to be pressed into the wall as if into putty, giving the room a soft, rubbery look that is one of the strangest effects ever achieved by classical architecture. It is almost as if Michelangelo purposely set out to defy his predecessors—intentionally to flout the conventions of the High Renaissance in order to see what kind of bizarre, mannered effect might result. His innovations were tremendously influential and produced a period of architectural experimentation, known as Mannerism, that eventually evolved into the Baroque. As his contemporary Giorgio Vasari put it, "Artisans have been infinitely and perpetually indebted to him because he broke the bonds and chains of a way of working that had become habitual by common usage."

Nobody has ever complained about the anteroom's staircase (best viewed head-on), which emerges from the library with the visual force of an unstoppable lava flow. In its highly sculptural conception and execution, it is quite simply one of the most original and fluid staircases in the world. ✉ *Piazza San Lorenzo 9, entrance to the left of San Lorenzo,* ☎ *055/213440.* 💳 *Free.* ⏲ *Mon.–Sat. 8:30–1.*

★ ⑰ **Cappelle Medicee** (Medici Chapels). This magnificent complex includes the **Cappella dei Principi,** the Medici chapel and mausoleum that was begun in1605 and kept marble workers busy for several hundred years, and the **Sagrestia Nuova** (New Sacristy) designed by Michelangelo, so called to distinguish it from Brunelleschi's Sagrestia Vecchia (Old Sacristy).

Michelangelo received the commission for the New Sacristy in 1520 from Cardinal Giulio de' Medici (1478–1534), who later became Pope Clement VII and who wanted a new burial chapel for his father, Giuliano (1478–1534), his uncle Lorenzo the Magnificent, and two recently deceased cousins. The result was a tour de force of architecture and sculpture. Architecturally, Michelangelo was as original and inventive here as ever, but it is, quite properly, the powerful sculptural compositions of the side wall tombs that dominate the room. The scheme is allegorical: on the wall tomb to the right are figures representing day and night, and on the wall tomb to the left are figures representing dawn and dusk; above them are idealized portraits of the two cousins, usually interpreted to represent the active life and the contemplative life. But the allegorical meanings are secondary; what is most important is the intense presence of the sculptural figures, the force with which they hit the viewer. Michelangelo's contemporaries were so awed by the impact of this force (in his sculpture here and elsewhere) that they invented an entirely new word to describe the phenomenon: *terribilità* (dreadfulness). To this day it is used only when describing his work, and it is in evidence here at the peak of its power. During his stormy relations with the Medici, Michelangelo once hid out in a tiny subterranean room that is accessed from the left of the altar. Ever the artist, he drew some charcoal sketches on the wall. If you want to see them, tell the ticket vendor and pay 1,000 lire extra; guided visit only. ✉ *Piazza di Madonna degli Aldobrandini,* ☎ *055/2388602.* 💳 *10,000 lire.* ⏲ *Daily 8:30–1:50. Closed 1st, 3rd, 5th Mon. of month and 2nd, 4th Sun. of month.*

★ ⑳ **Galleria dell'Accademia** (Accademia Gallery). The collection of Florentine paintings, dating from the 13th to the 18th centuries, is notable, but the statues by Michelangelo are renowned. The unfinished *Slaves,* fighting their way out of their marble prisons, were meant for the tomb of Michelangelo's overly demanding patron, Pope Julius II (1443–1513). But the focal point is the original *David,* moved here from Piazza della Signoria in 1873. The *David* was commissioned in 1501 by the Opera del Duomo (Cathedral Works Committee), which gave the 26-year-old sculptor a leftover block of marble that had been ruined by another artist. Michelangelo's success with the block was so dramatic that the city showered him with honors, and the Opera del Duomo voted to build him a house and a studio in which to live and work.

Today *David* is beset not by Goliath but by tourists, and seeing the statue at all—much less really studying it—can be a trial. After a 1991 attack upon it by a hammer-wielding artist who, luckily, inflicted only a few minor nicks on the toes, the sculpture is surrounded by a Plexiglas barrier. The statue is not quite what it seems. It is so poised and graceful and alert—so miraculously alive—that it is often considered the definitive embodiment of the ideals of the High Renaissance in sculpture. But its true place in the history of art is a bit more complicated.

As Michelangelo well knew, the Renaissance painting and sculpture that preceded his work were deeply concerned with ideal form. Perfection of proportion was the ever-sought Holy Grail; during the Renaissance, ideal proportion was equated with ideal beauty, and ideal beauty was equated with spiritual perfection. But *David,* despite its supremely calm and dignified pose, departs from these ideals. Michelangelo did not give the statue perfect proportions. The head is slightly too large for the body, the arms are too large for the torso, and the hands are dramatically large for the arms. By High Renaissance standards these are defects, but the impact and beauty of *David* are such that it is the *standards* that must be called into question, not the statue. Michelangelo, revolutionary because he brought a new expressiveness to art, created the "defects" of *David.* He knew exactly what he was doing, calculating that the perspective of the viewer would be such that, in order for the statue to appear proportioned, the upper body, head, and arms would have to be bigger as they are farther away from the viewer's line of vision. But he also did it to express and embody, as powerfully as possible in a single figure, an entire biblical story. David's hands *are* too big, but so was Goliath, and these are the hands that slew him. ✉ *Via Ricasoli 60,* ☎ *055/2388609.* 🎫 *12,000 lire.* ⏲ *Apr.–Oct., Tues.–Sat. 8:30–10, Sun. 8:30–6; Nov.–Mar., Tues.–Sat. 8:30–7, Sun. 8:30–1:50.*

OFF THE BEATEN PATH

MUSEO DELL'OPIFICIO DELLE PIETRE DURE – This fascinating small museum is attached to an Opificio, or workshop, established by Ferdinand I to train craftsmen in the art of working with precious and semiprecious stones and marble. It is internationally renowned as a center for the restoration of mosaics and inlays in semiprecious stones. Informative exhibits include some magnificent antique examples of this highly specialized craft. ✉ *Via degli Alfani 78,* ☎ *055/210101.* 🎫 *4,000 lire.* ⏲ *Tues.–Sat. 9–2.*

23 **Museo Archeologico** (Archaeological Museum). Of the Etruscan, Egyptian, and Greco-Roman antiquities here, the Etruscan collection is particularly notable—one of the largest in Italy. The famous bronze *Chimera* was discovered (without the tail, a reconstruction) in the 16th century. ✉ *Via della Colonna 36,* ☎ *055/23575.* 🎫 *8,000 lire.* ⏲ *Tues.–Sat. 9–2, Sun. 9–2, 1st, 3rd, and 5th Mon. of month 9–1. Closed 1st, 3rd, and 5th Sun. of month.*

OFF THE BEATEN PATH

TORRE DEI CORBIZI – The tower at the south end of the small Piazza San Pier Maggiore dates from the Middle Ages, when, during the Guelph-Ghibelline conflict of the 13th and 14th centuries, Florence was awash with such towers—more than 200 of them. Today only a handful survive. From the Museo Archeologico, follow Via della Colonna east to Borgo Pinti and turn right, following Borgo Pinti through the arch of San Piero into the piazza. ✉ *Piazza San Pier Maggiore.*

19 **Museo di San Marco.** A former Dominican monastery adjacent to the church of San Marco now houses this museum, which contains many stunning works by Fra Angelico (circa 1400–55), the Dominican monk famous for his piety as well as for his painting. When the monk's cells were restructured between 1439 and 1444, he decorated many of them with frescoes meant to spur religious contemplation. His paintings are simple and direct and furnish a compelling contrast to the Palazzo Medici-Riccardi chapel (☞ *below*). While Gozzoli's frescoes celebrate the splendors of the Medici, Fra Angelico's exalt the simple beauties of monastic life and quiet reflection. Both the cells and the museum are worth exploring, for Fra Angelico's works are everywhere from the monk's cells to the superb panel paintings on view in the museum. Don't miss the famous *Annunciation* in the upper-floor monks' cells and the

works in the gallery just off the cloister as you enter. Here you can see, among many other works, his beautiful *Last Judgment*; as usual, the tortures of the damned are far more inventive than the pleasures of the redeemed. ✉ *Piazza San Marco 1,* ☎ *055/2388608.* 🎫 *8,000 lire.* ⏲ *Daily 8:30–1:50. Closed 1st, 3rd, 5th Sun. and 2nd, 4th Mon. of month.*

OFF THE BEATEN PATH

CENACOLO DI SANT'APOLLONIA – The frescoes of the refectory of a former Benedictine monastery were painted in sinewy style by Andrea del Castagno, a follower of Masaccio (1401–28). The *Last Supper* is a powerful version of this typical refectory theme. From the entrance, walk around the corner to Via San Gallo 25 and take a peek at the lovely 15th-century cloister that belonged to the same monastery but is now part of the University of Florence. ✉ *Via XXVII Aprile 1,* ☎ *055/2388606.* ⏲ *Daily 8:30–1:50. Closed 1st, 3rd, 5th Sun. and 2nd, 4th Mon. of month.*

CHIOSTRO DELLO SCALZO – Often overlooked, this small, peaceful 16th-century cloister was frescoed in monochrome by Andrea del Sarto (1486–1530) with scenes from the life of St. John the Baptist, Florence's patron saint. ✉ *Via Cavour 69,* ☎ *055/2388604.* ⏲ *Mon.–Thurs. 9–1.*

21 **Ospedale degli Innocenti.** Built by Brunelleschi in 1419 to serve as a foundling hospital, it takes the historical prize as the very first Renaissance building. Brunelleschi designed the building's portico with his usual rigor, building it out of the two shapes he considered mathematically (and therefore philosophically and aesthetically) perfect: the square and the circle. Below the level of the arches, the portico encloses a row of perfect cubes; above the level of the arches, the portico encloses a row of intersecting hemispheres. The whole geometric scheme is articulated with Corinthian columns, capitals, and arches borrowed directly from antiquity. At the time he designed the portico, Brunelleschi was also designing the interior of San Lorenzo, using the same basic ideas. But since the portico was finished before San Lorenzo, the Ospedale degli Innocenti can claim the honor of ushering in Renaissance architecture. The 10 ceramic medallions depicting swaddled infants that decorate the portico are by Andrea della Robbia (1435–1525/28), done in about 1487. ✉ *Piazza di Santissima Annunziata 1.*

★ 18 **Palazzo Medici-Riccardi.** The main attraction of this palace, begun in 1444 by Michelozzo for Cosimo de' Medici, is the interior chapel, the so-called **Cappella dei Magi** on the upper floor. Painted on its walls is Benozzo Gozzoli's famous *Procession of the Magi,* finished in 1460 and celebrating both the birth of Christ and the greatness of the Medici family. Like his contemporary Ghirlandaio, Gozzoli was not a revolutionary painter and is today considered less than first rate because of his technique, old-fashioned even for his day. Gozzoli's gift, however, was for entrancing the eye, not challenging the mind, and on those terms his success here is beyond question. The paintings are full of activity yet somehow frozen in time in a way that fails utterly as realism, but succeeds triumphantly as soon as the demand for realism is set aside. Entering the chapel is like walking into the middle of a magnificently illustrated child's storybook, and this beauty makes it one of the most unpretentiously enjoyable rooms in the entire city. ✉ *Via Cavour 1,* ☎ *055/2760340.* 🎫 *6,000 lire.* ⏲ *Mon.–Tues. and Thurs.–Sun. 9–1 and 3–6.*

15 **San Lorenzo.** The facade of this church was never finished. Like Santo Spirito on the other side of the Arno, the interior of San Lorenzo was designed by Filippo Brunelleschi in the early 15th century. The two church interiors are similar in design and effect and proclaim with ringing clarity the beginning of the Renaissance in architecture. San Lorenzo pos-

sesses one feature that Santo Spirito lacks, however, which considerably heightens the dramatic effect of the interior: the grid of dark, inlaid marble lines on the floor. The grid makes the rigorous regularity with which the interior was designed immediately visible and offers an illuminating lesson on the laws of perspective. If you stand in the middle of the nave at the church entrance, on the line that stretches to the high altar, every element in the church—the grid, the nave columns, the side aisles, the coffered nave ceiling—seems to march inexorably toward a hypothetical vanishing point beyond the high altar, exactly as in a single-point-perspective painting. Brunelleschi's **Sagrestia Vecchia** (Old Sacristy) has stucco decorations by Donatello; it's at the end of the left transept. ✉ *Piazza San Lorenzo,* ☎ *055/216634.* ⏲ *Daily 7–noon and 3:30–6:30.*

OFF THE BEATEN PATH **MERCATO CENTRALE** – In this huge, two-story market hall, food is everywhere, some of it remarkably exotic. At the Mercato Nuovo (☞ *above*), near the Ponte Vecchio, you will see tourists petting the snout of the bronze piglet for good luck; here you will see Florentines petting the snout of a very real one. There is a coffee bar upstairs among the mountains of vegetables. ✉ *Piazza del Mercato Centrale.* ⏲ *Daily 7–2.*

24 **Santa Maria Maddalena dei Pazzi.** One of Florence's hidden treasures, Perugino's cool and composed *Crucifixion* is in the chapter hall of the monastery located below this church. Here we see the Virgin Mary and St. John the Evangelist with Mary Magdalen and Sts. Benedict and Bernard of Clairvaux posed against a simple but haunting landscape. The figure of Christ crucified occupies the center of this brilliantly hued fresco. Perugino's colors radiate—note the juxtaposition of the yellow-green cuff against the orange tones of the Magdalen's robe. ✉ *Borgo Pinti 58,* ☎ *055/2478420.* *Donation requested.* ⏲ *Daily 9–noon and 5–7.*

22 **Santissima Annunziata.** Dating from the mid-13th century, this church was restructured in 1447 by Michelozzo, who gave it an uncommon (and lovely) entrance cloister. The interior is an extreme rarity for Florence: a sumptuous example of the Baroque. But it is not really a fair example, since it is merely 17th-century Baroque decoration applied willy-nilly to an earlier structure—exactly the sort of violent remodeling exercise that has given the Baroque a bad name ever since. The **Cappella dell'Annuziata,** immediately inside the entrance to the left, illustrates the point. The lower half, with its stately Corinthian columns and carved frieze bearing the Medici arms, was built for Piero de'Medici in 1447; the upper half, with its erupting curves and impish sculpted cherubs, was added 200 years later. Each is effective in its own way, but together they serve only to prove that dignity is rarely comfortable wearing a party hat. ✉ *Piazza di Santissima Annunziata,* ☎ *055/2398034.* ⏲ *Daily 7–12:30 and 4–6:30.*

25 **Sinagoga.** Jews were well settled in Florence by 1396, when the first money-lending operations became officially sanctioned. Medici patronage helped Jewish banking houses to flourish, but by 1570 Jews were required to live within the large "ghetto," near today's Piazza della Repubblica (☞ *above*), by the decree of Pope Pius V (1504–72). Construction of the modern Moorish-style Synagogue, set in its lovely garden, began in 1874 as a bequest of David Levi, who wished to endow a synagogue "worthy of the city." Falcini, Michele, and Treves designed the building on a domed Greek cross plan with galleries in the transept and a roofline bearing three distinctive copper cupolas visible from all over Florence. The exterior features alternating bands of tan travertine and pink granite, reflecting an Islamic style repeated in Giovanni

Panti's ornate interior. Of particular interest are the cast-iron gates by Pasquale Franci, the eternal light by Francesco Morini, and the Murano glass mosaics by Giacomo dal Medico. The gilded doors of the Moorish ark, which fronts the pulpit and is flanked by extravagant candelabra, are decorated with symbols of the ancient Temple of Jerusalem and bear bayonet marks from vandals. The synagogue was used as a garage by the Nazis, who failed to inflict much damage in spite of an attempt to blow up the place with dynamite. Only the columns on the left side were destroyed, and even then, the Women's Balcony above did not collapse. Note the Star of David in black and yellow marble inlaid in the floor. The original capitals can be seen in the garden.

Some of the oldest and most beautiful Jewish ritual artifacts in all of Europe are held in the small **Museo Ebraico** upstairs, accessible by the stair or elevator in the main entrance. Exhibits document the Florentine Jewish community and the building of the Synagogue. The donated objects all belonged to local families, and date back to the late 16th century. Take special note of the exquisite needlework and silver items. A small but well-stocked gift shop is downstairs. Adjacent to the synagogue is **Ruth's** (✉ Via Farini 2/a, ☎ 055/2480888), the only kosher-vegetarian restaurant in Tuscany. Closed Friday dinner and Saturday lunch, it features inexpensive vegetarian and Mediterranean dishes and a large selection of kosher wines. *Synagogue and museum: ✉ Via Farini 4, ☎ 055/2346654. 6,000 lire. ⏲ Apr.–Sept., Sun.–Thurs. 10–1 and 2–5, Fri. 10–1; Oct.–Mar., Sun.–Thurs. 10–1 and 2–4, Fri. 10–1.*

Santa Maria Novella to the Arno

Piazza Santa Maria Novella is near the train station, and like the train stations of most other European cities, it is an area pervaded by a certain squalor, especially at night. Nevertheless, the streets in and around the piazza are an architectural treasure trove, lined with some of Florence's most tasteful palazzi.

A Good Walk

Start in the Piazza Santa Maria Novella, its north side dominated by the church of **Santa Maria Novella** ㉖, then take Via delle Belle Donne, which leads from the east side of Piazza Santa Maria Novella to a minuscule square, at the center of which a curious shrine, known as the Croce al Trebbio, stands. Take Via del Trebbio east and turn right onto Via Tornabuoni, Florence's finest shopping street. At the intersection of Via Tornabuoni and Via Strozzi is the overwhelmingly large **Palazzo Strozzi** ㉗. If you want a dose of contemporary art, head straight down Via Spada to the **Museo Marino Marini** ㉘. One block west from Via Tornabuoni and Palazzo Strozzi, down Via della Vigna Nuova, is Leon Battista Alberti's ground-breaking **Palazzo Rucellai** ㉙. Follow the narrow street opposite the palazzo (Via del Purgatorio) east almost to its end, then zigzag right and left, turning east on Via Parione to reach Piazza di Santa Trinità, where, in the middle, stands the **Colonna della Giustizia,** which Pope Pius IV (1499–1565) gave to Cosimo I in 1560. Halfway down the block to the south (toward the Arno) is the church of **Santa Trinità** ㉚, home to Ghirlandaio's glowing frescoes. Then go east on Borgo Santi Apostoli, a typical medieval street flanked by tower houses, and take a right on Via Por Santa Maria to get to the Ponte Vecchio. Alternatively, walk from Piazza Santa Trinità to Ponte Santa Trinità, which leads into the Oltrarno neighborhood.

TIMING

The walk takes about 30 minutes, plus 30 minutes for Santa Maria Novella and 15 minutes for Santa Trinità. A visit to the Santa Maria Novella museum and cloister takes about 30 minutes.

Sights to See

Croce al Trebbio. This little granite column was erected in 1338 by the Dominican friars (there is a Dominican church close to Santa Maria Novella) to commemorate a famous local victory: it was here in 1244 that they defeated their avowed enemies, the Patarene heretics, in a bloody street brawl. ⊠ *Via del Trebbio.*

28 **Museo Marino Marini.** The dates of Marino Marini (1901–80) are not a misprint. One of Marini's major works, a 21-ft-tall bronze horse and rider, dominates the space of the main gallery dedicated to the painter. The museum itself is an eruption of contemporary space in a deconsecrated 9th-century church, designed with a series of open stairways, walkways, and balconies that allow you to peer at Marini's work from all angles. In addition to Marini's Etruscanesque sculpture, the museum houses Marini's paintings, drawings, and engravings. ⊠ *Piazza San Pancrazio,* ☎ *055/219432.* 🎟 *8,000 lire.* ⊙ *Wed.–Mon. 10–5.*

29 **Palazzo Rucellai.** Architect Leon Battista Alberti (1404–72) designed perhaps the very first private residence inspired by antique models—which goes a step further than the Palazzo Strozzi. A comparison between the two is illuminating. Evident on the facade of the Palazzo Rucellai, dating between 1455 and 1470, is the ordered arrangement of windows and rusticated stonework seen on the Palazzo Strozzi, but Alberti's facade is far less forbidding. Alberti devoted a far larger proportion of his wall space to windows, which lighten the facade's appearance, and filled in the remainder with rigorously ordered classical elements borrowed from antiquity. The end result, though still severe, is less fortresslike, and Alberti strove for this effect purposely (he is on record as stating that only tyrants need fortresses). Ironically, the Palazzo Rucellai was built some 30 years *before* the Palazzo Strozzi. Alberti's civilizing ideas here, it turned out, had little influence on the Florentine palazzi that followed. To the Renaissance Florentines, power—in architecture, as in life—was just as impressive as beauty. ⊠ *Via della Vigna Nuova.*

27 **Palazzo Strozzi.** This is the most imposing palazzo on Via Tornabuoni. Based on a model by Giuliano da Sangallo (circa 1445–1535) dating from around 1489 and executed under Il Cronaca (1457–1508) and Benedetto da Maiaino (1442–97) between 1489 and 1504, it was inspired by Michelozzo's earlier Palazzo Medici-Riccardi (☞ Michelangelo Country, *above*). The exterior of the palazzo is simple and severe; it is not the use of classical detail but the regularity of its features, the stately march of its windows, that marks it as a product of the late 15th-century Renaissance. The interior courtyard, entered from the rear of the palazzo, is another matter altogether. It is here that the classical vocabulary—columns, capitals, pilasters, arches, and cornices—is given uninhibited and powerful expression. ⊠ *Via Tornabuoni.*

26 **Santa Maria Novella.** The facade of this church looks distinctly clumsy by later Renaissance standards, and with good reason: it is an architectural hybrid. The lower half of the facade was completed mostly in the 14th century; its pointed-arch niches and decorative marble patterns reflect the Gothic style of the day. About a hundred years later (around 1456), architect Leon Battista Alberti was called in to complete the job. The marble decoration of his upper story clearly defers to the already existing work below, but the architectural features he added evince an entirely different style. The central doorway, the four ground-floor half-columns with Corinthian capitals, the triangular pediment atop the second story, the inscribed frieze immediately below the pediment—these are classical features borrowed from antiquity, and they reflect the new Renaissance era in architecture, born some 35 years

earlier at the Ospedale degli Innocenti (☞ Michelangelo Country, *above*). Alberti's most important addition, however, the S-curve scrolls that surmount the decorative circles on either side of the upper story, had no precedent whatever in antiquity. The problem was to soften the abrupt transition between wide ground floor and narrow upper story. Alberti's solution turned out to be definitive. Once you start to look for them, you will find scrolls such as these (or sculptural variations of them) on churches all over Italy, and every one of them derives from Alberti's example here.

The architecture of the interior is, like the Duomo, a dignified but somber example of Florentine Gothic. Exploration is essential, however, because the church's store of art treasures is remarkable. Highlights include the 14th-century stained-glass rose window depicting *The Coronation of the Virgin* (above the central entrance); the Cappella Filippo Strozzi (right of the altar), containing late 15th-century frescoes and stained glass by Filippino Lippi; the *cappella maggiore* (the area around the high altar), displaying frescoes by Domenico Ghirlandaio (1449–94); and the Cappella Gondi (to the left of the altar), containing Filippo Brunelleschi's famous wood crucifix, carved around 1410 and said to have so stunned the great Donatello when he first saw it that he dropped a basket of eggs.

Of special attention, for its great historical importance and beauty, is Masaccio's *Trinity,* on the left-hand wall, almost halfway down the nave. Painted around 1426 and 1427 (at the same time he was working on his frescoes in Santa Maria del Carmine; (☞ The Oltrarno, *below*), it unequivocally announced the arrival of the Renaissance. The realism of the figure of Christ was revolutionary in itself, but what was probably even more startling to contemporary Florentines was the coffered ceiling in the background. The mathematical rules for employing perspective in painting had just been discovered (probably by Brunelleschi), and this was one of the first paintings to employ them with utterly convincing success. ✉ *Piazza Santa Maria Novella,* ☎ *055/210113. At press time closed for restoration until 2000.*

In the church's cloisters of the **Museo di Santa Maria Novella,** to the left of Santa Maria Novella, is the faded fresco cycle by Paolo Uccello depicting tales from Genesis, with a dramatic vision of the Deluge. Earlier and better-preserved frescoes painted between 1348 and 1355 by Andrea da Firenze are in the chapter house, or the **Cappellone degli Spagnoli** (Spanish Chapel), off the cloister. ✉ *Piazza Santa Maria Novella,* ☎ *055/282187.* 🎟 *5,000 lire.* ⏲ *Mon.–Thurs. and Sat. 9–2, Sun. 8–1.*

30 **Santa Trinità.** Originally Romanesque in style, started in the 11th century by Vallambrosian monks, the church underwent a Gothic remodeling during the 14th century (remains of the Romanesque construction are visible on the interior front wall). Its major work is the cycle of frescoes and the altarpiece in the Cappella Sassetti, the second to the high altar's right, painted by Domenico Ghirlandaio, around 1480 to 1485. Ghirlandaio was a wildly popular but conservative painter for his day, and generally his paintings exhibit little interest in the investigations into the rigorous laws of perspective that had been going on in Florentine painting for more than 50 years. But his work here possesses such graceful decorative appeal it hardly seems to matter. The wall frescoes illustrate the life of St. Francis, and the altarpiece, *The Adoration of the Shepherds,* nearly glows. ✉ *Piazza Santa Trinità,* ☎ *055/216912.* ⏲ *Mon–Sat. 8–12 and 4–6, Sun. 4:30–6.*

In the center of Piazza Santa Trinità is a column from Rome's Terme di Caracalla, given to the Medici Grand Duke Cosimo I by Pope Pius

IV in 1560. The column was raised here by Cosimo in 1565, to mark the spot where he heard the news that the Marciani had defeated the Sienese in the 1554 battle of Marciano near Prato; the victory made his power in Florence unchallengeable and all but absolute. The column is called, with typical Medici self-assurance, the **Colonna della Giustizia**, the Column of Justice.

The Oltrarno: Palazzo Pitti, Giardini Boboli, Santo Spirito

A walk through the Oltrarno takes in two very different aspects of Florence: the splendor of the Medici, manifest in the riches of the mammoth Palazzo Pitti and the gracious Giardini Boboli; and the charm of the Oltrarno, literally "beyond the Arno," a now-gentrified, fiercely proud working-class neighborhood with artisans and antiques shops.

A Good Walk

If you start from Santa Trinità, cross the Arno over Ponte Santa Trinità and continue south down Via Maggio until you reach the crossroads of Sdrucciolo dei Pitti (on the left) and the short Via Michelozzi (on the right). Turn left onto the Sdrucciolo dei Pitti. **Palazzo Pitti** ㉛, Florence's largest palace, lies before you as you emerge onto Piazza Pitti. Behind the palace are the **Giardini Boboli** ㉜. If you have time, walk through the gardens. At the top, the adjacent **Forte di Belvedere** ㉝ commands a wonderful view and sometimes has art exhibits. If you want to take a Mannerist detour to see the Pontormo *Deposition* at **Santa Felicita** ㉞, head northeast from Palazzo Pitti on Via Guicciardini back toward the Ponte Vecchio. Return to Via Maggio off of Piazza Pitti, take Via Michelozzi west to Piazza Santo Spirito, dominated at its north end by the unassuming facade of the church of **Santo Spirito** ㉟. Take Via Sant' Agostino, diagonally across the square from the church entrance, and follow it west to Via dei Serragli. Cross and follow Via Santa Monaca west through the heart of the Oltrarno to Piazza del Carmine and the church of **Santa Maria del Carmine** ㊱, where, in the attached Cappella Brancacci, is the famous Masaccio cycle. Go to the far end of Piazza del Carmine and turn right onto Borgo San Frediano, then follow Via di Santo Spirito and Borgo San Jacopo east to reach the Ponte Vecchio.

TIMING

The walk alone takes about 45 minutes; allow one hour to visit the Galleria Palatina in Palazzo Pitti, or more if you visit the other galleries. Spend at least 30 minutes to an hour savoring the graceful elegance of the Giardini Boboli. When you reach the crossroads of the Sdrucciolo dei Pitti and Via Michelozzi, you have a choice. If the noon hour approaches, you may want to postpone the next stop temporarily to see the churches of Santo Spirito, Santa Felicita, and Santa Maria del Carmine before they close for the afternoon. Otherwise, proceed to Palazzo Pitti. The churches can be visited in 15 minutes each.

Sights to See

33 **Forte di Belvedere** (Fort Belvedere). This impressive structure was built in 1590 to help defend the city against siege. But time has effected an ironic transformation, and what was once a first-rate fortification is now a first-rate exhibition venue. Farther up the hill is Piazzale Michelangelo (☞ From Santa Croce to San Miniato al Monte, *below*), but, as the natives know, the best views of Florence are right here. To the north, all the city's monuments are spread out in a breathtaking cinemascopic panorama, framed by the rolling Tuscan hills beyond. To the south, the nearby hills furnish a complementary rural view, in its way equally memorable. The fortress, occasionally a setting for art exhibitions, is adjacent to the top of the Giardini Boboli. ✉ *Porta San Giorgio.* 🎫 *Varies per exhibit.*

32 **Giardini Boboli** (Boboli Gardens). The main entrance to these landscaped gardens is in the right wing of Palazzo Pitti. The gardens began to take shape in 1549, when the Pitti family sold the palazzo to Eleanor of Toledo, wife of the Medici Grand Duke Cosimo I. The initial landscaping plans were laid out by Niccolò Tribolo (1500–50). After his death, work was continued by Vasari, Ammannati, Giambologna, Bernardo Buontalenti (circa 1536–1608), and Giulio (1571–1635) and Alfonso Parigi (1606–56), among others, which produced the most spectacular backyard in Florence. The Italian gift for landscaping—less formal than the French but still full of sweeping drama—is displayed here at its best. A copy of the famous *Morgante,* Cosimo I's favorite dwarf astride a particularly unhappy tortoise sculpted by Valerio Cioli (circa 1529–99), is near the exit. It seems to illustrate—very graphically, indeed—the perils of too much pasta. ⊠ *Enter through Palazzo Pitti, (☞ below),* ☎ *055/213440,* 🎟 *4,000 lire.* ⏲ *Apr.–Oct., daily 9–5:30; Nov.–Mar., daily 9–4:30. Closed 1st and last Mon. of each month.*

31 **Palazzo Pitti.** This enormous palace is one of Florence's largest—if not one of its best—architectural set pieces. The original palazzo, built for the Pitti family around 1460, comprised only the middle cube (the width of the middle seven windows on the upper floors) of the present building. In 1549 the property was sold to the Medici, and Bartolomeo Ammannati was called in to make substantial additions. Although he apparently operated on the principle that more is better, he succeeded only in producing proof that more is just that, more.

Today it houses several museums: the former **Apartamenti Reali** (Royal Apartments), containing furnishings from a remodeling done in the 19th century; the **Museo degli Argenti,** displaying a vast collection of Medici household treasures; the **Galleria del Costume,** a showcase of the fashions of the past 300 years; the **Galleria d'Arte Moderna,** holding a collection of 19th- and 20th-century paintings, mostly Tuscan; and, most famous of all, the **Galleria Palatina,** containing a broad collection of paintings from the 15th to 17th centuries. The rooms of the Galleria Palatina remain much as the Medici family left them. Their floor-to-ceiling paintings are considered by some as Italy's most egregious exercise in conspicuous consumption, aesthetic overkill, and trumpery. Still, the collection possesses high points, including a number of portraits by Titian and an unparalleled collection of paintings by Raphael, such as the famous *Madonna of the Chair.* ⊠ *Piazza Pitti,* ☎ *055/210323. Galleria Palatina and Appartamenti Reali:* 🎟 *12,000 lire;* ⏲ *Nov.–Mar., Tues.–Sat. 8:30–7, Sun. 8:30–1:50; Apr.–Oct., Tues.–Sat. 8:30–10, Sun. 8:30–8. Museo degli Argenti:* 🎟 *4,000 lire, also valid for Galleria del Costume;* ⏲ *Nov.–Mar., Wed., Fri., and Sat. 8:30–1:50, Tues. and Thurs. 8:30–5; Apr.–Oct., Wed., Fri., and Sat. 8:30–3:30 and Tues. and Thurs. 2–5. Galleria del Costume:* 🎟 *8,000 lire; closed for restoration. Galleria d'Arte Moderna:* 🎟 *4,000 lire; closed for restoration.*

34 **Santa Felicita.** This late Baroque church (its facade was remodeled 1736–39) contains the Mannerist Jacopo Pontormo's (1494–1557) tour de force, the *Deposition* centerpiece of the Cappella Capponi (executed 1525–28), regarded as a masterpiece of 16th-century Florentine art. The remote figures, which transcend the realm of Renaissance classical form, are portrayed in an array of tangled shapes and intense pastel colors (well preserved because of the low lights in the church), in space and depth that defy reality. Note, too, the exquisitely frescoed *Annunciation,* also by Pontormo, at a right angle to the *Deposition.* The granite column in the piazza was erected in 1381, and marks a Christian cemetery. ⊠ *Piazza Santa Felicita, Via Guicciardini.* ⏲ *Mon.–Sat. 9–12 and 3:30–6, Sun. 4:30–6.*

36 **Santa Maria del Carmine.** The Cappella Brancacci, at the end of the right transept of this church, houses a masterpiece of Renaissance painting: a fresco cycle that changed the course of Western art forever. Fire almost destroyed the church in the 18th century; miraculously, the Brancacci Chapel survived almost intact. The cycle is the work of three artists: Masaccio and Masolino (1383–circa 1440/47), who began it around 1424, and Filippino Lippi, who finished it some 50 years later, after a long interruption during which the sponsoring Brancacci family was exiled. It was Masaccio's work that opened a new frontier for painting; tragically, he did not live to experience the revolution his innovations caused, as he died in 1428 at the age of 27.

Masaccio collaborated with Masolino on several of the paintings, but by himself he painted *The Tribute Money* on the upper-left wall; *Peter Baptizing the Neophytes* on the upper altar wall; *The Distribution of the Goods of the Church* on the lower altar wall; and, most famous, *The Expulsion of Adam and Eve* on the chapel's upper-left entrance pier. If you look closely at the latter painting and compare it with some of the chapel's other works, you will see a pronounced difference. The figures of Adam and Eve possess a startling presence primarily due to the dramatic way in which their bodies seem to reflect light. Masaccio here shaded his figures consistently, so as to suggest emphatically a single, strong source of light within the world of the painting but outside its frame. In so doing, he succeeded in imitating with paint the real-world effect of light on mass, and he thereby imparted to his figures a sculptural reality unprecedented in its day.

These matters have to do with technique, but with *The Expulsion of Adam and Eve,* his skill went beyond technical innovation, and if you look hard at the faces of Adam and Eve, you will see more than just finely modeled figures. You will see terrible shame and suffering, and you will see them depicted with a humanity rarely achieved in art. ✉ *Piazza del Carmine,* ☎ *055/2382195.* 🎫 *5,000 lire.* ⊙ *Mon. and Wed.–Sat. 10–5, Sun. 1–5.*

35 **Santo Spirito.** The plain, unfinished facade gives nothing away, but the interior, although it appears chilly (cold, even) compared with later churches, is one of the most important examples of Renaissance architecture in all Italy. The interior is one of a pair designed in Florence by Filippo Brunelleschi in the early 15th century (the other is San Lorenzo). It was here that Brunelleschi supplied definitive solutions to the two main problems of interior Renaissance church design: how to build a cross-shape interior using classical architectural elements borrowed from antiquity and how to reflect in that interior the order and regularity that Renaissance scientists (of which Brunelleschi was one) were at the time discovering in the natural world around them.

Brunelleschi's solution to the first problem was brilliantly simple: turn a Greek temple inside out. To see this clearly, look at one of the stately arch-topped arcades that separate the side aisles from the central nave. Whereas the ancient Greek temples were walled buildings surrounded by classical colonnades, Brunelleschi's churches were classical arcades surrounded by walled buildings. This brilliant architectural idea overthrew the previous era's religious taboo against pagan architecture once and for all, triumphantly reclaiming that architecture for Christian use.

Brunelleschi's solution to the second problem—making the entire interior orderly and regular—was mathematically precise: he designed the ground plan of the church so that all its parts are proportionally related. The transepts and nave have exactly the same width; the side aisles are precisely half as wide as the nave; the little chapels off the side aisles are exactly half as deep as the side aisles; the chancel and transepts are exactly one-eighth the depth of the nave; and so on, with dizzying exactitude. For Brunelleschi, such a design technique would have been far more than a convenience; it would have been a matter of passionate conviction. Like most theoreticians of his day, he believed that mathematical regularity and aesthetic beauty were opposite sides of the same coin, that one was not possible without the other. The conviction stood unchallenged for a hundred years, until Michelangelo turned his hand to architecture and designed the Cappelle Medicee and the Laurentian Library across town, and thereby unleashed a revolution of his own that spelled the end of the Renaissance in architecture and the beginning of the Baroque. In the refectory of **Santo Spirito** (✉ Piazza Santo Spirito 29, ☎ 055/287043), adjacent to the church, you can see Andrea Orcagna's fresco of the *Crucifixion*. Admission is 4,000 lire; it's open Tuesday–Saturday 9–2 and Sunday 8–1. *Church:* ✉ *Piazza Santo Spirito,* ☎ *055/210030.* ⏲ *Thurs.–Tues. 8:30–12 and 4–6, Wed. 8:30–12, Sun. 4–6.*

From Santa Croce to San Miniato al Monte

The Santa Croce neighborhood, on the southwest fringe of the historic center, was built up in the Middle Ages just outside the medieval city walls. The centerpiece of the neighborhood was the church of Santa Croce, which could hold great numbers of worshipers and accommodate the overflow in the vast piazza, which also served as a fairground and playing field for traditional, no-holds-barred football games. A center of leather working since the Middle Ages, the neighborhood is still packed with leather craftsmen and leather shops.

A Good Walk

Begin your walk at the church of **Santa Croce** ㊲; from here you can take a quick jaunt up Via della Pinzochere to **Casa Buonarroti** ㊳ to see works by Michelangelo. Return to Santa Croce, and at the southwest end of the piazza go south on Via de' Benci and cross the Arno over Ponte alle Grazie. Turn left onto Lungarno Serristori and continue to Piazza Giuseppe Poggi; a series of ramps and stairs climbs to **Piazzale Michelangelo** ㊴, where the city lies before you like a painting. From Piazzale Michelangelo, climb the stairs behind La Loggia restaurant to the church of San Salvatore al Monte, and go south on the lane leading to the stairs that climb to **San Miniato al Monte** ㊵, cutting through the fortifications hurriedly built by Michelangelo in 1529 when Florence was threatened by the Holy Roman Emperor Charles V's (1500–58) troops. You can avoid the long walk by taking Bus 12 or 13 at the west end of Ponte alle Grazie and get off at Piazzale Michelangelo or at the stop after for San Miniato al Monte; you still have to climb the monumental stairs to San Miniato, but then the return trip will be downhill. You can take the bus from Piazzale Michelangelo back to town center.

TIMING

The walk alone takes about 1½ hours one way, plus 30 minutes in Santa Croce, 30 minutes in the Museo di Santa Croce, and 30 minutes in San Miniato. Depending on the amount of time you have, you can limit your sightseeing to Santa Croce and Casa Buonarroti or continue on to Piazzale Michelangelo. The walk to Piazzale Michelangelo is a long uphill hike, with the prospect of another climb to San Miniato from there. If you decide to take a bus, remember to buy your ticket before you board. Finally, since you go to Piazzale Michelangelo for the view, skip it if it's a hazy day.

Sights to See

㊳ **Casa Buonarroti.** If you are really enjoying walking in the footsteps of the great genius, you may want to complete the picture by visiting

Michelangelo's home, even though he never actually lived in the house. It was given to his nephew and it was the nephew's son, Michelangelo, who turned it into a gallery dedicated to his great-uncle. The artist's descendents filled it with art treasures, some by Michelangelo himself—a marble bas-relief, *The Madonna of the Steps,* carved when Michelangelo was just a teenager, and his wooden model for the facade of San Lorenzo—and some by other artists that pay homage to him. ⊠ *Via Ghibellina 70,* ☎ *055/241752.* 🎫 *10,000 lire.* ⏲ *Wed.–Mon. 9:30–1:30.*

39 **Piazzale Michelangelo.** From this lookout, you have a marvelous view of Florence and the hills around it, rivaling the vista from the Fort Belvedere (☞ The Oltrarno, *above*). It has a copy of Michelangelo's *David* and outdoor cafés packed with tourists during the day and with Florentines in the evening. In May, the **Giardino dell'Iris** (Iris Garden) off the piazza is abloom with more than 2,500 varieties of the flower. The **Giardino delle Rose** (Rose Garden) on the terraces below the piazza is also in full swing May and June.

40 **San Miniato al Monte.** This church, like the Baptistery, is a fine example of Romanesque architecture and one of the oldest churches in Florence, dating from the 11th century. The lively green-and-white marble facade has a 12th-century mosaic topped by a gilded bronze eagle, emblem of San Miniato's sponsors, the Calimala (Wool Merchant's Guild). Inside are a 13th-century inlaid marble floor and apse mosaic. Artist Spinello Aretino (1350–1410) covered the walls of the **Sagrestia** with frescoes of the life of St. Benedict. The adjacent **Cappella del Cardinale del Portogallo** (Chapel of the Portuguese Cardinal) is one of the richest Renaissance works in Florence. Built to hold the tomb of a Portuguese cardinal, Prince James of Lusitania, who died young in Florence in 1459, it has a glorious ceiling by Luca della Robbia, a sculptured tomb by Antonio Rossellino (1427–79), and inlaid pavement in multicolor marble. ⊠ *Viale Galileo Galilei, Piazzale Michelangelo,* ☎ *055/2342731.* ⏲ *Daily 8–7.*

★ 37 **Santa Croce.** Like the Duomo, this church is Gothic, but (also like the Duomo) its facade dates only from the 19th century. The interior is most famous for its art and its tombs. As a burial place, the church is a Florentine pantheon and probably contains more Renaissance-celeb skeletons than any church in Italy. Among others, the tomb of Michelangelo is immediately to the right as you enter; he is said to have chosen this spot so that the first thing he would see on Judgment Day, when the graves of the dead fly open, would be Brunelleschi's Duomo dome through Santa Croce's open doors. The tomb of Galileo Galilei (1564–1642), who produced evidence that the earth is not the center of the universe, and who was not granted a Christian burial until 100 years after his death because of it, is on the left wall, opposite Michelangelo. The tomb of Niccolò Machiavelli (1469–1527), the Renaissance political theoretician whose brutally pragmatic philosophy so influenced the Medici, is halfway down the nave on the right. The grave of Lorenzo Ghiberti, creator of the Gates of Paradise doors to the Baptistery, is halfway down the nave on the left. Composer Gioacchino Rossini (1792–1868), of "William Tell Overture" fame, is entombed at the end of the nave on the right. The monument to Dante Alighieri (1265–1321), the greatest Italian poet, is a memorial rather than a tomb (he is actually buried in Ravenna); it is on the right wall near the tomb of Michelangelo.

The collection of art within the church and church complex is by far the most important of that in any church in Florence. Historically, the most significant works are probably the Giotto frescoes in the two adjacent chapels immediately to the right of the high altar. They illustrate scenes from the lives of St. John the Evangelist and St. John the Baptist (in the right-hand chapel) and scenes from the life of St. Francis (in the left-hand chapel). Time has not been kind to them; over the centuries, wall tombs were introduced into the middle of them, whitewash and plaster covered them, and in the 19th century they underwent a clumsy restoration. But the reality that Giotto introduced into painting can still be seen. He did not paint beautifully stylized religious icons, as the Byzantine style that preceded him prescribed; he instead painted drama—St. Francis surrounded by grieving monks at the very moment of his death. This was a radical shift in emphasis, and it changed the course of art. Before him, the role of painting was to symbolize the attributes of God; after him, it was to imitate life. The style of his work is indeed primitive, compared with later painting, but in the proto-Renaissance of the early 14th century, it caused a sensation that was not equaled for another 100 years. He was, for his time, the equal of both Masaccio and Michelangelo.

Among the church's other highlights are Donatello's *Annunciation,* one of the most tender and eloquent expressions of surprise ever sculpted (on the right wall two-thirds of the way down the nave); Taddeo Gaddi's (circa 1300–66) 14th-century frescoes illustrating scenes from the life of the Virgin Mary, clearly showing the influence of Giotto (in the chapel at the end of the right transept); and Donatello's *Crucifix,* criticized by Brunelleschi for making Christ look like a peasant (in the chapel at the end of the left transept). Outside the church proper, in the **Museo dell'Opera di Santa Croce** off the cloister, is Cimabue's (circa 1240–1302) 13th-century *Triumphal Cross,* badly damaged by the flood of 1966. A model of architectural geometry, the **Cappella Pazzi,** at the end of the cloister, is the work of Brunelleschi. ✉ *Piazza Santa Croce 16,* ☎ *055/244619.* 🎫 *5,000 lire.* ⏲ *Church: Mon.–Sat. 8–6:45, Sun. 3–5:30. Cloister and museum: Mar.–Sept., Thurs.–Tues. 10–12 and 3–5; Oct.–Feb., Thurs.–Tues. 10–12:30 and 3–5.*

DINING

A typical Tuscan repast starts with an antipasto of *crostini* (grilled bread spread with various savory toppings) or cured meats such as prosciutto *crudo* (cured ham thinly sliced) and *finocchiona* (salami seasoned with fennel). *Primi piatti* (first courses) can consist of local versions of pasta dishes available throughout Italy. Peculiar to Florence, however, are the vegetable-and-bread soups such as *pappa al pomodoro* (bread and tomato soup), ribollita, or, in the summer, a salad called *panzanella* (tomatoes, onions, vinegar, oil, basil, and bread). Before they are eaten, these are often christened with *un "C" d'olio,* a generous C-shape drizzle of the sumptuous local olive oil.

Unparalleled among the *secondi piatti* (main courses) is *bistecca alla fiorentina*—a thick slab of local Chianina beef, grilled over charcoal, seasoned with olive oil, salt, and pepper, and served rare. *Trippa alla fiorentina* (tripe stewed with tomato sauce) and *arista* (roast loin of pork seasoned with rosemary) are also regional specialties, as are many other roasted meats that go especially well with Chianti. A *secondo* is usually served with a *contorno* (side dish) of white beans, sautéed greens, or artichokes in season, all of which can be drizzled with more of that fruity olive oil. Dining hours are earlier here than in Rome, starting at 1 for the midday meal and at 8 for dinner. Many of Florence's restaurants are small, so reservations are a must.

Centro Storico

$$ ✕ **Il Latini.** As soon as you spy the primary decoration pieces—innumerable slabs of prosciutto—you realize you're in hog lover's

heaven. This is not the place to come if you are a vegetarian. Four big rooms are lined with bottles of wine and prints, and somehow they manage to feel cozy—perhaps because there are always a lot of happy Florentines tucking into their *salsicce e fagioli* (sausage and beans) or, in season, *agnello fritto* (fried lamb). Portions are big—you'll think you won't be able to eat it all, but you will. This place packs them in, tourists and locals alike, with good reason. Reservations are advised. It's around the side of Palazzo Rucellai. ✉ *Via dei Palchetti 6/r,* ☎ *055/210916. AE, DC, MC, V. Closed Mon. and 15 days at Christmas.*

$$ ✕ **La Posta.** Only steps away from Piazza Repubblica, this restaurant has been around for over 100 years. Ceilings reach high above the cloth-covered tables in the three dining rooms. Now under the fine ministrations of owner Enzo Vocino, La Posta offers a large menu with typical Tuscan treats as well as less typical offerings such as *filetto alla tartara* (steak tartare) prepared tableside. The chef has a deft touch with fried vegetables, particularly the *fiori di zucca,* which are so light you'll forget that they're cholesterol bombs. Reserve in warmer months for the lovely outdoor tables. ✉ *Via dei Lamberti 20,* ☎ *055/212701. AE, DC, MC, V. Closed Tues.*

$$ ✕ **Osteria n. 1.** "*Osteria,*" nowadays, might be the only pretentious element in this romantic restaurant nestled in the ground floor of an old palazzo in the historic center. The place is suffused with a rosy glow from the tablecloths and cream-colored walls, lined with painted landscapes and the occasional coat of arms. The food is expertly handled—try, for example, the delicate artichoke ravioli with olive oil and Parmesan or the *crespelle,* a little package of pasta stuffed with zucchini puree and topped with a subtle walnut sauce, before moving on to any of their grilled meats. ✉ *Via del Moro 22,* ☎ *055/284897. AE, DC, MC, V. Closed Sun. and 15 days in Aug. No lunch Mon.*

$$ ✕ **Pasquini.** A spin-off sister to Angiolino (☞ *below*), Pasquini is a small, one-room trattoria in the heart of the centro storico. You might get the feeling you're in someone's Tuscan farmhouse kitchen—you can watch the chef cook behind garlands of garlic and hot peppers while you wait for a bowl of ribollita or a plate of carpaccio. Giacinto, who manages the place and also waits on tables, can, if in the mood, provide you with lots of laughs in between mouthfuls. ✉ *Via Val di Lamone, 2/r,* ☎ *055/218995. AE, DC, MC, V.*

San Lorenzo and Beyond

$$$ ✕ **Taverna del Bronzino.** Want to have a sophisticated meal in a 16th-century Renaissance artist's studio? There's nothing outstanding about the decor in the former studio of Santi di Tito, a student of Bronzino, save for its simple formality, with white tablecloths and place settings. Lots of classic, superb Tuscan food, however, the presentation often dramatic, graces the artful menu—which is rounded out by a wine list of solid, affordable choices. For starters try the *prosciutto di Serrano e tomino alla griglia* (cheese briefly broiled and served on cured serrano ham)—ham and cheese never tasted this good. The service is outstanding. Reservations are advised, especially for eating at the wine cellar's only table. ✉ *Via delle Ruote 27/r,* ☎ *055/495220. AE, DC, MC, V. Closed Sun. and Aug.*

$$ ✕ **Alfredo.** This place is just on the other side of Piazza della Libertà, which happily puts it somewhat off the beaten tourist path. The decor is simple—white walls and white tablecloths—and the feel lively. The cooks turn out a fine pizza, but even better are the primi and secondi—some are atypical Tuscan and pleasant surprises such as fettuccine *alla carbonara di mare* (with a carbonara sauce of squid rather than

Dining ●
Alfredo, **45**
Alle Murate, **33**
Angiolino, **30**
Baldovino, **35**
Caffè Concerto, **50**
Cammillo, **29**
Cantinetta Antinori, **10**
Cibrèo, **38**
Danny Rock, **34**
Enoteca Pinchiorri, **37**
Harry's Bar, **5**
Il Cestello, **4**
Il Latini, **7**
La Giostra, **39**
La Maremmana, **36**
La Posta, **22**
Le Fonticine, **16**
Mario, **17**
Maximilian, **42**
Osteria Antica Mescita San Niccolò, **51**
Osteria de'Benci, **31**
Osteria n. 1, **6**
Pallottino, **32**
Pasquini, **23**
Quattro Leone, **28**
Taverna del Bronzino, **46**
Toscano, **18**

Lodging ○
Albergo Ferretti, **12**
Albergo Firenze, **21**
Alessandra, **25**
Beacci Tornabuoni, **8**
Bellettini, **13**
Brunelleschi, **20**
Excelsior, **4**
Grand, **3**
Grand Hotel Villa Cora, **52**
Hermitage, **26**
J & J, **40**
Kraft, **2**
La Residenza, **9**
Le Vigne, **11**
Loggiato dei Serviti, **44**
Lungarno, **27**
Monna Lisa, **41**
Morandi alla Crocetta, **43**
Nuova Italia, **14**
Pendini, **19**
Plaza Hotel Lucchesi, **48**
Porta Faenza, **15**
Regency, **47**
Ritz, **49**
Torre Guelfa, **24**
Villa Azalee, **1**

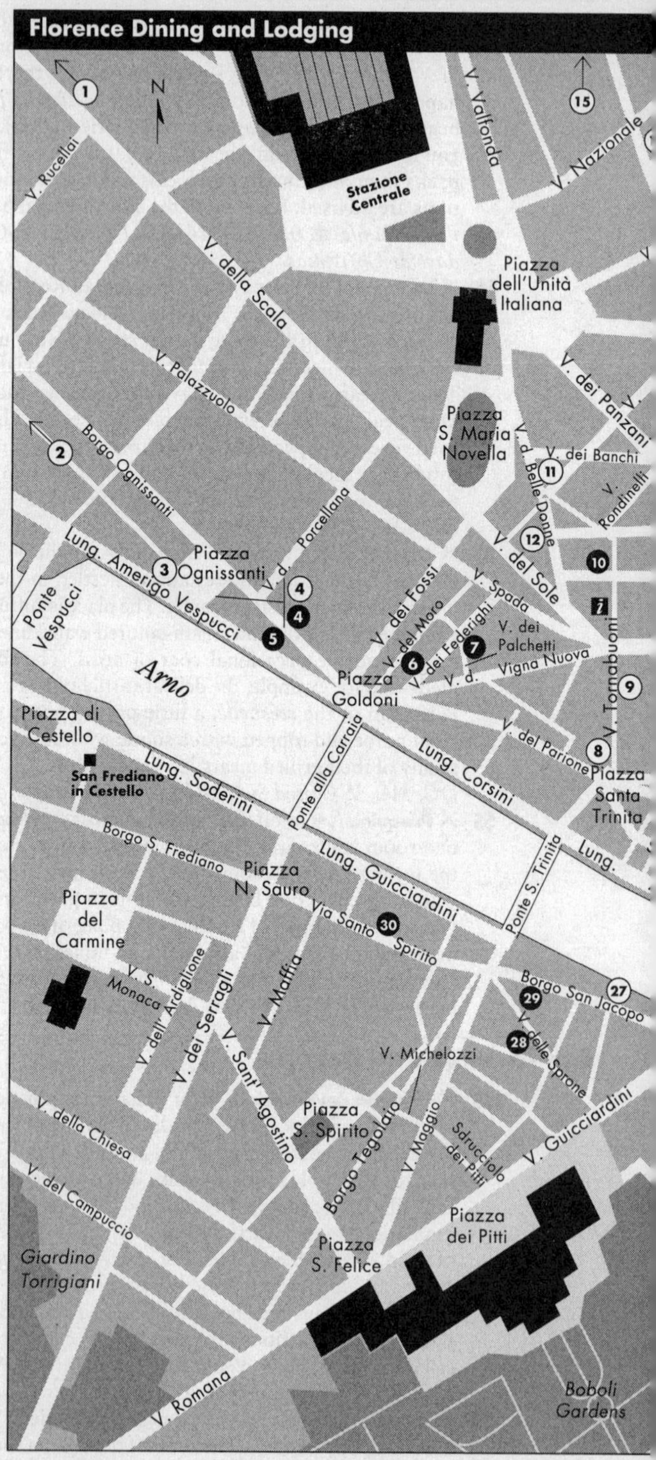

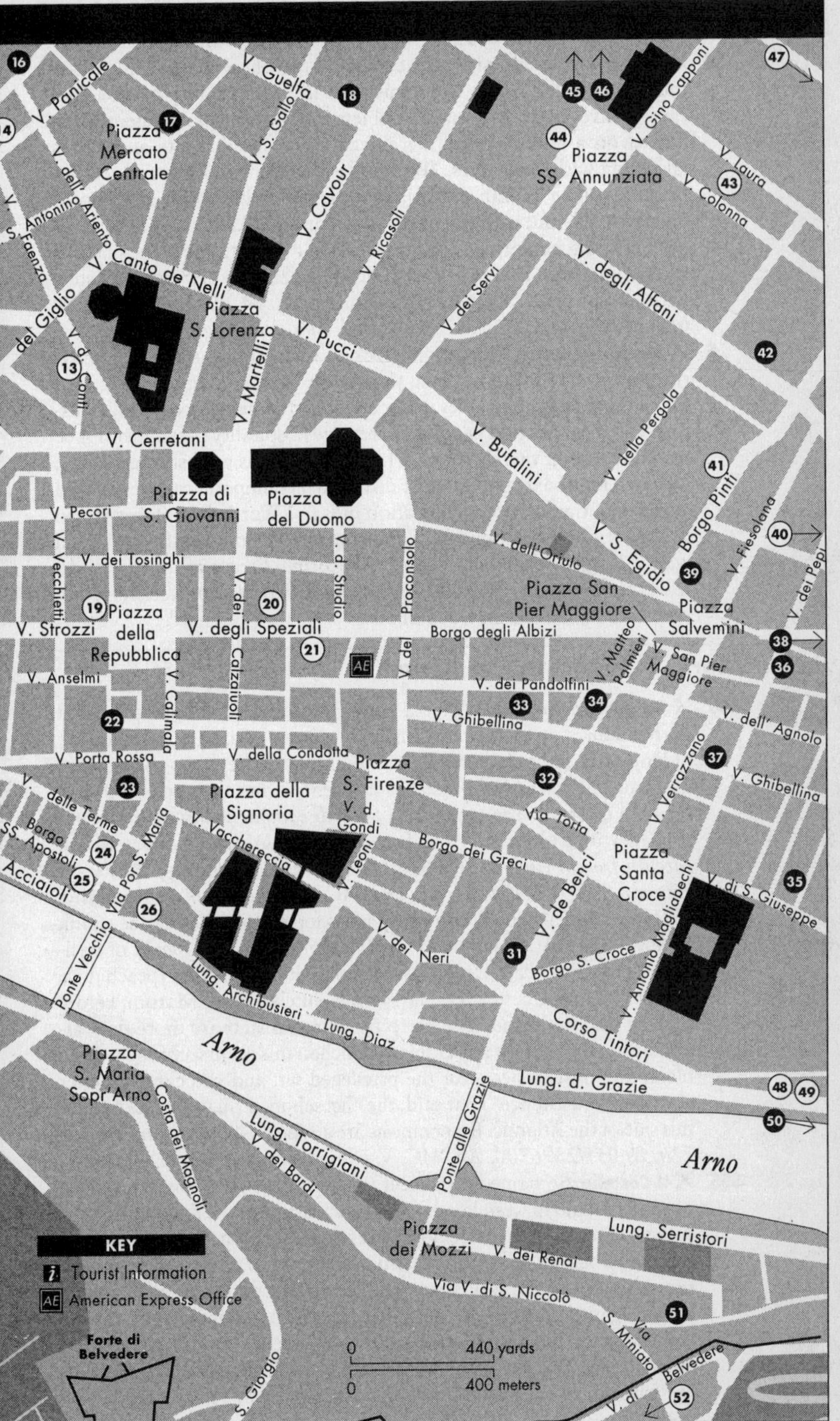
Piazza Mercato Centrale
Piazza S. Lorenzo
Piazza SS. Annunziata
Piazza di S. Giovanni
Piazza del Duomo
Piazza della Repubblica
Piazza San Pier Maggiore
Piazza Salvemini
Piazza S. Firenze
Piazza della Signoria
Piazza Santa Croce
Piazza S. Maria Sopr'Arno
Piazza dei Mozzi
V. Guelfa
V. Panicale
V. S. Gallo
V. Cavour
V. Ricasoli
V. dei Servi
V. Gino Capponi
V. Laura
V. Colonna
V. degli Alfani
V. dell'Ariento
V. S. Antonino
V. Faenza
V. Canto de Nelli
V. del Giglio
V. d. Conti
V. Martelli
V. Pucci
V. Cerretani
V. Bufalini
V. della Pergola
Borgo Pinti
V. Fiesolana
V. dei Pepi
V. S. Egidio
V. dell'Oriuolo
V. Pecori
V. dei Tosinghi
V. Vecchietti
V. dei Calzaiuoli
V. d. Studio
V. del Proconsolo
V. Strozzi
V. degli Speziali
Borgo degli Albizi
V. Matteo Palmieri
V. San Pier Maggiore
V. Anselmi
V. Calimala
V. dei Pandolfini
V. Ghibellina
V. dell' Agnolo
V. Verrazzano
V. Porta Rossa
V. della Condotta
V. d. Gondi
Via Torta
V. delle Terme
Borgo SS. Apostoli
Via Por S. Maria
V. Vacchereccia
V. Leoni
Borgo dei Greci
V. de Benci
V. di S. Giuseppe
Acciaioli
Ponte Vecchio
V. dei Neri
Borgo S. Croce
V. Antonio Magliabechi
Lung. Archibusieri
Lung. Diaz
Corso Tintori
Arno
Lung. d. Grazie
Costa dei Magnoli
Lung. Torrigiani
V. dei Bardi
Ponte alle Grazie
Lung. Serristori
V. dei Renai
Via V. di S. Niccolò
Via S. Miniato
V. di Belvedere
S. Giorgio
Forte di Belvedere
KEY
Tourist Information
AE American Express Office
0 440 yards
0 400 meters
13 14 16 17 18 19 20 21 22 23 24 25 26
31 32 33 34 35 36 37 38 39 40 41 42 43 44 45 46 47 48 49 50 51 52

pancetta). You'd be wise to reserve ahead. ✉ *Viale Don Giovanni Minzoni 3/r,* ☎ *055/578291. AE, DC, MC, V. Closed Mon.*

$$ ✕ **Toscano.** A small table attractively set in a show window identifies this restaurant, about a five minutes' walk from Palazzo Medici-Riccardi. It lives up to its name in ambience and cuisine. Prominently displayed on a counter near the entrance are cured meats and plates glistening with vegetables. Terra-cotta tile floors and beamed ceilings further typify a Tuscan trattoria, but the pink tablecloths, arty photos on the walls, and a touch of creative cuisine take it out of the ordinary. The kitchen prides itself on top-quality meat; this is the place to try *tagliata* (thin slivers of rare beef) or *spezzatino peposo* (beef stew with lots of black pepper and a wine sauce). ✉ *Via Guelfa 70/r,* ☎ *055/215475. AE, DC, MC, V. Closed Tues. and Aug.*

$ ✕ **Mario.** At lunch Florentines flock to this narrow, unfussy, family-run trattoria near San Lorenzo to feast on Tuscan favorites savored at a scattering of simple tables under a wooden ceiling dated 1536. A distinct cafeteria feel and genuine Florentine hospitality prevail: you'll be seated wherever there's room, which often means with strangers. Yes, there's a bit of extra oil in most dishes, which imparts calories as well as taste, but aren't you on vacation in Italy? Worth the splurge is *riso al ragù* (rice with ground beef and tomatoes). Come early to avoid a wait. It's open for lunch only. ✉ *Via Rosina 2/r, corner of Piazza del Mercato Centrale,* ☎ *055/218550. Reservations not accepted. No credit cards. Closed Sun. No dinner.*

Santa Maria Novella to the Arno

$$$ ✕ **Cantinetta Antinori.** After a rough morning of shopping on Via Tornabuoni, stop for lunch in this 15th-century palazzo in the company of Florentine ladies (and men) who lunch and come to see and be seen. The panache of the food matches its clientele, but be prepared to pay for such treats as *tramezzino con pane di campagna al tartufo* (country pâté with truffles served on bread) or the *insalata di gamberoni con carciofi freschi* (shrimp salad with shaved raw artichokes). ✉ *Piazza Antinori 3,* ☎ *055/292234. AE, DC, MC, V. Closed weekends and Aug.*

$$$ ✕ **Harry's Bar.** You don't come to Harry's for the food, but for the swank setting—it's cozy, with a tiny bar, pink tablecloths, and plenty of well-heeled customers captured in rosy lighting. Enjoy a Bellini (peach juice and Prosecco) or, better yet, Harry's absolutely superb Martini, before tucking into the menu. The perfectly bilingual staff are more than affable. But don't expect any culinary punches: this is nursery food—often bland and unseasoned—for the privileged set, and you can eat better elsewhere in Florence. That said, the cheeseburger might be the best on this side of the Atlantic. Reservations are advised. ✉ *Lungarno Vespucci 22/r,* ☎ *055/2396700. AE, MC, V. Closed Sun. and Dec. 15–Jan. 8.*

$$$ ✕ **Il Cestello.** So named because it is across the Arno from the church of San Frediano in Cestello, the restaurant is part of the Excelsior Hotel. A huge Florentine fireplace dominates the Renaissance tone of the dining room, but it's really the only rustic element in an otherwise formal room. Poised at the well-spaced tables arranged under a high ceiling is an elegantly dressed clientele. The Tuscan-based menu features delicious risotto and pasta dishes, a rare selection of seafood, and an ever-changing sampling of whatever is fresh from the market. Reservations are advised. ✉ *Excelsior Hotel, Piazza Ognissanti 3,* ☎ *055/264201. Jacket and tie. AE, DC, MC, V.*

$$ ★ ✕ **Le Fonticine.** This restaurant is a welcome oasis in a neighborhood near the train station not noted for its fine dining options. Here you dine very well since this place combines the best of two Italian cuisines: owner Silvano Bruci is from Tuscany and his wife Gianna is from Emilia-

Romagna. Start with the mixed vegetable antipasto plate or the delicate fried cauliflower balls before moving on to the osso buco *alla fiorentina* (in a hearty tomato sauce). The interior of the restaurant, filled with the Brucis' painting collection, provides a cheery space for the satisfying food. ✉ *Via Nazionale 79/r,* ☎ *055/282106. AE, DC, MC, V. Closed Sun.–Mon. and July 25–Aug. 25.*

The Oltrarno and Santo Spirito

$$ ✕ **Angiolino.** Though some fans have complained recently that standards are slipping here, there's no arguing with the arista served with fresh herbs, or the *acquacotta* (literally cooked water, a delicious Tuscan vegetable soup thickened with bread and topped with a fried egg). This and other good stuff is served in a room with wood-burning stove by a thoroughly wonderful waitstaff. Under the same management and equally pleasant is Pasquini (☞ *above*), in the centro storico. ✉ *Via Santo Spirito 36/r,* ☎ *055/2398976. AE, DC, MC, V. Closed Mon. No dinner Sun.*

$$ ✕ **Cammillo.** You'll be likely to hear a lot of languages (English included) bantered about at this lively, multiroom trattoria crammed with tables just on the other side of the Arno. The restaurant has been in the capable hands of the Masiero family for three generations, and in its present location since 1945. Their farm in the country supplies the olive oil and wines for the restaurant, which go along nicely with the wide-ranging list of Tuscan specialties. Reservations are advised. ✉ *Borgo Sant' Jacopo 57/r,* ☎ *055/212427. AE, DC, MC, V. Closed Wed., 15 days in Aug., and 15 days Dec.–Jan.*

$$ ✕ **Quattro Leone.** The eclectic staff at this trattoria nestled in a small piazza is an appropriate match for the eclectic menu. In winter, you can sample the wares in one of two rooms with high ceilings, and in the summer you can sit outside and admire the scenery. Traditional Tuscan favorites, such as *taglierini con porcini* (Long, thin, and flat pasta with porcini), are offered, but so, too, are less typical things like the earthy cabbage salad with avocado, pine nuts, and drops of *olio di tartufo* (truffle oil). Reservations are a good idea. ✉ *Piazza della Passera, Via dei Vellutini 1/r,* ☎ *055/218562. AE, DC, MC, V. Closed Thurs.*

$ ✕ **Osteria Antica Mescita San Niccolò.** This bustling osteria is directly next to the church of San Niccolò, and if you sit in the lower part of the restaurant, you will find yourself in what was once a chapel dating from the 11th century. Such subtle but dramatic background plays off nicely with the food, which is simple Tuscan style at its very best. The *pollo con limone* is tasty little pieces of chicken in a fragrant lemon-scented broth. In the winter, try the *spezzatino di cinghiale con aromi* (wild boar stew with herbs). Reservations are advised. ✉ *Via San Niccolo, 60/r,* ☎ *055/234 2836. No credit cards. Closed Sun.*

Santa Croce

$$$$ ★ ✕ **Enoteca Pinchiorri.** A sumptuous Renaissance palace with high, frescoed ceilings and bouquets in silver vases is the setting for this restaurant, one of the most expensive in Italy, and also considered one of the best. The enoteca part of the name comes from its former incarnation as a wineshop under owner Giorgio Pinchiorri, who still keeps a stock of vintage bottles in the cellar. A variety of fish, game, and meat dishes are always on the menu, along with splendid pasta combinations like the *ignudi*—ricotta and cheese dumplings with a lobster and coxcomb fricassee. ✉ *Via Ghibellina 87,* ☎ *055/242777. Reservations essential. Jacket and tie. AE, MC, V. Closed Sun., Aug., and 1 wk in Dec. No lunch Mon. or Wed.*

$$$ ✕ **Alle Murate.** This sophisticated restaurant features creative versions of classic Tuscan dishes—such as *zuppa di ceci e merluzzo* (pureed chickpeas with hints of cod). The main dining room has a rich, uncluttered look, with warm wood floors and paneling and soft lights. In a smaller adjacent room called the *vineria,* you get the same, splendid service and substantially reduced prices. Be warned that there's no middle ground with the wine list—only a smattering of inexpensive offerings before it soars to exalted heights. ✉ *Via Ghibellina 52/r,* ☎ *055/240618. AE, DC, MC, V. Closed Mon. No lunch.*

$$$ ✕ **Caffè Concerto.** You might feel like you're in California on the Arno while dining at this sleek, airy restaurant a short ride from the city center: the owner has spent some time in the United States, which shows in the plants that fill the interior as well as the creative touches on the menu, which changes monthly. It's a rare thing and a blessing in Florence to find such imagination in the *composta di cozze cavolo cinese e carciofi,* a mound of artichokes and Chinese cabbage garnished with mussels. Dessert is also enigmatic—try the sesame seed concoction with rum-soaked dates and papaya sorbet. ✉ *Lungarno Colombo 7,* ☎ *055/677377. Reservations essential. AE, DC, MC, V. Closed Sun.*

$$$ ★ ✕ **Cibrèo.** The food at this classic Florentine trattoria is fantastic, from the first bite of seamless, creamy crostini *di fegatini* (with savory Tuscan chicken liver spread) to the last bite of one of the meltingly good desserts. If you thought you'd never try tripe—let alone like it—this is the place to lay any doubts to rest: the *trippa in insalata* (cold tripe salad) with parsley and garlic is an epiphany. So is just about everything else on the menu. It's best to construe the owner Fabio Picchi's adamantly advising his customers on the A to Zs of Italian eating as a manifestation of his enthusiasm about his food—which is warranted as he has created some of the best, most creative food in town. ✉ *Via A. del Verrocchio 8/r,* ☎ *055/2341100. Reservations essential. AE, DC, MC, V. Closed Sun.–Mon., July 25–Sept. 5, and Dec. 31–Jan. 7.*

$$–$$$ ★ ✕ **La Giostra.** The clubby La Giostra, which means "carousel" in Italian, is owned and run by Prince Dimitri Kunz d'Asburgo Lorena and his way with mushrooms is as remarkable as his charm. The unusually good pastas may require explanation from Dimitri or Soldano, the prince's good-looking twin sons. In perfect English they'll describe a favorite dish, *carbonara di tartufo,* a decadently rich spaghetti with eggs and white truffles. Try the *spianata* (slices of thinly shaved beef baked quickly and served with fresh rosemary and sage). Leave room for dessert: this might be the only show in town with a sublime tiramisu and a wonderfully gooey Sacher torte. ✉ *Borgo Pinti 12/r,* ☎ *055/241341. AE, DC, MC, V.*

$$ ✕ **Danny Rock.** This place is always hopping with Italians eager to eat well-executed cheeseburgers and fries or one of the many tasty crepes (served both sweet and savory). You can also find a basic plate of spaghetti and other Italian dishes here, which makes it a perfect place to come to—it offers a little bit of everything. The place isn't high on atmosphere or on interior decor: you'll dine on a green metal table with matching chairs. The young-at-heart feel might explain why there's a big screen in the main dining room showing Looney Tunes. ✉ *Via Pandolfini 13/r,* ☎ *055/2340307. AE, DC, MC, V. No lunch.*

$$ ✕ **Maximilian.** "This is not fast food" appears on the menu outside the door of this intimate, white-walled trattoria (make reservations). Until recently, Adele, the chef-owner, was the sole employee. Though she has since hired a waitress, the service is still relaxed—slow, in fact. All complaints immediately dissipate with the first bite. The risotto *al tartufo nero* (with black truffle sauce) is a creamy, heavenly perfumed concoction. Don't miss her tagliata topped with raw arugula and an

olive-lemon juice dressing: it's the best in town. The menu is rich with vegetarian primi and secondi, a rarity in Florentine restaurants. ✉ *Via Alfani 10/r,* ☎ *055/2478080. AE, DC, MC, V. Closed Mon. and 3 wks in July and Aug.*

$$ ✕ **Pallottino.** With its tiled floor, photograph-filled walls, and wooden tables, Pallottino is the quintessential Tuscan trattoria, with hearty, heart-warming classics like pappa al pomodoro and *peposo alla toscana* (a beef stew laced with black pepper). Their lunch special could be, at 13,000 lire, the best bargain in town. ✉ *Via Isola delle Stinche 1/r,* ☎ *055/289573. AE, DC, MC, V. Closed Mon. and 2–3 wks in Aug.*

$ ✕ **Baldovino.** This lively, brightly hued trattoria across the street from the church of Santa Croce is the brainchild of David and Catherine Gardner, expat Scots. In addition to turning out fine pizzas, Baldovino offers some tasty *antipasti* (try the plate of smoked salmon and tuna) and *insalatone* (big salads). They also serve various pasta dishes and grilled meat until the wee hours. Save room for dessert; they're all winners. If you're pressed for time, duck into their lovely enoteca just across the street for a quick bite to eat and a glass of wine. ✉ *Via San Giuseppe 22/r,* ☎ *055/241773, AE, DC, MC, V. Closed Mon. and 2 wks in Aug.*

$ ★ ✕ **La Maremmana.** Owners Benedetto Silenu and Sergio Loria have owned this restaurant for the past 19 years, and their chef has been in place for the same amount of time. It shows. The space is light and cheery—with white walls, tile floor, and pink tablecloths. Dead center is a mixed antipasto table, with a formidable array of choices: cold squid salad, various marinated vegetables, fried whole anchovies, marinated salmon, and more. The spaghetti *alle vongole* (with tiny clams) is a winner, as are their grilled meats. ✉ *Via dei Macci 77/r,* ☎ *055/241226. AE, DC, MC, V. Closed Sun. and 3 wks in Aug.*

$ ✕ **Osteria de'Benci.** Just a few minutes from Santa Croce, this charming osteria serves some of the most eclectic food in Florence at remarkably low prices. Try the spicy spaghetti *degli eretici* (of the heretics), in a fresh tomato sauce laced with fresh herbs and a dash of *peperoncini* (hot chile peppers). When it's warm, you can dine outside with a view of the 13th-century tower belonging to the prestigious Alberti family. The English-speaking staff shouldn't scare you off: Florentines *do* eat here. ✉ *Via de' Benci 11/13/r,* ☎ *055/2344923. AE, DC, MC, V. Closed Sun.*

Pizzerias

Many pizza aficionados believe that the best pizza is town can be found at **Il Pizziauolo** (✉ Via dei Macci 113/r, ☎ 055/241171). In the Oltrarno, **Borgo Antico** (✉ Piazza S. Spirito, 6/r, ☎ 055/210437) serves up a good pizza and other trattoria fare. Others insist that the best pizza in town can be had at **I Tarocchi** (✉ Via de' Renai, 12/r, ☎ 055/2343912), also in the Oltrarno.

Enoteche

Just a hop, skip, and a jump from Orsanmichele in the heart of the historic center, the little enoteca (wine bar) **I Fratellini** (✉ Via dei Cimatori 38/r, ☎ 055/2396096) has been around since 1875. It sells wines by the glass and has a list of 27 sandwiches—try the pecorino with sun-dried tomatoes or the spicy wild boar *salame* with goat cheese if you're feeling brave. **Le Volpi e l'Uva** (✉ Piazza de' Rossi 1, ☎ 055/2398132), just off Piazza Santa Trinità, is an oenophile's dream: they pour significant wines by the glass and serve equally impressive cheeses and little sandwiches to accompany them; it's closed Sunday.

Caffè

Caffè in Italy serve not only coffee concoctions and pastries, but also sweets, drinks, *panini* (sandwiches), and some offer hot pasta and lunch dishes. They are usually open from early in the morning to late, and closed all day Sunday. All bars in Italy ought to be like **Caffetteria Piansa** (✉ Borgo Pinti 18/r, ☎ 055/2342362), great for breakfast, lunch, and drinks at night. After looking at the frescoes in Santissima Annunziata, cross the piazza towards the refined **Robiglio** (✉ Via dei Servi, 112/r, ☎ 055/212784). **Gilli** (✉ Piazza della Repubblica 39/r, ☎ 055/213896), closed Tuesday, has been a café, with all the amenities, since 1733. Try any of their chocolates. **Giacosa** (✉ Via Tornabuoni 83/r, ☎ 055/2396226), in the heart of Florence's ritzy shopping district, serves fancy sandwiches and sweets. The Negroni (a bombshell of a drink: gin, Campari, and sweet vermouth) was supposedly invented here before WWII.

Gelaterie and Pasticcerie

Though the *pasticceria* (bakery) **Dolci e Dolcezze** (✉ Piazza C. Beccaria 8/r, ☎ 055/2345458), closed Monday, is somewhat off the beaten path, if you walk down colorful Borgo La Croce, you'll be rewarded with the prettiest and tastiest cakes, sweets, and tarts in town. **Gran Caffè** (✉ Piazza San Marco 11/r, ☎ 055/215833) is down the street from the Accademia, so it's a perfect stop for a marvelous panino or sweet, while raving about the majesty of Michelangelo's *David*. Most people seem to think **Vivoli** (✉ Via Isola delle Stinche 7, ☎ 055/292334) is the best gelateria in town. What with their *cioccolata con caffè* (chocolate ice cream heavily dosed with coffee), they're probably right.

Salumerie

Salumerie are gourmet food shops strong on fine fresh ingredients, such as meats and cheeses, and are great for picking up a picnic lunch. If you find yourself in the Oltrarno and hungry for lunch or a snack, drop into **Azzarri Delicatesse** (✉ Borgo S. Jacopo, 27/b–27/c, ☎ 055/2381714), closed Sunday and Monday morning. They make sandwiches, or you can get the fixings to go. Its list of cheeses, some of which comes from France, is rather impressive. Looking for some cheddar cheese to pile in your panino? **Pegna** (✉ Via dello Studio 8, ☎ 055/282701 or 055/282702), closed Sunday and Saturday afternoon, has been selling Italian food and non-Italian food since 1860. **Perini** (✉ Mercato Centrale, enter at Via dell'Aretino, near San Lorenzo, ☎ 055/2398306), closed Sunday, sells everything from prosciutto and mixed meats to sauces for pasta and a wide assortment of antipasti. It's probably the nicest little food shop in all of Florence—bring a lot of money.

LODGING

Florence's importance not only as a tourist city but as a convention center and the site of the Pitti fashion collections throughout the year has guaranteed a variety of accommodations, many in former villas and palazzi. However, these very factors mean that, except during the winter, reservations are a must. If you do find yourself in Florence with no reservations, go to the **Consorzio ITA** office (✉ Stazione Centrale, ☎ 055/212245, FAX 055/2381226). For lodging choices in nearby Fiesole, *see* Lodging *in* Side Trips from Florence, *below*.

Centro Storico

$$$ ★ Brunelleschi. Architects united a Byzantine tower, a medieval church, and a later building in a stunning structure in the very heart of Renaissance Florence to make this a unique hotel. There's even a museum displaying the ancient Roman foundations and pottery shards found during restoration. Medieval stone walls and brick arches contrast pleasantly with the plush, contemporary decor. The comfortable, soundproof bedrooms are done in coordinated patterns and soft colors; the ample bathrooms feature beige travertine marble. ✉ *Piazza Sant'Elisabetta (off Via dei Calzaiuoli), 50122,* ☎ *055/290311,* FAX *055/219653. 96 rooms, 7 junior suites. Restaurant, bar, meeting rooms, parking (fee). AE, DC, MC, V. CP.*

$$$ Hermitage. Comfortable and charming are suitable adjectives for this hotel occupying the top six floors of a palazzo next to the Ponte Vecchio and the Uffizi. Bright breakfast rooms, a flowered roof terrace, and well-lighted bedrooms have the air and ease of a well-kept Florentine home. Double glazing and air-conditioning sustain the relaxing ambience. (The hotel has an elevator at the top of a short flight of stairs from the street.) ✉ *Vicolo Marzio 1 (Piazza del Pesce, Ponte Vecchio), 50122,* ☎ *055/287216,* FAX *055/212208. 28 rooms. Breakfast room. MC, V. CP.*

$$ Alessandra. The location, a block from the Ponte Vecchio, and clean, ample rooms make this a good choice. The place, known as the Palazzo Roselli del Turco, was designed in 1507 by Baccio d'Agnolo, a student of Michelangelo's. Though little remains of the original design save for the high wood ceilings, there's still an aura of grandeur. The English-speaking staff is friendly and helpful. ✉ *Borgo Santi Apostoli 17, 50123,* ☎ *055/283438,* FAX *055/210619. 25 rooms, 9 without bath. AE, MC, V. Closed Dec. 15–26. CP.*

$$ Pendini. The atmosphere of an old-fashioned Florentine pensione is intact at this find in the absolute center of Florence. Public rooms are delightful, complete with a portrait of Signora Pendini, who founded the hotel in 1879, and early 19th-century antiques or reproductions throughout. Most bedrooms have brass or walnut beds, pretty floral wallpaper, and pastel carpeting; baths are modern. Many rooms can accommodate extra beds. Rates are low for the category, and off-season rates are a real bargain. ✉ *Via Strozzi 2, 50123,* ☎ *055/211170,* FAX *055/281807. 42 rooms. AE, DC, MC, V. CP.*

$$ Torre Guelfa. Enter this hidden hotel through an immense wooden door on a narrow street, continue through an iron gate, and up a few steps where an elevator will take you to the third floor of this palazzo where the 12 guest rooms are. A few more steps will take you into the 13th-century Florentine *torre* (tower) itself. Each guest room is different, some with canopied beds, some with balconies. The Torre Guelfa once protected the fabulously wealthy Acciaiuoli family. Now it's one of the best-located small hotels in Florence, where you can have breakfast or sunset drinks on a rooftop that offers unmatched Florentine panoramas. ✉ *Borgo S.S. Apostoli 8, 50123,* ☎ *055/2396338,* FAX *055/2398577. 12 rooms. Bar, breakfast room. AE, MC, V. CP.*

$ Albergo Firenze. A block from the Duomo, this hotel is in one of the oldest piazzas in Florence. In fact, it is said that Dante's wife lived in one of the medieval houses in the piazza. The hotel is clean and bright, with a large lobby area and breakfast room. No frills but adequate furnishings are found in the guest rooms. ✉ *Piazza Donati 4, 50122,* ☎ *055/214203,* FAX *055/212370. 57 rooms. Breakfast room. No credit cards. CP.*

San Lorenzo and Beyond

$$ **Porta Faenza.** The 12th-century medieval well discovered during renovations has now become a focal point in the lobby. Two small pensiones were combined and a ground floor added to create this hotel, which offers good value in spacious rooms decorated in Florentine style. The friendly Italian-Canadian owners extend lots of little touches and services, including a no-smoking floor and breakfast room, baby-sitting, new bathrooms, and an E-mail station. ✉ *Via Faenza 77, 50123,* ☎ *055/284119,* FAX *055/210101. 25 rooms. Breakfast room, parking (fee). AE, DC, MC, V. CP.*

$ ★ **Bellettini.** You're in good hands here at this small, family-run hotel on three floors (the top floor has two nice rooms with a view). Sisters Marcia and Gina Naldini, along with their respective husbands, run the place and provide a relaxed atmosphere. Attractive public rooms have a scattering of antiques. Breakfast, featuring homemade cakes, and air-conditioning are included in the low room rate. The good-size rooms have Venetian or Tuscan provincial decor; bathrooms are bright and modern. ✉ *Via dei Conti 7, 50123,* ☎ *055/213561,* FAX *055/283551. 28 rooms. Bar, parking (fee). AE, DC, MC, V. CP.*

Near Piazza San Marco and Beyond

$$–$$$ ★ **Loggiato dei Serviti.** This hotel was not designed by Brunelleschi, Florence's architectural genius, but it might as well have been. A mirror image of the architect's famous Ospedale degli Innocenti across the way, the Loggiato is tucked away on one of the city's quietest and loveliest squares. Occupying a 16th-century former monastery, the building was originally a refuge for traveling priests. Vaulted ceilings, tasteful furnishings (some antique), canopy beds, and rich fabrics make this a find if you want to get the feel of Florence in an attractively spare Renaissance building, while enjoying modern creature comforts. ✉ *Piazza Santissima Annunziata 3, 50122,* ☎ *055/289592,* FAX *055/289595. 29 rooms. Bar, breakfast room, parking (fee). AE, DC, MC, V. CP.*

$$ ★ **Morandi alla Crocetta.** Near Piazza Santissima Annunziata, this is a charming and distinguished residence in which guests are made to feel like privileged friends of the family. It is close to the sights but very quiet, in a former monastery, and is furnished comfortably in the classic style of a gracious Florentine home. The Morandi is not only an exceptional hotel but also a good value. It's very small, so try to book well in advance. ✉ *Via Laura 50, 50121,* ☎ *055/2344747,* FAX *055/2480954. 10 rooms. AE, DC, MC, V. CP.*

Santa Maria Novella to the Arno

$$$$ ★ **Excelsior.** Traditional old-world charm finds a regal setting at the Excelsior, built as a convent in the 13th century, and once the private residence of Josephine Bonaparte. The neo-Renaissance palace has painted wooden ceilings, stained glass, and acres of Oriental carpets strewn over marble floors in the public rooms. The opulence of 19th-century Florentine antiques and fabrics is set off by charming old prints of the city and long mirrors of the Empire style. ✉ *Piazza Ognissanti 3, 50123,* ☎ *055/264201,* FAX *055/210278. 168 rooms. Restaurant, piano bar. AE, DC, MC, V. EP.*

$$$$ **Grand.** Across the piazza from the Excelsior, this Florentine classic provides all the luxurious amenities of its sister. Here most rooms and public areas are decorated in sumptuous Renaissance style with rich fabrics in distinctive Florentine style. You can choose between imperial- or Florentine-style rooms, many with frescoes or canopied beds. Baths are all marble. A few rooms have balconies overlooking the Arno.

✉ *Piazza Ognissanti 1, 50123,* ☎ *055/288781,* FAX *055/217400. 107 rooms. Restaurant, bar, parking (fee). AE, DC, MC, V. EP.*

$$$$ **Kraft.** The efficient and comfortable Kraft is modern, but it has many period-style rooms, all with polished wooden floors, some with balconies, and a rooftop terrace café. Its location near the Teatro Comunale (also next to the U.S. consulate) gives it a clientele from the music world. ✉ *Via Solferino 2, 50123,* ☎ *055/284273,* FAX *055/2398267. 75 rooms, 5 junior suites. Restaurant, bar, pool, parking (fee). AE, DC, MC, V. EP.*

$$–$$$ **Beacci Tornabuoni.** This is perhaps *the* classic Florentine pensione. Set in a 14th-century palazzo, it has old-fashioned style and just enough modern comfort to keep you happy. The food is good and can be served in the dining room, the garden, or in the rooms, most of which have views of the red-tile roofs in the neighboring downtown area. ✉ *Via Tornabuoni 3, 50123,* ☎ *055/212645,* FAX *055/283594. 28 rooms. Restaurant, bar. AE, DC, MC, V. CP, MAP.*

$$ **La Residenza.** On Florence's fanciest shopping street, on the upper floors of a restored 15th-century building, La Residenza has character and comfort. The roof garden and adjacent sitting room are added attractions. Paintings and etchings add interest to the rooms, which have soundproofing and satellite TV. ✉ *Via Tornabuoni 8, 50123,* ☎ *055/218684,* FAX *055/284197. 24 rooms, 4 without bath. Restaurant, bar, parking (fee). AE, DC, MC, V. CP, MAP.*

$$ **Villa Azalee.** In a residential area about five minutes from the train station, this century-old mansion is set in a large garden. It has a private-home atmosphere and comfortable living rooms. Rooms are decorated individually and are air-conditioned. ✉ *Viale Fratelli Rosselli 44, 50123,* ☎ *055/214242,* FAX *055/268264. 24 rooms. AE, DC, MC, V.*

$ **Albergo Ferretti.** Minutes away from the exquisite Renaissance piazza Santa Maria Novella, this family-run pensione offers views onto a tiny piazza containing the Croce di Trebbio, as well as quick and easy access to the historic center. English-speaking owner Luciano Michel and his South African-born wife, Sue, do just about anything to make you feel at home (which includes using their E-mail if you want). Though it's housed in a 16th-century palazzo, accommodations are simple and no-frills: it's a fantastic place for the budget-conscious traveler. ✉ *Via delle Belle Donne 17 50123,* ☎ *055/2381328,* FAX *055/219288. 16 rooms, 10 without bath. AE, DC, MC, V.*

$ **Le Vigne.** At this small hotel on one of Florence's most beautiful and central squares, the new owners have created the warm atmosphere of a private home. Complimentary afternoon tea and homemade breakfast jams and cakes are on offer, in addition to many other amenities such as a play area for children and an Internet connection. The spacious, air-conditioned rooms are furnished in 19th-century Florentine style. The caring management and reasonable rates make this a very special place. ✉ *Piazza Santa Maria Novella 24, 50123,* ☎ *055/294449,* FAX *055/2302263. 25 rooms. AE, DC, MC, V. EP.*

$ **Nuova Italia.** Near the train station and within walking distance of the sights, this hotel is run by a genial English-speaking family. It has a homey atmosphere; rooms are clean and simply furnished and have air-conditioning and triple-glazed windows to ensure restful nights. Some rooms can accommodate extra beds. Low bargain rates include breakfast. ✉ *Via Faenza 26, 50123,* ☎ *055/268430,* FAX *055/210941. 20 rooms. Parking (fee). AE, MC, V. CP.*

The Oltrarno

$$$$ **Grand Hotel Villa Cora.** Built near the Boboli Gardens in 1750, the Villa Cora retains the opulence of the 18th and 19th centuries. The decor of its remarkable public and private rooms runs the gamut from neoclassic to rococo and even Moorish, and reflects the splendor of such former guests as the Empress Eugénie, wife of Napoléon III, and Madame Von Meck, Tchaikovsky's mysterious benefactress. ✉ *Viale Machiavelli 18, 50125,* ☎ *055/2298451,* FAX *055/229086. 48 rooms. Restaurant, piano bar, pool, parking (fee). AE, DC, MC, V. CP.*

$$$$ **Lungarno.** The location couldn't be better—directly across the river from the Palazzo Vecchio and the Duomo. Rooms and suites have private terraces that jut out right over the Arno. Four suites in a 13th-century tower preserve atmospheric details like exposed stone walls and old archways and look out onto a little square with another medieval tower covered in jasmine. The very chic decor approximates a breezily elegant home, with lots of crisp white fabrics trimmed in blue. More than 100 paintings and drawings—from Picassos and Cocteaus to contemporary Italian artists—hang in hallways, bedrooms, even bathrooms. Great photographs by Cecil Beaton and pictures of famous figures like Eleanora Duse and Gabriele d'Annunzio hang in the restaurant. The lobby bar has a wall of windows and a sea of white couches that makes it one of the nicest places in the city to stop for a drink. ✉ *Borgo San Jacopo 14, 50125,* ☎ *055/27261,* FAX *055/268437. 61 rooms, 11 suites. Restaurant, bar, parking (fee). AE, DC, MC, V. CP.*

Santa Croce

$$$$ ★ **Plaza Hotel Lucchesi.** Fancy without being ostentatious, this hotel is right on the Arno near Santa Croce. Front bedrooms have views of the river and hills beyond; rear rooms on the top floor have balconies and knockout views of Santa Croce. Spacious, quiet bedrooms (double glazing throughout) are furnished comfortably in mahogany and pastel fabrics against creamy white walls. The roomy, welcoming lounges and piano bar are favorite meeting places for Florentines. ✉ *Lungarno della Zecca Vecchia 38, 50122,* ☎ *055/26236,* FAX *055/2480921. 97 rooms. Restaurant, bar. AE, DC, MC, V. EP.*

$$$$ **Regency.** In this stylish hotel in a residential district near the synagogue, the noise and crowds of Florence seem far away, though you are less than 10 minutes away from the Accademia and Michelangelo's *David.* The rooms are decorated in richly colored and tasteful fabrics and antique-style furniture faithful to the hotel's 19th-century origins as a private mansion. ✉ *Piazza Massimo D'Azeglio 3, 50121,* ☎ *055/245247,* FAX *055/2346735. 34 rooms. Restaurant, parking (fee). AE, DC, MC, V. CP.*

$$$ **J&J.** Away from the crowds, on a quiet street within walking distance of the sights, this unusual hotel is a converted 16th-century monastery. Its large, suitelike rooms are ideal for honeymooners, families, and small groups of friends. Some rooms are on two levels, and all are imaginatively arranged around a central courtyard and decorated with flair. The smaller rooms are more intimate, some opening onto their own little courtyard. The gracious owners chat with guests in the airy and light lounge; breakfast is served in a glassed-in Renaissance loggia or in the central courtyard. ✉ *Via di Mezzo 20, 50121,* ☎ *055/2345005,* FAX *055/240282. 20 rooms. Bar. AE, DC, MC, V. CP.*

$$$ ★ **Monna Lisa.** Housed in a Renaissance palazzo, the hotel has its original marble staircase, terra-cotta floors, and painted ceilings. Its rooms still have a rather homey quality, and though on the small side, many have contemplative views of a lovely garden. The ground-floor lounges give you the feel of living in an aristocratic town house. ✉ *Borgo Pinti 27, 50121,* ☎ *055/2479751,* FAX *055/2479755. 30 rooms. Bar. AE, DC, MC, V. CP.*

$$ 🏨 **Ritz.** Set amidst a row of buildings on the Arno, this old hotel has been given new energy by young owners who have worked to give it a comfortable family feeling. They've decorated to make clients feel as if they are guests in a very pretty 19th-century Florentine home with 20th-century amenities. Almost all the rooms have dramatic views of the river or the domed, red-roofed "skyline" of Florence. ✉ *Lungarno Zecca Vecchia 24, 50122,* ☎ *055/2340650,* FAX *055/240863. 30 rooms. Bar, breakfast room. AE, DC, MC, V. CP.*

NIGHTLIFE AND THE ARTS

The Arts

Festival

On June 24th, Florence grinds to a halt in order to celebrate the **Festa di San Giovanni** (Feast of St. John the Baptist) in honor of its patron saint. Many shops and bars close, and at night a fireworks display along the Arno attracts thousands. Though it's rather pretty, if you've ever been to the Mall in Washington, D.C. on the Fourth of July, you might be tempted to yawn.

Film

You can find movie listings in *La Nazione,* the daily Florence newspaper. American films are dubbed into Italian—no subtitles—so unless you command good knowledge of Italian, English-language movies are the way to go. English-language films are shown at the **Cinema Astro** (✉ Piazza San Simone near Santa Croce). Two films are shown evenings, Tuesday through Sunday; it's closed in August. English-language films are offered at the **Odeon** (✉ Piazza Strozzi, ☎ 055/214068) on Monday and on Wednesday at the **Goldoni** (✉ Via Serragli, ☎ 055/222437). The **Festival del Popolo,** held in late November or early December, celebrates documentaries and is held in the Fortezza da Basso. An international panel of judges gathers in late spring at the Forte di Belvedere for the **Florence Film Festival** to preside over new original-language releases.

Music

The **Maggio Musicale Fiorentina** series of internationally acclaimed concerts and recitals is held in the Teatro Comunale (✉ Corso Italia 16, ☎ 055/2779236 or 055/211158) from late April through June. From December to early June is the concert season of the **Orchestra Regionale Toscana** (✉ Via Ghibellina 99, ☎ 055/210804). **Amici della Musica** organizes concerts at the Teatro della Pergola (✉ Box office, Via della Pergola 10/r, ☎ 055/2479651).

Opera

Operas are performed in the **Teatro Comunale** (☞ *above*) from December through February.

Nightlife

Unlike the Romans and Milanese, the reserved Florentines do not have a reputation for an active nightlife; however, the following places attract a mixed crowd of Florentines and visitors.

Bars

Rex (✉ Via Fiesolana 23–25/r, Santa Croce, ☎ 055/2480331) has a trendy atmosphere and an arty clientele. June to September, Rex turns into **Via di Fuga** and moves its operations to the courtyard of Le Murate (✉ Via Ghibellina), a former Renaissance convent and 19th-century prison, hosting big bands, performance art, movies, and more. **Robin Hood's Tavern** (✉ Via dell'Oriuolo 58/r, ☎ 055/2340374) is the place to come when you're craving a dose of English beer, English chatter, and big plates of Buffalo chicken wings, of all things. **Sant'Ambrogio Caffè** (✉ Piazza Sant'Ambrogio 7–8/r, ☎ 055/241035) has outdoor summer seating with a view of an 11th-century church (Sant'Ambrogio) directly across the street.

The hip vibe at **La Dolce Vita** (✉ Piazza del Carmine 6/r, ☎ 055/284595) attracts the coolest Florentines and occasionally the visiting American movie star. **Danny Rock** (✉ Via Pandolfini 13/r, ☎ 055/2340307, also ☞ Dining, *above*) bills itself as a "pub restaurant"—you can enjoy their divine cheeseburger (or have a plate of pasta) while watching Bugs Bunny cartoons on a big screen. **Il Caffe** (✉ Piazza Pitti 9, ☎ 055/2396241) offers terrific cocktails, light lunches, and a view of Palazzo Pitti.

Nightclubs

Most clubs are closed either Sunday or Monday. **Yab** (✉ Via Sassetti 5/r, ☎ 055/215160) is one of the largest clubs, with a young clientele. **Hurricane Roxy** (✉ Via Il Prato 58/r, ☎ 055/210399) serves up a light lunch during the day, but in the evening there's a deejay, good music, and a welcoming atmosphere. **Space Electronic** (✉ Via Palazzuolo 37, ☎ 055/293082) has two floors with karaoke upstairs, and an enormous disco downstairs. Live music, a well-stocked bar, and a cavernous underground space make for a rollicking good evening at **Loonees** (✉ Via Porta Rossa 15, ☎ 055/212249).

Full Up (✉ Via della Vigna Vecchia 21/r, ☎ 055/293006) draws a very young clientele. **Meccanò** (✉ Viale degli Olmi 1, in Le Cascine park, ☎ 055/331371) is a multimedia experience in a high-tech disco with a late-night restaurant. **River Club** (✉ Lungarno Corsini 8, ☎ 055/282465) has winter-garden decor and a large dance floor. Young up-to-the minute Florentines drink and dance 'til the wee hours at **Maramao** (✉ Via dei'Macci 79/r, ☎ 055/244341).

OUTDOOR ACTIVITIES AND SPORTS

Participant Sports

Biking

Bikes are a good way of getting out into the hills, but the scope for biking is limited in town center. **Florence by Bike** (✉ Via della Scala 12/r, ☎ 055/264035) has designed some guided city tours that work quite well. They leave several times a day for one- to three-hour tours of major monuments or for tours with specific themes such as Renaissance Florence or 13th-century Florence. **I Bike Italy** (✉ Borgo degli Albizi 11, ☎ FAX 055/2342371) offers one-day tours of the Florence countryside. **The International Kitchen** (✉ 1209 N. Astor No. 11-N, Chicago, IL 60610, ☎ 800/945–8606) can arrange biking and walking tours of Tuscany that involve cooking and eating as well; the tours should be arranged in advance through the U.S. office. For information on where to rent bicycles, *see* Getting Around *in* Florence A to Z, *below.*

Golf

Golf dell'Ugolino (✉ Via Chiantigiana 3, Impruneta, ☎ 055/2301009) is a hilly 18-hole course in the heart of Chianti country just outside town. It is open to the public.

Health Clubs

Palestra Riccardi (✉ Borgo Pinti 75, ☎ 055/2478444 or 055/2478462), daily 20,000 lire or weekly 50,000 lire, has free weights, stretching, aerobics, and body building. **Centro Sportivo Fiorentino Indoor Club**

(✉ Via Bardazzi 15, ☎ 055/430275 or 430703), daily 30,000 lire or weekly 135,000 lire, has all the usual gym amenities plus sauna and pool. The only drawback is that it's far from the center. **Palestra Gymnasium** (✉ Via Palazzuolo 49/r, ☎ 055/293308), daily 20,000 lire, is your basic, run-of-the-mill gym.

Running

Don't even think of running on the skinny city streets, where tour buses and triple-parked Alfa Romeos leave precious little space for pedestrians. Instead, head for **Le Cascine,** the park along the Arno at the western end of the city. You can run to Le Cascine along the Lungarno (stay on the sidewalk), or take Bus 17 from the Duomo. A cinder track lies on the hillside just below **Piazzale Michelangelo,** across the Arno from the city center. The locker rooms are reserved for members, so come ready to run.

Swimming

Bellariva (✉ Lungarno Aldo Moro 6, ☎ 055/677521). **Circolo Tennis alle Cascine** (✉ Viale Visarno 1, ☎ 055/356651).

Tennis

Circolo Tennis alle Cascine (✉ Viale Visarno 1, ☎ 055/332651). **Tennis Club Rifredi** (✉ Via Facibeni, ☎ 055/432552).

Spectator Sport

Soccer

Italians are passionate about *calcio* (soccer), and the Florentines are no exception; indeed, *tifosi* (fans) of the Fiorentina team are fervent supporters. The team plays its home games at the **Stadio Comunale** (Municipal Stadium, ✉ Top of Viale Manfredo Fanti, northeast of the center) in Campo di Marte. Tickets for all games except those against their biggest rivals—Juventus of Turin and A. C. Milan—are difficult but not impossible to come by. Try the ticket booth **Chiosco degli Sportivi** (✉ Via Anselmi, the southwest side of Piazza della Repubblica, ☎ 055/292363). Games are usually played on Sunday afternoon, from about late August to May. A medieval version of the game, **Calcio Storico,** is played on or around the Festa di San Giovanni each year by teams dressed in costume representing the six Florence neighborhoods.

SHOPPING

Window-shopping in Florence is like visiting an enormous contemporary art gallery, for many of today's greatest Italian artists are fashion designers, and most keep shops in Florence. Except during the two sale seasons (January 7–March 7 and July 10–September 10), Florence is a very expensive shopping city. Discerning shoppers may find bargains in the street markets. Shops are generally open 9–1 and 3:30–7:30 but closed Sunday and Monday morning most of the year. Summer (June–September) hours are usually 9–1 and 4–8, and some shops close Saturday afternoon instead of Monday morning. When looking for addresses of shops, you will see two color-coded numbering systems on each street. The red numbers are commercial addresses and are indicated, for example, as 31/r. The blue or black numbers are residential addresses. Most shops take major credit cards and will ship purchases, but due to possible delays it's wiser to take your purchases with you.

Markets

Those with a tight budget or a sense of adventure may want to take a look at the souvenir stands under the loggia of the **Mercato Nuovo** (✉

Corner of Via Por San Maria and Via Porta Rossa; ☞ Centro Storico *in* Exploring Florence, *above*), or the clothing and leather goods stalls of the **Mercato di San Lorenzo** in the streets next to the San Lorenzo church. The **Mercato Centrale** (✉ Piazza del Mercato Centrale; ☞ Michelangelo Country *in* Exploring Florence, *above*) is the huge indoor food market in the midst of the San Lorenzo Market. You can find bargains at the **flea market** on Piazza dei Ciompi on the last Sunday of the month. An **open-air market** is held in Le Cascine park every Tuesday morning.

Shopping Districts

Florence's most fashionable shops are concentrated in town center. The fanciest designer shops are mainly on **Via Tornabuoni** and **Via della Vigna Nuova.** The city's largest concentration of antiques shops can be found on **Borgo Ognissanti** and the Oltrarno's **Via Maggio.** The **Ponte Vecchio** houses reputable jewelry shops, as it has since the 16th century. The area near **Santa Croce** is the heart of the leather merchants' district.

Specialty Stores

Antiques

At **Alberto Pierini** (✉ Borgo Ognissanti 22/r, ☎ 055/2398138) the rustic Tuscan furniture is all antique, and much of it dates from the days of the Medici. **Galleria Luigi Bellini** (✉ Lungarno Soderini 5, ☎ 055/214031) claims to be Italy's oldest antiques dealer, which may be true, since father Mario Bellini was responsible for instituting Florence's international antiques biennial. **Giovanni Pratesi** (✉ Via Maggio 13/r, ☎ 055/2396568) specializes in Italian antiques, in this case furniture, with some fine paintings, sculpture, and decorative objects turning up from time to time. Vying with Luigi Bellini as one of Florence's oldest antiques dealers, **Guido Bartolozzi** (✉ Via Maggio 18/r, ☎ 055/215602) deals in predominately period Florentine pieces. At **Paolo Paoletti** (✉ Via Maggio 30/r, ☎ 055/214728) look for Florentine antiques with an emphasis on Medici-era objects from the 15th and 16th centuries.

Books and Paper

Pineider (✉ Piazza della Signoria 13/r and Via Tornabuoni 76/r, ☎ 055/211605) now has shops throughout the world, but the business began in Florence and still does all its printing here. Personalized stationery and business cards are the mainstay, but the stores also sell fine leather desk accessories. **Centro Di** (✉ Via dei Renai 20/r, ☎ 055/2342666) publishes art books and exhibition catalogs for some of the most important organizations in Europe. One of Florence's oldest paper-goods stores, **Giulio Giannini e Figlio** (✉ Piazza Pitti 37/r, ☎ 055/212621) is *the* place to buy the marbleized stock, which come in a variety of shapes and sizes, from flat sheets to boxes and even pencils. Long one of Florence's best art bookshops, **Libreria Salimbeni** (✉ Via Matteo Palmieri 14–16/r, ☎ 055/2340905) specializes in publications on Tuscany. **FMR** (✉ Via delle Belle Donne 41/r, ☎ 055/283312), the shop of the world-famous art book editor and tastemaker Franco Maria Ricci, offers exquisite art books, handmade papers, and small works on paper. **Alberto Cozzi** (✉ Via del Parione 35/r, ☎ 055/294968) keeps an extensive line of Florentine papers and paper products, and the artisans in the shop rebind and restore books and works on paper.

Clothing

The surreal window displays at **Luisa Via Roma** (✉ Via Roma 19–21/r, ☎ 055/217826) hint at the trendy yet tasteful clothing that can be found inside this fascinating, *alta moda* boutique featuring the world's top designers as well as Luisa's own line. The sleek, classic **Giorgio Armani** (✉ Via della Vigna Nuova 51/r, ☎ 055/219041) boutique is a centerpiece of the dazzling high-end shops clustered in this part of town. Its sister store, **Emporio Armani** (✉ Piazza Strozzi 16/r, ☎ 055/284315), offers slightly more-affordable, funky, nightclub-friendly Armani threads.

Prada (Via Tornabuoni 67/r, ☎ 055/283439), known to mix schoolmarmish sensibility with sexy cuts and funky fabrics, appeals to an exclusive clientele. The signature **Gianni Versace** (Via Tornabuoni 13–15/r, ☎ 055/282638) couture collection revolutionized the catwalk with rubber dresses and purple leather pants; for a lighter bite, check out **Versus** (Via Vigna Nuova 36–38/r, ☎ 055/217619), the more playful line. You can take home a custom-made suit or dress from **Giorgio Vannini** (✉ Via Borgo SS Apostoli 43/r, ☎ 055/293037), who has a showroom for his pret-a-porter designs. **Bernardo** (✉ Via Porta Rossa 87/r, ☎ 055/283333) specializes in men's shirts (with details like mother-of-pearl buttons), trousers, and cashmere sweaters. **Gianfranco Ferré** (Via Tosinghi 52/r, ☎ 055/292003) captures beauty and luxury in various constructions and fabrics in his couture lines; he has also created a line of sleek jeans.

Jasmine (✉ Borgo San Jacopo 27/r, ☎ 055/213501) is an unpretentious yet sophisticated shop well worth taking a look at in the Oltrarno. If you're looking for something to turn heads in the Florence clubs, try **Metropole** (✉ Piazza Stazione 24/r, ☎ 055/295022). The aristocratic Marchese di Barsento, **Emilio Pucci** (✉ Via della Vigna Nuova, 97–99/r, ☎ 055/294028), became an international name in the early 1960s, when the stretch ski clothes he designed for himself caught on with the la-dolce-vita crowd—his pseudo-psychedelic prints and "palazzo pajamas" became all the rage. The showroom in the family palazzo and two boutiques (one wholesale) still sell the celebrated Pucci prints.

Embroidery and Linens

Signora **Loretta Caponi** (✉ Ponte Antinori 4/r, ☎ 055/213668) is synonymous with Florentine embroidery, and her luxury lace, linens, and lingerie have earned her worldwide renown. **Valmar** (✉ Via Porta Rossa 53/r, ☎ 055/284493) is filled with tangled spools of cords, ribbons, and fringes, plus an array of buttons, tassels, sachets, and hand-embroidered cushions you can take home—or bring in your own fabric, choose the adornments, and you can have your cushion or table runner made.

Gifts and Housewares

The essence of a Florentine holiday is captured in the sachets of the **Officina Profumo Farmaceutica di Santa Maria Novella** (✉ Via della Scala 16/r, ☎ 055/216276), an art nouveau emporium of herbal cosmetics and soaps that are made following centuries-old recipes created by monks. For housewares nothing beats **Bartolini** (✉ Via dei Servi 30/r, ☎ 055/211895) for well-designed practical items. **Sbigoli Terrecotte** (✉ Via Sant'Egidio 4/r, ☎ 055/2479713) carries traditional Tuscan terracotta and ceramic vases, pots, cups, and saucers. If you want to go one step further, you can even shop in the **Sbigoli Laboratorio** (✉ Via di Camaldoli 10/r, ☎ 055/229706), where the artisans are working on their wheels and glazing the pieces. For outstanding contemporary design housewares, check out **Open House** (✉ Via Barbadori 40/r, ☎ 055/211809).

Jewelry

Della Loggia (✉ Ponte Vecchio 52/r, ☎ 055/2396028) combines precious and semiprecious stones and metals in contemporary settings. **Gher-**

ardi (✉ Ponte Vecchio 5/r, ☎ 055/287211), Florence's king of coral, has the city's largest selection of finely crafted pieces, as well as cultured pearls, jade, and turquoise. **Carlo Piccini** (✉ Ponte Vecchio 31/r ☎ 055/292030) has been around for several generations, selling antique jewelry as well as making it to order; you can also get old jewelry reset. One of Florence's oldest jewelers, **Tiffany Faraone** (✉ Via Tornabuoni 25/r, ☎ 055/2396284) has supplied Italian (and other) royalty with finely crafted gems for centuries. Its selection of antique-looking classics has been updated with a choice of contemporary silver. To reach **C. O. I. Wholesale Jewelry** (✉ Via Por S. Maria 8/r, ☎ 055/283970), you must ring the doorbell at the street and take the elevator to the second floor, where the display cases are filled with handsome handmade Florentine designs.

Shoes and Leather Accessories

In the high tourist season, status-conscious shoppers often stand in line outside **Gucci** (✉ Via Tornabuoni 73/r, ☎ 055/264011), ready to buy anything with the famous designer's initials. **Ugolini** (✉ Via Tornabuoni 20/r, ☎ 055/216664) once made gloves for the Italian royal family, but now anyone can have the luxury of its exotic leathers, as well as silk and cashmere ties and scarves. Born near Naples, the late Salvatore **Ferragamo** (✉ Via Tornabuoni 2/r, ☎ 055/292123) made his fortune custom-making shoes for famous feet, especially Hollywood stars. His palace has since passed on to his wife, Wanda, and displays designer clothing and accessories, but elegant footwear still underlies the Ferragamo success. **Cellerini** (Via del Sole 37/r, ☎ 055/282533) is an institution in a city duded up in the finest of leathers, beloved by Florentines alike.

Giotti (✉ Piazza Ognissanti 3–4/r ☎ 055/294 265) has a full line of leather goods and its own leather clothing. **Leather Guild** (✉ Piazza Santa Croce 20/r, ☎ 055/241932) is one of many such shops that produce inexpensive, antique-looking leather goods of mass appeal, but here you can see the craftspersons at work. **Lily of Florence** (✉ Via Guicciardini 2/r, ☎ 055/294748) offers high quality, classic shoe designs at reasonable prices and in American sizes. **Il Bisonte** (✉ Via del Parione 31/r, just off Via della Vigna Nuova, ☎ 055/215722) is known for its natural-looking leather goods, all stamped with the store's bison symbol. The ultimate fine leathers are crafted into classic shapes at **Casadei** (✉ Via Tornabuoni 33/r, ☎ 055/287240), winding up as women's shoes and bags. **Madova** (✉ Via Guicciardini 1/r, ☎ 055/2396526) has a rainbow array of quality leather gloves.

SIDE TRIPS FROM FLORENCE

Fiesole and Gracious Gardens Around Florence

Fiesole

A half-day excursion to Fiesole, set in the hills 8 km (5 mi) above Florence, gives you a pleasant respite from museums and a wonderful vantage point of the city. From here, the view of Brunelleschi's Duomo, with its powerful cupola, will give you a new sense of appreciation of what he—and the Renaissance—accomplished. Fiesole began life as an ancient Etruscan and later Roman village that held some power until it succumbed to the barbarian invasions and eventually gave up its independence in exchange for Florence's protection. The medieval cathedral, ancient Roman amphitheater, and lovely old villas behind garden walls are clustered on a series of hilltops. A walk around Fiesole can take from one to two or three hours, depending on how far you stroll from the main piazza.

The **Duomo** reveals a stark medieval interior. In the raised presbytery, the **Cappella Salutati** was frescoed by 15th-century artist Cosimo Rosselli, but it was his contemporary, sculptor Mino da Fiesole (1430–84), who put the town on the artistic map. The Madonna on the altarpiece and the tomb of Bishop Salutati demonstrate the artist's work. ✉ *Piazza Mino da Fiesole,* ☎ *055/59400.* ⊙ *Daily 2:30–6:30.*

The nearby beautifully preserved 2,000-seat **Anfiteatro Romano** (Roman Amphitheater) dates from the 1st century BC and is still used for summer concerts. To the right of the amphitheater are the remains of the **Terme Romani** (Roman Baths), where you can see the gymnasium, hot and cold baths, and the rectangular chamber where the water was heated. A beautifully designed **Museo Archeologico,** an intricate series of levels connected by elevators, is built amidst the ruins and contains objects dating from 2000 BC. The nearby **Museo Bandini** is a small venue with a lot to offer. It is filled with the private collection of Canon Angelo Maria Bandini (1726–1803), who fancied 13th- to 15th-century Florentine paintings, terra-cotta pieces, and wood sculpture, which he bequeathed to the Diocese of Fiesole. ✉ *Via San Francesco 3,* ☎ *055/59477.* 🎫 *10,000 lire (1 ticket provides access to the archaeological park and the museums).* ⊙ *May–Oct., Wed.–Sun. 9:30–7; Nov.–Apr., Wed.–Sun. 9:30–5.*

Climb the hill to the church of **San Francesco** for a good view of Florence and the plain below enjoyed from the terrace and benches. Halfway up the hill, you'll see sloping steps to the right; they lead to a lovely wooded **park** with trails that loop out and back to the church.

If you really want to stretch your legs, walk 4 km (2½ mi) back toward Florence center along Via Vecchia Fiesolana, a narrow lane, to the church of **San Domenico.** Sheltered in the church is *Madonna and Child with Saints* by Fra Angelico, who was a Dominican monk at this church. ✉ *Piazza San Domenico, off Via Giuseppe Mantellini,* ☎ *055/59230.* ⊙ *Daily 4–6.*

From the church, it's only a five-minute walk northwest to the **Badia Fiesolana,** which was the original cathedral of Fiesole. ✉ *Via della Badia dei Roccettini,* ☎ *055/59155.* ⊙ *Mon.–Fri. 8:30–6, Sat. 9–noon, Sun. 10:30–12:30.*

Bus 7 (☞ Fiesole A to Z, *below*) goes from Florence to Fiesole, and also stops in San Domenico; from here you can walk the rest of the way to Fiesole along the narrow Via Vecchia Fiesolana, followed since the days of the Etruscans.

Lodging

$$$$ 🏨 **Villa San Michele.** The setting for this hideaway is so romantic—nestled in a luxuriant garden—that it once attracted Brigitte Bardot for her honeymoon. The villa was originally a monastery whose facade and loggia have been attributed to Michelangelo. Many of the rooms contain sumptuous statuary, paintings, and whirlpool baths. The restaurant is excellent. This is one of Italy's costliest hotels. ✉ *Via Doccia 4, 50014 Fiesole,* ☎ *055/59451,* FAX *055/598734. 41 rooms. Restaurant, piano bar, pool, exercise room. AE, DC, MC, V. Closed Dec.–mid-Mar. MAP.*

$$ 🏨 **Bencistà.** Below the luxurious Villa San Michele, this hotel has the same tranquil setting and is even two centuries older. The rooms are furnished with antiques, and breakfast and dinner are included with the price. The management requires that you take half pension. ✉ *Via*

Benedetto da Maiano 4, 50014 Fiesole, ☎ 055/59163, FAX 055/59163. 44 rooms, 12 without bath. Dining room. No credit cards. MAP.

$$ **Villa Aurora.** On the main piazza, this attractive hotel takes advantage of its hilltop spot, with beautiful views in many of the rooms, some of which are on two levels with beamed ceilings and balconies. The building, built as a theater in 1860, was transformed into a hotel in the late 19th century. It's fit for queens, and quite a few of them—Queen Victoria and Margherita di Savoia among others—have stayed here. Rooms are sophisticated but understated, as is the hotel. ✉ *Piazza Mino da Fiesole 39, 50014 Fiesole, ☎ 055/59100, FAX 055/59587. 25 rooms. Bar, restaurant, meeting rooms. AE, DC, MC, V. EP.*

Nightlife and the Arts

From June through August, **Estate Fiesolana** (✉ Teatro Romano, Fiesole, ☎ 055/59611) is a festival of theater, music, dance, and film that takes place in the churches and the archaeological park of Fiesole.

Fiesole A to Z

ARRIVING AND DEPARTING

The trip from Florence by car or bus takes 20–30 minutes. Take city Bus 7 from the Stazione Centrale di Santa Maria Novella, Piazza San Marco, or the Duomo. There are several possible routes for the two-hour walk from central Florence to Fiesole. One route begins in a residential area of Florence called Salviatino (Via Barbacane, near Piazza Edison, on Bus 7 route), and after a short time it offers glorious peeks over garden walls of beautiful villas, as well as the opportunity to look over your shoulder at the panorama of Florence nestled in the valley.

BIKING TOURS

If you have well-exercised legs and lungs, you can also take a guided half-day bicycle tour from Florence to Fiesole. For tour and bike rental information, *see* Guided Tours *in* Florence A to Z, *below.*

VISITOR INFORMATION

Tourist office (✉ Piazza Mino da Fiesole 37, 50014, Fiesole, ☎ 055/598720).

Gracious Gardens Around Florence

Like the Medici you can get away from Florence's hustle and bustle by heading for the hills. Take a break from city sightseeing to enjoy the gardens and villas set like jewels in the hills around the city. Villa di Castello and Villa La Petraia, both just northwest of the center in Castello, can be explored in one trip. The Italian garden at Villa Gamberaia is a quick 8-km (5-mi) jaunt east of the center near Settignano. Plan for a full-day excursion, picnic lunch included (☞ Salumerie *in* Dining, *above*), if visiting all three gardens. Spring and summer is the ideal time to visit the gardens, when flowers are in glorious bloom. For a prime taste of Medici living, venture farther afield to the family's Villa Medicea in Poggio a Caiano, just south of Prato (☞ Chapter 3).

Villa di Castello

A fortified residence in the Middle Ages, Villa di Castello was rebuilt in the 15th century by the Medici. The Accademia della Crusca, a 400-year-old institution that is the official arbiter of the Italian language, now occupies the palace, which is not open to the public. The gardens are the main attraction. From the villa entrance, walk uphill through the 19th-century park laid out in Romantic style, set above part of the formal garden. You'll reach the terrace, which affords a good view of the geometric layout of the Italian garden below; stairs on either side descend to the parterre.

Though the original garden design has been altered somewhat over the centuries, the allegorical theme of animals devised by Tribolo in the 1540s to the delight of the Medici is still evident. The artificial cave, Grotta degli Animali (Animal Grotto), displays an imaginative menagerie of sculpted animals by Giambologna and his assistants. An Ammanati sculpture, a figure of an old man representing the Appenines, is at the center of a pond on the terrace overlooking the Italianate garden. Two bronze sculptures by Ammanati, centerpieces of fountains studding the Italian garden, can now be seen indoors in Villa La Petraia (☞ *below*). Allow about 45 minutes to visit the garden; you can easily visit Villa La Petraia from here, making for a four-hour trip in total. ✉ *Via di Castello 47, Castello,* ☎ *055/454791.* 🎫 *4,000 lire (includes entrance to Villa La Petraia,* ☞ *below).* ⏲ *Garden: Nov.–Mar., daily 9–4, Apr.–Oct., daily 9–7. Closed 1st and 3rd Mon. of month. Palace closed to the public.*

Villa La Petraia

The splendidly planted gardens of Villa La Petraia sit high above the Arno plain with a sweeping view of Florence. The villa was built around a medieval tower and reconstructed after it was purchased by the Medici sometime after 1530. Virtually the only trace of the Medici having lived here is the 17th-century courtyard frescoes depicting glorious episodes of the clan's history. In the 1800s the villa served as a hunting lodge of King Vittorio Emanuele II (1820–78), who kept his mistress here, while Florence was the temporary capital of the newly united Kingdom of Italy.

An Italian-speaking guide will take you through the 19th-century-style salons. The Italian garden—also altered in the 1800s—and the vast park behind the palace suggest a splendid contrast between formal and natural landscapes. Allow 60 to 90 minutes to explore the park and gardens, plus 30 minutes for the guided tour of the so-called museum, the villa interior. This property is best visited after the Villa di Castello (☞ *above*). ✉ *Via della Petraia 40, Castello,* ☎ *050/454791.* 🎫 *4,000 lire (includes entrance to Villa di Castello).* ⏲ *Garden: Mar. and Oct., daily 9–5:30; Apr., May, and Sept., daily 9–6:30; June–Aug., daily 9–7:30; Nov.–Feb., daily 9–4:30. Villa: tours of the villa daily at 9:15, 10, 10:45, 11:30, 12:10, 1:30, 2:20, 3, 3:40, 4:45, 5:35, 6:35. Closed 2nd and 3rd Mon. of the month.*

Villa Gamberaia

Villa Gamberaia, near the village of Settignano on the eastern outskirts of Florence, was the rather modest 15th-century country home of Matteo di Domenico Gamberelli, the father of noted Renaissance sculptors Bernardo, Antonio, and Matteo Rossellino. In the early 1600s, the villa eventually passed into the hands of the wealthy Capponi family. They spared no expense in rebuilding it and, more importantly, creating its Italian garden, one of the finest near Florence. Festooned with statues and fountains, the garden suffered damage during World War II but has been restored according to the original 17th-century design. This excursion takes about 1½ hours, allowing 45 minutes to visit the garden. ✉ *Via del Rossellino 72, near Settignano,* ☎ *055/697205.* 🎫 *12,000 lire.* ⏲ *Garden: weekdays 9–noon and 1–6, weekends by appointment. Villa closed to the public.*

Gracious Gardens Around Florence A to Z

ARRIVING AND DEPARTING

Villa di Castello. By car, head northwest from Florence on Via Reginaldo Giuliani (also known as Via Sestese) to Castello, about 6 km (4 mi) northwest of city center in the direction of Sesto Fiorentino; follow signs to Villa di Castello. Or take Bus 28 from city center, and tell the driver you want to get off at Villa di Castello; from the stop, walk north about ½ km (¼ mi) up the tree-lined allée from the main road to the villa.

Villa La Petraia. By car, follow directions to Villa di Castello (☞ *above*), but take the right off Via Reginaldo Giuliani, following the sign for Villa La Petraia. You can walk from Villa di Castello to Villa La Petraia in about 15 minutes; turn left beyond the gate of Villa di Castello and continue straight along Via di Castello and the imposing Villa Corsini; take Via della Petraia uphill to the entrance.

Villa Gamberaia. By car, head east on Via Aretina, an extension of Via Gioberti, which is picked up at Piazza Beccaria; follow the sign to the turnoff to the north to Villa Gamberaia, about 8 km (5 mi) from the center. Take Bus 10 to Settignano. From Settignano's main Piazza Tommaseo walk east on Via di San Romano; the second lane on the right is Via del Rossellino, which leads southeast to the entrance of Villa Gamberaia. The walk from the piazza takes about 10 minutes.

VISITOR INFORMATION

☞ Visitor Information *in* Florence A to Z, *below.*

FLORENCE A TO Z

Arriving and Departing

By Bus

Long-distance buses offer inexpensive if somewhat claustrophobic service between Florence and other cities in Italy and Europe. One operator is **SITA** (✉ Via Santa Caterina da Siena 15/r, ☎ 055/214721). Also try **Lazzi Eurolines** (✉ Via Mercadante 2, ☎ 055/363041).

By Car

Florence is connected to the north and south of Italy by the Autostrada del Sole (**A1**). It takes about an hour of driving on scenic roads to get to Bologna (although heavy truck traffic over the Apennines often makes for slower going), about three hours to Rome, and three to three and a half hours by car to Milan. The Tyrrhenian Coast is an hour away on **A11** west.

By Plane

Although the Aeroporto A. Vespucci Airport, called **Peretola** (✉ 10 km/6 mi northwest of Florence, ☎ 055/373498), services flights from Milan, Rome, and some European cities, it is still a relatively minor airport. Pisa's **Aeroporto Galileo Galilei** (✉ 12 km/7 mi south of Pisa, 80 km/50 mi west of Florence, ☎ 050/500707) is used by most international carriers. For flight information, call the **Florence Air Terminal** (✉ Stazione Centrale di Santa Maria Novella, ☎ 055/216073) or Aeroporto Galileo Galilei.

International travelers flying on Alitalia to Rome's **Aeroporto Leonardo da Vinci** (☞ Chapter 1) and headed directly for Florence can make connections at the airport for a flight to Florence (the same holds true for Milan's Malpensa, ☞ Chapter 8), but if the layover is a long one, consider taking the FS airport train to Termini station in Rome, where fast trains for Florence are frequent during the day.

BETWEEN THE AIRPORTS AND DOWNTOWN

By Bus. There is a local bus service from Peretola to Florence. Buy a ticket at the second-floor bar; the bus shelter is beyond the parking lot. There is no direct bus service from Pisa's airport to Florence. Buses do go to Pisa itself, but then you have to change to a slow train service.

By Car. From Peretola take autostrada **A11** directly into the city. Driving from the airport in Pisa, take **S67,** a direct route to Florence.

By Train. There is no train service from downtown Florence to Peretola (☞ By Bus, *above*). A scheduled service connects the station at Pisa's Aeroporto Galileo Galilei with Florence's Stazione Centrale di Santa Maria Novella, roughly a one-hour trip. Trains start running about 7 AM from the airport, 6 AM from Florence, and continue service every hour until about 11:30 PM from the airport, 8 PM from Florence. You can check in for departing flights at the **air terminal** (✉ Track 5, Galileo Galilei Airport station, ☎ 055/216073).

By Train

Florence is on the principal Italian train route between most European capitals and Rome and within Italy is served frequently from Milan, Venice, and Rome by nonstop Intercity (IC) and Eurostar trains. **Stazione Centrale di Santa Maria Novella** (☎ 147/888088 toll-free) is the most convenient city-center station. Be sure to avoid trains that stop only at the Campo di Marte or Rifredi stations, which are not convenient to the center.

Getting Around

By Bicycle

Brave souls (cycling in Florence is difficult, at best) may rent bicycles at easy-to-spot locations at Fortezza da Basso, the Stazione Centrale di Santa Maria Novella, and Piazza Pitti. Otherwise try **Motorent** (✉ Via San Zanobi 9/r, ☎ 055/490113) or **Alinari** (✉ Via Guelfa 85r, ☎ 055/280500).

By Bus

Maps and timetables are available for a small fee at the **ATAF** booth (✉ Next to the train station; Piazza del Duomo 57/r), or for free at visitor information offices (☞ Contacts and Resources, *below*). Tickets must be bought in advance at tobacco stores, newsstands, from automatic ticket machines near main stops, or at ATAF booths. The ticket must be canceled in the small validation machine immediately upon boarding. Two types of tickets are available, both valid for one or more rides on all lines. One costs 1,500 lire and is valid for one hour from the time it is first canceled; the other costs 2,500 lire and is valid for two hours. A multiple ticket—four tickets, each valid for 60 minutes—costs 5,800 lire. A 24-hour tourist ticket costs 6,000 lire. Monthly passes are also available.

By Car

In the city, abandon all hope of using a car, since most of the downtown area is a pedestrian zone. For assistance or information, call the **ACI** (Automobile Club Firenze, ☎ 055/2486246).

By Moped

If you want to go native and rent a noisy Vespa (Italian for "wasp") or other make of motorcycle or moped, you may do so at Motorent (☞ By Bicycle, *above*). However unfashionable, helmets can be rented at either place.

By Taxi

Taxis usually wait at stands throughout the city (such as in front of the train station and in Piazza della Repubblica), or you can call for one (☎ 055/4390 or 055/4798). The meter starts at 4,500 lire, with a 7,000 lire minimum and extra charges for nights, Sunday, or radio dispatch. A tip of at least 10% is customary.

Contacts and Resources

Car Rentals

Eurodollar (✉ Via Termine 1, ☎ 055/310887). **Hertz Italiana** (✉ Via Finiguerra 33/r, ☎ 055/317543). **Maggiore-Budget Autonoleggio** (✉ Via Termine 1, ☎ 055/311256).

Consulates

U.S. Consulate (✉ Lungarno Vespucci 38, ☎ 055/2398276). **U.K. Consulate** (✉ Lungarno Corsini 2, ☎ 055/284133). **Canadians** should contact their consulate in Rome (☞ Chapter 1).

Doctors and Dentists

You can get a list of English-speaking doctors and dentists at the U.S. Consulate (☞ *above*). Contact the **Tourist Medical Service** (✉ Viale Lorenzo Il Magnifico, ☎ 055/475411).

Emergencies

Police (✉ Via Zara 2, near Piazza della Libertà, ☎ 055/49771). **Ambulance** (☎ 118). **Emergencies** (☎ 113). **Misericordia** (Red Cross, ✉ Piazza del Duomo 20, ☎ 055/212222). If you need hospital treatment and an interpreter you can call **AVO** (☎ 055/2344567), a group of volunteer interpreters; it's open Monday, Wednesday, and Friday 4–6 PM and Tuesday and Thursday 10–noon.

English-Language Bookstores

BM Bookshop (✉ Borgo Ognissanti 4/r, ☎ 055/294575). **Paperback Exchange** (✉ Via Fiesolana 31/r, ☎ 055/2478154). **Seeber** (✉ Via Tornabuoni 70/r, ☎ 055/215697).

Guided Tours

BIKING TOURS

See Outdoor Activities and Sports, *above*.

ORIENTATION TOURS

The major bus operators (☞ Arriving and Departing, By Bus, *above*) offer half-day itineraries, all of which use comfortable buses staffed with English-speaking guides. Morning tours begin at 9, when buses pick visitors up at the main hotels. Stops include the cathedral complex, the Galleria dell'Accademia, Piazzale Michelangelo, and the Palazzo Pitti (or, on Monday, the Museo dell'Opera del Duomo). Afternoon tours stop at the main hotels at 2 PM and take in Piazza della Signoria, the Galleria degli Uffizi (or the Palazzo Vecchio on Monday, when the Uffizi is closed), nearby Fiesole, and, on the return, the church of Santa Croce. A half-day tour costs about 48,000 lire, including museum admissions.

Late-Night Pharmacies

The following are open 24 hours a day, seven days a week. For a complete listing, call 192. **Comunale No. 13** (✉ Stazione Centrale di Santa Maria Novella, ☎ 055/289435).

Travel Agencies

American Express (✉ Via Guicciardini 49/r, near Piazza Pitti, ☎ 055/288751; ✉ Via Dante Alighieri 14/r, ☎ 055/2382876). **CIT** (✉ Via Cavour 56, ☎ 055/294306; ✉ Piazza Stazione 51/r, ☎ 055/284145 or 055/212606). **Micos Travel Box** (✉ Via dell'Oriuolo 50/52/r, ☎ 055/2340228), just down the street from the Duomo, has an English-speaking staff. **Thomas Cook** is represented by World Vision (✉ Via Cavour 158/r, ☎ 055/577185).

Villa Rentals

Chianti e Terre di Toscana (✉ Via Santa Maria Macerata 23/a, 50020 Montefiridolfi, ☎ 055/8244211, FAX 055/8244382). **Florence and**

Abroad (✉ Via San Zanobi 58, 50100 Florence, ☎ 055/470603). **The Best in Italy** (✉ Via Foscolo 72, 50124, Florence, ☎ 055/223064, FAX 055/2298912). **Ville e Casali Toscani** (✉ Via delle Scuole 12, 53010 Rosia (Siena), ☎ 0577/344901, FAX 0577/344800).

Visitor Information

Tourist offices (Agenzia Promozione Turistica, APT, ✉ Via Cavour 1/r, next to Palazzo Medici-Riccardi, 50100, ☎ 055/290832; ✉ Stazione Centrale di Santa Maria Novella 50100, ☎ 055/212245; ✉ Piazza della Signoria, Chiasso dei Baroncelli 17/r, 50100, ☎ 055/2302124; ✉ Borgo Santa Croce 29/r, ☎ 055/2340444).

3 TUSCANY

LUCCA, SIENA, CHIANTI, AND THE HILL TOWNS

Punctuated by thickly wooded hills, sun-warmed vineyards, olive groves, and dramatic hill towns, Tuscany's milk-and-honey vistas have changed little since Renaissance artists first beheld them. Siena, a maze of steep cobbled lanes spilling into its fan-shape piazza, rivals Florence in enchantment. Grape- and cypress-rich Chianti is the quintessence of Tuscany.

Updated by Patricia Rucidlo

ROME MAY BE THE CAPITAL OF ITALY, but Tuscany is the heart. Stretching from the Apennines to the sea, midway between Milan and Rome, the region is the essence of Italy, in both appearance and history. The variety in its landscapes is unmatched in Italy. Its past has been ignoble—it produced the Guelph-Ghibelline conflict of the Middle Ages—and glorious, for it gave birth to the Renaissance. Tuscany's towns are justly famous for their wealth of fine architecture and art, but visitors often go home even more enthusiastic about Tuscany's unspoiled hilly scenery, about the delicious Chianti wines produced by vineyards on those hills, and about the robust and flavorful Tuscan cooking. Be sure to allot some portion of your time here for leisurely strolls, unhurried meals, and aimless wandering around this stupendously beautiful countryside, where the true soul of Tuscany is to be found.

Tuscany also produced the Italian language. Thanks to the eminence of their writings, it was the Tuscan dialect of Dante, Boccaccio, and Petrarch, all native sons, that grew to be the national tongue, a fact of which the Tuscans are rightly proud. Today the purest Italian is said to be spoken in the area between Siena and Arezzo, and even with limited textbook Italian you might hear the difference. As you enter the region, the language suddenly becomes much easier to understand and takes on a bell-like clarity and mellifluous beauty unequaled throughout the rest of Italy.

It also takes on a notorious wit. As a common proverb has it, "Tuscans have Paradise in their eyes and the Inferno in their mouths" (a wry reference to Dante), and the sting of their wit is as famous throughout Italy as is the beauty of their speech. Happily, Tuscans usually reserve their wit for each other and treat visitors with complete and sincere courtesy.

For a long time, the Tuscan hill towns were notorious as well. Even their earliest civilized settlers, the Etruscans, chose their city-sites for defensive purposes (the fortress-town of Fiesole, above Florence, is a fine surviving example). With the end of the Roman Empire, the region fell into disunity, and by the 11th century, Tuscany had evolved into a collection of independent city-states, each city seeking to dominate, and sometimes forcibly overpower, its neighbors. The region then became embroiled in an apparently endless international quarrel between a long succession of popes and Holy Roman Emperors. By the 13th century, Tuscany had become a battleground: the infamous conflict between the Guelphs and the Ghibellines had begun.

The Guelphs and the Ghibellines are the bane of Italian schoolchildren; their infinitely complicated, bloody history is to Italy what the Wars of the Roses are to England. To oversimplify grossly, the Ghibellines were mostly allied with both the Holy Roman Emperor (headquartered over the Alps in Germany) and the local aristocracy (dominated by feudal lords); the Guelphs were mostly allied with both the pope (headquartered in Rome) and the emerging middle class (dominated by the new trade guilds). Florence, flourishing as a trade center, was (most of the time) Guelph; its neighboring city-states Pisa and Siena were (most of the time) Ghibelline. But the bitter struggles that resulted were so Byzantine in their complexity, so full of factional disputes and treachery, that a dizzying series of conflicts within conflicts resulted. (Dante, for instance, was banished from Florence not for being a Ghibelline but for being the wrong brand of Guelph.)

Eventually the Florentine Guelphs emerged victorious, and in the mid-16th century the region was united to become the Grand Duchy of Tuscany under Medici Grand Duke Cosimo I (1519–74). Today the hill towns are no longer fierce, although they retain a uniquely medieval air, and in most of them the citizens walk the same narrow streets and inhabit the same houses that their ancestors did 600 years ago.

Tuscan art, to most people, means Florence, and understandably so. The city is unique and incomparable, and an astonishing percentage of the great artists of the Renaissance lived and worked there. But there is art elsewhere in Tuscany, and too often it is overlooked in favor of another trip to the Uffizi. Siena, particularly, bears its own style of architecture and art quite different from the Florentine variety; the contrast is both surprising and illuminating. And even the smallest of the hill towns can possess hidden treasures, for the artists of the Middle Ages and the Renaissance took their work where they could find it. Piero della Francesca's fresco cycle in the church of San Francesco in Arezzo is perhaps the preeminent hidden treasure. Majestically placed in the high altar, the frescoes are currently undergoing restoration and cleaning, revealing Piero's fine palette and sense of geometrical symmetry.

Pleasures and Pastimes

Dining

Just as the ancient Etruscans introduced cypress trees to the Tuscan landscape, their influence on regional food—in the use of fresh herbs—still persists after more than three millennia. Earthy and austere, Tuscan food evolved from its peasant and noble past, resulting today in a host of fresh vegetables, wonderful peasant soups, and savory meats and game perfumed with sage, rosemary, and thyme. Day-old saltless Tuscan bread is grilled and drizzled with olive oil (*crostini*), or spread with chicken liver (*crostini di fegatini*), or rubbed with garlic, and topped with tomatoes (*bruschetta* or *fettunta*). For their love of beans—particularly *cannellini* (white kidney beans) simmered in olive oil and herbs until creamy—Tuscans have been disparagingly nicknamed *mangiafagioli* (bean eaters) by Italians from other regions. The region's sheep's milk pecorino cheese, delicious with ripe pears, is even seen at the breakfast table.

Grapes have been cultivated here since Etruscan times, and Chianti still rules the wine roost (almost literally when selected by the Gallo Nero Black Rooster label, a symbol of one of the region's most powerful winegrowing consortiums; the other is a putto, or cherub). The robust red wine is still a staple on most tables, and the discerning can select from a multitude of other varieties, including such reds as Brunello di Montalcino and Vino Nobile di Montepulciano, and whites such as Valdinievole and Vergine della Valdichiana. The dessert wine *vin santo* is produced throughout the region and is often sipped with *biscotti di Prato* (hard almond cookies), perfect for dunking.

Lodging

Staying in Tuscany is not a cheap enterprise, especially in well-traveled cities such as Siena, Lucca, San Gimignano, and Arezzo. But wonderful properties abound, including Renaissance and medieval palazzi, where you'll feel more like Lorenzo de Medici than a 20th-century visitor. To keep costs down, overnight in less-visited towns. You might want to consider staying at an *agriturismo* property, a farm and/or vineyard that has opened its rooms or apartments to guests; choices range from rustic to stately (note that some require a minimum stay). Villa rental can also be an economical and enjoyable option for groups and families.

Exploring Tuscany

It is best to have a car to travel in Tuscany to fully enjoy the region's riches—it's the only way to get to many of the vineyards and estates. If traveling by public transportation, however, plan on traveling by bus service rather than by train. The cities west of Florence—once embroiled in battle with Florence for control of the sea—are easily reached by the A1, which heads east from Florence towards Arezzo. Florence and Siena are connected by a superstrada and also the panoramic S222, which threads through the wine country of Chianti. The hill towns radiating from Siena lie along superstradas and winding local roads—all are well marked, but you should arm yourself with a good map.

Numbers in the text correspond to numbers in the margin and on the Tuscany, Lucca, Pisa, and Siena maps.

Great Itineraries

Although Tuscany is relatively small—no important destination is more than a few hours' drive from Florence—the desire to linger is strong: can you really get enough of sitting on a hillside *terrazza* (terrace) with a good espresso or a robust Chianti and watching the evening settle over a landscape of soft-edged hills, proud medieval towns, quiet villages, and cypress-ringed villas?

It only takes a few days for the region to leave an indelible mark on your memory, and even your soul. Seven days would allow for leisurely exploration of the main towns and for meandering along country roads to rustic, grand estates and wineries. In five days, you can see the most interesting towns, but you'll need to stick to the main sights and move briskly. If three days is the limit, you can take in all the highlights, if not the small corners.

IF YOU HAVE 3 DAYS

Florence is a practical starting point. See **Lucca** ④–⑩ and the **Leaning Tower** ⑪ in **Pisa** ⑪–⑱, then head for **San Gimignano** ㉑ to overnight. The next day, explore the tangle of medieval alleyways in **Siena** ㉖–㉝ for a few hours, then move on to **Montepulciano** ㊲ for the night. The following day, detour south to the thermal waters of **Saturnia** ㊹ and stroll through the medieval town of **Pitigliano** ㊺, then go north to **Arezzo** ㉞ and head back to Florence via the A1 or, if you have time, drive back to Florence through the twisting roads of **Chianti** ㉓–㉕ (on S69 west, S408 west, S429 west, and S222 north).

IF YOU HAVE 5 DAYS

From Florence, head for industrial **Prato** ① to see its striking medieval core; historic **Pistoia** ②, site of bitter Guelph-Ghibelline feuding; and, if you enjoy resorts, **Montecatini Terme** ③, one of Europe's most famous spas. Stay over in **Lucca** ④–⑩ and spend part of the next day exploring. Head for **Pisa** ⑪–⑱ to see the **Leaning Tower** ⑪, and then move on to the enchanting hilltop town of **San Miniato** ⑲ and either **Volterra** ⑳ or **San Gimignano** ㉑, the archetypal Tuscan town and a good place to spend your second night. On the third day, either while away the morning driving through **Chianti** ㉓–㉕ (where you will inevitably want to settle in for a night), or head directly to **Siena** ㉖–㉝, perhaps Italy's loveliest medieval city. From Siena see the **Abbazia di Monte Oliveto Maggiore** ㊱, **Montalcino** ㊴, the **Abbazia di Sant'Antimo** ㊵, and then **Montepulciano** ㊲, where you should overnight if you don't stay in Siena. On the morning of your fourth day drive to **Saturnia** ㊹ and enjoy a hot thermal bath before moving on to **Pitigliano** ㊺ to wander its quaint and narrow streets. Then head to **Pienza** ㊳, designed for Pope Pius II to be the perfect Re-

Tuscany
ITALY
Faenza
EMILIA-ROMAGNA
Firenzuola
Roncobilacci
Reno
Abetone
GARFAGNANA
ALPI APUANE
La Spezia
Carrara
Seravezza
Pietrasanta
Forte dei Marmi
Viareggio
Migliarino
Marlia
Lucca 4—10
Pisa 11—18
Livorno
Ligurian Sea
TO CORSICA
Montecatini Terme 3
Pistoia 2
Prato 1
Monte Albano
Monsummano Terme
Altopascio
TUSCANY
Empoli
Poggio a Caiano
Peretola
Fiesole
Florence
Arno
Impruneta
Strada
Monte Fioralle
Greve in Chianti 23
Volpaia
Radda in Chianti 24
Castellina in Chianti 25
Colle Val d'Elsa
Elsa
San Miniato 19
San Gimignano 21
Volterra
Arezzo
A1
A11
A12
S1
S2
S12
S64
S65
S67
S69
S71
S206
S222
S302
S324
S429
S435
S439
S445
S503
S610
N

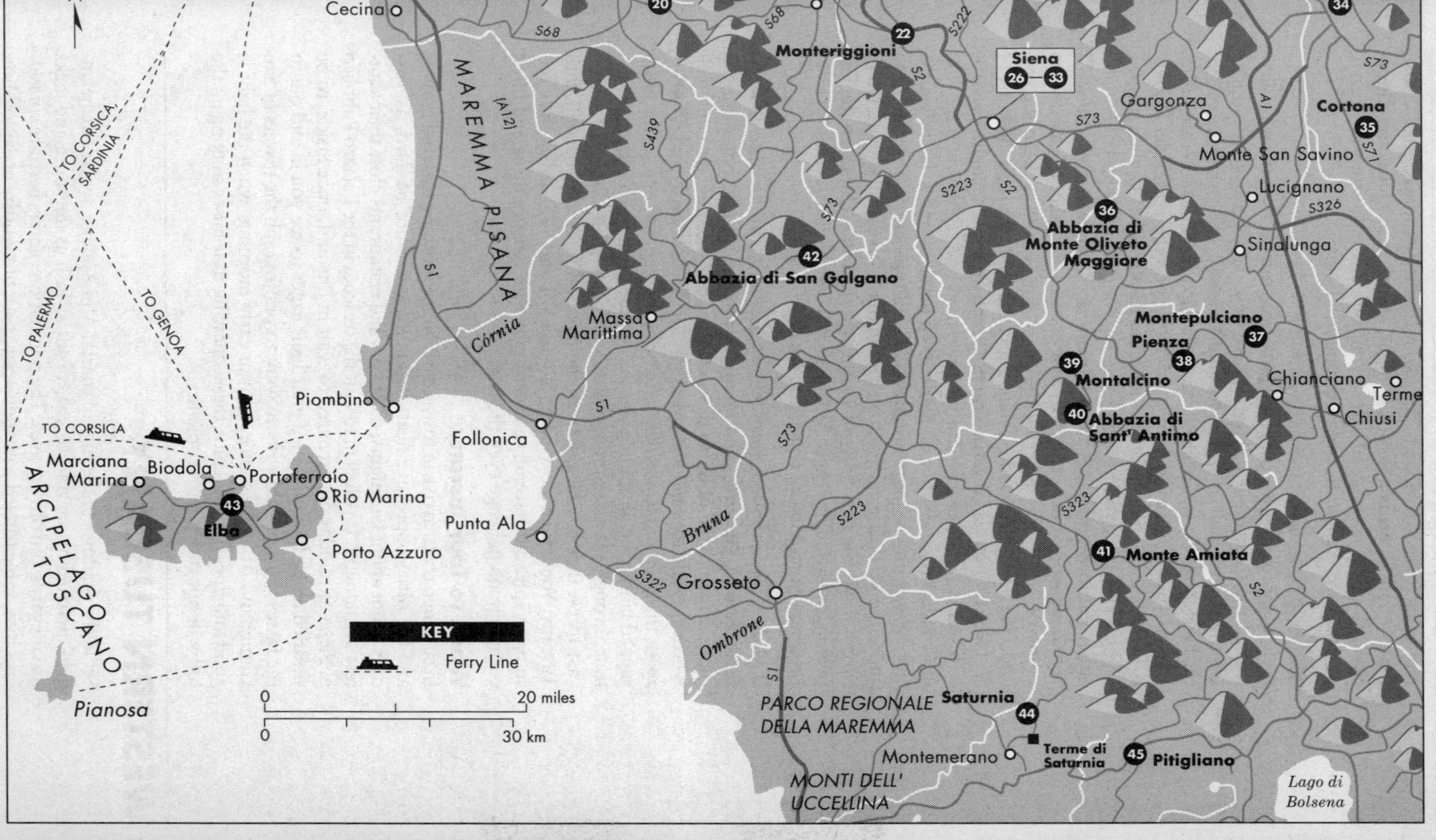

Cecina
20
S68
Monteriggioni
22
S222
Siena
26—33
34
S73
Gargonza
Cortona
35
S71
Monte San Savino
Lucignano
S326
Sinalunga
A1
MAREMMA PISANA
(A12)
S439
TO CORSICA
SARDINIA
TO PALERMO
TO GENOA
S1
S2
S223
36
Abbazia di Monte Oliveto Maggiore
42
Abbazia di San Galgano
Massa Marittima
Córnia
Montepulciano
37
Pienza
38
39
Montalcino
40
Abbazia di Sant' Antimo
Chianciano
Terme
Chiusi
Piombino
Follonica
TO CORSICA
Marciana Marina
Biodola
Portoferraio
Rio Marina
43
Elba
Punta Ala
Porto Azzuro
ARCIPELAGO TOSCANO
Pianosa
Bruna
S322
Grosseto
Ombrone
S323
41
Monte Amiata
KEY
Ferry Line
0
20 miles
30 km
PARCO REGIONALE DELLA MAREMMA
Saturnia
44
Terme di Saturnia
Montemerano
45
Pitigliano
MONTI DELL' UCCELLINA
Lago di Bolsena

naissance town. Move on to handsome but underappreciated **Cortona** ㉟ and **Arezzo** ㉞ for the night, stopping at **Chiusi** and **Chianciano** along the way. Spend part of your fifth day in Cortona or Arezzo, or exploring Chianti before returning to Florence.

IF YOU HAVE 7 DAYS

As you approach **Prato** ①, you'll have time to visit the modern collection at the Centro per l'Arte Contemporanea L. Pecci. If you opt to see the resort town of **Montecatini Terme** ③, take a cure in one of the local *terme* (spas) or ride the funicular up to older Montecatini Alto. Extend your **Pisa** ⑪–⑱ exploration beyond the Piazza del Duomo to include the Renaissance trio in **Piazza dei Cavalieri** ⑰, then stay the night. From Pisa, you have a choice for your next day and overnight: either explore timeless **San Miniato** ⑲, **Volterra** ⑳, and/or **San Gimignano** ㉑, or head east to wine country. Take the S67 east toward Florence, and before entering the city turn south to pick up the meandering S222, the Strada Chiantigiana that runs through the heart of **Chianti** ㉓–㉕ via **Castellina in Chianti** ㉕; stay the night, perhaps in **Radda in Chianti** ㉔. The next two days and nights, vineyard-hop in Chianti or settle into a **Siena** ㉖–㉝ hotel, taking a day to see the city. Be sure to visit **Monteriggioni** ㉒, a hilltop hamlet between Siena and Colle Val d'Elsa encircled by formidable 13th-century walls. Don't forget about the possibility of visiting the Tuscan archipelago the last two nights, including rugged **Elba** ㊸ and Montecristo, accessible from Livorno, Piombino (by boat), and Pisa (by air).

If you're not seabound, from Siena head south to discover **Montepulciano** ㊲, **Pienza** ㊳, and **Montalcino** ㊴ for a night. For a moving sight, detour to the **Abbazia di San Galgano** ㊷. East of Siena and well worth the side trip and last overnight are **Cortona** ㉟ and **Arezzo** ㉞, the main hill towns of the Arezzo province. For a taste of a more rugged landscape, don't take the autostrada back to Florence, but detour through the Casentino, a mountainous region blanketed with a vast forest that is a far cry from the pastoral images associated with Tuscany. You'll take the winding S70 (on S71 and S67), called the Consuma, a splendidly scenic road wrought with hairpin turns and blind corners that challenge even the best drivers.

When to Tour Tuscany

In summer, try to arrive in towns early in the morning to avoid crowds and the often oppressive heat. Rising early will not be hard, as Tuscany is not about late nights; most bars and restaurants close their shutters at midnight. If you plan to visit the frescoes in the Palazzo Pubblico in Siena at midday, be prepared to wait in line and, once inside, to be shuffled along by iron-willed guardians eager to see you in and out in the fastest time possible. If you want to photograph the towers of San Gimignano from a distance, do it in early morning, when the light is good and lines of neon-color, diesel-spewing tour buses snaking up the hill will not ruin a perfect picture.

WESTERN TUSCANY

Set in the shadows of the rugged coastal Alpi Apuane, where Michelangelo quarried his marble, this area isn't as lush as the south and lacks its vineyards and olive groves. The population centers here are sprawling cities, some fringed with industrial areas, but worthy of exploration for their stunning medieval and Renaissance centers.

Prato

❶ *17 km (11 mi) northwest of Florence, 60 km (37 mi) east of Lucca.*

The wool industry in this city, one of the world's largest manufacturers of cloth, was known throughout Europe as early as the 13th century. It was further stimulated in the 14th century by a local cloth merchant, Francesco di Marco Datini, who built his business, according to one of his surviving ledgers, "in the name of God and of profit."

Prato's **Centro per l'Arte Contemporanea L. Pecci** (L. Pecci Center of Contemporary Art) has acquired a burgeoning collection of works by Italian and other artists. ✉ *Viale della Repubblica 277,* ☎ *0574/570620.* 🎟 *12,000 lire.* ⏲ *Mon. and Wed.–Sun. 10–7.*

Prato's Romanesque **Duomo,** reconstructed from 1211, is famous for its **Pergamo del Sacro Cingolo** (Chapel of the Holy Girdle), to the left of the entrance, which enshrines the sash of the Virgin Mary. It is said that the girdle was given to the apostle Thomas by the Virgin Mary when she miraculously appeared after her Assumption. The Duomo also contains 15th-century frescoes by Prato's most famous son, Fra Filippo Lippi (1406–69), who executed scenes from the life of St. Stephen on the left wall and scenes from the life of John the Baptist on the right in the **Cappella Maggiore** (Main Chapel). Bring a flashlight: no illumination is provided. ✉ *Piazza del Duomo,* ☎ *0574/26234.* ⏲ *May–Oct., daily 7:30–noon and 3:30–7:30; Nov.–Apr., daily 7–noon and 3:30–6:30.*

A sculpture by Donatello (circa 1386–1466) that originally adorned the Duomo's exterior pulpit is now on display in the **Museo dell'Opera del Duomo.** ✉ *Piazza del Duomo 49,* ☎ *0574/29339.* 🎟 *8,000 lire (includes entry to Museo di Pittura Murale,* ☞ *below).* ⏲ *Mon. and Wed.-Sat. 9:30–12:30 and 3–6:30, Sun. 9:30–12:30.*

Installed in the **Museo di Pittura Murale** (Museum of Mural Painting) is a collection of paintings by Fra Filippo Lippi and other works from the 13th–15th centuries in a special exhibit called "Treasures of the City," on view until 2000. The permanent collection contains frescoes removed from sites in Prato and environs. ✉ *Piazza San Domenico,* ☎ *0574/445007.* 🎟 *8,000 lire (includes Museo dell'Opera del Duomo,* ☞ *above).* ⏲ *Mon. and Wed.–Sat. 10–1 and 3:30–7:30, Sun. 10–1.*

OFF THE BEATEN PATH

POGGIO A CAIANO – For a look at gracious country living, Renaissance style, detour south of Prato to the Villa Medicea in Poggio a Caiano. Lorenzo "Il Magnifico" (1449–92) commissioned Giuliano da Sangallo (circa 1445–1516) to redo the villa, which was lavished with frescoes by important Renaissance painters such as Andrea del Sarto (1486–1530) and Pontormo (1494–1557). You can take a walk around the austerely ornamented grounds while waiting for entry. ✉ *Poggio a Caiano, 7 km (4½ mi) south of Prato, follow signs,* ☎ *055/877012.* 🎟 *4,000 lire.* ⏲ *Apr.–May and Sept., Mon.–Sat. 9–5:30; June–Aug., Mon.–Sat. 9–6:30; Mar. and Oct., Mon.–Sat. 9–4:30; Nov.–Feb., Mon.–Sat. 9–3:30. Guided visits only, hourly on the half hr (9:30–1 hr before closing). Closed 2nd and 3rd Mon. of month. Ticket office closes 1 hr before villa and grounds.*

Dining

$$$ ★ ✕ **Da Delfina.** Veer off the autostrada (after making reservations) to this haven of Tuscan cooking nestled amid vineyards and olive trees past Poggio a Caiano in Artimino. Delfina began cooking for hungry area hunters, and now she has four comfortably rustic dining rooms

in a farmhouse where you can enjoy dishes centered around pure ingredients, seasonal vegetables, and savory meats accented with herbs. Everything is good: the fegatini; seasonal pasta—always homemade; and the *secondi* (second courses) such as *coniglio con olive e pignoli* (rabbit sautéed with olives and pine nuts). ✉ *Via della Chiesa 1, Artimino,* ☎ *055/8718074. Reservations essential. No credit cards. Closed Mon. and 1 wk in Dec.–Jan.*

$$$ ✕ **Piraña.** Oddly named for the cannibalistic fish swimming in an aquarium with a full view of the diners, this sophisticated restaurant, decorated in shades of blue with steely accents, is a local favorite. Seafood is the specialty and may take the form of ravioli *di branzino in crema di scampi* (stuffed with sea bass with a creamy shrimp sauce) and *rombo al forno* (baked turbot). It's a bit out of the way for sightseers but handy if you have a car, as it's near the Prato Est autostrada exit. ✉ *Via G. Valentini 110,* ☎ *0574/25746. AE, DC, MC, V. Closed Sun. and Aug. No lunch Sat.*

$$–$$$ ★ ✕ **Osvaldo Baroncelli.** Please do not come to this restaurant in shorts and sneakers—the food and atmosphere here are elegant and sophisticated. Polished wooden floors, subtly striped chairs, and pale sponged walls bespeak the seriousness of this restaurant, which has been in the Baroncelli family for 50 years, and in that time they've perfected their menu. You'll be tempted to eat all of the perfectly fried olives that arrive warm, but save room for what's to come. Try the *insalata tiepida di gamberi, calametti, e carciofi* (warm salad with shrimp, squid, and artichokes) or the colorful *flan di zucca gialla e ricotta* (yellow squash and ricotta flan) in a light fish sauce. The pastas are house made—the *tortelli di branzino in salsa di seppie and carciofi* (tortelli stuffed with sea bass in a sauce of cuttlefish and artichokes) is wonderful. Reservations are advised. ✉ *Via Fra Bartolomeo 13,* ☎ *0574/23810. AE, MC, V. Closed Aug. 7–21. No lunch Sat.*

$$ ✕ **Baghino.** In the heart of the historic center, Baghino serves typical Tuscan fare as well as atypical Tuscan fare like spaghetti *all'amatriciana* (with bacon in a spicy tomato sauce) and penne *con vongole e curry* (with clams and curry). You can dine in the lovely outdoor terrace in summer. ✉ *Via dell'Accademia 9,* ☎ *055/27920, AE, DC, MC, V. No dinner Sun., no lunch Mon.*

Shopping

Prato's biscotti (literally "twice cooked") have an extra-dense texture, lending themselves to submersion in your caffè or vin santo. The best in town are at **Antonio Mattei** (✉ Via Ricasoli 20/22).

Pistoia

❷ *18 km (11 mi) northwest of Prato, 36 km (22 mi) northwest of Florence.*

Pistoia saw the beginning of the bitter Guelph-Ghibelline conflict of the Middle Ages. Reconstructed after heavy bombing during World War II, it has preserved some fine Romanesque architecture. The **Cattedrale di San Zeno** in the main piazza houses the *Dossale di San Jacopo,* a magnificent silver altar. The two half figures on its left side were executed by Filippo Brunelleschi (1377–1446). ✉ *Piazza del Duomo,* ☎ *0573/25095,* 🎫 *Illumination of altarpiece 1,500 lire.* ⏲ *Daily 9–noon and 4–7.*

The **Palazzo del Comune,** begun around 1295, houses the Museo Civico, containing mostly works by local artists from the 14th to 20th centuries. ✉ *Museo Civico, Piazza del Duomo,* ☎ *0573/3711.* 🎫 *6,000 lire; free Sat. 3–7.* ⏲ *Tues.–Sat. 10–7, Sun. 9:30–12:30.*

Founded in the 13th century, the **Spedale del Ceppo** reveals a glorious early 16th-century exterior terra-cotta frieze begun by Giovanni della Robbia (1469–1529) and completed by the workshop of Santi and Benedetto Buglioni in 1527. ✉ *Piazza Ospedale, a short way down Via Pacini from Piazza del Duomo.*

In the church of **Sant'Andrea,** the pulpit by Giovanni Pisano (circa 1270–1348) depicts scenes from the life of Christ. ✉ *Via Pappe to Via Sant'Andrea,* ☎ *0573/21912.* ⏲ *Daily 8–1 and 3–5:30.*

A 20-minute drive out of town is the **Giardino Zoologico,** a small zoo especially laid out to accommodate the wiles of both animals and children. Take Bus 29 from the train station. ✉ *Via Pieve a Celle 160/a,* ☎ *0573/911219.* *13,000 lire.* ⏲ *Daily 9–5.*

Dining

$$ ✕ **Corradossi.** This lovely pan-Italian restaurant is a short walk from Piazza del Duomo, and makes an excellent place to break for lunch or dinner. The food is ornate yet simple, service quick and attentive, and the prices more than reasonable. Start with the *trofie e gamberi* (corkscrew-shape pasta sauced with perfectly cooked shrimp and sliced baby zucchini), then follow with their *fritte miste* (fish and seafood crisply fried). ✉ *Via Frosini 112,* ☎ *0573/25683. AE, DC, MC, V. Closed Sun.*

$$ ✕ **Rafanelli.** *Maccheroni all'anatra* (pasta with duck sauce) and other game dishes—the specialties here—have been prepared with attention to tradition and quality for more than half a century by the same family. The restaurant is just outside the old city walls in a garden setting with alfresco dining in summer. ✉ *Via Sant'Agostino 47,* ☎ *0573/532046. AE, DC, MC, V. Closed Mon. and Aug. No dinner Sun.*

$$ ✕ **S. Jacopo.** This charming restaurant, minutes away from the Piazza del Duomo, has white walls, tiled floors, and a gracious host in Bruno Lottini, a native Pistoian fluent in English. The food is as welcoming as he: bread, flecked with olives, is baked on the premises and arrives hot to the table. The menu has mostly regional favorites, such as the maccheroni S. Jacopo, wide ribbons of house-made pasta with a duck *ragù* (sauce), but they can turn out perfectly grilled squid as well. Save room for dessert, especially the apple strudel. ✉ *Via Crispi 15,* ☎ *0573/27786. AE, DC, MC, V. Closed Mon. No lunch Tues.*

Montecatini Terme

❸ *16 km (10 mi) west of Pistoia, 49 km (30 mi) west of Florence.*

Immortalized in Fellini's *8½*, Montecatini Terme is home to Italy's premier *terme* (spas), reputed for their curative powers and, at least once upon a time, for their great popularity among the wealthy. It is renowned for its mineral springs, which flow from five sources and are used to treat liver and skin disorders. Those "taking the cure" report each morning to one of the town's *stabilimenti termali* (thermal establishments; information: ✉ Via Verdi 41, ☎ 0572/778451) to drink their prescribed cupful of water, whose curative effects became known in the 1800s. The town's wealth of Art Nouveau buildings went up during its most active period of development, at the beginning of this century. Like most well-heeled resort towns, Montecatini attracts the leisured traveler; aside from taking the waters and people-watching in Piazza del Popolo, there's not a whole lot to do here. Of the town's Art Nouveau structures, the most attractive is the **Terme Tettuccio** (✉ Viale Verdi 4, ☎ 0572/778501), a neoclassic edifice with colonnades. Here Montecatini's healthful tonic spouts from fountains set up on marble counters, the walls are decorated with bucolic scenes depicted on painted ceramic tiles, and an orchestra plays under a frescoed dome.

The older town of **Montecatini Alto** sits on top of a hill above the spa town and is reached by a funicular from Viale Diaz. A medieval square is lined with restaurants and bars, the air is crisp, and the views of the Nievole, the valley below, are gorgeous.

Lodging

$$$ **Croce di Malta.** Taste and sophistication have been the calling cards of this hotel since 1911. It's a short walk on tree-lined streets from town center and it's even closer to the thermal baths. Rooms are spacious, with high ceilings; many have deep bathtubs with water jets. You can enjoy an *aperitivo* (aperitif) in the majestic lobby before dining at the hotel's Tuscan restaurant. ✉ *Viale IV Novembre 18, 51016,* ☎ *0572/9201,* FAX *0572/767516. 121 rooms, 19 suites. Restaurant, bar, pool, exercise room, convention center. AE, DC, MC, V.*

LUCCA

It was in this picturesque fortress town that Caesar, Pompey, and Crassus agreed to rule Rome as a triumvirate in 56 BC; it was later the first town in Tuscany to accept Christianity. Lucca still has a mind of its own, and when most of Tuscany was voting communist as a matter of course, its citizens rarely followed suit. Within the city's 16th- to 17th-century ramparts, the famous composer Giacomo Puccini (1858–1924) was born. He is celebrated, along with his peers, during the summer Opera Theater of Lucca Festival.

Exploring Lucca

The historic center of Lucca is walled and traffic, including motorbikes, is restricted. Walking is therefore the best, most enjoyable way to get around. You can rent bicycles (☞ Outdoor Activities and Sports, *below*), and, as the center is quite flat, getting around town on bike without the threat of traffic is easy.

A Good Walk

Start at the **Museo Nazionale di Palazzo Mansi** ④ on Via Galli Tassi, just within the walls. Walk down Via del Toro to Piazza del Palazzo Dipinto, and follow Via di Poggio to **San Michele** ⑤. From Piazza San Michele, walk down Via Beccheria through Piazza Napoleone, and make a left through the smaller Piazza San Giovanni, which leads directly to the **Duomo** ⑥. Check out the fun facade before going into the church and looking at the *Volto Santo* and the *Tomb of Ilaria del Carretto.* Walk down Via dell'Arcivescovado, which is behind the Duomo and turns into Via Guinigi. Climb into the tower of the **Palazzo Guinigi** ⑦ and admire the view. The **Museo Nazionale di Villa Guinigi** ⑧ is a 10- to 15-minute walk east through Piazza San Francesco on Via della Quarquonia. Backtrack to the Palazzo Guinigi; take Via Sant'Andrea to Via Fillungo to see the many Liberty-style buildings. At Via Fontana, take a left and follow it to Via Cesare Battisti. Make a right and head toward the church of **San Frediano** ⑨, with its incredibly mummified Santa Zita, the patron saint of domestic workers. From the church, walk on Via San Frediano back towards the Fillungo; make a right and then a left, and head into the **Piazza del Anfiteatro Romano** ⑩, where the Anfiteatro Romano once stood. Relax and have an aperitivo at one of the many sidewalk cafés.

TIMING

The walk will take about three hours; add a half hour for lingering in each of the museums.

Sights to See

★ ❻ **Duomo.** The round-arched facade of the cathedral is an example of the rigorously ordered Pisan Romanesque style, in this case happily enlivened by an extremely disordered collection of small carved columns. Take a closer look at the decoration of the facade and that of the portico below, making for one of the most entertaining church exteriors in Tuscany. The Gothic interior contains a moving wood crucifix (called the *Volto Santo,* or Holy Face), brought here, as legend has it, in the 8th century (though it probably dates from between the 11th and early 13th centuries). The masterpiece of the Sienese sculptor Jacopo della Quercia (1371/74–1438) is the marble *Tomb of Ilaria del Carretto* (1408). ✉ *Piazza del Duomo,* ☎ *0583/490530.* 🎟 *3,000 lire.* 🕘 *Duomo: Apr.–Oct., daily 7–7; Nov.–Mar., daily 7–5. Tomb: Apr.–Oct., daily 10–6; Nov.–Mar., Mon.–Fri. 10–4:45, Sat. 9:30–4:45, Sun. 9–5; Apr.–Oct., daily 10–6.*

❹ **Museo Nazionale di Palazzo Mansi.** Highlights are the lovely *Portrait of a Youth* by Pontormo and portraits of the Medici painted by Il Bronzino (1503–72) and others. ✉ *Palazzo Mansi, Via Galli Tassi 43, near the west walls of the old city,* ☎ *0583/55570.* 🎟 *8,000 lire.* 🕘 *Tues.–Sat. 9–7, Sun. 9–2.*

❽ **Museo Nazionale di Villa Guinigi.** On the eastern end of the historic center, the museum houses an extensive collection of local Romanesque and Renaissance art. ✉ *Villa Guinigi, Via della Quarquonia,* ☎ *0583/496033.* 🎟 *4,000 lire.* 🕘 *May–Sept., Tues.–Sun. 9–7; Oct.–Apr., Tues.–Sun. 9–2.*

❼ **Palazzo Guinigi.** The tower of the medieval palace contains one of the city's most curious sights: a grove of ilex trees has grown at the top of the tower, and their roots have grown into the room below. From the top, you will have a magnificent view of the city and the surrounding countryside. ✉ *Palazzo Guinigi, Via Guinigi.* 🎟 *4,500 lire.* 🕘 *Nov.–Feb., daily 10–4:30; Mar.–Sept., daily 9–7:30; Oct., daily 10–6.*

❿ **Piazza del Anfiteatro Romano.** This is the site where the **Anfiteatro Romano,** or Roman Amphitheater, once stood; some of the medieval buildings built over the amphitheater retain its original oval shape and brick arches. ✉ *Off Via Fillungo.*

❾ **San Frediano.** The church contains more works by Jacopo della Quercia, and, bizarrely, the lace-clad mummy of the patron saint of domestic servants, Santa Zita. ✉ *Piazza San Frediano,* ☎ *no phone.* 🕘 *Daily 7:30–12 and 3–5, holidays 9–1 and 3–6.*

❺ **San Michele.** Slightly west of town center is this church with a facade even more fanciful than the Duomo's. Check out the superb Filippino Lippi (1448/57–1504) panel painting of Saints Girolamo, Sebastian, Rocco, and Helen in the right transept. ✉ *Piazza San Michele,* ☎ *no phone.* 🕘 *Daily 7:30–12:30 and 3–6.*

OFF THE BEATEN PATH

VILLA REALE – Eight kilometers (5 mi) north of Lucca in Marlia, this villa was once the home of Napoléon's sister, Princess Elisa. Restored by the Counts Pecci-Blunt, this estate is celebrated for its spectacular gardens, originally laid out in the 16th century and redone in the middle of the 17th. Gardening buffs adore the legendary *teatro di verdura,* a theater carved out of hedges and topiaries; concerts are occasionally held here. One of Tuscany's most popular summer events, the Festival di Marlia, is held in Marlia in July and August; contact the Lucca tourist office (☞ Visitor Information *in* Tuscany A to Z, *below*) for details. ✉ *Villa Reale,* ☎ *0583/30108.* 🎟 *9,000 lire.* 🕘 *Mar.–Nov., guided visits at 10, 11, 3, 4, 5; Dec. 6–Feb., open by previous appointment only.*

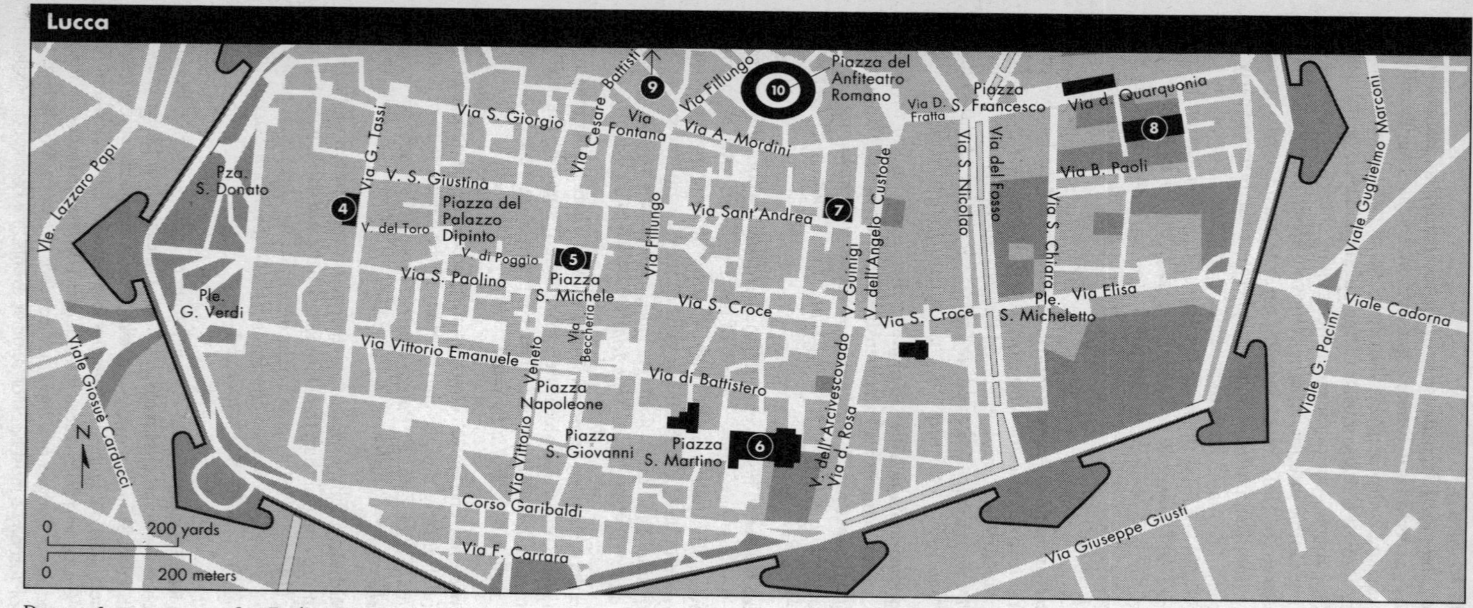

Duomo, **6**

Museo Nazionale di Palazzo Mansi, **4**

Museo Nazionale di Villa Guinigi, **8**

Palazzo Guinigi, **7**

Piazza del Anfiteatro Romano, **10**

San Frediano, **9**

San Michele, **5**

FORTE DEI MARMI – Tuscany's most exclusive summer beach resort is a favorite of moneyed Tuscans and Milanese, whose villas are neatly laid out in an extensive pinewood. In summer, a beachcomber's bonanza takes place on Wednesday mornings, when everything from faux designer sunglasses to plastic sandals and terry-cloth towels goes on sale. It's 35 km (22 mi) northwest of Lucca and 65 km (40 mi) northwest of Florence, and also near the marble-producing towns of Carrara (where Michelangelo also quarried his stone), Seravezza, and Pietrasanta.

Dining and Lodging

$$$ ✕ **Solferino.** About 6 km (4 mi) outside town along the road to Viareggio, this restaurant prepares elegant renditions of Tuscan country-style cooking. Amid silver, linens, and crystal, you'll be treated to ingredients from the family farm in such dishes as *tagliolini con pernice rossa* (fresh pasta with partridge sauce). Ask for a piece of *buccellato,* Lucca's dessert bread. Reservations are advised. ✉ *San Macario in Piano,* ☎ *0583/59118. AE, DC, MC, V. Closed Wed. and Jan. 7–15. No lunch Thurs.*

$$–$$$ ★ ✕ **La Mora.** Detour to this former stagecoach station, now a gracious, rustic country inn 9 km (5½ mi) outside Lucca, for local specialties—from *minestra di farro* (soup made with emmer, a wheat that resembles barley) with beans to homemade *tacconi* (a thin, short, wide pasta) with rabbit sauce and lamb raised in the nearby Garfagnana hills. You might be tempted by the varied crostini and delicious desserts. ✉ *Via Sesto di Ponte a Moriano 1748,* ☎ *0583/406402,* FAX *0583/406135. AE, DC, MC, V. Closed Wed. and 3 wks in Jan.*

$$ ★ ✕ **Buca di Sant'Antonio.** This restaurant has been around for more than two centuries, and it's easy to see why. The white-walled interior hung with copper pots, expertly prepared food, and an able staff make dining here a real treat. The menu offers something for everyone—from simple pasta meals to such daring dishes as roast *capretto* (kid) with herbs. ✉ *Via della Cervia 3,* ☎ *0583/55881. AE, DC, MC, V. Closed Mon. and last 3 wks in July. No dinner Sun.*

$$ ✕ **Da Giulio in Pelleria.** A large trattoria that is quintessentially Tuscan in atmosphere, food, and clientele, this tavern is in one of Lucca's characteristic old neighborhoods near the ramparts and Porta San Donato, and handy to the Pinacoteca Nazionale. The menu features Lucca's specialties, including hearty farro or wheat soups and roasted meats—beware, the portions are generous. ✉ *Via delle Conce 47,* ☎ *0583/555948. AE, DC, MC, V. Closed 3rd Sun. of every month.*

$$ ✕ **Il Giglio.** Just off Piazza Napoleone, this restaurant has quiet, late-19th-century charm and classic cuisine. It's a place for all seasons, with a big fireplace and an outdoor terrace in summer. Among the local specialties are *farro garfagnino* (a thick soup made with grain and beans), and *coniglio con olive* (rabbit stew with olives). ✉ *Piazza del Giglio 2,* ☎ *0583/494058. AE, DC, MC, V. Closed Wed. and 3 wks in Aug. No dinner Tues.*

$$$$ 🏨 **Locanda l'Elisa.** An intimate, refined hotel in a handsome blue neoclassic villa with white trim, this deluxe spin-off of the adjacent Villa La Principessa (☞ *below*) is a notch higher on the scale of style and comfort. One of the nonsuite rooms is a suite, and one a double. ✉ *Massa Pisana, 55050,* ☎ *0583/379737,* FAX *0583/379019. 2 rooms, 8 suites. Restaurant, bar, pool. AE, DC, MC, V.*

$$$$ 🏨 **Villa La Principessa.** This heavenly decorated 19th-century country mansion is found 3 km (2 mi) outside of Lucca. Some rooms have handsome beamed ceilings, and doors are individually decorated; antique furniture and portraits impart an aura of gracious living. The grounds are well manicured, the pool large and inviting. The restaurant is

closed Sunday. ✉ *Massa Pisana, 55050,* ☎ *0583/370037,* FAX *0583/379136. 37 rooms, 5 suites. Restaurant, pool. AE, DC, MC, V. Closed Nov.–Mar.*

$$ **Fattoria di Camporomano.** This agriturismo, nestled among rolling and tiered olive groves, consists of seven separate apartments scattered in and around the *casa padronale* (main house), which, in this case, is an 18th-century villa belonging to the Pecchioli family. The host is a baron and his son a count, and both are perfectly fluent in English. The apartments sleep from 2 to 6; all have kitchens and some have fireplaces. Unwind by the pool, walk in the woods, or explore Lucca, Viareggio, Carrara, and the Apuan Alps—all are a stone's throw away. ✉ *55054 Piano del Quercione, Massarosa,* ☎ *0584/92231,* FAX *0584/92231. 7 apartments. Pool. No credit cards.*

$$ **La Luna.** On a quiet, airy courtyard close to historic Piazza del Mercato, this family-run hotel occupies two renovated wings of an old building. The bathrooms are modern, but some of the rooms still have the atmosphere of Old Lucca. A parking lot for guests is a bonus. ✉ *Corte Compagni 12, corner of Via Fillungo, 55100,* ☎ *0583/493634,* FAX *0583/490021. 30 rooms. Parking (fee). AE, DC, MC, V. Closed last 3 wks in Jan.*

$$ **Piccolo Hotel Puccini.** Steps away from the busy square and church of San Michele, this little hotel is quiet, calm, and handsomely decorated. It also offers parking (which must be reserved in advance) at a reasonable fee, which is a great advantage. ✉ *Via di Poggio 9, 55100,* ☎ *0583/55421,* FAX *0583/53487. 14 rooms. Parking (fee). AE, DC, MC, V.*

Nightlife and the Arts

The **Estate Musicale Lucchese,** one of many music festivals throughout Tuscany, runs throughout the summer in Lucca. Contact the Lucca tourist office (☞ Visitor Information *in* Tuscany A to Z, *below*) for details. The **Opera Theater of Lucca Festival,** sponsored by the Opera Theater of Lucca and the music college of the University of Cincinnati, runs from mid-June to mid-July; performances are staged in open-air venues. Call the Lucca tourist office for information.

Outdoor Activities and Sports

One of the best ways to get around this lovely medieval town is on a bike. You can rent one at **Barbetti Cicli** (✉ Via Anfiteatro 23, ☎ 0583/954444) or at **Poli Antonio Biciclette** (✉ Piazza Santa Maria 42, ☎ 0583/493787).

Shopping

Lucca's olive oil, available throughout the city, is exported throughout the world. A particularly delicious version of buccellato, a sweet, anise-flavored bread with raisins that is a specialty of Lucca, is baked at **Pasticceria Taddeucci** (✉ Piazza San Michele 34). On the second Sunday of the month, there's a **flea market** in Piazza San Martino.

PISA

If you get beyond the kitschy atmosphere around the Leaning Tower, Pisa has much to offer. Pisa may have been inhabited as early as the Bronze Age. It was certainly populated by the Etruscans and, in turn, became part of the Roman Empire. In the early Middle Ages, it flourished as an economic powerhouse—along with Amalfi, Genoa, and Venice, it was one of the maritime republics. The city's economic and political power ebbed in the early 15th century as it fell under Florence's domination, though it enjoyed a brief resurgence under Cosimo I in the mid-16th century. Pisa endured heavy Allied bombing—miraculously, the Duomo and Tower were spared. Its cathedral-baptistery-tower complex on Piazza del Duomo is among the most dramatic in Italy. Pisa's treasures are more subtle than Florence's, to which it is inevitably compared. Though it sustained heavy damage during World War II, Pisa and its many beautiful Romanesque structures are still preserved.

Exploring Pisa

Pisa, like many Italian cities, is best seen on foot, and most of what you'll want to see is within walking distance. The views along the Arno are particularly grand and shouldn't be missed—there's a feeling of spaciousness that doesn't exist along the Arno in Florence. A combination ticket of 10,000 lire allows entry to two sights on the Piazza del Duomo, and a ticket for 15,000 lire allows entry to all four sights.

A Good Walk

Start in the Campo dei Miracoli, exploring the piazza complex containing the **Leaning Tower** ⑪, **Duomo** ⑫, **Battistero** ⑬, **Camposanto** ⑭, **Museo dell'Opera del Duomo** ⑮, and the **Museo delle Sinopie** ⑯. After a coffee or gelato, walk down Via Santa Maria—the Campanile will be behind you. At Piazza Felice Cavallotti, go left on to Via dei Mille. Continue straight on Via dei Mille to **Piazza dei Cavalieri** ⑰, a study in Renaissance symmetry. Go straight through the piazza to Via Dini, and make a right on to Borgo Stretto, a major thoroughfare lined with cafés. On the left, before the river, is the church of San Michele in Borgo that, with its ornate 14th-century Pisan Romanesque facade and columns, is vaguely reminiscent of a wedding cake. Walk up to Piazza Garibaldi and turn left along the Lungarno Mediceo. Practically at the Ponte alla Fortezza, on the left, is the **Museo Nazionale di San Matteo** ⑱.

TIMING

The walk takes a little more than an hour without stops—but there's lots to see along the way; stops could take a few of hours, depending upon how long you stay in the Museo Nazionale di San Matteo.

Sights to See

⓭ **Battistero.** The lovely Gothic Baptistery, which stands across from the Duomo's facade, is best known for the pulpit carved by Giovanni's father, Nicola, in 1260. Ask one of the ticket takers if he'll sing for you inside the baptistery. The acoustics are remarkable; a tip of 5,000 lire is appropriate. ✉ *Piazza del Duomo,* ☎ *no phone.* 🎫 *10,000 lire plus 1 other sight; combination ticket 15,000 lire.* ⏲ *Oct.–Mar., daily 9–5; Apr.–Sept., daily 8–8.*

⓮ **Camposanto.** The walled area on the northern side of the Campo dei Miracoli is the Cemetery, which is filled, according to legend, with earth brought back from the Holy Land during the Crusades. Its galleries contain numerous frescoes, notably *The Drunkenness of Noah,* by Renaissance artist Benozzo Gozzoli, and the disturbing *Triumph of Death* (14th century), whose authorship is disputed, but whose subject matter shows what was on people's minds in a century that saw the ravages of the Black Death. ✉ *Camposanto,* ☎ *050/560547.* 🎫 *10,000 lire plus 1 other sight; combination ticket 15,000 lire.* ⏲ *Oct.–Mar., daily 9–5; Apr.–Sept., daily 8–8.*

⓬ **Duomo.** Pisa's cathedral was the first building to use the horizontal marble stripe motif (borrowed from Moorish architecture in the 11th century) common to Tuscan cathedrals. It is famous for the Romanesque

Battistero, **13**
Camposanto, **14**
Duomo, **12**
Leaning Tower, **11**
Museo delle Sinopie, **16**
Museo dell'Opera del Duomo, **15**
Museo Nazionale di San Matteo, **18**
Piazza dei Cavalieri, **17**

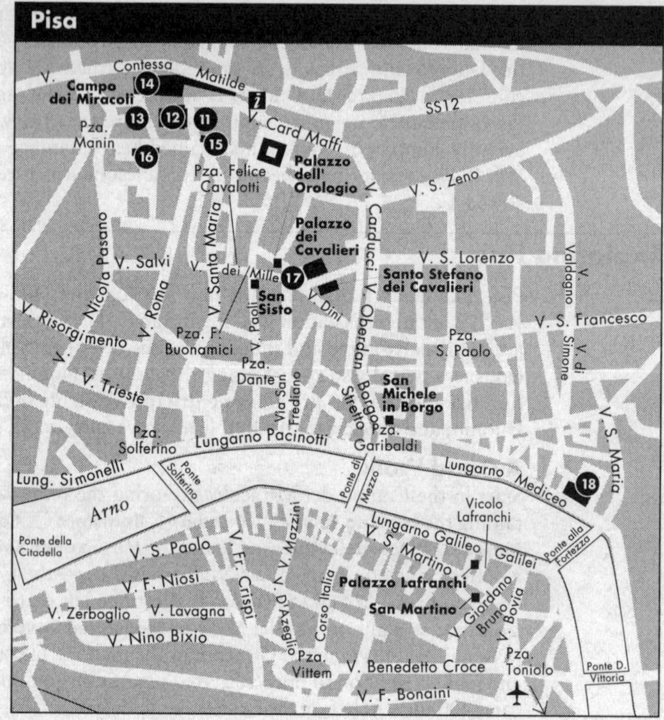

panels on the transept door facing the tower, which depict the life of Christ, and for its beautifully carved 14th-century pulpit, by Giovanni Pisano. ✉ *Piazza del Duomo,* ☎ *050/560921.* 🎫 *2,000 lire (free Oct.–Mar.).* ⏲ *Oct.–Mar., Mon.–Sat. 10–12:45 and 3–5, Sun. 3–5; Apr.–Sept., Mon.–Sat. 10–8, Sun. 1–8.*

11 **Leaning Tower.** Begun in 1174, the Leaning Tower (Torre Pendente) was the last of the three structures to be built, and the lopsided settling began when construction reached the third story. The tower's architects attempted to compensate by making the remaining floors slightly taller on the leaning side, but the extra weight only made the problem worse. The settling has continued, and a few years ago it accelerated to a point that led many to fear it would simply topple over, despite all efforts to prop the structure up. Now it has been firmly anchored to the earth. At press time, a project to stabilize (and eventually reopen) the tower was underway: digging machines were to remove soil from below the tower in the hopes that the angle at which it leans will be reduced by one degree (it now leans 6 degrees, or 13 ft, off-kilter). Legend holds that Galileo conducted an experiment on the nature of gravity by dropping metal balls from the top of the 187-ft-high tower; historians say this legend has no basis in fact (which is not quite to say that it is false). ✉ *Campo dei Miracoli.*

16 **Museo delle Sinopie.** The well-arranged museum on the south side of the Piazza del Duomo holds the *sinopie,* or preparatory drawings, for the Camposanto frescoes and is of limited interest to most tourists. ✉ *Piazza del Duomo,* ☎ *050/560547.* 🎫 *10,000 lire; combination ticket 15,000 lire.* ⏲ *Oct.–Mar., daily 9–5, Apr.–Sept., daily 8–8.*

15 **Museo dell'Opera del Duomo.** At the southeast corner of the sprawling Campo dei Miracoli, the museum holds a wealth of medieval sculptures and the ancient Roman sarcophagi that inspired Nicola

Pisano's (circa 1220–84) figures. ✉ *Via Arcivescovado,* ☎ *050/560547.* 🎫 *10,000 lire plus 1 other sight; combination ticket 15,000 lire.* ⏲ *Oct.–Mar., daily 9–5; Apr.–Sept., daily 10–7:30.*

18 **Museo Nazionale di San Matteo.** Along the northern side of the Arno, this museum contains some incisive examples of local Romanesque and Gothic art. ✉ *Lungarno Mediceo,* ☎ *050/541865.* 🎫 *8,000 lire.* ⏲ *Tues.–Sat. 9–7, Sun. 9–1:30.*

17 **Piazza dei Cavalieri.** The piazza, which holds the Renaissance **Palazzo dei Cavalieri, Palazzo dell'Orologio,** and **Santo Stefano dei Cavalieri,** was laid out by Giorgio Vasari in about 1560. The square was the seat of the Ordine dei Cavalieri di San Stefano (Order of the Knights of St. Stephen), a military and religious institution that was meant to defend the coast from possible invasion by the Turks. Also in this square is the prestigious **Scuola Normale Superiore,** founded by Napoléon in 1810 on the French model. Here graduate students pursue doctorates in literature, philosophy, mathematics, and science. In front of the school is an oversize statue of Ferdinando de' Medici dating from 1596.

Dining and Lodging

$$$ ✕ **Al Ristoro dei Vecchi Macelli.** The 18-year-old "Inn by the Old Slaughterhouse" got its name from being down the street from an old slaughterhouse, no longer in use today. Such earthy connotations aside, the food is complex and special, served in a room with low, subdued lighting, an old wooden ceiling, terra-cotta floors, and walls lined with stylish black-and-white photographs. You can order a fixed-price seafood or meat menu or choose dishes à la carte. The *gnochetti con broccoli e vongole veraci* (dumplings with broccoli and small clams) is a winner, as is the *coniglio disossato e farcito con salsa di tartufo* (boneless rabbit stuffed with truffle sauce). The place is calm and serene, a perfect backdrop for the food. Reservations are advised. ✉ *Via Volturno 49,* ☎ *050/20424. AE, DC, MC, V. Closed Wed. and Aug. 10–25. No lunch Sun.*

$$ ✕ **Bruno.** A pleasant restaurant with beamed ceilings and the look of a country inn, Bruno is just outside Pisa's old city walls, a short walk from the bell tower and cathedral. Dine on classic Tuscan dishes, from *zuppa alla pisana* (a thick vegetable soup) to *baccalà* (cod) with leeks. ✉ *Via Luigi Bianchi 12,* ☎ *050/560818. AE, DC, MC, V. Closed Tues. No dinner Mon.*

$$ ✕ **Osteria dei Cavalieri.** This charming white-walled *osteria* (restaurant), a few steps from Piazza dei Cavalieri, is reason enough to come to Pisa. The chef does it all—serves up grilled fish dishes, pleases vegetarians, and prepares *tagliata* (thin slivers of rare beef) for meat lovers. There are three set menus, from the sea, garden, and earth, or you can order à la carte—which can be agonizing because everything sounds so good. And it is. Finish your meal with a lemon sorbet bathed in Prosecco (dry sparkling wine), and walk away feeling like you've eaten like a king at plebeian prices. ✉ *Via San Frediano 16,* ☎ *050/580858. AE, DC, MC, V. Closed Sun. and July 25–Aug. 25. No lunch Sat.*

$$$$ 🏨 **Cavalieri.** Opposite the railway station, in an unremarkable 1950s building, this Jolly Group hotel offers functional, modern comforts in completely soundproof and air-conditioned rooms, all with color TVs and minibars. The restaurant specializes in homemade pasta and seafood. ✉ *Piazza della Stazione 2, 56125,* ☎ *050/43290,* FAX *050/502242. 100 rooms, 3 suites. Restaurant, bar, minibars. AE, DC, MC, V.*

$$ 🏨 **Fattoria di Migliarino.** Martino Salviati and his wife, Giovanna, have turned their working farm (soy, corn, sugar beets) 15 minutes northwest of Pisa into a working inn. Their *fattoria* (farm) is now seven charming, spacious apartments (putting up from two to eight people) with rustic decor, each complete with kitchen, and many with fireplaces. The pool is framed by fields, and the only sound you're likely to hear is the clucking of the hens they keep for eggs. The surrounding woods can be explored by horse or by mountain bike. There is a two-night minimum stay. Migliarino is convenient to Lucca and sandy beaches are a five-minute drive away. ✉ *Viale dei Pini 289, 56010 Migliarino,* ☎ *050/803046,* FAX *050/803170. 7 apartments. Pool. MC, V.*

$$ **Royal Victoria.** In a pleasant palazzo facing the Arno, a 10-minute walk from the Campo dei Miracoli, this hotel is about as close as Pisa comes to old-world ambience. It's comfortably furnished, with antiques and reproductions in the lobby and in some rooms, whose style ranges from the 1800s, complete with frescoes, to the 1920s. ✉ *Lungarno Pacinotti 12, 56126,* ☎ *050/940111,* FAX *050/940180. 48 rooms, 8 without bath. AE, DC, MC, V.*

Nightlife and the Arts

The **Luminaria** feast day on June 16 honors San Ranieri, the patron saint of the city. Palaces along the Arno are lit with white lights, and there's plenty of fireworks; this is the city at its best.

HILL TOWNS WEST OF SIENA

Submit to the draw of the enchanting fortified cities, many dating to the Etruscan period, crowning the hills west of Siena. San Gimignano, known as the "medieval Manhattan" because of the sprouting towers built by rival families, is perhaps the most touristed; but visitors are old hat to this Roman outpost, and with its tilted cobbled streets and stout medieval buildings, the days of the Guelph-Ghibelline conflicts can seem palpable. Rising from a series of bleak gullied hills and valleys, Volterra has always been popular for its minerals and stones, particularly alabaster, which was used by the Etruscans for many implements, some now displayed in the exceptional Museo Etrusco Guarnacci. Blissfully off the tour-bus circuit, San Miniato is a peaceful hill town with a pleasant local museum and a convent that boards guests.

San Miniato

★ 19 *42 km (26 mi) southeast of Pisa, 43 km (27 mi) southwest of Florence.*

Dating from Etruscan and Roman times, San Miniato was so named when the Lombards erected a church here in the 8th century and consecrated it to San Miniato. The Holy Roman Empire had very strong ties to San Miniato. Today the pristine, tiny hill town's narrow, cobbled streets are lined with austere 13th–17th century facades, some of them built over already centuries-old buildings. Its artistic treasures are somewhat limited in comparison with Florence, but it's well worth the trip simply because the town is so pretty. St. Francis founded the 1211 **Convento e Chiesa di San Francesco** (Convent and Church of St. Francis), containing two cloisters and an ornate wooden choir. For a dose of monastic living, you can stay overnight (☞ Lodging, *below*). ✉ *Piazza San Francesco,* ☎ *0571/43051.* ⏲ *Daily 9–noon and 3–7 (or ring bell).*

Although the **Museo Diocesano** is small, the modest collection displays a number of subtle and pleasant works of art. Note the rather odd Fra Filippo Lippi *Crucifixion,* Verrocchio's (1435–88) *Il Redentore,* and the small but sublime *Education of the Virgin* by Tiepolo (1696–1770). ✉ *Piazza del Castello,* ☎ *0571/418271.* 🎫 *3,000 lire.* ⏲ *Apr.–Oct., Tues.–Sun. 9–12 and 3–6:30; Nov.–Mar., weekends 9–12 and 3–5:30.*

Lodging

$ 🏨 **Convento San Francesco.** For a complete change of pace, you can stay in this 13th-century monastery in the company of five Franciscan friars. Rooms are simple, bordering on spartan, but clean and quiet. You are given keys, so you're not expected home by a certain time. You can partake in some spiritual activities, or skip them altogether. All rooms have baths, and there are five rooms that groups can rent. It's a short 10-minute walk from the town center. ✉ *Piazza San Francesco, 56020,* ☎ *0571/43051,* FAX *0571/4339898. 30 rooms. No credit cards.*

Volterra

20 *64 km (40 mi) southwest of Pisa, 50 km (31 mi) west of Siena.*

Unlike other Tuscan hill towns that rise above sprawling vineyards and rolling fields of green, Volterra—recorded by D. H. Lawrence in his *Etruscan Places* as standing "somber and chilly alone on her rock"—is surrounded by desolate terrain marred with industry and mining equipment. The fortress, walls, and gates still stand mightily over Le Balze, a stunning series of gullied hills and valleys to the west that were formed by irregular erosion. The town has long been known for its alabaster, which has been mined since Etruscan times; today the Volterrans use it to make ornaments and souvenirs sold all over town. A 12,000-lire combination ticket allows entry to the Museo Etrusco Guarnacci, Pinacoteca e Museo Civico, and the Museo di Arte Sacra.

Volterra is home to some of Italy's best small museums. The extraordinarily large and unique collection of the **Museo Etrusco Guarnacci** is an enigma in a region where many of the Etruscan artifacts have landed in state museums and at the Vatican. You'll find the usual Attic vases, *bucchero* (dark, reddish clay) ceramics, jewelry, and household items, but the bulk of the collection is made up of about 700 carved funerary urns found in nearby excavations. ✉ *Via Don Minzoni 15,* ☎ *0588/86347.* 🎫 *Combination ticket 12,000 lire.* ⏲ *Mid-Mar.–Oct., daily 9–7; Nov.–mid-Mar., daily 9–2.*

The **Pinacoteca e Museo Civico** houses a highly acclaimed collection of religious art, including Luca Signorelli's (1445/50–1523) *Madonna and Child with Saints* and Rosso Fiorentino's (1494–1541) *Deposition.* ✉ *Via dei Sarti 1,* ☎ *0588/87580.* 🎫 *Combination ticket 12,000 lire.* ⏲ *Mid-Mar.–Oct., daily 9–7; Nov.–mid-Mar, daily 9–2.*

The impressive facade of medieval **Palazzo dei Priori** is adorned with Florentine medallions and a large five-sided tower. ✉ *Piazza dei Priori,* ☎ *0588/86050.* 🎫 *Free.* ⏲ *Apr.–Oct., Mon.–Sat. 10–1 and 3–4; Nov.–Mar., Mon.–Sat. 10–1.*

Next to the altar in the town's unfinished **Duomo** are the overly restored 13th-century *Deposition.* Note the Benozzo Gozzoli (1420–97) fresco in the Cappella della Addolorata. Along the left nave you can see the arrival of the magi. ✉ *Piazza San Giovanni,* ☎ *0588/86192.* ⏲ *Daily 7–7.*

Original works from the Duomo and adjacent Baptistery are in the **Museo di Arte Sacra.** ✉ *Via Roma 7,* ☎ *0588/86290.* 🎫 *Combination ticket 12,000 lire.* ⏲ *Mid-Mar.–Oct., daily 9–1 and 3–6; Nov.–mid-Mar., daily 9–1.*

Two of Volterra's best-preserved ancient remains are the Etruscan **Porta all'Arco,** a 3rd-century arch incorporated into the city walls; and the ruins of the 1st-century BC **Teatro Romano,** one of the best-preserved Roman theaters in Italy, with the adjacent remains of the **Roman Terme** (baths). The theater complex is just outside the walls past Porta

Fiorentina. ✉ *Viale Francesco Ferrucci.* ⏲ *May–Oct., daily 11–4. Closed when it's raining.*

Dining and Lodging

$$ ✕ **Etruria.** Late-19th-century frescoes on the walls and outdoor dining in the warm weather denote this restaurant on the town's main square. An array of local game is used in such specialties as *pappardelle alla lepre* (broad noodles in hare sauce) and *cinghiale alla maremmana* (wild boar stewed with olives). ✉ *Piazza dei Priori 8,* ☎ *0588/86064. AE, DC, MC, V. Closed Thurs.*

$$ 🏨 **San Lino.** In a former convent with wood beams and terra-cotta floors, this hotel offers modern-day comforts. On top of this, it's within the town walls, a 10-minute walk from the main piazza. The restaurant serves regional specialties, including *zuppa alla volteranna,* a very thick vegetable soup. ✉ *Via San Lino 26, 56048,* ☎ *0588/85250,* FAX *0588/80620. 43 rooms. Restaurant, pool. AE, DC, MC, V. Closed Nov.*

Shopping

A number of shops in Volterra sell boxes, jewelry, and other objects made of alabaster. The **Cooperativa Artieri Alabastro** (✉ Piazza dei Priori 5, ☎ 0588/87590) has two large showrooms in a medieval building with an array of alabaster pieces. In a former medieval monastery, the **Galleria Agostiniane** showrooms (✉ Piazza XX Settembre 3, ☎ 0588/86868) craft alabaster objects of all kinds. You can see a free video on how the mineral is quarried and carved. At the **Rossi** (✉ Via Lungo Mura del Mandorlo 7, ☎ 0588/86133) you can actually see the craftsmen at work; there are objects for all tastes and budgets.

San Gimignano

★ ㉑ *27 km (17 mi) east of Volterra, 57 km (35 mi) southwest of Florence.*

When you're high on a hill surrounded by crumbling towers in silhouette against the blue sky, it's difficult not to fall under the medieval spell of San Gimignano. Its high walls and narrow streets are typical of Tuscan hill towns, but it is the surviving medieval "skyscrapers" that set the town apart from its neighbors and give the town a uniquely photogenic silhouette. Today 15 towers remain, but at the height of the Guelph-Ghibelline conflict there was a forest of more than 70, and it was possible to cross the town by rooftop rather than road. The towers were built partly for defensive purposes—they were a safe refuge and useful for pouring boiling oil on attacking enemies—and partly to bolster the egos of their owners, who competed with deadly seriousness to build the highest tower in town. When the Black Death devastated the population in 1348, power and independence faded fast and civic autonomy was ultimately surrendered to Florence.

Today, San Gimignano isn't much more than a gentrified walled city, amply prepared for its booming tourist trade, but still very much worth exploring. Unfortunately, tour groups arrive early and clog the wine-tasting rooms—San Gimignano is famous for its dry, light white wine called Vernaccia—and art galleries for the majority of the day, but most sights are open through late afternoon during summer. Escape midday to the uninhabited areas outside the city walls for a hike and a picnic, and return to explore the town in the afternoon and evening, when things quiet down and the long shadows cast by the imposing towers take on fascinating shapes. You can buy a 18,000-lire combination ticket valid for all San Gimignano museums and the Cappella di Santa Fina.

The town's most important medieval buildings are clustered around the central **Piazza del Duomo.** The imposing **Torre Grossa** is the biggest tower in town, with views that are well worth the climb. ✉ *Piazza del Duomo 1.* 🎫 *8,000 lire; Torre and Museo Civico* (☞ *below): 12,000 lire; combination ticket 18,000 lire.* ⏲ *Mar.–Oct., daily 9:30–7:30; Nov.–Feb., Tues.–Sun. 9:30–1 and 2:30–5.*

The **Palazzo del Popolo** houses the **Museo Civico,** featuring Taddeo di Bartolo's celebratory scenes from the life of San Gimignano. San Gimignano, a bishop of Modena, was sainted because he drove hordes of barbarians out of the city in the 10th century. Dante visited San Gimignano for only one day in 1300 as a Florentine ambassador, but it was long enough to get a room named after him, which now holds a *Maestà* by 14th-century artist Lippo Memmi. A small room contains frescoes by Memmo di Filippuccio (active 1288–1324) depicting the courtship, shared bath, and wedding of a young couple. The highly charged eroticism of the frescoes may be explained, in part, by the fact that they were located in what were probably the private rooms of the commune's chief magistrate. ✉ *Piazza del Duomo,* ☎ *0577/940008.* 🎫 *Museo Civico: 7,000 lire; Museo and Torre Grossa* (☞ *above): 12,000 lire (available Mar.–Oct., daily 12:30–3 and 6–7:30); combination ticket 18,000 lire.* ⏲ *Mar.–Oct., daily 9:30–7:30; Nov.–Feb., Tues.–Sun. 9:30–1 and 2:30–5.*

The Romanesque **Collegiata** is a treasure trove of frescoes, including Bartolo di Fredi's cycle of scenes from the Old Testament dating from 1367. Taddeo di Bartolo's otherworldly *Last Judgment,* on the arch just inside the facade, depicts distorted and suffering nudes—avant-garde stuff for the 1390s. The New Testament scenes on the right wall, which may have been executed by Barna da Siena in the 1330s, suggest a more reserved, balanced Renaissance manner. The **Cappella di Santa Fina** contains frescoes of the story of this local saint by Domenico Ghirlandaio (1449–94); at press time the frescoes were being restored. ✉ *Piazza del Duomo,* ☎ *0577/940316.* 🎫 *3,000 lire, combination ticket 18,000 lire.* ⏲ *Daily 9:30–12:30 and 3–5:30.*

The **Museo di Criminologia Medievale** (Museum of Medieval Criminology) displays what was on the cutting edge in medieval torture technology, replete with operating instructions and a clear description of the intended effect. The museum was in part created to illustrate the inherent racism and sexism in certain torture devices and to show how they've been updated for current use around the world. Some scholars discount the theories and attribute its creation for luring tourist dollars. ✉ *Via del Castello,* ☎ *0577/942243.* 🎫 *15,000 lire.* ⏲ *Mon.–Fri. 10–6 and weekends 10–7.*

Before leaving San Gimignano, be sure to see its most revered work of art, at the northern end of town, in the church of **Sant'Agostino:** Benozzo Gozzoli's utterly stunning 15th-century fresco cycle depicting the life of St. Augustine. ✉ *Piazza Sant'Agostino,* ☎ *0577/907012.* ⏲ *Daily 7–12 and 3–7.*

Dining and Lodging

$$–$$$ ✕ **Bel Soggiorno.** On the top floor of a 100-year-old inn, this rustic restaurant has a wall of windows from which to view the landscape. Tuscan specialties include *zuppa del granduca* (a medieval soup recipe of mushrooms, grain, and potatoes) and *sorpresa in crosta* (spicy rabbit stew with a bread crust). ✉ *Via San Giovanni 91,* ☎ *0577/940375. AE, DC, MC, V. Closed Wed. and Jan.–Feb.*

$$–$$$ ✕ **Le Terrazze.** Seasonal Tuscan classics are prepared in this restaurant in a time-honored inn in the heart of San Gimignano. A charming view of rooftops and the countryside and specialties like homemade pasta, a variety of grilled mushrooms, and grilled meats are in store. ✉ *Pi-*

azza della Cisterna 24, ☎ 0577/940328. AE, DC, MC, V. Closed Tues. and Nov.–Mar. 9. No lunch Wed.

$$ ✕ **La Mangiatoia.** In this rustic trattoria, near the church of Sant'Agostino, prices are more moderate than at places with a view, and the food is simple Tuscan country cooking. ✉ *Via Mainardi 5, off Via San Matteo, ☎ 0577/941528. MC, V. Closed Tues., 3 wks in Nov., and 1 wk in Jan.*

$$–$$$ ✕🏨 **Palazzo Mannaioni.** A 16th-century villa has been converted into a lovely, up-to-the-minute place set in a small village just 10 km (6 mi) northwest of San Gimignano. Rooms are spacious with high ceilings; there's a pool and an American-style bar and an atrium reminiscent of the 19th century. The hotel's restaurant is housed in the room where olive oil was once made; the dining room's high, ribbed vault ceilings are a perfect setting for chef Emanuele Bandini's food, which, though often typically Tuscan, achieves heights of sophistication rarely seen in such dishes. ✉ *Via Marconi 2 50050 Montaione, ☎ 0571/698300, FAX 0571/698299. 24 rooms, 5 suites. Restaurant, bar, pool, tennis court, conference room. AE, DC, MC, V.*

$$$ ★ 🏨 **Santa Chiara.** In a low contemporary building with a plethora of balconies and terraces on a panoramic hillside site just outside San Gimignano's walls, this hotel is an airy and spacious oasis, and an upscale base from which to explore the countryside and hill towns. The hotel has no restaurant but serves an ample buffet breakfast and light meals in summer. ✉ *Via Matteotti 15, 53037, ☎ 0577/940701, FAX 0577/942096. 39 rooms, 2 suites. Breakfast room, pool. AE, DC, MC, V. Closed Jan.–Feb.*

$$ ★ 🏨 **Pescille.** This rambling farmhouse 4 km (2½ mi) outside San Gimignano has been converted into a handsome hotel, in which restrained contemporary and country classic motifs blend well. ✉ *Località Pescille, Strada Castel San Gimignano, 53037, ☎ 0577/940186, FAX 0577/943165. 40 rooms. Pool, tennis court. AE, DC, MC, V. Closed Nov.–Feb.*

OFF THE BEATEN PATH — **COLLE VAL D'ELSA** – Pause in the town Colle Val d'Elsa and take time to make the lengthy detour around its workaday lower town to reach the upper town on the ridge, where the medieval center remains practically intact.

Monteriggioni

㉒ *20 km (12 mi) southeast of San Gimignano, 55 km (33 mi) south of Florence.*

Tiny Monteriggioni makes a nice stop for a quiet walk on the way north to Colle Val d'Elsa, San Gimignano, or Volterra. It's hard to imagine that this little town surrounded by open countryside and poppy fields was ever anything but sleepy. But in the 13th century, Monteriggioni served as Siena's northernmost defense against impending Florentine invasion. The town's formidable walls are in good condition, although the 14 square towers are not as tall as in Dante's time, when the poet likened them to the four giants who guarded the horrifying central pit of hell.

Dining

$$ ✕ **Il Pozzo.** On the village square, this rustic tavern serves hearty Tuscan country cooking and savory wines. The specialties are homemade fresh pasta, main courses of fillet of Tuscan beef with porcini mushrooms and *piccione ripieno* (stuffed squab), and homey desserts. ✉ *Piazza Roma 2, ☎ 0577/304127. AE, DC, MC, V. Closed Mon., Jan. 7–Feb. 7, and Aug. 1–7. No dinner Sun.*

Close-Up

HANDS-ON ITALY

COULD THERE POSSIBLY BE A BETTER WAY to get acquainted with Italy than by eating your way through it? Well, yes: imagine a hands-on cooking lesson with a famous chef in Tuscany's Palazzo Mannaioni, during which you unravel the complexities of making such luscious dishes as ***spuma di spinaci con tartufo,*** a spinach mousse laced with white truffle oil. Or a week-long course at Toscana Saporita, set in the tranquil Lucca countryside, where you learn the vagaries of multicolored ravioli under the tutelage of two profilic cookbook authors. If a cooking school seems too demanding, but an enlightening art and food-tasting tour does not, check out Esperienze Italiane, organized by celebrated restaurateur Lidia Bastianich. The International Kitchen represents these and a number of other cooking programs throughout Italy—from Lake Como to Catania—and will find the one that's right for you.

Other options include Bologna's International Cooking School of Italian Food and Wine, which arranges market visits and balsamic vinegar tastings. At Cooking Under the Tuscan Sun, outside Cortona, you prepare Tuscan food and match it with local wines. English-language cooking programs catering to amateur cooks are proliferating in Italy, and this is just a mere grazing of the pile. *Buon appetito*!

Cooking Under the Tuscan Sun (✉ Il Falconiere Relais, Località San Marco 370, 52044 Cortona, ☎ 0575/612679, FAX 0575/612927). **Esperienze Italiane** (✉ Lidia Bastianich, c/o Felidia Ristorante, 242 E. 58th St., New York, NY 10022, ☎ 800/480–2426, FAX 212/935–7687), or contact **The International Kitchen** (✉ 1209 N. Astor, 11–N, Chicago, IL 60610, ☎ 800/945–8606, FAX 847/295–0945). **International Cooking School of Italian Food and Wine** (✉ 201 E. 28th St., Suite 15B, New York, NY 10016-8538, ☎ 212/779–1921, FAX 212/779–3248).

CHIANTI

Directly south of Florence is the Chianti district, Italy's most famous wine-producing area; its hill towns, olive groves, and vineyards comprise the quintessential Tuscany. Many British and northern Europeans have relocated here, drawn by the unhurried life, balmy climate, and picturesque villages; there are so many Britons, in fact, that the area has been nicknamed Chiantishire. Still, it remains strongly Tuscan in character, and you'll be drawn to the vistas framing vine-quilted rolling hills and stout cypress.

The sinuous S222, known as the Strada Chiantigiana, runs from Florence through the heart of Chianti. Its most scenic section connects Strada in Chianti, 16 km (10 mi) south of Florence, and Greve in Chianti, whose triangular central piazza is surrounded by restaurants and vintners offering *degustazioni* (wine tastings), 11 km (7 mi) farther south.

Greve in Chianti

23 *27 km (17 mi) south of Florence, 40 km (25 mi) north of Siena.*

If there is a capital of Chianti, it is Greve, a friendly market town with no shortage of cafés, enoteche, and crafts shops along its pedestrian street. The sloping, asymmetrical **Piazza Matteotti** is attractively arcaded and has a statue of Giovanni da Verrazzano (circa 1480–1528), the explorer who discovered New York harbor, in the center. At the small end of the piazza is the **Chiesa di Santa Croce,** with works from the school of Fra Angelico (circa 1400–55). ✉ *Piazza Matteotti,* ☎ *no phone.* ⏲ *Daily 9–1 and 3–7.*

OFF THE BEATEN PATH **MONTEFIORALLE** – Just 2 km (1 mi) west, in the tiny hilltop hamlet of Montefioralle, you'll find the ancestral home of Amerigo Vespucci (1454–1512), the navigator and mapmaker who named America and whose niece Simonetta may have been the model for Sandro Botticelli's (1445–1510) *Venus*. Chianti's annual mid-September wine festival, **Rassegna del Chianti Classico,** takes place here.

Dining and Lodging

$$$ ✕ **Trattoria del Montagliari.** Typical home-style cooking is a big draw for locals, who eat around a wood-burning fireplace in the winter and in the garden in the summer. Ravioli in walnut sauce and fragrant apple pie await. ✉ *Via Montagliari 29,* ☎ *055/852184. MC, V. Closed Mon. and mid-Aug.*

$$ 🏨 **Castello Vicchiomaggio.** This castle, now a prestigious wine estate with a tasting facility you can visit, dates from 956 and was rebuilt during the Renaissance. Throughout the nine apartments and two farmhouses is wonderful heavy wooden furniture, in keeping with the estate's history. The restaurant serves homemade pastas and specialties such as *stracotto,* meat cooked in the farm's own prize-winning Chianti Classico. ✉ *Via Vicchiomaggio 4, 50022,* ☎ *055/854079,* FAX *055/853911. 9 apartments. Restaurant. MC, V.*

$$ 🏨 **Il Cenobio/Villa Vignamaggio.** This historic estate has guest rooms and apartments in a villa as well as two small houses and a cottage on the grounds. The villa, surrounded by manicured classical Italian gardens, dates from the 14th century, but was restored in the 16th. It's reputedly the birthplace of Leonardo da Vinci's *Mona Lisa,* and was the setting for Kenneth Branagh's film *Much Ado About Nothing.* ✉ *50022 Greve in Chianti,* ☎ *055/8544840,* FAX *055/8544468. 10 apartments, 2 rooms. 2 pools, tennis court. AE, DC, MC, V.*

Radda in Chianti

24 *33 km (20 mi) south of Greve, 52 km (32 mi) south of Florence.*

Radda in Chianti sits on a hill that separates Val di Pesa from Val d'Arbia. It's one of many tiny Chianti villages that invites you to stroll through its steep streets and to follow the signs that point you toward the *camminamento,* a covered medieval road that circles part of the city inside the walls. In Piazza Ferrucci, you'll find the **Palazzo del Podesta,** or Palazzo Comunale, the city hall that has served the people of Radda for more than four centuries and has 51 coats of arms imbedded in the facade. ✉ *Piazza Ferrucci.*

OFF THE BEATEN PATH **VOLPAIA** – Atop a hill 10 km (6 mi) north of Radda is this fairy-tale hamlet, a military outpost from the 10th to the 16th centuries and once shelter for religious pilgrims. Every July, for the Festa di San Lorenzo, people come to Volpaia to watch for falling stars and a traditional fireworks display put on by the family that owns the surrounding Castello di Volpaia (✉ Piazza della Cisterna 1, 53017, ☎ 0577/738066) wine estate and agritourist lodging. The 16th-century farmhouse of Podere Terreno (✉ Via della Volpaia, 53017, ☎ FAX 0577/738312), with seven well-sought-after agritourist rooms, was photographed by Helmut Newton for Pirelli tires.

Lodging

$$–$$$$ **Vescine.** Set on what was once an Etruscan settlement is this secluded complex of low-slung medieval stone buildings connected by cobbled paths, punctuated by cypress trees. Unfussy white rooms have terra-cotta tile floors, attractive woodwork, and comfortable furnishings typical to Tuscany. ✉ *53017 Radda in Chianti,* ☎ *0577/741144,* FAX *0577/740263. 20 rooms, 5 suites. Restaurant, breakfast room, pool, tennis court, library. AE, MC, V. Closed Dec. (except over Christmas)–Feb.*

$$$ **Relais Fattoria Vignale.** On the main road into town, this unadorned farmhouse with a annex across the street is English-country-house comfortable on the inside—with terra-cotta floors, sitting rooms, and nice stone- and woodwork. White rooms with exposed brick and wood beams contain simple wooden bed frames and furniture, lovely rugs and prints, modern white-tile bathrooms, and a bedside candle to promote relaxation. The grounds, lined with vineyards and plum and olive trees, are equally inviting, with various lawns, terraces, and a pool. The cavernous and rustic Ristorante Vignale serves excellent wines and various cold and warm Tuscan plates; it's perfect for a sampling of savory meats, pâtés, and cheeses. ✉ *53017 Radda in Chianti,* ☎ *0577/738300,* FAX *0577/738592. 34 rooms. Restaurant, breakfast room, wine shop, pool, library. AE, MC, V. Closed early Dec. 1–Dec. 25 and early Jan.–late Mar.*

Castellina in Chianti

25 *14 km (8 mi) west of Radda, 21 km (13 mi) north of Siena.*

Castellina in Chianti, or simply Castellina, is on a ridge above the Val di Pesa, Val d'Arbia, and Val d'Elsa, and the panorama is bucolic no matter which direction you look. The strong 15th-century medieval walls and fortified town gate give a hint of the history of this village, which was an outpost during the continuing wars between Florence and Siena.

Lodging

$$ **Hotel Belvedere di San Leonino.** There are wonderful gardens for strolling around this restored country complex that dates from the 14th century. The guest rooms are in two houses that look out upon vineyards to the north and upon Siena to the south. Homey rooms have antique furniture and exposed beams. There is a restaurant with a fixed menu, and in the summer you can eat dinner in the garden by the pool. ✉ *Località San Leonino, 53011,* ☎ *0577/740240,* FAX *0577/740924. 28 rooms. Restaurant, pool. AE, MC, V. Closed mid-Nov.–mid. Mar.*

SIENA

Italy's most enchanting medieval city, Siena is the one city you should visit in Tuscany if you visit no other. Florence's great historical rival was in all likelihood founded by the Etruscans. During the late Middle Ages, the city was both wealthy and powerful, for it saw the birth of the world's oldest bank, the Monte dei Paschi, still very much in business. It was bitterly envied by Florence, which in 1254 sent forces that besieged the city for over a year, reducing its population by half and laying waste to the countryside. The city was finally absorbed by the Grand Duchy of Tuscany, ruled by Florence, in 1559.

Sienese identity is still very much defined by its 17 medieval *contrade* (neighborhoods), each with its own church, museum, and symbol. Look for streetlights painted in the contrada's colors, plaques displaying its symbol, and statues embodying the spirit of the neighborhood. The various contrade uphold ancestral rivalries during the centuries-old Palio, a yearly horse race through the main square; civic pride rests on the outcome.

Exploring Siena

Practically unchanged since medieval times, Siena is laid out over the slopes of three steep hills, but you will find the most interesting sights in a fairly compact area. Be sure to leave some time to wander off the main streets. Most sights are concentrated in the pedestrian-only city center, so you will end up walking up and down a lot of steep streets. If you only have one day in Siena, see the Piazza del Campo, the Duomo and its Museo dell'Opera del Duomo, and the Palazzo Pubblico. If you are seeing more sights, it will probably be worth buying a cumulative ticket (valid for three days, 8,500 lire), good for entrance to the Duomo's Biblioteca Piccolomini, Battistero, and Museo dell'Opera del Duomo.

From Florence, there are two basic routes to Siena. The speedy modern S2 is good if you're making a day trip from Florence; for a jaunt through Chianti, take the narrower and more meandering S222, known as the Strada Chiantigiana.

A Good Walk

Begin at the **Piazza del Campo** ㉖, one of Italy's finest squares, and visit the **Palazzo Pubblico** ㉗ and its adjacent tower, the Torre del Mangia, which you can climb up. Cross the piazza and exit on the stairs to the left to Via di Città, one of Siena's main shopping streets. Up on the left is the enchanting Palazzo Chigi-Saracini, where concerts are often held. Step in to admire the especially well-preserved courtyard. Continue up the hill and take the next street on the right, Via del Capitano, which leads to Piazza del Duomo. The **Duomo** ㉘ is a must-see, along with its **Battistero** ㉙ (around the other side of the Duomo) and **Museo dell'Opera del Duomo** ㉚. Opposite the front of the Duomo is **Santa Maria della Scala** ㉛. Chief among Siena's other gems is the **Pinacoteca Nazionale** ㉜, several blocks straight back down Via del Capitano (becomes Via San Pietro). The church of **San Domenico** ㉝ lies in the other direction; you could take Via della Galluzza to Via della Sapienza.

TIMING

This walk should take a full day, taken at a leisurely pace and allowing some time to relax in the Piazza del Campo. Allow two days to really explore Siena. The *passeggiata* (evening stroll) along the main shopping streets should not be missed. Almost all shops are closed Sunday, and the Pinacoteca is closed Monday.

Sights to See

㉙ **Battistero.** The Duomo's 14th-century Gothic Baptistery was built to prop up one side of the Duomo. There are frescoes throughout, but the highlight is a large bronze 15th-century baptismal font, designed by Jacopo della Quercia and adorned with bas-reliefs by various artists, including two by Renaissance masters: the *Baptism of Christ* by Lorenzo Ghiberti (1378–1455) and the *Feast of Herod* by Donatello. ✉ *Piazza San Giovanni.* 🎫 *3,000 lire; combination ticket 8,500 lire.* ⏲ *Mid-Mar.–Sept., daily 9–7:30; Nov.–mid-Mar., daily 10–1 and 2:30–5.*

NEED A BREAK? Not far from the Duomo and the Pinacoteca, Siena's **Orto Botanico** (Botanical Gardens, ✉ V. Pier Andrea Mattioli 4, ☎ 0577/298874) is a great place to relax and enjoy views onto the countryside below. It's open Monday–Friday 8–5:30, Saturday 8–noon.

Battistero, **29**
Duomo, **28**
Museo dell'Opera del Duomo, **30**
Palazzo Pubblico, **27**
Piazza del Campo, **26**
Pinacoteca Nazionale, **32**
San Domenico, **33**
Santa Maria della Scala, **31**

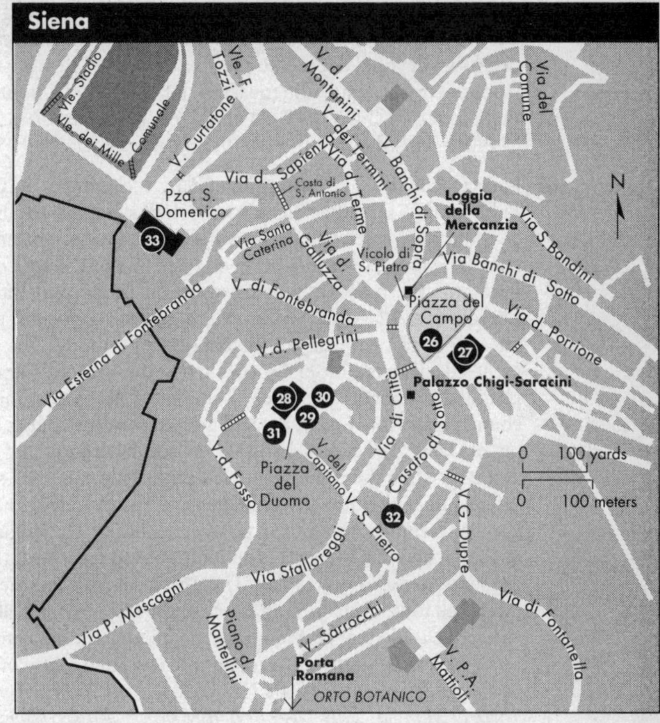

28 **Duomo.** Several blocks west of Piazza del Campo, Siena's Duomo is beyond question one of the finest Gothic cathedrals in Italy. The facade, with its multicolor marbles and painted decoration, is typical of the Italian approach to Gothic architecture, lighter and much less austere than the French. The cathedral as it now stands was completed in the 14th century, but at the time the Sienese had even bigger plans. They had decided to enlarge the building by using the existing church as a transept for a new church, with a new nave running toward the southeast. But in 1348 the Black Death decimated Siena's population, the city fell into decline, funds dried up, and the plans were never carried out. The beginnings of the new nave can be seen from the steps outside the Duomo's right transept.

The Duomo's interior, with its coffered and gilded dome, is simply striking. It is most famous for its unique and magnificent inlaid marble floors, which took almost 200 years to complete (beginning around 1370); more than 40 artists contributed to the work, made up of 56 separate compositions depicting biblical scenes, allegories, religious symbols, and civic emblems. The Duomo's carousel pulpit, also much appreciated, was carved by Nicola Pisano between 1266 and 1268; the life of Christ is depicted on the rostrum frieze. In the **Biblioteca Piccolomini,** a room painted by Pinturicchio (circa 1454–1513) between 1502–09, frescoes depict events from the life of native son Aeneas Sylvius Piccolomini, who became Pope Pius II (1405–64) in 1458. They are in excellent condition and reveal a freshness rarely seen in Renaissance frescoes. ✉ *Piazza del Duomo,* ☎ *0577/283048.* 🎫 *Biblioteca Piccolomini: 2,000 lire; combination ticket 8,500 lire.* ⊙ *Nov.–mid-Mar., daily 10–1 and 2:30–5; mid-Mar.–Oct., daily 9–7:30.*

30 **Museo dell'Opera del Duomo.** Built into part of the unfinished new cathedral's nave, the museum contains a small collection of Sienese art and

the cathedral treasury. Its masterpiece is unquestionably Duccio's (circa 1255–1318) *Maestà,* painted around 1310 and magnificently displayed in a room devoted entirely to the artist's work. There is a splendid view from the tower inside the museum. ✉ *Piazza del Duomo, next to the Duomo,* ☎ *0577/283048.* 🎟 *6,000 lire; combination ticket 8,500 lire.* ⏲ *Nov.–mid-Mar., daily 9–1:30; mid-Mar.–Oct., daily 9–7:30.*

27 **Palazzo Pubblico.** The focal point of Piazza del Campo, the Gothic Palazzo Pubblico has served as Siena's town hall since the 1300s. It now also contains the **Museo Civico,** its walls covered with pre-Renaissance frescoes. The nine governors of Siena once met in the *Sala della Pace,* famous for the most important medieval frescoes in Italy, Ambrogio Lorenzetti's *Allegories of Good and Bad Government,* painted in the late 1330s to demonstrate the dangers of tyranny. The good government side depicts a utopia, showing first the virtuous ruling council surrounded by angels and then scenes of a perfectly running city and countryside. Conversely, the bad government fresco tells a tale straight out of Dante. The evil ruler and his advisors have horns and fondle strange animals, while the town scene depicts the seven mortal sins in action. Interestingly, the bad government fresco is severely damaged, and the good government fresco is in terrific condition. The original bas-reliefs of the Jacopo della Quercia fountain, moved to protect them from the elements, are also on display. The **Torre del Mangia,** the palazzo's famous bell tower, is named after one of the tower's first bell ringers, Giovanni di Duccio (called Mangiaguadagni, or earnings eater). The climb up to the top is long and steep, but the view makes it worth every step. ✉ *Piazza del Campo,* ☎ *0577/292263.* 🎟 *6,000 lire for all sights.* ⏲ *Torre di Mangia: daily 10–1 hr before sunset. Museo Civico: Mar.–Oct., Mon.–Sat. 9:30–6:30; Nov.–early Jan., Mon.–Sat. 9:30–1:30.*

26 **Piazza del Campo.** Known simply as Il Campo (The Field), this fan-shape piazza is one of the finest in Italy. Constructed towards the end of the 12th century on a market area unclaimed by any contrada, it is still very much the heart of town. The bricks of the Campo are patterned in nine different sections—one for each of the medieval Government of Nine. At the top of the Campo is the **Fonte Gaia,** decorated in the early 15th century by Siena's greatest sculptor, Jacopo della Quercia, with 13 sculpted reliefs of biblical events and virtues. The sculptures now lining the rectangular fountain are 19th-century copies; the originals are in the Museo Civico. On Palio days (July 2 and August 16), Il Campo and all its surrounding buildings are packed with cheering, frenzied locals and tourists craning their necks to take it all in.

32 **Pinacoteca Nazionale.** The national picture gallery contains a supreme collection of Sienese art, including Ambrogio Lorenzetti's 14th-century depiction of a castle that is generally considered the first nonreligious painting—the first pure landscape—of the Christian era. ✉ *Via San Pietro 29,* ☎ *0577/281161.* 🎟 *8,000 lire.* ⏲ *Tues.–Sun. 8:30–1.*

33 **San Domenico.** In the church of San Domenico is the **Cappella di Santa Caterina,** with frescoes by Sodoma portraying scenes from the life of St. Catherine. Catherine was a much-respected diplomat, noted for ending the Great Schism by convincing the pope to return to Rome from Avignon. ✉ *Costa di Sant'Antonio,* ☎ *0577/280330.* ⏲ *Daily 9–12:30 and 3:30–6.*

31 **Santa Maria della Scala.** A former hospital, built beginning in the late 9th century, is now an exhibition space and restoration center, with a frescoed hall. ✉ *Piazza del Duomo, opposite the front of the cathedral,* ☎ *0577/586410.* 🎟 *8,000 lire.* ⏲ *Nov.–Mar., daily 10:30–4:30; Apr.–Oct., daily 10:30–6.*

Dining and Lodging

$$$–$$$$ ★ ✕ **Antica Trattoria Botteganova.** Just outside the city walls, along the road that leads north to Chianti, the Botteganova is arguably the best restaurant in Siena. Contemporary Italian food is rarely this successful; chef Michele Sonentino's cooking is all about clean flavors, balanced combinations, and inviting presentation. The interior, with high vaulting, is relaxed yet classy, and the service is first rate. There is a small room for nonsmokers. ✉ *Strada Chiantigiana di Montevarchi (S222) 29, 2 km (1 mi) north of Siena,* ☎ *0577/284230. AE, DC, MC, V. Closed Mon.*

$$ ★ ✕ **Le Logge.** Near Piazza del Campo, this classic Sienese trattoria has rustic dining rooms on two levels and tables outdoors from June to October. Tuscan dishes are the draw, such as *malfatti all'osteria* (ricotta and spinach dumplings in a cream sauce) and *anatra al finocchio* (roast duck with fennel). Reservations are advised. ✉ *Via del Porrione 33,* ☎ *0577/48013. AE, DC, MC, V. Closed Sun. and 2 wks in June and Nov.*

$$ ✕ **Osteria Castelvecchio.** The menu at this cheerful little restaurant with modern decor, set in an old stall near the Pinacoteca, is an intriguing mix of rare dishes not seen for centuries and updated Sienese standards. The choice of dishes is not ample, as chef Mauro prefers a change. He has chosen a solid selection of wines from Tuscany. ✉ *Via Castelvecchio 65,* ☎ *0577/49586. AE, MC, V. Closed Tues.*

$$ ✕ **Tullio Tre Cristi.** This is a typical and historic neighborhood trattoria, still reliable and filled with loyal customers. The paintings on the walls were executed by famous local artists of the 1920s, but the culinary tradition here goes back even further. Try spaghetti *alle briciole,* a poor-man's dish of pasta with bread crumbs, tomato, and garlic, or the *cinghiale alla chiantigiana* (wild boar cooked with an excellent local wine). You can eat outdoors in summer. ✉ *Vicolo di Provenzano 1, take Via dei Rossi from Via Banchi di Sopra,* ☎ *0577/280608. MC, V. Closed Tues.*

$ ✕ **Enoteca Italica.** Not far from the church of San Domenico, this fantastically stocked wine cellar is in the bastions of the Medici fortress. Here you can taste wines from all over Italy and have a snack, too. It's open until the wee hours (1 AM). ✉ *Fortezza Medicea, Viale Maccari,* ☎ *0577/288497, AE, MC, V.*

$ ✕ **Enoteca I Terzi.** Near the Campo and the main shopping streets, this *enoteca* (wine bar) is hard to beat for a good glass of wine from a list of several hundred and a little snack or a full meal. Fast but "passionate" service, very good value, and long opening hours (you can have lunch as early as 10:30 AM and dinner as late as 1 AM) gained the young owners a dedicated following among locals. The room at the back is for nonsmokers. ✉ *Via dei Termini 7,* ☎ *0577/44329. AE, DC, MC, V. Closed Sun.*

$$$$ ★ 🏨 **Certosa di Maggiano.** A former 14th-century monastery converted into an exquisite country hotel, this haven of gracious living is a little more than about 1½ km (1 mi) from the center of Siena, near the Porta Romana gate. The atmosphere is that of an exclusive retreat in which a select number of guests enjoy the style and comfort of an aristocratic villa. Guest rooms blend taste and comfort, with classic prints and bold colors such as a happy daffodil yellow. Common rooms are luxurious, replete with fine woods, leathers, and traditional prints. In warm weather, breakfast is served on the patio next to the garden aburst with roses, zinnias, and other blessed friends. ✉ *Via Certosa 82 (take the Siena Sud exit off superstrada), 53100,* ☎ *0577/288180,* FAX *0577/288189. 5 rooms, 12 suites. Restaurant, pool, tennis court, helipad. AE, DC, MC, V.*

$$$$ ★ **La Suvera.** This luxurious estate in the lovely valley of the River Elsa, 28 km (17 mi) west of Siena and 56 km (33 mi) south of Florence, was once owned by Pope Julius II. The papal villa and adjacent building accommodate guests in magnificently furnished rooms and suites appointed with antiques and modern comforts. With excellent facilities such as drawing rooms, a library, Italian garden, park, and the Oliviera restaurant (serving estate wines), guests find it hard to tear themselves away. ✉ *Pievescola (Casola d'Elsa), off S541, 53030,* ☎ *0577/960300,* FAX *0577/960220. 19 rooms, 13 suites. Restaurant, bar, pool, sauna, tennis court, horseback riding, library, meeting rooms. AE, DC, MC, V. Closed Nov.–Easter.*

$$$$ **Park.** Set among olive groves and gardens on a hillside just outside the city walls, this handsome hotel offers solid comfort and spacious double rooms with views of the grounds, which also includes a nine-hole practice golf course. Public rooms in the historic medieval villa lend an easy elegance and patrician antique charm. Comfortable guest rooms have bold, dark fabrics, mirrors, and modern appointments. The Olivo restaurant serves regional cuisine. ✉ *Via Marciano 18, 53100,* ☎ *0577/44803,* FAX *0577/49020. 69 rooms. Restaurant, bar, pool, 9-hole golf course, tennis court. AE, DC, MC, V.*

$$ **Antica Torre.** A restored 17th-century tower within the town walls in the southeast corner of Siena, Antica Torre is a 10-minute walk from Piazza del Campo. It is the work of a cordial couple who have created the atmosphere of a private home, furnished simply but tastefully and with only eight guest rooms. The old stone staircase, wooden beams, and original brick vaults here and there are reminders of the building's august age. ✉ *Via Fieravecchia 7, 53100,* ☎ FAX *0577/222255. 8 rooms. AE, MC, V.*

$$ **Chiusarelli.** In a well-kept neoclassic villa, built in the early 1900s complete with caryatids, this hotel has functional rooms that are airy and reasonably quiet. A handy location—near the long-distance bus terminal and a parking area and only a 10-minute walk from the main sights—is the big plus here. The small garden invites reading; a downstairs restaurant caters to tour groups. ✉ *Viale Curtatone 15, 53100,* ☎ *0577/280562,* FAX *0577/271177. 49 rooms. Restaurant. MC, V.*

$$ **Duomo.** Occupying the top floor of a 300-year-old building near Piazza del Campo, this quiet hotel is furnished in a neat contemporary style, with traces of the past showing in the artfully exposed brickwork in the breakfast room. Many bedrooms have views of the city's towers and the hilly countryside. Two rooms have balconies. ✉ *Via Stalloreggi 38, 53100,* ☎ *0577/289088,* FAX *0577/43043. 23 rooms. Breakfast room. AE, DC, MC, V.*

$$ **Pensione Ravizza.** Don't let the word "pensione" confuse you, as the Ravizza is a particularly elegant hotel. Rooms are large and furnished with antiques, and those in the back have great views over the garden and countryside. Just a few minutes' walk from Piazza del Campo, this is the best choice in town for location, and the free parking is also a great plus. ✉ *Pian dei Mantellini 34, 53100,* ☎ *0577/280462,* FAX *0577/221597. 30 rooms, 4 suites. Free parking. AE, DC, MC, V.*

$$ **Piccolo Hotel Oliveta.** This little hotel in a rejuvenated 18th-century brick farmhouse has lots of atmosphere. Just outside Porta Romana and only 10 minutes from Piazza del Campo on foot, it has simply furnished rooms and a garden overlooking olive groves and verdant hills. A Palio-time option includes tickets to the race. ✉ *Via Piccolomini 35, 53100,* ☎ *0577/283930,* FAX *0577/270009. 16 rooms. Free parking. AE, MC, V.*

$$ Santa Caterina. Just outside Porta Romana—10 minutes' walk to the Campo—the Santa Caterina is an extremely pleasant, well-run hotel. The rooms are nicely decorated with Tuscan country furniture and tapestries; half overlook the garden. Breakfast is served in a sunny room or out in the garden. ✉ *Via E. S. Piccolomini 7, 53100,* ☎ *0577/221105,* FAX *0577/271087. 19 rooms. Breakfast room. AE, DC, MC, V.*

Nightlife and the Arts

Music

In late July and August, Siena hosts the **Settimane Musicali Senesi,** a series of concerts held in churches and courtyards with performances of local and other music.

Outdoor Activities and Sports

Siena's **Palio** horse race takes place every year on July 2 and August 16, but its spirit lives all year long. Three laps around a makeshift track in Piazza del Campo earn participants of the Palio the respect or scorn of the other 16 contrade. The event is so important to the Sienese that bribery, brutality, and kidnapping of the jockeys are commonplace—sabotaging a horse's reins is the only thing that remains taboo. A horse doesn't even need its rider to be considered a valid winner. Festivities kick off three days prior to the main event, with trial races, banquets lining the streets, and late-night celebrations. As the Palio approaches, residents don scarves with their contrada's colors and march through city streets in medieval costumes. Tickets are usually sold out eight months in advance of the events; call the tourist office (☞ Visitor Information *in* Tuscany A to Z, *below*) for info. It is possible you might luck out and get an unclaimed seat or two; of course, the center of the piazza is free to all on a first-come, first-served basis, until just moments before the start.

Shopping

The city is known for a variety of cakes and cookies, their recipes of medieval origin—*cavallucci* (sweet spice biscuits), *panforte* (traditional Sienese Christmas fruitcake with honey, hazelnuts, almonds, and spices), and *ricciarelli* (almond-paste cookies)—as well as for its ceramics.

AREZZO AND CORTONA

The lovely hill towns of Arezzo and Cortona carry on age-old local traditions—each September Arezzo's beautiful Franciscan, Romanesque, and Gothic churches are enlivened by the Giostra del Saracino, a costumed medieval joust. Since ancient times, Arezzo has been home to important artists: from the Etruscan potters who produced those fiery-red vessels to the poet Petrarch and Giorgio Vasari, writer, architect, and painter. Fine examples of the work of native painter Luca Signorelli are preserved in Cortona.

Arezzo

34 *81 km (50 mi) southeast of Florence, 74 km (46 mi) northwest of Perugia.*

The birthplace of the poet Petrarch; of the Renaissance artist and art historian Giorgio Vasari; and of Guido d'Arezzo, the inventor of musical notation, Arezzo is today best known for the magnificent Piero ★ della Francesca (1420–92) frescoes in the church of **San Francesco.** Painted between 1452 and 1466, they depict *The Legend of the True*

Cross on three walls of the choir. What Sir Kenneth Clark called "the most perfect morning light in all Renaissance painting" may be seen in the lowest section of the right wall, where the troops of the Emperor Maxentius flee before the sign of the cross. Though part of the frescoes may be hidden from view while restoration work takes place, it is possible to go up onto the scaffolding to view part of this magnificent fresco cycle at eye level (reservations necessary). ✉ *Via Cavour, Piazza San Francesco,* ☎ *0575/20630.* ⏲ *Daily 2–7.*

With its irregular shape and sloping brick pavement, framed by buildings of assorted centuries, Arezzo's **Piazza Grande** echoes Siena's Piazza del Campo. Though not so grand, it is lively enough during the outdoor antiques fair every first Sunday of the month and when the **Giostra del Saracino** (Joust of the Saracen), featuring medieval costumes and competition, is held there on the first Sunday of September.

The curving, tiered apse on Piazza Grande belongs to **Santa Maria della Pieve,** one of Tuscany's finest Romanesque churches, built in the 12th century. To the left of the altar, there is a 16th-century Episcopal throne by Vasari. ✉ *Via dei Pileati, end of Corso Italia,* ☎ *0575/377678.* ⏲ *Daily 8–1 and 3–7.*

And Arezzo's medieval **Duomo** (at the top of the hill) contains a fresco of a tender *Magdalen* by Piero della Francesca; look for it next to the large marble tomb near the organ. ✉ *Via Ricasoli,* ☎ *0575/23991.* ⏲ *Daily 7–12:30 and 3–6:30.*

The church of **San Domenico,** just inside the walls, houses a 13th-century crucifix by Cimabue (circa 1240–1302). ✉ *Piazza Fossombroni, Piazza San Domenico,* ☎ *0575/22906.* ⏲ *Daily 7–1 and 3:30–6.*

The **Casa di Giorgio Vasari** (Giorgio Vasari house) was designed and decorated by the region's leading Mannerist artist around 1540 for his own use. ✉ *Via XX Settembre 55,* ☎ *0575/300301.* 🎟 *Free.* ⏲ *Mon.–Sat. 9–7, Sun. 9–1.*

The **Museo Archeologico,** on the south side of Arezzo in the **Convento di San Bernardo,** exhibits an impressive collection of Etruscan bronzes. ✉ *Via Margaritone 10,* ☎ *0575/20882.* 🎟 *8,000 lire.* ⏲ *Mon.–Sat. 9–2, Sun. 9–1.*

Dining and Lodging

$$ ✕ **Buca di San Francesco.** A frescoed cellar restaurant in a historic building next to the church of San Francesco, this *buca* (literally "hole," figuratively "cellar") has a medieval atmosphere and serves straightforward local specialties, including *ribollita* (minestrone thickened with beans and bread). Meat eaters will find the lean Chianina beef and the *saporita di Bonconte* (a selection of several meats) succulent treats. ✉ *Via San Francesco 1,* ☎ FAX *0575/23271. AE, DC, MC, V. Closed Tues. and 2 wks in July. No dinner Mon.*

$$ ✕ **Tastevin.** Tastevin has introduced creative cooking—risotto alla Tastevin (with a creamy truffle sauce) and seafood—to Arezzo, but also remains true to tradition. Two of the dining rooms are furnished in a warm Tuscan provincial style, one in more sophisticated bistro style. At the small bar the talented owner plays and sings Sinatra and show tunes. ✉ *Via dei Cenci 9, close to San Francesco and the central Piazza Guido Monaco,* ☎ *0575/28304. AE, MC, V. Closed Sun. (except the 1st Sun. of every month) and 1 wk in Aug.*

$ ✕ **L'Agania.** The main reason for coming to this central osteria, with plain wood paneling and rather cheap furniture, is the good food for less. Its specialties include boar meat, both as a second course and in a savory sauce with pasta. Also try the tasty *griffi,* which is actually veal cheek, with tomatoes and spices. ✉ *Via Mazzini 10,* ☎ *0575/295381. AE, DC, MC, V. Closed Mon.*

$$ 🏨 **Castello di Gargonza.** Enchantment reigns at this tiny 13th-century hamlet in the countryside near Monte San Savino, part of the fiefdom of the aristocratic Florentine Guicciardinis restored by the modern Count Roberto Guicciardini as a way to rescue a dying village. A castle, church, and the cobbled streets set the stage. Rooms can be had for a minimum of three nights. Cottages and apartments are for rent by the week; they have one to six rooms each, sleep two to seven people, and have as many as four baths. La Torre restaurant (closed Tuesday) serves local fare. ✉ *Monte San Savino, 52100,* ☎ *0575/847021,* FAX *0575/847054. 7 rooms, 25 apartments. Restaurant, pool. AE, DC, MC, V. Closed Jan. 10–31 and Nov.*

$ 🏨 **Continental.** Centrally located near the train station and within walking distance of all major sights, the Continental has been a reliable and convenient place to stay since it opened in the 1950s. Bright white furnishings with yellow accents are throughout; gleaming bathrooms complete with hair dryers, air-conditioning in most rooms, and a pleasant roof garden are welcome pluses. Breakfast is extra. ✉ *Piazza Guido Monaco 7, 52100,* ☎ *0575/20251,* FAX *0575/350485. 73 rooms. 3 conference rooms. DC, MC, V.*

Outdoor Activities and Sports

HORSEBACK RIDING

A well-reputed outfit is **Ippo Equitazione** (✉ Via Michelangelo da Caravaggio 34, just behind Piazza Giotto, ☎ 0575/300417).

Shopping

FLEA MARKET

The first Sunday of each month, a colorful flea market selling antiques and not-so-antiques takes place in the **Piazza Grande.**

GOLD

Gold production here is on an industrial scale. **Uno-A-Erre** is the biggest of several factories. Big-time baubles can be purchased on a small scale in town center. For gold jewelry set with precious or semiprecious stones, try **Il Diamante** (✉ Via Guido Monaco 69), **Borghini** (✉ Corso Italia 126), **Prosperi** (✉ Corso Italia 76), or **Aurea Monilia** (✉ Piazza San Francesco 15).

KNITWEAR

A cottage knitwear industry is burgeoning in Arezzo. For sweaters, try **Maglierie Mely's** (✉ Via Romana 190).

Cortona

35 *29 km (18 mi) south of Arezzo, 117 km (73 mi) southeast of Florence.*

Magnificently situated, with olive trees and vineyards creeping up to its walls, one of Tuscany's prettiest villages commands sweeping views over Lake Trasimeno and the plain of the Valdichiana. Its two galleries and scattering of churches are rarely visited; delightful medieval streets are a pleasure to wander for their own sake.

Cortona may be one of Italy's oldest towns—"Mother of Troy and Grandmother of Rome" in popular speech. Tradition claims that it was founded by Dardanus, the founder of Troy (after whom the Dardanelles are named). He was fighting a local tribe, so the story goes, when he lost his helmet (*corythos* in Greek) on Cortona's hill. In time a town grew up that took its name (Corito) from the missing headgear. By the 4th century BC the Etruscans had built the first set of town walls, whose cyclopean traces can still be seen in the 3-km (2-mi) sweep of the present fortifications. As a member of the Etruscans' 12-city Dodecapolis, it became one of the federation's leading northern cities. An important consular road, the Via Cassia, which passed the foot of its hill, maintained the town's importance under the Romans. Medieval fortunes waned, however, as the plain below reverted to marsh. After holding out against neighbors like Perugia, Arezzo, and Siena, the *comune* was captured by King Ladislas of Naples in 1409 and sold to the Florentines two years later.

The heart of Cortona is formed by **Piazza della Repubblica** and the adjacent **Piazza Signorelli.** Wander into the courtyard of the picturesque 13th-century **Palazzo Pretorio,** and, if you want to see a representative collection of Etruscan bronzes, climb its centuries-old stone staircase to the **Museo dell'Accademia Etrusca** (Gallery of Etruscan Art). ✉ *Piazza Signorelli 9,* ☎ *0575/630415.* 🎫 *8,000 lire.* ⏲ *Oct.–Mar., Tues.–Sun. 9–1 and 3–5; Apr.–Sept., Tues.–Sun. 10–1 and 4–7.*

The **Museo Diocesano** (Diocesan Museum) houses an impressive number of large and splendid paintings by native son Luca Signorelli, as well as a beautiful *Annunciation* by Fra Angelico, a delightful surprise to find in this small, eclectic town. ✉ *Piazza del Duomo 1,* ☎ *0575/62830.* 🎫 *8,000 lire.* ⏲ *Nov.–Mar., Tues.–Sun. 10–1 and 3–5; Apr.–Sept., Tues.–Sun. 9:30–1 and 3:30–7.*

Dining and Lodging

$$ ✕ **La Loggetta.** Above Cortona's main medieval square, this attractive restaurant is housed in a 16th-century wine cellar. In good weather you can eat outdoors, overlooking the 13th-century town hall, dining on regional dishes and such specialties as *gnudi,* "naked ravioli," made with spinach and ricotta but without pasta, and tagliata. The owners pride themselves on their selection of Tuscan wines. ✉ *Piazza Pescheria 3,* ☎ *0575/630575. AE, DC, MC, V. Closed Nov. 5–20 and Mon. Sept.–June.*

$$ ✕ **Tonino.** It must be host Tonino's own *antipastissimo*—an incredible variety of delectables—that make this large modern establishment noisy and crowded at times. But it is very satisfactory indeed when not, when you can enjoy the view of the Valdichiana and savor Chianina steak. Tonino requires that you order a *primo piatto* (first course) and a *secondo* (second course), a practice that has died a fortunate death in most of Italy. ✉ *Piazza Garibaldi,* ☎ *0575/630500. AE, DC, MC, V. Closed Tues.*

$$$ ✕🏨 **Il Falconiere.** This might be as close as you can come to dying and going to heaven in Italy. Run by the young husband-wife team of Silvia and Riccardo Baracchi, the hotel, just minutes outside of Cortona, consists of rooms in an 18th-century villa and suites in the *chiesetta* (little church) once belonging to an obscure 19th-century Italian poet and hunter. Rooms are spacious and many have sweeping views of the plain below. The restaurant's marvelous and inventive menu is complemented by the wine list, the product of Silvia's extensive sommelier training. Fragrant and massive rosemary bushes decorate the place. ✉ *Località San Martino, 52044,* ☎ *0575/612679,* FAX *0575/612927. 12 rooms. Restaurant, bar, pool. AE, DC, MC, V. Closed 1 month Jan.–Feb.*

SOUTHERN TUSCANY

Along the roads leading south from Siena, soft green olive groves give way to a blanket of oak and rich, dark-green cypress forests and reddish brown earth; here and there throughout this area are the vineyards that produce excellent wines, among them Brunello di Montalcino. Towns are the size of the roads—small—and as old as the hills. The scruffy mountain landscapes of Monte Amiata make up some of the wildest parts of Tuscany, and once across the mountains the landscape is still full of cliffs, like the one Pitigliano perches on. The deep south offers good wine—especially in Pitigliano—thermal baths at Saturnia, Etruscan ruins, and the strands and fishing villages of Elba.

Abbazia di Monte Oliveto Maggiore

36 *37 km (23 mi) southeast of Siena, 104 km (65 mi) south of Florence.*

This Benedictine abbey, Tuscany's most visited, is an oasis of olive and cypress trees amid the harsh landscape of a zone known as the Crete, where erosion has sculpted the hills starkly, laying open gashes of barren rock in lush farmland. Secluded amid thick woodlands in the deep-cut hills south of Siena, it is accessible by car but not easily by bus.

Olivetans, or "White Benedectines," founded the abbey in 1313; this breakaway group sought to return to the simple ideals of the early Benedictines. The monastery's mellow brick buildings, restored in the last century and set in one of Tuscany's most striking landscapes, protect a treasure or two. Only the **main cloister** and portions of the **park** are open to the public. The wooden choir in the church, with superfine inlay designs, is an understated work of art that dates from 1503 to 1505. In the main cloister of the abbey, the frescoes by Luca Signorelli and Sodoma on the walls of the portico relate the life of St. Benedict with earthy realism, a quality that came naturally to Sodoma, described by Vasari as "a merry and licentious man . . . of scant chastity." ✉ *S451 south of Asciano,* ☎ *0577/707611.* ⏲ *Daily 9:15–noon and 3:15–5:45.*

Dining

$–$$ ✕ **La Torre.** This pleasant restaurant and café in the massive tower at the abbey's entrance provides more than adequate sustenance. The local specialties—served in a cozy dining room in winter or on an attractive terrace under tall cypresses in good weather—include *pici ai funghi* (thick, short spaghetti with mushroom sauce) or *zuppa di funghi* (mushroom soup). The wine list is remarkably good, and the tourist menu is a good value. ✉ *Abbazia di Monte Oliveto Maggiore,* ☎ *0577/707022. AE, DC, MC, V. Closed Tues.*

Montepulciano

37 *13 km (8 mi) west of the A1, 119 km (74 mi) south of Florence.*

Perched high on a hilltop, Montepulciano is made up of a pyramid of redbrick buildings set within a circle of cypress trees. At an altitude of almost 2,000 ft, it is cool in summer and chilled in winter by biting winds that sweep its spiraling streets. The town has an unusually harmonious look, the result of the work of three architects, Sangallo (Il Vecchio 1455–1535), Giacomo da Vignola (1507–73), and Michelozzo (1396–1472), who endowed it with palaces and churches in an attempt to impose Renaissance architectural ideals on an ancient Tuscan hill town. ★ The pièce de résistance is the beautiful **Piazza Grande.** On the hillside below the town walls is the church of **San Biagio,** designed by Sangallo, a paragon of Renaissance architectural perfection considered to be his masterpiece. ✉ *Via di San Biagio,* ☎ *0578/7577761.* ⏲ *Daily 9–12:30 and 3:30–7:30.*

Dining and Lodging

$$$$ ★ ✕🏨 **Locanda dell'Amorosa.** This "inn" occupies the 14th-century stone-and-brick hamlet of Amorosa, in the hills crowning the Valdichiana, just south of Sinalunga. The stunning setting is matched by the

perfectly restored, gorgeous buildings. A lane lined with cypress trees brings you to the gateway of Amorosa, which still has its tiny little church and a group of farmers' houses for the staff. The bedrooms are handsomely decorated with antiques, the bathrooms seem like little sitting rooms. The restaurant, housed in the old stables, serves both traditional and contemporary dishes (stick to the former). ✉ *Località Amorosa, Sinalunga, 10 km (6 mi) off the Valdichiana exit of A1, 53048,* ☎ *0577/679497,* FAX *0577/632001. 13 rooms, 4 suites. Restaurant, wine bar. AE, DC, MC, V.*

$$ **Il Marzocco.** A 16th-century building within the town walls, this hotel is furnished circa 19th century, complete with dignified, old-fashioned parlors and a billiard room. Furnished in heavy late-19th-century style or in spindly white wood, many bedrooms have large terraces overlooking the countryside. Many rooms are large enough to accommodate extra beds. No breakfast is served. ✉ *Piazza Savonarola 18, 53045,* ☎ *0578/757262,* FAX *0578/757530. 16 rooms, 1 without bath. Restaurant. AE, DC, MC, V. Closed Jan. 20–Feb. 10.*

$$ **La Bandita.** This attractive old farmhouse possesses great charm, with terra-cotta floors throughout, lace curtains and antiques in the bedrooms, and a fireplace and 19th-century Tuscan provincial furniture in a large, brick-vaulted living room. Some rooms can accommodate an extra bed. A garden and meals are available to guests. The restaurant is closed Tuesday. ✉ *Via Bandita 72, 53048 Bettolle, 1 km (½ mi) from Valdichiana exit of A1 autostrada,* ☎ *0577/624649,* FAX *0577/624649. 7 rooms. Restaurant. AE, DC, MC, V.*

Nightlife and the Arts

The **Cantiere Internazionale d'Arte,** held in July and August, is a multifaceted festival of figurative art, music, and theater, ending with a major theatrical production in Piazza Grande. Contact the Montepulciano tourist office (☞ Visitor Information *in* Tuscany A to Z) for info.

Chianciano Terme

9 km (5½ mi) south of Montepulciano, 85 km (53 mi) southeast of Siena.

This small medieval town, surrounded by walls, has billboards proclaiming that Chianciano's restorative waters are indispensable for a *fegato sano* (healthy liver). Outside the old walls is a well-attended, top-of-the-line modern spa with neat parks and a host of hotels. The spa has grabbed attention away from the old city center, which nevertheless is worth a visit, mainly for its castle.

Chiusi

11 km (7 mi) east of Chianciano, 126 km (78 mi) south of Florence.

Known for the frescoed tombs that date from the 5th century BC in its necropolis, Chiusi was one of the most powerful of the 12 ancient cities in the Etruscan federation. It's a transportation hub accessible from either the main north–south rail line or by car or bus from the A1 autostrada.

Pienza

38 *22 km (14 mi) west of Chianciano Terme, 120 km (75 mi) south of Florence.*

Pienza owes its urban plan to Pope Pius II, who had grand plans to transform his home village of Corsignano—the town's former name—into a model Renaissance town. The man entrusted with the transformation was Bernardo Rossellino (1409–64), a protégé of the great

Renaissance architectural theorist Leon Battista Alberti (1404–74). His mandate was to create a cathedral, a papal palace, and a town hall (plus miscellaneous buildings) that adhered to the vainglorious pope's principles. Gothic and Renaissance styles were fused, and the buildings were decorated with Sienese and Florentine paintings. The net result was a project that expressed Renaissance ideals of art, architecture, and civilized good living in a single scheme: it stands as a sensational example of the architectural canons that Alberti formulated in the early Renaissance and which were utilized by later architects, including Michelangelo (1475–1564), in designing many of Italy's finest buildings and piazzas. Today the cool nobility of Pienza's center seems almost surreal in this otherwise unpretentious village, known locally for *pienzino,* also called *cacio,* a smooth sheep's-milk cheese.

The **Palazzo Piccolomini,** the seat of Pius II's papal court, was designed by Rossellino in 1459 using Florence's Palazzo Rucellai by Alberti as a model. You can visit the papal apartments, including a beautiful library, the **Sala delle Armi,** with an impressive weapons collection, and the music room, with its extravagant wooden ceiling. ✉ *Piazza Pio II, ☎ 0578/748503. 🎫 Free. ⏲ June–Oct., Tues.–Sun. 10–12:30 and 4–7; Nov.–May, Tues.–Sun. 10–12:30 and 3–6.*

The interior of the **Duomo** is simple but richly decorated with Sienese paintings. The facade is divided in three parts with Renaissance arches under the Pope's coat of arms encircled by a wreath of fruit. ✉ *Piazza Pio II. ⏲ June–Oct., Tues.–Sun. 10–12:30 and 4–7; Nov.–May, Tues.–Sun. 10–12:30 and 3–6.*

Dining

$ ✕ **La Chiocciola.** This restaurant offers typical Pienza fare, including homemade local pici (thick, short spaghetti) with hare or boar sauce, and baked pienzino cheese. It has a nice summer garden. ✉ *Via dell'Acero 2, ☎ 0578/748063. No credit cards. Closed Wed. and for about 10 days in mid-Nov.*

Montalcino

39 *24 km (15 mi) west of Pienza, 41 km (25 mi) south of Siena.*

Another medieval hill town with a special claim to fame, Montalcino is home to Brunello di Montalcino, one of Italy's most esteemed red wines. You can sample it in wine cellars in town or visit a nearby winery for a free guided tour and tasting; you must call ahead for reservations. One such winery is Fattoria dei Barbi e del Casato (☞ *below*). The 14th-century Sienese **La Fortezza** has an enoteca for tasting wines. *☎ 0577/849211. 🎫 3,500 lire. ⏲ Apr.–Sept., Tues.–Sun. 9–1 and 2:30–8; Oct.–Mar., Tues.–Sun. 9–1 and 2–6.*

Dining and Lodging

$$$ ✕ **Poggio Antico.** One of Italy's renowned gourmet chefs, Roberto Minnetti, abandoned his highly successful restaurant in Rome a few years ago and moved to the country just outside Montalcino. Now he and his wife, Patrizia, who is the hostess, serve Tuscan cuisine, masterfully interpreted by Roberto, in a relaxed but regal dining room replete with arches and beamed ceilings. The seasonal menu might suggest *pappardelle al ragù di agnello* (flat, wide noodles in a lamb sauce) or venison in a sweet-and-sour sauce. ✉ *Località I Poggi, 4 km (2½ mi) outside Montalcino on road to Grossetto, ☎ 0577/849200. MC, V. Closed Mon. and 20 days in Jan. No dinner Sun.*

$$ ★ ✕🏨 **Fattoria dei Barbi e del Casato.** The rustic taverna of this family-owned wine estate, which produces excellent Brunello, is set among vineyards and mellow brick buildings and features a beamed ceiling,

huge stone fireplace, and arched windows. The estate farm produces many of the ingredients used in such traditional specialties as *stracotto nel brunello* (braised veal cooked with beans in Brunello wine); big ravioli pillows filled with ricotta, swathed in butter, and dusted with Parmesan and herbs; and a dessert called ricotta *montata* (farm-fresh ricotta whipped with vin santo, sugar, and vanilla). Two comfortable, traditionally furnished agritourist apartments right next to the cantina—where you can take a tour and buy the fattoria's different labels (call ahead)—each sleep three. Reservations for a meal or a stay are essential. ✉ *Località Podernuovi, 53024,* ☎ *0577/849347 taverna; 0577/848277 fattoria.* FAX *0577/849356. 2 apartments. AE, DC, MC, V. Taverna closed Wed., last 2 wks Jan., and 1st 2 wks July.*

$$ **La Crociona.** A quiet and serene family-owned farm is in the middle of a small vineyard with glorious views and all the comforts of home, including antique iron beds and 17th-century wardrobes in the rooms. There's a big terrace and you are invited to hang out around the pool and use the family barbecue as well as to sample the owner's own wine supply. ✉ *Località La Croce, 53024 Montalcino,* ☎ FAX *0577/848007. 6 apartments. Pool, mountain bikes. AE, DC, MC, V.*

Abbazia di Sant'Antimo

40 *10 km (6 mi) south of Montalcino, 51 km (32 mi) south of Siena.*

It's well worth your while to visit this abbey, a 12th-century Romanesque gem of pale stone set in the silvery green of an olive grove. The exterior and interior sculpture is outstanding, particularly the nave capitals, a combination of French, Lombard, and even Spanish influences. According to legend, the **sacristy** (rarely open) forms part of the primitive Carolingian church (founded in AD 781), its entrance flanked by 9th-century pilasters. The small **vaulted crypt** dates from the same period. An unusual element is the ambulatory, whose three radiating chapels (rare in Italian churches) were probably copied from the French model. ✉ *Castelnuovo dell'Abate,* ☎ *0577/835659.* ⏲ *Apr.–Sept., daily 9–noon and 2–7; Oct.–Mar., daily 10–noon and 2–4.*

Monte Amiata

41 *86½ km (52 mi) southeast of Siena, 156½ km (94 mi) southeast of Florence.*

At 5,702 ft high, the benign volcano Monte Amiata is one of Tuscany's few ski resorts, but it's no match for the Alps or the Dolomites. Its main attraction is a wide-open view of Tuscany. From here, you can meander along panoramic mountaintop roads in your car and visit Castel del Piano, Arcidosso, Santa Flora, and Piancastagnaio, towns dating from the Middle Ages.

Abbazia di San Galgano

42 *33 km (20 mi) southwest of Siena, 70 km (43 mi) northwest of Montalcino.*

This Gothic cathedral missing its rooftop is truly a hauntingly beautiful sight to behold. The church was built in the late 12th century by Cistercian monks, who designed it after churches built by their order in France. But starting in the 15th century it fell into ruins, declining gradually over centuries. Grass has grown through the floor, and the roof and windows are gone. What's left of its facade and walls makes a grandiose and desolate picture. Behind it, a short climb up a hill brings you to the charming little **Chiesa di San Galgano,** with frescoes by 14th-century painter Ambrogio Lorenzetti (documented 1319–48), and a sword in stone. Legend has it that Galgano, a medieval warrior, was struck by a revelation on this spot to give up fighting. He thrust his sword into stone, where it remains to this day.

Elba

43 *Portoferraio 1 hr by ferry from Piombino.*

The largest island in the Tuscan archipelago, ringed with pristine beaches and pocked with rugged vegetation, Elba is an hour by ferry or a half hour by Hovercraft from Piombino, or a short hop by air from Pisa. Its main port is Portoferraio, fortified in the 16th century by the Medici Grand Duke Cosimo I. Be sure to sample the local wines, including Moscato and Aleatico.

Lively **Portoferraio** is the best base for exploring the island. Good beaches can be found at Biodola, Procchio, and Marina di Campo. From Elba, private visits can be arranged to the other islands in the archipelago, including **Montecristo,** which inspired Alexandre Dumas's 19th-century best-seller *The Count of Monte Cristo* and is now a wildlife refuge.

Victor Hugo spent his boyhood here, and Napoléon was here during his famous exile in 1814–15, which resulted in the building of **Palazzina Napoleonica dei Mulini.** More interesting is the **Villa San Martino,** a few kilometers outside town, whose grandiose neoclassic facade was built by the emperor's nephew. *Palazzina: ✉ Piazzale Napoleone 1, Portoferraio, ☎ 0565/915846. Villa: ✉ Località San Martino, ☎ 0565/914688. 8,000 lire for both if visited on same day. Both: ⏲ Apr.–Sept., Mon.–Sat. 9–7, Sun. 9–1; Oct.–Mar., Mon.–Sat. 9–4, Sun. 9–1; possible evening openings in summer.*

You can also visit the **Museo Archeologico,** which reconstructs the island's ancient history through a display of Etruscan and Roman artifacts recovered from shipwrecks. *✉ Calata Buccari, Portoferraio, ☎ 0565/937370. 4,000 lire. ⏲ Easter–June and Sept., Fri.–Wed. 9:30–12:30 and 4–7; July–Aug., Fri.–Wed. 9:30–12:30 and 6–midnight; Nov.–Easter, Fri.–Wed. 4–7.*

Dining and Lodging

$$$ ✕ **La Canocchia.** This is in the center of Rio Marina on the eastern shore of Elba, across the street from a public garden. Specialties include fish-stuffed ravioli with a red shellfish sauce, and *tagliolini* (thin spaghetti) with fresh shrimp. Reservations are essential in summer. *✉ Via Palestro 3, Rio Marina, ☎ 0565/962432. DC, MC, V. Closed Mon. and Nov.–Apr.*

$$$ ✕ **Trattoria da Lido.** In the historic center of Portoferraio, at the beginning of the road heading up to the old Medici walls, this restaurant serves specialties such as *gnocchetti di pesce* (bite-size potato and fish dumplings) with a white cream sauce, and *pesce all'elbana,* fresh white fish baked with vegetables and potatoes. Reservations are encouraged. *✉ Salita del Falcone 2, Portoferraio, ☎ 0565/914650. AE, DC, MC, V. Closed Mon. Nov.–Apr. and Dec. 15–Feb. 15.*

$$$–$$$$ ★ **Hermitage.** This hotel, on the most exclusive bay on Elba, 8 km (5 mi) from Portoferraio, is heavenly. It is composed of a central building with rooms and several little cottages, each with six to eight rooms with their own separate entrances. You have private access to a white sandy beach, and there are a bar and restaurant on the beach, all part of the hotel. *✉ 57037 Biodola, ☎ 0565/936911, FAX 0565/969984. 110 rooms. Restaurant, bar, 3 pools, 6-hole golf course, 9 tennis courts, soccer, volleyball, meeting rooms. AE, DC, MC, V. Closed Nov.–Apr.*

Saturnia

44 *47 km (30 mi) south of Monte Amiata, 129 km (77 mi) south of Siena.*

Etruscan and pre-Etruscan tombs cut into the local rock remain in this town, a lively center in pre-Etruscan times. Today it is known for its hot sulphur **thermal baths.** There is a modern spa with hotel called **Terme di Saturnia** (☞ Dining and Lodging, *below*), or you can bathe for free at the tiered natural pools of Cascate del Gorello by the road to Montemerano.

According to an oft-repeated local legend, the 3,000-year-old thermal baths were created when Saturn, restless with earth's bickering mortals, threw down a thunderbolt and created a hot spring whose miraculously calming waters created peace among them. Today, these mythic magnesium-rich waters bubble forth from the clay at a purported perfect 98.6°F, drawing Italians and Germans seeking relief for skin and muscular ailments as well as a bit (well, a lot) of relaxation. Unlike better-known spa centers like Montecatini Terme, nature still has her place here; just outside of the town's medieval center, the hot, sulfurous waters cascade over natural limestone shelves, affording bathers a sweeping view of the open countryside with not a nightclub in sight.

Dining and Lodging

$$$ ✕ **Da Caino.** This excellent restaurant in the nearby town of Montemerano (on the road to Scansano) is at the high end of the category. Its specialties include tomatoes and peppers on crisp phyllo dough, lasagna with pumpkin, and such hearty *cinghiale* (roast boar) meat dishes as cinghiale *lardolato con olive* (wild boar larded with olives). ✉ *Via della Chiesa 4, Montemerano, 7 km (4½ mi) south of Saturnia,* ☎ *0564/602817. Reservations essential. AE, DC, MC, V. No dinner Wed., no lunch Thurs.*

$$$ ★ ✕ **I Due Cippi–Da Michele.** Owner Michele Aniello has a terrific restaurant with a lengthy and creative menu; strong emphasis is placed on Maremman cuisine though there's other treats on the menu as well; try the *tortelli di castagne al seme di finocchio* (chestnut-stuffed tortelli lightly sauced with butter and fennel seeds). Eating on a terrace overlooking the town's main square can be enjoyed in good weather. Signor Aniello also runs a lovely hotel called Villa Garden ($$, ☎ 0564/601182). ✉ *Piazza Veneto 26/a,* ☎ *0564/601074. Reservations essential. AE, DC, MC, V. Closed Tues. (except July–Sept.) and Dec. 10–24.*

$$$$ ★ **Terme di Saturnia.** Cure takers looking for a more refined approach can don their bathrobes here, at the region's premier resort. The hotel, an elegant stone building, wraps around three tufa-rock pools built over the hot springs' source. Every imaginable type of health and beauty treatment is available here, supplemented by decidedly unspalike meals in the hotel restaurant. Half-pension prices are a good deal. ✉ *58050 Saturnia,* ☎ *0564/601061,* FAX *0564/601266. 82 rooms, 8 suites. Restaurant, bar, piano bar, in-room safes, minibars, in-room VCRs, 4 pools, beauty salon, sauna, spa, steam room, health club. AE, MC, V.*

$ **Villa Acquaviva.** This elegant villa painted antique rose is at the end of a long tree-lined driveway and perched on top of a hill on the main road 1 km (½ mi) from Montemerano. It has lovely views and quintessential Tuscan charm, with tastefully decorated rooms both in the main villa and in a guest house. The farm that fans out around it produces both wine and olive oil. ✉ *Strada Scansanese, 58050 Montemerano,* ☎ *0564/602890,* FAX *0564/602895. 16 rooms. AE, DC, MC, V.*

Pitigliano

45 *33 km (21 mi) east of Saturnia, 147 km (92 mi) southeast of Siena.*

From a distance the medieval stone houses of Pitigliano look as if they melt into the cliffs of soft tufa rock they are perched on. Etruscan tombs, which locals use to store wine, are connected by a network of caves and tunnels. In 1293, the Orsini family moved their base from Sovana to the more naturally fortified Pitigliano. They built up the town's defenses, and fortified their home, Palazzo Orsini. Later, starting in 1543, Antonio da Sangallo the Younger added more to the town's fortresslike aspect, building bastions and towers throughout the town, and adding the acqueduct as well.

Savory local specialties include the famous Pitigliano white wine, olive oil, cold cuts, and cheeses; local restaurants serve up good food at modest prices. Note the 16th-century **aqueduct** below the fortress. Wander down the narrow streets of the old **Jewish Ghetto.** Though Jews had settled in Pitigliano as early as the 15th century, they arrived in much greater numbers after Pope Pius IV's 1569 papal bull that threw the Jews out of Rome.

The 18th-century Baroque **Duomo** has a single nave with chapels and various paintings on the sides. There are two Zuccarelli altarpieces. ✉ *Piazza San Gregorio,* ☎ *0564/616090.* ⏲ *Daily 9–7.*

Inside the **Palazzo Orsini** is the Museo Zuccarelli, featuring paintings by local artist Francesco Zuccarelli (1702–88), as well as a *Madonna* by Jacopo della Quercia, a 14th-century crucifix, and other works of interest. ✉ *Piazza della Fortezza,* ☎ *0564/615568.* 🎫 *5,000 lire.* ⏲ *Mar. 21–Dec., Tues.–Sun. 10–1 and 3–6.*

TUSCANY A TO Z

Arriving and Departing

By Car

The Autostrada del Sole (**A1**) connects Florence with Bologna, 105 km (65 mi) north, and Rome, 277 km (172 mi) south, and passes close to Arezzo.

By Plane

The largest airports in the region are Pisa's **Aeroporto Galileo Galilei** (✉ Pisa, 80 km/50 mi west of Florence, ☎ 050/500707) and Florence's Aeroporto A. Vespucci, called **Peretola** (✉ 10 km/6 mi northwest of Florence, ☎ 055/333498).

By Train

The coastal line from Rome to Genoa passes through Pisa and all the beach resorts. The main line from Rome to Bologna passes through Arezzo, Florence, and Prato. Call 147/888088 for toll-free information.

Getting Around

By Bike

I Bike Italy (✉ Borgo degli Albizi 11, ☎ FAX 055/2342371) offers one-day tours of the Florence countryside.

By Boat

Boat services link the islands of Tuscany's archipelago with the mainland; passenger and car ferries leave from Piombino and Livorno for Elba.

Navarma (✉ Piazzale Premuda, 57025 Piombino, ☎ 0565/225211; ✉ Via Ninci 1, Portoferraio, 57100, ☎ 0565/918901). **Elba Ferries** (✉ Viale Regina Margherita, 57025 Piombino, ☎ 0565/220956; ✉ Nuova Stazione Marittima Calata Carrara, 57100 Livorno, ☎ 0586/898979, FAX 0586/896103; ✉ 57100 Portoferraio, ☎ 0565/930676). **Toremar** (✉ Porto Mediceo, 57025 Piombino, ☎ 0565/31100; ✉ Porto Mediceo, 57123 Livorno, ☎ 0586/896113 or 0586/886273; ✉ Piazzale A. Candi, 58019 Porto Santo Stefano, ☎ 0564/818506).

By Bus

Tuscany is crisscrossed by bus lines that connect the smaller towns and cities on the autostrade and superhighways. They are a good mode of transport for touring the hill towns around Siena, such as San Gimignano; you can then take a Tra-In or Lazzi bus from Siena to Arezzo and get back onto the main Rome–Florence train line. From Chiusi on the main train line you can get a bus to Montepulciano. Buses connect Florence and Siena with Volterra.

By Car

The best way to see Tuscany, making it possible to explore the tiny towns and country restaurants that are so much a part of the region's charm, is by car. Drivers should be prepared to navigate through bewildering suburban sprawls around Tuscan cities; to reach the historic sections where most of the sights are, look for the CENTRO STORICO signs. In many small towns you must park outside the walls.

A11 leads west from Florence and meets the coastal **A12** between Viareggio and Livorno. The **A1** autostrada links Florence with Arezzo and Chiusi (where you turn off for Montepulciano). A toll-free superstrada links Florence with Siena. For Chianti wine country scenery, take the **S222** south of Florence through the undulating hills between Strada in Chianti and Greve in Chianti.

By Train

Italy's main rail line, which runs from Milan to Calabria, links Florence and Arezzo in Tuscany and runs past Chiusi and Cortona on its way south. Another main line connects Florence with Pisa by way of Prato, Pistoia, and Lucca. There are a few other local lines. Call 147/888088 for toll-free information.

Contacts and Resources

Agritourist Agencies

Agriturist (✉ Piazza San Firenze 3, 50122 Florence, ☎ 055/295163). **Terranostra** (✉ Via dei Magazzini 2, 50122 Florence, ☎ 055/280539). **Turismo Verde** (✉ Via Verdi 5, Florence, ☎ 055/2344925).

Car Rentals

AREZZO

Avis (✉ Piazza della Repubblica 1/a, ☎ 0575/354232).

LUCCA

Avis (✉ Via Luporini 1411/a, ☎ 0583/513614).

PISA

Hertz (✉ Aeroporto Galileo Galilei, ☎ 050/49187).

PRATO

Hertz (✉ Via Valentini 60, ☎ 0574/611287).

SIENA

Avis (✉ Via Simone Martini 36, ☎ 0577/270305; **Hertz,** ✉ Viale Sardegna 37, ☎ 0577/45085).

Emergencies

Police, fire (☎ 113). **Ambulance, medical emergency** (☎ 118).

Guided Tours

From Florence, **American Express** (✉ Via Guicciardini 49/r, ☎ 055/288751) operates one-day excursions to Siena and San Gimignano and can arrange for cars, drivers, and guides for special-interest tours in Tuscany. **CIT** (✉ Via Cavour 56, ☎ 055/294306) has a three-day Carosello bus tour from Rome to Florence, Siena, and San Gimignano, as well as a five-day tour that also takes in Venice.

Horseback Riding

Rifugio Prategiano (✉ Montieri, Grosseto, ☎ 0566/997703) is a hotel that offers horseback riding daily. Also try **Le Cannelle** (✉ Parco dell'Uccellina, Talamone, Grosseto, ☎ 0564/887020).

Sailing

Charters in Tuscany are available through the **Centro Nautico Italiano** (✉ Piazza della Signoria 31/r, Florence, ☎ 055/287419).

Travel Agencies

In Florence: **American Express** (✉ Via Guicciardini 49/r, Florence, ☎ 055/288751). **CIT** (✉ Via Cavour 56, Florence, ☎ 055/294306). **Thomas Cook** (✉ c/o World Vision, Via Cavour 154/r, Florence, ☎ 055/579294).

Visitor Information

Tourist offices (✉ Piazza della Repubblica 22, Arezzo, ☎ 0575/377678; ✉ Piazza del Comune 1, Castellina in Chianti, ☎ 055/740201; ✉ Via Nazionale 42, Cortona, ☎ 0575/630352; ✉ Calata Italia 26, Portoferraio, ☎ 0565/914671; ✉ Via Luca Cini 1, Palazzo della Torre, Greve in Chianti, ☎ 055/8545243; ✉ Piazzale Verdi, Lucca, ☎ 0583/419689; ✉ Costa del Municipio 8, Montalcino, ☎ 0577/849331; ✉ Viale Verdi 66, 51016 Montecatini Terme, ☎ 0572/772244; ✉ Via Ricci 9, Montepulciano, ☎ 0578/758687; ✉ Strada Cassia 4, Località Colonna, Monteriggioni, ☎ 0577/304810; ✉ Palazzo Pubblico, Piazza Pio II, Pienza, ☎ 0578/749071; ✉ Piazza del Duomo 8, Pisa, ☎ 050/560464; ✉ Palazzo dei Vescovi, Via Roma 1, Pistoia, ☎ 0573/21622; ✉ Via Cairoli 48, Prato, ☎ 0574/24112; ✉ Piazza Ferrucci 1, Radda in Chianti, ☎ 0577/738494, open March–October only; ✉ Piazza del Duomo 1, San Gimignano, ☎ 0577/940008; ✉ Piazza del Popolo, San Miniato, ☎ 0571/42745; ✉ Piazza del Campo 56, Siena, ☎ 0577/280551; ✉ Via Turazza 2, Volterra, ☎ 0588/86150).

4 VENICE

It's easy to forgive Venice for its eternal preoccupation with its own beauty. All the picture books in the world won't prepare you for the city's exotic landmarks, such as the Basilica di San Marco and the Palazzo Ducale, rising like mirages from the lagoons. With sumptuous palaces and romantic waterways, Venice is straight out of an 18th-century Canaletto masterpiece.

Updated by
Carla Lionello
and Jon Eldan

IT IS CALLED LA SERENISSIMA. The literal translation of this name is ungainly: "the most serene." The term "Serene Republic" more successfully suggests the monstrous power and majesty of this city that was for centuries the unrivaled mistress of trade between Europe and the Orient and the staunch bulwark of Christendom against the tides of Turkish expansion. It suggests, too, the extraordinary beauty of the city—and surely Venice is the most beautiful city in the world (although the Florentines would surely disagree)—and its lavishness and fantasy, the result not just of its remarkable buildings but of the very fact that Venice is a city built on water, a city created more than 1,000 years ago by men who dared defy the sea, implanting their splendid palaces and churches on mud banks in a swampy and treacherous lagoon.

No matter how many times you have seen it in movies or TV commercials, the real thing is more surreal and dreamlike than you ever imagined. Its landmarks, the Basilica di San Marco and the Palazzo Ducale, seem hardly Italian: delightfully idiosyncratic, they are exotic mélanges of Byzantine, Gothic, and Renaissance styles. Sunlight shimmers and silvery mist softens every perspective here, a city renowned in the Renaissance for its artists' rendering of color. It is full of secrets, ineffably romantic, and—at times—given over entirely to pleasure.

Founded on the marshes by the Veneti escaping from the barbarians, Venice rose from the waters to dominate the Adriatic and hold the gorgeous East in fee. Early in its history the city called in Byzantine artists to decorate its churches with brilliant mosaics, still glittering today. Then the influence of Lombard-Romanesque architecture from the 11th to 13th centuries gave rise to the characteristic type of palace, typically built on two floors with a porticoed entrance at water level and a loggia on the first floor, for which Venice is famous the world over. Many of the sumptuous palaces along the Grand Canal were built at that time, strong reminders of Venice's control of the major trade routes to the East. Subsequently, Gothic styles from elsewhere in Europe were adapted to create a new kind of Venetian Gothic art and architecture.

Venice attained a peak of power and prosperity in the 15th and 16th centuries. It extended its domain inland to include all of what is now known as the Veneto region and even beyond. In the last half of the 15th century, the Renaissance arrived in Venice, and the city's greatest artists—Giovanni and Gentile Bellini and Carpaccio in the late 15th century; Giorgione, Titian, Veronese, and Tintoretto in the 16th century—played a decisive role in the development of Western art, and their work still covers walls and ceilings and altars all over the city today.

The decline of Venice came slowly. For 400 years the powerful maritime city-republic had held sway. After the 16th century the tide changed. The Ottoman Empire blocked Venice's Mediterranean trade routes, and newly emerging sea powers, such as Britain and the Netherlands, broke Venice's monopoly by opening oceanic trading routes. Like its steadily dwindling fortunes, Venice's art and culture began a prolonged decline, leaving only the splendid monuments to recall a fabled past, with the luminous paintings of Canaletto (1697–1768) and the beautiful frescoes of Giambattista Tiepolo striking a glorious swan song.

You must walk everywhere in Venice (Venezia in Italian) and where you cannot walk, you go by water. Occasionally, from fall to spring, you have to walk *in* water, when extraordinarily high tides known as *acque alte* invade the lower parts of the city, flooding Piazza San Marco for a few hours. The problem of protecting Venice and its lagoon from dangerously high tides has generated extravagant plans and so many committee reports (☞ Close-Up: Save La Serenissima, *below*), that the city may sink as much under the weight of paper as under water. Progress is being made, however. For centuries Venice's canals were regularly dredged to keep them clean and navigable. After nearly 30 years' neglect, the dredging of canals was finally resumed in 1993. It is hoped that waterless and malodorous canals (caused by *acqua bassa*—exceptionally low tides) will soon be a thing of the past. Today, Venetians are being encouraged by state subsidies to renovate their homes, rather than leave the city to live and work on the mainland—a trend that over the last three decades has drastically reduced Venice's resident population.

In spite of these problems, Venetians have mastered the art of living well in their singular city. You'll see them going about their daily affairs in *vaporetti* (water buses), crowded aboard the *traghetti* (traditional gondola ferries) that ply between the banks of the Grand Canal, in the *campi* (squares), and along the *calli* (narrow Venetian streets). They are nothing if not skilled—and remarkably tolerant—in dealing with the veritable armies of tourists from all over the world that at peak times inundate the city.

Pleasures and Pastimes

Carnevale

". . . All the world repaire to Venice to see the folly and madnesse of the Carnevall . . .'tis impossible to recount the universal madnesses of this place during this time of licence," commented traveler John Evelyn in 1646. Indeed, Carnevale (Carnival) was once an excuse for all manner of carnal indulgence. In its 18th-century heyday, festivities began on December 26 and lasted two months; the festival has since traded some of its more outlandish flavor for vast commercialization and lasts only for the 10 days preceding Ash Wednesday.

Dining

The general standard of Venetian restaurants has suffered from the onslaught of mass tourism, but it is still possible to eat well in Venice at moderate prices. A great Venetian tradition revolves around *bacari,* the local name for the little watering holes—called *osterie* elsewhere in Italy—where locals have gone for centuries to have a glass of wine, *cicchetti* (little savory snacks), and a chat. Venetian fish specialties include *sarde in saor* (layers of fried sardines, onions, pine nuts, and raisins), *baccalà mantecato* (dried cod with milk and olive oil) and *moeche* (soft-shell crabs), and *seppie in umido* (cuttlefish braised in tomato sauce).

Lodging

Most of Venice's hotels are in renovated palaces, but space is at a premium—and it comes for a price—with all Venice lodging. The most exclusive hotels are indeed palatial, although even they may have some small, dowdy Cinderella-type rooms. In lower categories, some rooms may be cramped, and not all hotels have lounging areas. Because of preservation laws, some hotels are not allowed to have elevators. Air-conditioning can be essential if you suffer in summer heat; some hotels charge a supplement for it. Although the city has no cars, it does have boats plying the canals and pedestrians chattering in the streets, even late at night, so ask for a quiet room if noise bothers you. During the summer months, don't leave your room lights on at night *and* your window wide open: mosquitoes can descend en masse.

EXPLORING VENICE

Piazza San Marco is unquestionably the heart of Venice. The city is made up of *sestiere,* or neighborhoods, among them San Marco, west of Piazza San Marco; Castello, east of San Marco; Cannaregio, to the northwest; Santa Croce and San Polo, roughly between the station and the Grand Canal; and Dorsoduro, diagonally across the Grand Canal from San Marco. Although the smaller canals (a canal is called a *rio*) are spanned by frequent bridges, the Grand Canal can only be crossed on foot at three points—Ponte degli Scalzi (near the train station), at the Ponte di Rialto, and at the Ponte dell'Accademia—which decidedly complicates matters. It's supremely maddening to find yourself on the wrong bank of a canal with no bridge in sight.

A street is called a *calle,* but a street that runs alongside a canal is called either a *riva* or a *fondamenta.* The closed-in streetscapes of Venice make it hard to see any reference point, such as the spire of the Campanile, above the rooftops, and the narrow backstreets often take unpredictable turns that confuse your sense of direction. Streets and canals may look deceptively familiar, only to make sudden dead ends. To get around Venice, you should use the vaporetti, which circulate through the city on set routes. A map of vaporetto routes, available at the train station, is always helpful.

A group of 13 Venetian churches selected for their artistic merit have begun charging admission (2,000 or 3,000 lire) for visitors during fixed hours that do not interfere with church services; they include Santa Maria del Giglio, Santo Stefano, Santa Maria Formosa, Santa Maria dei Miracoli, Santa Maria Gloriosa dei Frari, San Polo, San Giacomo dall'Orio, San Stae, Sant'Alvise, La Madonna dell'Orto, San Pietro di Castello, Il Redentore, and San Sebastiano. At these times there should always be someone to provide information there and a free leaflet (available in English). Postcards and booklets about these important sights are on sale. If you plan to visit more than a few, consider the cumulative ticket (one-day ticket for six churches, 10,000 lire; three-month ticket for all churches, 26,000 lire). New lighting systems have been installed in many sights; all take 500-lire coins. A combined ticket of 17,000 lire gains entry to the Palazzo Ducale, Museo Correr, Museo del Merletto on Burano, and Museo Vetrario on Murano.

Numbers in the text correspond to numbers in the margin and on the Venice map.

Great Itineraries

IF YOU HAVE 2 DAYS

Spend your first day visiting the sights in and around that most famous of squares, Piazza San Marco, including the Basilica di San Marco. Explore the adjoining neighborhoods San Zaccaria, the Mercerie (shopping district), and Sant'Angelo–Santo Stefano central quarters if you want to catch a glimpse of Venetian life. Make an early start the following day to explore the Rialto fish and produce market, then spend the rest of the morning cruising down the Grand Canal, stopping to visit the Gallerie dell'Accademia and the Ca' Rezzonico. Don't forget to walk over the Ponte di Rialto to the surrounding markets. End your day with a visit to San Stae, near Ca'Pesaro and the Chiesa di San Stae, a neighborhood particularly characteristic of Venice.

IF YOU HAVE 4 DAYS

Follow the itinerary above for the first two days. On the third day, visit the Campo dei Santi Giovanni e Paolo, northwest of the Castello, and the Campo dell'Arsenale, only a short walk from your next stop, the

Museo Storico Navale, in the Castello. Return to Piazza San Marco and take the 52 or 82 vaporetto line from San Zaccaria for a look at the impressive churches of San Giorgio Maggiore (on the island of San Giorgio Maggiore) and Redentore (on the Giudecca), both particularly beautiful at sunset. On your final day visit the islands of the lagoon: be sure not to miss Murano and its glass museums, along with the islands of Burano and Torcello.

IF YOU HAVE 6 DAYS

Start at Piazza San Marco, ending your day on the Ponte dei Sospiri next door. The next day cruise the Grand Canal, stopping at Santa Maria della Salute and the nearby Collezione Peggy Guggenheim, before visiting the Gallerie dell'Accademia. Next visit the Ca' Rezzonico and explore the Ponte di Rialto area. Spend the late afternoon walking through the neighborhood of San Stae. On the third day, visit Santa Maria dei Miracoli, Campo dei Santi Giovanni e Paolo, Campo dell'Arsenale, and finally the Museo Storico Navale. If you have time, try to visit San Pietro di Castello before returning to Piazza San Marco via the Scuola di San Giorgio degli Schiavoni. On the fourth day, take the 52 or 82 vaporetto line from San Zaccaria to explore San Giorgio Maggiore and the Giudecca. Head directly across from the Giudecca to the Zattere, a lively Dorsoduro promenade with lots of pizzerias. Spend the fifth day exploring Titian's works: start in Campo Santo Stefano and then head for the Scuola dei Carmini and the Chiesa di San Sebastiano. A must is the Frari, home of some of Titian's best. Next, visit the Scuola Grande di San Rocco, with delightful paintings by Tintoretto. On your final day explore the islands of the lagoon. If you can, squeeze in a visit to the cemetery island, Cimitero San Michele.

Piazza San Marco, the Heart of Venice

The most evocative square in the world, Piazza San Marco is the heart of Venice, a vast open square enclosed by an orderly procession of arcades marching toward the fairy-tale cupolas and marble lacework of the Basilica di San Marco. Perpetually animated during the day when it's filled with people and crowds of fluttering pigeons, it can be magical at night, especially in the winter, when melancholy mists swirl around the lampposts and bell tower.

A Good Walk

Start your day in the **Piazza San Marco** ① with a morning visit to the **Basilica di San Marco** ②, home of the Pala d'Oro and the Museo di San Marco. Next, get a bird's-eye view of the piazza and city from the **Campanile** ③. Move on to the smaller **Piazzetta San Marco** for a visit to the glorious **Palazzo Ducale** ④ and a look at the Ponte dei Sospiri at the east wing of the palace. Return to Piazza San Marco where directly opposite the facade of the basilica you will find the **Museo Correr** ⑤ in the Ala Napoleonica.

TIMING

You'll need a full day to visit each sight thoroughly. If you have limited time, you will need to discipline yourself from straying too far from the Piazza San Marco; a half day should be enough to see the essential sights, but do not miss the Pala d'Oro in the basilica, the Palazzo Ducale, and, of course, the piazza itself. If you come in summer, like the Venetians, you will have to adapt to the crowds, visiting at odd hours to avoid tour groups.

Sights to See

★ ❷ **Basilica di San Marco.** An opulent synthesis of Byzantine and Romanesque styles, Venice's gem is laid out in a Greek cross topped off with five plump domes. The basilica did not actually become the cathedral of Venice until as late as 1807, but its role as the church of the doge gave it immense power and wealth. It was begun in 1063, and inaugurated in 1094, to house the remains of St. Mark the Evangelist, which were filched from Alexandria two centuries earlier by two agents of the doge. The story goes that they stole the saint's remains and hid them in a barrel under layers of pickled pork to get them past the Muslim guards. The escapade is illustrated in a mosaic in the semicircular lunette over the farthest left of the front doors. This 13th-century mosaic is the earliest one on this heavily decorated facade; look at it closely to see a picture of the church as it appeared at that time.

Over the years this church stood as a symbol of Venetian wealth and power, and it was endowed with all the riches the Republic's admirals and merchants could carry off from the Orient, earning it the nickname Chiesa d'Oro (Golden Church). The four bronze horses that prance and snort over the central doorway (copies only, but the originals are on view indoors in the Museo di San Marco, (☞ *below*) were classical sculptures that victorious Venetians took away from Constantinople in 1204, along with a lot of other loot on display here. Just inside the central front doors in the church porch is a medallion of red porphyry set in the floor to mark the spot of another of Venice's political coups: the reconciliation between Barbarossa, the Holy Roman Emperor, and Pope Alexander III (circa 1105–81), brought about by Doge Sebastiano Ziani in 1177.

One of the innovations of this church was a roof of brick vaulting, rather than wood, which enabled the ceiling to be decorated with mosaics. As you enter the basilica, you'll find it surprisingly dark inside, compared to the soaring light-filled Gothic cathedrals of northern Europe. This is because many of the original windows were filled in and covered with even more mosaics. In the mysterious dusk, candles flicker and the gold tiles of mosaics glitter softly, sensuously. (The tiles were laid on at slight angles to achieve precisely this effect.) The earliest mosaics are from the 11th and 12th centuries; later ones were done as late as the 16th century, such as the *Last Judgment* on the arch between the porch and the nave, said to be based on drawings by Tintoretto (1518–94). The dim light, the galleries high above the naves—they served as the *matroneum* (women's gallery)—the massive altar screen, or iconostasis, the single massive Byzantine chandelier, even the Greek cross ground plan, give San Marco an exotic feel quite unlike that of most Christian churches. The effect is remarkable. Here the pomp and mystery of Oriental magnificence are wedded to Christian belief, creating an intensely awesome impression.

To the right, just off the porch, step into the **Cappella Zen** (Zen Chapel), named after a local cardinal rather than any form of Buddhism, to see some earlier (13th-century) mosaics, telling the story of the life of St. Mark. Next to it, the **Battistero** (Baptistery) contains a bronze font cover by Sansovino (1486–1570) and the tomb of Doge Andrea Dandolo (1307–54), a friend of Petrarch (1304–74) and a writer in his own right. Several of the earlier doges were buried here, while later ones were interred in the Chiesa dei Santi Giovanni e Paolo (☞ *below*). Two more chapels, both in the left transept, are worth a special look: the **Cappella della Madonna di Nicopeia** (Chapel of the Madonna of Nicopeia), which holds a precious icon (part of the loot from Constantinople) that many consider Venice's most powerful protector. Nearby is the **Cappella della Madonna dei Mascoli,** where the Virgin Mary was worshiped by a male confraternity (*mascoli*), with fine 15th-century mosaics depicting her life, possibly based on drawings by Jacopo Bellini (1400–70).

The **Santuario** (Sanctuary) in the Basilica of San Marco is well worth the modest admission fee. The main altar, with its green marble canopy lifted high on carved alabaster columns, covers the tomb of St. Mark. Behind this is the real attraction: the extraordinarily sumptuous **Pala d'Oro** (Golden Altarpiece), a dazzling gilded silver screen encrusted with 1,927 precious gems and 255 enameled panels. It was originally made in Constantinople in the 11th century, and then continually embellished over the next three centuries by Byzantine and Venetian master craftsmen. The bronze door leading from the sanctuary back into the sacristy is another work by Sansovino; check out the top left corner, where the artist included a self-portrait and, above that, a picture of his friend and fellow artist Titian (circa 1485–1576). Tickets for the Sanctuary also include admission to the **Tesoro** (Treasury), entered from the right transept. Many of the exquisite pieces are exotic treasures borne away from Constantinople and other vanquished places.

From the atrium, climb the steep stairway to the **Galleria** and the **Museo di San Marco** for a look at the interior of the church from the organ gallery and a sweeping view of Piazza San Marco and the Piazzetta dei Leoncini from the outdoor gallery. The highlight of the museum is the close-up of the four magnificent gilded bronze horses that once stood outside on the gallery. The originals were probably cast in Imperial Rome, and later transported to the New Rome, Constantinople. Napoléon hauled them off to Paris after he conquered Venice in 1797, but they were returned after the fall of the French Empire. Be warned: guards at the door turn away any visitors, male or female, wearing shorts, short skirts, tank tops, and other attire considered inappropriate. If you want to take a free guided tour in English in summer (with less certainty in winter, since the guides are volunteers), wait on the left in the porch for a group to form. ✉ *Piazza San Marco,* ☎ *041/5225205. Basilica:* 🎫 *Free.* ⏲ *Mon.–Sat. 9:45–4:30, Sun. 1–4:30. Sanctuary, Pala d'Oro, and Treasury:* 🎫 *3,000 lire, free for those with the combined church admission ticket.* ⏲ *Same as basilica, last entry 30 mins before closing. Gallery and Museum:* ☎ *041/5225205.* 🎫 *4,000 lire.* ⏲ *Same as basilica, last entry 30 mins before closing. Tours:* 🎫 *free.* ⏲ *June–Aug., Mon.–Sat. several tours daily.*

★ ❸ **Campanile.** The brick Bell Tower is a reconstruction of the original, which stood for 1,000 years before it collapsed one morning in 1912, practically without warning (miraculously none of the surrounding buildings suffered serious damage, and the only victim was a cat). In the 15th century, clerics found guilty of immoral behavior were suspended in wooden cages from the tower, sometimes to subsist on bread and water for as long as a year, other times to starve to death. The pretty marble loggia (covered gallery) at its base was built in the early 16th century by Sansovino. The view from the tower on a clear day—the Lido, the lagoon, and the mainland as far as the Alps—oddly doesn't include the myriad canals that snake through the 117 islets on which Venice is built. ✉ *Piazza San Marco,* ☎ *041/5224064.* 🎫 *8,000 lire.* ⏲ *June–Sept., daily 9:30–10; Oct.–May, daily 9:30–4:15; last entry 30 mins before closing. Closed 2 wks in Jan.*

❺ **Museo Correr.** In 1830 the aristocrat Teodoro Correr donated his private collection—a fascinating, diverse mix of historical items and old master paintings—to the city. Exhibits range from the absurdly high-soled shoes worn by 16th-century Venetian ladies (who had to be supported by a servant on each side to walk on these precarious perches) to fine art by the talented Bellini family of Renaissance painters. ✉ *Piazza San Marco, Ala Napoleonica,* ☎ *041/5225625.* 🎫 *17,000 lire combined ticket includes entrance to Palazzo Ducale, Museo Vetrario,* *and Museo del Merletto (☞ below). ⏲ Apr.–Oct., daily 9–7; Nov.–Mar., daily 9–5; last entry 1 hr before closing.*

★ 4 **Palazzo Ducale** (Doge's Palace). This Gothic-Renaissance fantasia of pink-and-white marble, a majestic expression of the prosperity and power attained by Venice during its most glorious period, rises above Piazzetta San Marco. Its top-heavy design (the dense upper floors rest on the graceful ground-floor colonnade) has always confounded architectural purists, who insist that proper architecture be set out the other way around. The building was much more than just a palace—rather it was a sort of combination White House, Senate, torture chamber, and prison rolled into one. Venice's government, set up sometime in the 7th century as a participatory democracy, provided for an elected ruler, the doge, to serve for life, but in practice he was simply a figurehead. Power really rested with the Great Council, originally an elected body but, from the 13th century on, an aristocratic stronghold, with members inheriting their seats from their noble ancestors. Laws were passed by the Senate, a group of 200 elected from the Great Council (which could have as many as 1,700 members). Executive powers belonged to the College, a committee of 25 leaders. In the 14th century, the Council of Ten was formed to deal with emergency situations; though it was often more powerful than the Senate, its members could only serve for limited terms.

A fortress for the doge existed on this spot in the early 9th century; the building you see today was a product of the 12th century, although, like the basilica next door, it was continually added to and transformed throughout the centuries. You enter the palace at the ornate Gothic **Porta della Carta** (Gate of the Paper), where official decrees were traditionally posted; it opens onto an immense courtyard. Ahead is the **Scala dei Giganti** (Stairway of the Giants), guarded by huge statues of Mars and Neptune by Sansovino. Ordinary mortals do not get to climb these stairs, however; after paying your fee, walk along the arcade to reach the central interior staircase. Its upper flight is called the **Scala d'Oro** (Golden Staircase), also designed by Sansovino, with its lavish gilded decoration. Although it may seem odd that the government's main council rooms and reception halls would be so far upstairs, imagine how effectively foreign emissaries must have been intimidated by this arduous climb.

Visitors must have also been overwhelmed by the sumptuous decoration of these apartments, their walls and ceilings covered with works by Venice's greatest artists. Among the grand rooms you can visit are the **Anticollegio,** a waiting room outside the Collegio's chamber with two fine paintings, Tintoretto's *Bacchus and Ariadne Crowned by Venus* and Veronese's (1528–88) *Rape of Europa;* the **Sala del Collegio** (College Chamber), its ceiling magnificently painted by Veronese; and the **Sala del Senato** (Senate Chamber), with Tintoretto's *Triumph of Venice* on the ceiling. The huge *Paradise* on the end wall of the **Sala del Maggior Consiglio** (Great Council Hall) is by Tintoretto; it is a dark, dynamic masterpiece. This is the world's largest oil painting (23 × 75 ft), a vast work commissioned for a vast hall. The massive carved and gilded ceiling is breathtaking, even dizzying, as you wheel around searching for the best vantage point from which to admire Veronese's majestic *Apotheosis of Venice* filling one of the center panels. Look at the frieze of portraits of the first 76 doges around the upper part of the walls. One portrait is missing: a black painted curtain near the left-hand corner of the wall opposite Tintoretto's painting marks the spot where the portrait of doge Marin Falier should be. A Latin inscription bluntly explains that Falier was executed for treason in 1355. The Republic never forgave him.

Venice

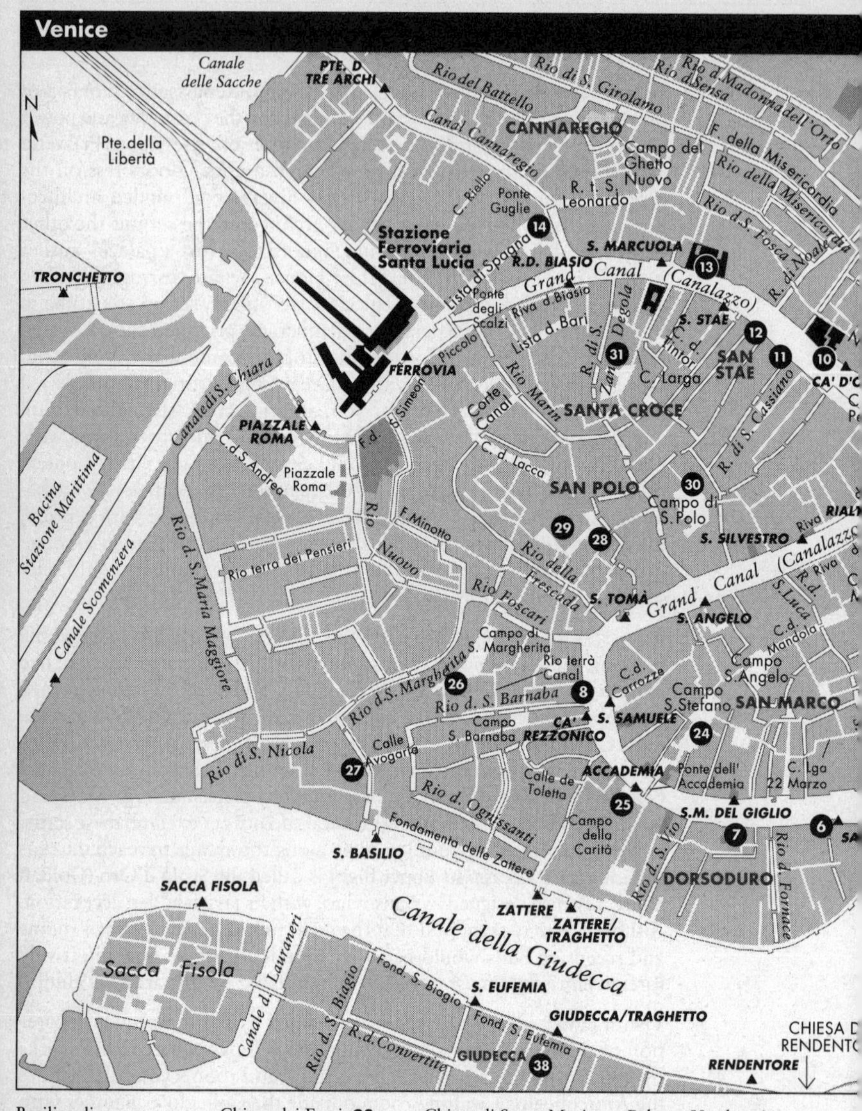

Basilica di San Marco, **2**
Ca' d'Oro, **10**
Ca' Pesaro, **12**
Ca' Rezzonico, **8**
Campanile, **3**
Campo dei Santi Giovanni e Paolo, **17**
Campo dell'Arsenale, **20**
Campo San Giacomo dall'Orio, **31**
Campo San Polo, **30**
Campo Santo Stefano, **24**
Chiesa dei Frari, **28**
Chiesa dei Gesuiti, **32**
Chiesa di San Francesco della Vigna, **19**
Chiesa di San Giorgio Maggiore, **37**
Chiesa di San Pietro di Castello, **22**
Chiesa di San Sebastiano, **27**
Chiesa di Santa Maria dei Miracoli, **16**
Chiesa di Santa Maria della Salute, **6**
Chiesa di Santa Maria Formosa, **15**
Collezione Peggy Guggenheim, **7**
Gallerie dell'Accademia, **25**
Giudecca, **38**
Museo Correr, **5**
Museo Storico Navale, **21**
Ospedaletto, **18**
Palazzo Corner della Regina, **11**
Palazzo Ducale, **4**
Palazzo Labia, **14**
Palazzo Vendramin-Calergi, **13**
Piazza San Marco, **1**
Ponte di Rialto, **9**
Scuola dei Carmini, **26**
Scuola di San Giorgio degli Schiavoni, **23**
Scuola Grande di San Rocco, **29**

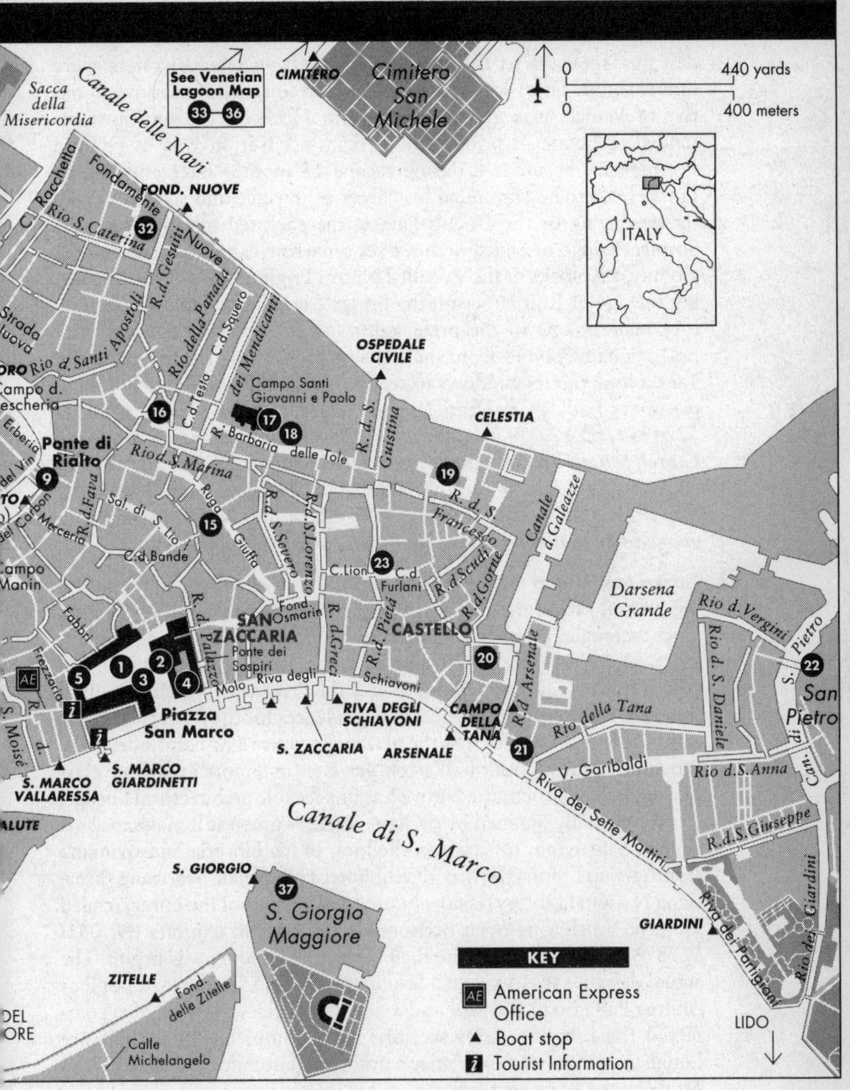

See Venetian Lagoon Map
33–36
CIMITERO
Cimitero San Michele
440 yards
400 meters
ITALY
Sacca della Misericordia
Canale delle Navi
FOND. NUOVE
Fondamente Nuove
OSPEDALE CIVILE
CELESTIA
Campo Santi Giovanni e Paolo
Ponte di Rialto
Darsena Grande
SAN ZACCARIA
CASTELLO
Ponte dei Sospiri
Piazza San Marco
RIVA DEGLI SCHIAVONI
S. ZACCARIA
ARSENALE
CAMPO DELLA TANA
S. MARCO GIARDINETTI
S. MARCO VALLARESSA
Canale di S. Marco
Riva dei Sette Martiri
V. Garibaldi
S. GIORGIO
S. Giorgio Maggiore
ZITELLE
Fond. delle Zitelle
Calle Michelangelo
GIARDINI
Riva dei Partigiani
San Pietro
LIDO
KEY
American Express Office
Boat stop
Tourist Information

A guided tour of the palace's secret rooms takes you to the doge's private apartments, up into the attic and Piombi prison, and through hidden passageways to the torture chambers, where prisoners were interrogated. The 18th-century writer and libertine, Casanova, a native of Venice, was imprisoned here in 1755, having somehow offended someone in power (the official accusation was of being a Freemason); he made a daring escape 15 months later and fled to France, where he continued his career of intrigue and scandal. From the east wing of the Doge's Palace, the enclosed marble **Ponte dei Sospiri** (Bridge of Sighs) arches over a narrow canal to the cramped, gloomy cell blocks of the so-called Nuova Prigione (New Prison). During the age of Romanticism, the bridge's tragic and melancholic history made it one of the prize sights for 19th-century tourists. The bridge's name comes from the sighs of those being led to execution. Take a look out its windows to see the last earthly view many of these prisoners had. ✉ *Palazzo Ducale, Piazzetta San Marco,* ☎ *041/5224951.* 🎫 *17,000 lire combined ticket includes entrance to Museo Correr, Museo Vetrario, and Museo del Merletto (☞ above and below).* ⏲ *Apr.–Oct., daily 9–7; Nov.–Mar., daily 9–5; last entry 1½ hrs before closing. "Secret Itineraries" tour:* 🎫 *24,000 lire.* ⏲ *English-language tours usually daily at 10:30, reservations mandatory.*

★ ❶ **Piazza San Marco** (St. Mark's Square). If you stand at the far end of the piazza, facing the basilica, you'll notice that rather than being a strict rectangle, it opens wider at the basilica end, enhancing the perspective and creating the illusion of being even larger than it is. On your left, the long arcaded building is the **Procuratie Vecchie,** built in the early 16th century as offices and residences for the powerful Procurators of San Marco. Across the piazza, on your right-hand side, is the **Procuratie Nuove,** built half a century later in a more grandiose classical style. The Procuratie Nuove has impeccable architectural lineage: it was originally planned by perhaps Venice's greatest Renaissance architect, Sansovino, to carry on the look of his **Libreria Sansoviniana** (Sansovinian Library), where the **Biblioteca Nazionale Marciana** (Marciana National Library) is now housed (an old part of the library, called Libreria Vecchia, is open occasionally for special exhibits (☎ 041/5208788), though Sansovino died before the building was begun. The actual designer was Vincenzo Scamozzi (circa 1552–1616), a pupil of Andrea Palladio (1508–80) and a devout neoclassicist who also completed the Libreria; later sections were completed by Baldassare Longhena (1598–1682), Venice's other great architect, who belonged firmly to the Baroque tradition.

When Napoléon (1769–1821) entered Venice with his troops in 1797, he called Piazza San Marco "the world's most beautiful drawing room"—and promptly gave orders to redecorate it. His architects demolished a 16th-century church, with a facade designed by Sansovino, that stood behind you, at the end of the square farthest from the basilica, and put up the **Ala Napoleonica** (Napoleonic Wing), or Fabbrica Nuova (New Building), to unite the two 16th-century buildings on either side.

NEED A BREAK?

On the Procuratie Vecchie side of Piazza San Marco is the historic **Caffè Quadri** (☎ 041/5289299), closed Mondays November–March, shunned by Venetians during the 19th century when the occupying Austrians made it their gathering place. **Caffè Florian** (☎ 041/5285338), closed Wednesdays November–March, on the Procuratie Nuove side, is where Casanova, Wagner, and Proust regularly visited.

Piazzetta San Marco. This square leads from Piazza San Marco down to the waters of the Bacino di San Marco (St. Mark's Basin). This landing stage, now crowded with excursion boats, was once the grand entrance to the Republic. Two tall columns rise here on the waterfront: one is topped by the winged lion, a traditional emblem of St. Mark that became by extension the symbol of Venice itself; the other bears aloft a statue of St. Theodore (the first patron saint of Venice) and his dragon.

Torre dell'Orologio. Erected in 1496, the Clock Tower has an enameled timepiece and animated figures of Moors that strike the hour (HORAS NON NUMERO NISI SERENAS says the inscription on the tower—"Only happy hours"). During Ascension Week (40 days after Easter) and on the Epiphany (January 6), an angel and three wise men go in and out of the doors and bow to the Virgin Mary. It is closed for restoration until at least 2000. ✉ *Northern side of Piazza San Marco.*

Along the Grand Canal

Venetians call it the Canalazzo, but to the rest of the world it's the Grand Canal, the city's main thoroughfare. A 3-km- (2-mi-) long, 40- to 76-yard-wide ribbon of water, wending its way from San Marco to the Stazione Ferroviaria Santa Lucia like an inverted letter *S,* it was, and to some extent still is, the Fifth Avenue of Venice. It was here, from the 14th to 18th centuries, that the city's richest families lived, building for themselves a series of magnificent Venetian Gothic and Renaissance palaces—200 at last count—remarkable even by the city's standards. Here, the combination of being surrounded by water and the most opulent, luxurious, and fantastic efforts of a people obsessed with opulence, luxury, and fantasy has created a seemingly endless unfolding panorama of unique architectural richness. It makes sense to attempt little more at first than to sample, to breathe in, the unparalleled magnificence of the Grand Canal, letting it wash over you—only metaphorically, of course; it may not be deep (average depth is 9 ft) but it's very dirty. To begin your exploration, catch Vaporetto 1 at the San Marco landing stage. Don't forget to return for a gondola ride an hour or so before sunset; this is the most romantic way to see Venice. However, for an overall sightseeing tour of the canal, you get a better, more extensive view from a vaporetto—which is both higher in the water and much less expensive. Try to get one of the coveted seats in the prow, where you have a clear view. Once off the vaporetto, keep in mind the two-man traghetti that allow you—at many points along the Canalazzo—to ferry across from one bank to the other for only 700 lire.

A Good Boat Trip

As you leave Piazza San Marco on the vaporetto, **Chiesa di Santa Maria della Salute** ⑥, the huge, white, domed 17th-century Baroque church designed by Longhena, is on the left. Not far from this stop is the small **Collezione Peggy Guggenheim** ⑦, filled with engaging 20th-century works, a nice departure from the cinquecento. Across the canal you can see the imposing terraced front of the **Gritti Palace** hotel (☞ Lodging, *below*), which occupies the former Palazzo Pisani. A few minutes farther on (after passing the Gallerie dell'Accademia, ☞ *below*), on the left bank at the Ca' Rezzonico stop is Longhena's Baroque **Ca' Rezzonico** ⑧. Be sure to visit the Museo del Settecento Veneziano, housed here in gilded salons. The canal narrows and boat traffic increases as you approach the **Ponte di Rialto** ⑨, arched high over the canal. The Ca' d'Oro landing on the right, just beyond the Rialto, marks the lovely Venetian Gothic palace of **Ca' d'Oro** ⑩. Across the canal from the Ca' d'Oro, you'll see the classical facade, with loggias on two stories, of the **Palazzo Corner della Regina** ⑪. Just beyond the Corner della Regina you can't miss the imposing bulk of the grand

Baroque **Ca' Pesaro** ⑫, designed by Longhena, and unfortunately closed for restoration until 2001. Not far beyond, on the left, another white church is adorned with Baroque statues; this is the Chiesa di San Stae, and the landing here is a gateway to an untrammeled San Stae neighborhood, with its narrow canals and airy squares. Back on the right bank, the Renaissance **Palazzo Vendramin-Calergi** ⑬ is now the winter home of Venice's glamorous Casino (☞ Nightlife and the Arts, *below*). Continuing along the Grand Canal, winding toward the railway station, you will see on your right the 16th-century Ponte delle Guglie, famed for its spires and adjacent to the elegant facade of **Palazzo Labia** ⑭.

TIMING

All these sights can be comfortably visited in one day. Jumping on and off the vaporetto is easy, although you may be tempted just to take the ride and view the sights from the canal.

Sights to See

⑩ **Ca' d'Oro.** This lovely Venetian Gothic palace is adorned with marble traceries and ornaments once embellished with pure gold. Today it houses the **Galleria Franchetti,** a fine collection of tapestries, sculptures, and paintings. ✉ *Calle della Ca' d'Oro, 3933 Cannaregio,* ☎ *041/5238790.* 🎫 *6,000 lire.* ⏲ *Daily 9–2.*

⑫ **Ca' Pesaro.** Designed by Longhena in grand Baroque style, the palace is now home to two rather dull art collections, the **Museo Orientale** (Oriental Art Museum) and the **Galleria d'Arte Moderna** (Modern Art Gallery), containing mostly 19th-century and some 20th-century works. ✉ *San Stae, Santa Croce,* ☎ *041/5241173.* 🎫 *4,000 lire.* ⏲ *Museo Orientale: Tues.–Sun. 9–2, last entry 30 mins before closing. Galleria d'Arte Moderna closed for restoration until 2001.*

★ ⑧ **Ca' Rezzonico.** In this huge Baroque mansion you'll find Venice's most magnificent ballroom—site of Venice's greatest costume ball, the last of which was held in the 1960s to honor Elizabeth Taylor and Richard Burton. Longhena began work on it in the 1660s, and it was completed by architect Giorgio Massari in the 1740s. This was the English poet Robert Browning's (1812–89) last home, where he died. The **Museo del Settecento Veneziano** (Museum of 18th-Century Venice), housed in gilded salons, is closed for restoration through about 2001. Pictures by the 18th-century Venetian painters Francesco (1712–93) and Gianantonio (1699–1760) Guardi and Pietro Longhi (1702–85), and a fine series of frescoes by their younger contemporary Giandomenico Tiepolo (1727–1804) at the back of the palace, really open a window onto that charming and delightfully frivolous social era. ✉ *Fondamenta Pedrocco, 3136 Dorsoduro,* ☎ *041/2410100.* 🎫 *12,000 lire. Museum closed until 2000.*

⑥ **Chiesa di Santa Maria della Salute.** Longhena designed this huge, white, domed 17th-century Baroque church. ✉ *Punta della Dogana, Dorsoduro.* ☎ *041/731268.* ⏲ *Daily 10–noon and 4–6.*

⑦ **Collezione Peggy Guggenheim.** Visit and delight in this small but choice gallery of 20th-century painting and sculpture in the heiress's lavish former apartments in the Palazzo Venier dei Leoni. Through wealth and social connections, Guggenheim (1898–1979) became a serious patron of art—she was once married to the painter Max Ernst—and her holdings include several works by Picasso, Kandinsky, Ernst, Pollock, and Motherwell. ✉ *Entrance on Calle San Cristoforo, 701 Dorsoduro,* ☎ *041/5206288.* 🎫 *12,000 lire.* ⏲ *Wed.–Mon. 11–6.*

⓫ **Palazzo Corner della Regina.** Now housing the Biennale's library, this palace is among the most beautiful in Venice. It was built in 1724 and named after the *regina* (queen) of Cyprus, Caterina Cornaro, who was born in an older palace on this site. On the second floor is a *portego*—a hall running the length of a palace, a feature typical of Venetian palazzi. ✉ *Calle della Regina, San Stae,* ☎ *041/5218701.* *Free. Closed for restoration until 2000.*

⓮ **Palazzo Labia.** Once the palatial stamping grounds of Venice's showiest 18th-century family, the palace today is the Venetian headquarters of RAI, the Italian radio and television giant. It is hard to imagine a broadcasting company in any other country establishing itself among such opulent splendor, however apt in Italy. The **Tiepolo Room,** a gorgeous ballroom in the palazzo, exhibits the final flowering of Venetian painting: Giambattista Tiepolo's (1696–1770) illusionistic frescoes of Antony and Cleopatra, teeming with dwarfs, Barbary pirates, and toy dogs. The artist's true sense of pleasure is evident. ✉ *Campo San Geremia, Cannaregio,* ☎ *041/5242812.* *Free.* *Wed., Thurs., and Fri. 3–4 (by appointment only).*

⓭ **Palazzo Vendramin-Calergi.** In 1883 the great German composer Wagner (1813–83) died in this Renaissance palazzo designed by Mauro Coducci (1440–1504) in white stone with red marble medallions and an imposing carved frieze. It is now the winter home of Venice's glamorous **Casino** (☞ Nightlife and the Arts, *below*).

★ ❾ **Ponte di Rialto** (Rialto Bridge). The canal narrows and boat traffic increases as you approach this bridge arched high over the canal. The windows are those of the shops inside. The surrounding area is a commercial hub, with open-air vegetable, fruit, and fish markets and an upscale shopping district.

Castello to San Pietro

Some of Venice's most beautiful churches and campi are north of Piazza San Marco and in the eastern part of town, in the picturesque sestiere of Castello, reachable by way of the Mercerie district. One of the city's busiest areas, this mesh of upscale shopping streets (Merceria dell'Orologio, Merceria di San Zulian, Merceria del Capitello, Merceria di San Salvador, and Merceria 2 Aprile) leads more or less directly from the Piazza San Marco north to Campo Santa Maria Formosa, or, alternatively, west to the Rialto Bridge. The island of San Pietro, farther east, is also home to one of these churches.

A Good Walk

Head out of Piazza San Marco under the clock tower onto the Mercerie. At Campo San Zulian and the church of San Giuliano, turn right onto Calle Guerra and Calle delle Bande to reach the white marble **Chiesa di Santa Maria Formosa** ⑮. Follow Calle Borgoloco into Campo San Marina, where you turn right, cross the little canal, and take Calle Castelli to the **Chiesa di Santa Maria dei Miracoli** ⑯. Behind the church, bear right to Calle Larga Giacinto Gallina, which leads to **Campo dei Santi Giovanni e Paolo** ⑰, site of the massive Dominican Chiesa dei Santi Giovanni e Paolo, or San Zanipolo. The powerful equestrian monument of Bartolomeo Colleoni, by Florentine sculptor Andrea del Verrocchio (1435–88), stands in the square.

Behind the east end of San Zanipolo, on Barbaria del le Tole, is the church of Santa Maria dei Derelitti, with its over-the-top Baroque facade by Longhena, and the attached **Ospedaletto** ⑱. Continue beyond the Ospedaletto to another large church, **Chiesa di San Francesco della Vigna** ⑲, with its stern classical Palladian facade. Go left as you leave the church to begin the 500-yard walk to the **Campo dell'Arsenale** ⑳, the main entrance to the immense arsenal dockyard. The **Museo Storico Navale** ㉑ on nearby Campo San Biagio has four floors of scale boat models. If you still have time and energy, go east to the island and the **Chiesa di San Pietro di Castello** ㉒; two footbridges lead to this island. About midway between the Arsenal and Piazza San Marco, on your way back from the eastern district, is the **Scuola di San Giorgio degli Schiavoni** ㉓.

TIMING

An exploration of this neighborhood and as far east as the island of San Pietro should take four to five hours. Try to avoid walking around this mostly open neighborhood during the hottest hours of the day if you plan to travel in summer. Allow some time to browse through the Mercerie district.

Sights to See

★ ⑰ **Campo dei Santi Giovanni e Paolo.** This large square has the massive Dominican Chiesa dei Santi Giovanni e Paolo—or San Zanipolo as it's known in Venetian dialect—on one side, and the powerful equestrian Monumento di Bartolomeo Colleoni by Florentine sculptor Andrea del Verrocchio on the other. Colleoni had served Venice well as a *condottiere,* or mercenary commander (the Venetians preferred to pay others to fight for them on land). When he died in 1475, he left his fortune to the city on the condition that a statue be erected in his honor "in the piazza before St. Mark's." The republic's shrewd administrators coveted Colleoni's ducats but had no intention of honoring anyone, no matter how valorous, with a statue in Piazza San Marco. So they commissioned the statue and put it up before the Scuola di San Marco, which is off to the side and the headquarters of a charitable confraternity, enabling them to collect the loot. San Zanipolo contains tombs of several doges, as well as a wealth of art. Don't miss the Cappella del Rosario (Rosary Chapel), off the left transept; with its Veronese ceiling paintings, it's a sumptuous study in decoration, built in the 16th century to commemorate the victory of Lepanto in western Greece in 1571, when Venice and a combined European fleet succeeded in destroying the Turkish navy. ✉ *Campo SS. Giovanni e Paolo,* ☎ *041/5237510.* ⊙ *Mon.–Sat. 8–12:30 and 3–6, Sun. 3–6.*

⑳ **Campo dell'Arsenale.** The immense Arsenale (Arsenal) dockyard was founded in 1104 to build and equip the fleet of the Venetian republic. It was augmented continually through the 16th century. For a republic founded on sea might, having a huge state-of-the-art shipyard was of paramount importance, and this one was renowned for its size and skill. All subsequent dockyards were named after it (the name comes from the Arabic *d'arsina,* meaning workshop). No wonder it has such a grandiose entrance, with four stone lions from ancient Greece guarding the great Renaissance gateway. ✉ *Arsenale, Castello.*

⑲ **Chiesa di San Francesco della Vigna** (St. Francis of the Vineyard). This large and austere classical Palladian church was built by Sansovino in 1534. A pretty cloister opens out from the severely simple and unadorned gray-and-white interior, its works of art minor and not particularly interesting. ✉ *Campo di San Francesco della Vigna, Castello,* ☎ *041/5206102.* ⊙ *Mon.–Sat. 8–noon and 3–7, Sun. 3–7.*

㉒ **Chiesa di San Pietro di Castello.** On the island of San Pietro, connected to the mainland by two footbridges, this church served as Venice's cathedral for centuries. It now presides over a picturesque workaday neighborhood, and its slanted bell tower leans over a grassy square. ✉ *Campo San Pietro Apostolo, Castello,* ☎ *041/5238950.* 🎫 *2,000 lire.* ⊙ *Mon.–Sat. 10–5, Sun. 1–5.*

(16) **Chiesa di Santa Maria dei Miracoli.** Perfectly proportioned and sheathed in marble, this church is an early Renaissance gem, decorated inside with exquisite marble reliefs. Notice how the architect, Pietro Lombardo (circa 1435–1515), made the church look bigger with various optical illusions: varying the color of the exterior marble to create the effect of distance; using extra pilasters to make the building's canal side look longer; slightly offsetting the arcade windows to make the arches look deeper. The church was built in the 1480s to house an image of the Virgin Mary that is said to perform miracles—look for this icon on the high altar. The church reopened in 1998 after a three-year restoration to slow down the effects of saltwater erosion (☞ Close-Up: Save La Serenissima, *below*). ⊠ *Calle delle Erbe, Castello,* ☎ *041/5235293.* *2,000 lire.* *Mon.–Sat. 10–5, Sun. 1–5.*

(15) **Chiesa di Santa Maria Formosa.** This graceful white marble church was inspired by a vision of *una Madonna formosa* (a buxom Madonna) that appeared to Saint Magno in the 7th century. The matronly Madonna told him to follow a small white cloud and build a church wherever it settled. The present building, built by Coducci in 1492, was grafted on to the foundations of an earlier 11th-century church that replaced Magno's original. The church's interior is a unique architectural blend, merging a welter of Renaissance decoration with Coducci's ersatz collection of Byzantine cupolas, barrel vaults, and narrow-columned screens. Of interest are two fine paintings, Bartolomeo Vivarini's *Madonna of the Misericordia* and Palma Vecchio's *Santa Barbara.* Outside there is a lively square with a few sidewalk cafés and a small vegetable market on weekday mornings. ⊠ *Campo Santa Maria Formosa, Castello,* ☎ *041/5234645.* *2,000 lire.* *Mon.–Sat. 10–5, Sun. 1–5.*

(21) **Museo Storico Navale** (Museum of Naval History). Four floors of scale boat models and an annex containing actual boats—from gondolas to doges' ceremonial boats—are guaranteed to fascinate children and boat lovers. ⊠ *Campo San Biagio, Arsenale, Castello,* ☎ *041/5200276.* *2,000 lire.* *Mon.–Fri. 8:45–1:30, Sat. 8:45–1.*

(18) **Ospedaletto.** Literally little hospital, this was founded in the 16th century and was one of Venice's four foundling hospitals. The church of **Santa Maria dei Derelitti** (St. Mary of the Destitute) is next to the Ospedaletto. Each hospital had an orchestra and choir of little orphans (one of which was presided over by Antonio Vivaldi). Note the large gallery above the Derelitti's altar, built to accommodate the young musicians. The orphanage is now an old people's home, but the beautiful 18th-century **Sala della Musica** (Music Room), where rehearsals took place and patrons and honored guests were received—the only one of its kind to survive—has been magnificently restored and can be visited (enter through the church). On the Music Room's end wall is a lovely fresco by Jacopo Guarana (1720–1808), depicting Apollo, the God of Music, surrounded by the orphan musicians conducted by their music master, Pasquale Anfossi. ⊠ *Barbaria de le Tole, Castello.* *Free; donations appreciated.* *Church and Music Room: Apr.–Sept., Thurs.–Sat. 4–7; Oct.–Mar., Thurs.–Sat. 3–6.*

(23) **Scuola di San Giorgio degli Schiavoni.** This is one of numerous *scuole* built during the time of the Republic. These weren't schools, as the present-day Italian word would imply, but confraternities devoted to charitable works. This one in particular is still run by a confraternity of 300 families, and is closed to visitors when the building is used for private ceremonies. Many scuole were decorated lavishly, both in the private chapels and in the meeting halls. The confraternity features works by Vittore Carpaccio (circa 1465–1525), a local artist who often filled

his otherwise devotional paintings with acutely observed details of Venetian life. Study the exuberance of his *St. George* as he slays the dragon or the vivid colors and details in *The Funeral of St. Jerome* and *St. Augustine in His Study.* ✉ *3259A Castello, near Ponte dei Greci,* ☎ *041/5228828.* *5,000 lire.* ⏲ *Nov.–Mar., Tues.–Sat. 10–12:30 and 3–6, Sun. 10–12:30; Apr.–Oct., Tues.–Sat. 10–12:30 and 3–6:30, Sun. 9:30–12:30.*

Dorsoduro, San Polo, and Santa Croce

If churches, further ramblings along dreamy canals, and masterpieces by great Venetian artists such as Titian and Tintoretto capture your interest, head out of Piazza San Marco under the arcades of the Fabbrica Nuova at the far end of the square.

A Good Walk

Leave Piazza San Marco via the Calle Bocca di Piazza. Next take Calle Larga XXII Marzo (or "wide street") to **Campo Santo Stefano** ㉔, dominated by the 14th-century church of Santo Stefano. Join the stream of pedestrians crossing the Grand Canal on the Ponte dell'Accademia to the district Dorsoduro (literally, "hard back" for its strong clay foundation). The bridge leads you directly to the **Gallerie dell'Accademia** ㉕, displaying an unparalleled collection of Venetian art. Continue toward Campo Santa Margherita, passing Mondonovo, one of Venice's best mask shops (☞ Shopping, *below*). At Campo Santa Margherita, a busy neighborhood shopping square, stop in to see Giambattista Tiepolo's ceiling paintings in the **Scuola dei Carmini** ㉖. Tiepolo was strongly influenced by Paolo Veronese, some of whose finest works can be seen if you take a short and rewarding canal-side detour along Fondamenta del Soccorso, making a sharp left turn along Fondamenta de San Sebastiano, and crossing the second bridge on the right, which leads to the **Chiesa di San Sebastiano** ㉗.

Retracing your steps, continue from Campo Santa Margherita (via Calle San Pantalon to Calle dei Preti to Calle della Scuola) to the Franciscan **Chiesa dei Frari** ㉘. To the left of the Frari is the **Scuola Grande di San Rocco** ㉙, filled with dark, dramatic canvases by Mannerist Tintoretto. In the area around San Rocco, narrow alleys and streets give way to small canals and lead to little squares, where posters advertising political parties and sports events might seem to be the only signs of life. From the Frari, head back to Campo San Tomà, to Calle di Nomboli, to Calle dei Saoneri to Salizzade San Polo to **Campo San Polo** ㉚, one of Venice's largest squares. From here you take Calle della Madonetta, Calle dell'Olio, Rugheta del Ravano, and Ruga Vecchia San Giovanni to the Rialto shopping district, where you can cross the Grand Canal for the shortcut back to San Marco. Alternatively, you can go north from Campo San Polo by way of Calle Bernardo, Calle dello Scaleter, Rio Terrà Parrucchetta, and Calle del Tintor to **Campo San Giacomo dall'Orio** ㉛, where the 13th-century church of San Giacomo stands in an enchanting square. Here you're not far from the San Stae vaporetto landing, so you can take the boat back along the Grand Canal to the heart of the city.

TIMING

Not including time spent in the Gallerie dell'Accademia and time to get totally lost (as always, arm yourself with a good map), walking this route will take approximately three to four hours. There are fewer people out and about in the early afternoon, which makes it easier to get around, but keep in mind that many of the shops and some churches are also closed at that time. Also remember: only three bridges span the Grand Canal—the Ponte degli Scalzi, Ponte di Rialto, and the

Ponte dell'Accademia—so be sure to be near one of them when you're ready to call it a day. If you're not, you may have to backtrack.

Sights to See

31 **Campo San Giacomo dall'Orio.** The 13th-century **Chiesa di San Giacomo dall'Orio** stands on this square, near a number of reasonably priced pizzerias. ⊠ *Campo San Giacomo dall'Orio.* 🎫 *2,000 lire.* ⏲ *Mon.–Sat. 10–5, Sun. 1–5.*

30 **Campo San Polo.** One of Venice's largest squares and a favorite playground for neighborhood children, this *campo* has a church of the same name, **Chiesa San Polo,** open to the public. ⊠ *Campo San Polo.* ⏲ *Mon.–Sat. 10–5, Sun. 1–5.*

24 **Campo Santo Stefano.** One of the nicest campi in all of Venice, this neighborhood square, until 1802, was used for bullfights, during which bulls (or oxen) were tied to a stake and baited by dogs. For years the square was grassy, all except for a stone avenue known as the *liston.* This became such a popular place to stroll that it led to a Venetian expression, *andare al liston,* which means "go for a walk." Check out the 14th-century **Chiesa di Santo Stefano** and its bell tower—the tipsiest in all Venice—and stop in to see the ship's-keel roof, a type found in several of Venice's older churches and the work of its master shipbuilders. *Church:* ⊠ *Campo Santo Stefano,* ☎ *041/5225061.* 🎫 *Sacristy: 2,000 lire.* ⏲ *Mon.–Sat. 10–5, Sun. 1–5. Sacristy closes 1 hr before church.*

NEED A BREAK? **Caffè Paolin** (⊠ 3464 Campo Santo Stefano, ☎ 041/5220710), closed Tuesday, makes some of the best gelato in Venice and is pleasant for watching the passing parade.

★ 28 **Chiesa dei Frari** (Church of the Friars). This immense Gothic church, with its russet-color brick, was built in the 14th century for the Franciscans. I Frari, as it is known locally, is deliberately austere and plain, befitting the simplicity of the Franciscans' lives, in which spirituality and poverty were key tenets. Paradoxically, however, the Frari also contains a number of the most sumptuous and brilliant pictures in any Venetian church. Chief among them are the magnificent **Titian altarpieces,** arguably the most dazzling works that the prolific artist produced. For its mellow luminosity, first check out Giovanni Bellini's *Madonna and Four Saints* in the sacristy, painted in 1488 for precisely this spot. The contrast with the heroic energy of Titian's large *Assumption* over the main altar—painted little more than 30 years later—is startling, and clearly illustrates the immense and rapid development of Venetian Renaissance painting. This work caused a sensation when unveiled in 1519 and was immediately acclaimed for its winning combination of Venetian color—especially the glowing reds—and classical Roman figure style.

The *Pesaro Madonna* over the first altar on the left nave near the main altar is also by Titian; his wife, who died shortly afterward in childbirth, posed for the figure of Mary. The Madonna was radical for its time because the main figure was not placed squarely in the center of the painting, creating a dynamic result. On the same side of the church, look at the spooky pyramid-shape monument to the sculptor Antonio Canova (1757–1822) containing his heart. Across the nave is a neoclassic 19th-century monument to Titian, executed by two of Canova's pupils. ⊠ *Campo dei Frari, San Polo,* ☎ *041/5222637.* 🎫 *3,000 lire.* ⏲ *Mon.–Sat. 9–6, Sun. 1–6.*

27 **Chiesa di San Sebastiano.** Veronese established his reputation with the frescoes he painted at this church when still in his twenties, after leaving his native Verona. He continued to embellish the interior for over

a decade with amazing perspective and trompe l'oeil scenes. In 1588 he was buried here. ✉ *Campo San Sebastiano, Dorsoduro,* ☎ *041/5282487.* 💰 *2,000 lire.* ⏲ *Mon.–Sat. 10–5, Sun. 3–5.*

★ 25 **Gallerie dell'Accademia** (Accademia Galleries). Housed in this magnificent museum is unquestionably the most extraordinary collection of Venetian art. Highlights include Giovanni Bellini's altarpiece from the church of San Giobbe (notice how he carried the church's architectural details right into the frame of the painting) and his moving *Madonna with St. Catherine and the Magdalen;* a fine *St. George* by Andrea Mantegna (1431–1506), Bellini's brother-in-law from Padua; and Veronese's monumental canvas, *Feast in the House of Levi.* Here is the Venetian High Renaissance in all its richness, even glamour. The painting was commissioned as a Last Supper, but the Inquisition took issue with Veronese's inclusion of jesters and German soldiers in the painting. Veronese avoided the charge of profanity by changing the title, and the picture was then supposed to depict the bawdy, but still biblical, feast of Levi. A room preserved from the Scuola della Carità—which previously occupied the museum's site—holds on one wall its original masterpiece, Titian's *Presentation of the Virgin.*

Don't miss the room containing various views of 15th- and 16th-century Venice by Vittore Carpaccio and Giovanni Bellini's brother Gentile—study them to see how little the city has changed since then. Room V holds one of the gallery's most famous paintings, the *Tempest,* by Giorgione (1477–1510), a work that has consistently baffled art historians as to its meaning, while charming all with its magical painterly qualities and exquisite landscape. The work is nothing if not ambiguous—what exactly is going on between this impassive young soldier and naked woman suckling a child?—but possesses a brooding sense of threat created by the gathering summer storm in the background. For the first time in art, the atmosphere of a painting became as important as the figures. The top floor displays paintings by Cima di Conegliano (circa 1459–circa 1517), Veronese, and Mansueti (died circa 1527) and hosts special exhibitions. ✉ *Campo della Carità, Accademia, Dorsoduro,* ☎ *041/5222247.* 💰 *12,000 lire.* ⏲ *Tues.–Sat. 9–7, Sun. and Mon. 9–2; longer hrs in summer.*

26 **Scuola dei Carmini.** This scuola is home to Giambattista Tiepolo's ceiling paintings, which were commissioned to honor the Carmelite order by depicting prominent Carmelites in conversation with saints and angels. Of the three great Venetian painters whose names start with *T* (Titian, Tintoretto, and Tiepolo), Tiepolo came last chronologically (he painted in the 18th century, the others in the 16th-century) and achieved the greatest international fame in his own time. An underlying melancholy in his ethereal, brightly colored paintings betrays a man of sober piety. Tiepolo's vivid techniques transformed some unpromising religious themes into flamboyant displays of color and movement. Mirrors on the benches make it easier to see the ceilings. ✉ *Campo dei Carmini, Dorsoduro,* ☎ *041/5289420.* 💰 *7,000 lire.* ⏲ *Mon.–Sat. 9–noon and 3–6, Closed Sun.*

29 **Scuola Grande di San Rocco.** This workshop is famed for its many dark, dramatic canvases by Tintoretto. Born some 30 years after Titian, Jacopo Robusti—called Tintoretto because his father was a dyer—was more mystical and devout than the sophisticated Titian. Though his colors are equally brilliant, he carried Titian's love of motion and odd composition to almost surreal effects, in the same Mannerist vein as El Greco (who was at one time a pupil of Titian's). In 1564, Tintoretto beat other painters competing for the commission to decorate this building by submitting not a sketch but a finished work, which he ad-

ditionally offered gratis. The series of more than 50 paintings he ultimately created took a total of 23 years to complete. These works, depicting Old and New Testament themes, were restored in the 1970s, and Tintoretto's inventive use of light has once more been revealed. ✉ *Campo San Rocco, Frari,* ☎ *041/5234864.* 🎫 *8,000 lire.* ⏲ *Dec.–Feb., Mon.–Fri. 10–1, weekends 10–4; Mar. and Nov., daily 10–4; Apr.–Oct., daily 9–5:30.*

Islands of the Lagoon

The perfect vacation from your Venetian vacation is an escape to the magical islands of the city's lagoon—Murano, Burano, and Torcello—which can provide a welcome relief after the brooding, enclosed charms of Venice itself. Far from the madding crowd, Torcello is the actual birthplace of Venice, today visited for its haunting melancholy, its great Byzantine-era church, and that famous outpost of elegance, the Locanda Cipriani. The island is also perfect for picnics, but bring food from Venice. Burano is a toy town of little houses all painted in a riot of color—blue, yellow, pink, ocher, and dark red; here, visitors love to shop for the best in Venetian lace. Murano is known the world over for its glass—but guided tours usually involve high-pressure attempts to make you buy, with little time left for anything else. It's worth the extra effort to make your own way around the islands, using the good vaporetto connections. There are several options in getting to these islands: lines 12 and 14 to Murano, Burano, and Torcello from the landing stage at Fondamente Nuove, almost due north of San Marco; and Line 52, which you can pick up in town (☞ Getting Around *in* Venice A to Z, *below*), runs to Fondamente Nuove, San Michele, and Murano, where you change to Line 14 to continue to Torcello and Santa Maria Elisabetta on the Lido.

Numbers in the text correspond to numbers in the margin and on the Venice and Venetian Lagoon maps.

A Good Boat Trip

Take Line 52 from Piazza San Marco to the Fondamente Nuove stop. Here, in the Campo dei Gesuiti, is the **Chiesa dei Gesuiti** ㉜. It's only a five-minute ride from there to **San Michele** ㉝, the cemetery island home to the church of San Michele in Isola. Another five minutes on Line 52 takes you to **Murano** ㉞. Cross the Ponte Vivarini and turn right onto Fondamenta Cavour. Follow the Fondamenta Cavour around the corner to the Museo Vetrario, one of the most famous glass factories in the world. Make your way back along the same route to the landing stage, and take Line 12 to **Burano** ㉟, where you can see traditional lace making at the Scuola di Merletti di Burano. Line 12 continues from the Burano landing stage to the sleepy green island of **Torcello** ㊱, about 10 minutes farther. A brick-paved lane leads up from the landing stage and follows the curve of the canal toward the center of the island. You pass the Locanda Cipriani, one of Hemingway's haunts. Just beyond is the grassy square that holds the island's only surviving monuments. Next to it is the cathedral of Santa Maria Assunta, also built in the 11th century.

TIMING

Boats leave every hour and the trip takes about 50 minutes each way. Stopping on every island and visiting the various sights will take a full day. If, however, you limit yourself to Torcello, Burano, and Murano, a full morning or a full afternoon will suffice.

Sights to See

★ ㉟ **Burano.** Dotting this fishing village are houses painted in cheerful colors and a raffishly raked bell tower on the main square, about 100 yards from the landing stage. Lace is to Burano what glass is to Murano, but be prepared to pay a lot for the real thing. Stalls line the way from the landing stage to Piazza Galuppi, the main square; the vendors, many of them fishermen's wives, are generally good-natured and blessedly unfamiliar with the techniques of the hard sell.

The **Museo del Merletto** (Lace Museum) is the best place to learn the intricacies of the lace-making traditions of Burano, plus the nature of the skills needed to make the more expensive lace. ✉ *Piazza Galuppi,* ☎ *041/730034.* 🎫 *8,000 lire, 17,000 lire combined ticket includes entry to Museo Correr, Museo Vetrario, and Palazzo Ducale (☞ above).* ⏲ *Apr.–Oct., Wed.–Mon. 9–5; Nov.–Mar., Wed.–Mon. 10–4.*

32 **Chiesa dei Gesuiti.** This 18th-century church dominating the Campo dei Gesuiti is extravagantly Baroque in style; the classical arches and straight lines of the Renaissance have been abandoned in favor of flowing, twisting forms. The marble of the gray-and-white interior is used like brocade, carved into swags and drapes. Titian's *Martyrdom of St. Lawrence,* over the first altar on the left, is a dramatic example of the great artist's feel for light and movement. ✉ *Campo dei Gesuiti,* ☎ *041/5231610.* ⏲ *Daily 10–noon and 5–7.*

★ 34 **Murano.** Like Venice, Murano is made up of a number of smaller islands linked by bridges. It is known for its glassworks, which you can visit to see how glass is made. Many of these line the **Fondamenta dei Vetrai,** the canal-side walkway leading away from the Colonna landing stage. The houses are simpler than many of their Venetian counterparts; traditionally they were workmen's cottages. Just before the junction with Murano's Grand Canal—250 yards up from the landing stage—is the **Chiesa di San Pietro Martire.** This 16th-century reconstruction of an earlier Gothic church has several works by Venetian masters: notably, the *Madonna and Child* by Giovanni Bellini and *St. Jerome* by Veronese.

The Venetian glass at the **Museo Vetrario** (Glass Museum) ranges from priceless antique to only slightly less-expensive modern. The museum details authentic Venetian styles and patterns and the history of Murano's glassworks, moved here from Venice in the 13th century because they were a fire hazard. ✉ *Murano,* ☎ *041/739586.* 🎫 *8,000 lire, 17,000 combined ticket includes entry to the Museo del Merletto, Palazzo Ducale, and Museo Correr (☞ above).* ⏲ *Apr.–Oct., Thurs.–Tues. 10–5; Nov.–Mar., Thurs.–Tues. 10–4.*

33 **San Michele.** Venice's cypress-lined cemetery island is home to the pretty Renaissance church of **San Michele in Isola,** designed by Coducci in 1478, and Venice's cemetery. It is a unique experience to walk among the gravestones with the sound of lapping water on all sides. The American poet Ezra Pound (1885–1972), the great Russian impresario and art critic Sergey Diaghilev (1872–1929), and the composer Igor Stravinsky (1882–1971) are buried here. For most Venetians, however, the stay here is short-lived, as the cemetery has a policy of transferring those interred more than 10 years to another, less grandiose cemetery, making room for more recent burials.

★ 36 **Torcello.** This is where the first Venetians landed in their flight from the barbarians 1,500 years ago. Even after many settlers left to found the city of Venice on the island of Rivo Alto (Rialto), Torcello continued to grow and prosper until its main source of income, wool manufacturing, was priced out of the marketplace. It's hard to believe now, looking at this almost deserted island, that in the 16th century it had 20,000 inhabitants and 10 churches.

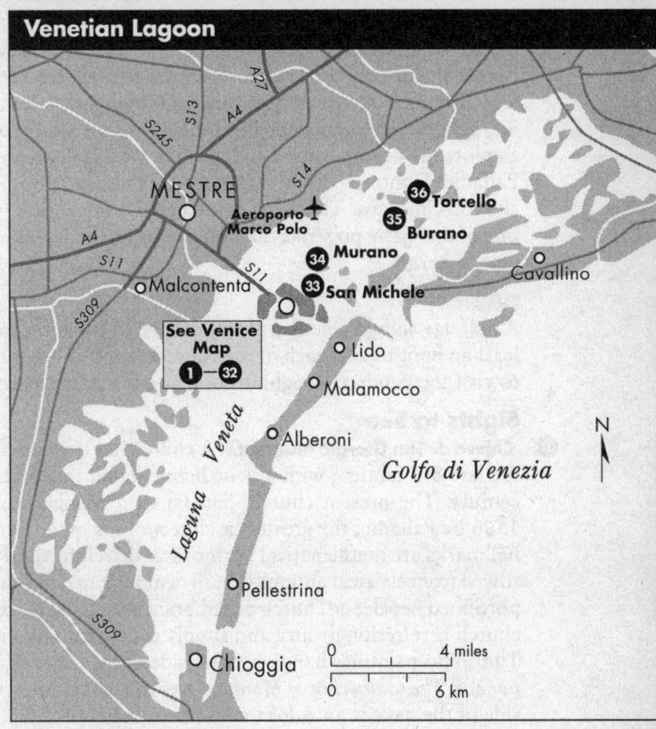

The island's cathedral, **Santa Maria Assunta,** dates from the 11th century. The ornate Byzantine mosaics are testimony to the importance and wealth of an island that could attract the best artists and craftsmen of its day. The vast mosaic on the inside of the facade depicts the *Last Judgment* as artists of the 11th and 12th centuries imagined it: figures writhe in vividly depicted contortions of pain. Facing it, as if in mitigation, is the calm mosaic figure of the Madonna, alone in a field of gold above the staunch array of Apostles. ✉ *Torcello,* ☎ *041/730084.* 🎫 *4,000 lire.* ⏲ *June–Sept., daily 10:30–5:45; Oct.–May, daily 10–12:15 and 2–4:45.*

NEED A BREAK? **Locanda Cipriani** (✉ Torcello, ☎ 041/730150), closed Tuesday and early January–early February, is an inn famous for its good food and the patronage of Ernest Hemingway, who often came to Torcello for the solitude. These days Locanda Cipriani—not to be confused by the Cipriani hotel on Giudecca—is about the busiest spot on the island, as well-heeled customers arrive on high-speed powerboats for lunch.

San Giorgio Maggiore and the Giudecca

Beckoning all travelers across the St. Mark's Basin like some sort of Venetian Bali Hai is the island of San Giorgio Maggiore, separated by a small channel from the Giudecca. A tall brick campanile on that distant bank perfectly complements the Campanile of San Marco. Behind it looms the stately dome of one of Venice's greatest churches, San Giorgio Maggiore. The island of Giudecca, a crescent cupped around the southern shore of Venice, is one of the most mysterious neighborhoods in all of Venice, with an obscure history and a somber feel.

Numbers in the text correspond to numbers in the margin and on the Venice map.

A Good Boat Trip

Take Line 82 from San Zaccaria near San Marco to head south for the island of San Giorgio Maggiore, across the lagoon. Here you should visit Palladio's **Chiesa di San Giorgio Maggiore** ㊲. Return to the pier and proceed by vaporetto (still Line 82) to the island of **Giudecca** ㊳. Explore the neighborhood and visit the Chiesa del Redentore, also by Palladio. Continue on the vaporetto to the next stop, Zattere, opposite the Giudecca. The promenade here is enchanting; you can eat in one of the many pizzerias that line the promenade, taking in the lively atmosphere.

TIMING

A half day should give you plenty of time to enjoy the sights. Allow at least an hour to visit each of the churches, and another hour to or two to visit the Giudecca neighborhood and the Zattere promenade.

Sights to See

37 **Chiesa di San Giorgio Maggiore.** A church has been on this island since the late 8th century, with a Benedictine monastery added in the 10th century. The present church, San Giorgio Maggiore, was begun in 1566 by Palladio, the greatest architect of his time. Two of Palladio's hallmarks are mathematical harmony and architectural elements borrowed from classical antiquity, both demonstrated in this superbly proportioned neoclassic church of red brick and white marble. Inside, the church is refreshingly airy and simply decorated. Two important late Tintoretto paintings hang on either side of the chancel: *The Last Supper* and *The Gathering of Manna.* Over the first altar on the right-hand side of the nave is an *Adoration of the Shepherds* by Jacopo Bassano (1517–92), a painter from Bassano del Grappa on the mainland who possessed considerable originality and was especially adept at portraying nature and country life. The campanile is so high that it was struck by a lightning bolt in 1993. The elevator ride to the top is well worth the 3,000 lire offering, as the views are some of the finest in town. ✉ *Isola di San Giorgio,* ☎ *041/5227827.* ⏲ *June–Sept., daily 9–12:30 and 2:30–6; Oct.–May, daily 10–12:30 and 3–5.*

The **Monastero di San Giorgio Maggiore** (Monastery of San Giorgio Maggiore), where the conclave that elected Pope Pius VII took place in 1800, later a barracks for the occupying Austrians, now houses an artistic and cultural foundation where conferences are often held. Palladio designed the monastery's first cloister, and Longhena was the architect for the grand Baroque library. It's usually closed to the public. ✉ *San Giorgio Maggiore.*

38 **Giudecca.** The island's name is something of a mystery; according to some, it derives from the possible settlement of Jews here in the 14th century, others believe it was so called because in the 9th century nobles condemned to exile (*giudicato* means judged or sentenced) were sent here. It became a pleasure garden for wealthy Venetians during the long and luxurious decline of the Republic. In one regard it is still the province of the wealthy: the exclusive Cipriani hotel (☞ Lodging, *below*) lies secluded on its eastern tip.

Palladio's **Chiesa del Redentore** is a tranquil, stately facade, actually a series of superimposed temple fronts topped by a dome and a pair of slim, almost minaret-like, bell towers. The interior, like San Giorgio Maggiore's (☞ *above*), is perfectly proportioned and airy, in contrast to the dusky Byzantine mystery of the Basilica di San Marco. ✉ *Fondamenta San Giacomo, Giudecca,* ☎ *041/5231415.* 🎫 *2,000 lire. Closed for restoration until 2000.*

Close-Up

SAVE LA SERENISSIMA

ON NOVEMBER 4, 1966, the Adriatic surrounding Venice swelled, barometric pressure dropped, and winds whipped the city. The watermark reached an unprecedented high of 6 ft, 4 inches and holes were punctured in the ***murazzi,*** artificial stone sea walls erected in the 18th century. Flood damage to the historic center alone was estimated at 13 billion lire, and it was in the storm's aftermath that a rethinking of the delicate relationship between the city, lagoon, and sea was born. Venice and her artistic treasures were in jeopardy.

Venice is built on some 118 islands in a 518-square-km (200-square-mi) lagoon. Rising from the lagoon are Byzantine, Gothic, and Renaissance buildings, aglitter with dazzling light, gold mosaics, and medieval works of art. Construction began slowly: in the 9th century thousands of wood pilings, sandwiched together, were driven into the land, mud banks, and ooze underneath the water to create the foundation for the first buildings, usually built of wood. After a devastating fire in the 12th century, brick and stone became the primary building materials.

Nature could claim some responsibility for the flood of '66; however, much of the damage wrought upon Venice is man-made. More and more today, Piazza San Marco finds itself knee-deep in the murky *acque alte* (high tides). A rise in the sea level, due to the creation of canals in the 1960s, as well as the deepening of channels throughout the 20th century, has rid the city of tidal flow–off areas. The city's ancient infrastructure is sinking, making flood conditions worse. Industrial development on the terra firma has virtually killed the ecological balance in the lagoon. Besides dioxins, there's algae, farm waste, and the threat of oil spills from tankers.

Works of art have always suffered through the passage of time, natural catastrophes such as earthquakes, floods, and fires notwithstanding. One of the biggest problems is the pervading dampness: the water seeping into the masonry brings with it salt and other impurities, which cause paintings to chip and flake, stones to crumble, and buildings to become unstable. Church paintings have blackened from centuries' worth of candle smoke, and the faulty work of well-intentioned restorers has also had a hand in the damage.

Saving Venice boils down to a few primary issues. To safeguard against flooding, the government and various environmental groups are moving to restore the lagoon to its original condition (this means putting a halt to further industrial development, among other things). The coastal defense system of sandbanks needs to be strengthened, and the flow of rivers must be regulated to counteract the continuous rise in sea level. The precious works of art and the buildings in which they stand must also be refurbished.

ONE OF THE LATEST EFFORTS has been the painstaking 10-year restoration of Santa Maria dei Miracoli, its colorful marble interior and exterior built 1481–89 to the design by Pietro Lombardo. The amounts of salt and moisture were measured, and the marbles were examined for cracks. The marbles were then removed from the brick and soaked in deionized water for a month to remove the salt, then reattached with metal hooks. (During a 19th-century restoration, the marbles had been detached and then reattached with cement.)

Who pays for these costly restorations? The Italian government cannot possibly pay for it all. Private organizations have come to La Serenissima's aid: at present, 23 in Italy and abroad defray costs through assiduous fund-raising. Perhaps the two most famous are **Save Venice** (⊠ 15 E. 74th St., New York, NY, USA 10021, ☎ 212/737–3141) and **Venice in Peril Fund** (⊠ 314–322 Regent St., London W1R 5AB, England, ☎ 020/7636–6138).

DINING

Venetian cuisine is based on seafood—*granseola* (crab), *moeche* (small, soft-shelled crabs), and *seppie* or *seppioline* (cuttlefish). It can be very expensive, usually priced by the *etto* (100 grams, or about ¼ pound). Antipasti may take the form of a seafood salad, *prosciutto di San Daniele* (cured ham of the Veneto region), or pickled vegetables. As a first course Venetians favor risotto, the creamy rice dish, prepared here with vegetables or shellfish. Pasta, too, is paired with seafood sauces—Venice is *not* the place to order spaghetti with tomato sauce. *Pasticcio di pesce* is pasta baked with fish, usually *baccalà* (salt cod). A classic first course here and elsewhere in the Veneto is *pasta e fagioli* (thick bean soup with pasta). *Bigoli* is strictly a local pasta shaped like short, fat spaghetti, usually served with *nero di seppia* (squid ink sauce). Polenta, a creamy cornmeal dish, is another pillar of regional cooking. It's often served as an accompaniment to *fegato alla veneziana* (liver with onions).

Though it originated on the mainland, tiramisu is Venice's favorite dessert, a heavenly concoction of mascarpone (a rich, soft double-cream cheese), espresso, chocolate, and *savoiardi* (ladyfingers). Local wines are the dry white Tocai and Pinot from the Friuli region and bubbly white Prosecco, a naturally fermented sparkling wine that is a shade less dry. The best Prosecco comes from the Valdobbiadene; Cartizze, which is similar, is considered superior by some but is expensive. Popular red wines include merlot, cabernet, Raboso, and Refosco. You can sample all of these and more in Venice's many bacari (local osterie), where wine is served by the glass (known as an *ombra* in Venetian dialect) and accompanied by cicchetti (assorted tidbits), often substantial enough for a light meal.

It's always a good idea to reserve your table or have your hotel *portiere* (concierge) do it for you. Dining hours are short, starting at 12:30 or 1 for lunch and ending at 2:30 or 3, when restaurants close for the afternoon, opening up again to start serving at about 8 and closing again at 11 or midnight. Most close one day a week and are also likely to close without notice for vacation or renovation. Few have signs on the outside, so when the metal blinds are shut tight, you can't tell a closed restaurant from a closed TV-repair shop.

Cannaregio

$$$ ✕ **Fiaschetteria Toscana.** This warm restaurant in a former Tuscan wine and oil storehouse merits a jaunt from terra firma to Cannaregio for its cheerful, courteous service, fine cucina, and rose-hue walls. Gastronomic highlights include a delicate *tagliolini* (noodles), perhaps prepared *alla buranella* (with shrimp), the zabaglione, and the wine list. In warm weather, the best tables are in the arbor on the square. ✉ *Campo San Giovanni Crisostomo 5719, Cannaregio,* ☎ *041/5285281. AE, DC, MC, V. Closed Tues. and 4 wks in July–Aug.*

$$ ★ ✕ **Vini da Gigio.** A quaint, friendly, family-run trattoria on the quay side of a canal just off the Strada Nuova, da Gigio is very popular with Venetians and other visiting Italians, who appreciate the affable service; excellently cooked homemade pasta, fish, and meat dishes; and imaginative and varied cellar and good-quality draft wine. It's good, too, for a cheap, simple lunch at tables in the barroom. ✉ *Fondamenta de la Chiesa 3628/a, Cannaregio,* ☎ *041/5285140. AE, DC, MC, V. Closed Mon., last 2 wks in Jan., last 2 wks in Aug.*

Castello

$$$ ★ ✕ **Al Covo.** This small and charming osteria changes its menu according to the day's bounty—mostly local seafood caught just hours before and specialties from other European waters. Cesare Benelli and his American wife, Diane, insist on only the freshest ingredients and claim to not use butter or animal fats. Try the *zuppa di pesce* (fish broth) followed by the fish of the day either grilled, baked, or steamed. Diane will guide you through some of her homemade desserts and the extensive wine selection. At lunch, only a fixed price menu (with several options) is served; dinner is served à la carte. ✉ *Campiello della Pescaria 3968, Castello,* ☎ *041/5223812. No credit cards. Closed Wed. and Thurs., 1 wk in Aug., and 1 month between Dec. and Jan.*

$$ ✕ **Al Mondo Novo.** In this informal, spacious fish restaurant you can get grilled *cape sante* (scallops) and *cape longhe* (razor clams), risottos and pastas, and the best of the day's catch. Meat dishes are also available. ✉ *Salizzada San Lio 5409, Castello,* ☎ *041/5200698. AE, MC, V.*

$$ ✕ **Da Remigio.** This very popular, family-run local trattoria near San Giorgio dei Greci turns out reliable and tasty fish and meat dishes. It's the ideal place to enjoy an informal meal in the company of hungry, chatty Venetians. ✉ *Salizzada dei Greci 3416, Castello,* ☎ *041/5230089. Reservations essential. AE, DC, MC, V. Closed Tues., 2 wks. July–Aug., and 4 wks in Jan. No dinner Mon.*

$ ✕ **Al Mascaron.** The convivial, crowded Al Mascaron, with its paper tablecloths and very informal atmosphere, is a regular stop for Venetians who drop in to gossip, drink, play cards, and eat cicchetti at the bar. You can bet on delicious seafood, pastas, risottos, and seafood salads. So popular has Mascaron become that the owners, Gigi and Momi, have opened an offshoot called Mascareta a few doors down the calle (at No. 5183), where you can enjoy a glass of wine and cold snacks. ✉ *Calle Lunga Santa Maria Formosa 5225, Castello,* ☎ *041/5225995. No credit cards. Closed Sun. and mid-Dec.–mid-Jan.*

Dorsoduro

$$ ✕ **Cantinone Storico.** On a quiet, romantic canal near the Accademia, this comfortable trattoria with tables alfresco serves excellently prepared specialties such as risotto *terra mare* (with seafood, vegetables, and porcini mushrooms) and *tagliolini alla granseola* (narrow fettuccine–shape pasta with crab sauce). Heavily advertised, the Cantinone draws mosty tourists, yet it's hard to beat the good location, and the prices are reasonable. The house wines are good. ✉ *Fondamenta di Ca' Bragadin 660/1, Dorsoduro,* ☎ *041/5239577. AE, MC, V. Closed Sun., last wk July–1st wk Aug., and Jan. 19–26.*

$$ ✕ **Locanda Montin.** Peggy Guggenheim used to take many of the leading artists of the day—including Jackson Pollock and Mark Rothko—to this archetypal Venetian inn, not far from her Palazzo Venier dei Leoni, in Dorsoduro. The walls are still covered with modern art, but it's far from the haute bohemian hangout it used to be, except for when the Biennale crowd takes charge. Outside, you can dine under an elongated arbor and enjoy such specialties as rigatoni *ai quattro formaggi* (with four cheeses), spaghetti *Adriatica* (with fish sauce), and antipasto *Montin* (seafood antipasto). ✉ *Fondamenta di Borgo 1147, Dorsoduro,* ☎ *041/5227151. AE, DC, MC, V. Closed Wed., Jan. 7–26, and 15 days in Aug. No dinner Tues.*

$ ★ ✕ **L'Incontro.** This trattoria has a faithful clientele of Venetians and visitors, attracted by flavorsome food, friendly service, and reasonable prices. Menu choices include freshly made Sardinian pastas, juicy steaks, wild duck, boar, and (with advance notice) roast suckling pig.

Venice Dining and Lodging

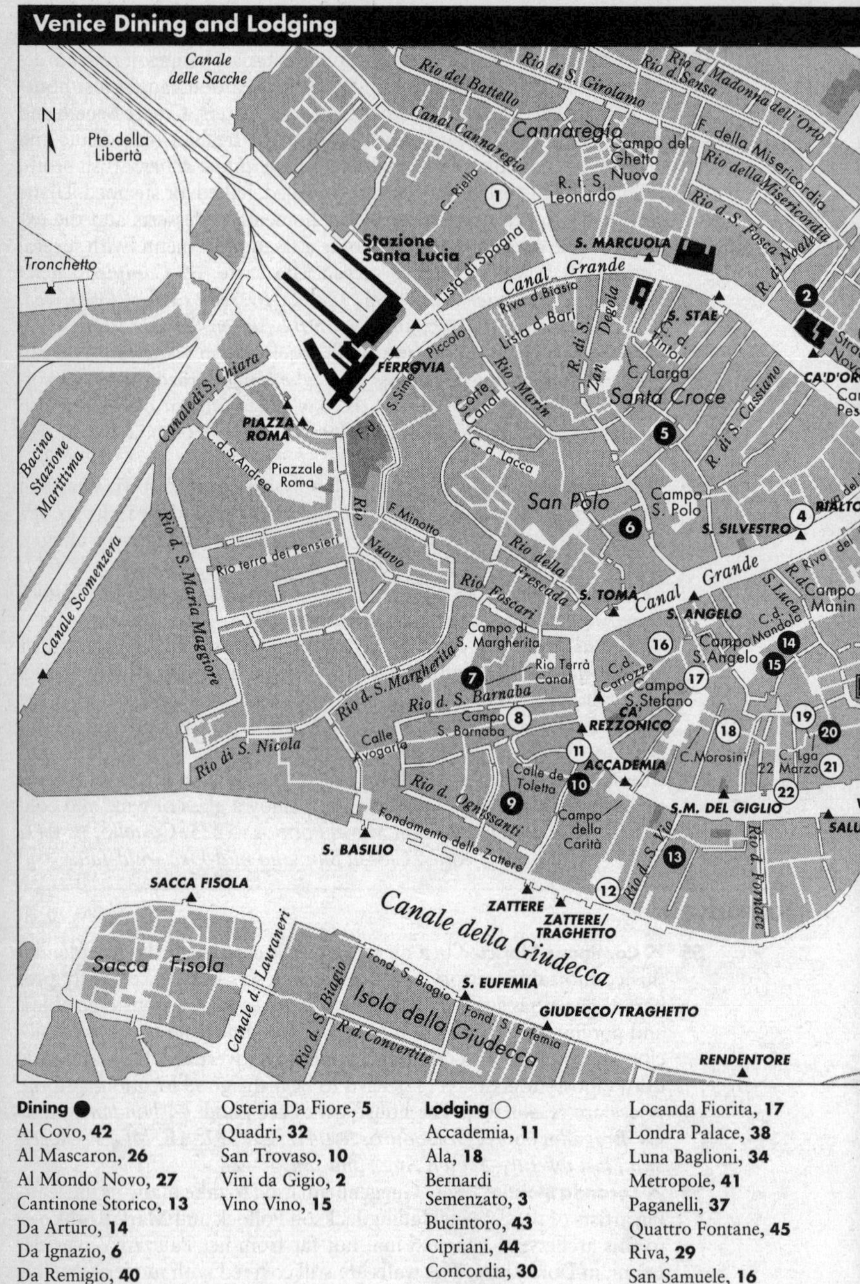

Dining ●
Al Covo, **42**
Al Mascaron, **26**
Al Mondo Novo, **27**
Cantinone Storico, **13**
Da Arturo, **14**
Da Ignazio, **6**
Da Remigio, **40**
Fiaschetteria Toscana, **23**
Grand Canal, **33**
Harry's Bar, **35**
La Caravella, **20**
Le Bistrot, **31**
L'Incontro, **7**
Locanda Montin, **9**
Osteria Da Fiore, **5**
Quadri, **32**
San Trovaso, **10**
Vini da Gigio, **2**
Vino Vino, **15**

Lodging ○
Accademia, **11**
Ala, **18**
Bernardi Semenzato, **3**
Bucintoro, **43**
Cipriani, **44**
Concordia, **30**
Danieli, **36**
Flora, **21**
Gritti Palace, **22**
Hesperia, **1**
Hotel Pausania, **8**
Istituto San Giuseppe, **28**
La Calcina, **12**
Locanda Fiorita, **17**
Londra Palace, **38**
Luna Baglioni, **34**
Metropole, **41**
Paganelli, **37**
Quattro Fontane, **45**
Riva, **29**
San Samuele, **16**
Santa Marina, **24**
Saturnia Internazionale, **19**
Scandinavia, **25**
Sturion, **4**
Wildner, **39**

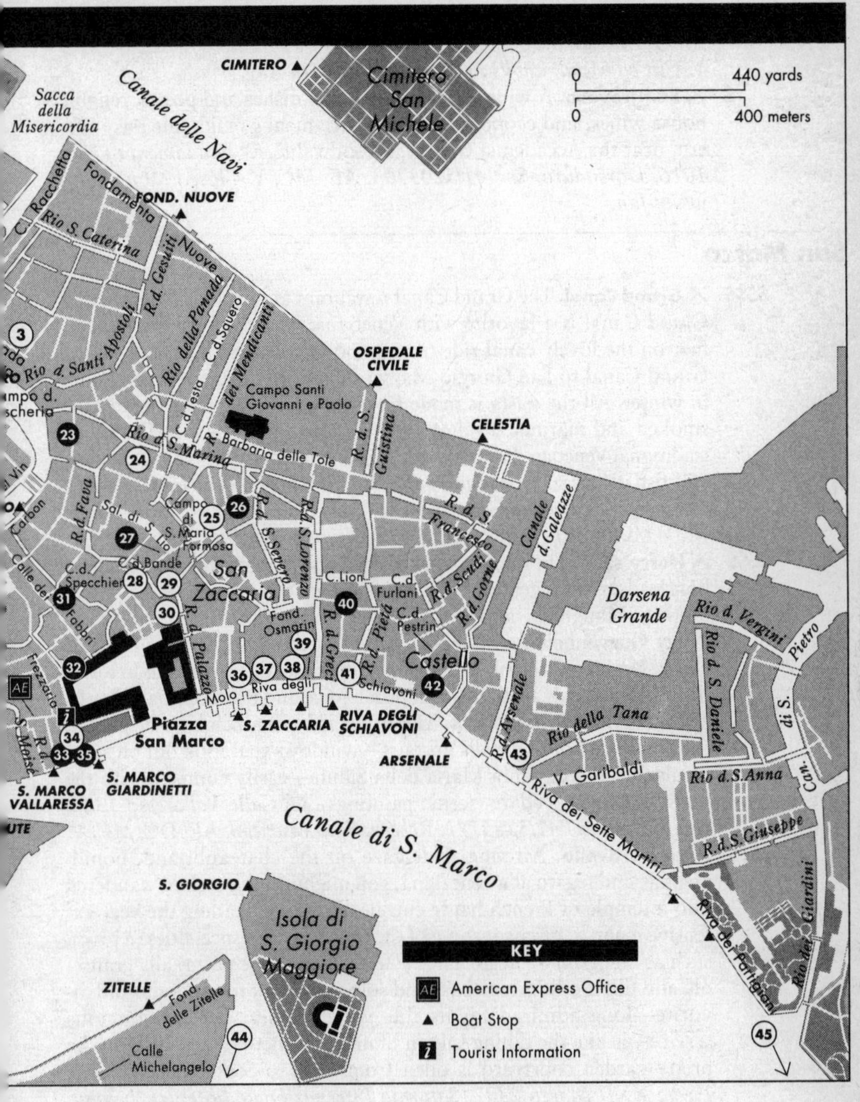

CIMITERO
Cimitero San Michele
0 440 yards
0 400 meters
Sacca della Misericordia
Canale delle Navi
FOND. NUOVE
Fondamenta Nuove
C. Racchetta
Rio S. Caterina
R. d. Gesuiti
Rio d. Santi Apostoli
Rio della Panada
C.d. Squero
Rio dei Mendicanti
C.d. Testa
Campo Santi Giovanni e Paolo
OSPEDALE CIVILE
R. d. S. Giustina
CELESTIA
Rio d. S. Marina
Barbaria delle Tole
Canale d. Galeazze
R. d. S. Francesco
R.d. Fava
Sal. di S. Lio
Campo di S. Maria Formosa
R.d. S. Severo
R.d. S. Lorenzo
C.d. Bande
C.d. Specchieri
Calle dei Fabbri
San Zaccaria
C. Lion
C.d. Furlani
R.d. Scudi
R.d. Gorne
Darsena Grande
Rio d. Vergini
Fond. Osmarin
R. d. Greci
C.d. Pestrin
R.d. Pietà
Rio d. S. Daniele
Rio di S. Pietro
Castello
R. d. Palazzo
Molo
Riva degli Schiavoni
Frezzeria
Piazza San Marco
S. ZACCARIA
RIVA DEGLI SCHIAVONI
ARSENALE
R. d. Arsenale
Rio della Tana
V. Garibaldi
Rio d. S. Anna
Can.
R. d. S. Moisè
S. MARCO VALLARESSA
S. MARCO GIARDINETTI
Riva dei Sette Martiri
R.d. S. Giuseppe
Canale di S. Marco
Rio dei Giardini
S. GIORGIO
Riva dei Partigiani
Isola di S. Giorgio Maggiore
ZITELLE
Fond. delle Zitelle
Calle Michelangelo
KEY
American Express Office
Boat Stop
Tourist Information
3
23
24
25
26
27
28
29
30
31
32
33
34
35
36
37
38
39
40
41
42
43
44
45

You'll find it between San Barnaba and Campo Santa Margherita. ✉ *Rio Terrà Canal 3062/a, Dorsoduro, ☎ 041/5222404. AE, D, MC, V. Closed Mon., 2 wks in Jan., and 2 wks in Aug.*

$ ✕ **San Trovaso.** A wide choice of Venetian dishes and pizzas, reliable house wines, and economical fixed-price menus make this busy tavern, near the Accademia Gallery, a good value. ✉ *Fondamenta Priuli 1016, Dorsoduro, ☎ 041/5203703. AE, MC, V. Closed Mon. and 1 wk in Jan.*

San Marco

$$$$ ✕ **Grand Canal.** The Grand Canal restaurant at the Hotel Monaco and Grand Canal is a favorite with Venetians, who enjoy eating in summer on the lovely canal-side terrace looking across the mouth of the Grand Canal to San Giorgio Maggiore, and in the cozy dining room in winter. All the pasta is made fresh daily on the premises, and the smoked and marinated salmon are also prepared on-site. The chef's traditional Venetian dishes are top-flight; you'll marvel over savory meat and fish dishes such as *scampi alla Buséra* (shrimp in a cognac sauce). ✉ *Hotel Monaco and Grand Canal, Calle Vallaresso 1325, San Marco, ☎ 041/5200211. Jacket required for dinner. AE, DC, MC, V.*

$$$$ ✕ **Harry's Bar.** The humble door of this very less-than-humble watering hole leads to the legendary Venetian hangout of such notables as Hemingway, Maugham, and Onassis, not to mention Barbara Hutton, Peggy Guggenheim, and Orson Welles. Such company doesn't come cheap, but Harry's is still known for the best and driest martinis in town, the most heavenly Bellinis (fresh peach juice and Prosecco), and for its kitchen's fine *cucina veneta.* The decor is boring beige-on-beige, but the "pictures" on the walls upstairs—windows that look out on spectacular Chiesa di Santa Maria della Salute—easily compete with the finest Canaletto *vedute* (scenic paintings). ✉ *Calle Vallaresso 1323, San Marco, ☎ 041/5285777. Reservations essential. AE, DC, MC, V.*

$$$$ ✕ **La Caravella.** Affixing your gaze on the chateaubriand, bouillabaisse, and fegato alla veneziana, you might think you had wandered into a temple of French haute cuisine. Continue reading the very extensive menu to discover some of the best Venetian specialties in town, such as *taglierini* (delicate narrow fettuccine-shape pasta) alla granseola and fillets of local sea bass and sole. The front room of this old favorite—long admired for its fine wine list and cordial, gracious service—is like the dining saloon of an old Venetian sailing ship. The pretty garden courtyard is open from May to September. ✉ *Calle Larga XXII Marzo 2397, Saturnia Internazionale hotel (☞ below), San Marco, ☎ 041/5208901. Reservations essential. AE, DC, MC, V.*

$$$$ ✕ **Quadri.** In the 19th century, princes, dukes, and countesses dined here, and you'll feel like one when you walk into the gilded salons of Venice's most beautiful restaurant. The decor is stunning—Quadri's second-floor aerie gives you a pigeon's-eye view of Piazza San Marco—and the four-star truffles-on-everything kitchen is also a major draw. Come September, when the Venice Film Festival is in session, the sequins-and-sunglasses set takes over. ✉ *Piazza San Marco 120–124, San Marco, ☎ 041/5289299. Reservations essential. AE, DC, MC, V. Closed Mon. No lunch Tues. or in July and Aug.*

$$$ ✕ **Da Arturo.** On the Calle degli Assassini—a name common to several Venetian streets and a reminder of the centuries gone by when violence and betrayal were everyday occurrences—this tiny restaurant can offer a most peaceful and enjoyable evening. It has the distinction (in Venice) of *not* serving seafood. Instead you'll choose from among fresh vegetable and salad dishes; tasty, tender, and generous meat courses, including the delicately pungent *braciola alla veneziana* (pork

chop schnitzel with vinegar); and an authentic creamy homemade tiramisu to finish. ✉ *Calle degli Assassini 3656, San Marco,* ☎ *041/5286974. Reservations essential. No credit cards. Closed Sun. and 4 wks in Aug.*

$ ✕ **Le Bistrot.** Live music, poetry readings, and art exhibits attract the younger crowd to this café-brasserie. Centrally located, it's open all day (until 1 AM) and features 16th-century Venetian cuisine, such as *l'ambrosino* (spiced chicken with nuts and raisins) and *biancomangiare* (soup with rice flour, almonds, pomegranates, and chicken). ✉ *Calle dei Fabbri 4685, San Marco,* ☎ *041/5236651. MC, V.*

$ ✕ **Vino Vino.** The annex of the extremely expensive Antico Martini restaurant is a highly informal wine bar where you can sample Italian vintages and munch on a limited selection of (microwaved) dishes from the kitchens of its upscale big sister next door. ✉ *Calle delle Veste 2007/a, near Campo San Fantin, San Marco,* ☎ *041/5237027. Reservations not accepted. AE, DC, MC, V. Closed Tues.*

San Polo

$$$ ★ ✕ **Osteria Da Fiore.** Tucked away in a little calle off the top of Campo San Polo, Da Fiore is always packed. It's imperative to reserve for a superlative seafood lunch or dinner, which might include delicate hors d'oeuvres of moeche, scallops, and tiny octopus, followed by a succulent risotto or tagliolini *con scampi e zucchine* (with shrimp and zucchini), and a perfectly cooked main course of *rombo* (turbot) or *branzino* (sea bass). ✉ *Calle del Scaleter 2202/a, San Polo,* ☎ *041/721308. Reservations essential. AE, DC, MC, V. Closed Sun.–Mon., Aug. 10–early Sept., and Dec. 25–Jan. 15.*

$$ ✕ **Da Ignazio.** In a smallish, pleasant, and unadorned space near Campo San Polo, Ignazio is reliable for good food at reasonable prices (except for the expensive fish dishes). The cuisine is classic Venetian, from seafood risotto to fegato alla veneziana, but there are standard Italian items as well. ✉ *Calle dei Saoneri 2749, San Polo,* ☎ *041/5234852. AE, DC, MC, V. Closed Sat., 2 wks during Christmas, and 2 wks in July.*

LODGING

Everyone loves Venice, and hotels here can cater to all tastes and price ranges. Rates are a little higher than in Rome and Milan, but you can save off-season (November–March, excluding Christmas and Carnevale). Most rates include breakfast. It is *essential* to know how to get to your hotel when you arrive, as transport can range from arriving in a water taxi or gondola direct to the front door or wandering down curious alleys and side streets—luggage in hand—with relapses of déjà vu. The busiest times for hotels are spring and autumn; December 20–January 2; and the two-week Carnival period leading up to Ash Wednesday. Book well in advance. If you don't have reservations, you can almost always get a room in any category by going to the **AVA** (Venetian Hoteliers Association, ✉ Stazione Ferroviaria Santa Lucia; Aeroporto Marco Polo; parking garage at Piazzale Roma, ☎ 1678/43006 toll-free) booths.

Cannaregio

$$ **Hesperia.** A quiet, friendly hotel with some rooms overlooking the wide (and clean!) Canale di Cannaregio, the Hesperia is convenient walking distance from the train station and right across from the Jewish Ghetto. The restaurant, Il Melograno, has tables outside come summertime. ✉ *459 Cannaregio, 30121,* ☎ *041/715251,* FAX *041/715112. 15 rooms, 2 without bath. Restaurant. AE, DC, MC, V.*

$ ★ **Bernardi Semenzato.** This is a particularly inviting little hotel just off Strada Nuova and near the Rialto. All rooms in the main hotel are well-maintained, making the Bernardi better value than ever. Prices are even lower in the nearby annex, with six rooms and a big room with a lovely canal view. ✉ *Calle dell'Oca, 4366 Cannaregio, 30121,* ☎ *041/5211052,* FAX *041/5222424. 24 rooms, 10 without bath. AE, MC, V. Closed 2 wks Nov.–Dec. and 2 wks before Carnevale.*

Castello

$$$$ **Danieli.** You'll feel like a doge in Venice's largest luxury hotel, a collage of newer buildings around a 15th-century palazzo, built for the Doge Dandolo—all oozing with sumptuous Venetian decor and atmosphere. Some suites are positively palatial, but some of the less attractive rooms are still overpriced. The four-story-high lobby is supreme, its chic salons and bar offering relaxation and celebrity sightings. The rooftop terrace restaurant is justly famous for top-notch cuisine and its heavenly view of San Giorgio Maggiore and St. Mark's Basin. Guests have access to a pool and tennis courts. ✉ *Riva degli Schiavoni 4196, Castello, 30122,* ☎ *041/5226480,* FAX *041/5200208. 219 rooms, 11 suites. Restaurant, bar, air-conditioning. AE, DC, MC, V.*

$$$$ **Metropole.** Only a few minutes' stroll from Piazza San Marco, the Metropole offers spacious rooms and sitting areas furnished with style and panache from the owner's impressive collection of antiques. Many rooms have a view of the lagoon, but the others overlooking a canal and peaceful gardens are also inviting. You can step from your water taxi or gondola directly into the hotel lobby. ✉ *Riva degli Schiavoni 4149, Castello, 30122,* ☎ *041/5205044,* FAX *041/5223679. 67 rooms, 7 suites. Restaurant, bar, air-conditioning. AE, DC, MC, V.*

$$$–$$$$ **Santa Marina.** In the small neighborhood campo home to this hotel, five minutes from the Rialto Bridge, you will probably see more Venetians than tourists passing by. Immaculate rooms are outfitted in pastel colors and laquered Venetian style furniture. The staff is helpful and kind, and breakfast is served on the veranda in summer. ✉ *Campo Santa Marina, 6068 Castello, 30122,* ☎ *041/5239202,* FAX *041/5200907. 20 rooms. Breakfast room. AE, DC, MC, V.*

$$$ **Londra Palace.** This grand hotel commands a fine view of San Giorgio and St. Mark's Basin and has a distinguished ambience. A neoclassic touch graces the rooms, with light pastel colors and plenty of marble. The Deux Lions restaurant offers fine Venetian and French cuisine, and the piano bar is open late. Perks include a complimentary Mercedes for one-day excursions, free entrance to the city Casino (☞ Nightlife and the Arts, *below*), and the therapeutic solarium. ✉ *Riva degli Schiavoni 4171, Castello, 30122,* ☎ *041/5200533,* FAX *041/5225032. 36 rooms, 17 suites. Restaurant, piano bar, air-conditioning. AE, DC, MC, V.*

$$$ **Scandinavia.** Central but off the main tourist arteries, the Scandinavia is housed in a medieval building dating from the 11th century. Despite the name, the rooms are done in Venetian style with brocade tapestry and Murano chandeliers. Ask for a room with a view onto the cheerful campo below. The top suite has a beautiful, private covered veranda with a view of the nearby church. ✉ *Campo Santa Maria Formosa, 5240 Castello, 30122,* ☎ *041/5223507,* FAX *041/5235232. 33 rooms, 1 suite. Breakfast room. AE, MC, V.*

$$ **Bucintoro.** Whistler once stayed here and, today, the Bucintoro is still favored by artists drawn by the lagoon views outside each room. Off the tourist track, this friendly, family-run hotel on the waterfront by the Arsenal has clean, simple rooms and prices that are unbeatable for such a spectacular location. ✉ *Riva San Biagio 2135, Castello, 30122,*

☎ *041/5223240,* FAX *041/5235224. 28 rooms, 3 without bath. Breakfast room. No credit cards. Closed mid-Dec.–early Feb.*

$$ **Paganelli.** The lagoon views here so impressed Henry James that he wrote the Paganelli up in the preface to his *Portrait of a Lady.* This enchanting, small hotel on the waterfront near Piazza San Marco, with an annex on the quiet square of Campo San Zaccaria (three rooms overlook the lagoon, six face the square), is tastefully decorated in the Venetian style. ✉ *Riva degli Schiavoni 4687, Castello, 30122,* ☎ *041/5224324,* FAX *041/5239267. 22 rooms, 3 without bath. Bar, breakfast room. AE, MC, V.*

$$ **Wildner.** Right between the super deluxe Danieli and Londra hotels, this pleasant family-run, unpretentious pensione enjoys the same views. The rooms are spread over four floors (no elevator), half with a view of San Giorgio, the quieter look out onto Campo San Zaccaria. ✉ *Riva degli Schiavoni, 4161 Castello, 30122,* ☎ *041/5227463,* FAX *041/5265615. 16 rooms. Breakfast room. AE, DC, MC, V.*

$ **Istituto San Giuseppe.** This is one of several religious institutions in Venice run by nuns—and it's in an excellent location north of Piazza San Marco. Rooms are spartan in decor, but spotless and very quiet, as they overlook the inner cloister. Book well ahead, as the unbeatable prices draw crowds of guests, mostly Italians in the know. Curfew is at 11 PM (10:30 in the winter), and no breakfast is served. ✉ *5402 Castello, 30122,* ☎ *041/5225352,* FAX *041/5224891. 16 rooms. No credit cards.*

$ **Riva.** This small hotel, close to San Marco, is at the junction of three canals much used by all manner of Venetian watercraft. Although they are endlessly fascinating to watch, the boats can be a little noisy early in the morning. ✉ *Ponte dell'Angelo 5310, Castello, 30122,* ☎ *041/5227034,* FAX *041/5285551. 12 rooms, 2 without bath. No credit cards. Closed mid-Nov.–Jan., except 2 wks at Christmas.*

Dorsoduro

$$–$$$ ★ **Accademia.** Probably the most enchanting hotel in Venice, the Accademia is also one of the most popular, so early reservations are a must. Just beyond an iron gate, a secret garden awaits, complete with mini Palladian-style villa, canal parterre, and verdant trees—all rarities in Venice. Lounges, the bar, and a wood-paneled breakfast room are cheery, and breakfast outside on the garden terrace is a special treat. ✉ *Fondamenta Bollani 1058, Dorsoduro, 30123,* ☎ *041/5210188,* FAX *041/5239152. 27 rooms. Bar, breakfast room, air-conditioning. AE, DC, MC, V.*

$$–$$$ **Hotel Pausania.** This 14th-century palazzo delivers all of the modern comforts with taste, from the moment you ascend the grand staircase rising above a fountain. Light-shaded rooms are spacious, with comfortable furniture and carpets with rugs thrown over them. Some rooms (which can be noisy at times) face the small and quiet canal in front of the hotel, others look out over the large garden courtyard. The hotel has a convenient car service (75,000 lire) to and from the airport. ✉ *2824 Dorsoduro, 30123,* ☎ *041/5222083,* FAX *041/5222989. 26 rooms. Bar, breakfast room, air-conditioning. AE, DC, MC, V.*

$$ ★ **La Calcina.** On a wonderful, if not particularly central, position on the Zattere with an enviable view on the Giudecca canal, this hotel is a must for those with a love of the lagoon and seagulls. There's an *altana* (wooden roof terrace) on which to rest and sunbathe, and in good weather, breakfast is served on a floating platform in front of the hotel. The hotel annex nearby offers bargain rooms without a view. ✉ *780 Dorsoduro, 30123,* ☎ *041/5206466,* FAX *041/5227045. 42 rooms. Breakfast room. AE, DC, MC, V.*

Giudecca

$$$$ **Cipriani.** It's impossible to feel stressed in this sybaritic oasis of stunning rooms and suites, some with garden patios. The hotel launch whisks you to Giudecca from San Marco and back at any hour; those just dining at the exceptional Ristorante Harry Cipriani can use it as well. Cooking courses and fitness programs are offered. The restored and subtly integrated 17th-century style Palazzo Vendramin, an annex of seven suites and three double rooms, is open all year. ✉ *Giudecca 10, 30133,* ☎ *041/5207744,* FAX *041/5203930. 54 rooms, 50 suites. Restaurant, bar, air-conditioning, pool, tennis court. AE, DC, MC, V. Closed Dec.–April.*

Lido

$$$ ★ **Quattro Fontane.** This fine hotel in a well-maintained mansion run by a Danish couple offers the serenity of the Lido, although you will be a walk or a 15-minute boat ride from the center. Well-decorated rooms overlook the surrounding garden. The library has books in many languages. ✉ *Via delle Quattro Fontane 16, Lido, 30126,* ☎ *041/5260227,* FAX *041/5260726. 59 rooms. Library. AE, DC, MC, V.*

San Marco

$$$$ **Concordia.** Half of the rooms in this central, attractive, and well-run hotel overlook the basilica of San Marco, as does the spacious breakfast room–bar, where light meals and snacks are also available all day. The romantic *mansarda* (rooftop room) has a panoramic view over the Piazza San Marco. The management offers good price deals at off-peak times, so check when booking. ✉ *Calle Larga San Marco 367, San Marco, 30124,* ☎ *041/5206866,* FAX *041/5206775. 54 rooms, 3 suites. Bar, breakfast room, air-conditioning. AE, DC, MC, V.*

$$$$ ★ **Gritti Palace.** Queen Elizabeth, Greta Garbo, and Winston Churchill made this their Venetian address. The feeling of being in an aristocratic private home pervades this legendary hotel, replete with fresh flowers, fine antiques, sumptuous appointments, and old-fashioned service. The dining terrace on the Grand Canal is best enjoyed in the evening when the boat traffic dies down. Guests have access to pool and tennis courts. ✉ *Campo Santa Maria del Giglio 2467, San Marco, 30124,* ☎ *041/794611,* FAX *041/5200942. 87 rooms, 6 suites. Restaurant, bar, café, air-conditioning. AE, DC, MC, V.*

$$$$ **Luna Baglioni.** Two minutes from San Marco, this handsome hotel has elegant rooms, several with a view of the Grand Canal. Breakfast is served in a salon fit for a king, with frescoes by the school of Tiepolo, 18th-century furniture, and Venetian floors. Most suites feature fireplaces, Jacuzzis, and terraces. Restaurant Canova offers modern Venetian cuisine. ✉ *1243 San Marco, 30124,* ☎ *041/5289840,* FAX *041/5287160. 111 rooms, 7 suites. Restaurant. AE, DC, MC, V.*

$$$–$$$$ **Saturnia Internazionale.** There's lots of patinated charm in this historic palace, near Piazza San Marco, but it's peaceful and tranquil. Its beamed ceilings, damask-hung walls, and authentic Venetian decor impart real character to the solid comfort of its rooms and salons. Many rooms are endowed with glamorous, large bathrooms. La Caravella restaurant (☞ Dining, *above*) is of special note. ✉ *Calle Larga XXII Marzo 2398, San Marco, 30124,* ☎ *041/5208377,* FAX *041/5207131. 95 rooms. Restaurant, bar, air-conditioning. AE, MC, V.*

$$ **Ala.** The Ala is between San Marco and Santo Stefano, a few steps from the Santa Maria del Giglio vaporetto stop. Some rooms are large with coffered ceilings and old-style furnishings, others are smaller, with more modern decor. Breakfast is served overlooking a small canal.

✉ *2494 San Marco, 30124,* ☎ *041/5208333,* FAX *041/5206390. 85 rooms. Breakfast room. AE, DC, MC, V.*

$$ **Flora.** This hotel has what many in this category lack: plenty of sitting rooms and a pretty courtyard. It's in a quiet but central spot near San Moisè and Piazza San Marco. Rooms have Venetian period decor and are a bit dark for some; a handful are small, with tiny bathrooms. Ask for a room with a view of the courtyard or the garden. ✉ *Calle Bergamaschi 2283 (off Calle Larga XXII Marzo), San Marco, 30124,* ☎ *041/5205844,* FAX *041/5228217. 44 rooms. Bar, air-conditioning. AE, DC, MC, V.*

$ **Locanda Fiorita.** This welcoming small hotel is tucked away in a sunny little square (where breakfast is served in the summer), just off Campo Santo Stefano, near the Accademia Bridge, a good position for sightseeing. The rooms have beamed ceilings and are simply furnished. Eight of the rooms are in an annex on Campo Santo Stefano. ✉ *Campiello Novo o dei Morti, 3457/a San Marco, 30124,* ☎ *041/5234754,* FAX *041/5228043. 18 rooms, 4 without bath. AE, MC, V. Closed 2 wks mid-Jan.*

$ **San Samuele.** Near the Grand Canal and Palazzo Grassi, this friendly hotel has clean, sunny rooms, in surprisingly good shape for the price. ✉ *Salizzada San Samuele 3358, San Marco, 30124,* ☎ FAX *041/5228045. 10 rooms, 8 without bath. No credit cards.*

San Polo

$$ **Sturion.** You might recognize the facade of the hotel in a painting by Carpaccio that hangs at the Gallerie dell'Accademia. Once frequented by merchants who traded at the nearby Rialto market, this small family-run hotel has two rooms overlooking the Grand Canal and a small but pretty breakfast room. Some rooms reserved for nonsmokers. ✉ *Calle del Sturion, 679 San Polo, 30125,* ☎ *041/5236243,* FAX *041/5228378. 11 rooms. Breakfast room. AE, DC, MC, V.*

NIGHTLIFE AND THE ARTS

The Arts

You'll find a list of current and upcoming events in the *Guest in Venice* booklet, free at your hotel. Venice hosts important temporary exhibitions in the Doge's Palace, in Palazzo Grassi at San Samuele on the Grand Canal, and in other venues. The **Biennale,** a cultural institution, organizes many events throughout the year, including the film festival, which begins at the end of August. The big Biennale international art exhibition, usually held from mid-June to the end of September, has been held since 1993 on odd-numbered years at the **Giardini di Castello** (Castello Gardens).

Festivals

Carnevale takes place the 10 or more days leading up to Ash Wednesday. Crowds of revelers make the city almost impossible to visit, so unless you are intent on joining in, stay away. For information on Carnival, check with the main IAT office (☞ Visitor Information *in* Venice A to Z, *below*). On the third Sunday of July, the **Festa del Redentore** (Feast of the Redeemer) is celebrated with the building of a pontoon bridge over the channel to the Giudecca, commemorating the doge's annual visit to this church to offer thanks for the end of a 16th-century plague. At midnight on Saturday fireworks explode over the lagoon as many Venetians take to the water in boats to enjoy the show. The following day there is procession to the church.

Music

Regular concerts at the **Chiesa della Pietà** (✉ Riva degli Schiavoni, San Zaccaria, Castello) have an emphasis on Vivaldi. Those in San Stae and surrounding churches tend to be high priced and the performance quality uneven. Concerts (sometimes free) are also performed in other churches by visiting choirs and musicians. For up-to-date information, ask at the **IAT offices** (☞ Visitor Information in Venice A to Z, *below*). **Kele e Teo Agency** (✉ Ponte dei Bareteri, 4930 San Marco, ☎ 041/5208722, FAX 041/5208913), closed weekends, handles tickets for some musical events.

Opera and Ballet

Teatro La Fenice (✉ Campo San Fantin) is one of Italy's oldest opera houses, a pilgrimage shrine for opera lovers everywhere, and scene of many memorable operatic premieres, including, in 1853, the dismal first-night flop of Verdi's *La Traviata.* The great opera house was badly damaged by fire in January 1996, and although restoration work has begun (helped in large part by donations from opera lovers around the world), the theater will not reopen until the year 2000. In the meantime, opera, symphony, and ballet performances are held year-round at the **Palafenice** (✉ Near the Tronchetto parking area, ☎ 041/5204010); call for ticket information or go to the Cassa di Risparmio bank (✉ Campo San Luca, ☎ 041/5210161).

Nightlife

Piazza San Marco in fair weather, when the cafés stay open late, is a meeting place, though young Venetians tend to gravitate toward Campi San Luca, San Salvador, and San Bartolomeo, near Rialto.

Bars

The **Martini Scala Club** (✉ Calle del Cafetier, 1007 San Marco, ☎ 041/5224121) is an elegant piano bar with a restaurant. Tunes start at 10 and go until the wee hours. **Devil's Forest Pub** (✉ Calle dei Stagneri 5185, off Campo San Bartolomeo, ☎ 041/5200623) is a favored hang-out of many young Venetians. **Fiddler's Elbow** (✉ Strada Nuova, Cannaregio 3847, ☎ 041/5239930) offers all the typical trappings of an Irish pub: gab, grub, and frothy Guinness. A nightspot with food, drinks, and music, **Paradiso Perduto** (✉ Fondamenta della Misericordia 2540, Cannaregio, ☎ 041/720581) serves up inexpensive fish dishes, plus live music usually on Sundays.

Casino

The city-run gambling **Casino** operates June to September in a modern building on the Lido (✉ Lungomare Marconi 4, ☎ 041/5297111). It's open June–September, daily 4 PM–2:15 AM and October–May, daily 3–2:15. At press time there are plans to move the Casino to Mestre in the summertime, into the splendorous **Palazzo Vendramin Calergi** (✉ Grand Canal, ☎ 041/5297111). Admission costs 10,000 lire, or 5,000 lire for the slot machines area.

Nightclubs

For dancing try the **Disco Club Piccolo Mondo** (✉ 1056/a Dorsoduro, near the Accademia, ☎ 041/5200371), next to the Gallerie dell' Accademia. Outside Venice on nearby Lido is **Piazza Caffè** (✉ Lungomare Marconi 22, Lido, ☎ 041/5260466), one of the more trendy, hip spots, with disco and live performances. It's open March–September, daily and October–April, Saturday only.

OUTDOOR ACTIVITIES AND SPORTS

Participant Sports

Golf

The 18-hole **Golf Club Lido di Venezia** (✉ Via del Forte, Alberoni, Lido, ☎ 041/731333), closed Monday, is on Lido island.

Horseback Riding

Circolo Ippico Veneziano (✉ Ca' Bianca, the Lido, ☎ 041/5265162), closed Sunday afternoon and Monday, rents horses for riding trails on the premises and can refer you to terra firma clubs around the Veneto.

Running

The best running route heads east from the Giardini Pubblici in the Castello district and over to the pine wood on Sant'Elena; it allows a magnificent view of the city as you run back toward the center.

Swimming

Venice's best public pool is the **Piscina Comunale** (✉ Island of Sacca Fisola, far end of Giudecca, ☎ 041/5285430), open daily mid-September–June; call ahead for hours. Take Line 82 to Sacca Fisola. A second public pool is in Cannaregio at Sant'Alvise (☎ 041/713567), housed in a well-preserved building that once served as the community laundry. The deluxe **Hotel des Bains** (✉ Lungomare Marconi, Lido, ☎ 041/5265921) opens its small pool to nonguests for a substantial fee (85,000–130,000 lire per day).

Tennis

The **Hotel des Bains** (☞ Swimming, *above*) rents tennis courts to nonguests. The exclusive **Sea Gull Club** of the Cipriani hotel (☞ Lodging, *above*) will also let nonguests play for a fee. There are several tennis clubs on the Lido, including **Lido Tennis Club** (✉ Via Sandro Gallo 163, ☎ 041/5260954). The Lido's **Club Ca' del Moro** (✉ Via F. Parri 6, ☎ 041/770965) has tennis and an outdoor pool in summer.

SHOPPING

You're sure to find plenty of pleasant shops and boutiques as you explore Venice. It's always a good idea to mark the location of a shop that interests you on your map; otherwise you may not be able to find it again in the maze of tiny streets. Regular store opening hours are usually 9–12:30 and 3:30 or 4–7:30 PM. Food shops are open 8–1 and 5–7:30, and are closed all day Sunday and on Wednesday afternoon (and sometimes on Monday morning). However, many tourist-oriented shops are open all day, every day. Some shops close for both a summer and a winter vacation.

Markets

The morning open-air fruit and vegetable market at **Rialto** offers animated local color and commerce. On Tuesday through Saturday mornings, the adjacent **fish market** teaches an impressive lesson in ichthyology, with species you've probably never seen before. In the Castello district is **Via Garibaldi,** the scene of another lively food market on weekday mornings. Another small market is near the train station.

Shopping Districts

The San Marco area is full of shops and couture boutiques such as Armani, Missoni, Valentino, Fendi, and Versace. Le Mercerie, along with the Frezzeria and Calle dei Fabbri, leading from Piazza San Marco, are some of Venice's busiest streets. Other good shopping areas surround Calle del Teatro and Campi San Salvador, Manin, San Fantin, and San Bartolomeo. Less-expensive shops are between the Rialto Bridge and San Polo.

Specialty Stores

Glassware

Glass, most of it made in Murano, is Venice's number-one product, and you'll be confronted by mind-boggling displays of traditional and contemporary glassware, often kitsch. Take your time and be selective. You will probably find that prices in Venice's shops and the showrooms of Murano's factories are pretty much the same. However, because of competition, shops in Venice with wares from various glassworks may charge slightly lower prices. **Galleria San Nicolò** (✉ Calle del Traghetto 2793, Dorsoduro, by the Ca' Rezzonico vaporetto stop, ☎ 041/5221535) is owned by the American glass expert Louise Berndt. It shows the best of contemporary glass, including superb work by Yoichi Ohira, a Japanese designer and long a resident in Venice. **Domus** (✉ Fondamenta dei Vetrai, Murano, ☎ 041/739215) has a selection of smaller objects and jewelry from the best glassworks. For chic, contemporary glassware designs, Carlo Moretti is a good choice; his signature designs are on display at **L'Isola** (✉ San Marco 2084, ☎ 041/5285263).

Marina Barovier's gallery (✉ Calle delle Botteghe 3172, San Marco, just off Campo Santo Stefano, ☎ 041/5236748) has an excellent selection of collectors' 20th-century glass. Go to Michel Paciello's **Paropàmiso** (✉ Frezzeria 1701, near Piazza San Marco, ☎ 041/5227120) for stunning Venetian glass beads and traditional jewelry from all over the world. **Pauly** (✉ Piazza San Marco 73–77, ☎ 041/5209899) is central, with a wide array of glassware. In a category all his own is **Gianfranco Penzo** (✉ Campo del Ghetto Nuovo 2895, ☎ no phone), who decorates Jewish ritual vessels in glass and makes commemorative plates; he takes special orders. **Salviati** (✉ Piazza San Marco 79/b, ☎ 041/5207075) is a reliable and respected firm. **Venini** (✉ Piazzetta dei Leoncini 314, ☎ 041/5224045) has been an institution since the 1930s, attracting some of the foremost names in glass design. **Vetri d'Arte** (✉ Piazza San Marco 140, ☎ 041/5200205) offers moderately priced glass jewelry.

Lace and Embroidered Fabrics

Venice's top name is **Jesurum** (✉ Piazza San Marco 60–61, ☎ 041/5229864). It is one of the few stores in Venice whose lace *is* made in and around the city. Go to **Lorenzo Rubelli** (✉ Campo San Gallo 1089, just off Piazza San Marco, ☎ 041/5236110) for the same sumptuous brocades, damasks, and cut velvets used by the world's most prestigious decorators. Much of the lace and embroidered linen sold in Venice and on Burano is really made in China or Taiwan. At **Norelene** (✉ Calle de la Chiesa 727, ☎ 041/5237605) you'll find wonderful hand-printed fabrics.

Masks

Mondonovo (✉ Rio Terrà Canal, ☎ 041/5287344) is a cut above most other mask stores. **Laboratorio Artigiano Maschere** (✉ Barbaria delle Tole, near Campo dei Santi Giovanni e Paolo, ☎ 041/5223110) is home to Giorgio Clanetti, credited with starting the current revival in mask making.

VENICE A TO Z

Arriving and Departing

By Bus

Buses connect the **bus terminal** (✉ Piazzale Roma, across the Grand Canal from the train station, near the vaporetto stop of that name) to Mestre, the Brenta Riviera, Padua, and other destinations in the region.

By Car

Venice is on the east–west **A4** autostrada, which connects with Padua, Verona, Brescia, Milan, and Turin. If you bring a car to Venice, you will have to pay for a garage or parking space. Warning: do not be waylaid by illegal touts—often wearing fake uniforms, and whose activities have in recent years become a scandal in a city generally remarkably free of con men and criminals—who may try to flag you down and offer to arrange parking and hotels; ignore them and continue on until you reach the automatic ticket machines. Do not leave valuables in the car. There is a left-luggage office, open daily 8 AM–8 PM, next to the Pullman Bar on the ground floor of the municipal garage at Piazzale Roma. You can take your car to the Lido; the car ferry (Line 17) makes the half-hour trip about every 50 minutes from a landing at Tronchetto, but in summer there can be long queues. It costs 12,000 to 30,000 lire, depending on the size of the car. Line 82 runs from Tronchetto to Piazzale Roma and Piazza San Marco and also goes on to the Lido in summer. (When there is thick fog or extreme tides, a bus runs to Piazzale Roma instead.) Avoid private boats—they are a rip-off.

Parking at **Autorimessa Comunale** (✉ Piazzale Roma, end of S11 road) costs between 15,000 and 25,000 lire for 24 hours. The private **Garage San Marco** (✉ Piazzale Roma, end of S11 road) costs between 34,000 and 46,000 lire per 24 hours, depending on the size of the car. To reach the privately run **Tronchetto** parking area, follow the signs to turn right before Piazzale Roma. Parking costs 25,000 lire per 24 hours. The AVA (☞ Lodging, *above*) has arranged a discount of around 5,000 lire per day for hotel guests who use the Tronchetto facility. Ask for a voucher upon checking into your hotel and present it at Tronchetto when you pay.

By Plane

Aeroporto Marco Polo (✉ Tessera, about 10 km/6 mi north of the city on the mainland, ☎ 041/2609260 information) is served by domestic and international flights, including connections from London, Amsterdam, Brussels, Frankfurt, Munich, Paris, Vienna, and Zurich.

BETWEEN THE AIRPORT AND DOWNTOWN

By Boat. This may be the best way to get to Venice from the airport. The most direct way is by the **Cooperativa San Marco** launch, with regular scheduled service until midnight; it takes about an hour to get to the landing (just off Piazza San Marco), stopping at the Lido on the way, and the fare is 17,000 lire per person, including bags. A **water taxi** (☎ 041/5415084), a sleek, modern motorboat known as a *motoscafo,* from the airport costs about 130,000 lire, but it is always essential to agree on a fare before boarding.

By Bus. Blue **ATVO** (☎ 041/929500) buses make the 25-minute nonstop trip from the airport to Piazzale Roma; from there you can get a vaporetto to the landing nearest your hotel. The ATVO fare is 5,000 lire, and tickets are available on the bus when the airport ticket booth is closed. The local **ACTV** bus (Line 5) runs from the airport to Piazzale Roma, but you need a ticket (1,500 lire) before boarding, which can only be purchased at the airport tobacconist-newsstand, open daily 6:30 AM–9 PM. Luggage can be a hassle on the bus, which is usually crowded with local commuters.

By Taxi. A yellow taxi from the airport to Piazzale Roma costs about 60,000 lire.

By Train

Venice has rail connections with every major city in Italy and Europe. Some trains do not terminate at **Stazione Ferroviaria Santa Lucia** (⌧ On the Grand Canal in the northwest corner of the city, ☎ 147/8880880 toll free). Instead, they stop only at the **Stazione Ferroviaria Venezia-Mestre** (⌧ On the mainland, ☎ 147/8880880 toll free). All trains traveling to and from Santa Lucia stop at Mestre; to get from Venezia-Mestre to Santa Lucia, or vice versa (a 10-minute trip), take the first available train, remembering there is a *supplemento* (extra charge) for traveling on Intercity and Eurocity and Eurostar trains, and that if you do not purchase it at the station booth and validate it in the machine on the platform before boarding, you are liable for a hefty fine.

Getting Around

First-time visitors find that getting around Venice presents some unusual problems: the layout is complex; the waterborne transportation can be bewildering; the house-numbering system is baffling; many street names in the *sestieri* (six districts) of San Marco, Cannaregio, Castello, Dorsoduro, Santa Croce, and San Polo, are duplicated; and often you must walk, whether you want to or not. It's essential to have a good map showing all street names and vaporetto routes; buy one at a newsstand. Signs are posted on many corners pointing you in the right direction for the nearest major landmark—San Marco, Rialto, Accademia, etc.—but don't count on finding such signs once you're deep into residential neighborhoods.

For those aged 14–29, the **"Rolling Venice"** youth card (5,000 lire) includes handy guidebooks to the city, and offers good discounts for ACTV vaporetto passes and a few museums, as well as some hotels, restaurants, and shops. It is available from the Assessorato alla Gioventù (⌧ Corte Contarini 1529, behind Piazza San Marco post office, ☎ 041/2747651), open Monday, Wednesday, and Friday 9:30–1, Tuesday and Thursday 9:30–1 and 3–5; Arte e Storia travel agency (⌧ Campo della Lana, ☎ 041/5240232), open Monday–Friday 9–12:45 and 3–6:15; and Associazione Italiana Alberghi per la Gioventù (⌧ Calle Castelforte, near San Rocco, ☎ 041/5204414), open Monday–Saturday 8:30–1:30. You must show your passport to qualify.

By Gondola

If you simply can't leave Venice without a gondola ride, the best time is in the late afternoon or early evening hours, when the Grand Canal isn't so heavily trafficked. Try to avoid low tide, when the foul odors of the canals are at their worst. It's best to start from a station on the Grand Canal because the lagoon is usually choppy. Make it clear that you want to see the smaller canals, and come to terms on the cost and duration of the ride before you start. Gondoliers are supposed to charge a fixed minimum of about 120,000 lire for up to six passengers for 50 minutes. After 8 PM and up to 8 AM the rate increases to approximately 150,000 lire. Bargaining may get you a better price.

By Motoscafo

These stylish powerboat water taxis are extremely expensive, and the fare system is as complex as Venice's layout. Plan on spending at least 80,000 lire for a short trip in town, 130,000 to or from the airport. Always agree on the fare before starting out, and beware of other additions such as handling luggage and late or early hours. Call Cooperativa San Marco (☎ 041/5222303) for 24-hour service.

By Traghetto

Few tourists know about the two-man gondolas that ferry people across the Grand Canal at various fixed points. They are the cheapest and shortest gondola ride in Venice and can save a lot of walking. The fare is 700 lire, which you hand to the gondolier when you get on. Look for TRAGHETTO signs.

By Vaporetto

ACTV water buses (☎ 041/5287886 information), open daily 7:30 AM–8 PM, run the length of the Grand Canal and circle the city. There are several lines, some of which connect Venice with the major and minor islands in the lagoon. The fare is 6,000 lire on all lines. A 24-hour tourist ticket costs 18,000 lire, a three-day ticket 35,000 lire, and a seven-day ticket 60,000 lire; these are especially worthwhile if you are planning to visit the islands. Free timetables are available at the ticket office at Piazzale Roma. Timetables are also posted at every landing stage, and there is a ticket booth at each stop. After 9 PM, tickets are available on the boats, but you must immediately inform the controller that you need a ticket. For this reason, it may be useful to buy a *blocchetto* (book of tickets) in advance. Be sure to validate tickets in the time-stamp machines before getting on board, or you could be subject to a fine.

Landing stages are clearly marked with name and line number, but check before boarding, particularly with Lines 52 and 82, to make sure the boat is going in your direction. **Line 1** is the Grand Canal local, calling at every stop, and continuing via San Marco to the Lido. (The trip takes about 45 minutes from the station to San Marco.) **Line 41** and **Line 42** follow long loop routes in opposite directions: take Line 41 from San Zaccaria to Murano, but Line 42 from Murano to San Zaccaria; Line 42 from San Zaccaria to the Redentore, but Line 41 from the Redentore back to San Zaccaria. **Line 51** runs from the railway station to San Zaccaria via Piazzale Roma and Zattere and continues to the Lido. **Line 52** goes along the same route but in the opposite direction, so from the Lido it makes stops at the Giardini, San Zaccaria, Zattere, Piazzale Roma, the train station, Fondamente Nuove (where boats leave for the islands of the northern lagoon), San Pietro, and back to the Lido. **Line 82** runs in a loop from San Zaccaria to Giudecca, Zattere, Piazzale Roma, the train station, Rialto, (with fewer stops along the Grand Canal than Line 1), and back to San Zaccaria, and out to the Lido.

Contacts and Resources

Car Rentals

Sixt Rent-a-Car (✉ Piazzale Roma, ☎ 041/5289551). **Avis** (✉ Piazzale Roma, ☎ 041/5225825; ✉ Aeroporto Marco Polo, ☎ 041/5415030). **Hertz** (✉ Piazzale Roma ☎ 041/5284091; ✉ Aeroporto Marco Polo ☎ 041/5416075).

Consulates

U.K. Consulate (✉ Campo della Carità 1051, Dorsoduro, ☎ 041/5227207). There is no U.S. or Canadian consular service.

Doctors and Dentists

The U.K. Consulate (☞ *above*) can recommend doctors and dentists. Your hotel or any pharmacy should also be able to offer advice.

Emergencies

General Emergencies (☎ 113). **Carabinieri** (☎ 112). **Ambulance** (☎ 118). **Venice Hospital First Aid** (☎ 041/5230000).

English-Language Bookstores

Fantoni (✉ On Salizzada San Luca, ☎ 041/5220700). **Emiliana Editrice** (✉ Calle Goldoni, between Piazza San Marco and Campo San Luca, ☎ 041/5220793). **Studium** (✉ Calle de la Canonica, off Piazzetta dei Leoncini, ☎ 041/5222382). **Libreria Editrice Filippi** (✉ On Casseleria, between Ponte de l'Anzolo, take the last left off Calle de la Canonica, ☎ 041/5236916). The newspaper stall to the right of the San Marco post office has English-language newspapers.

Guided Tours

EXCURSION

Islands of the Lagoon. The **Cooperativa San Marco** (✉ Just off San Marco, ☎ 041/5235775) organizes tours of the islands of Murano, Burano, and Torcello. April through November, the 3½-hour tours depart daily at 9:30 and 2:30 (December through March daily at 2) from the landing stage in front of the Giardini Reali, just off Piazza San Marco; they cost about 25,000 lire. Tours tend to be annoyingly commercial and emphasize glass-factory showrooms, pressuring you to buy, sometimes at higher prices than normal.

Veneto. American Express (✉ Salizzada San Moisè 1471, San Marco, ☎ 041/5200844, FAX 041/5229937) runs a day trip to Padova by boat along the Brenta River, with stops at three Palladian villas, and a return to Venice by bus. The tours run three days a week from March to November and cost 120,000 lire per person (170,000 lire with lunch); bookings need to be made the day before.

ORIENTATION

Two-hour walking tours of the San Marco area can be booked through **American Express** (✉ Salizzada San Moisè 1471, San Marco, ☎ 041/5200844, FAX 041/5229937). It's daily "Jewels of the Venetian Republic" tour (about 45,000 lire) ends with a glassblowing demonstration. From April 25 to November 15, American Express also offers an afternoon walking tour that ends with a gondola ride (about 50,000 lire).

PERSONAL GUIDES

Guides' Association (✉ San Marco 750, near San Zulian, ☎ 041/5209038, FAX 041/5210762). **American Express** (☞ *above*).

SPECIAL-INTEREST

Basilica di San Marco. From June through August, free guided tours (some in English) of the Basilica di San Marco are offered by the **Procuratoria** (☎ 041/5225205); information is available in the atrium of the church; no tours Sunday.

Gondola. American Express (☞ *above*) offers group gondola rides with serenades from May through October nightly (about 50,000 lire).

Late-Night Pharmacies

The nearest pharmacy is never far, and they take turns opening nights, Saturday afternoons, and Sundays; the weekly list of after-hours pharmacies is posted on the front of every pharmacy.

Travel Agencies

American Express (✉ Salizzada San Moisè 1471, San Marco, ☎ 041/5200844, FAX 041/5229937). **Sattis Viaggi** (✉ Calle Larga dell'Ascensione 1261, ☎ 041/5285101, 041/5285102, or 041/5285103). **Carlson Wagon-Lit Travel** (✉ Piazzetta dei Leoncini 289, ☎ 041/5223405).

Visitor Information

Tourist offices (✉ Santa Lucia train station, ☎ 041/5298727; ✉ San Marco 71/f, near the Museo Correr, ☎ 041/5298740; Lido: ✉ Gran Viale S. Maria Elisabetta 6/a, ☎ 041/5265721).

5 VENETIAN ARC

PADUA, VERONA, VICENZA, AND PALLADIO COUNTRY

The art and architecture of every city in the Venetian Arc—Verona, Vicenza, Padua, Treviso—echo in some way the graces and refinements of Venice. Here you'll find Asolo, the City of a Hundred Horizons; Padua, ennobled by Giotto's frescoes; Verona's romantic *Romeo and Juliet* settings; and the villas of Andrea Palladio, where 16th-century aristocrats led the privileged life.

Updated by Carla Lionello and Jon Eldan

AS ROME PRESIDES OVER LAZIO, the arc to the north of Venice that stretches from Verona east to Trieste falls under the historical and spiritual influence of its namesake city. No lagoons, perhaps, but the region's architecture, paintings, and way of life all bask in the reflected splendor of La Serenissima. Much of the pleasure of exploring this area comes from discovering the individual variations on the overall Venetian theme that confer special charm on each of the towns you'll visit. Some, such as Verona, Treviso, and Udine, have a solid medieval look; Asolo has an idyllic setting; Bassano combines a bit of both. If you are a confirmed or fledgling oenophile, you'll enjoy tasting local wines within view of the vineyards that produce some of the best-known Italian vintages—among them, Soave, Valpolicella, Bardolino, and Prosecco. But most of all, you'll find artistic jewels everywhere, from the great Venetian masters in Verona to Veronese's lighthearted frescoes in Villa Barbaro at Maser.

Pleasures and Pastimes

Concerts and Opera

The love of Italian culture need not stop at Venice. Verona, Trieste, and Vicenza offer some of the most spectacular opportunities for indulging in the passions of open-air operas and concerts.

Dining

In the main cities of the Veneto region, restaurants are in the middle to upper ranges of each price category, but in smaller towns and in the countryside you can find some real bargains. At the eastern end of the Arc, in less-trafficked Friuli-Venezia Giulia, prices are generally lower. Seafood is the specialty along the coast, of course, but inland the cuisine varies from the delicate risotto of the Veneto to the more decisively flavored cooking of the Trieste area, heavily influenced by Austria. San Daniele del Friuli, near Udine, is famous for its delicious prosciutto. Polenta, made of cornmeal, is a staple throughout the area; it is served with thick, rich sauces or grilled as an accompaniment to meat dishes. In the Veneto, a bowl of thick *pasta e fagioli* (pasta and bean soup), here typically prepared with the addition of wide pieces of fresh pasta, is all you might want to eat on a cold winter's night. Trieste's position near the Austrian and Slovenian borders has fostered a varied—and somewhat heavier—cuisine reflecting the tastes of those countries.

The best local wines are Soave, Tocai, Prosecco, Riesling, and pinot—all white; and reds Bardolino, Valpolicella, merlot, cabernet, and pinot nero. The Collio designation indicates wines from vineyards in the eastern part of Friuli, up against the Slovenian border. One of the best known and rarest wines produced here is the Picolit, similar to sauterne and made in very limited quantities. The Veneto and Friuli regions are renowned for their grappas. Justifiably popular are those made by the families Nardini, in Bassano, and Nonino, at Udine. Trieste is the home of the famous Stock liqueur.

Lodging

The area around Venice has been playing host to visitors for centuries, and the result is a range of comfortable accommodations at every price. As with dining, common sense should tell you that the slightly out-of-the-way small hotel will cost you less than its counterpart in a stylish Adriatic resort. Hotels in nearby Vicenza, Bassano del Grappa, along the Brenta, and in Venice are better in terms of variety and quality than in Padua itself, which caters primarily to business travelers.

Expect to pay more as you approach Venice, since many of the mainland towns absorb the overflow during the times when Venice becomes most crowded, such as Carnevale (Carnival, held two weeks preceding Lent) and throughout the summer.

Shopping

Many of the goods associated with Venice are actually produced in the surrounding areas of the Venetian Arc—which means that with a bit of diligence or luck you can pick up a bargain from the source. Mountain towns and villages such as Bassano del Grappa have the strongest handicraft tradition, and you can find a wide range of goods in artisans' shops on the side streets. The main towns on the coastal plain are often associated with one or two specialties, either because of traditional skills or because of ancient trading rights that set a pattern of importing specific items from other parts of the Mediterranean.

Villas and Palazzi

The countless villas and palaces sprinkled throughout the Venetian hinterland and the Palladian villas along the Brenta River should not be missed. These gracious country homes give insight into the way wealthy Venetians used to—and still do—spend leisure time. Many of the villas are privately owned but are open to the public at certain times or by special request. Local tourist offices can be helpful in providing information on visiting these jewels.

Exploring the Venetian Arc

The Venetian Arc comprises principally the coastal crescent and the inland plain that stretches from the mouths of the Po and Adige rivers southwest of Venice. In addition, the cities of Trieste and Udine lie east of Venice and close to the Slovenian border. They bridge two Italian regions—the Veneto and Friuli-Venezia Giulia—and landscapes of flat green farmland spotted with low hills that swell and rise steeply inland in a succession of plateaus and high meadows to the snow-tipped Alps.

Numbers in the text correspond to numbers in the margin and on the Venetian Arc and Verona maps.

Great Itineraries

Hard as it may seem to leave the unique beauty of Venice behind, the Venetian Arc is the perfect last course to round off your stay. The towns are all beautiful, mixing grandiose architecture and medieval aristocracy flawlessly. One of these towns, Verona, also unknowingly produced the most tragic of all *storie d'amore* (love stories)—*Romeo and Juliet.* The sorrow that this tale inspires can be drowned in the delights of some of the best-known Italian wines.

Many towns can be seen on one- or two-day excursions from Venice itself. A three-day itinerary will exclude Trieste and restrict you to the other principal sights. A five-day exploration will give you plenty to remember and even savor, but you will have to discipline yourself to keep up a swift pace. A seven-day trip will give you the time to fully experience the architecture, history, and culture of this beautiful region.

IF YOU HAVE 3 DAYS

Begin your drive at **Villa Pisani** ①, the most splendid of all Veneto villas. Move on to **Padua** ②, taking in the Cappella degli Scrovegni. Continue toward **Verona** ④–⑱, the city of *Romeo and Juliet.* The following day see some of Palladio's works in **Vicenza** ③ and head for **Marostica** ⑲, **Bassano del Grappa** ⑳, and **Asolo** ㉑. Save the last day for **Treviso** ㉓, **Conegliano** ㉔, and stop for a tour of **Udine** ㉕. Return to Venice along the A4.

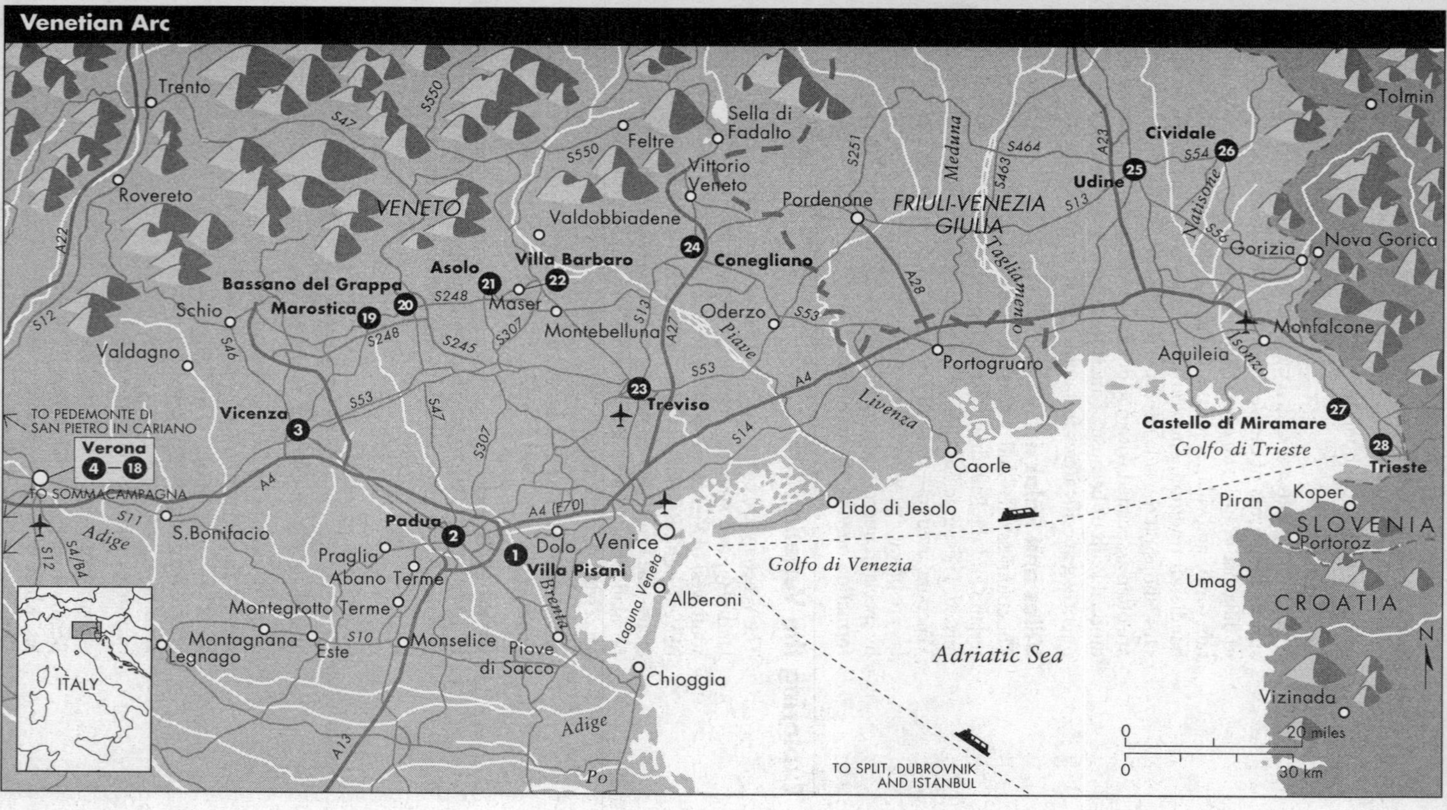
Venetian Arc
Trento
Rovereto
Feltre
Sella di Fadalto
Vittorio Veneto
Valdobbiadene
VENETO
Pordenone
FRIULI-VENEZIA GIULIA
Meduna
Tagliamento
Cividale
Udine
Natisone
Tolmin
Gorizia
Nova Gorica
Monfalcone
Isonzo
Aquileia
Asolo
Villa Barbaro
Conegliano
Bassano del Grappa
Marostica
Maser
Schio
Montebelluna
Oderzo
Piave
Portogruaro
Valdagno
Livenza
Treviso
Vicenza
TO PEDEMONTE DI SAN PIETRO IN CARIANO
Verona
TO SOMMACAMPAGNA
Caorle
Castello di Miramare
Golfo di Trieste
Trieste
Lido di Jesolo
Koper
Piran
SLOVENIA
Portoroz
Padua
Venice
Dolo
Villa Pisani
S.Bonifacio
Adige
Praglia
Abano Terme
Brenta
Laguna Veneta
Golfo di Venezia
Alberoni
Umag
CROATIA
Montegrotto Terme
Montagnana
Este
Monselice
Piove di Sacco
Legnago
Chioggia
Adriatic Sea
ITALY
Vizinada
Po
TO SPLIT, DUBROVNIK AND ISTANBUL
0
20 miles
0
30 km
N
A4
A4 (E70)
A13
A22
A23
A27
A28
S10
S11
S12
S13
S14
S4/B4
S46
S47
S53
S54
S56
S245
S248
S251
S307
S463
S464
S550

IF YOU HAVE 5 DAYS

Follow the 3-day itinerary until Asolo. Instead of moving on directly to Treviso, travel toward **Villa Barbaro** ㉒ in Maser and then on to **Treviso** ㉓. Visit **Conegliano** ㉔ and **Udine** ㉕, where you can overnight. The next day head for **Cividale** ㉖ and then down to **Trieste** ㉘. Spend a day in this border city and then move on to **Castello di Miramare** ㉗ before taking the A4 back to Venice.

IF YOU HAVE 7 DAYS

Follow the itinerary described above, but in **Bassano del Grappa** ⑳ take in a visit to the famous Nardini distillery on the edge of town. From **Treviso** ㉓, head to Oderzo on the magnificent Strada del Vino Rosso (Red Wine Road), which winds through the cabernet and merlot country along the Piave River.

When to Tour the Venetian Arc

There is no particular good or bad time to see the sights around the Venetian Arc. Most of the year, the area is relatively free from very heavy traffic and congestion. If, however, you want to get the most out of your stay, come during the late spring and early summer months (May, June, July) or in early September. Winter is a good time to avoid travel to the region, when in November through March foggy conditions and wet, bone-chilling cold are not unusual. Opera and theater buffs should come in spring and summer, when the outdoor performances are held.

ON THE ROAD TO PADUA AND VERONA

Foremost among the treasures of the Veneto region are the beautiful villas of Andrea Palladio (1508–80) built to render la vita all the more dolce for 16th-century aristocrats. Other important sights include Giotto's 14th-century frescoes in Padua's Cappella degli Scrovegni and many of Donatello's greatest statues.

Villa Pisani

❶ *10 km (6 mi) southeast of Padua.*

This extraordinary house, also called Villa Nazionale, in Stra is the most spectacular of all the villas in the region. Through the 16th to 18th centuries, wealthy Venetians sought to enjoy *villeggiatura*—a vacation and escape from harried city life—by building stately residences on their country estates throughout Venetia. Many of them were constructed on the Brenta River, the main waterway used by Venetians to go inland. Villa Pisani may remind you more of Versailles, for it's an imposing 18th-century edifice that once belonged to Napoléon, who appreciated its similarities to Versailles. See the grandiose frescoes by Giambattista Tiepolo (1696–1770) on the ceiling of the ballroom. If you have youngsters surfeited with the old masters in tow, explore the gorgeous **park** and the **maze** (open April to September only). ✉ *Stra,* ☎ *049/502074.* *Villa, maze, and grounds: 10,000 lire; maze and grounds: 5,000 lire.* ⏲ *Apr.–Sept., daily 9–7; Oct.–Mar., daily 9–4.*

Padua

❷ *37 km (23 mi) west of Venice, 92 km (57 mi) east of Verona.*

Bustling Padua (Padova in Italian), has long been one of the major cultural centers in northern Italy. It's home to the peninsula's second-oldest university, founded in 1222, which attracted the likes of Dante (1265–1321), Petrarch (1304–74), and Galileo Galilei (1564–1642). Three great artists—Giotto (1266/67–1337), Donatello (circa 1386–1466), and Mantegna (1431–1506)—left great works here. If you will be visiting many of the local sights, plan on getting the Padua Biglietto Unico, a cumulative ticket (10,000 lire).

★ The **Cappella degli Scrovegni** (Scrovegni Chapel) was erected in the 13th century by a wealthy Paduan, Enrico Scrovegno, to honor his deceased father. Scrovegni called on Giotto to decorate its interior, a task that occupied the great artist and his helpers from 1303 to 1305. They created a magnificent fresco cycle, arranged in typical medieval comic-strip fashion, illustrating the lives of Mary and Christ. The realism in these frescoes—which include the first blue skies in Western painting—was revolutionary. ✉ *Piazza Eremitani 8,* ☎ *049/8204550.* 🎫 *10,000 lire (includes admission to Museo Civico,* ☞ *below).* ⏲ *Feb.–Oct., daily 9–7; Nov.–Jan., daily 9–6.*

The 13th-century **Chiesa degli Eremitani** contains some fragments of frescoes—most, however, were destroyed by the Allied bombing of 1944—by Andrea Mantegna, the brilliant locally born artist, some of whose masterpieces are in nearby Mantua. The **Museo Civico di Padova** (Civic Museum of Padua), housed in what used to be the monastery of the church, has its quota of works by Venetian masters, as well as a fine collection of ancient relics. ✉ *Piazza Eremitani 10,* ☎ *049/8204550.* 🎫 *Museo Civico: 10,000 lire (includes admission to Cappella degli Scrovegni,* ☞ *above).* ⏲ *Feb.–Oct., daily 9–7; Nov.–Jan., daily 9–6.*

The 16th-century **Palazzo del Bo'** houses the **Università di Padova,** founded in 1222. The building, which now features an 18th-century facade, is named after the Osteria del Bo' (*bo* means ox), an inn which once stood on the site. This is worth a visit to see the exquisite and perfectly proportioned anatomy theater and a hall with a lectern used by Galileo. ✉ *Via VIII Febbraio,* ☎ *049/8209711.* 🎫 *5,000 lire.* ⏲ *Guided visits only; call for tour times.*

Palazzo della Ragione, also called Il Salone, was built in the Middle Ages as the seat of Padua's parliament. Today its street-level arcades shelter shops and cafés. In the frescoed **Salone** (Salon) on the upper level is an enormous wooden horse, a 15th-century replica of the bronze steed in Donatello's equestrian statue of Gattamelata. ✉ *Piazza della Ragione,* ☎ *049/8205006.* 🎫 *7,000 lire.* ⏲ *Tues.–Sun. 9–7.*

The huge **Basilica di Sant'Antonio** is a cluster of Byzantine domes and slender, minaretlike towers that gives the church an Asian-inspired style reminiscent of San Marco in Venice. The interior is sumptuous, too, with marble reliefs by Tullio Lombardo (circa 1455–1532), the greatest in a talented family of marble carvers who decorated many churches in the area, among them Santa Maria dei Miracoli in Venice. The artistic highlights here, however, all bear Donatello's name: the 15th-century Florentine master did the remarkable series of bronze reliefs illustrating the life of St. Anthony—whose feast day, Festa di Sant'Antonio on June 13, draws pilgrims from all over Europe—as well as the bronze statues of the Madonna and saints on the high altar. ✉ *Piazza del Santo,* ☎ *049/8242811.* ⏲ *Mon.–Sat. 6:30–7, Sun. 6:30–7:45.*

To mark the 800th anniversary of the birth of St. Anthony in 1195, a museum, the **Mostre Antoniane,** with 300 exhibits relating to the image of the saint and of the basilica, was opened in 1995 on the first floor of the church cloister building. Standing in front of the church is Donatello's powerful statue of the *condottiere* (mercenary general) *Gattamelata,* which was cast in bronze—a monumental technical achievement—in 1453 and was to have an enormous influence on the development of Italian Renaissance sculpture. ✉ *Piazza del Santo,* ☎ *049/8242811.* 🎫 *5,000 lire.* ⏲ *Easter–Oct., daily 9–1 and 2–6:30; Nov.–Easter, Tues.–Sun. 10–1 and 2–5.*

The **Orto Botanico** (Botanic Garden) was founded in 1545 by order of the Venetian Republic to supply the university with medicinal plants. The garden is in front of Sant'Antonio. ✉ *Via Orto Botanico 15,* ☎ *049/656614.* 🎫 *5,000 lire.* ⏲ *Apr.–Oct., daily 9–1 and 3–6; Nov.–Mar., Mon.–Sat. 9–1.*

Piazza dei Signori exhibits some fine examples of 15th- and 16th-century buildings. The **Cathedral** is just a few steps from Piazza dei Signori.

Laid out in 1775, **Prato della Valle** is an unusual and attractive piazza with a central wooded oval park, encircled by a canal, called Isola Memmia. A market is featured here weekends (☞ Shopping, *below*). At the southeast end of this immense square is the church of **Santa Giustina,** with finely inlaid choir stalls and Veronese's (1528–88) colossal altarpiece, *The Martyrdom of St. Justine.* ✉ *Prato della Valle.* ⏲ *Apr.–Oct., daily 8.30–noon and 3–7; Nov.–Mar., 9–noon and 3–6.*

OFF THE BEATEN PATH

ABANO TERME AND MONTEGROTTO TERME – These two spas, about 12 km (7 mi) south of Padua, are set in the dreamy landscape of the Euganean Hills. Colorful gardens and fresh summer breezes make them havens if you are looking for a respite from city life.

PRAGLIA – You can tour the evocative 15th-century halls and cloisters of this Benedictine monastery hidden in the hills. Wine and honey produced by the monks are for sale. Head 12 km (7 mi) southwest of Padua, following signs for Abano Terme on the south side of the city. ☎ *049/9900010.* 🎫 *Free; donations appreciated.* ⏲ *Tours: Apr.–Oct., Tues.–Sun. (except major religious holidays) every ½ hr 3:30–5:30; Nov.–Mar., Tues.–Sun. every ½ hr 2:30–4:30.*

MONTAGNANA – The surrounding walls of this medieval city 50 km (30 mi) southwest of Padua are remarkably well preserved, and there are 24 towers, a moat, and four city gates. Its former rivals, Este and Monselice, are only 20 km (12 mi) east on the same road.

Dining and Lodging

$$$ ✕ **Antico Brolo.** Housed in a 16th-century building not far from central Piazza dei Signori, charming Antico Brolo is one of the best restaurants in town. Seasonal specialties are prepared with a flair of creativity and might include starters like tiny flans with wild mushrooms and herbs or fresh pasta dressed with zucchini flowers. The wine list won't disappoint you. ✉ *Corso Milano 22,* ☎ *049/664555. AE, DC, MC, V. Closed Mon.*

$$ ✕ **Cavalca.** A family-run establishment with a long tradition, Cavalca is just off Piazza dei Signori in the heart of Padua. Classic decor and simple but courteous service are hallmarks here. The specialties are pasta e fagioli (pasta and bean soup), *capretto arrosto* (roast kid), or a platter of *arrosti misti* (assorted roast meats). ✉ *Via Manin 8,* ☎ *049/8760061. Reservations essential. AE, DC, MC, V. Closed Wed., 2 wks in mid-Jan., and 3 last wks in July. No dinner Tues.*

$–$$ ✕ **Angelo Rasi.** Perfect for a light dinner on a breezy summer evening, this wine bar with tables along the river offers delicious fish salads, but also a few pasta dishes and simple meat courses. ✉ *Riviera Paleocapa 7,* ☎ *049/8719797. V. Closed Mon. No lunch.*

$$$ 🏨 **Donatello.** Directly opposite the Basilica di Sant'Antonio, Donatello has rooms with a view of the square and church, but it can be noisy. Rooms are contemporary, with color TVs. ✉ *Via del Santo 102,*

35100, ☎ *049/8750634,* FAX *049/8750829. 49 rooms. Restaurant. AE, DC, MC, V. Closed mid-Dec.–mid-Jan.*

$$$ **Villa Ducale.** Set in its own statuesque gardens, one of the country residences built along the Brenta River by Venetian noblemen has been turned into a stylish hotel with stuccoed walls and ceilings, Murano glass chandeliers and mirrors, and Venetian-style marble flooring. This is not in Padua but in Dolo, halfway between Venice and Padua, and is connected to both by a regular local train service. ✉ *Riviera Martiri della Libertà 75, 30031 Dolo, 10 km (6 mi) east of Padua,* ☎ *041/5608020,* FAX *041/5608004. 11 rooms. Restaurant. AE, DC, MC, V.*

Nightlife and the Arts

CAFFÈ

The ever-popular **Caffè Pedrocchi** (✉ Piazzetta Pedrocchi, ☎ 049/8781231), in a monumental 19th-century neoclassic coffeehouse that looks like a cross between a museum and a stage set, serves up an excellent cappuccino. The upstairs rooms, with their frescoed ceilings brightly restored in 1998, are open only for art shows (☎ 049/8205007). The *caffè* downstairs is open daily until 11.

NIGHTCLUBS AND BARS

Big Club (✉ Via Armistizio 68, ☎ 049/680934), closed Monday–Wednesday, has pizza and live music on Thursday and Sunday, and on Friday and Saturday it becomes a disco. **Victoria** (✉ Via Savonarola 149, ☎ 049/8721530) is a *birreria* (a bar that serves primarily beer) with live jazz concerts on Thursday. **Limbo** (✉ Via San Fermo 44, ☎ 049/656882) has a pool table, a game room upstairs, and live music downstairs.

Outdoor Activities and Sports

GOLF

The 18-hole **Golf Club Padova** (✉ Via Noiera 57, Valsanzibio di Galzignano Terme, ☎ 049/9130078) is 23 km (15 mi) south of Padua.

Shopping

Padua's Saturday market in **Prato della Valle** has a wide range of goods. An antiques market is held the third Sunday of every month.

Vicenza

❸ *60 km (37 mi) east of Verona, 32 km (19 mi) west of Padua.*

Vicenza bears the distinctive signature of the 16th-century architect Andrea Palladio and was designated by UNESCO in 1994 as a preeminent site of world cultural heritage. The architect, whose name is the root of the style referred to as "Palladian," gracefully incorporated elements of classical architecture—columns, porticoes, and domes—into a style that reflected the Renaissance celebration of order and harmony. His elegant villas and palaces were influential in propagating classical architecture in Europe, especially Britain, and later in America—most notably at Thomas Jefferson's Monticello.

In the mid-16th century Palladio was given the opportunity to rebuild much of Vicenza, which had suffered great damage during the bloody wars waged against Venice by the League of Cambrai, an alliance of thePapacy, France, the Holy Roman Empire, and several neighboring city-states. He imposed upon the city a number of his grand Roman-style buildings—rather an overstatement, considering the town's status. With the basilica, begun in 1549 in the very heart of Vicenza, he ensured his reputation and embarked on a series of lordly buildings, all of which proclaim the same rigorous classicism.

FRANCAISE
REPUBLIQUE
5 CENTS
CANADA
1978
748599
PESOS
DIEZ PESOS
UN PESO
LIBERTY
058
VOLTA
747022 T
VINGT FRANCS
ELIZABETH II
D·G·REGINA
DIEZ PESOS
BANCA D'IT
LIRE CIN
CAISSIERE

The Gothic **Duomo** contains a gleaming altarpiece by Lorenzo Veneziano, a 14th-century Venetian painter. The cathedral itself was partly destroyed in World War II, but nearly all the damaged areas have been restored. ✉ *Piazza Duomo.* ⏲ *Daily 10:30–12 and 3:30–7.*

The **Corso Palladio** is lined with a succession of imposing palaces and churches that run the gamut from Venetian Gothic to Baroque. Many of these palaces were designed by Palladio. The church of **Santa Corona** holds an exceptionally fine *Baptism of Christ* (1500) by Giovanni Bellini (1430–1516) over the altar on the left, just in front of the transept. ✉ *Contrà S. Corona.* ⏲ *Daily 8:30–noon and 2:30–6.*

The exquisite and unmistakably Palladian **Palazzo Chiericati** houses the city municipal art gallery, with a representative collection of Venetian paintings. ✉ *Piazza Matteotti,* ☎ *0444/321348.* 🎫 *5,000 lire, 9,000 lire includes admission to Teatro Olimpico (☞ below).* ⏲ *Apr.–Sept., Tues.–Sat. 9:30–noon and 3–6, Sun. 9:30–noon and 2–7; Oct.–Mar., Tues.–Sat. 9:30–12:30 and 2:15–5, Sun. 9–12:30.*

★ The **Teatro Olimpico** is Palladio's last, and perhaps most exciting, work. Based closely on the model of the ancient Roman theater, it represents an important development in theater and stage design and is noteworthy for its acoustics and the cunningly devised false perspective of a classical street in the permanent backdrop. The anterooms are all frescoed with important figures in Venetian history. ✉ *Piazza Matteotti,* ☎ *0444/323781.* 🎫 *5,000 lire, 9,000 lire includes admission to Palazzo Chiericati (☞ above).* ⏲ *Mon.–Sat. 9:30–12:30 and 2:15–5, Sun. 9–12:30.*

At the heart of Vicenza is **Piazza dei Signori,** also the site of **Palazzo della Ragione,** or Palladio's "basilica"—a confusing way to refer to it, since it is not a church but a courthouse and public meeting hall. An early Palladian masterpiece, it was actually a medieval building that the architect modernized, and the skill with which he wedded the graceful two-story exterior loggias to the existing Gothic structure is remarkable. Also note the **Loggia del Capitaniato,** opposite, which Palladio designed, but never completed. ✉ *Piazza dei Signori,* ☎ *0444/323681.* ⏲ *Apr.–Sept., Tues.–Sat. 9:30–noon and 2:30–5, Sun. 9:30–noon and 2–7; Oct.–Mar., Tues.–Sat. 9:30–noon and 2:30–5, Sun. 9:30–noon (hrs might vary depending on exhibition).*

OFF THE BEATEN PATH

VILLA LA ROTONDA – This is the most famous Palladian villa of all. In truth, it can hardly be called a villa, since Palladio was inspired by ancient Roman temples. Serene and symmetrical, it was the model for Jefferson's Monticello. Take the time to admire it from all sides, and you'll see that it was the inspiration not just for Monticello, but for nearly every state capitol in the United States. The interior is typical of Palladio's grand style, with a unique juxtaposition of solids and voids. You can walk 3 km (2 mi) along the Riviera Berica from Vicenza, or take Bus 8 from Viale Roma and ask the driver to let you off at the Villa. Note that the interior is only open Wednesday, from March through November. ✉ *Via della Rotonda 29,* ☎ *0444/321793.* 🎫 *10,000 lire (grounds only, 5,000 lire).* ⏲ *Grounds: Mar. 15–Nov. 4, daily 10–noon and 3–6. Villa: Mid-Mar.–Nov. 4, Wed. only 10–noon and 3–6.*

VILLA VALMARANA AI NANI – A short walk from Villa La Rotonda, this 18th-century country house is decorated with a series of marvelous frescoes by Giambattista Tiepolo: these are fantastic visions of a mythological world, including one of his most stunning works, the *Sacrifice of Iphegenia.* The neighboring Foresteria, or guest house, holds more frescoes, showing vignettes of 18th-century Veneto life at its most charming, executed by Tiepolo's son, Giandomenico (1727–1804). ✉ *Via dei*

Nani 2/8, ☎ 0444/321803. 8,000 lire. ⊙ Mid-Mar.–mid-Nov., Wed.–Thurs. and weekends. 10–noon and 2–6, Tues. and Fri. 2–6.

Dining and Lodging

$$ ★ ✕ **Conte Negroni.** People come for the stupendous location (in front of the Basilica Palladiana), but you can eat reasonably well here. The small menu offers such appealing Italian classics as *tagliolini con tartufo* (narrow fettuccine sprinkled with truffle slivers) and *linguine alle vongole* (flat spaghetti with clams and parsley), as well as the city's specialty, *baccalà alla vicentina* (delicious stew of dried cod cooked with onions, anchovies, milk, and Parmesan). In warm weather you can reserve a table outside. ✉ *Piazza dei Signori 5,* ☎ *0444/542455. DC, V. Closed Wed.*

$$ ✕ **Da Remo.** About a kilometer (½ mi) or so outside town, Da Remo is worth the taxi ride simply because it is one of Vicenza's best restaurants. In an attractive country-house setting, with light, airy dining rooms and a garden terrace, you can enjoy a relaxing meal of Venetian specialties, among them *faraona* (guinea hen) with radicchio, and risotto with seasonal vegetables. ✉ *Via Ca'Impenta 14,* ☎ *0444/911007. AE, DC, MC, V. Closed Mon., over Christmas and Aug. No dinner Sun.*

$–$$ ✕ **Al Paradiso.** This pizzeria-trattoria just off the Piazza dei Signori is one of a pair right next door to each other and owned by two brothers; the other is **Vecchia Guardia** (✉ Via Vecchia Guardia 15, ☎ 0444/321231), closed Thursday. The setting is particularly attractive in summer, when you can sit at tables outside. The pizzas and other dishes are tasty and very reasonably priced. ✉ *Via Pescherie Vecchie 5,* ☎ *0444/322320. AE, DC, MC, V. Closed Mon.*

$$$ **Campo Marzio.** This elegant and luxurious hotel sits right in the center of the city. The rooms are furnished in different styles; choose from Chinese, modern, or floral themed, all with bathrooms that have nice ceramic sinks. A special perk is the free bicycle service. The price increases at trade fair times, but for it you'll always get a good buffet breakfast. ✉ *Via Roma 27, 36100,* ☎ *0444/545700,* FAX *0444/320495. 35 rooms. AE, DC, MC, V. Restaurant, bar, bicycles, free parking.*

$–$$ **Due Mori.** In the heart of Vicenza just off Piazza dei Signori, this small hotel is a favorite with regular visitors and very good value. It's light and airy, yet at the same time cozy. The rooms are individually furnished with nice antiques and wood detail in the bathrooms. ✉ *Contrá Do Rode 26, 36100,* ☎ *0444/321886,* FAX *0444/326127. 26 rooms. AE, MC, V.*

Nightlife and the Arts

MUSIC AND THEATER

Vicenza's **Teatro Olimpico** (☞ Exploring, *above*)has a concert season in May and June, as well as a classical drama season in September. Even if your Italian is dismal, it's thrilling to see a performance in Palladio's magnificent theater.

Shopping

JEWELRY

Vicenza is one of Italy's leading centers for the production and sale of jewelry. Each year, in January, June, and September, it hosts an international trade fair for goldsmiths that is open to the public only one day at a time (no purchases allowed). For details, inquire at **Ente Fiera** (Via Dell'Oreficeria 16, ☎ 0444/969111).

VERONA

On the banks of the fast-flowing Adige River, enchanting Verona lays claim to classical and medieval monuments, a picturesque town center where bright geraniums bloom in window boxes, and a romantic reputation, thanks to being the setting of Shakespeare's *Romeo and Juliet.* It is one of Italy's most alluring cities, despite extensive industrialization and urban development in its newer sections. Inevitably, with its lively Venetian air, proximity to Lake Garda, and renowned summer opera season, it attracts hordes of tourists, especially vacationing Germans and Austrians, who drive over the Brenner Pass to the north.

Verona grew to power and prosperity within the Roman Empire as a result of its key commercial and military position in northern Italy. After the fall of the Empire, the city continued to flourish under the guidance of Barbarian kings such as Theodoric, Alboin, Pepin, and Berenger I, reaching its cultural and artistic peak in the 13th and 14th centuries, under the della Scala dynasty. (You'll see the *scala,* or ladder, emblem all over town.) In 1404, however, Verona traded its independence for security and placed itself under the control of Venice. (The other recurring architectural motif is the lion of St. Mark, symbol of Venetian rule.) Verona remained under Venetian protection until 1797, when Napoléon invaded. In 1814 the entire Veneto region was won by the Austrians, and it was finally united with the rest of Italy in 1866.

Exploring Verona

Please note that the Duomo and churches in Verona enforce a strict dress code: no tanks, sleeveless shirts, shorts, or short skirts. You might want to consider buying the 8,000 lire-combined ticket that gives admittance to most churches in town, including the Duomo, San Zeno, and Sant'Anastasia.

A Good Walk

Start at the **Arena di Verona** ④ in Piazza Brà, the vast and airy square at the center of the city. Built by the Romans in the 1st century AD, the arena is one of the largest and best-preserved Roman amphitheaters anywhere. Take Via Mazzini, the main shopping street in town, to **Piazza delle Erbe** ⑤, a busy square with an open-air market. The **Casa di Giulietta** ⑥, with the most famous balcony in Italy, is a block down Via del Cappello. Return and take a few moments to stroll around **Piazza dei Signori** ⑦, and admire the **Palazzo della Ragione** ⑧, **Loggia del Consiglio** ⑨, and **Palazzo degli Scaligeri** ⑩. It's a short walk through Piazza Indipendenza to Ponte Nuova and across the river toward the church of **Santa Maria in Organo** ⑪ and the **Giardino Giusti** ⑫. Follow Via Santa Maria in Organo up to the Teatro Romano and **Museo Archeologico** ⑬. The Romanesque **Duomo** ⑭ is just over Ponte Pietra. From here either walk down Via Duomo to Corso Sant'Anastasia to **Sant'Anastasia** ⑮ and Via Forti and the **Galleria d'Arte Moderna** ⑯, or turn toward the riverbank and stroll (or alternately take Bus 76) down to the 14th-century **Castelvecchio** ⑰, looking like a fairy-tale castle guarding the bridge reaching over the Adige. The stunning Romanesque **San Zeno Maggiore** ⑱ church is another few minutes' walk downriver.

TIMING

It takes about 40 minutes to walk the route and three hours to see all the sights.

Sights to See

★ ❹ **Arena di Verona.** Only four arches remain of the outer rings of the arena, but the main structure is so complete that it takes little imagination to

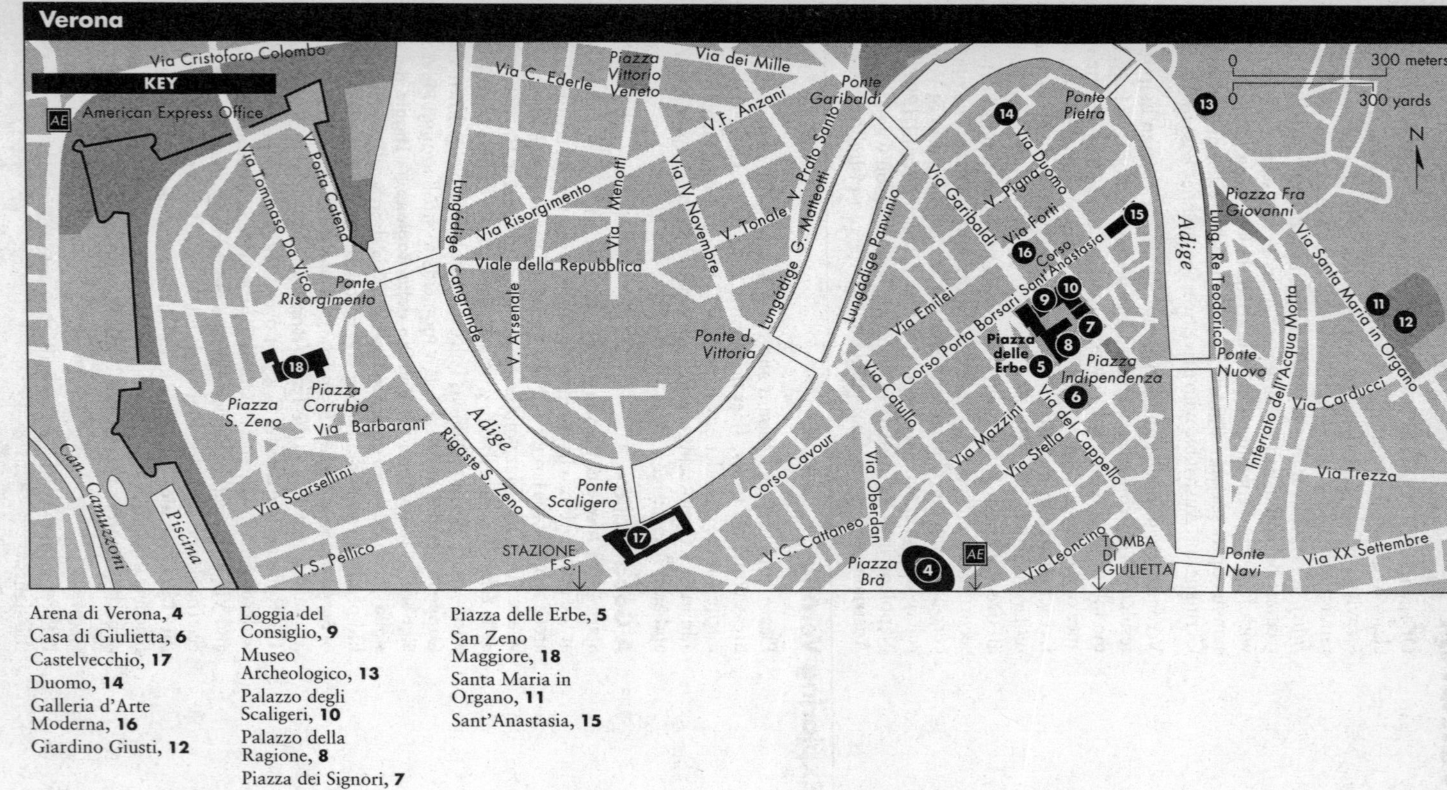

Arena di Verona, **4**
Casa di Giulietta, **6**
Castelvecchio, **17**
Duomo, **14**
Galleria d'Arte Moderna, **16**
Giardino Giusti, **12**
Loggia del Consiglio, **9**
Museo Archeologico, **13**
Palazzo degli Scaligeri, **10**
Palazzo della Ragione, **8**
Piazza dei Signori, **7**
Piazza delle Erbe, **5**
San Zeno Maggiore, **18**
Santa Maria in Organo, **11**
Sant'Anastasia, **15**

picture it as the site of the cruel deaths of countless gladiators, wild beasts, and Christians. Today it hosts Verona's summer opera, famous for spectacular productions and audiences of as many as 16,000. The best operas to see here are the big, splashy ones that demand huge choruses, Cinerama sets, lots of color and movement, and, if possible, camels, horses, and/or elephants. The music can be excellent, and the acoustics are fine, too. If you go, be sure to take or rent a cushion—four hours on 2,000-year-old marble can be an ordeal. ⊠ *Arena di Verona, Piazza Brà 5,* ☎ *045/8003204.* 🎫 *6,000 lire, 2,000 lire 1st Sun. of month.* ⏲ *July–Aug., Tues.–Sun. 8–2:30; Sept.–June, Tues.–Sun. 8–6:30.*

6 **Casa di Giulietta** (Juliet's House). The balcony in the small courtyard will help to bring Shakespeare's play to life, even if it was built this century. Historians now believe that the couple had no real-life counterparts, but this hasn't discouraged anyone from imagining that they did. After all, historians are not as renowned for their storytelling as Shakespeare is. ⊠ *Via Cappello 23,* ☎ *045/8034303.* 🎫 *6,000 lire.* ⏲ *Tues.–Sun. 9–6:30.*

OFF THE BEATEN PATH

TOMBA DI GIULIETTA – Romantic souls may want to see the pretty spot claimed to be Juliet's Tomb. Authentic or not, it is still popular with lovesick Italian teenagers, who leave notes for the tragic lover. ⊠ *Via del Pontiere 35,* ☎ *045/8000361.* 🎫 *5,000 lire, free 1st Sun. of month.* ⏲ *Tues.–Sun. 9–7.*

GIARDINI DI VILLA ARVEDI – Formal gardens surround a 17th-century villa 8 km (5 mi) northeast of town. ⊠ *Statale per Grezzana,* ☎ *045/907045.* 🎫 *10,000 lire.* ⏲ *By appointment, minimum 10 people.*

17 **Castelvecchio** (Old Castle). This crenellated, russet brick building with massive walls, towers, turrets, and a vast courtyard was built for Cangrande II della Scala in 1354. It presides over a street lined with attractive old buildings and palaces of the nobility. Inside, the **Museo di Castelvecchio** gives you a good look at the castle's vaulted halls and the treasures of Venetian painting and sculpture that they contain. ⊠ *Corso Castelvecchio,* ☎ *045/594734.* 🎫 *6,000 lire, free 1st Sun. of month.* ⏲ *Tues.–Sun. 9–6:30; hrs and admission may change during special exhibitions.*

14 **Duomo.** The ornate Romanesque Duomo has not only architectural characteristics typical of the Venetian style, but also some Byzantine attributes. A strict dress code is enforced (no tanks, sleeveless shirts, shorts, or short skirts). ⊠ *Via Duomo.* 🎫 *3,000 lire, combined ticket 8,000 lire.* ⏲ *Nov.–Feb., Tues.–Sat. 10–4, Sun. 1–5; Mar.–Oct., Tues.–Sat. 8:30–5:30, Sun. 1–5:30.*

16 **Galleria d'Arte Moderna** (Gallery of Modern Art). The handsome Palazzo Forti, where Napoléon once stayed, frequently hosts contemporary painting exhibitions of well-known artists such as Marcel Duchamp (1887–1968) and Andy Warhol (1928–87). ⊠ *Via Forti 1,* ☎ *045/8001903.* 🎫 *10,000 lire.* ⏲ *Tues.–Sun. Prices and hrs vary according to exhibition.*

12 **Giardino Giusti.** The formal Giusti Gardens, laid out on several levels around a 16th-century villa, is a symbol of things long past. There's a fine view of the city from the terrace, from which the German poet and dramatist Johann von Goethe (1749–1832) recorded his inspiration. ⊠ *Via Giardino Giusti 2,* ☎ *045/8034029.* 🎫 *7,000 lire.* ⏲ *Apr.–Sept., daily 9–8; Oct.–Mar., daily 9–sunset.*

9 **Loggia del Consiglio.** The graceful structure was built in the 12th century to house city council meetings and still serves as the seat of the provincial government. ✉ *Piazza dei Signori. Closed to the public.*

13 **Museo Archeologico.** The museum is housed in an old monastery above the Teatro Romano that was built in the same era as the Arena di Verona. The Roman Theater is sometimes used for dramatic productions. From here there are good views over the entire city. ✉ *Rigaste del Redentore,* ☎ *045/8000360.* *5,000 lire, free 1st Sun. of month.* ⏲ *Tues.–Sun. 9–6:30.*

10 **Palazzo degli Scaligeri.** This was the medieval stronghold from which the della Scalas ruled Verona with an iron fist. ✉ *Piazza dei Signori. Closed to the public.*

8 **Palazzo della Ragione.** The 12th-century palace has a somber courtyard, Gothic staircase, and medieval tower overlooking the piazza. ✉ *Piazza dei Signori. Closed to the public.*

7 **Piazza dei Signori.** Verona's great piazza has been at the center of things for over a thousand years, but the impressive facades and arched entrances surrounding it date from the early Renaissance.

5 **Piazza delle Erbe** (Vegetable Market Square). This square is the site of an ancient Roman forum and today a colorful morning market, with huge rectangular umbrellas raised to shade the neat ranks of fruits and vegetables.

18 **San Zeno Maggiore.** What is possibly the finest example of a Romanesque church in Italy, with a 13th-century rose window and 12th-century portal, is set between two medieval bell towers. The light-gray and white-brick color scheme—typical of Italy's Romanesque churches—is especially impressive here. Inside, look for Mantegna's *Madonna* over the main altar; a peaceful cloister is off the left nave. ✉ *Piazza San Zeno,* ☎ *045/8006120.* *3,000 lire, combined ticket 8,000 lire.* ⏲ *Nov.–Feb., Tues.–Sat. 10–4, Sun. 1–5; Mar.–Oct., Tues.–Sat. 8:30–5:30, Sun. 1–5:30.*

11 **Santa Maria in Organo.** The choir and sacristy of this medieval church are decorated with inlaid-wood masterpieces by the 15th-century monk Fra Giovanni. A series of panels depicts varied scenes—local buildings, an idealized Renaissance town, wildlife, and fruit—that radiate a love of life and reveal the artist's eye for detail. ✉ *Via Interrato dell'Acqua Morta,* ☎ *045/591440.* ⏲ *Apr.–Oct., daily 7:30–noon and 3–6; Nov.–Mar., daily 7:30–noon.*

15 **Sant'Anastasia.** Not far from the Duomo, Sant'Anastasia is Verona's largest church. In stark contrast to the simple, vaguely Romanesque facade, the impressive Gothic doorway is surrounded by elaborate carvings illustrating scenes from the New Testament, and down the steps you'll meet the famous *Gobbi,* two sculptures of crouching humpbacks supporting the holy water stoups. The highlight, on display inside the sacristy and sadly damaged, is a detached fresco painted in blue and gray pastel shades by Pisanello (1377–1455) called *St. George and the Princess. Vicolo Sotto Riva 4,* ☎ *045/8004325.* *3,000 lire.* ⏲ *Tues.–Sat. 10–1 and 1:30–4, Sun. 1–5.*

Dining and Lodging

$$$$ ✕ **Le Arche.** True to its name, this elegant restaurant is in a medieval building a step away from the della Scala tombs. The art-nouveau dining room features candlelight and flowers. Only seafood is served, absolutely fresh and superlatively prepared. Try the *raviolone al branzino* *e spinaci in salsa di foie gras e tartufo* (large ravioli stuffed with sea bass and spinach with foie gras and truffle sauce) and the unusual *salsiccia di pesce* (fish sausage made with sea scorpion, sea bass, and salmon). ✉ *Via Arche Scaligere 6,* ☎ *045/8007415. AE, DC, MC, V. Closed Sun., last 2 wks of Jan., and first 2 wks of Feb. No lunch Mon.*

$$$ ✕ **Dodici Apostoli.** Vaulted ceilings, frescoed walls, and a medieval ambience make this an exceptional place to enjoy classic local and regional dishes. Near Piazza delle Erbe, it stands on the foundations of a Roman temple. Specialties include *zuppa scaligera* (soup of meat stock with vegetables and bread) and *vitello Lessinia* (veal with mushrooms, cheese, and truffles). ✉ *Vicolo Corticella San Marco 3,* ☎ *045/596999. AE, DC, MC, V. Closed Mon., Jan. 1–7, and June 15–July 7. No dinner Sun.*

$$$ ✕ **Osteria All'Oste Scuro.** Two local gourmets turned this ex-family trattoria into a first-class fish restaurant. Specialties might include *spaghettini ai gamberetti e cannellini* (thin spaghetti with shrimp and Tuscan beans), and more traditional dishes like grilled crab and prawn or baked fish with potatoes are always on the menu. ✉ *Vicolo San Silvestro 10,* ☎ *045/592650. V. Closed Sun. and June. No lunch Mon.*

$$ ✕ **Al Calmiere.** This congenial trattoria on the lovely piazza in front of San Zeno Maggiore is the ideal place to enjoy Veronese specialties of tagliatelle *con fegatini di pollo* (with chicken-liver sauce), various types of pasta in *brodo* (broth), meats, and local wines—there are some 20 different Valpolicellas alone available—at reasonable prices. The interior, with an enormous open fireplace used for cooking, is especially cozy in winter. ✉ *Piazza San Zeno 10,* ☎ *045/8030765. AE, DC, MC, V. Closed Thurs., 1st wk in Jan., and 2–3 wks in July. No dinner Wed.*

$$ ✕ **La Greppia.** The classic decor with vaulted ceilings sets the tone in this bustling restaurant off Via Mazzini between the Arena and Piazza delle Erbe. The kitchen produces fine versions of local and regional dishes, especially *tortelli di zucca* (pasta filled with squash) and *bolliti* (assorted boiled meats served with a choice of sauces). Service is courteous and efficient. ✉ *Vicolo Samaritana 3,* ☎ *045/8004577. AE, DC, MC, V. Closed Mon., 2nd wk of Jan., last 2 wks in June.*

$$ ✕ **La Stueta.** Perhaps the best bargain in town (prices are at the lowest end of this category), La Stueta is a friendly trattoria not far from the Giardino Giusti across the river. Try the gnocchi *con la pastisada* (with a horse-meat sauce), *baccalà* (salt cod), or *maiale all'amarone* (pork shin in a red wine sauce and served with polenta). ✉ *Via del Redentore 4/b,* ☎ *045/8032462. AE, DC, MC, V. Closed Mon. No lunch Tues.*

$ ✕ **Pizzeria Vesuvio.** Between Castelvecchio and San Zeno Maggiore, this authentic Neapolitan pizzeria has tables on the riverbank in summer and a lovely, breezy view of the Adige. ✉ *Via Rigaste 41,* ☎ *045/595634. No credit cards. Closed Mon.*

$$$$ 🏨 **Colomba d'Oro.** This attractive four-star hotel right by the Arena occupies a building that dates from the 14th century. It has retained its clubby atmosphere and European charm while providing up-to-date comfort. ✉ *Via Cattaneo 10, 37121,* ☎ *045/595300,* FAX *045/594974. 41 rooms, 10 suites. Parking (fee). AE, DC, MC, V.*

$$$$ ★ 🏨 **Gabbia d'Oro.** Set in a historic building off Piazza delle Erbe in the ancient heart of Verona, this hotel is a tasteful fantasia of romantic ornamentation, lavish trimmings, exquisite fabrics, and gorgeous period pieces. Rooms—each one different and more attractive than the next—have frescoes, beamed ceilings, pretty wallpaper, antique prints and furnishings, canopy beds, and some are festooned with flying cupids and rosy-cheeked cherubs. You can relax outdoors in the medieval courtyard, in the comfortable orangerie, or on the roof terrace. The breakfast spread is to die for. ✉ *Corso Porta Borsari 4/a, 37121,* ☎ *045/*

8003060, FAX 045/590293. 19 rooms, 8 suites. Breakfast room. AE, DC, MC, V.

$$$$ ★ **Villa del Quar.** This tranquil 16th-century villa is surrounded by gardens and vineyards in the Valpolicella country, 10 minutes by taxi from the city. Architect Leopoldo Montresor and his wife, Evelina, who live here with their children, converted part of the villa into a stylish and sophisticated hotel. No expense has been spared: all rooms have marble bathrooms (some with whirlpool baths) and European antiques. ✉ *Via Quar 12, 37020 Pedemonte di San Pietro in Cariano, 5 km (3 mi) northwest of Verona,* ☎ *045/6800681,* FAX *045/6800604. 18 rooms, 4 suites. Restaurant, pool. AE, DC, MC, V.*

$$ ★ **Torcolo.** The warm welcome extended by the owners, Signoras Diana and Silvia, the pleasant rooms decorated unfussily, and the central location on a peaceful street close to Piazza Brà and the Arena make the Torcolo outstanding value in its class. Breakfast is served outside on the terrace in front of the hotel in summer. ✉ *Vicolo Listone 3, 37121,* ☎ *045/8007512,* FAX *045/8004058. 19 rooms. AE, MC, V.*

Nightlife and the Arts

Nightclubs

Alter Ego (✉ Via Torricelle 9, ☎ 045/915130) packs a twentysomething crowd that might call itself alternative. **Berfi's** (✉ Via Lussemburgo 1, ☎ 045/508024) is a popular and expensive spot with a restaurant and piano bar.

Opera

Of all the venues for enjoying opera in the region, pride of place must go to the summer opera season in the **Arena di Verona.** The season runs from July through August, and the 16,000 in the audience sit on the original stone terraces that date from the time when gladiators fought to the death. The opera stage is huge and best suited to grand operas such as *Aïda,* but the experience is memorable no matter what is being performed. Sometimes, while sipping a drink in a café at **Piazza Brà**, you can overhear the opera. A 15% advance-sale fee is added to the price of a ticket for bookings made more than 24 hours before performance. *Contact: Ente Lirico Arena di Verona,* ✉ *Piazza Brà 28, 37121 Verona; Box office:* ✉ *Via Dietro Anfiteatro 6B,* ☎ *045/8005151.* ⏲ *Mon.–Fri. 9–noon and 3:15–5:45, Sat. 9–noon.*

Outdoor Activities and Sports

Golf

The 18-hole **Golf Club Verona** (✉ Ca' del Sale 15, Sommacampagna, ☎ 045/510060), closed Tuesday, is 16 km (10 mi) west of Verona and 2 km (1 mi) from the Sommacampagna exit on the A4 autostrada.

Shopping

Antiques and Housewares

The area around the Gothic church of Sant'Anastasia is full of antiques shops, most of them catering to serious collectors. You can picnic on the Piazza dei Signori in the cool breeze after a strenuous day of antiques hunting. The perfect place to splurge on a modern gift or imaginative decorative piece is the diminutive boutique **Fornasetti** (✉ Via Rosa 8/d, ☎ 045/8000064), with the dreamy, geometric black-and-white designs of the namesake artist imparted onto everything from ties, umbrellas, and pillowcases to lacquer furniture, plates, and postcards.

Market

Verona's **Piazza delle Erbe** daily market, open Monday–Saturday 8–1 and 3:30–sundown, has a selection of food, wine, clothing, antiques, and even pets.

VILLA BARBARO, TREVISO, AND THE HILLSIDE TOWNS

Northern Arc

In this area directly north of Venice, market towns cling to the steep foothills of the Alps and the Dolomites alongside streams that rage down from the mountains. Villa Barbaro, Palladio's most beautiful creation, is here, as are the arcaded streets of Treviso and the graceful Venetian Gothic styles of the smaller hill towns.

Marostica

19 *7 km (4½ mi) west of Bassano del Grappa, 26 km (16 mi) northeast of Vicenza.*

The first and most evident feature of Marostica is its Castello Superiore, perched on the hillside overlooking the surrounding countryside. But the most famous sight in town is Piazza Castello, the main square, paved in checkerboard fashion.

Outdoor Activities and Sports

A game of **human-scale chess** is acted out here by players in medieval costume on the second Sunday in September in even-numbered years (tickets go on sale in April); for information and bookings, contact Marostica's tourist office (☞ Venetian Arc A to Z, *below*).

Bassano del Grappa

20 *7 km (4½ mi) east of Marostica, 37 km (23 mi) north of Venice.*

Beautifully positioned directly above the swift-flowing waters of the Brenta River at the foot of the Mt. Grappa massif (5,880 ft), Bassano has old streets lined with low-slung buildings flanked by wooden balconies and pretty flowerpots. Bright ceramic wares produced here and in nearby Nove are displayed in shops along byways that curve uphill toward a centuries-old square, and, even higher, to a belvedere with a good view of Mt. Grappa and the beginning of the Val Sugana.

Bassano's most famous landmark is the **covered bridge** that has spanned the Brenta since the 13th century. Rebuilt countless times (floods are frequent), the present-day bridge is a postwar reconstruction using Andrea Palladio's 16th-century design. The great architect astutely chose to use wood as his medium, knowing that it could be replaced quickly and cheaply. Almost as famous is the liquor distillery **Nardini,** where grappa has been distilled for more than a century. Stop in for a sniff or a snifter at any of the local cafés.

Dining and Lodging

$$ ✕ **Da Renzo.** This popular, family-run restaurant has a view of the hills and olive groves of Bassano and a pleasant terrace used year-round. Seafood antipasto and grilled fish fresh from the Adriatic are the specialty. You can also enjoy regional dishes made with fresh seasonal ingredients. ✉ *Via Santissima Trinità 9,* ☎ *0424/503055. AE, D, MC, V. Closed Tues. and 2 wks in Aug. No lunch Wed.*

$$ ✕ **Ristorante Birreria Ottone.** This old-world restaurant in town center is a favorite with the locals, who tout the excellent cuisine, draft wine and beer, and the friendly Wipflinger family, headed by Otto, whose Austrian forebear founded this beer hall about 100 years ago. Equally good for a simple lunch or a more elaborate dinner, Ottone's specialties include a delicious goulash cooked with cumin. ✉ *Via Matteotti 47/50, ☎ 0424/522206. AE, D, MC, V. Closed Tues. and 3–4 wks between June and July. No dinner Mon.*

$$$–$$$$ **Villa Palma.** This gracefully refurbished 18th-century country villa, only a short drive from Asolo (10 km/6 mi) and Bassano (5 km/3 mi), combines modern comforts and conveniences with rural calm and old-fashioned style and charm—wooden beams, vaulted brick ceilings, and tasteful furnishings. Creature comforts include whirlpool baths or sauna showers and fax and computer facilities. In summer, meals are served on the terrace, overlooking the splendid garden. ✉ *Via Chemin Palma 30, Mussolente, 36065, ☎ 0424/577407, FAX 0424/87687. 20 rooms, 1 suite. Restaurant. AE, DC, MC, V.*

$$$ ★ **Belvedere.** This historic hotel has richly decorated public rooms with period furnishings and Oriental rugs. A fireplace and piano music in the lounge and an excellent restaurant with a garden make for a very pleasant stay. The rooms are decorated in traditional Venetian or chic contemporary style. ✉ *Piazzale G. Giardino 14, 36061, ☎ 0424/529845, FAX 0424/529849. 81 rooms, 6 suites. Restaurant. AE, DC, MC, V.*

$$ **Al Castello.** In a restored town house at the foot of the medieval Torre Civica (Civic Tower), the Cattapan family's Castello is a reasonable, attractive choice. Rooms are well equipped and furnished simply. ✉ *Piazza Terraglio 19, 36061, ☎ 0424/523462, FAX 0424/228665. 11 rooms. Café. AE, MC, V.*

Shopping

Bassano del Grappa and nearby Nove are the best bets for ceramic items. A large number of shops in town feature wrought-iron and copper utensils, many of them made on the premises.

Asolo

★ 21 *11 km (7 mi) east of Bassano del Grappa, 33 km (20½ mi) northwest of Treviso.*

The romantic, charming hillside hamlet of Asolo was the consolation prize of an exiled queen. At the end of the 15th century, Venetian-born Caterina Cornaro was sent here by Venice's doges to keep her from interfering with their administration of her former kingdom of Cyprus, which she had inherited. To soothe the pain of exile, she established a lively and brilliant court in Asolo. Over the centuries, Venetian aristocrats continued to build gracious villas on the hillside, and in the 19th century Asolo once again became the idyllic haunt of musicians, poets, and painters. From the outside, you can explore villas once inhabited by Robert Browning and the actress Eleonora Duse. Be warned that Asolo's old-world atmosphere vaporizes on holiday weekends when the crowds pour in. In town center is **Piazza Maggiore,** with its Renaissance palaces and fin-de-siècle cafés. Uphill from the piazza, past Caterina's ruined castle and some Gothic-style houses, is **La Rocca,** the fortress standing on the summit.

Dining

$$ ✕ **Hosteria Ca'Derton.** Right on the main square, Ca'Derton has a pleasant, old-fashioned ambience, with early photos of Asolo and bouquets of dried flowers. The friendly proprietor takes pride in the homemade pasta and desserts and offers a good selection of both local

and international dishes. ✉ *Piazza D'Annunzio 11,* ☎ *0423/952730. AE, DC, MC, V. Closed Tues., last wk in July, and 1st wk in Aug.*

Shopping

Asolo center hosts an antiques market on the second Sunday of the month (except July and August).

Villa Barbaro

22 *7 km (4½ mi) northeast of Asolo, 33 km (20½ mi) northwest of Treviso.*

Villa Barbaro is one of the most gracious Renaissance creations of Palladio. The fully furnished villa just outside the town of Maser is still inhabited by its owners, who make you slip heavy felt scuffs over your shoes to protect the highly polished floors. The elaborate stuccos and opulent frescoes by Paolo Veronese bring the 16th century to life. After La Rotonda, this is Palladio's greatest villa and is definitely worth going out of your way to see (before making the trip, note restricted hours, *below*). ✉ *Via Cornuda 2,* ☎ *0423/923004.* *9,000 lire.* ⏲ *Apr.–Sept., Tues. and weekends 3–6; Oct.–Mar., weekends 2:30–5.*

Dining and Lodging

$$ ★ ✕ **Agnoletti.** In the town of Giavera del Montello, about 25 km (16 mi) east of Maser, Agnoletti is an 18th-century inn of a bygone era with a lovely summer garden. The kitchen can produce an all-mushroom menu; but if you order something else, at least try the mushroom zuppa or *crostata di funghi* (mushroom tart). ✉ *Via della Vittoria 190, Giavera del Montello,* ☎ *0422/776009. No credit cards. Closed Mon. and Tues. and 3 wks in Jan.*

$$ ✕ **Da Bastian.** A good place to stop in Maser for lunch before visiting the Villa Barbaro, this contemporary place has a pleasant garden for outdoor dining. Varied antipasto of pâtés, homemade vegetarian ravioli, and broiled meat with tasty sauces top the menu. ✉ *Via Cornuda (follow signs),* ☎ *0423/565400. No credit cards. Closed Thurs. and Aug. No dinner Wed.*

$$$$ **Villa Cipriani.** This historic villa is set in a romantic garden on the hillside and surrounded by other gracious country homes. Tastefully furnished with 19th-century antiques, it offers oldfangled atmosphere, creature comforts, and attentive service. The superb restaurant has a terrace overlooking the garden. ✉ *Via Canova 298, 31011,* ☎ *0423/952166,* FAX *0423/952095. 31 rooms. Restaurant. AE, DC, MC, V.*

Treviso

23 *35 km (22 mi) southeast of Maser, 30 km (19 mi) north of Venice.*

The arcaded streets, frescoed houses, and channeled streams that run through the center of Treviso date mostly from the 15th century. The most important church in Treviso is **San Nicolò,** an impressive Gothic building with an ornate vaulted ceiling. San Nicolò has frescoes of the saints by 14th-century artist Tommaso da Modena on the columns. But the best is the remarkable series of 40 portraits of Dominican friars by the same artist in the seminary next door. They are astoundingly realistic, considering that some were painted as early as 1352, and include one of the earliest-known portraits of a subject wearing glasses. ✉ *Capitolo dei Domenicani, Seminario Vescovile, Via San Nicolò,* ☎ *0422/3247.* ⏲ *Mon.–Sat. 9–noon and 3–6:30, Sun. 3–6:30. To enter, ring at custodian's desk at seminary entrance.*

Inside the **Duomo,** on the altar of one of the chapels to the right, is an *Annunciation* by Titian (circa 1488–1576). ✉ *Piazza del Duomo.* ⏲ *Daily 10:30–12:30.*

Piazza dei Signori is the heart of medieval Treviso and still the town's social center, with outdoor cafés and some impressive public buildings. One of these, the **Palazzo dei Trecento,** has a small alley leading behind it. Follow the alley for about 200 yards to the *pescheria* (fish market), on an island in one of the small rivers that flow through town. Shops in Treviso feature wrought-iron and copper utensils.

Dining and Lodging

$$$ ★ ✕ **Da Alfredo.** This restaurant belongs to the El Toulà group, a small chain of well-known, high-class restaurants in Italy and abroad. This is your chance to enjoy the art nouveau decor and classic international cuisine for which it became famous. Among regional dishes are risotto *con funghi* (with mushrooms) or asparagus in season. For cooking, ambience, and service, it's one of the region's best. ✉ *Via Collalto 26,* ☎ *0422/540275. AE, DC, MC, V. Closed Mon. and Aug. No dinner Sun.*

$$ ★ ✕ **Beccherie.** In a town known for good eating, this rustic inn is a favorite. It's in the heart of old Treviso, behind the main square, and there are tables outside for fair-weather dining under the portico. Specialties vary with the season. In winter, look for *crespelle al radicchi* (crepes with radicchio) and *faraona in salsa peverada* (guinea hen with a peppery sauce); spring heralds risotto with spring vegetables, *stinco di vitello* (veal shin), and *pasticcio di melanzane* (eggplant casserole). ✉ *Piazza Ancilotto 10,* ☎ *0422/56601. AE, DC, MC, V. Closed Mon. and 2 wks in July. No dinner Sun.*

$$$$ 🏨 **Continental.** You'll find this hotel within the old city walls, between the train station and the sights. It is a traditional four-star hotel offering solid comfort. Rich fabrics and Oriental rugs lend an air of opulence. ✉ *Via Roma 16, 31100,* ☎ *0422/411216,* FAX *0422/55054. 80 rooms. Parking (fee). AE, DC, MC, V.*

$$$ 🏨 **Al Fogher.** On the outskirts of town, Al Fogher is handy if you're traveling by car. This part of the Best Western chain has a bright contemporary look, with lots of modern art and room decor about equally divided between classic and modern. ✉ *Viale della Repubblica 10, 31100,* ☎ *0422/432950,* FAX *0422/430391. 54 rooms, 1 suite. AE, DC, MC, V.*

Conegliano

㉔ *23 km (14 mi) north of Treviso, 60 km (37 mi) north of Venice.*

Conegliano is in the heart of wine-producing country. The town itself is attractive, with Venetian-style villas and frescoed houses, but the real draw is the wine, particularly the effervescent Prosecco di Conegliano.

Lodging

$$ 🏨 **Canon d'Oro.** The town's oldest inn, the Canon d'Oro is in a 15th-century building in a central location near the train station. The restaurant's tranquil decor lets you concentrate on the good food, mainly regional specialties such as risotto, Canon d'Oro gnocchi (with a rich meat sauce), baccalà *alla vicentina* (dry cod prepared in a creamy stew with anchovies and Parmesan), and *fegato alla veneziana* (liver with onions). ✉ *Via XX Settembre 129, 31015,* ☎ *0438/34246,* FAX *0438/34246. 35 rooms. Restaurant. AE, MC, V.*

En Route Well marked and leading southeast from Conegliano, the **Strada del Vino Rosso** (Red Wine Road) wends its way through cabernet and merlot country along the Piave River, and there are dozens of places to stop, sample, and buy the red—and some rosé—wines. The road ends at Oderzo.

UDINE AND TRIESTE

Eastern Arc

Italy's northeastern corner is an ethnically jumbled cocktail of Italian, Slavic, and central European cultures. A peripheral position usually puts this potentially fascinating area beyond the range of most visitors. The old Hungarian port of Trieste—a symbol of Italian nationalist aspirations for so long—and the medieval city of Udine are perfect bases for local excursions.

Udine

25 *71 km (44 mi) east of Conegliano, 127 km (79 mi) northeast of Venice.*

Udine, in Italy's Friuli-Venezia Giulia region, commands a view of the surrounding plain and the Alpine foothills; according to legend, it stands on a mound erected by Attila the Hun so he could watch the burning of the important Roman center of Aquileia to the south. Udine flourished in the Middle Ages, thanks to its good location for trade and the rights it gained from the local patriarch to hold regular markets. There is a distinct Venetian feel to the city, noticeable in the architecture of Piazza della Libertà, under the stern gaze of the lion of St. Mark, symbol of Venetian power.

The **Galleria d'Arte Antica** is the best place to trace the history of the area and the importance of Cividale and Udine in the formative period following the collapse of the Roman Empire. A large collection of Lombard artifacts includes weapons, jewelry, and domestic wares from this warrior race, which swept into what is now Italy in the 6th century. ✉ *Piazza Duomo 7,* ☎ *0432/700700.* 🎫 *4,000 lire.* ⏲ *Daily 8–2 (longer hrs in summer).*

Dining and Lodging

$$ ✕ **Alla Buona Vite.** This traditional restaurant in town center specializes in seafood. *Tagliolini dello chef* (noodles with a creamy scampi sauce) and *rombo al limone e capperi* (turbot with lemon and capers) are among the many choices here. ✉ *Via Treppo 10,* ☎ *0432/21053. AE, DC, MC, V. Closed Mon. and Aug. No dinner Sun.*

$$ ★ ✕ **Antica Maddalena.** Just a few steps from Udine's pretty Piazza dell'Unità is where you'll find this elegant eating place, defined by its owner as a deluxe trattoria. Lots of warm wood tones, fresh flowers, and stained glass complement a menu of regional and Italian specialties, among them *zuppa di funghi porcini* (porcini mushroom soup) and gnocchi *con zucca e ricotta* (with squash and ricotta cheese). ✉ *Via Pelliccerie 4,* ☎ *0432/25111. AE, DC, MC, V. Closed Sun. and 2 wks in Aug. No lunch Mon.*

$$ ✕ **Trattoria al Lepre.** A characteristic *focolare* (hearth) in one of the dining rooms is a symbol of traditional local cooking, and that's what you'll enjoy in this simple establishment. The specialties include tagliatelle con funghi and *stinco di maiale* (roast pork shin served with polenta). ✉ *Via Poscolle 27,* ☎ *0432/295798. AE, DC, MC, V. Closed Tues. and 2 wks in Aug.*

$$$ 🏨 **Astoria Hotel Italia.** Centrally located, the Italia offers soundproofed rooms furnished in traditional style. Public rooms have Venetian glass chandeliers and comfortable armchairs. ✉ *Piazza XX Settembre 24, 33100,* ☎ *0432/505091,* FAX *0432/509070. 73 rooms, 2 suites. Restaurant, minibars. AE, DC, MC, V.*

En Route From Udine, the road eastward follows the coast under the shadow of the huge geological formation called the Carso, a large, barren expanse of limestone that forms a giant ledge, most of which is across the border in Slovenia. Italian territory goes only a few kilometers inland in this strip, and Italy's small Slovenian minority ekes out an agricultural existence in the region, which has changed hands countless times since the final days of Imperial Rome.

Cividale

26 *17 km (11 mi) east of Udine, 144 km (89 mi) northeast of Venice.*

Cividale dates from the time of Julius Caesar. It is popularly supposed (particularly by locals) that it was built by Caesar when he was commander of Roman legions in the area. The city straddles the Natisone River and contains many examples of Venetian Gothic buildings, particularly the **Palazzo Comunale** and the Renaissance **Duomo,** with a striking silver-gilted altar. ✉ *Piazza Duomo,* ☎ *0432/731144.* ⏲ *Daily 9–noon and 3:30–6.*

Castello di Miramare

★ 27 *78 km (48 mi) south of Cividale, 7 km (4½ mi) north of Trieste.*

This seafront castle in Miramare is a 19th-century extravaganza in white stone, built for the Archduke Maximilian of Habsburg (brother of Emperor Franz Josef). Maximilian spent a brief, happy time here until Napoléon III of France took Trieste from the Habsburgs and sent the poor archduke packing. He was given the title of Emperor of Mexico in 1864 as a compensation, but met his death before a Mexican firing squad in 1867. You can visit the lush grounds and admire the memorable views over the Adriatic. ✉ *Miramare,* ☎ *040/224143.* 🎫 *Castle: 8,000 lire, plus 3,000 lire for guided visit.* ⏲ *Grounds: daily, 8–1 hr after closing of the castle; castle: Oct.–May, Mon.–Sat 9–4; June–Sept., daily 9–6.*

Trieste

28 *64 km (40 mi) southeast of Udine, 163 km (101 mi) east of Venice.*

Surrounded by rugged countryside and beautiful coastline, Trieste is built on a hillside above what was once the chief port of the Austro-Hungarian Habsburg Empire. Typical of Trieste are its belle epoque cafés (☞ Close-Up: Caffè Culture, *below*). Like Vienna's coffeehouses, these are social and cultural centers of the city, and much-beloved refuges from the city's prevailing northeast wind, the "*bora.*"

The sidewalk cafés on the vast seaside **Piazza dell'Unità d'Italia** are popular meeting places in the summer months. The square is similar to Piazzetta San Marco in Venice; both are focal points of architectural interest that command the best views of the sea. Behind **Palazzo Comunale** (Town Hall, ✉ At the end of Piazza dell'Unità d'Italia), going away from the sea, steps lead uphill, following the city's pattern of upward expansion from its roots as a coastal fishing port in Roman times.

Civico Museo Revoltella e Galleria d'Arte Moderna (Revoltella Museum and Gallery of Modern Art) was founded in 1872 when the Venetian Baron Revoltella left the city his palazzo, library, and art collection. The gallery has one of the most important collections of 19th- and 20th-century art in Italy, with Italian artists particularly well represented. ✉ *Via Diaz 27,* ☎ *040/311361.* 🎫 *10,000 lire.* ⏲ *Wed.–Mon 9–7.*

The solid Romanesque construction of **San Silvestro** church (✉ Via San Silvestro), open Monday–Saturday 10–1, dates from the 11th century. Just beyond it is the Baroque extravagance of **Santa Maria Maggiore,** which backs onto a network of alleys closed to traffic.

The 14th-century **Cattedrale di San Giusto** incorporates two much-older churches, one dating from as far back as the 5th century. The exterior adds even more to the jumble of styles involved by using fragments of Roman tombs and temples: you can see these most clearly on the pillars of the main doorway. The highlights of the interior are the 13th-century mosaics and frescoes. ✉ *Piazza Cattedrale.* ⏲ *Apr.–Sept., Mon.–Sat. 8–noon and 3:30–7:30, Sun. 8–1 and 3:30–8; Oct.–Mar., Mon.–Sat. 8–noon and 2:30–6:30, Sun. 8–1 and 3:30–8.*

From the hilltop **Castello di San Giusto** you can take in some of the best views of the area. In the 15th century this castle was built by the Venetians, who always had an eye for the best vantage point in the cities they conquered or controlled. The Habsburgs, subsequent rulers of Trieste, enlarged it to its present size. Some of the best exhibits in the **Museo Civico del Castello di San Giusto** are the displays of weaponry and armor. ✉ *Piazza Cattedrale,* ☎ *040/309362.* 🎟 *Museum and castle: 2,000 lire.* ⏲ *Museum: Tues.–Sun. 9–1. Castle: June–Sept., daily 9–7; Oct.–May, daily 9–5.*

Piazza della Borsa is the square containing Trieste's original stock exchange, the **Borsa Vecchia,** a neoclassic building now serving as the chamber of commerce. The **statue of Leopold I** is at one end of the square.

OFF THE BEATEN PATH

GROTTA GIGANTE – More than 300 ft high, 900 ft long, and 200 ft wide, this gigantic cave is dripping with spectacular stalactites and stalagmites. Reserve 45 minutes for the tour. It is not far from Trieste, about 10 km (6 mi) north of the city (take Bus 42 from Piazza Oberdan). ☎ *040/327312.* 🎟 *13,000 lire.* ⏲ *Nov.–Feb., daily 10–noon and 2:30–4:30; Mar. and Oct., daily 9–noon and 2–5; Apr.–Sept., daily 9–noon and 2–7.*

Dining and Lodging

$$ ★ ✕ **Suban.** Though in the hills on the edge of town, this historic trattoria is worth the taxi ride. The rustic decor is rich in dark wood, stone, and wrought iron, and you'll find typical regional fare with imaginative variations. Among the specialties are *jota carsolina* (typical local minestrone made of cabbage, potatoes, and beans) and duck breast in Tokay sauce. ✉ *Via Emilio Comici 2,* ☎ *040/54368. AE, DC, MC, V. Closed Tues., 3 wks in Aug., and 1 wk in Jan. No lunch Mon.*

$$$–$$$$ 🏨 **Duchi d'Aosta.** On the spacious Piazza dell'Unità d'Italia, this hotel is beautifully furnished in lavish Venetian-Renaissance style. Its restaurant, Harry's Grill, is one of the city's most elegant. ✉ *Piazza dell'Unità d'Italia 2, 34121,* ☎ *040/7600011,* FAX *040/366092. 53 rooms, 2 suites. Restaurant, bar. AE, DC, MC, V.*

$$–$$$ 🏨 **Colombia.** Unpretentious but adequate, this small hotel caters mainly to a business clientele. There is no restaurant, but there's a typical beer cellar restaurant close by. ✉ *Via della Geppa 18, 34121,* ☎ *040/369333,* FAX *040/369644. 40 rooms. AE, DC, MC, V.*

Nightlife and the Arts

The opera season in Trieste runs from October through May, with a brief operetta festival in July and August. Contact the **tourist information office** (✉ Stazione Centrale, ☎ 040/420182) for further details on events.

Outdoor Activities and Sports

GOLF

The 9-hole **Golf Club Trieste** (✉ Padriciano 80, ☎ 040/226159), closed Tuesday, is 6 km (4 mi) from town center.

Close-Up

CAFFÈ CULTURE

TRIESTE BEING ONE OF THE most famous coffee towns in the world, perhaps it's no coincidence that its mayor is Riccardo Illy, patriarch of the famous *über*-roaster, Illycaffè, which can be credited with supplying caffeine fixes to most Italians and much of the free world. The elegant civility of Trieste plays out beautifully in a caffè culture that rivals Vienna. Know that in Trieste your cappuccino will come in an espresso cup, with only half as much frothy milk and a dollop of whipped cream. Many caffè are part of a *torrefazione* (roasting shop), so you can sample the beans before you buy. Few caffè in Trieste, in Italy, or in the world, can rival **Antico Caffè San Marco** (✉ Via Cesare Battisti 18, ☎ 040/363538) for its glimmering art deco style and old-world atmosphere. On Friday and Saturday there is live music. **Cremecaffè** (✉ Piazza Goldoni 10, ☎ 040/636555) may not be the place to sit down and read the paper, but it's nonetheless one of the most frequented caffè in town, with 20 different blends to choose from. One of the city's finest roasting shops, **Caffè La Colombiana** (✉ Via Carducci 12, ☎ 040/370855) has stood here since the 1940s. There is no better locale in town than at **Caffè Piazza Grande** (✉ Piazza dell'Unità d'Italia 5, ☎ 040/369878), with a great view of the great piazza. **Il Gran Bar Malabar** (✉ Piazza San Giovanni 6, ☎ 040/3636226) is yet another wonderful stop for a coffee or aperitif, with an excellent wine list and tastings every Friday.

Shopping

Trieste's busy shopping street, **Corso Italia,** is reached from Piazza della Borsa. There are antiques markets on the streets of the city's old center on the third Sunday of each month. Trieste has some 60 antiques dealers, jewelers, and secondhand shops, and a large antiques fair is held in the city at the end of October.

VENETIAN ARC A TO Z

Arriving and Departing

By Car

The main access roads to the Venetian Arc from southern Italy are both linked to the A1 (Autostrada del Sole), which connects Bologna, Florence, and Rome. They are the A13, which culminates in Padua, and the A22, which passes through Verona in a north–south direction. The road linking the region from east to west is the A4, the primary route from Milan to as far as Trieste.

By Plane

The main airport serving the Venetian Arc is **Aeroporto Marco Polo** (☎ 041/2609260), 10 km (6 mi) north of Venice (☞ Venice A to Z *in* Chapter 4), which handles international and domestic flights to the region. A few European airlines schedule flights to **Aeroporto di Villafranca** (✉ 11 km/7 mi southwest of Verona, ☎ 045/8095666), also served by a number of charter flights. A regular bus service connects Villafranca with Verona's Porta Nuova railway station.

Treviso's **Aeroporto San Giuseppe** (✉ 5 km/3 mi southeast of Treviso, 32 km/19 mi north of Venice, ☎ 0422/315131) is also served by charter flights. Flights to Treviso usually include transportation from the airport to Venice or other destinations; otherwise there is ATVO local bus service to Treviso every 20 minutes during the day, or a taxi (☎ 0422/431515) will come from Treviso, only 6 km (4 mi) away, to pick you up. There are domestic flights to **Aeroporto Ronchi dei Legionari** (✉ 35 km/22 mi northwest of Trieste, ☎ 0481/773224), linked with Via Flavio Gioia near Trieste's train station by regular SAITA (☎ 040/425001) bus service.

By Train

The most important train routes arriving from the south will stop almost every hour in either Verona, Padua, or Venice. From northern Italy and the rest of Europe, trains usually enter via Milan to the west or through Porta Nuova station in Verona. Call (☎ 147/888088) for train information.

Getting Around

By Bus

There are interurban and interregional connections throughout the Veneto and Friuli. Local tourist offices may be able to provide details of timetables and routes; otherwise contact the local bus station, or in some cases the individual bus companies operating from the station.

Bus stations (✉ Piazzale Trento, Bassano, ☎ 0424/30850; ✉ Piazzale Boschetti, Padua, ☎ 049/8206811; ✉ Via Lungosile Mattei, Treviso, ☎ 0422/577311; ✉ Piazza Libertà, Trieste, ☎ 040/425001; ✉ Piazzale Roma, Venice, ☎ 041/5287886 for buses to Brenta Riviera; 041/5205530 for buses to Cortina, weekends only; ✉ Porta Nuova, Verona, ☎ 045/8004129; Stazione FS, ✉ Piazzale della Stazione, near Campo Marzio, Vicenza, ☎ 0444/223115).

By Car

The main highway in the region is A4, which connects Verona, Padua, and Venice with Trieste. The distance from Verona, in the west, to Trieste is 263 km (163 mi). Branches link A4 with Treviso (A27), Pordenone (A28), and Udine (A23).

By Train

To the west of Venice, on the main line running across the north of Italy, are Padua (20 mins), Vicenza (1 hr), and Verona (1½ hrs); to the east is Trieste (2 hrs). Local trains link Venice to Bassano del Grappa (1 hr), Padua to Bassano del Grappa (1 hr), Vicenza to Treviso (1 hr), and Udine to Trieste (1 hr). Treviso and Udine both lie on the main line from Venice to Treviso, on which Eurocity trains continue to Vienna and Prague. Call for train information (☎ 147/888088).

Contacts and Resources

Car Rentals

PADUA

Avis (✉ Piazzale della Stazione 1, ☎ 049/664198). **Hertz** (✉ Piazzale della Stazione 5/4, ☎ 049/657877).

TRIESTE

Avis (✉ Stazione Marittima, Molo Bersaglieri, ☎ 040/300820; ✉ Aeroporto Ronchi dei Legionari, ☎ 0481/777085). **Hertz** (✉ Piazza della Libertà, c/o Silos, ☎ 040/422122; ✉ Aeroporto Ronchi dei Legionari, ☎ 0481/777025).

UDINE

Avis (✉ Viale Leopardi 5/a, ☎ 0432/501149). **Hertz** (✉ Via Crispi 17, ☎ 0432/511211).

VERONA

Avis (✉ Stazione FS, ☎ 045/8006636). **Hertz** (✉ Stazione FS, ☎ 045/8000832).

VICENZA

Avis (✉ Viale Milano 88, ☎ 0444/321622). **Hertz** (✉ Stazione FS, ☎ 0444/321313).

Emergencies

Police, Ambulance, Fire (☎ 113). For first aid, ask for *"pronto soccorso"* and be prepared to give your address. **Ospedale Civile e Policlinico dell'Università** (✉ Padua, ☎ 049/8211111). **Late-Night Pharmacies:** all pharmacies post signs on the door with addresses of pharmacies that stay open at night, on Saturday afternoon, and on Sunday.

Guided Tours

EXCURSION

Many of the best tours begin and end in Venice because so much of the region is accessible from there (☞ Venice A to Z *in* Chapter 4). The Burchiello excursion boat makes an all-day villa tour along the Brenta River Canal; contact **American Express** (Salizzada San Moisè, 1471 San Marco, Venice, ☎ 041/5200844, FAX 041/5229937; also ☞ Guided Tours *in* Venice A to Z *in* Chapter 4). For those who prefer to go it alone, the most practical way is to hire a car for the day. Local tourist offices will be able to put you in contact with the Tourist Guides Association or provide you with a list of authorized guides, for whom there is an official tariff rate.

PACKAGES

Trieste and Vicenza offer special weekend package deals ("T for you" and "Vicenza Weekend") that include discounts in hotels and restaurants, free or reduced-price entrance to a selection of the cities' main tourist attractions, and some guided tours. Contact the Trieste and Vicenza tourist offices (☞ *below*).

Travel Agencies

For agencies in Venice, *see* Venice A to Z *in* Chapter 4.

American Express (✉ Tiarè Viaggi/American Express, Via Risorgimento 20, Padua, ☎ 049/666133; ✉ Paterniti Viaggi/American Express, Corso Cavour 7, Trieste, ☎ 040/366161; ✉ Fabretto Viaggi/American Express, Corso Porta Nuova 11/f, Verona, ☎ 045/8009040).

Visitor Information

Tourist offices (✉ Stazione Ferroviaria, 35100 Padua; ✉ Piazza Castello, 36063 Marostica, ☎ 0424/72127; ✉ Piazzetta Monte di Pietà 8, 31100 Treviso, ☎ 0422/547632; ✉ Stazione Centrale, 34100 Trieste, ☎ 040/420182; ✉ Piazza Primo Maggio 7, 33100 Udine, ☎ 0432/295972; ✉ Inside the yard of the Tribunale, Piazza dei Signori, 37100 Verona, ☎ 045/8068680; ✉ Piazza delle Erbe 38, 37121 Verona, ☎ 045/8000065; ✉ Stazione FS, Verona, ☎ 045/8000861; ✉ Piazza Matteotti 12, 36100 Vicenza, ☎ 0444/320854; ✉ Consorzio di Promozione Turistica "Vicenza è," Vicenza, ☎ 0444/327141 for info about hotel-restaurant discounts).

6 ITALIAN RIVIERA

GENOA, PORTOFINO, AND CINQUE TERRE

It was the Italians who perfected il dolce far niente—the sweet art of idleness—and all signs show they did it in Liguria. Flanking Genoa, an art-filled city of long-decaying splendor, the twin rivieras bask in the sun, dotted with seaside summer resorts and quaint pastel villages. Rapallo, Portovenere, and the Cinque Terre glisten like pearls on a string, but Portofino still wins the beauty contest, as it has since the days of Bogie and Bacall.

LIKE THE FAMILY JEWELS THAT BEDECK its habitual visitors, the Italian Riviera is glamorous, but in the old-fashioned way. The resort towns and tiny coastal villages that stake intermittent claims on the rocky shores of the Ligurian Sea have much more in common than their analogues in other, newer, or more overbuilt seaside paradises. Here, the grandest palazzi share space with frescoed, angular, late-19th-century apartment buildings, and high-rise glitz seems as foreign as the Maine lobster some of the region's tiniest restaurants incongruously fly in for dinner. The rustic and elegant, the provincial and smart set, the cosmopolitan and the small-town are blended together here in a sun-drenched pastiche that makes up this, the "other" Riviera.

Updated by Robin S. Goldstein

The serpentine arc of Liguria's coastline, sweeping serenely from Ventimiglia to La Spezia, is the defining mark of the region's identity. Although it technically extends inland to the tops of the Ligurian Alps, Liguria is Italy's seaside region, and its greatest charms are those of the sea. For centuries, the region has inspired poets and artists. For this is where a captivated Percy Shelley praised the "soft blue Spezian bay"; here is where daredevil English poet Lord Byron swam from Portovenere to Lerici. Today, travelers escaping the conceits of civilization still head for the Italian Riviera for a cure. Mellowed by the balmy breezes blowing off the sea, they bask in the sun and explore the tiny coastal towns whose greatest treasures—peace, quiet, and dramatic natural beauty—remain for the most part undiscovered.

Liguria's narrow strip of mountain-protected coastline varies considerably between the two rivieras. The western Riviera di Ponente (Riviera of the Setting Sun), which reaches from the French border to Genoa, has protected bays and wide sandy beaches, and is generally more developed and commercialized than its counterpart to the east, the Riviera di Levante (Riviera of the Rising Sun). Beginning at the French border, the Ponente is home to the glamorous seaside resorts of San Remo and Bordighera, similar to their glittery francophone cousins to the west in their unabashed civic dedication to the pursuit of pleasure. Much of the eastward sweep of the Ponente coastline has been developed for the packs of sun worshippers who descend upon it in the summer. The minuscule bays and inlets spanning the coastline from Genoa to Portovenere become steeper, sculpted by nature into rocky cliffs.

If this coastline is a necklace, hung with jewels, the most dazzling pendant is the Portofino promontory. This must be the most photographed village in the world, and one look is enough to tell you why—if you pull up to the port by boat, chances are you'll shoot all your film before you disembark. Smooth-faced, brightly painted houses frame the port in a burst of color that becomes sheer enchantment at sunset, when the houses are reflected in the dancing waters of the harbor. Despite what all the shops and restaurants worldwide named "Portofino" would have you believe, however, once you've landed, there's not much to see or do in Portofino. The people here, at least in summer, are the real attractions—it was, after all, Bogart and Bacall and Taylor and Burton who put the place on the map.

Farther along the coast is a second peninsula; here the road weaves inland, leaving you to hike or take a train or boat to explore the Cinque Terre, a collective community of five fishing villages perched on bluffs above the sea. Here are some of Liguria's most uncrowded beaches, picturesque village squares, and certainly its best views. From the hiking trails that link the Cinque Terre, the tiny villages seem like colorful blooms of flowers clinging to hulking black cliffs that plunge into the sea. Though this is still the Italian Riviera at its unbuttoned best, Vernazza's growing trinket-shop trade and Monterosso's ever-booked hotels are signs that even Cinque Terre has been "discovered" in recent years.

Set in the heart of the region is Genoa, Italy's largest commercial port, where magnificent Renaissance palaces wearing the dusty patina of time attest to the wealth of the city's seafaring past. Every schoolchild knows Genoa as the birthplace of Christopher Columbus, and many would become wide-eyed in knowing it's the home of Europe's largest aquarium. Despite the city's considerable charms, most visitors to Liguria are more interested in the less-historic waters found along the coast—not surprising, given the relaxed, easy lifestyle found alongside them.

Pleasures and Pastimes

Boating

With so much coastline—350 km (217 mi)—and so many pretty little harbors, it's no wonder that the Riviera attracts pleasure craft of all shapes and sizes, from rowboats to megayachts. San Remo, Rapallo, Santa Margherita Ligure, Chiavari, Finale Ligure, and Sestri Levante have large, well-equipped marinas, and nearly every town has a harbor and at least one marine shop. Kayaking is also popular along Ligurian shores on calmer days. Every October Genoa hosts a mammoth international boat show.

Dining

Liguria's cooking might surprise you. It employs all sorts of seafood—especially anchovies, sea bass, squid, and octopus—but it makes even wider use of vegetables and the aromatic herbs that grow wild on the hillsides, together with liberal amounts of olive oil and garlic. Basil- and garlic-rich pesto is Liguria's classic pasta sauce. You will also find *pansoti* (round pockets of pasta filled with a cheese mixture) and *trofie* (doughy, short pasta twists sometimes made with chestnut flour) with *salsa di noci,* an intense sauce of garlic, walnuts, and cream that, as with pesto, is often pounded with a mortar and pestle. *Vitello* (veal) and *porcho* (pork) are the most popular meats; *cima alla Genovese,* breast of veal stuffed with a mixture of eggs and vegetables, is served as a cold cut. You should also try the succulent *agnello* (lamb) and fresh wild mushrooms foraged from the hills.

When not snacking on pizza sold by the slice or by weight, the Genovese and other Ligurians eat *torta pasqualina* (vegetable pie), or focaccia, the salty and oily pizzalike bread with various toppings. *Focaccia alla Genovese* is usually served plain, and the delectable *focaccia al formaggio* is topped with stracchino cheese. Local vineyards produce mostly light and refreshing whites such as Pigato, Vermentino Ligure, and Cinque Terre. Reds called Rossese and Dolceacqua actually resemble whites in their light, crisp flavor; they go well with the lighter meat dishes of the region. *Vini frizzanti* (sparkling wines), both red and white, are ubiquitous in the region, though their quality varies. Sweets are less rich than those in other parts of Italy; *panna cotta* (creamy egg custard, often flavored with caramel, served cold) and gelato are favorites for dessert, and *canestralli* (light almond cookies with powdered sugar) and various *frittelle* (crispy fried sweet dough cookies) are perfect with a *caffè* (espresso).

Hiking and Walking

Liguria's hilly terrain makes walking strenuous but rewarding, with stunning views of the sea and castles and little villages dotting the coast.

Portofino invites walking, whether you opt for the popular and relatively easy walk from Portofino to the Abbazia di San Fruttuoso or the more challenging hike from Ruta to the top of Monte Portofino. One of the best treks is along the five Cinque Terre fishing towns, all the while thumbing your nose at the tourists on the sightseeing boats. Everywhere in Liguria, roads, mule paths, or footpaths lead into the hills, where you can discover the region at its unspoiled best.

Lodging

Most good hotels in Genoa are set in pretty modern buildings and interiors, not the sort of grand, old restored villa you might hope for. When choosing a hotel in Genoa, you should know that in its center it is one of Italy's noisiest cities; make sure your windows are double-glazed (*doppi vetri*). Lodging in Genoa and Liguria is somewhat expensive, at least compared to lodging in other parts of Italy like Rome, Florence, and down south. This is partly due to its seasonality—Genoa and Liguria absolutely come alive in summer, but are dead in winter. The best bargains and the warmest welcomes can be found in the less-visited inland areas; there are few hotels in this part of Liguria, but many of them are family-run and special because of it. Reserve ahead year-round for Genoa, and during peak Easter and summer seasons for resorts. Note that many hotels and resorts in the area close for a number of weeks each year, usually late fall and early winter, and some in summer; it's best to call ahead.

Exploring the Italian Riviera

Liguria's cities, towns, and resorts are nestled into the elongated coastal strip and connected by a highway stretching 260 km (161 mi) from Ventimiglia on the French border to La Spezia and Sarzana. At the center, Genoa separates the western (Ponente) from the eastern (Levante) Riviera, forming two distinct geographic areas to explore (three, including Genoa itself). The hilly and mountainous hinterland, very different in scenery and character from the Riviera, can easily be explored from towns along the coast. From the sea, a series of narrow valleys extend inland, giving access to the sparsely settled interior.

Getting around the Riviera is an expedient affair, though the pace here is leisurely. Public transportation in the region is excellent: trains connect all sights along the coast and buses snake inland. It takes two hours for a fast train to cover the entire coast (though local trains make innumerable stops and take upwards of five hours). With the freedom of a car, you could drive from one end of the Riviera to the other on the autostrada in less than three hours. The A10 and A12 autostrade on either side of Genoa skirt the coast, avoiding local traffic on the Via Aurelia, which was laid out by the ancient Romans. The Via Aurelia, now known as national highway S1, connects practically all the towns along the coast.

Numbers in the text correspond to numbers in the margin and on the Italian Riviera and Genoa maps.

Great Itineraries

If urban artistic and historic treasures are your passion but you also want some seaside relief, stay in Genoa and make it your base for exploring the rest of the region on day trips. For a more relaxed approach, sea views, and recreation, settle into a resort and take a day trip into Genoa. In seven days you can visit the prettiest resorts and fishing villages, spend a day or two in Genoa, and perhaps make an excursion inland. Five days would allow you to see the highlights, but you will probably want to see Genoa in a day so that you can visit more of the smaller towns. In three days you will be able to see Genoa and perhaps two major resorts and two or three of the smaller, more picturesque towns.

IF YOU HAVE 3 DAYS

Tour time is limited, and you should rent a car and concentrate on select towns. On your first day begin on the eastern Riviera di Levante. Stop at the delightful fishing villages of **Portovenere** ㊼ and **Camogli** ㊲, detouring for a look at romantic **Portofino** ㊵. For a more cosmopolitan resort atmosphere, opt instead for **Rapallo** ㊳ or **Santa Margherita Ligure** ㊴, with a short jaunt from Santa Margherita to Portofino. On the second day see **Genoa** ⑭–㉟, exploring the historic center and old harbor. The western Riviera should be the focus of the third day; head for glitzy **San Remo** ④ or the more sedate **Bordighera** ③, but allow about a half day along the way to visit the medieval centers of **Albenga** ⑧, **Cervo** ⑦, and **Taggia** ⑤. Naturally, you should follow this itinerary in the opposite direction if you are arriving in the region from the west.

IF YOU HAVE 5 DAYS

In five days you can go from one end of the Riviera to the other, or start in Genoa and head east or west from there. If you make Genoa your base you can alternate excursions along the coast and into the interior with city sightseeing. On your first day explore **Genoa** ⑭–㉟. If the day is a clear one, take the **Zecco-Righi funicular** ⑯ to the top for an aerial view of the city. On the second day head west, making a detour to Spotorno, and proceed to Noli, one of the best-preserved medieval towns on the entire Riviera. Then see the medieval delights of Cervo before going on to sophisticated **San Remo** ④ and palm-studded **Bordighera** ③ for the night. Bask in the sun on the third day or venture inland to the well-preserved medieval villages of Dolcedo and Valloria instead. On the fourth and fifth days explore the eastern Riviera, starting with stately **Nervi** ㊱, near Genoa. Among the many allurements on the Portofino promontory, explore the fishing village of **Camogli** ㊲ and chichi **Portofino** ㊵; don't miss the hamlets of San Rocco, San Niccolò, and Punta Chiappa, accessible by foot from Camogli. You can overnight in a stylish resort such as **Santa Margherita Ligure** ㊴ or **Rapallo** ㊳; or you can go for lower-key **Sestri Levante** ㊷, an industrial town with a charming medieval center, or the secluded town of **Levanto** ㊹, closer to the Cinque Terre. If you have time on your fifth day, a daylong excursion by train or boat to the five rock-perched coastal villages of the **Cinque Terre** ㊺ is highly recommended. If you don't go to Cinque Terre, proceed to **Portovenere** ㊼. Then, bypass industrialized La Spezia and wind up in the pretty port village of **Lerici** ㊽.

IF YOU HAVE 7 DAYS

If you begin your visit of the region in **Genoa** ⑭–㉟, spend two days there. You will have time for an excursion to **Nervi** ㊱. On the third day head west from Genoa, either working your way gradually to Ventimiglia or going directly to Ventimiglia and then heading back to Genoa. See the extraordinary cactus collection in the **Giardino Hanbury** ① near **Ventimiglia** ②, then turn inland to medieval Dolceacqua, only 10 km (6 mi) away. Stop for tea in genteel **Bordighera** ③ before continuing on to the much busier and more commercial resort of **San Remo** ④; stay overnight in San Remo or **Finale Ligure** ⑨. On the fourth day, discover Noli and Spotorno (bus transport to Noli is via Spotorno). With the exception of **Albisola Marina** ⑪ and **Pegli** ⑬, you can skip the industrialized coast between **Savona** ⑩ and Genoa.

On the fifth day, see the offhand charm of **Camogli** ㊲. Take the turnoff for **Rapallo** ㊳ and **Santa Margherita Ligure** ㊴ and, if the traffic isn't

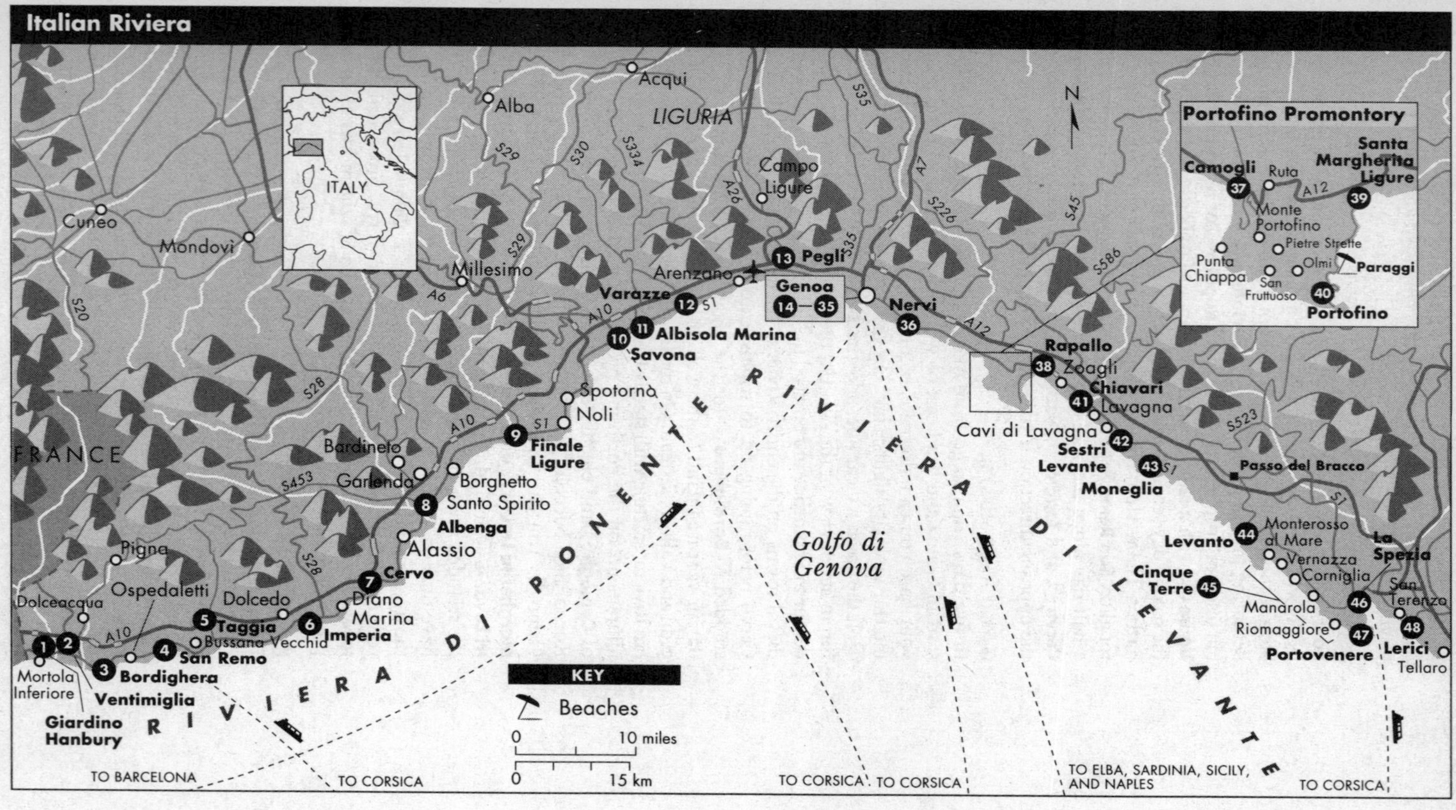
Italian Riviera
Portofino Promontory
Camogli
Ruta
Monte Portofino
Pietre Strette
Santa Margherita Ligure
Paraggi
Olmi
San Fruttuoso
Punta Chiappa
Portofino
LIGURIA
Acqui
Alba
Mondovi
Cuneo
Millesimo
Campo Ligure
Arenzano
Varazze
Albisola Marina
Savona
Pegli
Genoa
Nervi
Rapallo
Zoagli
Chiavari
Lavagna
Cavi di Lavagna
Sestri Levante
Moneglia
Passo del Bracco
Levanto
Monterosso al Mare
Vernazza
Corniglia
Manarola
Riomaggiore
Cinque Terre
La Spezia
San Terenzo
Lerici
Tellaro
Portovenere
Spotorno
Noli
Finale Ligure
Borghetto Santo Spirito
Albenga
Alassio
Bardineto
Garlenda
Cervo
Diano Marina
Imperia
Dolcedo
Bussana Vecchia
Taggia
San Remo
Ospedaletti
Bordighera
Pigna
Ventimiglia
Dolceacqua
Mortola Inferiore
Giardino Hanbury
FRANCE
ITALY
Golfo di Genova
RIVIERA DI PONENTE
RIVIERA DI LEVANTE
TO BARCELONA
TO CORSICA
TO ELBA, SARDINIA, SICILY, AND NAPLES
KEY
Beaches
0 10 miles
0 15 km
N

heavy, head for Portofino ⑩. At the height of the season an excursion boat to Portofino from Camogli, Santa Margherita Ligure, or Rapallo may avoid the traffic jams on the narrow access road and parking problems once you arrive. You may want to consider staying in **Chiavari** ⑪, a good hub for forays into the mountains on your sixth day, or spend a night in Monterosso or Vernazza and absorb the **Cinque Terre's** ⑮ magical nocturnal calmness. Regardless, hike the paths in Cinque Terre on your sixth or seventh day, then head east to **La Spezia** ⑯ and look for signs to **Portovenere** ⑰. Doubling back to La Spezia, take the coast road to charming **Lerici** ⑱. The La Spezia turnoff on the A12 and S1 highways is only about 15 km (9 mi) from the border of Tuscany.

When to Tour the Italian Riviera

Though shops, cafés, clubs, and restaurants stay open late in resorts during high season (at Easter and during the summer), during the rest of the year they close early. You should keep in mind that Liguria is one of the most seasonal places in the world, and everything from the yacht-dotted playground of Portofino to the rows of seaside restaurants and bars that line the Riviera's quieter shores become ghost towns from October to February, with the occasional exception of the week around Christmas. Avoid driving through Ventimiglia on Friday, the busy market day.

RIVIERA DI PONENTE

The Riviera di Ponente stretches from Ventimiglia on the French border to Genoa. For the most part it is an unbroken chain of popular beach resorts sheltered from the north by the Ligurian and Maritime Alps, mountain walls that guarantee mild winters and a long growing season—resulting in its other nickname, the Riviera dei Fiori (Riviera of Flowers). Actually, the name is more evocative than the sight of once-verdant hillsides now swathed in plastic to form massive greenhouses. Many towns on the western Riviera have suffered from an epidemic of overdevelopment, but most have preserved their historic cores, usually their most interesting features. In major resorts large new marinas cater to the pleasure-craft crowd. The Riviera di Ponente has both sandy and pebbly beaches with some quiet bays. Varazze, with a wide, sandy beach and many tall palm trees, is perhaps the last pleasant beach resort on the Riviera di Ponente to resist the encroachment of greater Genoa's industrial influence and the unwelcome effects of the tourist boom.

Giardino Hanbury

★ ❶ *165 km (102 mi) southwest of Genoa.*

Mortola Inferiore, only 2 km (1 mi) from the French border, is site of the world-famous Giardino Hanbury (Hanbury Garden), one of the largest botanical gardens in Italy. Planned and planted by a wealthy English merchant, Sir Thomas Hanbury, and his botanist brother, Daniel, in 1867, the terraced gardens contain a variety of species from five continents, including many palms and succulents (plants of the cactus group). There are panoramic views of the sea from the gardens, which descend right down to the beach. ✉ *Giardino Hanbury, Mortola Inferiore,* ☎ *0184/229507.* *8,500 lire.* ⏲ *Mar.–mid-June, daily 10–6; mid-June–Sept., daily 9–7; Oct.–Mar., Thurs.–Tues. 10–5. Ticket office closes 1 hr before garden.*

OFF THE BEATEN PATH **BALZI ROSSI** – At the French border, 7 km (4½ mi) from Ventimiglia and 2 km (1 mi) from the Giardino Hanbury, are the Balzi Rossi (Red Rocks), caves carved in the sheer rock in which prehistoric humans left traces of their lives and magic rites. You can visit the caves and a small museum displaying some of the objects found there. ✉ *Via Balzi Rosso 9,* ☎ *0184/38113.* 🎟 *4,000 lire.* ⏲ *Tues.–Sun. 9–7.*

Ventimiglia

❷ *6 km (4 mi) east of Giardino Hanbury, 159 km (98 mi) southwest of Genoa.*

From its past life as a pre-Roman settlement known as Albintimilium, Ventimiglia possesses some important archaeological remains, including a 2nd-century AD amphitheater. A vital trade center for hundreds of years, Ventimiglia declined in prestige as Genoa grew, and is now little more than a frontier town that lives on tourism and the cultivation of flowers. The town is divided in two by the Roia River. The well-preserved medieval **Città Vecchia** (Old City) on the western bank is what you'll see first. The 11th-century **Duomo** (Cathedral) has a Gothic portal dating from 1222. Walk up Via del Capo to the **ancient walls,** which offer fine views of the coast. On Friday the large flower market, open to trade only, is chaotic with bargain hunters from France, creating traffic gridlock; it's best to avoid Ventimiglia on that day.

OFF THE BEATEN PATH **DOLCEACQUA** – From Ventimiglia, a provincial road swings up the Nervia River valley to this lovely-sounding medieval town, whose name translates as Sweetwater, with its ruined castle. Beyond is **Pigna,** another medieval village built in concentric circles on a hilltop.

Lodging

$$ ★ 🏨 **La Riserva.** Just 5 km (3 mi) west of Ventimiglia, but more than 1,100 ft above sea level, is the village of Castel d'Appio, where you'll find this innlike establishment. The staff is very helpful, providing, for example, regular lifts into town for those without cars. Apart from its excellent restaurant, La Riserva offers numerous activities and a lovely terrace for drinks or sunbathing or candlelight dinners. Full-board rates are a good deal. Reservations for the hotel are recommended. ✉ *Castel d'Appio, 18039,* ☎ *0184/229533,* FAX *0184/229712. 25 rooms. Restaurant, bar, pool. AE, DC, MC, V. Closed Sept. 30–Easter (except Dec. 20–Jan. 6). FAP.*

Bordighera

❸ *5 km (3 mi) east of Ventimiglia, 155 km (96 mi) southwest of Genoa.*

Bordighera, on a lushly vegetated, large promontory, wears its genteel past as a famous winter resort with unstudied ease. A large English colony, attracted by the mild climate, settled here in the second half of the 19th century and is still very much in evidence today. In fin-de-siècle Bordighera, you'll regularly find people taking afternoon tea in the cafés. This garden spot was the first town in Europe to grow date palms, and its citizens still have the exclusive right to provide the Vatican with palm fronds for Easter celebrations. Walk along the **Lungomare Argentina,** the magnificent 1½-km (1-mi) -long seafront promenade beginning at the western end of the town, for a good view westward to the French Côte d'Azur. Thanks partly to its year-round English residents, Bordighera does not close down entirely in the winter like many Riviera resorts, but it's nevertheless very quiet in that season. With plenty of fine hotels and restaurants, it makes a good base for excursions and is quieter and less commercial than San Remo.

Dining and Lodging

$$–$$$ ✕ **La Reserve Restaurant.** This traditional and informal trattoria has access to the beach and excellent views of the sea from the dining room. There are even changing rooms for anyone who wants a post-lunch dip. Concentrate on the seafood here: specialties are seafood ravioli *al finocchio selvatico* (with wild fennel) and assorted grilled seafood. Reservations are recommended. ✉ *Via Arziglia 20,* ☎ *0184/261322. AE, DC, MC, V. Closed Mon. (except July–Aug.) and Nov.*

$$–$$$ ✕ **Le Chaudron.** The charming rustic interior, with ancient Roman arches, has the look of restaurants across the French border in Provence. Ligurian specialties are featured on the predominantly seafood menu of this centrally located restaurant: try the cheese pansoti con salsa di noci and *branzino* (sea bass) with artichokes or mushrooms. A café annex serves a daily lunch special. ✉ *Piazza Bengasi 2,* ☎ *0184/263592. Reservations essential. DC, MC, V. Closed Mon., Feb., and July 1–15.*

$$ ✕ **Piemontese.** Only a block from the seaside and five minutes from the train station, this simple restaurant features the typical cooking of the neighboring Piedmont region, including *risotto al Barolo* (rice cooked with Barolo wine, sausage, and porcini mushrooms) and *bagna cauda* (raw vegetables with a garlic and oil sauce). Ligurian dishes and seafood are also prepared. ✉ *Via Roseto 8, off Via Vittorio Veneto,* ☎ *0184/261651. AE, MC, V. Closed Tues., mid-June–mid-July, and Nov. 20–Dec. 20.*

$$$–$$$$ 🏨 **Grand Hotel del Mare.** This tasteful hotel at the top of a steep hill rising from the beach lives up to its name, with impeccable service and facilities. The large rooms have panoramic views of the coastline; ask for one facing the water. One floor is filled with beautiful antique furnishings. ✉ *Via Portico della Punta 34, 18012,* ☎ *0184/262201,* FAX *0184/262394. 104 rooms, 3 suites. Restaurant, piano bar, saltwater pool, beauty salon, mineral baths, tennis court, exercise room, beach. AE, DC, MC, V. Closed Oct. 15–Dec. 23.*

$$$ 🏨 **Grand Hotel Capo Ampelio.** This hotel occupies a converted villa on a hill overlooking the town and the coastline. Traditional architectural details in the reception rooms and staircases are paired with convenient modern features in the rooms, all with balconies. The hotel is somewhat outside the town center, so the rooms are quiet. ✉ *Via Virgilio 11, 18012,* ☎ *0184/264333,* FAX *0184/264244. 104 rooms. Restaurant, bar, pool, massage, exercise room, recreation room. DC, MC, V. Closed Oct. 10–Dec. 22.*

San Remo

★ ❹ *12 km (7 mi) east of Bordighera, 146 km (90 mi) southwest of Genoa.*

The self-styled capital of the Riviera di Ponente is San Remo, also the area's largest resort, lined with polished world-class hotels, exotic gardens, and seaside promenades. Renowned for its royal visitors, famous casino, and romantic setting, San Remo still maintains some of the glamour of its heyday from the late 19th century to World War II. Among the rich and famous who flocked to San Remo, drawn by the mild climate and pleasant countryside, were Alfred Nobel, who built a summer house here, and Russian Empress Maria Alexandrovna, wife of Czar Alexander II.

The onion-domed Russian Orthodox church of **San Basilio** stands at one end of the Corso dell'Imperatrice and, like this imposing seafront promenade, is a legacy of the empress. San Remo is famous for the **Mercato dei Fiori,** Italy's most important wholesale flower market, held in a market hall between Piazza Colombo and Corso Garibaldi and open to dealers only. More than 20,000 tons of carnations, roses, mimosa flowers, and innumerable other cut flowers are dispatched from here each year.

In the old part of San Remo, **La Pigna,** or pinecone, explore the warren of alleyways that climb upward to Piazza Castello, with a splendid view of the town. The newer parts of San Remo suffer from the same epidemic of overbuilding that changed so many towns on the western Riviera for the worse. And as the center of northern Italy's flower-growing industry, the resort is surrounded by hills where once-verdant terraces are now blanketed with plastic to form immense greenhouses.

The Art Nouveau **San Remo Casino** is reminiscent of the turn of the century, with a restaurant, nightclub, and a theater that hosts concerts and the annual San Remo Music Festival. ✉ *Corso Inglese, San Remo,* ☎ *018/45951.* *Slot machines free; tables 15,000 lire weekends.* *Daily 2:30 PM–3 AM.*

OFF THE BEATEN PATH

BUSSANA VECCHIA – About 8 km (5 mi) east of San Remo, in the hills where flowers are cultivated for export, is Bussana Vecchia, a self-consciously picturesque ghost town largely destroyed by an earthquake in 1877. The inhabitants packed up and left en masse after the quake, and for almost a century, the houses, church, and crumbling bell tower were empty shells, overgrown by weeds and wildflowers. Since the 1960s, an artist's colony has evolved among the ruins. Painters, sculptors, artisans, and bric-a-brac dealers have restored dwellings for themselves and sell their wares to visitors.

Dining and Lodging

$ ★ ✕ **Nuovo Piccolo Mondo.** This small, central trattoria has plenty of charm and a homey atmosphere, found in such details as the old wooden chairs dating from the 1920s, when the place opened. Family-run, it has a faithful clientele, so get there early to grab a table and order Ligurian specialties such as *sciancui* (a mixture of beans, tomatoes, vegetables, and pesto) and *polpo e patate* (stewed octopus with potatoes). ✉ *Via Piave 7,* ☎ *0184/509012. No credit cards. Closed Sun., Mon., and 1st 3 wks in July.*

$$$$ **Royal.** It would take a dedicated hedonist to determine whether this deluxe hotel or the Splendido in Portofino (☞ Dining and Lodging *in* Portofino, *below*) is the most luxurious in Liguria. One major difference is the location: only a few paces from the casino and the train station, the Royal is definitely part of San Remo, unlike the Splendido, which is set above Portofino. Rooms here have a mixture of modern equipment and antique furnishings. The heated seawater swimming pool, open April–September, is dug into a subtropical garden. On the terrace, candlelight dining and music get underway each night under the stars in season. ✉ *Corso Imperatrice 80, 18038,* ☎ *0184/5391,* FAX *0184/661445. 136 rooms, 6 suites. Restaurant, bar, saltwater pool, miniature golf, tennis court. AE, DC, MC, V. Closed Oct. 10–Dec. 20.*

$$ **Paradiso.** This small central hotel is adjacent to a lush public park near the Royal (☞ *above*). A quiet, palm-fringed garden gives it an air of seclusion, a plus in this sometimes hectic city. Rooms are modern and bright, and many have a little terrace. The hotel restaurant has a good fixed-price menu. ✉ *Via Roccasterone 12, 18038,* ☎ *0184/571211,* FAX *0184/578176. 41 rooms. Restaurant, bar. AE, DC, MC, V.*

Outdoor Activities and Sports

GOLF

The 18-hole **San Remo Golf Club** (✉ Via Campo Golf, ☎ 0184/557093), closed Tuesday, is 5 km (3 mi) north of town.

Taggia

5 *10 km (6 mi) east of San Remo, 135 km (84 mi) southwest of Genoa.*

The town of Taggia has a medieval core and one of the most imposing medieval stone bridges in the area. The church of **San Domenico,** on a rise south of Taggia, was part of a monastery founded in the 15th century, and was a beacon of faith and learning in western Liguria for 300 years. An antiques market is held here on the fourth weekend of the month.

Imperia

6 *20 km (12 mi) east of Taggia, 116 km (71 mi) southwest of Genoa.*

Imperia actually consists of two towns: **Porto Maurizio,** a medieval town built on a promontory, and **Oneglia,** now an industrial center for oil refining and pharmaceuticals. Obviously, Oneglia can be skipped entirely. Porto Maurizio has a virtually intact medieval center, the Parasio quarter, an intricate spiral of narrow streets and stone portals, and some imposing 17th- and 18th-century palaces.

OFF THE BEATEN PATH

MUSEO DELL'OLIVO – Imperia is king when it comes to olive oil, and the story of the olive—its cultivation and pressing into oil—is the theme of this small museum set up by the Carli olive oil company. Displays of farm implements, types of presses, and utensils demonstrate how olive oil has been made in many countries throughout history. ✉ *Via Garessio 11, Imperia,* ☎ *0183/295762.* *Free.* *Sept.–July, Mon. and Wed.–Sat. 9–noon and 3–6:30; Aug., Mon. and Wed.–Sat. 3–6:30.*

Dining

$ ★ ✕ **Candidollo.** This charming and good-value restaurant is worth a detour to the village of Diano Borello, on the valley road a couple of kilometers north of Diano Marina, 6 km (4 mi) east of Imperia. In his rustic country inn, with checkered tablecloths and worn terra-cotta floors, host Bruno Ardissone depends upon locally grown ingredients and seasonal traditional recipes. The menu usually includes *coniglio al timo* (rabbit with thyme and other herbs) and *lumache all'agliata* (grilled snails in piquant sauce). Reservations are recommended. ✉ *Diano Borello,* ☎ *0183/43025. No credit cards. Closed Tues. and Nov.–Mar. No lunch Mon.*

Cervo

7 *12 km (7 mi) east of Imperia, 106 km (65 mi) southwest of Genoa.*

Cervo is the quintessential sleepy Ligurian coastal village, nicely polished for the tourists who come to explore its narrow byways and street staircases. It is a remarkably well-preserved medieval town, crowned with a big Baroque church.

Nightlife and the Arts

In July and August the square in front of the church is the setting for **chamber music** concerts.

Albenga

8 *23 km (14 mi) northeast of Cervo, 90 km (55 mi) southwest of Genoa.*

Albenga has a medieval core, with narrow streets laid out by the ancient Romans. A network of alleys is punctuated by centuries-old towers surrounding the 18th-century Romanesque **cathedral,** with a late 14th-century campanile, and **baptistery** dating back to the 5th century AD.

OFF THE BEATEN PATH **BARDINETO** – For a look at some of the Riviera's mountain scenery, make an excursion by car to this attractive village in the middle of an area rich in mushrooms, chestnuts, and raspberries, as well as local cheese. A ruined castle stands high above the village. From Borghetto Santo Spirito (between Albenga and Finale Ligure), drive inland 25 km (15 mi).

Lodging

$$$$ **La Meridiana.** An oasis of Italian hospitality and refinement lies 8 km (5 mi) off the Albenga exit of the A10. The handsome farmhouse compound is spread on a bucolic garden. The interiors are that of a comfortably luxe home, with tasteful, bright prints and colors, fresh flowers, and a mix of traditional and period-style furniture in the common and guest rooms. Il Rosmarino restaurant serves fine wine and seafood dishes. Nearby are the Golf Club Garlenda, a tennis club, and a country club for horseback riding. ✉ *Via ai Castelli, Garlenda 17033,* ☎ *0182/580271,* FAX *0182/580150. 16 rooms, 15 suites. Restaurant, pool. AE, MC, V. Closed Nov.–early Mar.*

Finale Ligure

9 *20 km (12 mi) northeast of Albenga, 72 km (44 mi) southwest of Genoa.*

Palms, sand strips, *gelaterie* (gelato shops), and good rock-climbing terrain make Finale Ligure a good break from gaudiness and pastel villages. Finale Ligure is made up of three villages: Finalborgo, Finalmarina, and Finalpia. The latter two have fine sandy beaches and modern resort amenities. The most attractive village is **Finalborgo,** a medieval settlement, planned to a rigid blueprint, with 15th-century walls. The village is crowned by the impressive ruins of the huge **Castel Gavone.** The Baroque church of **San Biagio** houses many works of art. The 14th- to 15th-century Dominican convent of **Santa Caterina** can be visited for the shade of the courtyard or to see the museum of paleontology and natural history, which houses prehistoric remains found in the area. ✉ *Museo Civico,* ☎ *019/690020.* *5,000 lire.* ⏲ *July–Oct., Tues.–Sat. 9–noon and 3–6, Sun. 9–noon; Sept.–June, Tues.–Sat. 9–noon and 2:30–4:30, Sun. 9–noon.*

The countryside around Finale Ligure is pierced by deep, narrow valleys and caves; the limestone outcroppings provide the warm pinkish stone found in many buildings in Genoa. Here lurk rare reptiles and exotic flora.

Dining

$$–$$$ ✕ **Ai Torchi.** You could easily become a homemade pesto snob at this restaurant in the center of Finalborgo. It is set in a restored 5th-century olive oil refinery. ✉ *Via dell'Annunziata 12,* ☎ *019/690531. AE, DC, MC, V. Closed Mon. (Oct.–May), Tues. (except in Aug.), and Jan. 7–Feb. 11.*

OFF THE BEATEN PATH **NOLI** – Just 9 km (5½ mi) northeast of Finale Ligure, picturesque ruins of a castle loom benevolently over the tiny medieval gem of Noli. It is hard to imagine this charming village was—like Genoa, Venice, Pisa, and

Amalfi—a prosperous maritime republic in the Middle Ages. If you don't have a car, you can get a bus for Noli at Spotorno, where local trains stop.

Savona

10 *44 km (27 mi) northeast of Albenga, 46 km (29 mi) southwest of Genoa.*

Savona is the fifth-largest seaport in Italy and handles vast oil and coal cargoes, as well as car and truck ferries. Much of the town is modern and not very interesting, although a small, austere older quarter near the harbor contains some fine homes of the town's merchant class. The large **Palazzo della Rovere** (⊠ Via Pia) was designed for Pope Julius II by the Florentine Giuliano da Sangallo in 1495. Other medieval monuments include the 14th-century **Palazzo degli Anziani,** and three 12th-century towers. Every other year (next in 2000) on Good Friday, antique wooden carvings depicting the Passion of Christ are carried in procession.

Shopping

Watch for shops selling crystallized fruit, a local specialty. In Millesimo, a town 4 km (2½ mi) west and 36 km (18 mi) inland of Savona, little rum chocolates known as *millesimi* are produced. Look for bargains, too, in wrought-iron work, relief work on copper plate, and pieces in local sandstone.

Albisola Marina

11 *4½ km (3 mi) northeast of Savona, 43 km (26 mi) west of Genoa.*

Albisola Marina has preserved its centuries-old tradition of ceramic making. Numerous shops here sell these distinctive wares, and even a whole sidewalk, **Lungomare degli Artisti,** has been transformed by the colorful ceramic works of well-known artists. It runs along the beachfront. The 18th-century **Villa Faraggiana** has interesting antique ceramics and exhibits on the history of the craft. ⊠ *Near the parish church on Via dell'Oratorio.* ☎ *019/480622.* *Free.* ⊙ *Apr.–Sept., Wed.–Mon. 3–7.*

Shopping

Ceramiche San Giorgio (⊠ Corso Matteotti 5, ☎ 019/482747) has been producing ceramics since the 17th century and is known for both classic and modern designs. **Mazzotti** (⊠ Corso Matteotti 25, ☎ 019/481626) has an exclusive selection and a small in-house museum. In Albisola Superiore, **Ernan** (⊠ Corso Mazzini 77, ☎ 019/489916) features the classic blue-and-white Old Savona patterns typical of the 18th century.

Varazze

12 *11 km (7 mi) northeast of Albisola Marina, 35 km (22 mi) west of Genoa.*

Varazze, known for its fine sandy beach, is a good place to stop for some sea and sun. The town, nicknamed the "city of the woman," also has well-preserved ancient ramparts, with a 10th-century church facade built into one of the rampart walls.

Pegli

13 *23 km (14 mi) northeast of Varazze, 13 km (8 mi) west of Genoa.*

Once a popular summer home for many patrician Genovese families, Pegli has museums, parks, and some regal old villas with well-tended gardens. This residential suburb manages to maintain its dignity despite industrial development and the proximity of airport and port facilities. Two lovely villas make it worth an excursion. Pegli can be reached conveniently by commuter train from Stazione Porta Principe in Genoa.

Villa Doria, near the Pegli train station, has a large park. The villa itself, built in the 16th century by the Doria family, has been converted into a **naval museum.** ✉ *Piazza Bonavino 7, Pegli,* ☎ *010/6969885.* *Villa 6,000 lire; park free.* ⏲ *Villa Tues.–Thurs. 9–1, Fri.–Sat. 9–7, 1st and 3rd Sun. of month 9–1; park daily 10–noon and 2–6.*

Villa Durazzo Pallavicini is set in 19th-century gardens with temples and artificial lakes. The villa has an **archaeological museum.** ✉ *Via Pallavicini 11, Pegli,* ☎ *010/6981048.* *Museum 6,000 lire; park 7,000 lire.* ⏲ *Apr.–Sept., Tues.–Thurs. 9–7, Fri.–Sat. 9–1; Oct.–Mar., Tues.–Thurs. 9–5, Fri.–Sat. 9–1; 2nd and 4th Sun. of month 9–1.*

GENOA

Ligurian beach bums beware: Genoa (Genova in Italian) is a busy, sprawling, and cosmopolitan city, apt to break the spell of the coastal towns in a hurry. This isn't necessarily bad news, though; with over a millennium of history under its belt, magnificent palaces and art, and an elaborate network of ancient hilltop fortresses, Genoa may be just the dose of curious culture you were looking for. Genoa's downfall began over 500 years ago, when it began to be eclipsed by other Mediterranean ports and northern Italian powerhouses, but the city's faded splendor can still be seen through dark shadows and centuries of grime in the narrow alleyways of the city's brooding historic center.

Genoa's streets haven't always been so haunted and obscure. This is the birthplace of Columbus—a historical tidbit of which you'll be reminded at every turn, due to the somewhat ill-fated citywide sprucing-up that took place in 1992 for the Columbus Quincentennial celebrations—but the city's proud history of trade and navigation predates Columbus by several hundred years.

Known as *La Superba* (The Proud), Genoa was from the 13th century a great maritime center rivaling Venice and Pisa in power and splendor. Loud and modern container ships unload at docks that centuries before served galleons and vessels bound for the spice routes. By the 3rd century BC, when the Romans conquered Liguria, Genoa was already an important trading station. The Middle Ages and the Renaissance saw the rise of Genoa into a jumping-off place for the Crusaders, a commercial center of tremendous wealth and prestige, and a strategic bone of international contention. A network of fortresses defending the city connected by a wall second only in length to the Great Wall of China was constructed in the hills above, and Genoa's bankers, merchants, and princes adorned the city with palaces, churches, and impressive art collections.

By the 17th century, however, Genoa had declined as a sea power. Although it brims with historical curiosities and buildings, it is also a city which has fought with—and often lost to—every enemy associated with industrialization and urbanity. Crammed into a thin crescent of land sandwiched between sea and mountains, Genoa has expanded up rather than out, taking on the form of a multilayer wedding cake, with streets, highways, churches, and entire neighborhoods built on others' rooftops; public elevators and funiculars are now as common as buses and trains in this vertical metropolis. Traffic-, pollution-, and crime-ridden (by Italian standards), Genoa has lost precious tourist and business revenues due both to its urban-planning follies and the ever-falling shipping demand for overtaxed Italian products.

And yet, Europe's biggest boat show, the annual Salone Nautico Internazionale, takes place here, as does the Euroflora flower show (held every five years—next in 2001). Classical dance and music are richly represented; the Teatro Carlo Felice is the local opera venue. The internationally renowned annual Niccolò Paganini Violin Contest also takes place in Genoa.

The historic harbor area was given a face-lift for the Columbus celebrations in 1992, and some of the fair installations, such as the new portside promenade and Bigo elevator ride with harbor view, and Europe's largest aquarium, have become a permanent part of the city scene, though they have attracted far fewer patrons than the government had hoped. It will take a lot more than that to rescue this once proud, still fascinating city.

Exploring Genoa

The ancient center of Genoa, threaded with little streets flanked by 11th-century portals, is roughly the area between the port and Piazza de Ferrari; this pedestrian-only zone goes by many names: *centro storico* (historic center), Caruggi District, and the Vicoli. Stazione Principe marks the west end of the center, and Stazione Brignole more or less marks the east end. In the middle are the Old Port and Piazza de Ferrari, which you can use as a jumping-off point for city walks.

A Good Walk: Medieval and Renaissance Genoa

The best way to start your exploration of Genoa is to see it from above. From Piazza Acquaverde, behind Stazione Principe, start your walk along Via Balbi, which runs southeast from Stazione Principe toward the medieval town. On Via Balbi you pass Palazzo Balbi Durazzo, also known as **Palazzo Reale** ⑭, and **Palazzo dell'Università** ⑮. Continue straight ahead to Piazza della Nunziata, from where you can take the **Zecco-Righi Funicular** ⑯ up to a marvelous lookout point on the edge of Genoa's network of fortresses. From Righi you can also walk along the ancient city walls in either direction. After descending, cross Piazza della Nunziata past **Santissima Annunziata** ⑰ to Via P. Bensa and continue southeast on Via Cairoli to reach the famed **Via Garibaldi,** a majestic street where you can pause to see the collections in the museums of **Palazzo Rosso** ⑱ and **Palazzo Bianco** ⑲. Stop in at **Palazzo Tursi** ⑳, Genoa's town hall, and ask the guard at the door if it happens to be open to visitors that day; if it is you can see one of Paganini's violins. At the end of Via Garibaldi go left and left again to Piazza del Portello, where you can take the **Castelletto** ㉑ elevator for another view of the city, this one offering a closer look at the new port. Returning to Piazza Fontane Marose at the end of Via Garibaldi, turn southwest, taking Via Luccoli into the medieval Caruggi District. Beyond Piazza Soziglia, detour to the left, taking Via Campetto to Piazza San Matteo, flanked by the well-preserved houses of the Dorias and the church of **San Matteo** ㉒. Follow Salita Arcivescovado and turn right on Via Reggio to the cathedral of **San Lorenzo** ㉓, medieval Genoa's religious heart. North of the cathedral is Vico degli Indoratori, onto which you turn northwest. Follow it to Via degli Orefici, on which you turn left to reach the **Loggia dei Mercanti** ㉔. Head north on **Via San Luca,** Genoa's best shopping street (hopping on weekend afternoons), to the **Galleria Nazionale** ㉕. At the northern end of Via San Luca is the spooky church of **San Siro** ㉖.

TIMING

Allow a full day for this walk. Note that the Galleria Nazionale is open until 7 every day except Monday, when it closes at 1 PM.

Sights to See

Caruggi District. The winding, picturesque alleys—known as *caruggi*—that make up the popular side of medieval Genoa are the city's heart and soul. Wealthy Genovese built their homes in this quarter in the 16th century, and prosperous guilds, such as the goldsmiths for whom Vico dei Indoratori and Via Orefici were named, set up shop here. In this warren of narrow, cobbled streets, extending north from Piazza Caricamento, you'll find the city's oldest churches punctuating unbroken blocks of 500-year-old apartment buildings, and tiny shops selling antique furniture, coffee, rifles, cheese, wine, gilt picture frames, camping gear, even live fish. When exploring, however, do bear in mind that this quarter is also the city's most disreputable. Don't come here at night, or on holidays, when shops are closed and the alleys deserted, unless you're willing to part with your valuables.

21 **Castelletto.** One of Genoa's handy municipal elevators whisks you skyward from Piazza Portello, at the end of Via Garibaldi, for a good view of the old city. ⊠ *Piazza Portello.* 🎫 *600 lire one way.* ⊙ *Continuous service 6:40 AM–midnight.*

OFF THE BEATEN PATH

MUSEO D'ARTE ORIENTALE CHIOSSONE – In the Villetta di Negro park on the hillside above Piazza Portello, the Chiossone Oriental Art Museum has one of Europe's most extensive and noteworthy collections of Japanese, Chinese, and Thai objects. You can get a fine view of the city from the museum's terrace. ⊠ *Piazzale Mazzini (Piazza Corvetto),* ☎ *010/542285.* 🎫 *6,000 lire, free Sun.; guided tour 7,000 lire.* ⊙ *Tues. and Thurs.–Sat. 9–1; 1st and 3rd Sun. of month 9–1.*

25 **Galleria Nazionale** (National Gallery). This collection, housed in the richly adorned **Palazzo Spinola** north of Piazza Soziglia, contains masterpieces by Luca Giordano and Guido Reni. The *Ecce Homo,* by Antonello da Messina, is a hauntingly beautiful painting and is also of historical interest because it was the Sicilian da Messina who first brought Flemish oil paints and techniques to Italy from his voyages in the Low Countries. ⊠ *Piazza Pellicceria 1,* ☎ *010/2477061.* 🎫 *8,000 lire.* ⊙ *Tues.–Sat. 9–7, Sun. 2–7.*

Granarolo funicular. Actually a cog railway, this tram takes you up the steeply rising terrain to another part of the city's fortified walls. It takes 15 minutes to hoist you from Stazione Principe, on Piazza Acquaverde, to **Porta Granarolo,** 1,000 ft above, where the sweeping view gives you a sense of Genoa's size. ⊠ *Piazza del Principe.* 🎫 *1,600 lire; bus tickets valid.* ⊙ *Departs on the ¼ hr, 6 AM–11:45 PM.*

24 **Loggia dei Mercanti.** This merchants' row dating from the 16th century is lined with shops selling local foods and gifts as well as raincoats, rubber boots, and fishing line. ⊠ *Piazza Banchi.*

19 **Palazzo Bianco.** Originally white, as its name suggests, this palace—a mainstay of the regal Via Garibaldi—has become considerably darkened from age and grime. It has a fine art collection, with the Spanish and Flemish schools well represented. ⊠ *Via Garibaldi 11,* ☎ *010/2476377.* 🎫 *6,000 lire, or 10,000 lire in combination with Palazzo Rosso (☞ below).* ⊙ *Tues. and Thurs.–Fri. 9–1, Wed. and Sat. 9–7, Sun. 10–6.*

15 **Palazzo dell'Università.** Built in the 1630s as a Jesuit college, this institution has been Genoa's university since 1803. The exterior is unas-

suming, but climb the stairway flanked by lions to visit the handsome courtyard, with its portico of double Doric columns. ⊠ *Via Balbi 5.*

★ 14 **Palazzo Reale.** In a city where conspicuous consumption was a hobby of high society, this sumptuous 17th-century palace—also known as Palazzo Balbi Durazzo—contains lavish, frivolous Rococo rooms displaying paintings, sculptures, tapestries, and Oriental ceramics. The former royal digs were inhabited by Italy's rulers, then bought by the Royal House of Savoy in the early 19th century. The gallery of mirrors and the ballroom on the upper floor are particularly decadent. You'll also find works by Sir Anthony Van Dyck, who lived in Genoa for six years, from 1621, and painted many fine portraits of the Genovese nobility. ⊠ *Via Balbi 10,* ☎ *010/27101.* 🎫 *8,000 lire.* ⏲ *Sun.–Tues. 9–1:45, Wed.–Sat. 9–6:30.*

18 **Palazzo Rosso.** The 17th-century Baroque palace was named for the red stone used in its construction. It now contains, apart from a number of lavishly frescoed suites, works by Titian, Veronese, Reni, and Van Dyck. ⊠ *Via Garibaldi 18,* ☎ *010/5574741.* 🎫 *6,000 lire, or 10,000 lire in combination with Palazzo Bianco (☞ above).* ⏲ *Tues. and Thurs.–Fri. 9–1, Wed. and Sat. 9–7, Sun. 10–6.*

20 **Palazzo Tursi.** In the 16th century, wealthy Nicolò Grimaldi had this palace built of pink stone quarried in the region. It's been reincarnated as Genoa's Palazzo Municipale (Municipal Building), and so most of the goings-on inside are the stuff of local politics and quickie weddings. When the rooms aren't in use by Genovese officialdom, however, you are welcome to view the richly decorated rooms and the famous Guarnerius violin that belonged to Niccolò Paganini (1782–1840) and is played once a year on Columbus Day (October 12). ⊠ *Via Garibaldi 9,* ☎ *010/557111.* 🎫 *Free.* ⏲ *Mon.–Fri. 8–noon (call in advance).*

23 **San Lorenzo.** This cathedral, at the heart of medieval Genoa's political and religious center, is embellished inside and out with the contrasting black slate and white marble so common in Liguria. It was consecrated in 1118 to St. Lawrence, who passed through the city on his way to Rome in the 3rd century; the last campanile dates from the early 16th century. For hundreds of years the building was used for state and religious purposes such as civic elections. Note the 13th-century Gothic portal, fascinating twisted barbershop columns, and the 15th- to 17th-century frescoes inside. The **Museo del Tesoro di San Lorenzo** (San Lorenzo Treasury Museum) has some stunning pieces from medieval goldsmiths and silversmiths, for which medieval Genoa was renowned. ⊠ *Piazza San Lorenzo,* ☎ *010/311269.* 🎫 *Museum 10,000 lire.* ⏲ *Mon.–Sat. 9–noon and 3–6; guided visits every ½ hr (last visits at 11:30 and 5:30).*

22 **San Matteo.** This typically Genovese, black-and-white-striped church dates from the 12th century; its crypt contains the tomb of Andrea Doria (1466–1560), the Genovese admiral and statesman who maintained the independence of his native city. ⊠ *Piazza San Matteo.* ☎ *010/2474361.* ⏲ *Mon.–Sat. 8–12 and 4–7, Sun. 9:30–10:30 and 4–5.*

26 **San Siro.** Genoa's oldest church served as the city's cathedral from the 4th to the 9th centuries. It was rebuilt in the 16th and 17th centuries, and it now feels like a haunted house—imposing Christian-fear frescoes line the dank hallways and chandeliers with crooked candles iterate through the darkness. ⊠ *Via San Luca.* ☎ *010/22461468.* ⏲ *Daily 7:30–12 and 4–7.*

17 **Santissima Annunziata.** The 16th- to 17th-century church has exuberantly frescoed vaults and is an excellent example of Genovese

Acquario di Genova, **35**
Castelletto, **21**
Childhood home of Christopher Columbus, **28**
Galleria Nazionale, **25**
Il Bigo, **34**
Loggia dei Mercanti, **24**
Palazzo Bianco, **19**
Palazzo dell' Università, **15**
Palazzo Ducale, **30**
Palazzo Reale, **14**
Palazzo Rosso, **18**
Palazzo Tursi, **20**
Porta Soprana, **27**
San Donato, **31**
San Lorenzo, **23**
San Matteo, **22**
San Siro, **26**
Sant'Agostino, **32**
Santa Maria di Castello, **33**
Santissima Annunziata, **17**
Teatro Carlo Felice, **29**
Zecco-Righi funicular, **16**

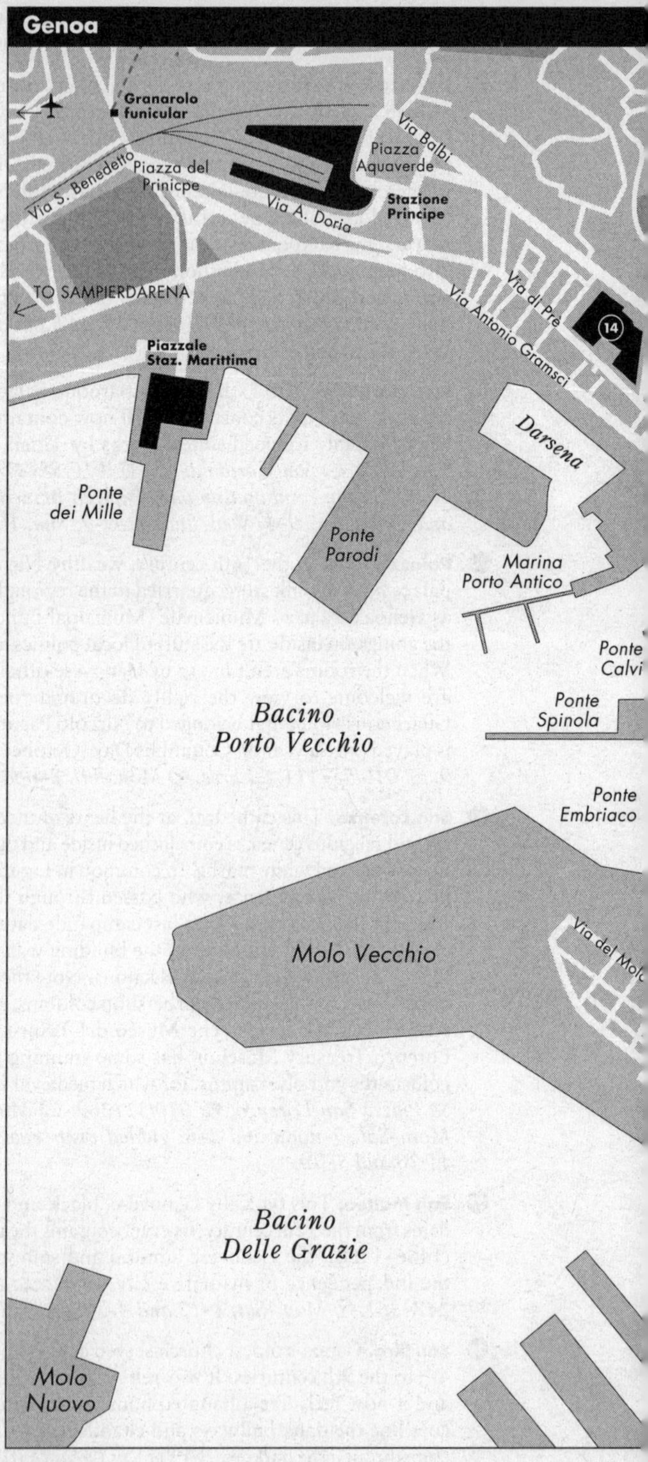

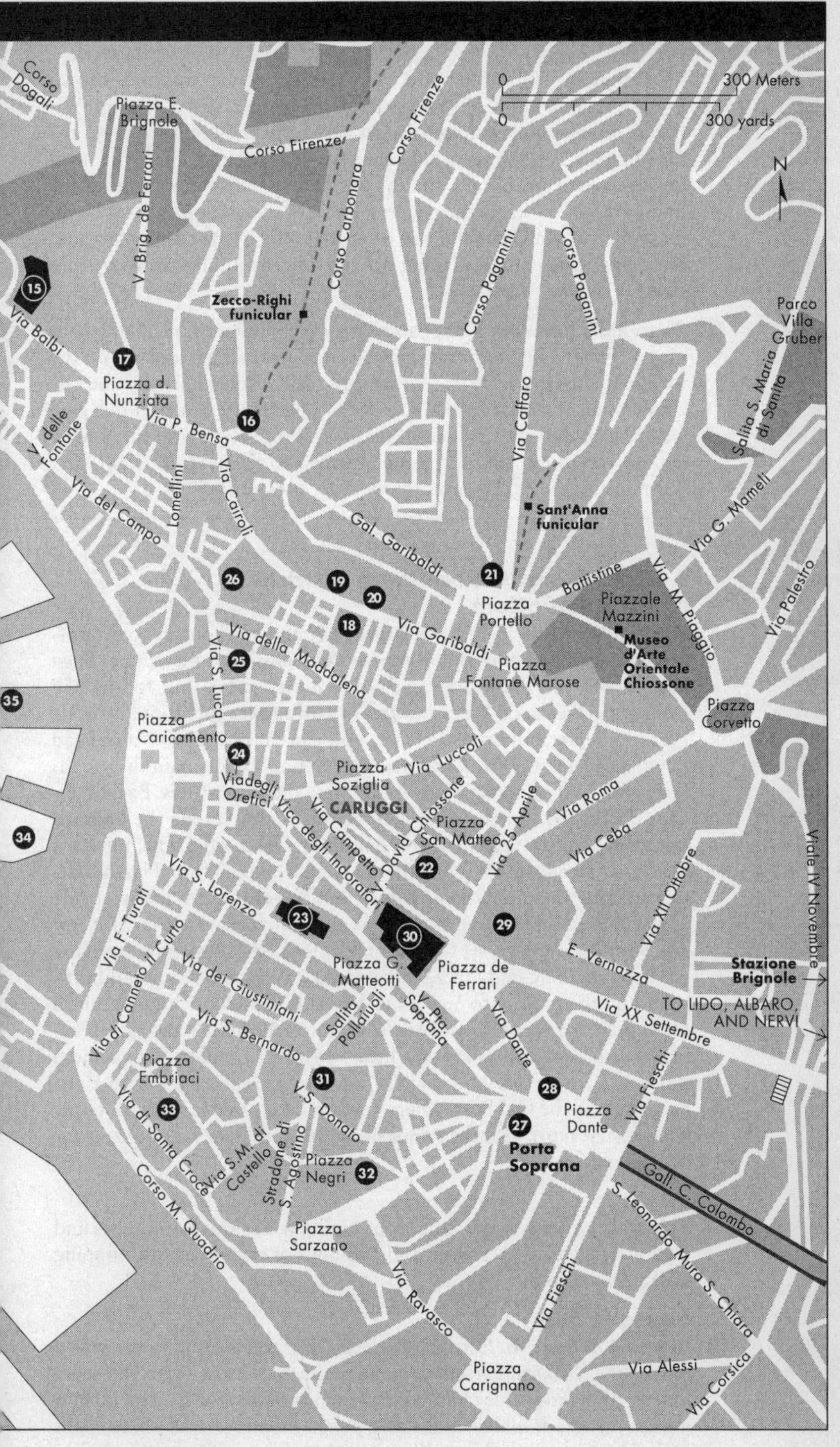

300 Meters
300 yards
N
Corso Dogali
Piazza E. Brignole
Corso Firenze
V. Brig. de Ferrari
Corso Carbonara
Corso Firenze
Corso Paganini
Corso Paganini
Zecco-Righi funicular
Via Balbi
Piazza d. Nunziata
Via P. Bensa
V. delle Fontane
Via del Campo
Lomellini
Via Cairoli
Via Caffaro
Sant'Anna funicular
Gal. Garibaldi
Parco Villa Gruber
Salita S. Maria di Sanità
Via G. Mameli
Battistine
Piazza Portello
Piazzale Mazzini
Museo d'Arte Orientale Chiossone
Via M. Piaggio
Via Palestro
Via Garibaldi
Via della Maddalena
Via S. Luca
Piazza Fontane Marose
Piazza Corvetto
Piazza Caricamento
Via degli Orefici
Piazza Soziglia
Via Luccoli
CARUGGI
Vico degli Indoratori
Via Campetto
V. David Chiossone
Piazza San Matteo
Via 25 Aprile
Via Roma
Via Ceba
Via XII Ottobre
Viale IV Novembre
Via S. Lorenzo
Via F. Turati
Via di Canneto il Curto
Via dei Giustiniani
Piazza G. Matteotti
Piazza de Ferrari
E. Vernazza
Stazione Brignole
TO LIDO, ALBARO, AND NERVI
Via XX Settembre
Via S. Bernardo
Salita Pollaiuoli
V. Pta. Soprana
Via Dante
Piazza Embriaci
Via di Santa Croce
V. S. Donato
Via S.M. di Castello
Stradone di S. Agostino
Piazza Negri
Piazza Dante
Porta Soprana
Via Fieschi
Gall. C. Colombo
S. Leonardo
Mura S. Chiara
Corso M. Quadrio
Piazza Sarzano
Via Ravasco
Via Fieschi
Piazza Carignano
Via Alessi
Via Corsica
15
16
17
18
19
20
21
22
23
24
25
26
27
28
29
30
31
32
33
34
35

Baroque architecture. ✉ *Piazza della Nunziata.* ☎ *010/297662.* ⏲ *Daily 9–12 and 3–7.*

★ **Via Garibaldi.** Thirteen palaces were built along what was once known as the Via Aurea (Golden Street) in just 10 years. Genoa's leading patrician families built their residences here from 1554 onward to escape the cramped conditions of the medieval section. It is one of the most impressive streets in Italy, and the palace-museums house some of the finest art collections in the country. Most of the other palaces without museums on Via Garibaldi can be visited only by special application, but many have courtyards that are open to the public. ✉ *West from Piazza Fontane Marose.*

⑯ **Zecco-Righi funicular.** This is a seven-stop commuter funicular, beginning at Piazza della Nunziata, which ends up at a high lookout on the fortified gates in the 17th-century city walls. Ringed around the circumference of the city are a number of huge fortresses, and this gate was part of the city's system of defenses. From Righi you can undertake scenic all-day hikes from one fortress to the next. 🎫 *1,600 lire; bus tickets valid.* ⏲ *Departs on the ¼ hr, 6 AM–11:45 PM.*

A Good Walk: The Southern Districts and the Aquarium

Start just downhill from **Porta Soprana** ㉗ and pay homage to the purported **childhood home of Christopher Columbus** ㉘ on the square. Then head under the Porta Soprana (ancient city gate), and follow Via Dante into Piazza de Ferrari to **Teatro Carlo Felice** ㉙. From Piazza de Ferrari, Genoa's unofficial center, you can make a detour and head down and back up **Via XX Settembre,** Genoa's wide main thoroughfare, with leading-name boutiques, cafés, and bookstores. Back in Piazza de Ferrari, on the west side of the piazza stands the **Palazzo Ducale** ㉚. Follow the Palazzo around to its back side, which bears a neoclassic facade on Piazza Matteotti. Leading uphill from Piazza Matteotti, Salita Pollaiuoli takes you to **San Donato** ㉛. On the west side of the church is Stradone Sant'Agostino, which leads to Piazza Negri and **Sant'Agostino** ㉜. At the top of Stradone Sant'Agostino, from the west end of elongated Piazza Sarzano, take Via Santa Croce and turn right and then left onto Via Santa Maria di Castello, climbing up to the church of **Santa Maria di Castello** ㉝ atop the hill. From Piazza Embriaci turn west and follow the little streets downhill to Via Canneto il Curto, turning downhill on Via San Lorenzo to reach Piazza Caricamento and the Old Port, where you can take a ride in the panoramic **Il Bigo** ㉞ elevator, visit the **Acquario di Genova** ㉟, or take a boat tour of the port.

TIMING

This walk will take from 2½ to four hours, with stops at churches and the museum at Sant'Agostino; add an hour or two if you are stopping at the Acquario di Genova.

Sights to See

㉟ **Acquario di Genova.** Europe's biggest aquarium, second in the world only to the Osaka aquarium in Japan, is the third-most-visited museum in Italy and a must for children. Fifty tanks of marine species, including sea turtles, dolphins, seals, eels, penguins, and sharks, share space with educational displays and re-creations of marine ecosystems, including a new tank for live corals from the Red Sea. An annexed eco-simulation of Madagascar was a recent exhibit. ✉ *Ponte Spinola,* ☎ *010/2481205.* 🎫 *19,000 lire.* ⏲ *Apr.–Sept., Mon.–Fri. 9:30–7, week-*

ends 9:30–8; Oct.–Mar., Tues.–Fri. 9:30–7. Ticket office closes 1–1½ hrs before aquarium.

28 **Childhood home of Christopher Columbus.** The ivy-covered ruins of this fabled medieval house stand, strangely all alone, in the gardens adjacent to the Porta Soprana. ⊠ *Piazza Dante.*

Harbor. A boat tour gives you a good perspective on the layout of the harbor, which dates to Roman times. The Genoa inlet, the largest along the Italian Riviera, was also used by the Phoenicians and Greeks as a harbor and a vantage point from which they could penetrate inland to form settlements and to trade. The port is guarded by the Diga Foranea, a striking 5-km- (3-mi-) long wall built into the ocean. Boat tours are available for 10,000 lire (☞ Guided Tours in Italian Riviera A to Z, *below*). The **Lanterna,** a lighthouse more than 360 ft high, was built in 1544 at the height of Andrea Doria's career; it is one of Italy's oldest lighthouses and a traditional emblem of Genoa.

34 **Il Bigo.** This bizarre white structure, erected as a symbol of the 1992 Columbus Quincentennial events, looks like either a radioactive spider or an overgrown potato spore, depending on your point of view. Fortunately, its scenic **Ascensore Panoramico Bigo** (Bigo Panoramic Elevator) takes in the harbor, city, and sea. ⊠ *Ponte Spinola, next to Acquario,* ☎ *010/2485710.* 🎫 *4,000 lire, 3,000 lire with Acquario (☞ above) ticket.* ⊙ *Tues.–Fri. 11–1 and 2–5, Sat.–Sun. 11–1 and 2–6.*

30 **Palazzo Ducale.** This palace was built in the 16th century over a medieval hall, and its facade was rebuilt in the late 18th century and later restored. It now houses temporary exhibitions. ⊠ *Piazza Matteotti and Piazza de Ferrari,* ☎ *010/562440.* 🎫 *12,000 lire.* ⊙ *Tues.–Sun. 9:30–12:30 and 2:30–7:30.*

Piazza San Matteo. The excellently preserved medieval square was, for 500 years, the seat of the Doria family, who ruled Genoa and much of Liguria from the 16th to the 18th century. The square is bounded by 13th- to 15th-century houses decorated with portals and loggias. ⊠ *South of Piazza Soziglia.*

27 **Porta Soprana.** The striking, twin-towered, 12th-century edifice also known as Porta di Sant'Andrea stands at the old gateway to the Roman road that led through Genoa. Just uphill from Columbus' boyhood home, Porta Soprana supposedly employed the explorer's father as a gatekeeper. ⊠ *Piazza Dante.*

31 **San Donato.** The 12th-century Romanesque church with its original portal and octagonal campanile is slightly north of Sant'Agostino. ⊠ *Piazza San Donato.* ☎ *010/2468869.* ⊙ *Mon.–Sat. 8–12 and 3–5:30, Sun. 9–12 and 3:30–7.*

32 **Sant'Agostino.** This 13th-century Gothic church was damaged during World War II, but it still has a fine campanile and two well-preserved cloisters, which now house an excellent sculpture museum. ⊠ *Piazza Sarzano 35/r,* ☎ *010/2511263.* 🎫 *6,000 lire, Sun. free.* ⊙ *Tues.–Sat. 9–7, Sun. 9–12:30.*

33 **Santa Maria di Castello.** One of Genoa's greatest religious buildings, an early Christian church, was rebuilt in the 12th century and finally completed in 1513. You can visit the adjacent cloisters and see the fine artwork contained in the museum. ⊠ *Salita di Santa Maria di Castello 15,* ☎ *010/2549511.* ⊙ *Daily 9–noon and 3:30–6; call ahead.*

29 **Teatro Carlo Felice.** The World War II–ravaged opera house in Genoa's modern center, Piazza de Ferrari, was rebuilt and reopened in 1991 to host the fine Genoese opera company (☞ Nightlife and the Arts,

below); its massive tower has been the subject of much criticism. It stands next to the **Accademia delle Belle Arti** (Academy of Fine Arts), which contains a collection of Ligurian paintings from the 13th to the 19th centuries. *Theater:* ✉ *Passo al Teatro 4,* ☎ *010/53811. Academy:* ✉ *Largo Pertini 4,* ☎ *010/581957.* 🎫 *Free.* ⏲ *Mon.–Sat. 9–1.*

Dining and Lodging

$$$–$$$$ ✕ **Gran Gotto.** Innovative classic regional dishes are served in this posh, spacious restaurant festooned with contemporary paintings. The service is quick and helpful. Try *pesce in salsa di zucca e parri* (fish in squash and leek sauce) and the sumptuous *flan di cioccolato* (dark chocolate flan with white chocolate sauce), one of the many excellent homemade desserts. It's in Piazza della Vittoria, near Stazione Brignole, in the modern part of town. ✉ *Viale Brigata Bisagno 69/r,* ☎ *010/564344. Reservations essential. Jacket and tie. AE, DC, MC, V. Closed Sun. and last 2 wks Aug. No lunch Sat.*

$$$–$$$$ ★ ✕ **Zeffirino.** The five Belloni brothers share the chef's duties at this remarkable restaurant, which is full of odd combinations. The decor is a mixture of styles and materials, ranging from rustic wood to modern metallic. Try the *passutelli* (ravioli stuffed with ricotta cheese and fruit) or any of the homemade pasta dishes. ✉ *Via XX Settembre 20,* ☎ *010/591990. Reservations essential. Jacket and tie. AE, DC, MC, V.*

$$–$$$ ✕ **Sette Nasi.** The historic Quarto dei Mille district is the setting for this large establishment, with accents of gray slate and pink marble. The chef, Fausto Nasi, specializes in a wide range of Ligurian seafood dishes and makes some mean homemade desserts. Top off a lovely day spent at the annexed pool and beach club with a dinner of ravioli *di pesce* (seafood) or lasagna with pesto. Reservations are recommended. ✉ *Via Quarto 16,* ☎ *010/3731344. AE, DC, MC, V. Closed Tues. and Nov.*

$$ ✕ **Bakari.** Hip styling and ambient lighting hint at the creative, even daring, takes on Ligurian classics offered at this casual centro storico restaurant. Sure bets are the stuffed spinach-and-cheese gnocchi, any of several carpaccios, and the delicate beef dishes. Reserve ahead, requesting a table on the ground floor for a better atmosphere. ✉ *Vico del Fieno 16/r, northwest of P. San Matteo,* ☎ *010/291936. AE, MC, V. Closed Sun. No dinner Wed. and Fri.*

$$ ✕ **Da Genio.** At the top of a pedestrian stairway near Piazza Dante in the Caruggi District, this classic trattoria serves equally classic Genovese dishes, including *trenette al pesto* (pasta with pesto sauce) and minestrone, finished off with a dollop of pesto. Reservations are recommended. ✉ *Salita San Leonardo 61/r,* ☎ *010/588463. AE, MC, V. Closed Sun. and Aug.*

$$$$ 🏨 **Bristol Palace.** This grand hotel was built in the last century and maintains the old-fashioned traditions of courtesy and discretion. The rooms are large, with high ceilings; paintings decorate the large reception rooms. There's no restaurant, but you're in the heart of the shopping district. ✉ *Via XX Settembre 35, 16121,* ☎ *010/592541,* FAX *010/561756. 133 rooms. Bar, café, snack bar, meeting rooms. AE, DC, MC, V.*

$$$ 🏨 **Novotel.** Built in 1994, this hotel—an anonymous gray structure with a large glassy lobby—is a good choice if you value comfort over atmosphere. Rooms are clean and modern, typical of a chain hotel. It is in a semicentral area just beyond one end of the harbor; you can take a bus or taxi to the heart of town. ✉ *Via Cantore 8/c, 16126,* ☎ *010/64841,* FAX *010/6484844. 223 rooms. Restaurant, bar, pool, free parking. AE, DC, MC, V.*

$$ ★ **Agnello d'Oro.** In Genoa's centro storico, about 100 yards from Stazione Principe and next to the Palazzo Reale, this hotel has simple and modern rooms, and several have a balcony with a view. The friendly owner does double duty as a travel agent and is happy to help you with plane reservations and travel plans. It's a bit outside of the heart of the modern city. ✉ *Vico delle Monachette 6, 16126,* ☎ *010/2462084,* FAX *010/2462327. 30 rooms. Bar. AE, DC, MC, V.*

$$ **Cairoli.** This family-run, central hotel is on a historic street near Stazione Principe and the aquarium. It is neatly furnished and has a roof terrace. Happily, the rooms have been soundproofed so you'll get a good night's sleep—not always the easiest thing to do in this noisy city. ✉ *Via Cairoli 14, 16124,* ☎ *010/2461524,* FAX *010/2467512. 12 rooms. Bar, breakfast room. AE, DC, MC, V.*

Nightlife and the Arts

Opera

The opera season (October–May) at **Teatro Carlo Felice** (✉ Passo al Teatro 4, ☎ 010/5381) attracts many lavish productions and occasionally sees the debut of a new work. Genoa's opera company, Fondazione Teatro Carlo Felice, is well respected.

Shopping

Liguria is famous for its fine laces, silver and gold filigree work, and ceramics. Look also for bargains in velvet, macramé, olive wood, and marble. Genoa is the best spot to find all these specialties. In the heart of the medieval quarter, **Via Soziglia** is lined with shops selling handicrafts and tempting foods. **Via XX Settembre** is famous for its wide range of exclusive shops. Fine shops also line **Via Luccoli.** The best shopping area for trendy (read: black) but inexpensive Italian clothing is near San Siro, on **Via San Luca,** which runs through the centro storico parallel to the port.

Clothing and Leather Goods

At the fancy **Pescetto** (✉ Via Scurreria 8, ☎ 010/2473433), you'll find designer clothes, perfumes, and gift ideas. **Pimkie** (✉ 215 Via XX Settembre, ☎ 010/584206) and **Stefanel** (✉ 36–39 Via XX Settembre, ☎ 010/714755) are the venues of choice for modern Italian women's clothing. Bologna-based **Bruno Magli** (✉ Via XX Settembre 135, ☎ 010/561890) makes an impeccable line of leather shoes and boots for men and women, beautiful handbags, and leather jackets.

Jewelry

The well-established **Codevilla** (✉ Via Orefici 53, ☎ 010/2472567) is one of the best jewelers on a street swarming with goldsmiths.

Wines

Vinoteca Sola (✉ Piazza Colombo 13, near Stazione Brignole, ☎ 010/561329) stocks a good selection of Italian and Ligurian wines.

Side Trip from Genoa

Nervi

36 *11 km (7 mi) east of Genoa, 23 km (14 mi) northwest of Chiavari.*

The true identity of this stately late-19th-century-style resort, famous for its 1½-km- (1-mi-) long seaside promenade, Passegiata Garibaldi, palm-lined roads, and 300 acres of parks rich in orange trees and exotics, is given away only by the sign on the sleepy train station in the center of town: it's technically part of the city of Genoa. Nervi's secret is an easy one to keep, though: its attractions are peace and quiet, the natural beauty of its lush gardens, and the dramatic black cliffs that drop into the sea, as different from Genoa's hustle and bustle as Nervi's clear blue water is from Genoa's crowded port. Despite the contrast, it's easy to visit this remarkable part of the city for a stroll along the water or a day at the beach. Frequent trains take 15 minutes from Stazione Principe or Brignole (buy a ticket for Genova–Nervi), or Buses 15 or 17 will take you from Brignole or Piazza de Ferrari to Nervi. Alternatively, a taxi from town center will run about 25,000 lire one way. From the Nervi train station, walk along the seaside promenade east to reach beach stations, a cliff-hanging restaurant, and the 2,000 varieties of roses in the **Parco Villa Grimaldi,** all the while enjoying one of the most breathtaking views on the Riviera.

DINING AND LODGING

$$ ✕ **Marinella.** This restaurant is perched on seaside shoals a few minutes outside Genoa. Competing for attention are an impressive wrought-iron chandelier and great sea views from windows and terrace. (There's an inexpensive hotel annex, too.) Try the *zuppa di pesce* (fish soup); main dishes change according to the day's catch. Reservations are a good idea. ✉ *Passeggiata Anita Garibaldi 18,* ☎ *010/3728343. MC, V. Closed Mon. and Nov. 1–15.*

$$$ ★ **Romantik Hotel Villa Pagoda.** This small, top-quality hotel in seaside Nervi is a majestic choice that offers the best of both worlds—luxurious peace and quiet, with the city's attractions just 15 minutes away. Housed in a gated 19th-century merchant's mansion designed after a Chinese pagoda, the hotel comes with a private park, private access to Nervi's famed cliff-top seawalk, and magnificent sea views. Request a tower room. ✉ *Via Capolungo 15, 16167,* ☎ *010/3726161,* FAX *010/321218. 13 rooms, 5 suites. Restaurant, piano bar, in-room safes, minibars, meeting rooms. AE, DC, MC, V.*

NIGHTLIFE AND THE ARTS

An **International Ballet Festival** is held every July in the Villa Gropallo park, drawing performers and audiences from all over the world. Contact the Genoa APT office (☎ 010/2462633) for ticket and schedule information.

RIVIERA DI LEVANTE

On the Road to Portofino

Of the two Ligurian Rivieras, the Riviera di Levante, east of Genoa, is overall the wilder and more rugged, yet here you will also find towns like Portofino and Rapallo, world famous for their classic, elegant style. Around every turn of this area's twisting roads, the hills plummet sharply to the sea, forming deep, hidden bays and inlets. Beaches on this coast are rocky, backed by spectacular sheer cliffs. The Portofino promontory has one sandy beach, on the east side, at Paraggi. From Chiavari to Cavi di Lavagna, the coast becomes a bit gentler, with a few sandy areas. Sailing conditions along the rugged coast from Sestri Levante down to Portovenere are good. Waterskiing, tennis, and golf are also popular. You may want to choose a base and take short day trips or explore the area by boat from the larger towns. You can anchor your boat in the relatively calm waters of small *ciazze* (coves) found all along the coast.

Camogli

★ 37 *20 km (12 mi) east of Genoa, 23 km (14 mi) west of Chiavari.*

Camogli, at the edge of the large promontory and nature reserve known as the Portofino peninsula, has always been a town of sailors.

By the 19th century this small village was leasing its ships throughout the continent. Today multicolor houses and the massive 17th-century seawall mark this picturesque harbor community, perhaps as beautiful as Portofino but without the glamour.

The **Castello Dragone,** built onto the sheer rock face near the harbor, is home to the Acquario (Aquarium), which has display tanks of local marine life actually built into the ramparts. *4,000 lire. May–Sept., daily 10–noon and 3–7; Oct.–Apr., Fri.–Sun. 10–noon and 2:30–6, Tues.–Thurs. 10–noon.*

OFF THE BEATEN PATH

SAN ROCCO, SAN NICCOLÒ, AND PUNTA CHIAPPA – You can reach these hamlets along the western coast of the peninsula by foot or boat from Camogli. They are more natural and less fashionable than those facing south on the eastern coast. In the small Romanesque church at San Niccolò, sailors who survived dangerous voyages came to offer thanks.

ABBAZIA DI SAN FRUTTUOSO – On the sea at the foot of Monte Portofino, 30 minutes by boat from Camogli (20 minutes by boat from Portofino), the medieval Abbey of San Fruttuoso—built by the Benedictines of Monte Cassino—protects a minuscule fishing village and can be reached only on foot or by boat from Camogli, Portofino, Santa Margherita Ligure, or Rapallo. The restored abbey is now property of a national conservation fund (FAI). The church holds the tombs of some illustrious members of the Doria family. The historic abbey and its grounds are a delightful place to spend a few hours, perhaps lunching at one of the modest beach trattorias nearby. But boatloads of visitors can make it very crowded very fast; you might appreciate it most off-season. ☎ *0185/772703. 6,000 lire. May–Oct., Tues.–Sun. 10–5:45; Dec.–Feb., weekends 10–5:45; Mar.–Apr., Tues.–Sun. 10–3:45; call ahead to check hours.*

Dining and Lodging

$$$ ✕ **Vento Ariel.** This tiny, friendly restaurant is right on the port, and it has informal but impressive decor and place settings. It serves seafood only and regularly runs out of items because it relies on the day's catch. Try the spaghetti *alle vongole* (with clams) or the grilled mixed fish. ✉ *Calata Porto,* ☎ *0185/771080. AE, DC, MC, V. Closed Wed. and Jan.*

$$$–$$$$ ★ **Cenobio dei Dogi.** Although this hilltop villa perched over the town was once the summer home of Genoa's doges, it now has a modern look. You can relax in the well-kept park affording outstanding views of the Portofino peninsula, or enjoy numerous sporting activities. ✉ *Via Cuneo 34, 16032,* ☎ *0185/7241,* FAX *0185/772796. 107 rooms. Restaurant, bar, pool, tennis courts, beach. AE, DC, MC, V.*

Nightlife and the Arts

During the festival of San Fortunato, held on the second Sunday of May each year, is the **Sagra del Pesce,** a crowded, festive, and free-to-the-public feast of freshly caught fish, cooked outside at the port in a frying pan 12 ft wide.

Ruta

4 km (2½ mi) east of Camogli, 24 km (15 mi) east of Genoa.

The footpaths that leave from Ruta up to and around Monte Portofino and Camogli thread through rugged terrain, home to a wide variety of plant species. Weary hikers will be sustained by stunning views of the Riviera di Levante from the various vantage points along the way.

Rapallo

38 *12 km (7 mi) east of Camogli, 28 km (17 mi) east of Genoa.*

Rapallo was once one of Europe's most fashionable resorts, but it passed its heyday before World War II and has suffered from the building boom brought on by tourism. Ezra Pound and D. H. Lawrence lived here, and many other writers, poets, and artists have been drawn to it. Today, the town's harbor is filled with yachts. A single-span bridge on the eastern side of the bay is named after Hannibal, who is said to have passed through the area after crossing the Alps. Two ancient buildings are highlights in town center: the cathedral of **Santi Gervasio e Protasio,** at the western end of Via Mazzini, founded in the 6th century. ☎ *0185/52375.* ⏲ *Mon.–Fri. 7–6, weekends 7–7.*

Across the road is the Leper House of **Lazzaretto di Banna,** which still retains parts of its original medieval frescoes on its exterior walls. The **Museo del Pizzo a Tombolo,** in a 19th-century mansion, has a collection of antique lace for which Rapallo was renowned. ✉ *Villa Tigullio.* ☎ *0185/50234.* 🎫 *Free.* ⏲ *Oct.–Aug., Tues.–Wed., Fri.–Sat. 3–6, Thurs. 10–12:30.*

Dining and Lodging

$$ ✕ **Roccabruna.** In a splendid villa outside Rapallo, seafood specialties adorn an abundant menu that changes constantly. Take the Casello–Savagna highway from Rapallo; Savagna is only about 2 km (1 mi) away. Reservations are recommended. ✉ *Via Sotto la Croce 6, Savagna,* ☎ *0185/261400. No credit cards. Closed Mon. and part of Nov.*

$$$$ 🏨 **Grand Hotel Bristol.** This large Victorian showcase is in an elevated position overlooking road and sea outside Rapallo, and is set in lush gardens with a huge seawater pool. Spacious rooms, many with balcony and sea view, are decorated in soft colors in a smart, contemporary style and have extra-large beds. Dinner is served on the roof terrace. ✉ *Via Aurelia Orientale 369, 16035,* ☎ *0185/273313,* FAX *0185/55800. 85 rooms, 6 suites. Restaurant, bar, pool, horseback riding, meeting rooms. AE, DC, MC, V. Closed Dec.–Feb.*

$$ 🏨 **Giulio Cesare.** Only a block from the sea, this old town house was transformed into a hotel that offers rooms with modern furnishings and sea views. Many rooms have balconies, but noise may be a problem, since the hotel is on a main street. ✉ *Corso Colombo 52, 16035,* ☎ *0185/50685,* FAX *0185/60896. 33 rooms. AE, MC, V. Closed Nov.–Dec. 18.*

Outdoor Activities and Sports

GOLF

The **Rapallo Golf Club** (☎ 0185/261777) has a lush 18-hole course about 2 km (1 mi) northwest of town center.

Shopping

The attractive coastal village of **Zoagli** (✉ On S1, 4 km/2½ mi east of Rapallo) has been famous for silk, velvet, and damask since the Middle Ages.

Santa Margherita Ligure

39 *3 km (2 mi) south of Rapallo, 31 km (19 mi) southeast of Genoa.*

A pretty resort favored by well-to-do Italians, Santa Margherita Ligure has everything a Riviera playground should have—plenty of palm trees and attractive hotels, cafés, and a marina packed with yachts. Some of the older buildings here are still decorated on the outside with the trompe l'oeil frescoes typical of this part of the Riviera. This is a pleasant and convenient base for excursions by land and by sea.

Dining and Lodging

$$$ ✕ **La Paranza.** As befits a spot just off of Santa Margherita's port, the specialty here is fresh seafood in every shape and form, from the piles of tiny *bianchetti* (whitebait) in oil and lemon in the antipasto *di mare* (of the sea) to a simple, perfectly grilled whole sole. In between you'll find mussels, clams, octopus, salmon, and whatever else is fresh that day. Locals say this is the town's best restaurant (make reservations), but if you're looking for a stylish evening out, look elsewhere—La Paranza is about food, not fashion. ✉ , ☎ *0185/283686. Reservations essential. AE, DC, MC, V. Closed Thurs. and Nov.*

$$ ✕ **Il Frantoio.** The large, hand-carved wooden screws that turned the olive press for which this rather stylish little restaurant is named stand at the entrance. And here you not only select from the wine list, you can also choose from the olive oil list for just the right piquancy or mellowness. Quality is a keynote in the food, too, as in the specialties: spaghetti with shellfish cooked in a pastry crust, and either rabbit or seafood with pomegranate sauce. ✉ *Via del Giunchetto 23/a,* ☎ *0185/286667. Reservations essential. AE, DC, MC, V. Closed Tues. and last 3 wks of Nov.*

$$$$ 🏨 **Continental.** This stately seaside mansion with a columned portico was built in the early 1900s and is set in a lush garden shaded by tall palms and pine trees. The decor is a blend of traditional furnishings, mostly in 19th-century style, with some more functional pieces. There is also a modern wing. The hotel's own cabanas and swimming area are at the bottom of the garden. ✉ *Via Pagana 8, 16038,* ☎ *0185/286512,* FAX *0185/284463. 76 rooms. Restaurant, bar. AE, DC, MC, V. Closed Nov.–Dec. 23.*

$$$$ ★ 🏨 **Grand Hotel Miramare.** Take the shore road south from town to reach this palatial old-world hotel overlooking the bay. It has a lush garden and swimming pool, and a private swimming area on the sea. The bright and airy rooms are furnished with antique furniture and marble bathrooms. ✉ *Lungomare Milite Ignoto 30, 16038,* ☎ *0185/287013,* FAX *0185/284651. 75 rooms, 9 suites. 2 restaurants, bar, in-room safes, minibars, pool, beach, waterskiing, meeting rooms. AE, DC, MC, V.*

$$$$ 🏨 **Imperial Palace.** Via Pagana climbs north out of Santa Margherita Ligure on its way toward Rapallo; just outside town it passes this old-world luxury hotel, set in an extensive park. Reception rooms with tall windows, plush chairs, and potted plants create a warm welcome. The rooms are furnished with antiques; many overlook the shore drive to the sea. ✉ *Via Pagana 19, 16038,* ☎ *0185/288991,* FAX *0185/284223. 83 rooms, 14 suites. Restaurant, 2 bars, pool. AE, DC, MC, V. Closed Nov.–Mar.*

$$ ★ 🏨 **Fasce.** A good value, this small, modern hotel is on one of the town's main thoroughfares, but from its pleasant roof garden you have views of the sea and surrounding hills. The Italian owner and his British wife take cordial interest in their guests' well-being and comfort, providing free bus passes and bicycles. Rooms are attractive, with satellite TVs. ✉ *Via Bozzo 3, 16038,* ☎ *0185/286435,* FAX *0185/283580. 16 rooms. Restaurant. AE, DC, MC, V. Closed Jan.–early Mar.*

Portofino

★ 40 *5 km (3 mi) south of Santa Margherita Ligure, 36 mi (22 km) east of Genoa.*

One of the most picturesque villages along the coast, with a decidedly romantic and affluent aura, is also precious, in the true sense of the word. Unless you are traveling on a deluxe level and can keep up with the Agnellis and Berlusconis, you should probably choose a hotel in Rapallo or Santa Margherita Ligure rather than one of Portofino's few and very expensive hotels, restaurants, and cafés (don't expect to have a beer here for much under 20,000 lire). Some of Europe's wealthiest lay anchor in Portofino in the summer, but they stay out of sight by day, appearing in the evening after buses and boats have carried off the day-trippers.

Portofino has long been a popular destination for foreigners. Once an ancient Roman colony and taken by the Republic of Genoa in 1229, Portofino has also been ruled by French, English, Spanish, and Austrian empires, as well as marauding bands of 16th-century pirates. Elite British tourists first flocked to the lush harbor in the mid-1800s. At first glance, you may wonder what all the fuss is about. There's little to do in Portofino, other than stroll around the wee harbor, see the castle, walk to Punta del Capo, and look at the pricey boutiques. However, weaving through picture-perfect cliffside gardens and gazing at yachts on a field of pastel-color houses and awnings, framed by the turquoise Ligurian Sea and the cliffs of Santa Margherita, can make for quite a relaxing afternoon. There are also several tame but photogenic hikes into the hills from Portofino to nearby villages. Trying to reach Portofino by bus or car on the single narrow road can be a nightmare in the summer and on holiday weekends. No trains go directly to Portofino; if traveling by rail, you must stop at Santa Margherita and take the public bus from there (5,000 lire). An alternative is to take a boat from Santa Margherita.

From the harbor, follow the signs for the climb to the **Castello di San Giorgio,** by far the most worthwhile sight in Portofino, with its medieval relics, impeccable gardens, and sweeping views. The castle was founded in the Middle Ages but restored in the 16th to 18th centuries; in true Portofino form, it was owned by Genoa's English Consul from 1870 until its opening to the public in 1961. 🎫 *3,000 lire.* ⏲ *Apr.–Sept., Wed.–Mon. 10–6; Oct.–Mar., Wed.–Mon. 10–5.*

Sitting on a ridge above the harbor is the small church of **San Giorgio,** rebuilt four times in WWII, which is supposed to contain the saint's relics, brought back from the Holy Land by the Crusaders. Portofino enthusiastically celebrates St. George's Day every April 23. ☎ *0185/269337.* ⏲ *Daily 7–6.*

Other pristine views can be seen from the deteriorating lighthouse, or **Faro,** at **Punta Portofino,** a 15-minute walk along a marked path from the village. Along the seaside path you can see some of the numerous impressive and sprawling private residences that stand behind high iron gates.

The only sand beach near Portofino is at **Paraggi,** a cove on the road between Santa Margherita and Portofino (the bus will stop there on request).

Dining and Lodging

$$$$ ✕ **Il Pitosforo.** A chic, tan clientele, many with luxury yachts in the harbor, gives this waterfront restaurant a glamorous atmosphere augmented by outlandish prices. Spaghetti *ai frutti di mare* (with seafood) is recommended; adventurous diners might want to try *lo stocco accomodou* (dried cod in a savory sauce of tomatoes, raisins, and pine nuts). ✉ *Molo Umberto I, 9,* ☎ *0185/269020 or 0335/5615833. Reservations essential. AE, DC, MC, V. Closed Mon.–Tues. and Jan.–mid-Feb. No lunch June–Sept.*

$$$ ★ ✕ **Ristorante Puny.** A table at this tiny restaurant is next to impossible to get, as the manager actively discourages tourist lire (shunning credit cards, for example) and caters almost exclusively to regulars and his own friends. If you are lucky enough to get in, however, the food will not disappoint, nor will the cozy but elegant yellow interior. The delicate *pappardelle portofino* masterfully blends two of Liguria's tastes: tomato and pesto. Otherwise, go with Ligurian seafood specialties like baked fish with laurel, potatoes, and olives, or the inventive *moscardini al forno,* baked octopus with lemon and rosemary in tomato sauce. ✉ *P. Martiri dell'Olivetta, 5 (on the harbor),* ☎ *0185/269037. Reservations essential. No credit cards. Closed Thurs.*

$$$$ **Eden.** If you must stay in Portofino, this is the only affordable option in town. Comfortable if unexciting and small rooms have all the basic amenities, with clean bathrooms, working showers, pinkish walls, and views onto the street but not the bay. Anywhere else, this hotel would be overpriced. But in Portofino, it's a good deal. ✉ *Vico Dritto 18, near the harbor, 16034,* ☎ *0185/269091,* FAX *0185/269047. 12 rooms. Restaurant (closed mid-Sept.–mid-June), breakfast room. AE, MC, V. Closed Dec. 1–Dec. 25.*

$$$$ **Splendido.** Most people resort to superlatives when trying to describe this luxury hotel, built in the 1920s on a hill overlooking the sea. The abiding theme is color, from the coordinated fabrics and furnishings of the rooms to the fresh flowers in the reception rooms and on the large terrace. It's like a Jazz Age film set, and you almost expect to see a Bugatti or Daimler roll up the winding drive from Portofino below. Even more grand than the hotel are its prices, making this a place for very special occasions indeed. Rates are off the charts (about 900,000–1,100,000 lire per night). ✉ *Viale Baratta 13, 16034,* ☎ *0185/269551,* FAX *0185/269614. 64 rooms. Restaurant, 2 bars, pool, tennis court. AE, DC, MC, V. Closed Jan.–mid-Mar.*

Outdoor Activities and Sports

HIKING

If you have the stamina, you can hike to the Abbazia di San Fruttuoso (☞ Off the Beaten Path *in* Camogli, *above*) from Portofino. It's a steep climb at first, and the walk takes about 2½ hours one way. By boat, the trip takes about 20 minutes. If you are extremely ambitious and want to make a whole day of it, you can then hike another 2½ hours all the way to Camogli. Much more modest hikes from Portofino include a one-hour uphill walk to Cappella delle Gave, a bit inland in the hills, from where you can continue the hike by walking back downhill to Santa Margherita Ligure (another 1½ hours). Finally, there is a 2½-hour hike from Portofino that heads farther inland to Ruta, through Olmi and Pietre Strette.

Chiavari

41 *22 km (13 mi) east of Portofino, 38 km (23 mi) southeast of Genoa.*

Chiavari is a fishing town, rather than village, and it has considerable character, with narrow, twisting streets and a good harbor. Chiavari's citizens were intrepid explorers, and many emigrated to South America in the 19th century. The town boomed, thanks to the wealth of the returning voyagers, but Chiavari still retains many medieval traces in its buildings.

In town center, the **Museo Archeologico** (Archaeological Museum) displays objects from an 8th-century BC necropolis, or ancient cemetery, excavated nearby. ✉ *Palazzo Rocca, Piazza Matteotti.* ☎ *0185/320829.* *Free.* *Tues.–Thurs. 9–1, Fri.–Sun. 2–7.*

Outdoor Activities and Sports

HORSEBACK RIDING

Riding is a rewarding way to explore the wooded hills framing Chiavari. **Rivarola Carasco** (✉ Via Veneto 212, ☎ 0185/382204) provides mounts.

Shopping

The traditional, light—they weigh only 3 pounds—*campanine* chairs made of olive wood or walnut are still produced by a few Chiavari craftsmen. Macramé lace can also be found here.

Sestri Levante

42 *8 km (5 mi) southeast of Chiavari, 59 km (36 mi) northwest of La Spezia.*

Though industrialized, with steelworks and shipyards, Sestri Levante has good views and an interesting medieval district surrounding what is known as the Baia del Silenzio (Bay of Silence), the small harbor just behind Piazza Matteotti. Walk up one of the alleyways to see some of the worked slate doorways of the older houses.

En Route From Sestri, S1 turns inland past the spectacular Passo del Bracco and does not reach the coast again until the large port of La Spezia (☞ *below*), more than 60 km (37 mi) southeast. The Cinque Terre, five towns that lie on the less accessible coastal strip between Levanto and Portovenere (near La Spezia) could be reached only by boat or on foot until about 50 years ago.

Moneglia

43 *12 km (7 mi) southeast of Sestri Levante, 58 km (36 mi) northwest of La Spezia.*

The town of Moneglia, sheltered by the wooded hills of a nature preserve, faces a little bay guarded by ruined castles. An out-of-the-way alternative to fussier resorts, it's a quiet base for walks and excursions by boat, car, or train to Portofino and the Cinque Terre towns. A classical guitar festival is held here in September.

Lodging

$$ **Villa Edera.** Ingeniously merging an older building on a verdant hillside with a smart contemporary stone and glass wing, the family that owns this small hotel offers guests their personal and caring attention. Terraces, a garden, luminous bedrooms, and lounges with stylish wicker armchairs are among the comforts. Mamma Ida's cooking is special, too. ✉ *Via Venino 12, 16030,* ☎ *0185/49291,* FAX *0185/49470. 27 rooms. Restaurant. AE, MC, V. Closed Nov. 5–Mar. 12.*

Levanto

44 *25 km (15 mi) southeast of Sestri Levante, 32 km (20 mi) northwest of La Spezia.*

Secluded Levanto has good beaches and a few graceful buildings dating from the 13th century. Take a closer look at the buildings; some are adorned with clever trompe l'oeil frescoes that give the impression that real town folk are looking at you from their windows.

Dining and Lodging

$$$ ★ ✕ **Araldo.** Arches and frescoes festooned throughout this little restaurant are coupled with outstanding food and service. Seasonal, creative Mediterranean cuisine is complemented by more than 100 wines. Try *pesce con patate alla ligure* (fillets of fish baked with potatoes in wine with olives and fresh thyme), or put your faith in the chef and order the tasting menu, a good deal and a real treat. ✉ *Via Jacopo 24,* ☎ *0187/807253. AE, DC, MC, V. Closed Tues. (except July–Aug.) and Nov.*

$$$$ ★ **Stella Maris.** In Levanto center and only a 10-minute walk from the beach, this is a real find. It takes up one floor of a 19th-century palazzo (the ground floor houses a bank). Seven rooms are decorated with original frescoes and 19th-century furniture, and seven are modern; the couple who run the hotel have an infectious enthusiasm for the building's history and decoration. A half-board plan is included in the price, but that's no sacrifice because the home cooking features Ligurian seafood specialties; you can have your homemade gelato in the sunny garden. ✉ *Via Marconi 4, 19015,* ☎ *0187/808258,* FAX *0187/807351. 16 rooms. Restaurant, bar. AE, DC, MC, V. Closed Nov. MAP.*

Cinque Terre

★ 45 *Monterosso al Mare 93 km (58 mi) southeast of Genoa, Riomaggiore 14 km (9 mi) west of La Spezia.*

The aura of isolation that has surrounded five coastal villages known as the Cinque Terre, together with their dramatic coastal scenery, has made them one of the eastern Riviera's most stunning attractions. However, that aura has been rapidly disappearing (especially in summer) for the past five years, as the Cinque Terre have turned into a common, if not requisite, stop on Italy's tourist trail, in spite of their relative inaccessibility. Clinging haphazardly to steep cliffs, these five enchanting villages are linked by oceanside footpaths, by train, and now by narrow, unasphalted and rather tortuous roads, a fairly recent development. The local train on the Genoa–La Spezia line stops at each town between Levanto and Riomaggiore. The westernmost village is Monterosso, but the easiest to reach by car is Riomaggiore, easternmost of the villages and closest to La Spezia and the A12 autostrada.

All five of the tiny Cinque Terre enclaves are linked by well-established and groomed hiking footpaths—for much of their history, these were the only way to get from town to town on land. Although today the train, and to a certain extent the road, have surpassed the footpaths, they still showcase breathtaking ocean views as well as access to the rugged, secluded beaches and grottoes that will never have a train station. The most famous and easiest of these trails is the **Via dell'Amore** (Lover's Lane), which links Riomaggiore with Manarola (2 km/1 mi, 30 mins) by a flat path cut into the cliffside. The same trail continues to Corniglia (3 km/2 mi, 1 hr), then becomes more difficult between Corniglia and Vernazza (3 km/2 mi, 1½ hrs) and even more difficult from Vernazza to Monterosso (2 km/1 mi, 1½ hrs). Still, because of the relative elevations, walking east to west is easier than walking west to east. Additionally, trails lead from Monterosso up the mountainside and back down to Vernazza, and into the mountains from Corniglia, Manarola, and Riomaggiore, with historic churches and great views along the way. Trail maps are available at the Monterosso tourist office. Be sure to wear sturdy shoes (hiking boots are best) and a hat, and bring a water bottle, as there is little shade. But also check weather reports before hiking; especially in fall and winter, frequent thunderstorms flying in off the coast can send townspeople running for cover and make the shelterless trails slippery and dangerous.

Monterosso al Mare

12 km (7 mi) east of Levanto.

Monterosso is the largest, most developed, and least pretty of the five fishing towns, with the Cinque Terre's only sizable hotels and most of its restaurants. The narrow alleys and colorful houses of the historic center are clustered on a hilltop above the port and its seaside promenade. Stone stairways link the two areas of town, affording lovely views of the mountains that tumble down onto a wide, sandy beach below, which is mobbed in summer. In the historic center, the 12th-century **church** (✉ Piazza Garibaldi) is striped black and white in the Ligurian Gothic fashion. On Thursday morning the town comes alive with its weekly **market**, where you can pick up local anchovies and lemons among other delicacies. The **Pro Loco** tourist office (✉ Via Fegina 38, below train station, ☎ 0187/817506) can help with trail maps and boat schedules.

DINING AND LODGING

$$$ ✕ **Il Gigante.** A good introduction to Ligurian seafood is the zuppa di pesce served at this traditional trattoria in Monterosso. This soup is usually served as a first course, but is filling enough to be an entrée. Daily specials might include risotto di frutti di mare and spaghetti with an octopus sauce. ✉ *Monterosso al Mare,* ☎ *0187/817401. Reservations essential weekends and summer. AE, DC, MC, V. Closed Mon.*

$$–$$$ ★ ✕ **Il Pirata.** Bright and rustic, this trattoria near the port should be the first stop for lunchtime visitors, especially those who make it in time to grab a seat at the long tables on the front porch outside. Specialties are those of the region, with a few surprising gourmet touches, like the French wines lining the shelves and Maine lobster. ✉ *Via Molinelli 6/8,* ☎ *0187/817536. Reservations essential weekends and summer. MC, V. Closed Wed. and mid-Jan.–mid.-Feb.*

$$$ ★ **Porto Roca.** In a panoramic position above the sea, Porta Roca is set slightly apart, blessedly removed from the crowds who visit, especially on weekends. It has the look of a well-kept villa; its interiors have authentic antique pieces and there are ample terraces. The rooms are bright and airy, with sea breezes. Porto Roca is on a network of not-too-demanding hill walks and has a faithful American clientele. ✉ *Via Corone 1, 19016,* ☎ *0187/817502,* FAX *0187/817692. 43 rooms. Restaurant, bar. AE, MC, V. Closed Nov. 4–Mar. 18.*

Vernazza

3½ km (2 mi) east of Monterosso.

A few kilometers to the east of Monterosso is lovely Vernazza, with the largest and best-equipped port of the Cinque Terre towns. The town's pink, slate-roofed houses and picturesque squares contrast with the remains of a medieval fort and castle. The castle's tower was struck by lightning in 1896; it's been rebuilt and today offers some of the best views in Cinque Terre. Summertime in Vernazza brings smart-set Italians to the town's cafés and restaurants. Stay in town and delve right in, or escape on one of the many footpaths leading up through the hillsides' terraced vineyards.

DINING

$$$ ✕ **Gambero Rosso.** On Vernazza's main square, looking out at the church, this fine trattoria serves such delectable dishes as shrimp salad, vegetable torte, and squid-ink risotto; for dessert don't miss the Cinque Terre's own *schiacchetrà*, a dessert wine served with hard, semisweet *biscotti* (hard cookies). Don't drink it out of the glass—dip the biscotti in the wine and eat them instead. ✉ *Piazza Marconi 7,* ☎ *0187/812265. AE, DC, MC, V. Closed Mon. (Oct.–Mar.) and first 3 wks of Nov.*

Corniglia

3 km (2 mi) east of Vernazza.

Tiny, isolated Corniglia is unquestionably the most difficult of the Cinque Terre to visit: it has no port and no (usable) access road for automobiles, so you will have to arrive by local train or on foot, using the difficult trail from Vernazza or the easy one from Manarola. The town is strung back from a hilltop overlooking the sea to the mountainside behind it; within you'll find pretty pastel squares and the 14th-century **San Pietro church.** The rose window of marble imported from Carrara is particularly impressive considering the work it must have taken merely to get it to Corniglia.

Manarola

3 km (2 mi) east of Corniglia.

In photogenic Manarola, multicolor houses spill down a dark hillside to town squares that hang over the port like balconies overlooking the tiny turquoise harbor. This is also the center of the Cinque Terre's wine making, and you can taste the fruits of local labor in a number of *cantine,* as well as the **Cooperativa Agricoltura di Riomaggiore, Manarola, Corniglia, Vernazza e Monterosso** (Groppo, ☎ 0187/920435), just outside town.

Riomaggiore

1½ km (1 mi) east of Manarola, 116 km (72 mi) east of Genoa.

Civilization and all that goes with it begins to resurface in Riomaggiore, where you'll find the same sorts of flowery little squares that bedeck the town's four siblings, interspersed with modern stucco houses and a sense that the population is less isolated here. This may be because Riomaggiore is comparatively convenient to La Spezia; get here via car, following signs from La Spezia's port.

La Spezia

46 *14 km (9 mi) west of La Spezia, 103 km (64 mi) southeast of Genoa.*

La Spezia is a large industrialized naval port on routes to the Cinque Terre and to Portovenere. La Spezia lacks the quiet charm of the smaller towns. However, its palm-lined Morin promenade, fertile citrus parks, the remains of the massive 13th-century **Castel San Giorgio** (✉ Via XX Settembre), and lively, balcony-lined streets make parts of La Spezia surprisingly beautiful. La Spezia is a reasonable jumping-off point for trips to the smaller Riviera villages.

Outdoor Activities and Sports

WATERSKIING

La Spezia Motorboat Club (✉ Via della Marina 224, ☎ 0187/50401) will get you up and skiing.

Portovenere

★ 47 *12 km (7 mi) south of La Spezia, 114 km (70 mi) southeast of Genoa.*

Portovenere's small colorful houses, some dating from the 12th century, were once all connected to the 12th- to 16th-century citadel, so that in times of attack the villagers could reach the safety of the battlements. The town commands a strategic position at the end of a peninsula that extends southeast from the Cinque Terre and forms the western border of the Gulf of La Spezia. Lord Byron (1788–1824) is said to have written *Childe Harold's Pilgrimage* here. Near the entrance to the huge, strange **Grotto Arpaia** at the base of the sea-swept cliff is a plaque recounting the poet's strength and courage as he swam across the gulf to the village of San Terenzo, near Lerici, to visit his friend Percy Shelley (1792–1822); the feat is commemorated as well by the name of the stretch of water, "Golfo dei Poeti," or Poets' Gulf. Above the grotto, on a formidable solid mass of rock, is **San Pietro,** a 13th-century Gothic church built on the site of an ancient pagan shrine. With its black-and-white-stripe exterior, it is a landmark recognizable from far out at sea. ⏲ *Daily 7–6.*

Dining and Lodging

$$ ✕ **Da Iseo.** Try to get one of the tables outside at this waterfront restaurant, with bistro accents and paintings of Portovenere. Seafood is the only choice, and it's fresh and plentiful. Pasta courses are inventive; try spaghetti *alla Giuseppe* (with shellfish and fresh tomato) or spaghetti *alla Iseo* (with a seafood curry sauce). ✉ *Waterfront,* ☏ *0187/790610. AE, DC, MC, V. Closed Wed. and Jan. 2–Feb. 15.*

$ ✕ **Antica Osteria del Carrugio.** Near the castle built to defend the coast from Pisan incursions is this 100-year-old tavern with maritime decor. The menu features seafood, which varies with the catch of the day. Specialties include *mescina* (soup of beans, chickpeas, and wheat) and *polpo in insalata* (octopus salad). ✉ *Via Cappellini 66,* ☏ *0187/790617. Reservations not accepted. No credit cards. Closed Thurs. and Nov.–Dec.*

$$$ ★ **Royal Sporting.** Appearances are deceptive at this modern hotel on the beach about a 10-minute walk from the village. From the outside, the stone construction seems austere and unwelcoming, but the courtyards and interior—with fresh flowers, potted plants, and cool, airy rooms—are colorful and vibrant. The sports facilities are among the best in the area. ✉ *Via dell'Olivo 345, 19025,* ☏ *0187/790326,* FAX *0187/777707. 62 rooms. Restaurant, bar, saltwater pool, tennis court, beach. AE, DC, MC, V. Closed mid-Oct.–Apr. (except Easter wk).*

Lerici

48 *11 km (7 mi) east of La Spezia, 65 km (40 mi) west of Lucca.*

Lerici, near Liguria's border with Tuscany, is set on a magnificent coastline of gray cliffs and pine forests. The town once belonged to Tuscan Pisa, and the 13th-century Pisan **Castello Doria** standing above the splendid bay has attracted lovers of nature for centuries. Shelley was one of Lerici's best-known visitors and spent some of the happiest months of his life in the lovely white village of **San Terenzo,** 2 km (1 mi) away. The **Villa Magni,** where he lived, has a museum devoted to him. After Shelley drowned at sea here in 1822, the bay was renamed Golfo dei Poeti, in his and Byron's honor.

Dining and Lodging

$$$ ✕ **Miranda.** Perched amid the clustered old houses in the seaside hamlet of Tellaro, 4 km (2½ mi) southeast of Lerici, this small family-run inn has become a pricey gourmet's destination because of chef Angelo Cabani's imaginative way with Ligurian cooking. His unusual seafood dishes include *insalata di gamberoni e aragosta con finocchio* (shrimp and lobster salad with fennel) and *involtino di branzino farcito di spinaci* (fish roulade stuffed with spinach). If you stay in one of the seven comfortable rooms with bath, you can take half board for 180,000 lire per person. ✉ *Via Fiascherino 92,* ☏ *0187/964012. 7 rooms. Restaurant, bar. Reservations essential. AE, DC, MC, V. Restaurant closed Mon. Hotel closed Jan. 10–mid-Feb. MAP.*

$$ **Florida.** This seafront family-run establishment has bright rooms with all the extras you would expect in a higher category, including soundproofing and a balcony with a sea view. For an even better view, loll in one of the deck chairs on the roof terrace. The Florida overlooks a small beach area and is close to tennis courts and a golf course; a solarium is also on the premises. ✉ *Lungomare Biaggini 35, 19032,* ☏ *0187/967332,* FAX *0187/967344. 37 rooms. Breakfast room, bar, minibar, beach. AE, DC, MC, V. Closed Jan. 6–Mar. 15.*

ITALIAN RIVIERA A TO Z

Arriving and Departing

By Boat

Genoa is Italy's largest port and can be reached from the United States as well as other parts of Liguria and Italy (Sardinia, La Spezia, and Savona). Ships berth in the heart of Genoa, including cruise ships of the Genoa-based **Costa Cruise Line** (✉ Via Gabriele D'Annunzio 2, ☎ 010/54831). Ferries to various ports around the Mediterranean are operated by **Tirrenia Navigazione** (✉ Stazione Marittima, ☎ 010/2758041), whose most popular route is Sardinia (a 13-hour trip), and **Grimaldi Lines** (✉ Stazione Marittima, ☎ 010/589331), which sends cruise-ship-like overnight ferries to Barcelona (a 17-hour trip) and Palermo, Sicily (a 20-hour trip).

By Bus

The main bus station in Genoa is at Piazza Principe. Several bus lines provide connections along the Ligurian coast and link Genoa with other parts of Italy, the French Riviera, and other cities in Europe. PESCI provides reliable bus service to the Nice airport. **PESCI** (✉ Piazza della Vittoria 94/r, Genoa, ☎ 010/564936). **Geotravels** (✉ Piazza della Vittoria 302/r, Genoa, ☎ 010/587181). **Guimar Tours** (✉ Via Balbi 192, Genoa, ☎ 010/256337).

By Car

Autostrada **A12** southeast from Genoa links up with the autostrada and superstrada network for all northern and southern destinations; Rome is a six-hour drive from Genoa. The 150-km (93-mi) trip north to Milan on **A7** takes two hours. Nice is 2½ hours west on **A10.**

By Plane

Aeroporto Internazionale Cristoforo Colombo (✉ Sestri Ponente, ☎ 010/60151) is only 6 km (4 mi) from the center of Genoa. It has daily service to Zurich (on Crossair), London (on British Airways), and Milan and Rome (on Alitalia). The nearest airports for direct U.S. flights are Nice, in France, about 2½ hours west of Genoa (and an easy bus connection from Genoa, ☞ PESCI, *above*), and Milan's Linate and Malpensa, about two hours northeast.

BETWEEN THE AIRPORT AND DOWNTOWN

Volabus (☎ 010/5997414) services from Cristoforo Colombo connect with Genoa's Stazione Brignole, stopping also at Piazza Acquaverde (Stazione Principe).

By Train

Frequent and fast train service connects Liguria with the rest of Italy. Genoa is 1½ hours from Milan and five hours from Rome. Many services from France (in particular, the French Riviera) pass along the Ligurian Coast on the way to all parts of Italy.

Getting Around

By Boat

This is the most pleasant—and, in some cases, the only—way to get from place to place within Liguria. A busy network of local services connects many of the resorts. For general information about availability of services in Liguria, contact **Servizio Marittimo del Tigullio** (✉ Via Palestro 8/1b, Santa Margherita Ligure, ☎ 0185/284670). Another source is **Alimar** (✉ Calata Zingari, Genoa, ☎ 010/256775). Or contact **Servizio Marittimo Camogli–San Fruttuoso** (✉ Società Golfo Paradiso, Via Scalo 2, Camogli, ☎ 0185/772091), which runs between

Camogli and San Fruttuoso (on the Portofino promontory), as well as between Recco and Punta Chiappa, two towns close to Camogli. **Navigazione Golfo dei Poeti** (✉ Viale Mazzini 21, La Spezia, ☎ 0187/967676 or 0336/258037) runs frequent ferry-shuttle services between Portofino, Portovenere, and the Cinque Terre.

By Bus

PESCI (✉ Piazza della Vittoria 94/r, Genoa, ☎ 010/564936) buses run the length of the Ligurian Coast in both directions. Local buses serve the steep valleys that run to some of the towns along the western coast. Tickets may be bought at local bus stations, or at newsstands for local buses. Buy your ticket before you board the bus.

By Car

Two good roads run parallel to each other along the coast of Liguria. Closer to shore and passing through all the towns and villages is **S1,** which has excellent views at almost every turn but which gets crowded in July and August. More direct and higher up than S1 is the autostrada, **A10** west of Genoa and **A12** to the east. This route saves a lot of time on weekends, in summer, and on days when festivals slow traffic in some resorts to a standstill.

By Train

Regular service, connecting all parts of Liguria, operates from Genoa's two stations, **Stazione Principe** (points west, ✉ Piazza Principe, ☎ 147/888088 toll free) and **Stazione Brignole** (points east, ✉ Piazza Giuseppe Verdi, ☎ 147/888088 toll free). All the coastal resorts are on this line, and many international trains stop along the coast west of Genoa on their way from Paris to Milan or Rome.

Contacts and Resources

Car Rentals

GENOA

Avis (✉ Piazza Acquaverde, ☎ 010/564412). **Budget** (✉ Aeroporto Internazionale Cristoforo Colombo, ☎ 010/6503822). **Hertz** (✉ Via delle Casacce 3, ☎ 010/564412).

LA SPEZIA

Avis (✉ Via Fratelli Rosselli 86/88, ☎ 0187/770270). **Hertz** (✉ Via Casaregis 76/r, ☎ 010/592101).

SAN REMO

Avis (✉ Corso Imperatrice 96, ☎ 0184/532462). **Hertz** (✉ Via XX Settembre 17, ☎ 0184/500470).

Emergencies

Police, Doctor (☎ 113). **Genoa municipal police** (☎ 112). **Ambulance** (☎ 118). **Ospedale Generale Regionale San Martino** (✉ Viale Benedetto XV, Genoa, ☎ 010/5551).

Guided Tours

ORIENTATION TOURS

Informal harbor cruises or excursion cruises among coastal towns are scheduled and operated by the main ferry lines (☞ Getting Around by Boat, *above*), but you can have as much fun—if not more—negotiating a price with a boat owner at one of the smaller ports. You're likely to get a boat operator who commands rudimentary English at best.

Boat Tours: You can also take a boat tour of Genoa harbor. The tour costs 10,000 lire, lasts about an hour, and includes a visit to the breakwater outside the harbor, the Bacino delle Grazie, and the Molo Vecchio (Old Port). You can see extensive views of the city throughout the tour. For information, contact the **Cooperativa Battellieri** (✉ Stazione Marittima, Ponte dei Mille, Genoa, ☎ 010/265712).

Bus Tours: A three-hour bus tour of Genoa with an English-speaking guide is the best way to see the city and its panoramic upper reaches. A coach with a multilingual guide aboard leaves every day at 3 from Piazza Caricamento, by the port, and does a 1¾-hour narrated loop of the city, operated by **Between Sea and Sky Tours** (☎ 010/2543431), for 25,000 lire. Call first to check times. Another option is the 45-minute loop (without a guide) run by **AMT** (the municipal bus company, ✉ Piazza della Vittoria, ☎ 010/5582414), stopping to pick up and drop off passengers at several points around town. The municipal tour bus costs 1,600 lire and runs from 9 AM to 3:30 PM, starting at Piazza Caricamento.

Late-Night Pharmacies

Genoa: Europa (✉ Corso Europa 676, Genoa, ☎ 010/380239). **Ghersi** (✉ Corte Lambruschini, Tower A, Genoa, ☎ 010/541661).

Visitor Information

Genoa (✉ Palazzina Santa Maria, Old Port, Genoa, ☎ 010/24871; ✉ Stazione Principe, Genoa, ☎ 010/2462633; ✉ Aeroporto Internazionale Cristoforo Colombo, Genoa, ☎ 010/6015247). In certain seasons, a provisional office is set up at the Terminale Crociere for the arrival of major ferries (☎ 2463686).

Local tourist offices (✉ Palazzo Hanbury, Via Gibb 26, 17021 Alassio, ☎ 0182/647027; ✉ Via B. Ricci, corner of Piazza San Michele, 17031 Albenga, ☎ 0182/559058; ✉ Via Roberto 1, 18012 Bordighera, ☎ 0184/262322; ✉ Via XX Settembre 33/r, 16032 Camogli, ☎ 0185/771066; ✉ Via Matteotti 54/a, 18100 Imperia, ☎ 0183/294947; ✉ Via Mazzini 47, 19100 La Spezia, ☎ 0187/770900; ✉ Via Biaggini 3, 19032 Lerici, ☎ 0187/967346; ✉ Piazza Cavour 12, 19015 Levanto, ☎ 0187/808125; ✉ Via Fegina 38, 19016 Monterosso, ☎ 0187/817506; ✉ Via Roma 35, 16034 Portofino, ☎ 0185/269024; ✉ Via A. Diaz 9, 16035 Rapallo, ☎ 0185/230346; ✉ Corso Nuvoloni, 18038 San Remo, ☎ 0184/571571; ✉ Via Biaggini 3, 16038 Santa Margherita Ligure, ☎ 0185/287485; ✉ Viale Nazioni Unite, 17019 Varazze, ☎ 019/934609; ✉ Via Cavour 61, 18039 Ventimiglia, ☎ 0184/351183).

7 PIEDMONT/ VALLE D'AOSTA

FROM TURIN TO THE ALPS AND ACROSS THE PO PLAIN

Italy's windows on France and Switzerland are delightful surprises even in a land of natural beauty. Snowcapped Monte Bianco and Monte Cervino climb to the highest heights in Europe, and below them, Alpine valleys cradle storybook castles. From here come Alba's truffles, Barolo's wine, and the FIATs, Borsalino hats, and Asti Spumante of Turin, the city sparkling at the center of it all.

Updated by Robin S. Goldstein

FROM ALPINE VALLEYS hemming the highest mountains in Europe to the mist-shrouded lowlands skirting the Po River, from pulsating industrial centers turning out the best of Italian design to tiny stone villages isolated above the clouds, and from hearty peasant cooking in farmhouse kitchens to French-accented delicacies *accompagné* by some of Italy's finest wines, Piedmont and the spectacular Valle d'Aosta promise the traveler a store of historical, cultural, and natural riches.

The Valle d'Aosta's Italian Alps afford excellent skiing and climbing at renowned resort towns such as Courmayeur and Breuil-Cervinia. In the Piedmontese lowlands, Turin, the regional capital, is a historical center that today also serves as the heart of Italy's booming auto industry. Don't be put off by Turin's industrial reputation—it's also home to elegant piazzas, high fashion, fine chocolate, and worthwhile museums. Nearby are Alba, home of fragrant Italian white truffles, seasonal delicacies that sell for more than $1,000 per pound; Asti, Barolo, and Barbaresco, the famous wine centers; and the modern business hubs Ivrea, Novara, and Alessandria.

Tucked away at the foot of the Pennine, Graian, Cottian, and Maritime Alps (Piemonte, in Italian, means "foot of the mountains"), Piedmont and the autonomous region of Valle d'Aosta just north of it seem more akin to neighboring France and Switzerland. Well-dressed women in the refined cafés of Turin are addressed more often as *madama* than *signora,* and French is often used in the more remote mountain hamlets.

Piedmont was originally inhabited by Celtic tribes who were absorbed by the conquering Romans. As allies of Rome, the Celts held off Hannibal when he came down through the Alpine passes with his elephants but were eventually defeated, and their capital—Taurasia, the present Turin—was destroyed. The Romans rebuilt the city, giving its streets the grid pattern that survives today. Roman ruins can be found throughout both regions and are particularly conspicuous in the town of Aosta. With the fall of the Roman empire, Piedmont suffered the fate of the rest of Italy and was successively occupied and ravaged by barbarians from the east and the north. In the 11th century, a feudal French family named Savoy ruled Turin briefly; toward the end of the 13th century they returned to the area, where they would remain, almost continuously, for 500 years. In 1798 the French Republican armies invaded Italy, but when Napoléon's empire fell, the House of Savoy returned to power.

Beginning in 1848, Piedmont was one of the principal centers of the Risorgimento, the movement for Italian unity. In 1861 the Chamber of Deputies of Turin declared Italy a united kingdom. Rome became the capital in 1870, marking the end of Piedmont's importance in the political sphere. Nevertheless, the architectural splendors of Turin, together with some unheralded but excellent museums, continue to draw travelers.

Piedmont became one of the first industrialized regions in Italy, and the automotive giant FIAT—the Fabbrica Italiana Automobili Torino—was established here in 1899. Today the region is the center of Italy's automobile, metalworking, chemical, and candy industries, having attracted thousands of workers from Italy's impoverished south. The FIAT dynasty has been perhaps the most important player in the region's rise to power and affluence; *The Economist* once commented that were prosperous northwestern Italy to secede and form its own country, it would be richer than Switzerland.

The Valle d'Aosta, to the north, is famous for its impressive fortified castles and splendid Alpine beauty. It was settled in the 3rd millennium BC by people from the Mediterranean and later by a Celtic tribe known as the Salassi, who eventually fell to the Romans. The Saracens were here in the 10th century; by the 12th century, the Savoy family had established itself, and the region's feudal nobles moved into the countryside, building the massive castles that still stand. Valle d'Aosta enjoyed relative autonomy as part of the Savoy kingdom and was briefly ruled by the French four separate times. The region is still officially bilingual, so you will hear both Italian and French.

Pleasures and Pastimes

Dining

These two regions offer rustic specialties, from farmhouse hearths to fine cuisine with a French accent—and everything in between. The region's best-known food is probably polenta, a creamy cornmeal concoction often served with *carbonada* (veal stew), local sausages, melted cheese, or wild mushrooms, among other things. The favorite form of pasta is *agnolotti,* similar to ravioli and filled with meat, spinach, or ricotta cheese, often served in a delectably simple coating of melted butter and shaved truffles. Another regional specialty is *fonduta,* a local version of fondue, made with melted Fontina (a cheese from the Valle d'Aosta), eggs, and sometimes grated truffles. Fontina and ham also often deck out the ubiquitous, French-style *crepes alla valdostana,* served piping hot and casserole style. Alba is the home of *tartufi bianchi* (white truffles), much rarer and more expensive than black ones and considered the tastiest by connoisseurs. They sell for at least $1,000 a pound wholesale. Another local dish is *bagna cauda*(literally hot bath), a heated sauce made from butter, oil, anchovies, cream, and shredded garlic; it is served with *cardi* (edible thistles) or other raw vegetables for dipping.

Although as a rule desserts here are less sweet than in some other Italian regions, treats like *panna cotta,* a cooked milk custard, and *torta di nocciole* (hazelnut torte) still delight. Turin is renowned for its delicate pastries and fine chocolates, especially for the hazelnut *gianduiotti.* Valle d'Aosta is famous for a variety of schnappslike brandies made from fruits or herbs. Piedmont is one of Italy's most important wine-producing regions. Most of the wines are full-bodied reds, such as Barolo, Nebbiolo, Freisa, Barbera, and the lighter Barbaresco. Asti Spumante, a sparkling wine, comes from the region, as does vermouth, which was developed in Piedmont by A. B. Carpano in 1786. Many prefer dry (brut) Spumante to the sweet Asti varietal.

Lodging

There is a high standard of old-world opulence in Turin's better hotels, and it is translated into the Alpine idiom in the top resort hotels in the mountains. Less-expensive hotels in cities and towns are generally geared to business travelers. You can usually count on a measure of charm at resorts and the Italian brand of gemütlichkeit even in more modest resort hotels. Summer and winter occupancy rates and prices are usually quite high at resorts, with summer vacationers and skiers, respectively, monopolizing available accommodations. Hotels in mountain resorts may offer attractive half-board or off-season rates that can sometimes reduce the cost by a full price category. Many mountain resort hotels cater primarily to half- or full-board guests only, for stays of at least a week. It's a good idea to take a package deal on a ski vacation; it may give you a break on the price of lift tickets.

Skiing

This is the major sport in both Piedmont and the Valle d'Aosta. Resorts with excellent facilities abound near the highest mountains in Europe—Monte Bianco (Mont Blanc), Monte Rosa, Monte Cervino (the Matterhorn), and the Gran Paradiso. Lift tickets, running around 50,000 lire for a day's pass, are significantly less expensive than at major U.S. resorts (though often for fewer trails).

Exploring Piedmont/Valle d'Aosta

The vast Po Plain that stretches eastward in a wide belt across the top of the Italian peninsula begins in Piedmont, where the Po River has its source in the Coolidge Glacier on 11,000-ft-high Monviso. But Piedmont is primarily a mountainous region. The Maritime Alps lie to the south of Turin, and the rolling hills of the Monferrato and Langhe districts fold the landscape southeast of Turin. High Alpine crests of the Valle d'Aosta rise to the north and west of the plain. As you wind your way northeast into the Valle d'Aosta, you are in the Italian Loire, where solid, imposing castles sit in the shadow of Europe's most impressive peaks, Mont Blanc and the Matterhorn. Nature has endowed Piedmont and the Valle d'Aosta with some of the most striking scenery in Italy.

Like any rugged, mountainous region, the Alps of Piemonte and the Valle d'Aosta can be tricky to navigate. Roads that look like superhighways on the map can be narrow and twisting, with steep slopes and cliffside drops. Generally, roads are well maintained, but the sheer distance covered by all of those curves tends to take longer than you might have anticipated, and so it's best to figure in extra time for getting around. This is especially true in winter, when weather conditions can cause slow traffic and road closings. Be sure to check with local tourist offices and police before venturing off the beaten path, and find out whether you may need tire chains for snowy and icy roads. Train routes, on the other hand, are more or less reliable in the region.

Numbers in the text correspond to numbers in the margin and on the Piedmont/Valle d'Aosta and Turin maps.

Great Itineraries

With the exception of the mountain resorts, which may be packed at the height of the season, much of Piedmont and Valle d'Aosta is off the beaten track. These regions of Italy offer the pleasures of discovery: uncrowded, unhurried samplings of scenery, art, food, and some of Italy's finest wines. The amount of time you choose to spend here depends on your interests. If you want to admire the highest mountains in the Alps from the pistes or the deck of a chalet, sneak up on the chamois in the Parco Nazionale del Gran Paradiso, and still have time to devote to Turin and the wine country, a total of seven days should be ideal. Five days would give you a chance to visit Turin's attractions, make an excursion into the mountains, and discover some of the smaller cities. In three days you can see Turin and then head to Aosta for a look at some impressive Roman ruins and a quick trip into the mountains. If you budget your time carefully, you can spend half a day in Asti.

IF YOU HAVE 3 DAYS

Visitors with limited time should concentrate first on **Turin** ①–⑮, including the **Duomo di San Giovanni** ①, where the famous shroud is housed; the 17th-century **Palazzo Reale** ②, former residence of the Savoy royal family; and the churches of **San Carlo** ⑤ and **Santa Cristina** ⑥, which flank the impressive **Piazza San Carlo** ⑦, considered by many to be Italy's finest square. Take time to enjoy one or more of the city's authentic old-world cafés and walk by the striking **Mole Antonel-**

liana ⑩, an odd structure that was once the world's tallest building. On the second day, head northeast along the A5 motorway to **Aosta** ㉘ to see its large and well-preserved Roman ruins and enjoy some regional French-influenced cooking. If you have a couple hours to spare on your way to Aosta, see **Castello Fénis** ㉗, well worth the detour. On the third day, continue on to **Courmayeur** ㉙ for magnificent views of **Monte Bianco** ㉚, and, if time allows, **Breuil-Cervinia** ㉖ for a look at the Matterhorn. Alternatively, you can catch a glimpse of one or the other and then double back through Aosta to **Cogne** ㉛, where you can make a foray into the Parco Nazionale Gran Paradiso. Another alternative is to return to Turin and head southeast into the vineyard-blanketed hills around medieval **Asti** ㉜.

IF YOU HAVE 5 DAYS

Spend two days in **Turin** ①–⑮, then head for the Roman city of **Aosta** ㉘, perhaps stopping on the way to see the fairy-tale **Castello Fénis** ㉗. On the third day, you can drink in the views of the **Monte Bianco** ㉚ from **Courmayeur** ㉙, see the Matterhorn from **Breuil-Cervinia** ㉖, or follow the trails from **Cogne** ㉛ into the Parco Nazionale Gran Paradiso. On the fourth day double back to Turin and make an excursion to **Saluzzo** ㉑, an old town steeped in 15th-century atmosphere. Alpine fans might choose instead to spend the fourth day in the mountains, at Gran Paradiso. On the fifth day continue southeast to **Asti** ㉜, exploring the rolling hills where great wines and good food make this a gourmet's paradise.

IF YOU HAVE 7 DAYS

Make **Turin** ①–⑮ your base for three days, from which you can explore the city and the outlying towns, including **Saluzzo** ㉑, with its picturesque hilltop center and castles. Another second-day excursion from Turin takes you to the castle at **Rivoli** ⑰, a sanctuary of contemporary art, and then over a pilgrim's route to two medieval abbeys, **Abbazia di Sant'Antonio di Ranverso** ⑱ and Umberto Eco's inspiration, the **Sacra di San Michele** ⑳. Alternatively, travel westward to Piedmont's high mountains and see the resorts of **Sestriere** ㉒ and **Bardonecchia** ㉓ close to the French border. On the third day head for the mountains of the Valle d'Aosta; visit the **Castello Fénis** ㉗ on the way to **Aosta** ㉘, a good base for excursions into the mountains that will keep you moving on the fourth and fifth days between **Courmayeur** ㉙, **Breuil-Cervinia** ㉖, and **Cogne** ㉛. Devote the better part of a day to the stunning Gran Paradiso national park, near Cogne. Head south on the sixth day, doubling back past Turin and continuing southeast to **Asti** ㉜. Follow the provincial roads through the vineyards of the hilly Monferrato and Langhe districts of south-central Piedmont, delving into their culinary and enological delights. On the seventh day head east across the fertile Po Plain toward the rice-growing capital of **Vercelli** ㉞, making sure you see the Duomo, the final resting place of several Savoy rulers. The easternmost city of Piedmont is **Novara** ㉟, of little interest, but a rest stop on the way to Milan, only 50 km (30 mi) away.

When to Tour Piedmont/Valle d'Aosta

Unless you are dead set on skiing, the region can be visited in either summer or winter (and for that matter, there's summer skiing at Monte Cervino). In winter, road conditions can be treacherous, especially higher up in the mountains, requiring the use of snow tires or chains. The ski resorts of the Valle d'Aosta are popular with Italians and non-Italians alike, so book your accommodations in advance. Snow conditions for skiing vary drastically year to year—there is nothing approaching the consistency of, say, the Colorado and Utah Rockies—so keep apprised of weather conditions. If you are visiting in summer, try to avoid coming in August, the holiday month for the vast majority of Italians, many of whom will come here for an Alpine holiday of walking, hiking, and relaxation.

TURIN

Turin—in Italian, Torino—is roughly in the center of Piedmont/Valle d'Aosta and is 128 km (80 mi) west of Milan; it is on the Fiume Po River, on the edge of the Po plain that stretches eastward all the way to the Adriatic. Turin's flatness and wide, angular, tree-lined boulevards are a far cry from Italian *metropoli* (cities) to the south; the region's decidedly northern European bent is quite evident in its nerve center. Apart from its role as northwest Italy's major industrial, cultural, and administrative hub, Turin is a center of education, science, and the arts. It also has a reputation as Italy's capital of black magic and the supernatural. This distinction is enhanced by the presence of Turin's most famous, controversial, and unsettling relic, the Sacra Sindone (Holy Shroud), still believed by many Catholics to be the cloth in which Christ's body was wrapped when he was taken down from the cross.

Downtown Turin

Many of Turin's major sights are clustered around Piazza Castello, and others are on or just off the porticoed Via Roma, one of the city's main thoroughfares, which leads 1 km (½ mi) from Piazza Castello south to Piazza Carlo Felice, a landscaped park with a fountain in front of the train station. First opened in 1615, Via Roma was largely rebuilt in the 1930s, during the time of Premier Benito Mussolini.

A Good Walk

Start on Piazza San Giovanni at the **Duomo di San Giovanni** ①, the hushed and shadowy repository of a controversial relic. Step into the **Palazzo Reale** ②, adjacent to the Duomo, to see the sumptuous interiors and, in a separate wing also on Piazza Castello, the **Armeria Reale.** The massive building occupying an entire block at the center of Piazza Castello is **Palazzo Madama** ③ (closed for restoration). In the northwest corner of the same square, take time to observe Guarini's lively architectural vision in the church of **San Lorenzo** ④. Go southwest on Via Roma, a street rebuilt with arcades in the 1930s, during the time of Premier Benito Mussolini. Continuing a few blocks down Via Roma, you come to **Piazza San Carlo** ⑦, with its twin churches of **San Carlo** ⑤ and **Santa Cristina** ⑥. Just off the northeast end of Piazza San Carlo is the imposing **Palazzo dell'Accademia delle Scienze** ⑧, where you may devote upward of an hour or two to the collections in the Museo Egizio and Galleria Sabauda. To the east, across the street is the graceful **Palazzo Carignano** ⑨, not only historic but also an example of Piedmontese Baroque. The east facade of the palace faces Piazza Carlo Alberto, where you turn into Via Po, heading east to Via Montebello, where you turn left to reach the **Mole Antonelliana** ⑩, Turin's oddest and most conspicuous building.

TIMING

This walk takes the better part of a day if you allow plenty of time for the museums. Since it includes the most important of Turin's sights, it can constitute a satisfactory, albeit speedy, visit.

Sights to See

❶ **Duomo di San Giovanni.** The most impressive piece in Turin's 15th-century cathedral is the shadowy, black marble–walled **Cappella della Sacra Sindone** (Chapel of the Holy Shroud), where the Holy Shroud was housed before a fire in 1997. The chapel was designed by the priest and architect Guarino Guarini (1604–83), a genius of the Baroque style

Piedmont/Valle d'Aosta

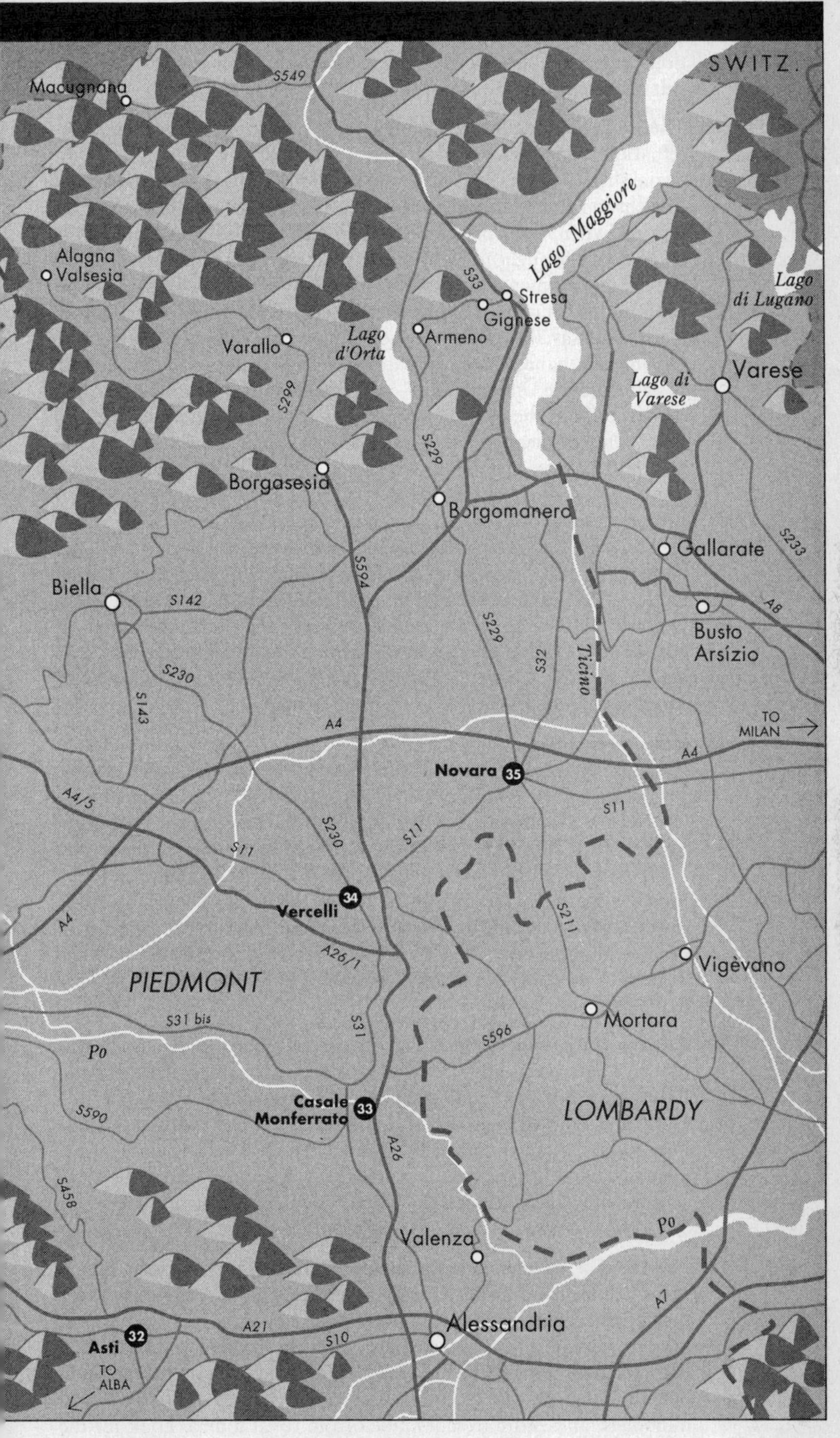

SWITZ.
Macugnana
S549
Alagna Valsesia
Lago Maggiore
Lago di Lugano
S33
Stresa
Gignese
Lago d'Orta
Armeno
Varallo
Lago di Varese
Varese
S299
S229
Borgasesia
Borgomanero
Gallarate
S233
Biella
S142
S594
A8
S229
S32
Ticino
Busto Arsízio
S230
S143
A4
TO MILAN
A4
Novara 35
A4/5
S11
S230
S11
S11
Vercelli 34
S211
A4
A26/1
Vigèvano
PIEDMONT
Mortara
S31 bis
S31
S596
Po
Casale Monferrato 33
S590
LOMBARDY
A26
S458
Po
Valenza
A7
Alessandria
A21
Asti 32
S10
TO ALBA

who was official engineer and mathematician to the court of Duke Carlo Emanuele II of Savoy. The fire was a major setback to ongoing restorations; the chapel is expected to remain closed for many years as a result of the damage.

The Sacra Sindone (Holy Shroud) is a 4-yard-long sheet of linen, unremarkable except for the fact that it is thought by millions to be the burial shroud of Christ, bearing the light imprint of His crucified body. The shroud first made an appearance around the middle of the 15th century, when it was presented to Ludovico of Savoy in Chambéry. In 1578 it was brought to Turin by another member of the Savoy royal family, Duke Emanuele Filiberto. It is only in the last few years that the Catholic Church has allowed rigorous scientific study of the shroud. Needless to say, the results have come in on both sides of the argument. On the one hand, three separate university teams—in Switzerland, Britain, and the United States—have concluded, as a result of carbon 14 dating, that the cloth is a forgery dating from between 1260 and 1390. On the other hand, they are unable to explain how medieval forgers could have created the shroud's image, which is like a photographic negative, and how they could have had the knowledge or means to incorporate traces of Roman coins covering the eyelids and endemic Middle Eastern pollen woven into the cloth. Either way, the shroud continues to be revered as a holy relic. It was on display only four times during the last 100 years, but it will be exhibited again from August 26 to October 22, 2000 to mark the beginning of the third millennium. If you want to catch a glimpse, it is essential to call and reserve a viewing slot well in advance. ✉ *Piazza San Giovanni,* ☎ *011/4361540.* ⏲ *Mon.–Sat. 7–noon and 3–7, Sun. 8–noon and 3–7.*

★ ⑩ **Mole Antonelliana.** You won't miss the unusual square dome and thin, elaborate spire tower of this Turin landmark above the city's rooftops. This odd structure, built between 1863 and 1897, was originally intended to be a synagogue, but costs escalated and eventually it was bought by the city of Turin. In its time it was the tallest building in the world. There is an excellent view of the city, the plain surrounding it, and the Alps beyond from a terrace at the top of the dome. The inside of the tower and the elevator to the top are closed indefinitely for renovations—call the tourist office (☞ Visitor Information *in* Piedmont/Valle d'Aosta A to Z, *below*) for the latest. ✉ *Via Montebello 20,* ☎ *011/8170496.*

⑨ **Palazzo Carignano.** Another one of Guarini's Baroque triumphs, this redbrick palace was built from 1679 to 1685 and is one of Turin's and Italy's most historic buildings. Kings of Savoy, Carlo Alberto (1798–1849) and Vittorio Emanuele II (1820–78), were born within its walls. Italy's first parliament met here from 1860 to 1865. The palace is now inhabited by the **Museo del Risorgimento,** a museum honoring the 19th-century movement for Italian unity. ✉ *Piazza Carignano,* ☎ *011/5621147.* 🎟 *Free.* ⏲ *Tues.–Sat. 9–7, Sun. 9–1.*

⑧ **Palazzo dell'Accademia delle Scienze** (Palace of the Academy of Sciences). Guarini's large Baroque tour de force, prefiguring the 18th century's preoccupation with logic and science, houses two of Turin's most famous museums, the Museo Egizio and the Galleria Sabauda. The **Museo Egizio** (Egyptian Museum) is considered to be one of the finest outside Cairo. Its superb collection includes statues of pharaohs and mummies, and entire frescoes taken from royal tombs. Look for the 13th-century BC statue of Ramses II, which still glistens in its original colors. ✉ *Via Accademia delle Scienze 6,* ☎ *011/5617776.* 🎟 *12,000 lire.* ⏲ *Tues.–Sat. 9–10, Sun. 9–2.*

Borgo Medioevale, **14**
Castello del Valentino, **13**
Duomo di San Giovanni, **1**
Gran Madre di Dio, **11**
Mole Antonelliana, **10**
Museo dell'Automobile, **15**
Palazzo Carignano, **9**
Palazzo dell'Accademia delle Scienze, **8**
Palazzo Madama, **3**
Palazzo Reale, **2**
Piazza San Carlo, **7**
San Carlo, **5**
San Lorenzo, **4**
Santa Cristina, **6**
Santa Maria del Monte, **12**

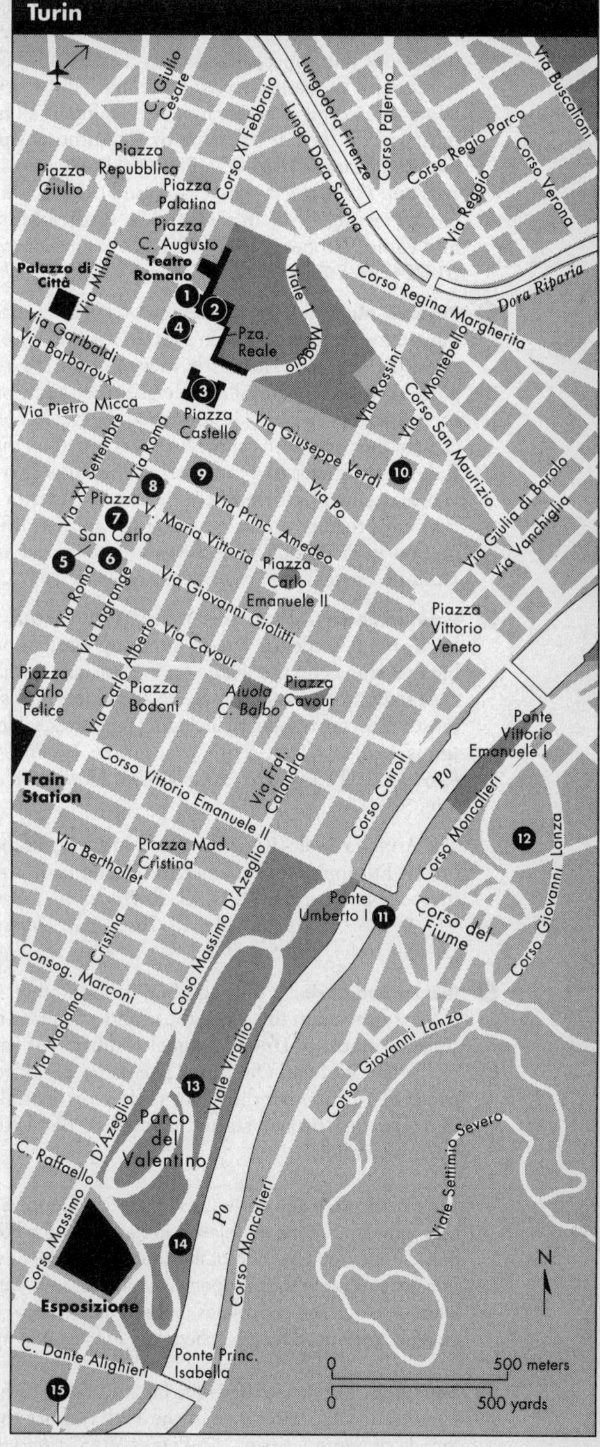

The **Galleria Sabauda** houses the collections of the house of Savoy. It is particularly rich in 16th- and 17th-century Dutch and Flemish paintings: note Jan Van Eyck's (before 1395–1441) *St. Francis with Stigmata,* with the saint receiving the marks of Christ's wounds while a companion cringes beside him as if feeling it all himself. Other Dutch masterpieces include paintings by Sir Anthony Van Dyck (1599–1641) and Rembrandt (1606–69). Piero del Pollaiuolo's (circa 1443–96) *Tobias and the Angel* is showcased, and other Italian artists featured include Fra Angelico (circa 1400–55), Andrea Mantegna (1431–1506), and Paolo Veronese (1528–88). ✉ *Via Accademia delle Scienze 6,* ☎ *011/547440.* 🎫 *8,000 lire.* ⏲ *Fri.–Wed. 9–2, Thurs. 10–7.*

3 **Palazzo Madama.** In the center of Piazza Castello, this castle was named for the French queen Maria Cristina, who made it her home in the 17th century. The castle incorporates the remains of a Roman gate, as well as medieval and Renaissance additions. The architect Filippo Juvarra (1678–1736) designed the castle's elaborate Baroque facade in the early 18th century: he was intent on dispelling the idea that Italy's importance as a producer of contemporary art and architecture was in decline. Unfortunately, the castle's interior is closed for restoration until further notice—contact the tourist office (☞ Visitor Information *in* Piedmont/Valle d'Aosta A to Z, *below*) for an update. ✉ *Piazza Castello.*

2 **Palazzo Reale** (Royal Palace). This 17th-century palace is the former Savoy royal residence. It is an imposing work of brick, stone, and marble that stands on the site of Turin's ancient Roman city gates. In contrast to its austere exterior, the palace's interior is swathed in luxurious, mostly Rococo, trappings, including tapestries, gilded ceilings, and sumptuous 17th- to 19th-century furniture. ✉ *Piazza Castello,* ☎ *011/4361455.* 🎫 *8,000 lire.* ⏲ *Groups of 15 allowed every 40 mins Tues.–Sun. 9–6:15.*

The **Armeria Reale** (Royal Armory), in a wing of the Royal Palace, holds one of Europe's most extensive collections of arms and armor. It is a must-see for connoisseurs. ✉ *Entrance at Piazza Castello 191,* ☎ *011/543889.* 🎫 *8,000 lire.* ⏲ *Tues. and Thurs. 1:30–7; Wed., Fri. (groups only), and Sat. 9–2.*

7 **Piazza San Carlo.** While standing in the stately, formal expanse, you too may proclaim this to be the grandest square in Italy. In the center stands a **statue of Duke Emanuele Filiberto of Savoy,** victor, in 1557, of the battle of San Quintino. The melee heralded the peaceful resurgence of Turin under the Savoys, after years of bloody dynastic fighting. The fine bronze statue, erected in the 19th century, is one of Turin's symbols.

NEED A BREAK?

The historic **Café San Carlo** (✉ Piazza San Carlo) is usually lively with locals, gathered at the marble-top tables under the huge crystal chandelier. On the opposite side of the square, **Stratta,** one of Turin's most famous chocolate shops, open since 1836, sells confections of all kinds—not just the chocolates in the lavish window displays, but fancy cookies, rum-laced fudges, chocolate truffles, and magnificent cakes.

5 **San Carlo.** The ornate Baroque facade of this 17th-century church was enhanced in the latter part of the 19th century to harmonize with the facade of Santa Cristina. ✉ *Piazza San Carlo, entrance to the southern end of the square.*

4 **San Lorenzo.** The cupola and vividly painted interior of this church are standouts. Guarino Guarini was in his mid-sixties when he began

work on the church in 1668, but the sprightly collection of domes, columns, and florid Baroque features seems more the work of a younger architect cutting his teeth with a daring display of mathematical invention. ✉ *Piazza Castello.*

NEED A BREAK? **Baratti e Milano** (✉ Just to the east of Piazza Castello), in the glass-roofed gallery between Via Lagrange and Via Po, is another one of Turin's charming old-world cafés. It's famous for its chocolates, so you can indulge your sweet tooth here or buy some gianduiotti or candied chestnuts to take home to friends.

6 **Santa Cristina.** Built in the mid-17th century, this church received a Baroque-style face-lift by Juvarra in 1715. ✉ *Piazza San Carlo.* ⏲ *Daily 7–12 and 3–7.*

Along the Po

The Po River is narrow and unprepossessing here in Turin, only a hint of the broad and mighty watercourse that it becomes as it flows eastward toward the Adriatic. It is flanked, however, by formidable edifices, a park, and a lovely pedestrian path.

A Good Tour

Start at the east end of Piazza Vittorio Veneto, at the end of Via Po. Cross the river on Ponte Vittorio Emanuele I, the bridge leading to the church of **Gran Madre di Dio** ⑪, a replica of Rome's Pantheon. To reach the church of **Santa Maria del Monte** ⑫, follow Corso Moncalieri south and then wend your way upward to the top of the hill. Then return to Corso Moncalieri and cross the next bridge downstream, Ponte Umberto I, to the **Parco del Valentino,** opened in 1856. One of the city's many pretty pedestrian paths, **Viale Virgilio** runs parallel to the river and leads to the **Castello del Valentino** ⑬, reminiscent of castles on the Loire. Go south on Viale Virgilio to the **Borgo Medioevale** ⑭, replica of a medieval hamlet and castle. From the park, catch a bus or taxi or just keep on walking south on Corso Massimo d'Azeglio to the **Museo dell'Automobile** ⑮, a low modern building that sweeps you into a world of nostalgia for the sleek, glamorous cars of yesteryear.

TIMING

Three hours should be enough to allow you to cover the ground with ease, but if you are an automobile buff, allow well over an hour for the Museo dell'Automobile.

Sights to See

14 **Borgo Medioevale** (Medieval Village). This was a veritable forerunner of today's theme parks. The village, a faithful reproduction of medieval Piedmontese buildings, was created for the Turin Exposition of 1884. A visit here is like stepping back into the Middle Ages, with craftsmen's shops, houses, churches, and stores clustered along narrow streets and lanes. The centerpiece is the **Rocca Medievale,** a medieval castle in the heart of the village. ✉ *By the riverside, southern edge of the Parco del Valentino,* ☎ *011/6699372.* *Rocca Medievale 5,000 lire.* ⏲ *Village: daily 9–8; Rocca Medievale: Tues.–Sun. 9–7.*

13 **Castello del Valentino.** The design of this 17th-century castle, built more for appearance than for defense, is based on models of 16th-century French châteaux. It stands on the left bank of the Po, in the pretty **Parco del Valentino,** laid out in 1856, which includes botanical gardens. The interior is elaborate, with frescoed walls and rich decoration, but is only open for occasional art exhibits; the real attraction of the castle is its riverside setting amid the greenery of the park. ✉ *Parco del Valentino,*

☎ *Castello 011/6692545, botanical gardens 011/6707446.* ⏲ *Castello open for exhibits.*

11 **Gran Madre di Dio** (Great Mother of God). This 19th-century church was built in a neoclassic style based on the Pantheon in Rome. ✉ *East bank of the Po, west of Piazza Castello.* ⏲ *Daily 7–12 and 3–7.*

15 **Museo dell'Automobile** (Car Museum). No visit to car-manufacturing Turin would be complete without a pilgrimage to see perfectly conserved Bugattis, Ferraris, and Isotta Fraschinis. Here you'll get an idea of the importance of FIAT—and automobiles in general—to Turin's economy. There's a collection of antique cars dating from 1893, and displays show how the city has changed over the years as a result of its premier industry. ✉ *Corso Unita d'Italia 40,* ☎ *011/677666.* 🎫 *10,000 lire.* ⏲ *Daily 10–6:20.*

12 **Santa Maria del Monte.** The church and convent standing on top of 150-ft Monte dei Cappuccini date from 1583. Don't be surprised if you find yourself in the middle of a wedding party: local couples often come here to have their pictures taken. *Monte dei Cappuccini, above Corso Montcalieri.* ⏲ *Daily 9–12 and 2:30–6.*

Dining and Lodging

$$$$ ★ ✕ **Del Cambio.** The setting and atmosphere of this town-center restaurant in a palace dating from 1757 is nearly unmatched. It is probably one of Europe's most beautiful and historic restaurants, with decorative moldings, mirrors, and hanging lamps that look just as they did when Italian national hero Cavour dined here more than a century ago. The cuisine draws heavily on Piedmontese tradition and is paired with a wide array of fine Piedmontese wines. Great pastas might include agnolotti in an *arrosto* (roast veal) sauce; the carbonada is another savory treat. ✉ *Piazza Carignano 2,* ☎ *011/546690. Reservations essential. Jacket and tie. AE, DC, MC, V. Closed Sun. and Aug.*

$$$$ ★ ✕ **La Cloche.** This restaurant, stationed up on a hillside overlooking Turin and the Alps, follows the Piemontese tradition of many small courses, with equally careful attention paid to each, which at night numbers into the teens. The decor is typically overdone, with wine bottles, pictures, and pianos covering every inch, but the food is top-notch. Courses might include a typical *corne all'albese* (slivers of raw veal with Parmesan and white truffles) or rabbit pâté. ✉ *Strada Traforo del Pino 106,* ☎ *011/8994213 or 011/8992851.* FAX *011/8981522. Reservations essential. Jacket and tie. AE, DC, MC, V. Closed Mon. and Aug. No dinner Sun.*

$$$–$$$$ ✕ **Balbo.** This relaxing Piedmontese restaurant is elegantly set in an 18th-century palace in Turin's historic center. Some of the more creative takes on traditional regional fare include *tagliatelline al rosso d'uovo con intingolo di verdure, pinoli e uvetta* (fresh pasta with egg yolk, vegetables, pine nuts, and raisins) and *insalata di astice e riso selvaggio* (crawfish and wild rice salad). In spite of Turin's inland position, Balbo has a nice array of seafood. ✉ *Via Andrea Doria 11,* ☎ *011/8395775. Reservations essential. AE, DC, MC, V. Closed Mon. and July 25–Aug. 20.*

$$$ ★ ✕ **La Prima Smarrita.** Intimate and elegant, this restaurant is widely recognized by critics as one of Turin's best. It is on the fringes of the Lingotto neighborhood, a short taxi ride from the city center. Host Moreno Grossi's light, innovative versions of Mediterranean dishes are a departure from the usual Piedmontese fare. Try *tortelli di borragine* (fresh pasta filled with borage and served with fresh tomato sauce) or sea bass with artichokes, potatoes, and olives. And for dessert try the *gianduia* (hazelnut chocolate) mousse. Wine lovers will revel in this restaurant's cellar, one of the best in town. ✉ *Corso Unione Sovietica*

244, ☎ 011/3179657. Reservations essential. Jacket and tie. AE, DC, MC, V. Closed Mon. and sometimes Aug.

$$–$$$ ✕ **Taverna delle Rose.** The cooking of the Piedmont and Veneto regions, with some creative touches, dominates in this quirky restaurant near the train station. One dining room has walls covered with paintings; the other is done in old bricks and candlelight. Specialties include *faraona farcita di carciofi* (guinea fowl stuffed with artichokes) and roast venison with raspberry sauce. From the Veneto comes *bigoli con ragù d'anatra* (whole wheat pasta with duck sauce). ✉ *Via Massena 24,* ☎ *011/538345. AE, DC, MC, V. Closed Sun. and Aug. No lunch Sat.*

$$ ✕ **Da Mauro.** Try the Tuscan dishes in this lively, popular family-run trattoria. Specialties include cannelloni *alla Mirella* (baked with mozzarella cheese, prosciutto, and tomato), *involtini di Gorgonzola* (veal roulades with Gorgonzola cheese and a sauce of peppers and olives), and famous grilled Florentine beef. ✉ *Via Maria Vittoria 21,* ☎ *011/8170604. No credit cards. Closed Mon. and July.*

$$ ✕ **Ostu Bacu.** You'll find this small wood-paneled restaurant, in the same family for three generations, on the edge of town near the autostrada to Milan. Regional Piedmontese dishes are the draw, such as agnolotti and *fritto misto di carne* (a typical Piedmontese specialty of fried mixed meats, vegetables, and sweet morsels). ✉ *Corso Vercelli 226,* ☎ *011/2464579. AE, DC, MC, V. Closed Sun. and Aug.*

$$ ✕ **Tre Galline.** Set in a portion of the ancient Roman wall only a few blocks northwest of Piazza Castello, this trattoria has a long history of serving good Piedmontese cooking. The menu changes regularly, but whatever's available will be flavorfully prepared. The *insalata di gallina* (chicken salad) has the tang of mustard, and the *stinco di vitello* (veal shin) is redolent of thyme. ✉ *Via Bellezia 37,* ☎ *011/4366553. AE, DC, MC, V. Closed Sun. and 1st week Aug. No lunch Mon.*

$–$$ ✕ **Porto di Savona.** Look for this centuries-old tavern under the arcades of vast Piazza Vittorio Veneto, where it once served as a terminal for the Turin–Savona stagecoach line. The small street-level and upstairs dining rooms have a decidedly old-fashioned air; the marble stairs are well worn and the walls are decked with photos of Old Turin. Customers sit at long wooden tables to eat home-style Piedmontese cooking, including gnocchi with the owner's handmade Gorgonzola and *bollito misto* (mixed boiled meats, appropriately served only in winter). The Barbera house wine is good. ✉ *Piazza Vittorio Veneto 2,* ☎ *011/8173500. MC, V. Closed Mon., 1st 2 wks Jan., and last 2 wks Aug. No lunch Tues.*

$ ✕ **Arcardia.** Japanese food, especially sushi, is a rare find in Italy, and until recently, Milan had a near-monopoly. This quiet, centrally located restaurant is Turin's new entry. The restaurant's surprising popularity and inexpensive sushi and sashimi (relative to its Milanese counterparts) is a testimony to the slowly but steadily growing popularity of Asian food in the country. The lunch menu is a particular bargain. ✉ *Galleria Subalpina 16,* ☎ *011/5613898. AE, MC, V. Closed Sun.*

$$$$ 🏨 **Jolly Hotel Principi di Piemonte.** Over a half century old, the central Principi is one of the best hotels in town and often caters to a famous clientele. The rooms, elegantly furnished in antique style, are spacious and light, with high ceilings. ✉ *Via Gobetti 15, 10123,* ☎ *011/5629693,* FAX *011/5620270. 99 rooms, 8 suites. Restaurant, bar, minibars. AE, DC, MC, V.*

$$$ 🏨 **Turin Palace.** You're right across from the train station at this grand, century-old building in the center of town. Quiet, spacious, and well-furnished rooms have high ceilings and feature either leather-and-wood classic modern style or Imperial Louis XV furnishings. ✉ *Via Sacchi 8, 10128,* ☎ *011/5625511,* FAX *011/5612187. 123 rooms. Restaurant, bar, minibars. AE, DC, MC, V.*

$$$ ★ **Victoria.** Uncommon style and comfort are the hallmarks of this boutique hotel, personally decorated and supervised by the caring management to create the atmosphere of a refined town house. The newer wing has a grand marble staircase and rooms individually decorated according to a theme, from romantic to clubby. The same attention to detail is given to the older rooms and to the attractive sitting room and breakfast room overlooking a small park. ✉ *Via Nino Costa 4, 10123,* ☎ *011/5611909,* FAX *011/5611806. 94 rooms, 4 suites. Bar, breakfast room. AE, DC, MC, V.*

$$–$$$ **Liberty.** Liberty is the Italian term that refers to the Art Nouveau style, and this small, conveniently located hotel maintains that style in old-world furnishings and an old-world atmosphere, enhanced by the Anfossi family's attentive courtesy. The hotel is a favorite of academics, artists, and others who appreciate its solid, old-fashioned comfort. You must reserve ahead for the restaurant. ✉ *Via Pietro Micca 15, 10121,* ☎ *011/5628801,* FAX *011/5628163. 35 rooms. Restaurant, bar. AE, DC, MC, V.*

$$ **Genio.** This 120-year-old building is done in a smart, modern style. The rooms are large and bright, with big, comfortable beds. There's no restaurant, but you're in the hub of town center. ✉ *Corso Vittorio Emanuele 47, 10125,* ☎ *011/6505771,* FAX *011/6508264. 100 rooms, 9 suites. Bar, minibars, 2 meeting rooms. AE, DC, MC, V.*

Nightlife and the Arts

The Arts

MUSIC

Classical music concerts are held in the famous **Conservatorio Giuseppe Verdi** (✉ Via Mazzini 11, ☎ 011/8121268, and Piazza Bodoni, ☎ 011/888470) throughout the year, but mainly in the winter months. The **Salone della Musica Torino** (☎ 011/4424715) music festival (September 3–24) also highlights classical music; call for specifics. Sacred music and some modern religious pieces are performed in the **Duomo** (☞ Sights to See, *above*) on Sunday evening; these are usually advertised in the vestibule or in the local edition of Turin's nationally distributed daily, *La Stampa.*

OPERA

The **Teatro Regio** (☎ 011/88151, FAX 011/8815214), one of Italy's leading opera houses, begins its season in December. You can buy tickets for most performances (premieres are sold out well in advance) at the box office.

Nightlife

NIGHTCLUBS

A plush after-hours venue for Turin's smart set, **Hennessy** (✉ Strada Traforo del Pino 23, ☎ 011/8998522) is in a large hotel in the upscale Superga residential district; it's open Thursday, Friday, and Saturday nights until late. The aptly named **Big Club** (✉ Corso Brescia 28, ☎ 011/2485656) is a roomy disco that also hosts rock concerts. Hot Latin music, often live, is dished up with gusto at **Sabor Latino** (✉ Via Stradella 10, ☎ 011/852327). **Pick Up** (✉ Via Barge 8, ☎ 011/4472204) caters to a mixed crowd of young Turinese, university students, and visitors.

Outdoor Activities and Sports

Boating

Turin makes good use of the Po's recreational potential for boating. The **Lega Navale di Torino** (Turin Boating League, ✉ Corso Unione

Sovietica 316, ☎ 011/6197643), open 3:30–7 PM, organizes courses and special races throughout the summer.

Golf

There are several courses in the Turin area. Three 18-hole courses are northwest of the city, one at **La Mandria** (☎ 011/9235719), 18 km (11 mi) northwest, and two at **Fiano Torinese** (☎ 011/9235440), 20 km (12 mi) northwest.

Soccer

Turin's two professional soccer clubs, Juventus and Torino, play their games in the **Stadio delle Alpi** (✉ 6 km/4 mi northwest of city), a stadium that was used during the World Cup of 1990. Until recently, Juventus was one of Italy's best teams, and there is fierce rivalry among its supporters and those of visiting clubs, especially with Inter Milan and AC Milan. Home matches are usually played on Sunday afternoon during the season, which runs from late August to mid-May. The **tourist office** (✉ Via Roma 226, ☎ 011/535901) can provide information on where to find tickets, which are difficult to get.

Shopping

Markets

Go to the famous **Balon Flea Market** (✉ Piazza Repubblica) on a Saturday morning for some excellent bargains in secondhand books and clothing and some stalls selling local specialties such as gianduiotti. The second Sunday of every month, a special **antiques market** sets us shop in Piazza Repubblica.

Specialty Stores

Most people know that Turin produces more than 75% of Italy's cars, but they are often unaware that it is also a clothing manufacturing city. Top-quality boutiques stocking local, national, and international lines are clustered along Via Roma and Via Garibaldi. Piazza San Carlo, Via Po, and Via Maria Vittoria are lined with **antiques shops,** some—but not all—specializing in 18th-century furniture and domestic items.

THE COLLINE AND SAVOY PALACES

Heading west from Turin toward France, into the Colline (little hills), castles and medieval fortifications begin to pepper the former dominion of the House of Savoy, and the Alps come into better and better focus. In the region lie the storybook medieval towns of Avigliana, Rivoli, and Saluzzo, 12th-century abbeys, and farther west and into the mountains, the venerable, if not flashy, ski resorts of Bardonecchia and Sestriere.

Stupinigi

16 *8 km (5 mi) southwest of Turin.*

The **Palazzina di Caccia,** in the town of Stupinigi, is an elaborate building built by Juvarra in 1729 as a hunting lodge for the House of Savoy. It is more like a royal villa, with its many wings, landscaped gardens, and surrounding forests. This regal aspect was not lost on Napoléon, who lived here before claiming the crown of Italy. The castle interior is sumptuously decorated and today houses a collection of art and furniture in the matter-of-factly named **Museo d'Arte e Ammobiliamento** (Museum of Art and Furniture). Take Bus 41 from Stazione Porta Nuova. *Stupinigi,* ☎ *011/3581220.* *10,000 lire.* *Daily 10–4:20.*

Rivoli

17 *16 km (10 mi) north of Stupinigi, 13 km (8 mi) west of Turin.*

The Savoy court was based in Rivoli in the Middle Ages. The 14th- to 15th-century **Casa del Conte Verde,** right in the center of town, is a good example of medieval architecture of the transitional period, when its defensive function was giving way to the decorative. To get to Rivoli, take Tram 1 from downtown Turin, then Bus 36. The 18th-century Savoy castle, built in the Baroque style under the direction of Juvarra, now houses the **Museo d'Arte Contemporaneo** (Modern Art Museum), which contains many examples of 20th-century Italian art. The Futurist movement is particularly well represented. ✉ *Piazzale Masalda di Savoia,* ☎ *011/9581547.* 🎫 *12,000 lire.* ⏲ *Tues.–Fri. 10–5, weekends 10–7, 1st and 3rd Thurs. of month 10–10.*

Abbazia di Sant'Antonio di Ranverso

18 *10 km (6 mi) west of Rivoli, 23 km (14 mi) west of Turin.*

The abbey was originally an abbey hospital, founded in the 12th century by the Hospitalers of St. Anthony to care for victims of St. Anthony's Fire, a crippling disease contracted by eating contaminated grains. Pilgrims came here over the centuries for cures or, sometimes, to offer thanks for a miraculous recovery. The 15th-century fresco decorations, with their lifelike depictions of pilgrims and saints, retain their original colors. ✉ *Buttigliera Alta, Rosta exit off autostrada and Buttigliera Alta exit off S25,* ☎ *011/9367450.* 🎫 *5,000 lire.* ⏲ *Sept.–June, Tues.–Sun. 9–12 and 2–6:30; July and Aug., Tues.–Sun. 9–12 and 2:30–4:30.*

Avigliana

19 *6 km (4 mi) west of the Abbazia di Sant'Antonio di Ranverso, 29 km (18 mi) west of Turin.*

Perhaps due to its attractive setting, medieval Avigliana was a favorite of the Savoys up until the mid-15th century. Medieval houses still line the twisting and narrow streets. **Casa della Porta Ferrata,** on the street of the same name, is a well-preserved example of Piedmont Gothic domestic architecture: notice how the fascination with narrow, pointed arches is carried through even to private houses.

Outdoor Activities and Sports

GOLF

Avigliana has a well-laid-out 18-hole golf course, **Le Fronde** (☎ 011/935083), closed January and February.

Sacra di San Michele

★ 20 *14 km (8½ mi) west of Avigliana, 43 km (27 mi) west of Turin.*

Unless you plan a 14-km (7-mi) day hike from Avigliana, a car is essential for an excursion to the Abbey of St. Michael, perhaps best known as the dramatic setting for Umberto Eco's *The Name of the Rose.* San Michele was built on Monte Pirchiriano in the 11th century to stand out: it is the most prominent location for miles around, and it hangs over a 1,000-m (3,280-ft) bluff. When monks came to enlarge the abbey, they had to build part of the structure on supports more than 90 ft high—an engineering feat that was famous in medieval Europe and still impressive today. By the 12th century, this important abbey controlled 176 churches in Italy, France, and Spain, and one of the abbeys under its influence was Mont Saint-Michel in France. Because of the abbey's strategic position, it came under numerous attacks over the next five centuries, and it was eventually abandoned in 1622. It was restored in the late 19th and early 20th centuries.

From **Porta dello Zodiaco,** a splendid Romanesque doorway decorated with the signs of the zodiac, you climb 150 steps, past 12th-century sculptures, to reach the church. On the left side of the interior 16th-century frescoes are religious subjects representing New Testament themes; on the right are stories depicting the founding of the church. Go down to the crypt to see the 9th- to 12th-century chapels. *4,000 lire. Apr.–Sept., Tues.–Sun. 9:30–12:30 and 3–7; Oct.–Mar., Tues.–Sun. 9:30–12:30 and 3–6.*

Saluzzo

21 *58 km (36 mi) southwest of Turin.*

Saluzzo is a well-preserved medieval gem. The older and more interesting part of the town hugs a hilltop in the Po Valley and is crowned by a castle. This town of time-worn russet brick was once a flourishing medieval center and was seat of a ducal court during the Renaissance. The narrow, winding streets and frescoed houses, the Gothic cathedral and the church of **San Giovanni,** and the 15th-century **Casa Cavassa,** a richly decorated palace that now houses a museum, take you back in time to the age of chivalry.

Knights and damsels of old, heroes and heroines of an allegorical poem written by Marquis Tommaso III of Saluzzo, humanist lord of the castle, parade in full costume in the 15th-century frescoes in the **Sala del Barone** (Baron's Hall) of the **Castello di Manta** (Castle of Manta), only 4 km (2½ mi) south of Saluzzo. The castle's exterior is austere, but inside are frescoes and other interior decorations. ✉ *Via al Castello, Manta,* ☎ *0175/87822. 6,000 lire. Tues.–Sun. 10–1 and 2–6. Closed last 2 wks in Dec.–Jan.*

Sestriere

22 *32 km (20 mi) east of Briançon, 93 km (58 mi) west of Turin.*

In the early 1930s, before skiing became a sport for the commoners, the patriarch of the FIAT automobile dynasty had this resort built, with two distinctive tower hotels and ski facilities that have been developed into some of the best in the Alps. The resort lacks the charm of other, older Alpine centers, overdevelopment added some eyesores, and the mountains don't have the striking beauty of those in the Valle d'Aosta. But skiers have an excellent choice of trails, some of them crossing the border into France.

Lodging

$$$$ **Principi di Piemonte.** Large and elegant, this luxurious hotel is on the slopes above the town, near the lifts and golf course. Its secluded location heightens the sense of exclusivity, a quality appreciated by a very stylish clientele. The restaurant and a cozy bar invite après-ski relaxation. ✉ *Via Sauze, 10058,* ☎ *0122/7941,* FAX *0122/755411. 95 rooms, 5 suites. Restaurant, bar. AE, DC, MC, V. Closed Easter–May and Sept.–Nov.*

$$ **Miramonti.** Nearly every room has a terrace at this pleasant, central, modern chalet. The ample, comfortable rooms are done in traditional mountain style, featuring lots of wood paneling and coordinated floral-print fabrics. ✉ *Via Cesana 3, 10058,* ☎ *0122/755333,* FAX *0122/755375. 30 rooms. Restaurant, bar, minibars. DC, MC, V.*

Outdoor Activities and Sports

GOLF

Sestriere's 18-hole **golf course** (☎ 0122/755170) is open from mid-June to mid-September.

SKIING

At 6,670 ft, this resort was built in the late 1920s under the auspices of Turin's Agnelli clan. Although it's near the French border, it is just 93 km (58 mi) west of Turin. The slopes get good snow some years from November through May, others from February through May. A quaint village with slate-roof houses, **Claviere** (✉ 17 km/11 mi west of Sestriere) is one of Italy's oldest ski resorts. Its slopes overlap with those of the French resort of Montgenèvre.

Bardonecchia

23 *36 km (22 mi) northwest of Sestriere, 89 km (55 mi) west of Turin.*

This sunny town is one of Italy's oldest winter ski resorts, attracting hardy sports enthusiasts from Turin ever since the 1920s. It is near the entrance to the Fréjus train and automobile tunnels.

Lodging

$$ ★ **Asplenia.** Skiers love this small, modern version of a mountain chalet, near the town center and the ski lifts. The ample rooms are comfortably furnished, with a small entryway and a balcony affording beautiful views. ✉ *Viale della Vittoria 31, 10052,* ☎ *0122/999870,* FAX *0122/96192. 19 rooms, 4 suites. MC, V. Closed Easter–May and Sept.–Nov.*

$$ **Des Geneys-Splendid.** One of the best hotels in the area is in a private park near the town center. Its 1930s style is evident in the arched windows on the ground floor, the stucco walls, and the long wrought-iron balconies. The public rooms are spacious and comfortable, and there's a playroom for children. ✉ *Via Einaudi 21, 10052,* ☎ *0122/99001,* FAX *0122/999295. 57 rooms. Restaurant, bar. DC, MC, V. Closed mid-Apr.–mid-June and mid-Sept.–mid-Dec.*

$$ **Riky.** This central, modern hotel has lots to offer: good service, comfy and spacious rooms, a good restaurant, and pleasant public rooms, including a children's playroom equipped with video games. There's a solarium and a piano bar with a cozy fireplace. It caters mainly to longer stays at half-board rates, and offers excellent low-season rates (nearly half price) for people staying at least a week. ✉ *Via della Vittoria 22, 10052,* ☎ *0122/999353,* FAX *0122/980580. 76 rooms. Restaurant, bar, piano bar, recreation room, video games. AE, DC, V. Closed Apr.–June and Sept.–mid-Dec. MAP.*

VALLE D'AOSTA, THE MATTERHORN, AND MONT BLANC

The unspoiled beauty of the highest peaks in the Alps competes with the magnificent scenery of Italy's oldest national park in the Valle d'Aosta, a semiautonomous, French-speaking region tucked away at the border with France and Switzerland. Luckily, you don't have to choose—the region is small, so you can fit ski, après-ski, and wild ibex into one memorable trip. The main Aosta Valley, largely on an east–west axis, is hemmed in by high mountains where glaciers have gouged out 14 tributary valleys, six to the north and eight to the south. A car is very helpful here, but take care: distances here are relative, short horizontally, as the crow flies, and much longer vertically, on steep slopes over winding roads.

En Route Coming up from Turin, beyond Ivrea, the road takes you through countryside that becomes hillier and hillier, passing through steep ravines guarded by brooding, romantic castles. Pont St. Martin, about 18 km (11 mi) north of Ivrea, is the beginning of French-speaking territory.

Bard

24 *65 km (40 mi) north of Turin.*

A few minutes beyond the French-speaking village of Pont St. Martin, you pass through the narrow Gorge de Bard and reach the **Forte di Bard** (closed to the public), a 19th-century reconstruction of a fort that stood for eight centuries, serving the Savoys for six of them. In 1800 Napoléon entered Italy through this valley and used the cover of darkness to get his artillery units past the castle unnoticed. Ten years later he remembered this inconvenience and had the fortress destroyed.

St. Vincent

25 *28 km (17 mi) north of Bard, 93 km (58 mi) north of Turin.*

The town of St. Vincent has been a popular spa resort since the late 18th century. Its main game these days is the **Casinò de la Vallée,** one of Europe's largest gambling casinos. Remember to pack your black tie—and plenty of lire.

Dining and Lodging

$$$$ ★ ✕ **Batezar.** With only eight tables, this restaurant is considered by some to be one of Italy's best. The ambience is rustic yet elegant, with arches and beamed ceilings enhanced by local antiques and fine crystal and silver place settings. The menu is seasonal Valdostana and Piemontese, with the accent on mushrooms, fish, and truffles, and the chef prepares set menus if you have trouble choosing. For a starter, try the *tazzarella* (a small pizza with porcini mushrooms, mozzarella, and truffles) or fettuccine with herbs, artichokes, and fillet of rabbit. Book well in advance for weekends. ✉ *Via Marconi 1, steps from casino,* ☎ *0166/513164. Reservations essential. Jacket and tie. AE, DC, MC, V. Closed Wed., June 10–30, and Nov. 15–30. No lunch weekdays.*

$$$$ 🏨 **Billia.** A luxury belle-epoque hotel with pseudo-Gothic touches, the Billia is in a park in the middle of town and connected directly to the casino by a passageway. Half the rooms are done in modern and half in period decor, replete with all creature comforts. The hotel has extensive facilities, including a conference center and a private fishing reserve on a nearby mountain stream. ✉ *Viale Piemonte 72, 11027,* ☎ *0166/5231,* FAX *0166/523799. 239 rooms, 6 suites. 3 restaurants, bar, pool, sauna, tennis courts, health club, fishing, billiards, casino, nightclub, convention center. AE, DC, MC, V.*

$–$$ 🏨 **Elena.** The central location is the selling point of this hotel near the casino. The spacious rooms, some with balconies and/or king-size beds, are decorated with color-coordinated fabrics in a comfortable modern style and have air-conditioning. ✉ *Via Biavaz 2 (Piazza Zerbion), 11027,* ☎ *0166/512140,* FAX *0166/537459. 48 rooms. Restaurant, bar. AE, DC, MC, V.*

Breuil-Cervinia

26 *30 km (18 mi) north of St. Vincent, 116 km (72 mi) north of Turin.*

Breuil-Cervinia is a village at the base of the Matterhorn (Monte Cervino, in Italian; Mont Cervin in French). Like the village, the famous peak straddles the border between Italy and Switzerland, and all sightseeing and skiing facilities are operated jointly. Splendid views of the peak can be seen from **Plateau Rosa** and the **Cresta del Furggen,** both of which can be reached by cable car from the center of Breuil-Cervinia. While many locals complain that the tourist facilities and the condominiums in the village have changed the face of their beloved Breuil, most would agree that the cable car has given them access to climbing and off-trail skiing in ridges that were once inaccessible.

Dining and Lodging

$$–$$$ ✕ **Cime Bianche.** This calm, quiet restaurant-inn-mountain lodge is one of the few dining spots in town to offer regional Valdostana cuisine in a rustic setting. The wood beams and tables are reminiscent of a lodge, only meals are much less chaotic than your average apres-ski affairs. The commanding view covers the Matterhorn and Grandes Murailles. Reservations are strongly recommended. ✉ *Località La Vieille, toward the ski area, near the base lift,* ☎ *0166/949046. MC, V. Closed Mon. and mid-May–mid-July.*

$$$ ★ ✕🏨 **Les Neiges D'Antan.** In a pine wood at Perrères, just outside Cervinia, this small, rustic family-run inn is quiet and cozy, with lots of wood, three big fireplaces, and a nice view of the Matterhorn. There are no TVs in the rooms: "It disturbs the atmosphere," says one of the proprietors. An excellent restaurant serves local specialties, such as fonduta, *zuppa Valpellinentze* (a peasant soup of bread, cabbage, and Fontina cheese), and an opulent antipasto (local salami, country pâté, and tomino cheese). ✉ *Località Perrères, 3½ km (2 mi) outside Cervinia, 11021,* ☎ *0166/948775,* FAX *0166/948852. 28 rooms. Restaurant, bar. AE, MC, V. Closed May 15–June 25 and Sept. 8–Dec. 5.*

$$$$ ★ 🏨 **Hermitage.** A marble relief of St. Theodolus at the entrance reminds you that this was the site of the saint's hermitage. But asceticism has given way to sybaritic comfort and elegance in what is now one of the most exclusive hotels in this Alpine region. It has the look and atmosphere of a relaxed but posh family chalet, with a fire always glowing in the enormous hearth and a romantic, candlelit dining room. The decor includes rustic antiques, petit-point upholstery, and the Neyroz family's collection of paintings of the Matterhorn. The bright bedrooms have balconies; suites have antique fireplaces and 18th-century furnishings. ✉ *Strada Cristallo, 11021,* ☎ *0166/948998,* FAX *0166/949032. 36 rooms. Restaurant, bar, indoor pool, sauna, health club, meeting rooms. AE, DC, MC, V. Closed May–June and Sept.–Nov.*

$$$–$$$$ 🏨 **Bucaneve.** This small, central hotel, catering to longer stays, is decorated in typical mountain style, with lots of wood paneling throughout, cheery floral upholstery in spacious lounges, and terraces dripping with geraniums. Après-ski, there's a restaurant (with half board) and a cozy bar with a big fireplace and pianist in the evening. ✉ *Piazza Jumeaux 10, 11021,* ☎ *0166/949119,* FAX *0166/948308. 19 rooms, 7 suites. Restaurant, bar, piano bar, sauna, exercise room. AE, MC, V. Closed May–mid-June and Sept.–Oct. MAP.*

$$$–$$$$ 🏨 **Gran Hotel Cristallo.** An elegantly modern hotel high above town, the Cristallo has spectacular views. You can try local specialties like fonduta at the two restaurants and relax poolside year-round in this place noted for its feeling of pampered comfort. ✉ *Via Piolet 6, 11021,* ☎ *0166/943411,* FAX *0166/948377. 92 rooms, 15 suites. 2 restaurants, 2 bars, indoor pool, outdoor pool, 2 tennis courts, health club, 2 meeting rooms. AE, DC, MC, V. Closed May–June and Sept.–Nov.*

$$$ 🏨 **Chalet Valdotain.** About 2 km (1 mi) outside the town on the road from Châtillon, this Alpine chalet has wooden balconies and snug rooms with terrific views of the Matterhorn. It is known for good food and a friendly atmosphere. ✉ *Località Lago Bleu 2, 11021,* ☎ *0166/949428,* FAX *0166/948874. 35 rooms. Restaurant, bar, pool, sauna, exercise room. AE, MC, V. Closed May and mid-Sept.–Nov.*

Outdoor Activities and Sports

CLIMBING

Serious climbers can make the ascent of the Matterhorn from Breuil-Cervinia after registering with the local mountaineering officials at the tourist office (☞ Visitor Information *in* Piedmont/Valle d'Aosta A to Z, *below*). This climb is for skilled and experienced climbers only.

SKIING

Because its slopes border the Cervino glacier, this resort at the foot of the Matterhorn offers year-round skiing.

Castello Fénis

★ 27 *11 km (7 mi) west of St. Vincent, 104 km (65 mi) north of Turin.*

The best-preserved fortress in the Valle d'Aosta, the many-turreted castle of Castello Fénis was built in the mid-14th century by Aimone di Challant, a member of a prolific family that was related to the Savoys. This castle is the sort imagined by schoolchildren, with pointed turrets, portcullises, and spiral staircases. The 15th-century courtyard has a stairway leading to a loggia (open walkway) with wooden balconies. Inside you can see the medieval kitchen, with much of the original cooking equipment, and a collection of weapons in the armory. If you have time to visit only one castle in the Valle d'Aosta, this should be it, even though parts of it may be closed for restoration. ☎ *0165/764263.* 🎫 *6,000 lire.* ⏲ *Apr.–Sept., Wed.–Mon. 9–6:30 (25-person tour every ½ hr); Oct.–Mar., daily 10–5 (25-person tour every hr).*

En Route The highway continues climbing through the Valle d'Aosta to the town of Aosta itself. The road at this point is heading almost due west, with rivulets from the wilderness reserve Parco Nazionale del Gran Paradiso streaming down from the left to join the Dora Baltea River, one of the major tributaries of the Po. Be careful driving here in late spring, when melting snow can turn some of these streams into torrents.

Aosta

28 *12 km (7 mi) west of Castello Fénis, 113 km (70 mi) north of Turin.*

Aosta stands at the junction of two important trade routes from France to Italy—from the valleys of the Rhône and the Isère. Its significance as a trading post was recognized by the Romans, who built a garrison here in the 1st century BC. The present-day layout of streets in this small city, tucked away in the Alps more than 644 km (400 mi) from Rome, is the clearest example of Roman street planning in Italy. Well-preserved Roman walls form a perfect rectangle around the center of Aosta, and the regular pattern of streets reflects its role as a military stronghold. St. Anselm was born in Aosta, and later became archbishop of Canterbury in England. At the eastern entrance to town, in the Piazza Arco d'Augusto commanding a fine view over Aosta and the mountains, is the **Arco di Augusto** (Arch of Augustus), built in 25 BC to mark Rome's victory over the Celtic Salassi tribe. The sloping roof, quite clearly, is not original—an early effort at preservation of the site, it was added in 1716 in an attempt to keep rain from seeping between the stones.

The **Collegiata di Sant'Orso** (Collegiate Church of St. Orso) is the sort of church that has layers of history in its architecture. Originally there was a 6th-century chapel on this site, founded by the Archdeacon Orso, a local saint. Most of this structure was destroyed or hidden when an 11th-century church was erected over it. This church, in turn, was encrusted with Gothic, and later Baroque, features, leaving the church a jigsaw puzzle of styles, but, surprisingly, not a chaotic jumble. The

11th-century features are almost untouched in the crypt, and if you go up the stairs on the left from the main church you can see the 11th-century frescoes (ask the sacristan for entrance). These restored frescoes depict the life of Christ and the Apostles: although only the tops are visible, you can see the expressions on the faces of the disciples. Take the outside doorway to the right of the church's main entrance to see the crowning glory of Sant'Orso, the 12th-century **cloister.** Next to the church, it is enclosed by some 40 stone columns with masterfully carved capitals representing Old and New Testament themes and scenes from the life of St. Orso. The turrets and spires of Aosta peek out above. ✉ *Via Sant'Orso,* ☎ *0165/362026.* ⏲ *Wed.–Fri. and Sun. 9:30–noon and 2–5:30, Sat. 9–7.*

The huge **Roman Porta Pretoria,** regally guarding over the city, is a remarkable relic of the Roman era. The area between the inner and outer gates was used as a mini–parade ground for the changing of the guard. ✉ *Western end of Via Sant'Anselmo.*

The 72-ft-high ruin of the facade of the **Teatro Romano** (Roman Theater) guards the ruins of the 1st-century BC **amphitheater,** which once held 20,000 spectators. Only a bit of the outside wall and seven of the amphitheater's original 60 arches remain, and these are built onto the facade of the adjacent convent of the sisters of San Giuseppe. The convent usually allows visitors in to see these arches (ask at the entrance or call to set up in advance). ✉ *Via de Baillage,* ☎ *0165/362149.*

Aosta's **Duomo** dates from the 10th century, but all that remains from that period are the campaniles. The decoration inside is mainly Gothic, but the main attraction of the cathedral predates that era by 1,000 years: a carved ivory diptych (devotional work with two images) showing the Roman Emperor Honorius and dating from AD 406 is among the many ornate objects housed in the **treasury.** ✉ *Via Monsignor de Sales,* ☎ *0165/40251.* ⏲ *Treasury Mon.–Sat. 10–noon and 3–6, Sun. 3–5:45.*

Dining and Lodging

$$ ★ ✕ **Piemonte.** A small restaurant in the center of town, the Piemonte has a welcoming atmosphere and rustic decor. Heartwarming dishes might include *crespelle alla valdostana* (crepes with cheese and ham) and *camoscio* (chamois) with polenta. ✉ *Via Porta Pretoria 13,* ☎ *0165/40111. MC, V. Closed Sun. and Feb.*

$$ ✕ **Vecchio Ristoro.** The chef-proprietor of this central converted mill furnished with antiques and a large ceramic stove takes pride in creative versions of regional favorites. Among them may be *petto di faraona in crosta* (breast of guinea hen in a crisp potato crust) and *pizzoccheri* (buckwheat pasta), a specialty of his native Lombardy. ✉ *Via Tourneuve 4,* ☎ *0165/33238. AE, DC, MC, V. Closed Sun. No lunch Mon.*

$ ✕ **La Brasserie du Commerce.** Small, lively, and informal, this place is in the heart of Aosta, near central Piazza E. Chanoux. On a sunny summer day try to get a table on the terrace. Typical valley dishes, such as fonduta, are on the menu, together with a wide range of vegetable dishes and salads. ✉ *Via de Tillier 10,* ☎ *0165/35613. Reservations not accepted. AE, DC, MC, V. Closed Sun.*

$ ✕ **Taverna Nando.** A wine cellar with wooden floors and vaulted ceilings, this family-run tavern is in the center of Aosta, and it has a terrace for outdoor dining. Try regional specialties such as fonduta, carbonada, and *cervo* (venison) with mushrooms. Reservations are recommended. ✉ *Via de Tillier 41,* ☎ *0165/44455. AE, DC, MC, V. Closed Mon. and June 20–July 10.*

$$$ **Holiday Inn Aosta.** This modern, comfortable, and highly regarded hotel has the advantages of a central location and rooms with the chain's predictable amenities. There's local color, however, in the attractive Provençal fabrics and the views of the mountains. There are rooms equipped for people with disabilities. ✉ *Corso Battaglione Aosta 30, 11100,* ☎ *0165/236356,* FAX *0165/236337. 45 rooms, 5 suites. Restaurant, bar. AE, DC, MC, V.*

$$ ★ **Milleluci.** A small, cozy, family-run hotel, Milleluci is set in its own garden on a hillside overlooking Aosta, next to Castello Jocteau and with good views of the city and mountains. A huge brick hearth and rustic wooden beams highlight the lounge. Bedrooms are bright, with prints *de Provence* and attractive wood fittings. The hotel provides breakfast only. ✉ *Località Roppoz 15, 11100,* ☎ *0165/235278,* FAX *0165/235284. 15 rooms. Bar, tennis court. AE, MC, V.*

Nightlife and the Arts

Each summer a series of **concerts** is held in different venues around the city. Organ recitals in July and August attract performers of world renown. Call the **tourist board** (✉ Piazza E. Chanoux 8, ☎ 0165/236627) for information.

Shopping

Aosta and the surrounding countryside are famous for wood carvings and wrought-iron work. There is a permanent **crafts exhibition** in the arcades of Piazza E. Chanoux, in the heart of Aosta; it's a good place to pick up a bargain. Each year, on the last two days of January, the whole town turns out for the **Sant'Orso Fair,** when all sorts of crafts are on sale, including handmade lace from nearby Cogne, carved wood and stonework, and brightly colored woolens.

Courmayeur

★ 29 *35 km (21 mi) northwest of Aosta, 150 km (93 mi) northwest of Turin.*

The main attraction of Courmayeur is a knock-'em-dead view of Europe's tallest peak, Monte Bianco, better known as Mont Blanc. The jet-set celebrities who flock here are following a tradition that dates from the late 17th century, when Courmayeur's natural springs first began to draw visitors. The scenic spectacle of the Alps gradually surpassed the springs as the biggest drawing point (the Alpine letters of the English poet Shelley were almost advertisements for the region), but the biggest change in the history of Courmayeur came in 1965, when the Mont Blanc tunnel opened. (The tunnel was closed indefinitely at press time due to a devastating fire in March, 1999; for alternatives ☞ Arriving and Departing, By Car *in* Piedmont/Valle d'Aosta A to Z, *below.*) Thus, not only does Courmayeur attract much of northern Italy's vacationing elite, but it also now stands on one of the main routes from France into Italy. Luckily, planners have managed to keep some restrictions on wholesale development within the town, and its angled rooftops and immaculate cobblestone streets maintain a cozy (if prepackaged) feel. There is no train directly into Courmayeur, so if you don't have a car, you'll have to bus it from nearby Pré-Saint-Didier, accessible by train from Aosta.

Dining and Lodging

$$–$$$ ★ ✕ **Cadran Solaire.** This warm and inviting restaurant in town center, in what was the oldest tavern in Courmayeur, has been renovated by the Garin family, owners of the Maison de Filippo (☞ Monte Bianco, *below*), to highlight the 17th-century stone vault, old wooden floor, and huge fireplace. The menu offers seasonal specialties and innova-

tive interpretations of regional dishes, such as gnocchi *gratinati* (potato and ricotta dumplings) and *filetto di trota alle nocciole* (fillet of trout with hazelnuts). The stylish bar-lounge is also a relaxing place for a before-dinner drink. ✉ *Via Roma 122,* ☎ *0165/844609. AE, DC, MC, V. Reservations essential. Closed Tues., May, and Oct.*

$–$$ ★ ✕ **Snack Bar du Tunnel.** This cozy restaurant near the center of town had to convert one room into two neck-ducking minifloors in order to accommodate some more of the hungry throngs who show up each night and beg for tables. Still, many are turned away. Those in the know come from miles around for the pizza, which is by consensus among the best in northern Italy. Valdostana specialties, such as carbonada with polenta, are also served. Reserve at least two days in advance. ✉ *Via Circonvallazione 80,* ☎ *0165/841705. Reservations essential. AE, DC, MC, V. Closed 2nd half of June; closed Wed. Easter–Oct. No lunch Wed.*

$$$$ ✕🏨 **Royal.** A grand Courmayeur landmark in the town center, the Royal rises high above the modest surrounding townscape. Decorated with terraces, flowers, and wood paneling, it is the most elegant and upscale spot in town, with modern rooms and an evening piano bar. The hotel caters to longer stays with half- or full-board service. The restaurant, Grill Royal e Golf, is a sight in itself, locally renowned for its culinary creations like frog's legs in a basil fish broth. Reservations are required at the restaurant, which is open for dinner only and is closed Monday. ✉ *Via Roma 87, 11013,* ☎ *0165/846787,* FAX *0165/842093. 71 rooms, 15 suites. Restaurant, bar, piano bar, minibars, pool, sauna, health club. Jacket and tie at restaurant. AE, DC, MC, V. Closed wk after Easter–mid-June and mid-Sept.–Dec. 1. FAP, MAP.*

$$$–$$$$ 🏨 **Pavillon.** This is an elegant modern version of rustic chalet architecture, complete with warm golden-toned wood paneling, stylish furnishings, a clubby bar, and some stunning contemporary stained glass in the public areas and in the well-equipped health center. Full-board rates are a good value. ✉ *Strada Regionale 62, 11013,* ☎ *0165/846120,* FAX *0165/846122. 40 rooms, 10 suites. Restaurant, bar, indoor pool, sauna, health club, meeting room. AE, DC, MC, V. Closed May–June 15 and Oct. 8–Nov. FAP.*

$$$ 🏨 **Cresta et Duc.** A bright, modern Alpine hotel in town center, the Cresta features plenty of wooden terraces, flowers, and wooden furnishings. For fun and relaxation there's a billiards room and lounges. The rooms are large and warm, and the hotel offers good full- and half-board rates. Be forewarned that Alpine Adventures, an American package-tour group, books up large blocks of rooms for much of the winter, dominating both the reservation list and the social atmosphere. ✉ *Via Circonvallazione 7, 11013,* ☎ *0165/842585,* FAX *0165/842591. 39 rooms. Restaurant, bar, minibars, billiards. AE, DC, MC, V. Closed Easter–June and mid-Sept.–mid-Dec. MAP, FAP.*

$$$ ★ 🏨 **Palace Bron.** Set in a lovely pinewood above the town, this posh, comfortable hotel is an ideal spot to relax. Guest rooms are bright and pretty, furnished with period pieces and local designs. The sitting room has picture windows with magnificent views of Mont Blanc, and for chilly winter nights, the recommended restaurant offers a cozy fireplace. There's a free shuttle between the hotel, town center, and ski lifts. ✉ *Via Plan Gorret 41, 11013,* ☎ *0165/846742,* FAX *0165/844015. 27 rooms. Restaurant, bar, piano bar, minibars, meeting room. AE, DC, MC, V. Closed May–June and Oct.–Nov.*

$$ 🏨 **Croux.** This bright, comfortable hotel is near the town center on the road leading to Mont Blanc. Friendly management makes it feel like a more intimate place for its size. Half the rooms have balconies, the other half have great views of Mont Blanc. ✉ *Via Circonvallazione 94, 11013,* ☎ *0165/846735,* FAX *0165/845180. 33 rooms. Bar. AE, DC, MC, V. Closed mid-Apr.–June and Sept. 15–Dec. 20.*

Monte Bianco (Mont Blanc)

30 *3 km (2 mi) north of Courmayeur.*

At La Palud you can catch the cable car up to the top of Monte Bianco. In the summertime, if you get the inclination, once up top you can switch cable cars and descend into Chamonix in France. In winter, you can ski parts of the route off-piste. The Funivie La Palud whisks you up to the viewing platform at **Punta (Pointe) Helbronner** (more than 11,000 ft), which is also the border post with France. Mont Blanc's attraction is not so much its shape (much less distinctive than the Matterhorn) as its expanse and the vistas from the top. The next stage, on the **Telepherique de L'Aiguille du Midi,** as you pass into French territory, is particularly impressive: you dangle over a huge glacial snowfield (more than 2,000 ft below) and make your way slowly to the viewing station above Chamonix. It is one of the most dramatic rides in Europe. From this point you're looking down into France, and if you change cable cars at the Aiguille du Midi station, you can make your way down to Chamonix itself. The return trip covers the same route, and the total time should be 90 minutes, weather permitting. Schedules are unpredictable; call in advance or inquire at the Courmayeur tourist office (☞ Visitor Information *in* Piedmont/Valle d'Aosta A to Z, *below*). ✉ *Funivie La Palud,* ☎ *0165/89925 for the Italian side (La Palud); 33/04/50536210 for the French side (Aiguille du Midi).* 🎫 *46,000 lire round-trip to Punta Helbronner; 110,000 lire to complete the ride to Aiguille du Midi and back to La Palud; 290 FF from Punta Helbronner to Chamonix and back.* ⏲ *Hrs change throughout year: daily from 7:20 to 8:50 AM–4:20 to 5:50 PM (Aug. 24–July 24, closed 12:40–2). Jan.–Mar., closed daily 1–2; closed mid-Oct.–mid-Dec., depending on demand.*

Dining and Lodging

$$ ✕ **Maison de Filippo.** Here you'll find country-style home cooking in a picturesque mountain house furnished with antiques. Reserve in advance, for it's one of the most popular restaurants in the Valle d'Aosta. There is a set menu only, featuring a daily selection of specialties including a wide choice of antipasti and pasta dishes, such as agnolotti in various sauces and spaghetti *affumicata* (with salami and bacon). ✉ *Entreves,* ☎ *0165/869797,* FAX *0165/869705. Reservations essential. MC, V. Closed Tues., June, and Nov.–mid-Dec.*

$–$$ ✕🏨 **Rifugio Montebianco Cai-Uget.** You won't find a more dramatic setting for a lodge or a restaurant than this ski-in/ski-out refuge, set at 1,666 m (5,464 ft) along the Courmayeur ski slopes with a sweeping vista of the peak. Surprisingly for such an unassuming, Club Alpino Italiano–run locale, the food is spectacularly good—you can enjoy traditional Valle d'Aostan dishes like *polenta con funghi selvaggi e salsiccia* (hot polenta with wild mushrooms and local sausage) at picnic tables outside or in the warmer dining room. The refuge offers very basic ($) rooms with up to six beds and shared bathrooms, a good choice for hardy skiers who want to stay on the mountain itself and aren't fussy about creature comforts. ✉ *Val Veny, Courmayeur, near the top of the Zerotta lift, 11013,* ☎ *0165/869097. 16 without bath. Restaurant, ski storage. MC, V.*

Outdoor Activities and Sports

SKIING

The famous Courmayeur, for the well-heeled, is well equipped and easy to reach, just outside the Italian end of the Mont Blanc tunnel (not passable at press time; ☞ Arriving and Departing, By Car *in* Piedmont/Valle d'Aosta A to Z, *below*). With only 24 trails, Courmayeur pales in comparison to its French neighbor, Chamonix, in both number and quality of trails. However, especially with good natural snow cover, trails and alpine vistas are nevertheless spectacular. A huge gondola leads from the center of Courmayeur to Plan Checrouit, from where gondolas and lifts lead to the actual ski slopes. The skiing around Mont Blanc is particularly good, and the off-piste options are among the best in Europe. The off-piste routes from Cresta d'Arp (the local peak) to Dolonne, and from the La Palud area into France, should be done with a guide (☞ Guided Tours *in* Piedmont/Valle d'Aosta A to Z, *below*).

Cogne and the Parco Nazionale del Gran Paradiso

31 *52 km (32 mi) southeast of Courmayeur, 134 km (83 mi) northwest of Turin.*

Cogne is the gateway to the Parco Nazionale del Gran Paradiso. This huge park, once the domain of King Vittorio Emanuele II (1820–78) and bequeathed to the nation after World War I, is one of Europe's most rugged and unspoiled wilderness areas, with wildlife and many plant species protected by law. Try to visit in May, when spring flowers are in bloom and most of the meadows are clear of snow. This is one of the few places in Europe where you can see the ibex (a mountain goat with horns up to 3 ft long) or the chamois, a small soft-skin antelope.

Outdoor Activities and Sports

HIKING

There's wonderful hiking to be done here, both on daylong excursions and longer journeys with overnight stops in the park's mountain refuges. The Cogne tourist office (☞ Visitor Information *in* Piedmont/Valle d'Aosta, *below*) has a wealth of information and trail maps to help.

FORTIFIED CITIES OF THE PO PLAIN

Southeast of Turin, in the hilly wooded area around Asti known as the Monferrato and farther south in a similar area around Alba known as the Langhe, the rolling landscape is a patchwork of vineyards spotted with dark woods and dotted with little hill towns and castles. This is wine country, producing some of Italy's most famous reds and sparkling whites. And hidden away in the woods are the secret places where hunters and their dogs unearth the precious, aromatic truffles worth their weight in gold at Alba's truffle fair. To the north of these hills, across the Po, are the cities of the plain. Beyond them lies Lago Maggiore and eastward, across the Ticino River, is Milan.

Asti

32 *60 km (37 mi) southeast of Turin.*

Asti is best known to Americans for its wines—excellent reds as well as the famous sparkling white Spumante—but its strategic position on trade routes between Turin, Milan, and Genoa has given it a broad economic base. In the 12th century, Asti began to develop as a republic, at a time when other Italian cities were also flexing their economic and military muscles. It flourished in the following century, when the inhabitants began erecting lofty towers for its defense, giving rise to the medieval nickname "city of 100 towers." In the center of Asti, some of these remain, among them the 13th-century **Torre Cometini** and the well-preserved **Torre Troyana,** a tall, slender tower attached to the **Palazzo Troya.**

Corso Vittorio Alfieri is Asti's main thoroughfare, running west–east across the city. This road, known in medieval times as Contrada Maestra, was built by the Romans. The 18th-century church of **Santa Caterina** (✉ Western end of Corso Vittorio Alfieri) has incorporated one of the medieval towers, the **Torre Romana** (itself built on an ancient Roman base), as its bell tower.

The **Duomo** is an object lesson in the evolution of the Gothic architectural style. The cathedral, built in the early 14th century, is decorated mainly in a Gothic style that emphasizes geometry and verticality: pointed arches and narrow vaults are counterbalanced by the earlier, Romanesque attention to balance and symmetry. The porch, on the south side of the cathedral facing the square, was built in 1470 and represents Gothic at its most florid and excessive. *Piazza Catedrale,* ☎ *0171/592924.* ⏲ *Daily 8–noon and 3–7.*

The Gothic church of **San Secondo** (✉ South of Corso Alfieri) is dedicated to Asti's patron saint, reputedly decapitated on the spot where the church now stands. Secondo is also patron of the city's favorite folklore and sporting event, the annual **Palio,** the colorful medieval-style horse race (evocative of Siena's), held each year on the third Sunday of September in the vast Campo del Palio to the south of the church.

OFF THE BEATEN PATH

ALBA – Thirty kilometers (18 mi) southwest of Asti, this small town has a compact core studded with medieval towers and Gothic buildings, and a gracious old-world atmosphere. In addition to being a wine center of the region, Asti is known as the "City of the White Truffle" for the dirty little tubers that command more per ounce than diamonds. After picking out your truffle and enjoying the few wisps shaved onto your dish, you shell out an extra $16 per course for the pleasure—which is well worth it. Visit in October for the Fiera del Tartufo (National Truffle Fair), Cento Torri Joust (a medieval jousting festival), and the Palio degli Asini (donkey races), held the first Sunday in October.

BAROLO – Some of Italy's finest wines are made within a radius of about 16 km (10 mi) of Alba. The zone is dotted with castles, and every town has a wineshop where you can sample the local vino. The Castello di Barolo houses a wineshop and a museum of wine making. ⏲ *Fri.–Wed. 10–12:30 and 3–6:30. Closed Jan. and part of Feb.*

Dining and Lodging

$$$$ ★ ✕ **Gener Neuv.** Family-run and one of Italy's top restaurants, the Gener Neuv offers a sumptuous menu of regional specialties in a warm, welcoming atmosphere of rustic-style elegance, highlighted by excellent service, fine linen, silver, and crystal. The setting in a park on the bank of the Tanaro River is splendid, although it resulted in severe flood damage in 1994; the restaurant had to be rebuilt. Your choices may include agnolotti *ai tre stufati* (with a filling of ground rabbit, veal, and pork), and you can finish with *composta di prugne e uva* (prune and grape compote). The prix-fixe menu is good value ($$$) but does not include beverages. ✉ *Lungo Tanaro 4,* ☎ *0141/557270,* FAX *0141/436723. AE, DC, MC, V. Closed Sun. and Mon. in Jan.–July, Mon. in Sept.–Dec., and all of Aug. No dinner Sun.*

$$$ ✕ **Falcon Vecchio.** There's been a restaurant in this ancient house in the historic center of Asti since the year 1670. Today, in intimate surroundings, the Falcon Vecchio serves rich local dishes that vary with the season. In fall and winter there are mushroom, truffle, and game dishes. Otherwise, there's a big selection of antipasti, grilled vegetables, and *bollito misto* (seven types of boiled meat, served with various sauces and heaped on a steaming tray). ✉ *Via San Secondo 8,* ☎

0141/593106. Reservations essential. AE, DC, MC, V. Closed Mon., 15 days in Aug., and 10 days in Jan. No dinner Sun.

$$$ **Palio.** The hotel is in the historic heart of Asti and, though in an ultramodern building, it also has considerable character in individually decorated rooms featuring authentic antiques. Bathrooms in the minisuites have whirlpool baths. ✉ *Via Cavour 106, 14100,* ☎ *0141/34371,* FAX *0141/34373. 25 rooms, 5 suites. AE, DC, MC, V. Closed July 25–Aug. 10 and Dec. 23–Jan. 10.*

$–$$ **Rainero.** An older hotel in the town center, near the station, Rainero has been under the same family management for three generations. It's fitted with cheerful modern furnishings, but has no restaurant. ✉ *Via Cavour 85, 14100,* ☎ *0141/353866,* FAX *0141/594985. 55 rooms. DC, MC, V. Closed Jan. 1–8.*

Nightlife and the Arts

September is a month of fairs and celebrations in this famous wine city, and the **Asti Competition** in the middle of the month brings musicians, who perform in churches and concert halls. For 10 days in September, Asti is host to the **Douja d'Or National Wine Festival**—an opportunity to see Asti and celebrate the product that made it famous.

Shopping

The **Enoteca** on Piazza Alfieri, a square adjacent to Campo del Palio, is a wine center and shop, open Monday–Saturday 9–4:30, where you can try the range of Asti vintages, buy some as souvenirs or picnic ingredients, and even have a light snack. Be aware, though, that prices for Spumante in Asti are not necessarily lower than those elsewhere.

En Route From Alba double back to Asti to pick up the A21 autostrada. The road east from Asti to Alessandria is straight, skirting the southern edge of the Po plain, but for the first half of the drive you see to the south the green hillsides covered with vineyards. If you find yourself driving along this road during a thunderstorm (quite common on late summer afternoons), don't be surprised by the sound of explosions. Wine growers will often let off cannons loaded with blanks to persuade heavy clouds to rain, rather than build up and develop destructive hailstones.

Casale Monferrato

33 *42 km (26 mi) northeast of Asti, 75 km (46½ mi) southwest of Milan.*

Casale Monferrato, strategically situated on the southern banks of the Po, was held by the Gonzagas, rulers of Mantua, before falling into the hands of the Savoys. The 16th-century **Torre Civica,** marking the heart of Casale Monferrato in Piazza Mazzini, commanded extensive views up and down the Po. From March 19 through March 29, the **Festa di San Giuseppe** brings artisans, musicians, and vendors of traditional sweets to the central Piazza del Castello.

Casale's most enlightening sight is the **Museo Israelitico** (Jewish Museum) in the women's section of the synagogue. Inside is a collection of documents and sacred art of a community that was vital to the prosperity of this mercantile city. The synagogue dates from the late 16th century, and neighboring buildings on the same street formed the Jewish ghetto of that period. ✉ *Vicolo Olper 44, south of the Torre Civica,* ☎ *0142/71807.* ⏲ *Mid-Feb.–Dec., Sun. 10–noon and 3:30–6; at other times by appointment only. Closed Sat.*

Vercelli

34 *23 km (14 mi) north of Casale Monferrato, 80 km (50 mi) northeast of Turin.*

Vercelli is the rice capital of Italy and of Europe itself. Northern Italy's mainstay, risotto, owes its existence to the crop that was introduced to this fertile area in the late Middle Ages. **Piazza Cavour** is the heart of the medieval city and former market square. It was to this small square that merchants across northern Italy came in the 15th century to buy bags of the novelty grain from the East. Rising above the low rooftops around the square is the **Torre dell'Angelo** (Tower of the Angel), whose forbidding military appearance reflects its origins as a watchtower. ✉ *Piazza Cavour.*

The **Duomo,** a mainly late 16th-century construction on the site of what was a 5th-century church, contains tombs of several Savoy rulers in an octagonal chapel along the south (right) wall. The cathedral's **Biblioteca** (chapter library; for entrance, see cathedral office) contains the "Gospel of St. Eusebius," a 4th-century document, and the *Codex Vercellensis,* an 11th-century book of Anglo-Saxon poetry. ✉ *Piazza Sant' Eusebio,* ☏ *0161/255205.* ⏲ *Daily 8–12:30 and 3–6:30, except during mass on Sun.*

The **Basilica di Sant'Andrea,** a Cistercian abbey church built in the early 13th century with funds from another Abbey of St. Andrew (in England), witnessed the growing influence of northern Europe on Italy. Sant'Andrea is one of Italy's earliest examples of Gothic architecture, which spread from the north but ran out of steam before getting much farther south than the Po plain. The church interior is a soaring flight of Gothic imagination, with slender columns rising up to the ribbed vaults of the high ceiling. The gardens on the north side (Corso de Gasperi side) of the basilica hold the remains of the abbey itself and some of the secondary buildings. It is only here that the Gothic style is interrupted. The buildings surround a cloister in which you can see the pointed Gothic arches resting on the severe and more solid 12th-century Romanesque column bases. ✉ *Piazza G. Bicheri,* ☏ *0161/255513.* ⏲ *Daily 8–noon and 3–6:30.*

The **Città Vecchia** is a collection of narrow streets and alleys. Many of the houses are five centuries old, and you can see partly hidden gardens and courtyards beyond the wrought-iron gates.

OFF THE BEATEN PATH

BORSA MERCI – On weekdays, you can take an unusual guided tour of the commodities market (✉ Via Zumaglini 4, ☏ 0161/5981), where rice has been traded for centuries. Call first to check on tour times.

Novara

35 *23 km (14 mi) northeast of Vercelli, 95 km (59 mi) northeast of Turin.*

Novara is the easternmost city in Piedmont, only about 10 km (6 mi) west of the Ticino River, forming the border with Lombardy. Milan is only 32 km (20 mi) beyond the border, and over the centuries the opposing attractions of this neighboring giant and of the regional capital, Turin, have given Novara a bit of an identity crisis. In the Middle Ages, Novara's pivotal position actually made it a battlefield. A major engagement took place as recently as 1849, when the Austrian forces from the east defeated the Piedmontese armies.

Much of the present city dates from the late 19th and early 20th centuries, although there are interesting buildings from earlier periods scattered around Novara. Novara's most famous landmark is the tall, slender cupola of **San Gaudenzio.** The church itself, built between 1577 and 1690, conforms to a Baroque design, with twisted columns and sumptuous statues. The main attraction for most people, though, is its cupola, built from 1840 to 1888 and soaring to a height of just under 400 ft. This spire is visible from everywhere in the city and the surrounding countryside, and has become as much a symbol of Novara as the Mole Antonelliana is of Turin—not overly coincidental since Antonelli designed this cupola and spire as well. ☎ *0321/629894.* ⊙ *Daily 8–12 and 3–7.*

The **Broletto,** a cluster of well-preserved late-medieval buildings, is next to the **Duomo,** of medieval origins but reconstructed in neoclassic style. The Battistero (Baptistery), just outside the entrance to the cathedral, shows its august age in a much more evident manner. This rotunda-shape building dates from the 5th century, although it was substantially enlarged in the 10th and 11th centuries. Recent restoration work has uncovered pre-Romanesque frescoes, more than 1,000 years old, decorating the inside walls. Their flat, two-dimensional style reflects the influence of Byzantine icons, and their restored colors add a frightening feel to the apocalyptic scenes depicted. *Piazza Martiri della Libertà,* ☎ *0321/35634.* ⊙ *Daily 8–12.*

Lodging

$$ **Italia.** This modern hotel in the center of the city offers comfortable rooms and efficient service. The facilities cater mainly to businesspeople and include a restaurant. Some rooms have extensive views of the town. ✉ *Via Solaroli 8, 28100,* ☎ *0321/399316,* FAX *0321/399310. 59 rooms, 4 suites. Restaurant, bar. AE, DC, MC, V.*

PIEDMONT/VALLE D'AOSTA A TO Z

Arriving and Departing

By Bus

Turin's main bus station is on the corner of Corso Inghilterra and Corso Vittorio Emanuele. The Turin-based **SADEM** line (✉ Via della Repubblica 14, 10095 Grugliasco, Turin, ☎ 011/3111616) services the autostrada network to Milan and other, more distant destinations in Italy. The Turin-based **SAPAV** line (✉ Corso Torino 396, 10064 Pinerolo, Turin, ☎ 0121/322032) services the same area. **SITA** buses, part of the nationwide system, also connect Turin with the rest of Italy. There is also a major bus station at Aosta, right across the street from the train station. General bus info for a 1,400-lire-per-minute fee is available at ☎ 166/845010.

By Car

Italy's autostrada network links the region with the rest of Italy and neighboring France. Aosta, Turin, and Alessandria all have autostrada connections, with the A4 heading east to Milan and the A6 heading south to the Ligurian coast and Genoa. If you drive in from France or Switzerland, you pass through either the Mont Blanc or Grand St. Bernard tunnels: These are two of the most scenically dramatic entrances to Italy.

For travel between the French and Italy borders, only a few passes are usable year-round in Piedmont/Valle d'Aosta: the Colle del Gran San Bernardo/Col du Grand St. Bernard (Martigny to Aosta on Swiss Highway E27 to Italian Highway S27, with 6-km/4-mi tunnel) and the Traforo del Fréjus, which follows the Italian S335 west through a 13-km (8-mi) tunnel. The 12-km (7 mi) Mont Blanc Tunnel from Chamonix to Courmayeur was closed indefinitely at press time due to fire in March, 1999. There are plenty of other passes, but they are not reliable from at least November through April. Bear in mind this is very rough country, so no matter what time of year and what route, you are always advised to check with the tourist office (☞ Visitor Information *in* Piedmont/Valle d'Aosta A to Z, *below*) or, in a pinch, with the police, to make sure roads are passable and safe.

By Plane

The region's only international airport, **Aeroporto Torino Caselle** (☎ 011/5676361 information), is 18 km (11 mi) north of Turin. The airport is notoriously foggy in winter, and many flights are diverted to Genoa, on the coast, with bus connections provided to Turin.

BETWEEN THE AIRPORT AND DOWNTOWN

From Aeroporto Caselle, local buses to Turin arrive at the bus station on Corso Inghilterra in the city center.

By Train

Turin is on the main Paris–Rome TGV express line and is also connected with Milan, only 90 minutes away on the fast train. The fastest (Eurostar) trains cover the 667-km (400-mi) trip to Rome in about six hours, but most take about nine.

Getting Around

By Bus

SADEM and SAPAV (☞ Arriving and Departing, By Bus, *above*) are the specialists in bus transportation in Piedmont and the Valle d'Aosta. **SAVDA** (✉ Strada Ponte Suaz 6, 11100 Aosta, ☎ 0165/361244) specializes in mountain service, providing frequent links between Aosta, Turin, and Courmayeur.

By Car

Turin is the hub of all the transportation systems in Piedmont, with autostrada connections to the north, south, and east. Well-paved secondary roads (superstrade) run through the rest of the region, following the course of mountain valleys in many places. Sudden winter storms can close off some of the mountain stretches; contact local tourist offices (☞ Visitor Information, *below*) for up-to-date road information before you set out.

By Train

Services to the larger cities east of Turin are part of the extensive and reliable train network serving the Lombard Plain. West of the region's capital, however, the train services soon peter out in the steep mountain valleys. Continuing connections by bus serve these valleys, and information about train-bus mountain services can be obtained from train stations and tourist information offices.

Contacts and Resources

Car Rentals

TURIN

Avis (✉ Corso Turati 15, ☎ 011/500852; ✉ Aeroporto Torino Caselle, ☎ 011/4701528). **Hertz** (✉ Via Magellano 12, ☎ 011/502080; ✉ Aeroporto Torino Caselle, ☎ 011/5678166).

Emergencies

Emergencies (☎ 113). **Police** (☎ 112).

Guided Tours

Turin's group and personally guided tours are organized by the city's tourist office (☞ Visitor Information, *below*).

ALPINE GUIDES

Alpine guides are not only recommended, they're essential if you're planning to traverse some of the dramatic ranges outside St. Vincent, Courmayeur, or Breuil-Cervinia. Before embarking on an excursion (however short) into the mountains in these areas, contact the representative of the **CAI** (Club Alpinisti Italiani; ✉ Piazza E. Chanoux 8, Aosta, ☎ 0165/40194) about the risks involved and the availability of an experienced guide. CAI information is also available at each tourist information office (☞ Visitor Information, *below*).

Late-Night Pharmacies

Pharmacies throughout the region take turns staying open late and on Sunday. Call ☎ 192 for the latest information, in Italian, on which are open.

Aosta Farmacia Centrale (✉ Piazza E. Chanoux 35, Turin, ☎ 0165/262205). **Turin Farmacia Internazionale** (✉ Via Carlo Alberto 24, Turin, ☎ 011/535144).

Visitor Information

Tourist offices (✉ Piazza Medford, 12051 Alba, ☎ 0173/35833; ✉ Piazza E. Chanoux 8, 11100 Aosta, ☎ 0165/236627; ✉ Piazza Alfieri 34, 14100 Asti, ☎ 0141/530357; ✉ Viale Vittoria 44, 10052 Bardonecchia, ☎ 0122/99032; ✉ Via Carrel 29, 11021 Breuil-Cervinia, ☎ 0166/949136; ✉ Piazza E. Chanoux, 11012 Cogne, ☎ 0165/74040; ✉ Piazzale Monte Bianco 13, 11013 Courmayeur, ☎ 0165/842060; ✉ Via Dominioni 4, 28100 Novara, ☎ 0321/623398; ✉ Via Griselda 6, 12037 Saluzzo, ☎ 0175/46710; ✉ Piazza Castello 161, 10122 Turin, ☎ 011/535901; ✉ Stazione Porta Nuova, 10121 Turin, ☎ 011/531327; ✉ Viale Garibaldi 90, 13100 Vercelli, ☎ 0161/58002).

8 MILAN, LOMBARDY, AND THE LAKES

Old and new are often unexpectedly fused in Italy, and in Lombardy, they marry magnificently. The 19th-century Lakes Como, Maggiore, and Garda—of opulent villas, exotic gardens, and Alpine vistas—remain the perfect escapes from Milan, Italy's business hub and crucible of chic. Pavia, Cremona, and Mantua, once proud medieval fortress towns dictating the fortunes of northern Italy, are today bustling centers of industry and commerce, still playing a key role in Italy's richest region.

Updated by Fionn Davenport

ONE IS TEMPTED TO DESCRIBE LOMBARDY as a place with something for everyone—Milan, capital of all that is new in Italy; the great Renaissance cities of the Po plain, Pavia, Cremona, and Mantua, where even the height of summer can be comparatively peaceful; and the lakes, where glacial waters framed by the Alps have been praised as the closest thing to Paradise by writers as varied as Virgil, Tennyson, and Hemingway.

"Nothing in the world," wrote Stendhal in 1817, "can be compared to the fascination of those burning summer days passed on the Milanese lakes, in the middle of those chestnut groves so green that they immerse their branches in the waves . . ." Millions of travelers have since agreed that, for sheer beauty, the lakes of Northern Italy—Como, Maggiore, Garda, and Orta—have few equals. Where else can you find magnificent 18th- and 19th-century villas on the shores of lakes bordered by toy villages and nestled under the foothills of mountains of almost Scandinavian grandeur? From Pliny to d'Annunzio, visitors have found this region—to quote Stendhal—"elegant, picturesque, and voluptuous."

The truth, of course, is more complicated. The lakes, home to dozens of resorts that were once Italy's—and Europe's—most fashionable, have preserved an astonishingly unspoiled beauty, often enhanced by sumptuous summer palaces and exotic formal gardens. Still, one cannot imagine Catullus returning to his "jewel" Sirmione, on Lago di Garda (Lake Garda), without being a little daunted by its development as a lively resort town. Milan can be disappointingly modern—rather too much like the place you have come here to escape—but it is also the perfect blend of old and new, with historic buildings and art collections rivaling those in Florence and Rome.

More than 3,000 years ago—the date and the details are lost in the mysteries of Etruscan inscriptions—explorers from the highly civilized realm of Etruria in central Italy wandered northward beyond the River Po. The Etruscans extended their dominance into this region for hundreds of years but left little of their culture. They were succeeded by the Cenomanic Gauls, who, in turn, were conquered by the legions of Rome in the latter days of the Republic. The region became known as Cisalpine Gaul, and under the rule of Augustus it became a Roman province. Its warlike, independent people became citizens of Rome. Virgil, Catullus, and both the Plinys were born in the region during this relatively tranquil era.

The decline of the Roman Empire was followed by the invasions of the Huns and the Goths. Attila and Theodoric, in turn, gave way to the Lombards, who ceded their iron crown to Charlemagne as the emblem of his vast but unstable empire. Even before the fragile bonds that held this empire together had begun to snap, the cities of Lombardy were erecting walls in defense against the Hungarians and against each other. These communes did, however, form the Lombard League, which, in the 12th century, finally defeated Frederick Barbarossa.

Once the invaders had been defeated, new and even bloodier strife began. In each city the Guelphs (bourgeois supporters of the popes) and the Ghibellines (noble adherents to the so-called emperors) clashed with each other. The communes declined, and each fell under the yoke of powerful local rulers. The Republic of Venice dominated Brescia and Bergamo. Mantua was ruled by the Gonzaga, and the Visconti and Sforza families took over Como, Cremona, Milan, and Pavia.

The Battle of Pavia in 1525, when the generals of Charles V (1500–58) defeated the French (and gave Francis I the chance to coin the famous phrase "All is lost save honor"), brought on 200 years of Spanish occupation. The Spaniards were, on the whole, less cruel than the local tyrants and were hardly resisted by the Lombards. The War of the Spanish Succession, in the early years of the 18th century, threw out the Spaniards and brought in the Austrians instead, whose dominion was "neither liked nor loathed" during the nearly 100 years of its existence.

Napoléon and his generals routed the Austrians. The Treaty of Campoformio resulted in the proclamation of the Cisalpine Republic, which quickly became the Republic of Italy and, just as rapidly, the Kingdom of Italy, which lasted only until Napoléon's defeat brought back the Austrians. But Milan, as the capital of Napoléon's republic and of the Kingdom of Italy, had a taste of glory, and the city's inherently independent citizens, along with those of the other Lombardian cities, were not slow to resent and combat the loss of "national" pride.

From 1820 on, the Lombards joined the Piedmontese and the House of Savoy in a long struggle against the Habsburgs and, in 1859, finally defeated Austria and brought about the re-creation of the Kingdom of Italy two years later.

Milan and other cities of Lombardy have not lost their independence and their hatred of domination. Nowhere in Italy was the partisan insurrection against Mussolini—to whom they first gave power—and the German regime better organized or more successful. Milan was liberated from the Germans by its own partisan organization before the entrance of Allied troops; escaping Allied prisoners could find sanctuary there when fighting was still going on far to the south. Today, the Milanesi independent spirit is demonstrated through the increasingly popular separatist movement known collectively as the Lega Nord (Northern League), whose aims are to divide the northern regions from the rest of Italy and create a new state called Padania, with Milan as its capital. Although it seems unlikely that secession will occur, the movement maintains a strong voice of protest against the government in Rome, whom it accuses of squandering revenue from the prosperous north on ill-fated projects in the poorer south.

New and Noteworthy

Milan's new **Malpensa 2000** (MXP) airport, now Italy's biggest aerial gateway to the rest of the world, finally opened amid much hoopla in late 1998. Much to the chagrin of many major European and American airlines, most international flights on foreign carriers were immediately forced to fly through Malpensa 2000 rather than Linate, Milan's other airport, which is closer to the city. Malpensa 2000 was almost immediately plagued by problems ranging from sticky runway tar to lost luggage, topped off by reliably long delays that have continued into 1999. The rail link from Milano Centrale was slated for completion by the millennium, but progress has been slow. Well into 1999, the inconvenient bus was still the only link to Milan's train station.

Pleasures and Pastimes

Car Racing

Though the fortunes of Italy's beloved Ferrari have waned in recent years, passion for the sport is undiminished here. A Formula 1 race is held in Monza, 15 km (9 mi) from Milan, every September. The track was built in 1922 in the Parco di Monza, where there is also a hippodrome, golf course, and other facilities.

Dining

Unlike most Italian regions, Lombardy exhibits a northern European preference for butter rather than oil as its cooking medium, which imparts a rich and distinctive flavor to the cuisine. *Alla milanese*–style cooking means the food is usually dipped in egg and bread crumbs mixed with grated Parmesan, then sautéed in butter. One of the most popular specialties here, osso buco, is almost always paired with risotto—its alla milanese preparation enriching it with chicken broth and saffron, imparting a rich flavor and yellow hue. The lakes are a good source of fish, particularly trout and pike. Gorgonzola, a strong, creamy, veined cheese, and panettone, a sweet yeast bread with raisins, citron, and anise, both hail from the Milan area and can be enjoyed throughout Lombardy. Although most of the wines in Lombardy can be paired well with the cuisine, search the local wine lists for red Grumello or Sangue di Giuda (blood of Judas) wines or the delicious light sparkling whites from the Franciacorta area.

Golf

Golf is a recent addition to Italy's sporting roster, and the success of Italy's most famous professional golfer, Constantino Rocca, has added to the sport's popularity among Italians. Facilities have improved dramatically over the last decade, resulting in a proliferation of courses groomed into northern Italy's landscape. Five courses are convenient to Milan, and seven courses are near Lago di Como (Lake Como).

Lodging

Lombardy is one of Italy's most prosperous regions, and hotels cater to a clientele of high standards, willing to pay for extra comfort. Many Lombardy hotels are converted from handsome old villas with well-landscaped grounds. Try to visit one or two, even if they are out of your price range as accommodations. Most of the famous lake resorts are expensive, although more basic—and reasonably priced—accommodations can be found in the smaller towns and villages. Milan may seem to have fewer tourists than other large Italian cities, but there is always competition for rooms, generated by the nearly year-round trade fairs and other business-related bookings. It is best—and almost essential in spring and summer—to make reservations.

Soccer

Like the rest of Italy, the region is soccer-mad, with fans from all over Italy exhibiting fierce support for Milan's soccer teams, AC Milan and Inter Milan, two of the most successful in Europe. Matches are usually played on Sunday, with both teams sharing the San Siro soccer stadium in Milan for home matches. On match day, close to 85,000 fans pile into the San Siro to watch, cheer, and boo the performances of each team. For the rest of the week, Sunday's performance is debated and scrutinized in bars, cafés, and restaurants (not to mention the home, workplace, barbershop . . .).

Water Sports

Schools for sailing, scuba diving, waterskiing, and windsurfing are in Riva del Garda, on Lake Garda. Torbole, 5 km (3 mi) east of Riva del Garda on S240, is a prime spot for windsurfing. At Lake Como, there are well-equipped sailing and windsurfing schools as well as waterskiing.

Exploring Milan, Lombardy, and the Lakes

This area of northern Italy is dominated by the region of Lombardy and especially by Milan, which lies at its heart. Many of the region's most important cities—Pavia, Cremona, and Mantua—are to the south and southeast of Milan. These cities all have in common flat geographical surroundings bordered by the Po River, hence they are categorized here as cities of the plain. "The lakes" actually denotes a vast region spread over the middle third of the northern border region. The roads that connect major cities are excellent and are supported by several major highways (autostrade) as well as by secondary routes.

From the north to the east of Milan lie all of the region's lakes. Some border Switzerland; others are at the foot of the Dolomites, Italy's foremost mountain range. The best way to see the lake country is to rent a car in fall or spring and thread a path, at as leisurely a pace as possible, along the small mountain roads that link the lakes' least-spoiled northern tips. This is splendid mountain-driving country, with some of the most beautiful and challenging roads in the world. Without a car, however, it is still possible to see many of the region's sights, thanks to extensive bus routes and the many *vaporetti* (water taxis) that ferry the lakes. The throngs that descend upon the lakes in July and August, weekends particularly, make reservations absolutely necessary—especially so at Lake Como, the quintessential Italian lake resort.

Numbers in the text correspond to numbers in the margin and on the Milan and Lombardy and the Lakes maps.

Great Itineraries

Traveling by car is usually the best way to get around and to fully appreciate the beauty of the landscape. Allow plenty of time to travel the winding lake roads at leisure, as photo opportunities abound. A week is enough to see the area thoroughly, and although five days will not exclude any sights, you have to keep on the move. Three days will give you a taste of the major sights in the area, but time will be precious and morning starts will have to be early.

IF YOU HAVE 3 DAYS

Begin in **Milan** ①–⑮, taking in the city's major sights, before heading south on the A7 autostrada to the cities of **Pavia** ⑯ and **Cremona** ⑰, home to Stradivari, violin maker extraordinaire. End your day in **Mantua** ⑲. The next day head north on the A22 as far as **Riva del Garda** ㉓ and make your way back through **Gargnano** ㉔, **Gardone Riviera** ㉕, and down into the jewel of Lake Garda's crown, **Sirmione** ㉖. Overnight in **Bergamo** ㉘. The next day go as far as **Madonna del Ghisallo** ㉙ and **Bellagio** ㉚ on Lake Como. Finally, move on to Lake Maggiore via **Cernobbio** ㉝, taking time out to cruise the lake on one of the steamers.

IF YOU HAVE 5 DAYS

Travel south along the A7 to **Pavia** ⑯ and **Cremona** ⑰, and then move on to the star-shape fortress city of **Sabbioneta** ⑱, ending your day in **Mantua** ⑲, where you can enjoy Mantegna's masterpieces. The next day head north to Lake Garda through the lakefront towns of **Punta di San Vigilio** ㉑, **Malcesine** ㉒, and, at the top of the lake, the pretty town of **Riva del Garda** ㉓. Head down the western side of the lake through **Gargnano** ㉔ and **Gardone Riviera** ㉕, where you should visit Gabriele d'Annunzio's former home, Il Vittoriale, before reaching **Sirmione** ㉖. The next day pass through the wealthy city of **Brescia** ㉗ and on to **Bergamo** ㉘. From here head via **Madonna del Ghisallo** ㉙ to **Bellagio** ㉚ on Lake Como, said to be the prettiest town in Europe. Take time in the afternoon to explore the lake towns of **Varenna** ㉛ and **Tremezzo** ㉜, where you'll find the magnificent Villa Carlotta. If you can manage an early start the following morning, head for **Cernobbio** ㉝ and then west to **Orto San Giulio** ㉟ on Lake Orto. It's only a short hop to Lake Maggiore. You can explore the area from here by steamer, traveling north to **Stresa** ㊱ on the western side of

Lombardy and the Lakes

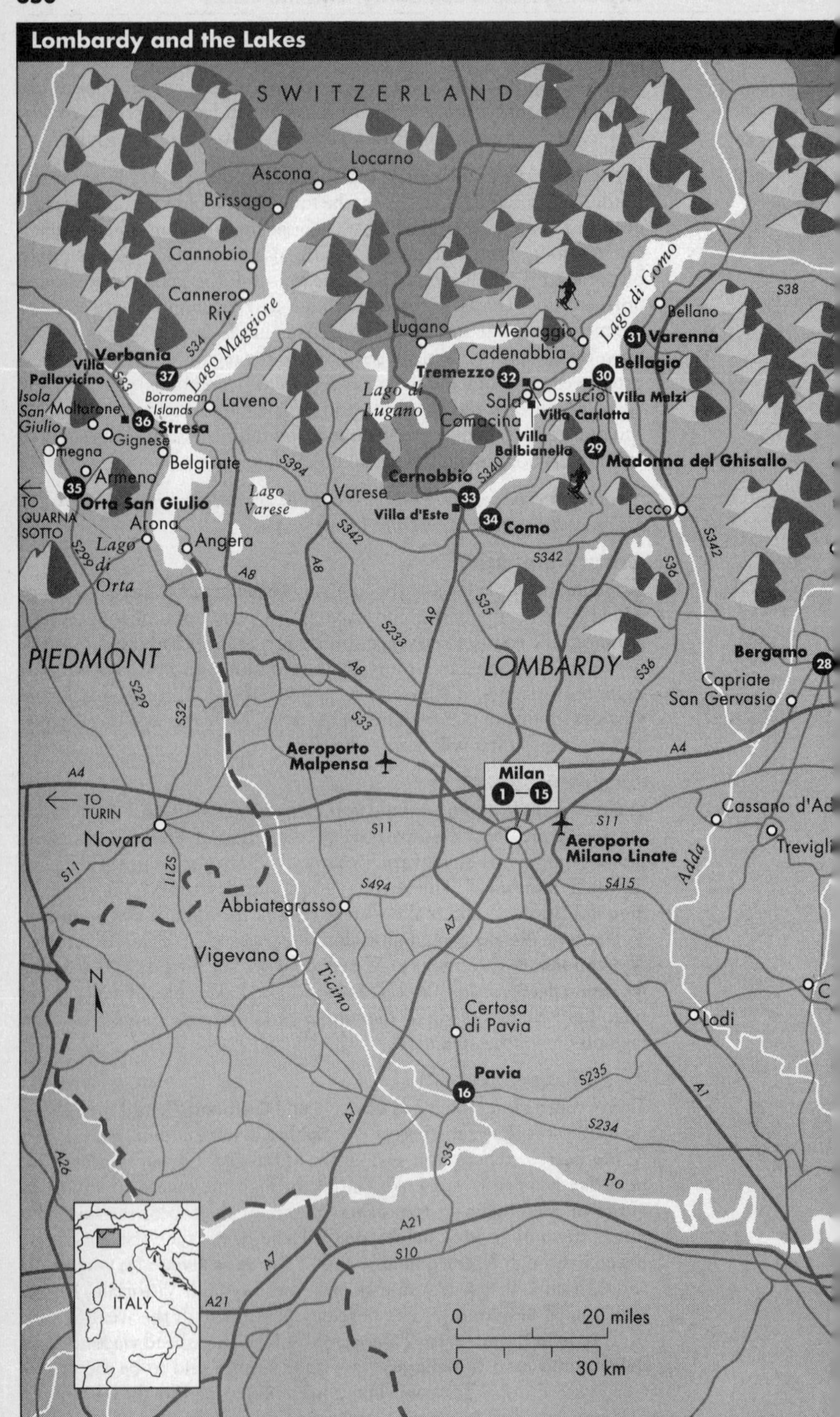

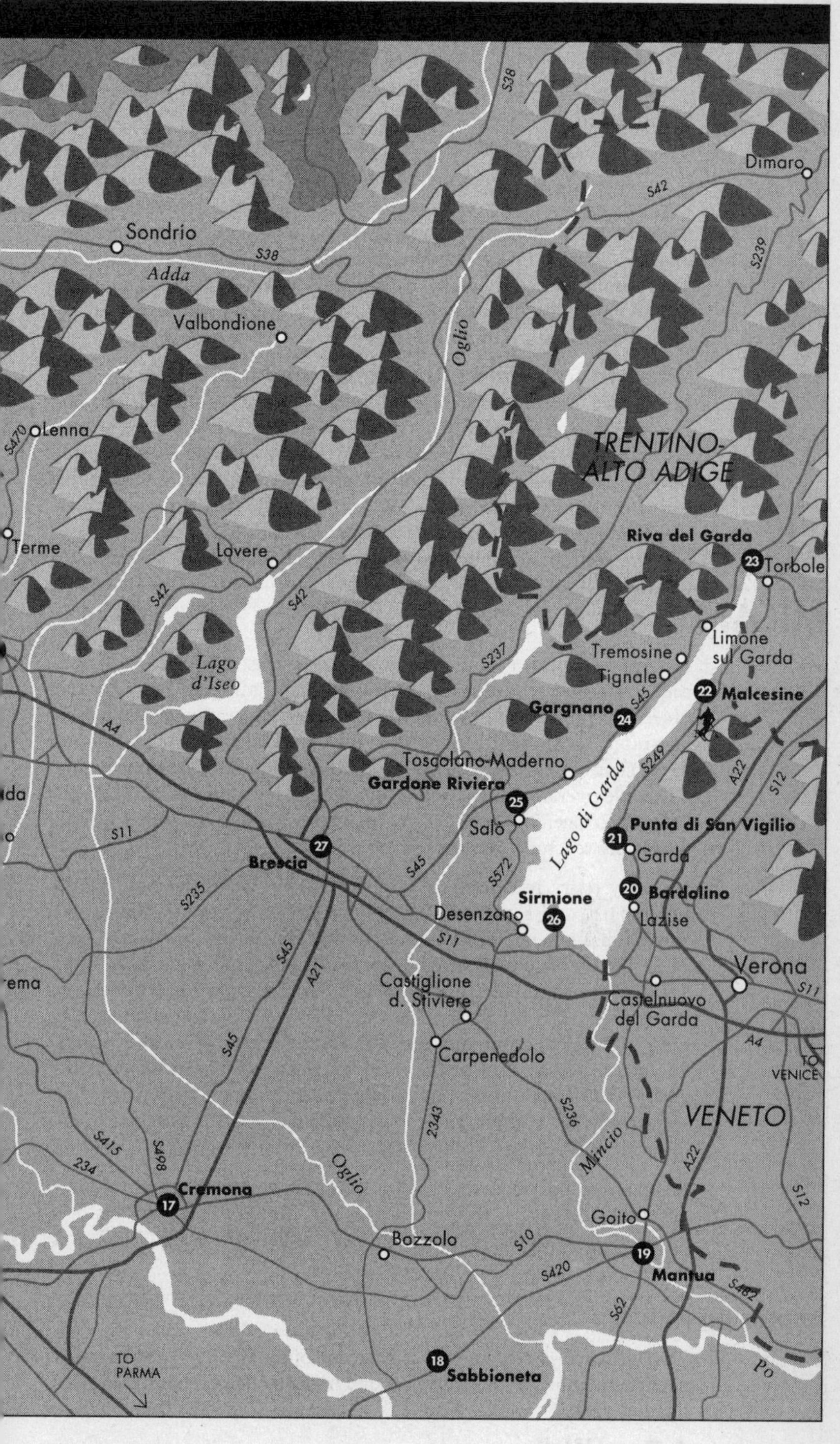
Sondrio
Adda
Valbondione
Oglio
S38
S42
S239
Dimaro
Lenna
S470
Terme
Lovere
Lago d'Iseo
TRENTINO-ALTO ADIGE
Riva del Garda
23
Torbole
Limone sul Garda
Tremosine
Tignale
22
Malcesine
Gargnano
24
S45
S237
Toscolano-Maderno
Gardone Riviera
25
Salò
Lago di Garda
S249
A22
S12
Punta di San Vigilio
21
Garda
20
Bardolino
Lazise
Sirmione
26
Desenzano
S572
A4
S11
27
Brescia
S235
A21
Verona
Castiglione d. Stiviere
Castelnuovo del Garda
Carpenedolo
TO VENICE
VENETO
2343
S236
Mincio
S415
S498
234
Cremona
17
Oglio
Goito
19
Bozzolo
S10
S420
Mantua
S482
S62
Po
18
Sabbioneta
TO PARMA
rema
da

the lake. From here it's a short excursion to the town of **Verbania** ㊲, across the bay of the same name. That afternoon or the following day (alternately staying in Stresa) head for **Milan** ①–⑮ to see the main sights. You could also visit Milan first before setting off on your tour of the rest of the region.

IF YOU HAVE 7 DAYS

If you have the luxury of seven days to tour the area, make sure you linger in some of the lake towns, especially **Riva del Garda** ㉓ and **Sirmione** ㉖, **Bellagio** ㉚ on Lake Como, and Lake Maggioire's **Verbania** ㊲, where you can explore the magnificent botanical gardens of Villa Taranto. Take an extra day to visit **Milan** ①–⑮, which may appear to be yet another industrialized city at first glance but reveals artistic and architectural treasures once you scratch its surface.

When to Tour Milan, Lombardy, and the Lakes

In summer months, particularly July and August, lake roads can become congested, especially on evenings and weekends. Fewer people visit in fall, winter, and spring, so many of the lakeside towns are deserted and some restaurants and hotels close. Note that many of the ferry and steamer boat services stop running in October and recommence in May. Early summer, late summer, and early fall are the best times to see the area, but October can be a tad chilly for swimming.

MILAN

Milan's history as a capital city goes back at least 2,500 years. Its fortunes ever since—both as a great commercial trading center and as the object of regular conquest and occupation—are readily explained by its strategic position at the center of the Lombard plain. Directly south of the central passes across the Alps, Milan is bordered by three highly navigable rivers—the Po, Ticino, and Adda—for centuries the main arteries of an ingenious network of canals crisscrossing all Lombardy (and ultimately reaching most of northern Italy).

Virtually every invader in European history—Gaul, Roman, Goth, Longobard, and Frank—as well as every ruler of France, Spain, and Austria, has taken a turn at ruling the city and the region. Milan's glorious heyday of self-rule proved comparatively brief, from 1277 until 1500, when it was ruled by its two great family dynasties, the Visconti and subsequently the Sforza. These families were known, justly or not, for a peculiarly aristocratic mixture of refinement, classical learning, and cruelty, and much of the surviving grandeur of Gothic and Renaissance art and architecture is their doing. Be on the lookout in your wanderings for the Visconti family emblem—a viper, its jaws straining wide, devouring a child.

If you are wondering why so little seems to have survived from Milan's antiquity, the answer is simple—war. Three times in the city's history, partial or total destruction has followed conflict—in AD 539, 1157, and 1944.

Exploring Milan

The subway system, known as the Metropolitana, is a good way to get around, but staying above ground in the trolley cars or buses gives a better view.

A Good Walk

Start at the **Duomo** ① and visit its roof, museum, and the **Battistero Paleocristiano** ②. Then move on to **Galleria Vittorio Emanuele** ③, just beyond the northern tip of the cathedral's facade. Continue across the transepts of the Galleria and head north to **Teatro alla Scala** ④, where Verdi attained his fame. Head northeast on Via Manzoni, stopping in to the **Museo Poldi-Pezzoli** ⑤ to see some fine Renaissance paintings. Via Manzoni leads to the **Giardini Pubblici** (great for kids), with the **Museo Civico di Storia Naturale** ⑥ on the eastern side of the park. Via Manzoni leads to Via Fatebenefratelli; follow it west to Via Pontaccio and then to Via Brera to the **Pinacoteca di Brera** ⑦. Next, a brisk walk west along Via Pontaccio will bring you to the imposing **Castello Sforzesco** ⑧. A few blocks southwest of the Castello on Corso Magenta is **Santa Maria delle Grazie** ⑨, home to the renowned *Last Supper.* Go east on Corso Magenta, across Via Carducci, to visit the city's **Museo Civico Archeologico** ⑩. Next to the Museo Civico Archeologico, Via Sant'Agnese leads to the **Basilica di Sant'Ambrogio** ⑪. Across from the church's main doors, turn left on Via San Vittore to see the **Museo Nazionale della Scienza e Tecnica** ⑫. From the museum, take a right and walk down Via Edmondo de Amicis, then take a left on Corso Porta Ticinese to reach the church of **San Lorenzo Maggoire** ⑬. Down Corso Porta Ticinese is the laid-back **Navigli district** ⑭. From San Lorenzo Maggiore, take Corso Porta Ticinese north to Via Torino, where, after a few blocks, you'll find **San Satiro** ⑮, yet another of Bramante's Renaissance masterpieces.

TIMING

To visit each sight in Milan will take a couple of days, but the most important ones can be seen in one day. Note that some churches and museums are closed Monday, including Santa Maria delle Grazie (*The Last Supper*). Expect long lines waiting to see *The Last Supper,* even in the early morning.

Sights to See

⓫ **Basilica di Sant'Ambrogio** (Basilica of St. Ambrose). Noted for its medieval architecture, the church was consecrated by St. Ambrose in AD 387, and is the model for all Lombard Romanesque churches. The **Museo della Basilica di Sant'Ambrogio** contains ancient pieces such as a remarkable 9th-century altar in precious metals and enamels. The museum trove also includes paintings, sculptures, and a couple of Flemish tapestries. ✉ *Piazza Sant'Ambrogio 15,* ☎ *02/86450895.* 🎫 *Museum: 3,000 lire.* ⏲ *Basilica: Mon.–Sat. 9:30–12 and 2:30–6:30. Museum: Sept.–July, Mon.–Sat. 10–12 and 3–5. Metro: Sant'Ambrogio.*

❷ **Battistero Paleocristiano.** This subterranean ruin of the baptistery dating from the 4th century is beneath the Duomo's piazza. Although opinion remains divided, it is widely believed that this may have been where Ambrose, Milan's first bishop and patron saint, baptized Augustine. ✉ *Enter through Duomo, Piazza Duomo.* ⏲ *Tues.–Sun. 10–noon and 3–5. Metro: Duomo.*

❽ **Castello Sforzesco.** For the serious student of Renaissance military engineering, the imposing Castello must be something of a travesty, so often has it been remodeled or rebuilt since it was begun in 1450 by the *condottiere* (hired mercenary) who founded the city's second dynastic family, Francesco Sforza, fourth duke of Milan. Though today the word "mercenary" has a strongly pejorative ring, during the Renaissance all Italy's great soldier-heroes were professionals hired by the cities and principalities that they served. Of them—and there were thousands—Francesco Sforza (1401–66) is considered to have been one of the greatest and most honest. It is said he could remember not only the names of all his men, but of their horses as well. And it is with his era, and the building of the Castello, that we know we have entered the enlightened age of the Renaissance. It took barely half a century before it and the city were under foreign rule.

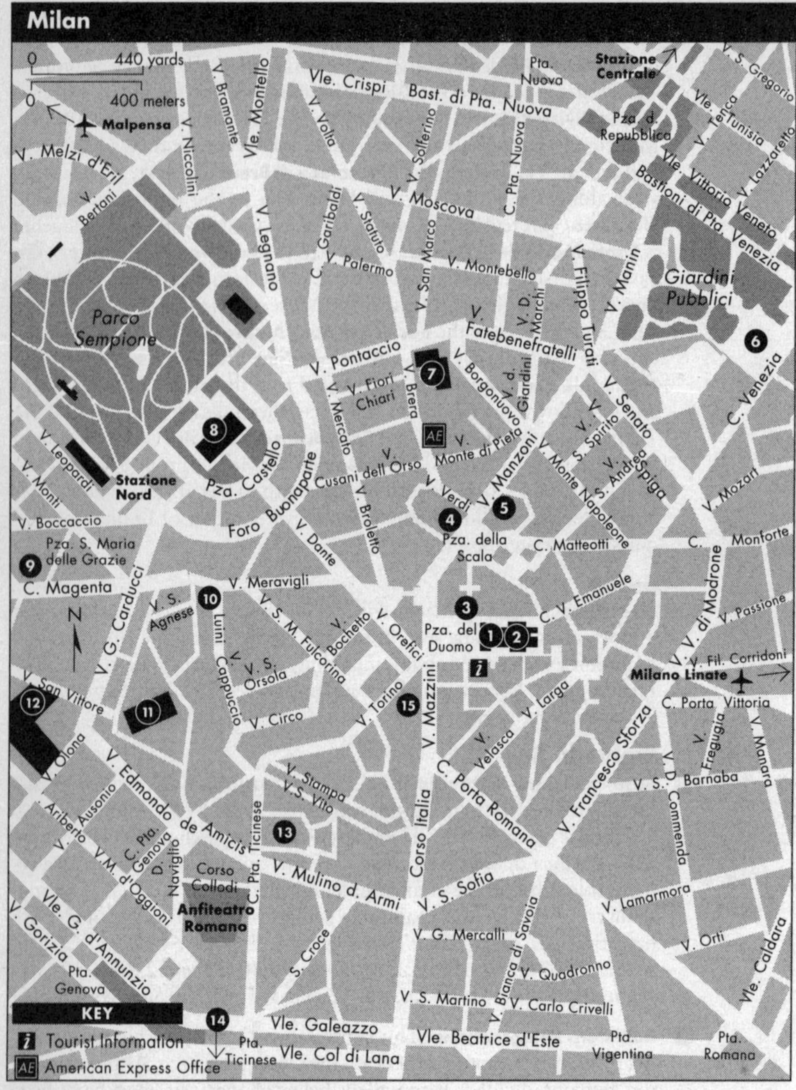

Basilica di Sant'Ambrogio, **11**

Battistero Paleocristiano, **2**

Castello Sforzesco, **8**

Duomo, **1**

Galleria Vittorio Emanuele, **3**

Museo Civico Archeologico, **10**

Museo Civico di Storia Naturale, **6**

Museo Nazionale della Scienza e Tecnica, **12**

Museo Poldi–Pezzoli, **5**

Navigli district, **14**

Pinacoteca di Brera, **7**

San Lorenzo Maggiore, **13**

San Satiro, **15**

Santa Maria delle Grazie, **9**

Teatro alla Scala, **4**

Today, the Castello houses municipal museums devoted variously to Egyptian and other antiquities, musical instruments, paintings, and sculpture. Highlights are the **Salle delle Asse,** a frescoed room still sometimes attributed to Leonardo da Vinci (1690–1730), and Michelangelo's (1475–1564) unfinished *Rondanini Pietà,* believed to be his last work—an astounding achievement for a man nearly 90 and a moving coda of his life. ✉ *Piazza Castello,* ☎ *02/76002378.* *Free.* *Tues.–Sun. 9:30–5:30. Metro: Cairoli.*

NEED A BREAK? **Viel** (✉ Largo Cairoli), just across the road from Castello Sforzesco, is said to be the best *gelateria* in northern Italy.

★ ❶ **Duomo.** This intricate Gothic structure—Italy's largest—has been fascinating and exasperating visitors and conquerors alike since it was begun by Galeazzo Visconti III (1351–1402), first duke of Milan, in 1386. Consecrated in 1577, it was not wholly completed until 1897. Whether you concur with travel writer H. V. Morton, writing some 30 years ago that the cathedral is "one of the mightiest Gothic buildings ever created," or regard it as a spiny pastiche of centuries, there is no denying that for sheer size and complexity it is unequaled; its very size and appearance suggest Gotham rather than Milan. Its capacity—though it is hard to imagine the church filled—is reckoned to be 40,000. Usually it is empty, a perfect sanctuary from the frenetic pace of life outside and the perfect place for solitary contemplation. The poet Shelley swore by it—claiming it was the only place to read Dante.

The building is adorned with 135 marble spires and 2,245 marble statues. The oldest part is the **apse** (the end of the cruciform opposite the portals). Its three colossal bays of curving and counter-curved tracery, especially the bay adorning the exterior of the stained-glass windows, should not be missed. Step inside and walk down the right aisle to the southern transept, to the **tomb of Gian Giacomo Medici.** The tomb owes something to Michelangelo, but is generally considered its sculptor's (Leone Leoni's, 1509–90) masterpiece; it dates from the 1560s. Directly ahead is the Duomo's most famous sculpture, the rather gruesome but anatomically instructive figure of **San Bartolomeo** (St. Bartholomew), whose glorious martyrdom consisted of being flayed alive. It is usually said the saint stands "holding" his skin, but this is not quite accurate. It would appear more that he is luxuriating in it, much as a 1950s matron might have shown off a new fur stole.

As you enter the apse to admire those splendid windows, glance at the **sacristy doors** to the right and left of the altar. The lunette on the right dates from 1393 and was decorated by Hans von Fernach. That on the left also dates from the 14th century and is ascribed jointly to Giacomo da Campione and Giovanni dei Grassi. Don't miss the view from the Duomo's **roof;** walk out the left (north) transept to the stairs and elevator. Sadly, late 20th-century air pollution, on all but the rarest days, drastically reduces the view. As you stand among the forest of marble pinnacles, remember that virtually every inch of this gargantuan edifice, including the roof itself, is decorated with precious white marble. ✉ *Piazza del Duomo,* ☎ *02/86463456.* *Stairs to roof 7,000 lire, elevator 10,000 lire.* *Mar.–Oct., daily 9–5:30; Nov.–Feb., daily 9–4:30. Metro: Duomo.*

Exhibits at the **Museo del Duomo** shed more light on the cathedral's history and include some of the treasures removed for safety from the exterior. ✉ *Piazza del Duomo 14,* ☎ *02/860358.* *8,000 lire.* *Tues.–Sun. 9:30–12:30 and 3–6. Metro: Duomo.*

NEED A BREAK? The best alternative to a conventional restaurant is **Peck** (✉ Via Spadari 9, ☎ 02/860842), one of Italy's, if not the world's, most irresistible food emporiums. In the Duomo area, it is something better than a shop—it's six shops. **Peck Rosticceria** (✉ Via Cantù 3, ☎ 02/8693017), closed Monday, offers grilled takeout. Best for a quick stand-up lunch is **Bottega del Vino** (✉ Via Victor Hugo 4, ☎ 02/861040), which pours almost 200 wines by the glass. For a relaxed lunch, try **Il Restaurant** (✉ Via Victor Hugo 4, ☎ 02/876774); closed Sunday. For do-it-yourself, try the **Delicatessen** (✉ Via Spadari 11, ☎ 02/86461158).

★ 9 **Galleria Vittorio Emanuele.** Anyone who has grown up on the periphery of a contemporary American city should recognize this spectacularly extravagant late 19th-century glass-topped, barrel-vaulted tunnel for what it is—one of the planet's earliest and most select of shopping malls. It may be rivaled perhaps only by GUM, off Red Square in Moscow, for sheer Belle Epoque splendor. Its architect, Giuseppe Mengoni, accidently lost his footing while on the roof and tumbled to his death on the floor of his own creation, just days before its opening.

Like its suburban American cousins, the Galleria fulfills a variety of social functions vastly more important than its ostensible commercial purpose. This is the city's heart, midway between the cathedral and La Scala opera house, and it is sometimes called *Il Salotto* (the Living Room). It teems with life, inviting people-watching from the tables that spill from the Galleria's bars and restaurants, where you can enjoy a ridiculously overpriced coffee.

Like the cathedral, the Galleria is a cruciform. The space at the crossing, however, forms an octagon. If this is where you're standing, don't be afraid to look up and gawk. Even in poor weather, the great glass dome makes for a splendid sight. And the mosaics, usually unnoticed, are a vastly underrated source of pleasure, even if they are not to be taken too seriously. They represent Europe, Asia, Africa, and America; those at the entrance arch are devoted to science, industry, art, and agriculture.

Books, clothing, food, wine, pens, jewelry, and myriad other goods are all for sale in the Galleria, and one of Milan's most traditional restaurants, Savini, is here (☞ Dining and Lodging, *below*). There is, in addition, one of those curious Italian institutions, an *albergo diurno* (daytime hotel), where you can take an hour's nap or a bath, get a haircut or a pedicure, and have your suit pressed or a button replaced. Most of its patrons are Italian, but it is hard to think of a better oasis for a vacationer worn out from sightseeing. ✉ *Piazza del Duomo, beyond northern tip of cathedral's facade.* ⏲ *Shops open 9:30–1 and 3:30–7. Metro: Duomo.*

10 **Museo Civico Archeologico** (Civic Archaeological Museum). Housed in a former monastery, this museum has some enlightening relics from Milan's Roman past—from everyday utensils and jewelry to several fine examples of mosaic pavement. ✉ *Corso Magenta 15,* ☎ *02/86450011.* *Free.* ⏲ *Tues.–Sun. 9–5:30. Metro: Cadorna.*

6 **Museo Civico di Storia Naturale** (Civic Natural History Museum). Exhibits here appeal to animal and nature lovers. Just behind the museum is the **Giardini Pubblici** (Public Gardens), a refuge for active young children. ✉ *Corso Venezia 55,* ☎ *02/62085405.* *Free.* ⏲ *Tues.–Fri. 9:30–5:30, weekends 9:30–6:30. Metro: Sant'Ambrogio.*

12 **Museo Nazionale della Scienza e Tecnica** (National Museum of Science and Technology). Models based on technical projects by Leonardo da Vinci and collections of locomotives, planes, and cars hold your at-

tention. ✉ *Via San Vittore 21, near Sant'Ambrogio,* ☎ *02/485551.* 🎫 *10,000 lire.* ⏲ *Tues.–Fri. 9:30–5, weekends 9:30–6:30. Metro: Sant'Ambrogio.*

5 **Museo Poldi-Pezzoli.** The highlight of this extraordinary museum is undoubtedly Antonio Pollaiuolo's (circa 1431–98) *Portrait of a Lady,* one of the city's most prized treasures. The collection also includes masterpieces by Andrea Mantegna (1431–1506), Giovanni Bellini (1430–1516), and Fra Filippo Lippi (circa 1406–69), whose uncomplicated, heartrending style won him the favor and patronage of Piero de'Medici, son of Cosimo and father of Lorenzo Il Magnifico (1449–92). ✉ *Via Manzoni 12,* ☎ *02/794889.* 🎫 *10,000 lire.* ⏲ *Tues.–Fri. 9:30–12:30 and 2:30–6, Sat. 9:30–12:30 and 2:30–7:30, Sun. 9:30–12; Oct.–Mar. also 2:30–6. Metro: Duomo.*

14 **Navigli district.** This romantic, bohemian neighborhood in the southern part of the city was, in medieval times, a network of navigable canals, called *navigli,* crisscrossing Milan. Almost all have been covered over, except for two long canals, Naviglio Grande and Naviglio Pavese, and part of a third, Darsena. The canals are lined with quaint shops, art galleries, cafés, restaurants, and clubs. ✉ *Corso Porta Ticinese.*

★ 7 **Pinacoteca di Brera** (Brera Gallery). The picture collection in this art gallery is star studded, even by Italian standards. Start with the best, while you're still fresh, and leave the charming minor masterpieces for afterward. In Room 22, note that Raphael (1483–1520) painted *Betrothal of the Virgin* when he was 22. The other painting, Piero della Francesca's *Madonna with Saints and Angels,* is just as lovely, much aided by its skillful restoration and cleaning.

The somber, beautiful, and moving *Dead Christ* by Mantegna, in Room 6, is by far the smallest painting in the room, but it dominates, with its sparse palette of gray and terra-cotta, and especially for its original perspective. Mantegna's shocking, almost surgical, precision—in the rendering of Christ's wounds, the face propped up on a pillow, the day's growth of beard—tells of an all-too-human agony. It is one of Renaissance painting's most quietly wondrous achievements, finding an unsuspected middle ground between the excesses of conventional gore and beauty in representing the Passion's saddest moment. On your way out, pause a moment to view the fine paintings by Carlo Carrà (1881–1966)—especially *La Musa Metafisica,* or *Metaphysical Muse*—suggesting Italy's confident and stylish response to the likes of Picasso and Max Ernst and to the schools of Cubism and Surrealism. ✉ *Via Brera 28,* ☎ *02/722631.* 🎫 *8,000 lire.* ⏲ *Tues.–Sat. 9–5:30, Sun. 9–12:45. Metro: Cairoli or Monte Napoleone.*

OFF THE BEATEN PATH

LATIN QUARTER – Take time to wander around the lively quarter surrounding the Pinacoteca di Brera. The narrow streets, lined with boutiques, crafts shops, cafés, restaurants, and music clubs, comprise what is often referred to as Milan's Greenwich Village. A longtime haunt of artists and musicians, it has a number of clubs and cafés offering live music until late at night.

MINITALIA PARK – Between Milan and Bergamo, this theme park has a 1:500-scale relief model of Italy, with about 200 replicas of the country's most important monuments. ✉ *A4 autostrada toward Bergamo, Capriate San Gervasio, 35 km (22 mi) east of Milan,* ☎ *02/9091341.* 🎫 *17,000 lire.* ⏲ *Mar.–Oct., daily 9–dusk.*

PARCO DELLA PREISTORIA – Kids of all ages marvel at the 70-ft-long brontosaurus, the fierce tyrannosaurus, and the 4-km (2½-mi) path with 20 more full-size replicas of prehistoric animals. There is a picnic area and two cafés. ✉ *25 km (16 mi) east of Milan on S11 near Cassano d'Adda,* ☎ *0363/78184.* 🎫 *11,000 lire.* ⏲ *Mar.–Nov., daily 9–dusk; ticket office closes at 6.*

13 **San Lorenzo Maggiore.** Sixteen ancient Roman columns line the front of this sanctuary; 4th-century mosaics still survive in the Cappella di Sant'Aquilino (Chapel of St. Aquilinus). ✉ *Corso di Porta Ticinese.* ⏲ *Daily 9–1 and 3–7.*

15 **San Satiro.** This church is another architectural gem in which Bramante's (1444–1514) perfect command of proportion and perspective, keynotes of Renaissance architecture, makes a small interior seem extraordinarily spacious and airy. ✉ *Via Torino.* ⏲ *Daily 9–dusk.*

★ 9 **Santa Maria delle Grazie.** H. V. Morton once noted that Milan might well be the only city on earth where you could give a taxi driver the title of a painting as your destination. If this appeals to you, flag one down and say, *"L'Ultima Cena,"* since this is how *The Last Supper* is known here.

The Last Supper, housed in the church and former Dominican monastery of Santa Maria delle Grazie, has had an almost unbelievable history of bad luck and neglect—its near destruction in an American bombing raid in August 1943 was only the latest chapter in a series of misadventures, including, if one 19th-century source is to be believed, being whitewashed by the monks. Well-meant but disastrous attempts at restoration have done little to rectify the problem of the work's placement: it was executed on a wall unusually vulnerable to climatic dampness. Yet the artist chose to work slowly and patiently in oil pigments—which demand dry plaster—instead of proceeding hastily on wet plaster according to the conventional fresco technique. Novelist and critic Aldous Huxley (1894–1963) called it "the saddest work of art in the world." After years beneath a scaffold, with restorers patiently shifting from one square centimeter to another, Leonardo's famous masterpiece is free of the shroud of scaffolding—and centuries of retouching, grime, and dust. Astonishing clarity and luminosity have been regained.

Despite Leonardo's carefully preserved preparatory sketches in which the apostles are clearly labeled by name, there still remains some small debate about a few identities in the final arrangement. But there can be no mistaking Judas, small and dark, his hand calmly reaching forward toward the bread, isolated from the terrible confusion that has taken the hearts of the others. One critic, Professor Frederick Hartt, offers an elegantly terse explanation for why the composition works: it combines "dramatic confusion" with "mathematical order." Certainly, the amazingly skillful and unobtrusive repetition of threes, when first you see it—in the windows, in the grouping of the figures, and in their placement—adds a mystical aspect to what at first seems simply the perfect observation of spontaneous human gesture.

Santa Maria delle Grazie is the **Cenacolo Vinciano** (Vincian Refectory), which used to be the order's refectory. Take at least a moment to visit Santa Maria delle Grazie itself. It's a handsome church, with a fine dome by Bramante, which was added along with a cloister about the time that Leonardo was commissioned to paint *The Last Supper.* If you're wondering how two such giants came to be employed decorating and remodeling the refectory and church of a comparatively modest religious order, and not, say, the Duomo, the answer lies in the ambitious but largely unrealized plan to turn Santa Maria delle Grazie into a magnificent Sforza family mausoleum. Though Ludovico il Moro

Sforza (1452–1508), seventh duke of Milan, was but one generation away from the founding of the Sforza dynasty, he was its last ruler. Two years after Leonardo finished *The Last Supper,* Ludovico was defeated and was imprisoned in a French dungeon for the remaining eight years of his life.

Lines to view Leonardo's fading masterpiece are, inevitably, exceedingly long; the situation is exacerbated by the strict procedures to gain entry. You are admitted in groups of 30 and for only 15 minutes; you must first pass through two antechambers intended to remove pollutants from clothing and, before leaving, are directed through two additional filtration chambers. In short, the key is patience. ✉ *Corso Magenta, Cenacolo Vinciano,* ☎ *02/4987588.* 🎫 *12,000 lire.* ⏲ *Tues.–Sun. 8–1:45. Metro: Cadorna.*

NEED A BREAK? For those who don't scream for ice cream, a venerable neighborhood institution, the **Bar Magenta** (✉ Via Carducci 13 at Corso Magenta) provides an excellent alternative en route. Beyond lunch, beer, or coffee, the real attraction is its casual but civilized, quintessentially Milanese ambience.

4 **Teatro alla Scala.** You need know nothing of opera to sense that, like Carnegie Hall, La Scala is something rather more than an auditorium—here Verdi established his reputation and Maria Callas sang her way into opera lore. It looms as a symbol—both for the performer who dreams one day of singing here and for the buff who knows every note of *Rigoletto* by heart. Audiences here can be notoriously fickle, and have been known to jeer performers who do not do appropriate justice to their beloved *opera lirica,* as it is known in Italian. The opera house was completely renovated after its destruction by Allied bombs in 1943 and reopened at a performance led by the great Arturo Toscanini in 1946.

If you are lucky enough to be here during the opera season, which runs for approximately six months beginning each December 7, St. Ambrose Day, do whatever is necessary to attend—even if it requires perching among the rafters in one of the dreaded gallery seats. Hearing a Verdi or Puccini opera sung in Italian by Italians in Italy is a magical experience. It appears that plans for a renovation of the theater's stage—intended to bring it into line with the more modern stages at l'Opéra Bastille in Paris and New York's Met—have finally been agreed upon after several years of political machinations. Following the special events to mark the 100th anniversary of Verdi's death in 2001, the theater will be closed for a season. During a quick stroll through the theater's small **Museo Teatrale alla Scala,** you will get a peek at the gilded grandeur of the boxes and admire the excellent collection of original, hand-painted Art Nouveau posters. Also on display are original scores by Giuseppe Verdi and a small gallery devoted to Toscanini. ✉ *Piazza della Scala,* ☎ *02/8053418.* 🎫 *5,000 lire.* ⏲ *May.–Oct., Mon.–Sat. 9–noon and 2–6, Sun. 9:30–noon and 2:30–5; Nov.–Apr., Mon.–Sat. 9–noon and 2–6 (except during rehearsals). Metro: Duomo.*

Dining and Lodging

$$$$ ★ ✕ **L'Antica Osteria del Ponte.** Rich, imaginative seasonal cuisine at the whim of chef Ezio Santin is reason enough to make your way 20 km (12 mi) southwest of Milan to one of Italy's finest (and most expensive) restaurants. It is set in a traditional country inn, its interior a cozy combination of wooden ceiling beams with a blazing fire in chilly weather. Inventive recipes include ravioli *di aragosta* (filled with lobster meat) in summer and, in the fall, a range of heartwarming spe-

cialties, many using the prized wild porcini mushrooms. ✉ *Cassinetta di Lugagnano, 3 km (2 mi) north of Abbiategrasso,* ☎ *02/9420034. Reservations essential. Jacket and tie. AE, DC, MC, V. Closed Sun.–Mon., Dec. 25–Jan. 15, and Aug.*

$$$$ ✕ **Savini.** Red carpets and glass chandeliers characterize the classy Savini, in the Galleria Vittorio Emanuele. It's a typical old-fashioned Milanese restaurant, with dining rooms on three floors, including a "winter garden," with views of the Galleria. Try the Milanese specialty risotto *al salto* (grilled in the pan) or *costoletta di vitello* (veal cutlets). ✉ *Galleria Vittorio Emanuele,* ☎ *02/72003433. AE, DC, MC, V. Closed Aug. 10–20, Jan. 1–Jan. 6, and Sun.*

$$$$ ✕ **Scaletta.** The restaurant's name means "little stairway" in Italian, perhaps inspired by its own stairway ascending to culinary paradise. This tiny restaurant could be the dining room of a gracious home, with cool pastels, book-lined walls, and a superb collection of blown glass. Host-sommelier Aldo Bellini and genius cook Mamma Pina in the kitchen treat you with cordiality and take time to discuss wines and menus, if you like. Pina's cooking is a light, personalized version of traditional Italian cuisine. ✉ *Piazzale Stazione Porta Genova 3,* ☎ *02/58100290. AE, DC, MC, V. Closed Sun. and Aug. No lunch Mon.*

$$$–$$$$ ★ ✕ **Boeucc.** Milan's oldest restaurant (pronounced "birch") is in the same square as novelist Alessandro Manzoni's house, not far from La Scala. Subtly lit, with cream-color fluted columns, chandeliers, thick carpets, and a garden for warm-weather dining, it has come a long way from the time when it was simply a basement "hole" (*boeucc* is old Milanese for *buco,* or hole). Typical Milanese and Italian dishes served include penne *al branzino e zucchini* (with sea bass and zucchini sauce) and *gelato di castagne con zabaglione caldo* (chestnut ice cream with hot zabaglione). ✉ *Piazza Belgioioso 2,* ☎ *02/76020224. Reservations essential. AE. Closed Sat. and Aug. No lunch Sun.*

$$$ ✕ **Giannino.** Although not quite as old as Boeucc, Giannino celebrated its 100th anniversary in 1999, and it has been a very successful century by any standards. The cuisine concentrates on Milanese specialties, such as the ubiquitous *milanesa* (breaded veal cutlet), which you would be hard pressed to find a better version of anywhere in the city, and a particularly fine risotto. But you'll also find other regional dishes within the vast menu, including some excellent Florentine dishes, among them a succulent version of the *bistecca alla fiorentina* (grilled Chianina beef). ✉ *Via Amatore Sciesa 8,* ☎ *02/55195582. Reservations essential. AE, DC, MC, V. Closed Sun.*

$$–$$$ ✕ **Antica Trattoria della Pesa.** Fin de siècle decor, dark wood paneling, and old-fashioned lamps re-create the atmosphere of this restaurant at its opening more than 100 years ago. This is authentic Old Milan, as the menu confirms, offering risotto, minestrone, and osso buco. ✉ *Viale Pasubio 10,* ☎ *02/6555741. AE, DC, MC, V. Closed Sun., 2 wks in Aug., and Dec. 23–Jan. 6.*

$$ ✕ **Al Cantinone.** Opera enthusiasts still come here for an after-theater drink, just as they did a century ago. The decor is classic Milanese, the service is fast, and the food is homey and reliable. Try the homemade *pappardelle* (thick, flat noodles) or Tuscan ravioli with meat sauce. There's a wide selection of grilled meats and a staggering choice of wines. ✉ *Via Agnello 19, entrance on Via Ragazzi del 99,* ☎ *02/86461338. AE, DC, MC, V. Closed Sun., Aug., and Dec. 24–Jan. 5. No lunch Sat.*

$$ ✕ **La Capanna.** Signora cooks and her husband pours wine and sees that everything goes smoothly in this popular trattoria near the Piola Metro stop (and the university). The food is predominantly Tuscan—Tuscan salami, pappardelle, fish, and steak—but some Milanese specialties are also on the menu. ✉ *Via Donatello 9,* ☎ *02/29400884. AE, DC, MC, V. Closed Sat. and Aug.*

$$ ✕ **La Libera.** Although this establishment in the heart of Brera bills itself as a *birreria con cucina* (beer cellar with kitchen), its young clientele comes here for the excellent food and convivial atmosphere. A soft current of jazz soothes the ripple of conversation amid restful dark green decor. Sample the creative cooking, including the *insalata esotica* (avocado, chicken, rice, and papaya salad) or *rognone di vitello con broccoletti e ginepro* (veal kidneys with broccoli and juniper berries). ✉ *Via Palermo 21,* ☎ *02/8053603. Reservations not accepted. No credit cards. Closed Sat., Aug., and Dec. 22–Jan. 1. No lunch Sun.*

$$ ✕ **Nabucco.** This smart, tasteful restaurant in the Brera offers such delights as risotto *con porcini,* an excellent range of salads, and homemade pastries and desserts. It serves good fixed-price lunches ($). ✉ *Via Fiori Chiari 10,* ☎ *02/860663. AE, DC, MC, V. Closed Tues.*

$$ ✕ **Trattoria Milanese.** Between the Duomo and the Basilica of Sant'Ambrogio, this small, popular trattoria has been run by the same family for more than 60 years and is crowded with businesspeople for lunch and with regulars, and the occasional Milanese celeb, at dinner. Food is authentic regional, with risotto and *costoletta alla milanese* (milanese-style breaded veal cutlet) good choices. ✉ *Via Santa Marta 11,* ☎ *02/86451991. DC, MC, V. Closed Tues. and Aug.*

$–$$ ✕ **Bistrot di Gualtiero Marchesi/Brunch.** Atop the Rinascente department store off Piazza del Duomo, this brunch eatery, bar, and bistro is supervised by the well-known chef Gualtiero Marchesi and offers a variety of menus with a full range of prices. A bonus is a great view of the Duomo's spires. ✉ *La Rinascente, Piazza Duomo,* ☎ *02/877120. AE, DC, MC, V. Closed Sun. No lunch Mon.*

$–$$ ✕ **La Bruschetta.** You'll find this tiny, busy pizzeria off Corso Vittorio Emanuele, behind the Duomo; it is run by a partnership of Tuscans and Neapolitans. The woodstove is in full view, so you can see your pizza cooking in front of you, although there are plenty of nonpizza dishes available, too, such as spaghetti *alle cozze e vongole* (with a clam and mussel sauce). ✉ *Piazza Beccaria 12,* ☎ *02/8692494. MC, V. Closed Mon., 3 wks in Aug., and 1st wk in Jan.*

$ ✕ **Al Tempio d'Oro.** It may be noisy, it may have the ambience of an Italian pub, but the food is very good, filling, and—for Milan—surprisingly cheap. It is also near the train station, which makes it a great place to eat before embarking on a journey or, indeed, before beginning your visit to Milan. The food is hardly haute cuisine, but here you'll find an excellent selection of Mediterranean dishes, ranging from a plain pasta to a more exotic Maghrebin couscous. The paella is delicious. ✉ *Via delle Leghe 23,* ☎ *02/26145709. No credit cards. Closed Sun. and 2 wks in Aug.*

$ ✕ **La Giara.** The quality of the food from the limited menu in this simple Pugliese restaurant is a revelation. Here you eat tavern style, at wooden tables and benches, often sharing a table with other diners. Start with the antipasto *sott'olio* (eggplant, artichokes, mushrooms, and tomatoes preserved in olive oil), and try one of the grilled-meat courses, cooked on a range at the front of the restaurant. ✉ *Viale Monza 10,* ☎ *02/26143835. No credit cards. Closed Wed.*

$ ✕ **San Tomaso.** The informality of a beer hall, a trendy young clientele, and a self-service counter here add up to pleasant, easy eating. Very busy at lunch, it's usually quieter at night. ✉ *Via San Tomaso 5,* ☎ *02/874510. No credit cards. Closed Sun.*

$ ✕ **Taverna Moriggi.** Near the stock exchange, this is a dusky, wood-paneled wine bar serving a fixed-price lunch for about 30,000 lire, or cold cuts and cheeses in the evening. ✉ *Via Moriggi 8,* ☎ *02/86450880. Reservations essential. DC, MC, V. Closed Sun. No lunch Sat.*

$$$$ **Carlton-Senato.** This hotel is the ideal choice for visitors who intend to spend time shopping—or window shopping—in the nearby high-fashion streets, Via della Spiga, Via Sant'Andrea, and Via Monte Napoleone. The hotel is very light and airy, with double-thick windows, a garage with direct access to the hotel, and lots of little touches—gratis chocolates and liqueurs—to make up for the rather functional rooms. Some have terraces large enough for a table, chair, and potted shrubs. ✉ *Via Senato 5, 20124,* ☎ *02/77077,* FAX *02/783300. 79 rooms. Restaurant, bar, parking (fee). AE, DC, MC, V.*

$$$$ **Duomo.** Your comfort is the important thing at this spacious, modern hotel: celebrities have been turned away when it was thought they would attract noisy fans and paparazzi. This is the obvious choice if a central location is also your priority: you're only 20 yards from the cathedral itself, yet within a quiet pedestrian-only zone. Air-conditioned rooms and duplex suites are swankily done in golds, creams, and browns. If in a room on the second, fourth, or fifth floor, you'll be eye to eye with the Gothic gargoyles and pinnacles of the Duomo. ✉ *Via San Raffaele 1, 20121,* ☎ *02/8833,* FAX *02/86462027. 153 rooms. Restaurant, bar, parking (fee). AE, DC, MC, V.*

$$$$ **Four Seasons.** The renaissance of a 14th-century monastery on an exclusive shopping street in the center of Milan has produced a precious gem, for which you'll pay dearly. The hotel blends European sophistication with American comfort. Individually decorated rooms have opulent marble bathrooms; most rooms face the quiet courtyard. Downstairs is the hotel's well-regarded Il Teatro restaurant. ✉ *Via Gesù 8, 20121,* ☎ *02/77088,* FAX *02/7708500. 98 rooms. 2 restaurants, bar, business services, meeting rooms. AE, DC, MC, V.*

$$$$ ★ **Palace.** The rather unprepossessing 1950s Milanese exterior is no indication of what lies within, a truly superior hotel with personalized service. Beyond the sumptuous Renaissance and postmodern lobby, rooms reveal precious Empire-style antiques. Exquisite bathrooms are done in Portugal pink and Issoire green marble. It's aim is to be Milan's premier business hotel, with Internet and modem connections in every room, and more. Mediterranean cuisine is served in the Casanova Grill. You can putt on the computer-simulated golf center or avail yourself of lessons on the putting green and driving range at the City Golf Center. ✉ *Piazza della Repubblica 20, 20124,* ☎ *02/6336,* FAX *02/654485. 216 rooms. Restaurant, bar, breakfast room, in-room data ports, in-room safes, minibars, laundry service, business services, meeting rooms, parking (fee). AE, DC, MC, V.*

$$$$ **Pierre.** No expense was spared to furnish each room of this luxury hotel in a different style with the lavish color-coordinated fabrics and a variety of modern and antique furniture. Everything is electronic: you can open the curtains, turn off the lights, get personal messages on your TV screen—all with the touch of a button. It's on the inner beltway, near the medieval church of Sant'Ambrogio. ✉ *Via De Amicis 32, 20123,* ☎ *02/72000581,* FAX *02/8052157. 49 rooms. Restaurant, bar, in-room safes, minibars, parking (fee). AE, DC, MC, V.*

$$$$ ★ **Principe di Savoia.** Of the three deluxe ITT-Sheraton Luxury Collection hotels here, this is the most posh. Opened in 1923, it has set and borne the standards for European hotels. Behind the Liberty-style facade, the prevailing style is 19th-century Lombard, with lavish mirrors, drapes, and carpets. The understated, gracious bedrooms are designed to reflect the eclectic architectural styles of the fin de siècle. If you want to spoil yourself in full Roman-emperor fashion, book the Presidential Suite, complete with private marbled pool. The hotel isn't cheap, but if you stay here you're in good company: this is the favorite Milanese destination of such notables as the Sultan of Brunei, George Bush, Demi Moore, and Woody Allen. You can dine alfresco in the re-

fined Galleria restaurant. ✉ *Piazza della Repubblica 17, 20124,* ☎ *02/62301,* FAX *02/6595838. 299 rooms. Restaurant, bar, health club, dry cleaning, laundry service, business services, convention center, meeting rooms. AE, DC, MC, V.*

$$$ **Canada.** This friendly small hotel is close to Piazza del Duomo on the edge of a district full of shops and restaurants. It offers good value in rooms that are furnished in a nondescript fashion but have the usual modern trappings. ✉ *Via Santa Sofia 16, 20122,* ☎ *02/58304844,* FAX *02/58300282. 35 rooms. Bar. AE, DC, MC, V.*

$$$ **Casa Svizzera.** A faithful clientele considers this one of Milan's best small hotels in its price category, so it's advisable to reserve early. Adjacent to the Duomo and a few yards from the Galleria, it's central and handy to Metro and bus lines. The hotel is soundproofed; air-conditioned rooms have refrigerator-bars and cheery floral-print fabric. ✉ *Via San Raffaele 3, 20121,* ☎ *02/8692246,* FAX *02/72004690. 45 rooms. Bar, minibars. AE, DC, MC, V. Closed Aug. and Dec. 24–Jan. 6.*

$$$ **Gritti.** The Picassos, Matisses, and van Goghs in the lobby here are originals—so the manager will tell you—except that they were painted quite recently "in the spirit." The Gritti is a bright hotel with a cheerful atmosphere, adequate rooms, and good views (from the inside upper floors) of tiled roofs and the gold Madonnina statue on top of the Duomo, only a few hundred yards away. ✉ *Piazza Santa Maria Beltrade 4, north end of Via Torino, 20123,* ☎ *02/801056,* FAX *02/89010999. 48 rooms. Bar, breakfast room. AE, DC, MC, V.*

$$$ **Hotel Vittoria.** This family-owned hotel is in a quiet residential street only minutes from the Galleria Vittorio Emanuele and the Duomo. The guest rooms are tiny, but in pristine condition. The staff are courteous and extremely friendly, eager to do whatever they can to ensure their guests' comfort and satisfaction. In summer, breakfast is served in the small garden at the back. ✉ *Via Pietro Calvi 32, 20129,* ☎ *02/5456520,* FAX *02/55190246. 20 rooms. Breakfast room, in-room safes, minibars. AE, DC, MC, V.*

$$–$$$ ★ **London.** Close to the Duomo, the London has clean, spacious rooms and a staff unfailing in their politeness and efficiency, attending to their guests' every need. ✉ *Via Rovello 3, 20121,* ☎ *02/72020166,* FAX *02/8057037. 29 rooms. Bar. MC, V. Closed Dec. 23–Jan. 3 and Aug.*

$$ **Hotel Garda.** This modern hotel can claim the best location in Milan: it's a two-minute walk from the main train station, three subway lines, and a multistory parking lot. Although the lobby looks spartan, rooms beyond are well furnished, comfortable, and clean. Most rooms overlook the busy center streets, thankfully quieter at night. ✉ *Via Napo Torriani 21, 20124,* ☎ *02/66982626,* FAX *02/66982576. 55 rooms. Bar, breakfast room. AE, DC, MC, V.*

$$ **San Francisco.** Near Metro stations on two lines (Loreto, Piola, or Pasteur stops) and not far from the Central Station, this modern hotel has a functional, flag-bedecked lobby, simply furnished rooms, and a small garden. ✉ *Viale Lombardia 55, 20131,* ☎ *02/2361009,* FAX *02/26680377. 31 rooms. AE, DC, MC, V.*

Nightlife and the Arts

The Arts

MUSIC

Teatro alla Scala opera house (☞ Exploring, *above,* and Opera, *below*) features a two-month season of classical concerts in October and November. The **Conservatorio** (✉ Via del Conservatorio 12, ☎ 02/7621101) is the best place in the city for classical concerts and is a popular venue for the well-heeled all year long.

OPERA

The season at Milan's famous **Teatro alla Scala** opera house runs from December 7 (St. Ambrose Day) through May or later. Seats are usually sold out well in advance, but if you are prepared to pay the desk clerk at your hotel, you will probably be able to get hold of a pair of tickets. For information on schedules, ticket availability, and how to buy tickets, there is an **Infotel Scala Service** (with English-speaking staff) at the ticket office (✉ Teatro alla Scala, Ufficio Biglietteria, Via Filodrammatici 2, ☎ 02/72003744), open daily noon–6. Telephone bookings are not accepted. From abroad you can book in advance, within a short specified period for each presentation (the dates are published at the beginning of the season; these tickets are allocated on a first-come, first-served basis), by applying for a reservation by mail or fax (transmitted 9–6 local time, with time and date of transmission, and sender's fax number indicated on the fax, to 02/8607787 or 02/861778), or at CIT or other travel agencies (at agencies, no more than 10 days before performance). Consult the listings in the informative monthly *Milano Mese,* free at APT (tourist board) offices, or the weekly *Viva Milano.*

THEATER

Milan's **Piccolo Teatro** (✉ Via Rovello 2, ☎ 02/877663) is noted for its excellent productions, given in Italian, of course. **Teatro Manzoni** (✉ Via Manzoni 40, ☎ 02/790543) is equally renowned.

Nightlife

BARS

El Brellin (✉ Vicolo Lavandai at Alzaia Naviglio Grande, ☎ 02/58101351), closed Sunday, is one of the many bars in the Navigli district. In the Brera quarter, **Momus** (✉ Via Fiori Chiari 8, ☎ 02/8056227), closed Monday, is upscale and intimate.

NIGHTCLUBS

Head to the hot spot of late, **Le Scimmie** (✉ Via Ascanio Sforza 49, ☎ 02/89402874), closed Tuesday, for cool jazz and a relaxed atmosphere. **Capolinea** (✉ Via Ludovico II Moro 119, ☎ 02/89122024) is open every night of the week and features an eclectic range of jazz, from Dixieland to the ultramodern New Beat style. Milan clubs are good bets for dancing, but don't expect to get them for a song. Club kids with plenty of money crowd **Stage** (✉ Galleria Manzoni off Via Monte Napoleone, ☎ 02/76021071), closed Sunday. **Rock Hollywood** (✉ Via Como 15/c, ☎ 02/6598996) is the in place for the fashion set.

Killer Plastic (✉ Viale Umbria 120, ☎ 02/733996), closed Monday–Wednesday, is one of Milan's trendiest nightclubs. Saturday night is glamour night, with the beautiful people in strict attendance. Thursday night is gay night. **Lizard** (✉ Largo La Foppa, ☎ 02/6590890), closed Sunday–Tuesday, is trendy, loud, and expensive—a formula that doesn't deter the young Milanese crowd. **Nepentha** (✉ Piazza Diaz 1, ☎ 02/804837), closed Sunday, is also a popular spot.

Outdoor Activities and Sports

Participant Sports

GOLF

The **Parco di Monza** (✉ 15 km/9 mi from Milan) has 18- and 9-hole courses. Contact the Golf Club Milano (☎ 039/303081). For information and bookings for other golf clubs in the Milan area, contact **City Golf Club** (✉ Hotel Palace, Piazza della Repubblica 20, ☎ 02/29030075).

HEALTH CLUB

The best equipped of Milan's many sport centers is the **Centro Saini** (✉ Via Corelli 136, ☎ 02/7561280), in the vast Parco Forlanini.

Much like a municipal gym, it offers squash and volleyball facilities and weight rooms. It's outside the city center; take Bus 38.

Spectator Sport

SOCCER

AC Milan and Inter Milan share the use of the **San Siro Stadium** (Via Piccolomini, ☎ 02/48707123). With more than 60,000 of the 85,000 seats allocated to season ticket holders, and another couple of thousand tickets made available to visiting fans (which means they are on sale outside of Milan), tickets can be notoriously difficult to come by, especially for the high profile games such as the local AC Milan–Inter derby or between either team and their rivals from Turin (Juventus) or the capital (Roma or Lazio). However, the stadium does have tickets on sale weekdays from 9 AM to 5 PM and for a couple of hours before each game, usually played on Sunday.

Shopping

Milan's fortissimo occurs twice a year, in the end of February and October (for women) and June and January (for men), when the world's fashion elite descend upon the city for the famous ready-to-wear designer shows that invariably set next season's international styles (☞ Close Up: Clothes Make the City, *below*).

Department Stores

La Rinascente (✉ Piazza del Duomo) is one of the bigger department stores in Milan. **Coin** (✉ Piazza Loreto) is smaller but stylish.

Markets

Markets selling food and a vast array of items, new and old, are displayed in open-air stalls all over Milan. In many markets, bargaining is no longer the custom. You can try to haggle, but if you fear getting ripped off, go to the stalls where prices are clearly marked. On Saturday there is the huge **Mercato Papiniano** (✉ Viale Papiniano, and the Fiera di Senigallia, on Via Calatafimi) with old and new bargains. If you collect coins or stamps, go on Sunday morning to the specialized market at **Via Armorari** (✉ Near Piazza Cordusio). The best antiques markets are held on the last Sunday of each month along the Navigli and the third Saturday of each month on **Via Fiori Chiari** (✉ Near Via Brera).

Shopping Districts

At the northern end of Piazza della Scala, Via Manzoni leads straight into the heart of Milan's most luxurious shopping district, perhaps the most luxurious shopping district in all of Italy. Right here, in a few small streets laid out like a game of hopscotch—Via Monte Napoleone, Via Sant'Andrea, Via della Spiga—exist the shops of the great Italian designers, such as Armani, Versace, and Gianfranco Ferré. Don't come here looking for affordable fashion—that has been relegated to the other side of the Duomo. Shops are usually open 9–1 (except Monday morning) and 4–7:30; many are closed in August. A good locator map (posted on a pole) of the best boutiques in the area can be found at the corner of Via della Spiga and Via Borgospesso.

Brera is a Milanese neighborhood with many unique shops. Walk along Via Brera, Via Solferino, Corso Garibaldi, and Via Paolo Sarpi. **Corso Buenos Aires** is a wide avenue with a variety of shops, several offering moderately priced items. **Corso Vittorio Emanuele** has clothing, leather goods, and shoe shops, some with items at reasonable prices. **Via Monte Napoleone** has 10 top-notch jewelers and a profusion of antiques stores and designer fashion boutiques, as well.

Specialty Stores

CLOTHING

For the constant redefinition of cut, design, and style, **Giorgio Armani** (✉ Via Sant'Andrea 9, ☎ 02/76003234) is the fashion temple. Hip, sleek, less formal Armani wear is sold at **Emporio Armani** (✉ Via Durini 24, ☎ 02/76003030), at less formal prices. **Cerruti 1881** (✉ Via della Spiga 20, ☎ 02/76009777) has elegant styles with an edge for men and women. Head to **Prada** (✉ Via della Spiga 1, ☎ 02/76002019) for Miucca's bewitching, chic spartan design found on everything from celebrities to runways these days, smart leather goods, and a look at the famous series of fin de siècle murals with a travel theme. **Gianfranco Ferré** (✉ Via Sant'Andrea 19, ☎ 02/782212) concentrates on swank, ready-to-wear apparel. Daring design and color on the cutting edge is the fashion at **Gianni Versace** (✉ Via Monte Napoleone 2 and 11, ☎ 02/76001982 and 02/76008528). **Moschino** (✉ Via Sant'Andrea 7, ☎ 02/76000832 or 02/76009404) counters the conventional. **Guiseppe Falzone** (✉ Corso Cristotoro Colombo 5, ☎ 02/58103673) is a great place to find designer gear at massive discounts, sometimes two-thirds off of the retail price. **Primavera** (✉ Via Torino 47, ☎ 874565) also offers substantial reductions on its clothing.

HOUSEWARES

L'Utile e il Dilettevole (✉ Via della Spiga) sells enchanting Italian country-style items for the home.

SHOES AND LEATHER ACCESSORIES

Beltrami (✉ , ☎ 02/76006660; ✉ Piazza San Babila 4/a) *scarpe* (shoes) enjoy the fashion limelight, with assurance of good quality. For top-quality, classic design in the finest of hides, choose **Ferragamo** (✉ Via Monte Napoleone 3, ☎ 02/76000054). For a taste of style mixed with tradition, head to **Fratelli Rossetti** (✉ Corso Matteotti 9, ☎ 02/76021650). Shoe addicts would be hard pressed not to find a gorgeous pair from **Lario 1898** (✉ Via Monte Napoleone 21, ☎ 02/76002641) in their closets.

PAVIA, CREMONA, AND MANTUA

Cities of the Po Plain

Great Lombard cities of the Po River plain south of Milan are worthy of discovery. Pavia is celebrated for its Certosa, the Carthusian monastery. In Cremona, history's great violin makers lived and worked. A diminutive utopian Renaissance city, Sabbioneta was the fruit of one man's lifelong obsession. Mantua was home for almost 300 years of the fantastically wealthy Gonzaga dynasty.

Pavia

16 *57 km (35 mi) west of Cremona, 38 km (24 mi) south of Milan.*

Pavia was once Milan's chief local rival. The city dates at least from the Roman era and was the capital of the Lombard kings for two centuries (572–774). Pavia came to be known as "the city of a hundred towers" (of which only a handful have survived). Its prestigious university was founded in 1361 on the site of a 10th-century law school but has claims dating from antiquity.

The 14th-century **Castello Visconteo** now houses the local **Museo Civico** (Civic Museum), with an interesting archaeological collection and a picture gallery featuring works by Correggio. ✉ *Viale 11 Febbraio, near Piazza Castello,* ☎ *0382/33853.* *5,000 lire.* ⏲ *Tues.–Sun. 9–1:30.*

Close-Up

CLOTHES MAKE THE CITY

WHEN DESIGNER MARIUCCIA Mandelli decided in 1954 to stamp her collection with the name "Krizia" she anticipated fashion-mad 1990s Milan with an uncanny foresight. The name adopted by the former teacher is derived from a character in one of Plato's dialogues who spends all of his money on clothes and jewelry for fatuous and vain women; while this may be a designer's dream consumer, the name remains an ironic reminder of the fashion world's constant clash of art and commerce. Nowhere do the two come together as tumultuously as in Milan's Golden Triangle, the 1-km (½-mi) area spanning Via della Spiga, Via Monte Napoleone, and Via Sant'Andrea that is home to most of Italy's high-fashion houses and the source of several billion dollars of revenue each year. It's here that top designers like Donatella Versace, Gianfranco Ferré, and Giorgio Armani have their workshops, and here that the fashion world's attention is focused four weeks a year for the men's and women's summer and winter collection shows. The city has grown out of its long-standing rivalry with Florence, home to Gucci and Salvatore Ferragamo, over the title of Italy's fashion capital, and in the 1990s has become a rival to Paris and New York for the presentation of top-quality, top-price *alta moda*.

Milan's designers, Mandelli among them, are known for a subversive attitude toward the conventions of fashion. Legends abound: Missoni's famous 1967 show in which the black silk dresses of braless models became transparent on the catwalk; Moschino's 1980s-era anti-fashion Minnie Mouse dresses and fried-egg buttons; the late Gianni Versace's rock and roll aesthetic that put chains and leather on the catwalk. Italian style is still Italian style, however; one notable exception to this revolutionary fervor is Giorgio Armani, the former medical student whose fluid, elegant designs have made him not only one of the world's leading stylists but also a top Hollywood designer, for films including *American Gigolo* (1980), *True Romance* (1993), *Rising Sun* (1993), and *Prêt-à-Porter* (1994), the Robert Altman fashion world spoof that, coincidentally, featured another Milanese designer, Nicola Trussardi.

Unfortunately, it's all but impossible for the general public to get in to watch fashion history being made at the collections, held mid-January (Men's Spring-Summer), at the end of February (Women's Spring-Summer), at the beginning of October (Women's Fall-Winter), and the end of June (Men's Fall-Winter). Houses hold their own lavish, celebrity-studded presentations, and admission is by jealously guarded invitation only. The national trade organization, the **Camera Nazionale della Moda Italiana** (✉ Largo Domodossola 1, ☎ 02/48008286) suggests giving it a go anyway. If you contact design houses in Milan directly before the shows, you may be able to wheedle your way in among the glitterati. **Missoni** (✉ Via T. Salvini 1, 20122, ☎ 02/76001479), **Dolce & Gabbana** (✉ Piazza Umanitaria 2, 20122, ☎ 02/54108152), **Trussardi** (✉ Piazza Duse 4, 20122, ☎ 02/760641), **Gianfranco Ferré** (✉ Via San Andrea 18, 20121, ☎ 02/784460), **Prada** (✉ Via A. Maffei 2, 20122, ☎ 02/546701), **Krizia** (✉ Palazzo Melzi d'Eril, Viale Manin 19, 20121, ☎ 02/6596415), **Moschino** (✉ Via Ceradini 11/a, 20129, ☎ 02/7610200), **Giorgio Armani** (✉ Via Borgonuovo 11, 20121, ☎ 02/76003118), **Gianni Versace** (✉ Via Gesu 12, 20121, ☎ 02/760931).

In the Romanesque church of **San Pietro in Ciel d'Oro,** you can visit the tomb of Christianity's most celebrated convert, St. Augustine, housed in a Gothic marble ark on the high altar. ✉ *Via Matteotti.* ⊙ *Mon.–Sat. 9–5 and for Sun. Mass.*

The main reason for stopping in Pavia is the **Certosa** (the Carthusian monastery) 8 km (5 mi) north of Pavia city center. Its facade is stupendous, with much the same relish as the Duomo in Milan, which follows the delightful first commandment of Victorian architecture: always decorate the decoration. The Certosa's extravagant grandeur was due, in part, to the plan to have it house the tombs of the family of the first duke of Milan, Galeazzo Visconti III (he died during a plague, at age 49, in 1402). And extravagant it was—almost unimaginably so in an age before modern roads and transport. Only the very best marble was used in construction, transported, undoubtedly by barge, from the legendary quarries of Carrara, roughly 240 km (150 mi) away. Though the ground plan may be Gothic—a cruciform planned in a series of squares—the gorgeous fabric that rises above it is triumphantly Renaissance. On the facade, in the lower frieze, are medallions of Roman emperors and Eastern monarchs; above them are low reliefs of the life of Christ, as well as that of Galeazzo Visconti III.

The first duke was the only Visconti to be interred here, and then only some 75 years after his death, in a tomb designed by Gian Cristoforo Romano. Look for it in the right transept. In the left transept is a tomb of greater human appeal—that of a rather stern middle-aged man and a beautiful young woman. The man is Ludovico il Moro Sforza (1452–1508), seventh duke of Milan, who commissioned Leonardo da Vinci to paint *The Last Supper.* The woman is his wife, one of the most celebrated women of her day, Beatrice d'Este (1475–97), the embodiment of brains, culture, birth, and beauty. Married when he was 40 and she was 16, they had enjoyed six happy years of marriage when she died suddenly, while giving birth to a stillborn child. Ludovico commissioned the sculptor Cristoforo Solari to design a joint tomb for the high altar of Santa Maria delle Grazie in Milan. Originally much larger, the tomb for some years occupied the honored place in Santa Maria delle Grazie as planned. Then, for reasons that are still mysterious, the Dominican monks, who seemed to care no more for their former patron than they did for their faded Leonardo fresco, sold the tomb to their Carthusian brothers to the south. Sadly, part of the tomb, and its remains, were lost. ✉ *Certosa, 8 km (5 mi) north of Pavia,* ☎ *0382/925613.* 🎫 *Free, donation requested.* ⊙ *Oct.–Mar., Tues.–Sat. 9–11:30 and 2:30–4:30; Apr. and Sept., Tues.–Sun. 9–11:30 and 2:30–5:30; May–Aug., Tues.–Sun. 9:30–11:30 and 2:30–6.*

Dining

$$$ ★ ✕ **Locanda Vecchia Pavia.** At this sophisticated, art-nouveau style restaurant, you'll find creative versions of traditional regional cuisine, including *rane* (frogs), the local specialty, in risotto or on a spit. *Casoncelli* (stuffed pasta), *petto d'anatra* (breast of duck), and veal cutlet alla milanese are done with style, as are more imaginative seafood dishes. For dessert, choco-addicts will relish the hot chocolate pudding with white chocolate sauce. It's next to the Duomo. ✉ *Via Cardinale Riboldi 2,* ☎ *0382/304132. Reservations essential. AE, DC, MC, V. Closed Mon., Jan. 1–9, and Aug. No lunch Wed.*

Nightlife and the Arts

During the first half of September, Pavia's **Settembre Pavese** festival presents street processions, displays, and concerts.

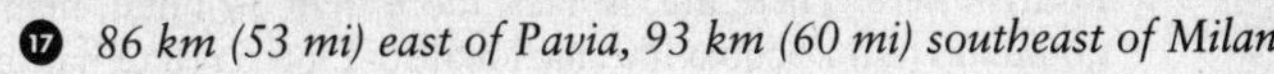

Cremona

17 *86 km (53 mi) east of Pavia, 93 km (60 mi) southeast of Milan.*

If there is only one place in Italy to buy a violin, it's Cremona—as true today as when Andrea Amati (1510–80) opened up shop here in the middle of the 16th century. Though cognoscenti continue to revere the Amati name, it was the apprentice of Amati's nephew, Nicolo (1596–1684), for whom the fates had reserved a wide and lasting international fame. In a career that spanned an incredible 68 years, Antonio Stradivari (1644–1737) made more than 1,200 instruments—including violas, cellos, harps, guitars, and mandolins, in addition to his fabled violins. Labeled simply with a small printed slip, "Antonius Stradivarius Cremonensis. Faciebat anno . . ." (the date added in a neat italic hand), they remain the best, most coveted, and most expensive stringed instruments in the world.

Cremona's Romanesque **Duomo** was consecrated in 1190 and is home to the beautiful *Story of the Virgin Mary and the Passion of Christ,* the central fresco of an extraordinary cycle commissioned in 1514 and featuring the work of primarily local artists, including Boccacio Boccancino, Giovan Francesco Bembo, and Altobello Melone. ⊠ *Piazza del Comune.* ⏲ *Mon.–Sat. 7–noon and 3:30–7, Sun. 7:30–1 and 3:30–7.*

If you would like to see the original Stradivarius instruments, go to the second floor of **Palazzo del Comune** (City Hall), where five masterpieces by Cremonese *liutai* (violin makers), dating from the 16th to the 18th centuries, are on view. ⊠ *Piazza del Comune,* ☎ *0372/4071.* 🎫 *6,000 lire, valid for all other Cremona museums, including the Museo Stradivariano (☞ below).* ⏲ *Tues.–Fri. 8:30–1 and 2:30–4:30, Sat. 9–11:30.*

Piazza del Comune, with its Duomo (☞ *above*), campanile, baptistery, and city hall, is particularly distinctive and harmonious. The combination of old brick, rose- and cream-color marble, terra-cotta, and old copper roofs brings Romanesque, Gothic, and Renaissance together with unusual success.

The large campanile that dominates the square is the **Torrazzo** (Big Tower), perhaps the tallest bell tower in the country, visible for a considerable distance across the Po plain. Its height, however, was the source of tragedy in 1997, when three people committed suicide by throwing themselves from the top; consequently, the tower was closed for renovation, so check with the tourist authority for its eventual reopening. ⊠ *Piazza del Comune.* 🎫 *6,000 lire.* ⏲ *Apr.–Oct., Mon.–Sat. 10:30–noon and 3–6, Sun. 10:30–12:30 and 3–6:30.*

At No. 1 **Piazza Roma,** Antonio Stradivari lived, worked, and died. It's a lovely square of gardens, trees, and lawns. It is said that in addition to knowing all there was to know about woods, varnish, and the subtleties of assembling the 70-odd component parts that make up a violin, Stradivari liked to keep each new instrument in his bedroom for a month before varnishing it. This way, he claimed, by virtue of some mysterious somnolent transmigration, he gave a soul to each of his creations. In the center of the park is **Stradivari's grave,** marked by a simple tombstone.

The small **Museo Stradivariano** (Stradivarius Museum) has an informative display of Stradivari's plans and models, and violins made by Cremona's more modern masters. ⊠ *Via Palestro 17,* ☎ *0372/461886.* 🎫 *6,000 lire valid for Palazzo del Comune (☞ above).* ⏲ *Tues.–Sat. 9–6, Sun. 10–6.*

Strolling about town, you may notice that violin making continues to flourish here. There are, in fact, more than 50 liutai, many of them graduates of the Scuola Internazionale di Liuteria (International School of Violin Making), who continue to work by traditional methods in small shops scattered throughout Cremona. You are usually welcome to these ateliers, especially if contemplating the acquisition of their own ready-made or custom-built Cremonese violin.

Dining

$$$$ ★ ✕ **Ceresole.** This unobtrusive restaurant just off the Piazza del Comune is Cremona's best—and most expensive—place. It offers a variety of elegant international dishes but concentrates on local delights: *cotecchino* (rich boiled sausage) and risotto, to name a couple. ✉ *Via Ceresole 4,* ☎ *0372/30099. AE, DC, MC, V. Closed Mon. No dinner Sun.*

$$–$$$ ★ ✕ **Centrale.** Close to the cathedral, this rustic canteen-like restaurant is a favorite among the locals for traditional Cremonese fare, such as cotecchino *con mostarda* (with mustard-hot crystallized fruit), at moderate prices. ✉ *Vicolo Pertusio 4,* ☎ *0372/28701. AE, DC, MC, V. Closed Thurs. and July.*

Shopping

Cremona is famous throughout Europe as the home of nougat, known here as *torrone.* If the thought of sweet, tooth-crunching nougat is too much to resist, go to **Spellari** (✉ Via Solferino 26), home of *the* best nougat in the world. The store also sells all kinds of mostarda.

Sabbioneta

18 *53 km (33 mi) southeast of Cremona, 142 km (88 mi) southeast of Milan.*

Vespasiano Gonzaga (1531–91), Sabbioneta's lord, founder, and chief architect, was not a particularly sympathetic man. The glory of his attainments in a life of public service is said to have been excelled only by the ignominy of his treatment of three wives and his only son. Upon retiring from military life at 47, he resolved to turn an old castle and a few squalid cottages into the Perfect City—a tiny, urbane metropolis where the most gifted artists and greatest writers would live in perfect harmony with a perfect patron. After some five years of planning and another five of work, the village was transformed into an elegant, star-shape, walled fortress, with a rational grid of streets, two palaces, two squares, two churches, an exquisite theater (said to be the first in Europe with a roof) by Vincenzo Scamozzi (1552–1616), and a noble Gallery of Antiquities (a forerunner of today's art galleries). Gonzaga died four years later, survived only by the last of his wives.

When Aldous Huxley and his wife visited Sabbioneta in 1924, the town had reached an appalling state of neglect and decay. The Huxleys were given a tour (still the only way of seeing the interiors of most of Sabbioneta's buildings) much like the tour you can take today. Arrange tours through the tourist office (☞ Visitor Information *in* Milan, Lombardy, and the Lakes A to Z, *below*). *Tours:* ✉ *Piazza Ducale.* 🎫 *Tour 10,000 lire.* ⏲ *Apr.–Sept., Tues.–Sun. 9–noon and 2:30–7; Oct.–Mar., Tues.–Sat. 9–noon and 2:30–5, Sun. 9–noon and 2:30–5:30.*

In the majestic **Palazzo Ducale** (Ducal Palace) are four fine equestrian figures of Vespasiano and his Gonzaga forebears. The Huxleys were led through what had once been the Cabinet of Diana, the ducal saloon, and other rooms, only to discover that the rooms had been converted to serve the structure's new function as the town hall. They were shown the little **theater** (an adaptation of Palladio's, at Vicenza, by the man who helped him build it), but it lacked its stage, and its frescoes were covered with whitewash. Today you will find the theater restored and its frescoes uncovered. The third building on the tour, the **Palazzo del Giardino,** has a dusty but impressive gallery of antique sculptures. Tours (☞ *above*) begin whenever enough interested people have assembled. The **synagogue** is now a shuttered and derelict building, the sole surviving trace of Sabbioneta's prosperous 16th-century Jewish community. You'll have to ask someone to point it out. ✉ *Town center.*

Mantua

⓳ *37 km (23 km) east of Sabbioneta, 160 km (102 mi) southeast of Milan.*

Mantua (Mantova to Italians) is known as the seat of the Gonzagas, who, like the Viscontis and Sforzas of Milan (with whom they intermarried), lived with the regal pomp and circumstance befitting one of Italy's richest family dynasties. Their reign, first as marquesses, and later as dukes, was a long one—stretching from the first half of the 14th century into the beginning of the 18th.

Even if you've had enough of old palaces, you may still wish to come to Mantua. First, Virgil was born near here. Second, Mantegna (painter of the poignant *Dead Christ* in Milan's Pinacoteca di Brera, (☞ Exploring Milan, *above*) was the Gonzaga court painter for 50 years, and his best-known and only large surviving fresco cycle can be seen here. In addition, there are two fine churches by Leon Battista Alberti (1404–72). Much like Mantegna's work here, both proved highly influential and were widely emulated by lesser architectural lights later in the Renaissance.

Home to the Gonzagas for centuries, the 500-room **Palazzo Ducale** gives one the sense that the palace took centuries to build. From a distance, the group of buildings dominates the skyline, and the effect is fascinating. The **Appartamento dei Nani** (Dwarfs' Apartments) were literally that, dwarf collecting being one of the more amusing occupations of Renaissance princes. According to historians, the dwarfs were not mistreated but were considered to be something between members of the family and celebrity comics. The apartments were built both for the dwarfs' enjoyment and for that of the court.

The **Appartamento del Paradiso** is praised for its view but is somewhat more interesting for its decorator and first resident, Isabella d'Este (1474–1539). Not only was she married at 16, like her younger sister Beatrice (the beautiful young woman of the tomb in the Certosa at Pavia, (☞ *above*), she was apparently also Ludovico il Moro Sforza's first choice for a wife—until he learned she was already affianced to a Gonzaga rival. Isabella, too, was one of the great patrons of the Renaissance. She survived her sister by more than 40 years, and the archives of her correspondence, totaling more than 2,000 letters, are considered some of the most valuable records of the era.

The high point of all 500 rooms, if not of the city, is the **Camera degli Sposi**—literally, "Chamber of the Wedded Couple," because Duke Ludovico and his wife are the focus of attention; it was actually an audience chamber. It was painted by Mantegna over a nine-year period, when he was at the height of his power, and finished when he was 44. Here, Mantegna made a startling advance in painting by organizing the picture's plane of representation in a way that systematically mimics the experience of human vision. Even now, more than five centuries later, you can almost sense the excitement of a mature artist, fully aware of his painting's great importance, expressing his vision with a masterly, joyous confidence. The interiors of Mantua's Palazzo Ducale may be seen today only on a rigorous guided tour normally conducted in

Italian by the museum. However, if you wish to be accompanied by an English-speaking guide, call the Tourist Guide Association or the tourist office (☞ Contacts and Resources *in* Milan, Lombardy, and the Lakes A to Z, *below*). ✉ *Piazza Sordello,* ☎ *0376/320283.* 12,000 *lire.* ⏲ *Tues.–Sat. 9–1 and 2:30–6, Sun.–Mon. 9–1.*

The most serious Mantegna aficionado will want to visit the **Casa di Andrea Mantegna,** designed by the artist himself and built around an intriguing circular courtyard, usually open to view (the interior can only be seen by appointment or occasional art exhibitions). ✉ *Via Acerbi 47,* ☎ *0376/360506.* *Free.* ⏲ *Daily 9–12:30 and 3–6.*

The artist's tomb is in the first chapel on the left in another church, **Sant'Andrea** (1471, some sections earlier or later), a masterwork of the architect Alberti, which itself is considered Mantua's most important Renaissance creation. ✉ *Piazza delle Erbe, south of Piazza Sordello.* ⏲ *Daily 8–12:30 and 3–6.*

Palazzo Tè is one of the greatest of all Renaissance palaces, built by Isabella d'Este's son, Federigo II Gonzaga (1500–40), between 1525 and 1535, for his mistress. It is the singular Mannerist creation of artist-architect Giulio Romano, decorated with mythological trompe l'oeil paintings not to every visitor's taste. Nevertheless, as the magnificently frescoed Sala dei Giganti (Room of Giants) proves, the palace does not skimp on pictorial drama. ✉ *Viale Tè, south of town walls,* ☎ *0376/365886.* *12,000 lire.* ⏲ *Mon. 1–6, Tues.–Sun. 9–6.*

Dining and Lodging

$$$$ ★ ✕ **Al Bersagliere.** One of Lombardy's best restaurants can be found in this rustic four-room inn, in the tiny riverside hamlet of Goito, some 16 km (10 mi) north of Mantua on Route 236 (the main Mantua–Brescia road). It has been run by a single family for more than 150 years. The fish in particular is excellent, as is a Mantuan classic, frog soup. ✉ *Via Goitese 258, Goito,* ☎ *0376/60007. Reservations essential. AE, DC, MC, V. Closed Mon., 15 days in Jan., and 15 days in Aug. No lunch Tues.*

$$$ ✕ **L'Aquila Nigra.** Down a small side street opposite the Palazzo Ducale, this popular restaurant is set in a former medieval convent. Frescoes grace the walls while diners make their way through local dishes, such as *frittata di zucchine* (zucchini frittata) and *faraona al pepe verde* (guinea fowl with green pepper). ✉ *Vicolo Bonacolsi 4,* ☎ *0376/327180. Reservations essential. AE, DC, MC, V. Closed Sun.–Mon., 3 wks in Aug., and Dec. 24–Jan. 5.*

$$–$$$ ✕ **Trattoria dei Martini–Il Cigno.** In a romantic 16th-century palazzo featuring some period frescoes, this restaurant scores well with atmosphere. The menu features local specialties such as *tortelli di zucca* (pasta stuffed with squash), *insalata di cappone* (capon salad), and local variations on the Lombard favorite, risotto. ✉ *Piazza Carlo d'Arco 1,* ☎ *0376/327101. Reservations essential. AE, DC, MC, V. Closed Mon.–Tues., 1 wk in Jan., 3 wks in Aug.*

$–$$ ✕ **Cento Rampini.** In a square in the heart of medieval Mantua, this friendly, family-run trattoria is a local favorite. Among the tasty traditional dishes are risotto, *agnoli* (meat-filled pasta dumplings), and *costoletta d'agnello al timo* (lamb cutlet with thyme). ✉ *Piazza Erbe 11,* ☎ *0376/366349. AE, DC, MC, V. Closed Mon., 1 wk in late Jan., and Aug. 1–15. No dinner Sun.*

$$$ 🏨 **San Lorenzo.** Rooms in this center city hotel are large, with authentic early 19th-century decor. Although there is no restaurant, you're within easy walking distance of many. Some people may find the rooms in the front a little noisy at night, when locals perform their ritualistic *passeggiata,* or early evening promenade. The San Lorenzo has a

rooftop terrace and exudes comfort and individual attention. ✉ *Piazza Concordia 14, 46100,* ☎ *0376/220500,* FAX *0376/327194. 32 rooms. Minibars, parking (fee). AE, DC, MC, V.*

Nightlife and the Arts

Each year on the feast of the Assumption (August 15), a contest is held in Mantua to determine who is the best *madonnaro* (street artist). Some of the painters can re-create masterpieces in a matter of minutes.

LAKE GARDA, BRESCIA, BERGAMO

Of all the curious things to be noted about Lake Garda, one is its perennial attraction for writers. Even the 16th-century essayist Michel de Montaigne (1533–92), whose 15 months of travel journals contain not a single other reference to nature, paused to admire the view down the lake from Torbole, which he called "boundless."

Lake Garda is 50 km (31 mi) long, ranges from roughly 1–16 km (½–10 mi) wide, and is as much as 1,135 ft deep. The terrain is flat at the lake's southern base, and mountainous at its northern tip. As a consequence, the standard descriptions of it vary from stormy inland sea to crystalline Nordic fjord. It is the biggest lake in the region and by most accounts the cleanest. If you are traveling by car, you should be particularly careful when driving in and out of the hairpin turns on the lake road, as there have been several fatal accidents in recent years.

Bardolino

20 *64 km (40 mi) north of Mantua, 147 km (91 mi) northeast of Milan.*

Bardolino, which makes unremarkable but famous red wine, is one of the biggest summer resorts on the lake. It stands on the eastern shore at the widest end of the lake. Here there are two handsome Romanesque churches: **San Severo,** from the 11th century, and **San Zeno,** from the 9th. Both are in the center of the small town. Bardolino is very lively at night, especially compared to other towns on the lake.

Punta di San Vigilio

21 *6 km (4 mi) north of Bardolino, 70 km (44 mi) north of Mantua.*

Punta di San Vigilio, which just about everyone agrees is the prettiest spot on Garda's eastern shore, is full of cypresses from the gardens of the 15th-century **Villa Guarienti di Brenzone.**

Nightlife and the Arts

Bardolino is host to several festivals, but the best one is the **Cura del Grappolo** (Grape Cure Festival), a great excuse to indulge in some of the local vino, since the idea is that the more you drink the better the cure will be. Bring aspirin, just in case.

Malcesine

22 *28 km (17 mi) north of Punta di San Vigilio, 179 km (111 mi) northeast of Milan.*

One of the loveliest areas along the upper eastern shore of Lake Garda, Malcesine is principally known as a summer resort with sailing and windsurfing schools. The 13 campsites and tourist villages do tend to make the town a little crowded in summer. There are however, some nice walks from the town toward the mountains behind. Dominating the town is the 13th- to 14th-century **Castello Scaligero,** built by the Della Scalas.

OFF THE BEATEN PATH **MONTE BALDO** – You're in the Veneto now, and if you are fond of cable cars, take the 15-minute *funivia* (funicular) ride to the top of Monte Baldo (5,791 ft) for a great view of the whole lake in summer, or possibly a short ski run in winter.

Outdoor Activities and Sports

SKIING

Malcesine (☎ 045/7400555) is a well-equipped resort with six lifts and more than 11 km (7 mi) of runs of varying degrees of difficulty.

Riva del Garda

23 *21 km (13 mi) north of Malcesine, 170 km (106 mi) northeast of Milan.*

One of the biggest towns on the northern tip of the lake, Riva del Garda is large and prosperous, and if you're there in summer, you may want to lodge there if the towns farther south seem too crowded. Many of the town's public buildings date from the 15th century, when it was a strategic outpost of the Venetian Republic. The heart of town, the lakeside **Piazza 3 Novembre,** is surrounded by medieval *palazzi.* The newly cleaned **Torre Apponale,** predating the Venetian period by three centuries, looms above the medieval residences of Riva del Garda's main square; its crenellations recall its defensive purpose. Standing in the piazza and looking out onto the lake, you can understand Riva del Garda's importance as a windsurfing center. Mountain air currents ensure good breezes on even the sultriest midsummer days. The fortress of La Rocca, formerly a residence of the Scaligeri princes of Verona, is now a small museum, which frankly is only worth going into if you have nothing else to do. Inside you'll find work of varying quality by local artists. ☎ *0464/573869.* 🎫 *4,000 lire.* ⏲ *Easter–Sept., Tues.–Sun. 9–12:30 and 4:30–8:30; Oct.–Easter, Tues.–Sun. 9–12:30 and 2–6.*

OFF THE BEATEN PATH **TORBOLE** – Take the 10-minute boat ride from Riva del Garda to Torbole (5 km/3 mi east), with a slightly less-resorty feel, quaint waterfront, and colorful windsurfers as far as the eye can see. For lovely Italian-made items such as unique costume jewelry and decorative fixtures, find your way to the little store called Pescicoltura (✉ Piazza Alpini 16, ☎ 0335/283858), great for gifts.

CASCATA DEL VARONE – This waterfall, some 295 ft high, is 4 km (2½ mi) north of town on the road to Tenno. You can walk up to an observation platform and look up at the water plummeting down the cavity it has carved over time; bring a waterproof jacket.

CASTEL TOBLINO – A lovely stop for a lakeside drink or a romantic dinner is this castle, right on a lake in Sarche, about 20 km (12 mi) north of Riva towards Trento (☞ Chapter 9). The compound is fabled to be a prehistoric, then Roman village, and then later associated with the Church of Trento. Bernardo Clesio had it rebuilt in the 16th century in the Renaissance style. It is now a sanctuary of fine food, serving such dishes as *garganelli alla salsa di carciofi* (grooved tubular-shape pasta with artichoke sauce) and *filetto di cavalli ai finferli* (horse meat fillet with wild mushrooms). ✉ *Via Caffaro 1, Sarche,* ☎ *0461/864036. MC, V. Closed Tues. No dinner Mon.*

Lodging

$$$ **Hotel du Lac et du Parc.** Perhaps the French name is intended to evoke the lake's 19th-century grandeur, when it was a favorite destination of the European aristocracy. Whatever the reason, it works: Riva's most splendid hotel oozes elegance, the highest quality of personalized service, and a luxury found in few places on Lake Garda. The airy, com-

fortable public spaces include a large dining room, a delightful bar, and a beautifully manicured private garden that leads to the private beach. The rooms are well appointed and comfortable; be sure to ask for an air-conditioned one, as it can make all the difference. ✉ *Viale Rovereto 44, 38066,* ☎ *0464/551500,* FAX *0464/555200. 170 rooms, 8 suites. 2 restaurants, bar, dining room, pool, beauty salon, sauna, 2 tennis courts, exercise room, beach. AE, DC, MC, V.*

$ **Hotel Sole.** Occupying a restored 15th-century palazzo, this understated, lovely hotel offers comfortable, well-appointed rooms at affordable rates, which these days is a rare combination for the ever-popular Lake Garda. The terraced rooms in front have breathtaking views of the lake, mountains, and the medieval rooftops of the town. In summer, sun worshipers who despair at the often-crowded beaches can sun themselves in the secluded privacy of the roof terrace. ✉ *Piazza 3 Novembre, 38066,* ☎ *0464/552686,* FAX *0464/552811. 49 rooms, 3 suites. Restaurant, bar, in-room safes, refrigerators, room service, sauna, steam room. AE, DC, MC, V.*

Outdoor Activities and Sports

WINDSURFING

Contact **Circolo Surf Torbole** (✉ Colonia Pavese, ☎ 0464/505385) for news on windsurfing in the area.

En Route After passing the town of Limone—where it is said the first lemon trees in Europe were planted—take the fork to the right about 5 km (3 mi) north of Gargnano and head to Tignale. The view from the Madonna di Monte Castello church, some 2,000 ft above the lake, is spectacular. Adventurous travelers will want to follow this pretty inland mountain road to Tremosine; the road winds its way up the mountain through hairpin turns and blind corners that can test even the most experienced drivers.

Gargnano

24 *27 km (17 mi) south of Riva del Garda, 141 km (88 mi) northeast of Milan.*

This small port town was an important Franciscan center in the 13th century. One of the two houses owned and lived in by Mussolini is now a language school; the other, **Villa Feltrinelli,** has not yet been opened to the public, but plans for a high-end spa are in the works. An Austrian flotilla bombarded the town in 1866 and some of the houses still bear signs of cannon fire. The town comes alive in the summer months when mostly German tourists, many of whom have villas here, invade the small pebble beach.

Dining and Lodging

$$$–$$$$ ★ **La Tortuga.** This highly acclaimed restaurant may have the appearance of a rustic trattoria, but the decor belies the sophisticated, nouvelle-style twists on local dishes. The six-course meals are divine: highlights include *pasta fresca gamberi e radicchio Trevisano* (fresh pasta with shrimp and radicchio from Treviso) and *branzino e lenticchio* (sea bass covered in marinated lentils). Tempting desserts include hot chocolate soufflé smothered in white-and-dark chocolate sauce. Wines surface from the owner's extensive cellar; try the local white Lugana. ✉ *Via XXIV Maggio,* ☎ *0365/71251. AE, MC, V. Closed Tues. and Jan.–Feb. No dinner Mon. Oct.–May.*

$ **Hotel Bartabel.** This cozy hotel on the main street offers comfortable, basic accommodations at a reasonable price. The restaurant has an elegant terrace overlooking the lake. ✉ *Via Roma 39, 25084,* ☎ *0365/71330,* FAX *0365/790009. 10 rooms. Restaurant. AE, DC, MC, V.*

Outdoor Activities and Sports

HIKING

Tremosine, some 17 km (11 mi) north of Gargnano, is known as the "Garda Terrace," and is a mountain forest area that is an ideal place for nature hikes. For more information, write or call the **Ufficio Comunale** (✉ Via Papa Giovanni XXIII, ☎ 0365/953185).

En Route Going from Gargnano to Gardone you pass the small town of **Toscolano-Maderno,** which has a delightful lakefront piazza and one of the oldest paper-recycling factories in Italy. The town itself hails from Etruscan times but there are also remnants of Roman influence.

Gardone Riviera

25 *12 km (7 mi) south of Gargnano, 90 km (56 mi) north Mantua.*

Gardone Riviera is a once-fashionable 19th-century resort, now delightfully faded, and the former home of the flamboyant Gabriele d'Annunzio (1863–1938), one of Italy's greatest modern poets. D'Annunzio's estate, **Il Vittoriale,** perched on the hills above the town, is an elaborate memorial to himself, clogged with the trappings of conquests in art, love, and war (of which the largest is a ship's prow in the garden), and complete with a mausoleum. ✉ *Gardone Riviera,* ☎ *0365/20130.* 🎫 *16,000 lire (includes tour of house).* ⏲ *Oct.–Mar., Tues.–Sun. 9–12:30 and 2–5:30; Apr.–Sept., Tues.–Sun. 8:30–8.*

OFF THE BEATEN PATH **SALÒ MARKET** – 4 km (2½ mi) south of Gardone Riviera is the pretty lakeside town of Salò, which history buffs may recognize as the capital of the ill-fated Social Republic, set up in 1943 by the Germans after they liberated Mussolini from the Gran Sasso. Every Saturday morning, in the Piazza dei Martiri della Libertà, an enormous market is held, with great bargains on everything from household items to clothing to foodstuffs. In August or September, a lone vendor often sells locally unearthed *tartufi neri* (black truffles) at affordable prices.

Dining and Lodging

$$$–$$$$ ★ ✕🏨 **Villa Fiordaliso.** The pink-and-white lakeside Villa Fiordaliso—once home to Claretta Petacci, given to her by her lover Benito Mussolini—is a high-quality restaurant, but it also has seven tastefully furnished rooms, some overlooking the lake. The art-nouveau style restaurant (no lunch Tuesday) features seasonal ingredients like zucchini flowers or porcini mushrooms, paramount in salads and soups. ✉ *Via Zanardelli 132, 25083,* ☎ *0365/20158,* FAX *0365/290011. 7 rooms. Restaurant. AE, DC, MC, V. Closed Mon. and Jan.–Feb.*

$$$–$$$$ ★ 🏨 **Villa del Sogno.** A small, winding road takes you from the village to this imposing villa, which surveys the valley and the lake below it. The large hotel terrace and the quiet surrounding grounds add to the feeling of getting away from it all, and you'll probably think twice about a busy sightseeing itinerary once you've settled into position in the sun, cool drink in hand. ✉ *Corso Zanardelli 107, 25083,* ☎ *0365/290181,* FAX *0365/290230. 33 rooms, 5 suites. Restaurant, pool, tennis court. AE, DC, MC, V. Closed Oct. 21–Easter.*

$$$ 🏨 **Grand Hotel Fasano.** A former 19th-century hunting lodge on the lakefront, the Fasano has matured into a seasonal hotel of a high standard. The hotel has had several celebrity guests in the past, including Winston Churchill, who came here in 1948 for a lengthy stay. Writers W. Somerset Maugham and Vladimir Nabokov also stayed here; a local rumor that the latter wrote *Lolita* after observing a local girl may not be true, but it makes for interesting speculation while sunbathing. The staff is friendly, as are most of the guests, who seem to be keen on mak-

ing the most use of the water sports at their disposal. It's worth paying a bit extra to get one of the larger rooms with a lake view and balcony. ✉ *Corso Zanardelli 160, 25083,* ☎ *0365/290220,* FAX *0365/290221. 75 rooms. Restaurant, bar, pool, beach, windsurfing, waterskiing. MC, V. Closed Nov.–mid-May.*

Nightlife and the Arts

BAR

Although it may appear that Gardone's nightlife is reserved strictly for the pacemaker set, it is the tranquility of the place that is its greatest attraction. Visitors and locals alike relish partaking in the passeggiata along the lakefront, stopping perhaps to enjoy an ice cream or aperitif at a bar. **Winnie's Bar,** in the Grand Hotel Fasano (☞ *above*), is particularly elegant, and is named after Winston Churchill, who reputedly enjoyed more than just a couple of brandies in the Belle Epoque surroundings.

CONCERTS

Il Vittoriale (☎ 0365/20130, ☞ *above*) holds a series of concerts in its outdoor theater during July and August.

Sirmione

★ 26 *32 km (19 mi) south of Gardone Riviera, 127 km (79 mi) east of Brescia.*

The ruins at this enchanting town on an isthmus at the southwestern shore of Lake Garda, complete with narrow, cobbled streets that wind their way through medieval arches, are a reminder that Garda has been a holiday resort for the leisurely well-to-do since the height of the Roman era. Most of the historic town, which stretches the length of the spit, is inaccessible to cars, so you must park the car at the bottom of the historic center and walk the rest of the way. The locals will almost certainly tell you that the so-called **Grotte di Catullo** (Grottoes of Catullus) were once the site of the villa of Catullus, one of the greatest pleasure-seeking poets of all time. Present archaeological wisdom, however, does not concur, and there is some consensus that this was the site of two villas of slightly different periods, dating from about the 1st century AD. But never mind—the view through the cypresses and olive trees is lovely, and even if Catullus didn't have a villa here, he is closely associated with the area and undoubtedly did have a villa somewhere nearby. The ruins are at the top of the isthmus and are badly signposted: walk through the historic center and past the various villas to the top of the spit; the grottoes are on the right. ✉ *Grotte di Catullo,* ☎ *030/916157.* 🎫 *8,000 lire.* ⏲ *Mar.–Sept., Tues.–Sun. 8:30–6; Oct.–Feb., Tues.–Sat. 8:30–4:30, Sun. 9–4:30.*

The **Castello Scaligera** was built, along with almost all the other castles on the lake, by the Della Scala family. As hereditary rulers of Verona for more than a century before control of the city was seized by the Visconti in 1402, they counted Garda among their possessions. You may wish to go inside, since there is a nice view of the lake from the tower. Or you may want to go for a swim at the nearby beach before continuing on. Entry to the old part of town is gained through the castle's gates, over what was originally a drawbridge. ✉ *Piazza Castello, Sirmione,* ☎ *030/916468.* 🎫 *8,000 lire.* ⏲ *June–Sept., Tues.–Sat. 9–6, Sun. 9–1; Oct.–Apr., Mon.–Sat. 9–1.*

OFF THE BEATEN PATH

GARDALAND AMUSEMENT PARK – This park has more than 40 different rides and water slides and is one of Italy's biggest amusement parks to thrill your children. It is 16 km (10 mi) east of Sirmione. ✉ *Castelnuovo del Garda,* ☎ *045/6449777.* 🎫 *27,000 lire.* ⏲ *July–mid-Sept., daily*

9 AM–midnight; Apr.–June, daily 9–6 (some days until 7 or 8); mid- to late Mar. and Oct., weekends 9–6.

Dining and Lodging

$$$ ★ ✕ **Vecchia Lugana.** At the base of the peninsula and outside the town, this restaurant is oft touted to be among Italy's best. Fish from the lake, grilled trout, and fillet of perch with artichokes are especially good. There's also an elegant garden. ✉ *Piazzale Vecchia Lugana 1, Lugana di Sirmione,* ☎ *030/919012. AE, DC, MC, V. Closed Tues. and Jan. No dinner Mon.*

$$ ✕ **Ristorante Al Pescatore.** The specialty of this simple rustic looking, but very popular restaurant is lake fish. Try grilled trout with a bottle of local white wine and finish your meal with a walk in the nearby public park. ✉ *Via Piana 20,* ☎ *030/916216. DC, MC, V. Closed Jan.–Feb. and Wed. Oct.–May.*

$$$$ ★ 🏨 **Villa Cortine Palace.** A formidably decorative former private villa in a secluded park, Villa Cortine is in danger of being just plain ostentatious, but only just: it is saved by the sheer luxury of its setting and the extraordinary professionalism of its staff, which, although a little too formal and cold, will leave you wanting for virtually nothing. The hotel dominates a low hill, and the grounds—a colorful mixture of lawns, trees, statues, and fountains—go down to the lake. The villa itself dates from the early part of the 19th century, although a wing (1952) was added: the trade-off is between the more charming old-world decor in the older rooms and the better lake views from the newer ones. ✉ *Via Grotte 6, 25019,* ☎ *030/9905890,* FAX *030/916390. 51 rooms, 6 suites. Restaurant, bar, pool, tennis court, beach. AE, DC, MC, V. Closed Oct.–Apr. 10.*

$$–$$$ 🏨 **Continental.** On the lakefront, right next to a spa, the Continental operates on a half-pension basis only. This works to keep the cost in check, and the hotel has the amenities and feel of a much more expensive establishment. Most rooms have balconies, but ask specifically for a lake view. ✉ *Via Punta Staffalo 7, 25019,* ☎ *030/9905711,* FAX *030/916278. 51 rooms. Pool, beach. MAP. AE, DC, MC, V. Closed Dec.–Mar.*

$$ ★ 🏨 **Hotel Sirmione.** Just inside the city walls, near the Castello, this hotel and spa sits amid lakeside gardens and terraces. Some rooms display superb execution, with comfortable Scandinavian slat beds, matching floral draperies and wall coverings, and built-in white furniture. Many guests have been returning for years, largely due to the homespun feel and the attentiveness of its staff. Full and half pension are offered. ✉ *Piazza Castello 19, 25019,* ☎ *030/916331,* FAX *030/916558. 76 rooms. Restaurant, bar, pool, spa, meeting rooms. AE, DC, MC, V. MAP, FAP.*

Brescia

㉗ *40 km (25 mi) west of Sirmione, 50 km (31 mi) east of Milan.*

The ruins of the **Capitolino,** a Capitoline temple built by the Emperor Vespasian in AD 73, testify to Brescia's Roman origin. The adjoining **Museo Romano** is closed indefinitely for restortation, but its outstanding exhibits—including the famed 1st-century bronze *Winged Victory*—can be viewed in the **Monasterio di Santa Giulia** down the street. ✉ *Via dei Musei 81/b,* ☎ *030/2977833.* 🎫 *10,000 lire.* ⏲ *Tues.–Sun. 10–6.*

In addition to the Brescia School, the **Pinacoteca Civica Tosio-Martinengo** houses paintings by Raphael, Tintoretto (1518–94), Tiepolo (1727–1804), and Jean Clouet (1485–1540). ✉ *Piazza Moretto,* ☎ *030/3774999.* 🎫 *5,000 lire.* ⏲ *June–Sept., Tues.–Sun. 10:30–7; Oct.–May, Tues.–Sun. 9–1 and 2:30–5.*

Palladio (1508–80) and Sansovino (1486–1570) contributed to the splendid **Palazzo della Loggia,** the Lombard-Venetian palace of marble overlooking the Piazza della Loggia. The **Torre dell'Orologio** (Clock Tower, ✉ Piazza della Loggia) dates from the 16th century and is modeled on the campanile in Venice's Piazza San Marco. In the church of **Madonna del Carmine** are a flight of stairs that climb to the ramparts of the Venetian Castello, high enough to give a panoramic view over the town and across the plain to the distant Alps. ✉ *Piazza del Duomo. Closed Mon. and Wed.*

Dining and Lodging

$$$$ ★ ✕ **Gualtiero Marchesi.** Never afraid to try something new, owner-chef Gualtiero Marchesi is celebrated as the founder of *la cucina nuova* (nouvelle cuisine). Since 1993 the kitchen in this deluxe hotel villa has been revered for its spectacular flights of fantasy grounded with classic Lombardian finesse. Tiny lake fish are served within white paper, folded origami fashion, soups are garnished with caviar, and ravioli are served *aperto* (open and unsealed at the edges) or *fazzoletto,* handkerchief-style. You can easily become Romeo to Marchesi's dazzling Juliet—*a rombo in crosta di sale* (turbot in salt crust). The desserts—and prices—are stellar. ✉ *Via Vittorio Emanuele 11, Erbusco, part of the Albereta Hotel,* ☎ *030/7760562. Reservations essential. Jacket and tie. AE, DC, MC, V. Closed Mon. and Jan. 12–Feb. 12. No dinner Sun.*

$$$ ✕ **La Sosta.** Just south of Brescia's cathedral, La Sosta occupies a 17th-century building. The cuisine and service suggest a more expensive establishment. A Brescian specialty is *casonsei* (large meat-filled ravioli). *Capretto alla bresciana* (roast kid with polenta) is an outstanding main course, but make sure you have room for it. ✉ *Via San Martino della Battaglia 20,* ☎ *030/295603,* FAX *030/292589. AE, DC, MC, V. Closed Mon., 1st wk in Dec., and 3 wks in Aug. No dinner Sun.*

$$$ 🏨 **Vittoria.** Centrally located among 16th-century buildings, Vittoria has more than its share of atmosphere. Erected in 1933, the hotel is in the Venetian style, with a hint of Byzantium and the Spice Routes in its pointed arches and windows. Many of the rooms are adorned with antiques. ✉ *Via delle X Giornate 20, 25019,* ☎ *030/280061,* FAX *030/280065. 66 rooms. Restaurant, bar, meeting rooms. AE, DC, MC, V.*

Nightlife and the Arts

Brescia's **Teatro Grande** (☎ 030/3750459) has a series of classical music concerts from May to November.

Bergamo

㉘ *49 km (30 mi) west of Brescia, 58 km (36 mi) southeast of Bellagio.*

Bergamo is two cities—**Bergamo Bassa** (Lower Bergamo) and **Bergamo Alta** (Upper Bergamo), connected by a funicular railway. High up on the hillside, walled in by the ruins of ancient Venetian fortifications, surmounted by a fortress, is Bergamo Alta. The old city of Bergamo, one of northern Italy's most charming medieval centers, lies at the foot of the Bergamese Alps.

The massive **Torre Civica** offers a great view of the two cities. ✉ *Piazza Vecchia,* ☎ *035/262566.* ⊙ *Apr.–Sept., Mon.–Thurs. and Sun. 9–noon and 2–8, Fri.–Sat. 9–noon and 2–11; Oct., weekends 10–noon and 2–6; Nov.–Feb., weekends 10–noon and 2–4; Mar., Mon.–Sun. 10–noon and 2–6.*

The **Duomo** of Bergamo and the **Battistero** are the most notable buildings in Piazza Vecchia. But the most impressive is the **Cappella Colleoni,** with resplendently elaborate marble decoration. ✉ *Piazza Vecchia,* ☎

035/217317. ⏲ *Cappella Colleoni weekdays 7:30–noon and 3–6:30. Baptistery visits by arrangement with Duomo parish priest.*

★ In the **Accademia Carrara** you will find one of Italy's greatest and most important art collections. Many of the Venetian masters are represented—Mantegna, Carpaccio (circa 1460–1525/26), Tiepolo, Francesco Guardi (1712–93), Canaletto (1697–1768)—and there are some magnificent Bellinis and Botticellis (1445–1510) as well. ✉ *Bergamo Bassa, Piazza Carrara,* ☎ *035/399426.* 🎫 *5,000 lire, Sun. free.* ⏲ *Wed.–Mon. 9:30–noon and 2:30–5:30.*

Dining and Lodging

$$$$ ★ ✕ **Dell'Angelo–Taverna del Colleoni.** Angelo Cornaro closed the celebrated Antico Ristorante dell'Angelo to concentrate all his attention on the Taverna del Colleoni, on the 15th-century Piazza Vecchia, right behind the Duomo, where he continues to serve a wide and imaginative range of fish and meat dishes, all expertly prepared. ✉ *Piazza Vecchia 7,* ☎ *035/232596. AE, DC, MC, V. Closed Mon., 1 wk in Jan., and 2 wks in Aug.*

$$ ✕ **Agnello d'Oro.** A 17th-century tavern on a main street in Upper Bergamo, with wooden booths and walls hung with copper utensils and ceramic plates, Agnello d'Oro is a good place to imbibe the atmosphere as well as the good local wine. Specialties are typical Bergamasque risotto and varieties of polenta served with game and mushrooms. The same establishment also has 20 modestly priced rooms. ✉ *Via Gombito 22,* ☎ *035/249883. AE, DC, MC, V. Closed Mon. and Jan. No dinner Sun.*

$$ ✕ **Da Ornella.** On the main street in the upper town, this trattoria is well attended, so reservations are a must. Vaulted ceilings, wooden beams, and antique ceramic ware on the walls enhance the old worldliness. Ornella herself is in the kitchen, turning out casonsei in butter and sage and platters of assorted roast meats. ✉ *Via Gombito 15,* ☎ *035/232736. Reservations essential. AE, DC, MC, V. Closed Thurs. and July. No lunch Fri.*

$$ ✕ **La Trattoria del Teatro.** Traditional regional food tops the bill at this good-value restaurant in the Upper Town. The polenta is a silky delight, and game is recommended in season. Fettuccine *con funghi* (with mushrooms) is a deceptively simple but rich and memorable specialty. ✉ *Piazza Mascheroni 3,* ☎ *035/238862. No credit cards. Closed Mon. and July 15–30.*

$$$ 🏨 **Cristallo Palace.** On the periphery of town, the Cristallo Palace offers the amenities of a modern, efficient hotel, plus the bonus of being on the *tangenziale* (the road that bypasses the center). The rooms are large and well equipped, and the service is polished and prompt. The hotel's restaurant, L'Antica Perosa, is very good. A shuttle runs into town in the mornings and late afternoon. ✉ *Via Betty Ambiveri 35, 24126,* ☎ *035/311211,* FAX *035/312031. 90 rooms. Restaurant, bar. AE, DC, MC, V.*

$$$ 🏨 **Excelsior San Marco.** The most comfortable hotel in the lower part of Bergamo, the Excelsior San Marco is only a short walk from the walls of the Upper Town. The rooms are surprisingly quiet, considering the central location of the hotel. Its restaurant, Tino Fontana, has a rooftop terrace. ✉ *Piazza della Repubblica 6, 24126,* ☎ *035/366111,* FAX *035/223201. 162 rooms. Restaurant, bar. AE, DC, MC, V.*

Nightlife and the Arts

The **Festival Internazionale del Pianoforte** (International Piano Festival), an event of more than 30 years' standing, is held in Bergamo's Teatro Donizetti (✉ Piazza Cavour 14, ☎ 035/4160611) in summer.

LAKE COMO

For those whose idea of heaven is palatial villas, rose-laden belvederes, operetta towns, hanging gardens of wisteria and bougainvillea, flickering lanterns casting a glow over lakeshore restaurants, and dreamy alpine vistas, heaven exists at Lake Como. Virgil liked Como at least as much as Garda, calling it simply our "greatest" lake. Stendhal described it as an "enchanting spot, unequaled on earth for loveliness," in his *Charterhouse of Parma*. Though summer crowds do their best to vanquish the lake's dreamy mystery and civilized, slightly faded, millionaire's-row gentility, they fail. Como remains a place of consummate partnership between the beauties of nature and those of humanity. Like so many of Italy's most beautiful villa gardens, those of Como owe their beauty to the landscape architecture of two eras: Renaissance Italian, with its taste for order; and 19th-century English, with its fondness for illusions of natural wildness. The two are often framed by vast areas of the most picturesque farmland—notably olive groves, fruit trees, and vineyards.

Lake Como is some 47 km (30 mi) long north to south, and it is also Europe's deepest lake (almost 1,350 ft). Rarely out of sight to visitors, it looks like a burnished mirror—until a breeze ruffles its incandescence. Here, in the *centro di lago* (center region of the lake), travelers have long headed for Bellagio. This alluring town is known as the "punta di Bellagio" because it's at the point that divides Lake Como into three branches. It's an enchanting location, one that inspired Gabriel Faure to call Bellagio "a diamond contrasting brilliantly with the sapphires of the three lakes in which it is set." After just a few days on Lake Como, you'll understand why Verdi chose to compose *La Traviata* in Cadenabbia, across the lake from Bellagio. Today, for Milanese weekend-trippers, countless honeymooners, and visitors from around the world, going to Lake Como is not so much escape, as return; not so much getting away from it all, but returning to that *douceur de vie,* that sweetness of life rarely encountered today.

If you're not going by car, you arrive at the lake by pulling into the railway station at Como, a leading textile center, famous for its silks. Most of you hasten to the vaporetti waiting to take you to the centro di lago, the most beautiful part of the lake. Art lovers, however, should note that 15 or so blocks south of the station is one of the greatest Italian Romanesque churches, Sant'Abbondio—a detour you will consider well worth making once you've seen its awe-inspiring, gigantic nave interior. Although you can take a bus up either shoreline, most people take a ferry to Bellagio, the key town of the centro di lago; be sure to take an express ferry, as the local vaporetti can turn a half-hour ride into a three-hour ordeal. Once at Bellagio, vaporetti and car ferries traverse the lake, making it easy for travelers to get to the other main towns, Cernobbio, Cadenabbia, and Varenna.

Madonna del Ghisallo

29 *18 km (11 mi) north of Cernobbio, 48 km (30 mi) northwest of Bergamo.*

The **Chiesa della Madonna del Ghisallo** (Church of the Patroness of Bicyclists) is not far from the shores of Lake Como and offers a fine view. You will often see cyclists parked outside taking a breather after their uphill struggle, but many come just as a homage to this unique Madonna. From Bergamo you pass it on the road to Bellagio. ✉ *Magreglio.* ⏲ *Mar.–Nov., daily 8–7.*

Bellagio

★ 30 *58 km (36 mi) northwest of Bergamo, 28 km (17 mi) north of Cernobbio.*

Sometimes called the prettiest town in Europe, Bellagio also has ferry services to most towns on the lake. Here, buildings always seem to be flag bedecked, geraniums rustle from every window, and bougainvillea veils the staircases, or *montées,* that thread through the town. At dusk, Bellagio's nightspots—including the wharf where an orchestra serenades dancers under the stars—beckon vacationers to come and make merry.

★ **Villa Serbelloni,** a property of the Rockefeller Foundation, can also be visited for its celebrated gardens on the site of Pliny the Elder's villa overlooking Bellagio. As there are only two guided visits per day restricted to 30 people each, and these tend to be commandeered by group bookings especially during May, you'd do well to book far in advance with the Bellagio tourist office (☞ Visitor Information *in* Milan, Lombardy, and the Lakes A to Z, *below*). *5,000 lire. Guided visits mid-Apr.–mid-Oct., Tues.–Sun. at 10:30 and 4.*

The famous gardens of the **Villa Melzi** are open to the public and were once a favorite picnic spot for Franz Lizst, who advised author Louis de Ronchaud in 1837: "When you write the story of two happy lovers, place them on the shores of Lake Como. I do not know of any land so conspicuously blessed by heaven." High praise, indeed. Although you can't get into the 19th-century villa, don't miss the lavish Empire-style family chapel. The Melzi were Napoléon's greatest allies in Italy (the family has passed down the name of Josephine to the present). Directly across the lake is the Villa Carlotta (☞ Tremezzo, *below*), once residence of Count Sommariva, Napoléon's worst Italian enemy. ✉ *3 km (2 mi) outside Bellagio,* ☎ *031/950318. 5,000 lire. Late Mar.–early Nov., daily 9–6:30.*

OFF THE BEATEN PATH **VILLA BALBIANELLO** – This may be the most magical house in all of Italy. It sits on its own little promontory, Il Dosso d'Avedo—separating the bays of Venus and Diana—around the bend from the tiny fishing village of Ossuccio. Relentlessly picturesque, the villa is comprised of loggias, terraces, and *palazzetini* (tiny palaces), all of which spill down verdant slopes to the lakeshore where an old Franciscan church, magnificent stone staircase, and statue of San Carlo Borromeo blessing the waters welcome visitors. Designed in 1596 by Pellegrino Pelligrini, it was enlarged by Count Lambertenghi (who insisted on calling all his guests "Count," but refused the title himself). In 1974 it was sold to Count Monzino, who graciously willed it to the Fondo Ambiente Italiano, which has opened it to the public. The only access to the villa is by launch, which leaves Ossuccio and Sala Comacina several times a week. Check with the Bellagio tourist office (☞ Visitor Information *in* Milan, Lombardy, and the Lakes A to Z, below) for the hours of launch tours. ✉ *Il Dosso d'Avedo. 5,500 lire. Tues. and weekends 10–12:30 and 4–6:30.*

Dining and Lodging

$$ ✕ **Silvio.** At the edge of town, this family-owned trattoria with a terrace on the lakeshore is for those who love fresh lake fish. Served cooked or marinated, with risotto or as a ravioli stuffing, the fish is caught by Silvio's family. This is local cooking at its best. There are also 17 modestly priced rooms. ✉ *Lòppia di Bellagio, Via Carcano 12,* ☎ *031/950322. MC, V. Closed Jan.*

$–$$ ✕ **La Pergola.** In Pescallo, about 1 km (½ mi) from Bellagio, on the other side of the peninsula, La Pergola is a popular lakeside restaurant. Of course, try to reserve a table on the lakeside terrace and order the daily special of freshly caught lake fish. You can also stay in one of the inn's 13 rooms, all of which have baths. ✉ *Pescallo,* ☎ *031/950263. AE, DC, MC, V. Closed Tues. and Nov.–Feb.*

$$$$ ★ **Grand Hotel Villa Serbelloni.** They used to say that those who drove Rolls-Royces stayed at the Villa d'Este hotel in Cernobbio and those who drove Bentleys came here. Once designed to cradle dukes and duchesses in high luxury, this hotel is now a refined haven for the discreetly wealthy. Just down the road from the punta di Bellagio, the hotel is set within a pretty park. Inside, the atmosphere is one of 19th-century luxury that has not so much faded as mellowed: the rooms are immaculate and plush. The public rooms are a mix of gilt, marble, and thick, colorful carpets. Service is unobtrusive, and the staff is particularly good about arranging transportation across and around the lake. The best rooms—in which Churchill and Kennedy have stayed—face the lake and the Tremezzina, a group of towns on the shores opposite Bellagio. ✉ *Lungolago Bellagio, Via Roma 1, 22021,* ☎ *031/950216,* FAX *031/951529. 95 rooms. Restaurant, pool, beauty salon, tennis court, health club. AE, DC, MC, V. Closed end Oct.–early Apr.*

$$ **Belvedere.** In Italian, the name means "beautiful view," and from the gardens of this enchanting hotel there is indeed a view worthy of Stendhal's epithet that the vista was equal to that of the Bay of Naples, the 19th century's most famous and favorite. The hotel has been in the Martinelli-Manoni family since 1880, and it is perhaps this unbroken tradition of service that makes it one of the best places to stay in town. The house itself is simple and unadorned, though never plain; the rooms are understated but comfortable. Antique chairs and eye-catching rugs complement the modern fittings. The bathrooms are all expertly designed for maximum comfort. Once upon a time, vineyards surrounded the house; these have been transformed into the hotel's outstanding feature, the terraced gardens. The restaurant is very good. ✉ *Via Valassina 31, 22021,* ☎ *031/950410,* FAX *031/950102. 58 rooms, 5 suites. Restaurant, bar, pool, meeting rooms. AE, DC, MC, V.*

$$ **Du Lac.** In the center of Bellagio, by the Lake Como landing dock, Du Lac is a comfortable medium-size hotel owned by an Anglo-Italian family who set a relaxed and congenial tone. Most rooms have views of the lake and mountains, and there is a rooftop terrace garden for drinks or just unwinding. ✉ *Piazza Mazzini 32, 22021,* ☎ *031/950320,* FAX *031/951624. 48 rooms. Restaurant, bar. MC, V. Closed late Oct.–late Mar.*

$$ **Excelsior-Splendide.** Chances are you'll be lulled to sleep at night here by the lilting sounds of an orchestra directly under your window—this hotel is opposite Bellagio's enchanting quay, where live music beckons one and all on summer nights. It's in town center, handy to restaurants, and just a five-minute walk from the stunning gardens of Villa Melzi. ✉ *Lungo Lalio Mazzoni, 22021,* ☎ *031/950225,* FAX *031/951224. 47 rooms. Restaurant, pool. AE, DC, MC, V. Closed Oct. 21–May 1.*

$$ **Hotel Florence.** If there is a bargain to be had amid all of Bellagio's opulence, then this lakeside villa is it. Originally constructed at the beginning of the 18th century, the mainstay of the house as it appears today dates from the 1880s, including the impressive lobby with its vaulted ceiling and imposing Florentine fireplace. Most of the rooms, furnished with interesting antiques, are large and comfortable and have splendid views of the lake. The restaurant and bar are new additions to the hotel, with live music at weekends drawing locals and visitors alike. ✉ *Piazza Mazzini 45, 22021,* ☎ *031/950342,* FAX *031/951722. 36 rooms. Restaurant, bar. AE, MC, V.*

Varenna

31 *10 km (6 mi) north of Bellagio, 78 km (48 mi) north of Milan.*

Using the ferry boat services in Bellagio, make your way to the town of Varenna. The principal sight here is the spellbindingly beautiful garden of the **Villa Monastero,** which, as its name suggests, was a monastery before it was a villa. Now it's an international science center. ✉ *Varenna.* 🎫 *4,000 lire.* ⏲ *Apr.–Oct., daily 9–noon and 2–5.*

Tremezzo

 32 *34 km (21 mi) north of Cernobbio, 78 km (48 mi) north of Milan.*

If you are lucky enough to visit this small lakeside town in late spring or very early summer, you will find the magnificent **Villa Carlotta** a riotous blaze of color, with more than 14 acres of azaleas and dozens of varieties of rhododendrons in full bloom. The villa itself was built between 1690 and 1743 for the luxury-loving Marquis Giorgio Clerici. The range of the garden's collection is remarkable, particularly when you consider the difficulties of transporting delicate, exotic vegetation before the age of aircraft. Palms, banana trees, cactus, eucalyptus, a sequoia, orchids, and camellias are only the beginning of a list that includes more than 500 species.

According to local lore, one motive for the Villa Carlotta's magnificence was a keeping-up-with-the-Joneses sort of rivalry between the marquis's ambitious, self-made son-in-law, who inherited the estate, and the son-in-law's arch rival, who built *his* summer palace directly across the lake. Whenever either added to his villa and garden, it was tantamount to taunting the other in public. Eventually the son-in-law's insatiable taste for self-aggrandizement prevailed. The villa's last (and final) owners were Prussian royalty (including the "Carlotta" of the villa's name), and the property was confiscated during World War I.

The villa's interior is worth a visit, particularly if you have a taste for Antonio Canova's (1757–1822) most romantic sculptures. The best known is his *Cupid and Psyche,* which depicts the lovers locked in an odd but graceful and passionate embrace, with the young god above and behind, his wings extended, while Psyche, her lips willing, waits for a kiss that will never come. Check with the Bellagio tourist office (☞ Visitor Information *in* Milan, Lombardy, and the Lakes A to Z, *below*) for the hours of the launch from Tremezzo. ✉ *Tremezzo,* ☎ *0344/40405.* 🎫 *Villa and gardens 8,000 lire.* ⏲ *Apr.–Sept., daily 9–6; mid- to late Mar. and Oct.–early Nov., daily 9–11:30 and 2–4:30.*

Cernobbio

 33 *34 km (21 mi) south of Tremezzo, 53 km (3 mi) north of Milan.*

Cernobbio is the first town you come to as you head north from the town of Como. Although many of the villas of the southwest branch—the lake's most overbuilt district—remain private and closed to the public, they can be enjoyed from a boat. If you're planning to say "budget be damned" in only one place, the **Villa d'Este** (☞ Lodging, *below*) could be it. If you can't stay at this legendary lakeside resort hotel, call ahead and ask to see the grounds or enjoy a wonderful meal in the hotel's restaurant.

Originally built for Cardinal Tolomeo Gallio, who began life humbly as a fisherman, over the course of approximately 45 years (it was completed in 1615), the Villa d'Este has had a colorful and somewhat checkered history, swinging wildly between extremes of grandeur and dereliction. Its tenants have included the Jesuits, two generals, a ballerina, the disgraced and estranged wife of a future king of England (Caroline of Brunswick and George IV, respectively), a family of ordinary Italian nobles, and, finally, a czarina of Russia. Its life as a private summer residence ended in 1873, when it was turned into the fashionable hotel it has remained ever since.

Though the gardens are not as grand as they are reputed to have been during the villa's best days as a private residence and though they have suffered some modification in the course of the hotel's building of tennis courts and swimming pools, they still possess an aura of stately, monumental dignity. The alley of cypresses is a fine example of a proudly repeated Italian garden theme. The fanciful pavilions, temples, miniature forts, and mock ruins make for an afternoon's walk of quietly whimsical surprises.

Lodging

$$$$ ★ **Villa d'Este.** From Napoléon to the Duchess of Windsor, this grand establishment has welcomed the rich and famous of several centuries. One of the most luxurious hotels in Italy, the 16th-century Villa d'Este provides just about every conceivable comfort, even a nightclub. The sparkling chandeliers in the vast lobby cast their light on the broad, marble staircases that lead to the guest rooms. Indeed, they are so regal that one could be forgiven for ascending them as Napoléon surely did, one hand on the banister, the other placed inside the coat. The rooms are furnished in the manner of wealthy Italians, Empire-style: walnut paneling, sofas striped in silk, and plenty of gorgeous antiques. A broad veranda sweeps out to the lakefront, where a large swimming pool juts out above the water. Across the lake blue, snowcapped mountains gradually blend into the deep green of the slopes that lead down to the shore. ✉ *Via Regina 40, 22010,* ☎ *031/3481,* FAX *031/348844. 158 rooms. Restaurant, bar, indoor pool, outdoor pool, sauna, 8 tennis courts, squash, nightclub. AE, DC, MC, V. Closed Nov.–Feb.*

Como

34 *5 km (3 mi) south of Cernobbio, 61 km (38 mi) north of Milan.*

Como, on the shores of the eponymous lake, is part elegant resort, with cobbled pedestrian streets that wind their way elegantly past parks and bustling cafés and away from the lakefront. The other part is industrial town, renowned throughout the world for its production of silk. If you're traveling by car leave it outside town center, as traffic can be mayhem and streets are often closed.

The splendid 15th-century Renaissance-Gothic **Duomo** was begun in 1396, the facade was added in 1455, and the transepts completed in the mid-18th century. The dome was designed in 1744 by Filippo Juvara (1678–1736), who was the chief architect of many of the sumptuous palaces of Italy's royal family, the Savoys (☞ Chapter 7). On the facade there are statues of two of Como's most famous sons, Pliny the Elder and Pliny the Younger, whose chronicles are some of the most important documents of antiquity. Inside, the works of art include Luini's *Holy Conversation,* a fresco cycle by Morazzone, and the *Wedding of the Virgin Mary* by Ferrari. ✉ *Piazza del Duomo.* ⏲ *Daily 9–6.*

At the heart of Como's medieval quarter, the city's first cathedral, **San Fedele,** is also worth a peek, if only for the fact that it is one of the oldest churches in the region. ✉ *Piazza San Fedele.* ⏲ *Easter–Sept., daily 8:30–8; Oct.–Easter, daily 9–7.*

If you can brave Como's industrial quarter, you will find the beautiful church of **Sant'Abbondio,** a gem of Romanesque architecture begun by Benedictine monks in 1013 and consecrated by Pope Urban II (circa 1035–99) in 1095. Inside, the five aisles of the church converge on a presbytery with a semicircular apse decorated with a cycle of 14th-century frescoes—all of which have been restored to their original magnificence—by Lombard artists heavily influenced by the Sienese school. In the nave, the cubical capitals supporting the pillars are the first example of this style in all of Italy. ✉ *Via Sant'Abbondio.* ⏲ *Daily 9–6.*

OFF THE BEATEN PATH

CASTIGLIONE OLANA – Just 18 km (11 mi) west of Como is a Gothic Collegiata and baptistery, with superlative frescoes by Giotto's pupil Masolino da Panicale.

Dining and Lodging

$$$ ✕ **Da Angela.** Reservations are a must at this small and intimate restaurant serving Piedmontese specialties. Owner Angela and her staff are attentive, and the waiters will help you select from a menu that includes various homemade pasta dishes and tasty *coniglio alle olive e alloro* (rabbit with olives and bay leaves). ✉ *Via Ugo Foscolo 16,* ☎ *031/304656. Reservations essential. AE, DC, MC, V. Closed Mon. and Aug.*

$$$ ✕ **La Locanda dell'Isola.** Isola Comacina, Lake Como's only island, five minutes by regular boat from Sala Comacina, is rustic and restful, but at times crowded. The same could be said for the Locanda. Forget any notions of choosing from a menu, because here the deal is a set price for a set meal, with drinks included. The good news is that the food is delicious, the service friendly, and the setting magnificent. You'll have to pace yourself through a mixed antipasto, salmon, trout, chicken, salad, cheese, coffee, and dessert. ✉ *Isola Comacina, Sala Comacina,* ☎ *0344/55083. No credit cards. Closed Nov.–Feb. and Tues. Sept.–May.*

$$$ 🏨 **Barchetta Excelsior.** Despite its rather unprepossessing exterior, this central, modern hotel is comfortable, with many rooms looking directly across Piazza Cavour over to Lake Como. The rooms are airy and spacious, with those on the upper floors commanding the best views. Ask for a lake view because not all rooms have one, although the noise of the piazza can be a distraction. ✉ *Piazza Cavour 1, 22021,* ☎ *031/3221,* FAX *031/302622. 85 rooms. Restaurant, bar, breakfast room, minibars. AE, DC, MC, V.*

$$$ 🏨 **Palace.** This well-run, refurbished grand 19th-century hotel on the waterfront has fine lake views and the advantage of being set back in its own gardens, where there is an outside bar in summer. The rooms, however, are a little disappointing: the simple, almost plain, furnishings do little justice to the magnificent exterior. ✉ *Lungo Lario Trieste 16, 22100,* ☎ *031/303303,* FAX *031/303170. 100 rooms. Restaurant, bar, meeting rooms, travel services. AE, DC, MC, V.*

$$–$$$ ★ 🏨 **Terminus.** Commanding a panoramic view over Lake Como, this early 20th-century, Liberty-style building is perhaps the city's finest hotel. The public spaces have a quiet, understated elegance, with plenty of marble and high ceilings. The guest rooms are done in floral patterns and are tastefully furnished with large, walnut wardrobes and silk-covered sofas. The best room in the hotel is Room 500, in a small tower: the split-level room is divided by a thin spiral staircase and the three-sided view from the bedroom is magnificent. In summer, the garden terrace is perfect for relaxing over a drink. ✉ *Lungo Lario Trieste 13, 22100,* ☎ *031/329111,* FAX *031/302550. 41 rooms. Restaurant, bar, breakfast room, in-room data ports, in-room safes, minibars, no-smoking rooms, massage, sauna, meeting rooms. AE, DC, MC, V.*

$$ **Tre Re.** This clean, spacious, and welcoming hotel is just a few steps west of the cathedral and convenient to the lake. Although the exterior gives away the age of this 16th-century former convent, the rooms inside are airy, comfortable, and modern. The moderately priced restaurant shares an ample terrace with the hotel. ✉ *Via Boldoni 20, 22021,* ☎ *031/265374,* FAX *031/241349. 34 rooms, 4 without bath. Restaurant, bar. MC, V. Closed Dec. 10–Jan. 15.*

Outdoor Activities and Sports

SEAPLANES

The school at the **Seaplane Club Como** (✉ Viale Masia 44, ☎ 031/574495) gives seaplane flying lessons in Como.

SKIING

In the province of Como, fine skiing facilities abound at Valsassina, Val Lesina, Valvarrone, Valcavargna, and Val d'Intelvi. For information, call the Provincial Tourist Board in Como (☞ Visitor Information *in* Milan, Lombardy, and the Lakes A to Z, *below*).

WATERSKIING

Various facilities for waterskiing and all water sports can be found on the lake; contact the Provincial Tourist Board in Como (☞ Visitor Information *in* Milan, Lombardy, and the Lakes A to Z, *below*).

Shopping

MARKET

Every Saturday (except the first Saturday of every month), Piazza San Fedele holds a **crafts market** featuring local crafts from 9 to 7.

SILK

Como is renowned for its production of high-quality silk. **Mantera** (✉ Via Volta) sells a wide range of locally made silks. **In Seta** (✉ Piazza Cavour) offers the latest in silk fashions for both men and women. **Binda** (✉ Viale Geno) is a silk wholesale store, with great prices on a variety of items, including shirts, ties, and scarves.

LAKE MAGGIORE AND LAKE ORTA

Magnificently scenic, Lake Maggiore has its less mountainous eastern shore in Lombardy, its higher western shore in Piedmont, and its northern tip in Switzerland. Never more than 5 km (3 mi) wide, the lake is almost 50 km (30 mi) long. The better-known resorts are on the Piedmontese shore, particularly Stresa, a well-established tourist town that partly provided the setting for Hemingway's *A Farewell to Arms.* A mountainous strip of land separates Lake Maggiore from Lago di Orta (Lake Orta), its smaller neighbor to the west, in Piedmont. Orta attracts fewer visitors than the three larger lakes, and consequently a tour around this lake can be a pleasant alternative in the summer. Stresa is the main town on Lake Maggiore, and Orta San Giulio is the largest center on Lake Orta; all points of interest on the two lakes are reached from these towns.

Orta San Giulio

35 *15 km (9 mi) west of Stresa, 76 km (47 mi) northwest of Milan.*

Orta San Giulio is at the end of a small peninsula that juts out into Lake Orta about a third of the way up its eastern shore. Intricate wrought-iron balustrades and balconies adorn the 18th-century buildings of this small and charming town. The shady main square looks out across the lake to the small island of San Giulio. There are few more relaxing experiences than sipping a drink at one of the piazza cafés and looking out at the languid waters being stirred by a mountain breeze, with sailboats busily making their way to nowhere in particular.

OFF THE BEATEN PATH **SACRO MONTE** – Rising up behind Orta and looking down on the lake, Sacred Mountain offers an enjoyable and interesting hike up from Orta. Pass the church of the Assumption, and just ahead you see a gateway marked Sacro Monte. This leads to the path up the hill, a comfortable climb that takes about 40 minutes for the round-trip. As you approach the top, you pass no fewer than 20 17th-century chapels, all devoted to St. Francis of Assisi. They are decorated with frescoes and striking, life-size terra-cotta statue groups (a total of almost 400 figures) that illustrate incidents in the saint's life. You can climb the campanile of the last chapel for a panoramic view over the whole lake and the town, about 350 ft below.

The island of **San Giulio,** just offshore, is accessible by hiring a boatman. The lake is no more than 2 km (1 mi) wide, and most boats charge about 10,000 lire for up to four people to make the round-trip. The island takes its name from the 4th-century St. Julius, who—like St. Patrick in Ireland—is said to have banished snakes from the island. Julius is also said to have founded the Basilica in AD 390, although the present building shows more signs of its renovations in the 10th and 15th centuries. Inside, there is a black marble pulpit (12th century) with elaborate carvings, and downstairs you'll find the crypt containing relics of the saint. In the sacristy of the church is a large bone said to be from one of the beasts destroyed by the saint, but on closer examination it seems to be a whalebone.

Since much of the area is taken up by the grounds of private villas, it only takes a few minutes to walk around the parts of the island that are open to the public. The view back across the lake to Orta, with Sacro Monte behind it, is memorable, particularly in the late afternoon, when the light picks up the glint of the wrought-iron traceries.

Lodging

$$$ **Hotel San Rocco.** Half of the rooms in this converted 17th-century convent in a lakeside garden on the edge of town have views of the lake, garden, and surrounding mountains. Many have balconies and are furnished in modern style. The restaurant features international cuisine and beautiful views of the lake. Among the specialties is *pesce persico* (perch). ✉ *Via Gippini da Verona 11, 28016,* ☎ *0322/905632,* FAX *0322/905635. 74 rooms. Restaurant, bar, pool, health club. AE, DC, MC, V.*

En Route Follow the shore drive from Orta San Giulio north to Omegna, at the head of Lake Orta. A couple of kilometers west of Omegna, in the village of Quarna Sotto, there's a musical instrument factory that's worth a stop. The shore drive continues around the rest of the lake, and at the southern end you can pick up S229, which will take you back to the A4 autostrada.

If you're going to Stresa from Lake Orta, take the twisting mountain road past Mottarone, the tallest peak between the lakes, to Gignese, where you'll be about 2,300 ft above sea level and can take in a last dramatic view of Maggiore. Follow the road up to Lake Orta, through the town of Armeno, shaded first by forests of evergreens, then oaks. In the late summer and early fall, you're likely to see whole families out in these woods, crouched down in their hunt for wild mushrooms, or—if they're particularly lucky—truffles.

Stresa

 *16 km (10 mi) east of Orta San Giulio, 80 km (50 mi) northwest of Milan.*

Stresa, which has capitalized on its central lakeside position and its good connections to the Isole Borromee (Borromean Islands) in Lake Maggiore, has to some extent become a victim of its own success. The luxurious elegance that distinguished it in its heyday has grown somewhat faded; the grand hotels are still grand but their surrounding parks and gardens are now encroached by traffic. Even the undeniable loveliness of the lakeshore drive has been threatened by the roar of diesel trucks and BMW traffic. One way to escape is to head for the Isole Borromee just off Stresa.

As you wander around the grounds of **Villa Pallavicino,** with their palms and semitropical shrubs, don't be surprised if you're followed by a peacock or even an ostrich: they're part of the zoological garden, and they are allowed to roam almost at will. From the top of the hill on which the villa stands, you can see the gentle hills of the Lombardy shore of Lake Maggiore and, nearer and to the left, the jewel-like Borromean Islands. In addition to a bar and restaurant, the grounds also have picnicking spots. ✉ *Via Sempione Sund 8,* ☎ *0323/31533.* 🎟 *11,500 lire.* ⏲ *Mid-Mar.–Oct. 30, daily 9–6.*

Boats to the **Borromean Islands** leave every 15–30 minutes from the dock at Stresa's Piazza Marconi. Although you can hire a boatman to take you, it's cheaper and just as convenient to use the regular service. Make sure you buy a ticket allowing you to visit all the islands—Bella, Dei Pescatori, and Madre. The islands take their name from the Borromeo family, which has owned them since the 12th century. **Isola Bella** (Beautiful Island) is the most famous of the three, and the first that you'll visit. Its name is actually a shortened form of Isabella, wife of the 16th-century Count Carlo III Borromeo (1538–84), who built the palace and terraced gardens for her. Few wedding presents anywhere have been more romantic. Wander up the 10 terraces of the gardens, where peacocks roam among the scented shrubs, statues, and fountains. The view of the lake is splendid from the top terrace. Before Count Carlo began his project, the island was rocky and almost devoid of vegetation, and the soil for the garden had to be transported from the mainland. Visit the palazzo to see the rooms where famous guests—including Napoléon and Mussolini—stayed in 18th-century splendor. ☎ *0323/30556.* 🎟 *Garden and palazzo 10,000 lire.* ⏲ *Apr.–Oct., daily 9–noon and 1:30–5:30.*

Stop for a while at the tiny **Isola dei Pescatori** (Island of the Fishermen), less than 100 yards wide and only about ½ km (¼ mi) long. Of the three islands, this is the one that has remained closest to the way they all were before the Borromeos began their building projects. The island's little lanes, strung with fishing nets and dotted with shrines to the Madonna, are so picturesque they practically drip off the canvas. Little wonder that this tiny fishing village is crowded with postcard stands in high season.

Isola Madre (Mother Island) is the largest of the three and, like Isola Bella, has a large botanical garden. Even dedicated nongardeners should stop to appreciate the profusion of exotic trees and shrubs running down to the shore in every direction. Two special times to visit are April (for the camellias) and May (when azaleas and rhododendrons are in bloom). Also on the island is a 16th-century palazzo, where an antique puppet theater is on display, complete with string puppets, prompt books, and elaborate scenery designed by Alessandro Sanquirico, who was a scenographer at La Scala in Milan. 🎟 *12,000 lire.* ⏲ *Apr.–Oct., daily 8:30–noon and 2–5:30.*

For more information about the islands and how to get there, contact the tourist office in Stresa (☞ Visitor Information *in* Milan, Lombardy, and the Lakes, *below*) or ask at the landing stages (look for Navigazione Lago Maggiore signs).

Lodging

$$$$ 🏨 **Grand Hotel des Iles Borromees.** A palatial old-world hotel, this princely establishment has catered to a demanding European clientele since 1863. And though it still has the spacious salons and lavish decor of the turn of the century, it has also been discreetly modernized; rooms have luxurious bathrooms, and there is an exercise room. ✉ *Lungolago Umberto I 67, 28049 Stresa,* ☎ *0323/30431,* FAX *0323/32405. 172 rooms. Restaurant, bar, indoor pool, spa, golf privileges, tennis courts, exercise room, convention center. AE, DC, MC, V.*

$–$$ 🏨 **Primavera.** In a plain 1950s building in the heart of Stresa, Primavera has balconies embellished with flower boxes. It has the advantage of a location in a quiet pedestrian zone only three minutes from the lake and embarcadero. Rooms are compact and simply furnished. ✉ *Via Cavour 39, 28049 Stresa,* ☎ *0323/31286,* FAX *0323/33458. 32 rooms. AE, MC, V. Closed Jan.–Feb. and mid-Nov.–mid-Dec.*

Verbania

37 *16 km (10 mi) north of Stresa, 95 km (59 mi) northwest of Milan.*

Verbania lies across the Gulf of Pallanza from Stresa. It's known for the **Villa Taranto,** which has magnificent botanical gardens containing some 20,000 species. Created by the enthusiastic Scotsman Captain Neil McEachern, these gardens rank among Europe's finest. ✉ *Verbania,* ☎ FAX *0323/404555.* 🎟 *8,000 lire.* ⏲ *Apr.–Oct., daily 8:30–7:30.*

Dining

$$$–$$$$ ★ ✕ **Ristorante del Sole.** Chef Carlo Brovelli presides over this lakeside inn with a cheerfulness that is infectious. The lake figures into the menu, in the form of carpaccio made of fine slices of trout and perch. The seasonal menu is heavy on artichoke dishes in spring and eggplant in summer. Squab caramelized in honey might also top the menu. There are also nine sizable apartments. ✉ *Piazza Venezia 5, Ranco, near Angera,* ☎ *0331/976507,* FAX *0331/976620. Reservations essential. AE, DC, MC, V. Closed Tues. and Jan.–mid-Feb. No dinner Mon. mid-Feb.–mid-Mar.*

$$ ✕ **Monferrato.** Off Piazza Cadorna and close to the embarcadero, this hotel restaurant serves tasty risotto *con filetti di persico* (with perch fillets) and typical Piedmontese meat dishes, such as beef braised in Barolo wine. ✉ *Via Mazzini 14,* ☎ *0323/31386. AE, DC, MC, V. Closed Tues. and mid-Dec.–late Feb.*

MILAN, LOMBARDY, AND THE LAKES A TO Z

Arriving and Departing

By Bus

Italian bus service is best avoided on intercity routes, since it is neither faster, cheaper, nor more convenient than the railways. Most bus companies use Piazza Castello as a terminus, because Milan has no central bus terminal. For bus information, call **Autostradale** (☎ 166/845010). You can also try **Zani Viaggi** (☎ 02/867131).

By Car

Two major autostrada routes cross at Milan: the A1, which leads south to Bologna, Florence, and Rome, and the A4, which runs west–east from Turin to Venice. A7 angles southwest down to Genoa from Milan. Milan is ringed by a bypass road (the tangenziale). The A8 travels northwest to Lago Maggiore and beyond to Domodossola. The A9 leads north past Como to Chiasso and the Saint Gottard Pass into Switzerland.

By Plane

Aeroporto Malpensa (✉ About 50 km/31 mi northwest of Milan, ☎ 02/74851) services intercontinental flights. **Aeroporto Milano Linate** (✉ Less than 10 km/6 mi east of Milan, ☎ 02/74851) handles international and domestic flights. **Air Pullman** (☎ 02/40099260) coaches run twice daily in the morning between Malpensa and Linate airports. The fare is 20,000 lire, and the trip takes about 75 minutes.

BETWEEN THE AIRPORT AND DOWNTOWN

By Bus. There is bus service from Malpensa to the bus station at Stazione Centrale. **Air Pullman** (☎ 02/40099260) shuttle buses usually leave Malpensa every half hour on the half hour from 7 AM to 5 PM (excluding a bus at 1:30) and hourly 5–9 PM, the last bus leaving at 10:15 PM. Buy your ticket inside the airport before embarking. Buses leave the Stazione Centrale every half hour on the half hour 5:30 AM–7:30 PM (excluding a bus at 3) and hourly on the half hour 7:30–10:30 PM. A trip either way costs 13,000 lire and takes about one hour. Buses leave Linate every 20 minutes for Milan's Stazione Centrale. The trip takes about 20 minutes; the cost is 5,000 lire. You can also take ATM municipal Bus 73 to Piazza San Babila (every 15 minutes); the cost is 1,500 lire. Alternatively, there is a bus-service link between the airport and an airport terminal at **Lumpagnano** (☎ 02/74851). The trip costs 10,000 lire. Lumpagnano is on the subway route to the city center.

By Car. From Malpensa, take Route S336 east to the A8 autostrada southeast toward Milan. The drive takes about 40 minutes, depending on traffic and destination. From Linate, take what was once the Old Brescia Road west into the central downtown area.

By Taxi. A taxi stand is directly outside the arrivals building doors at Malpensa. Approximate fare is 130,000 lire; the trip takes 40 minutes. From Linate, the approximate fare is 30,000 lire; the trip takes less than 20 minutes.

By Train

Although Milan has a bewildering number of railway stations, only one is of concern, **Milano Centrale** (About 5 km/3 mi northwest of the Duomo and Galleria, ☎ 1478/88088 for toll-free information; 02/72524370 for APT office), unless you travel on local routes at peculiar hours—in which case service can begin or terminate in suburban stations (most notably **Milano Lambrate** for Bergamo, and **Stazione Nord** for Como). Premium international (EC) service and premium (IC) domestic service connect Milano Centrale with major European cities. Metro line 3 links Milano Centrale with Piazza de Duomo.

Getting Around

By Bicycle

As part of its campaign to ban cars from Milan's center, the city government has begun to set up a network of one-way bicycle rental stations. At first, rentals were free; now there is a small charge. Though the bicycles are clearly intended for residents who would otherwise use cars, current opinion is that tourists may use them, too (although individual proprietors of stands may arbitrarily decide to disagree, especially if you are unable to explain your rights in Italian). Look for yellow stands filled with yellow bicycles.

By Boat

There is frequent daily ferry and hydrofoil service between towns on the lakes, and a range of round-trip excursions, with a dining service (optional) aboard. **Navigazione Laghi** (✉ Via Ariosto 21, Milan, ☎ 02/4676101). **Navigazione Lago di Garda** (✉ Piazza Matteotti 2, Desenzano, ☎ 030/9149511). **Navigazione Lago di Como** (✉ Via Per Cernobbio 8, Tavernola, near Como, ☎ 031/579211). **Navigazione Lago Maggiore** (✉ Viale Baracca 1, Arona, ☎ 0322/46651).

By Bus

Trains are generally better than buses for getting around the cities of the plain. There is regular bus service between the small towns on the lakes, and it tends to be a cheaper way of getting around than ferry or hydrofoil service. The bus service around Lake Garda serves mostly towns on the western coast. Call **SIA** (☎ 0365/3774237) for information.

Milan has an excellent system of public transport (for information, call ATM, ☎ 02/48032403) consisting of trolley cars, buses, and a subway system, the **Metropolitana,** which runs on three lines. Tickets for each must be purchased before you board and must be canceled by machines at underground station entrances and mounted on poles inside trolleys and buses. Tickets cost 1,500 lire and can be purchased from news vendors, tobacconists, and machines at larger stops. Buy several at once—they remain valid until canceled. One ticket is valid for 75 minutes on all surface lines, or for one subway trip. A 24-hour ticket valid on all public transport lines costs 5,000 lire, and one ticket valid for 48 hours costs 9,000 lire; they are sold at Duomo Metro and Stazione Centrale Metro stations.

By Car

The A4 autostrada is the main east–west highway for this region. The A22 is a major north–south highway running just east of Lake Garda. Although these major highways will allow you to make good time between the cities of the plain, you'll have to follow secondary roads—often of great beauty—around the lakes. S572 goes along the southern and western shores of Lake Garda, S45b is along the northernmost section of the western shore, and S249 along the eastern shore. Around Lake Como, follow S340 along the western shore, S36 on the eastern coast, and S583 on the lower arms. S33 and S34 trace the western shore of Lake Maggiore.

Serious pollution is responsible for a rigorously enforced effort to control excessive traffic in and out of the city center. Cars lacking a special resident's permit will be stopped and ticketed. Parking in city center is possible 7 AM–8 PM for a fee. For **taxi service,** call ☎ 02/6767, 02/8585, or 02/8388. For **limousine service,** call Autonoleggio Pini (☎ 02/29400555, FAX 02/2047843). If age or infirmity entitle you to special dispensation, ask your rental agency or hotel concierge about car permits for special cases.

By Taxi

Taxi fares in Milan seem expensive compared with those in American cities, but drivers are honest (to an extreme, compared with those in some cities). A short downtown hop averages 16,000 lire. Taxis wait at stands or can be called (☎ 02/6767, 02/8585, or 02/8388).

By Train

From Milan, there is frequent direct service to Cremona, Bergamo, Pavia, Brescia, Mantua, Desenzano del Garda–Sirmione, and Como. Call 1478/88088 for toll-free information.

Contacts and Resources

Car Rental

MILAN

Avis (✉ Via Carlo D'Adda 19, ☎ 02/58106247; ✉ Aeroporto Milano Linate, ☎ 02/717214; ✉ Aeroporto Malpensa, ☎ 02/400099375). **Hertz** (✉ Via Novegro 49, ☎ 02/70200258; ✉ Aeroporto Milano Linate, ☎ 02/70200256; ✉ Aeroporto Malpensa, ☎ 02/40099022). **Europcar** (✉ Via Galbani 12, ☎ 02/66710491; ✉ Aeroporto Milano Linate, ☎ 02/76110277; ✉ Aeroporto Malpensa, ☎ 02/40099351).

Consulates

Australia Consulate (✉ Via Borgogna 2, Milan, ☎ 02/777041). **Canada Consulate** (✉ Via Vittorio Pisani 19, Milan, ☎ 02/67581). **U.K. Consulate** (✉ Via San Paolo 7, Milan, ☎ 02/723001). **U.S. Consulate** (✉ Via Principe Amedeo 2, Milan, ☎ 02/290351).

Emergencies

Carabinieri (☎ 112); English-speaking officers are available 24 hours a day to deal with every kind of emergency. **Police** (☎ 62261). **Ambulance** (☎ 113). You can dial this number wherever you are and it will connect you to the nearest local emergency service. For first aid, ask for *"pronto soccorso,"* and be prepared to give your address.

English-Language Bookstores

MILAN

American Bookshop (✉ Largo Cairoli at Via Camperio, ☎ 02/878920). **English Bookshop** (✉ Via Ariosto at Mascheroni, ☎ 02/4694468). **Feltrinelli Bookstore** (✉ Via Manzoni 12, ☎ 02/76000386). **Hoepli** (✉ Via Hoepli 5, ☎ 02/864871).

Guided Tours

For tours in Milan, contact the tourist office (☞ Visitor Information *below*). Lake tours can often be arranged by private launches at lakeside hotels (also ☞ Getting Around, By Boat, *above*). Contact the Tourist Guide Association (☎ 0376/368917) for English-speaking guides.

Late-Night Pharmacies

There are a number of pharmacies open 24 hours a day, including one on the upper level of **Stazione Centrale** (☎ 02/6690735). The **Cooperativa Farmaceutica** (✉ Piazza Duomo, ☎ 02/86460936 and 72022799) is also open 24 hours. Others take turns staying open late and on weekends; to find the nearest one, check the roster outside any chemist or the list published in the *Corriere della Sera.* Alternatively, you can call ☎ 0661/14471 for medical information.

Travel Agencies

MILAN

Compagnia Italiana Turismo (✉ CIT, Galleria Vittorio Emanuele, ☎ 02/863701). **American Express Travel Agency** (✉ Via Brera 3, ☎ 02/809645).

Visitor Information

Tourist offices (✉ Piazza della Chiesa 14, Bellagio, ☎ 031/950204; ✉ Vicolo Aquila Nera at Piazza Vecchia, Upper Bergamo, Bergamo, ☎ 035/232730; ✉ Viale Papa Giovanni 106, Bergamo Bassa, Bergamo, ☎ 035/213185; ✉ Corso Zanardelli 34, Brescia, ☎ 030/43418; ✉ Piazza Cavour 16, Como, ☎ 031/3300111; ✉ Train station, Como, ☎

031/267214; Provincial Tourist Board, ✉ Via Borgovico 148, Como, ☎ 031/230329 or 031/230111; ✉ Piazza del Comune 8, Cremona, ☎ 0372/23233; ✉ Via Capitanato del Porto 6, Malcesine, ☎ 045/7400555; ✉ Piazza A. Mantegna 6, Mantua, ☎ 0376/328253; ✉ Via Marconi 1, Milan, ☎ 02/72524300; ✉ Stazione Centrale, Milan, ☎ 02/72524370; ✉ Municipal Information Office, Galleria Vittorio Emanuele, Piazza della Scala, Milan, ☎ 02/8690734; ✉ Via Fabio Filzi 2, Pavia, ☎ 0382/22156; ✉ Giardini di Porta Orientale 8, Riva del Garda, ☎ 0464/554444; ✉ Via Vespasiano Gonzaga 31, Sabbioneta, ☎ 0375/52039; ✉ Viale Marconi 2, Sirmione, ☎ 030/916245 or 030/916114; ✉ Via Principe Tomaso 70, Stresa, ☎ 0323/30150).

9 THE DOLOMITES: TRENTINO-ALTO ADIGE

TRENTO, ROVERETO, BOLZANO, AND CORTINA D'AMPEZZO

Little wonder Leonardo da Vinci depicted the Dolomites behind his Mona Lisa. Nature's skyscrapers, they are hemmed in by stupefying cliffs, emerald-green meadows, and crystal-clear lakes. Dramatic rose-color peaks take on a purple hue at summer's sunset; in winter, the lure is the see-and-be-seen ski resort of Cortina d'Ampezzo. In the valleys bustle the history-rich cities of Trento, Rovereto, and Bolzano.

Updated by Fionn Davenport

UNLIKE OTHER FAMOUS ALPINE RANGES, this vast mountainous domain in northeast Italy has remained relatively undeveloped. The virginal landscape is the ultimate playground for the family or traveler on a quest for an original adventure. Ski fanatics travel across the world to dare some of the steep slopes that test Olympic champions. Mountaineers risk the climb up sheer rock faces. For calmer souls the seduction of a landscape painted from a palette of extreme colors prevails. The lowland valleys are laced with rivers spanned by awkward bridges and are dotted with secluded villages, picture-book castles, and unexpected historic sites.

The Dolomites, sprawling over the Trentino-Alto Adige region and into parts of Lombardy by the Swiss border and the Veneto along the Austrian border, became known to Americans as a winter sports center after Cortina d'Ampezzo catapulted to fame by hosting the Winter Olympics of 1956. Today, scores of funiculars, chairlifts, and ski lifts provide access to 1,200 km (750 mi) of ski runs, as well as ski jumps and bobsled runs.

Then there are the "untouchable" zones—inaccessible by means of chairlift or ski lift. These are the famous plateaus topping some of the highest mountains, from which you can see Italy on one side and Austria or Switzerland on the other. To enjoy such a rare spectacle, you must spend arduous hours climbing beyond where the lifts leave you, and when you reach the top, you will probably see cows casually grazing on the grass. It can make you dizzy just thinking of how they got there, but contradictions are common in the Dolomites.

Called "the most beautiful work of architecture ever seen" by Le Corbusier, this expansive land of rocks and valleys has long attracted Italians and other Europeans seeking a diverse natural environment. What they—and you—find is a profusion of brilliant colors, architectural styles, and languages. A meander through the valleys becomes a botanical escapade, with rare plant species abounding; high above you on the cliffs are castles, protected by their size and position. The serious climber will get a closer view of these remote fortresses. There, on the higher levels, are some rarely seen animals: bears, deer, mountain goats, and birds of prey. It's perhaps not surprising that Reinhold Messer, the first man to climb Everest without oxygen, lives in the Dolomites.

Straddling the Brenner Pass—the main access point to Italy from central Europe—the Dolomites play host to a mixture of cultures and languages. The people of the Alto Adige are predominantly German speaking, and their crafts and food have an Austrian accent (until World War I, the area was Austria's South Tyrol). The region of Trentino, on the other hand, is Italian speaking. Reflecting this diversity, the area, since 1848 has enjoyed special status as the Autonomous Region of Trentino-Alto Adige, made up of the independent provinces of Trento and Bolzano. But there is still another language to be heard in the area: Ladin, an offshoot of Latin still spoken by a small Ladin community primarily in the Val Gardena, can credit centuries of isolation in mountain strongholds for its survival. Signs throughout much of the Dolomites are bilingual. Place-names are given in Italian with German equivalents, where useful, in parentheses below.

Pleasures and Pastimes

Cross-Country Skiing

The Dolomites are an ideal place to learn or improve your *sci di fondo* (cross-country skiing). The major Alpine resorts, and even many out-of-the-way villages, have prepared trails (usually loops marked off by kilometers) appropriate for differing degrees of ability. Two of the best are at Ortisei and Dobbiaco. You can have a lot of fun blazing new trails across virgin snowfields; you can usually get permission by asking at the nearest farmhouse or by inquiring at local tourist offices.

Dining

Encompassing the Germanic Alto Adige province and the Italian Trentino province, the Dolomites region combines Italian cuisine with local Tyrolean specialties, which are much like the dishes of Austria and central Europe. Local *alimentari* (food shops) stock a bounty of regional cheeses, pickles, salami, and smoked meats—perfect for picnics—and local bakeries turn out a wide selection of crusty dark rolls and caraway-studded rye breads. Local dishes vary from one isolated mountain valley to the next. Don't miss *speck,* the local smoked ham. Other specialties include *canederli,* or *knoedel,* a type of dumpling with many variations, served either in broth or with a sauce; hot sauerkraut; ravioli made from rye flour, stuffed with spinach, and fried; and apple or pear strudel. And—as befits a wine-producing region—the local vintages (and fruit brandies) are delicious. In the fall in the South Tyrol, when autumn colors beautify the mountains and valleys, it's a tradition to make a tour of the cozy country wine taverns to drink the new wine and eat hot roasted chestnuts.

Downhill Skiing

The Dolomites command some of the best downhill skiing environments and facilities in Europe, with some centers equipped for summer skiing. Generally the ski season runs from late November to April, by which time some people prefer to ski in shirtsleeves. The most comprehensive centers are Cortina d'Ampezzo, in the heart of the Dolomites to the east of Bolzano, and Madonna di Campiglio, west of Trento. These resorts are unabashedly upscale, but you get the extras you expect from world-class centers: kilometers of interconnecting runs linked by cable cars and lifts, plus skating rinks, heated indoor pools, and lively après-ski. Less-expensive adventures can be had at Val di Badia (Badia Valley), south from Brunico, and Ortisei, a modern, popular resort.

Folk Festivals

Essentially rural in character, the Dolomites offer a rich selection of folk festivals, harvest fairs, and religious celebrations. Chief among these is Trento's weeklong festival of San Vigilio held the last week of June, when marching bands and costumed choirs perform in the streets and squares of the heart of the city. The other major towns have similar festivals, but equally enjoyable are the more informal and low-key celebrations in the villages of the many valleys, sometimes amounting to nothing more than excuses for hardworking mountain farmers to get together for some local wine and song.

Hiking and Climbing

The Dolomites have a well-maintained network of trails for hiking and rock climbing, with *rifugi* (huts) in both hiking terrain and near the most difficult ascents. At these spartan accommodations you can just refuel with a meal or stay overnight in a dormitory-style room. Routes are designated by grades of difficulty (T, tourist path; H, hiking path; EE for expert hikers; EEA, for equipped expert hikers). It is important to follow safety procedures, have the necessary equipment, and obtain the latest information on trails and conditions. For information, call the **Club Alpino Italiano** (✉ Piazza delle Erbe 46, Bolzano, ☎ 0471/978172; ✉ Corso della Libertà 188, Merano, ☎ 0473/448944).

Lodging

Accommodations in the Dolomites range from restored castles to spick-and-span chalet guest houses, from stately 19th-century hotels to chic modern ski resorts. Even a small village may have scores of lodging places, many of them very inexpensive. Hotel information offices at train stations and tourist offices can help you avoid the language problem if you arrive without reservations: Bolzano train station has a 24-hour hotel service, and tourist offices will give you a list of all the hotels in the area, arranged by location and price. We've tried to mention here a few hotels in towns that make good bases for travel, as well as some notable hotels found along the road. Remember that many hotels in ski resorts cater primarily to longer stays at full or half board: it's wise to book ski vacations as a package in advance. A word of warning: although spring and fall are wonderful times to travel in the region, many mountain hotels are closed for a month or two after Easter and for about six weeks before Christmas.

Shopping

Shopping is an event in the Dolomites, where larger towns such as Bolzano, Bressanone, and Brunico have shops clustered in arcaded shopping streets designed to keep shoppers dry on rainy or snowy days. The ethnic mixture, with its strong Tyrolean influence, makes for local products and crafts that are quite different from those elsewhere in Italy. Tyrolean clothing—loden goods, lederhosen, dirndls, and linen suits with horn buttons—is a good buy and costs less than in neighboring Austria. Local crafts, such as embroidered goods, wood carvings, figures for nativity scenes, pottery, and handcrafted copper and iron objects, make good gifts.

Exploring the Dolomites

The best—and only—way to get around in this mountainous region is by following the course of the valleys that find their way to the heart of the massifs of the Dolomites. Two of the most important valleys are those formed by the Isarco and Adige rivers. The Isarco River begins at the Brenner Pass and runs due south to Bolzano where it joins the Adige River. The Adige itself originates near the Swiss border and also runs south through Bolzano. Italy's main road and rail connections to north central Europe follow the same rivers northward en route to the Brenner Pass.

Numbers in the text correspond to numbers in the margin and on the Dolomites: Trentino-Alto Adige and Bolzano maps.

Great Itineraries

The area of the Dolomites is a vast expanse of valleys, mountain roads, and hillside towns. Unfortunately, most roads, although of excellent quality, can be hazardous, especially during the winter months. Instead of rushing to get all the sights into your travels, try to be discerning and stick to the areas you would most like to see. A further note of caution involves the closure of some roads during the winter season, which can begin as early as November and continue until May, in particular the high mountain passes such as Passo di Gavia and Passo dello Stelvio in the east.

IF YOU HAVE 3 DAYS

Start in **Trento** ① and head south to **Rovereto** ② and **Riva del Garda** on the tip of Lake Garda (☞ Chapter 8), then on to the quaint towns of **Pinzolo** ③ and **Madonna di Campiglio** ④ for a bird's-eye view of the Dolomites, ending your day via Dimaro in **Bolzano** ⑨–⑮. The next day head for the lovely town of **Bressanone** ⑱ and onward via

Brunico ⑲ to the exclusive resort of **Cortina d'Ampezzo** ㉑. The last day take the Grande Strada delle Dolomiti, passing **Lago di Carezza** ㉖, and return to Trento.

IF YOU HAVE 5 DAYS

Follow the three-day itinerary above as far as Dimaro, but instead of going directly to Bolzano, swing east and head for the dizzily high Passo di Gavia and down then to the small town of **Bormio** ⑤. The next day proceed to the breathtaking **Passo dello Stelvio** ⑥ and on down to **Naturno** ⑦ before stopping in one of the pearls of the Alto Adige region, **Merano** ⑧. Continue on to **Bolzano** ⑨–⑮, the principal city in this region. The next day head for **Cornedo** ⑯, **Chiusa** ⑰, and **Bressanone** ⑱. Move on to Brunico and **Cortina d'Ampezzo** ㉑. The next day head to **Canazei** ㉒ via the breathtaking Passo di Sella and on down into **Ortisei** ㉓ in the heart of the Val Gardena. Return to Trento via **Fiè** ㉔ and **Caldaro** ㉕.

IF YOU HAVE 8 DAYS

Follow the five-day itinerary as far as Brunico. The following day stroll through **Dobbiaco** ⑳ before moving on to **Cortina d'Ampezzo** ㉑. From here follow the Grande Strada delle Dolomiti through the Passo di Falzarego and slightly north through the Passo di Sella and into the Val Gardena and **Ortisei** ㉓. On the last day, drive to **Fiè** ㉔ and south on the A22. Just south of Cornedo, turn left onto the S241 to get to **Lago di Carezza** ㉖. Continue along the road until you reach Vigo di Fassa, veering south onto the S48, passing through the small towns of Predazzo, Cavalese, and Ora, until you rejoin the A22 and continue south back to **Trento** ①.

When to Tour the Dolomites

If you are here for the skiing, most resorts open from mid-December to April. With the exception of the main bargain period known to Italians as *settimane bianche* (white weeks), ski-package weeks usually running from January to February, the slopes are relatively crowd free. Booking well in advance of your ski holiday is highly recommended, as lack of snow in the early part of the season can sometimes cause overcrowding later on. During the rest of the year accommodations are easier to find, but booking is still recommended. Note that nearly all hotels and guest houses outside the main urban centers close from early November to mid- or late December.

WESTERN TRENTINO

The areas east and west of Trento are collectively known as Trentino, a region shaped roughly like a butterfly. The west side includes the peaks of the Brenta Massif, the Stelvio Pass, and the Val Venosta. Some of the passes in this region close during the winter months, so if you are traveling during this period you will not be able to follow the entire itinerary. Towns are given in order as you come upon them by road.

Trento

❶ *51 km (32 mi) south of Bolzano, 24 km (15 mi) north of Rovereto.*

Capital of the autonomous Trentino province, Trento has somehow escaped the ravages of commercialization and retains its architectural charm, artistic attractions, and historic importance. It was here, from 1545 to 1563, that the structure of the Catholic Church was redefined at the famous Council of Trent. This was the starting point of the Counter-Reformation, which brought half of Europe back to Catholicism. Trento itself was ruled by prince-bishops until 1803 when they

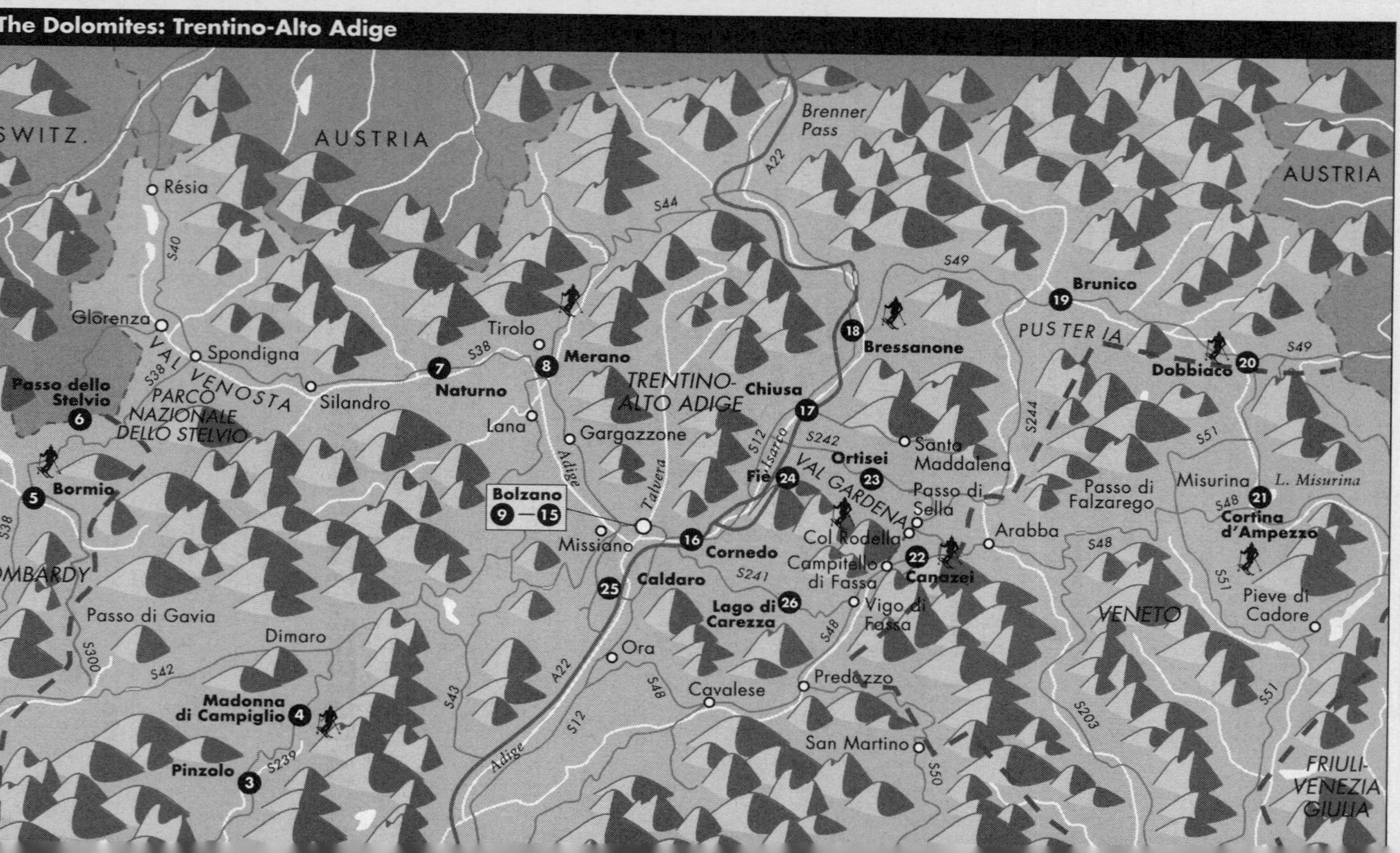
The Dolomites: Trentino-Alto Adige
SWITZ.
AUSTRIA
Brenner Pass
A22
AUSTRIA
Résia
S40
S44
S49
Brunico
19
Glorenza
Tirolo
18
Bressanone
PUSTERIA
S49
Spondigna
S38
7
8
Merano
Dobbiaco
20
Passo dello Stelvio
6
S38
VAL VENOSTA
Silandro
Naturno
TRENTINO-ALTO ADIGE
Chiusa
17
S244
PARCO NAZIONALE DELLO STELVIO
Lana
Gargazzone
S242
Santa Maddalena
S51
Adige
S12
Isarco
Ortisei
Fiè
24
23
VAL GARDENA
Misurina
L. Misurina
Bormio
5
Bolzano
9—15
Talvera
Passo di Sella
Passo di Falzarego
S48
21
Cortina d'Ampezzo
S38
Missiano
16
Cornedo
Col Rodella
Arabba
S48
LOMBARDY
Campitello di Fassa
22
Canazei
S51
25
Caldaro
S241
Lago di Carezza
26
Vigo di Fassa
VENETO
Pieve di Cadore
Passo di Gavia
S48
Dimaro
S300
Ora
S42
A22
S48
Predazzo
S43
Cavalese
S203
S51
Madonna di Campiglio
4
S12
San Martino
Pinzolo
3
S239
Adige
S50
FRIULI-VENEZIA GIULIA

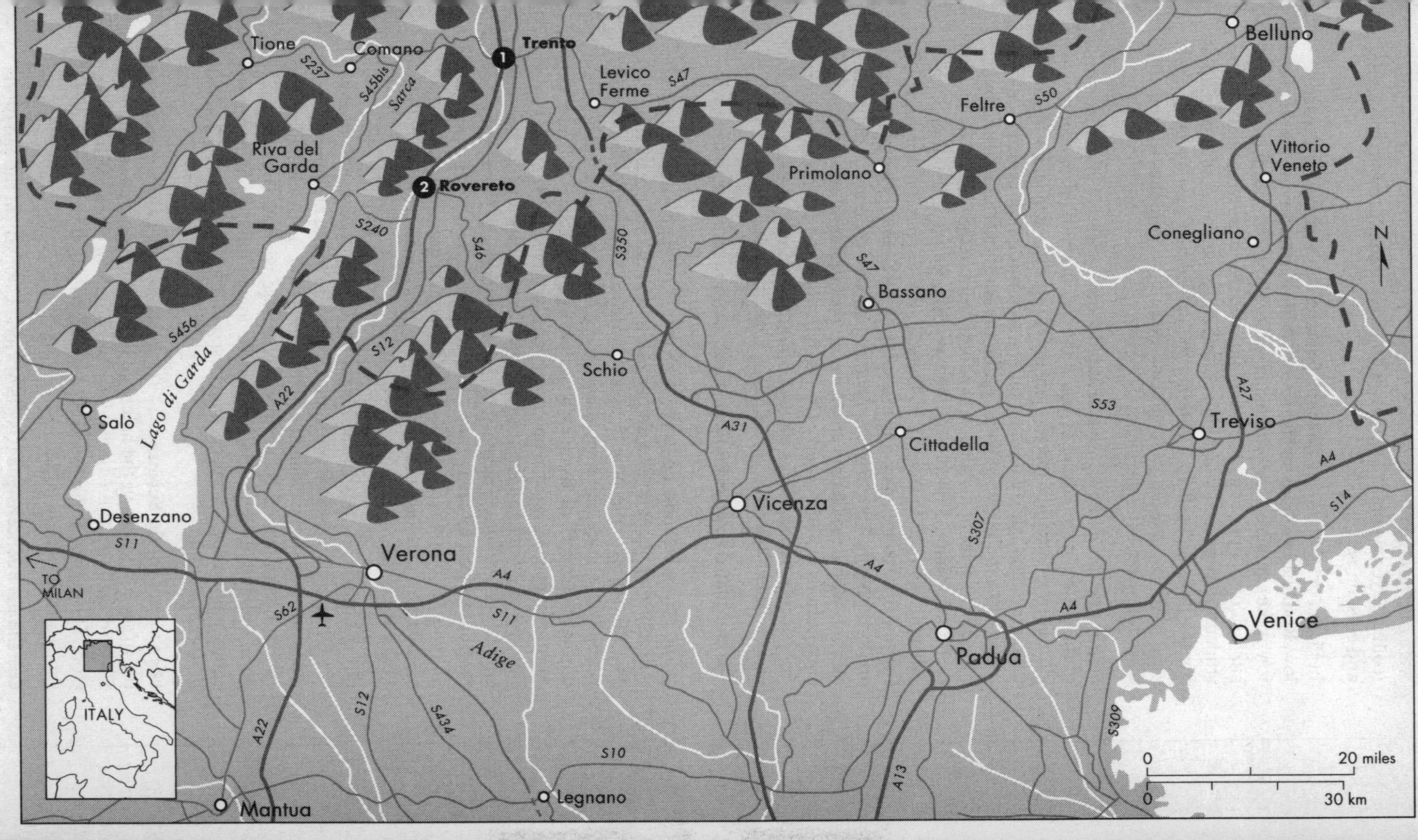
Tione
Comano
Trento
Levico Ferme
S47
Belluno
S237
S45bis
Sarca
Feltre
S50
Riva del Garda
Rovereto
Primolano
Vittorio Veneto
S240
S46
S350
Conegliano
N
S47
Bassano
S456
S12
Schio
Lago di Garda
A22
S53
A27
Salò
A31
Cittadella
Treviso
A4
Vicenza
S14
S307
Desenzano
S11
Verona
A4
A4
TO MILAN
S62
S11
A4
Venice
Adige
Padua
ITALY
S12
S434
S309
A22
S10
A13
0
20 miles
0
30 km
Mantua
Legnano

were overthrown by Napoléan's armies. You'll see the word *consiglio* (council) everywhere in Trento—in hotel, restaurant, and street names, and even on wine labels.

In Piazza del Duomo is a Baroque **Fontana del Nettuno**. The massive, low, Romanesque **Duomo,** also known as the Cathedral of San Virgilio, forms the southern edge of the square. Locals refer to the piazza as the city's *salotto,* or sitting room, as in fine weather it is always filled with students and residents drinking coffee, enjoying an aperitif, or reading the newspaper. Before entering the cathedral, pause to savor the view of the mountaintops ranged majestically around the city in every direction when skies are clear.

Step inside to see the unusual arcaded stone stairways on either side of the austere nave. Ahead of you is the *baldacchino* (altar canopy), a clear copy of Bernini's masterpiece in St. Peter's in Rome. In the small Chapel of the Crucifix to the right is a mournful 15th-century Crucifixion, with the Virgin Mary and John the Apostle. This crucifix, built by German artist Sixtus Frei, was a focal point of the Council of Trent: each decree agreed on during the two decades of deliberations was solemnly read out in front of it. Outside, walk around to the back of the cathedral to see an exquisite display of 14th-century stonemasons' art, from the small porch to the intriguing knotted columns on the graceful apse. Within the Duomo grounds is an **archaeological area,** displaying ancient ruins of a 6th-century Christian basilica and a gate dating from the 9th century. ✉ *Piazza del Duomo.* 💳 *Archaeological area 2,000 lire.* ⏲ *Weekdays 10–noon and 2–6, Sat. 10–noon.*

The crenellated **Palazzo Pretorio,** which seems to be a wing of the cathedral, was built in the 13th century as the prudently fortified residence of the prince-bishops. Endowed with considerable power and autonomy, these clerics enjoyed a unique position in the medieval hierarchy. The Palazzo Pretorio now houses the **Museo Diocesano Tridentino,** where you can see paintings showing the seating plan of the prelates during the Council of Trent; early 16th-century tapestries by Pieter van Aelst, the Belgian artist who carried out Raphael's (1483–1520) designs for the Vatican tapestries; carved wood altars and statues; and an 11th-century sacramentary, or book of services. These and other precious objects all come from the cathedral's treasury. ✉ *Piazza del Duomo 18,* ☎ *0461/234419.* 💳 *6,000 lire includes Duomo archaeological area* (☞ *above).* ⏲ *Mid-Feb.–mid-Nov., Mon.–Sat. 9:30–12:30 and 2:30–6.*

Off the northwest side of the Piazza del Duomo, about 650 ft down Via Cavour, is the Renaissance church of **Santa Maria Maggiore,** where many sessions of the Council of Trent were held. The only light in the church comes from a beautifully simple rose window over the main door, so you'll have to strain to see the magnificent ceiling, an intricate combination of stucco and frescoes. ✉ *Via Cavour.* ⏲ *Daily 8:30–12 and 2:30–8.*

Locals refer to **Via Belenzani** as Trento's outdoor gallery because of the frescoed facades of the hallmark Renaissance palazzi. It's an easy 50-yard walk up the lane behind the church of Santa Maria Maggiore.The climb up **Via Manci** is pleasant, past 200 yards of souvenir shops and glassware outlets.

Castello del Buonconsiglio (Castle of Good Counsel), at the end of Via Manci, was once the stronghold of the prince-bishops; its position and size made it easier to defend than the Palazzo Pretorio. As you stand facing it, you can see the evolution of architectural styles, starting with the medieval fortifications of the Castelvecchio section on the far left, down to the more decorative Renaissance **Magno Palazzo,** built three centuries later in 1530. The Castello now houses the **Museo Provinciale d'Arte** (Provincial Art Museum), where permanent and visiting exhibits of art and archaeology are displayed in Renaissance frescoed medieval halls or under Renaissance coffered ceilings. The 13th-century **Torre dell'Aquila** (Eagle's Tower) holds the highlight of the museum, a medieval fresco cycle of the months of the year called the *Ciclo dei Mesi.* It is full of charming and informatively detailed scenes of 15th-century life in both court and countryside. ✉ *Via Bernardo Clesio 5,* ☎ *0461/233770.* 🎫 *10,000 lire July–Oct., 7,000 lire Nov.–June.* ⏲ *May–Sept., Tues.–Sun. 9–6; Oct.–Apr., Tues.–Sun. 9–12:15 and 2–5:15. Admission and hrs vary when exhibitions are held.*

The emphasis of the **Museo Storico di Trento** (Trento Historical Museum), housed in the former joiner's shop inside the castle walls, is on modern Trentino history, with displays, dioramas, and the occasional exhibition on the region from the unification of Italy in 1861 up to and including World War II. ✉ *Via Bernardo Clesio 3,* ☎ *0461/230482.* 🎫 *7,000 lire, 10,000 during an exhibition.* ⏲ *Apr.–Sept., Tues.–Sun. 9–noon and 2–6; Oct.–Mar., Tues.–Sun. 9–noon and 2–5.*

The **Torre Verde,** or Green Tower (✉ Piazza Raffaello Sanzio), is part of Trento's 13th-century fortifications standing alongside other fragments of the city walls. The **Torre Vanga** (✉ Via Torre Vanga) is another 13th-century fortification, this time guarding the medieval bridge across the Adige, Ponte San Lorenzo.

The progressive, modern works in the **Museo d'Arte Moderna e Contemporanea di Trento** collection are installed in a Renaissance villa, Palazzo delle Albere, next to the Adige river. Permanent works date from the 19th and 20th centuries; rotating exhibitions feature the work of modern and contemporary artists. ✉ *Palazzo delle Albere, Via Ruggero da Sanseverino 45,* ☎ *0461/234860.* 🎫 *4,000–10,000 lire.* ⏲ *Tues.–Sun. 10–6.*

OFF THE BEATEN PATH

BELVEDERE DI SARDAGNA – Take the cable car from the station at the Ponte San Lorenzo bridge to this scenic spot, a vantage point 1,200 ft above Trento.

LEVICO TERME – About 20 km (13 mi) southeast of Trento and just east of the summer resorts of Lago di Caldonazzo is the undiscovered Levico Terme, a medieval *terme* (thermal bath) town nestled in the Val Sugana; the valley was inhabited by the Celts and then conquered by the Romans, and today the Latin-derived Ladin is still spoken by remote peoples in a valley enclave. Today, settle into a hotel here for summer sports and relaxation. For cosseting, spa treatment, and modern comforts, the gracious **Imperial Grand Hotel Terme** (✉ Via Silva Domini 1, 38056, Levico Terme, ☎ 0461/706104, FAX 0261/706350) is in a lordly restored Austrian noble estate, with a beautiful indoor pool, garden, and a fine Tuscan restaurant.

Dining and Lodging

$$$ ✕ **Chiesa.** Near the castle in a building that dates from about 1400 is this bright but nicely lit restaurant with a mix of antiques and modern detail, and power lunchers. Bright red chairs with black trim, apple prints, and even risotto *alle mele* (with apples) celebrate the local produce. The food is traditional: *maccheroncini con salsiccia e verze* (short, narrow pasta tubes with sausage and cabbage) and *tonco de Pontesel* (a stew of mixed meat served with polenta and made according to a 15th-century recipe). ✉ *Via San Marco 64,* ☎ *0461/238766. AE, DC, MC, V. Closed Sun.*

$$$ ★ ✕ **Le Due Spade.** Near the Duomo, small and cozy, with wood paneling and chairs and an antique stove, this typical Tyrolean tavern has an atmosphere of warmth and comfort, able service, and superb locally inspired food. You can sample heartwarming, traditional *gnocchetti di ricotta* (ricotta cheese dumplings) and polenta *con funghi* (with mushroom sauce) and such savory *secondi* (second courses) as *tagliata di Angus alla griglia* (grilled slivers of beef) served with an aromatic herb sauce. Given its deserved popularity with locals and limited seating, reservations are a must. ✉ *Via Don Arcangelo Rizzi 11,* ☎ *0461/234343. Reservations essential. AE, DC, MC, V. Closed Sun. No lunch Sun. or Mon.*

$ ✕ **Trattoria Pizzeria Laste.** Owner Guido Rizzi invented pizza Calabrese, a white pizza with garlic, mozzarella, and hot red pepper flakes. He's also a national pizza champion. Well, the proof is in the pudding. Each of his 35 pies—including the *sedano* (mozzarella, celery root, *grana* cheese, oregano)—is delectable. Save room for dessert: pizza *dolce,* with bananas, strawberries, kiwi, and caramel. The trattoria is housed in a pleasant villa in the hills above city center. ✉ *Via alle Laste 39, Cognola,* ☎ *0461/231570. MC, V. Closed Tues.*

$$ ✕🏨 **Castel Pergine.** On a hilltop outside of town toward Levico looms this castle, which in the 13th century was transformed into a fort, and in the 16th century was occupied by the prince-bishop Bernardo Clesio. Today, the involved Swiss Schneider-Neffs manage it. In the labyrinth of brooding stone and brick chambers, prisons, and chapels are sparse, rustic rooms with carved wood trim, lace curtains, and heavy wooden beds, some canopied. The grounds often have brightly colored modern-art installations—an interesting juxtaposition. The candlelit restaurant, which serves age-old seasonal recipes from Trento in lighter guises, is a favorite of locals and visitors alike. Lodging rates are happily at the bottom of this category. ✉ *38057 Pergine Val Sugana, about 10 km (6 mi) east of Trento* ☎ *0461/531158,* FAX *0461/531329. 21 rooms, 14 with bath. Restaurant, horseback riding, library. AE, MC, V. Closed Nov. 2–Thurs. before Easter.*

$$$ 🏨 **Accademia.** This friendly character-filled hotel occupies an ancient house in the historic center of Trento, close to Piazza del Duomo. The public rooms retain the ancient vaulting, but the bedrooms are modern and comfortably equipped. There's a good but expensive restaurant and a courtyard garden. ✉ *Vicolo Colico 4/6, 38100,* ☎ *0461/233600,* FAX *0461/230174. 42 rooms. Restaurant, wine bar. AE, DC, MC, V.*

$$$ 🏨 **Buonconsiglio.** Near the train station, this elegant, modern hotel offers well-kept, sizable rooms and an efficient service, perfect for the business traveler. The public spaces are replete with modern art, which is in keeping with the hotel's insistence on a modern approach to the art of hostelry. ✉ *Via Romagnosi 16–18, 38100,* ☎ *0461/272888,* FAX *0461/272889. 46 rooms, 2 suites. Restaurant, bar. AE, DC, MC, V.*

$$$ 🏨 **Grand Hotel Trento.** Its contemporary facade amid ancient palaces makes this hotel on Piazza Dante an anomaly. Inside it's lush with modern appointments, from the marble and woodwork in the lobby and lounges to the Clesio restaurant's rich drapery. Rooms are ample and have thick carpets in blues and creams with clubby, wood-trim furniture and remote controls. ✉ *Via Alfieri 1/3, 38100,* ☎ *0461/271000,* FAX *0461/271001. 136 rooms. Restaurant, bar, meeting rooms, parking (fee). AE, DC, MC, V. Closed Dec. 24–Jan. 6.*

$$ 🏨 **Aquila d'Oro.** This small hotel offers comfort, efficiency, and a prime location in the historic town center. Most rooms have modern furniture in somber colors. The owner is more then willing to pitch in names of places for lunch and dinner. ✉ *Via Belenzani 76, 38100,* ☎ FAX *0461/986282. 20 rooms. Bar, breakfast room. AE, DC, MC, V. Closed Dec. 24–Jan. 6.*

Nightlife and the Arts

FESTIVALS

From late June to late September a regional **Superfestival** highlights historic castles as venues for performances and evocations of fact and legend. Trains taking passengers on excursions to the castles are part of it, as are music, costumes, and banquets. The **Festivale di Musica Sacra** (Sacred Music Festival)—a monthlong series of concerts held in the churches of Trento and the Trentino—is held in May and June; for information, call ☏ 0462/983880.

A summer bonus is the weeklong **Festive Vigiliane,** a spectacular pageant in the Piazza del Duomo, culminating on June 26, when townspeople don medieval clothing in honor of their patron saint. For more than 60 years the May wine festival **Mostra dei Vini** has attracted every Bacchus, from farmers of surrounding hillside towns to sommeliers from all over Italy. The weeklong festival includes tastings, sommelier tours, and prizes; for information, call ☏ 0461/983880.

Shopping

FOODSTUFFS

The **Enoteca di Corso** (✉ Corso 3 Novembre 54) is an extraordinary shop laden with local produce including cheese, salami, and wine.

MARKETS

The small morning **Mercato di Piazza Lodron** is now held in Piazza Alessandro Vittoria, where you can pick up meats, cheeses, produce, and local truffles and porcini mushrooms. On **Piazza Arogno** is a flea market held the third Sunday of every month; there is also a crafts market every Friday and Saturday, but the big shopping day is Thursday, when the weekly market spreads out around this piazza and winds down next to the cathedral.

WOODEN CRAFTS AND CERAMICS

Il Pozzo (✉ Piazza Pasi 14/l) sells excellent handcrafted wooden objects. **Il Laboratorio** (✉ Via Roma 12) specializes in terra-cotta pieces molded by local artists.

Rovereto

❷ *24 km (15 mi) south of Trento, 75 km (47 mi) south of Bolzano.*

The 15th-century **Castello di Rovereto** looks down on the medieval town of Rovereto, on the main north–south valley of the Adige. Some of the fiercest fighting of World War I took place in the wooded hills around Rovereto, with Italian and Austrian troops bogged down in prolonged and costly conflict. Every evening at nightfall you're reminded of the thousands who fell by the ringing of the Campana dei Caduti (Bell of the Fallen). Today, it's a noble, peaceful city filled with baby carriages and bright geraniums. Crumbling pastel-color medieval villas inhabit long-shadowed piazzas and winding streets.

Among the city's brooding history, a Futurist vision explodes at the **Museo Depero.** This small installment of native Fortunato Depero's (1892–1960) dynamic works, from 1914 to 1950, includes his hectic New York impressions. ✉ *Via della Terra 53,* ☏ *0464/434393.* 🎫 *5,000.* ⏲ *Tues.–Sun. 9–12:30 and 2:30–6.*

Dining

$$–$$$ ✕ **Ristorante Novecento.** Owner Marco Zani can't for the life of him persuade his grandmother, Wanda, to stop cooking. But after a superb dinner in this airy, candlelit restaurant, you'll be happy she still reigns in the kitchen. Luscious dishes, paired with local wines, include *tortelli con fonduta di formaggi* (pasta squares with spinach and ricotta bathed

in a butter sauce) and *petto di faraona con finferli su fonduta di porri* (guinea fowl with wild mushrooms and leek puree). ✉ *Corso Rosmini 82/d,* ☎ *0464/435222. AE, D, MC, V. Closed Sun.*

$–$$ ✕ **La Lanterna.** Up the stairs from the sprawling piazza is this homey, simple, wood-trim trattoria, perfect for a hearty meal among locals. You can start with plates of polenta, *crostini* (grilled bread with toppings), and *trippe en brodo* (tripe in broth), and move on to the rich pastas and meats. ✉ *Piazza Malfatti 12,* ☎ *0464/436612. AE, MC, V. Closed Thurs. No dinner Wed.*

Nightlife and the Arts

The **Rovereto Festival** (☎ 0464/452159) in early September celebrates modern dance and art exhibitions. Late September welcomes the **Festival Internazionale W. A. Mozart** (☎ 0464/452159), with classical performances at the exquisite **Teatro Zadonai** (✉ Corso Bettini 82, ☎ 0464/452159).

En Route Traveling south from Rovereto, head west on S240, passing the lovely lakeside town of Riva del Garda (☞ Chapter 8), and then north on S45 bis to Comano, a small but locally renowned spa. The road continues to Tione, a small farming community. From here head north on S239 to reach Pinzolo.

Pinzolo

❸ *75 km (47 mi) northwest of Rovereto, 59 km (37) mi northwest of Trento.*

In this quaint mountain village you can see a remarkable 16th-century fresco on the side of a small church. Follow the signs for the church of **San Vigilio,** which you'll come to after a short walk through the pines. On an exterior wall, a vivid fresco painted in 1539 by the artist Simone Baschenis describes the Dance of Death, with 40 ghoulish figures offering a stern rebuke to potential sinners. Unfortunately, the church is usually closed to the public.

Madonna di Campiglio

★ ❹ *14 km (9 mi) north of Pinzolo, 88 km (55 mi) southwest of Bolzano.*

The chichi winter resort of Madonna di Campiglio grooms more than 130 km (80 mi) of ski runs and operates some 39 lifts. The resort itself is at a 5,000-ft altitude, and some of the ski runs, summer hiking paths, and mountain biking routes venture onto the surrounding peaks, including Pietra Grande, more than 9,700 ft up. An excursion to the Punta Spinale (Spinale Peak) on the year-round chairlift affords magnificent views of the Brenta Dolomites.

Lodging

$$$$ ★ 🏨 **Golf.** You'll have to make your way up to Campo Carlo Magno, the famous pass just north of town, to reach this grand hotel, the former summer residence of Habsburg Emperor Franz Joseph. A modern wing has been added to the more-than-a-century-old structure, but old-world charm remains: Rooms 114 and 214 are still lavished in the old imperial style. Replete with verandas, Persian rugs, and bay windows, it's practically on the fairway of a golf course that draws a tony summer crowd. A shuttle bus makes runs into town. ✉ *Campo Carlo Magno, 38084,* ☎ *0465/441003,* FAX *0465/440294. 124 rooms. Restaurant, bar, 9-hole golf course. AE, DC, MC, V. Closed mid-Apr.–June, mid-Sept.–mid-Dec.*

$$$$ 🏨 **Savoia Palace.** One of the more traditional hotels at the resort is full of mountain-style furnishings with lots of carved wood and an intimate atmosphere. Two fireplaces blaze away in the bar, where guests recall the day's exploits on the ski slopes. The elegant restaurant serves a mixture of local specialties and rich dishes drawing on Italian and Austrian influences. Guests stay on full- or half-board terms only. ✉ *Via Dolomiti di Brenta, 38084,* ☎ *0465/441004,* FAX *0465/440549. 55 rooms. Restaurant, bar. AE, DC, MC, V. Closed mid-Apr.–June, mid-Sept.–Nov. FAP, MAP.*

$$$ 🏨 **Grifone.** A comfortable hotel that catches the sun, the Grifone has distinctive wood paneling on the outside, flower-decorated balconies, and rooms with views of the forested slopes. The restaurant serves home cooking as well as international dishes. ✉ *Via Vallesinella 7, 38084,* ☎ *0465/442002,* FAX *0465/440540. 40 rooms. Restaurant, bar. AE, DC, MC, V. Closed mid-Apr.–June, mid-Sept.–Nov.*

Outdoor Activities and Sports

GOLF

On **Campo Carlo Magno** (☎ 0465/41003) is a 9-hole course, set in the mountains near Madonna di Campiglio, open from July through mid-September.

HIKING

The local **tourist office** (☞ Visitor Information *in* The Dolomites: Trentino-Alto Adige A to Z, *below*) supplies maps of the dozen or so treks for walking amid waterfalls, lakes, and stupefying views.

SKIING

This quaint resort is one of the better-skied resorts in the Dolomites, with kilometers of interconnecting runs linked by cable cars and lifts. The popularity of this town is due to the well-organized lodging, skiing, and trekking facilities it provides.

En Route Just a few kilometers north of Madonna di Campiglio is one of the highest points in the Dolomites, the **Campo Carlo Magno** pass. This is where Charlemagne is said to have stopped in AD 800 on his way to Rome to be crowned emperor. Stop here to glance over the whole of northern Italy. Resume your descent with caution (in the space of a couple of kilometers, you descend more than 2,000 ft via hairpin turns and switchbacks). The strange, rocky pinnacles of the Dolomites, which jut straight up like chimneys and look at times more like Utah's Monument Valley than any European ranges, loom over scattered mountain lakes. Turn left at Dimaro, and continue 37 km (23 mi) east to Ponte di Legno through another high pass, **Passo del Tonale** (5,600 ft). Here turn right on S300 and, passing the so-called Black Lake on your left, head for Bormio, the famous Lombard skiing center, through the **Passo di Gavia,** which also must be approached carefully and attentively when open to traffic.

Bormio

❺ *20 km (12 mi) south of Passo dello Stelvio, 100 km (60 mi) southwest of Merano.*

At the foot of the Stelvio Pass, in the Valtellina, Bormio is one of the most famous ski resorts on the western side of the Dolomites, with 38 km (24 mi) of pistes. It differs greatly from Madonna di Campiglio in that it is both a town and a summer resort. With an altitude of close to 4,000 ft, Bormio has clean, fresh air that in summer draws Italians escaping the humidity of the cities. There are plenty of shops, restaurants, and hotels throughout the town. Bormio has also been known for the therapeutic qualities of its waters since the Roman era. You'll find spas throughout the town.

Bormio is the place to enter the Alps' biggest national park, the **Parco Nazionale dello Stelvio,** spread over 1,350 square km (520 square mi) and four provinces. Opened in 1935 with the express intent to preserve flora and protect fauna, today it thrives with over 1,200 types of plants—not to mention 600 different mushrooms—and over 160 species of animals, including the chamois, ibex, and roe deer. ✉ *Visitor center, Via Monte Braulio 56,* ☎ *0342/901582.* *Free.*

Lodging

$$$ **Posta.** Ostelli della Posta hotels, staging inns of days gone by, are a time-honored tradition in northern Italy. The warm reception and atmosphere of this town-center hotel will temper the cold, with its warm wood detail in the low-vaulted areas. The rooms are cozy and comfortable, with heavy drapery and bed linens. Perks include a small health center with a pool, sauna, gym, and Turkish bath and a slopes shuttle bus. ✉ *Via Roma 66, 23032,* ☎ *0342/904753,* FAX *0342/904484. 50 rooms. Restaurant, pub, indoor pool, sauna, Turkish bath, health club. AE, DC, MC, V. Closed Oct.–Dec. 19.*

$$ **Nazionale.** Bordering the Stelvio National Park, this central hotel caters to the winter and summer crowd. Rooms are small but well equipped, with TVs and safes. The exterior is, for the most part, wood, with balconies on nearly all floors except the top. The hotel operates a shuttle bus to and from the cable cars. ✉ *Via al Forte 28, 23032,* ☎ *0342/903361,* FAX *0342/905294. 48 rooms. 2 restaurants, bar, sauna, shops, recreation room. AE, DC, MC, V. Closed Oct.–Dec.*

Passo dello Stelvio

★ ❻ *20 km (12 mi) north of Bormio, 80 km (48 mi) west of Merano.*

At just over 9,000 ft, the Passo dello Stelvio (Stelvio Pass) is the second-highest pass in Europe. The view from the top is worth the effort because the pass connects the Val Venosta with the Valtellina in neighboring Lombardy. Just to the left as you enter the pass is Switzerland. Stelvio is a year-round skiing center, with summer skiing on many of its runs.

En Route Between the Stelvio Pass and Spondigna is 30 km (19 mi) of picturesque, winding road, with 48 hairpin turns. This section of road can be a bit hair-raising if you don't like mountain driving. In Spondigna keep to the right for the road to Naturno.

ALTO ADIGE AND CORTINA

Alto Adige (Südtirol), the northern half of the region, was ceded to Italy at the end of World War I, hitherto having been part of the Austro-Hungarian Empire. As a result, everything here has more than a tinge of the Teutonic, which is none more apparent than in the fact that the majority of the inhabitants speak German. Ethnic differences have led to inevitable tensions (including, alas, acts of terrorism), though a large measure of autonomy has, for the most part, kept the lid on nationalist ambitions. Towns are listed in order as you come upon them by road.

Naturno

❼ *61 km (38 mi) east of Passo dello Stelvio, 44 km (27 mi) northwest of Bolzano.*

Naturno is a large horticultural center, with streets lined with colorful houses that display painted murals on their walls. Art lovers will appreciate the church of **San Procolo,** which is frescoed inside and out, and has wall paintings that are the oldest in the German-speaking world, dating from the 8th century. ⏲ *Sun. 8–8.*

Above the town, a short distance away, is the 13th-century **Castello Juval,** since 1983 the home of the South Tyrolese climber and polar adventurer Reinhold Messner—the first man to conquer Everest solo, and the first to scale all 14 of the world's highest peaks without oxygen. Since 1995, part of the castle has been a museum, showing Messner's collection of Tibetan art, mountaineering illustrations, and masks from around the world. ✉ *Viale Europa 2,* ☎ *0473/221852.* 🎫 *12,000 lire.* ⏲ *Mid-Apr.–June and Sept.–mid-Nov., daily 10–5.*

Dining

$$ ✕ **Juval Inn.** Just below Castello Juval, Reinhold Messner's Juval Inn is an old-style hostelry in a restored farmhouse, serving traditional local dishes and wines provisioned from his own farm. ✉ *Schlosswirt-Juval,* ☎ *0473/668238. No credit cards. Closed Wed., July, and mid-Nov.–Easter.*

Merano

★ 8 *24 km (15 mi) north of Bolzano, 100 km (62 mi) northeast of Bormio.*

The second-largest town in the Alto Adige, Merano was once the capital of the Austrian region of Tirol; when the town and surrounding area were ceded to Italy as part of the 1919 Treaty of Versilles, Innsbruck became the capital—its fame however, was as a spa town attracting the European nobility to enjoy its therapeutic waters and take the peculiar grape cure, which consisted simply of eating the grapes grown on the surrounding hillsides! Sheltered by mountains, Merano has an unusually mild climate, with summer temperatures rarely exceeding 80°F and winters that usually stay above freezing, despite the skiing that is within easy reach. Chairlifts and cable cars connect Merano with the high Alpine slopes of Avelengo and San Vigilio. Along the narrow streets of Merano's old town, houses have little towers and huge wooden doors, and the pointed arches of the Gothic cathedral sit with harmony next to neoclassic and art nouveau–style buildings.

In the heart of the old town, **Piazza del Duomo,** is the 14th-century Gothic **Cathedral,** with a crenellated facade and an ornate campanile. The **Cappella di Santa Barbara,** just behind the cathedral, is an octagonal church containing a 15th-century Pietà. *Piazza del Duomo.* ⏲ *Easter–Sept., daily 8–12 and 2:30–8; Oct.–Easter, daily 8–12 and 2:30–7.*

The **Terme di Merano** (thermal baths) is a huge complex and nerve center for spa facilities; although some hotels have their own, these are unique. Technicians are trained to treat you with mud packs, massages, and inhalation and sauna routines, or just with the thermal waters, which are said to be especially good for coronary and circulatory problems. Other cures include the famous grape cure at harvest time in the fall, when a two-week diet of fresh grapes has, since Roman times, been reputed to tone up digestive, liver, and urinary tract functions. ✉ *Via Piave 9.* ☎ *0473/237724.*

Overlooking the town atop of the Mt. Tappeinerweg is a castle that was the home of poet Ezra Pound from 1958 to 1964. Still in the Pound family, the castle now houses the **Brunnenburg Agrarian Museum,** devoted to Tyrolean country life. Among its exhibits are a blacksmith's shop and, not surprisingly, a room with Pound paraphernalia. To get there, take Bus No. 3 from Merano to Dorf Tirol, which departs every hour on the hour. ✉ *Ezra Pound Weg 6,* ☎ *0473/923533.* 🎫 *4,000 lire.* ⏲ *Wed.–Mon. 9:30–5. Closed Nov.–Mar.*

Dining and Lodging

$$$$ ✕ **Andrea.** This relaxed but splendid showcase for fine cuisine and service is just off Via dei Portici and right by a cable-car station. Surrounded by wood paneling and lots of green plants, you can dine on local and international cuisine, such as risotto *alle erbe* (with herbs) and *filetto di vitello con salsa di alloro* (veal fillet with bay leaf sauce). A set menu (about 100,000 lire) offers a complete five-course dinner, including superb wine. ✉ *Via Galilei 44,* ☎ *0473/237400. Reservations essential. Jacket and tie. AE, DC, MC, V. Closed Mon. and 2 wks in Feb. No dinner Sun. Nov.–Mar.*

$$$ ✕ **Flora.** There's room for only about 20 diners in this intimate candlelit restaurant under the historic arched arcades of Merano's ancient center. Chef Louis Oberstolz describes his cooking as "fresh, spontaneous, and natural, using only the finest ingredients." He offers a seven-course set menu. Among the specialties are *quaglia ripiena con fegato d'oca grasso* (boned quail stuffed with foie gras), and *schlutzkrapfen* (fresh pasta ravioli with various fillings). ✉ *Via dei Portici 75,* ☎ *0473/231484. Reservations essential. AE, DC, MC, V. Closed Sun. and mid-Jan.–mid-Feb. No lunch Mon.*

$$$ ★ ✕ **Schloss Maur.** Stained-glass lamps and wood paneling create a warm art nouveau effect in this restaurant in the Hotel Palace (☞ *below*). Schloss Maur is the height of elegance, with huge marble columns, high ceilings, and crystal chandeliers. Italian and international dishes include the signature spaghetti with a sauce of zucchini, sage, and green pepper or roast saddle of lamb and lobster. ✉ *Hotel Palace, Via Cavour 2/4,* ☎ *0473/211300. Reservations essential. AE, DC, MC, V.*

$–$$ ✕ **Terlaner Weinstube Putz.** This local favorite is an old rustic *stube* (Tyrolean-style drinking hall) in Merano's old town. The seasonal menu focuses on Tyrolean specialties. Try *zuppa al vino bianco* (soup with white wine) and the various risottos, including one with asparagus in the spring, and with Barolo in chillier months. ✉ *Via dei Portici 231,* ☎ *0473/235571. No credit cards. Closed Wed. Feb.–Mar., and July.*

$$$$ 🏨 **Castel Labers.** On a hilltop amid forested slopes about 3 km (2 mi) east of Merano's center, this castle hotel with red-tile gables, towers, and turrets is unmistakably Tyrolean in style. Ceiling beams, painted fresco decorations, and crossed halberds on the walls complete the look. The hospitable Stapf-Neubert family owns the hotel and takes an active part in its management. ✉ *Via Labers 25, 39012,* ☎ *0473/234484,* FAX *0473/234146. 32 rooms. Restaurant, pool, tennis court. No credit cards. Closed Nov.–Mar.*

$$$$ ★ 🏨 **Hotel Palace.** Merano's grandest hotel is an opulent old-world institution set in an extensive garden. Rooms are spacious, decorated in a stately modern classic design. The public rooms are attractive and comfortable with art-nouveau touches, Tiffany glass, marble pillars, and high ceilings. The impressive spa features various baths, massages, mud treatments, and other cures. A lovely fountain gurgles with thermal Merano water. The excellent Tiffany Grill Restaurant serves a wide variety of local and international dishes. ✉ *Via Cavour 2/4, 39012,* ☎ *0473/211300,* FAX *0473/234181. 136 rooms. 2 restaurants, bar, indoor-outdoor pool, spa. AE, DC, MC, V.*

$$ 🏨 **Hotel Minerva.** If you don't feel like dishing out for the prices charged by Merano's better-known resort hotels but still want a bit of luxury, then this classic hotel might be your best bet. All rooms are done in the Germanic, heavy wood style of the area, and are very warm in winter; most have balconies that afford lovely views over the town. ✉ *Via Cavon 95, 39012,* ☎ *0473/236712,* FAX *0473/230460. 46 rooms. Restaurant, bar, outdoor pool. AE, DC, MC, V.*

Nightlife and the Arts

There are plenty of nighttime options in and around Merano. Younger visitors might enjoy a night at the **Manhattan Disco** (Corso della Libertà, ☎ 0471/449655), which has the latest in dance music. If you can do without ultra-modern sound and you have a car, you might want to check out **Dancing Club Exclusif** (☎ 0471/561711), 10 km (6 mi) east in the tiny village of Lana, which caters to an older, more sedate crowd. The **Grape Festival** on the second Sunday of October has parades and wine tastings in Piazza del Duomo.

Outdoor Activities and Sports

Farmers test their horses in the highly charged **horse race** that is the highlight of Easter Monday. **Tennis Club Merano** (⊠ Via Piave 46, ☎ 0473/236550) maintains nine clay courts (four indoor) and two hard courts that are open to the public. Lessons are given at the tennis university.

Shopping

Merano's main shopping street, the narrow, arcaded **Via dei Portici** (Laubengasse) runs west from the cathedral. It features most of the best regional products: wood carvings, Tyrolean-style clothing, embroidery, cheeses, salami, and fruit schnapps. From the end of November until Christmas Eve, Merano holds a traditional ***Christkindlmarkt*** (Christmas market) in the main square.

Bolzano

32 km (19 mi) south of Merano, 50 km (31 mi) north of Trento.

Bolzano (Bozen) is the capital of the autonomous province of Alto Adige. It is protected by the mountains to the north and the east and is on the main north–south artery between northern Europe and Italy. This quiet city at the confluence of the Isarco (Eisack) and Talvera rivers has retained a provincial appeal, with no high-rises. With the highest per capita earnings of any city in Italy and a standard of living that is second to none, Bolzano was voted the best place to live in Italy in a 1996 poll conducted by *L'Espresso* magazine.

9 Bolzano's heart is pedestrian-only **Piazza Walther,** named after the 12th-century German wandering minstrel Walther von der Vogelweide, whose songs lampooned the papacy and praised the Holy Roman Emperor. The square serves as an open-air living room where locals and tourists alike can be found at all hours sipping a drink (perhaps a glass of chilled Riesling) at the café tables.

10 The city's Gothic **Duomo** was built between the 12th and 14th centuries; its lacy spire looks down on the mosaic-like tiles covering its pitched roof. Inside the church are 14th- and 15th-century frescoes and an intricately carved stone pulpit dating from 1514. ⊠ *Piazza Walther.* ⊙ *Weekdays 9:30–6, Sat. 9:30–noon.*

11 The 13th-century **Chiesa Domenicana** (Dominican Church) in Piazza Domenicani is renowned as Bolzano's main repository for paintings, especially frescoes. In the adjoining **Cappella di San Giovanni** you can see frescoes of the Giotto school, one of which is the *Triumph of Death* (circa 1340). Despite its macabre title, this fresco shows the birth of a pre-Renaissance sense of depth and individuality. ⊠ *Piazza Domenicani.* ⊙ *Church and chapel Mon.–Sat. 9–6:30, Sun. mass.*

12 In **Piazza delle Erbe,** a bronze statue of Neptune presides over a bountiful fruit and vegetable market. The stalls spill over with colorful displays of local produce; bakeries and grocery stores showcase hot breads, pastries, cheeses, and delicatessen meats—a complete range of picnic supplies. Try the speck and the Tyrolean-style apple strudel. The

Bolzano

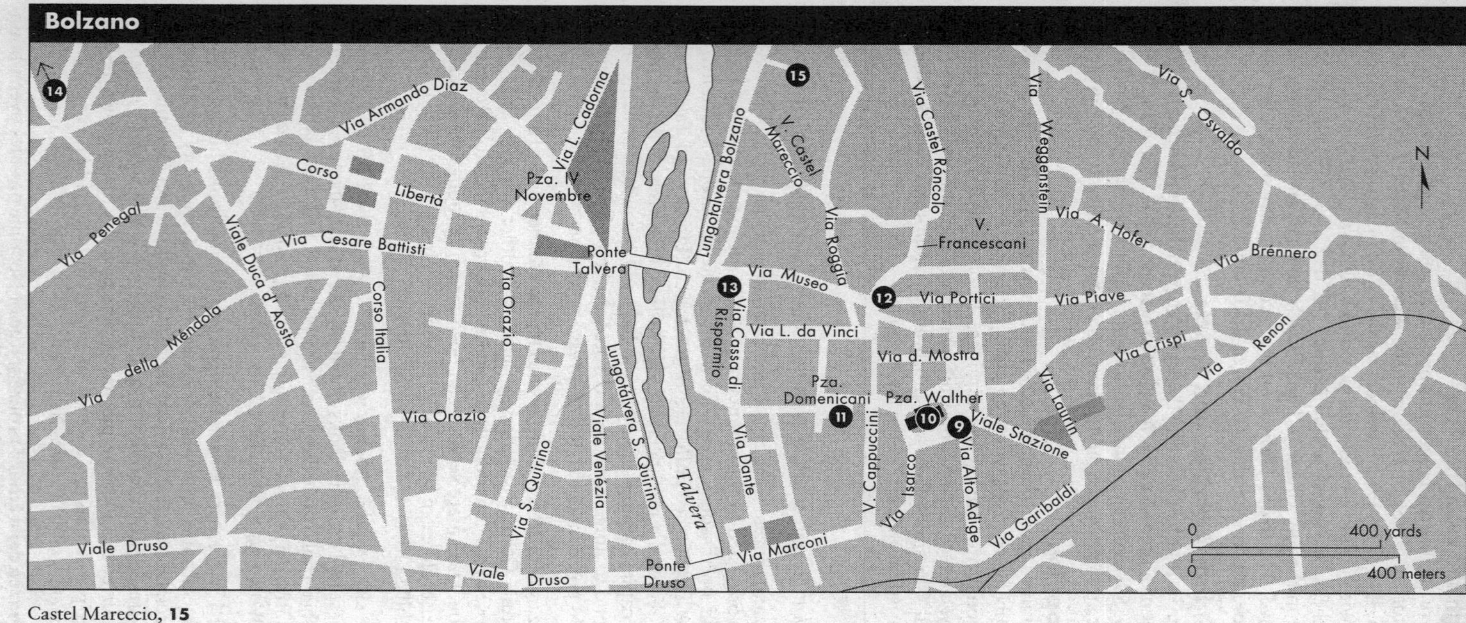

Castel Mareccio, **15**
Chiesa Domenicana, **11**
Duomo, **10**
Museo Civico, **13**
Parrocchiale, **14**
Piazza delle Erbe, **12**
Piazza Walther, **9**

market is at the beginning of Bolzano's best-known shopping street, Via dei Portici (Laubengasse).

13 The **Museo Civico** (Civic Museum) houses a rich collection of traditional costumes, wood carvings, and archaeological exhibits. The mixture of styles is a reflection of the region's cultural cross-fertilization. ✉ *Via Cassa di Risparmio 14,* ☎ *0471/974625.* *7,000 lire.* *June–Sept., Tues.–Sat. 9–12:30 and 2:30–5:30, Sun. 10–1; Nov.–May, Tues.–Sat. 9–noon and 2–5.*

14 The **Parrocchiale** (parish church) of Gries is worth a visit, if only for the elaborately carved 15th-century wooden Altar of Michael Pacher, considered a masterpiece of the Gothic style. The 11th-century wooden Romanesque crucifix was probably brought here from France. ✉ *Corso della Libertà.* *Apr. 21–Oct., weekdays 10:30–noon and 2–4, Sun. mass.*

Passeggiata del Guncina (✉ Quartiere di Gries) is an 8-km (5-mi) botanical promenade, dating from 1892, that culminates in a panoramic view of Bolzano.

15 **Castel Mareccio** (Schloss Maretsch) dates from the 13th century and is nestled under mountains and surrounded by vineyards. The castle is now a well-equipped conference center with a restaurant and bar, all open to the public. ✉ *Lungotalvera Promenade,* ☎ *0471/976615. Closed Tues.*

OFF THE BEATEN PATH **RENON (RITTEN) PLATEAU** – The Earth Pyramids of Renon Plateau make up a bizarre geological formation where erosion has left a forest of tall, thin, needlelike spires of rock, each topped with a boulder. The Soprabolzano funicular leaves from Via Renon, about 300 yards left of the Bolzano train station. At the top, an electric train takes you to the site, which is at Collalbo, just above Bolzano.

Dining and Lodging

$$–$$$ ✕ **Abramo.** Although outside Bolzano's attractive old center, this restaurant is the best in town. Chef Abramo Pantezi offers an Italian variation of nouvelle cuisine in an attractive, modern Renaissance setting. At tables set with crystal and silver, you'll choose among seafood dishes such as *salmone allo champagne* (salmon in champagne sauce). There's a vegetarian antipasto selection. The extensive wine cellar features top-quality California vintages, among others. ✉ *Piazza Gries 16,* ☎ *0471/280141. AE, DC, MC, V. Closed Sun. and Aug. 1–25.*

$$ ✕ **Alexander.** Typical Tyrolean dishes are served up in a convivial atmosphere at this city-center restaurant. The venison ham and the lamb cutlets *al timo con salsa all'aglio* (with thyme and garlic sauce) are particularly delicious, but make sure to leave room for the rich chocolate cake. ✉ *Via Aosta 37,* ☎ *0471/918608. AE, DC, MC, V. Closed Sat.*

$$ ✕ **Gostner Flora's Bistrot.** In a medieval tower on Bolzano's market square, this tiny tavern has been around for centuries, and it has been lovingly restored. There is no menu; you choose from a limited number of typical homey Tyrolean specialties, different every day. They may include canederli or *schlutzkrapfen* (ravioli). The desserts are homemade, too. The young owner takes pride in a selection of good wines. ✉ *Piazza delle Erbe 17,* ☎ *0471/974086. No credit cards. Closed Sun. No dinner Sat.*

$ ✕ **Batzenhausl.** A medieval building in the center of town houses this crowded stube. It's a popular hangout for the local intellectual set, who hold long, animated conversations over glasses of local wine and tasty local South Tyrolean specialties, such as *herrngröstl* (beef on a bed of boiled potatoes) and apple pancakes with ice cream. Try the fried

Camembert. ✉ *Via Andreas Hofer 30,* ☎ *0471/976183. No credit cards. Closed Tues. and 3 wks in June–July. No lunch.*

$$$–$$$$ ★ 🏨 **Park Hotel Laurin.** This hotel, an exercise in art-nouveau opulence, is set in a large park in the middle of town. Its history is speckled with visits from Europe's grand nobility, including the Archduke Franz Ferdinand (whose murder in Sarajevo sparked World War I), King Leopold of Belgium, and Field Marshall Montgomery. Today, it is considered the finest hotel in all of Alto Adige. Some rooms carry through the Belle Epoque decor; others are classic modern; all have original paintings by artists including Oskar Kokoschka, Max Klinger, and Ernst Nepo. A room upgrade has added modern connections. The popular Belle Epoque restaurant prides itself on its use of fresh seasonal ingredients. ✉ *Via Laurin 4, 39100,* ☎ *0471/980500,* FAX *0471/970953. 96 rooms. Restaurant, bar, no-smoking rooms, pool, convention center. AE, DC, MC, V.*

$$$ ★ 🏨 **Schloss Korb.** It's worth the 5-km (3-mi) drive west from Bolzano to reach this hotel. It's set in a romantic 13th-century castle with a crenellated roof and a massive central tower, perched in a park amid vine-covered hills. Much of the ancient decor is preserved, and the public rooms are filled with Tyrolean antiques, elaborate wood carvings, old paintings, and attractive plants. The rooms are comfortably furnished—some tower rooms have the old Romanesque arched windows. ✉ *Missiano, Strada Castel d'Appiano 5, 39056,* ☎ *0471/636000,* FAX *0471/636033. 56 rooms. Indoor pool, sauna, 2 tennis courts. No credit cards. Closed Nov.–Easter.*

$$–$$$ 🏨 **Luna/Mondschein.** This central yet secluded hotel was built in 1798. Set in a lovely garden, it washes a tranquil, friendly calm over its guests. The rooms are comfortable, with classic style using wood paneling throughout. Some rooms overlooking the garden have balconies, but even the rooms overlooking the garage have good views of the mountains. The two restaurants include a typical Tyrolean weinstube that serves inexpensive local specialties in a cozy, convivial setting. ✉ *Via Piave 15, 39100,* ☎ *0471/975642,* FAX *0471/975577. 85 rooms. Restaurant, weinstube. AE, DC, MC, V.*

Nightlife and the Arts

Spring is heralded each May with large flower markets and events, including concerts and folklore and art exhibits.On August 24 is the **Bartolomeo Horse Fair,** on Renon Mountain just northeast of the town. Hundreds of farmers converge for a day of serious trading and frivolous merriment.

Outdoor Activities and Sports

HIKING

Club Alpino Italiano (✉ Piazza delle Erbe 46, ☎ 0471/978172) is a helpful organization that provides information for hiking and rock climbing. It is important to follow safety procedures and to have all the latest information on trails and conditions.

TENNIS

Courts can be found in Bolzano at **Circolo Tennis Bolzano** (✉ Via M. Knoller 8, ☎ 0471/280587).

Shopping

LOCAL CRAFTS

The long, narrow arcades of **Via dei Portici** house shops that specialize in Tyrolean crafts and clothing—lederhosen, loden goods, linen suits, and dirndls. The best store for locally made handcrafted goods is **Artigiani Atesini** (✉ Via Portici 39).

MARKETS

From the end of November until Christmas Eve there are traditional **Christkindlmarkt** in the main square of Bolzano with stalls selling all kinds of Christmas decorations and local handcrafted goods. The outdoor fruit and vegetable market is held in the central **Piazza delle Erbe** (☞ *above*) from Monday through Saturday 8–1. The big weekly flea market takes place Saturday morning in **Piazza della Vittoria.**

Cornedo

⓰ *6 km (4 mi) east of Bolzano.*

At the mouth of the Ega Valley (Eggental), Cornedo is a place to savor the view of the Catinaccio Mountains. Craggy peaks seem to be props for a lighting display, as pink and purple reflections dance over huge rocks. Their creation is the subject of a local German legend that tells of King Laurin, who lived in a vast palace on the Catinaccio, at a time when the mountain was covered with roses. King Laurin became infatuated with the daughter of a neighboring king, Similde, and kidnapped her, but Similde, searching for his daughter, recognized her place of imprisonment by the red roses that grew there. Laurin freed the girl and was made Similde's prisoner. When Laurin finally escaped he decreed that the betraying roses should be turned to rocks, so that they could be seen neither by day nor by night. Today, the spectacular pinkish-red display is at its best at dawn and at sunset.

Chiusa

⓱ *24 km (15 mi) north of Cornedo, 30 km (19 mi) northeast of Bolzano.*

Beautiful narrow streets lined with houses built in the 15th and 16th centuries best characterize Chiusa (Klausen), the main town in the Val Isarco. Geraniums and begonias fill window boxes beneath the carved wooden shutters. From here you can catch a bus east to Val di Funes, where Santa Maddalena is spectacularly hemmed in by the Geisler Peaks and offers good walking terrain and hotels.

Above the town of Chiusa is the Benedictine monastery of **Saviona** (Saeben), built as a castle in the 10th century but occupying a site that was fortified in Roman times. The monastery buildings date from the late Middle Ages and are a mixture of Romanesque and Gothic architecture, surrounded by walls and turrets. Guided visits are organized by the Tourist Association in Chiusa; contact the local **tourist office** (☞ Visitor Information *in* The Dolomites: Trentino-Alto Adige A to Z, *below*).

Bressanone

⓲ *14 km (9 mi) north of Chiusa, 40 km (25 mi) northeast of Bolzano.*

Bressanone (Brixen) is an important artistic center of the Alto Adige and for centuries was the seat of prince-bishops. Like their counterparts in Trento, these medieval administrators had the delicate task of serving two opposing masters—the pope (the ultimate spiritual supervisor) and the Holy Roman Emperor (the civil and military leader). Since the papacy and the Holy Roman Empire were virtually at war throughout the Middle Ages, Bressanone's prince-bishops became experts at tact and diplomacy in order to survive. As you arrive from Brunico, you enter the town on Via Mercato Vecchio, a broad road leading to the imposing **Duomo.** It was built in the 13th century but acquired a Baroque facade 500 years later, and its 14th-century cloister is decorated with medieval frescoes. *Piazza Duomo.* ⏲ *Easter–Sept., daily 8–8; Oct.–Easter, daily 8–7.*

The Bishop's Palace, which now houses the **Museo Diocesano** (Diocesan Museum), is a treasure trove of local medieval art, particularly Gothic wood carving. The wooden statues and liturgical objects were all collected from the cathedral treasury. During the Christmas season, the curators highlight displays of the museum's large collection of antique nativity scenes; look for the shepherds wearing Tyrolean hats. ✉ *Palazzo Vescovile,* ☎ *0472/830505.* 🎫 *7,000 lire (3,000 lire for nativity scenes exhibition only).* ⏲ *Mid-Mar.–Oct., Mon.–Sat. 10–5; nativity scenes Dec. 15–Feb. 10, Mon.–Sat. 2–5.*

Dining and Lodging

$$ ★ ✕ **Fink.** This restaurant under the arcades in the pedestrians-only town center has a friendly staff and offers an affordable daily set menu. It has a rustic ambience upstairs with lots of wood paneling, and serves international as well as hearty Tyrolean specialties. Try the *carré di maiale gratinato* (pork roasted with cheese and served with cabbage and potatoes) or the *castrato alla paesana* (a kind of lamb stew). ✉ *Via Portici Minori 4,* ☎ *0472/834883. AE, DC, MC, V. Closed Wed. and July. No dinner Tues. Oct.–June.*

$$–$$$ ★ 🏨 **Elefante.** This cozy inn, one of the area's best hotels, is in a historic 15th-century building. The hotel takes its name from an incident in 1550, when King John of Portugal stopped here for a few days while leading an elephant over the Alps as a present for Austria's Emperor Ferdinand. Each room is different, many with antiques and paintings. Housed on the park property is the separate Villa Marzari, with 14 rooms. The hotel restaurant is known as one of the region's best. ✉ *Via Rio Bianco 4, 39042,* ☎ *0472/832750,* FAX *0472/836579. 44 rooms. Restaurant, pool. DC, MC, V. Closed Nov. 15–Dec. 25 and Jan. 10–Feb. 28.*

$$ 🏨 **Croce d'Oro** (Goldenes Kreuz). A five-centuries-old tradition of hospitality is still practiced by staff at this centrally placed hotel. Shops line the ground floor of the pink building, with styles inside ranging from the more modern, tasteful reception area to the tavern-style bar. The rooms are spacious with sturdy wood appointments. ✉ *Bastioni Minori 8, 30042,* ☎ *0472/836155,* FAX *0472/834255. 72 rooms. Restaurant, bar. No credit cards.*

Outdoor Activities and Sports

Tennis can be played at **Club Bressanone** (✉ Via Von Kemter 1, ☎ 0472/834792).

Shopping

From the end of November until Christmas Eve there are traditional **Christkindlmarkt** (Christmas markets) in the main square of Bressanone, with stalls selling all kinds of Christmas decorations and local handcrafted goods.

Brunico

★ ⓳ *33 km (20 mi) east of Bressanone, 65 km (40 mi) northwest of Cortina d'Ampezzo.*

With its medieval quarter nestling below the 13th-century bishop's castle, Brunico (Bruneck) is within the heart of the Val Pusteria. This picturesque little town, often noted for its quiet and relaxing qualities, is divided by the Rienza River with the old quarter on one side and the modern quarter on the other.

The **Museo degli Usi e Costumi della Provincia di Bolzano** (Bolzano Province Customs and Costumes Museum, or Ethnographic Museum) re-creates a typical local village and is built around an authentic 300-year-old mansion. It examines the functions and significance of tradi-

tional architecture. The wood-carving displays are particularly interesting. It's in the district of Teodone, just outside the town. ✉ *Via Duca Teodone 24,* ☎ *0474/550781.* 🎫 *6,000 lire.* ⏲ *Mid-Apr.–Oct., Tues.–Sat. 9:30–5:30, Sun. 2–6.*

Lodging

$–$$ **Andreas Hofer.** There's a Tyrolean feel to this comfortable hotel set in a large garden outside the center of town. Rooms are modern, with chalet-style balconies overlooking the Val Pusteria. ✉ *Via Campo Tures 1, 39031,* ☎ *0474/551469,* FAX *0474/551284. 54 rooms. Restaurant, weinstube, sauna. MC, V. Closed Apr.–May and mid-Nov.–mid-Dec.*

$–$$ **Post.** Locals recommend this traditional, homey hotel for its friendly rates and restaurant, café, and pastry shop. It has its own parking, which is important because of the pedestrians-only rules in effect throughout much of the central area. ✉ *Via Bastioni 9, 39031,* ☎ *0474/555127,* FAX *0474/551603. 54 rooms, 45 with bath. Restaurant, café, weinstube, free parking. MC, V. Closed Nov.*

Outdoor Activities and Sports

On January 22 locals turn up for the **dogsled race,** and there seems nary a soul without a flask of hot mulled wine to back their favorites. A comparatively inexpensive **ski area** is at Badia Valley, reached by heading south on S244 from Brunico.

Dobbiaco

20 *25 km (16 mi) east of Brunico, 34 km (21 mi) north of Cortina d'Ampezzo.*

In Dobbiaco (Toblach), just 12 km (7 mi) to the east along the Drau Valley, Austria's influence intensifies. Italian is spoken grudgingly here, Austrian money is accepted at most shops and restaurants, and the locals appear more blond and blue-eyed than the average Italian. It is not surprising that Gustav Mahler (1860–1911), the great Austrian composer, would have come here often for inspiration.

Lodging

$–$$ ★ **Alpino Monte Rota/Alpengasthof Ratsberg.** To reach this hotel, you take the 10-minute cable-car ride to Monte Rota. It is in traditional style, with the timeless look of local chalets. Front rooms have stunning mountain views from balconies, and those in the back look out over the dense mountain forest. You needn't take the cable car back down for sustenance: the Alpino has a good restaurant, a bar, and a Tyrolean-style stube. ✉ *Monte Rota 10, 39034,* ☎ *0474/972916,* FAX *0474/972213. 30 rooms. Restaurant, bar, pool, sauna. No credit cards. Closed Easter–May and Oct. 20–mid-Dec.*

$–$$ **Cristallo.** Wood beams and paneling lend an Old Tyrolean patina to this small hotel set in a garden just outside town. The architecture and furnishings reflect the local preference for combining traditional chalet design with functional, but comfortable, modern furniture. You can relax in the cozy and informal stube. ✉ *Viale S. Giovanni 37, 39034,* ☎ *0474/972138,* FAX *0474/972755. 30 rooms. Restaurant, bar, indoor pool. AE, MC, V. Closed mid-Apr.–mid-May and mid-Oct.–mid-Dec.*

Outdoor Activities and Sports

SKIING

Prepared trails for cross-country skiing (usually loops marked off by kilometers) accommodate differing degrees of ability. One of the best of this kind can be found at **Dobbiaco.** Inquire at the local tourist office. Downhill skiing can be found at **Monte Rota** slopes, accessible from Dobbiaco. These offer considerably lower rates than in many of the more exclusive resorts.

Cortina d'Ampezzo

★ 21 *30 km (19 mi) south of Dobbiaco, 140 km (87 mi) east of Bolzano.*

"The Pearl of the Dolomites" is set in a lush meadow 4,000 ft above sea level. Dense forests adjoin the town, and mountains encircle the whole valley. The town sprawls on the slopes along a fast-moving stream; a public park extends along one bank. Luxury hotels and the villas of the rich are conspicuously scattered over the slopes above the town—identifiable by their attempts to hide behind stands of firs and spruces.

The bustling center of Cortina d'Ampezzo has little nostalgia for old-time atmosphere, despite its Alpine appearance. The tone is set by fancy shops and stylish cafés, as opulent as their well-dressed patrons, whose corduroy knickerbockers may well have been tailored by Armani. Cortina is the place to go for a whiff of the heady aroma of wealth and sophistication; if you want authentic Tyrolean gemütlichkeit, pass through Cortina and stop at one of the more low-key resorts.

Dining and Lodging

$$$ ✕ **De la Poste.** The exclusive restaurants of the hotel on Cortina's main square have a casually chic clientele and a lively atmosphere. There's a refined, high-ceiling main dining room with three big chandeliers where you can dine on soufflés and nouvelle cuisine dishes (every Friday fresh fish is served). There's also a more informal grill room with wood paneling and the family pewter collection. ✉ *Piazza Roma 14,* ☎ *0436/4271. Reservations essential. Jacket and tie. AE, DC, MC, V.*

$$–$$$ ✕ **Tavernetta.** Near the Olympic ice-skating rink, this popular restaurant has an authentic Tyrolean ambience, with wood-paneled dining rooms and a local clientele. Here you can try Cortina specialties such as *zuppa di porcini* (porcini mushroom soup), ravioli *di cervo* (stuffed with venison), and game. ✉ *Via dello Stadio 27/a,* ☎ *0436/867494. AE, DC, MC, V. Closed mid-June–mid-July, Nov., and Wed. No lunch Thurs. May and Sept.*

$$$$ 🏨 **Miramonti Majestic.** This imposing and luxe hotel, nearly a century old, has a magnificent mountain valley position about 1 km (½ mi) south of town. A touch of old-world formality accompanies the imperial Austrian design, and the interior reflects the period style throughout. There's always a roaring fire in the cozy bar. ✉ *Località Peziè 103, 32043,* ☎ *0436/4201,* FAX *0436/867019. 128 rooms. Restaurant, pool, sauna, golf course, tennis courts, exercise room. AE, DC, MC, V. Closed Easter–June and Sept. 15–Dec. 20.*

$$$ 🏨 **De la Poste.** Skiers who want to be seen keep returning to this lively hotel on the main square in a pedestrian zone. It's been under the same family management since 1826, and the furnishings feature antiques in characteristic Dolomite style. Almost all rooms have wooden balconies. One of Cortina's social centers, the hotel's main terrace bar is always crowded. ✉ *Piazza Roma 62, 32043,* ☎ *0436/4271,* FAX *0436/868435. 83 rooms. Restaurant, bar. AE, DC, MC, V. Closed mid-Apr.–mid-June and mid-Oct.–mid-Dec.*

Nightlife and the Arts

At **Europa** hotel (✉ Corso Italia 207, ☎ 0436/3221) you can expect to mingle with the couture set at the VIP disco; nonguests are welcome, but don't expect to spend less than 50,000 lire.

Outdoor Activities and Sports

In Cortina d'Ampezzo's several accessible mountain ranges you will be challenged by slopes of all degrees of difficulty for **skiing.** Public **tennis courts** (☎ 0436/2937) can be used at Via Sopiazes.

En Route As you enter the Crepa Tunnel along the S48 from Cortina d'Ampezzo, the ascent for the Passo di Falzarego begins. The **Passo Pordoi** will lead to the so-called heart of the Dolomites. The roads around this region of the Sella mountains are deemed to be among the most spectacular in Europe and many consider their rugged beauty to be unparalleled. A fork in the road farther ahead will lead left to Canazei and right into Val Gardena.

HEART OF THE DOLOMITES

The area between Cortina d'Ampezzo and east to Bolzano is dominated by two major valleys, the Val di Fassa and the famous Val Gardena. Both share the spectacular panorama of the Sella mountain range, known because of its circular shape as the Heart of the Dolomites. Val di Fassa is made up primarily of the Grande Strada delle Dolomiti (Great Dolomites Road), which runs from the mountain resort of Cortina d'Ampezzo as far as Bolzano. The route, opened in 1909, now comprises 110 km (68 mi) of easy grades and smooth driving between the two cities.

With some of the best views of the Dolomites, Val Gardena is famous as a ski resort, freckled with well-equipped, picturesque towns overlooked by the oblong Sasso Lungo (Long Rock), which is more than 10,000 ft above sea level. It is also home of the Ladins, descendants of soldiers sent by the Roman Emperor Tiberius to conquer the Celtic population of the area in the 1st century AD. Forgotten in the narrow cul-de-sacs of isolated mountain valleys, the Ladins have developed their own folk traditions and speak an ancient dialect that is derived from Latin and is similar to Romansch, which is spoken in some high valleys in Switzerland.

Canazei

22 *60 km (37 mi) west of Cortina d'Ampezzo, 52 km (32 mi) east of Bolzano.*

Of the towns in the Val di Fassa, Canazei is the most popular ski resort as well as a summer haven. The slopes around this small town are threaded with mountain trails and ski slopes, surrounded by large pockets of conifers.

OFF THE BEATEN PATH **COL RODELLA** – An excursion from Campitello di Fassa to the vantage point at Col Rodella is a must. The cable car rises some 3,000 ft up the mountain to this most panoramic of vistas. From the balcony at the top you can see full circle around the region, including the Sasso Lungo and the rest of the Sella range.

En Route **Passo di Sella** is one of the most famous mountain passes in the Dolomites. It can be approached from the S48 and continues into Val Gardena among the most panoramic mountain scenery in Europe. The road descends to Ortisei, passing the small ski resort of Santa Cristina.

Lodging

$$$ **Alla Rosa.** Facilities are modern, and good for a big family. Centrally located, the hotel has a modest restaurant with a choice of either local or international cuisine, and a cozy bar. The three-story building has balconies in half of all rooms and large reception areas. The bedrooms are well laid out with a pleasant rustic and modern mix, but the real attraction is the view over the imposing Dolomites. ✉ *Via Dolomite 142, 39046,* ☎ *0462/601107. 37 rooms. Restaurant, bar, recreation room. MC, V. Closed Oct.*

Ortisei

23 *28 km (17 mi) north of Canazei, 35 km (22 mi) northeast of Bolzano.*

Ortisei (St. Ulrich), the jewel in the crown of Val Gardena's ski resorts, is a hub of activity both in summer and, especially, in winter. There are hundreds of miles of hiking trails as well as several hundred miles of accessible ski slopes, including the Siusi slopes to the south. Hotels are everywhere and facilities are excellent, with swimming pools, ice rinks, health spas, tennis courts, and bowling. Most impressive of all is the location, a valley surrounded by formidable views in all directions. For further information on activities in Val Gardena, contact the main tourist office in Ortisei (☞ Visitor Information *in* The Dolomites: Trentino-Alto Adige A to Z, *below*).

For centuries Ortisei has also been famous for the expertise of its wood-carvers and there are still numerous workshops here. Apart from making religious sculptures—particularly the wayside Calvaries you come upon everywhere in the Dolomites—Ortisei's carvers were long famous for producing wooden dolls, horses, and other toys. As itinerant peddlers, every spring they traveled by foot with their loaded packs as far as Paris, London, and St. Petersburg to sell their wares. Fine historic and contemporary examples of all kinds of locally carved wooden sculptures and artifacts can be seen at the **Museo della Val Gardena** at Cesa di Ladins. ✉ *Via Rezia 83, Ortisei,* ☎ *0471/797554.* 🎫 *5,000 lire.* ⏲ *July–Aug., daily 10–noon and 3–7; June, Sept., Dec. 28–30, Jan. 4–7, and Feb. 8–Mar., Tues.–Fri. 3–6:30.*

Lodging

$$$ 🏨 **Adler.** Since 1810, this hotel, one of the best in the valley, has been under the same family management. Set in a large park, the original building has been enlarged several times in the intervening years, yielding spacious guest rooms, but it retains a lot of the old turreted-castle appeal. The Tyrolean character is carried through in special parties held once a week for guests. ✉ *Via Rezia 7, 39046,* ☎ *0471/796203,* FAX *0471/796210. 94 rooms, most with bath. Restaurant, bar, pool, beauty salon, sauna, tennis courts, health club. AE, DC, MC, V. Closed mid-Apr.–mid-May and mid-Oct.–mid-Dec.*

$$–$$$ 🏨 **Posta Cavallino Bianco.** In town center and a five-minute walk from the main ski facilities, this hotel looks more like a gigantic dollhouse, with delicate wooden balconies and an eye-catching wooden gable. Inside, the decor is full of deep colors and ornate carpets and drapery. Wood is incorporated throughout the interior, most notable in the cozy hotel bar with a large handcrafted fireplace. The rooms are a good size with all amenities. ✉ *Via Rezia 22, 39046,* ☎ *0471/796392,* FAX *0471/797517. 99 rooms. Restaurant, bar, coffee shop, dance club. MC, V. Closed mid-Apr.–mid-May and mid-Oct.–mid-Dec.*

Outdoor Activities and Sports

The Val Gardena comes alive with a parade of **horse-drawn sleighs** on January 1. With almost 600 km (370 mi) of accessible downhill slopes, Ortisei is one of the most popular **skiing** resorts in the Dolomites. Prices are good and facilities are among the most modern. There are more than 90 km (56 mi) of cross-country skiing lanes. **Tennis courts** can be found in Roncadizza (☎ 0471/797275).

Fiè

24 *26 km (16 mi) southwest of Ortisei, 18 km (11 mi) east of Bolzano.*

Fiè (Voels) is set in a valley with the Renon mountains on one side and the Siusi on the other. The town is surrounded by acres of green coniferous forests. In the town is the parish church of **Santa Maria Assunta** in the late Gothic style, built in the 16th century. The church is being perpetually restored, and is closed to the public.

Lodging

$$$ ★ **Turm.** The *turm* (tower) that houses this welcoming hotel on the edge of the Sciliar National Park dates from the 13th century and has been used as a courthouse, prison, and tavern. Now owned and run by the Pramstrahler family, it's furnished with their charming collection of paintings and antiques. The picturesque hostelry also has an excellent restaurant. ✉ *Piazza della Chiesa 9, Fiè allo Sciliar (Voels am Schlern), 39040,* ☎ *0471/725014,* FAX *0471/725474. 26 rooms. Restaurant, indoor and outdoor pools, sauna. MC, V. Closed early Nov.–Dec. 19.*

Outdoor Activities and Sports

The **Oswald von Wolkenstein Cavalcade,** named after the medieval South Tyrolese knight and troubadour, is held every year over the first or second weekend of June. After a colorful procession, teams of local horsemen and -women compete in fast-paced events.

Caldaro

25 *22 km (14 mi) south of Fiè, 15 km (9 mi) south of Bolzano.*

Caldaro is a vineyard village with clear views of castles high up on the surrounding mountains, a backdrop that reflects the centuries of division that forged the unique character of the area. Caldaro architecture is famous for the way it blends Italian Renaissance elements of balance and harmony with the soaring windows and peaked arches of the local Gothic tradition. The church of **Santa Caterina,** on the main square, is a good example. ⏲ *Daily dawn–dusk.*

Close to the main square is the **Museo Alto Adegino del Vino** (South Tyrolean Museum of Wine) illustrating the history of wine production in this region. To further your wine tour, take a ramble along the **Strada del Vino** (Wine Road) that starts in Caldaro. ✉ *Via dell'Oro 1,* ☎ *0471/963168.* 🎫 *5,000 lire.* ⏲ *Easter–Oct., Tues.–Sat. 9:30–noon and 2–6, Sun. 10–noon.*

Lago di Carezza

26 *35 km (22 mi) east of Caldaro, 29 km (18 mi) east of Bolzano.*

A lake of icy cold glacial waters, Lake Carezza is some 5,000 ft above sea level. The azure blue of the waters can at times change to magical greens and purples, reflections of the surrounding forest and rosy peaks of the Dolomites.

THE DOLOMITES: TRENTINO-ALTO ADIGE A TO Z

Arriving and Departing

By Bus

Only a handful of buses link Bolzano with Milan and Venice; the service between these cities and Trento is more frequent (for instance, there is an hourly bus service between Riva del Garda and Trento), but if you want to get to Merano or Cortina d'Ampezzo you will have to change in either Trento or Bolzano. For information, call ☎ 0471/974292.

By Car

The most important route in the region, **A22,** is the main north–south autostrada linking Italy with northern Europe by way of the Brenner Pass. It connects Bressanone, Bolzano, Trento, and Rovereto, and at Verona joins the **A4,** running east–west across northern Italy from Trieste to Turin.

By Plane

The nearest airports are Verona's **Aeroporto Villafranca** (11 km/7 mi southwest of Verona, ☎ 045/8095666) and Munich's **Franz Josef Strauss (FJS) Airport** in Germany, both well connected by road and rail with the Dolomite area.

By Train

The express train line that links the towns of Bolzano, Trento, and Rovereto connects with other main lines at Verona, just south of the region. Eurocity trains on the Dortmund–Venice and Munich–Rome routes also stop at these stations. Call (☎ 147/888088) for toll-free FS (Italian State Railways) information.

Getting Around

By Bus

Local buses connect the train stations at Trento, Bolzano, and Merano with the mountain resorts. The service is fairly frequent between most main towns during the day. Though some parts of the region remain out of the reach of public transportation, it is possible to visit even the remotest villages without a car if you are equipped with the local bus timetables (and lots of time), available from regional and local tourist offices (☞ Visitor Information *in* Contacts and Resources, *below*).

By Car

Autostrada **A22** connects Bressanone, Bolzano, Trento, and Rovereto. Roads in the broad mountain valleys are usually wide two-lane routes, but the roads up into the highest passes can be narrow and subject to sudden closure, even in the months when they are open to drivers. Call **Autostrada Weather Information Service** (☎ 0471/993810 or 0471/978577) in Bolzano for information on weather-related closures.

By Train

An express train line follows the course of the Adige Valley from the Brenner Pass southward past Bolzano, Trento, and Rovereto. Branch lines from Trento and Bolzano go to some of the smaller valleys, but most of the mountain attractions described above are beyond the reach of trains. Call (☎ 147/888088) for toll-free information.

Contacts and Resources

Car Rentals

BOLZANO

Avis (✉ Piazza Verdi 18, ☎ 0471/971467). **Hertz** (✉ Via Garibaldi 34, ☎ 0471/981411).

Emergencies

Carabinieri (☎ 112). **Police, Ambulance** (☎ 113). For first aid, ask for "Pronto Soccorso," and be prepared to give your address.

Guided Tours

If you are without a car or if you don't care to drive over mountain roads, guided tours from Bolzano or Trento can show you the Dolomites the easy way. However, the sudden and frequent snowfalls mean that tours are offered in summer only.

SIGHTSEEING

In Bolzano, city sightseeing and local excursions are organized by the **SAD** bus company (✉ Via Conciapelli 60, near the train station, ☎ 167/846047). In July and August, full-day mountain tours include a "Great Dolomites Tour" from Bolzano to Cortina and a tour of the Val Venosta that climbs over the Stelvio Pass into Switzerland. A tour of the Val Gardena and the Siusi Alps is available from April to October.

In Trento, city sightseeing can be arranged through the city **APT** office (☞ Visitor Information, *below*). From June through September, the **Calderari e Moggioli** travel agency (✉ Via Manci 46, ☎ 0461/980275) offers a full-day guided bus tour of the Brenta Dolomites and the "Great Dolomites Tour," a full-day drive over the Pordoi and Falzarego passes to Cortina d'Ampezzo and Lake Misurina. The Trentino **APT** (☞ Visitor Information, *below*) also organizes guided tours and excursions by train to castles in the region.

Hiking and Climbing

Local tourist offices can provide information on less-demanding trails (☞ Visitor Information, *below*). **Società degli Alpinisti Tridentini** (✉ Via Manci 57, 38100 Trento, ☎ 0461/981871). **Club Alpino Italiano** (✉ Piazza delle Erbe 46, Bolzano, ☎ 0471/978172; ✉ Corso della Libertà 188, Merano, ☎ 0473/448944). **Associazione Rifugi del Trentino** (✉ Piazza Centa 13/7, 38100 Trento, ☎ FAX 0461/826066).

Late-Night Pharmacies

Pharmacies take turns staying open late or on Sunday; for the latest information, consult the current list posted on the front door of each pharmacy or ask at the local tourist office (☞ Visitor Information, *below*).

Visitor Information

Alto Adige province (✉ Piazza Parrocchia 11–12, Bolzano, ☎ 0471/993808, FAX 0471/975448). **Trentino Tourist Board** (✉ Via Alfieri 4, Trento, ☎ 0461/983880, FAX 984508).

Local tourist offices (✉ Piazza Walther 8 Bolzano, ☎ 0471/975656; ✉ Via Roma 131/b Bormio, ☎ 0342/903300; ✉ Viale Stazione 9 Bressanone, ☎ 0472/836401; ✉ Piazza Tinne 6 Chiusa, ☎ 0472/847424; ✉ Piazzetta San Francesco 8 Cortina d'Ampezzo, ☎ 0436/3231; ✉ Via Dolomiti 3 Dobbiaco, ☎ 0474/972132; ✉ Via Pradalago 4 Madonna di Campiglio, ☎ 0465/442000; ✉ Corso della Libertà 45 Merano, ☎ 0473/212404; ✉ Via Municipio 1 Naturno, ☎ 0473/666077; ✉ Via Rezia 1 Rezia 1 Ortisei, ☎ 0471/796328. ✉ Via Dante 63 Rovereto, ☎ 0464/430363; ✉ Via Alri 4 Trento, ☎ 0461/983880).

10 EMILIA-ROMAGNA

PARMA, BOLOGNA, RIMINI, AND RAVENNA

Gourmets the world over claim that Emilia-Romagna's greatest contribution to humankind has been gastronomic. Birthplace of fettuccine, tortellini, and lasagna, Bologna offers a bevy of great restaurants. But there are also many cultural riches here: Parma's Correggio paintings, Verdi's villa at Sant'Agata, the Renaissance splendors of Ferrara, and the Byzantine beauty of mosaic-rich Ravenna—glittering today as brightly as it did 1,500 years ago.

Updated by Robin S. Goldstein

EMILIA-ROMAGNA OWES ITS BEGINNINGS to a road. In 187 BC the Romans laid out the Via Aemelia, a long highway running straight northwest from the Adriatic port of Rimini to the central garrison town of Piacenza, and it was along this central spine that the primary towns of the region developed. The old Roman road is called Via Emilia (S9) today, and the autostrada (A1 and A14) runs parallel to it.

Despite the unifying factor of the Via Emilia, as the highway is now called, the region has had a fragmented history. The eastern portion of the region, roughly the area from the city of Faenza to the coast, known as Romagna, has looked first to the east and then to Rome for art, political power, and, some say, national character. The western portion, Emilia, from Bologna to Piacenza, had a more northern, rather dour sense of self-government and dissent. Italians say that in Romagna a stranger will be offered a glass of wine; in Emilia, a glass of water—if anything at all.

The principal city of the region is Bologna. It was founded by the Etruscans but eventually came under the influence of the Roman Empire. The Romans established a garrison there, renaming the old Etruscan settlement Bononia, the Bologna of today. It was after the fall of Rome that the region began its fragmentation. Romagna, centered in Ravenna, was ruled from Constantinople. Ravenna eventually became capital of the empire in the West in the 5th century, passing to papal rule in the 8th century. The city today, however, is still filled with reminders of two centuries of Byzantine rule.

The other cities of the region, from the Middle Ages on, became the fiefs of important noble families—the Este in Ferrara and Modena, the Pallavicini in Piacenza, the Bentivoglio in Bologna, and the Malatesta in Rimini. Today all these cities bear the marks of their noble patrons. When in the 16th century the papacy managed to exert its power over the entire region, some of these cities were divided among the families of the reigning popes—hence the stamp of the Farnese family on Parma, Piacenza, and Ferrara.

In the 19th century, the region was one of the first to join the fight for a unified Italy, pledging itself to the king of Italy and the forces of Garibaldi in the 1840s. Loyalty to the crown did not last long, however. The Italian socialist movement was born in the region, and throughout Italy Emilia-Romagna has been known for rebellion and dissent. Benito Mussolini was born here, although in keeping with the political atmosphere of his home state, he was a firebrand socialist during the early part of his career. Despite being the birthplace of Il Duce, Emilia-Romagna did not take to fascism: It was in this region that the antifascist resistance was born, and during World War II the region suffered terribly at the hands of the Fascists and the Nazis.

Despite a long history of bloodletting, turmoil, and rebellion, the arts—both decorative and culinary—have always flourished in Emilia-Romagna. The great families financed painters, sculptors, and writers (Dante found a haven in Ravenna after being expelled from his native Florence). In modern times, Emilia-Romagna has given to the arts such famous sons as painter Giorgio Morandi, writer Giorgio Bassani (author of *The Garden of the Finzi-Continis*), filmmaker Federico Fellini, and tenor Luciano Pavarotti.

Bologna is the acknowledged leading city of Italian cuisine, and the rest of the region follows—eating is a seminal part of any Emilia-Romagnan experience. The area's history is replete with culinary chronicles that raise food to the level of legend: the original tortellino, modeled on the shape of Venus's navel; the original *tagliolini* (long, thin egg pasta) served at the wedding banquet of Annibale Bentivoglio and Lucrezia d'Este; and Bologna's centuries-old, anything-but-pejorative nickname, "The Fat." It's impossible to eat badly here, and everything is worth trying. Parma's famed prosciutto and Parmigiano di Reggiano cheese; Modena's *zampone* (pig's feet stuffed with minced meat) and jet-black, sweet balsamic vinegar; and Bologna's tortellini, fettuccine, mortadella, and *ragù* (meat sauce) are all served throughout the region, along with *tortelli alla zucca* (dumpling- or ravioli-shape pasta stuffed with squash), fresh fruits and vegetables, ancient Roman *piadina* (chewy, flat griddle bread), and a number of fine, robust wines.

New and Noteworthy

Bologna will serve as one of Europe's nine official Cultural Capitals for the year 2000, along with Kraków, Brussels, Prague, and others. The nine cities will collaborate to establish improved public access to each of their museum and exhibition collections, and use technology to help create a "virtual cultural infrastructure" linking their resources electronically.

Pleasures and Pastimes

Dining

Emilia-Romagna's reputation as Italy's gourmet region is well deserved, ever more so as the spreading of its reputation spurs the region's chefs onto even greater heights of gastronomic achievement. For you, this means a virtual moral obligation to eat lots and eat well: a trip through Emilia-Romagna wouldn't be complete without sampling what the region does best.

Emilia-Romagnan *cucina* is not without its drawbacks, however. What the region does best, for example, does not include preparing light meals—in Emilia-Romagna, eating light means leaving half of your *tortellini con noci e panna* (tortellini with walnuts and cream) on your plate. Ravioli stuffed with spinach and ricotta cheese, tortelli and *cappellacci* (triangular pasta dumplings) stuffed with squash, tortellini stuffed with minced pork and beef all have in common one key word—and you'll inevitably be stuffed, too.

This is not to say that the uninitiated should be wary of the culinary delights of Bologna the Fat and its sister cities. The specialties are nothing new in name, they're just better here, where they were born: Parma's crumbly Parmigiano di Reggiano cheese and world-famous Parma ham (look for prosciutto di Parma); Bologna's pasta (especially tagliatelle) *al ragù,* a heavenly, slow-cooked mix of onions, carrots, minced pork and beef, and fresh tomatoes that in no way resembles the Bolognese sauce served worldwide; likewise the rich, soft, garlicky mortadella sausage that has been reincarnated elsewhere to its detriment as "baloney." Although most local specialties are served throughout the region, traditionalists will have their zampone and *aceto balsamico* (sweet, black-herb balsamic vinegar) in Modena, their risotto *in padella* (with fresh herbs and tomatoes) in Piacenza, their *brodetto* (tangy seafood stew) in Rimini, their *cappellacci di zucca* in Ferrara, and everything else in Bologna.

Emilia-Romagna's wines, fittingly, are meant to accompany the region's fine food rather than vie with it for attention and accolades. The best-known wine of the region is Lambrusco, a sparkling red produced on the flat, expansive Po plain that has some admirers and many detractors. Some praise it for its tartness; others condemn it for the same quality. The region's best wines include Barbera, produced in the Colli Piacetini and Apennine foothills, and Sangiovese di Romagna, which can be very similar to Chianti, from the Romagnolan hills.

Lodging

In Italy, the region of Emilia-Romagna has a reputation for an efficiency uncommon in most of the rest of the country. Consequently, even the smallest hotels are well run, with high levels of service and quality. Bologna is very much a businessperson's city, and most of the hotels cater to travelers of this type. There are, of course, smaller, more intimate hotels that cater to the tourist.

The business of Rimini, on the other hand, is tourism. There are hundreds of hotels, grand ones with all sorts of luxury facilities and modest pensions with only a few rooms. Many offer full- or half-board plans—an economical alternative to eating in Rimini's many, but not particularly distinguished, restaurants. Despite the abundance of lodging, however, you should not go to Rimini during tourist season without confirmed hotel reservations: in July and August the city is filled to overflowing. Hotels in Rimini are closed off-season.

Exploring Emilia-Romagna

A tour through Emilia-Romagna has something for everyone: great art, fascinating history, fabulous food, and even a day at the beach at the seaside resort of Rimini. The best way to see the region is to begin your tour in the west, in Piacenza, and to proceed east along the Via Emilia (S9) to the sea. The major towns are either on that route or just off it, the longest detours being no more than 48–65 km (30–40 mi) off the main road.

Numbers in the text correspond to numbers in the margin and on the Emilia-Romagna and Bologna maps.

Great Itineraries

Although Emilia-Romagna has a geographical logic—following the Via Emilia through the Po Valley and Romagna plain—it is not a compact area, making it hard to cover much of it in a short time. If you are traveling straight through, then you should confine your stops to places along the main north–west artery north of Bologna. Alternatively, you could base yourself in the regional capital, Bologna, and make forays from this hub. From Bologna there are three choices of itineraries: head north on A13 to Ferrara and then southeast on S16 to Ravenna, or continue east or west along the Via Emilia (S9), stopping for short visits at some of the smaller towns en route northwest to Piacenza or southeast to Rimini and the sea.

IF YOU HAVE 3 DAYS

Given three days, you should set aside two nights to see **Bologna** ⑤–⑭ and its environs, including **Dozza** ⑮. The city itself has enough to fill much more than this, but while you are there, make a point of seeing the sights in and around Piazza Maggiore, including **Santo Stefano** ⑩, the **Basilica di San Petronio** ⑤, **Palazzo Comunale** ⑥, and the nearby two towers. On day two, take a train or drive the short distance to **Ferrara** ⑲, a calm, unspoiled Renaissance city. Where you spend your third day will depend on your route out of Emilia-Romagna. If you are going to Milan or Turin, make a stop about 100 km (62 mi) northwest of Bologna at **Parma** ③, where you could cover the major sights in two or three hours. If you are heading toward the Adriatic coast, **Ravenna** ⑱ should be your priority stop. Of course, if you are heading north toward Venice, you should see Ferrara on this leg of the trip and see Parma and Ravenna on the other days.

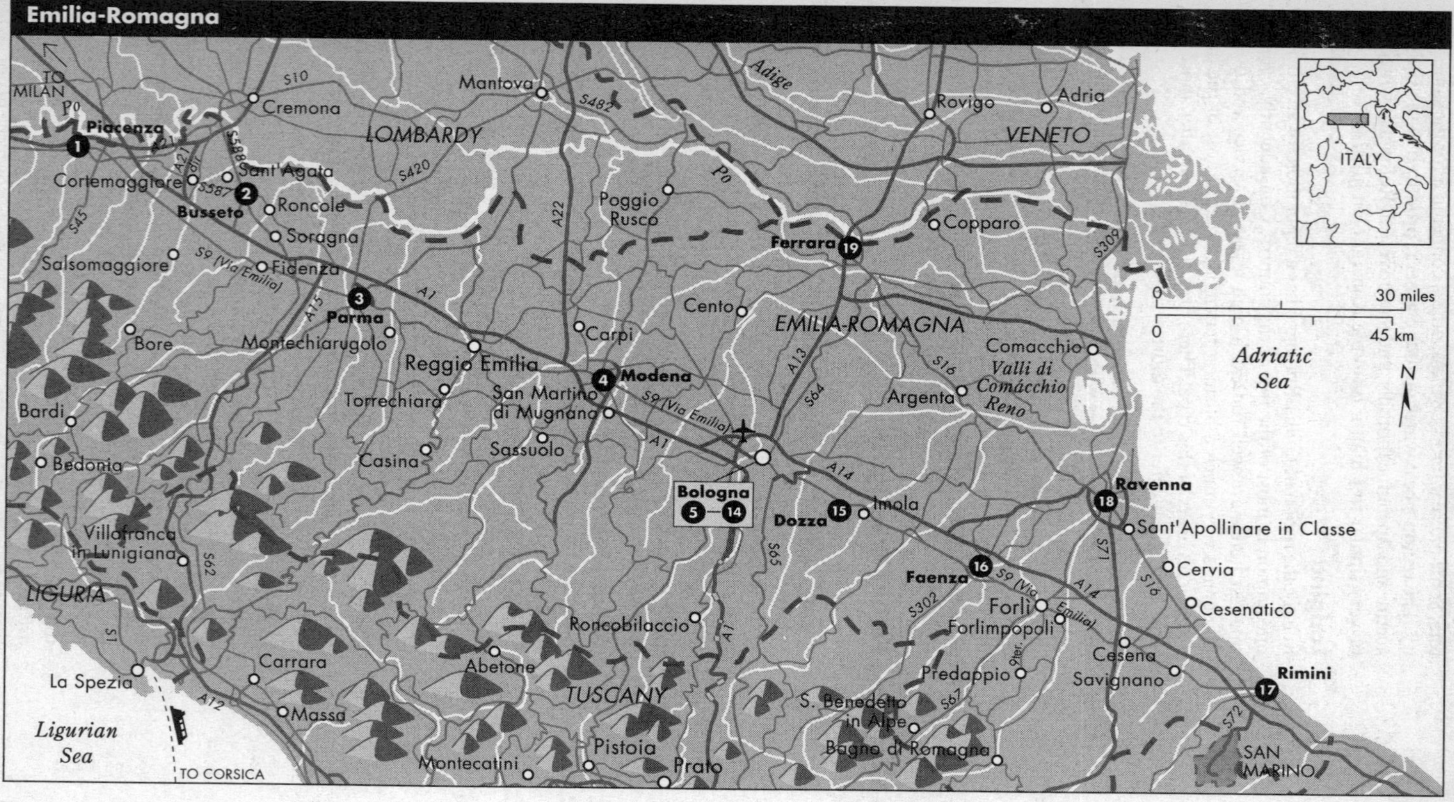
Emilia-Romagna
ITALY
0
30 miles
0
45 km
N
Adriatic Sea
Ligurian Sea
TO MILAN
TO CORSICA
LOMBARDY
VENETO
EMILIA-ROMAGNA
TUSCANY
LIGURIA
SAN MARINO
Po
Adige
Reno
Valli di Comácchio
Piacenza 1
Busseto 2
Parma 3
Modena 4
Bologna 5—14
Dozza 15
Faenza 16
Rimini 17
Ravenna 18
Ferrara 19
Cortemaggiore
Sant'Agata
Roncole
Soragna
Fidenza
Salsomaggiore
Cremona
Mantova
Bardi
Bedonia
Bore
Villafranca in Lunigiana
La Spezia
Carrara
Massa
Montechiarugolo
Torrechiara
Casina
Reggio Emilia
San Martino di Mugnano
Sassuolo
Carpi
Poggio Rusco
Cento
Abetone
Montecatini
Pistoia
Prato
Roncobilaccio
Rovigo
Adria
Copparo
Comacchio
Argenta
Imola
Forlì
Forlimpopoli
Predappio
S. Benedetto in Alpe
Bagno di Romagna
Cesena
Savignano
Cervia
Cesenatico
Sant'Apollinare in Classe
A1
A12
A13
A14
A15
A21
A22
S1
S9 (Via Emilia)
S10
S16
S45
S62
S64
S65
S67
S71
S72
S302
S309
S420
S482
S587
S588

IF YOU HAVE 5 DAYS

Bother with chaotic **Rimini** ⑰ only if you must get a taste of a hardcore resort and disco scene, in which case you should start here. But we recommend skipping it altogether and heading straight for **Ravenna** ⑱, being sure to see Sant'Apollinare in Classe, outside the city proper but well worth the excursion. On your way to Bologna on day two, drop in on a factory in the ceramic center of **Faenza** ⑯, famed for its faience pottery. Stay two to three nights in **Bologna** ⑤–⑭ itself, savoring meals and taking in the siights. From Bologna, take a day or overnight trip to **Ferrara** ⑲, enjoying the pleasures ambling around its turreted and towered medieval streets. Spend the last night or two sampling the fine food and wine in **Parma** ③, stopping in **Modena** ④, another culinary capital, along the way. Northwest of Parma, make a slight detour from the autostrada or Via Emilia to see the cluster of places associated with the composer Verdi, centered in the village of **Busseto** ②. Still heading northwest, spend your last morning or afternoon in **Piacenza** ①, its elegance and harmony typical of Emilia-Romagna's centers of culture, and a fitting exit or entrance to the region. From here, it's a mere 66 km (41 mi) to Milan.

When to Tour Emilia-Romagna

You would never visit Emilia-Romagna for the weather. In this predominantly flat landscape, the winters are gray and cold, and summers are airless and hot, though sea breezes on the coast offer some respite. If you are here in summer, get up early and do as much as you can in the morning. Ideally, mid-afternoons in summer should be left unplanned; the hours after five are best for sightseeing and traveling. In winter, make sure you are equipped for the frequent rain and damp, penetrating cold. Fog is common throughout the low-lying areas of the region and can be starkly beautiful, but it can also be very hazardous on the road. No matter what the season, make sure you reserve ahead for rooms: the cities are often awash with commercial conventions and business conferences. Note that restaurants and hotels in Rimini are usually closed up tight during the off-season.

ON THE ROAD TO PARMA AND MODENA

The Via Emilia runs through Emilia's heart in a straight shot from medieval Piacenza to thoroughly modern Modena. On the way from the past to the present you'll pass through the homes of many of Italy's famous cultural riches—from the culinary and artistic treasures of Parma to the opera country around Bussetto, birthplace and home of Giuseppe Verdi. It may be tempting to imitate Modena's Ferraris and zoom over the short (113-km/70-mi) stretch of highway spanning the region, but if you take the time to detour into the countryside or stop for a taste of prosciutto di Parma, you will be richly rewarded.

Piacenza

❶ *66 km (41 mi) southeast of Milan, 150 km (94 mi) northwest of Bologna.*

The city of Piacenza has always been associated with industry and commerce. Its position on the River Po has made it an important inland port since the earliest times; the Etruscans, and then the Romans, had thriving settlements on this site. As you approach the city today, you could be forgiven for thinking that it holds little of interest. Piacenza is surrounded by ugly industrial suburbs (with particularly unlovely cement factories and a power station), but forge ahead and you'll discover that they surround a delightfully preserved medieval downtown.

The heart of the city is **Piazza dei Cavalli** (Horses' Square), dominated by the massive 13th-century **Palazzo del Comune.** This severely Gothic turreted and crenellated building was the seat of town government before Piacenza fell under the respective iron fists of the ruling Pallavicini and Farnese families. The flamboyant **equestrian statues** from which the piazza takes its name are depictions of members of the last and greatest of the Farnese: on the right is Ranuccio Farnese (1569–1622); on the left is his father, Alessandro (1545–92). Alessandro was a beloved ruler, enlightened and fair; Ranuccio, his successor, was less successful. Both statues are the work of Francesco Mochi, a master sculptor of the Baroque period.

Attached like a sinister balcony to the bell tower of Piacenza's 12th-century **Duomo** is a *gabbia* (iron cage), where miscreants were incarcerated naked and subjected to the scorn (and missiles) of the crowd in the marketplace below. Inside the cathedral, a less-evocative but equally impressive array of fine medieval stonework decorates the pillars and the crypt, and there are extravagant frescoes by Il Guercino (a.k.a. Giovanni Barbieri, 1591–1666) in the dome of the cupola. The Duomo can be reached by following Via XX Settembre down from Piazza dei Cavalli. ✉ *Piazza Duomo,* ☎ *0523/335154.* ⏲ *Daily 8:30–noon and 4–7.*

The **Museo Civico** (Civic Museum), the city-owned collection of Piacenzan art and antiquities, is housed in the vast **Palazzo Farnese.** The ruling family originally commissioned a monumental palace, but the construction, begun in 1558, was never completed. The highlight of this rather eclectic exhibit is the 2nd century BC *Etruscan Fegato di Piacenza,* a bronze tablet in the shape of a *fegato* (liver), with the symbols of the gods of good and ill fortune marked on it. By comparing this master "liver" with one taken from the body of a freshly slaughtered sacrifice, the priests could predict the future. On a more humanistic note, the collection also contains a painting by Botticelli (1445–1510), the *Madonna with St. John the Baptist,* and a series of Roman bronzes and mosaics. There is also a collection of carriages, arms and armor, and other paraphernalia owned by the Farnese, which give life to the history of that powerful family. ✉ *Piazza Cittadella,* ☎ *0523/330567.* 🎫 *10,000 lire for all exhibits, 4,000–8,000 lire for individual sections.* ⏲ *Tues.–Wed. 9–12:30, Thurs.–Sat. 9–12:30 and 3–6, Sun. 9:30–12:30 and 3–6.*

Dining

$$$ ★ ✕ **Antica Osteria del Teatro.** Set on a lovely piazza in the center of town, this restaurant is generally touted to be the best in Piacenza. Set in a typical 15th-century building with lacunar ceilings and sober period furniture, the Osteria effuses elegance, with excellent service and an impeccable wine list. Try the rich liver with chutney and figs. ✉ *Via Verdi 16,* ☎ *0523/323777. Reservations essential. AE, DC, MC, V. Closed Mon., Aug. 1–25, and Jan. 1–10. No dinner Sun.*

$ ✕ **Agnello.** Central (on the corner of Piazza dei Cavalli), simple, small, and cheap, with paintings hung here and there, Agnello is an excellent place to plop down for lunch. Try the tortelli *alla Piacentina* (stuffed with ricotta and spinach and bathed in butter and Parmesan) or the *coniglio alla cacciatore* (rabbit in a tomato and white-wine sauce). Reservations are a good idea. ✉ *Via Calzolai 2,* ☎ *0523/320874. No credit cards. Closed Mon. and Aug.*

En Route If you are driving from Piacenza, take the S10 northeast for Cremona (☞ Chapter 8, but turn off it just a few kilometers out of Piacenza and follow the signs for S587 to the town of Cortemaggiore. From Cortemaggiore, turn right onto a smaller rural road (not numbered) and follow the signs for Busseto, some 10 km (6 mi) away.

Busseto

❷ *30 km (19 mi) southeast of Piacenza, 15 km (9 mi) south of Cremona.*

Busseto's main claim to fame is the **Villa Pallavicino,** where Giuseppe Verdi (1813–1901), Italian opera composer of *Aïda, Rigoletto, La Traviata,* and *Otello,* worked and lived with his mistress (and later wife), Giuseppina Strepponi. The small **Verdi museum** here displays such relics of the maestro as his piano, scores, composition books, walking sticks, and other bits of memorabilia. If you plan to visit all the area's Verdi sights, invest in an 8,000-lire ticket valid for Villa Pallavicino, Palazzo Orlandi, Teatro Verdi, and Verdi's birthplace (but not Villa Sant'Agata). Call the Busseto tourist office (☞ Visitor Information *in* Emilia-Romagna A to Z, *below*) for more information. *4,000 lire. Apr.–Sept., daily 9:30–12:30 and 3–7; Mar., Tues.–Sun. 9:30–12:30 and 3–7; Oct.–Nov. and Feb., Sat. 2:30–5:30, Sun. 9:30–12:30 and 2:30–5:30.*

Palazzo Orlandi, owned for the past century by the Orlandi family, was Verdi's home for a few years from 1845. Only a few of its stately rooms are open to the public; it's a good idea to call ahead to confirm it's open. *Via Roma 56, ☎ 0524/92708. 2,000 lire. Apr.–Sept., Tues.–Sun. 9:30–12:30 and 3–7; Oct.–Nov., Tues.–Sun. 9:30–noon and 2:30–5.*

In the center of Busseto is the lovely **Teatro Verdi,** dedicated, as one may expect, to the works of the hamlet's famous son. Once inside the well-preserved, ornate 19th-century-style theater, use your imagination to get a feel for where he worked. Call the Busseto tourist office for the latest theater performances and visiting hours. *Piazza Verdi 10. 5,000 lire. Feb.–Nov., Tues.–Sun. 9:30–12:30 and 3–7.*

OFF THE BEATEN PATH

VILLA SANT'AGATA – Five kilometers (3 mi) north of Busseto, Villa Sant'Agata, also known as Villa Verdi, is the grand country home Verdi built for himself in 1849 and where some of his greatest works were composed. For Verdi lovers, Sant'Agata is a veritable shrine. ✉ *3 km (2 mi) north of Busseto on S588 toward Cremona. 8,000 lire. Apr.–Oct., Tues.–Sun. 9–11:40 and 3–6:40.*

RONCOLE – Giuseppe Verdi was born in a simple farmhouse on the edge of the town of Roncole, 3 km (2 mi) southeast of Busseto. Equally modest is the church in which he took some of his earliest steps in a musical career; he was the church organist here when still in his teens. ✉ *5 km (3 mi) east of Busseto on local road to Soragna (follow signs). Verdi's birthplace: 3,000 lire. Apr.–Sept., daily 9:30–12:30 and 3–7; Mar., Tues.–Sun. 9:30–12:30 and 3–7; Oct.–Nov. and Feb., Sat. 2:30–5:30, Sun. 9:30–12:30 and 2:30–5:30.*

Parma

❸ *40 km (25 mi) southeast Busseto, 97 km (61 mi) northwest of Bologna.*

Dignified, delightful Parma stands on the banks of a tributary of the River Po. Much of the lively historic center has been untouched by modern times, despite heavy damage during World War II. Almost every major European power has had a hand in ruling Parma at one time or another. The Romans founded the city—it was little more than a garrison on the Via Emilia—and then a succession of feudal lords held sway here. In the 16th century came the ever-avaricious Farnese family (who are still the dukes of Parma) and then, in fast succession, the

Spanish, French, and Austrians (after the fall of Napoléon). The French influence is strong. The French novelist Stendhal (1783–1842) lived in the city for several years and set his classic novel *The Charterhouse of Parma* here.

Thanks to the efforts being made by the city fathers to control traffic—and the city's enormous economic prosperity—strolling Parma's cobbled streets along with the teeming masses of locals is a charming experience. The traffic regulations, although a boon to pedestrians, are a nightmare for motorists. Every obstacle is put in the way of motor traffic—one-way streets, no-turning zones, and the like—so it is best to leave your car outside the center and see the town on foot.

★ The **Piazza del Duomo,** site of the cathedral, the baptistery, the church of San Giovanni, and the palaces of the bishop and other notables, is the heart of the city. This square and its buildings make up one of the most harmonious, tranquil city centers in Italy. The focal point of the piazza is the magnificent 12th-century **Duomo,** with its two vigilant stone lions standing guard beside the main door. The arch of the entrance is decorated with a delicate frieze of figures representing the months of the year, a motif repeated inside the baptistery on the right-hand side of the square. Some of the original artwork still exists in the church, notably the simple yet evocative *Descent from the Cross,* a carving in the right transept by Benedetto Antelami (1150–1230), a sculptor and architect whose masterwork is this cathedral's Baptistery (☞ *below*).

It is odd to turn from this austere work of the 12th century to the exuberant fresco in the dome, the *Assumption of the Virgin,* by the 16th-century painter Antonio Correggio (1494–1534). The fresco was not well received when it was unveiled in 1530. "A mess of frogs' legs," the bishop of Parma is said to have called it. In contrast to the rather dark, somber interior of the cathedral, though, the beauty and light of the painting in the dome are a welcome relief. Today, of course, Correggio is acclaimed as one of the leading masters of Baroque painting; his many works on view in Parma now constitute one of the greatest draws of the city. ☒ *Piazza del Duomo,* ☎ *0521/235886.* ⏲ *Daily 7–12:30 and 3–7.*

The **Baptistery** is a solemn, simple Romanesque building on the exterior and an uplifting Gothic building within. The doors of the Baptistery are richly decorated with figures, animals, and flowers, and the interior is adorned with figures carved by Antelami showing the months and seasons. ☒ *Piazza del Duomo,* ☎ *0521/235592.* 🎫 *4,000 lire.* ⏲ *Daily 9–12:30 and 3–6.*

Once beyond the elaborate Baroque facade of **San Giovanni Evangelista,** the Renaissance interior reveals several works by Correggio; his *St. John the Evangelist* (left transept) is considered the finest of them. Also in this church (in the second and fourth chapels on the left) are works by Girolamo Parmigianino (1503–40)—a contemporary of Correggio's and the spearhead of the astonishing Mannerist art movement. Once seen, Parmigianino's anorexic and swan-necked Madonnas are never forgotten: they pose with all the precious élan of today's high-fashion models. ☒ *Piazzale San Giovanni,* ☎ *0521/235592.* ⏲ *Daily 6:30–noon and 3:30–8.*

Next door to the church of San Giovanni Evangelista, in the adjoining monastery, is the **Spezieria di San Giovanni**—once a pharmacy where Benedictine monks mixed medicines and herbals. The 16th-century decorations still survive, although the potions, which people of Parma swore would cure almost every malady, are, alas, gone—the pharmacy stopped production in 1881. ☒ *Borgo Pipa 1, off Piazzale San Giovanni,* ☎ *0521/233309.* 🎫 *4,000 lire.* ⏲ *Daily 9–1:45.*

★ Works by Parma's own Correggio and Parmigianino as well as Leonardo da Vinci (1452–1519), El Greco (1541–1614), and Il Bronzino (1503–72) are the highlights of the **Galleria Nazionale,** housed in the vast but rather grim-looking **Palazzo della Pilotta,** on the banks of the river. The palace was built in about 1600 and is so big that from the air it is Parma's most recognizable sight—hence the destruction done to it when it was bombed by Allied forces in 1944. Much of the building has been restored, but not all. The palazzo takes its name from the ball game *pilotta,* a sort of handball played within the palace precincts in the 17th century.

To enter the Galleria Nazionale, on the ground floor of the palace, you pass through the magnificent and elaborately Baroque **Teatro Farnese,** built in 1628 and based on Palladio's theater in the northern Italian town of Vicenza (☞ Chapter 5). Built entirely of wood, the theater was burned badly during Allied bombing but has been flawlessly restored. ✉ *Palazzo della Pilotta, Piazza Pilotta,* ☎ *0521/233309.* 🎟 *Teatro Farnese 4,000 lire; Teatro and Galleria Nazionale 12,000 lire.* ⏲ *Daily 9–1:30.*

The **Camera di San Paolo** is the former dining room of the abbess of the Convent of St. Paul. It was extensively frescoed by Correggio, and despite the religious character of the building, the decorations are entirely secular, with ravishingly beautiful (and very worldly) depictions of mythological scenes—the *Triumphs of the Goddess Diana,* the *Three Graces,* and the *Three Fates.* It is near the Palazzo della Pilotta, off Strada Garibaldi. ✉ *Via Melloni,* ☎ *0521/233309.* 🎟 *4,000 lire.* ⏲ *Daily 9–1:45.*

Near the central Piazza Garibaldi is **Madonna della Steccata,** a delightful 16th-century domed church famous for a wonderful fresco cycle by Parmigianino. The painter took so long to complete it that his exasperated patrons imprisoned him briefly for breach of contract before releasing him to complete the work. ✉ *Via Dante,* ☎ *0521/234937.* ⏲ *Daily 10:30–noon and 3–6.*

Dining and Lodging

$$$ ★ ✕ **La Greppia.** The most elegant and most talked-about restaurant in the city is also the best. The service is extremely personal and friendly, thanks to the place's tiny size. Taste from whence come the plaudits with innovative treats like the *tortino vegetale di melanzane* (eggplant and vegetable tartlet) and the *fegato di vitello ore due* (two-hour veal liver), a recipe of the Farnese kitchen. ✉ *Via Garibaldi 39,* ☎ *0521/233686. Reservations essential. AE, DC, MC, V. Closed Mon.–Tues. and July.*

$$ ✕ **Croce di Malta.** The premises of this appealing old-world restaurant once housed a convent, then an inn. Traditional local fare includes light, delicate homemade pasta—try the tortelli with squash filling or tagliatelle in any fashion. Second courses are well-prepared, filling versions of classic veal and cheese dishes. ✉ *Borgo Palmia 8,* ☎ *0521/235643. Reservations essential. AE, DC, MC, V.*

$$ ✕ **Gallo d'Oro.** Warmly colored and warmly lit rooms upstairs and a multilevel bodega downstairs each house dozens of tables—and they all fill most nights. To go along with the atmosphere, the menu features traditional Parma specialties, like antipasti with local hams and several varieties of tortelli. ✉ *Via Borgo della Salina 3,* ☎ *0521/208846. AE, DC, MC, V. Closed Sun.*

$$ ★ ✕ **Parma Rotta.** An old inn about 2 km (1 mi) from downtown Parma, the Parma Rotta remains an informal neighborhood trattoria serving hearty dishes like spit-roasted lamb and roast pork, topped off with a wide array of homemade desserts. ✉ *Via Langhirano 158,* ☎ *0521/966738. AE, DC, MC, V. Closed Sun. June–Sept. and Mon. Oct.–May.*

$-$$ ★ ✕ **Sant'Ambrogio.** This is an ideal spot for informal dining in the center of town. Duck and quail are the best bets, but don't overlook the *crauti spinaci* (boiled pork sausage with pickled cabbage or spinach). ✉ *Vicolo Cinque Piaghe 1/a,* ☎ *0521/234482. AE, DC, MC, V. Closed Mon.*

$$$$ **Palace Hotel Maria Luigia.** A top-quality hotel convenient to old Parma and the train station, the Maria Luigia has large, well-furnished rooms and is popular with business travelers. ✉ *Viale Mentana 140, 43100,* ☎ *0521/281032,* FAX *0521/231126. 102 rooms, 11 suites. Restaurant, bar, minibars, meeting rooms. AE, DC, MC, V.*

$$$$ **Park Hotel Stendhal.** The Stendhal is again one of the best hotels in Parma. It is on the edge of the historic center of town and convenient for the tourist and business traveler alike. Rooms are thickly carpeted and spacious, some with chandeliers and period furniture. Some rooms have views of the Palazzo della Pilotta. ✉ *Via Bodoni 3, 43100,* ☎ *0521/208057,* FAX *0521/285655. 65 rooms. Restaurant, bar, meeting rooms. AE, DC, MC, V.*

$$$ **Hotel Torino.** A warm reception and pleasant, relaxed surroundings are the best reasons for staying in this former convent, tucked away in a quiet pedestrian zone in the heart of town. It has modern, smallish rooms with Correggio reproductions on the walls. ✉ *Via Mazza 7, 43100,* ☎ *0521/281046,* FAX *0521/230725. 33 rooms. Bar. AE, DC, MC, V. Closed Jan. 9–17 and Aug. 1–20.*

Nightlife and the Arts

ENOTECA

Before and after dinner, locals flock to **Enoteca Antica Osteria Fontana** (✉ Via Farini 24/a, ☎ 0521/286037), an atmospheric *enoteca* (wine bar) that serves up several varieties of good local wines like the sparkling Lambrusco or Sangiovese di Romagna to a crowd that is gregarious whether standing or sitting.

OPERA AND THEATER

Parma is the region's opera center, with performances held at the **Teatro Regio** (✉ Via Garibaldi, ☎ 0521/218910). Opera here is taken just as seriously as in Milan, although tickets are a little easier to come by. Playwright Dario Fo, the recipient of the 1997 Nobel prize in Literature, helped found the **Teatro Due** (✉ Viale Basetti 12, ☎ 0521/230242), a theater whose productions still maintain a mixture of comedy and politics—though your understanding of the themes will be limited without a knowledge of Italian.

Modena

❹ *56 km (35 mi) southeast of Parma, 38 km (23 mi) northwest of Bologna.*

Old town Modena has today gained recognition for being home to three very contemporary names. The luxury high-performance cars Maserati and Ferrari come from Modena, and so does the world-famous opera star Luciano Pavarotti. But one should not forget about Modena's herb-infused balsamic vinegar, perhaps the city's most perfect achievement. The modern town that encircles the historic center is extensive, and although the old quarter is small, it is filled with narrow medieval streets and pleasant piazzas.

The 12th-century **Duomo,** also known as the Basilica Metropolitana, is one of the finest examples of Romanesque architecture in the country. As in Parma, the exterior is decorated with medieval sculptures depicting scenes from the life of San Geminiano, the patron saint of Modena, and fantastic beasts, as well as a realistic-looking scene of the sacking of a city by barbarian hordes, a reminder to the faithful to be ever vigilant in defense of the church. The bell tower is made of white marble and is known as **La Ghirlandina** (The Little Garland) because of its distinctive garland-shape weather vane on the summit. The somber church interior is divided by an elaborately decorated gallery carved with scenes of the *Passion of Christ.* The carvings took 50 years to complete and are by an anonymous Modenese master of the 12th century. The tomb of San Geminiano is in the crypt. ✉ *Piazza Grande,* ☎ *059/216078.* ⏲ *Daily 7–12:30 and 3:30–7.*

The principal museum of the town is housed in the **Palazzo dei Musei,** a short walk from the Duomo. The collection was assembled in the mid-17th century by Francesco d'Este(1610–58), Duke of Modena, and the **Galleria Estense** is named in his honor. The first room displays his portrait bust done by Bernini (1598–1680). The duke was a man of many interests, as you can see from the collection of objets d'art—ivories, coins, medals, and bronzes, as well as fine art dating from the Renaissance to the Baroque. There are works here by Correggio and by masters from other parts of Italy, such as the Venetians Tintoretto (1518–94) and Veronese (1528–88), the Bolognese Guido Reni (1575–1642) and the Carracci brothers (Annibale, 1560–1609, and Agostino, 1557–1602), and the Neapolitan Salvator Rosa (1615–73).

The gallery also houses the duke's **Biblioteca Estense,** a huge collection of illuminated books, of which the best known is the beautifully illustrated bible of the 15th century, the *Bible of Borso d'Este.* A map dated 1501 was one of the first in the world to show Columbus's discovery of America. Follow Via Emilia, the old Roman road that runs through the heart of the town, to Via di Sant'Agostino. ✉ *Piazza Sant'Agostino,* ☎ *059/222145.* *8,000 lire.* ⏲ *Tues. and Fri.–Sat. 9–7, Wed.–Thurs. 9–2, Sun. 9–1.*

The huge Baroque **Palazzo Ducale** of the dukes of Modena now houses a military academy; once the province of the dukes only, it is still off-limits, except to flocks of cadets in elaborate uniforms. Behind the academy are Modena's large **Giardini Pubblici** (Public Gardens). ✉ *Piazza degli Estensi.*

Dining and Lodging

$$$ ★ ✕ **Borso d'Este.** One of the city's most highly regarded restaurants—particularly with the *crema* of the region's monied set—offers some delicious variations on old themes, like ravioli stuffed with game and Parmesan. The space is ultra trendy and modern, achieved with antiques throughout. In season don't miss the *tartufo* (truffle) specialties: ricotta- and spinach-stuffed *tortelloni* (pasta squares) in a truffle-mushroom sauce, and the mushroom tart laced with the perfumy tubers. ✉ *Piazza Roma 5,* ☎ *059/214114. Reservations essential. AE, DC, MC, V. Closed Sun. and Aug. No lunch Sat.*

$$$ ✕ **Fini.** A Modena institution, fancy, modern Fini is widely held to be the best restaurant the city has to offer. It's Pavarotti's favorite—and you could easily gain a Pavarottiesque figure by making a habit of the excellent local wines, *gran bollito misto,* a groaning board of boiled meats in a *salsa verde* (vegetable sauce), and homemade desserts. ✉ *Piazzale San Francesco,* ☎ *059/223314. Reservations essential. AE, DC, MC, V. Closed Mon.–Tues., July 20–Aug. 20, and last wk in Dec.*

$$ ✕ **Da Enzo.** This cheerful, well-patronized trattoria is in the old town's pedestrian zone, close by the synagogue and a few steps from Piazza Mazzini. All the classic Modenese specialties are here, including zampone and *cotechino* (animal bladders stuffed with pork). For starters, try the tortelloni *di ricotta e spinaci* (stuffed with ricotta and spinach).

✉ *Via Coltellini 17,* ☎ *059/225177. Reservations essential weekends. AE, DC, MC, V. Closed Mon. and Aug. No lunch Sun.*

$$$ **Canal Grande.** Once a ducal palace, the Canal Grande offers large, airy, well-appointed rooms with minibars. The hotel's restaurant, La Secchia Rapita (closed Wednesday and August), gets rave reviews. ✉ *Corso Canalgrande 6, 41100,* ☎ *059/217160,* FAX *059/221674. 72 rooms, 3 suites. Restaurant, bar, in-room safes, minibars. AE, DC, MC, V.*

$$ **La Torre.** Not particularly exciting, La Torre is nonetheless the best hotel choice in the low end of this price category, thanks to its being in town center just off the Via Emilia. The somewhat stuffy rooms are functional, comfortable, and well equipped. ✉ *Via Cervetta 5, 41100,* ☎ *059/222615,* FAX *059/216316. 26 rooms. Bar. AE, DC, MC, V.*

BOLOGNA

Through its long history, first as an Etruscan city, then a Roman one, then as an independent city-state in the Middle Ages, Bologna has always been a power in the north of Italy. Over the centuries, the city has acquired a number of nicknames: Bologna the Learned, in honor of its venerable university, the oldest in the world; Bologna the Red, for its rosy rooftops and political leanings; Bologna the Turreted, recalling the forest of medieval towers that once rose from the city center (two remarkable examples still exist); and Bologna the Fat, a tribute to its preeminent position in the world of cuisine.

Today one might be tempted to dub it Bologna the Prosperous for its immaculately kept streets, trendy boutiques, and revered restaurants exuding impeccable class. Centuries of wars, sackings, rebellions, and aerial bombing that left such dramatic evidence in other cities of the region have not taken their toll on Bologna's old city center: the narrow cobblestone streets remain as they were hundreds of years ago (except cleaner), as do the ancient churches, massive palaces, medieval towers, and famous porticoed arcades lining many of the main thoroughfares, shading the walkways to such an extent that you can stroll around town in a rainstorm for hours without feeling a drop. The noticeable lack of foreign visitors in the city is one of the more bizarre anomalies in the world of Italian tourism. Bologna's vitality is entirely locally driven.

This is due in large part to its student population. The university was founded in about the year 1088 and by the 13th century already had more than 10,000 students. It was a center for the teaching of law and theology, and it was ahead of its time in that many of the professors were women. Today the university has one of the most prominent business schools in Italy and the finest faculty of medicine in the country. Guglielmo Marconi, the inventor of the wireless telegraph, first formulated his groundbreaking theories in the physics labs of the university.

Exploring Bologna

Piazza Maggiore and the adjacent Piazza del Nettuno make up the heart of the city. Arranged around these two squares are the imposing Basilica di San Petronio, the massive Palazzo Comunale, the Palazzo del Podestà, the Palazzo di Re Enzo, and the Fontana del Nettuno—one of the most visually harmonious groupings of public buildings in the entire country. From here, sights that aren't on one of the piazzas are but a short walk away, along delightful narrow cobbled streets or under the ubiquitous porticoes that double as municipal umbrellas in case of rain.

A Good Walk

Start at the southern end of sprawling Piazza Maggiore at the 14th-century **Basilica di San Petronio** ⑤, peeking into its museum to see the church's original designs, some never realized. On the west side of Piazza Maggiore is the **Palazzo Comunale** ⑥, especially great if you like the work of modern artist Giorgio Morandi. Next, on to the **Palazzo del Podestà** ⑦ and its Torre dell'Arengo, at the north end of Piazza Maggiore in the adjoining Piazza Nettuno, where stands the Fontana del Nettuno, a.k.a. Il Gigante. To the left (west) is **Palazzo di Re Enzo** ⑧ with its dark medieval associations. The busy, chic Via Rizzoli runs east from Piazza Nettuno directly into the medieval section of the city to Piazza di Porta Ravegnana, where you can climb the slightly off-kilter **Torre degli Asinelli** ⑨, next to the smaller **Torre Garisenda.** From Piazza di Porta Ravegnana, you have two choices of routes if you want a shorter walk: head south and southwest to **Santo Stefano** ⑩ and **San Domenico** ⑪, or continue northeast along Via Zamboni for the last three important sights (bullets ⑫–⑭). If you want a long walk, explore all five sights. From the piazza, walk five minutes southeast down Via Santo Stefano to the remarkable church of Santo Stefano, actually several churches in one. From there, head west on Via Farini and take a left on Via Garibaldi; a few blocks down take a left to reach Piazza San Domenico and San Domenico, containing the saint's tomb and a minor work by Michelangelo. Retrace your steps back to Piazza di Porta Ravegnana, and walk northeast on Via Zamboni a few blocks to **San Giacomo Maggiore** ⑫, haunt of the Bentivoglio. Continue up Via Zamboni to Via delle Belle Arte and the **Pinacoteca Nazionale** ⑬, with works of Raphael, Giotto, Parmigianino, and Bolognese masters. Stroll north to the **Università di Bologna** ⑭ district for a *caffe* and snack.

TIMING

You'll want at least a full day to explore Bologna; it's compact, but it lends itself to easy exploration. This walk, allowing a little time to explore each sight, should take at least four hours, not including the hour you should devote to the Pinacoteca Nazionale, a half hour to climb the Torre degli Asinelli, and a lunch break for a sampling of Bologna's culinary bounty. Note that the Pinacoteca closes at 1 or 2 PM, so plan your exploration accordingly.

Sights to See

❺ **Basilica di San Petronio.** Construction on this cathedral began in the 14th century, and work was still in progress on this vast building some 300 years later. It is still not finished, as you can see: the wings of the transept are missing and the facade is only partially decorated, lacking most of the marble face the architects planned several hundred years ago. The main doorway was carved by the great Sienese master of the Renaissance, Jacopo della Quercia. Above the center of the door is a Madonna and Child, flanked by Saints Ambrose and Petronius, patrons of the city.

The interior of the basilica is huge and echoing, 432 ft long, 185 ft wide, and 144 ft high. It is so vast that it's sobering to note that originally the Bolognans had planned an even bigger church—you can still see the columns erected to support the larger church outside the east end—but had to tone down construction when the University seat was established next door in 1561. The **Museo di San Petronio** contains models to show how the original church was intended to have looked. The most important artworks in the church are in the left aisle, frescoes by Giovanni di Modena dating from the first years of the 1400s. Also in the left aisle, laid out in the pavement of the church, is a huge sundial, placed there in 1655, showing the time, date, and month. ✉ *Piazza Maggiore.* ☎ *051/225442.* ⏲ *Basilica: Apr.–Sept., daily 7:30–*

Basilica di San Petronio, **5**
Palazzo Comunale, **6**
Palazzo del Podestà, **7**
Palazzo di Re Enzo, **8**
Pinacoteca Nazionale, **13**
San Domenico, **11**
San Giacomo Maggiore, **12**
Santo Stefano, **10**
Torre degli Asinelli/Torre Garisenda, **9**
Università di Bologna, **14**

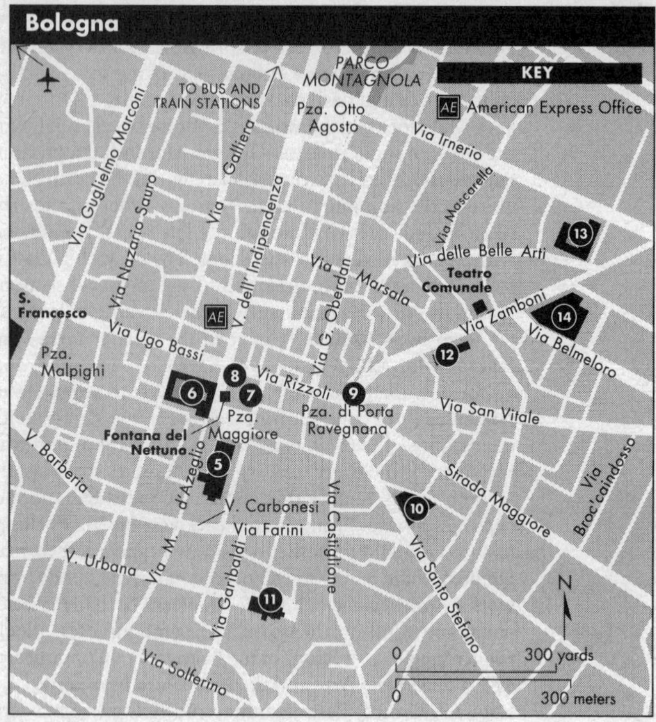

1:30 and 2:30–7:30; Oct.–Mar., daily 7–1 and 2–7. Museo di San Petronio: Mon. and Wed.–Sun. 10–12:30.

Fontana del Nettuno. Sculptor Giambologna's elaborate 1566 Baroque monument to Neptune in stone occupying Piazza Nettuno has been aptly nicknamed Il Gigante (The Giant). Its exuberantly sensual mermaids and undraped God of the Sea drew fire when it was constructed, but not enough, apparently, to dissuade the populace from using the fountain as a public washing stall for centuries. ✉ *Piazza Nettuno, next to the Palazzo di Re Enzo.*

❻ **Palazzo Comunale.** A mélange of building styles and constant modifications characterize this palace, dating from the 13th to 15th centuries. When Bologna was an independent city-state, this huge palace was the seat of government, a function it still serves today. Over the door is a statue of Bologna-born Pope Gregory XIII, most famous for his reorganization of the calendar. The "Gregorian" system remains in use today. ✉ *Piazza Maggiore.*

The **Collezioni Comunali d'Arte** exhibits paintings from the Middle Ages as well as some Renaissance works by Luca Signorelli (1445/1450–1523) and Tintoretto. On the same floor, a separate **Museo Morandi** is dedicated to the 20th-century still-life artist Giorgio Morandi; in addition to his paintings, you'll see a re-creation of his studio and living space. An equally good reason to come is to get a look at the views of the piazza from the upper stories of the palace. ✉ *Piazza Maggiore, west side,* ☎ *051/203629.* 🎫 *8,000 lire each museum, 12,000 lire for both.* ⏲ *Tues.–Sun. 10–6.*

❼ **Palazzo del Podestà.** This classic Renaissance palace facing the Basilica di San Petronio was erected in 1484, and attached to it is the soaring **Torre dell'Arengo.** The bells in the tower have rung since 1453, whenever the city has celebrated, mourned, or called its citizens to arms. ✉ *Piazza Nettuno,* ☎ *051/224500.* ⏲ *Call for entry and group tours.*

8 **Palazzo di Re Enzo.** King Enzo of Sardinia was imprisoned in this 13th-century medieval palace for 23 years until his death in 1272. He had been unwise enough to wage war on Bologna and was captured after the fierce battle of Fossalta in 1249. The palace has other macabre associations: common criminals received the last rites of the church in the tiny chapel in the courtyard before being taken out to be executed in Piazza Maggiore. ✉ *Piazza Nettuno, next to the Palazzo del Podestà,* ☎ *051/224500.*

13 **Pinacoteca Nazionale.** Bologna's principal art gallery contains many works by the immortals of Italian painting, including Raphael's famous *Ecstasy of St. Cecilia.* There is also a beautiful multipaneled painting by Giotto and a Parmigianino *Madonna and Saints.* The centerpieces of the collection, however, are the many rooms devoted to the two most important late 16th-century Bolognese masters, painters Guido Reni and Annibale Carracci. Some of the most interesting works, from a historical point of view, are by Giuseppe Crespi (circa 1575–1632), a Bolognese painter who avoided grand religious or historical themes, preferring instead to paint scenes of daily life in his native city. These small canvases convey marvelously the boisterous, earthy life of old Bologna. ✉ *Via delle Belle Arti 56,* ☎ *051/243222.* 🎫 *8,000 lire.* ⏲ *Tues.–Sat. 9–2, Sun. 9–1.*

11 **San Domenico.** The tomb of Saint Dominic, who died here in 1221, is called the **Arca di San Domenico** and found in the sixth chapel on the right. Many artists participated in the decoration, notably Niccolò di Bari, who was so proud of his contribution that he changed his name to Niccolò dell'Arca to recall this famous work. The young Michelangelo carved the angel on the right. In the right transept of the church is a tablet marking the last resting place of the hapless King Enzo, whose prison you saw in Piazza Maggiore (☞ Palazzo di Re Enzo, *above*). In the square in front of San Domenico are two curious tombs raised above the ground on pillars, commemorating two famous 14th-century lawyers. ✉ *Piazza San Domenico 13, off Via Garibaldi,* ☎ *051/640–0411.* ⏲ *Daily 7:30–1 and 2–8.*

12 **San Giacomo Maggiore.** Inside this church is the burial chamber of the Bentivoglio family, the leading family in Bologna in the Middle Ages. The crypt is connected by underground passage to the Teatro Comunale across the street—a rather odd feature, until you realize that the family palazzo of the Bentivoglio used to stand on that spot. The most notable tomb is that of Antonio Bentivoglio (died 1435), carved by Jacopo della Quercia (circa 1374–1438) in 1435. You can tell his profession—lecturer in law—from the group of students carved on the base, all listening intently to their professor. ✉ *Piazza Rossini, off Via Zamboni,* ☎ *051/6493594.* ⏲ *Daily 6–noon and 3:30–6.*

★ 10 **Santo Stefano.** This splendid and unusual basilica actually contains between four and seven connected churches (authorities differ). The oldest is **Santi Vitale e Agricola,** which dates from the 8th century and contains a 14th-century nativity scene much loved by Bologna's children, who come at Christmastime to pay their respects to the baby Jesus. The church of **San Sepolcro** (12th century) contains the **Cortile di Pilato** (Courtyard of Pontius Pilate), so named for the basin in the center of the courtyard that's said to be the place where Pilate washed his hands after condemning Christ. Also in the building is a **museum** displaying various medieval religious works where you can buy sundry items made by the monks, such as honey, shampoo, and jam. ✉ *Via*

Santo Stefano 24, Piazza Santo Stefano, ☎ 051/223256. ⏲ Daily 9–noon and 3:30–6.

9 **Torre degli Asinelli/Torre Garisenda.** The taller (320 ft) of the twin towers in the compact Piazza di Porta Ravegnana, Torre degli Asinelli leans an alarming 7½ ft out of the perpendicular. The Torre Garisenda, now tilting 10 ft, was shortened to 165 ft for safety in the 1500s. The towers were built at the same time (1488) and are mentioned by Dante in *The Inferno.* They are two of the only 60 towers that remain of the more than 200 that presided over the city: every family of any importance had a tower as a symbol of its prestige and power, and as a fortified retreat when that prestige and power were threatened. For a fine view of Bologna's rooftops, climb up the 500 steep stairs of Torre degli Asinelli. ✉ *Piazza di Porta Ravegnana.* 🎟 *Torre degli Asinelli 3,000 lire.* ⏲ *Apr.–Sept., daily 9–6; Oct.–Mar., daily 9–5.*

14 **Università di Bologna.** Take a stroll through the adjoining streets in the university district, a jumble of buildings, some dating as far back as the 15th century and most to the 17th and 18th centuries. This neighborhood, like neighborhoods in most college towns, is full of bookshops, coffee bars, and cheap restaurants. None of them is particularly distinguished, but they're all characteristic of student life in the city. Try eating at the *mensa universitaria* (cafeteria) if you want to strike up a conversation with local students (most speak English). Political slogans and sentiments are scrawled on walls all around the university and tend, for the most part, to be ferociously leftist. ✉ *Via Zamboni.*

Dining and Lodging

$$$ ✕ **Al Pappagallo.** Almost directly beneath Bologna's famous Asinelli and Garisenda towers, the Pappagallo, facing stiff competition today, retains enough of its reputation and quality cuisine to merit at least one feast, served in a stylish, semiformal atmosphere. Try the first-course specialty, lasagna *del Pappagallo,* made with veal, sirloin of pork, and porcini mushrooms. The *filetto di tacchino al Pappagallo* (turkey stuffed with truffles, ham, and Parmesan cheese) is decadently rich. ✉ *Piazza della Mercanzia 3/c,* ☎ *051/232807. Reservations essential. AE, DC, MC, V. Closed Sun., Dec. 25–Jan. 5, and Aug. 7–Sept. 3.*

$$$ ✕ **I Carracci.** Classic, old-world elegance reaches its artistic height here, at meticulously laid tables under a magnificent ceiling frescoed in the 16th century with scenes of the four seasons. That the restaurant takes its name from the family of artists who decorated it invites a critical eye to its cuisine; some question whether the kitchen is on a par with the decor. Food or no food, this is the most exquisite room in the city. The restaurant closes some Sundays. ✉ *Grand Hotel Baglioni* (☞ *below*), *Via dell'Indipendenza 8 (hotel guests) or Via Manzoni 2,* ☎ *051/225445. Reservations essential. AE, DC, MC, V.*

$$$ ✕ **Luciano.** A changing list of daily specials at this art-deco style restaurant augments what is already one of Bologna's most varied menus. Some of the best offerings are grilled lamb and beef, breast of duck, and excellent guinea fowl. Among the desserts, the *ricottina al forno* (charcoal-flavored oven-baked ricotta) is worth the splurge. ✉ *Via Nazario Sauro 19,* ☎ *051/231249. Reservations essential. AE, DC, MC, V. Closed Wed., Aug., Dec. 23–Jan. 2.*

$$$ ✕ **Nuovi Notai.** If you get the time just right, you'll hear the Angelus ring from the cathedral at this spot, just off beautiful Piazza Maggiore. The building is 14th-century, the decor 19th-century, and the food a rich, complex blend of classic regional specialties and imaginative uses of seasonal ingredients. The *tortino tiepido* (warm tartlet) of porcini mushrooms makes a good starter. ✉ *Via de' Pignattari 1,* ☎ *051/228694. Reservations essential. AE, DC, MC, V. Closed Sun.*

$$ ✕ **Bertino.** Happy, gregarious diners don't seem to mind the crammed quarters in the large, bustling room here. Maybe it's because popularity hasn't spoiled this traditional neighborhood trattoria and its simple, home-style dishes. Tried-and-true highlights are the *paglia e fieno* (yellow and green pasta) with sausage and the choices on the steaming tray of bollito misto. ✉ *Via delle Lame 55,* ☎ *051/522230. AE, DC, MC, V. Closed Sun. and Aug. No dinner Sat. (June–Aug.); no dinner Mon. (Sept.–May).*

$$ ✕ **Da Carlo.** Dining on the medieval terrace in summer is a treat in this attractive restaurant, so be sure to reserve a table outside. The delicate game dishes, such as braised pigeon with artichokes, are favorites. ✉ *Via Marchesana 6,* ☎ *051/233227. Reservations essential. AE, DC, MC, V. Closed Sun., Tues., Jan. 1–22, Aug. 23–Sept. 3.*

$$ ★ ✕ **Da Cesari.** Wine made by the owner's family, famous Bolognese dishes such as *gramigna alla salsiccia* (Q-shaped tubular pasta with a sauce of sausage and tomato) and tortellini *in broda* (in broth), and excellent entrées such as duck with rosemary make this one of the best restaurants in Bologna in its price category. What's more, appetizers—including white truffles with celery and shaved Parmesan and various quiches—invariably amaze. ✉ *Via de' Carbonesi 8,* ☎ *051/237710. Reservations essential. AE, DC, MC, V. Closed Sun. and Aug.*

$$ ★ ✕ **Osteria Du Madon.** Young chef Lorenzo Boni, formerly of San Domenico in Imola(☞ Dining *in* Dozza, *below*) and New York, brought this country *osteria*—its interior undistinguished and clientele academic—to the University district and is now quietly turning out some of the city's most sophisticated food. Dishes such as fresh tortellini in a capon broth are cosmopolitan takes on traditional ingredients, with a light touch and an emphasis on truffles (in season) and mushrooms. Not so light but equally gratifying are the pear mousse with chocolate sauce and the *semifreddo* (soft ice cream) with pine nuts and honey in an apricot sauce (don't miss it if it's available). ✉ *Via San Vitale 73/d,* ☎ *051/226221. AE, DC, MC, V. Closed Sun. and 1st 3 wks in Aug. No lunch Sat.*

$$ ✕ **Rostaria Antico Brunetti.** Housed next door to a Romanesque tower and steps away from Piazza Maggiore, this wood-paneled restaurant was founded in 1873 and is known as Bologna's oldest. Specialties here range from "Mama's tortellini" to veal in a white-wine sauce, but most diners opt for the pizzas or simple pastas with seafood sauces. Dining is on two floors, but even then the restaurant fills quickly. ✉ *Via Caduti di Cefalonia 5,* ☎ *051/234441. AE, DC, MC, V. Closed Wed. and last 3 wks in Aug.*

$$ ★ ✕ **Victoria.** It is not unusual for this unpretentious and charming trattoria-pizzeria off Via dell'Indipendenza to have lines, so reserve ahead. Although locals come for the wide choice of cheap pizzas, the rest of the menu is not to be overlooked, particularly the tortellini *con noci e speck,* a ridiculously rich treatment of Bologna's classic pasta in a sauce of cream, ground walnuts, and cured ham. The back room has a lovely 17th-century painted wooden ceiling. ✉ *Via Augusto Righi 9/c,* ☎ *051/233548. Reservations essential. AE, DC, MC, V. Closed Thurs.*

$ ✕ **Tamburini.** Aptly dubbing itself an *antica salumeria Bolognese,* this gourmet deli–cum–self-service lunch spot sends the smells of all that is good about Bolognese food wafting through the room and out into the streets. Breads, numerous cheeses, Parma and Bologna hams and prosciuttos, roasted peppers, inventive salads, balsamic vinegars, local olive oils, smoked salmon, and fresh pasta are among the delights. ✉ *Via Vaprarie 1,* ☎ *051/234726. AE, MC, V. July–Aug.: closed Thurs., no dinner Sat. Sept.–June: closed Tues., no dinner Wed.*

$$$$ ★ **Corona d'Oro.** A medieval printing house in a former life, this hotel has delightful, lyrical art-nouveau decor in its public space, an atrium, and enough flowers for a wedding. Guest rooms make opulent use of original 15th- and 16th-century decorations, like painted wood ceilings and Gothic-vault windows. The morning English breakfast buffet is worth getting up for. ✉ *Via Oberdan 12, 40126,* ☎ *051/236456,* FAX *051/262679. 35 rooms. Bar, breakfast room, in-room safes, minibars, meeting room. AE, DC, MC, V. Closed 1st 3 wks in Aug.*

$$$$ ★ **Dei Commercianti.** Rooms in this hotel were designed to retain the structural integrity of the 11th-century palace and tower the hotel occupies and are therefore cozy and unique, with original wood beams built into the walls. Tower rooms and suites have balconies with magnificent views of the church; all rooms are stylishly furnished with, among other things, Carrara marble desks custom-built on a 15th-century design. ✉ *Via dei Pignattari 11, 40124,* ☎ *051/233052,* FAX *051/224733. 32 rooms, 2 suites. Bar, breakfast room, in-room safes, minibars. AE, DC, MC, V.*

$$$$ ★ **Grand Hotel Baglioni.** Sixteenth-century paintings and frescoes by the Bolognese Carracci brothers are rarely seen outside a museum or church, but in this 15th-century palazzo they provide the stunning backdrop for the public rooms and restaurant (☞ I Carracci, *above*) of one of Italy's most glamorous hotels. Lady Di slept here, and you'll feel no less royal in a handsome room with antique furniture and brocaded walls. ✉ *Via dell'Indipendenza 8, 40121,* ☎ *051/225445,* FAX *051/234840. 131 rooms. Restaurant, bar, breakfast room, in-room safes, minibars, no-smoking rooms, meeting rooms, parking (fee). AE, DC, MC, V.*

$$$ **Orologio.** Under the same management as the Corona d'Oro and the Dei Commercianti (☞ *above*), the Orologio is in a quiet pedestrian zone off Piazza Grande and is in an ideal sightseeing location. The hotel occupies a palazzo that was originally a public building, but the interior achieves a contemporary effect. Top-floor rooms have good views of Bologna's skyline. ✉ *Via IV Novembre 10, 40123,* ☎ *051/231253,* FAX *051/260552. 32 rooms. Minibars. AE, DC, MC, V.*

$$ **Accademia.** This small hotel is right in the middle of the university quarter, a comfortable base for exploring the area. The rooms are adequate, the staff friendly. ✉ *Via delle Belle Arti 6, 40126,* ☎ FAX *051/232318. 28 rooms. Bar. No credit cards.*

$$ **San Vitale.** Modern furnishings and a garden distinguish this modest hostelry, a five-minute walk from the center of town. The service is courteous, and rooms are clean and bright. Rates fall at the bottom end of the price category. ✉ *Via San Vitale 94, 40125,* ☎ *051/225966,* FAX *051/239396. 17 rooms. No credit cards.*

Nightlife and the Arts

Ballet

Ballet can be enjoyed at the historic **Arena del Sole** (✉ Via Indipendenza 44, ☎ 051/270790).

Festival

The **Festa di San Petronio,** held each year the during the first weekend in October, features bands, fireworks, and free *mortadella di bologna* in Piazza Maggiore.

Music

The city hosts a wide selection of orchestral and chamber music concerts. The 18th-century **Teatro Comunale** (✉ Largo Respighi 1, ☎ 051/529999) presents concerts by Italian and international orchestras throughout the year. Check concert schedules for the **Sala Bossi** (✉

Piazza Rossini 2, ☎ 051/233975) and the **Sala Mozart** in the Accademia Filarmonica (✉ Via Guerazzi 13, ☎ 051/222997), the principal music school of the city.

Opera

The acclaimed opera performances in Bologna dominate the **Teatro Comunale** (☞ *above*) in the winter season. All events sell out quickly, so be sure to reserve seats well in advance.

Theater

The winter season at the **Europa Auditorium** (✉ Piazza Costituzione, ☎ 051/372540) features shows from comedy to cabaret, and an occasional pop concert thrown in for good measure. A wide range of theatrical productions are staged throughout the winter at the **Teatro Duse** (✉ Via Cartoleria 42, ☎ 051/231836). Theater productions are staged at the **Arena del Sole** (☞ *above*). **Teatro delle Moline** (✉ Via delle Moline 1, ☎ 051/235288) is just one of the many small venues where contemporary drama, dance, and comedy productions are performed. Children learning Italian may enjoy the kids' productions at the **Teatro Testoni** (✉ Via Matteotti 16, ☎ 051/377968).

Outdoor Activities and Sports

Swimming

The public **indoor swimming pool** (✉ Via Costa 174, ☎ 051/519107) is open June–September, Wednesday and Monday 10:30–7 and Tuesday 2–7, and October–May, weekdays noon–3, Saturday 10:30–1:30, and Sunday 9:30–12:30; admission is 9,000 lire.

RIMINI, RAVENNA, AND FERRARA

Byzantine Splendors and Simple Pleasures

After taking the Via Emilia (S9) to Dozza, Faenza, and Savignano, the road leads to the next three important destinations: Rimini, Ravenna, and Ferrara, hooking back northwest along the S16.

Dozza

15 *31 km (19 mi) southeast of Bologna.*

As you head southeast out of Bologna, the first port of call is the little hamlet of Dozza, just off the Via Emilia (S9). It is a small village on a hill crowned with a splendid restored medieval castle, the **Rocca di Dozza.** Artists from all over the world flock to the town in September of odd years to take part in the mural competition that has left virtually every square foot of the town covered with colorful scenes executed with varying degrees of skill. The castle is home to the **Enoteca Regionale,** the wine "library" for the region. Here you can sample the different vintages from the surrounding countryside, particularly Dozza's own Albana, a white wine that comes dry or sweet. ☎ *0542/678240 Rocca di Dozza; 0542/678089 Enoteca Regionale.* 🎫 *Rocca di Dozza 6,000 lire.* ⏲ *Apr.–Sept., Tues.–Sat. 10–noon and 3–6, Sun. 10–noon and 3–7; Oct.–Mar., Tues.–Sat. 10–noon and 2–5, Sun. 10–noon and 2–6.*

Dining

$$$$ ★ ✕ **San Domenico.** Leading food critics still count San Domenico among Italy's top 10 restaurants, and so dedicated gourmands will want to make the trip to the luxe town of Imola (about 15 km/9 mi east). Majestic decor reflects the truly royal prices you'll pay for homemade pâté with white truffles, a delicious breast of duck in a sauce of black olives,

and hand-stuffed tortellini. With more than 3,000 wines, the wine list is touted as the second most extensive in Europe, after the Tour d'Argent in Paris. Make reservations well in advance. ✉ *Via Sacchi 1, Imola,* ☎ *0542/29000. Reservations essential. AE, DC, MC, V. Closed Mon. No dinner Sun.*

Faenza

16 *23 km (14 mi) southeast of Dozza, 49 km (30 mi) southeast of Bologna.*

The renowned style of pottery called faience has been produced in Faenza, on the Via Emilia, since the 12th century. In the central **Piazza del Popolo** are dozens of shops selling the native wares. Faenza is unsurprisingly home to the **Museo delle Ceramiche** (Museum of Ceramics), one of the largest of its kind in the world, covering the potter's art in all phases of history the world over. ✉ *Viale Baccarini 19,* ☎ *0546/21240.* *10,000 lire.* ⏲ *Apr.–Oct., Tues.–Sat. 9–7, Sun. 9:30–1; Nov.–Mar., Tues.–Fri. 9–1:30, Sat. 9–1:30 and 3–6, Sun. 9:30–1.*

OFF THE BEATEN PATH

PREDAPPIO – From Faenza continue on S9 to the town of Forlì, 14 km (9 mi) southeast, and turn off onto the rural Route 9ter (in Italian travel parlance, the abbreviation "ter" means a third, variant highway). This leads you through hilly country to the small town of Predappio, the birthplace and final resting place of Benito Mussolini. The cemetery on the outskirts of town contains the crypt of the Mussolini family, with the former dictator himself in the place of honor. A spotlighted bust glowers at visitors, and glass cases contain some of his decorations and medals. It is a chilling place and has become the object of pilgrimage for followers of fascism, young and old, who write repugnant political slogans in the visitors' book. ✉ *Cimitero Municipale.* ⏲ *Daily 8 am–sunset.*

SAVIGNANO – On S9 beyond Forlì, you pass through the modern towns of Forlimpopoli, Cesena, and Savignano. At this last town, there is a reminder that no matter how new the towns might look, you are still traveling in a place of great history—just outside the town is a small stream, the Rubicone. Cross it and you, too, have crossed the Rubicon, the river made famous by Julius Caesar when, in 49 BC, he defied the Senate of Rome by bringing his army across the river and plunging the country into civil war.

Rimini

17 *58 km (36 mi) southeast of Faenza, 121 km (76 mi) southeast of Bologna.*

Rimini is the principal summer resort on the Adriatic Coast and one of the most popular holiday destinations in Italy. Every summer, beginning in June, the city is flooded with vacationers, not just from Italy, but from France, Austria, Germany, Scandinavia, and Great Britain, as well. Be warned: the city is given over almost exclusively to tourism, with hundreds of hotels, grand and modest, and restaurants catering to virtually every national palate: you are just as likely to find a *bierkeller* (beer cellar) or an English tea shop as you are an Italian restaurant. The waterfront is lined with beach clubs that rent deck chairs and umbrellas by the day, week, month, or the entire season. Hotels along the beachfront have staked out their own private turf, so the chance of swimming without having to pay for privilege is had only by going to one of the public beaches. Swimming on public beaches is possible, but prepare for sand that packs sunbathers in like sardines. Prepare also for murky seawater; tourists come to Rimini for the company, not an idyllic setting. In the off-season (October–March), Rimini is a ghost town. Some hotels and restaurants are open, but the majority are closed tight, hibernating until the return of the spendthrifty tourists. Summers are so crowded here that it is most unwise to go to Rimini without confirmed hotel reservations.

The **new town** has just about swallowed the **old town,** but there is evidence here and there of Rimini's long and turbulent history. Rimini stands at the junction of two great Roman consular roads: the Via Emilia and the Via Flaminia. In addition, in Roman times, it was an important port, making it a strategic and commercial center. From the 13th century onward, the city was controlled by the Malatesta family, an unpredictable group capable of grand gestures and savage deeds. The famous lovers immortalized in Dante's *Inferno,* Paolo and Francesca, were Malatestas. Paolo was the brother of Gianciotto Malatesta (died 1304); Francesca Polenta (died 1283 or 1284) was Gianciotto's wife. Gianciotto murdered them both for having betrayed him. Sigismondo Malatesta (1417–68), lord of the city in the middle of the 15th century, was considered a learned man of great wit and culture. He also banished his first wife, strangled his second, and poisoned his third. He lived with his beautiful mistress, Isotta, until her death. He was so grief stricken that he raised a magnificent monument in her honor, the ★ **Tempio Malatestiano,** the principal sight in the town.

Despite the irregular—from the church's point of view—nature of Sigismondo's relationship with Isotta, Sigismondo's memorial to his great love is today the cathedral of Rimini. The building was in fact originally a Franciscan church before Sigismondo took it over to make it into a monument to his beloved. The Renaissance facade by Leon Battista Alberti (1404–72) is in the shape of a Roman triumphal arch and is considered to be one of Alberti's masterpieces.

The interior is light and spacious and contains the tombs of both the lovers. The intertwined *I,* for Isotta, and *S,* for Sigismondo, are placed everywhere and look rather like dollar signs. The carvings of elephants and roses recall the coat of arms of the Malatesta family. Sigismondo's tomb, on the right of the entrance door, is some distance from Isotta's in the second chapel on the right. (Her tomb is on the left wall of the chapel; the original inscription in marble had a pagan twist and was covered with another in bronze.) To the right of the entrance, in what is now the Tempio's book and gift shop, is a wonderful but badly damaged fresco by Piero della Francesca (1420–92) showing Sigismondo paying homage to his patron saint. When the shop is closed, one of the cathedral's staff will unlock the room containing the fresco. Over the main altar of the church is a crucifix attributed to Giotto (1266–1337); the painted feet are all but worn off from years when it was hung low enough for curious visitors to touch. ✉ *Via Quattro Novembre 35,* ☎ *0541/51130.* ⏲ *Daily 9–1 and 3:30–6.*

Rimini's oldest monument is the **Arco d'Augusto** (Arch of Augustus), now stranded in the middle of a square just inside the city ramparts. It was erected in 27 BC, making it the oldest Roman arch in existence, and it marks the meeting of the Via Emilia and the Via Flaminia. To reach the Arch of Augustus from the Tempio Malatestiano, walk up Via Quattro Novembre to Piazza Tre Martiri (where, legend says, the mule carrying Saint Anthony suddenly stopped and knelt in honor of the Holy Sacrament that was being carried past at the time) and turn left onto Corso d'Augusto. ✉ *Largo Giulio Cesare.*

Dining and Lodging

$$ ✕ **Picnic.** Take a break from Rimini's seaside crowds in the leafy garden of this casual restaurant in the city center, near Tempio Malatestiano. The menu is varied, with choices such as *pappardelle al sugo di carciofi* (pasta with artichoke sauce), *faraona ripiena alla castagna* (guinea hen with chestnut stuffing), or even just a simple pizza. ✉ *Via Tempio Malatestiano 30,* ☎ *0541/21916. AE, DC, MC, V. Closed Mon. Sept.–June.*

$$ ★ ✕ **Taverna degli Artisti.** The row of stylish glass-and-wood doors that enclose this restaurant give it the air of a French bistro, but once in the door, the atmosphere is abundantly Italian. A local clientele of resort types and expatriates chat table-to-table over such specialties as *crudaiola* (spicy spaghetti with tomatoes, basil, tuna, olives, and anchovies) or the Chianina steaks. An enormous wood oven and marble pizza-making counter provide a centerpiece to the sunny dining room. ✉ *Viale Vespucci 1,* ☎ *0541/28519. AE, DC, MC, V.*

$$ ★ ✕ **Zio.** Nothing but seafood is served here, and all of it is good value for the money. Two small rooms are unpretentiously furnished, one with antiques. Recommended treats are the *brodetto dell'Adriatica* (deliciously tangy shellfish broth), tortellini *al salmone* (in a salmon sauce), and simple grilled sole. ✉ *Vicolo Santa Chiara 16,* ☎ *0541/786160. Reservations essential. AE, DC, MC, V. Closed Wed. and mid-July–mid-Aug.*

$$$$ ★ 🏨 **Grand Hotel.** This fin de siècle extravaganza, made famous by Fellini in his *Amarcord,* is grander than ever. The hyper-luxe atmosphere begged by enormous crystal chandeliers in the lobby and inlaid wood in the rooms seems playful, rather than formal; with bright pink hallways, potted trees, and spotless adjacent beach, the Grand is a beach resort above all else. While entourages and steamer trunks will never be out of place here, neither would it be any surprise to see a greyhound loping through the restaurant on her way to the pool. ✉ *Parco Federico Fellini, 47900,* ☎ *0541/56000,* FAX *0541/56866. 117 rooms, 8 suites. 2 restaurants, 2 bars, minibars, 2 pools, beauty salon, sauna, tennis court, health club, beach, nightclub, meeting rooms. AE, DC, MC, V.*

$$$ 🏨 **Club House Hotel.** The Club House is a bit of a double-edged sword: for some, the suburban office building architecture may be off-putting; however, thanks to the design, all rooms have balconies, an asset right on the sea. Likewise with the hotel's location: for some, right on the main commercial strip and next door to McDonald's is a good thing. The hotel's rooms and facilities invite less debate: lovely, clean, airy rooms with green-and-white striped ticking and across-the-street private beach access will spell summer vacation to all. ✉ *Viale Vespucci 52, 47900,* ☎ *0541/391460,* FAX *0541/391442. 28 rooms. Restaurant, bar, minibars, pool, beach. AE, DC, MC, V.*

$ 🏨 **Annarita.** Set back on a residential road leading off the main Viale Vespucci, this hotel is small but comfortable, with a loyal clientele (availability may consequently be limited). Facilities are rudimentary, rooms are basic (though all have TVs and phones), but the main benefits here are its proximity to the beach promenade and the friendly price. ✉ *Viale Misurata 24, 47900,* ☎ *0541/391044. 14 rooms. Restaurant, bar. No credit cards.*

En Route There are two routes from Rimini to Ravenna. The coast road, S16, clings to the shoreline as far as Cervia before edging inland. Although its distance, 52 km (32 mi), is not great, the scenic route is slower by nature. The coast north of Rimini is lined with dozens of small resort towns, only one having any charm, the seaport of Cesenatico; the others are mini-Riminis, and during summer the narrow road is hopelessly clogged with traffic. A faster route is to head inland on A14 and then turn off onto the inland S71, which leads directly into Ravenna; the distance is 64 km (39 mi).

Ravenna

18 *52 km (32 mi) northwest of Rimini, 76 km (47½ mi) east of Bologna.*

Ravenna is a small, quiet city of brick palaces and cobbled streets, whose magnificent monuments are the only indicators of its storied past. The high point in Ravenna's history was 1,500 long years ago, when the city became the capital of the Roman Empire. The honor was short-lived—the city was taken by the barbarian Ostrogoths in the 5th century; in the 6th century it was conquered by the Byzantines, who ruled the city from Constantinople.

Because Ravenna spent much of its history looking to the East, its greatest art treasures show much Byzantine influence: above all, Ravenna is a city of mosaics, the finest in Western art. A single combination 10,000-lire ticket (available at ticket offices of all included sights) will admit you to six of Ravenna's most important monuments: the Tomba di Galla Placidia, the Basilica di San Vitale, the Battistero Neoniano, and Sant'Apollinare Nuovo (☞ *below*), as well as the church of Spirito Santo and the Museo Arcivescovile e Cappella Sant'Andrea.

★ The **Tomba di Galla Placidia and the Basilica di San Vitale** are decorated with the best-known, and most elaborate, mosaics in the city. The little tomb and the great church stand side by side, but the tomb predates the church by at least a hundred years. Galla Placidia was the sister of the last emperor of Rome, Honorius, the man who moved the imperial capital to Ravenna in AD 402. She is said to have been beautiful and strong willed, and to have taken an active part in the governing of the crumbling empire. One of the most active Christians of her day, she endowed churches and supported priests and their congregations throughout the realm. This tomb, constructed in the mid-5th century, is her memorial.

Outside, the tomb is a small, unassuming building of red brick, whose seeming poverty of charm only serves to enhance the richness of the interior mosaics, in deep midnight blue and glittering gold. The tiny, low central dome is decorated with symbols of Christ and the evangelists, and over the door is a depiction of the Good Shepherd. Eight of the Apostles are represented in groups of two on the four inner walls of the dome; the other four appear singly on the walls of the two transepts. Notice the small doves at their feet, drinking from the water of faith. Also in the tiny transepts are some delightful pairs of deer (which represent souls), drinking from the fountain of resurrection. There are three sarcophagi in the tomb, and, it is thought, not one contains the remains of Galla Placidia. She died in Rome in AD 450, and there is no record of her body having been transported back to the place where she wished to lie.

The mosaics of the Galla Placidia tomb are simple works that do not yet show the full impact of Byzantine influence. Quite the opposite is the case of the mosaics in the church of San Vitale, next door. The octagonal church was built in AD 547, after the Byzantines conquered the city, and its interior style shows a strong Byzantine influence. In the area behind the altar are the most famous works in the church, accurate portraits of the emperor of the East, Justinian, attended by his court and the bishop of Ravenna, Maximian. Facing him, across the chancel, is the emperor's wife, Theodora, with her entourage, holding a chalice containing the communion wine. The elaborate headdresses and heavy cloaks of the emperor and empress convey a marvelous sense of the grandeur of the imperial court, and of the mastery of the artisans responsible for the depictions. Presiding over the royal couple from the apse is Christ the King with San Vitale (the saint for whom the church was named) and the founder of the church, Bishop Ecclesio, who holds a model of the building. Unfortunately, these mosaics are currently undergoing a lengthy restoration expected to continue until the year 2000, and will be covered for most of the time until then. ✉ *Via San Vitale off Via Salara, near Piazza del Popolo,* ☎ *0544/216292.* 💳 *6,000 lire tomb and basilica, 5,000 lire for ticket holders for adjacent Museo Nazionale, 10,000 combination ticket (☞ below).* ⏲ *July–Aug., daily 9–7; Apr.–June, daily 9–6; Sept.–Mar., daily 9–4:30.*

Next to the Church of San Vitale, the **Museo Nazionale** of Ravenna contains artifacts of ancient Rome, Byzantine fabrics and carvings, and other pieces of early Christian art. The collection is housed in a former monastery but is well displayed and artfully lit. ✉ *Piazza Fiandrini,* ☎ *0544/34424.* 💳 *8,000 lire, 10,000 lire combination ticket.* ⏲ *Tues.–Sat. 8:30–7, Sun. 8:30–10. Ticket office closes ½ hr before museum.*

Next door to Ravenna's 18th-century cathedral, the **Battistero Neoniano** is one of the town's most important mosaic sights. In keeping with the purpose of the building, the great mosaic in the dome shows the baptism of Christ, and beneath that scene are the apostles. The lowest band of mosaics contains Christian symbols, the Throne of God and the Cross. ✉ *Via Battistero,* ☎ *0544/216292.* 💳 *5,000 lire (includes Museo Arcivescovile and Cappella Sant'Andrea), 10,000 lire combination ticket.* ⏲ *Apr.–Sept., daily 9:30–7; Oct.–Mar., daily 9:30–4:30.*

The **Mausoleo di Dante** (tomb of Dante) is in a small neoclassic building next door to the large church of St. Francis. Exiled from his native Florence, the great poet, author of *The Divine Comedy,* died here in 1321. The Florentines have been trying to reclaim their famous son for hundreds of years, but the Ravennans refuse to give him up, arguing that Florence did not welcome Dante in life, so it doesn't deserve him in death. In the church courtyard next door, note the site that served as temporary, less-grand quarters for the poet's distinguished bones: a plaque identifies the mound of earth under which the Franciscan brothers put Dante's remains for safekeeping from March 1944 to December 1945. A small **museum** is also on the site. ✉ *Via Dante Alighieri 9,* ☎ *0544/30252.* 💳 *Tomb free; museum 5,000 lire (free on Sun. and holidays); 10,000 lire combination ticket.* ⏲ *Tomb Apr.–Sept., daily 9–7; Oct.–Mar., daily 9–noon and 2–5. Museum Apr.–Sept., Tues.–Sun. 9–noon and 3:30–6; Oct.–Mar., Tues.–Sun. 9–noon.*

The last great mosaic display in the city proper is the church of **Sant'Apollinare Nuovo.** Since the left side of the church was reserved for women, it is only fitting that the mosaic decoration on that side is a scene of 22 virgins offering crowns to the Virgin Mary. On the right wall are 26 men carrying the crowns of martyrdom. They are approaching Christ, who is surrounded by angels. The mosaics in Sant'Apollinare Nuovo date from the early 6th century and are slightly older than the works in San Vitale. ✉ *Via Roma, at intersection of Via Guaccimanni,* ☎ *0544/216292.* 💳 *5,000 lire (includes church of Spirito Santo), 10,000 lire combination ticket.* ⏲ *July–Aug., daily 9–5:30; Sept.–June, daily 9:30–12 and 2–4:30.*

OFF THE BEATEN PATH

SANT'APOLLINARE IN CLASSE – This church, about 5 km (3 mi) southeast of Ravenna, is landlocked now but when it was built it stood in the center of the busy shipping port of Classis. The arch above and the area around the high altar are rich in mosaics. Those on the arch, older than those behind it, are considered superior to the rest. They show Christ in judgment and the 12 lambs of Christianity leaving the cities of Jerusalem and Bethlehem. In the apse is the figure of Sant'Apollinare himself, a bishop of Ravenna, and above him is a magnificent Transfiguration decorated with flowers, trees, and little birds. ✉ *Classe,* ☎ *0544/527004.* 🎫 *4,000 lire.* ⏲ *Apr.–Sept., daily 9–7; Oct.–Mar., daily 9–6.*

Dining and Lodging

$$$ ✕ **Bella Venezia.** Graceful low archways lead into this attractive restaurant's two small dining rooms. Try the owner's special risotto *Bazzani* (with butter, Parmesan, cured ham, mushrooms, and peas) and, for the entrée, *bistecca all'ortolana* (veal in cream sauce with cured ham and zucchini). A good-value tourist menu is available. ✉ *Via IV Novembre 16,* ☎ *0544/212746. Reservations essential weekends. AE, DC, MC, V. Closed Sun. and Dec. 25–Jan. 21.*

$–$$ ✕ **Ca' de Ven.** A vaulted wine cellar in the heart of the old city, the Ca' de Ven is great for a hearty lunch or dinner. You sit at long tables with the other diners and feast on platters of delicious cold cuts; *piadine* (griddle breads); and cold, heady white wine. If you're here in chilly weather, try the *pasta e fagioli* (pasta and bean soup). ✉ *Via C. Ricci 24,* ☎ *0544/30163. AE, DC, MC, V. Closed Mon., Jan. 23–Feb. 10, and 1st wk of June.*

$$$ 🏨 **Hotel Bisanzio.** Just steps from San Vitale and the Tomb of Galla Placidia, this Best Western hotel is the most convenient lodging for mosaic enthusiasts. Rooms are comfortable and modern, and the lobby's Florentine lamps add a touch of style. Ask for a room on the top floor and you may get a view of the basilica. ✉ *Via Salara 30, 48100,* ☎ *0544/217111,* FAX *0544/32539. 38 rooms. 2 bars, breakfast room, in-room safes, minibars, meeting rooms. AE, DC, MC, V.*

$$ 🏨 **Hotel Centrale Byron.** In the heart of Ravenna's old town, this is an old-fashioned, well-managed hotel, its rooms spotless if uninspiring. Because it's in a pedestrian zone, tranquility is assured, though you will have to leave your car in one of the nearby garages. ✉ *Via IV Novembre 14, 48100,* ☎ *0544/33479,* FAX *0544/34114. 54 rooms. Bar, in-room safes, minibars. AE, DC, MC, V. Closed Dec. 20–Jan. 25.*

$ 🏨 **Hotel Ravenna.** A functional stopover near the train station but still only a few minutes' walk from the center of town, this modern hotel offers smallish rooms with TVs and telephones. Two rooms are equipped for people with disabilities. ✉ *Viale Maroncelli 12, 48100,* ☎ *0544/212204,* FAX *0544/212077. 25 rooms. Bar, parking (fee). MC, V.*

Ferrara

19 *74 km (46 mi) northwest of Ravenna, 47 km (29 mi) northeast of Bologna.*

Ferrara is a city of turrets, towers, and marvelous pleasure palaces, all presided over by a mighty castle protected by a deep moat. Although the site was settled before Christ and was once ruled by Ravenna, the history of Ferrara begins in the 13th century, with the coming of the Este family. From 1259 until 1598 the dukes of the Este family reigned in Ferrara, and in those 3½ centuries the city was stamped indelibly with their mark.

It was during the Renaissance that the court of the Este came into full flower. In keeping with their time, the dukes could be politically ruthless—brother killed brother, son fought father—but they were avid scholars and enthusiastic patrons of the arts. The cultivated Duke Nicolò III (1384–1441) murdered his wife and her lover. The greatest of all the dukes, Ercole I (1433–1505), tried to poison the nephew who challenged his power, and when that didn't work, Ercole I beheaded him, but it is to this pitiless man that Ferrara owes its great beauty. One of the most celebrated villains in Italian history, Lucrezia Borgia, married into the Este family—and unlike that of her in-laws, it seems that her infamous reputation is not at all deserved. Beloved by the Ferrarese people and mourned greatly when she died, she is buried in the church of Corpus Domini in the city.

★ Naturally enough, the building that was the seat of Este power dominates the town: it is the massive **Castello Estense,** placed square in the center of the city in Piazza Castello. It is a suitable symbol for the Este family: cold and menacing on the outside, lavishly decorated within. The public rooms are grand, but deep in the bowels of the fortress are chilling dungeons where enemies of the state were held in wretched conditions—a function these quarters served as recently as 1943, when antifascist prisoners were detained there.

The castle was established as a fortress in 1385, but work on its luxurious ducal quarters continued into the 16th century. Representative of the Este grandeur are the **Sala dei Giochi** (the Games Room), extravagantly painted with pagan athletic scenes, and the **Sala dell'Aurora,** decorated to show the times of the day. From the terraces of the castle and from the hanging garden, reserved for the private use of the duchesses, are fine views of the town and surrounding countryside. ✉ *Piazza Castello,* ☎ *0532/299233.* 🎫 *8,000 lire.* ⏲ *Tues.–Sun. 9:30–5.*

A few steps from the castle is the magnificent Gothic **Duomo,** with its facade of three tiers of arches and beautiful carvings over the central door. It was begun in 1135 and took more than a hundred years to complete. The interior was completely remodeled in the 17th century, and very little of the original decoration remains in place, much of it residing instead in the **cathedral museum** above the church (entrance inside the church). Displayed here are some of the lifelike carvings taken from the cathedral doors, dating from the 13th century and showing the months of the year. Also in the museum are a statue of the Madonna by the Sienese master Jacopo della Quercia (1374–1438) and two masterpieces by the Ferrarese painter Cosimo Tura, an *Annunciation* and *St. George Slaying the Dragon.* ✉ *Piazza Cattedrale,* ☎ *0532/207449.* ⏲ *Duomo: Mon.–Sat. 8–noon and 3–6:30, Sun. 8–1 and 3:30–7:30. Museum: Tues.–Sat. 10–noon and 3–5, Sun. 10–noon and 3:30–6.* 🎫 *Museum free, but donation appreciated.*

The area behind the Duomo, the southern part of the city stretching between the Corso Giovecca and the ramparts of the city above the river, is the oldest and most characteristic part of Ferrara. In this part of the old town various members of the Este family built themselves pleasure palaces, the most famous of which is the **Palazzo Schifanoia** (*schifanoia* means carefree, or literally, "fleeing boredom"). Begun in the 14th century, the palace was remodeled in 1466 and is the first Renaissance palazzo in the city. The interior is lavishly decorated, particularly the **Salone dei Mesi,** with an extravagant series of frescoes showing the months of the year and their mythological attributes. The **Museo Civico** has a collection of coins, statuary, and paintings. ✉ *Via Scandiana 23,* ☎ *0532/64178.* 🎫 *8,000 lire, free 2nd Mon. of each month, 10,000 lire in combination with Palazzina Marfisa d'Este.* ⏲ *Daily 9–7.*

The grand but unfinished courtyard is the most interesting part of the luxurious **Palazzo di Ludovico il Moro,** a magnificent 15th-century palace built for Ludovico Sforza, husband of Beatrice d'Este. The palazzo also houses the region's **Museo Archeologico,** a repository of the relics of early man, the Etruscans, and Romans found in the country surrounding the city. ✉ *Near the Palazzo Schifanoia* (☞ *above*), ☎ *0532/66299.* 🎫 *8,000 lire.* ⏲ *Tues.–Fri. 9–2, weekends 9–2.*

The courtyard of the peaceful palace called the **Palazzo del Paradiso** contains the tomb of the great writer Ariosto (1474–1533), author of the most popular work of literature of the Renaissance, the poem "Orlando Furioso." The building now houses the city library. ✉ *Via Scienze,* ☎ *0532/206977.* *Free.* ⏲ *Weekdays 9–7, Sat. 9* AM*–10:30* PM.

The Estes were patrons of Ariosto, and he passed a good deal of his life in Ferrara. The interior of **Casa Ariosto** (✉ Via Ariosto 67) has been converted into an office building and is not open to the public. One of the best preserved of the Renaissance palaces scattered along Ferrara's old streets is the charming **Casa Romei.** Downstairs are rooms with 15th-century frescoes and several sculptures collected from destroyed churches. The house lies not far from the Palazzo del Paradiso, in the area behind Ferrara's castello. ✉ *Via Savonarola 30,* ☎ *0532/240341.* *4,000 lire.* ⏲ *Tues.–Sun. 8:30–2 (schedule varies with exhibits).*

On the busy Corso Giovecca is the **Palazzina di Marfisa d'Este,** a grandiose 16th-century home that belonged to Marfisa d'Este, a great patron of the arts. The house has painted ceilings, fine 16th-century furniture, and a garden containing a grotto and an outdoor theater. ✉ *Corso Giovecca 170,* ☎ *0532/207450.* *3,000 lire, free 2nd Mon. of month, 10,000 lire in combination with Palazzo Schifanoia* (*☞ above*). ⏲ *Daily 9:30–1 and 3–6.*

The collection of ornate religious objects in the **Museo Ebraico** (Jewish Museum) bears witness to the long and dramatic history of the city's Jewish community. This history had its high points—Ercole I d'Este's (1433–1505) 1492 invitation to Sephardic Jews exiled from Spain to come settle in Ferrara—and its lows, notably the papal government's 1624 closure of the Ghetto, which was reopened only with the advent of a united Italy in 1859. The triangular warren of narrow, cobbled streets that made up the ghetto originally extended as far as Corso Giovecca (from Corso Giudecca, or Ghetto Street); with the closure, the neighborhood was restricted to the area between Via Scienze, Via Contrari, and Via di San Romano. The museum, in the center of the ghetto, is also home to Ferrara's synagogue. ✉ *Via Mazzini 95,* ☎ *0532/210228.* *7,000 lire.* ⏲ *Hour-long guided tours only, Sun.–Thurs. at 10, 11, and 12.*

The **Palazzo dei Diamanti** (Palace of Diamonds) is so called for the 12,600 blocks of diamond-shape stone that stud the facade. The palace was built in the 15th and 16th centuries and today contains an extensive art gallery devoted primarily to the painters of Ferrara. ✉ *Corso Ercole I d'Este 21,* ☎ *0532/209988.* *10,000 lire.* ⏲ *Tues.–Sat. 9–2, Sun. 9–1.*

Dining and Lodging

$$$ ✕ **La Provvidenza.** One of the best-known restaurants in Ferrara, Provvidenza is a pleasant country-style inn with a lovely garden for summertime alfresco dining. The local specialties—fish grilled over charcoal (Thursday and Friday) and the bollito misto (weekends in winter)—are the best. ✉ *Corso Ercole d'Este 92,* ☎ *0532/205187. Reservations essential. AE, DC, MC, V. Closed Mon. and 10 days in mid-Aug.*

$$$ ★ ✕ **Trattoria La Romantica.** The former stables of a 17th-century merchant's house have been transformed into this casually elegant, welcoming restaurant that is the unanimous choice among well-fed locals. While the decor (warm light and wood-beam ceilings marred by incongruous prints and a piano) seems to be in perpetual transition, the haute-rustic food is fully realized: Ferrarese specialties like *cappellacci di zucca* in a cream-tomato-walnut-Parmesan sauce are served side by side with Texan beef and French oysters. Reservations are recommended. ✉ *Via Ripagrande 36,* ☎ *0532/765975. AE, DC, MC, V. Closed Wed., Jan. 7–17, and July 1–17.*

$–$$ ✕ **Guido Ristorante.** Down a long cobbled street in an atmospheric part of the old Jewish ghetto, this restaurant is a leading choice of locals. The menu is made up of Ferrarese specialties, plus some inventive dishes you won't find anywhere else. To wit: gnocchi with black olives and zucchini in curry sauce. ✉ *Via Vignatagliata 61,* ☎ *0532/761052. Reservations essential. AE, DC, MC, V. Closed Thurs. and June 20–mid-July.*

$$$$ **Duchessa Isabella.** Live out your Marie Antoinette fantasies, if you have them, at this converted 16th-century mansion near Piazza Ariostea. The exceptionally splendid dining rooms and entryway are sumptuously decorated in authentic style; the lacy, satiny rooms, however, teeter on the border between royal and ridiculous. Some may find the formality wearying and the tone somewhat bogus; others will find a stay here marvelous. A horse and carriage are available. ✉ *Via Palestro 70, 44100,* ☎ *0532/202121,* FAX *0532/202638. 22 rooms, 6 suites. Restaurant, bar, in-room safes, minibars, meeting rooms. AE, MC, V.*

$$$ ★ **Hotel Ripagrande.** The courtyards, vaulted brick lobby, and breakfast room of this 15th-century noble palazzo retain much of their lordly pre-Renaissance flavor, but rooms are decidedly more down-to-earth. Standard doubles as well as the many bi- and tri-level suites have faux-Persian rugs, tapestries, and cozy period-style furniture; top-floor rooms and suites with terraces are like a Colorado ski lodge. Unlike in many hotels, the Ripagrande's suites are a good deal and remain in this price category. ✉ *Via Ripagrande 21, 44100,* ☎ *0532/765250,* FAX *0532/764377. 20 rooms, 20 suites. Restaurant, bar, breakfast room, in-room safes, minibars, meeting rooms. AE, DC, MC, V.*

$$ **Locanda Borgonuovo.** This lovely B&B is set in a 17th-century monastery on a quiet but central pedestrian-only street, and since then has been booking up months in advance, partly due to the musicians and actors from the local theater who make this their home away from home. Individually named rooms are furnished with antiques, and one room has its own kitchen available for longer stays. Summer breakfasts are taken in the leafy courtyard. ✉ *Via Cairoli 29, 44100,* ☎ *0532/211100,* FAX *0532/248000. 4 rooms. Breakfast room, in-room safes, minibars, library. AE, MC, V.*

$–$$ **Hotel San Paolo.** On the edge of the old city, San Paolo is the best inexpensive choice in town. The 10-minute walk from the heart of Ferrara's medieval quarter is effortless in a town so amenable to strolling, and there are some good restaurants in the vicinity. There are 15 brand-new rooms in an annex—try for one of those. ✉ *Via Baluardi 9, 44100,* ☎ *0532/762040,* FAX *0532/762040. 47 rooms. AE, DC, MC, V.*

EMILIA-ROMAGNA A TO Z

Arriving and Departing

By Bus

Thanks to the autostrada bisecting the region and Emilia-Romagnan efficiency, bus travel in the region is easy—although the train, blessed with the same benefits but no traffic, is still easier. In Bologna, **ATC** (☎ 051/290290) buses leave from the terminal in Piazza XX Settembre, on the left from the train station. In Modena, contact **ATCM** (Via Fabriani, ☎ 059/218226); Ferrara, **ACFT** (☎ 0532/599492), near the train station; and Rimini, **TRAM** (☎ 0541/390444), on Via Roma.

By Car

Bologna is on the autostrada network, allowing direct and quick driving from cities.

By Plane

Bologna is an important business and convention center and is therefore served by air routes that link it with other Italian cities, as well as by direct flights to European capitals. The airport, **Guglielmo Marconi** (☒ Viale dell'Aeroporto, ☎ 051/6479615) is 10 km (6 mi) northwest of town.

BETWEEN THE AIRPORT AND DOWNTOWN

Half-hourly bus service (6,000 lire) connects Guglielmo Marconi with a downtown air terminal at Bologna's central train station.

By Train

Bologna is an important rail hub for the entire northern part of Italy and has frequent, fast train service to Rome, Milan, Florence, and Venice. For information about train departures, call (☎ 1478/88088) (toll-free).

Getting Around

By Bus

Private bus service (☞ Arriving and Departing, By Bus, *above*) links all the cities of Emilia-Romagna, with Bologna being the central hub. The ***autostazione*** (bus terminal, ☒ In Piazza XX Settembre, ☎ 051/290290 information), is at the top of Via dell'Indipendenza. City-run bus routes connect major towns with smaller villages and hamlets in the district, but routes are roundabout, and schedules vary from place to place.

By Car

The Via Emilia (**S9**) runs through the heart of the region. It is a straight, low-lying modern road, the length of which can be traveled in a few hours. Ferrara and Ravenna are joined to it by good modern highways. Although less scenic, the **A14** autostrada, which runs parallel to the S9, will get you where you're going even more quickly.

By Train

The railway follows the Via Emilia (S9), and all the cities covered can be reached by train. Call (☎ 147/888088) toll-free for train information.

Contacts and Resources

Car Rentals

BOLOGNA

Avis (☒ Via del Triumvirato 84, ☎ 051/6472032). **Europcar** (☒ Via Amendola 12/f, ☎ 051/247101). **SIXT Autonoleggio** (☒ Viale Mazzini 4/3, ☎ 051/255546).

PARMA

Avis (☒ Viale Frati 24, ☎ 0521/772418). **Europcar** (☒ Hotel Baglioni, Viale Piacenza 51/c, ☎ 0521/293035).

RIMINI

Avis (☒ Viale Trieste 16, ☎ 0541/51256). **Europcar** (☒ Via Giovanni XXIII 126, ☎ 0541/54746).

Emergencies

Police (☎ 112). **Ambulance** (☎ 113). **Doctors and Dentists** (☎ 113).

Late-Night Pharmacies

Pharmacies post the schedule of pharmacies open after hours, which functions on a rotating basis.

Travel Agencies

Bologna: Marconi Tours (✉ Via Marconi 47, Bologna, ☎ 051/235783). **Rimini: Viaggi Urbinati** (✉ Viale Vespucci 127, Rimini, ☎ 0541/391660).

Visitor Information

Tourist offices (✉ Aeroporto Gugliemo Marconi Bologna, ☎ 051/6472036; ✉ Stazione Centrale, 40121, ☎ 051/246541; ✉ Piazza Maggiore 6, 40124, ☎ 051/239660; ✉ Comune, Piazza Giuseppe Verdi 10, 43011 Busseto, ☎ 0524/92487; ✉ Via XX Settembre, 40050 Dozza, ☎ 0542/678052; ✉ Piazza del Popolo 1, 48018 Faenza, ☎ 0546/691602; ✉ Corso Giovecca 21, 44022 Ferrara, ☎ 0532/249751; ✉ Piazza Grande 17, 41100 Modena, ☎ 059/206660; ✉ Via Melloni 1/b, 43100 Parma, ☎ 0521/234735; ✉ Palazzo Farnese, Piazza Citadella, 29100 Piacenza, ☎ 0523/329324; ✉ Via Salara 8, 48100 Ravenna, ☎ 0544/35404; ✉ Via Danta 86, 47037 Rimini, ☎ 0541/51331; ✉ Piazzale Fellini 3, 47037 Rimini, ☎ 0541/56902).

11 UMBRIA AND THE MARCHES

PERUGIA, URBINO, ASSISI, AND ABRUZZO

Legends linger in smiling Umbria, ethereal birthplace of the saints. Here await Gothic treasures—Assisi's Basilica di San Francesco and Orvieto's awe-inspiring cathedral—and the more urbane pleasures of Spoleto's Festival dei Due Mondi and timeless, Renaissance-stamped Urbino. Above serpentine hills toward the Adriatic are Le Marche and its noble Urbino. Vying for elbow room is craggy, wild, and undiscovered Abruzzo.

Updated by Jon Eldan and Carla Lionello

BIRTHPLACE OF SAINTS AND CONDOTTIERI, Umbria has remained true to its name: "land of shadows." The hills, olive groves, and terraced vineyards of this mystic province are often wrapped in a bluish haze that gives its landscape an ethereal painted look—a landscape often recognized in the frescoes of its celebrated local artists, even when they were decorating churches far from their native soil. Blessed with steep, austere hills, deep valleys, and fast-flowing rivers, the region—roughly halfway between Florence and Rome—has not yet been swamped by tourism and has escaped the unplanned industrial expansion that afflicts much of central Italy. No town in Umbria boasts the extravagant wealth of art and architecture of Florence, Rome, or Venice, but this works in your favor. Cities can be experienced whole, rather than as a series of museums and churches, forced marches through 2,000 years of Western culture; in Umbria the visitor comes to know the towns as people live in them today. This is not to suggest that the cultural cupboard is bare—far from it. Perugia, the capital of the region, and Assisi, Umbria's most prominent city, are rich in art and architecture, as are Orvieto, Todi, and Spoleto. Virtually every small town in the region has a castle, church, or museum worth a stop.

The earliest inhabitants of Umbria, the Umbri, were thought by the Romans to be the most ancient inhabitants of Italy. Little is known about them, since with the coming of Etruscan culture, the tribe fled into the mountains in the eastern portion of the region. The Etruscans, who founded some of the great cities of Umbria, were in turn supplanted by the Romans. Unlike Tuscany and other regions of central Italy, Umbria had few powerful medieval families to exert control over the cities in the Middle Ages—its proximity to Rome ensured that Umbria would always be more or less under papal domination.

The relative political stability of the region did not mean that Umbria was left in peace. Located in the center of the country, it has for much of its history been a battlefield where armies from north and south clashed. Hannibal destroyed a Roman army on the shores of Lago Trasimeno, and the full and bloody course of the interminable Guelph-Ghibelline conflict of the Middle Ages was played out in Umbria. Dante considered it the most violent place in Italy. Trophies of war still decorate the facade of the Palazzo dei Priori in Perugia, and the little town of Gubbio continues a warlike rivalry begun in the Middle Ages—every year it challenges the Tuscan town of Sansepolcro to a crossbow tournament. Today, of course, the bowmen shoot at targets, but neither side has forgotten that 500 years ago its ancestors shot at each other. In spite of—or perhaps because of—this bloodshed, Umbria has produced more than its share of Christian saints. The most famous is St. Francis, the decidedly unmartial saint whose life shaped the Church and the history of his time. His great shrine at Assisi is visited by hundreds of thousands of pilgrims each year. St. Clare, his devoted follower, was Umbria-born, as were St. Benedict, St. Rita of Cascia, and, ironically, the patron saint of lovers, St. Valentine.

East of Umbria, the Marches (Le Marche to Italians) stretch between the hills of the southern Apennines down to the Adriatic sea. It is a scenic region of mountains and valleys, with great turreted castles standing on high peaks defending passes and roads—silent testament to the region's bellicose past. The Marches have passed through numerous hands. First the Romans supplanted the native civilizations; then Charlemagne supplanted the Romans (and gave the region its name—it was divided into "marks," or provinces, under the rule of the Holy Roman Emperor); then began the seemingly never-ending struggle between popes and local lords. Cesare Borgia (circa 1475–1507) succeeded in wresting control of the Marches from the local suzerains, annexing the region to the papacy of his father, Alexander VI. Despite all this martial tussling, it was in the lonely mountain town of Urbino that the Renaissance came to its fullest flower; that small town became a haven of culture and learning that rivaled the greater, richer, and more powerful city of Florence, and even Rome itself. Still a land of shepherds and wolves, the mountainous center of Abruzzo preserves much of its local traditions and culture. Medieval L'Aquila is a pleasant, walkable town yet undiscovered by tourists, and the Parco Nazionale d'Abruzzo, with its hiking trails and protected wildlife, is a favorite camping resort in central Italy.

Pleasures and Pastimes

Dining

Umbria is mountainous, and its food is hearty and straightforward, with a stick-to-the-ribs quality that sees hardworking farmers and artisans through a long day's work and helps them make the steep climb home at night. The region has made several important contributions to Italian cuisine. Particularly prized are *tartufi neri* (black truffles) from the area around Spoleto (☞ Close-Up: Truffle Trouble, *below*) and from the hills around the tiny town of Norcia. The local pasta specialty—thick, handmade *ciriole* (roughly shaped, fat spaghetti) or *strangozzi* (pasta like ciriole, *above,* but with holes in the middle)—is even better prepared *al tartufo,* enriched with excellent local olive oil and truffles. Norcia's pork products—especially sausages, salami, and *arista* (roast loin perfumed with rosemary)—are so famous that pork butchers throughout Italy are called *norcini,* no matter where they hail from, and pork butcher shops are called *norcinerie.*

In the coastal Marches, fish in various forms is the thing to look for. One of the characteristic dishes in Ancona is *brodetto,* a rich fish chowder containing as many as nine types of Adriatic saltwater fish. Ascoli Piceno, inland, is known for two dishes: *olive ascolane* (olives stuffed, rolled in batter, and deep fried) and *vincisgrassi* (lasagna with innards to enrich the sauce, sometimes with black truffles, and more sauce than usual), far richer than you're likely to find elsewhere in Italy. Ascoli Piceno is also the home of the licorice-flavored liqueur anisette.

Hiking

Magnificent scenery makes Umbria excellent hiking and mountaineering country. The area around Spoleto is particularly good, and the tourist office supplies itineraries of walks and climbs to suit all ages and levels of ability. With a bit of luck, and an early start, the shy chamois of the Parco Nazionale d'Abruzzo might cross your path. Find out their favorite routes on the maps sold at any of the information points inside the park, or join a guided tour to the wildlife of this beautiful protected area.

Lodging

Virtually every historic town in Umbria has some kind of hotel, no matter how small the place may be. A popular trend is the conversion of old villas and monasteries into first-class hotels. These tend to be outside the towns, in the countryside, and the splendor of the settings often outweighs the problem of getting into town. In all cases, these country hotels are comfortable, often luxurious, and offer a mixture of old-world charm and modern convenience. Reservations at any hotel are recommended, and traveling in high season to Perugia, Assisi, Spoleto, or Orvieto without advance bookings is a chancy proposition.

Shopping

Pottery and wine are the two most celebrated Umbrian exports, and examples of both commodities are excellent and unique to the region. Torgiano, south of Perugia, is one of the best-known centers of wine making, where you can watch the process and buy the product; you can find some of the best ceramics at Gubbio, Perugia, and Assisi. Those with the most flair are found in Deruta, south of Torgiano on S3bis. The red glazes of Gubbio pottery have been renowned since medieval times. The secret of the original glaze died with its inventor some 500 years ago, but some contemporary potters produce a fair facsimile.

Exploring Umbria and the Marches

The steep hills and deep valleys that make Umbria and the Marches so picturesque also make them difficult to explore. Driving routes must be chosen carefully to avoid tortuous mountain roads; major towns are not necessarily linked to each other by train, bus, or highway. A convenient base for exploring the region is Perugia, the largest city in Umbria, but to see the region properly you would still need to stay overnight in other towns along the way.

Numbers in the text correspond to numbers in the margin and on the Umbria and the Marches, Perugia, Spoleto, and Assisi maps.

Great Itineraries

The region of Umbria is particularly suited to touring in a limited time. Basing yourself in Perugia, you can see all the major sights in the regional capital in the equivalent of a day, making easy excursions to the hill villages on your other days without feeling stressed out by constant travel. East of Perugia, the Marches invite leisurely exploring, but expect some lengthy rides in between the main points of interest. L'Aquila is easily reachable from Rome and southern Umbria, and is only a couple of hours away from the wilderness of Abruzzo's national park.

IF YOU HAVE 3 DAYS

In 🏨 **Perugia** ①–④, your main stops will be the refurbished Galleria Nazionale dell'Umbria and the Collegio del Cambio, both contained in the atmospheric **Palazzo dei Priori** ②; much of the rest of your time will be spent alternately ambling along Corso Vannucci and toiling up and down the steep lanes on either side. Devote your second day to 🏨 **Assisi** ⑲–㉒, where the spiritual and the material are fused in a place that remains in essence a small medieval Umbrian town. The choice for a third excursion is a tough one, and you won't be disappointed by whichever place you opt for. Consider **Spoleto** ⑫–⑱: a tight-knit hill town whose narrow streets abound with evocative views and delightful surprises.

IF YOU HAVE 5 DAYS

Given five days, you will be able to spend a couple of them exploring the neighboring region of Le Marche. How you enter these rather inaccessible parts will depend on your mode of transport. In any case, start your tour in 🏨 **Perugia** ①–④, and follow the itinerary above for your first two days. If you are traveling by public transportation, spend your third night in 🏨 **Spoleto** ⑫–⑱, from which you can jump on a train bound for 🏨 **Ancona** ⑨; from here you can board a bus or a train for Pésaro and 🏨 **Urbino** ⑧. This hilltop gem retains its proud, self-contained character, almost untouched by 20th-century construction. Plan for at least half a day for reaching Urbino from Spoleto, and it's not much shorter by car, crossing the Marches border from 🏨 **Gubbio** ⑦, where you might spend your last day appreciating the views, shops, and choice hotels and restaurants.

IF YOU HAVE 7 DAYS

Reserve four days for Umbria and three for the Marches or Abruzzo. With greater flexibility you can choose how many nights you want to spend in Umbria's capital, **Perugia** ①–④, and how many in the region's smaller centers. More time in Perugia will allow you to explore the city thoroughly, including the archaeological museum, and you might take in the easy excursion to the wine village of **Torgiano** ⑤ or the ceramics town of **Deruta** ⑥. **Spoleto** ⑫–⑱ and **Assisi** ⑲–㉒ are essential stops farther afield, where you might stay for a night in each. **Gubbio** ⑦ is also worth overnighting in. From Spoleto, you can explore the quintessential hill town of **Todi** ㉓, unspoiled **Narni** ㉔, and the wine mecca **Orvieto** ㉕; they can also be seen on your way to or from Rome, only about 90 minutes away. From here you can drive north to the Marches region, or south to the undiscovered region of Abruzzo for the last three days. **Urbino** ⑧ is the premier destination in the Marches. The region's biggest city, **Ancona** ⑨ has little of interest, but good facilities—sleep here if you must; otherwise head south for the infinitely preferable inland town of **Ascoli Piceno** ⑪. There is little in the way of hotels, galleries, or sophisticated shops here, but it's marvelously quaint. On the way, or en route back, drop in at the holy sanctuary of **Loreto** ⑩, nestled in the mountains 24 km (15 mi) south of Ancona. If you are venturing to Abruzzo instead, **L'Aquila** ㉖ makes an excellent base for visiting the central part of the Abruzzo region, including the woods of the national park.

When to Tour Umbria and the Marches

The forested hills of Umbria and the Marches ensure beguiling colors in the fall and an explosion of greenery in spring—and fewer crowds. From a culinary standpoint, winter is best: January to April heralds the Norcia and Spoleto truffle season; October to December brings a bounty of fresh local mushrooms. Book accommodations far in advance if you are planning to visit in June and July, when the Spoleto Festival dei Due Mondi and the Jazz Festival of Perugia take place. Sightseers and pilgrims throng the streets of Assisi year-round; the religious festivals of Christmas, Easter, the feast of St. Francis (October 4), and the Calendimaggio Festival (May 1) draw even more visitors.

PERUGIA

Perugia is the venerable capital of a region rich in history, art, tradition, and beautiful landscapes—those depicted by Perugino in his paintings: hills with a few sparse trees, flat land, lakes. Despite rather grim fringe modern suburbs, Perugia's location on a series of hills high above the suburban plain has ensured that the medieval city remains almost completely intact. Perugia is the best well-preserved hill town of its size, and few other places in Italy illustrate better the concept of the self-contained city-state that so shaped the course of Italian history.

Exploring Perugia

The best approach to the city is by train—the station is in the unlovely suburbs, but there are frequent buses running directly to Piazza d'Italia, the heart of the old town. If you are driving to Perugia, it is best to leave your car in one of the parking lots near the station and then take the bus or the escalator, Piazza Partigiani to the Rocca Paolina, which passes through fascinating subterranean excavations of the Roman foundations of the city.

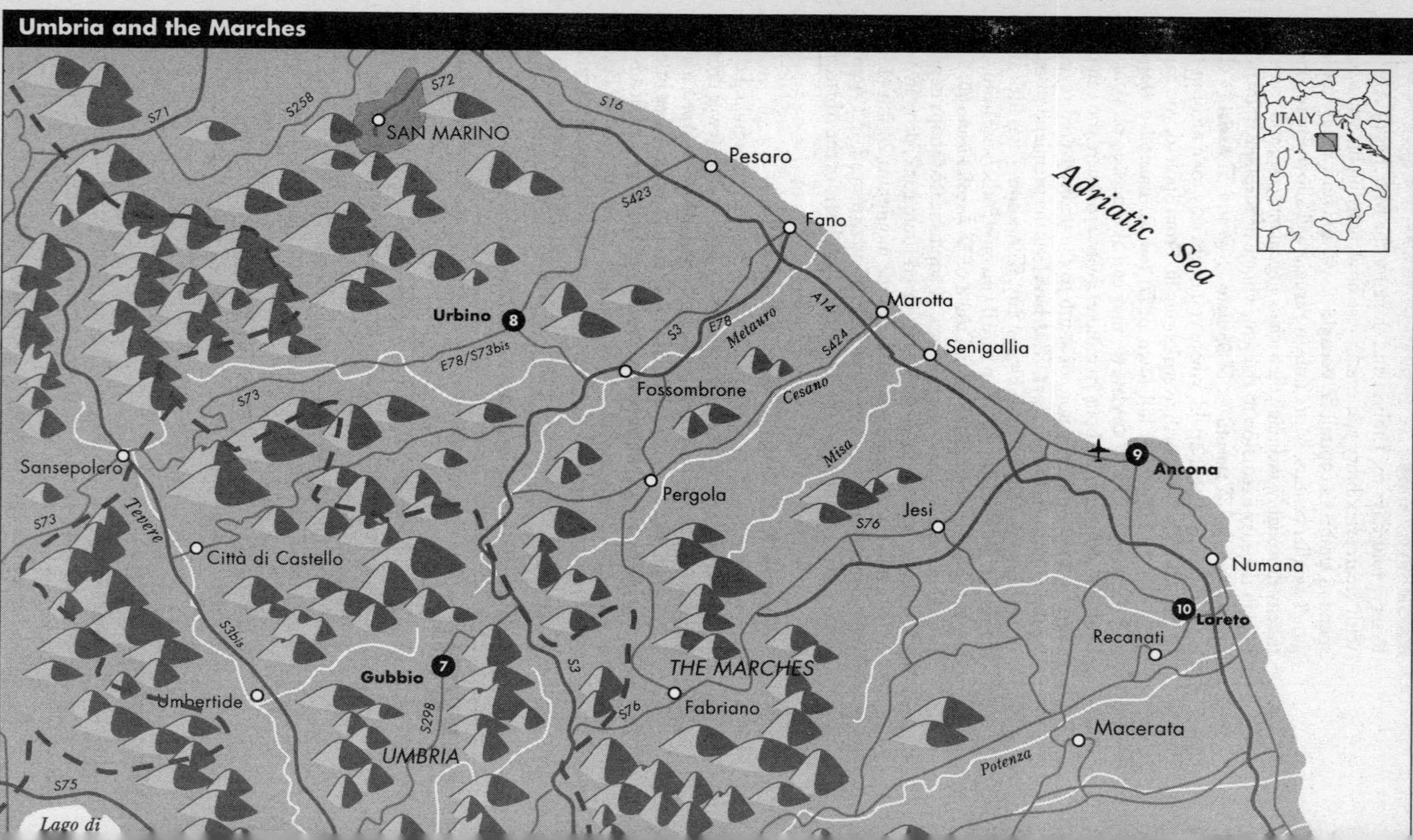
Umbria and the Marches
ITALY
Adriatic Sea
SAN MARINO
S72
S258
S71
S16
Pesaro
S423
Fano
Marotta
Senigallia
A14
S424
E78
S3
Metauro
Cesano
Misa
8 Urbino
E78/S73bis
Fossombrone
S73
Sansepolcro
Tevere
Città di Castello
Pergola
Jesi
S76
9 Ancona
Numana
10 Loreto
Recanati
S3bis
7 Gubbio
S298
Umbertide
THE MARCHES
Fabriano
UMBRIA
Macerata
Potenza
S75
Lago di

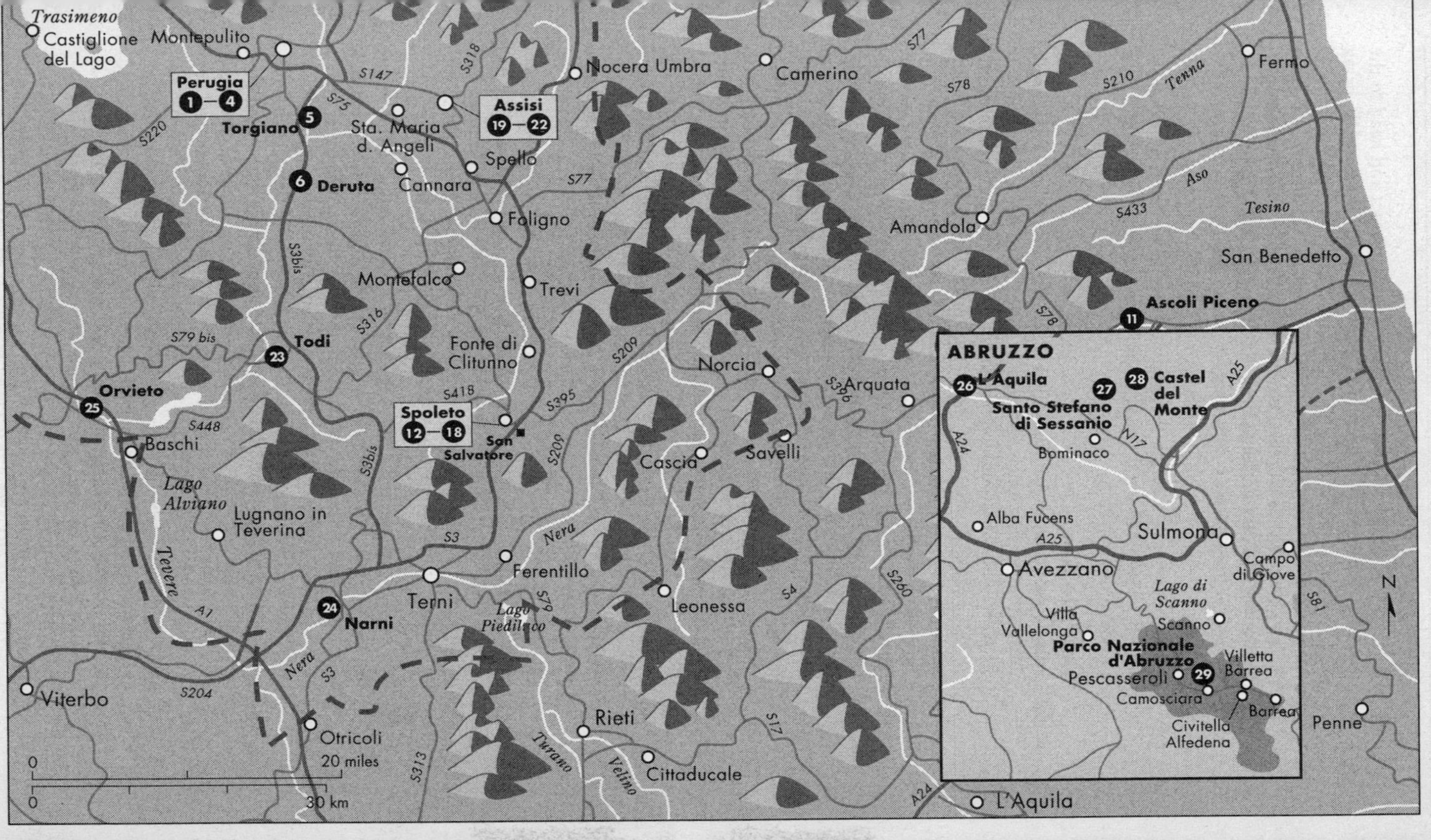
Trasimeno
Castiglione del Lago
Montepulito
Perugia 1—4
5 Torgiano
S147
S75
S220
Sta. Maria d. Angeli
Assisi 19—22
Spello
S318
Nocera Umbra
Camerino
S77
S78
S210
Tenna
Fermo
6 Deruta
Cannara
Foligno
Aso
Tesino
S433
Amandola
San Benedetto
S3bis
Montefalco
Trevi
S316
S79 bis
23 Todi
Fonte di Clitunno
S209
Ascoli Piceno
11
S78
Norcia
S396
Arquata
25 Orvieto
S418
Spoleto 12—18
S395
San Salvatore
S448
Baschi
Lago Alviano
Lugnano in Teverina
Cascia
Savelli
S3
Nera
Ferentillo
Tevere
A1
Terni
24 Narni
Lago Piediluco
S79
Leonessa
S4
S260
Nera
S3
Viterbo
S204
Otricoli
0
20 miles
30 km
S313
Turano
Rieti
Velino
Cittaducale
S17
A24
L'Aquila
ABRUZZO
26 L'Aquila
27 Santo Stefano di Sessanio
28 Castel del Monte
A25
A24
N17
Bominaco
Alba Fucens
A25
Sulmona
Campo di Giove
Avezzano
Lago di Scanno
Scanno
Villa Vallelonga
Parco Nazionale d'Abruzzo
29
Pescasseroli
Villetta Barrea
Camosciara
Barrea
Civitella Alfedena
S81
N
Penne

A Good Walk

Starting in Piazza Italia, stroll down Corso Vannucci and head to the **Duomo** ① in Piazza IV Novembre. Visit the **Palazzo dei Priori** ②, being sure to explore the Galleria Nazionale dell'Umbria, and the **Collegio del Cambio** ③, with its fine Perugino frescoes. A 10-minute walk south of the center along Corso Cavour leads to the **Museo Archeologico Nazionale** ④. After perusing the Etruscan relics in the museum, return to Piazza IV Novembre, breaking for lunch or an espresso at a café.

TIMING

A thorough walk through Perugia takes about an hour, and if stopping at all sights along this whole walk, you should plan on at least a half day, plus a stop for lunch.

Sights to See

★ ❸ **Collegio del Cambio** (Bankers' Guild Hall). The series of elaborate rooms housed the meeting hall and chapel of the guild of bankers and money changers. The walls were frescoed from 1496 to 1500 by the most important Perugian painter of the Renaissance, Pietro Vannucci, better known as Perugino (circa 1450–1523). The iconography prevalent in the works includes common religious themes, like the *Nativity* and the *Transfiguration* (on the end walls), but also figures intended to inspire the businessmen who congregated here. On the left wall are female figures representing the virtues, beneath them the heroes and sages of antiquity. On the right wall are the prophets and sibyls—said to have been painted in part by Perugino's most famous pupil, Raphael (1483–1520), whose hand, the experts say, is most apparent in the figure of Fortitude. On one of the pilasters is a remarkably honest self-portrait of Perugino, surmounted by a Latin inscription and contained in a faux frame. The Collegio is attached to Palazzo dei Priori, but entered on Corso Vannucci. ✉ *Corso Vannucci 25* ☎ *075/5728599.* 💳 *5,000 lire.* ⏲ *Mar.–Oct., Mon.–Sat. 9–12:30 and 2:30–5:30, Sun. 9–12:30; Nov.–Feb., Tues.–Sat. 8–2, Sun. 9–12:30. Dec. 20–Jan. 6, museum follows summer timetable.*

Corso Vannucci. The nerve center of the city is the broad, stately pedestrian street that runs from Piazza d'Italia to Piazza IV Novembre. As evening falls, Corso Vannucci is filled with Perugians out for their evening *passeggiata,* a pleasant predinner stroll that may include a pause for an aperitif at one of the many bars that line the street.

❶ **Duomo.** The cathedral is a large and rather plain building dating from the Middle Ages but with many additions from the 15th and 16th centuries. The interior is vast and echoing, with little in the way of decoration. There are some elaborately carved choir stalls, executed by Giovanni Battista Bastone in 1520. The great relic of the church—the wedding ring of the Virgin Mary that the Perugians stole from the nearby town of Chiusi—is kept in a chapel in the left aisle. The ring is the size of a large bangle and is kept under lock—15 locks, actually—and key every day of the year except July 30, when it is exposed to view. A large array of precious objects associated with the cathedral are on display at the Museo Capitolare, including vestments, vessels, manuscripts, and gold work. An early masterpiece by Luca Signorelli (circa 1450–1523) is the altarpiece showing the Madonna with St. John the Baptist, St. Onophrius, and St. Lawrence (1484). The museum was closed for restoration at press time and due to reopen in the fall of 1999. ✉ *Piazza IV Novembre,* ☎ *075/5723832.* ⏲ *Daily 7–noon and 4–7.*

❹ **Museo Archeologico Nazionale.** This museum next to the imposing church of San Domenico contains an excellent collection of Etruscan artifacts from throughout the region. Perugia was a flourishing Etr-

Collegio del Cambio, **3**
Duomo, **1**
Museo Archeologico Nazionale, **4**
Palazzo dei Priori, **2**

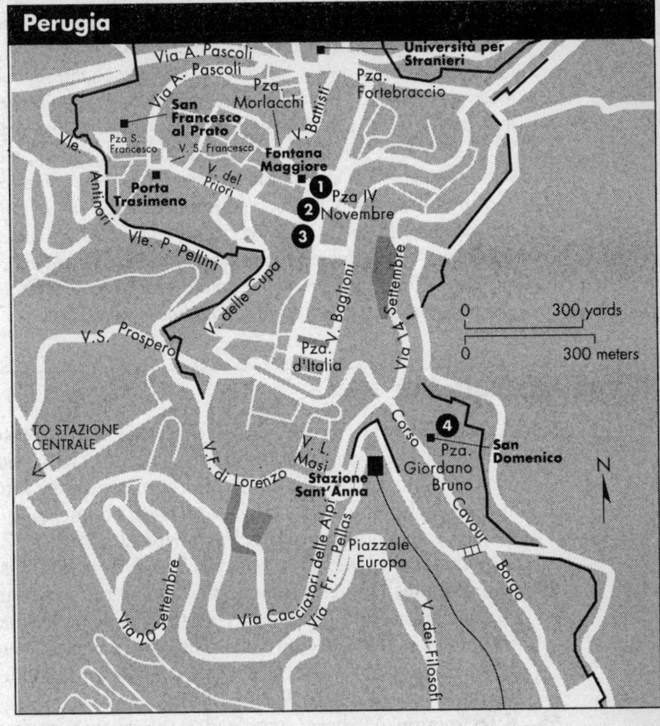

uscan site long before it fell under Roman domination in 310 BC. Other than this collection, little remains of Perugia's mysterious ancestors, although the **Arco di Augusto** (Arch of Augustus), in Piazza Fortebraccio, the northern entrance to the city, is of Etruscan origin. ✉ *Piazza Giordano Bruno 10,* ☎ *075/5727141.* 🎫 *4,000 lire.* ⏲ *Mon.–Sat. 9–7, Sun. 9–1.*

★ ❷ **Palazzo dei Priori.** The imposing palace, begun in the 13th century, has an unusual staircase that fans out into Piazza IV Novembre. The facade is decorated with symbols of Perugia's pride and past power: the griffin is the city's symbol; the lion denotes Perugia's allegiance to the Guelph (or papal) cause. Both figures support the heavy chains of the gates of Siena, which fell to Perugian forces in 1358.The fourth floor of the Palazzo dei Priori contains the region's most comprehensive art gallery, the **Galleria Nazionale dell'Umbria.** Enhanced by skillfully lit displays and computers allowing you to focus on details of the works and background information on them, the collection includes work by native artists—most outstandingly Pinturicchio (1454–1513) and Perugino—and others of the Umbrian and Tuscan schools, including Gentile da Fabriano (1370–1427), Duccio (circa 1255–1318), Fra Angelico (1387–1455), Fiorenzo di Lorenzo (1445–1525), and Piero della Francesca (1420–92). In addition to paintings, the gallery has frescoes, sculptures, and some superb examples of crucifixes from the 13th and 14th centuries; other rooms are dedicated to the city of Perugia itself, showing how the medieval city evolved. Although at press time the highlights were all visible, a great part of the "minor" works had to be put in storage for lack of space, as over half of the 33 rooms were undergoing restoration following the 1997 quake. ✉ *Corso Vannucci 19, Piazza IV Novembre.* 🎫 *8,000 lire.* ⏲ *Mon.–Sat. 9–7, Sun. 9–2; last admission 1 hr before closing. Closed 1st Mon. of each month.*

OFF THE BEATEN PATH

LA CITTÀ DELLA DOMENICA – Umbria's only attraction aimed directly at the younger set is La Città della Domenica, a Disney-style playground in the town of Montepulito, just west of Perugia on the secondary road that leads to Corciano. The 500 acres of parkland contain a variety of buildings based on familiar fairy-tale themes—Snow White's House, the Witches' Wood—as well as a reptile house, aquarium, medieval museum, an exhibit of shells from all over the world, game rooms, and a choice of restaurants. ✉ *Località Montepulito, 8 km (5 mi) west of Perugia,* ☎ *075/5054941.* 🎫 *16,500 lire (17,500 lire Sun. and holidays; 6,000 lire when playground is closed).* ⏲ *Apr.–mid-Sept., daily 10–7; mid-Sept.–Oct., weekends and holidays only 10–7; Nov.–mid-Mar. (game rooms, aquarium, and reptile house only), Sat. 2–7, Sun. 10–7.*

Dining and Lodging

$$ ✕ **Il Falchetto.** Here you'll find exceptional food at reasonable prices, making this Perugia's best restaurant bargain. The service is smart but relaxed in the two medieval dining rooms, with the kitchen and chef on view. The house specialty is *falchetti* (homemade gnocchi with spinach and ricotta cheese). ✉ *Via Bartolo 20,* ☎ *075/5731775. Reservations essential. AE, DC, MC, V. Closed Mon. and last 2 wks in Jan.*

$$ ✕ **La Rosetta.** This restaurant, in the hotel of the same name, is a peaceful, elegant spot. In the winter you dine inside under medieval vaults; in summer, in the cool courtyard. The cuisine is simple but reliable and flawlessly served. ✉ *Piazza Italia 19,* ☎ *075/5720841. Reservations essential. AE, DC, MC, V. Closed Mon.*

$$ ✕ **La Taverna.** Medieval steps lead to this rustic restaurant on two levels, where lots of wine bottles and artful clutter heighten the tavern atmosphere. The menu features regional specialties and better-known Italian dishes. Good choices include *chitarrini* (extra-thick spaghetti), with either *funghi* (mushrooms) or *tartufi* (truffles), and grilled meats. ✉ *Via delle Streghe 8, next to the Teatro Pavone, off Corso Vannucci,* ☎ *075/5724128. Dinner reservations essential. AE, DC, MC, V. Closed Mon.*

$$$$ 🏨 **Brufani Hotel.** The two hotels (this one and the Palace Hotel Bellavista) in this 19th-century palazzo were once one. The Brufani's public rooms and first-floor guest rooms have high ceilings and are done in the grand belle-epoque style. The second-floor rooms are more modern, and many on both floors have a marvelous view of the Umbrian countryside or the city. ✉ *Piazza Italia 12, 06121,* ☎ *075/5732541,* FAX *075/5720210. 27 rooms. Restaurant, bar, meeting rooms. AE, DC, MC, V.*

$$$ ★ 🏨 **Locanda della Posta.** This luxuriously decorated small hotel in the center of Perugia's historic district is a delight to behold, from its faux-marble moldings, paneled doors, and tile bouquets in the baths to the suede-upholstered elevator and fabric-covered walls. Architectural details of the 18th-century palazzo are beautiful, and views of city rooftops from windows and balconies are soothing. Breakfast is included here. ✉ *Corso Vannucci 97, 06121,* ☎ *075/5728925,* FAX *075/5732562. 39 rooms. Breakfast room, lobby lounge. AE, DC, MC, V.*

$$ 🏨 **Priori.** On an alley leading off the main Corso Vannucci, this unpretentious but elegant hotel has spacious and cheerful rooms with modern furnishings. There is a panoramic terrace where breakfast (included in the price) is served in summer. The hotel is difficult to find if you're driving, and a car is an encumbrance wherever you are in Perugia's historic center—but, there is a garage you can pay extra for. ✉ *Via dei Priori, 06123,* ☎ *075/5723378,* FAX *075/5723213. 56 rooms. Bar, parking (fee). V.*

$ Rosalba. This is a bright and friendly choice on the fringes of Perugia's historic center. Basic rooms are scrupulously clean, and the ones at the back enjoy a view. Although somewhat out of the way, the hotel is only a matter of minutes from Corso Vannucci by virtue of the nearby escalator stop, saving a good deal of legwork. Parking is easy, too. ✉ *Via del Circo 7, 06121,* ☎ *075/5728285,* FAX *075/5720626. 11 rooms. Free parking. No credit cards.*

Nightlife and the Arts

The monthly *Viva Perugia* (sold at newsstands), with a section in English, is a good source of information about what's going on in town.

Music Festivals

Summer sees two international music festivals in Perugia: the **Jazz Festival of Umbria** (10 days in July) and the **Sagra Musicale Umbra** (10 days in September). Call the **festival office** (☎ 075/5732432, FAX 075/572256), open year-round, for information about the Jazz Festival or to pre-buy tickets with a credit card as early as the end of April.

A lover of music should consider the lengthy trek to the **Festival Nazioni Musica da Camera** (Chamber Music Festival of Umbria), a two-week chamber music festival held between August and September in the town of Città di Castello, about 80 km (50 mi) north of Perugia on the S3bis. For information year-round, contact the festival office (☎ 075/8521142, FAX 075/8552461).

Shopping

Chocolate

The best and most typical thing to buy in Perugia is some of the famous **Perugina chocolate,** although there's no immediate need to load yourself with presents to bring home, as the brand (a Nestlè corporation since the early '90s) is easily found all over Italy. *Cioccolato al latte* (milk chocolate) and *fondente* (dark chocolate), set in tiny jewel-like boxes or in giant gift boxes the size of serving trays, are sold all over town. But the best-known chocolates made by Perugina are the round hazelnut-filled chocolate candies called Baci (literally kisses), which come wrapped in silver paper and, like fortune cookies, contain multilingual romantic sentiments or sayings.

Shopping District

Perugia is a well-to-do town, and judging by the array of expensive shops on **Corso Vannucci,** the Perugians are not afraid to part with their lucre. The main streets of the town are lined with clothing shops selling the best-known Italian designers, in luxurious shops such as Gucci, Ferragamo, Armani, and Fendi.

NORTHERN ARC TO GUBBIO

Umbrian Heights

In the rich countryside south of Perugia, along the Tiber River valley, are the two towns of Deruta and Torgiano, best known for their hand-painted ceramics and wine—go to Deruta to buy a pitcher, and to Torgiano to fill it, as they say locally. Nearby Gubbio climbs straight up a mountain, filling the bottom half with its houses and churches. Costumed runners, outsize pillars in hand, climb the rest of the way, up to the church of San Ubaldo, during Gubbio's bizarre Festa dei Ceri.

Torgiano

❺ *15 km (9 mi) southeast of Perugia, 60 km (37 mi) north of Orvieto.*

Wine aficionados are certain to want to visit this home to the winery **Cantine Lungarotti,** best known for delicious Rubesco Lungarotti, San Giorgio, and chardonnay. ✉ *Via Mario Angeloni 12,* ☎ *075/9880348.* ⏲ *Tours Mon.–Fri. 8–1 and 3–6, by appointment only.*

The fascinating **Museo del Vino** (Wine Museum) has a large collection of ancient wine vessels, presses, documents, and tools that tell the story of viticulture in Umbria and beyond. The museum traces the history of wine in all its uses—for drinking at the table, as medicine, and in mythology. At the Osteria del Museo (☎ FAX 075/9880069), you can taste and buy Lungarotti's award-winning reds or whites. ✉ *Corso Vittorio Emanuele 11,* ☎ *075/9880200.* *5,000 lire.* ⏲ *Apr.–Oct., daily 9–1 and 3–7; Nov.–Mar., daily 9–1 and 3–6.*

Deruta

❻ *7 km (4 mi) south of Torgiano, 20 km (12 mi) southeast of Perugia.*

Deruta has been distinguished since the 16th century for its ceramics. Notable in the medieval hill town are the 14th-century church of San Francesco and the Palazzo Comunale, but its main attraction is the magnificent ceramics collection in the **Museo delle Ceramiche.** ✉ *Via Largo San Francesco,* ☎ *075/9711000.* *5,000 lire.* ⏲ *Apr.–June, daily 10:30–1 and 3–6; Oct.–Mar., Wed.–Mon. 10:30–1 and 2:30–5.*

Lodging

$$$ **Nel Castello.** This little turretted castle, which the owner says dates from the 5th century, has nine guest rooms and a good Umbrian restaurant. Atop a hill 5 km (3 mi) outside Deruta, it is surrounded by grass and trees, and is a quiet, tranquil place to stay. The restaurant serves local dishes laced with *cinghiale* (boar meat) and truffles. ✉ *Castelleone, Deruta, 06503,* ☎ *075/9711302. 9 rooms. Restaurant, pool. AE, DC, MC, V.*

Shopping

CERAMICS

There are about 70 ceramics workshops and shops in and around this small town. Start your browsing in the central Piazza dei Consoli, where you can find a nice selection at **Maioliche Cynthia** (✉ Via Umberto I 1, ☎ 075/9711255), specializing in reproductions of antique Deruta ceramics. **Ceramiche El Frate** (✉ Piazza dei Consoli 29, ☎ 075/9711435) sells unusual tiles and jugs. If you want to visit a workshop, try **Fabbrica Maioliche Tradizionali** (✉ Via Tiberina Nord 37, ☎ 075/9711220), open Monday–Saturday 7–noon and 2–5 (call ahead), where there's also one of the largest shops in the area.

Gubbio

❼ *40 km (25 mi) northeast of Perugia, 92 km (57 mi) east of Arezzo.*

There is something otherworldly about this small jewel of a medieval town tucked away in a rugged, mountainous corner of Umbria. Even at the height of summer, the cool serenity of the City of Silence's streets remains intact. The town is perched on the slopes of Monte Ingino, and the streets are dramatically steep. Parking in the central Piazza dei Quaranta Martiri, named for 40 hostages murdered by the Nazis in 1944, is easy and secure, and it is wise to leave your car there and explore the narrow streets on foot.

★ The striking Piazza Grande is dominated by the **Palazzo dei Consoli** (Palace of the Consuls), the 14th-century meeting place of the parliament of Gubbio. The palace is attributed to a local architect known as Gattapone (died 1376), a man still much admired by today's residents—every other hotel, restaurant, and bar has been named after him—though studies have suggested that the palazzo was in fact the work of another architect, Angelo da Orvieto. The Palazzo dei Consoli houses a small museum, famous chiefly for the **Tavole Eugubine** (Gubbio Tablets), seven bronze tablets written in the ancient Umbrian language, employing Etruscan and Latin characters, and providing the best key to understanding this obscure tongue. Also in the museum are a captivating miscellany of coins, medieval arms, paintings, and majolica and earthenware pots, not to mention the exhilarating views over Gubbio's roofscape and beyond from the lofty loggia. For a few days at the beginning of May, the palace also displays the famous *ceri,* the ceremonial pillars at the center of Gubbio's annual festivities (☞ Nightlife and the Arts, *below*). ✉ *Piazza Grande,* ☎ *075/9274298.* 🎫 *7,000 lire.* ⊙ *Apr.–Sept., daily 10–1:30 and 3–6; Oct.–Mar., daily 10–1 and 2–5.*

The **Duomo,** on a narrow street on the highest tier of the town, dates from the 13th century, with some Baroque additions—in particular, a lavishly decorated bishop's chapel. ✉ *Via Ducale.* ⊙ *Daily 8–12:45 and 3–7:30.*

The **Palazzo Ducale** (Ducal Palace) is a scaled-down copy of the Palazzo Ducale in Urbino (Gubbio was once the possession of that city's ruling family, the Montefeltro). Gubbio's palazzo contains a small **museum** and a **courtyard.** There are magnificent views from some of the public rooms. ✉ *Via Ducale,* ☎ *075/9274298.* 🎫 *4,000 lire.* ⊙ *Mon.–Sat. 9–7, Sun. 9–1:30. Closed 1st Mon. of each month.*

Just outside the city walls at the eastern end of town (follow Corso Garibaldi or Via XX Settembre to the end), a **funicular** provides a bracing ride to the top of Monte Ingino. Aside from the spectacular views, the mountain has the basilica of **Sant'Ubaldo,** repository of Gubbio's famous ceri, three 16-ft-high poles crowned with statues of Sts. Ubaldo, George, and Anthony. The pillars are transported to the Palazzo dei Consoli on the first Sunday of May to honor the Festival of the Ceri (☞ Nightlife and the Arts, *below*). ✉ *Top of Monte Ingino.* ⊙ *Daily 9–12 and 4–7.*

Dining and Lodging

$$ ✕ **Bosone Garden.** This restaurant is in the former stables (note the stone arches inside) below the palace that houses the Hotel Bosone (☞ *below*) and has a summer garden that seats 200. It features dishes laced with truffles in season: two-mushroom salad with truffles and risotto *alla porcina* (with porcini mushrooms, sausage, and truffles). Another savory treat is the leg of pork. ✉ *Mastro Giorgio 1,* ☎ *075/9221246. AE, DC, MC, V. Closed Wed. and Jan.*

$$ ✕ **Grotta dell'Angelo.** This rustic trattoria is in the lower part of the old town, near the main square and tourist information office. The menu features simple local specialties, including salami, strangozzi pasta, and lasagna *tartufate* (with truffles). A few tables welcome outdoor dining. Inexpensive guest rooms are also available. ✉ *Via Gioia 47,* ☎ *075/9273438. Reservations essential. AE, DC, MC, V. Closed Tues. and Jan. 7–Feb. 7.*

$$ ✕ **Taverna del Lupo.** The "Tavern of the Wolf" is one of the city's best, and one of the largest—it seats 200 people and can still get a bit hectic during the high season. Lasagna made in the Gubbian fashion, with ham and truffles, is the menu's best pasta. You'll also find excellent desserts

and an extensive wine list. ✉ *Via Giovanni Ansidei 21,* ☎ *075/9274368. Reservations essential. AE, DC, MC, V. Closed Mon. Oct.–July.*

$$ **Hotel Bosone.** Occupying the old central Palazzo Raffaelli, this hotel in a former palace has preserved many original frescoes in the guest rooms. The suites furnished with period detail are particularly lavish. ✉ *Via XX Settembre 22, 06024,* ☎ *075/9220688,* FAX *075/9220552. 30 rooms. Bar. AE, DC, MC, V. Closed Jan.*

$$ **Hotel Gattapone.** Right in town center is this hotel with wonderful views of the sea of rooftops. It is casual and family run, with good-size, modern, comfortable rooms, some with well-preserved timber-raftered ceilings. ✉ *Via Ansidei 6, 06024,* ☎ FAX *075/9272489. 18 rooms. AE, DC, MC, V.*

Nightlife and the Arts

Every May 15, teams of Gubbio's young men dressed in medieval costumes race up the steep slopes to the basilica of Sant'Ubaldo carrying its heavy, fabled pillars to celebrate the **Festa dei Ceri.** This festival, enacted faithfully every year since 1151, is to thank the town's patron saints for their assistance in a miraculous Gubbian victory over a league of 11 other towns.

Outdoor Activities and Sports

Among the region's other historical pageants, Gubbio's costumed **Palio della Balestra** (crossbow tournament) takes place on the last Sunday in May; contact the Gubbio tourist office (☞ Visitor Information *in* Umbria and the Marches A to Z, *below*) for details.

THE MARCHES

Mirror to the Renaissance

An excursion from Umbria into the region of the Marches is recommended if you want to get off the beaten track and see a part of Italy rarely visited by foreigners. Not as wealthy as Tuscany or Umbria, the Marches has a diverse landscape of mountains and beaches, and marvelous views. Like its neighbors to the west, Le Marche's patchwork of rolling hills is stitched with grapevines and olive trees, bearing delicious wine and olive oil.

Traveling in the Marches is not as easy as in Umbria or Tuscany. Beyond the narrow coastal plain and away from major towns, the roads are steep and twisting. There's an efficient bus service from the coastal town of Pésaro to Urbino, the other principal tourist city of the region. Train travel in the region is slow, and stops are limited, although you can reach Ascoli Piceno by rail.

Urbino

❽ *101 km (63 mi) northeast of Perugia, 107 km (66 mi) northeast of Arezzo.*

Majestic Urbino, atop a steep hill with a skyline of towers and domes, is something of a surprise to come upon—it's oddly remote—and it is even stranger to reflect that it was once a center of learning and culture almost without rival in western Europe. The town looks much as it did in the glory days of the 15th century, a cluster of warm brick and pale stone buildings, all topped with russet-color tiled roofs. The focal point is the immense and beautiful Palazzo Ducale.

The tradition of learning in Urbino continues to this day. The city is the home of a small but prestigious Università di Urbino—one of the oldest in the world—and during school term the streets are filled with lively students. It is very much a college town, with the usual array of bookshops, record stores, bars, and coffeehouses. During the summer, the Italian student population is replaced by foreigners who come to study Italian language and arts at several prestigious private fine-arts academies.

Urbino's fame rests on the reputation of three of its native sons: Duke Federico da Montefeltro (1422–82), the enlightened warrior-patron who built the Palazzo Ducale; Raphael, one of the most influential painters in history and an embodiment of the spirit of the Renaissance; and the architect Donato Bramante (1444–1514), who translated the philosophy of the Renaissance into buildings of grace and beauty. Why three of the greatest men of the age should have been born within a generation of one another in this remote town has never been explained. Oddly enough, there is little work by either Bramante or Raphael in the city, but the duke's influence can still be felt strongly, even now, some 500 years after his death.

★ The **Palazzo Ducale** holds the place of honor in the city, and in no other palace of its era are the principles of the Renaissance stated quite so clearly. If the Renaissance was, in ideal form, a celebration of the nobility of man and his works, of the light and purity of the soul, then there is no place in Italy, the birthplace of the Renaissance, where these tenets are better illustrated. From the moment you enter the peaceful courtyard, you know that you are in a place of grace and beauty, the harmony of the building reflecting the high ideals of the artists who built it.

Today the palace houses the **Galleria Nazionale delle Marche** (National Museum of the Marches), with a superb collection of paintings, sculpture, and other objets d'art, well arranged and properly lit. Some works were originally the possessions of the Montefeltro family, others brought to the museum from churches and palaces throughout the region. Perhaps the most famous is Piero della Francesca's enigmatic work, long known as *The Flagellation of Christ.* Much has been written about this painting, and few experts agree on its meaning. Legend had it that the three figures in the foreground represented a murdered member of the Montefeltro family (the barefoot young man) and his two murderers. Others claimed the painting was a heavily veiled criticism of certain parts of Christian Europe—the iconography is obscure and the history extremely complicated. However, Sir John Pope-Hennessy—the preeminent scholar of Italian Renaissance art—has proved that it represents the arcane subject of the Vision of St. Lawrence. All the experts have always agreed that the painting is one of Piero della Francesca's masterpieces. Piero himself thought so. It is one of the few works he signed (on the lowest step supporting the throne). Other masterworks in the collection are Paolo Uccello's *Profanation of the Host,* Piero della Francesca's *Madonna of Senigallia,* and Titian's *Resurrection* and *Last Supper.* Duke Federico's study is an astonishingly elaborate but tiny room decorated with inlaid wood, said to be the work of Botticelli. ✉ *Piazza Duca Federico,* ☎ *0722/2760.* 🎫 *8,000 lire.* ⏲ *Tues.–Sun. 9–7 (on slow winter Sun. the Galleria might close at 2), Mon. 9–2.*

The **Casa di Raffaello** (House of Raphael) really is the house in which he was born and where he took his first steps in painting, under the direction of his artist father. There is some debate about the fresco of the Madonna here; some say it is by Raphael, others attribute it to the father—with Raphael's mother and the young painter himself standing in as models for the Madonna and Child. ✉ *Via Raffaello,* ☎ *0722/320105.* 🎫 *5,000 lire.* ⏲ *Mar.–Sept., Mon.–Sat. 9–1 and 3–7, Sun. 9–1; Oct.–Jan., Thurs.–Sat. and Mon.–Tues. 9–2, Sun. 10–10.*

Dining and Lodging

$ ✕ **La Vecchia Fornarina.** These two small rooms just down from Urbino's central Piazza della Repubblica are often filled to capacity. The trattoria specializes in meaty country fare, such as rabbit and *vitello alle noci* (veal cooked with walnuts) or *ai porcini* (with mushrooms). There is also a good range of pasta dishes. ✉ *Via Mazzini 14,* ☎ *0722/320007. Reservations essential. AE, DC, MC, V.*

$ **Hotel San Giovanni.** This hotel is in the old town and is housed in a renovated medieval building. The rooms are basic, clean, and comfortable—with a wonderful view from rooms 24 to 30—and there is a handy restaurant-pizzeria below. ✉ *Via Barocci 13, 61029,* ☎ *0722/2827,* FAX *0722/329055. 33 rooms, 16 without bath. No credit cards. Closed July and Christmas wk.*

Ancona

9 *87 km (54 mi) southeast of Urbino, 139 km (87 mi) northeast of Perugia.*

Ancona was probably once a lovely city. It is set on an elbow-shape bluff (hence its name; *ankon* is Greek for "elbow") that juts out into the Adriatic. Ancona was the object of serious aerial bombing during World War II—it was, and is, an important port city—and was reduced to rubble. The city has been rebuilt in the unfortunate postwar poured-concrete style, practical and inexpensive but not aesthetically pleasing. Unless you are taking a ferry to Venice, there is little reason to visit the city—with a few exceptions. Once in a while, glimpses of old architectural detail are redeeming, as seen in the **Duomo San Ciriaco** and the **Loggia dei Mercanti.** In addition, Ancona can be the base for an excursion to Loreto or to Ascoli Piceno, farther south along the Adriatic coast.

Dining and Lodging

$$ ✕ **La Moretta.** This family-run trattoria is on the central Piazza del Plebiscito. In summer there is dining outside in the square, which has a fine view of the Baroque church of San Domenico. Among the specialties here are *stoccafisso all'Anconetana* (stockfish baked with capers, anchovies, potatoes, and tomatoes) and the famous brodetto fish stew. ✉ *Piazza del Plebiscito 52,* ☎ *071/202317. Reservations essential. AE, DC, MC, V. Closed Sun. and first 10 days in Jan.*

$$$ **Grand Hotel Palace.** In town center, near the entrance to the port of Ancona, and widely held to be the best in town, this is an old-fashioned place well run by a courteous staff. ✉ *Lungomare Vanvitelli 24, 60100,* ☎ *071/201813,* FAX *071/2074832. 40 rooms. Bar, parking (fee). AE, DC, MC, V.*

Loreto

10 *31 km (19 mi) south of Ancona, 118 km (73 mi) southeast of Urbino.*

Loreto is famous for one of the best-loved shrines in the world, that ★ of the **Santuario della Santa Casa** (House of the Virgin Mary), within the Basilica. The legend is that angels moved the house from Nazareth, where the Virgin Mary was living at the time of the Annunciation, to this hilltop in 1295. The reason for this sudden and divinely inspired move was that Nazareth had fallen into the hands of Muslim invaders, not suitable landlords, the angelic hosts felt. More recently, following archaeological excavations made at the behest of the Church, evidence has come to light proving that the house did once stand elsewhere and was brought to the hilltop by human means around the time the angels are said to have done the job.

The house itself consists of three rough stone walls contained within an elaborate marble tabernacle; built around this centerpiece is the giant basilica of the Holy House, which dominates the town. Millions of visitors come to the site every year (particularly at Easter and on the Feast of the Holy House, December 10), and the little town of Loreto can become uncomfortably crowded with pilgrims. Many great Italian architects, including Bramante, Antonio da Sangallo (the Younger, 1483–1546), Giuliano da Sangallo (circa 1445–1516), and Sansovino (1467–1529), contributed to the design of the basilica. The basilica was begun in Gothic style in 1468 and continued in Renaissance style through the late Renaissance. The bell tower is by Luigi Vanvitelli (1700–73). Inside the church are a great many mediocre 19th- and 20th-century paintings but also some fine works by Renaissance masters such as Luca Signorelli and Melozzo da Forlì. ✉ *Piazza della Madonna,* ☎ *071/970104.* ⏲ *June–Sept., daily 8–8; Oct.–May, daily 6 AM–7 PM. The Santuario della Santa Casa closes from 12:30 to 2:30 year-round.*

If you're a nervous air traveler you can take comfort in the fact that the Holy Virgin of Loreto is the patroness of air travelers and that Pope John Paul II has composed a prayer for a safe flight—available in the church in a half dozen languages.

Ascoli Piceno

⓫ *105 km (65 mi) south of Ancona, 175 km (109 mi) southeast of Perugia.*

Ascoli Piceno is not a hill town; rather, it sits in a valley ringed by steep hills and cut by the fast-racing Tronto River. The town is almost unique in Italy, in that it seems to have its traffic problems—in the historic center, at any rate—pretty much under control; you can drive *around* the picturesque part of the city, but driving *through* it is most difficult. This feature makes Ascoli Piceno one of the most pleasant large towns in the country for exploring on foot. True, there is traffic, but you are not constantly assaulted by jams, noise, and exhaust fumes the way you are in other Italian cities.

★ The heart of the town is the majestic **Piazza del Popolo,** dominated by the Gothic church of **San Francesco** and the **Palazzo dei Capitani del Popolo,** a 13th-century town hall that contains a graceful Renaissance courtyard. The square itself functions as the living room of the entire city. At dusk each evening the piazza is packed with people strolling and exchanging news and gossip—the sweetly antiquated ritual called the passeggiata, done all over the country. Ascoli Piceno's **Giostra della Quintana** (Joust of the Quintana) takes place on the first Sunday in August. Children should love this medieval-style joust and the richly caparisoned processions that wind through the streets of the old town. Contact the Ascoli tourist office (☞ Visitor Information *in* Umbria and the Marches A to Z, *below*) for details.

Dining and Lodging

$$ ★ ✕ **Ristorante Tornasacco.** In this family-run restaurant with modern decor, you can sample Ascoli's specialties, like *olive ascolane* (stuffed with minced meat, breaded, and deep-fried), as well as *maccheroncini alla contadina* (a homemade pasta in a thick meat sauce). ✉ *Piazza del Popolo 36,* ☎ *0736/254151. AE, DC, MC, V. Closed Fri. and July 1–15.*

$ 🏨 **Piceno.** This modest hostelry is one of the few lodgings in the historic center. It offers clean, basic amenities—no frills at all here. The staff is helpful and courteous, and the setting is perfect. ✉ *Via Minucia 10, 63100,* ☎ *0736/252553. 30 rooms, 6 without bath. AE, DC, MC, V. Closed Jan.*

En Route The 175-km (108-mi) drive from Ascoli Piceno to Spoleto takes you out of the Marches and back into Umbria. The route—S4 southwest to Rieti, then S79 north to Terni, then S3 into Spoleto—is roundabout but vastly preferable to a series of winding mountain roads that connect Ascoli Piceno with Umbria.

SPOLETO

"Quaint" may be an overused term, but it is the most appropriate word to describe this city 50 km (30 mi) south of Perugia, still enclosed by stout medieval walls. From the churches set among silvery olive groves on the outskirts of town to the imposing fortress at it's peak, Spoleto radiates grandeur and hushed charm. You can simply delight in the enchanting mazes of twisting streets and cobbled stairways, and wonderful peace and quiet.

Quiet, that is, except when Spoleto is hosting the Festival dei Due Mondi (Festival of Two Worlds, ☞ Nightlife and the Arts, *below*), an arts festival held every year from mid-June to mid-July. During that month the sleepy town is swamped with visitors who come to see world-class plays and operas, to hear concerts, and to see extensive exhibitions of paintings and sculpture. It is unwise to arrive during this period without confirmed hotel reservations.

Exploring Spoleto

Spoleto is small, and its noteworthy sights are clustered in the upper part of town. Like most towns made up of narrow, winding streets, Spoleto is best explored on foot. Several pedestrian walkways cut down the hill, crossing the Corso Mazzini, which turns up the hill. Parking in Spoleto is always difficult; park outside the walls in Piazza della Vittoria.

A Good Walk

Begin at Piazza del Duomo, and visit the **Duomo** ⑫, which stands against a backdrop of hill and sky with La Rocca towering overhead. Cross the piazza and go up the stairs to Via Saffi and the church of **Sant'Eufemia** ⑬ and its museum (both closed for restoration at press time). If you are short on time, skip Sant'Eufemia and head straight up to **La Rocca** ⑭ and **Ponte delle Torri** ⑮. Retrace your steps back to the picturesque Via Fontesecca (Sant'Eufemia), with its tempting shops selling local pottery and other handicrafts; it descends to the **Pinacoteca** ⑯ and **Casa Romana.** Have a visit or continue on to Piazza del Mercato, built on the site of the Roman Forum and home to Spoleto's open-air produce market, open daily Monday–Saturday 8–1:30. At the narrow end of Piazza del Mercato is the **Arco di Druso** ⑰. Turn right on Via Brignone and cross Piazza della Libertà to Via Sant'Agata, which leads to the **Teatro Romano** ⑱ and **Museo Archeologico.**

TIMING

Spoleto is not the most demanding town in terms of sights. A day will allow you to see all of the highlights, leaving time for leisurely strolls and a walk to the Ponte delle Torri.

Sights to See

⑰ **Arco di Druso** (Arch of Drusus). This structure was built in the 1st century AD by the Senate of Spoleto to honor the Roman general Drusus (circa 13 BC–AD 23), son of the emperor Tiberius. It once marked the entrance to the Foro Romano (Roman Forum). ✉ *Piazza del Mercato.*

⑫ **Duomo.** The church's rather dour 12th-century Romanesque facade is lightened up by the addition of a Renaissance loggia and eight rose win-

Arco di Druso, **17**
Duomo, **12**
La Rocca, **14**
Pinacoteca, **16**
Ponte delle Torri, **15**
Sant' Eufemia, **13**
Teatro Romano, **18**

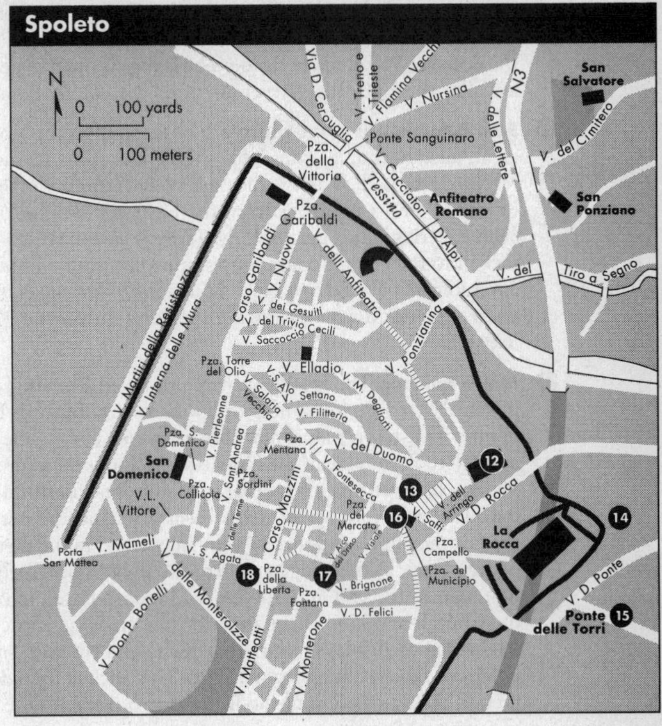

dows. The contrast demonstrates the difference in style and philosophy of the two eras: the earlier was strong and ungiving, the later, human and open-minded. The Duomo's interior holds the best art in town, most notably the immaculately restored frescoes in the apse by Fra Filippo Lippi (1406–69), showing the *Annunciation*, the *Nativity*, and the *Death of Mary*, with a marvelous *Coronation of the Virgin* adorning the dome; be ready with a 500-lire coin to illuminate the masterpiece. The Florentine artist died shortly after completing the work, and his tomb—designed by his son, Filippino Lippi (1457–1504)—lies in the church's right transept. Another fresco cycle, including work by Pinturicchio, can be seen in the **Cappella Eroli** off the right aisle. ✉ *Piazza Duomo.* ⏲ *Mar.–Oct., daily 8–1 and 3–6:30; Nov.–Feb., daily 8–1 and 3–5:30.*

⓮ **La Rocca.** Built in 1359–63 by the Gubbio-born architect Gattapone, the fortress dominates Spoleto. Until recently it served as a high-security prison, but at press time it was undergoing restoration and was to open in 1999 as a museum about medieval Spoleto, art restoration center, and exhibition space. You can admire the formidable exterior from the road that circles around it. ✉ *Take Via Saffi (off Piazza del Duomo) to Via del Ponte.*

⓰ **Pinacoteca.** The town picture gallery has a small collection of works from the 12th to the 18th centuries. Admission to the 1st-century AD **Casa Romana,** around the corner, is included on the same ticket. *Pinacoteca:* ✉ *Palazzo del Municipio, Via Aurelio Saffi. Casa Romana:* ✉ *Palazzo del Municipio, Via Visiale 9. Both:* ☎ *0743/2181.* 🎫 *5,000 lire.* ⏲ *Oct.–Apr., Tues.–Sun. 10–1 and 3–6; May–Sept., daily 10–1 and 4–7.*

⓯ **Ponte delle Torri.** La Rocca was built to protect the town's most famous monument, the massive Bridge of the Towers. It was built in the

14th century by Gattapone over the foundations of a Roman-era aqueduct, and stands 262 ft above the gorge at its highest point—taller than the dome of St. Peter's in Rome. The bridge is open to pedestrians, and a walk over it affords marvelous views. ✉ *Via del Ponte.*

13 **Sant'Eufemia.** Set in the courtyard of the archbishop's palace, this ancient, austere church dates from the 11th century. Its most interesting feature is the gallery above the nave where female worshipers were required to sit—a holdover from the Eastern Church—one of the few such galleries in this part of Italy. There is also a **Museo Diocesano** attached to the church containing some important paintings, including a Madonna by Fra Filippo Lippi. ✉ *Via Saffi, between Piazza del Duomo and Piazza del Mercato. Closed for restoration due to 1997 earthquake damage.*

18 **Teatro Romano.** The small but well-preserved Roman Theater is used in summer for performances of Spoleto's arts festival. It was the site of one of the town's most macabre incidents. During the Middle Ages, Spoleto took the side of the Holy Roman Emperor in the interminable struggle between Guelph (papal) and Ghibelline (imperial) factions over the question of who would control central and northern Italy. Four hundred of the pope's supporters were massacred in the theater, and their bodies were burned in an enormous pyre. The Guelphs were triumphant in the end and Spoleto was incorporated into the states of the Church in 1354. Through a door in the west portico, the **Museo Archeologico** displays assorted artifacts and the *Lex Spoletina* (Spoleto Law) tablets dating from 315 BC. This ancient legal document prohibited the destruction of the Bosco Sacro (Sacred Forest), just south of town on Monteluce, a pagan prayer site later frequented by St. Francis. ✉ *At the southern end of Corso Mazzini, in Via Sant'Agata,* ☎ *0743/223277.* 🎫 *4,000 lire.* ⏲ *Mon.–Sat. 9–7, Sun. 9–1.*

OFF THE BEATEN PATH

SAN SALVATORE – You may already have seen a lot of old churches in Italy, but few are as old as this one. It needed renovation in the 9th century—by that time it was already 500 years old. Nestled under cypresses and surrounded by Spoleto's cemetery, it's quiet, cool, and peaceful. The church was built by Eastern monks in the 4th century, and little has been added (or removed) since its renovation. San Salvatore has an air of timelessness and antiquity rarely found in churches so close to major towns. ✉ *Via della Basilica di San Salvatore, just out of town on the Via Flaminia.* ⏲ *Nov.–Feb., daily 7–5; Mar.–Apr. and Sept.–Oct., daily 7–6; May–Aug., daily 7–7.*

Dining and Lodging

$$$–$$$$ ✕ **Il Tartufo.** Spoleto's most famous restaurant has a smart modern dining room on the second floor and a rustic dining room downstairs—both of which incorporate the ruins of a Roman villa. The traditional cooking is spiced up in summer to appeal to the cosmopolitan crowd that is attending (or performing in) the Festival dei Due Mondi. As its name indicates, the restaurant specializes in dishes prepared with truffles ($$$$), though there is a second menu from which you can choose items not perfumed with this expensive delicacy ($$$). ✉ *Piazza Garibaldi 24,* ☎ *0743/40236. Reservations essential. AE, DC, MC, V. Closed Mon. and last 2 wks in July. No dinner Sun.*

$$ ✕ **Il Pentagramma.** Just off the central Piazza della Libertà, this modern restaurant features such local dishes as fresh ravioli *alle noci* (stuffed with butter and sage) and lamb in a truffle sauce. ✉ *Via Martani 4,* ☎ *0743/223141. Reservations essential during the festival and on weekends. DC, MC, V. Closed Mon.*

Close-Up

TRUFFLE TROUBLE

UMBRIA IS RICH WITH TRUFFLES—more are found here than anywhere else in Italy—and those not consumed fresh are processed into pastes or flavored oils. The primary truffle areas are around Spoleto (signs warning against unlicensed truffle hunting are posted at the base of the Ponte delle Torri) and the hills around the tiny town of Norcia, which holds a truffle festival every February. Even if they grow locally, the rare delicacy can nonetheless cost a small fortune, up to $200 for a quarter pound (fortunately, a little goes a long way). At such a price, there is great competition among the nearly 10,000 registered truffle hunters in the province, who use specially trained dogs to sniff them out among the roots of several trees, including oak and ilex. Although there have been recent incidences of poisoning truffle-hunting dogs and the importing of inferior tubers from China, you can be reasonably assured that the truffle shaved onto your pasta has been unearthed locally. The kind of truffle you taste will depend on the season: in summer, there's the *scorzone* (rough-skinned, dark gray–brown tuber); the fall rains bring out the *bianchetto* (small-sized, smoother, and dirty-white truffle variety); and the prized black *tartufo nero* (black truffle) appears from December through March. Out of season, restaurants rely on preserved truffles (in olive oil, vacuum sealed, frozen, or ground into a paste).

$$ ✕ **Trattoria Panciolle.** In the heart of Spoleto's medieval quarter, this restaurant has one of the most romantic settings you could wish for. Dining outside in summer is a welcome respite, in a small piazza filled with lemon trees. Specialties include strangozzi pasta with mushroom sauce and *agnello scottadito* (grilled lamb chops). Seven guest rooms are also available here. ✉ *Via del Duomo 3,* ☎ *0743/45598. Reservations essential. AE, MC, V. Closed Wed. and last 2 wks in Jan.*

$$$ **Hotel Gattapone.** The tiny four-star Hotel Gattapone at the top of the old town, near the Ponte delle Torri, has wonderful views of the ancient bridge and the wooded slopes of Monteluco. The rooms are modern and tastefully decorated. ✉ *Via del Ponte 6, 06049,* ☎ *0743/223447,* FAX *0743/223448. 16 rooms. Bar. AE, DC, MC, V.*

$$ **Dei Duchi.** This excellent, well-run hotel is a favorite among performers in the Festival dei Due Mondi. It's in town center, near the Roman amphitheater. Some rooms have fine views of the city. ✉ *Viale Matteotti 4, 06049,* ☎ *0743/44541,* FAX *0743/44543. 49 rooms. Restaurant, bar, meeting rooms, free parking. AE, DC, MC, V.*

$$ **Nuovo Clitunno.** A renovated 18th-century building houses this pleasant hotel, a five-minute walk from the town center. Bedrooms and public rooms, some with lovely timber-beamed ceilings, have a mixture of period as well as less characterful modern furniture. ✉ *Piazza Sordini 6, 06049,* ☎ *0743/223340,* FAX *0743/222663. 40 rooms. Restaurant, bar. AE, DC, MC, V.*

Nightlife and the Arts

The **Festival dei Due Mondi** (Festival of Two Worlds) in Spoleto, held mid-June to mid-July, features accomplished artists in all branches of the arts—particularly music, opera, and theater—and draws thousands of visitors from all over the world. Tickets for all performances should be ordered in advance from the festival's box office (✉ Piazza Duomo 8, ☎ 0743/220320, FAX 0743/220321) which has full program information starting in April.

OFF THE BEATEN PATH

VALNERINA – This is the name of the area southeast of Spoleto, and it is the most beautiful of central Italy's many well-kept secrets. The roads that serve the rugged landscape are poor, but a drive through the region, even with all those time-consuming twists and turns, will be worth it to see forgotten medieval villages and dramatic mountain scenery.

CASCATA DELLE MARMORE – The first stop should be these waterfalls, said to be the highest in Europe. You'll find them a few kilometers east of Terni, on the road to Lake Piediluco and Rieti. The waters are diverted on weekdays to provide hydroelectric power for the town of Terni, so check with the tourist office (☞ Visitor Information *in* Umbria and the Marches A to Z, *below*) in Spoleto before heading here. On summer evenings, when the falls are in full spate, the cascading water is floodlit (June–August, nightly 8–10; mid-March–May and September, weekends nightly 8–9).

SAN PIETRO IN VALLE – Close to the picturesque town of Ferentillo (northeast of Terni on S209) is the outstanding 8th-century abbey of San Pietro, with fine frescoes in the church nave and a peaceful cloister. As a bonus, one of the abbey outbuildings houses an excellent restaurant with moderate prices.

NORCIA – East of Spoleto in the Valnerina is this town, most famous for Umbrian food specialties. It is also the birthplace of St. Benedict. Norcia exports truffles to France and hosts a truffle festival, Mostra Internazionale del Tartufo Nero di Norcia, every November.

ASSISI

The legacy of St. Francis, founder of the Franciscan monastic order, pervades the rose-color hills of Assisi, 47 km (30 mi) north of Spoleto and 25 km (16 mi) east of Perugia. Each year, several million pilgrims come here to pay homage to the man who made God accessible to commoners. But not even the steadily massive flow of visitors to this town with just 3,000 residents can spoil the singular beauty of Italy's most significant religious center. The hill on which Assisi sits rises dramatically from the flat plain, and the town is dominated at the top of the mount by a medieval castle; on the lower slopes of the hill is the massive Basilica di San Francesco, rising majestically on graceful arched supports. From a distance, St. Francis's birthplace looks—to use an evocative phrase of travel essayist James Reynolds—"calm, white, pure as the fresh-washed wool from the Pascal Lamb."

St. Francis was born here in 1181, the son of a well-to-do merchant. After a sinful youth, he gave up the pleasures of the flesh and adopted a life of austerity. His mystical approach to poverty, asceticism, and the beauty of man and nature struck a responsive chord in the medieval mind, and he quickly attracted a vast number of followers. The compassion and humility of this humble and unassuming man brought him great love and veneration in his own lifetime. Without actively seeking power, as did many clerics of his day, he amassed great influence and political power, changing the history of the Catholic Church. He was the first person to receive the stigmata (wounds in his hands, feet, and side corresponding to the torments of Christ on the cross), injuries that caused him great pain and suffering, which he bore with characteristic patience. Today the Franciscans are the largest of all the Catholic orders. And among the mass of clergy at Assisi, you can identify the saint's followers by their simple, coarse brown habits bound by sashes of knotted rope.

A series of severe earthquakes in late September and October 1997 centered in nearby Foligno did devastating damage to Assisi and many towns in Umbria and the Marche. Particularly hard hit was the Basilica di San Francesco; frescoes by Giotto, widely held to be masterpieces of Western art, were destroyed when the vault of the Upper Basilica collapsed. Since then Assisi has risen again. At press time the other sights in town have been reopened, with the exception of Santa Maria degli Angeli, San Rufino, and San Francesco's Upper Basilica, Tesoro, and Chiostro dei Morti.

Exploring Assisi

The train station is 4 km (2½ mi) from town, with bus service about every half hour. The walled town is closed to outside traffic, so cars must be left in the parking lots at Porta San Pietro, near Porta Nuova or beneath Piazza Matteotti. Frequent city buses run between the parking lots and the center of town.

A Good Walk

Much of your visit to Assisi will likely be spent in churches and walking through the quiet streets. You'll want to set aside a good portion of your time for the **Basilica di San Francesco** ⑲, even if only the Lower Basilica is open. Via San Francesco leads back to Piazza del Comune and its Pinacoteca, Museo Civico, and the **Tempio di Minerva** ⑳. From the piazza, Via di San Rufino leads to **San Rufino** ㉑, which serves as Assisi's Duomo. Double back to the piazza and take Corso Mazzini to **Santa Chiara** ㉒, then continue through the Porta Nuova to the church of **San Damiano,** a 1-km (½-mi) walk a few minutes outside the walls. Also of interest outside the walls are the **Eremo delle Carceri,** east of the center along Via Santuario delle Carceri, and the church of **Santa Maria degli Angeli,** near the train station.

TIMING

Devote a half day or good part of the day for this walk. After seeing the Basilica di San Francesco, you can stroll along the length of town, stopping in at churches and shops.

Sights to See

★ ⑲ **Basilica di San Francesco.** One wonders what St. Francis would have made of a church—begun just a few years after his death—of such size, wealth, and grandeur, the opposite of all he preached and believed. His coffin, unearthed from its secret hiding place in 1818, is on display in the crypt below the Lower Basilica in a place of piety. The basilica is not one church but two huge structures built one over the other. Both are magnificently decorated artistic treasure houses: the Lower Basilica is dim and full of candlelit shadows, the Upper Basilica bright and airy. The Upper Basilica suffered extensive damage in the wake of the 1997 earthquakes and is closed to the public through 1999.

The first chapel in the **Lower Basilica** on the left of the nave was decorated by the Sienese master Simone Martini (1284–1344). Frescoed in 1322–26, the paintings show the life of St. Martin—the sharing of his cloak with the poor man, the saint's knighthood, and his death. There is some dispute about the paintings in the third chapel on the right. Experts have argued for years as to their authorship, with many saying that they were done by Giotto (1266–1337). The paintings depict the life of St. Mary Magdalen. There is a similar dispute about the works above the high altar—some say they are by Giotto; others claim them for an anonymous pupil. They depict the marriage of St. Fran-

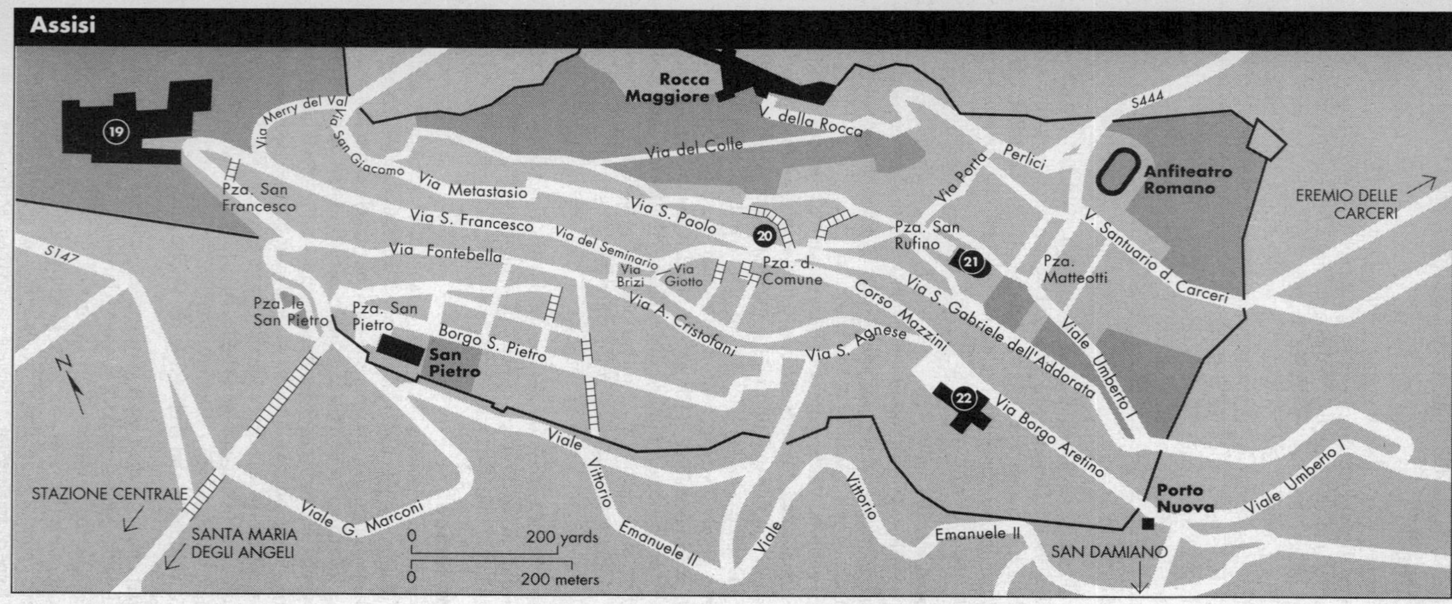

Basilica di San Francesco, **19**

San Rufino, **21**

Santa Chiara, **22**

Tempio di Minerva, **20**

cis to poverty, chastity, and obedience. In the right transept are frescoes by Cimabue (circa 1240–1302), a Madonna and saints, one of them St. Francis himself. In the left transept are some of the best-known works of the Sienese painter Pietro Lorenzetti (circa 1280–1348). They depict the *Madonna with Sts. John and Francis,* a *Crucifixion,* and a *Descent from the Cross.*

It is quite a contrast to climb the steps next to the altar and emerge into the bright sunlight and airy grace of the double-arched Renaissance **Chiostro dei Morti** (Cloister of the Dead). A door to the right leads to the **Tesoro** (Treasury) of the church and contains relics of St. Francis and other holy objects associated with the order. Both are closed through 1999 due to earthquake damage.

The **Upper Basilica,** at press time also closed through 1999, is dominated by Giotto's 28 frescoes (some damaged or obliterated from the earthquake), each portraying incidents in the life of St. Francis. Although the artist was only in his twenties when he painted this cycle, the frescoes show that Giotto was the pivotal artist in the development of Western painting, breaking away from the stiff, unnatural styles of earlier generations and moving toward a realism and grace that reached their peak in the Renaissance. The paintings are viewed left to right, starting in the transept. The most beloved of all the scenes is probably *St. Francis Preaching to the Birds,* a touching painting that seems to sum up the gentle spirit of the saint. It stands in marked contrast to the scene of the dream of Innocent III (1160/61–1216). The pope dreams of a humble monk who will steady the church. Sure enough, in the panel next to the sleeping pope, you see a strong Francis supporting a church that seems to be—bitterly ironic today—on the verge of tumbling down. ⊠ *Piazza di San Francesco,* ☎ *075/819001.* ⏲ *Lower Basilica: Easter–Oct., daily 7–7; Nov.–Easter, daily 7–12:30 and 2–6. Upper Basilica (church, Cloister, and Treasury) closed through 1999 for restoration.*

21 **San Rufino.** St. Francis and St. Clare were among those baptized in Assisi's Duomo, the principal church in town until the 12th century. The baptismal font has since been redecorated, but it is possible to see the **crypt** of San Rufino, the martyred 3rd-century bishop who brought Christianity to Assisi. Admission to the crypt includes a look at the small **Museo Capitolare,** which features detached frescoes and artifacts. ⊠ *Piazza San Ruffino. Closed through 1999 due to earthquake damage.*

22 **Santa Chiara.** This 13th-century church is dedicated to St. Clare, one of the earliest and most fervent of St. Francis's followers and the founder of the order of the Poor Ladies, or Poor Clares, in imitation of the Franciscans. The church contains the body of the saint, and in the **Cappella del Crocifisso** (Chapel of the Crucifix) is the cross that spoke to St. Francis and led him to a life of piety. A heavily veiled member of St. Clare's order is stationed before the cross in perpetual adoration of the image. ⊠ *Piazza Santa Chiara.* ⏲ *Daily 8–noon and 2:30–sunset.*

20 **Tempio di Minerva** (Temple of Minerva). Bits and pieces of a Roman temple dating from the time of Augustus (63 BC–AD 14) make up this sanctuary dedicated to the Roman goddess of wisdom. The expectations raised by the perfect classical facade are not met by the interior, subjected to a thorough Baroque assault in the 17th century. ⊠ *Piazza del Comune.* ⏲ *Daily 7–noon and 2:30–sunset.*

OFF THE BEATEN PATH

EREMO DELLE CARCERI – Just 4 km (2½ mi) east of Assisi is this monastery set in dense woodlands on the side of Monte Subasio. In the caves on the slope of the mountain, Francis and his followers established their first home, to which he returned often during his lifetime to pray and meditate. The church and monastery retain the tranquil contemplative air St. Francis so prized. From a vantage point within the monastery, visitors can take in one of the most beautiful vistas over the Umbrian countryside. True to their Franciscan heritage, the friars here are entirely dependent on alms from visitors. ✉ *Via Santuario delle Carceri.* *Donations accepted.* ⏲ *Nov.–Mar., daily 6:30–5; Apr.–Oct., daily 6:30–7.*

SANTA MARIA DEGLI ANGELI – On the outskirts of the town, near the train station, this Baroque church was built over the **Porziuncola,** a little chapel restored by St. Francis. The shrine is much venerated because it was here, in the **Cappella del Transito,** then a humble cell, that St. Francis died (1226). ✉ *Località Santa Maria degli Angeli. Closed indefinitely for restoration due to earthquake damage.*

CANNARA – A pleasant excursion from Assisi leads to this tiny town; a half-hour walk outside the town are the fields of Pian d'Arca, which legend claims as the site of St. Francis's sermon to the birds.

Dining and Lodging

$$ ✕ **Buca di San Francesco.** This central restaurant is Assisi's busiest—it's no wonder, for the setting is lovely no matter what the season. In summer you dine outside in a cool green garden; in winter, in the cozy cellars of the restaurant. The food is first rate, and the *filetto al rubesco* (fillet steak cooked in a heady red wine) is the specialty of the house. ✉ *Via Brizi 1,* ☎ *075/812204. Reservations essential. AE, DC, MC, V. Closed Mon. and July.*

$$ ✕ **La Fortezza.** Parts of the walls of this modern, family-run restaurant were built by the Romans. The service is personable and the kitchen reliable. A particular standout is *anatra al finocchio selvatico* (duck cooked with wild fennel). La Fortezza also has seven simple but clean guest rooms available. ✉ *Vicolo della Fortezza 19/b,* ☎ *075/812418. Reservations essential. AE, DC, MC, V. Closed Thurs. and Feb.*

$ ✕ **La Stalla.** A kilometer or two (½–1 mi) outside the town proper, this onetime stable has been turned into a simple and rustic restaurant. In summer, lunch and dinner are served outside under a trellis shaded with vines and flowers. In keeping with the decor, the kitchen turns out hearty country fare. ✉ *Via Santuario delle Carceri 8,* ☎ *075/812317. AE. Closed Mon. Oct.–June.*

$$$ **Hotel Subasio.** This hotel, close to the Basilica of St. Francis, has counted Marlene Dietrich and Charlie Chaplin among its guests. It is housed in a converted monastery and has plenty of atmosphere. Some of the rooms remain a little monastic, but the views, comfortable old-fashioned sitting rooms, flowered terraces, and a lovely garden more than make up for the simplicity. Ask for a room with a view of the valley. ✉ *Via Frate Elia 2, 06081,* ☎ *075/812206,* FAX *075/816691. 61 rooms. Restaurant, bar. AE, DC, MC, V.*

$$$ **San Francesco.** You can't beat the location—some of the rooms look out onto Basilica di San Francesco, which is just opposite the hotel. Rooms are rather basic, but with nice touches like slippers and a good-night piece of chocolate. This is also one of the few hotels with air-conditioning in every room. The breakfast is first-rate, with fruit, homemade tarts, and fresh ricotta. ✉ *Via di San Francesco 48, 06082,* ☎ *075/812281,* FAX *075/816237. 44 rooms. Restaurant, bar. AE, DC, MC, V.*

$$ ★ **Hotel Umbra.** A 16th-century town house is home to this hotel, which is in a tranquil part of the city, an area closed to traffic, near Piazza del Comune. The rooms are arranged as small apartments, each with a tiny living room and terrace. The restaurant does not serve lunch Tuesday or Wednesday. ✉ *Via degli Archi 6, 06081,* ☎ *075/812240,*

FAX 075/813653. 25 rooms. Restaurant, bar. AE, DC, MC, V. Closed mid-Jan.–mid-Mar. and Dec. 1–20.*

SOUTHERN UMBRIA

Save room for Orvieto, built on a tufa mount, with one of Italy's greatest cathedrals and most compelling fresco cycles. Nearby Narni and Todi are two pleasant medieval hill towns. The former stands firm over a steep gorge, its Roman pedigree evident in the dark alleyways and winding streets; the latter a fairy-tale town with incomparable Umbrian views and one of Italy's most perfect piazzas.

Todi

23 *60 km (37 mi) southwest of Assisi, 45 km (28 mi) south of Perugia.*

Standing on **Piazza del Popolo,** it's easy to see why Todi is often described as Umbria's prettiest hill town. The square is a model of spatial harmony with stunning views onto the surrounding countryside. On one end is the 12th-century Romanesque-Gothic **Duomo,** with a famous choir stall by Antonio Bencivenni da Mercatello and his son Sebastiano dating from 1521 to 1530. Its simple square facade is echoed by the solid Palazzo dei Priori across the way. Narrow cobblestone streets go winding around the hill, every so often finishing in a tiny, quiet piazza. Quite unexpected is the Renaissance church of **Santa Maria della Consolazione,** with an elegant pale-green dome, on the outskirts of town.

Dining and Lodging

$$ ✕ **Ristorante Umbria.** Todi's most popular restaurant for over four decades, Umbria is reliable for sturdy country food, plus a wonderful view from the terrace. There's always a hearty soup simmering away, as well as homemade pasta with truffles, game, and the specialty of the house, *palombaccio alla ghiotta* (roasted squab). ✉ *Via San Bonaventura 13,* ☎ *075/8942390. AE, D, MC, V. Closed Tues. and July.*

$$–$$$ **Tenuta di Canonica.** The affable hosts, Daniele and Maria Fano, scoured Tuscany and Umbria and returned to the first place they saw, a brick farmhouse and medieval tower, with a foundation dating from the Roman period, in the Tiber Valley 5 km (3 mi) northwest of Todi. The Fanos have tastefully retained the architectural integrity: you're bound to marvel at the exposed stone walls, high-beamed ceilings, brick floors, and terra-cotta tiles, all soothed by cool colors. Guest rooms are filled with family furniture and antique pieces. You can hike or horseback ride among the olive groves, orchards, and forest on the grounds, which includes two apartments that each sleep two to three people. ✉ *Località La Canonica, 75–76, follow signs to Titignano and Cordigliano, 06059,* ☎ *075/8947545,* FAX *075/8947581. 11 rooms, 2 apartments. Dining room, pool, library. No credit cards.*

Narni

24 *35 km (22 mi) south of Todi, 84 km (46 mi) southeast of Perugia.*

At the edge of a steep gorge, Narni—like so many other towns in Umbria—is a medieval city of Roman origins. Below its finely paved streets and pretty Romanesque churches, excavations have revealed parts of its fascinating past. The **Lacus,** under Piazza Garibaldi, is a large cistern with remnants of a Roman floor that was in use until the late Middle Ages. Two more cisterns and Roman fragments are visible in the crypt of the 12th-century church of **Santa Maria in Pensole** (✉ Via Mazzini), open daily 9:30–noon and 4:30–6:30. More interesting are the rooms under the ex-church of **San Domenico,** where the prisoners of the Inquisition engraved mysterious symbols and dates. The best day to visit is Sunday, when the excavated sites are open and tours are given in English. Contact Associazione Culturale Subterranea or call the tourist office (☞ Visitor Information *in* Umbria and the Marches A to Z, *below*) to book a visit of the excavations during the week. ✉ *Associazione Culturale Subterranea, Giardini di San Bernardo,* ☎ *0744/722292.* ⏲ *Excavations: Sun. and holidays 11–1 and 3–5.*

Dining

$ ✕ **Il Cavallino.** Run by the third generation of the Bussetti family, Il Cavallino is a first-rate trattoria about 2 km (1 mi) outside Narni. There are always several pastas to choose from, but it's the meat that makes this a worthy detour. Rabbit roasted with rosemary and sage and juicy grilled T-bone steaks are house favorites. The wine list features the best of what's local. ✉ *Via Flaminia Romana 220,* ☎ *0744/761020. AE, D, MC, V. Closed Tues. and 2 wks in July.*

Orvieto

25 *52 km (32 mi) northeast of Narni, 86 km (53 mi) south of Perugia.*

Sitting atop an enormous plateau of volcanic rock high above the valley below, Orvieto's natural defenses eliminated the need for high walls. The Etruscans were the first to take advantage of this and settled here, carving a network of 1,200 wells and storage caves out of the soft stone. The Romans attacked, sacked, and destroyed the city in 283 BC. From that time, Orvieto has had close ties with Rome. It was solidly Guelph in the Middle Ages, and for several hundred years popes sought refuge in the city, at times needing protection from their enemies, at times fleeing from the summer heat of Rome.

Orvieto is known for its white wines. Some of the region's finest wines are produced here (Signorelli, when painting the Duomo, asked that part of his contract be paid in wine), and the rock on which the town sits is honeycombed with caves used to ferment the Trebbiano grapes that are used in making Orvieto wines.

★ Orvieto's **Duomo** is one of the most dazzling in all of Italy, a triumph of Romanesque-Gothic architecture. Legend has it that a priest in the nearby town of Bolsena suddenly found himself assailed by doubts about the transubstantiation—he could not bring himself to believe that the body of Christ was contained in the consecrated communion host. His doubts were put to rest, however, when a wafer he had just blessed suddenly started to drip blood. Drops of blood fell onto the linen covering the altar, and this cloth and the host itself are the principal relics of the miracle. The pope seized the opportunity to proclaim a new religious holiday—the Feast of Corpus Christi—and the duomo was built to celebrate the miracle and house the stained altar cloth. The stunning facade is the work of some of Italy's finest artists and took 300 years to complete. The bas-reliefs on the lower parts of the pillars were carved by Lorenzo Maitani (circa 1275–1330), one of the original architects of the building, and show scenes from the Old Testament and some particularly gruesome renderings of the Last Judgment and Hell, as well as a more tranquil Paradise. (They have been covered with Plexiglas following some vandalizing in the 1960s.)

The major works inside are the two chapels in the transepts. To the left is the **Cappella del Corporale,** where the famous altar cloth is kept in a golden reliquary modeled on the cathedral, inlaid with enamel images of the miracle. The cloth is removed for public viewing on Easter and on Corpus Christi (the ninth Sunday after Easter). A trio of local artists executed frescoes depicting the miracle on the chapel walls. The **Cap-**

pella Nuova (a.k.a. Cappella della Madonna di San Brizio), in the right transept, is the artistic jewel of Orvieto. It contains Luca Signorelli's fresco cycle *Stories of the Antichrist,* among the most delightfully gruesome works in Italy. As the damned fall to hell, demons with green buttocks bite off ears, step on heads, and spirit away young girls. Dante would surely have approved; in the chapel, his portrait accompanies *Scenes from Purgatorio.* Signorelli and Fra Angelico, who also worked on the chapel, witness the gory scene. ✉ *Piazza del Duomo,* ☎ *0763/342477.* 🎫 *Cappella Nuova: 3,000 lire (buy tickets at tourist office across the piazza).* ⏲ *Nov.–Feb., daily 7:30–12:45 and 2:30–5:15; Mar. and Oct., daily 7:30–12:45 and 2:30–6:15; Apr.–Sept., daily 7:30–12:45 and 2:30–7:15.*

Next door, the **Museo dell'Opera del Duomo** (✉ Piazza del Duomo, ☎ 0763/342477), closed for restoration through 1999, contains original and later plans for the cathedral, as well as some paintings and sculptures. Right across the piazza, the **Museo Claudio Faina** holds Etruscan and Roman artifacts; the museum is designed in a way that makes its Roman coins, bronze pieces, and sarcophagi accessible and interesting. ✉ *Palazzo Faina,* ☎ *0763/341511.* 🎫 *7,000 lire.* ⏲ *Oct.–Mar., Tues.–Sun. 10–1 and 2:30–5; Apr.–Sept., daily 10–1 and 2–6.*

On Piazza Cahen, the **Fortezza,** built in the mid-14th century, encloses a public park with grass, benches, shade and an incredible view. The nearby **Pozzo di San Patrizio,** or Well of St. Patrick, was commissioned by Pope Clement VII (1478–1534) in 1527 to ensure a plentiful water supply. Descend into the well on a pair of zigzagging mule paths designed to avoid animal traffic jams. ✉ *Via Sangallo, off Piazza Cahen,* ☎ *0763/343768.* 🎫 *6,000 lire.* ⏲ *Oct.–Feb., daily 10–5:45; Mar.–Sept., daily 9:30–6:45.*

Dining and Lodging

$$ ★ ✕ **Le Grotte del Funaro.** This restaurant has an extraordinary spot, deep in a series of caves within the volcanic rock beneath Orvieto. Once you have negotiated the steep steps, typical Umbrian specialties like tagliatelle *al vino rosso* (with red wine sauce) and grilled beef with truffles await. Sample the fine Orvieto wines, either the whites or the lesser-known reds. ✉ *Via Ripa Serancia 41,* ☎ *0763/343276. Reservations essential. AE, DC, MC, V. Closed Mon.*

$$ ★ ✕ **Maurizio.** In the heart of Orvieto, just opposite the cathedral, this warm and welcoming restaurant gets its share of tourists and has a local clientele as well. The decor is unusual, with wood sculptures by Orvieto craftsman Michelangeli. The menu offers hearty soups and homemade pastas such as *tronchetti* (a pasta roll with spinach and ricotta filling). ✉ *Via del Duomo 78,* ☎ *0763/341114. Reservations essential in summer. AE, MC, V. Closed Tues.*

$$$ 🏨 **Hotel La Badia.** This is one of the best-known country hotels in Umbria. The 700-year-old building, a former monastery, is set in rolling parkland that provides wonderful views of the valley and the town of Orvieto in the distance. The rooms are well appointed. ✉ *Località La Badia, 4 km (2½ mi) south of Orvieto, 05018,* ☎ *0763/90359,* FAX *0763/92796. 26 rooms. Restaurant, bar, pool, 2 tennis courts, meeting rooms. AE, MC, V. Closed Jan.–Feb.*

$$–$$$ 🏨 **Grand Hotel Reale.** This hotel is in the center of Orvieto, across a square that hosts a lively market. Facing the impressive Gothic-Romanesque Palazzo del Popolo, rooms are spacious and adequately furnished, with a traditional accent. ✉ *Piazza del Popolo 25, 05018,* ☎ *0763/341247,* FAX *0763/341247. 32 rooms. Bar. MC, V.*

$$–$$$ 🏨 **Villa Bellago.** Outside Orvieto, in a tranquil setting on a spit of land overlooking Lake Corbara, three farmhouses have been completely overhauled. The result is welcome: the hotel now includes well-lighted and

spacious guest rooms, generous facilities, and a fine restaurant (closed Tuesday) specializing in imaginatively prepared Umbrian and Tuscan dishes. Fresh fish is always on the menu. ✉ *Outside the village of Baschi, 7½ km (4½ mi) south of Orvieto on S448, 05018,* ☎ *0744/950521,* FAX *0744/950524. 12 rooms. Restaurant, bar, pool, tennis court, exercise room. AE, DC, MC, V. Closed 4 wks Jan.–Feb.*

$$ 🏨 **Virgilio.** The modest Hotel Virgilio is right in Piazza del Duomo, and the views of the cathedral are wonderful. The rooms are small but nicely furnished. ✉ *Piazza del Duomo 5, 05018,* ☎ *0763/341882,* FAX *0763/343797. 13 rooms. Bar. MC, V. Closed Feb.*

Shopping

EMBROIDERY AND LACE

Minor arts such as embroidery and lace making flourish in Orvieto. One of the best shops for *merletto* (lace) is **Duranti** (✉ Corso Cavour 107).

WINE

Excellent Orvieto wines are justly prized throughout Italy and in foreign countries. The whites pressed from the region's Trebbiano grapes are fruity, with a tart finish. Orvieto also produces its own version of the Tuscan dessert wine *vin santo.* It is darker than its Tuscan cousin and is aged five years before bottling.You may stop for a glass of vino at the **wine cellar** (✉ No. 2, Piazza del Duomo), where there's also a good selection of sandwiches and snacks and vin santo is on sale.

WOODWORKING

Orvieto is a center of woodworking, particularly fine inlays and veneers. The Corso Cavour has a number of artisan shops specializing in woodwork, the best known being the **Michelangeli family studio** (✉ Corso Cavour), crammed with a variety of imaginatively designed objects ranging in size from a giant *armadio* (wardrobe) to a simple wooden spoon.

ABRUZZO

Central Italy isn't all tranquil rolling hills dotted with picturesquehill towns and vineyards; just south of Umbria the terrain of the often-overlooked Abruzzo region quickly turns more rugged and mountainous, with isolated mountain villages and some of the country's best-preserved wildlife. Abruzzo is a place to enjoy nature in the rough, and there's no better place than the Parco Nazionale d'Abruzzo, which is well organized for hiking, skiing, and horseback riding. L'Aquila, a walkable town well worth an afternoon stroll, can also serve as a good base to explore the central part of the region.

L'Aquila

 *58 km (36 mi) southeast of Rieti, 167 km (104 mi) southeast of Orvieto.*

Arguably the youngest regional capital in Italy, L'Aquila was founded when Emperor Frederick II (1482–1556) united the 99 surrounding kingdoms under one flag (which bore an eagle, or *l'aquila*). The town's most famous fountain, **Fontana Delle 99 Canelle,** commemorates the event with 99 spouts, and the church bells in the Duomo ring 99 times each night. A good place to start a walk through L'Aquila is Piazza Battaglione Alpini, which serves as a bus terminal. The town's austere **Castello** (fortress) looms above, offering sweeping vistas of the nearby Gran Sasso mountain range. Built by the Spanish rulers in the 16th century to discourage popular revolt, the Castello also served as a prison. Today it is home to the **Museo Nazionale dell'Abruzzo,** which has a good collection drawn from the region's earthquake-ravaged churches and a gallery of modern art on the top floor. The highlight of the visit is a skeleton of a million-year-old mammoth, discovered nearby in 1954. ✉ *Viale delle Medaglie d'Oro,* ☎ *0862/6331.* 🎫 *8,000 lire.* ⏲ *Tues.–Sat. 9–2, Sun. 9–1.*

The main road from Piazza Battaglione Alpini leads to the center of town. Up on the right is the small Piazza Santa Maria Paganica. A little farther ahead is Via di San Bernardino, which climbs to the left to the Renaissance church of **San Bernardino,** with a facade featuring the classical orders of columns. The church, dating from the 15th century, was built in honor of St. Bernardine of Siena. The mausoleum that holds the saint's remains was built by a pupil of Donatello (circa 1386–1466), and the altarpiece is by Andrea della Robbia (1435–1525). The rest of the interior got a Baroque makeover in the early 18th century. ✉ *Via di San Bernardino.* ⏲ *Daily 8–12 and 4–6.*

Retrace your steps to Corso Vittorio Emanuele, which widens to become the arcaded main drag that finishes in Piazza del Duomo. A short walk from the piazza along Via Fontebella brings you just outside the city walls, to what is probably the most famous church in Abruzzo, **Santa Maria di Collemaggio.** It was built toward the end of the 13th century by the hermit Peter of Morrone, who was later elected pope. He was so attached to the church that he insisted on being crowned and buried here rather than in Rome (his remains rest in the mausoleum to the right of the altar). The simple Romanesque facade is strikingly laced with a geometric pattern of white and pink marble. Gothic elements include the rose windows and decorative portals. The interior is rather bare, although the floor has decorative patterns and several fine 15th-century frescoes. *Piazzale Collemaggio 1,* ☎ *0862/26744.* ⏲ *Daily 9–6:30.*

Dining and Lodging

Abruzzese cooking often involves hearty preparations and simple, strong, long-cooked flavors. You are likely to find plenty of lamb, mutton, and pork, pecorino cheese and ricotta, and wild mushrooms and lentils on restaurant menus, along with several dishes with saffron, which is grown near L'Aquila. The local wines tend toward the robust and the spicy; white Trebbiano and red Montepulciano d'Abruzzo are the best-known types.

$–$$ ✕ **Elodia.** A local favorite for classic Abruzzese cooking, with hard-to-find dishes like *crespelle di ricotta alla montanara* (thin ricotta pancakes) and simple flavors like chickpea and chestnut soup (in winter). Portions are large. Delicious homemade desserts such as apple and chocolate cake or pears baked in red wine should not be missed. Tables are set outside when the weather permits. ✉ *Frazione Camarda, S17bis del Gran Sasso,* ☎ *0862/606219. AE, DC, MC, V. Closed Mon. and first 2 wks in July. No dinner Sun.*

$ ✕ **Trattoria del Giaguaro.** In the most evocative square of town, this trattoria will welcome you with an array of homemade pasta dishes, one more tempting than the other, like *maccheroni a chitarra al sugo* (macaroni with lamb sauce) or ravioli filled with first-rate fresh sheep's milk ricotta. A selection of grilled meat or the popular *osso buco agli ortaggi* (veal shank in a tomato sauce, served with mixed vegetables) will fill you up fast, although you should try to save room for the house custard pudding with caramelized sugar. ✉ *Piazza Santa Maria Paganica 4,* ☎ *0862/28249. MC, V. Closed Tues., 2 wks between July and Aug., and over Christmas.*

$$ 🏨 **Duomo.** There is not much of a choice for hotels in L'Aquila (several are along the roads that lead to the winter resorts), but the quiet Duomo, housed in 18th-century quarters, is as central as it can be. Many rooms have a view of the lovely square below, and the decor is a nice blend of traditional touches and modern comforts: expect terra-cotta floors and wrought-iron beds matched with practical wooden furniture. Buffet breakfast includes local honey, cakes, and cookies. ✉ *Via Dragonetti 10, 67100,* ☎ *0862/410893,* FAX *0862/413058. 27 rooms. Bar. AE, MC, V.*

Shopping

Piazza Santa Maria Paganica hosts a good **antiques market** the second weekend of each month. Piazza del Duomo hosts the town's daily **produce market** Monday–Saturday 8–1.

Santo Stefano di Sessanio

27 *27 km (17 mi) east of L'Aquila.*

Santo Stefano di Sessanio, was first the property of the powerful Roman Piccolomini family, and then passed to the Medici family. It features the most sophisticated guard tower in the area, built with rounded instead of squared sides to make an attack more difficult. You can climb to the top to enjoy a panoramic view of the Campo Imperatore valley and its unusual rock formations.

Castel del Monte

28 *13 km (8 mi) east of Santo Stefano di Sessanio, 40 km (25 mi) east of L'Aquila.*

The country landscape surrounding L'Aquila is studded with old castles, guard towers, and tiny hamlets, some perfectly preserved and still inhabited, others in ruins, haunted by the ghosts of past battles.Castel del Monte and Santo Stefano di Sessanio (☞ *below*) are two medieval *borghi* (hamlets) east of L'Aquila on the S17bis that will make a pleasant half-day excursion. The first is an unusual example of a *ricetto,* a type of fortified village without external walls. A single steep access road rises to the center of the town, which is crossed by narrow alleys and dark tunnels leading to the more distant houses. In case of attack, the inhabitants could barricade themselves in their houses, block the narrow streets, and pour hot oil down the main street.

Parco Nazionale d'Abruzzo

29 *Pescasseroli 109 km (68 mi) southeast of L'Aquila.*

Italy does not have an elaborate national park system, but the National Park of Abruzzo has one of its best, full of lakes, streams, ruined castles, wildlife, and rugged terrain crossed by hiking trails and ski runs. Helpful information offices in the towns of Pescasseroli, Civitella Alfedena, and Villetta Barrea (☞ Visitor Information *in* Umbria and the Marches A to Z, *below*) have all the information you will need for a hike through the scenery and can also arrange guided tours in English. The "Carta Turistica," on sale just about everywhere, is a comprehensive topographical map with nearly 150 trails marked and identified with symbols that correspond to their relative difficulty and the animals that are most likely to meet on the way. One of the most popular short walks (2½ hours) begins near Opi (path F2) and crosses the lovely Valle Fondillo, with chamois and brown bears to be spotted in the early morning. For a full-day loop in the green, try path I1 to the Val di Rosa forest, then head up to Passo Cavuto and return to town via Valle Ianna'nghera (path K6). The park is open year-round, although it is best appreciated in the off-season, as during Easter week and between July and September the crowds of visitors often scare the animals away, and popular hiking routes are accessible by reservation only, to hold down congestion on the trails.

Dining

$$ ✕ **Plistia.** Pescasseroli's oldest inn, the Plistia has a lovely, low-key, small restaurant with a mission to keep old, traditional recipes alive. Get the eight-course tasting menu for a full session on Abruzzese cuisine, or select from a list of unheard of dishes like *carratelli* (pasta with wild spinach) or *cotturo* (lamb slowly simmered in a spiced broth). For dessert, the apple cake and almond tart are delightful. ✉ *Via Principe di Napoli 28, Pescasseroli,* ☎ *0863/910732. AE, DC, MC, V. Closed Mon.*

UMBRIA AND THE MARCHES A TO Z

Arriving and Departing

By Bus

Perugia is served by the **Sulga Line** (☎ 075/5009641) with daily departures from Rome's Stazione Tiburtina and from Piazza Adua in Florence. The central bus station in Abruzzo's L'Aquila sends hourly ARPA buses to Rome; buy tickets in the small ARPA kiosk on the piazza.

By Car

On the western edge of the region is the Umbrian section of the Autostrada del Sole (A1), the principal north–south highway in Italy. It links Florence and Rome with the important Umbrian town of Orvieto and passes near Todi and Terni. The S3 intersects with A1 and leads on to Assisi and Urbino. The Adriatica superhighway (A14) runs north–south along the coast, linking the Marches to Bologna and Venice. The A24 runs from Rome to L'Aquila and up to the Adriatic.

By Plane

The closest airports are Rome's **Fiumicino** (☎ 06/65953640), Pisa's **Aeroporto Galileo Galilei** (☎ 050/500707), and Florence's **Peretola** (☎ 055/333498).

By Train

Assisi lies on the Terontola–Foligno rail line, with almost hourly connections to Perugia and direct trains to Rome and Florence several times per day. The main rail line from Rome to Ancona passes through Narni, Terni, Spoleto, and Foligno. Travel time from Rome to Spoleto is a little less than 90 minutes on intercity trains. The main Rome–Florence line stops at Orvieto. With a change of trains at the small town of Terontola, one can travel by rail from Rome or Florence to Perugia and Assisi. Trains run to L'Aquila via Sulmona, which is on the Rome–Pescara line (the bus from Rome's Stazione Tiburtina is much faster, however, ☞ *above*). For train information, dial ☎ 147/888088 toll-free.

Getting Around

By Bus

There is good local bus service between all the major and minor towns of Umbria. Some of the routes in rural areas, especially in the Marches, are designed to serve as many destinations as possible and are, therefore, quite roundabout and slow. Schedules often change, so consult with local tourist offices before setting out.

By Car

Umbria has an excellent and modern road network. Central Umbria is served by a major highway, S75bis ("bis" means alternative highway), which passes along the shore of Lake Trasimeno and ends in Perugia. Assisi is well served by the modern highway S75; S75 connects to S3 and S3bis, which cover the heart of the region. Major inland routes connect coastal A14 to large towns in the Marches, including Urbino, Jesi, Macerata, and Ascoli Piceno, but inland secondary roads in mountain areas can be tortuous and narrow.

By Train

Branch lines link the central rail hub, Ancona, with the inland towns of Fabriano and Ascoli Piceno. Dial ☎ 147/888088 for toll-free train information. In Umbria, a small, privately owned railway, run by Ferrovia Centrale Umbra (FCU), runs from Città di Castello in the north to Terni in the south via Perugia.

Contacts and Resources

Agritourist Agencies

Turismo Verde (✉ Via Campo di Marte 14/1, 06100 Perugia, ☎ 075/5002953, FAX 075/5002956).

Car Rentals

ORVIETO

Hertz (✉ Via dell'Arcone 13, ☎ 0763/301303).

PERUGIA

Avis (✉ Sant'Egidio airport, ☎ 075/6929796; ✉ Stazione Ferroviaria Fontivegge, ☎ 5000395). **Hertz** (✉ Piazza Vittorio Veneto 4, ☎ 075/5002439).

SPOLETO

Avis (✉ Località S. Chiodo 164, ☎ 0743/46272). **Hertz** (✉ Via Cerquiglia 144, ☎ 0743/46366).

TERNI

Avis (✉ Via XX Settembre 80/d, ☎ 0744/287170).

Emergencies

☎ 113.

Visitor Information

Tourist offices (✉ Via Thaon de Revel 4, 60100 Ancona, ☎ 071/33249; ✉ Stazione FS, Piazza Fratelli Rosselli, 60100 Ancona, ☎ 071/41703, open June–September only; ✉ Piazza del Popolo 1, 63100 Ascoli Piceno, ☎ 0736/257288; ✉ Piazza del Comune 12, 06081 Assisi, ☎ 075/812534; ✉ Via Santa Lucia, 67030 Civitella Alfedena, ☎ FAX 0864/890141; ✉ Piazza Oderisi 6, 06024 Gubbio, ☎ 075/9220693; ✉ Via XX Settembre 8, 67100 L'Aquila, ☎ 0862/22306; ✉ Centro Turistico del Gran Sasso, Corso Vittorio Emanuele 49, L'Aquila 67100, ☎ 0862/22146; ✉ Via Solari 3, 60025 Loreto, ☎ 071/977139; ✉ Piazza dei Priori 3, 05035 Narni, ☎ 0744/715362; ✉ Piazza Duomo 24, 05018 Orvieto, ☎ 0763/341772; ✉ Piazza IV Novembre, 06123 Perugia, ☎ 075/5042546; ✉ Via Mazzini 21, 06100 Perugia, ☎ 075/5725341; ✉ Via Vico Consultore, 67032 Pescasseroli, ☎ 0863/91955; ✉ Piazza della Libertà 7, 06049 Spoleto, ☎ 0743/220311; ✉ Piazza Umberto I 6, 06059 Todi, ☎ 075/8943395; ✉ Piazza Rinascimento 1, 61029 Urbino, ☎ 0722/2613; ✉ Via Roma 1, 67030 Villetta Barrea, ☎ 0864/89102).

12 CAMPANIA

NAPLES, POMPEII, AND THE AMALFI COAST

Emperors, kings, and artists have all made Campania's sea-wreathed resorts and starlit isles their abodes for more than 2,000 years. And well they might, for this region is a compact realm of undiluted beauty. Naples—the most operatic of cities—rules over its breathtaking bay. Nearby, ancient Romans once led carefree lives at Pompeii just as today's travelers now soak up the 24-karat sun in Capri, Positano, and Ravello.

Updated by Robert Andrews

CAMPANIA IS A REGION OF NAMES—Capri, Sorrento, Pompeii, Paestum—that evoke visions of cliff-shaded coves, sun-dappled waters, and mighty ruins. And Naples, a tumultuous, animated city, the very heart of Campania, stands guard over these treasures. Campania stretches south in flat coastal plains and low mountains from Baia Domizia, Capua, and Caserta to Naples and Pompeii on the magnificent bay; past the isles of Capri and Ischia; along the rocky coast to Sorrento, Amalfi, and Salerno; and farther still past the Cilento promontory to Sapri and the Calabria border. Inland lie the bleak fringes of the Apennines and the rolling countryside around Benevento.

On each side of Naples the earth fumes and grumbles, reminding us that all this beauty was born of cataclysm. Toward Sorrento, Vesuvius smolders sleepily over the ruins of Herculaneum and Pompeii, while west of Naples, beyond Posillipo, the craters of the Solfatara spew steaming gases. And nearby are the dark, deep waters of Lago d'Averno, legendary entrance to Hades. With these reminiscences of death and destruction so close at hand, it's no wonder that the southerner in general, and the Neapolitan in particular, takes no chances, plunging enthusiastically into the task of living each moment to its fullest.

Campania was probably settled by the ancient Phoenicians, Cretans, and Greeks. Traces of their presence here date from approximately 1000 BC, some 300 years before the legendary founding of Rome. Herculaneum is said to have been established by Hercules himself, and as excavation of this once-great city—Greek and later Roman—progresses, further light will be thrown on the history of the whole Campania region. The origin of Naples, once called Parthenope and later Neapolis, presumably can be traced to what are now the ruins of Cumae nearby, which legend tells us was already in existence in 800 BC. Here, in a dark vaulted chamber, the Cumaean Sybil rendered her oracles. Greek civilization flourished for hundreds of years all along this coastline, but there was nothing in the way of centralized government until centuries later, when the Roman Empire, uniting all Italy for the first time, surged southward and, with little opposition, absorbed the Greek colonies. The Romans were quick to appreciate the sybaritic possibilities of such a lovely land, and it was in this region that the wealthy of the empire built their palatial country residences. Generally, the peace of Campania was undisturbed during these centuries of Roman rule.

Naples and Campania, with the rest of Italy, decayed with the Roman Empire and collapsed into the abyss of the Middle Ages. Naples itself regained some importance under the rule of the Angevins in the latter part of the 13th century and continued its progress in the 1440s under Aragonese rule. The nobles who served under the Spanish viceroys in the 16th and 17th centuries, when their harsh rule made all Italy quail, enjoyed their pleasures, and taverns and gaming houses thrived, even as Spain milked the area with its taxes. After a short-lived Austrian occupation, Naples—Napoli in Italian—became the capital of the Kingdom of the Two Sicilies, which the Bourbon kings established in 1738. Their rule was generally benevolent, as far as Campania was concerned, and their support of the papal authority in Rome was an important factor in the development of the rest of Italy. Their rule was important artistically, too, for not only did it contribute greatly to the architectural beauty of the region, but it attracted great musicians, artists, and writers, who were only too willing to enjoy the easy life of court in such magnificent natural surroundings. Finally, Giuseppe Garibaldi launched his famous expedition, and in 1860 Naples was united with the rest of Italy.

Times were relatively tranquil through the years that followed—with visitors of one nation or another thronging to Capri, to Sorrento, to Amalfi, and, of course, to Naples—until World War II. Allied bombings did considerable damage in Naples and the bay area. At the fall of the fascist government, the sorely tried Neapolitans rose up against Nazi occupation troops and in four days of street fighting drove them out of the city. A monument was raised to the *scugnizzo* (the typical Neapolitan street urchin), celebrating the youngsters who participated in the battle. The war ended. Artists, tourists, writers, and other lovers of beauty began to flow again into the Campania region that one ancient writer called "most blest by the Gods, most beloved by man." As the years have gone by, some parts gained increased attention from knowing visitors, while others lost the cachet they once had. The balance is maintained, with a steady trend toward more and more tourist development.

Pleasures and Pastimes

Dining

Campania's simple cuisine relies heavily on the bounty of the region's fertile farmland. Locally grown tomatoes are exported all over the world, but to try them here is a new experience. Even during the winter you can find tomato sauce made with small sun-dried tomatoes plucked from bright red strands that you can see hanging outdoors on kitchen balconies. Pasta is a staple here, and spaghetti *al pomodoro* (with tomato sauce) and spaghetti *alle vongole* (with clam sauce, either white or red, depending on the cook's whim) appear on most menus.

Naples—the homeland of pizza—produces a simple pizza: *alla margherita* (with tomato, mozzarella, and basil) and marinara (with tomato, garlic, and oregano; ☞ Up-Close: Disciplined Pizzas, *below*). Locally produced mozzarella is used in many dishes; one of the most gratifying on a hot day is *insalata caprese* (salad with mozzarella, tomatoes, and basil). *Melanzane* (eggplant) and even zucchini are served parmigiana (fried and layered with tomato sauce and mozzarella). Meat may be served *alla pizzaiola* (cooked in a tomato-and-garlic sauce). Fish and seafood in general can be expensive, though fried calamari and *totani* (cuttlefish) are usually reasonably priced. Among the region's wines, Gragnano, Falerno, Lacrima Cristi, and Greco di Tufo are fine whites. Ischia and Ravello also produce good white wine. Campania's best-known reds are Aglianico, Taurasi, and the red version of Falerno.

Lodging

Although Capri, Ischia, Sorrento, and the Amalfi Coast have fine accommodations in all categories, good establishments in Naples are scarce, so reserve well in advance. High-season rates apply at all coastal resorts from April or May through September, and Christmas and Easter also draw crowds and command top rates. Whereas coastal resorts elsewhere close up tight from fall to spring, at least some hotels and restaurants are open in Sorrento and on the Amalfi Coast year-round. It's always a good idea to book ahead, and it's imperative in high season (July and September). During the summer, hotels on the coast that serve meals almost always require that you take half board.

Exploring Campania

Many of Campania's attractions are on the Golfo di Napoli (Bay of Naples)—including the city itself and its satellite islands, Capri and Ischia, and the archaeological sites of Pompeii, Herculaneum, and the Campi Flegrei (Phlegrean Fields) at the northern end of the bay. At the south-

Close-Up

DISCIPLINED PIZZAS

THERE'S NO PIZZA LIKE REAL Neapolitan pizza. If you don't believe it, try one at **Ciro a Santa Brigida** (✉ Via Santa Brigida 71, ☎ 081/5524072). This restaurant is a little more upscale than a typical Neapolitan pizzeria, but its pizza is the real thing, and it's proper to eat it with your napkin stuffed into your shirt to avoid tomato stains. The restaurant's owner, Antonio Pace, president of the True Neapolitan Pizza Association, is behind an unusual initiative to upgrade the quality of pizza worldwide. Mr. Pace and Professor Carlo Mangoni di Santo Stefano, a nutritionist at the University of Naples, have written what they call a Pizza Discipline, a treatise that discusses everything from the history of pizza to the perfect ingredients for the perfect Neapolitan pie. Based on the Pizza Discipline, the city of Naples recently registered a logo that pizzerias can hang in their window if, and only if, they serve true Neapolitan pizza. That means using sinfully luscious buffalo-milk mozzarella made in certain areas near Naples, kneading the dough for exactly 30 minutes, and letting it rise for four hours. (The "discipline" includes photos of dough taken through a microscope before and after it has risen.)

It may take a while before pizzerias around the globe actually hang the logo in their windows. But the city of Naples wants it to eventually be a sign of quality as distinctive as the DOC (Denominazione di Origine Controllata, or denomination of controlled origin) on wine labels. The logo will be blue, with Mt. Vesuvius in the background, a red pizza with mozzarella in the center, and PIZZA NAPOLETANA written across the foreground. Make sure you're the first to spot it!

Some pizza history, as recounted by Professor Mangoni (who scoffs at claims that pizza was invented in the United States): Pizza marinara, which doesn't have mozzarella at all but is simply a pie with tomatoes, garlic, oregano, and olive oil, first appeared in Naples around 1760. King Ferdinand of Naples liked the pizza, but his wife, a Habsburg princess, wouldn't allow pizza in the palace. The king would often sneak out to one of the world's first pizzerias, making the places famous. Even earlier, there's a mention of plates of flour with other food on top in Homer's *Iliad,* but Professor Mangoni says this was just a precursor to pizza, not the real thing. Tomato sauce, says Mangoni, dates back to 1733.

Mozzarella came later. The pizza margherita was invented in 1889, when Naples chef Raffaele Esposito was called on to prepare a meal for the Italian Queen, Margherita. He made a pizza with tomato sauce and mozzarella, and his wife had the idea of adding basil to honor Italy's red, white, and green flag.

ACCORDING TO THE PIZZA Discipline, the only true pizzas are marinara and margherita. Anchovies, pepperoni, and so on are heresy. So don't expect to see the logo with Mt. Vesuvius at your local pizza joint anytime soon.

In Antonio Pace's family, pizza goes back a long way. He claims his grandfather's grandfather made pizza in 1856. Pizza fact or fiction aside, at Ciro a Santa Brigida, everything is delicious. Ask for a taste of plain buffalo mozzarella and just savor it in your mouth. If you have a lactose intolerance, there's still hope—Professor Mangoni and his team of scientists are developing lactose-free mozzarella. If they manage to match the taste of real mozzarella, he says, pizzerias will be allowed to use it and still display the Pizza Napoletana logo. Go figure.

ern end, Sorrento also lies within this charmed circle, within easy distance of Positano, Amalfi, and the pleasures of the Amalfi Coast. Farther afield, Paestum offers more classical sights, and inland, Caserta and Benevento have a Bourbon palace and more majestic Roman remains.

Numbers in the text correspond to numbers in the margin and on the Campania, Naples, and Pompeii maps.

Great Itineraries

If art and antiquity are high on your list, consider spending a few days in Naples before retreating to the beauty of Capri, Ischia, or the Amalfi Coast. Few fall in love with Naples at first sight, and many complain about its obvious flaws: urban decay and delinquency. But practically everyone who takes the time and trouble to discover its artistic riches and appreciate its vivacious nature considers it worth the effort. Naples is close to Italy's most fabled classical ruins, and you should dedicate at least a morning or afternoon to Pompeii or Herculaneum.

IF YOU HAVE 3 DAYS

In **Naples** ①–⑰, a visit to the **Museo Archeologico Nazionale** ⑯ is an essential preparation (or follow-up) for an expedition to **Herculaneum** ㉒ and **Pompeii** ㉔–㊵, indispensable sights for anyone visiting Campania. The islands of **Ischia** ㊹ and **Capri** ㊺ can also be reached from Naples, and make an ideal antidote to the city's noise. It is worth spending at least one night out of Naples, and a good alternative to the islands would be **Sorrento** ㊻, an easy hydrofoil ride away and a good base from which to tour the nearby Amalfi Coast, where you could visit small towns—**Positano** ㊼, **Amalfi** ㊽, **Ravello** ㊾, and/or **Vietri sul Mare** ㊿, for instance—on a third day's excursion.

IF YOU HAVE 5 DAYS

In **Naples** ①–⑰, more time will enable you to take in one of the region's greatest palace-museums, the **Museo Capodimonte** ⑰, housed in one of the Bourbon royal palaces. Outside town, you could also see more than just one of the classical sights, including a visit to the Greek temples of **Paestum** (52), highly recommended for a glimpse at some of Magna Graecia's most stunning relics. You might also venture north to **Caserta** ㊶ to wander around the royal palace. Back in the Bay of Naples, spend your fourth and fifth days exploring **Ischia** ㊹ and **Sorrento** ㊻, both undemanding holiday resorts with plenty of natural beauty.

IF YOU HAVE 7 DAYS

A week in Campania will allow you to discover some of the more esoteric pleasures that Naples has to offer. Apart from the sheer vibrancy of its shopping streets and alleys, and the glorious views over the waterfront, **Naples** ①–⑰ has plenty of diversions within its tight mesh of streets, and you should make time for visiting some of its many famous churches—the **Duomo** ⑭, of course, but also **Santa Chiara** ⑪, **Santa Maria Donnaregina** ⑮, and the **Cappella Sansevero** ⑫, with its 18th-century sculptures. Outside town, head west to the volcanic region of the **Phlegrean Fields** ⑱–㉑, where Roman remains lie within a smoking, smoldering area rich with classical history. Spend three nights on the Amalfi Coast, making sure to visit inland **Ravello** ㊾ and pass some time in pretty **Positano** ㊼, which requires at least a day and a half. **Capri** ㊺, too, deserves a couple of nights to appreciate fully its beauty—of secluded coves and beaches, not to mention the famous Blue Grotto—easily eclipsing the island's more lurid tourist trappings. You might pass a last day, perhaps en route out of Campania, in **Benevento** ㊸, which holds a well-preserved Roman theater and the renowned Arco di Traiano.

Campania

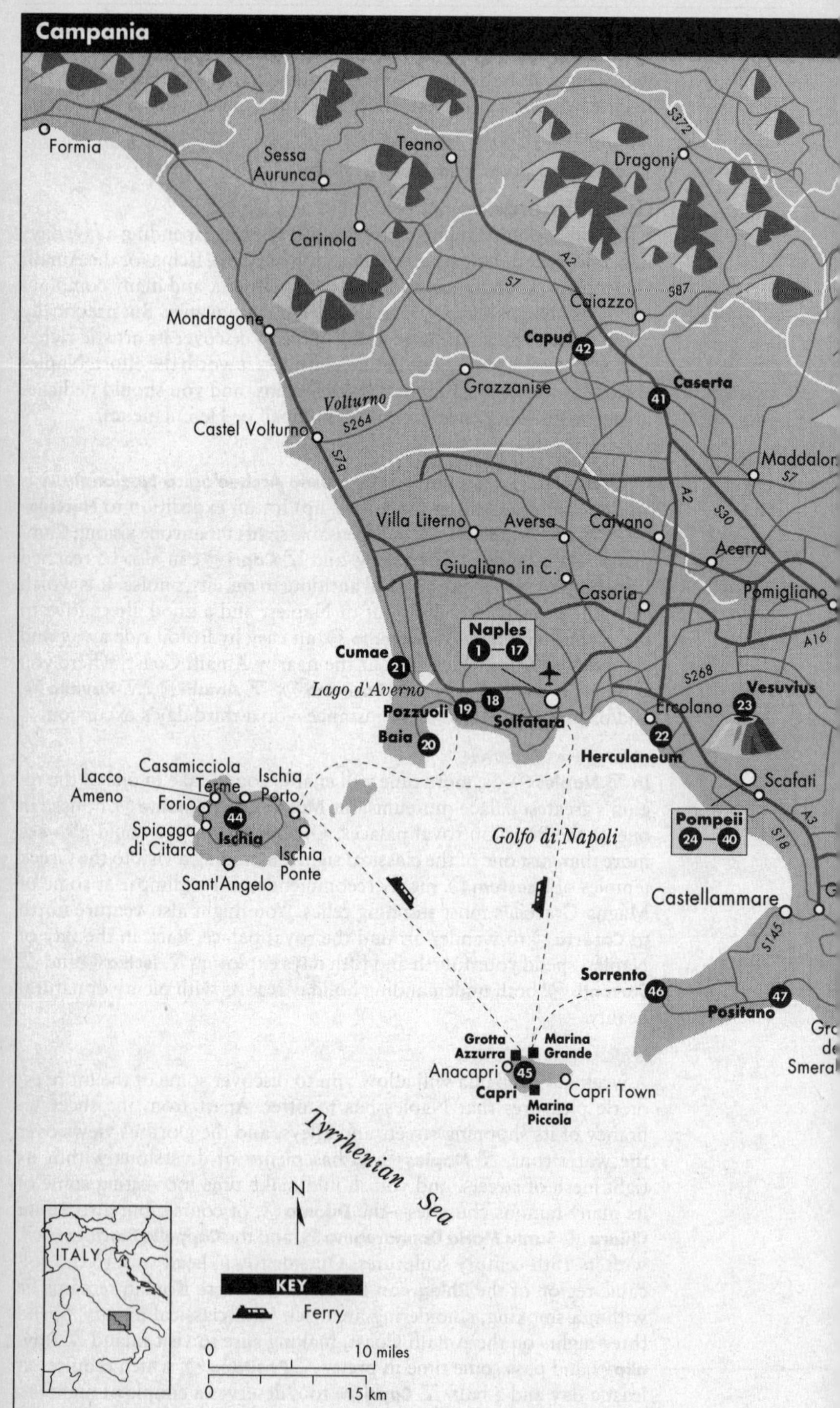

Formia
Sessa Aurunca
Teano
Dragoni
S372
Carinola
A2
S7
S87
Caiazzo
Mondragone
Capua
42
Grazzanise
Caserta
41
Volturno
Castel Volturno
S264
S7a
Maddalon
S7
A2
S30
Villa Literno
Aversa
Caivano
Acerra
Giugliano in C.
Casoria
Pomigliano
Naples
1
17
A16
Cumae
21
S268
Vesuvius
Lago d'Averno
18
Ercolano
23
Pozzuoli
19
Solfatara
22
Baia
20
Herculaneum
Casamicciola Terme
Lacco Ameno
Ischia Porto
Scafati
Forio
44
Spiaggia di Citara
Ischia
Pompeii
24
40
Golfo di Napoli
Ischia Ponte
S18
A3
Sant'Angelo
Castellammare
S145
Sorrento
46
47
Positano
Grotta Azzurra
Marina Grande
Anacapri
45
Capri
Capri Town
Marina Piccola
Tyrrhenian Sea
N
ITALY
KEY
Ferry
10 miles
15 km
0
0

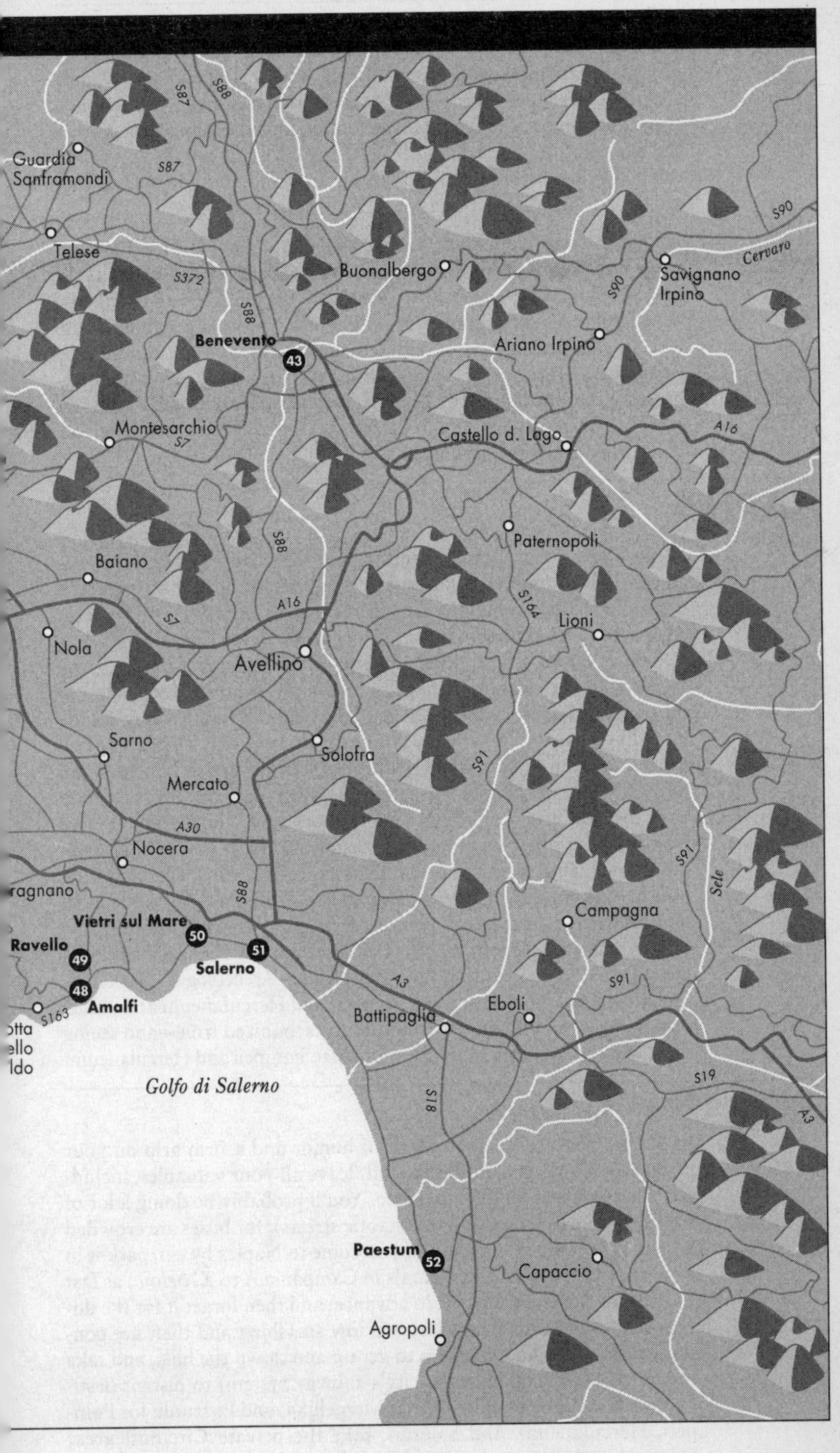
Guardia
Sanframondi
S87
S88
S87
Telese
S372
S88
Buonalbergo
S90
Savignano
Irpino
Cervaro
S90
Benevento
43
Ariano Irpino
Montesarchio
S7
Castello d. Lago
A16
S88
Paternopoli
Baiano
A16
S7
S164
Lioni
Nola
Avellino
Sarno
Solofra
S91
Mercato
A30
Nocera
S88
S91
Sele
Vietri sul Mare
50
Ravello
49
51
Salerno
Campagna
48
Amalfi
S163
A3
S91
Battipaglia
Eboli
Golfo di Salerno
S18
S19
A3
Paestum
52
Capaccio
Agropoli

When to Tour Campania

Campania is not at its best in high summer: Naples is a sweltering inferno, the archaeological sites swarm, and the islands and Amalfi Coast resorts are similarly overrun with tour buses and bad tempers. Any other time of year would be preferable, including even winter, when the temperature rarely falls below the comfort threshold and rain is relatively rare. Swimming is possible year-round, though you will only see the hardiest bathers out between October and May.

Summer is also the worst time for ascents to Vesuvius; the best visibility occurs around spring and fall. Watch the clock, however, as the days get shorter; excursions to Vesuvius, Pompeii, Herculaneum, and the islands all require some traveling, and it's easy to get caught with little daylight left. At most archaeological sites, you are rounded up two hours before sunset, so the earlier you arrive the better. Remember, too, that the majority of hotels, restaurants, and other tourist facilities in Sorrento, the Amalfi Coast, and the islands close down from November until around Easter.

NAPLES

"Built like a great amphitheater around her beautiful bay, Naples is an eternally unfolding play acted by a million of the best actors in the world," Herbert Kubly observes in his *American in Italy.* "The comedy is broad, the tragedy violent. The curtain never rings down." Is it a sense of doom, living in the shadow of Vesuvius, that makes many Neapolitans so volatile, perhaps so seemingly blind to everything but the pain or pleasure of the moment? Poverty and overcrowding are the more likely causes, but whatever the reason, Naples is a difficult place for the casual tourist to quickly like. The Committee of Ninety-Nine, formed to counter Naples's negative image, has its work cut out. If you have the time and if you're willing to work at it, you'll come to love Naples as a mother loves her reprobate son; but if you're only passing through and hoping to enjoy a hassle-free vacation, spend as little time here as you can. Why visit Naples at all? First, Naples is the most sensible base—particularly if you're traveling by public transportation—from which to explore Pompeii, Herculaneum, Vesuvius, and the Phlegrean Fields. Second, it's the home of the Museo Archeologico Nazionale. The most important finds from Pompeii and Herculaneum are on display here—everything from sculpture to carbonized fruit—and seeing them will add to the pleasure of your trip to Pompeii and Herculaneum.

Exploring Naples

In Naples you need a good sense of humor and a firm grip on your pocketbook and camera. Better still, leave all your valuables, including your passport, in the hotel safe. You'll probably be doing a lot of walking (take care crossing the chaotic streets), for buses are crowded and taxis get stalled in traffic. If you come to Naples by car, park it in a garage (for a list, ☞ Car Rentals *in* Campania A to Z, *below*) as fast as you can, agree on the cost in advance, and then forget it for the duration of your stay (otherwise, window smashing and theft are constant risks). Use the funiculars to get up and down the hills, and take the quick Metropolitana (the city's subway system) to distant destinations (Piazza Garibaldi, Chiaia, Mergellina, and Pozzuoli; for Pompeii, Herculaneum, and Salerno, take the private Circumflegrea, Cumana, and Circumvesuviana lines). Bus or funicular fares are 1,200 lire, valid for 90 minutes; 4,000 lire buys a ticket for the whole day. Subway tickets cost 1,500 lire each. The tourist information office (☞ Campania A to Z, *below*) at Piazza del Gesù can provide pamphlets with itineraries tracing the city's development in ancient, medieval, and modern times.

A Good Tour

Start at the **Castel Nuovo** ①, facing the harbor on Piazza Municipio, housing a museum of mainly religious art. Pass the **Teatro San Carlo** ② on your way to the imposing **Palazzo Reale** ③, a royal palace rich with the indulgences of Naples's past rulers. Next, turn back to the seafront where, a few minutes' walk south, is another royal fortress, the **Castel dell'Ovo** ④, overlooking the Santa Lucia waterfront. Walking or taking a bus farther along the seafront, you might drop into the extensive **Acquario** ⑤ before visiting the **Villa Pignatelli** ⑥, a small museum holding a low-key collection of aristocratic knickknacks. Walk up Via Ascensione, turn right onto Via Santa Teresa a Chiaia, left onto Via Bausan, and a left onto Via Colonna, leading to the funicular stop at Piazza Amedeo; take a ride up to the **Museo Nazionale della Ceramica Duca di Martina** ⑦, another museum—though you might be content to take in the extraordinary views from the slopes of the Vomero neighborhood. Also on Vomero are the **Castel Sant'Elmo** ⑧ and the **Certosa di San Martino** ⑨, again, set in the same parkland and commanding magnificent vistas over city and sea to Vesuvius. Take a funicular ride down—this time to Piazza Montesanto—from which you are well placed to stroll northeast along Spaccanapoli, a group of streets cutting a straight line through the heart of Old Naples, taking in the churches of **Gesù Nuovo** ⑩ and **Santa Chiara** ⑪ en route. Farther up Spaccanapoli, you need only detour a few steps off this ancient artery to see some other art-rich religious monuments: **Cappella Sansevero** ⑫, **San Lorenzo Maggiore** ⑬, the **Duomo** ⑭, and **Santa Maria Donnaregina** ⑮. Continuing north on Via Duomo, take a left onto Via Foria, and you will end up at one of Italy's most important museums, the **Museo Archeologico Nazionale** ⑯, packed with archaeological relics of the classical era, and a must before venturing out of town to see Pompeii and Herculaneum. From here, footsore and weary, you deserve a taxi or bus to reach **Museo Capodimonte** ⑰, the greatest of the Bourbon palaces, where, after ogling at the artistic masterpieces on display here, you can siesta in the Bosco di Capodimonte (park) and admire the wonderful views over the Bay of Naples.

TIMING

You should start early to fit all these sights into just one day: the best option would be to split it between two days, ending one at the Certosa di San Martino (seeing sights ①–⑨), then tackling Spaccanapoli, the Museo Archeologico Nazionale (where you really need half of a day), and Museo Capodimonte the next (area spanning sights ⑩–⑰). Make sure you do not end up at any churches at lunchtime, when they close for two or three hours. The views over the bay are good at any time, but especially at sunset. If it is winter, when the Museo Archeologico Nazionale closes for the afternoon, spend the morning here and the afternoon visiting either the Phlegrean Fields or Herculaneum and Vesuvius. Return to Naples for the evening, perhaps best spent at the world-famous Teatro San Carlo; the following morning, set out for Pompeii.

Sights to See

5 **Acquario** (Aquarium). Children and art-exhausted adults adore the aquarium in the public gardens on Via Caracciolo. Founded by a German naturalist in the late 19th century, it's the oldest in Europe. About 200 species of fish and marine plants thrive in large tanks, undoubtedly better off here than in the highly polluted Bay of Naples, their natural habitat. ✉ *Stazione Zoologica, Viale A. Dohrn,* ☎ *081/5833111.* 🎟 *3,000*

Naples
CATACOMBE DI SAN GENNARO
Via della Sanità
Corso Amedeo di Savoia
S. Margherita a Fonseca
Via Antonio Villari
Via Stella
Via Materdei
Salita S. Raffaele
V. S. Teresa degli Scalzi
Via Cristallini
Via Miracoli
Via Foria
Via Cesare Rosaroll
Via S. Antonio Abate
Via Benedetto
Giuseppi
Via Carbonara
Pza. E. De Nicola
Pza. Principe Umberto
Stazione Centrale
Via P.S. Mancini
Pza. Garibaldi
Garibaldi
Via Poerio
Pza. Cavour
Via Matteo Renato Imbriani
Via Gracinio
Vico Nocelle
Via S. Mandato
Via Salvator Rosa
V. Battistello Caracciolo
Via S. Giuseppi dei Nudi
Via Salvator Tommasi
Via F.S. Carrera (Cavone)
Via E. Pessina
Via S. Maria di Constantinopoli
Via L. de Crecchio
Via Pisanelli
Via Lucano Armani
V. S. Paolo
Via Anticaglia
Via S. Apostoli
Via Duomo
Via P. Colletta
Via Atri
Via Tribunali
Via Nilo
Via de Sanctis
Via S. Biagio d. Librai
V. Vicaria Vecchia
Corso Umberto I
V. Nolana
Museo Filangeri
V. Grand Archivio
(SPACCANAPOLI)
Via Benedetto Croce
Piazza Dante
San Domenico Maggiore
Via Toledo
Tarsia
Salita Pontecorvo
Salita Tarsia
Via Ventaglieri
Corso Vitt. Emanuele
Via U. Nutta
Via G. Orsi
Via Giotto
Piazza Med D'oro
Piazza Leonardo
Via Tino di Camaino
Via M. Fiore
Viale Michelangelo
Viale Raffaello
V.S. Gennaro al Vomero
Via G.L. Bernini
Via Luca Giordano
VOMERO
Via Solimente
Via F. Cilea
Via A. Scarlatti
Via R. Morghen
Via Tito Angelini
FUNICOLARE DI MONTESANTO
Via Cimarosa
Villa Floridiana
Via Luigia Sanfelice
Stazione Cumana
Piazza del Gesù
Via di Capitelli
Via Pasquale Scura
Via F. Girardi
QUARTIERI SPAGNOLI
Via E. De Dio
Toledo
Via Roma
Piazza Carita
Via G. Oberdan
Via Monteoliveto
SANTA CHIARA
Via S. Chiara
V. S. Geronimo
Via Mezzocanone
Via Giovanni Paladino
Piazza Matteotti
Via A. Diaz
Via R. Bracco
Via M. Cervantes
Via Medina
Via G. Sanfelice
V. Sedile di Porto
V. Donnalbina
Via A. Depretis
Via A. De Gasperi
V. A. di Costanzo
Via Nuova Marina
V. Marotta
V. A. Troya
Pza. N. Amore
V.L. Bianchini
V. Giacomo Savarese
Via Geraldo
Beato
Via Lavinaio
Cesare Carmigiano
Pza. del Mercato
V.S.Giovanni a Mare
Pza. Masanieollo
Bacino del Pilier

Acquario, **5**
Cappella Sansevero, **12**
Castel dell'Ovo, **4**
Castel Nuovo, **1**
Castel Sant'Elmo, **8**
Certosa di San Martino, **9**
Duomo, **14**
Gesù Nuovo, **10**
Museo Archeologico Nazionale, **16**
Museo Capodimonte, **17**
Museo Nazionale della Ceramica Duca di Martina, **7**
Palazzo Reale, **3**
San Lorenzo Maggiore, **13**
Santa Chiara, **11**
Santa Maria Donnaregina, **15**
Teatro San Carlo, **2**
Villa Pignatelli, **6**

lire. ⏲ *May–Sept., Tues.–Sat. 9–6, Sun. 9:30–7:30; Oct.–Apr., Tues.–Sat. 9–5, Sun. 9–2.*

OFF THE BEATEN PATH

EDENLANDIA – This is the largest amusement park in Campania. It's in the Mostra d'Oltremare area of Naples, near the Stadio San Paolo, southwest of the center. ✉ *Viale Kennedy,* ☎ *081/2391182.* 🎫 *3,000 lire admission, 15,000 lire all rides.* ⏲ *Oct.–Mar., weekdays noon–8, weekends 10:30 AM–midnight; Apr.–Sept., weekdays 3–10, weekends 10:30 AM–midnight.*

MUSEO NAZIONALE FERROVIARIO – Children love to see the old-fashioned engines, cars, and railroad equipment on display in the restored railway works, east of the center, founded by the Bourbon rulers of Naples in the last century. ✉ *Corso San Giovanni a Teduccio,* ☎ *081/472003.* 🎫 *Free.* ⏲ *Mon.–Sat. 8:30–1:30.*

⑫ **Cappella Sansevero.** Off Spaccanapoli, the Cappella di Santa Maria della Pietà dei Sangro, better known as the Cappella Sansevero, holds the tombs of the noble Sangro di San Severo family. Much of it was designed in the 18th century by Giuseppe Sammartino, including the centerpiece, a strikingly carved *Dead Christ,* hewn from a single block of alabaster. If you can stomach it, take a peek in the crypt, where some of the anatomical experiments conducted by Prince Raimondo, a scion of the family and noted 18th-century alchemist, are gruesomely displayed. ✉ *Via de Sanctis.* 🎫 *8,000 lire.* ⏲ *Wed.–Mon. 10–7.*

④ **Castel dell'Ovo.** Dangling over the Porto Santa Lucia on a thin promontory, this 12th-century fortress built over the ruins of an ancient Roman villa commands a view of the whole harbor—proof, if you need it, that the Romans knew a premium location when they saw one. For the same reason, some of the city's top hotels share the same site. ✉ *Santa Lucia waterfront. Closed to the public.*

① **Castel Nuovo.** Also known as the Maschio Angioino, this massive fortress was built by the Angevins (related to the French monarchy) in the 13th century and completely rebuilt by the Aragonese rulers (descendants of an illegitimate branch of Spain's ruling line) who succeeded them. The decorative marble triumphal arch that forms the entrance was erected during the Renaissance in honor of King Alfonso V of Aragón (1396–1458), and its rich bas-reliefs are credited to Francesco Laurana (circa 1430–circa 1502). Set incongruously into the castle's heavy stone walls, the arch is one of the finest works of its kind. Within the castle, you can see sculptures and frescoes from the 14th and 15th centuries, as well as the city's **Museo Civico,** comprising mainly local artwork from the 15th to the 19th centuries. It's hard to avoid the impression that these last were rejects from the much finer collection at the Museo Capodimonte (☞ *below*), though there are also regular exhibitions worth visiting, and the windows offer views over the piazza and the port below. ✉ *Castel Nuovo, Piazza Municipio,* ☎ *081/7952003.* 🎫 *10,000 lire.* ⏲ *Mon.–Sat. 9–7, Sun. 9–1.*

⑧ **Castel Sant'Elmo.** Perched on Vomero, the castle in Vomero was built by the Spanish to dominate the port and the old city. The stout fortifications are still in use today by the military, and are the occasional venue for performances, exhibitions, and fairs. ✉ *Largo San Martino,* ☎ *081/5784020.* 🎫 *4,000 lire.* ⏲ *Tues.–Sun. 9–2.*

⑨ **Certosa di San Martino.** A Carthusian monastery restored in the 17th century in exuberant Neapolitan Baroque style, this structure now houses the **Museo Nazionale di San Martino,** an eclectic collection of ships' models, antique *presepi* (Christmas crèches), and Neapolitan landscape paintings. The main reason to come, however, is to see the splendidly decorated church and annexes, the pretty garden, and the view from the balcony off Room 25. There's another fine view from the square in front of the Certosa. Take the funicular from Piazza Montesanto to Vomero. ⊠ *Museo Nazionale di San Martino,* ☎ *081/5781769.* 🎟 *9,500 lire.* ⏲ *Tues.–Sun. 9–2.*

⓮ **Duomo.** Though established in the 1200s, the building you see was erected a century later and has since undergone radical changes, especially during the Baroque age. Inside the cathedral, 110 ancient columns salvaged from pagan buildings are set into the piers that support the 350-year-old wooden ceiling. Off the left aisle, you step down into the 4th-century church of **Santa Restituta,** which was incorporated into the cathedral; though Santa Restituta was redecorated in the late 1600s in the prevalent Baroque style, a few very old mosaics remain in the **Battistero** (Baptistery). The chapel also gives access to a an archeological zone, a series of paleochristian rooms dating from the Roman era.

On the right aisle of the cathedral, in the **Cappella di San Gennaro,** are multicolor marbles and frescoes honoring St. Januarius, miracle-working patron saint of Naples, whose altar and relics are encased in silver. Three times a year—on September 19 (his feast day); on the Saturday preceding the first Sunday in May, which commemorates the transference of his relics to Naples; and on December 16—his dried blood, contained in two sealed vials, is believed to liquefy during rites in his honor. On these days large numbers of devout Neapolitans offer up prayers in his memory. ⊠ *Via del Duomo,* ☎ *081/449097.* 🎟 *Duomo and Cappella di San Gennaro: free; Battistero: 2,000 lire; Battistero and archaeological zone: 5,000 lire.* ⏲ *Duomo and Cappella di San Gennaro: daily 8–12:30 and 4:30–7; Battistero and archaeological zone: Mon.–Sat. 9–noon and 4:30–7, Sun. 8–1:30 and 5–7.*

OFF THE BEATEN PATH

MUSEO FILANGIERI – This Neapolitan museum contains Prince Gaetano Filangieri's private collection of arms, armor, furniture, paintings, and fascinating memorabilia. It's housed in the Florentine-style Renaissance Palazzo Cuomo. ⊠ *Palazzo Cuomo, Via Duomo 288,* ☎ *081/203175.* 🎟 *5,000 lire.* ⏲ *Tues.–Sat. 9:30–2 and 3:30–7, Sun. 9:30–1:30.*

---

❿ **Gesù Nuovo.** The oddly faceted stone facade of the church was designed as part of a palace dating from between 1584 and 1601, but plans were changed as construction progressed, and it became the front of an elaborately decorated Baroque church. ⊠ *Piazza Gesù Nuovo,* ☎ *081/5518613.* ⏲ *Daily 9–1 and 4–7.*

Molo Beverello. This pier is a hive of activity from which boats and hydrofoils leave for Sorrento and the islands. ⊠ *On the harbor behind the Castel Nuovo.*

OFF THE BEATEN PATH

SEAFRONT TOURS – Summer evening boat tours take in the waterfront of Naples, from the port at Mergellina to Cape Posillipo, with a view of Castel dell'Ovo (☞ *above*) on the way back. Ask at the port or in the tourist office (☞ Visitor Information *in* Campania A to Z, *below*).

★ ⓰ **Museo Archeologico Nazionale** (National Archaeological Museum). The huge red building, a cavalry barracks in the 16th century, is dusty and unkempt, but it holds one of the world's great collections of Greek and Roman antiquities, including such extraordinary sculptures as the *Hercules Farnese,* an exquisite Aphrodite attributed to the 4th-century BC Greek sculptor Praxiteles, and an equestrian statue of Roman Emperor Nerva. Vividly colored mosaics and countless artistic and household objects from Pompeii and Herculaneum provide insight into the life and art of ancient Rome. The most recent addition to the treasures on permanent display is an entire fresco sequence—more than 300 ft wide—discovered in 1765 in perfect condition at the Temple of Isis in Pompeii. Invest in an up-to-date printed museum guide because exhibits are poorly labeled. ✉ *Piazza Museo,* ☎ *081/440166.* 🎫 *12,000 lire.* ⏲ *Aug.–Sept., Mon.–Sat. 9–10, Sun. 9–6; Oct.–July, Wed.–Mon. 9–2.*

★ 17 **Museo Capodimonte.** The grandiose 18th-century neoclassic Bourbon royal palace, in the vast Bosco di Capodimonte (Capodimonte Park) that served as the royal hunting preserve and later as the site of the Capodimonte porcelain works, houses an impressive collection of fine and decorative art. Capodimonte's greatest treasure is the excellent collection of paintings well displayed in the **Galleria Nazionale** on the palace's first and second stories. Before you arrive at this remarkable collection, a magnificent staircase leads to the **royal apartments,** where you'll find beautiful antique furniture, most of it on the splashy scale so dear to the Bourbons, and a staggering collection of porcelain and majolica from the various royal residences. The walls of the apartments are hung with numerous portraits, providing a close-up of the unmistakable Bourbon features, a challenge to any court painter. The main galleries on the first floor are devoted to work from the 13th to the 18th centuries, including many familiar masterpieces by Dutch and Spanish masters, as well as by the great Italians. Look out for some stunning paintings by Caravaggio (1573–1610), originally gracing the city's churches. The second floor features mainly Neapolitan works of the 19th century, including plenty of dramatic renditions of Vesuvius in all its raging glory. When you've had your fill of these, take time to admire the genuine article from the shady parkland outside, which affords a sweeping view of the bay. ✉ *Parco di Capodimonte,* ☎ *081/7441307.* 🎫 *9,500 lire.* ⏲ *Tues.–Sun. 10–7.*

OFF THE BEATEN PATH

CATACOMBE DI SAN GENNARO – Many of these catacombs in Naples predate the Christian era by two centuries. The church was inspired by St. Peter's in Rome. The niches and corridors of the catacombs are hung with early Christian paintings. ✉ *Via Capodimonte, next to Madre di Buon Consiglio church on Via Capodimonte,* ☎ *081/7411071.* 🎫 *5,000 lire.* ⏲ *Guided tours daily every 45 mins 9:30–11:45 AM.*

7 **Museo Nazionale della Ceramica Duca di Martina.** The lushly shaded park and the view over Naples are two reasons to venture up the Chiaia funicular from Via del Parco Margherita. Set on the slopes of the Vomero hill in a park known as Villa Floridiana, it houses thousands of ceramic pieces such as local majolica and a fine collection of European and Asian porcelain, and other objets d'art in a neoclassic residence built in the early 19th century by King Ferdinand I for his wife, Lucia Migliaccio. Their portraits greet you as you enter. Enjoy the view from the terrace behind the museum. ✉ *Via Cimarosa 77,* ☎ *081/5788418.* 🎫 *5,000 lire.* ⏲ *Mon.–Sat. 9–2.*

3 **Palazzo Reale** (Royal Palace). Dominating Piazza del Plebiscito, the huge palace—best described as overblown imperial—dates from the early 1600s. It was renovated and redecorated by successive rulers, including Napoléon's sister Caroline and her ill-fated husband, Joachim Murat (1767–1815), who reigned briefly in Naples after the French emperor had sent the Bourbons packing and before they returned to reclaim their kingdom. Don't miss seeing the **royal apartments,** sumptuously furnished and full of precious paintings, tapestries, porcelains, and other objets d'art. The monumental marble staircase gives you an idea of the

scale on which Neapolitan rulers lived. ✉ *Piazza del Plebiscito,* ☎ *081/5808111.* *8,000 lire.* ⏲ *Thurs.–Tues. 9–2; Sat. and Sun. 9–7.*

NEED A BREAK? Besieged by the traffic swirling around the Teatro San Carlo and Palazzo Reale, the **Caffè Gambrinus** (✉ Piazza Trieste e Trento, ☎ 081/417582) is a haven of old-style Naples, and the onetime haunt of artists and intellectuals of every persuasion. Gilded and mirrored, this *gran caffè* continues to serve top-quality pastries and gelato alongside savories and the never-ending cappuccinos.

Piazza Dante. Students from the nearby music conservatory hang out in this semicircular hub, though presently fenced off for long-term work on the subway system, in an area bursting with inexpensive trattorias and pizzerias.

Piazza del Plebiscito. The vast square next to the Palazzo Reale was laid out by order of Murat, whose architect was clearly inspired by the colonnades of St. Peter's in Rome. The large church of **San Francesco di Paola** in the middle of the colonnades was added as an offering of thanks for the Bourbon restoration by Ferdinand I, whose titles reflect the somewhat garbled history of the Kingdom of the Two Sicilies—made up of Naples (which included most of the southern Italian mainland) and Sicily, which were united in the Middle Ages, then separated and unofficially reunited under Spanish domination during the 16th and 17th centuries. In 1816, with Napoléon out of the way on St. Helena, Ferdinand IV (1751–1825) of Naples, who also happened to be Ferdinand III of Sicily, officially merged the two kingdoms, proclaiming himself Ferdinand I of the Kingdom of Two Sicilies. His reactionary and repressive rule earned him a few more colorful titles among his rebellious subjects.

NEED A BREAK? Walking up the fashionable Via Chiaia, behind Piazza del Plebiscito, you'll come upon **Caflisch** (✉ Via Chiaia 144, ☎ 081/416477), closed Monday, a historic café serving snacks and high-quality chocolates and pastries to nibble over a cappuccino or espresso.

Quartieri Spagnoli (Spanish Quarter). The Spanish garrison was quartered inthe now-decaying tenements aligned in a tight-knit grid along incredibly narrow alleys in this neighborhood roughly between Via Toledo (downhill border) and Via Pasquale Scura (western leg of Spaccanapoli). It's a hectic, impoverished (sometimes dangerous) area—chock-full of local color—brooding in the shadow of Vomero, but it's showing signs of improvement. This area is a five-minute walk west of Piazza Municipio, accessible from Via Toledo.

13 **San Lorenzo Maggiore.** It is unusual to find the Gothic style in Naples, but it has survived to great effect in this church. Built in the Middle Ages and decorated with 14th-century frescoes, it is supposed to be where the poet Boccaccio (1313–75) first saw the model for his *Fiammetta.* ✉ *Via Tribunali,* ☎ *081/454948.* ⏲ *Daily 9–noon and 5–7:30*

11 **Santa Chiara.** The monastery church is a Neapolitan landmark and the subject of a famous old song. It was built in the 1300s in Provençal Gothic style, and it's best known for the quiet charm of its cloister garden, with columns and benches sheathed in 18th-century ceramic tiles painted with delicate floral motifs and vivid landscapes. An adjoining museum traces the history of the convent; the entrance is off the courtyard at the left of the church. ✉ *Piazza Gesù Nuovo,* ☎ *081/5526209.* ⏲ *Church: Apr.–Sept., daily 8:30–noon and 4–7; Oct.–Mar., daily 8:30–noon and 4–6. Museum: Thurs.–Tues. 9:30–1:30 and 3:30–5:30.*

15 **Santa Maria Donnaregina.** The towering Gothic funeral monument of Mary of Hungary, wife of Charles II of Anjou (circa 1254–1309), who is said to have commissioned the frescoes in the church at a cost of 33 ounces of gold, is contained within this church. Don't confuse this church with another, nearby in the piazza, of the same name, but Baroque. ✉ *Vico Donnaregina.* ⏲ *Daily 9–1.*

Spaccanapoli. Nowhere embodies the spirit of backstreet Naples better than the arrow-straight street divided into tracts bearing several names. It runs through the heart of the old city (*spacca* means "cut through") from west to east, retracing one of the main arteries of the Greek, and later Roman, settlement. ✉ *Beginning with Via Pasquale Scura, just west of Via Toledo, and ending with Via Vicaria Vecchia just east of Via del Duomo.*

2 **Teatro San Carlo.** In 1737, 40 years earlier than Milan's La Scala, this large 18th-century theater was first built—though it was destroyed by fire and rebuilt in 1816. You can visit the impressive interior, decorated in the white-and-gilt stucco of the neoclassic era, as part of a guided group, and visitors are sometimes allowed in during morning rehearsals. ✉ *Via San Carlo, between Piazza Municipio and Piazza Plebiscito,* ☎ *081/7972111.* 🎫 *5,000 lire.* ⏲ *Tours Sat. and Sun. at 2 and 4.*

NEED A BREAK? Across from the Teatro San Carlo, towers the imposing entrance to the glass-roofed neoclassic **Galleria Umberto** (✉ Via San Carlo), a shopping arcade where you can sit at one of several cafés and watch the vivacious Neapolitans as they go about their business.

Via Benedetto Croce. This section of Spaccanapoli was named in honor of the illustrious philosopher born here in 1866, in the building at No. 12. Continue past peeling palaces, dark workshops where artisans ply their trades, and many churches and street shrines. Where the street changes to **Via San Biagio dei Librai,** the shops stage a special fair of hand-carved crèche figures during the weeks before Christmas.

Via Toledo. Sooner or later you'll wind up at one of the busiest commercial arteries, also known as Via Roma, in this perennially congested city. However, don't avoid dipping into this parade of shops and coffee bars where plump pastries are temptingly arranged.

6 **Villa Pignatelli.** A small dignified museum on the grounds are of limitedinterest to anyone who doesn't like 19th-century furniture. But the collection of antique coaches and carriages in a pavilion on the grounds is worth a look. And a stroll in the park is a pleasant respite from the noisy city streets. ✉ *Riviera di Chiaia 200; museum near the lower station of the Chiaia funicular,* ☎ *081/669675.* 🎫 *Museum: 5,000 lire.* ⏲ *Tues.–Sun. 9–2.*

Vomero. Heart-stopping views of the Bay of Naples are framed by this gentrified neighborhood on a hill served by the Montesanto, Centrale, and Chiaia funiculars. Stops for all three are an easy walk from Piazza Vanvitelli, a good starting-point for exploring this thriving district with no shortage of smart bars and trattorias to pause in.

Dining and Lodging

$$$ ✕ **Casanova Grill.** Soft lights and a trendy art-deco look set the tone at Hotel Excelsior's restaurant. The seasonal specialties and antipasti arranged on the buffet will whet your appetite for such traditional Neapolitan dishes as the simple spaghetti al pomodoro and the classic *carne* (meat) alla pizzaiola. ✉ *Hotel Excelsior, Via Partenope 48,* ☎ *081/7640111. Jacket and tie. AE, DC, MC, V.*

$$$ ★ ✗ **La Sacrestia.** Neapolitans flock to this upscale patrician villa for the restaurant's location—on the slopes of the Posillipo hill—and high standards of food quality. The seafood and meat specialties range from tasty antipasti to linguine in *salsa di scorfano* (scorpion-fish sauce). ✉ *Via Orazio 116,* ☎ *081/7611051. AE, DC, MC, V. Closed Sun. (July–Aug.), and 2 wks in mid-Aug. No lunch Mon., no dinner Sun.*

$$ ✗ **Ciro a Santa Brigida.** Off Via Toledo near the Castel Nuovo, Ciro is a straightforward restaurant popular with business travelers, artists, and journalists who prefer food over frills. In dining rooms on two levels, customers enjoy classic Neapolitan cuisine, pizza especially. The *scaloppe alla Ciro* (veal scallops with prosciutto and mozzarella) is wonderful. ✉ *Via Santa Brigida 71,* ☎ *081/5524072. AE, DC, MC, V. Closed Sun. and 2 wks in Aug.*

$$ ✗ **La Bersagliera.** You'll inevitably be drawn to eating at the Santa Lucia waterfront, in the shadow of the looming medieval Castel dell'Ovo. This spot is big and touristy but fun, with an irresistible combination of spaghetti and mandolins. The menu suggests uncomplicated timeworn classics, such as spaghetti *alla pescatora* (with seafood sauce) and melanzane alla parmigiana. ✉ *Borgo Marinaro 10,* ☎ *081/7646016. AE, DC, MC, V. Closed Tues.*

$$ ✗ **Mimì alla Ferrovia.** Near the central station, this bustling fish restaurant has scooped plenty of plaudits in recent years. The service is polite without being obsequious, the atmosphere relaxed, sometimes noisy. Try the *céfalo* (mullet) when it's in season, or the lobster. Other sure bets are *peperoni ripieni* (stuffed peppers) and grilled mushrooms. ✉ *Via Alfonso D'Aragona 21,* ☎ *081/5538525. AE, DC, MC, V. Closed Sun. and 10 days mid-Aug.*

$$$$ 🏨 **Excelsior.** The lobby and lounges of this ITT-Sheraton Luxury Collection hotel in Santa Lucia are lavishly imbued with Oriental carpets and gilt or glass chandeliers. Rooms are done in Empire style, with neoclassic furniture and brocades, or are of a Neapolitan floral-print persuasion. Off the large semicircular lounge are a chic little bar and the Casanova restaurant. ✉ *Via Partenope 48, 80121,* ☎ *081/7640111,* FAX *081/7649743. 136 rooms. Restaurant, bar, free parking. AE, DC, MC, V.*

$$$$ 🏨 **Parker's.** Gracefully old-fashioned, this is a sumptuous home away from home, tucked away halfway between the Spanish Quarter and Vomero. Its hillside location affords wonderful views, which can be appreciated from the rooftop restaurant. The lobby and guest rooms reflect the general finery, and you can indulge bookish pursuits in the library filled with rare editions. ✉ *Corso Vittorio Emanuele, 80121,* ☎ *081/7612474,* FAX *081/663527. 83 rooms. Restaurant, bar, library. AE, DC, MC, V.*

$$$ 🏨 **Belvedere.** In the center of the airy Vomero district, opposite the Carthusian monastery of San Martino, the Belvedere makes the most of its position high above the Spanish Quarter. Each of the spacious, comfortable rooms—half with balconies—comes equipped with a minibar. The garden restaurant also offers a peaceful respite from the bustle downtown. ✉ *Via Tito Angelini 51, 80129,* ☎ *081/5788169,* FAX *081/5785417. 27 rooms. Restaurant, bar, minibars. AE, DC, MC, V.*

$$$ ★ 🏨 **Paradiso.** You can take a taxi or funicular from downtown to the modern air-conditioned building perched on a hill above the port of Mergellina. Huge window walls in the lobby and front rooms reveal gorgeous views. The decor, in tones of blue and beige, is restful and attractive. Smallish rooms are smart, with built-in furnishings of rosy wood with marble surfaces. A roof terrace invites sitting, dining, and contemplating the entire bay and Vesuvius. ✉ *Via Catullo 11, 80122,* ☎ *081/7614161,* FAX *081/7613449. 74 rooms. Restaurant, bar, air-conditioning, minibars, free parking. AE, DC, MC, V.*

$$ **Rex.** This hotel has a fairly quiet location near the Santa Lucia waterfront. On the first two floors of an art-nouveau building, the decor ranges from 1950s modern to fake period pieces and even some folk art, haphazardly combined. It has no restaurant or elevator. ✉ *Via Palepoli 12, 80132,* ☎ *081/7649389,* FAX *081/7649227. 38 rooms. Bar. AE, DC, MC, V.*

Nightlife and the Arts

The Arts

MUSIC

A classical music festival known as **International Music Weeks** takes place throughout May in Naples. Concerts are held at the Teatro San Carlo, the Teatro Mercadante, and in the neoclassic Villa Pignatelli. For information, contact the Teatro San Carlo box office (☞ *below*).

OPERA

Naples has a full opera season from fall through spring. The **Teatro San Carlo** (✉ Via San Carlo, ☎ 081/7972111), where the season runs throughout the year apart from July and August, is one of Italy's top opera houses.

Nightlife

NIGHTCLUBS

A sophisticated crowd heads to the fashionable **Gabbiano** (✉ Via Partenope 26, ☎ 081/7645717), where live music is usually on tap. **Tongue** (✉ Via Manzoni 207, ☎ 081/7690800) appeals especially to gays and techno-heads. The sophisticated **Chez Moi** (✉ Via del Parco Margherita 13, ☎ 081/407526) has a dress code and is popular with the fashion jet set.

Outdoor Activities and Sports

Fishing

For information on licenses and water quality, contact **Federazione Italiana Pesca Sportiva** (✉ Piazza Santa Maria degli Angeli, ☎ 081/7644921).

Horseback Riding

For riding in Campania, contact the **Centro Ippico Agnano** (✉ Via Circumvallazione, Agnano, between Naples and Pozzuoli, ☎ 081/5702695).

Sailing

Club Nautico (✉ Borgo Marinari, ☎ 081/7646162) offers courses for sailors or would-be sailors all year round. **Canottieri Savoia** (✉ Banchina Santa Lucia, ☎ 081/7646162) offers courses from October through June.

Waterskiing

Sci Nautico Partenopeo (✉ Lago d'Averno, Pozzuoli, ☎ 081/8662214) offers sessions and courses on what was once believed the mouth of hell, at Lago d'Averno, west of Naples.

Shopping

Leather goods, coral, jewelry, and cameos are some of the best items to buy in Campania. In Naples, where many of the top leather and fashion houses have their factories, you'll find good buys in handbags, shoes, and clothing, but it's often wise to make purchases in shops rather than from street vendors, who often fancy sewing on famous labels and logos to their inferior merchandise. Most boutiques and department stores are closed until about 4:30 on Monday (hours are roughly Monday 4:30 to 8, Tuesday to Saturday 9:15 to 1 and 4:30 to 8), though food shops are open Monday morning, too.

Shopping Districts

The area immediately around **Piazza dei Martiri** is the heart of luxury shopping, with perfume shops, fashion outlets, and antiques on display. **Via Toledo** is a better bet for bargains. Also try **Via Chiaia** for good deals.

Shopping Mall

The **Galleria Umberto** (✉ Via San Carlo) is a good introduction to shopping in Naples; a wide variety of retail outlets trade in the four glass-roofed arcades.

Specialty Stores

Arte Antica (✉ Via Domenico Morelli 6, ☎ 081/7643704) is long famous for Italian antiques, especially flamboyant, richly decorated porcelain. **Eddy Monetti** (✉ Piazza Santa Caterina, ☎ 081/403229; for women, ✉ Via dei Mille, ☎ 081/407064) offers a range of elegantly tailored togs.

THE PHLEGREAN FIELDS

The name Campi Flegrei—the fields of fire—was once given to the entire region west of Naples, including the island of Ischia. The whole area floats freely on a mass of molten lava very close to the surface. The fires are still smoldering. Greek and Roman notions of the Underworld were not the blind imaginings of a primitive people; they were the creations of poets and writers who stood on this very ground and wrote down what they saw. Today, it should take about a half of a day to assess it yourself.

Solfatara

18 *8 km (5 mi) west of Naples.*

Here at the sunken volcanic crater Solfatara you can experience first-hand the volcanic nature of this otherworldly terrain. In fact, the only eruption of this semiextinct volcano was in 1198, though according to one legend, every crater in the Phlegrean Fields is one of the mouths of a hundred-headed dragon named Typhon that Zeus hurled down the crater of Epomeo on the island of Ischia. According to another, the sulfurous springs of the Solfatara are poisonous discharges from the wounds the Titans received in their war with Zeus. Both legends, of course, are efforts to dramatize man's struggle to overcome the mysterious and dangerous forces of nature. The stark, scorched area, slightly marred by the modern apartment blocks peering over the rim, exerts a strange fascination. The area is safe for walking if you stick to the path. 🎟 *8,000 lire.* ⏲ *Apr.–Sept., daily 8:30–6:30; Oct.–Mar., daily 8:30–4:30.*

Pozzuoli

19 *2 km (1 mi) west of Solfatara, 8 km (5 mi) west of Naples.*

The **Anfiteatro Flavio** (Flavian Amphitheater) here is the third-largest arena in Italy, after the Colosseum and Santa Maria Capua Vetere, and once held 40,000 spectators, who were sometimes treated to mock naval battles when the arena was filled with water. The well-preserved underground passages and chambers are fascinating, and give a good sense of how the wild animals were hoisted up into the arena. ☎ *081/5266007.* 🎟 *4,000 lire.* ⏲ *Daily 9–1 hr before sunset.*

You may want to make a short side trip to the town's harbor and imagine St. Paul landing here in AD 61 en route to Rome. His own ship had been wrecked off Malta, and he was brought here on the *Castor and*

Pollux, a grain ship from Alexandria that was carrying corn from Egypt to Italy only 18 years before the eruption at Vesuvius.

Baia

20 *7 km (4½ mi) south of Pozzuoli, 12 km (7 mi) west of Naples.*

Now largely under the sea, this was once the most opulent and fashionable resort area of the Roman Empire, the place where Sulla, Pompey, Julius Caesar, Tiberius (42 BC–AD 37), Nero, and Cicero built their holiday villas. Petronius's *Satyricon* is a satire on the corruption and intrigue, the wonderful licentiousness of Roman life at Baia. (Petronius was hired to arrange parties and entertainments for Nero, so he was in a position to know.) It was here at Baia that Emperor Claudius built a great villa for his wife Messalina (who spent her nights indulging herself at public brothels); here that Agrippina poisoned her husband and was, in turn, murdered by her son Nero; and here that Cleopatra was staying when Julius Caesar was murdered on the ides of March (March 15, 44 BC). You can visit the excavations of the famous **terme** (baths). ✉ *Via Fusaro 35,* ☎ *081/8687592.* 🎫 *4,000 lire.* ⏲ *Daily 9–1 hr before sunset.*

En Route Follow the southern loop around Lago Miseno (a volcanic crater believed by the ancients to be the Styx, across which Charon ferried the souls of the dead) and Lago del Fusaro. You'll take in some fine views of Golfo di Pozzuoli (Bay of Pozzuoli).

Cumae

21 *5 km (3 mi) north of Pozzuoli, 16 km (10 mi) west of Naples.*

Perhaps the oldest Greek colony in Italy, Cumae overshadowed the Phlegrean Fields, including Naples, in the 6th and 7th centuries BC. The **Antro della Sibilla** (Sibyl's Cave) is here—one of the most venerated sites in antiquity. In the 5th or 6th century BC, the Greeks hollowed the cave from the rock beneath the present ruins of Cumae's acropolis. You walk through a dark, massive stone tunnel that opens into a vaulted chamber where the Sibyl rendered her oracles. Standing here, the sense of mystery, of communication with the invisible, is overwhelming. "This is the most romantic classical site in Italy," wrote H. V. Morton (1892–1979), the English travel writer. "I would rather come here than to Pompeii."

Virgil (70–19 BC) wrote the epic *The Aeneid,* the story of the Trojan prince Aeneas's wanderings, partly to give Rome the historical legitimacy that Homer had given the Greeks. On his journey, Aeneas had to descend to the Underworld to speak to his father, and to find his way in, he needed the guidance of the Cumaean Sibyl. Virgil did not dream up the Sibyl's cave or the entrance to Hades—he must have stood both in her chamber and along the rim of Lago d'Averno, as you yourself will stand. When he wrote, *"Facilis descensus Averno"*—"The way to hell is easy"—it was because he knew the way. In Book VI of *The Aeneid,* Virgil described how Aeneas, arriving at Cumae, sought Apollo's throne (remains of the **Tempio di Apollo** can still be seen) and "the deep hidden abode of the dread Sibyl / An enormous cave . . ."

The Sibyl was not necessarily a charlatan; she was a medium, a prophetess, an old woman whom the ancients believed could communicate with the Other World. The three most famous Sibyls were at Erythrae, Delphi, and Cumae. Foreign governments consulted the Sibyls before mounting campaigns. Wealthy aristocrats came to consult with their dead relatives. Businessmen came to get their dreams interpreted or to seek favorable omens before entering into financial agreements or setting off on journeys. Farmers came to remove curses on their cows. Love potions were a profitable source of revenue. Women from Baia lined up for potions to slip into the wine of handsome charioteers who drove up and down the street in their gold-plated four-horsepower chariots.

With the coming of the Olympian gods, the earlier gods of the soil were discredited or given new roles and names. Ancient rites, such as those surrounding the Cumaean Sibyl, were now carried out in secret and known as the Mysteries. The Romans—like the later Soviets—tried in vain to replace these Mysteries by deifying the state in the person of its rulers. Yet even the Caesars appealed to forces of the Other World. And until the 4th century AD, the Sibyl was consulted by the Christian bishop of Rome. ✉ *Via Acropoli,* ☎ *081/8543060.* 🎫 *4,000 lire.* ⏲ *Jan.–Oct., daily 9–1 hr before sunset; Nov. and Dec., daily 9–3:30.*

Lago d'Averno

4 km (2½ mi) south of Cumae, 11 km (7 mi) west of Naples.

The best time to visit the fabled Lago d'Averno (Lake Avernus) is at sunset or when the moon is rising. There's a restaurant on the west side, where you can dine on the terrace. Forested hills rise on three sides; the menacing cone of Monte Nuovo rises on the fourth. The smell of sulfur hangs over this sad, lonely landscape seemingly at the very gates of hell. No place evokes Homer, Virgil, and the cult of the Other World better than this silent, mysterious setting. ✉ *Drive west from Pozzuoli on S7 toward Cumae and then turn left (south) on the road to Baia. About 1 km (½ mi) along, turn right and follow signs to Lake Avernus.*

HERCULANEUM, VESUVIUS, POMPEII

Ancient Inspirations

Volcanic ash and mud preserved the Roman towns of Herculaneum and Pompeii almost exactly as they were on the day Mt. Vesuvius erupted in AD 79, leaving them not just archaeological ruins but testimonies of daily life in the ancient world. All three sights can be visited from either Naples or Sorrento, thanks to the Circumvesuviana (☞ Getting Around *in* Campania A to Z, *below*), the suburban railway that provides fast, frequent, and economical service.

Herculaneum

★ ㉒ *10 km (6 mi) south of Naples.*

Lying more than 60 ft below the town of Ercolano, the ruins of Herculaneum are set among the acres of greenhouses that make this area one of Europe's principal flower-growing centers. Hercules himself is said to have founded the town, which became a famous weekend retreat for the Roman elite. It had about 5,000 inhabitants when it was destroyed; many of them were fishermen, craftsmen, and artists. A lucky few patricians owned villas overlooking the sea. Herculaneum was damaged by an earthquake in AD 63, and repairs were still being made 16 years later when the gigantic eruption of Vesuvius (which also destroyed Pompeii) sent a fiery cloud of gas and pumice hurtling onto the town, which was completely buried under a tide of volcanic mud. This semiliquid mass seeped into the crevices and niches of every building, covering household objects and enveloping textiles and wood—sealing all in a compact, airtight tomb.

Casual excavation—and haphazard looting—began in the 18th century, but systematic digs were not initiated until the 1920s. Today less than half of Herculaneum has been excavated; with present-day Ercolano and the unlovely Resina Quarter (famous among bargain hunters as the area's largest secondhand clothing market) sitting on top of the site, progress is limited. From the ramp leading down to Herculaneum's neatly laid out streets and well-preserved edifices, you get a good overall view of the site, as well as an idea of the amount of rock that had to be removed to bring it to light.

If you feel closer to the past at Herculaneum than at Pompeii, it's in part because there are fewer hawkers here. Also, though Herculaneum had only one-fourth the population of Pompeii and has only been partially excavated, what has been found is generally better preserved. In some cases, you can even see the original wooden beams, staircases, and furniture. Much excitement is presently focused on one excavation in a corner of the site, the Villa dei Papiri, built by Julius Caesar's father-in-law. The building is named for the 1,800 carbonized papyrus scrolls dug up here in the 18th century, leading scholars to believe that this may have been a study center or library. Now Italian geologists and archaeologists have uncovered part of the villa itself and hope to unearth more of the library—given the right funds and political support. Little of the site can be seen above ground, though visitors to the J. Paul Getty Museum in Malibu, California, can see a modern version of the villa, according to drawings made by the Swiss archaeologist Carl Weber in the 18th century.

At the entrance to the archaeological park you should pick up a map showing the gridlike layout of the dig. Decorations are especially delicate in the **Casa del Atrio Mosaico** (House of the Mosaic Atrium), with a pavement in a black-and-white checkerboard pattern, and in the **Casa del Nettuno ed Anfitrite** (House of Neptune and Amphitrite), named for the subjects of a still-bright mosaic on the wall of the nymphaeum (a recessed grotto with a fountain). Annexed to the latter house is a remarkably preserved wineshop, where amphorae still rest on carbonized wooden shelves. And in the **Casa del Tramezzo di Legno** (House of the Wooden Partition), one of the best-preserved of all, there is a carbonized wooden partition with three doors. In the **terme** (baths), where there were separate sections for men and women, you can see benches; basins; and the hot, warm, and cold rooms, embellished with mosaics. The **Casa del Bicentenario** (House of the Bicentenary) was a patrician residence with smaller rooms on the upper floor, which may have been rented out to artisan-tenants who were probably Christians because they left an emblem of the cross embedded in the wall. The palaestra and 2,500-seat theater, the sumptuously decorated suburban baths, and the **Casa dei Cervi** (House of the Stags), with an elegant garden open to the sea breezes, are all evocative relics of a lively and luxurious way of life.

Until a few years ago it was believed that most of Herculaneum's inhabitants had managed to escape by sea, since few skeletons were found in the city. Excavations at Porta Marina, the gate in the sea wall leading to the beach, have revealed instead that many perished there, a few steps from the only escape route open to them. Most important buildings can be seen in about two hours. The site entrance is a short walk south from the Circumvesuviana station. ✉ *Corso Ercolano,* ☎ *081/7390963.* 🎟 *12,000 lire.* ⏲ *Daily 9–1 hr before sunset (ticket office closes 2 hrs before sunset).*

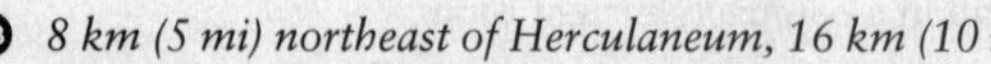

Vesuvius

23 *8 km (5 mi) northeast of Herculaneum, 16 km (10 mi) east of Naples.*

The profile of Vesuvius is so inseparable from the Bay of Naples area, and the ferocious power it can unleash so vivid as you tour the sights of the cities that it destroyed, you may be overwhelmed by the urge to explore the crater itself. In summer especially, the prospect of rising above the sticky heat of the city and sights below is a heady one. The view when clear is magnificent, with the curve of the coast and the tiny white houses among the orange and lemon blossoms. If the summit is lost in mist, you'll be lucky to see your hand in front of your face. When you see the summit clearing—it tends to be clearer in the afternoon—head for it. If possible, see Vesuvius after you've toured the ruins of buried Herculaneum to appreciate the magnitude of the volcano's awesome power.

Reaching the crater takes some effort. From the Ercolano stop of the Circumvesuviana, take scheduled buses (trip takes one hour; departures currently four or five times a day—check locally for the latest times) or your own car to the Seggovia station, the lower terminal of the defunct chairlift. (Though there's talk of putting it back in working order, no one is optimistic about the possibility.) From here you must climb the soft, slippery cinder track on foot, a 30-minute ascent, and you must pay about 5,000 lire for compulsory guide service, though the guides don't do much more than tell you to stay away from the edge of the crater. If you're not in shape, you'll probably find the climb tiring. Wear nonskid shoes (not sandals). *Guide service 5,000 lire.*

Pompeii

★ *11 km (7 mi) northeast of Herculaneum, 24 km (15 mi) southeast of Naples.*

Ancient Pompeii was much larger than Herculaneum; a busy commercial center with a population of 10,000–20,000, it covered about 160 acres on the seaward end of the fertile Sarno Plain. In 80 BC the Roman General Sulla turned Pompeii into a Roman colony, where wealthy patricians came to escape the turmoil of city life. The town was laid out in a grid pattern, with two main intersecting streets. The wealthiest took a whole block for themselves; those less fortunate built a house and rented out the front rooms, facing the street, as shops. The facades of these houses were relatively plain and seldom hinted at the care and attention lavished on the private rooms within. When a visitor entered, he passed the shops and entered an open atrium. In the back was a receiving room. Behind was another open area, called the peristyle, with rows of columns and perhaps a garden with a fountain. Only good friends ever saw this private part of the house, which was surrounded by the bedrooms and the dining area.

Pompeiian houses were designed around an inner garden so that families could turn their backs on the world outside. Today we install picture windows that break down visual barriers between ourselves and our neighbors; the people in these Roman towns had few windows, preferring to get their light from the central courtyard—the light within. How pleasant it must have been to come home from the forum or the baths to one's own secluded kingdom, with no visual reminders of a life outside one's own. Not that public life was so intolerable. There were wineshops on almost every corner, and frequent shows at the amphitheater. The public fountains and toilets were fed by huge cisterns, connected by lead pipes beneath the sidewalks. Since garbage and rainwater collected in the streets of Pompeii, the sidewalks were raised, and huge stepping stones were placed at crossings so pedestrians could keep their feet dry. Herculaneum had better drainage, with an underground sewer that led to the sea.

The ratio of freemen to slaves was about three to two. A small, prosperous family had two or three slaves. Since all manual labor was considered degrading, the slaves did all housework and cooking, including the cutting of meat, which the family ate with spoons or with their hands. Everyone loved grapes, and figs were popular, too. Venison, chicken, and pork were the main dishes. People ate quinces (a good source of vitamin C) to guard against scurvy. Bread was made from wheat and barley (rye and oats were unknown) and washed down with wine made from the grapes of the slopes of Vesuvius.

The government was considered a democracy, but women, children, gladiators, and Jews couldn't vote. They did, however, express their opinions on election day, as you'll see in campaign graffiti left on public walls. Some 15,000 graffiti were found in Pompeii and Herculaneum. Many were political announcements—one person recommending another for office, for example, and spelling out his qualifications. Some were bills announcing upcoming events—a play at the theater, a fight among gladiators at the amphitheater. Others were public notices—that wine was on sale, that an apartment would be vacant on the Ides of March. A good many were personal, and lend a human dimension to the disaster that not even the sights can equal. Here are a few:

At the baths: "What is the use of having a Venus if she's made of marble?"

At a hotel: "I've wet my bed. My sin I bare. But why? you ask. No pot was anywhere."

At the entrance to the front lavatory at a private house: "May I always and everywhere be as potent with women as I was here."

24 Enter through **Porta Marina,** so called because it faces the sea. It is near
the Pompeii–Villa Misteri Circumvesuviana Station. Past the Temple
25 of Venus is the **Basilica,** the law court and the economic center of the
city. These oblong buildings ending in a semicircular projection (apse)
were the model for early Christian churches, which had a nave (central aisle) and two side aisles separated by rows of columns. Standing
in the Basilica, you can recognize the continuity between Roman and
Christian architecture.

26 The Basilica opens onto the **Foro** (Forum), the public meeting place,
surrounded by temples and public buildings. It was here that elections
were held and speeches and official announcements made. At the far
27 (northern) end of the forum is the **Tempio di Giove** (Temple of Jupiter).
28 The renowned **Casa del Fauno** (House of the Faun) displays wonderful mosaics, though the originals are in the Museo Archeologico
Nazionale in Naples.

29 The **Terme di Foro** (Forum Baths) on Via delle Terme, is smaller than
the Terme Stabiane (☞ *below*) but with more delicate decoration. The
30 **Casa del Poeta Tragico** (House of the Tragic Poet) is a typical middle-
class house from the last days of Pompeii. On the floor is a mosaic of
a chained dog and the inscription CAVE CANEM ("Beware of the dog").

31 The beautiful **Porta Ercolano** (Gate of Herculaneum) was a main gate
32 that led to Herculaneum and Naples. The **Villa dei Misteri** (Villa of the
Mysteries), outside Pompeii's walls, contains what some consider the greatest surviving group of paintings from the ancient world, telling the story
of a young bride (Ariadne) being initiated into the mysteries of the cult
of Dionysus. Bacchus (Dionysus), the god of wine, was popular in a town
so devoted to the pleasures of the flesh. But he also represented the triumph of the irrational—of all those mysterious forces that no official
state religion could fully suppress. The cult of Dionysus, like the cult of
the Cumaean Sibyl, gave people a sense of control over fate, and in its
focus on the Other World, helped pave the way for Christianity.

Pompeii

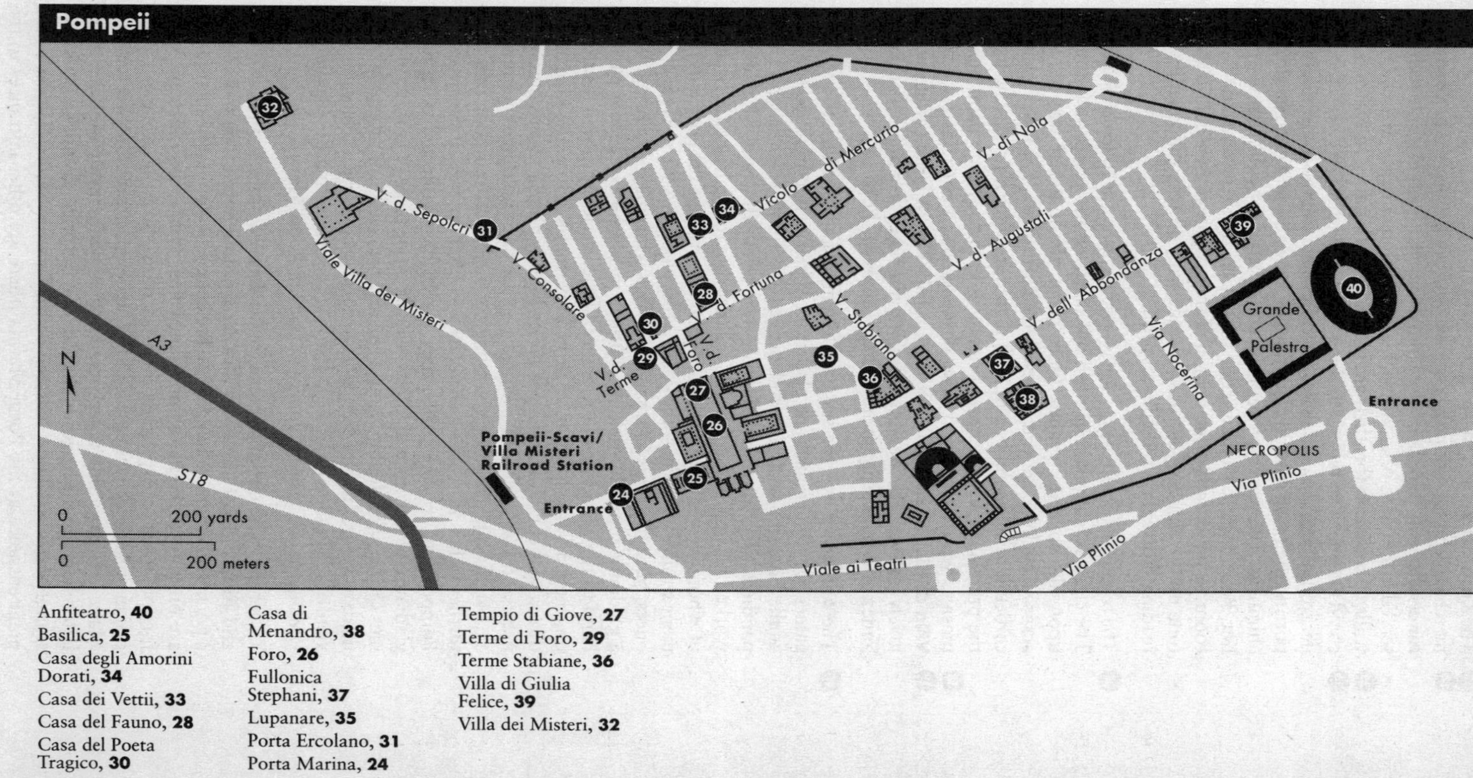

Anfiteatro, **40**
Basilica, **25**
Casa degli Amorini Dorati, **34**
Casa dei Vettii, **33**
Casa del Fauno, **28**
Casa del Poeta Tragico, **30**
Casa di Menandro, **38**
Foro, **26**
Fullonica Stephani, **37**
Lupanare, **35**
Porta Ercolano, **31**
Porta Marina, **24**
Tempio di Giove, **27**
Terme di Foro, **29**
Terme Stabiane, **36**
Villa di Giulia Felice, **39**
Villa dei Misteri, **32**

33 The **Casa dei Vettii** (House of the Vetti) is the best example of a rich
34 merchant's house, faithfully restored with vivid murals. The **Casa degli
Amorini Dorati** (House of the Gilded Cupids) is an elegant, well-preserved home with original marble decorations in the garden. On the
35 walls of **Lupanare** (brothel) are scenes of erotic games in which clients
36 could engage. The **Terme Stabiane** (Stabian Baths) were heated by underground furnaces whose heat circulated among the stone pillars supporting the floor, rose through flues in the walls, and escaped through
chimneys. The water temperature could be set for cold, lukewarm, or
hot. Bathers took a lukewarm bath to prepare themselves for the hot
room. A tepid bath came next, and then a plunge into cold water to
tone up the skin. A vigorous massage with oil was followed by rest,
reading, horseplay, and conversation.

37 The required Roman dress—togas—were washed at **Fullonica Stephani.**
The cloth was dunked in a tub full of water and chalk and stomped
upon like so many grapes. Once clean, the material was stretched
across a wicker cage and exposed to sulfur fumes. The fuller (cleaner)
carded it with a long brush, then placed it under a press. The harder
the pressing, the whiter and brighter it became. Many paintings and
38 mosaics were executed at **Casa di Menandro,** a patrician's villa. The
39 **Villa di Giulia Felice** (House of Julia Felix) has a large garden with a
lovely portico. The wealthy woman living here ran a public bathhouse
annex and rented out ground-floor rooms as shops.

40 The **Anfiteatro** was the stage for Olympic games, chariot races, and games between animals and gladiators. When an important person such as the Emperor was in attendance, exotic animals—lions and tigers, panthers, elephants, and rhinos—were released. Teams of gladiators worked for impresarios, who hired them out to wealthy citizens, many of whom were running for office and hoping that the gory entertainment would buy them some votes. Most gladiators were slaves or prisoners, but a few were Germans or Syrians who enjoyed fighting. When a gladiator found himself at another's mercy, he extended a pleading hand to the president of the games. If the president turned his thumb up, the gladiator lived; if he turned his thumb down, the gladiator's throat was cut. The arena got pretty bloody after a night's entertainment and was sprinkled with red powder to camouflage the carnage. The victorious gladiator got money or a ribbon exempting him from further fights. If he was a slave, he was often set free. If the people of Pompeii had trading cards, they would have collected portraits of gladiators; everyone had his favorite. Says one piece of graffiti: "Petronius Octavus fought thirty-four fights and then died, but Severus, a freedman, was victor in fifty-five fights and still lived; Nasica celebrates sixty victories." Pompeii had a gladiator school (Caserma dei Gladiatori), which you can visit on your way back to Porta Marina.

To get the most out of Pompeii, buy a detailed printed guide and map and allow plenty of time—at least three or four hours. You should have a pocketful of small change (500 lire coins) for tipping the guards who are on duty at the most important villas. They will unlock the gates for you, insist on explaining the attractions, show you some soft Pompeiian pornography if you ask for it, and expect a tip for their services. Make sure the guide is registered and standing inside the gate; agree beforehand on the length of the tour and the price. Pompeii has its own stop (Pompeii–Villa dei Misteri) on the Circumvesuviana, close to the main entrance at the Porta Marina (there are other entrances to the excavations at the far end of the site, near the amphitheater). ✉ *Pompeii Scavi,* ☎ *081/8610744.* 🎫 *12,000 lire.* ⏲ *Daily 9–1 hr before sunset (ticket office closes 2 hrs before sunset).*

Nightlife and the Arts

Pompeii's late-summer festival of the performing arts, known as the **Panatenee Pompeiane,** hosts a series of classical plays in July and August. For information, contact one of the tourist offices in Naples (☞ Visitor Information *in* Campania A to Z, *below*).

CASERTA AND BENEVENTO

From Caserta, the Italian answer to Versailles, if you proceed to Benevento you'll view an almost perfectly preserved Roman arch. Benevento was badly damaged by World War II bombings, but among the modern structures there are some medieval and even older relics still standing in the old town. If you go by car, make a brief detour to the medieval hamlet of Caserta Vecchia on the hillside, where there is a very old cathedral and one or two good restaurants.

Caserta

★ 41 *11 km (7 mi) northeast of Herculaneum, 25 km (16 mi) northeast of Naples.*

The royal palace known as the **Reggia** is exemplary of mid-18th-century Bourbon royalty living. Architect Luigi Vanvitelli devoted 20 years to its construction under Bourbon ruler Charles II, whose son, Charles III (1716–1788), moved in when it was completed in 1774. Both king and architect were inspired by Versailles, and the rectangular palace was conceived on a massive scale, with four interconnecting courtyards, 1,200 rooms, and a vast park. Though not as well maintained as its French counterpart, the main staircase puts the one at Versailles to shame, and the **royal apartments** are sumptuous. It was here, in what Eisenhower called "a castle near Naples," that the Allied High Command had its headquarters in World War II, and here German forces in Italy surrendered in April 1945. Most enjoyable are the gardens and parks, particularly the Cascades, where a life-size Diana and her maidens stand. ✉ *Piazza Carlo III,* ☎ *0823/321400.* 🎫 *Royal apartments: 8,000 lire; park: 4,000 lire; minibus: 1,500 lire.* ⏲ *Royal apartments: Apr.–Sept., Tues.–Sun. 9–6; Oct.–Mar., Tues.–Sun. 9–1:30; park: Apr.–Sept., Tues.–Sun. 9–1 hr before sunset; Oct.–Mar., Tues.–Sun. 9–3.*

Capua

42 *11 km (7 mi) northwest of Caserta, 33 km (20 mi) north of Naples.*

The nondescript town of Capua is home to the **Museo Campano,** a provincial museum collection that includes Le Madri (the Mothers), 200 eerily impressive stone votive statues representing highly stylized mother figures. They were found on the site of a sanctuary devoted to Matuta, the ancient goddess of childbirth, and date from the 7th to the 1st century BC. ✉ *Via Roma,* ☎ *0823/961402.* 🎫 *8,000.* ⏲ *Tues.–Sat. 9–1:30, Sun. 9–1.*

Benevento

43 *35 km (22 mi) east of Caserta, 60 km (37 mi) northeast of Naples.*

Benevento owes its importance to its establishment as the capital of the Lombards, a northern tribe that invaded and settled what is now Lombardy when they were ousted by Charlemagne in the 8th century. Tough and resourceful, the Lombards moved south and set up a new duchy in Benevento, later moving its seat south to Salerno, where they saw the potential of the natural harbor. Under papal rule in the 13th century, Benevento built a fine cathedral and endowed it with bronze doors that were a pinnacle of Romanesque art. The cathedral, doors, and a large part of the town were blasted by World War II bombs. The **Duomo** has been rebuilt, with the remaining panels of the original bronze doors in the chapter library. Fortunately, the majestic 2nd-century AD **Arco di Traiano** survived unscathed. Roman emperor Trajan, who sorted out Rome's finances, brought parts of the Middle East into the empire, and extended the Appian Way through Benevento to the Adriatic. The ruins of the **Teatro Romano,** which had a seating capacity of 20,000, is still in good enough shape to host a summer opera and theater season. ✉ *Take Via Carlo from the Duomo.* *4,000 lire.* ⏲ *Daily 9–1 hr before sunset.*

ISCHIA AND CAPRI

Swept Away

History's hedonists have long luxuriated on Campania's famous islands. The Roman emperor Tiberius built a dozen villas on Capri to indulge his sexual whims. Later residents have included dancer Rudolf Nureyev and droves of artists and writers. These days day-trippers make up the bulk of the visitors, diminishing the islands' social cachet but unable to tarnish their incomparable beauty. Ischia, less pretty and less chic than Capri, is still a popular landing point on account of spas, beaches, and hot springs.

Ischia

44 *45 mins by hydrofoil, 90 mins by car ferry from Naples; 60 mins by ferry from Pozzuoli.*

While Capri wows you with its charm and beauty, Ischia takes its time to cast its spell. In fact, an overnight stay is probably not long enough for the island to get into your blood. It does have its share of wine-growing villages beneath the lush volcanic slopes of Monte Epomeo and, unlike Capri, it enjoys a life of its own that survives when the tourists head home. But there are few signs of antiquity here, the architecture is unremarkable, the beaches are small and pebbly, there's little shopping beyond the high-trash gift shops, and most visitors are either German (off-season) or Italian (in-season). On the other hand, some of you will delight in discovering an island not yet discovered by Americans. Ischia also has some lovely hotel-resorts high in the mountains, offering therapeutic programs and rooms with breathtaking views. Should you want to plunk down in the sun for a few days and tune out the world, this is an ideal place to go; the mistake you shouldn't make is expecting Ischia to be an unspoiled, undiscovered Capri. When Augustus gave the Neapolitans Ischia for Capri, he knew what he was doing.

Unlike Capri, Ischia is volcanic in origin. From its hidden reservoir of seething molten matter come the thermal springs said to cure whatever ails you. As early as 1580, a doctor named Lasolino published a book about the mineral wells at Ischia. "If your eyebrows fall off," he wrote, "go and try the baths at Piaggia Romano. Are you unhappy about your complexion? You will find the cure in the waters of Santa Maria del Popolo. Are you deaf? Then go to Bagno d'Ulmitello. If you know anyone who is getting bald, anyone who suffers from elephantiasis, or another whose wife yearns for a child, take the three of them immediately to the Bagno di Vitara; they will bless you." Today the island is covered with thermal baths surrounded by tropical gardens.

Ischia Porto is the largest town on the island and the usual point of debarkation. It's no workaday port, however, but a pretty resort with plenty of hotels and low flat-roofed houses on terraced hillsides above the water. Its narrow streets often become flights of steps that scale the hill, and its villas and gardens are framed by pines.

Most of the hotels are along the beach in the part of town called **Ischia Ponte,** which gets its name from the *ponte* (bridge) built by Alfonso of Aragón in 1438 to link the picturesque castle on a small islet offshore with the town and port. For a while, the castle was the home of Vittoria Colonna, poetess and platonic soul mate of Michelangelo, with whom she carried on a lengthy correspondence, and granddaughter of Renaissance Duke Federico da Montefeltro (1422–82). You'll find a typical resort atmosphere: countless cafés, shops, and restaurants, and a 1-km (½-mi) stretch of fine sandy beach. Another popular beach resort, just 5 km (3 mi) west of Ischia Porto, is **Casamicciola.** Next is chic and upscale **Lacco Ameno,** distinguished by a mushroom-shape rock offshore and some of the island's best hotels. Here, too, you can enjoy the benefits of Ischia's therapeutic waters.

The far western and southern coasts of the island are more rugged and attractive. **Forio,** at the extreme west, is an ideal stop for lunch or dinner. The sybaritic hot pools of the **Giardini Poseidon Terme** (Poseidon Gardens) spa establishment are on the Citara beach, south of Forio. You can sit like a Roman senator on a stone chair recessed in the rock and let the hot water cascade over you—all very campy, and fun. **Sant' Angelo,** on the southern coast, is a charming village; the road doesn't reach all the way into town, so it's free of traffic, and it's a five-minute boat ride from the beach of Maronti, at the foot of cliffs. The inland towns of **Serrara, Fontana,** and **Barano** are all high above the sea; Fontana, most elevated of the three, is the base for excursions to the top of **Monte Epomeo,** the long-dormant volcano that dominates the island landscape. You can reach its 2,585-ft peak in less than 1½ hours of relatively easy walking.

A good 35-km (22-mi) road makes a circuit of the island; the ride takes most of a day at a leisurely pace, if you're stopping along the way to enjoy the views and perhaps have lunch. You can book a **boat tour** around the island at the booths in various ports along the coast; there's a one-hour stop at Sant'Angelo. The information office is at the harbor. Remember that Ischia is off-limits to visitors' cars from April through September; there's fairly good bus service, and you'll find plenty of taxis.

Dining and Lodging

$$ ✕ **Gennaro.** This small family restaurant on the seafront at Ischia Porto serves excellent fish in a convivial atmosphere. Specialties include spaghetti alle vongole and linguine *all'aragosta* (with lobster). ✉ *Via Porto 66, Ischia Porto,* ☎ *081/992917. AE, DC, MC, V. Closed Nov.–mid-Mar.*

$$$$ **Hotel San Montano.** Modern San Montano, replete with nautical motifs and ceramic-tile floors, overlooks the sea in a quiet spot. The rooms have compact English-navy furnishings, color TVs, and minibars. The San Montano has all resort facilities and provides spa treatments, too. ✉ *Via Montevico 1, 80076 Lacco Ameno,* ☎ *081/994033,* FAX *081/980242. 67 rooms. Restaurant, minibars, pool, spa, tennis court. AE, DC, MC, V. Closed Nov.–Mar.*

$$$$ ★ **Regina Isabella.** Tucked away in an exclusive corner of the beach in Lacco Ameno, Ischia's top luxury hotel has full resort facilities and pampers you with spa treatments as well. The rooms are ample and decorated in warm Mediterranean colors, and most have terraces or balconies. Don't miss the fun of socializing with chic vacationers in the elegant bar or restaurant or at poolside. ✉ *Lacco Ameno, 80076 Lacco Ameno,* ☎ *081/994322,* FAX *081/900190. 134 rooms. Restau-*

rant, bar, indoor pool, outdoor pool, spa, tennis court, beach. AE, DC, MC, V. Closed Oct.–Mar.

$$$ ★ **Villarosa.** A highlight at this gracious family-run hotel, in a villa with bright and airy rooms, is the thermally heated pool in the villa garden. In high season, half board is required, and you must reserve well in advance. Prices fall into the lower end of this category. It's in the heart of Ischia Porto and only a short walk from the beach. ✉ *Via Giacinto Gigante 3, 80077 Ischia Porto,* ☎ *081/991316,* FAX *081/992425. 37 rooms. Restaurant, pool. AE, MC, V. Closed Nov.–Mar.. MAP.*

$–$$ **Del Postiglione.** This attractive, pink, Mediterranean-style edifice is smaller than it appears, with only 15 guest rooms. Its aura of understated luxury is created by marble floors, tropical plants adorning the outside, and generous balconies overlooking one of Ischia Porto's quiet back streets, a couple of minutes from the seafront. Half board only is accepted in August. ✉ *Via Giacinto Gigante 19, 80077 Ischia Porto,* ☎ *081/991579,* FAX *081/985956. 15 rooms. Restaurant, bar. MC, V. MAP.*

Capri

45 *74 mins by boat, 40 mins by hydrofoil from Naples.*

Erstwhile pleasure dome to Roman emperors, and now Italy's most glamorous seaside getaway, Capri (pronounced with an accent on the first syllable) is a craggy island at the southern approach to the Bay of Naples. The summer scene on Capri calls to mind the stampeding of bulls through the narrow streets of Pamplona: if you can visit in the spring or fall, do so. Yet even the crowds are not enough to destroy Capri's very special charm. The town is a Moorish opera set of shiny white houses, tiny squares, and narrow medieval alleyways hung with flowers. You can take a bus or the funicular to reach the town, which rests on top of rugged limestone cliffs, hundreds of feet above the sea, and on which huge herds of *capre* (goats) once used to roam (giving the name to the island). Unlike the other islands in the Bay of Naples, Capri is not of volcanic origin but is an integral part of the limestone chain of the Apennines, left above water when some subterranean cataclysm sank its connecting link with the mainland.

The Phoenicians were the earliest settlers of Capri. The Greeks arrived in the 4th century BC and were followed by the Romans, who made it their playground. Emperor Augustus vacationed here; Tiberius built 12 villas, scattered over the island, and here he spent the later years of his life, refusing to return to Rome even when he was near death. Capri was one of the strongholds of the 16th-century pirate Barbarossa, who first sacked it and then made a fortress of it. Moors and Greeks had previously established their citadels on its heights, and pirates from all corners of the world periodically raided it. In 1806 the British wanted to turn it into another Gibraltar and were beginning to build fortifications when the French took it away from them in 1808. However, the Roman influence has remained the strongest, reflecting a sybaritic way of life inherited from the Greek colonists on the mainland.

Thousands of legends concerning the lives and loves of mythological creatures, Roman emperors, Saracen invaders, and modern eccentrics combine to give Capri a voluptuous allure—sensuous and intoxicating—like the island's rare and delicious white wine. (Most of the wine passed off as "local" on Capri comes from the much more extensive vineyards of Ischia.)

You may have to wait in line for the cog railway (3,000 lire roundtrip) to **Capri Town.** If it's not operating, there's bus and taxi service.

From the upper station, walk out into Piazza Umberto I, much better known as the Piazzetta, the island's social hub. You can window-shop in expensive boutiques and browse in souvenir shops along Via Vittorio Emanuele, which leads south toward the many-domed **Certosa di San Giacomo.** The church and cloister of this much-restored monastery can be visited, and you should also pause long enough to enjoy the breathtaking view of Punta Tragara and the Faraglioni, three towering shoals, from the viewing stand at the edge of the cliff. ✉ *Via Certosa.* ⏲ *Tues.–Sun. 9–2.*

All boats for Capri Town dock at Marina Grande, where you can also board an excursion boat for the 90-minute tour to the **Grotta Azzurra** (Blue Grotto). If you're pressed for time, however, skip this sometimes frustrating and disappointing excursion. You board one boat to get to the grotto, and you have to transfer to another smaller boat in order to get inside the grotto. If there's a backup of boats waiting to get in, you'll be given precious little time to enjoy the gorgeous color of the water and its silvery reflections. Adventurists can hike to the grotto area from Anacapri. ✉ *Marina Grande.* 🎫 *About 23,000 lire, including 8,000-lire admission to grotto.* ⏲ *Apr.–Sept., daily 9:30–2 hrs before sunset; Oct.–Mar., daily 10–noon.*

OFF THE BEATEN PATH

BELVEDERE AND ARCO NATURALE – A short walk along Via Tragara leads to a belvedere overlooking the Faraglioni; another takes you out of town on Via Matermania to the so-called Natural Arch, an unusual rock formation near a natural grotto that the Romans transformed into a shrine. The 20-minute walk from the Piazzetta along picturesque Via Madre Serafina and Via Castello to the belvedere at Punta Cannone gives you a panoramic view of the island.

From the terraces of **Giardini di Augusto** (Gardens of Augustus), a beautifully planted public garden with excellent views, you can see the village of Marina Piccola below—restaurants, cabanas, and swimming platforms huddle among the shoals. This is the best place on the island for swimming; you can reach it by bus or by following the steep and winding Via Krupp, actually a staircase cut into the rock, all the way down. (Friedrich Krupp, the German arms manufacturer, loved Capri and became one of the island's most generous benefactors.) ✉ *Via Matteotti, beyond the monastery of San Giacomo.* ⏲ *Daily dawn–dusk.*

OFF THE BEATEN PATH

VILLA JOVIS – From Capri town, the 45-minute hike east to Villa Jovis, the grandest of those built by Tiberius, is strenuous but rewarding. Follow the signs for Villa Jovis, taking Via Le Botteghe from the Piazzetta, then continuing along Via Croce and Via Tiberio. At the end of a lane that climbs the steep hill, with pretty views all the way, you come to the precipice over which the emperor reputedly disposed of the victims of his perverse attentions. From a natural terrace above, near a chapel, are spectacular views of the entire Bay of Naples and (on clear days) part of the Gulf of Salerno. Below are the ruins of Tiberius's palace. Allow 45 minutes each way for the walk alone. ✉ *Via Tiberio,* ☎ *081/8370381.* 🎫 *4,000 lire.* ⏲ *Daily 9–1 hr before sunset.*

A tortuous road up leads to **Anacapri,** the island's only other town. Crowds are thickest around the square that is the starting point of the chairlift (6,000 lire) to the top of **Monte Solaro.** Elsewhere, Anacapri is quiet and appealing. Look for the church of **San Michele,** where a climb to the choir loft rewards you with a perspective of the magnificent 18th-century majolica tile floor showing the Garden of Eden. To get to

Anacapri, you can take a bus from Marina Grande (1,700 lire) or a taxi (about 15,000 lire one way; agree on the fare before starting out).

Anacapri is good for walks: try the 80-minute round-trip walk to the **Migliara Belvedere** and the one-hour walk to the ruins of the Roman **Villa di Damecuta.** From Piazza della Vittoria, picturesque Via Capodimonte leads to **Villa San Michele,** the charming former home of Swedish scientist Axel Munthe (1857–1949), now a museum of his antiques and furniture. ✉ *Via Axel Munthe,* ☎ *081/837401.* 🎫 *8,000 lire.* ⏲ *May–Sept., daily 9–6; Mar., daily 9:30–4:30; Apr. and Oct., daily 9:30–5; Nov.–Feb., daily 10:30–3:30.*

Dining and Lodging

$$–$$$ ★ ✕ **La Capannina.** Known as one of Capri's best restaurants, La Capannina is only a few steps from the busy social hub of the Piazzetta. It has a vine-draped veranda for dining outdoors by candlelight in a garden setting. The specialties, aside from an authentic Capri wine with the house label, are homemade ravioli alla caprese and regional dishes. ✉ *Via Le Botteghe 14, Capri Town,* ☎ *081/8370732. Reservations essential. AE, DC, MC, V. Closed Wed. (Oct.–May) and mid-Jan.–mid-Mar.*

$$–$$$ ✕ **La Pigna.** Ensconced in a glassed-in veranda and offering outdoor dining in a garden shaded by lemon trees, the Pigna is one of Capri's favorite restaurants. The specialties are a house-produced wine, *farfalle impazzite* (bow-tie pasta with seafood and tomato), and aragosta *alla luna caprese* (with mozzarella, tomato, and basil). The cordial host organizes party evenings with feasts of seasonal specialties and seafood. ✉ *Via Lo Palazzo 30, Capri Town,* ☎ *081/8370280. Reservations essential. AE, DC, MC, V. Closed Tues.*

$$ ✕ **Al Grottino.** This small and friendly family-run restaurant, which is handy to the Piazzetta, has arched ceilings and lots of atmosphere; autographed photos of celebrity customers cover the walls. House specialties are gnocchi with tomato sauce and mozzarella, and linguine *ai gamberetti* (with shrimp and tomato sauce). ✉ *Via Longano 27, Capri Town,* ☎ *081/8370584. Reservations essential. AE, MC, V. Closed Tues. and Nov. 3–Mar. 20.*

$$$$ 🏨 **Europa Palace Hotel.** A modern resort atmosphere pervades this large Mediterranean-style hotel set in lovely gardens. Each of four junior suites has a private swimming pool and terrace. The bedrooms are tastefully decorated in bright contemporary style, with white predominating, and marble bathrooms. The position in Anacapri offers relative seclusion from the summer crowds. ✉ *Via Capodimonte, 80071 Anacapri,* ☎ *081/8373800,* FAX *081/8373191. 91 rooms. Restaurant, bar, air-conditioning, pool, spa. AE, DC, MC, V.*

$$$$ 🏨 **Quisisana.** Catering largely to Americans, this is the most luxurious and traditional hotel in the center of town. Spacious rooms are done in traditional or modern decor with some antique accents. Many have arcaded balconies with views of the sea or the charming enclosed garden, surrounding a swimming pool. ✉ *Via Camerelle 2, 80073 Capri Town,* ☎ *081/8370788,* FAX *081/8376080. 149 rooms. Restaurant, bar, pool, sauna, tennis court. AE, DC, MC, V. Closed Nov.–mid-Mar.*

$$$$ ★ 🏨 **Scalinatella.** The name means "little stairway," and that's how this charming but modern small hotel is built, on terraces following the slope of the hill, overlooking the gardens, pool, and sea. The bedrooms are intimate, with alcoves and fresh, bright colors; the bathrooms feature whirlpool baths. ✉ *Via Tragara 8, 80073 Capri Town,* ☎ *081/8370633,* FAX *081/8378291. 30 rooms. Bar, air-conditioning, pool, tennis court. AE, MC, V. Closed Nov.–mid-Mar.*

$$$$ 🏨 **Villa Brunella.** This quiet family-run gem nestles in a garden setting just below the lane leading to the Faraglioni. Comfortable and tastefully furnished, the hotel also has spectacular views, a swimming pool, and a terrace restaurant known for good food. ✉ *Via Tragara 24, 80073 Capri Town,* ☎ *081/8370122,* FAX *081/8370430. 20 rooms. Restaurant, bar, pool. AE, DC, MC, V. Closed Nov.–Mar.*

$$$ **Villa Sarah.** This whitewashed Mediterranean building has a homey look and bright, simply furnished rooms. It's close enough to the Piazzetta (a 10-minute walk) to give easy access to the goings-on there, yet far enough away to ensure restful nights. There's a garden and a small bar. ✉ *Via Tiberio 3/a, 80073 Capri Town,* ☎ *081/8377817,* FAX *081/8377215. 20 rooms. Bar. AE, DC, MC, V. Closed Nov.–Mar.*

$$–$$$ **Aida.** A 10-minute walk from town center in a tiny lane that borders the Gardens of Augustus, the Aida offers a tranquil haven from Capri's bustle and hard sell. The staff is sociable, and the rooms, which look onto a small garden, are spacious, comfortably furnished, and immaculately clean. The beach at Marina Piccola is only 20 minutes away. ✉ *Via Birago, 80073 Capri Town,* ☎ *081/8370366. 10 rooms. No credit cards. Closed mid-Oct.–Apr.*

$$–$$$ **San Michele.** You'll find this large white villa-hotel next to Axel Munthe's home. Surrounded by luxuriant gardens, the San Michele offers solid comfort and good value along with spectacular views. It's modern, with some Neapolitan period pieces adding atmosphere. Most rooms have a terrace or balcony overlooking either the sea or island landscapes. ✉ *Via G. Orlandi 5, 80071 Anacapri,* ☎ *081/8371427,* FAX *081/8371420. 59 rooms. Restaurant, pool. AE, DC, MC, V. Closed Nov.–Mar.*

$$–$$$ **Villa Krupp.** Occupying a quiet location overlooking the Gardens of Augustus, this historic hostelry was the onetime home of Maxim Gorky, whose guests included Lenin. Rooms are plain but spacious. ✉ *Viale Matteotti 12, 80073 Capri Town,* ☎ *081/8370362,* FAX *081/8376489. 12 rooms. MC, V. Closed Nov.–Feb.*

Nightlife and the Arts

Capri's New Year's Eve celebrations last all evening with dancing and music culminating in a magnificent fireworks display. On New Year's Day there are marching bands, pageants, and all the revelry you would expect on this exuberant island.

THE AMALFI COAST

Sorrento to Salerno

As travelers journey down the fabled Amalfi Coast, their route takes them past rocky cliffs plunging into the sea and small boats lying in sandy coves like brightly colored fish. Erosion has contorted the rocks into mythological shapes and hollowed out fairy grottoes where the air is turquoise and the water an icy blue. White villages, dripping with flowers, nestle in coves or climb like vines up the steep, terraced hills. The road must have a thousand turns, each with a different view, on its dizzying 69-km (43-mi) journey from Sorrento to Salerno.

Sorrento

46 *50 km (31 mi) south of Naples, 50 km (31 mi) west of Salerno.*

Sorrento is across the Bay of Naples, on autostrada A3 and S145. The Circumvesuviana railway, which stops at Herculaneum and Pompeii, provides another connection. The coast between Naples and Castellammare, where road and railway turn off onto the Sorrento peninsula, seems at times depressingly overbuilt and industrialized. Yet Vesuvius looms to the left, you can make out the 3,000-ft-high mass of Monte Faito ahead, and on a clear day you can see Capri off the tip of the peninsula. The scenery improves considerably as you near Sorrento, where the coastal plain is carved into russet cliffs rising perpendicularly from the sea. This is the Sorrento (north) side of the peninsula; on the other side is the Amalfi Coast, more dramatically scenic. But Sorrento has at least two advantages over Amalfi: the Circumvesuviana railway terminal and a fairly flat terrain.

Until the mid-20th century Sorrento was a small, genteel resort favored by central European princes, English aristocrats, and American literati. Now the town has grown and spread out along the crest of its famous cliffs, and apartments stand where citrus groves once bloomed. Like most resorts, Sorrento is best off-season, either in spring and early autumn or in winter, when Campania's mild climate can make a stay pleasant anywhere along the coast. Highlights include a stroll around town, with views of the Bay of Naples from the **Villa Comunale** or from the terrace behind the **Museo Correale.** The museum features a collection of decorative antiques, from precious porcelain to furniture to landscape paintings of the Neapolitan school. Lush gardens festooned with citrus groves and a belvedere with outstanding views back the villa. ✉ *Via Correale,* ☎ *081/8781846.* *Museum and gardens 8,000 lire.* *Wed.–Mon. 9–2.*

Explore the town's churches and narrow alleys and follow **Via Marina Grande,** which turns into a pedestrian lane and stairway, to Sorrento's only real beach, where the fishermen pull up their boats. You can take a bus or walk a kilometer or so to Capo Sorrento, then follow the signs to the **Villa di Pollio Felice,** the scattered seaside remains of an ancient Roman villa, where you can swim off the rocks or simply admire the setting. Before you leave Sorrento, consider a side trip west along the road that skirts the tip of the peninsula; if you enjoy dramatic seascapes, this will be worth the extra time.

Dining and Lodging

$$ ✕ **Antica Trattoria.** An old-world dining room inside and garden tables in fair weather make this a pleasant place to enjoy the local cooking. The atmosphere is homey and hospitable. The menu is voluminous and your choice will be difficult, but the specialties include spaghetti alle vongole and *gamberetti Antica Trattoria* (shrimp in tomato sauce). You can also opt for one of the four fixed-price menus. ✉ *Via Giuliani 33,* ☎ *081/8071082. AE, DC, MC, V. Closed Mon. and 4 wks in Jan.–Feb.*

$$ ✕ **Parrucchiano.** Central and popular, this is one of Sorrento's oldest and best restaurants. You walk up a few steps to glassed-in veranda dining rooms filled, like greenhouses, with vines and plants. The menu offers classic local specialties, among them *panzerotti* (pastry shells filled with tomato and mozzarella) and *scaloppe alla sorrentina* (scallops with tomato and mozzarella). ✉ *Corso Italia 71,* ☎ *081/8781321. MC, V. Closed Wed. Nov.–Mar.*

$$$$ **Bellevue Syrene.** This exclusive hotel is set in a cliff-top garden close to the center of Sorrento. It retains its solid, old-fashioned comforts and sumptuous charm, with Victorian nooks and alcoves, antique paintings, and exuberant frescoes. You can find interior-facing rooms in the $$$ category, if you are willing to forgo the splendid views over the sea. The Villa Pompeiana bar has a garden terrace and an ancient-Roman setting, and is the venue for music in summer. ✉ *Piazza della Vittoria 5, 80067,* ☎ *081/8781024,* FAX *081/8783963. 73 rooms. Restaurant, bar, beach. AE, DC, MC, V.*

$$$$ ★ **Cocumella.** A grand hotel in every sense, the Cocumella seems little changed from the days when Goethe and Napoléon's enemy, the Duke of Wellington, used to stay here. Set in the blissfully tranquil hamlet of Sant'Agnello in a cliff-top garden overlooking the Bay of Naples, this extraordinary hotel occupies a historic 17th-century monastery, complete with frescoed ceilings, antique reliquaries, and a marble cloister. The Del Papa family has seen fit to gild this lily with the last word in luxuries: a spectacular pool area, a beauty farm and workout room, a summer season of concerts held in the hotel's Baroque church, and palatial suites that offer fireplaces and Empire-style ambience. Lucky guests can use the hotel's 90-ft-long 19th-century yacht. ✉ *Via Cocumella 7, Sant'Agnello (Sorrento), 00187,* ☎ *081/8782933,* FAX *081/878–3712. 45 rooms, 15 suites. Restaurant, bar, spa, exercise room, pool. AE, DC, MC, V.*

$$$$ ★ **Excelsior Vittoria.** Magnificently set overlooking the Bay of Naples, this is a Belle Epoque dream come true. Gilded salons worthy of a Proust heroine, stunning gardens, and an impossibly romantic terrace where orchestras lull you with equal doses of Cole Porter and Puccini: in all, a truly intoxicating experience. Caruso stayed here, and now so does Pavarotti and Princess Margaret. Save your pennies, splurge—but come! ✉ *Piazza Tasso 34, 80067,* ☎ *081/8071044,* FAX *081/8771206. 100 rooms, 10 suites. Restaurant, bar, pool. AE, DC, MC, V.*

$$$$ **Imperial Hotel Tramontano.** The birthplace of the poet Torquato Tasso—the first of an impressive list of literary credentials—this palatial villa lies within a semitropical garden in the center of Sorrento. The sumptuous furnishings and Belle Epoque tone are set off by the spectacular views out to sea. ✉ *Via Veneto 1, 80067,* ☎ *081/8782588,* FAX *081/8072344. 120 rooms. Restaurant, bar, beach, meeting rooms. AE, MC, V. Closed Jan.–Feb.*

$–$$ **City.** The convenient location and excellent value for the money are the best reasons to stay in this modest establishment, close to the bus and train stations. Bedrooms are small and functional. The atmosphere is relaxed, and the management is always ready with information and advice. ✉ *Corso Italia 221, 80067,* ☎ FAX *081/8772210. 13 rooms. AE, MC, V.*

Nightlife and the Arts

BAR

At **Circolo dei Forestieri** (✉ Via de Maio 35, ☎ 081/8773263), closed January–February, you'll get a memorable view of the Bay of Naples from the terrace. Drinks are moderately priced, and there is live music nightly in summer and every weekend the rest of the year.

FILM

Every October–December, the **International Cinema Convention** in Sorrento draws an elite collection of producers, directors, and stars in a less frantic atmosphere than that of the festival in Cannes. While much of the activity revolves around deal making, a number of previews are screened. For details, contact the Sorrento tourist office (☞ Campania A to Z, *below*).

Shopping

LOCAL CRAFTS

Around **Piazza Tasso** are a number of shops selling embroidered goods and intarsia (wood inlay) work, a centuries-old tradition here. Along narrow **Via San Cesareo,** where the air is pungent with the perfumes of fruit and vegetable stands, there are more shops selling local and Italian crafts—everything from jewelry boxes to trays and coffee tables with intarsia decorations. **Ferdinando Corcione,** in his shop on Via San Francesco, gives demonstrations of his intarsia work, producing decorative plaques with classic or contemporary motifs.

Positano

★ 47 *14 km (9 mi) east of Sorrento, 57 km (34 mi) south of Naples.*

When John Steinbeck lived here in 1953, he wrote that it was difficult to consider tourism an industry because "there are not enough [tourists]." Alas, Positano, a village of white Moorish-type houses clinging dramatically to slopes around a small sheltered bay, has since been discovered. The artists came first, and, as happens wherever artists go, the wealthy followed and the artists fled. What Steinbeck wrote, however, still applies: "Positano bites deep. It is a dream place that isn't quite real when you are there and becomes beckoningly real after you have gone. Its houses climb a hill so steep it would be a cliff except that stairs are cut in it. I believe that whereas most house foundations are vertical, in Positano they are horizontal. The small curving bay of unbelievably blue and green water laps gently on a beach of small pebbles. There is only one narrow street and it does not come down to the water. Everything else is stairs, some of them as steep as ladders. You do not walk to visit a friend, you either climb or slide."

In the 10th century Positano was part of Amalfi's Maritime Republic, which rivaled Venice as an important mercantile power. Its heyday was in the 16th and 17th centuries, when its ships traded in the Near and Middle East, carrying spices, silks, and precious woods. The coming of the steamship in the mid-19th century led to the town's decline, and some three-fourths of the town's 8,000 citizens emigrated to America, mostly to New York. One major task of Positano's mayor has been to find space in the overcrowded cemetery for New York Positanesi who want to spend eternity here.

What had been reduced to a forgotten fishing village is now the number-one attraction on the coast, with hotels for every budget, charming restaurants, and dozens of boutiques. From here, you can take hydrofoils to Capri during the summer, escorted bus rides to Ravello, and tours of the Grotta dello Smeraldo. If you're staying in Positano, check whether your hotel has a parking area. If not, you will have to pay for space in a parking lot, which is almost impossible to find during the high season, from Easter to September. The best bet for day-trippers is to get to Positano early enough so that space is still available. No matter how much time you spend in Positano, make sure you have some comfortable walking shoes—no heels, please!—and that your back and legs are strong enough to negotiate steps.

Dining and Lodging

$$ ✕ **Buca di Bacco.** After an aperitif at the town's most famous and fashionable café downstairs, you dine on a veranda overlooking the beach. The specialties include spaghetti alle vongole and *grigliata mista* (mixed grilled seafood). ✉ *Via Rampa Teglia 8,* ☎ *089/875699. AE, DC, MC, V. Closed Nov.–Mar.*

$$ ✕ **'O Capurale.** Among the popular restaurants on the beach promenade, this one just around the corner has the best food and lowest prices. Tables are set under vines on a breezy sidewalk in the summer, indoors and upstairs in winter. Spaghetti *con melanzane* (with eggplant) and crepes *al formaggio* (with cheese) are among the specialties. ✉ *Via Regina Giovanna 12,* ☎ *089/875374. AE, DC, MC, V. Closed Nov.–mid-Feb.*

$$$$ ★ **Le Sirenuse.** A handsome 18th-century palazzo in the center of town is the setting for this luxury hotel in which bright tiled floors, precious antiques, and tasteful furnishings are featured in ample and luminous salons. The bedrooms have the same sense of spaciousness and comfort; most have splendid views from balconies and terraces. The top-floor suites have huge bathrooms and whirlpool baths. One

side of a large terrace has an inviting swimming pool; on the other is an excellent restaurant. ✉ *Via Cristoforo Colombo 30, 84017,* ☎ *089/875066,* FAX *089/811798. 62 rooms. Restaurant, bar, pool, sauna. AE, DC, MC, V.*

$$$$ **Palazzo Murat.** The location is perfect—in the heart of town, near the beachside promenade, but set in a quiet, walled garden. The old wing is a historic palazzo with tall windows and wrought-iron balconies; the new wing is a whitewashed Mediterranean building with arches and terraces. You can relax in antiques-accented lounges or in the charming vine-draped patio, and enjoy gorgeous views from the comfortable bedrooms. ✉ *Via dei Mulini 23, 84017,* ☎ *089/875177,* FAX *089/811419. 32 rooms. Restaurant, bar. AE, DC, MC, V. Closed Jan.–Mar.*

$$$$ ★ **San Pietro.** Extraordinary is the word for this luxurious oasis for the affluent international set. Outside the town and set high above the sea with garden terraces, the San Pietro has sumptuous Neapolitan Baroque decor and masses of flowers in the lounges, elegantly understated rooms (most with terraces), and marvelous views. There's a pool on an upper level, and an elevator whisks you to the private beach and beach bar. The proprietors organize boating excursions and parties and provide car and minibus service into town. ✉ *Via Laurito 82, 84017,* ☎ *089/875455,* FAX *089/811449. 60 rooms. Restaurant, 2 bars, pool, tennis court, beach, dock. AE, DC, MC, V. Closed Nov.–Mar.*

$$–$$$ ★ **La Fenice.** Paradise found. This tiny and unpretentious hotel on the peaceful outskirts of town beckons with bougainvillea-laden vistas, castaway cottages, and a turquoise pool, all perched over a private beach. Guest rooms—accented with coved ceilings, whitewashed walls, and native folk art—are simple havens of tranquillity (book the best, those closest to the sea, only if you can handle *very* steep walkways). ✉ *Via G. Marconi 4, 84017,* ☎ *089/875513,* FAX *089/811309. 10 rooms. Pool. No credit cards.*

Nightlife

L'Africana (✉ Vettica Maggiore, Praiano, 10 km/6 mi east of Positano on the coast road, ☎ 089/874042) is the premier nightclub on the Amalfi Coast and is built into a fantastic grotto above the sea.

Grotta dello Smeraldo

13 km (8 mi) east of Positano, 27 km (17 mi) east of Sorrento.

A peculiar green light that casts an eerie emerald glow over impressive formations of stalagmites and stalactites, many of them underwater, inspired the name for Grotta dello Smeraldo (Emerald Grotto). You can park at the signposts for the grotta along the coast road and take an elevator down, or you can drive on to Amalfi and return to the grotto by the more romantic route—via boat. Boat tours leave from the Amalfi seafront regularly, according to demand; the charge is 10,000 lire per person. Call ahead, as hours are subject to change. *5,000 lire.* ⌚ *Apr.–Sept., daily 9–5; Oct.–Mar., daily 10–4.*

Amalfi

48 *4 km (2½ mi) east of Grotta dello Smeraldo, 35 km (22 mi) east of Sorrento.*

"The sun—the moon—the stars and—Amalfi," Amalfitans used to say. During the Middle Ages, Amalfi was an independent maritime state—a little Republic of Venice—with a population of 50,000. The ship compass, trivia fans will be pleased to know, was invented here in 1302. The town is romantically situated at the mouth of a deep gorge and has some good-quality hotels and restaurants. It's also a convenient base for excursions to Capri and the Emerald Grotto. The parking problem here is as bad as that in Positano. The small lot in the center of town fills quickly; if you can afford the steep prices, make a luncheon reservation at one of the hotel restaurants and have your car parked for you.

Amalfi's main historical sight is its **Duomo** (Cathedral of St. Andrew), which shows an interesting mix of Moorish and early-Gothic influences. The interior is a 10th-century Romanesque skeleton in an 18th-century Baroque dress. The transept and the choir are 13th century. The handsome 12th-century campanile has identical Gothic domes at each corner. Don't miss the beautiful late 13th-century Moorish **cloister,** with its slender double columns. At least one critic has called the cathedral's facade the ugliest piece of serious architecture in Italy—decide for yourself. The same critic snickers at the tourists who fail to note the cathedral's greatest treasure, the 11th-century bronze doors from Constantinople. Turn right out of the doors for the cloister, with white-washed arches and palms, and a small **museum** in the adjoining crypt. *Piazza del Duomo, ☎ 089/871059. Cloister and museum: 3,000 lire. ⏲ Duomo: Apr.–Oct., daily 7:30 AM–8 PM; Nov.–Mar., daily 7:30–noon and 3–7. Cloisters and museum: Apr.–Oct., daily 9–9; Nov.–Mar., daily 10–12:30 and 2:30–5:30.*

Dining and Lodging

$$ ★ ✕ **La Caravella.** You'll find this welcoming establishment tucked away under some arches lining the coast road, next to the medieval Arsenal, where Amalfi's mighty fleet once was provisioned. La Caravella has a nondescript entrance but a pleasant interior decorated with paintings of Old Amalfi. It's small and intimate; specialties include linguine *alla colatura di alici* (with anchovies, based on a medieval recipe) and *calamari ripieni* (stuffed squid). ✉ *Via M. Camera 12, ☎ 089/871029. AE, MC, V. Closed Nov. and Tues. (except Aug.).*

$$$$ ★ **Santa Caterina.** A large mansion perched above terraced and flowered hillsides on the coast road just outside Amalfi proper, the Santa Caterina is one of the best hotels on the entire coast, attracting the great and the good from far and wide (Claudia Schiffer, Karl Lagerfeld, Hillary Clinton to name drop a few). The rooms are tastefully decorated; most have small terraces or balconies with great views. There are lovely lounges and terraces for relaxing, and an elevator delivers you to the seaside saltwater pool, bar, and swimming area. On grounds lush with lemon and orange groves, there are two romantic villa annexes. ✉ *Strada Amalfitana 9, 84011, ☎ 089/871012, FAX 089/871351. 54 rooms. Restaurant, bar, pool, saltwater pool. AE, DC, MC, V.*

$$$ **Miramalfi.** A modern building perched above the sea, the Miramalfi has wonderful views, simple but attractive decor, terraces, swimming pool, and a sunning-swimming area on the sea, as well as a quiet setting just below the coast road, only 1 km (½ mi) from the center of town. Almost all rooms have balconies with sea views. ✉ *Via Quasimodo 3, 84011, ☎ 089/871588, FAX 089/871287. 48 rooms. Restaurant, pool, beach. AE, DC, MC, V. Closed mid-Nov.–mid-Mar..*

$$–$$$ **Hotel dei Cavalieri.** This terraced, white, Mediterranean-style hotel on the main road outside Amalfi has three villa annexes on grounds just across the road that extend all the way to a beach below. Bright rooms are air-conditioned and functionally furnished, with splashy majolica tile floors. An ample buffet breakfast is served, and, though half board is mandatory during high season, you can dine either at the hotel or at several restaurants in Amalfi by special arrangement. ✉ *Via M. Comite 32, 84011, ☎ 089/831333, FAX 089/831354. 54 rooms. Restaurant, bar, air-conditioning. AE, DC, MC, V. MAP.*

Ravello

★ 49 *5 km (3 mi) northeast of Amalfi, 40 km (25 mi) east of Sorrento.*

Perched on a ridge high above Amalfi and the neighboring town of Atrani, the enchanting village of Ravello has stupendous views, quiet lanes, two important Romanesque churches, and several irresistibly romantic gardens. Set "closer to the sky than the sea," according to Andre Gide, the town has been the ultimate aerie ever since it was founded as a smart suburb for the richest families of Amalfi's 12th-century maritime republic. Rediscovered by English aristocrats a century ago, the town now hosts one of Italy's most famous music festivals.

★ Directly off the main piazza is the **Villa Rufolo,** built in the 13th century by Landolfo Rufolo, whose immense fortune stemmed from trade with Moors and Saracens. Within is a scene from the earliest days of the Crusades. Norman and Arab architecture mingle in profusion in a welter of color-filled gardens so lush that composer Richard Wagner used them as inspiration for the Home of the Flower Maidens in his opera *Parsifal.* Beyond the Arab-Sicilian cloister and the Norman tower are two flower-bedded terraces that offer a splendiferous vista of the Bay of Salerno; the lower "Wagner Terrace" is the site for the year-long **Festival Musicale di Ravello** (for information, contact the Ravello Concert Society, ☎ 089/858149, FAX 089/857977. *Piazza Vescovado, 84010, ☎ 089/857866.* 🎫 *4,000 lire.* ⏲ *Daily 9–sunset.*

$$ ★ From Ravello's main piazza head west along Via San Francesco and Via Santa Chiara to the **Villa Cimbrone,** a medieval-style fantasy that sits 460 m (1,500 ft) over the sea. Created in 1905 by England's Lord Grimthrope and made world-famous when Greta Garbo stayed here in 1937, the Gothic *castello-palazzo* is set in fragrant rose gardens that lead to the **Belvedere of Infinity,** a grand stone parapet that overlooks the impossibly blue Gulf of Salerno and frames a panorama that noted writer and Ravello resident Gore Vidal has called "the most beautiful in the world." The villa itself is now a hotel (☞ *below*). *Via Santa Chiara 26, 84010, ☎ 089/857459.* 🎫 *6,000 lire.* ⏲ *Daily 9–sunset.*

Dining and Lodging

$$ ★ ✕ **Cumpa Cosimo.** This family-run restaurant a few steps from the cathedral square offers a cordial welcome in two simple but attractive dining rooms. There's no view, but the food is excellent. Among the specialties are cheese crepes and roast lamb or kid. ✉ *Via Roma 44, ☎ 089/857156. AE, DC, MC, V.*

$$$$ 🏨 **Hotel Palumbo.** Occupying a 12th-century patrician palace furnished with antiques and endowed with modern comforts, this hotel has an elegant, warm atmosphere that gives you the feeling of being a guest in a lovely private home, under the personal care of courtly host Signor Vuilleumier. With lovely garden terraces, breathtaking views, and a sumptuous upstairs dining room, the hotel is a memorable one. Guest rooms in the modern annex are considerably cheaper. Note that half-board lodging is compulsory. ✉ *Palazzo Confalone, Via San Giovanni del Toro 28, 84010, ☎ 089/857244, FAX 089/858133. 8 rooms. Restaurant, bar. AE, DC, MC, V. MAP.*

$$$$ 🏨 **Palazzo Sasso.** In this 12th-century home of the aristocratic Sasso family, Wagner penned part of his opera *Parsifal* in the 1880s, and in the fashionable 1950s, the Sasso hosted Ingrid Bergman and Roberto Rossellini. On reopening in July 1997, after a 20-year hiatus, the hotel is still luring the glitterati—its first guests were Placido Domingo and his entourage. Ordinary mortals, too, can come to sightsee for a peek at the marble atrium and lofty coastal views. All the individually designed guest rooms are immaculately furnished, with the latest computer-

operated lighting systems, but extra-special ones include 201, for its wide terrace, and 213 for its architectural detail. The rooftop terrace has two hot tubs and a bar—one of Ravello's prime watering holes. The Rossellini restaurant is also not to be sniffed at. ✉ *Via San Giovanni del Toro 28, 84010,* ☎ *089/818181,* FAX *089/858900. 38 rooms, 5 suites. Restaurant, bar, pool, outdoor hot tub, library. AE, DC, MC, V.*

$$$$ ★ **Villa Cimbrone.** This magical place takes the breath away: suspended over the azure sea and set amid rose-laden gardens, it was once the home of Lord Grimthorpe and the holiday hideaway of Greta Garbo. Now exquisitely transformed into a hotel, the Gothic-style *castello* (castle) has guest rooms ranging from palatial to cozy (opt for the Peony Room, which has its own terrace). The villa is a strenuous hike from town center. ✉ *Via Santa Chiara 26, 84010,* ☎ *089/857459,* FAX *089/857777. 19 rooms. Breakfast room, minibars, library. AE, MC, V. Closed Nov.–Mar.*

$$$–$$$$ ★ **Caruso Belvedere.** Charmingly old-fashioned, spacious, and comfortable, this rambling villa hotel has plenty of character and a full share of Ravello's spectacular views from its terraces and balconied rooms. Relax in the garden belvedere with its memorable vistas. The restaurant is known for fine food and locally made house wine. ✉ *Via Toro 52, 84010,* ☎ *089/857111,* FAX *089/857372. 24 rooms. Restaurant, room service, baby-sitting, laundry service, free parking. AE, DC, MC, V.*

$$ **Villa Amore.** A 10-minute walk from the main Piazza Duomo, this hotel is family run, with a garden and an exhilarating view from most of its bedrooms. If you're looking for tranquillity, you've found it, especially at dusk, when the valley is tinged with a glorious purple light. Rooms are small, with modest if modern furnishings, and one of the treats at breakfast is delicious homemade jam. Full board is available here and may be required in the summer. Reserve ahead, and specify time of arrival if you need help with luggage from the parking lot or bus stop (you pay 7,000 lire per bag). ✉ *Via Santa Chiara, 84010,* ☎ FAX *089/857135. 12 rooms. Restaurant, bar. DC, MC, V. FAP.*

Vietri sul Mare

50 *20 km (12 mi) east of Amalfi, 60 km (37 mi) east of Sorrento.*

This Amalfi Coast town is a major ceramics center, and its distinctive pottery, with sunny motifs and bright colors, is sold in towns along the coast. The shops and factories are concentrated in the lively old town, grouped around a majolica-domed church, but the seafront below is dull.

Shopping

CERAMICS

Many small shops in Vietri sul Mare offer goods from local pottery workshops. You can pick over all kinds of dusty wares at the **Solimene works** (✉ Vietri sul Mare).

Salerno

51 *6 km (4 mi) east of Vietri sul Mare, 56 km (35 mi) southeast of Naples.*

Spread out along its bay, Salerno is a sad testimony to years of neglect and overdevelopment. An imposing **Romanesque cathedral,** built in 1085 and remodeled in the 18th century, has Byzantine doors (1099) from Constantinople and an outstanding 12th-century pulpit. ✉ *Via Duomo.* ⏲ *Daily 9–7:30.*

In the **Museo Diocesano** behind the cathedral is a collection of medieval carved tablets. ✉ *Piazza Plebiscito,* ☎ *089/239126.* 🎫 *Free.* ⏲ *Daily 9–6.*

Occupying two floors of the **Abbazia di San Benedetto** (San Benedetto Monastery), the **Museo Provinciale** holds a handsome bronze head of Apollo fished out of the bay in the 1930s. ✉ *Via San Benedetto,* ☎ *089/231135.* ⏲ *Mon.–Sat. 9–7:30, Sun. 9–1.*

Paestum

★ 52 *42 km (26 mi) southeast of Salerno, 99 km (62 mi) southeast of Naples.*

One of Italy's most majestic sights lies on the edge of a flat coastal plain: the remarkably well-preserved **Greek temples** of Paestum. S18 from the north passes the train station (Stazione di Paestum), which is about 800 yards from the ruins, through the perfectly preserved archway **Porta Sirena.** The ruins stand on the site of the ancient city of Poseidonia, founded by Greek colonists in the 7th century BC. When the Romans took over the colony in 273 BC and called it Paestum, they enlarged the settlement, adding an amphitheater and a forum. Much of the archaeological material found on the site is displayed in the **Museo Nazionale,** and several rooms are devoted to the unique tomb paintings discovered in the area, rare examples of Greek and pre-Roman pictorial art. About 200 yards from the museum (in front of the main entrance), framed by banks of roses and oleanders, is the **Tempio di Poseidone** (Temple of Poseidon), a magnificent Doric edifice, with 36 fluted columns and an extraordinarily well-preserved entablature (area above the capitals). Not even Greece itself possesses such a fine monument of Hellenic architecture. On the left of the temple is the so-called **Basilica,** the earliest of Paestum's standing edifices; it dates from very early in the 6th century BC. The name is an 18th-century misnomer, for the structure was in fact a temple sacred to Hera, the wife of Zeus. Behind it an ancient road leads to the **Foro Romano** (Roman Forum) and the single column of the **Tempio della Pace** (Temple of Peace). Beyond is the **Tempio di Cerere** (Temple of Ceres). Try to see the temples in the late afternoon, when the light enhances the deep gold of the stone and the air is pierced with the cries of the crows that nest high on the temples. ☎ *0828/811023.* *Excavations: 8,000 lire; Museum: 8,000 lire.* ⏲ *Excavations: July–Sept., daily 9 AM–10 PM; Oct.–June, daily 9–1 hr before sunset. Museum: July–Sept., daily 9 AM–10 PM; Oct.–June, daily 9–6:30; closed 1st and 3rd Mon. of each month.*

Lodging

$$ **Helios.** Directly across the road from the Porta della Giustizia and only a few steps from the temples, the Helios has cottage-type rooms, each with a minibar, in a garden setting. Suites are also available. A pleasant restaurant serves local specialties and seafood. The home-produced ricotta and mozzarella are especially recommended. ✉ *Via Principe di Piemonte 1, Zona Archeologica, 84063,* ☎ *0828/811451,* FAX *0828/721047. 30 rooms. 2 restaurants, minibars. AE, DC, MC, V.*

CAMPANIA A TO Z

Arriving and Departing

By Bus

Marozzi (☎ 06/4076140 or 06/44249519), a Rome-based line, runs direct, air-conditioned buses from Rome to Pompeii, Salerno, Sorrento, and Amalfi. Buses leave Rome's Stazione Tiburtina daily: Monday–Thursday 3 PM; Friday, Saturday, and Sunday 7 AM.

By Car

Italy's main north–south route, A2 (also known as the Autostrada del Sole), connects the capital with Naples and Campania. In good traffic the ride takes less than three hours.

By Plane

Aeroporto Capodichino (☎ 081/7896259), 8 km (5 mi) north of Naples, serves the Campania region. It handles domestic and international flights, including several flights daily between Naples and Rome (flight time 45 minutes). From May to September there is direct **helicopter service** (☎ 081/5841481) between Aeroporto Capodichino and Capri or Ischia.

International travelers flying Alitalia to Rome's **Aeroporto Leonardo da Vinci** can go directly from the airport to Naples's Mergellina train station via Alitalia's twice-daily airport train. Luggage is checked through to Naples, and meals are available on the train. Airport-train arrangements must be made when you buy your plane ticket. The service also operates in the other direction, returning from Naples to the Aeroporto Leonardo da Vinci.

BETWEEN THE AIRPORT AND DOWNTOWN

Taxis are available at the airport for the ride downtown (about 50,000 lire), or else there is a private bus service leaving once or twice hourly with stops at Piazza Garibaldi and Piazza Muncipio (3,000 lire). The more frequent but slightly slower city Bus 14 also plies the route to Piazza Garibaldi (tickets from the newsagent inside the airport, 1,500 lire).

By Train

There are trains every hour between Rome and Naples. Intercity trains make the trip in less than two hours. Trains take either the inland route (through Cassino) or go along the coast (via Formia). Intercity and express trains to Naples stop at **Stazione Centrale** (✉ Piazza Garibaldi, ☎ 147/888088 toll-free).

Getting Around

By Boat

Hydrofoil and passenger and car ferries connect the islands of Capri and Ischia with Naples and Pozzuoli year-round. In summer, Capri and Ischia are serviced by boats from the Amalfi Coast. Boats and hydrofoils for these islands and for Sorrento leave from Naples's **Molo Beverello** (✉ Southeast of Piazza Municipio). They also leave from **Mergellina** (✉ About 1½ km/1 mi to the west of Piazza Municipio).

Information on departures is available at the tourist office (☞ Visitor Information *in* Campania A to Z, *below*) or at the port, or contact the companies directly. Always double-check schedules in stormy weather. **Caremar** (☎ 081/5513882). **Linee Marittime Veloci** (LMV, ☎ 081/5527209). **SNAV** (☎ 081/7612348).

By Bus

There is an extensive network of local buses in Naples and throughout Campania. **ACTP** (☎ 081/7005091) buses connect Naples with Caserta in one hour, leaving every 20 minutes from Piazza Garibaldi in Naples (every 40 minutes on Sunday). There are about six buses a day Monday to Saturday from Piazza Garibaldi to Benevento. The trip takes 90 minutes. **SITA** (✉ Via Pisanelli, near Piazza Municipio, ☎ 081/5522176) buses for Salerno leave every 30 minutes Monday to Saturday and every two hours on Sunday from the SITA terminal on Via Pisanelli. SITA buses also serve the Amalfi Coast, connecting Sorrento with Salerno. **Curreri** (☎ 081/8015420) operates a service between Sorrento and Aeroporto Capodichino.

By Car

Autostrada A3, a southern continuation of A2 from Rome, runs through Campania and into Calabria. It also connects with autostrada A16 to Bari, which passes Avellino and is linked with Benevento by expressway. Take S18 south from Naples for Herculaneum, Pompeii, and the Sorrento peninsula; for the Sorrento peninsula and the Amalfi Coast, exit at Castellammare di Stabia. To get to Paestum, take A3 to the Battipaglia exit and take the road to Capaccio Scalo–Paestum. All roads on the Sorrento peninsula and Amalfi Coast are narrow, serpentine, and tortuous, although they have outstanding views. In summer hydrofoil and ferry lines have a residents-only policy for cars going on Ischia and Capri. Cars are not allowed on Ischia and Capri during high season, from about April through October.

By Train

Naples's rather old **Metropolitana** (subway system) provides frequent service and can be the fastest way to get across the traffic-clogged city. Lines are currently being extended, including a stop linking Vomero, but the project could take years.

Frequent local trains connect Naples with Caserta and Salerno. Travel time between Naples and Sorrento on the Circumvesuviana line (☞ *below*) is one hour. Benevento is on the main line between Naples and Foggia. A network of suburban trains connects Naples with several points of interest. The line used most by visitors is the **Circumvesuviana** (☏ 081/7722444), which runs from Corso Garibaldi Station and stops at Stazione Centrale before continuing to Ercolano (Herculaneum), Pompeii, and Sorrento. The **Circumflegrea** (☏ 081/5513328) runs from Piazza Montesanto Station in Naples to the archaeological zone of Cumae, with three departures in the morning. The **Ferrovia Cumana** (☏ 081/5513328) runs from Piazza Montesanto Station to Pozzuoli and Baia.

Contacts and Resources

Car Rentals

CASERTA

Avis (✉ Stazione FS, ☏ 0823/443756). **Hertz** (✉ Via G. Bosco, ☏ 0823/356383).

NAPLES

Avis (✉ Stazione Centrale, ☏ 081/5537171; ✉ Via Piedigrotta 44, ☏ 081/7611365). **Hertz** (✉ Aeroporto Capodichino, ☏ 081/7802971; ✉ Piazza Garibaldi 93, ☏ 081/206228).

Garages: Near Villa Pignatelli, **Garage dei Fiori** (✉ Via Colonna 21, ☏ 081/414190). Near Stazione Centrale, **Grilli** (✉ Via Ferraris 40, ☏ 081/264344). Near the port, **Turistico** (✉ Via de Gasperi 14, ☏ 081/5525442).

SORRENTO

Avis (✉ Viale Nizza 53, ☏ 081/8782459). **Hertz** (✉ Garage Di Leva, Via degli Aranci 9, ☏ 081/8071646).

Emergencies

Police (☏ 112). In Naples, **Ambulance** (☏ 081/7520696). **Doctors and Dentists** (☏ 081/7513177).

Guided Tours

Carrani Tours (✉ Via Vittorio Emanuele Orlando 95, Rome, ☏ 06/4880510 or 06/4742501). **Milleviaggi** (✉ Riviera di Chiaia 252, Naples, ☏ 081/7642064). **Tourcar** (✉ Piazza Matteotti 1, Naples, ☏ 081/5520429). **STS** (✉ Piazza Medaglie d'Oro 41, Naples, ☏ 081/5789292).

Late-Night Pharmacies

Farmacia Helvethia (✉ Piazza Garibaldi 11, opposite Stazione Centrale, ☏ 081/5548894).

Visitor Information

EPT (Naples, ✉ Piazza dei Martiri 58, 80100 Naples, ☎ 081/405311; ✉ Stazione Centrale, 80142 Naples, ☎ 081/268779; ✉ Stazione Mergellina, 80122 Naples, ☎ 081/7612102; ✉ Aeroporto Capodichino, 80133 Naples, ☎ 081/7805761).

Tourist offices (✉ Corso delle Repubbliche 27, 84011 Amalfi, ☎ 089/871107; ✉ Piazza Roma, 82100 Benevento, ☎ 0824/319938; ✉ Marina Grande pier, 80073 Capri, ☎ 081/8370634; ✉ Capri Town, Piazza Umberto I, 80073 Capri, ☎ 081/8370686; ✉ Piazza Dante, 81100 Caserta, ☎ 0823/321137; ✉ Piazza del Gesù, 80135 Naples, ☎ 081/5523328; ✉ Via Iasolino, Porto Salvo, 80077 Porto d'Ischia, ☎ 081/991146; ✉ Piazza Duomo, 84010 Ravello, ☎ 089/857096; ✉ Via Roma 258, 84100 Salerno, ☎ 089/224744; ✉ Circolo Forestieri, Via de Maio 35, 80067 Sorrento, ☎ 081/8074033).

13 APULIA

BARI, BRINDISI, AND THE GARGANO PROMONTORY

The gateway to Italy's south, Apulia is steeped in relics from antiquity that are only now coming to the surface. The region invites intrepid exploration of its whitewashed ports, imposing castles, and *trulli,* strange igloo-shape dwellings. The cities of Brindisi, Bari, and Lecce possess many fascinations, and the coastline is rich with seductions—unspoiled coves, bougainvillea-draped vistas, and seas shimmering under a blazing sun.

Updated by Robert Andrews

IT'S A PITY THAT MOST TOURISTS see Apulia (called Puglia by the Italians—English speakers are really using the Latin term) as merely a blur outside their car or train windows as they hurtle toward Bari or Brindisi for ferry connections to Greece.

This ancient land, the heel and spur of Italy's boot, possesses some of the country's most unspoiled scenery, interesting artistic and historicl sites, and finest beaches. What's more, beyond the increasingly popular seaside resorts and the few major sights lies sunbaked countryside where expanses of silvery olive trees and giant prickly-pear cacti fight their way through the rocky soil, as if in defiance of the relentless summer heat. Local buildings, too, do their best to dispel the effects of the sun: whitewashed ports stand coolly over the turquoise Mediterranean; the landscape is studded with the odd stone *trulli,* curious limestone structures dating from the Middle Ages.

Apulia had long before then been inhabited, conquered, and visited. The Greeks and later the Romans were quick to recognize the importance of this strategic peninsula, and among the nations later to raid or colonize Apulia were the Normans, Moors, and Spaniards, each leaving their mark. Romanesque churches and the powerful castles built by 13th-century Holy Roman Emperor Frederick II of Swabia (part of present-day Bavaria), king of Sicily and Jerusalem, are among the most impressive of buildings in the region. Frederick II, dubbed Wonder of the World for his wide-ranging interests in literature, science, mathematics, and nature, was an outstanding personality in the Middle Ages.

The last 50 years have seen a huge economic revival after the centuries of neglect that followed Apulia's golden age under the Normans and Swabians. Having benefited from EU and state subsidies for irrigation and incentive programs, Apulia is now Italy's biggest producer of wine, with most of the rest of the land devoted to olives, citrus fruits, and vegetables. The main ports of Bari, Brindisi, and Taranto are lively and economically thriving centers, though there remain serious problems of unemployment and poverty. However, the much publicized arrival of thousands of asylum seekers from Albania has not significantly destabilized these cities, as had been feared, and the economic and political refugees have been dispersed throughout Italy. Enjoying good communications networks for road and rail travelers, Apulia is blessed with plenty of quality restaurants testifying to the region's comparative prosperity, though don't expect to find the same abundance of accommodation facilities outside the business circuit.

Pleasures and Pastimes

Beaches

Italians and visitors return each summer for the draw of the sea, one of the major attractions of Apulia. Though no longer "undiscovered," the beaches along the Gargano Promontory offer safe swimming and sandy beaches. The whole coastline between Bari and Brindisi is well served with beach facilities. In even the smallest villages you'll find beaches where there are changing rooms and—essential in the blazing Apulian sun—beach umbrellas. If you don't mind venturing farther afield, Gallipoli, on the south coast of the heel, has exceptional strands.

Dining

Anyone who likes to eat will love Apulia, whose cuisine has evolved from more than 2,000 years of foreign influences. Southern cuisine is hearty and healthy, based around homemade pastas and cheeses, fresh vegetables, seafood, and local olive oil. Open-air markets and delicatessens overflow with local fruits, vegetables, pastries, sausages, smoked meats, and cheeses. Here you will find dishes unavailable elsewhere in Italy, such as *'ncapriata,* also called *favi e fogghi* (a first course fava-bean puree with bitter chicory or other cooked vegetables). Focaccia *barese* (stuffed with fried onions, black olives, anchovies, and ricotta) makes a great snack or lunch.

Apulia's pasta specialties include *orecchiette* (ear-shape pasta), *troccoli* (homemade noodles cut with a special ridged rolling pin), and *strascenate* (rectangles of pasta with one rough side and one smooth side). Among the many typical sauces is *salsa alla Sangiovanniello* (sauce of olive oil, capers, anchovies, parsley, and hot peppers) from Brindisi. Don't miss the dairy products, such as ricotta and buttery *burrata* cheese. Sample Apulia's wealth of excellent local wines, ranging from the strong white wine of Martina Franca to the sweet white Moscaro di Trani and the rich dry red Castel del Monte to the sweet red Aleatico di Puglia.

Festivals

In keeping with the provincial nature of Apulia, the arts take on a folk flavor, with processions on religious occasions more prevalent than performing arts in theaters or opera houses. Still, there are some good festivals and pageants to help broaden your experience of life in Italy's deep south. The best newspaper for listings is the daily *Gazzetta del Mezzogiorno,* which covers the entire region. Local crafts range from lace, wood carvings, and baskets to ceramic pots and painted clay whistles.

Lodging

Outside the big cities, hotel accommodations are limited and modest—both in amenities and price—though this may be more than compensated for by friendly service. Along the kilometers of sandy beaches on the Gargano spur and elsewhere on the coast, big, white Mediterranean-style beach hotels have sprung up in profusion. Most are similar in design, price, and quality. In summer, many cater only to guests paying full board (lodging plus three meals per day) or half board (lodging plus breakfast and one other meal) for longer stays. If you are traveling to the Gargano Promontory in summer, you should reserve through a travel agent to avoid complications with limited lodging and public transportation. During Easter, rooms in the Alberobello area may be at a premium.

In some cases, such as visiting Bari during the annual Trade Fair in September, you must make reservations. Throughout the region, hotels are often booked up with commercial travelers, so reserve well in advance. Many establishments, particularly the beach resorts, close during the winter months. And remember that in a region like this—blazing hot in summer and bitter cold in winter—air-conditioning and central heating are important.

Shopping

Apulia is rich in folk art, reflecting the influences of the many nations that have passed through the region or ruled it. Don't expect boutiques; instead, snatch up handmade goods, such as pottery with traditional designs, baskets, textiles, and carved wood figures, for nice gifts and souvenirs. These are on sale in shops and in open markets, where some bargaining can enter into the purchase.

Exploring Apulia

Driving is the best way to get around the region. The autostrada and superstrada networks connect the hubs of Bari and Brindisi and the smaller towns. If you are mainly interested in spending time at the beach, the Gargano Promontory is lined with some of Apulia's best coastline, although there are pleasant beach resorts within easy reach of most of the region's attractions. Convenient travel bases include Alberobello or Martina Franca in the trulli country; Lecce, near the tip of the heel; and the small ports of Barletta, Molfetta, and Trani, up the coast from Bari.

Bari and Brindisi are notorious for purse-snatchings, car thefts, and break-ins. If you are driving in these cities, do not leave valuables in the car or trunk, and find a guarded parking space if possible.

Numbers in the text correspond to numbers in the margin and on the Apulia and Bari maps.

Great Itineraries

Apulia's attractions are so varied and scattered that you may want to take a full week or more to explore it at a leisurely pace, selecting two or three bases in different parts of the region and taking day trips to nearby sights.

IF YOU HAVE 3 DAYS

With three days in Apulia, you will need to focus on one stop per day, starting with a morning stroll in the old town of **Bari** ①–③. After lunch, head south as far as **Lecce** ㉔, spending the next day in this glorious Baroque town. On the morning of the third day, retrace your steps northwest to **Brindisi** ㉓, stopping at the famous column marking the end of the Via Appia. Veer west along the Via Appia (S7) and head to **Taranto** ㉒ for your last night, to take in the Museo Nazionale. If you are heading back to Bari, drive on the S172 through the **trulli district** ⑰–㉑ to get an impression of the dwellings.

IF YOU HAVE 5 DAYS

Spend a couple of days exploring the forested **Gargano Promontory** ⑧–⑯, northwest of **Bari** ①–③, where you'll need about two hours to absorb the flavor of this old center. Take the coastal road (S16) from the city northwest toward **Molfetta** ④, **Trani** ⑤, and **Barletta** ⑥, with old ports reminiscent of Venetian ports such as Dubrovnik, across the Adriatic Sea in Croatia. The seaside fishing villages-cum-resorts of the Gargano Promontory—**Vieste** ⑪, **Peschici** ⑫, and **Rodi Garganico** ⑬—offer the best choice of accommodations, although **Foggia** ⑧ or **Manfredonia** ⑨ make good bases. Aim to spend your fourth night in **Alberobello** ⑰, the capital of trulli country—touristy but engaging—or in whitewashed **Ostuni** ⑳. From Alberobello, it's a short run to **Taranto** ㉒ to whip around the archaeological museum. Break your journey for an hour or two in **Brindisi** ㉓, but save your last night for **Lecce** ㉔, a treat that will provide some of your most abiding memories of Apulia.

IF YOU HAVE 7 DAYS

If your base is **Bari** ①–③, devote about a half day to the city before venturing to the Gargano Promontory. A car is indispensable since transport connections are tortuous and slow, but be prepared to abandon it for a half-day ramble through the **Foresta Umbra** ⑭ and **Monte Sant'Angelo** ⑮, dominated by a large Norman castle that was once host to crusaders setting off for the East, and **San Giovanni Rotondo** ⑯. Proceed down the Adriatic Coast back toward Bari, landing at the pretty fishing villages of **Barletta** ⑥, **Trani** ⑤, and **Molfetta** ④, and making an inland detour to view the fascinatingly geometrical **Castel del Monte** ⑦. Head southeast toward trulli country, spending a night in **Alberobello** ⑰ or **Martina Franca** ㉑. At some point take a trip underground at the **Grotte di Castellana** ⑱, a soothing respite from the summer heat. The bustling cities of **Taranto** ㉒ and **Brindisi** ㉓ are

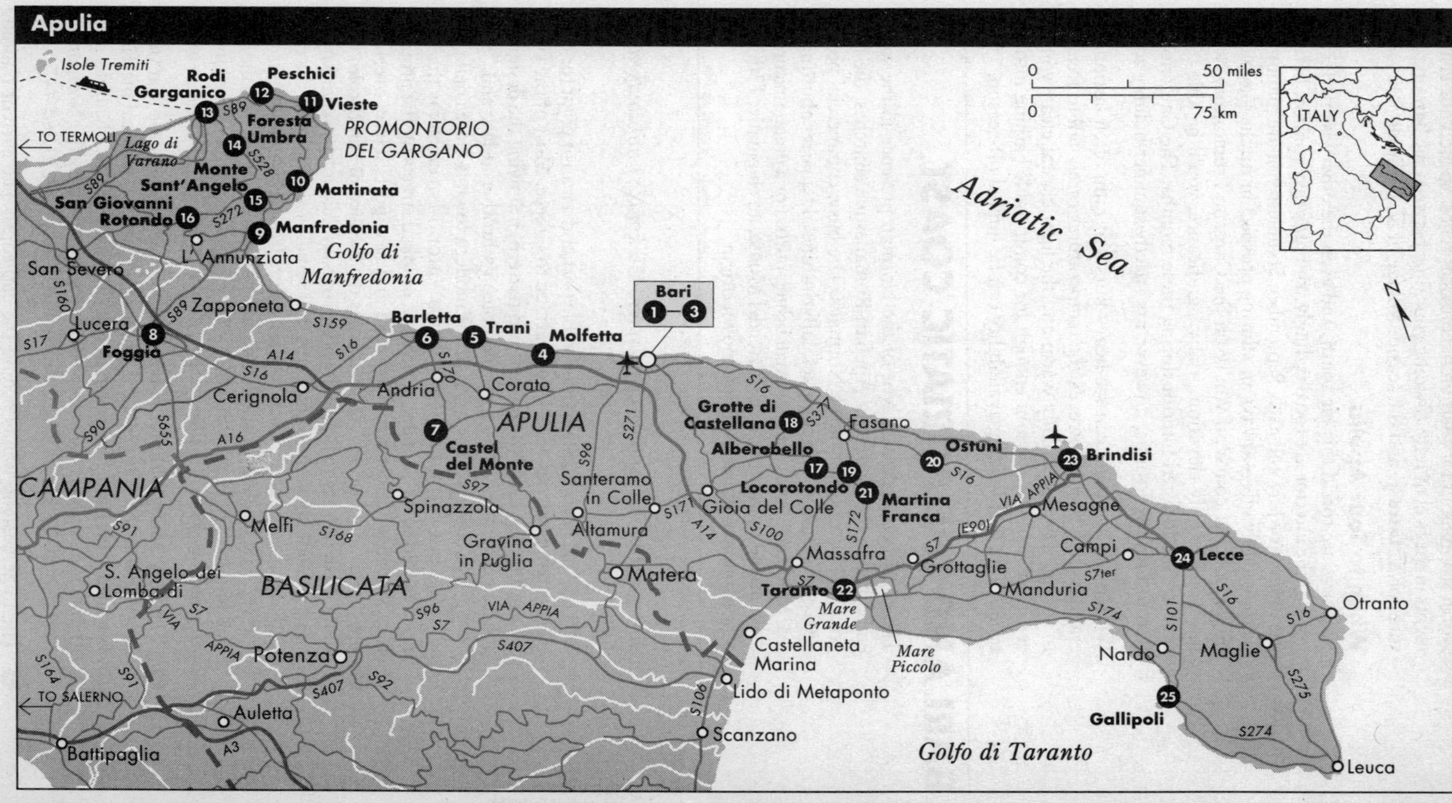
Apulia
Isole Tremiti
Rodi Garganico
Peschici
Vieste
Foresta Umbra
PROMONTORIO DEL GARGANO
TO TERMOLI
Lago di Varano
Monte Sant'Angelo
Mattinata
San Giovanni Rotondo
Manfredonia
L'Annunziata
Golfo di Manfredonia
San Severo
Zapponeta
Lucera
Foggia
Barletta
Trani
Molfetta
Bari 1—3
Adriatic Sea
0 50 miles
0 75 km
ITALY
N
Cerignola
Andria
Corato
APULIA
Castel del Monte
Grotte di Castellana
Fasano
Alberobello
Ostuni
Brindisi
Locorotondo
Martina Franca
CAMPANIA
Spinazzola
Santeramo in Colle
Gioia del Colle
Mesagne
Melfi
Altamura
Gravina in Puglia
Massafra
Grottaglie
Campi
Lecce
S. Angelo dei Lombardi
BASILICATA
Matera
Taranto
Mare Grande
Manduria
Otranto
Castellaneta Marina
Mare Piccolo
Nardo
Maglie
Potenza
Lido di Metaponto
Gallipoli
TO SALERNO
Auletta
Scanzano
Golfo di Taranto
Battipaglia
Leuca
VIA APPIA
S89
S528
S272
S160
S17
S159
S16
A14
S170
S655
S90
A16
S96
S271
S377
S97
S171
S100
S172
S7
E90
S7ter
S174
S101
S91
S168
S407
S92
S164
S106
S275
S274
A3

worth stopping in for their archaeological relics. Spend your last two nights in the heel of Italy, dividing your time between the Baroque pleasures of **Lecce** ㉔ and the seaside village of **Gallipoli** ㉕.

When to Tour Apulia

Summers are torrid this far south, and even the otherwise perfect villages of the interior are too dazzlingly white for easy comfort between the months of July and early September. So unless you are planning to be thoroughly idle—always an alluring prospect in Apulia—avoid the hot season. Of course, if you're on the Gargano Promontory, which has Apulia's only elevation of any significance, you'll be able to appreciate the forested interior during these months. The Gargano and Bari to Brindisi littorals, however, are strictly summer-holiday zones.

Wintertime in Apulia can see heavy bursts of rain, often lasting several days at a time. However, the temperatures rarely fall to freezing. In spring, days are usually warm and the light crystal clear; you can generally find water warm enough for comfortable bathing into October. Note that lodging availability can be limited off-season.

BARI AND THE ADRIATIC COAST

The coast has a strong flavor of the Norman presence in the south, embodied in the distinctive Apulian-Romanesque churches, the most graceful contribution of the Normans. The busy, commercial port of Bari offers charm in its compact, labyrinthine old quarter abutting the sea. Molfetta and Barletta are small fishing ports. For a unique excursion, drive inland to the imposing Castel del Monte, an enigmatic, 13th-century octagonal structure of unknown origin.

Bari

260 km (162 mi) southeast of Naples, 450 km (281 mi) southeast of Rome.

Bari is a big, hectic, rough-and-tumble port and a transit point for travelers catching ferries across the Adriatic to Greece. Most of the city is set out in a logical 19th-century grid pattern, following the designs of Joachim Murat (1767–1815), Napoléon's brother-in-law and "King of the Two Sicilies." The heart of the modern town is Piazza della Libertà, but just beyond it, across Corso Vittorio Emanuele, is the *città vecchia* (old town), a maze of narrow, crooked streets on the promontory that juts out between Bari's old and new ports. Here, overlooking the sea and just off Via Venezia, is the **Basilica di San Nicola**, built in the 11th century to house the bones of Saint Nicholas, better known to us as Saint Nick, or Santa Claus. His remains are buried in the crypt and said to have been stolen by Bari sailors from Myra, in what is now Turkey. The basilica, of solid and powerful construction, was the only building to survive the otherwise wholesale destruction of Bari by the Normans in 1152. ✉ *Piazza San Nicola.* ⏲ *Daily 7–12 and 4–6:30.*

❷ A century younger than the basilica, the **Cattedrale** is the seat of the local bishop and was the scene of many significant political marriages between important families in the Middle Ages. The cathedral's solid architecture reflects the Romanesque style favored by the Normans of that period. ✉ *Piazza dell'Odegitria.* ⏲ *Daily 7–1:30 and 4–7.*

❸ The huge **Castello** looms behind the cathedral. The current building dates from the time of Holy Roman Emperor Frederick II (1194–1250), who rebuilt an existing Norman-Byzantine castle to his own exacting specifications. Designed more for power than beauty, it looks out beyond the cathedral to the small Porto Vecchio (Old Port). Inside

Basilica di San Nicola, **1**
Castello, **3**
Cattedrale, **2**

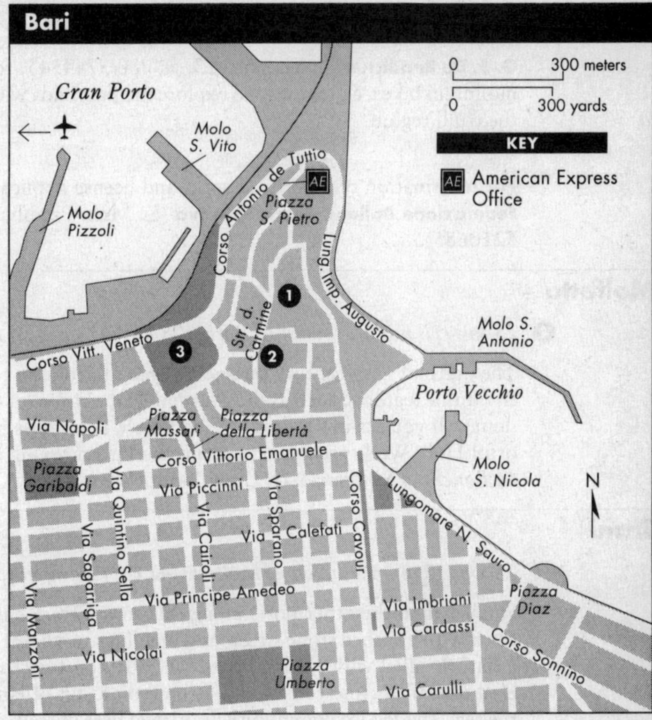

is a collection of medieval Apulian art. ⊠ *Piazza Federico II di Svevia.* 🎫 *4,000 lire.* ⏲ *Tues.–Sat. 8:30–1 and 2:30–7, Sun. 8:30–2.*

Dining and Lodging

$$ ✕ **Ristorante al Pescatore.** This is one of Bari's best fish restaurants, in the old town opposite the castle and just around the corner from the cathedral. Summer cooking is done outside, where you can sit amid a cheerful clamor of quaffing and dining. Try the *céfalo* (mullet) if it is available, accompanied by crisp salad and a carafe of invigorating local wine. ⊠ *Piazza Federico II di Svevia,* ☎ *080/5237039. Reservations essential in high season. AE, DC, MC, V. Closed Mon.*

$$$$ 🏨 **Sheraton Nicolaus.** This large, modern hotel on the edge of the city is easily reached by car from Highway S16, which skirts the congested town center. It caters mainly to businesspeople and is well equipped for meetings, conferences, and banquets. Rooms are spacious and comfortable, with the usual Sheraton amenities. There's even an indoor pool and a sauna. ⊠ *Via Agostino Ciasca 9, 70124,* ☎ *080/5042626,* FAX *080/5042058. 170 rooms. Restaurant, bar, indoor pool, sauna, convention center, meeting rooms. AE, DC, MC, V.*

$$ 🏨 **Adria.** This two-star's virtues are its convenience to the train station and relative low cost in a city sadly short on inexpensive lodgings. Facilities are adequate if undistinguished (rooms have showers only, not baths, for instance), but this is primarily a one-night stopover. Guest rooms are basic but fine. Turn right out of the station to find it. ⊠ *Via L. Zuppetta 10, 70121,* ☎ *080/5246699,* FAX *080/5213207. 35 rooms. Restaurant, bar. AE, DC, MC, V.*

Nightlife and the Arts

Bari's famous **Teatro Petruzzelli** (⊠ Corso Cavour) features performances of drama, opera, and ballet. The theater is still being restored after a devastating fire in 1991.

Outdoor Activities and Sports

BIKING

G. S. De Bendictus (✉ Via Nitti 23, ☎ 080/5744345) rents bikes and mountain bikes, a great way to explore the flat roads winding through the trulli region.

FISHING

For information on approved spots and license applications, contact **Federazione Italiana Pesca Sportiva** (✉ Molo Pizzoli, Bari, ☎ 080/5210685).

Molfetta

❹ *25 km (16 mi) northwest of Bari, 108 km (67 mi) east of Foggia.*

The unusual 12th-century **Duomo Vecchio** of Molfetta reveals distinct Byzantine features, such as the pyramid-shape covers of the three main domes. If you are in the area around Easter, don't miss Molfetta's colorful Holy Week processions, a surefire hit for young and old alike. ✉ *Banchina Seminario.* ⏲ *Daily 7–noon and 4–7.*

Trani

❺ *18 km (11 mi) northwest of Molfetta, 43 km (27 mi) northwest of Bari.*

Smaller than the other ports along this coast, Trani has a quaint old town with polished stone streets and buildings, medieval churches, and a harbor filled with fishing boats. The 11th-century **Duomo,** considered one of the finest in Apulia, is built on a spit of land jutting into the sea. The Jewish community flourished here in medieval times, and on Via Sinagoga (Synagogue Street) two of the four synagogues still exist: the 13th-century **Santa Maria Scolanova** and **Santa Anna,** which still bears a Hebrew inscription.

Dining and Lodging

$$ ★ ✕ **La Regia.** Just in front of the cathedral, on a swath of land jutting out into the sea, La Regia has an antique feel, with stonework, vaulted ceilings, and terra-cotta tile floors. Regional specialties are presented imaginatively: try the baked crepes (similar to cannelloni); risotto made with salmon, crab, and cream; lobster; or grilled fish. ✉ *Piazza Archivio 2,* ☎ *0883/584444. Reservations essential Sun. lunch and dinner on summer weekends. AE, DC, MC, V. Closed Mon. and 3 wks in Nov. or Dec.*

$$ 🏨 **Royal.** This is an unpretentious and modern four-star hotel near the train station. Furnishings are trim and tidy, suited to brief stopovers rather than extended sojourns. ✉ *Via De Robertis 29, 70059,* ☎ *0883/588777,* FAX *0883/582224. 40 rooms. Restaurant. AE, DC, MC, V.*

$ 🏨 **La Regia.** This small hotel occupies a 17th-century palazzo; it's above the restaurant of the same name (☞ *above*) and under the same ownership. Don't expect grand or spacious rooms, though they are perfectly adequate; the best of them take full advantage of the hotel's superb setting opposite Trani's cathedral. ✉ *Piazza Duomo 2, 70059,* ☎ FAX *0883/584444. 10 rooms. Restaurant, bar. AE, DC, MC, V. Closed Mon. and 3 wks in Nov. or Dec.*

Barletta

❻ *13 km (8 mi) northwest of Trani, 56 km (35 mi) northwest of Bari.*

The **Colossus,** a bronze statue more than 15 ft tall, is thought to be of the Byzantine emperor Valentinian and date from the 5th century AD. Part of Venice's booty after the sack of Byzantium's capital, Constantinople, in the 1200s, the Colossus was abandoned on the beach near Barletta when the ship carrying it to Venice foundered in a storm. ✉ *Next to the church of San Sepolcro, Corso Vittorio Emanuele.*

Dining

$$ ✕ **La Casaccia.** Near a picturesque castle, this simple restaurant serves such local dishes as homemade orecchiette and penne *piccanti* (spicy). There's nothing fancy here: the tone is calm and down-home, most tables occupied by discriminating regulars who appreciate the good Apulian cooking and the very moderate prices. ✉ *Corso Cavour 40,* ☎ *0883/533719. Reservations not accepted. No credit cards.*

Nightlife and the Arts

The **Disfida a Barletta,** held on the last Sunday in August, is a reenactment of an event of the same name, which took place in 1503. Every Italian child is taught in school that the *disfida* (challenge) of a duel was issued by 13 Italian officers to 13 French officers, after one of the French insulted the Italians by stating that Italy would always be under foreign domination. The Italians taught the rash Frenchman and his compatriots a lesson.

Castel del Monte

★ ❼ *30 km (19 mi) south of Barletta, 56 km (35 mi) southwest of Bari.*

Built on an isolated hill in the first half of the 13th century by Frederick II, Castel del Monte is a huge, bare, octagonal castle with eight towers. Very little is known about the structure, since virtually no records exist. It has none of the usual defense features associated with medieval castles, so it probably had little military significance. Some theories suggest it might have been built as a hunting lodge or may have served as an astronomical observatory or a stop for pilgrims on their quest for the Holy Grail. ✉ *On signposted minor road 18 km (11 mi) south of Andria.* 🎫 *4,000 lire.* ⏲ *Apr.–Oct., Tues.–Sat. 8:30–2 and 2:30–7, Sun. 9–1; Nov.–Mar., Tues.–Sat. 8:30–2, Sun. 9–1.*

Dining

$$ ✕ **Ostello di Federico.** This large, beautifully positioned restaurant, at the foot of the hill on which the celebrated Castel del Monte rises, has a terrace overlooking splendid scenery, plus a bar and a pizzeria with a wood oven. The restaurant serves local dishes, including orecchiette *a rape* (with bitter greens), and local cheeses, such as ricotta and creamy burrata. ✉ *Castel del Monte,* ☎ *0883/569877. Reservations essential. AE, DC, MC, V. Closed Mon., 2 wks in mid-Nov., and last 2 wks in Jan.*

Shopping

In Andria, between Castel del Monte and Barletta, **copper** objects and containers are made and sold by local craftsmen.

GARGANO PROMONTORY

Lining the spur of Italy's boot—the Gargano Promontory (Promontorio del Gargano)—are the region's most beautiful and popular beaches. Until a few years ago, this rocky peninsula of whitewashed coastal towns, wide sandy beaches, and craggy limestone cliffs topped by deep-green scrub pine was practically unknown, and some parts of the interior are still well off the usual tourist track. The resort business here has boomed in the past decade, though, and beaches can become crowded in midsummer. For the kids, the beaches and forests of the Gargano Promontory are great places for letting off steam, and many towns stage puppet shows in their public gardens.

Foggia

8 *95 km (60 mi) west of Bari.*

Foggia, the chief city in Apulia's northernmost province, is not the most inspiring destination, though it makes a useful overnight stop for visitors to the Gargano. On the main line from Rome and Naples, and easily accessible from the autostrada, Foggia has all the amenities one might expect from a major commercial center, the venue for numerous fairs and conventions throughout the year. This means that while it enjoys a decent selection of lodgings and restaurants, you'll need to reserve to make sure of accommodations. This is the place to get or exchange cash or rent a car for excursions to the Gargano.

Dining and Lodging

$$ ★ ✕ **Mangiatoia.** In an old farmhouse, this rustic restaurant has lovely arches, white walls, and wood-beamed ceilings. You can dine outdoors in a large garden, where tables made from wagon wheels surround an old well. Seafood is the specialty; fish and shellfish are displayed live in tanks. The chef will supply recipes for dishes, such as spaghetti *ai datteri di mare al cartoccio* (with razor clams), and fettuccine in a creamy scampi sauce. It's on the main road to Bari, near the Foggia Agricultural Fairgrounds. ✉ *Via Virgilio 2,* ☎ *0881/634457. Reservations essential on weekends. AE, DC, MC, V. Closed Mon.*

$$$ **Cicolella.** This 1920s hotel near the station has modern amenities and tasteful rooms with floor-length curtains, regal wallpaper, restful, discreet lighting, and some have balconies. The suites, which fall into the $$$$ category, are particularly recommended. The restaurant (closed weekends) specializes in international dishes and well-prepared local dishes. ✉ *Via Ventiquattro Maggio 60, 71100,* ☎ *0881/688890,* FAX *0881/778984. 106 rooms. Restaurant, meeting rooms. AE, DC, MC, V.*

Manfredonia

9 *39 km (24 mi) northeast of Foggia, 60 km (37 mi) northwest of Barletta.*

This lazy resort town on the southern lip of the promontory was once a flourishing port ferrying crusaders across the Adriatic to Greece and beyond. It now makes an excellent starting point for expeditions into the peninsula. The small **Museo Nazionale** in the Angevin castle on the seafront contains relics of the Daunian people who once inhabited the Gargano. ✉ *Corso Manfredi,* ☎ *0884/587838.* *4,000 lire.* ⊙ *Tues.–Sun. 8:30–1:30 and 3:30–7:30; closed 1st and last Sun. of the month.*

Apart from some adequate hotels and a buzz of the evening *passeggiata*—the most Mediterranean of pageants when locals stroll through the streets—there is little else.

Lodging

$$ **Gargano.** The functional, rather boxy rooms in this typical, white beach hotel are decorated in blue and white and have terraces. The public rooms are spacious and scattered with seating areas, and the dining area overlooks the pool and the sea. ✉ *Viale Beccarini 2, 71043,* ☎ *0884/587621,* FAX *0884/586021. 46 rooms. Restaurant, bar, pool. MC, V. Closed 2 wks in Jan. or Feb.*

Outdoor Activities and Sports

BIKING

There are no bike trails here per se, but the forest and interior is exciting biking terrain. Bicycles can be serviced at **G. S. Cicli Castriotta** (✉ Viale Beccarini 7, ☎ 0884/583424).

En Route From Manfredonia, take the winding coastal road (S89), which threads through kilometers of silvery olive groves interspersed with almond trees and prickly-pear cacti. Along the way you'll come across many local craftsmen's stalls, selling homemade preserves, baskets, and carved olive-wood bowls and utensils.

Mattinata

10 *15 km (9 mi) northeast of Manfredonia, 138 km (86 mi) northwest of Bari.*

Just inland of a fine sandy beach, where you'll find most of the campsites and hotels, this is a generally quiet village that comes into its own in the summer season.

Lodging

$$ **Baia delle Zagare.** On the shore road around the Gargano Promontory, north of Mattinata, Baia delle Zagare is a secluded, modern group of cottages overlooking an inlet. An elevator takes you down to a private beach, and the hotel restaurant is good enough to warrant staying on the premises all day. (You're expected to take full board in August.) ✉ *Strada Litoranea (17 km/10 mi northeast of Mattinata), 71030,* ☎ *0884/550155,* FAX *0884/550884. 144 rooms. Restaurant, pool, tennis court, beach. MC, V. Closed Oct.–May. FAP.*

$–$$ **Alba del Gargano.** Although it's in the town center, the modern Alba provides a restful atmosphere. Large balconies overlook a quiet courtyard garden, and a frequent (and free) bus service connects with a private beach, where you can use the hotel's beach chairs and umbrellas. Rooms are comfortably furnished, and there is a good restaurant. ✉ *Corso Matino 102, 71030,* ☎ *0884/550771,* FAX *0884/550772. 40 rooms, 3 suites. Restaurant, bar, beach. MC, V.*

Vieste

11 *50 km (30 mi) northeast of Manfredonia, 179 km (111 mi) northwest of Bari.*

This large town on the tip of the spur is the Gargano's main commercial center and an attractive place to wander around. Make for the **castle,** not open to the public but offering good views from its high position overlooking the beaches and town. The resort attracts legions of tourists in summer, some bound for the **Isole Tremiti** (☞ Off the Beaten Path *in* Rodi Garganico, *below*), a tiny archipelago connected to Vieste by regular ferries.

Lodging

$$$$ ★ **Pizzomunno.** Probably the most luxurious resort on the Gargano, Pizzomunno is right on the beach and is surrounded by an extensive park. It is large, white, modern, air-conditioned, and well equipped. The rooms are ample and plush, all with terraces. Here you can unwind, or try your hand at tennis or archery. ✉ *Lungomare di Pizzomunno, 71019,* ☎ *0884/708741,* FAX *0884/707325. 208 rooms. 3 restaurants, air-conditioning, 2 pools, sauna, 3 tennis courts, archery, health club, cinema, dance club, children's programs. AE, DC, MC, V. Closed Oct.–Mar.*

Peschici

12 *22 km (14 mi) northwest of Vieste, 199 km (124 mi) northwest of Bari.*

You may want to make this pleasant resort on Gargano's north shore your base for spending a few days exploring the surrounding beaches and coast. Development has not wreaked too much havoc on this whitewashed town, and the mazelike center retains its characteristic low houses topped with little domes.

Rodi Garganico

⓭ *20 km (12 mi) west of Peschici, 40 km (25 mi) west of Vieste.*

This fishing village squeezed between the hills and the sea takes its name from the island of Rhodes, recalling its former Greek population. Ringed by pine woods and citrus groves, Rodi is linked by hydrofoils with the Isole Tremiti, and things can get pretty hectic in high summer.

OFF THE BEATEN PATH **ISOLE TREMITI** – A ferry service from Termoli, west of the Gargano (1 hr, 40 mins), and hydrofoil service from Vieste, Peschici, Rodi Garganico, and Manfredonia (40 mins to 1 hr, 40 mins) connect the mainland with these three small islands north of the Gargano. Although somewhat crowded with Italian tourists in summer, they are famed for their sea caves, pine forests, and craggy limestone formations. Interesting medieval churches and fortifications dot the islands.

Dining

$$ ✕ **Gabbiano.** Admire the view facing the sea in Rodi Garganico at this cheerful restaurant while savoring freshly caught seafood. ✉ *Via Trieste 14,* ☎ *0884/965283. MC, V. Closed Thurs.*

Foresta Umbra

★ ⓮ *25 km (16 mi) south of Rodi Garganico, 30 km (19 mi) southwest of Vieste.*

In the middle of the peninsula is the majestic Foresta Umbra (Shady Forest), a dense growth of beech, maple, sycamore, and oak generally found in more northerly climates, thriving here because of the altitude, 3,200 ft above sea level. Between the trees are occasional dramatic vistas opening out over the Golfo di Manfredonia. From the north coast, take S528 (midway between Peschici and Rodi Garganico) south to head through the interior of the Gargano, where you'll discover a different world.

Monte Sant'Angelo

★ ⓯ *16 km (10 mi) north of Manfredonia, 60 km (19 mi) southwest of Vieste.*

Perched amid olive groves on the rugged white limestone cliffs overlooking the gulf is the town of Monte Sant'Angelo. Pilgrims have flocked here for nearly 1,500 years—among them, St. Francis of Assisi and the crusaders setting off for the Holy Land from the then-flourishing port of Manfredonia. The town is centered on the **Santuario di San Michele** (Sanctuary of San Michele), built over the grotto where the archangel Michael is believed to have appeared before shepherds in the year 490. Walk down a long series of steps to get to the grotto itself—on the walls you can see the hand tracings left by pilgrims as votive symbols.

Steps lead left from the sanctuary down to the **Tomba di Rotari** (Tomb of Rotari), believed to have been a medieval baptistery, with some remarkable 12th-century reliefs. More steep steps lead up to the large, ruined **Castello Normano** (Norman Castle) that dominates the town, with a view of the intricate pattern of the streets and steps winding their way up the side of the valley. The town's medieval quarter, the

Rione Junno, is a maze of little white houses squeezed into a corner of the narrow valley.

Lodging

$$ 🏨 **Hotel Rotary.** This simple but welcoming modern hotel is set amid olive and almond groves just outside town. Most rooms have basic decor and terraces with a good view of the Golfo di Manfredonia. ✉ *Via per Pulsano, 71037,* ☎ FAX *0884/562146. 24 rooms. Restaurant. AE, MC, V.*

Shopping

Most food shops in the Junno sell a local specialty called *ostia piena* (filled host), a pastry made with candied almonds and wafers of the type similar to communion hosts. The best place to get—or munch on—them is at the southern end of the Junno, by the Villa Comunale. Shoemaker **Domenico Palena** displays his unique leather sculptures at his tiny shop in the Junno quarter. Local wood craftsmen make and sell wooden utensils, furniture, and wrought-iron goods.

San Giovanni Rotondo

⓰ *25 km (16 mi) west of Monte Sant'Angelo, 85 km (52 mi) southwest of Vieste.*

The ancient village of San Giovanni Rotondo, on the winding S272, has gained importance in recent years as a center of religious pilgrimage. Devotees have flocked here to pay their respects to the shrine and **Tomba di Padre Pio** (1887–1968), a monk revered for his pious life, for miraculous intercessions, and for his having received the stigmata, the signs of Christ's wounds. The **Casa Sollievo della Sofferenza** (Foundation for the Mitigation of Suffering), supported through contributions from around the world, is a testament to the enduring appeal of this holy man.

En Route A short ride south on S273, and then east (left) at L'Annunziata, will take you back to Manfredonia, where you can link up with the coastal road to return to Bari.

TRULLI DISTRICT

Alberobello, Locorotondo, Ostuni, and Martina Franca

The inland area to the southeast of Bari is one of Italy's oddest enclaves, a flat land given over to olive cultivation and interspersed with the idiosyncratic habitations that have lent their name to the district. The origins of the igloo-shape trulli go back to the 13th century and maybe further. The trulli are built of local limestone, without mortar, and with a hole in the top for escaping smoke. Some are painted with mystical or religious symbols; some are isolated, and others are joined together with roofs on various levels. The center of trulli country is Alberobello, hosting the greatest concentration of the buildings, though you will spot scores of them all over this region, some in states of disrepair but always adding a quirky charm to the landscape.

Alberobello

★ ⓱ *59 km (37 mi) southeast of Bari, 45 km (28 mi) north of Taranto.*

The trulli zone of Alberobello, where more than 1,000 trulli huddle together along steep, narrow streets, is a national monument. It is also one of the most popular tourist destinations in Apulia and a gold mine if you like picking up local crafts (☞ Shopping, *below*).

Dining and Lodging

$$–$$$ ✕ **Il Poeta Contadino.** Proprietor Marco Leonardo serves "creative regional cooking" in this rustic-style restaurant. In the heart of the attractive trulli zone, it features candlelit tables and a refined, understated ambience. Specialties to look for are fish platters and antipasti. ✉ *Via Indipendenza 21,* ☎ *080/4321917. Reservations essential. AE, DC, MC, V. Closed Mon. (Oct.–June), Jan. 7–22, and 10 days at end of June.*

$$ ★ ✕ **Trullo d'Oro.** This welcoming, rustic restaurant set in five trulli houses has dark wood beams, whitewashed walls, and an open hearth. Local country cooking includes dishes using lamb and veal, vegetable and cheese antipasti, pasta dishes with crisp raw vegetables on the side, and almond pastries. Among the specialties are roast lamb with *lampasciuni* (a type of wild onion) and spaghetti *al trullo,* made with tomatoes, *rughetta* (arugula), and four cheeses. ✉ *Via F. Cavallotti 27,* ☎ *080/4321820. Reservations essential. AE, DC, MC, V. Closed Mon. and Jan. 7–Feb.*

$$$ **Dei Trulli.** Trulli-style cottages in a pine wood near the trulli zone make this a pleasant hotel, decorated with rustic furnishings and folk-art rugs. The modestly priced restaurant serves local specialties. You're expected to take half or full board in high season. ✉ *Via Cadore 28, 70011,* ☎ *080/4323555,* FAX *080/4323560. 33 rooms. Restaurant, pool. AE, MC, V. FAP, MAP.*

Shopping

In the trulli zone, you'll find small shops selling hand-painted clay figurines. Rugs and fabrics are the best bets here, but there is also a good deal of shoddy merchandise.

Grotte di Castellana

18 *20 km (12 mi) northwest of Alberobello, 63 km (52 mi) southeast of Bari.*

The Grotte di Castellana is a huge network of caves discovered in 1938. You can take one of the hourly guided tours through the grottoes, filled with fantastically shaped stalagmites and stalactites. The grottoes constitute the largest network of caves on the Italian mainland. ☎ *080/4965511.* *15,000 lire (1-hr tour), 20,000 lire (2-hr tour).* *Apr.–Oct., daily 8:30–12:30 and 2:30–6:30; Nov.–Mar., daily 8:30–12:30.*

Dining

$$ ✕ **Al Parco Chiancafredda.** The refined ambience and cuisine of this restaurant, set apart from the tourist haunts, make it pricier than its neighbors. But the food and service are worth it: try such regional dishes as *sformato di verdura* (vegetable stew) and *agnello alla castellanese* (local lamb). ✉ *Via Chiancafredda 12,* ☎ *080/4968710. Reservations essential. AE, MC, V. Closed Tues. and Nov.*

$ ✕ **Taverna degli Artisti.** Near the caves, this rustic tavern-style restaurant with a big garden specializes in local home cooking, such as roast lamb, homemade orecchiette, and dishes with ominous names like *timballo fine del mondo* (end-of-the-world timbale) and *involtini al purgatorio* (purgatory roulades). ✉ *Via Vito Matarrese 27,* ☎ *080/4968234. AE, DC, MC, V. Closed Thurs. (Oct.–June) and mid-Dec.–mid-Jan.*

Locorotondo

19 *9 km (5½ mi) southeast of Alberobello, 40 km (25 mi) north of Taranto.*

Still inside the trulli district, Locorotondo is an attractive hillside town in the Itria Valley (take S172 from Alberobello). The *rotondo* in the town's name refers to the circular pattern of the houses, apparent from any vantage point at the top of the town.

Ostuni

20 *50 km (30 mi) west of Brindisi, 40 km (25 mi) northeast of Locorotondo.*

This sun-bleached, picturesque medieval town lies on three hills a short distance from the coast. The **old center,** on the highest of the hills, has steep cobbled lanes and stupendous views out over the coast and the surrounding plain.

Dining and Lodging

$$ ✕ **Vecchia Ostuni.** Enjoy regional dishes from this well-established trattoria in the heart of the old town, whose grills and seafood dishes are renowned among locals. Let yourself go on the antipasti table before settling down with a *sarago alle brace* (char-grilled bream) or *lombate e salsicce alle brace* (loin and sausages char-grilled). The homemade desserts are also worth some attention, and there is a good selection of local wines. Reservations are recommended weekends. ✉ *Largo Lanza 9,* ☎ *0831/303308. AE, MC, V. Closed Tues. and Jan.*

$$ 🏨 **Incanto.** At this modest yet modern hotel outside the old town, you can admire the countryside and the sea in the distance from many of its rooms. It makes a basic, but adequate, overnight base for seeing the area. ✉ *Via dei Colli, 72017,* ☎ *0831/301781,* FAX *0831/338302. 70 rooms. 2 restaurants, 2 bars. AE, DC, MC, V.*

Martina Franca

21 *6 km (4 mi) south of Locorotondo, 36 km (22 mi) north of Taranto.*

Martina Franca is an appealing town with a dazzling mixture of medieval and Baroque architecture in the light-color local stone. Ornate balconies hang above the twisting, narrow streets, with little alleys leading off into the surrounding hills. Martina Franca was developed as a military stronghold in the 14th century, when a surrounding wall with 24 towers was built, but now all that remains of that role are the four gates that had been the only entrances to the town. Each July and August Martina Franca holds a music festival.

Dining and Lodging

$$ ✕ **La Tavernetta.** This small restaurant with a vaulted ceiling in the old town center serves large portions of good home cooking, starting with a pottery bowl full of local olives and excellent house wine. Specialties include favi e fogghi and, in summer, orecchiette with *cocomero* (a vegetable that looks like a miniature round watermelon but tastes like a cross between a cucumber and a honeydew melon). Main courses include mixed grilled lamb, liver, and spicy local sausage. ✉ *Corso Vittorio Emanuele 30,* ☎ *080/4306323. MC, V. Closed Mon.*

$$–$$$ 🏨 **Park Hotel San Michele.** This garden hotel makes a pleasant base in the warm months, thanks to its pool. The two categories of rooms have a small price difference; opt for the higher-priced ones. All are spacious, some embellished with handsome furniture and bowls of fruit. ✉ *Viale Carella 9, 74015,* ☎ *080/4807053,* FAX *080/4808895. 86 rooms. Restaurant, bar, pool. AE, DC, MC, V.*

Nightlife and the Arts

Martina Franca concentrates on music in its annual **Festa della Valle Itria** (Festival of the Itria Valley) each July and August.

ACROSS THE HEEL AND SOUTH TO LECCE

Taranto, Brindisi, Lecce, Gallipoli

This far south, the mountains run out of steam and the land is uniformly flat although agriculturally quite important. The monotonous landscape, however, is redeemed by some of the region's best sandy coastline and a handful of alluring small towns. Taranto and Brindisi don't quite fit this description: both are big ports where historical importance is obscured by unsightly heavy industry. Nonetheless, Taranto has its special attractions, not the least its archaeological museum; Brindisi marks the end of the Via Appia. Farther south, in Il Salentino (Salentine peninsula), Lecce is an unexpected oasis of grace and sophistication, and its swirling architecture will melt even the most uncompromising critic of the Baroque.

Taranto

22 *100 km (62 mi) southeast of Bari, 40 km (25 mi) south of Martina Franca.*

Taranto—the stress is on the first syllable—was an important port even in Roman times. It lies toward the back of the instep of the boot on the broad Mare Grande bay, which is connected to a small internal Mare Piccolo basin by two narrow channels, one artificial and one natural. The old town is on an island between the larger and smaller bodies of water; the modern city stretches inward along the mainland. Little remains of Taranto's past except the 14th-century church of **San Domenico,** at one end of the island, and its famous naval academy, betraying the city's maritime heritage.

★ A shining beacon to shed light on the millennia of local history is the **Museo Nazionale,** whose large collection of prehistoric, Greek, and Roman artifacts came mainly from the immediate vicinity. The museum is just over the bridge from the old town on the promontory. Some of the prehistoric items from Apulian tombs date from before 1000 BC, but more plentiful are the examples of intricate craftsmanship in the Greek jewelry dating from around 500 BC. The museum is a testament to the importance of this ancient port, which has always taken full advantage of its unique trading position at the end of the Italian peninsula. ✉ *Corso Umberto 41,* ☎ *099/4532112.* 🎫 *8,000 lire.* ⏲ *Mon.–Sat. 8:30–1:30 and 2–8, Sun. 8:30–1:30 and 2:30–7:30.*

Dining and Lodging

$ ✕ **Da Basile.** Here's an ideal spot just a couple of blocks from the museum for a quick lunch or a good, straightforward (and cheap!) evening meal. You'll be sharing the four small rooms with a motley crew—families, crowds of youths, solitary businessmen, and groups of women—and you may have to wait for a table. Pizzas with fresh vegetables, no-frills pasta dishes, fish and meat, and delicious homemade gelato round out the menu. Service is fast and attentive. ✉ *Via Pitagora 76,* ☎ *099/4526240. MC, V. Closed Sat.*

$$$ 🏨 **Golf Hotel.** Less than an hour's drive along the coast from Taranto, this hotel, as its name implies, caters to golf enthusiasts, with suites in a modern, well-equipped annex right overlooking the links. Guests are entitled to a 20% reduction on fees for the 18-hole course, and a shuttle-bus plies between hotel, golf course, and beaches. Guests are required to take half or full board in high season. ✉ *Località Riva dei Tessali, Castellaneta Marina, 74011,* ☎ *099/8439251,* FAX *099/8439255. 70*

rooms, 20 suites. Dining room, bar, pool, golf privileges, tennis court. AE, DC, MC, V. FAP, MAP.

$$$ 🏨 **Grand Hotel Delfino.** This big, modern, well-equipped hotel downtown caters to business clients. Airy rooms have balconies. The restaurant features regional seafood. Rates fall into the bottom half of this price category. ✉ *Viale Virgilio 66, 74100,* ☎ *099/7323232,* FAX *099/7304654. 198 rooms. Restaurant, minibars, pool. AE, DC, MC, V.*

Nightlife and the Arts

Taranto has Easter processions on Holy Thursday and Good Friday, the Processione dei Misteri (Procession of the Mysteries) and the Processione dell'Addolorata.

Outdoor Activities and Sports

GOLF

Apulia's only 18-hole golf course is the **Riva dei Tessali** (✉ Marina di Castellaneta, 40 km/25 mi west of Taranto along the coast road, ☎ 099/8431844).

SAILING

Sailors should contact the **Lega Navale** (✉ Lungomare Vittorio Emanuele II, ☎ 099/4593801).

Brindisi

23 *114 km (71 mi) southeast of Bari, 72 km (45 mi) east of Taranto.*

Occupying the head of a deep inlet on the eastern Adriatic coast, Brindisi (stress placed on first syllable) has long been one of Italy's most important ports, and today most people think of the town only as a terminus for the ferry crossing that links Italy with Greece. Although this impression fails to give credit to the broader importance of the city (it has a population of nearly 100,000), it is a present-day reminder of the role Brindisi has always played as gateway to the eastern Mediterranean and beyond. Brindisi has seen a constant flow of naval and mercantile traffic over the centuries, and in the Middle Ages it was an important departure point for several Crusades to the Holy Land.

The core of the city is at the head of a deep channel, which branches into two harbors with the city between them. Look for the steeple of the cathedral to get your bearings, but go beyond it and down the steps to the water's edge. Just to the left is a tall **Roman column** and the base of another one next to it. These were built in the 2nd century AD and marked the end of the **Via Appia** (Appian Way), the Imperial Roman road that led from the capital to this important southern seaport. ✉ *Viale Regina Margherita.*

A short walk from the column, the mosaic floor in the apse of the **Duomo** is worth stopping to have a look at; the floor dates from the 12th century, although much of the rest of the cathedral was rebuilt in the 18th. ✉ *Piazza Duomo.* ⏲ *Daily 7–noon and 4–8.*

The **Castello Svevo,** another of the defense fortifications built by the illustrious Frederick II in the 13th century, guards the larger of Brindisi's two inner harbors, though it is inaccessible to the public. ✉ *Piazza Castello.*

Lodging

$$$ 🏨 **Majestic.** A modern hotel across from the train station and near the port, the Majestic is fully air-conditioned and furnished in a unfussy and rather uninspired style. The hotel is somewhat overpriced for what it offers. ✉ *Corso Umberto 151, 72100,* ☎ *0831/597941,* FAX *0831/524071. 68 rooms. Restaurant. AE, DC, MC, V.*

$$$ 🏨 **Mediterraneo.** Comfort and a convenient central location are the advantages of this modern, air-conditioned hotel—though it is less accessible from the port than the Majestic. Most rooms have balconies. ✉ *Viale Aldo Moro 70, 72100,* ☎ *0831/582811,* FAX *0831/587858. 65 rooms. Restaurant. AE, DC, MC, V.*

Nightlife and the Arts

The **Festa della Città di Brindisi** (City of Brindisi Festival), July–September, is a citywide display of art and folklore; contact the **tourist office** (✉ Piazza Dionisi, ☎ 0831/523072).

Outdoor Activities and Sports

SAILING

Contact Brindisi's **Lega Navale** (✉ Via Vespucci, ☎ 0831/418824), which offers canoe and sailing courses.

Lecce

24 *40 km (25 mi) southeast of Brindisi, 87 km (54 mi) east of Taranto.*

Although Lecce, the crowning jewel on the tour of Apulia, was founded before the time of the ancient Greeks, it is almost always associated with the term Lecce Baroque. This is because of a citywide impulse in the 17th century to redo the town in the Baroque fashion. But this was Baroque with a difference. Although Baroque architecture is often heavy and monumental, here it took on a lighter, more fanciful tone.
★ Just look at the **Basilica di Santa Croce,** with the **Palazzo della Prefettura** abutting it. Although every column, window, pediment, and balcony is given a curling Baroque touch—and then an extra one for good measure—the overall effect is lighthearted. The scale of the buildings is unintimidating and the local stone is a glowing honey color: it couldn't look menacing if it tried. ✉ *Via Umberto I.* ⏲ *Daily 7:30–noon and 5–7:30.*

In the middle of **Piazza Sant'Oronzo** is a **Roman column** of the same era and style as the one in Brindisi. Next to the column the shallow rows of seats in the **Anfiteatro Romano** suggest a small-scale Roman Colosseum or Verona's arena.

Dining and Lodging

$ ✕ **Plaza.** Tucked away behind Lecce's castle, this high-quality restaurant has been keeping the city's gourmets happy for 30 years. Regional dishes reveal a personal touch. Try the *tubettini alle cozze* (pasta with clams) and the antipasti, worth dipping into. ✉ *Via 140 Fanteria 10,* ☎ *0832/305093. AE, MC, V. Closed Sun. and Aug.*

$$ 🏨 **Risorgimento.** An old-fashioned hotel in a converted palace in the heart of the Baroque old town, the Risorgimento combines historic charm with modern comfort. The roof garden has great town views. ✉ *Via Augusto Imperatore 19, 73100,* ☎ *0832/242125,* FAX *0832/245571. 56 rooms. Restaurant, lounge, meeting rooms. AE, DC, MC, V.*

$ 🏨 **Cappello.** This popular hotel is close to the train station but outside the old city walls, about a 10-minute walk from the town center. Space is confined in the upstairs guest rooms, but they are perfectly fine for a short stay, and fully equipped with TV, telephone, and air-conditioning. Those at the back can get noisy from the nearby railroad. Reservations are advised. ✉ *Via Montegrappa 4, 73100,* ☎ *0832/308881,* FAX *0832/301535. 32 rooms. Bar. AE, DC, MC, V.*

Nightlife and the Arts

In July, the public gardens are venues for productions of drama and, sometimes, opera. A **Baroque music festival** in September is held in churches throughout the city.

Shopping

Wrought-iron work is the local specialty. Also look for works in papier-mâché, especially nativity scenes.

Gallipoli

25 *37 km (23 mi) south of Lecce, 190 km (118 mi) southeast of Bari.*

The modern section of the town of Gallipoli, on the Golfo di Taranto, lies on the mainland; turn right on the main street at the end of the central square and cross a 17th-century bridge to the old town, crowded onto its own small island in the gulf. The Greeks called it Kallipolis, the Romans Anxa. Like the famous Turkish town of the same name on the Dardanelles, the Italian Gallipoli occupies a strategic location and thus was repeatedly attacked through the centuries—by the Normans in 1071, the Venetians in 1484, the British in 1809. The historic quarter, a mesh of narrow alleys and squares, is guarded by a formidable **Castello Aragonese,** a massive fortification that grew out of an earlier Byzantine fortress that you can still see at the southeast corner. Notable churches in town are the Baroque **Duomo** and the church of **La Purissima,** with a stuccoed interior as elaborate as a wedding cake (note especially the tiled floor).

Dining and Lodging

$$ ★ ✕ **Marechiaro.** You have to cross a little bridge to this simple port-side restaurant, actually not far from the town's historic center. It's built out onto the sea, replete with wood paneling, flowers, and terraces with panoramic coastal views. Try the renowned *zuppa di pesce alla gallipolina* (fish stew), succulent shellfish, and linguine with seafood. ✉ *Lungomare Marconi,* ☎ *0833/266143. AE, DC, MC, V. Closed Tues. (Oct.–May).*

$$$ ★ 🏨 **Costa Brada.** The rooms all have terraces with sea views at this modern white beach hotel of classic Mediterranean design. The interiors are uncluttered and tasteful; rooms 110–114 are particularly spacious and overlook the beach. The hotel accepts only half-board or full-board guests in the high season. ✉ *Baia Verde beach, Litoranea Santa Maria di Leuca, 73014,* ☎ *0833/202551,* FAX *0833/202555. 89 rooms. Restaurant, snack bar, indoor and outdoor pools, sauna, tennis court, exercise room. AE, DC, MC, V. FAP, MAP.*

$$ 🏨 **Le Sirenuse.** There is a private beach and pine forest at this gleaming white Mediterranean-style beach hotel complex. The pleasant rooms are air-conditioned and have terraces. Half or full board is required in high season. ✉ *At Baia Verde beach, 73014,* ☎ *0833/202536,* FAX *0833/202539. 120 rooms. Pool, tennis court, beach. MC, V. Closed Nov.–Apr. FAP, MAP.*

Outdoor Activities and Sports

BEACHES

Ample swimming, clean, fine sand, and water sports make Gallipoli a good choice for families.

APULIA A TO Z

Arriving and Departing

By Boat

Ferries ply the waters from Bari and Brindisi to Greece (Corfu, Igoumenitsa, Patras, and Kephalonia), Turkey, Albania, even Egypt and Croatia. Contact **Adriatica di Navigazione** (agents at A. Galli e Figlio, ✉ Corso Manfredi 4, 71043 Manfredonia, ☎ 0884/582520; Intercontinental Viaggi, ✉ Corso Umberto I 26, 86039 Termoli, ☎ 0875/

705341; Cafiero Emilio, ✉ Via Degli Abbati 10, 71040 Tremiti, ☎ 0882/663008; Gargano Viaggi, ✉ Piazza Roma 7, 71019 Vieste, ☎ 0884/708501). **European Seaways** (✉ Corso Garibaldi 97, 72100 Brindisi, ☎ 0831/527684).

By Plane

Alitalia flies regularly from other Italian cities to Bari and Brindisi. **Aeroporto Palese** (☎ 080/5382370) is 8 km (5 mi) west of Bari. **Aeroporto Papola Casale** (☎ 0831/418805) is 5 km (3 mi) north of Brindisi.

BETWEEN THE AIRPORT AND DOWNTOWN

Regular bus service connects the two airports with the cities. Alitalia buses provide service from the cites to arrivals and departures at both airports.

By Train

Bari is a transit hub for train connections with northern Italy. Call (☎ 147/888088) for toll-free FS (Italian State Railways) information.

Getting Around

By Boat

☞ **Adriatica di Navigazione** *in* Arriving and Departing, *above.*

By Bus

Direct, if not always frequent, connections operate between most destinations in Apulia. **SITA** (✉ Piazza Aldo Moro 15/a, ☎ 080/5213714) is the main bus company operating in Apulia. In many cases the bus service is actually the backup to the train service (☞ *below*).

By Car

Driving is the best way to get around Apulia and the only way to see remote sights. Apulia is linked with the Italian autostrada system making it just a four- or five-hour drive from Rome to the Gargano Promontory or Bari. Roads are good, and major cities are linked by fast autostrade. Secondary roads (superstrade) connect the whole region; more direct—but sometimes less scenic—routes provide a convenient link between Bari, Brindisi, and Lecce. Don't plan on any night driving in the countryside, because the roads can become confusing without the aid of landmarks or large towns.

By Train

Good train service, operated by **FS** (Italian State Railways), links Bari to Brindisi, Lecce, and Taranto, but smaller destinations can often be reached only by completing the trip on a connecting bus operated by the railroad. The private **Ferrovie Sud-Est** (FSE) line connects the trulli area and Martina Franca with Bari and Taranto, and the fishing port of Gallipoli with Lecce.

Contacts and Resources

Car Rentals

BARI

Avis (✉ Via Zuppetta 5/a, ☎ 080/5316168). **Hertz** (✉ Aeroporto Palese, ☎ 080/5316172).

BRINDISI

Avis (✉ Via del Mare 26, ☎ 0831/526407). **Hertz** (✉ Aeroporto Papola, ☎ 0831/413060).

FOGGIA

Avis (✉ Train station, ☎ 0881/778912). **Maggiore-Budget** (✉ Viale Ventiquattro Maggio 76, ☎ 0881/773173).

TARANTO

Avis (✉ Corso Umberto 61, ☎ 099/4532278). **Hertz** (✉ Viale Virgilio 51, ☎ 099/7362290).

Emergencies

☎ 113.

Guided Tours

The **CIT** office in Bari(☞ Visitor Information, *below*) is the best connection for guided tours in Apulia, otherwise poorly served by tour operators. The CIT office can put you in touch with one of a number of local operators that offer everything from chauffeur-driven cars to a quick regional primer as part of a longer excursion.

Late-Night Pharmacies

Pharmacies take turns staying open late and on Sunday. A list of hours is posted on each *farmacia* (pharmacy).

Travel Agencies

BARI

Sestante (✉ Via Abate Gimma 150, ☎ 080/5213552). **Carlson Wagonlit Travel** (✉ Via Cardassi 56, ☎ 080/5540588).

BRINDISI

Silver Viaggi (✉ Corso Garibaldi 95, 72100, ☎ 0831/528333). **Utac Viaggi** (✉ Via Santa Lucia 11, 72100, ☎ 0831/560780, FAX 0831/529040).

Visitor Information

Tourist offices (✉ Piazza Moro 32/a, 70122 Bari, ☎ 080/5242244; ✉ Piazza Dionisi, 72100 Brindisi, ☎ 0831/523072; ✉ Via Perrone 17, 71100 Foggia, ☎ 0881/723650; ✉ Via Vittorio Emanuele 24, 73100 Lecce, ☎ 0832/248092; ✉ Piazza Europa 104, 71013 San Giovanni Rotondo, ☎ 0882/456240; ✉ Corso Umberto I 113, 74100 Taranto, ☎ 099/4532392; ✉ Via Cavour 140, 70059 Trani, ☎ 0883/588830; ✉ Kiosk in Piazza della Repubblica, summer only, ☎ 0883/43295; ✉ Piazza Kennedy, 71019 Vieste, ☎ 0884/708806).

14 BASILICATA AND CALABRIA

The lure of Italy's deep south, a magical combination of mountain and sea, has eluded visitors so far. It's their loss, for here sprawls untrammeled scenery that's hardly been altered since the city-states of Magna Graecia ruled the coasts. Their vestiges are here, as are the bizarre cave dwellings of Matera, a shining example of Byzantine church-building at Stilo, and the tranquil, sun-drenched beaches of Tropea and Scilla.

By Robert Andrews

THE *MEZZOGIORNO,* the informal name for Italy's south, reaches its full apotheosis in the regions of Basilicata and Calabria, often referred to the heel and toe of Italy's boot. Here, in an area of Italy off most tourist itineraries, the southern sun burns on a sparsely populated landscape where government neglect and archaic social patterns have prevented the kind of industrialization and rush to modernity experienced in other parts of the country. Despite the undeveloped state of large tracts of these two regions, however, Basilicata and Calabria have become increasingly popular among Italians, and a good infrastructure of hotels and leisure facilities won't make your stay in any sense deprived. On the contrary, the combination of superlative beaches with spectacular mountain ranges, plus the ubiquitous relics of Magna Graecia—the name given to the Greek colonies of southern Italy—and from the Norman and Spanish occupations, make a visit here an essential complement to any trip to Italy.

Pleasures and Pastimes

Beaches

The lack of industry in Basilicata and Calabria has one positive result for beach fans—acres of sand and a largely unpolluted sea running almost continuously down both coasts of the peninsula. This is not the place for you if you like your beaches impeccably tended but crowded with regimented lines of sunbathers and ranks of uniform beach umbrellas. Here, you can pick and choose strands at whim and spread out. What's more, there is a pronounced difference between the two coasts: the more developed Tyrrhenian littoral, on the western side, has more villages and facilities and is more scenic, with the mountains a constant backdrop; the eastern Ionian shore, on the other hand, is flatter, wilder, has fewer towns and villages, and holds less visual interest. The best Tyrrhenian spots are around Maratea, Praia a Mare, Amantea, Tropea, and Scilla. On the Ionian, head for Lido di Metaponto, Sibari, Capo Rizzuto, and Soverato. Remember that, if you don't have your own beach umbrella, the summer sun can be oppressive and even dangerous: borrow or buy one if you can, and arm yourself with plenty of sunscreen. Alternatively, stick to your hotel beach or seek out those few spots where there are lidos and facilities to rent, such as at Metaponto, Soverato, and around Tropea.

Dining

The food of Basilicata and Calabria is renowned both for its seafood—calamari, bream, sea bass, and swordfish to name a few—and for its produce from the land. In the latter category, look out for the various types of *funghi* (mushrooms), particularly in the fall, and pork in its many incarnations. Food production has not reached the industrial level of Italy's north, and consequently you will find much greater variety in the methods of preparing and even naming of the dishes, leaving much scope for adventurous eating and the discovery of new tastes. One taste experience you will find universally available, however, is that of *peperoncini* (small dried hot chile peppers), whose sweat-inducing seeds are often added to pasta dishes.

Hiking and Skiing

Most vacationers in Basilicata and Calabria think of only swimming and sunbathing as the main pastimes, unaware of the hiking and skiing that can be done in the forested or craggily bare peaks and valleys of the predominantly mountainous landscape. Three zones have been made into nature reserves with facilities set up to cater to outdoors enthusiasts. All three areas see plenty of cross-country and downhill skiing; the best slopes are at Camigliatello and Gambarie, where you can rent equipment. Farthest north, Parco Nazionale del Monte Pollino, riddled with lush canyons and marked paths, straddles the boundary between Basilicata and Calabria and is a good place to spot eagles and even wild boars. The villages of Morano Calabro, off the A3 autostrada to the south, and San Severino Lucano, off S653 to the north, are good starting points for these mountains, which reach up to 7,435 ft. Occupying the widest part of the Calabrian peninsula, the Sila Massif (reaching up to 6,324 ft) attracts most visitors, though the thick pine, beech, and chestnut forests are vast enough for you to find your own space. The Sila Grande, accessible from Lorica or Camigliatello, offers the most rewarding exploring within this extensive range. Farthest south, the Aspromonte massif, soaring above Reggio di Calabria, is a welcome retreat from summer temperatures, with peaks reaching a maximum of 6,412 ft; access is easiest from the S183 between Melito di Porto Salvo and Gambarie. For further information, including walking and hiking itineraries and the state of the slopes, contact the local tourist offices (☞ Visitor Information *in* Basilicata and Calabria A to Z, *below*).

Lodging

Hotels are generously distributed throughout this region. They range from high-class, professionally run complexes with pools, tennis courts, and copious grounds to family-run places where the famous southern hospitality compensates for a lack of amenities. Note that many hotels close during the winter months, especially those by the sea, and hotels in skiing areas will be open in summer and winter but are closed for the rest of the year. Children are welcomed everywhere, and are usually a prominent presence in the region's hotels. Many families holiday in the numerous campsites dotted along both coasts, usually fully equipped and often with bungalows or apartments for rent by the week or less; these can get pretty congested in August. Most campsites and some hotels are closed in the winter months.

Exploring Basilicata and Calabria

The regions of Basilicata and Calabria can be toured as either brief side trips from Campania, Apulia, or Sicily, or as a series of select stops en route to these other regions. The best and fastest way to explore these regions is to stick to the coasts, making inland jaunts from there. West of Taranto, follow the Ionian coast for the classical remains at Metaponto, Locri, and other Greek sights strung along the S106, making brief detours to visit such curiosities as the troglodyte city of Matera and the Norman stronghold of Gerace. South of Salerno, the route along the Tyrrhenian coast takes in a brief stretch of Basilicata—among whose cliffs nestles the smart resort of Maratea—before swooping down into Calabria, where you can divide your time between first-class beaches on the Tropea promontory, or at Scilla, and the high inland ranges of Sila and Aspromonte.

Basilicata and Calabria are well served by transport connections, and drivers and bus and train passengers alike will find no difficulty circulating within these regions. The toll-free A3 autostrada gives a clear run from Salerno all the way down to Reggio di Calabria; the S106 traces the Ionian coast from Taranto to Reggio and is often empty of traffic. Trains also follow these coastal routes, with frequent connections on the Naples–Villa San Giovanni line and fewer trains on the Ionian side. Things get much busier, of course, in mid-summer, when beaches and resorts that can be dead quiet in winter burst into buzzing activity and available hotels can be hard to find.

Numbers in the text correspond to numbers in the margin and on the Basilicata and Calabria map.

Great Itineraries

Your itinerary while exploring Basilicata and Calabria will depend entirely on the direction you are traveling. An ideal route is to come from the north either along the Tyrrhenian coast—from Campania on the S18 or the faster A3 highway—or from Apulia on the S106. If you're traveling in Basilicata, you can cross over to the Tyrrhenian coast without any difficulty on the panoramic S653, passing through the Pollino range and enabling you to make a stop at Maratea. Farther south, you can change coasts at Sibari, Catanzaro, Stilo, and Locri. From the Tyrrhenian coast, head inland at Paola to go through the Sila range to Crotone on the Ionian Sea.

IF YOU HAVE 2 OR 3 DAYS

If heading south from Campania you should consider a night in the beautifully sited resort of **Maratea** ④, a perfect marriage of cliffs and beaches. On your second day, stop for lunch at **Diamante** ⑤, then move on to your next hotel stop at **Tropea** ⑦, close to some of Calabria's best beaches. From here, it's a short run down to the Sicily ferries at Villa San Giovanni. Coming from Apulia, make a stop at the archaeological site at **Metaponto** ① before crossing over to Basilicata's west coast for an overnight at Maratea, then continue south as above. With an extra day at your disposal, you might return to the Ionian coast to see the lovely Byzantine La Cattólica church at **Stilo** ⑮. Spend the night here, then drive the brief distance down the coast to see the classical ruins of **Locri** ⑬ before heading west to the archaeological museum at **Reggio di Calabria** ⑪.

IF YOU HAVE 4 OR 5 DAYS

A greater amount of time should allow you to form a closer acquaintance with Basilicata and Calabria. Having first made a stop at **Metaponto** ① for its classical remains, you might head inland on the fast S407 to wander among the intriguing *sassi*, prehistoric rock dwellings piled one on top of another, of **Matera** ②, spending your first night here. The next day, cross over to the Tyrrhenian side, making a brief diversion to see **Aliano** ③, the minuscule village made famous by Carlo Levi, who was interned here. Spend your second night at **Maratea** ④, then head south via **Diamante** ⑤ and **Pizzo** ⑥. You could hole up for the night in this attractive seaside town; otherwise find a hotel farther along the coast at **Tropea** ⑦. The following day, pause at the eclectic museum at **Palmi** ⑧, lunch by the harborside at **Bagnara Calabra** ⑨, siesta on the beach at **Scilla** ⑩, and check in for the night at **Reggio di Calabria** ⑪, where the archaeological museum is one of southern Italy's best. If you have any time left over, either make an excursion on to the brooding massif of **Aspromonte** ⑫, or skirt south around this range to the Greek site at **Locri** ⑬ and the nearby Norman town of **Gerace** ⑭. Otherwise, it's just a short hop over the Straits to Messina and Sicily.

When to Tour Basilicata and Calabria

The regions of Basilicata and Calabria suffer from intense heat in summer and, away from the coasts, bitter winter cold. If you don't mind sacrificing the Ferragosto celebrations in the middle of the month, avoid August at all costs, since accommodation can be limited and facilities generally strained, but any time on either side would be ideal for touring these regions. Beaches are comparatively empty and the water temperature is comfortable in June, July, and September. Avoid the coastal resorts in winter if you want to find hotels open and anything more than a lonely dog on the streets. The months of January and February

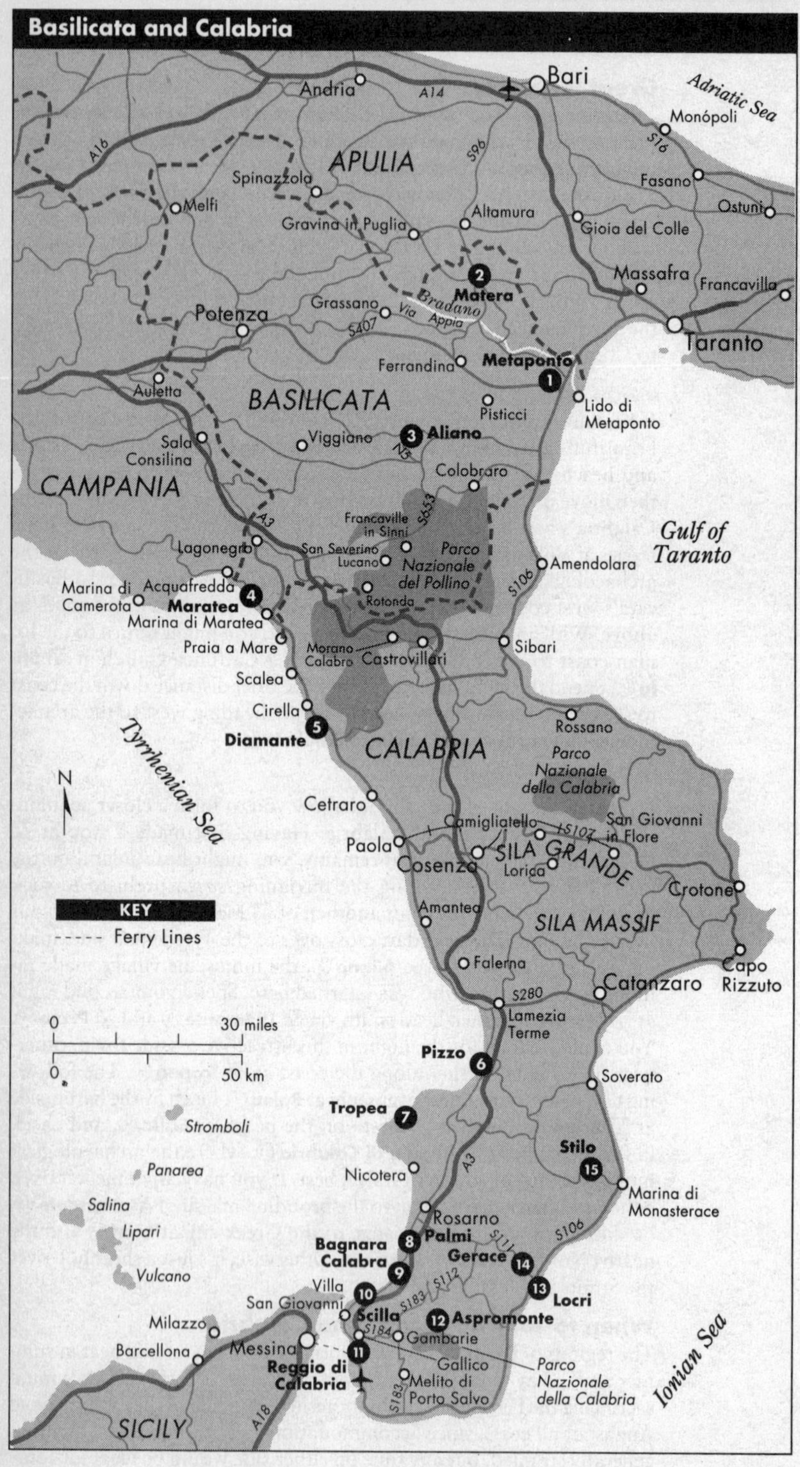
Basilicata and Calabria
Bari
Andria
A14
Adriatic Sea
Monópoli
S16
A16
APULIA
S96
Spinazzola
Fasano
Melfi
Ostuni
Altamura
Gravina in Puglia
Gioia del Colle
Massafra
Francavilla
Matera
Bradano
Grassano
Via Appia
Potenza
S407
Taranto
Ferrandina
Metaponto
Auletta
BASILICATA
Lido di Metaponto
Pisticci
Sala Consilina
Viggiano
Aliano
Colobraro
CAMPANIA
A3
Francaville in Sinni
S653
Gulf of Taranto
Parco Nazionale del Pollino
Lagonegro
San Severino Lucano
Amendolara
Marina di Camerota
Acquafredda
Maratea
Rotonda
S106
Marina di Maratea
Praia a Mare
Morano Calabro
Castrovillari
Sibari
Scalea
Cirella
Rossano
Diamante
Tyrrhenian Sea
CALABRIA
Parco Nazionale della Calabria
N
Cetraro
Camigliatello
S107
San Giovanni in Flore
Paola
Cosenza
SILA GRANDE
Lorica
Crotone
KEY
Ferry Lines
Amantea
SILA MASSIF
Falerna
Capo Rizzuto
Catanzaro
S280
Lamezia Terme
0
30 miles
0
50 km
Pizzo
Soverato
Stromboli
Tropea
Stilo
Panarea
Nicotera
A3
Marina di Monasterace
Salina
Rosarno
Palmi
Lipari
Bagnara Calabra
S111
S106
Gerace
Vulcano
Villa San Giovanni
S112
Locri
S183
Scilla
Aspromonte
Milazzo
S184
Gambarie
Barcellona
Messina
Reggio di Calabria
Gallico
Parco Nazionale della Calabria
Ionian Sea
Melito di Porto Salvo
S183
A18
SICILY

see snow inland, which is great if you want to ski, but can make for dangerous driving conditions. Spring and fall see the forests of Basilicata and Calabria at their best.

BASILICATA

Occupying the instep of Italy's boot, Basilicata has long been one of Italy's poorest regions, memorably described by Carlo Levi in his *Christ Stopped at Eboli,* a book that brought home to the majority of the Italians the depths of deprivation to which this forgotten region was subject (the tale of Levi's internment was poignantly filmed by Francesco Rosi in 1981). Basilicata was not always so desolate, however, for the ancient Greeks. The area formed part of Magna Graecia, the loose collection of colonies founded along the coasts of southern Italy whose wealth and military prowess rivaled the city-states of Greece itself. Metaponto (formerly Metapontion or Metapontum) was one of the most important of these colonies, the remains of which are easily reached along the coastal S106. You could visit the sights and museum en route to Matera, inland from here. The town is built on the side of an impressive ravine that is honeycombed with prehistoric dwellings (sassi), some of them still occupied, forming a separate enclave that contrasts vividly with the attractive Baroque town above.

Metaponto

❶ *48 km (30 mi) southwest of Taranto, 114 mi south of Bari.*

Greek Metapontion was founded around 700 BC by an Achaean colony from the city-states of Sybaris and Kroton (farther down the coast, in what is now Calabria). The great mathematician and philosopher Pythagoras, banished from Kroton, established a school here in about 510 BC, later dying in the city. Punished for its support of the Carthaginian general Hannibal (247–183 BC) after his victory over Rome at Cannae (216 BC), Metapontum, as it was known by the Romans, endured long years of decline—sacked by the slave-rebel Spartacus (died 71 BC) and subsequently ravaged both by malaria and Saracen raids. Most of what remained was used for building elsewhere in the region, but the *zona archeologica* (archaeological zone), which covers a vast area, retains enough interest to merit a visit. You'll need a car: allow an hour or two for the excavations, and about an hour for the museum, which is best seen before the sight, to view the plans and maps and put it all into context. When you've finished here, you might be tempted to take a dip at Lido di Metaponto, where there are sandy, well-equipped beaches.

The modern **Museo Archeologico Nazionale** displays 4th- and 5th-century statuary, ceramics, jewelry, and coins on a rotating basis—sadly, representing only a tiny fraction of the total number of finds until work on a new wing is completed. Perhaps most interesting are examples of coins stamped with ears of corn, symbolizing the cereal production to which Metapontion owed its prosperity. Also noteworthy is the section showing how the study of fingerprints on shards found in the artisans' quarter has revealed new information on the social makeup of the ancient city. Maps and aerial photographs of the site with accounts of the excavations are useful for your visit. The museum lies about 2 km (1 mi) outside Lido di Metaponto (it's well signposted). ✉ *Metaponto Borgo,* ☎ *0835/745327.* 🎫 *4,000 lire.* ⏲ *Apr.–Sept., daily 9–1 and 3:30–10; Oct.–Mar., daily 9–7:30.*

The sprawling and dispersed **zona archeologica** is accessible right opposite the museum, where the **Santuario di Apollo Licio** (Sanctuary of

Apollo Lykaios), a 6th-century BC Doric temple dedicated to Apollo Lykaios stands. Archaeologists have deduced that this structure once boasted 32 columns, though only the foundations and a few capitals and shafts are to be seen today. Nearby, encircled by an expanse of grass, lie the remains of a 4th-century BC **Teatro,** much restored. More compelling is the better-preserved Tempio di Hera (Temple of Hera), commonly known as **Tavole Palatine.** This is outside the area of the ancient city, 2–3 km (1–2 mi) north, where the main S106 crosses the Bradano River. With 15 of its fluted Doric columns surviving, it is the most evocative remnant of this once mighty state. ✉ *Metaponto Borgo,* ☎ *0835/745327.* *Free.* *Daily 9–1 hr before sunset.*

Lodging

$$ **Sacco.** Right in the center of Lido di Metaponto, yet never overwhelmed by the bustle that pervades the area in high summer, the Sacco is the best of the lodgings in the vicinity. It offers comfortably furnished, air-conditioned rooms and a patch of private beach in front. ✉ *Piazzale Lido 7, 75010,* ☎ *0835/741955,* FAX *0835/741975. 76 rooms. Restaurant, bar, beach. AE, MC, V. Closed Oct.–May.*

Matera

❷ *45 km (28 mi) north of Metaponto, 62 km (39 mi) south of Bari.*

Matera is one of southern Italy's most curious towns. On their own the elegant Baroque churches, palazzi, and broad piazzas—filled to bursting during the evening *passeggiata,* when the locals turn out to stroll the streets—would mark Matera out in Basilicata's impoverished landscape, but what really sets this town apart is its **sassi,** rock-hewn dwellings piled chaotically on top of each other and straggling along the sides of a steep ravine. Until relatively recently, these troglodytic abodes presented a Dante-esque vision of squalor and poverty, graphically described in Carlo Levi's *Christ Stopped at Eboli,* but in the 1960s most of them were emptied of their inhabitants, who were largely consigned to the ugly blocks you saw on your way into town. Today, however, having been designated a World Heritage Site in 1993, the area has been cleaned up and is gradually being populated once again. A Strada Panoramica highway leads you safely through this desolate region, which still retains its eerie atmosphere and panoramic views. To get the most out of the whole area, pick up an *itinerario turistico* (tourist itinerary) from the tourist office. For a commentary and access to parts of the sassi you might otherwise miss, you can join a guided tour (☞ Outdoor Activities and Sports, *below*) or hire a guide (☞ Guided Tours *in* Basilicata and Calabria A to Z, *below*).

There are two areas of sassi, the **Sasso Caveoso** and the **Sasso Barisano,** and both can be viewed from vantage points in the upper town. Follow the Strada Panoramica down and feel free to ramble among the strange structures, which, in the words of H. V. Morton in his *A Traveller in Southern Italy,* "resemble the work of termites rather than of man." Among them, you will find several *chiese rupestri,* or rock-hewn churches, some of which have medieval frescoes, notably **Santa Maria de Idris,** perched on the conical Monte Errone in the midst of the sassi, or the 10th-century **Santa Lucia alle Malve** in the so-called Albanian quarter (settled by refugees in the 15th century), which has Byzantine-style frescoes dating from 1250. Hours for both churches may vary, as you have to get the custodian to open them up. ✉ *Sasso Caveoso.* *Gratuity expected.* *Daily 9–1 and 3:30–dusk.*

When you've had your fill of the sassi, take a leisurely stroll around the upper town, starting with the **Duomo,** which occupies a prominent position between the two areas of sassi. Built in the late 13th century, the church has a pungent Apulian-Romanesque flavor; inside, some of the columns originate from Metaponto, and there is a recently recovered fresco, probably painted in the 14th century, showing scenes from the *Last Judgment*. On the Duomo's facade, the figures of Saints Peter and Paul stand on either side of a sculpture of Matera's patron, Madonna della Bruna. Her feast day, the Sagra di Santa Bruna, is celebrated on July 2, when her statue is carried in procession three times around the piazza before being stormed by the onlookers, who are allowed to break up the float and carry off bits as mementos. ✉ *Via Duomo.* ⏲ *Daily 8–noon and 4–7.*

Elsewhere in town, look out for the 17th-century church of **San Francesco d'Assisi,** which contains eight panels of a polyptych by Bartolomeo Vivarini (circa 1432–99), set above the altar. The church's ornate Baroque style was superimposed on two older churches that can be visited through a passage in the third chapel on the left; inside are traces of some 11th-century frescoes. ✉ *Piazza San Francesco.* ⏲ *Daily 8–noon and 4–7.*

Behind San Francesco, the graceful **conservatory** is dedicated to the 18th-century composer Egidio Duni (1708–75), a native of Matera who settled in Paris, where he helped to popularize Neapolitan comic opera among the ancien régime. The building was formerly a convent, then the town hall, before assuming its present role. ✉ *Piazza Sedile.*

Above all, allow some time to view Matera's excellent **Museo Ridola,** housed in the ex-monastery of Santa Chiara. Illustrating the human and geological history of the area, the museum includes an extensive selection of prehistoric and classical finds, notably an array of Bronze Age weaponry and beautifully decorated Greek plates and amphoras. ✉ *Via Ridola 24,* ☎ *0835/311239.* 🎟 *4,000 lire.* ⏲ *Daily 9–7, longer hours in summer. At press time all but two rooms were closed through 2000.*

At the end of Via Ridola, the **Palazzo Lanfranchi** holds a Pinacoteca with an assortment of 17th- and 18th-century paintings, but the real draw here is the Centro Carlo Levi, containing a good cross section of Levi's vivid canvases, as well as the long mural, *Lucania 1961.* ✉ *Piazzetta Pascoli,* ☎ *0835/310468.* 🎟 *Free.* ⏲ *Tues.–Sat. 9–1, Sun. 9–noon.*

Dining and Lodging

$$ ✕ **Il Terrazzino.** The main reason to eat here is for dining alfresco with an unrivaled view over the sassi, which isn't hampered by the airy and attractive space. The food isn't bad either—specialties include *coscia di maiale al forno* (roast pork) and *salsiccia* (sausage), and the spumoni ice cream is homemade. A very reasonable tourist menu is offered. Book ahead to get one of the best tables. ✉ *Vico San Giuseppe 7,* ☎ *0833/332503. AE, DC, MC, V. No dinner Tues.*

$$ ✕ **Trattoria Lucana.** This trattoria is a simple, family-run place in the center of town, where you can enjoy local recipes in a friendly, rustic trattoria environment—try out the *agnello allo spiedo* (lamb on the spit). It's advisable to reserve ahead. ✉ *Via Lucana 48,* ☎ *0835/336117. MC, V.*

$$ 🏨 **Albergo Italia.** Central and stylish, the Italia is an ideal base for staying in Matera, just steps away from the sassi and Museo Ridola. Rooms are smallish and unfussy, with pastel color-coordinated curtains and comforters, and some with balconies. Though the hotel is housed in a well-preserved old building, the restaurant and bar have a cool, modern tone, and there's a wood-fired oven for pizzas. Guest rooms are small but fully equipped. ✉ *Via Ridola 5, 75100,* ☎ *0835/333561,* FAX *0835/330087. 31 rooms. Restaurant, bar. AE, DC, MC, V.*

Outdoor Activities and Sports

WALKING TOUR

The agency **Nuovi Amici dei Sassi** (✉ Piazza Sedile 20, 75100, ☎ 0835/331011) arranges up to four tours of the sassi area a day, charging around 15,000 lire per person for a group of four or more. There are also independent guides who offer their services on the spot, asking from 15,000 lire to 30,000 lire, according to length of tour and the number in your party.

Aliano

3 *127 km (79 mi) southwest of Matera, 102 km (63 mi) southeast of Potenza.*

This remote village off S598 in the center of Basilicata's empty interior was the site of Carlo Levi's internment during 1936 and 1937. After the war, Levi (1902–75) published his account of that time in his classic *Christ Stopped at Eboli,* later filmed by Francesco Rosi. Not significantly different from any of the countless villages scattered over the featureless clay gullies and outcrops stretching out on all sides, Aliano (called Gagliano by Levi) has not altered much, and fans can identify the church, the piazza where the Fascist mayor addressed the impassive peasants, and the timeless views. The house where Levi stayed has been preserved as the **Museo Storico Carlo Levi,** displaying some personal items of Levi's as well as other articles of local interest. It's best to phone first or stop in the Bar Centrale in the center of the village for the custodian. ✉ *Palazzo Caporale,* ☎ *0835/568208.* *Free.* *By appointment.*

Maratea

4 *103 km (64 mi) southwest of Aliano, 217 km (135 mi) south of Naples.*

Anyone encountering Maratea for the first time might be forgiven for assuming they've somehow arrived at the French Riviera. The high, twisty road resembles nothing so much as a Corniche, complete with glimpses of a turquoise sea below. Divided by the craggy rocks into various separate localities—Maratea, Maratea Porto, Maratea Marina—the sequence ends above the main inland village (*paese*) where the ruins of a much older settlement can be seen (Maratea Antica), and, at the summit of the hill, a dramatic, gigantic Christ stands, reminiscent of that of Rio de Janeiro. Most of the area's hotels and restaurants lie in the Fiumicello–Santa Venere neighborhood, a short walk from an enticing arc of beach. But there's no shortage of secluded sandy strips in between the rocky headlands, which can get crowded in August. A summer minibus service connects all of the various points once or twice an hour.

Dining and Lodging

$$ ✕ **Taverna Rovita.** Housed in a former convent with exposed original beams, this restaurant in the heart of the old town offers a menu based on traditional local recipes, though the food here is altogether in a different league from Maratea's other eateries. The *antipasti,* for a start, are various and abundant, and the homemade pasta comes with a selection of rich sauces that change according to the season. Choose a locally caught fish or else a grand and meaty mixed grill for the main course, then succumb to a Lucanian dessert. Reservations are advised. ✉ *Via Rovita, Maratea,* ☎ *0973/876588. AE, DC, MC, V. Closed Tues. and Nov.–Feb.*

$$$$ **Santavenere.** This five-star hotel is worth fasting for, the high tab justified by the opulent architectural style of the public and guest rooms. The best feature, however, is the incredible panorama of rock and sea, as enjoyed by most rooms including the restaurant, with its enormous windows. A tennis court, private beach, and round outdoor

pool fill out the picture. ✉ *Località Fiumicello, 85046,* ☎ *0973/876910,* FAX *0973/877654. 38 rooms. Restaurant, bar, pool, tennis court, beach. AE, DC, MC, V.*

CALABRIA

Italy's southernmost mainland region has seen more than its fair share of oppression, poverty, and natural disaster, but the region of Magna Graecia, mountains, and *mare* (sea) also has more than its share of fantastic scenery and great beaches. The accent here is on the landscape, the sea, and the constantly changing dialogue they create together. Don't expect much in the way of high culture in this most neglected of regions, but be open to the simple pleasures to be enjoyed—the food, the friendliness, the disarming hospitality of the people. But this little-traveled region also boasts some superb sights worth going out of your way for, from the vividly colored murals of Diamante to the ruins of Magna Graecia at Locri. The drive on the southbound autostrada alone is a breathtaking experience, the more so as you approach Sicily, whose image is glimpsed tantalizingly as the road dips in and out of long tunnels through the mountain. This is the road you should take for the big picture—but don't forget to stop awhile to get a closer view of this fascinating land.

Diamante

5 *51 km (32 mi) south of Maratea, 225 km (140 mi) south of Naples.*

One of the most fashionable of the string of small resorts lining Calabria's north Tyrrhenian coast, Diamante makes a good stop for its whitewashed maze of narrow alleys, brightly adorned with a startling variety of large-scale murals. The work of various local artists, the murals depict a range of subjects and give a sense of wandering through a huge open-air art gallery. Flanking the broad seaside promenade are sparkling beaches to the north and south.

Dining and Lodging

$$ ✕ **Taverna del Pescatore.** This is one of a pair of good, moderately priced fish restaurants down by the seafront at Diamante's Spiaggia Piccola. Amid the spartan, bright, and modern interior, a more relaxed atmosphere pervades. Phone first to secure a table outside. Fish, naturally, predominates, whatever's hauled in, cooked in a variety of ways. ✉ *Via Calvario,* ☎ *0985/81482. MC, V. Closed Tues. Oct.–May.*

$$$–$$$$ 🏨 **Grand Hotel San Michele.** A survivor from a vanishing age of hotels, the San Michele occupies a belle-epoque-style, cliff-top ex-hunting lodge near the village of Cetraro, 20 km (12 mi) south of Diamante. Mingling Mediterranean charm with old-style elegance, this beautifully proportioned building is set within extensive grounds that include semitropical gardens and a small golf course. An elevator takes you down to the private beach at the base of the cliff. The only possible downside is the hotel's isolation—you need a car to do anything, if you can ever be lured away from this palatial paradise. ✉ *Località Bosco, 87022 Cetraro,* ☎ *0982/91012,* FAX *0982/91430. 73 rooms. Restaurant, bar, tennis court, 9-hole golf course, beach. AE, MC, V. Closed Nov.*

Pizzo

6 *148 km (92 mi) south of Diamante, 107 km (66) mi north of Reggio di Calabria.*

Overlooking the coast and fishing port, Pizzo has a good selection of seafood restaurants and a small cliff-top Aragonese castle near the center of town. Here, the French general Joachim Murat (1767–1815) was imprisoned, tried, and shot in October, 1815, after a bungled attempt to rouse the people against the Bourbons and reclaim the throne of Naples given to him by his brother-in-law Napoléon.

A couple of kilometers north of the castle, a flight of steps leads down to the beach and to the **Chiesetta di Piedigrotta,** a 17th century church hewn out of rock by the shipwrecked Neapolitan sailors, in thanks for their rescue, and filled with statues depicting Biblical figures. These were added to by a local father-and-son team at the beginning of this century, and in 1969 another scion of the family contributed some of his own, including a bizarre ensemble showing Fidel Castro kneeling before Pope John XXIII (1881–1963) and President Kennedy (1917–63). Before you leave Pizzo, make sure you sample the renowned gelato *di Pizzo,* a rich, creamy delight available in many flavors at any of the outdoor bars in the central Piazza della Repubblica. ✉ *Via Nazionale.* ⏲ *Daily 9–1 and 3–7:30.*

Lodging

$$ **Hotel Murat.** Here's a good, central choice of accommodation should you decide to overnight in Pizzo. Right in the town's main square, a stone's throw from the castle, the Murat has comfortable rooms with period trappings. ✉ *Piazza della Repubblica 41, 88026,* ☎ *0963/534201,* FAX *0963/534469. 12 rooms. Restaurant, bar. MC, V.*

Tropea

7 *28 km (17 mi) southwest of Pizzo, 140 km (87 mi) north of Reggio di Calabria.*

Ringed by cliffs and wonderful sandy beaches, the Tropea promontory is still undiscovered by the big tour operators. The main town, Tropea, easily wins the contest for prettiest town on Calabria's Tyrrhenian coast, its old palazzi built in simple golden stone on an elevation above the sea. On a clear day, the seaward views extend to embrace Stromboli's cone and perhaps some of the other Aeolians, too—the islands can be visited by motorboats, departing daily from Tropea in summer. Beach addicts will not be disappointed by the choice of magnificent sandy bays within easy reach of here—some of the best are south at Capo Vaticano and north at Briatico—and there are numerous hotels and restaurants in town to satisfy every taste.

Among Tropea's harmonious warren of lanes, seek out the old Norman **Cattedrale,** whose interior displays a couple of unexploded U.S. bombs from World War II, with a grateful prayer to the Madonna attached to each. ✉ *Piazza Sedile.* ⏲ *Daily 7–noon and 4–6.*

From the belvedere at the bottom of the main square, Piazza Ercole, the church and Benedictine monastery of **Santa Maria della Isola** glistens on a rocky promontory above an aquamarine sea. Stroll out to visit the church on a path lined with fishermen's caves. Of Basilian origins, the church was remodeled in the Gothic style, then given another face-lift after an earthquake in 1905. The interior has an 18th-century nativity and some fragments of medieval tombs. ✉ *Santa Maria della Isola.* ⏲ *Daily 7–noon and 4–7.*

Dining and Lodging

$$$ ✕ **Pimm's.** Centrally located in Tropea's historic center, this offers the town's best dining experience. Fish is top menu choice, with such specialties as pasta with sea urchins, smoked swordfish, and stuffed squid also to be savored. The splendiferous sea views are an extra enticement. ✉ *Largo Migliarese 2,* ☎ *0963/666105. AE, DC, MC, V. Oct.–Mar., closed Mon.*

$$ **Torre Ruffa.** Near the beach 6 km (4 mi) south of Tropea, this whitewashed hotel has everything you need for a quiet sojourn away from the madding crowds. Cane furniture, banana trees, and bright wisteria help to create a luxurious enclave. ✉ *Località Torre Ruffa 1, 88036 Ricadi,* ☎ *0963/663006,* FAX *0963/663942. 32 rooms. Restaurant, bar, tennis court, beach. AE, MC, V.*

Palmi

8 *60 km (37 mi) south of Tropea, 64 km (38 mi) north of Reggio di Calabria.*

The small town of Palmi is worth a stop for its excellent **Casa della Cultura Leonida Repaci** museum complex. Named after a local writer and artist, the wide-ranging collection includes an archaeological section, displaying pottery and other items dredged up from the sea bed; paintings by old masters, including work by Tintoretto (circa 1518–94) and Il Guercino (1591–1666); a gallery of modern art and sculpture, mainly by southern Italian artists such as Renato Guttuso but also by Amedeo Modigliani (1884–1920), Giorgio De Chirico, (1888–1978), and Carlo Levi; a section devoted to local composer Francesco Cilea (1866–1950); and Calabria's best collection of folklore items. The museum is a little way above the town, close to the S18. ✉ *Via San Giorgio, Palmi,* ☎ *0966/262250.* *3,000 lire.* ⏲ *Tues. and Thurs.–Sun. 8–2, Mon. and Wed. 8–2 and 3–6.*

Bagnara Calabra

9 *11 km (7 mi) south of Palmi, 34 km (21 mi) north of Reggio di Calabria.*

Fishing is in the blood of the local villagers, particularly when in pursuit of swordfish, for which the town has long enjoyed a wide fame. The casual trattorias here make this a great lunch stop.

Dining

$$ ✕ **Taverna Kerkira.** Centrally located on Bagnara's main street, this restaurant owes its name to the chef, who hails from Corfu. Accordingly, you'll see such Greek dishes as moussaka slipped in among the local choices on the menu, though in season (April–September) you can be sure of finding *pescespada,* or swordfish, prepared in a variety of ways. ✉ *Corso Vittorio Emanuele 217,* ☎ *0966/372260. AE, MC, V. Closed Mon. and Tues.*

Scilla

10 *10 km (6 mi) south of Bagnara Calabra, 42 km (26 mi) north of Reggio di Calabria.*

According to Homer's *Odyssey,* ancient Scylla was where one of two monsters resided (possibly whirlpools), dreaded by passing sailors. The other was Charybdis, modern-day Cariddi, on the Messina side of the Straits. Today, nothing in Scilla looks remotely threatening, especially in summer, when the broad sandy beach is the focus for sunning and swimming by day, and carousing by night. At the northern end of the bay, a castle rises loftily on a rocky spur—a grand vantage point for watching the tall-masted *felucche* swordfish boats patrolling the Straits. Most of these are based in Bagnara Calabra, to the north.

Reggio di Calabria

11 *22 km (14 mi) south of Scilla, 499 km (311 mi) south of Naples.*

Reggio di Calabria, the city on Italy's toe tip, was laid low by the same catastophic earthquake that struck Messina in 1908. The city has a rundown, nondescript appearance, though it does possess one of southern Italy's most important archaeological museums, the **Museo Nazionale della Magna Grecia.** Prize exhibits here are two statues, known as the Bronzi di Riace, found by accident by an amateur deep-sea diver off Calabria's Ionian coast in 1972. Black of color and vaunting physiques that gym enthusiasts would die for, the pair are thought to date from the 5th century BC and have been attributed to Phidias and Polyclites, possibly destined for the temple at Delphi when the vessel that carried them was shipwrecked. Coins and votive tablets are among the numerous other treasures from Magna Graecia contained in the museum, and there are also prehistoric remnants, Byzantine items, and some fine medieval artwork. ✉ *Piazza de Nava, Corso Garibaldi,* ☎ *0965/812255.* *8,000 lire.* ⏲ *Daily 9–6:30. Closed 1st and 3rd Mon. of the month.*

Lodging

$$ **Diana.** This moderately priced hotel lies just off Reggio's main Corso Garibaldi. There's not much in the way of imaginative decor, but the spacious guest rooms are perfectly adequate. The absence of a restaurant is no great problem in Reggio, which has a plethora of dining possibilities. ✉ *Via Vitrioli 12, 89100,* ☎ FAX *0965/891522. 12 rooms. Bar. No credit cards.*

Aspromonte

12 *Gambarie: 45 km (28 mi) northeast of Reggio di Calabria.*

Rising to the east of Reggio di Calabria, Aspromonte is the name of the sprawling massif that dominates mainland Italy's southern tip. Long the haunt of brigands and still the refuge of modern-day kidnappers—for whom industrialists, not tourists, are the usual targets—this thickly forested range reaches a height of nearly 6,560 ft and is popular with skiers in winter. In summer, it makes a cool respite from the heat of the coast, offering endless opportunities for hiking and shady picnics. On a clear day, you can see right across to Mt. Etna, 60 km (40 mi) south. Ask at Reggio's tourist office (☞ Visitor Information *in* Basilicata and Calabria, *below*) for walking itineraries. To get here going north from Reggio, turn inland off the autostrada or coast road at Gallico, 12 km (7 mi) north of town; driving east from Reggio on S184, turn left onto the S183 at Melito di Porto Salvo.

En Route The fast S106 hugs Calabria's Ionian coast, leading south out of Reggio di Calabria and curving around Aspromonte to your left. Having rounded Capo Spartivento, the road proceeds north. If you don't want to continue farther northward, turn left on to the S112dir, shortly before Bovalino and 14 km (9 mi) before reaching Locri. This winding mountain road takes you round the rugged northern slopes of Aspromonte, a highly scenic route but not one recommended for anyone who suffers from car sickness.

Locri

13 *98 km (61 mi) east of Reggio di Calabria.*

Just south of the seaside town of Locri, visit the excavations of **Locri Epizefiri,** where one of the most important of Magna Graecia's city-states stood. Founded around the 7th century BC, Locris became a regional power when—apparently assisted by Castor and Pollux—10,000

Locrians defeated a 130,000-strong army from Kroton on the banks of the Sagra River, 25 km (16 mi) north. Founding colonies and gathering fame in the spheres of horse rearing and music, Locri was responsible for the first written code of law throughout the Hellenic world. The walls of the city, parts of which are still visible, measured some 8 km (5 mi) in circumference, and the archaeological site within is spread over a wide area among farms and orchards. The best-preserved remains are a 5th-century BC Ionic temple, a Roman necropolis, and a Graeco-Roman theater. There's also an on-site museum, though you will have seen some of the best finds at Reggio's Museo Nazionale (☞ *above*). *Site:* 🎫 *Free.* ⏲ *Daily 9–1 hr before sunset. Museum:* 🎫 *4,000 lire.* ⏲ *Daily 9–7. Closed 1st and 3rd Mon. of month.*

Gerace

⓮ *12 km (7 mi) west of Locri, 149 km (93 mi) east of Reggio di Calabria.*

When the Saracens plundered Locri in the 7th century AD (☞ *above*), the survivors fled inland to found Gerace, on an impregnable site which was later occupied and strengthened by the Normans. It's worth the short detour to visit this redoubt, its ruined castle tottering precariously on a jagged outcrop. The **Duomo** is in better shape, founded in 1045 by Robert Guiscard (circa 1015–85), enlarged by Frederick II (1194–1250) two centuries later, and today still the biggest church in Calabria. Its simple, well-preserved interior has 20 columns of granite and marble, each different, and the tenth on the right in verd antique changes tone according to the weather. ✉ *Piazza Vittorio Emanuele.* ⏲ *Apr.–Sept., daily 9:30–8:30; Oct.–Mar., daily 9:30–1:30 and 3–7.*

Stilo

⓯ *38 km (24 mi) north of Locri, 138 km (86 mi) northeast of Reggio di Calabria.*

Grandly positioned on the side of the rugged Monte Consolino, the village of Stilo is famous on two accounts. As the birthplace and home of the philosopher Tommaso Campanella (1568–1639), whose magnum opus was the socialistic *La Città del Sole* (The City of the Sun, 1602)—for which he spent 26 years as prisoner of the Spanish Inquisition—Stilo would have already earned a name for itself, but the village also has a more tangible reason to visit, the tiny 10th-century Byzantine temple, **La Cattólica.** This tiled and turreted building, standing on a ledge above the town, is reckoned to be the best-preserved monument of its kind. ✉ *Via Cattolica.* 🎫 *Free (donation).* ⏲ *Easter–Sept., daily 8–8; Oct.–Easter, daily 7–7.*

Lodging

$$ 🏨 **San Giorgio.** Tucked away off Stilo's main Via Campanella, this hotel is housed in a 17th-century cardinal's palace and decked out in period style, with elegantly furnished guest rooms. There are exhilarating views seaward from the garden. Half- or full-board only is accepted—there's nowhere else in town to eat anyway. ✉ *Via Citarelli 8, 89049,* ☎ FAX *0964/775047. 15 rooms. Restaurant, bar, pool. Closed Oct.–mid-Apr. MC, V. MAP, FAP.*

En Route From Stilo, you can take the S110 inland—a long, twisty road that takes you through the high Serra region, covered with a thick mantle of chestnut forest. There are terrific views to be enjoyed over the Ionian coast, and you can continue across the peninsula to Calabria's Tyrrhenian littoral, emerging at Pizzo. The total road distance between Stilo and Pizzo is around 97 km (60 mi).

BASILICATA AND CALABRIA A TO Z

Arriving and Departing

By Boat

Hydrofoils and fast ferries ply the Straits of Messina once or twice hourly, day and night. Crossings take about 20 minutes. In Reggio contact **SNAV** (☎ 0965/29568), **FS** (☎ 0965/863754), and **Meridiano Ferries** (☎ 0347/9100118).

By Bus

Frequent bus connections link Matera with Bari; the main company is **Ferrovie Appulo-Lucane** (☎ 0835/332861). In Calabria, various bus companies make the north–south run with stops along both coasts. In Reggio di Calabria, contact **Lirosi** (☎ 0965/575552) for buses to Naples and Rome.

By Car

Metaponto is a major road and rail junction for routes along the coast and inland. To get to Metaponto by car from Apulia's Taranto, take the S106 southwest for 45 km (28 mi). From Apulia's Bari, take the S96 south for 44 km (28 mi) to Altamura, then the S99 south 19 km (12 mi) to Matera. The A3 Autostrada del Sole runs between Salerno and Reggio di Calabria, taking an inland route as far as Falerna, then tracking the Tyrrhenian coast south of here (excepting the bulge of the Tropea promontory). Take the S18 for coastal destinations on the Tyrrhenian side, S106 for the Ionian. Drivers crossing the Straits of Messina can do so from Villa San Giovanni or Reggio.

By Plane

Twenty-seven kilometers (17 mi) north of Pizzo, **Aeroporto di Lamezia** (☎ 0968/53083 or 0968/51205) caters to international charters in summer and internal flights year-round, with connections to Milan, Bologna, and Rome. Reggio di Calabria's **Aeroporto dello Stretto** (☎ 0965/642722) handles internal flights only, with four departures daily to Rome, three to Milan.

By Train

The main **FS** (Italian State Railways) line from Taranto stops in Metaponto, from which there are regular departures to Matera on **Ferrovie Appulo-Lucane** (FAL) trains. FAL also links Matera to Bari. South of Metaponto, FS trains run into Calabria, either following the Ionian coast as far as Reggio di Calabria, or swerving inland to Cosenza and the Tyrrhenian coast at Paola. The main north–south FS line has hourly services from Reggio north to Palmi, Pizzo, Diamante, and Maratea, continuing on as far as Salerno, Naples, and Rome. There are nine daily Intercity or Eurocity trains linking Reggio di Calabria with Naples (4–5 hours) and Rome (6–7 hours). All trains, which are run by FS, also stop at Villa San Giovanni (for connections to Sicily), a 20-minute ride from Reggio. Two fast FS trains daily run between Metaponto and Naples (about 4 hours) and Rome (5½–6 hours), and three others connect Metaponto and Salerno (about 3½ hours), from which there are frequent connections to Naples and Rome. Two trains daily go as far as Milan, fastest time 13¼ hr. Call ☎ 147/888088 for toll-free information for all FS services.

Getting Around

By Bus

Buses belonging to **Ferrovie Appulo-Lucane** (☎ 0835/332861) link Metaponto with Matera. In Calabria, **Ferrovie della Calabria** (☎ 0984/

36851) operate many of the local services. From Reggio di Calabria, **Salzone** (☎ 0965/751586) runs to Scilla, and **Federico** (☎ 0965/590212) to Locri and Stilo.

By Car

To drive from Basilicata's Metaponto to Matera, take the S175 northwest for 45 km (28 mi). The A3 autostrada runs up Calabria's Tyrrhenian (western) coast with exits at Scilla, Palmi, Rosarno (for Tropea), and Pizzo. The S106 along Calabria's Ionian (eastern) coast is uncongested and fast.

By Train

Matera is on the local **Ferrovie Appulo-Lucane** (FAL) rail line, linked to Altamura in Apulia (for connections to Bari) and to Ferrandina (for connections to Metaponto or Potenza). Main **FS** (Italian State Railways) services run along both coasts but can be crowded along the Tyrrhenian. Call ☎ 147/888088 for toll-free information on times and frequencies.

Contacts and Resources

Car Rentals

Cars can be rented at airports and downtown locations in Matera and Reggio di Calabria, also from Cosenza and Lamezia airport.

MATERA

Avis (✉ Vico XX Settembre 8, ☎ 0835/336632). **Damasco** (✉ Vico XX Settembre 12, ☎ 0835/334604).

REGGIO DI CALABRIA

Avis (✉ Aeroporto dello Stretto, ☎ 0965/643023). **Hertz** (✉ Aeroporto dello Stretto, ☎ 0965/643093; ✉ Via Florio 17, ☎ 0965/332222). **Maggiore-Budget** (✉ Aeroporto dello Stretto, ☎ 0965/643148).

Emergencies

Police, Ambulance, Fire (☎ 113). **Hospital** (☎ 0965/8501 Reggio di Calabria; 0835/2431 Matera).

Guided Tours

Foderaro (✉ Corso Mazzini 185, 88100 Catanzaro, ☎ 0961/726006) organizes bus tours of Reggio di Calabria, Scilla, Pizzo, Locri, and Gerace and boat tours to the Aeolian Islands. The tourist office recommends touring Matera with an official guide agency, preferably the English-language **Itinera** (✉ Via La Martella 43, Matera, ☎ 0835/334761 or 0335/8185461), which always has access to sights.

Late-Night Pharmacies

In Reggio di Calabria, **Curia** (✉ Corso Garibaldi 455, ☎ 0965/332332) and **Caridi** (✉ Corso Garibaldi 437, ☎ 0965/24013) are open at night. Elsewhere, late-night pharmacies are open on a rotating basis; information on current schedules is pinned up on any pharmacy door.

Travel Agency

Simonetta (✉ Corso Garibaldi 521, Reggio di Calabria, ☎ 0965/331444).

Visitor Information

Tourist offices (✉ Via de Viti de Marco 9, off Via Roma, 75100, Matera, ☎ 0835/333541, open Monday–Saturday 8–2, and Monday and Thursday 3:30–6; ✉ Piazza della Repubblica, 88026 Pizzo, ☎ 0963/531310; ✉ Corso Garibaldi 329, 89100, Reggio di Calabria, ☎ 0965/892012; ✉ Piazza Ercole, 88038 Tropea, ☎ 0963/61475).

15 SICILY

On this fabled island, you can ski down a snow-muffled volcano, wander through palm and orange groves, and swim within sight of majestic ruins. It has a stubborn personality: cynical yet passionate, languorous yet industrious. But the ethereal subtleties of this seemingly far-off kingdom reveal themselves in panoramic Taormina, the Valley of the Temples, and the unforgettable rose-tinted moon rising over Mt. Etna.

Updated by Robert Andrews

ARRIVING IN SICILY for the first time, you may be surprised to see so many people with blond hair and blue eyes and to learn that two of the most popular boys' names are Ruggero (Roger) and Guglielmo (William), but that is what Sicily is all about. For 2,000 years it has been an island where unexpected contrasts somehow come together peacefully. Lying in a strategic position between Europe and Africa, Sicily at one time hosted two of the most advanced and enlightened capitals of Europe—a Greek one in Siracusa and an Arab-Norman one in Palermo. (The Normans are responsible for the blond-haired Rogers and blue-eyed Williams.) Sicily was one of the great melting pots of the ancient world and home to every great civilization that existed in the Mediterranean: Greek and Roman; then Arab and Norman; and, finally, French, Spanish, and Italian. Something of all of these peoples was absorbed into the island's artistic heritage, a rich tapestry of art and architecture that includes massive Romanesque cathedrals, two of the best-preserved Greek temples in the world, Roman amphitheaters, and delightful Baroque palaces and churches.

Modern Sicily is still a land of surprising contrasts. The traditional graciousness and nobility of the Sicilian people exist side by side with the atrocities and destructive influences of the Mafia, although recent events suggest that the Mafia's grip on the island is being slowly loosened. Alongside some of the most exquisite architecture in the world are the shabby products of some of the worst speculation imaginable. In recent years, Sicily, like much of the Mediterranean coast, has experienced a boom in tourism and a surge in condominium development that has only now begun to be checked. The chic boutiques purveying lace and linen in jet-set resort towns like Taormina give no clue to the poverty in which their wares are produced.

In Homer's *Odyssey,* Sicily represented the unknown end of the world, yet the region eventually became the center of the known world under the Normans, who recognized a paradise in its deep blue skies and temperate climate, its lush vegetation, and rich marine life. Much of this paradise does still exist today. Add to it Sicily's unique cuisine—another harmony of elements—which mingles Arab and Greek spices with Spanish and French dishes, using some of the world's tastiest seafood, and you can understand why those who arrived here were often reluctant to leave.

You do not have to be paranoid about safety in Sicily, but you do have to be careful: do not flaunt jewelry, and keep your handbag securely strapped across your chest. Leaving valuables visible in your car while you go sightseeing is inviting trouble. Be careful; then enjoy the company of the Sicilians. You will find them to be friendly and often willing to go out of their way to help tourists. It is not uncommon in small towns for visitors to receive invitations to a local's house for dinner. It doesn't matter if you don't speak Italian or speak only a little: they aren't usually offended if your pronunciation isn't perfect. One of the reasons for this, no doubt, is the fact that many Sicilians or their close relatives have themselves been strangers in foreign lands, and empathy goes a long way.

Pleasures and Pastimes

Beaches

There is a surfeit of beaches in Sicily, but many of them are too rocky, too crowded, or too dirty to be enjoyed for long. Among the exceptions are Mondello, near Palermo, a popular sandy beach on a tiny peninsula jutting out into the Mediterranean; Sant'Alessio and Santa Teresa, north of Taormina (the beaches just below Taormina itself are disappointing); and Capo San Vito, on the northern coast, near Erice, a sandy beach on a promontory overlooking a bay in the Gulf of Castellammare.

Camping

Sicily has excellent camping facilities on both the main island and its satellite islands. The two best are El Bahira, in San Vito Lo Capo, and Bazia, in Furnari Marina, west of Milazzo. Both have restaurants and showers, as well as swimming pools, tennis courts, and discos.

Dining

Sicilian cooking reflects the various Mediterranean influences that have left their mark on the island. Fish, vegetables, and grains are used in imaginative combinations, sometimes served with Italian pastas or Arab or North African ingredients, such as couscous. Sweet and sour tastes are deftly mingled, and cooks have distinctive touches, so that *caponata* (an antipasto of eggplant, capers, olives, and, in eastern Sicily, peppers) is different at every restaurant.

Sicily has always been one of Italy's poorest areas, so meat is not the centerpiece on menus. It is usually prepared *alla brace* (skewered) or in *falso magro* (a thin slice of meat rolled around sausage, onion, bacon, bits of egg, and cheese). In Sicily, naturally, you'll enjoy the freshest seafood in all of Italy, and you'll also find the most variety. *Tonno* (tuna) is a staple in many coastal areas, and *pesce spada* (swordfish) is equally common, if more expensive. Try *ricci* (sea urchins), a specialty of Mondello, near Palermo. Fish sauces are often tossed on pasta: pasta *con le sarde* is made with fresh sardines, olive oil, anchovies, raisins, and pine nuts, and has the distinctive flavor of wild fennel. In Catania, spaghetti *alla Norma,* named for the heroine in the opera by local composer Vincenzo Bellini, is prepared with a sauce of tomato and fried eggplant.

Desserts from Sicily are famous. The traditional Easter cake is the *cassata siciliana,* a rich sponge cake with candied fruit, marzipan, and icing. From behind bakery windows and glass cases all over beam tiny marzipan sweets, fashioned into bright-color apples, cherries, corncobs, hamburgers, and more. Local gelato is excellent and is usually homemade, as are brilliant *granite* (granitas) in flavors such as lemon. Gooey cakes and very sweet desserts such as chestnut ice cream covered with hot zabaglione provide a sugar fix. The sweet dessert wine, Marsala, is Sicily's most famous, but there is a range of other local wines, from the dark red Faro to the sparkling dry Regaleali, excellent with fish.

Kids' Stuff

Almost every major city in Sicily has a theater giving performances of the world-famous Sicilian *pupi* (marionettes). The most popular are in Palermo, Acireale, and Taormina. Stories center on heroes from the Norman fables, distressed damsels, and Saracen invaders. Even if you can't understand Italian, the action is fast and furious, so it's easy to figure out what's going on. Palermo has an international museum dedicated to these and other types of marionettes. If you are in Sicily at Carnival time (the week before Ash Wednesday, about 45 days before Easter), Acireale has one of Italy's best celebrations, when dozens of colorful torch-lit floats, papier-mâché characters aboard, are pulled through the streets by costumed revelers.

Lodging

Though Sicily is Italy's largest region, it has some of the most remote countryside and only a limited number of good-quality hotels. The major cities and resorts of Palermo, Taormina, and Agrigento are the only spots with a real range of accommodations. There are, of course, some superb establishments, such as converted villas with sea views and well-equipped modern hotels, but it is best not to expect to come across some enchanting oasis in the middle of nowhere. If you want to get away from the major centers, make reservations well in advance.

Hotels in the $$$$ category provide comfort and services to match those in other Italian regions; they are usually the older, more established hotels. In the $$–$$$ range, you'll find newer hotels built to cater to the increased tourist trade of the past 20 years. Chains, such as Jolly Hotels, are predictable but reliable. Inexpensive establishments are usually family-run and offer a basic level of comfort: although the bathroom will be clean, it will probably also be down the hall.

Scuba Diving

The island of Ustica, north of Palermo, is an international center for scuba diving and snorkeling. Its rugged coast is dotted with grottoes that are washed by crystal-clear waters and filled with an incredible variety of interesting marine life. In July Ustica hosts an International Meeting of Marine Fishing that attracts sportsmen as well as marine biologists from all over the world.

Shopping

Sicily is one of the leaders in the Italian ceramics industry, with important factories at Caltagirone, in the interior, and Santo Stefano di Camastra, along the northern coast between Messina and Cefalù. Colorful Sicilian folk pottery can still be bought at bargain prices. Place mats, tablecloths, napkins, and clothing decorated with fine petit point are good buys in Cefalù, Taormina, and Erice, but they are not cheap. Make sure that any linen you buy is produced in Sicily and not on another continent. Collectors have been combing Sicily for years for pieces of the colorful *carretti siciliani* (Sicilian carts). Before the automobile, these were the major form of transportation in Sicily, and they were decorated in bright primary colors and in primitive styles, with scenes from the Norman troubadour tales. The axles of these carts were ornamented with open filigree work, which was also brightly painted.

Skiing

Skiing is fast becoming a popular sport in Sicily. Ski areas can be found on the slopes on the north side of Mt. Etna. The most popular is at Linguaglossa, in a magnificent pine forest about 45 km (27 mi) from Catania. The other area for skiing in Sicily is in the Le Madonie mountains, south of Cefalù.

Exploring Sicily

Sicily is about 180 km (112 mi) north to south and 270 km (168 mi) across. Sicily is so dense with places of interest that not even a week is sufficient to explore the island in depth, though with a car at your disposal you will be able to cover all the most important sights. The best way to visit it is to travel counterclockwise along the coast by car, bus, or train, making occasional detours inland. You needn't visit all seven of the Isole Eolie individually. In summer, hydrofoils and ferries connect all seven, so one or two of them can be admired from the sea. Lipari is the most equipped of the islands for tourism, though all of the islands except Stromboli offer some kind of accommodation, from small, family-run guest houses to beds in private homes.

Numbers in the text correspond to numbers in the margin and on the Sicily, Palermo, Agrigento, and Siracusa maps.

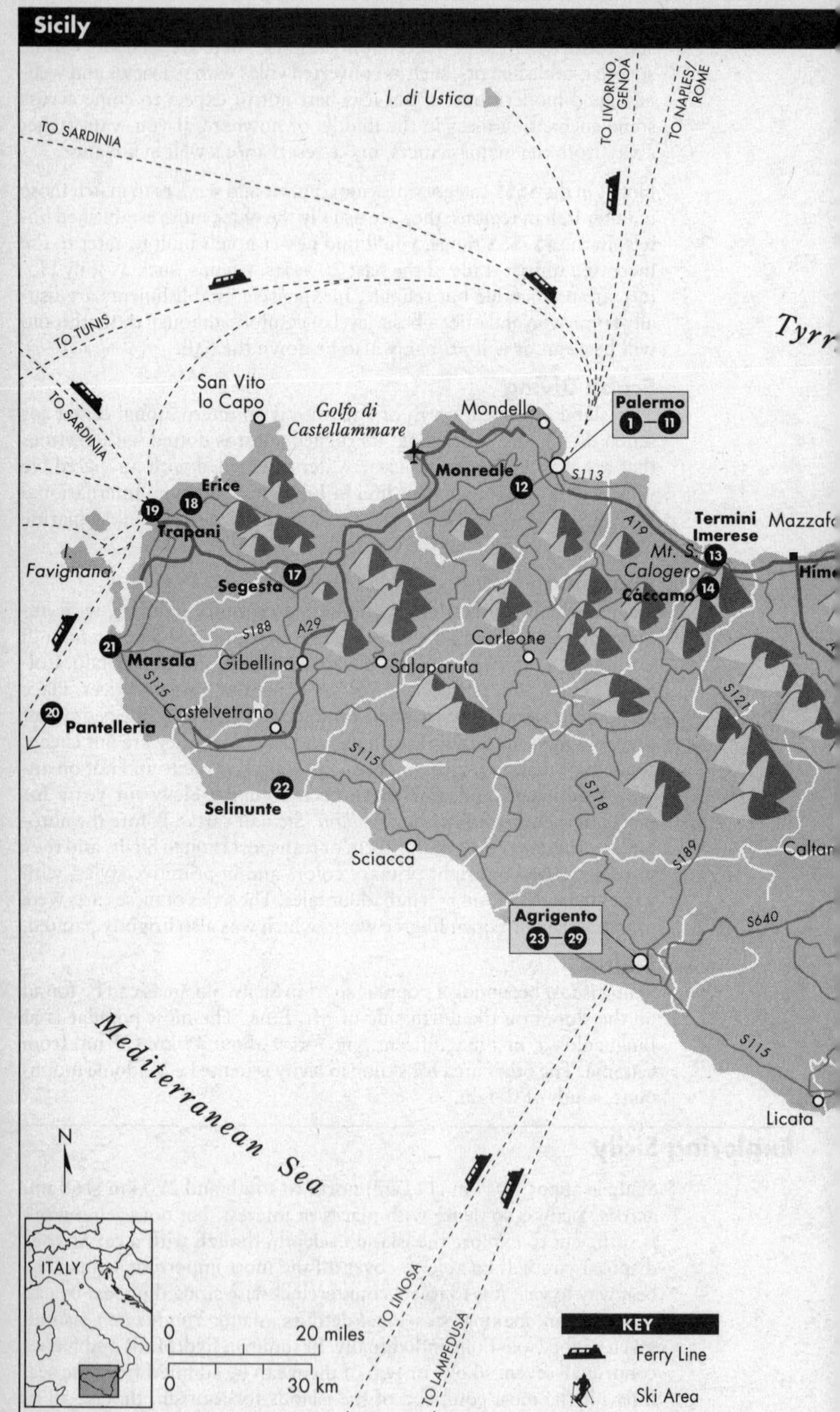
Sicily
I. di Ustica
TO LIVORNO, GENOA
TO NAPLES/ ROME
TO SARDINIA
TO TUNIS
TO SARDINIA
San Vito lo Capo
Golfo di Castellammare
Mondello
Palermo 1—11
Monreale 12
S113
Erice 18
19
Trapani
I. Favignana
Segesta 17
Termini Imerese 13
Mazzafa
Mt. S. Calogero
Càccamo 14
A19
Tyrr
S188
A29
21 Marsala
Gibellina
Salaparuta
Corleone
S115
20 Pantelleria
Castelvetrano
S115
S121
22 Selinunte
S118
Sciacca
S189
Caltan
Agrigento 23—29
S640
S115
Licata
Mediterranean Sea
N
ITALY
0 20 miles
0 30 km
TO LINOSA
TO LAMPEDUSA
KEY
Ferry Line
Ski Area

TO NAPLES
Stromboli 60
Panarea 59
Alicudi 61
Filicudi 62
Salina 58
ISOLE EOLIE
56 Lipari
57 Vulcano
TO NAPLES
Golfo di Gióia
enian Sea
Mortelle
Milazzo
Capo d'Orlando
S113
Patti
A20
Messina 55
Reggio di Calabria
Cefalù
15 Caldura
Santo Stefano di Camastra
16
S113
S117
A18
Castelmola
54
Taormina
Bronte
Mt. Etna 53
Riposto
Giarre
Adrano
Biancavilla
Acireale
Paterno
46
Enna
etta
S192
A19
Catania 52
Golfo di Catania
Ionian Sea
S288
47 Piazza Armerina
48 Casale
S114
49
Caltagirone
S124
Palazzolo Acreide
50
Euryalus
Gela
S124
Comiso
Golfo di Gela
Ragusa
Siracusa
30—45
Noto
51
Avola
Modica
Golfo di Noto
S115
Capo Passero
TO MALTA

Great Itineraries

In nine days, you can do a thorough loop around the island, which starts in Palermo, moves west and south to the stunning Greek cities of Selinunte and Agrigento, then dips inland and continues southeast to Siracusa, and finally heads north to picturesque Taormina and the Isole Eolie. Smaller explorations concentrated around Palermo and environs can be done in three or five days.

IF YOU HAVE 3 DAYS

A three-day sojourn on the island should not necessitate renting a car if you base yourself in Sicily's capital, **Palermo** ①–⑪. In this hub of Norman Sicily, the highlights include the **Palazzo dei Normanni** ① and the **Museo Archeologico Regionale** ⑩, as well as a handful of churches. Head out to **Monreale** ⑫ to admire the splendid cathedral, and compare it with the slightly earlier mosaic-laden monument at **Cefalù** ⑮. Spend your last day exploring this seaside resort.

IF YOU HAVE 5 DAYS

A longer time on the island will allow you to add choice excursions to the three-day itinerary. From **Cefalù** ⑮ proceed westward along the northwestern coast to panoramic **Erice** ⑱, a good spot to overnight. Just up the road is **Trapani** ⑲, a port-city that has little to offer the visitor. Heading east through the interior, drop in on the imposing half-finished temple of **Segesta** ⑰, then swing south to the ruins of **Selinunte** ㉒, whose remarkable metopes you will have seen in Palermo's archaeological museum. Following the coast down, aim for the Greek temple site at **Agrigento** ㉓–㉙. Allow a full day to explore Agrigento before heading north on the S189, back to Palermo.

IF YOU HAVE 9 DAYS

This itinerary is an extension of the 5-day itinerary above. From Agrigento, head inland toward **Enna** ㊻, worth a quick whirl around, then make a lunch stop at **Piazza Armerina** ㊼ before viewing the exuberant mosaics of the Roman villa at **Casale** ㊽. If you have time, stop off to see the Museo della Ceramica at **Caltagirone** ㊾ before continuing on the S124 to **Siracusa** ㉚–㊺ for a full day. Head north up the coast—a visit to **Catania** 52 is of limited interest—and keep going until you can see the silhouette of **Mt. Etna** 53 (most fog-free in the morning), an essential stop on any Sicilian tour. Spend the night in **Taormina** 54. A couple of hours are enough for a drive up to the village of **Castelmola,** above Taormina; otherwise, go directly to **Messina** 55. If you can, see the Museo Regionale here for your last blast of Sicilian art, before crossing the Straits to the seven islands of the Aeolian archipelago: **Lipari** 56, the biggest and most developed island, with a superb Museo Archeologico, **Vulcano** 57, **Salina** 58, **Panarea** 59, **Stromboli** 60, **Alicudi** 61, and **Filicudi** 62. Then, it's back to reality and the mainland.

When to Tour Sicily

Sicily comes into its own in the spring, but you're not alone in knowing this. Taormina and Erice attract a flood of visitors around Easter, and any visit scheduled for this time should be backed up by solid advance bookings. Many sights, such as inland Segesta, are at their best in the clear spring light, and are far enough off the beaten track to ensure a fairly hassle-free time. August, on the other hand, is hellish wherever you choose to roam—not just for the presence of fellow travelers, but for the extreme, uncomfortably hot temperatures. Cities should be avoided. Beaches don't necessarily offer refuge from the sizzling temperatures; they can get pretty clogged with Italian and foreign vacationers. Come in September or October, and you'll find acres of beach space. Cefalù, like Taormina, sees year-round tourism, though some

of the luxury hotels close down for the winter. As with Easter, Christmas and New Year's draw visitors to the island, and reservations should always be made as early as possible. Other festivals, such as Agrigento's almond festival in February, can also mean a dearth of vacancies.

PALERMO

The heritage of the past encompasses all ages, but Palermo's most unique aspect is its Arab-Norman identity, an improbable marriage that, mixed in with Byzantine and Jewish elements, created some unforgettable and resplendent works of art. These are most notable in the churches, small jewels such as San Giovanni degli Eremiti or larger-scale works such as the cathedral.

Once the intellectual capital of southern Europe, Palermo has always been at the crossroads of civilization. Favorably situated on a crescent-shape bay at the foot of Monte Pellegrino, it has attracted almost every people and culture touching the Mediterranean world. To Palermo's credit, it has absorbed these diverse cultures into a unique personality that is at once Arab and Christian, Byzantine and Roman, Norman and Italian. Palermo was first colonized by Phoenician traders in the 6th century BC, but it was their descendants, the Carthaginians, who built the important fortress here that caught the covetous eye of the Romans. After the First Punic War, the Romans took control of the city, in the 3rd century BC. After several invasions by the Vandals, Sicily was settled by Arabs, who made the country an emirate and made Palermo a showpiece capital that rivaled both Cordoba and Cairo in Asian splendor. Nestled in the fertile Conca d'Oro (Golden Conch) plain; full of orange, lemon, and carob groves; and enclosed by limestone hills, Palermo became a magical world of palaces and mosques, minarets and palm trees.

It was so attractive and sophisticated a city that the Norman ruler Roger de Hauteville (1031–1101) decided to conquer it and make it his capital (1072). The Norman occupation of Sicily resulted in the Golden Age of Palermo (from 1072 to 1194), a remarkable period of enlightenment and learning in which the arts flourished. The city of Palermo, which in the 11th century counted more than 300,000 inhabitants, became the center of the Norman court in all Europe and one of the most important ports of trade between East and West. Eventually the Normans were replaced by the Swabian ruler Frederick II, the Holy Roman Emperor, and incorporated into the Kingdom of the Two Sicilies. You will also see evidence in Palermo of the Baroque art and architecture of the Spanish viceroys, who came to power after the bloody Sicilian Vespers uprising of 1282, in which the French Angevin dynasty was overthrown. The Aragonese viceroys also brought the Inquisition to Palermo, which some historians believe helped foster the protective secret societies that eventually evolved into today's Mafia.

Exploring Palermo

The Sicilian capital is a multilayered, vigorous metropolis, packed with interest. Approach the city with an open mind, and you'll find it an enriching and enjoyable place to explore, with a strong historical profile. Regulate your pace, don't attempt to see too much too quickly, and keep your head. If you have a car, park it in a garage as soon as you can, and don't take it out until you are ready to depart.

Palermo is easily explored on foot, though you may choose to spend a morning taking a city bus tour to help you get oriented. The Quattro Canti, or Four Corners, is the hub that separates the four sections of the city: La Kalsa is southeast; southwest is Albergheria; Capo is the northwest quadrant; and Vucciria is northeast. Each of these is a tumult of activity during the day, though at night the narrow alleys empty out and are best avoided altogether, in favor of the more animated avenues of the new city, north of Piazza Castelnuovo. Sights you will want to see by day are scattered along three major streets: Corso Vittorio Emanuele, Via Maqueda, and Via Roma. The tourist information office in Piazza Castelnuovo will give you a map and a valuable handout that lists opening and closing times, which sometimes change with the seasons.

A Good Tour

Start at the **Palazzo dei Normanni** ①, at the far west end of Corso Vittorio Emanuele, to see the mosaics in the Cappella Palatina and the royal apartments. Walk down Via dei Benedettini, following the five pink domes of **San Giovanni degli Eremiti** ②. Back east on the Corso stands Palermo's **Cattedrale** ③, a cacophony of Arab, Norman, and Gothic influences. Farther east is Piazza Vigliena, better known as **Quattro Canti** ④, the intersection of Via Maqueda and Corso Vittoria Emanuele. Just east off Quattro Canti is **Piazza Pretoria.** Just south is Piazza Bellini, holding a trio of eminent churches: the Baroque **Santa Caterina** ⑤, and up the stairs, **San Cataldo** ⑥ and **La Martorana** ⑦ form a delightful Norman complex. Walk northeast along Via Alloro to **Palazzo Abatellis** ⑧ and its Galleria Regionale. If you like puppets, take Via Alloro east and go northwest (left) in Via Butera to the **Museo delle Marionette** ⑨. Then, either take Bus 104 or 105 (to 101) or take a 40-minute walk: cross Corso Vittorio Emanuele to reach Via Cala, follow this busy road around the old port, which becomes Via Barilai, turning left at Piazza XIII Vittime onto Via Cavour. Follow this as far as Via Roma, where you turn left, walking south 50 m (165 ft) to the **Museo Archeologico Regionale** ⑩. (If you're more adventurous and want a short cut, you can turn left off the noisy Via Cala, though you need a good sense of direction to negotiate the labyrinth of the Vucciria.) Cut through Via Bara all'Olivella to Piazza Verdi and the **Teatro Massimo** ⑪.

TIMING

Allow the best part of a day for this tour, with lunch around the Quattro Canti. Check first with the tourist office if all the sights on your itinerary are open, as they tend to close at short notice, national holidays, renovations, or staff shortages usually being the causes.

Sights to See

❸ **Cattedrale.** A lesson in Palermitan eclecticism—originally Norman (1182), then Catalan Gothic (14th–15th century) and Baroque and neoclassic interior (18th century)—sums up this church: turrets, towers, dome, and arches come together in the kind of meeting of diverse elements that King Roger II (1095–1154), whose tomb is inside along with that of Frederick II, fostered during his reign. Be sure to walk outside and look at the back of the apse, which is gracefully decorated with interlacing Arab arches, inlaid with limestone and black volcanic tufa. ✉ *Corso Vittorio Emanuele.* ⏲ *Mon.–Sat. 7–7, Sun. 8–1:30 and 4–7.*

❼ **La Martorana.** Distinguished by an elegant campanile, this church was erected in 1143 but had its interior altered considerably during the Baroque period. High along the western wall, however, is some of the oldest mosaic artwork of the Norman period. Near the entrance is an interesting mosaic of Roger being crowned by Christ. In it, Roger is dressed in a bejeweled Byzantine stole, reflecting the Norman court's

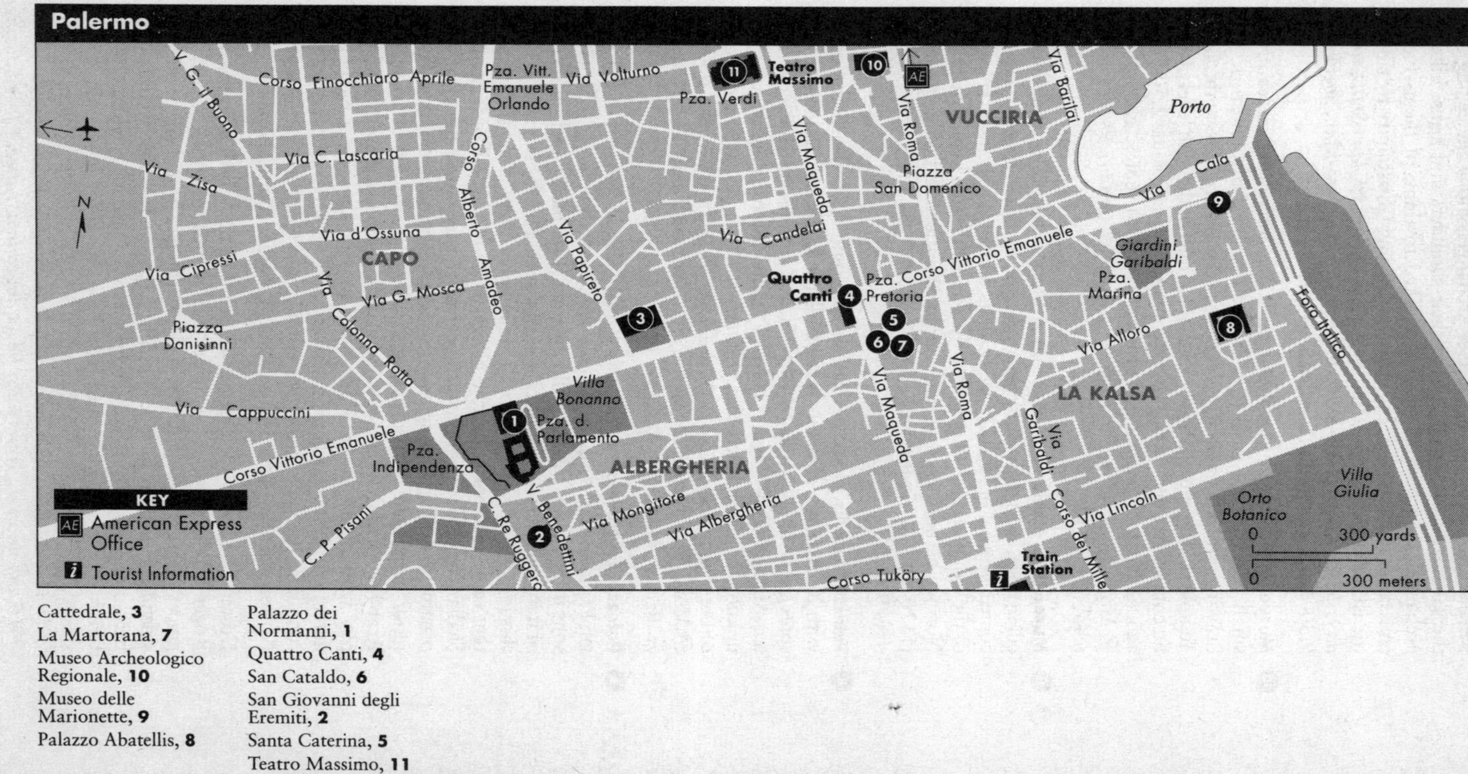

Cattedrale, **3**
La Martorana, **7**
Museo Archeologico Regionale, **10**
Museo delle Marionette, **9**
Palazzo Abatellis, **8**
Palazzo dei Normanni, **1**
Quattro Canti, **4**
San Cataldo, **6**
San Giovanni degli Eremiti, **2**
Santa Caterina, **5**
Teatro Massimo, **11**

penchant for all things Byzantine. Archangels along the ceiling wear the same stole, wrapped around their shoulders and arms. Like the archangels, the Norman monarchs liked to think of themselves as emissaries from heaven, engaged in defending Christianity by ridding the island of infidel invaders. ✉ *Piazza Bellini.* *Apr.–Sept., weekdays 9:30–1 and 3:30–6:30, weekends 9–1; Oct.–Mar., weekdays 9:30–1 and 3:30–5:30, weekends 9–1.*

10 **Museo Archeologico Regionale.** Especially interesting pieces in this small but excellent collection are the examples of prehistoric cave drawings and a marvelously reconstructed Doric frieze from the Greek Temple at Selinunte that gives you a good idea of the high level of artistic culture attained by the Greek colonists in Sicily some 2,500 years ago. ✉ *Piazza Olivella 24, Via Roma,* ☎ *091/6116805.* *8,000 lire.* *Mon., Tues., Thurs., and Sat. 9–1:45, Wed. and Fri. 9–1:45 and 3–6:45, Sun. 9–12:45.*

9 **Museo delle Marionette** (Museum of Marionettes). The traditional Sicilian pupi, with their glittering armor and fierce expressions, have become a symbol of Norman Sicily. Plots center on the chivalric legends of the troubadours, who, before the puppet theater, kept alive tales of Norman heroes in Sicily, such as Orlando Furioso and William the Bad (1120–66). ✉ *Via Butera 1,* ☎ *091/328060.* *5,000 lire.* *Weekdays 9–1 and 4–7, Sat. 9–1.*

8 **Palazzo Abatellis.** Housed in this late 15th-century Catalan Gothic palace with Renaissance elements is the **Galleria Regionale.** Among its treasures is an Annunciation (1474) by Sicily's prominent Renaissance master, Antonello da Messina (1430–79), and an arresting fresco by an unknown painter, titled *The Triumph of Death,* a macabre depiction of the plague years. ✉ *Via Alloro 4,* ☎ *091/6164317.* *8,000 lire.* *Mon., Wed., Fri., and Sat. 9–1:30; Tues. and Thurs. 9–1:30 and 3–7:30; Sun. 9–12:30.*

★ 1 **Palazzo dei Normanni** (Norman Royal Palace). The seat of the Sicilian Parliament was, unfortunately, closed to the public for security reasons in 1992, but the **Cappella Palatina** (Palatine Chapel) inside, one of Italy's greatest art treasures, remains open. Built by Roger II in 1132, this is a dazzling example of the unique harmony of artistic elements that came together under the Normans. In it, the skill of French and Sicilian masons was brought to bear on the decorative purity of Arab ornamentation and the splendor of Greek Byzantine mosaics. The interior is covered with glittering mosaics and capped by a splendid Arab honeycomb stalactite wooden ceiling. Biblical stories blend happily with scenes of Arab life—look for one showing a picnic in a harem—and Norman court pageantry. Stylized Moorish palm branches run along the walls below the mosaics and recall the battlements on Norman castles—each one a different mosaic composition.

Upstairs are the royal apartments, including the **Sala di Ruggero** (King Roger's Hall), decorated with medieval murals of hunting scenes. Tour guides escort you around these halls, which once hosted one of the most splendid courts in Europe. French, Latin, and Arabic were spoken here, and Arab astronomers and poets exchanged ideas with Latin and Greek scholars in what must have been one of the most unique marriages of culture in the Western world. ✉ *Piazza Indipendenza,* ☎ *091/7054317.* *Free.* *Weekdays 9–noon and 3–5, Sat. 9–noon, Sun. 9–10 and noon–1. Tours must be arranged in advance. Closed during religious services and for weddings.*

Piazza Pretoria. The square's centerpiece, a lavishly decorated fountain, was originally intended for a Florentine villa. Its abundance of nude figures so shocked some Palermitans when it was unveiled in 1575 that it got the nickname the "Fountain of Shame." It is even more of a sight at night, when illuminated. ✉ *Just east of Piazza Pretoria.*

4 **Quattro Canti.** The Four Corners is the converging point of Corso Vittorio Emanuele and Via Maqueda. Four rather traffic-blackened Baroque palaces from the Spanish rule meet at concave corners, each with its own fountain and representations of a Spanish ruler, patron saint, and one of the four seasons.

6 **San Cataldo.** Orange-red domes mark this church, built in 1160. Its spare but intense interior, punctuated by antique Greek columns, retains much of its original medieval simplicity. If the church is closed, the custodian at La Martorana (☞ *above*) will let you in during public hours. ✉ *Piazza Bellini.* ⏲ *Tues.–Fri. 9–5, weekends 9–1.*

2 **San Giovanni degli Eremiti.** Distinguished by its five pink domes, this 12th-century church was built by the Normans on the site of an earlier mosque—one of 200 that once stood in Palermo. The emirs ruled Palermo for almost two centuries and brought to it their passion for lush gardens and fountains. One is reminded of this while sitting in San Giovanni's delightful cloister of twin half-columns, surrounded by palm trees, jasmine, oleander, and citrus trees. ✉ *Via dei Benedettini.* ⏲ Mon.–Sat. 9–1 and 3–7, Sun. 9–12:30.

5 **Santa Caterina.** The walls of this splendid Baroque church (1596) in Piazza Bellini are covered in decorative 17th-century inlays of precious marble. ✉ *Piazza Bellini.* ⏲ *Daily 9–noon and 3–6.*

11 **Teatro Massimo.** Construction of this formidable neoclassic theater was started in 1875 by Giovanni Battista Basile and completed by his son, Ernesto, in 1897. Claimed to be Italy's largest, the theater was featured in scenes in *The Godfather Part III,* under Francis Ford Coppola's direction. ✉ *Piazza Verdi, at the top of Via Maqueda,* ☎ *091/6053315.*

★ **Vucciria outdoor market.** "Vucciria," in dialect, means "voices" or "hubbub," and it's easy to see why. In the maze of side streets around Piazza San Domenico, hawkers everywhere deliver their unceasing chants from behind stands brimming with mounds of olives, blood oranges, wild fennel, and long-stemmed artichokes. One of them goes at the trunk of a swordfish with a cleaver, while across the way another holds up a giant squid or dangles an octopus. It may be Palermo, but this is really the Casbah. Morning is the best time to see the market in full swing. ✉ *Around Piazza San Domenico.* ⏲ *Daily dawn–dusk.*

NEED A BREAK? If you're a street-food fanatic, Vucciria is your Eden. Stalls around the neighborhood sell everything from *calzoni* (deep-fried meat- or cheese-filled pockets of dough) to *panelle* (chickpea-flour fritters). If you're feeling adventurous for something typically Palermitan, look for a stall with a big cast-iron pot selling delicious *guasteddi* (fresh buns filled with thin strips of calf's spleen, ricotta cheese, and a delicious hot sauce).

Dining and Lodging

$$$ ★ ✕ **Charleston.** You'll feel pampered by the discreet service and elegant surroundings in this famous Palermo restaurant. Impeccably outfitted waiters coast effortlessly through the high-ceiling rooms, producing a range of Sicilian and international dishes, with an emphasis on seafood. Try the delicious spaghetti *all'aragosta* (with lobster sauce), or the pesce spada *arrosto* (roasted), but leave room for the house dessert, *semifreddo alle mandorle*(a soft ice cream made with almonds). The whole restaurant operation moves 8 km (5 mi) north to Mondello in summer,

where it sets up shop in a pavilion on the sea. ✉ *Piazza Ungheria 30,* ☎ *091/321366. Mondello:* ✉ *Charleston le Terrazze, Viale Regina Elena,* ☎ *091/450171. Reservations essential. Jacket and tie. AE, DC, MC, V. Closed Sun.*

$$$ ★ ✕ **Da Renato.** The view from this top-quality restaurant on the sea road toward Cefalù is enough out of the way to make it the insider's choice. And the well-heeled locals know their way around a good seafood and grills menu. *Frutti di mare* (mixed seafood) makes a good antipasto, and the *zuppa di mare* (fish soup) is hearty enough to be a meal in itself. ✉ *Via Messina Marina 224,* ☎ *091/6302881. AE, DC, MC, V. Closed Mon. and Aug. 10–25.*

$$ ✕ **Santandrea.** A chic clientele frequents this trattoria where home cooking is the rule, and most ingredients come from the Vucciria market just round the corner. There is no written menu, the dishes available depend on what is in season, but if lucky you'll find the delectable *tagliatelli con triglie, zucchini e mandorle* (pasta with red mullet, zucchini, and almonds). You can always count on a good choice of fresh fish for main course and some delicious homemade desserts, such as black chocolate mousse. It's a few steps down from Piazza San Domenico. ✉ *Piazza Sant'Andrea 4,* ☎ *091/334999. AE, DC, MC, V. Closed Tues. and Jan.*

$$ ✕ **Strascinu.** The specialty in this informal and busy restaurant is pasta con le sarde, the region's ubiquitous Arab-Sicilian dish. Amphoras, Sicilian ceramics, and even a miniature, electrically-operated puppet theater enliven the rustic decor, and there's a large garden with gazebos. ✉ *Viale Regione Siciliana 2286,* ☎ *091/401292. AE, DC, MC, V.*

$$ ✕ **Trattoria ai Normanni.** Here's a good place for lunch after visiting the Palazzo dei Normanni, just off Piazza Indipendenza. Amid the tall-ceilinged interior with internal balcony are casual ambience and polite service. Try the house specialty, spaghetti *ai Normanni* (with fresh tomatoes, shrimps, eggplant, and grated peanuts, the whole smothered with fennel); other choices include *zuppa di cozze* (mussel soup) and there are pizzas in the evening. Sit inside or out—but arrive early or reserve if you want an outdoor table. ✉ *Piazza della Vittoria 25,* ☎ *091/6516011. AE, MC, V.*

$ ✕ **Antica Focacceria San Francesco.** This place in Palermo's heart is an institution, as you can see from the turn-of-the-century wooden cabinets and fixtures of what is still a neighborhood bakery. It bakes and fries the snacks that locals love—and from which you can make an inexpensive meal. You can sit at marble-topped tables or take food out. The good gelateria in the piazza is under the same management. ✉ *Via Paternostro 58,* ☎ *091/320264. Reservations not accepted. No credit cards.*

$ ✕ **Bellini.** The pizzas are good, the pastas are better, but the best reason to eat in this former theater is the location, overlooking the churches of San Cataldo and La Martorana in the heart of old Palermo. Get a seat next to the window—or better still, in summer, eat alfresco. Trade is brisk, and so is the service, which can be offhand. ✉ *Piazza Bellini 6,* ☎ *091/6165691. AE, MC, V. Closed Wed.*

$ ✕ **Shangai.** There is nothing Chinese about this Palermo institution in the busy Vucciria market. It's on a terrace above the market (the source of all the ingredients); lookdown and order your fish from the displays below, and it will be hoisted up in a wicker basket. The atmosphere can get jovial and frantic, with lots of teasing and shouting. Although the fare here has become quite mediocre in recent years, the calamari *al forno* (baked in the oven) is always a good bet. ✉ *Vicolo Mezzani 34,* ☎ *091/589702. No credit cards. Closed Sun.*

$$$–$$$$ ★ 🏨 **Villa Igiea.** A short taxi ride through some rough-looking districts of Palermo takes you to this oasis of luxury and comfort, in its own tropical garden at the edge of the bay. A meander through the grounds

reveals such relics as an ancient Greek temple at the water's edge. Large rooms are furnished individually, the nicest with an Italian art-nouveau flavor. Spacious lobbies and public rooms unfold onto a terrace and restaurant. Sports facilities help make this elegant villa a self-contained enclave in frenetic Palermo. ✉ *Salita Belmonte 43, Acquasanta, 3 km/2 mi north of Palermo, 90142,* ☎ *091/543744,* FAX *091/547654. 117 rooms, 6 suites. Restaurant, bar, pool, tennis court. AE, DC, MC, V.*

$$$ **Hotel Principe di Villafranca.** A new hotel in Palermo, not far from the glitzy shopping district, has put a great deal of thought into creating the feel of a private home—and with fine Sicilian antiques, imperial striped silks, creamy marble floors, and vaulted ceilings, a museum-quality home indeed. But you will feel comfortable in the understated surroundings: relax in the library with an aperitif or savor an authentic meal in the rustic adjoining Ristorante dei Vecchi Monsù. Rooms are replete with pure linens, wardrobes painted by local artists, lovely handmade porcelain pieces (which you can order for your own casa), and more antiques. The hotel is a smart choice for business travelers. ✉ *Via G. Turrisi Colonna 4, 90140,* ☎ *091/6118523,* FAX *091/588705. 24 rooms. Restaurant, breakfast room, café, sauna, exercise room, library, meeting room, free parking. AE, DC, MC, V.*

$$–$$$ **Grand Hotel et des Palmes.** There is a faded charm about this grande dame, whose public rooms suggest the elegant life of Palermo society before World War I, when tea dances and balls were held here. Guest rooms are uneven—some are charming period pieces stuffed with antiques and heavy fabrics, others are dark and cramped. There is an American-style cocktail bar and a rooftop terrace. ✉ *Via Roma 398, 90139,* ☎ *091/583933,* FAX *091/331545. 187 rooms, 5 suites. Restaurant, bar, parking (fee). AE, DC, MC, V.*

$$–$$$ ★ **Mondello Palace.** This is the leading hotel at the Mondello resort, making the best use of its location near the beach. The private beach has cabins and changing rooms for the use of Mondello Palace guests, as well as sailing and windsurfing facilities and an exercise room. The rooms are well equipped and large, and most have balconies. In summer you can choose between the hotel's own restaurant or the beachside venue of Palermo's excellent Charleston (☞ *above*)—just across the road. ✉ *Viale Principe di Scalea, 90139 Mondello Lido, just north of Palermo,* ☎ *091/450001,* FAX *091/450657. 84 rooms, 9 suites. Restaurant, bar, pool, exercise room, beach, windsurfing, boating. AE, DC, MC, V.*

$$ **Grande Albergo Sole.** The main attractions of this three-star are the central location, just steps away from the Quattro Canti and Piazza Pretoria, and the extensive roof-terrace from which the major sights of Palermo are visible. The downside is some traffic-rumble on street-facing rooms, though in other respects they are comfortable enough, if somewhat old-fashioned, and some have period furnishings. The public rooms are right out of the 1950s. ✉ *Corso Vittorio Emanuele 291, 90133,* ☎ *091/581811,* FAX *091/6110182. 154 rooms. Restaurant, bar. AE, DC, MC, V.*

$$ **Massimo Plaza Hotel.** Opened in 1998, this hotel boasts one of Palermo's best locations—right opposite the renovated Teatro Massimo. It is small and select, the few rooms spacious, comfortably furnished, and—most important—well insulated from the noise on Via Maqueda. Service is personal and polite. ✉ *Via Maqueda 437, 90133,* ☎ *091/325657,* FAX *091/325711. 11 rooms. Bar, parking (fee). AE, DC, MC, V.*

$ **Principe di Belmonte.** This is a tasteful choice among Palermo's cheaper hotels. It is family-run, friendly, and central—a convenient walk both from the port and Piazza Castelnuovo—but is on a relatively quiet street. Rooms are smallish. Advance reservations are advised. ✉ *Via Principe* *di Belmonte 25, 90139, ☎ 091/331065, FAX 091/6113424. 17 rooms, 3 without bath. Bar. AE, DC, MC, V.*

Nightlife and the Arts

The Arts

CONCERTS AND OPERA

Teatro Massimo (✉ Piazza Verdi, at the top of Via Maqueda, ☎ 091/6053315) finally reopened in summer 1997, after 23 years of restoration. A program of concerts and operas is presented throughout the year. The grandiose **Politeama Garibaldi** (✉ Piazza Ruggero Settimo, ☎ 091/6053315) stages a winter season of opera and orchestral works. Choral and chamber recitals are performed at the **Teatro Golden** (✉ Via Terrasanta, ☎ 091/305217).

FESTIVALS

Palermo stages the **Festa di Santa Rosalia,** a street fair held July 11 through 15 in honor of the city's patron saint. There are fireworks displays in the evenings. **Epiphany** (January 6) is celebrated with Byzantine rites and a procession of townspeople in local costume through the streets of Piana degli Albanesi, near Palermo. The village, 24 km (15 mi) south of the island's capital, is named for the Albanian immigrants who first settled there, bringing with them the Byzantine Catholic rites.

PUPPET SHOW

Bring children to the **Opera dei Pupi** (✉ Via Bara all'Olivella 95, ☎ 091/323400). Check with the tourist office for details.

THEATER

Palermo's **Teatro Biondo** (✉ Via Roma, ☎ 091/582364) is Sicily's foremost theater, featuring a winter season of plays from November to May.

Nightlife

NIGHTCLUBS

Apart from some trendy bars lining Via Principe del Belmonte, intersecting with Via Roma and Via Ruggiero Settimo (a northern extension of Via Maqueda), nightlife is concentrated in the nightclubs and discotheques scattered around the northern, newer end of town, a taxi ride away. Check out **Il Cerchio** (✉ Viale Strasburgo 312, ☎ 091/6885421) and **Paramatta** (✉ Viale Lazio 51, ☎ 091/513621). In summer, the scene shifts to Mondello, Palermo's seaside satellite on the other side of Monte Pellegrino.

Shopping

Markets

Looking to pick up antique marionettes of the Norman cavaliers or brilliantly colored pieces from the carretti siciliani? Head to the flea market, behind Palermo's Cattedrale, on Via Papireto, held daily. Don't miss the raucous outdoor market around Vucciria's Piazza San Domenico, every day but Sunday.

Specialty Stores

ANTIQUES

The area behind the Cattedrale, in the midst of the flea market on Via Papireto and spreading to the next street, Corso Amedeo, is also the antiques-store neighborhood.

CERAMICS

De Simone has a wide selection of ceramics decorated in a modern style that remind many of Picasso. You can browse through the workshop (✉ Via Lanza di Scalea 698,) or get a glimpse of what's on offer at a more central retail outlet (✉ Via Daita 13/b, near Piazza Ruggero Settimo).

MONREALE AND THE TYRRHENIAN COAST

Palermo's Arab-Norman theme is continued in the cathedral at nearby Monreale and in Cefalù, a viable alternative to staying in the capital itself.

Monreale

12 *10 km (6 mi) southwest of Palermo.*

★ Don't miss the splendid **Duomo,** lavishly executed with mosaics depicting events from the Old and New Testaments. After the Norman conquest of Sicily, the new princes showcased their ambitions through monumental building projects. William II (1154–89) built the church complex with a cloister and palace between 1174 and 1185, and it is today regarded as the finest example of Norman architecture in Sicily. A fusion of Eastern and Western stylistic influences by Byzantine craftsmen developed into a glorious Sicilian decorative attitude.

The major attraction is the 6,340 square m (68,220 square ft) of glittering gold mosaics decorating the cathedral interior. The commanding image of Christ Pantocrator overlooks the apse area, which also contains mosaics of the *Virgin and Child,* the archangels, prophets, and saints. The nave contains two narrative bands, starting adjacent to the central apse, illustrating the book of Genesis from the *Creation of Heaven and Earth* and continuing through *Jacob Wrestling with the Angel.* Scenes from the *Life of Christ* adorn the walls of the aisles and the transept. The painted wooden ceiling, a reconstruction of the original following a fire in 1811, dates from 1816 to 1837. Bring 500-lire coins to illuminate the mosaics. A small pair of binoculars will make it easier to read the Latin inscriptions. The roof commands a great view if you are up to climbing the 172 stairs.

★ Bonnano Pisano's **bronze doors**, completed in 1186, depict 42 biblical scenes and are considered among the most important of medieval artifacts. Note the Norman heraldic symbols of lions and griffins on the bottom of the doors. Barisano da Trani's 42 panels on the north door, dating from 1179, show saints and evangelists. ✉ *Piazza del Duomo,* ☎ *091/6404413.* ⏲ *Daily 8–12:10 and 3:30–6:30.*

Don't miss the lovely **cloister** of the adjacent abbey. It was built at the same time as the church, but enlarged in the 14th century. The beautiful square enclosure is surrounded by 216 double columns, every other one decorated in a unique glass mosaic pattern. Note the intricate carvings on the bases and the capitals of the columns. In one of the corners, by the stylized palm-tree fountain, look for a capital showing William II offering the cathedral to the Virgin Mary. ✉ *Piazza del Duomo,* ☎ *091/6404403.* 🎫 *4,000 lire.* ⏲ *Mon.–Sat. 9–1 and 3–7, Sun. 9–12:30.*

Dining

$$ ✕ **La Botte.** It's worth the short drive or inexpensive taxi fare to reach this restaurant, a good value for well-prepared local specialties. Dine alfresco on daily specials, such as *pennette agli odori* (little penne with tomato, garlic, parsley, basil, mint, and oregano), or regular favorites, such as *involtini* (meat or fish roulades). Local wines are a good bet.

⊠ *Contrada Lenzitti 20, S186,* ☎ *091/414051. AE, DC, MC, V. Closed Mon.–Thurs. and Aug.*

Termini Imerese

⓭ *40 km (25 mi) east of Palermo.*

This port town takes its name from the the Greeks who founded it (refugees from nearby Himera, ☞ *below*), and the natural spa baths, or *terme,* that helped to make it an important Roman city. Termini's upper town, occupying a high promontory above the port, holds the few survivals from the town's classical period—the ruins of an amphitheater and the foundations of a public building, enveloped among the trees of the public gardens. More compelling are the outstanding vistas to be enjoyed from the belvedere, the extensive views along the coast only partly marred by the industry surrounding the port below. Have a gelato and a sit-down here before wandering around Termini's elegant Baroque churches, making a stop at the **Museo Civico,** housed in a 14th-century palazzo that incorporates a self-contained chapel. There is some impressive religious art to be seen here, including sculpture by 15th-century artist Antonello Gagini and a triptych of the *Madonna with Child and Saints* attributed to Gaspare da Pésaro (active 1413–60). Other rooms in this well-displayed collection hold prehistoric and archaeological material, including finds from Himera. ⊠ *Via Civico,* ☎ *091/8128279.* *Free.* ⏲ *Apr.–mid-Oct., Tues. and Fri. 9–1, Wed.–Thurs. and Sat.–Sun. 9–1 and 3–7; mid-Oct.–Mar., Tues. and Fri. 9–1, Wed.–Thurs. and Sat.–Sun. 9–1 and 3:30–6:30.*

OFF THE BEATEN PATH

HIMERA – From Termini Imerese, drive or take a taxi to the site of ancient Himera, 15 km (8 mi) east along the coast, site of the original 7th-century BC Chalcidinian (Greek) settlement. All that's left of the city that once stood here is the massive **Tempio della Vittoria** erected to commemorate the Greek victory over a huge Carthaginian army in 480 BC, and built by the Carthaginian prisoners themselves. The Carthaginian leader Hamilcar had intended to take Himera and probably the rest of Sicily too, but his defeat by the combined armies of Akragas (Agrigento), Gela, and Syracuse led him to throw himself onto the pyre. The victory marked the beginning of the Greek ascendancy in Sicily, though, for Himera, the celebrations were short lived: Hamilcar's nephew, Hannibal, wreaked his revenge in 409 BC by razing the city to the ground, forcing the surviving citizens west to what is now Termini Imerese. Little remains above knee-level of the original Doric monument, but it's a poignant sight, redolent of ancient glory. Above the temple on the site of Himera's acropolis, a modern **antiquarium** shows diagrams of the temple as it once appeared, together with some remnants of the Greek city; the rest is in the museums at Termini and Palermo. ⊠ *Buonfornello,* ☎ *091/8140128.* *4,000 lire.* ⏲ *Mon.–Sat. 9–1 and 3–6, Sun. 9–1.*

Lodging

$$$ **Grand Hotel delle Terme.** Dominating Termini's lower town, this hotel was built at the end of the 19th century right over the spring from which Termini's famous spa waters—praised by Plutarch, among others—gush forth. You can take full advantage of the curative waters in the classically styled thermal complex in the basement, where treatment includes massage and mud therapy. Above ground, public rooms are sumptuously furnished, with a grand staircase and a wealth of paintings and potted plants scattered around, though guest rooms tend to be on the small side. A rooftop pool provides an alfresco lounging area, if you are not tempted to take a dip. ⊠ *Piazza delle Terme, 90018,* ☎ *091/8113557,* FAX *091/8113107. 69 rooms, 11 suites.*

Restaurant, bar, pool, beauty salon, massage, spa, health club. AE, DC, MC, V.

Cáccamo

14 *12 km (8 mi) south of Termini Imerese, 52 km (32 mi) southeast of Palermo.*

The quiet village of Cáccamo rises on an inland spur which the Normans could not resist fortifying, and the mighty **Castello** that they raised here in the 12th century still stands, superbly restored, its sheer white walls a landmark from miles around. It's one of Sicily's largest and most impressive bastions, bristling with turrets and crenellations, and among its 130 rooms is the **Sala della Congiura,** where a baron's plot against William I was hatched in 1160. If the castle's entrance gate isn't open, ring at Corso Umberto 6 (the door nearest the war memorial opposite the main entrance). ✉ *Corso Umberto,* ☎ *091/8148402.* *Free (gratuity).* *Daily 9–1 and 3:30–1 hr before sunset.*

Dining

$ ✕ **A Castellana.** For a meal right by the castle, this medieval-looking pizzeria-restaurant is ideal. Have a simple pizza or pasta con le sarde. ✉ *Piazza Monumento 4,* ☎ *091/8148667. MC, V. Closed Mon.*

Cefalù

★ 15 *38 km (24 mi) northeast of Termini Imrese, 70 km (42 mi) east of Palermo.*

Cefalù is a charming town built on a spur jutting out into the sea and dominated by a massive 12th-century Romanesque **Duomo,** one of the finest Norman cathedrals in Italy. King Roger began it in 1131 as an offering of thanks for having been saved here from a shipwreck. Its mosaics rival those of Monreale. Both cathedrals are dominated by colossal mosaic figures of the Byzantine Pantocratic Christ, high in the bowl of their apses. The Monreale figure is an austere and powerful image, emphasizing the divinity of Christ, while the Cefalù Christ, softer and more compassionate, seems to stress his humanity. The traffic going in and out of Cefalù town can be heavy in summer; you may want to take the 50-minute train ride or 40-minute bus ride from Palermo instead of driving. ✉ *Piazza Duomo,* ☎ *0921/722021.* *Daily 8–noon and 3:30–8. No shorts or beachwear.*

Dining and Lodging

$$ ✕ **Gabbiano.** "Seagull" is an appropriate name for a harborside seafood restaurant with a nautical theme. House specialties are *involtini di pesce spada* (swordfish roulades) and spaghetti marinara. ✉ *Via Lungomare Giardina 17,* ☎ *0921/421495. AE, DC, MC, V. Closed Wed.*

$$ ✕ **La Brace.** This bistro-style restaurant near the cathedral has been serving upscale dishes and a lively atmosphere since 1977. Graceful ceiling arches and rustic walls lend an informal air. Dutch proprietor Dietmar Beckers and his team pride themselves on creatively reworking local ingredients. Savor the excellent grills, and save room for the homemade cassata siciliana. ✉ *Via Venticinque Novembre 10,* ☎ *0921/423570. AE, DC, MC, V. Closed Mon. and mid-Dec.–mid-Jan.*

$$ ★ **Baia del Capitano.** The peaceful district of Mazzaforno, about 5 km (3 mi) outside town, sets the stage for this handsome hotel with great amenities. The building is less than 30 years old, but it blends in with the traditional homes nearby. The colorful gardens, extending to the surrounding olive groves, are ideal for quiet reading or an afternoon siesta in the shade. A good sandy beach is an easy walk away. The rooms

are large and quiet. You must pay half board in high season. ✉ *Contrada Mazzaforno, 90015 Mazzaforno,* ☎ *0921/420005,* FAX *0921/420163. 39 rooms. Restaurant, bar, pool, tennis court. AE, MC, V. MAP.*

$$ ★ **Kalura.** Caldura, 3 km (2 mi) east along the coast, is the setting for this modern hotel on a small promontory that is hard to reach without a car. Taxis from Cefalù take only a few minutes, though. Sports facilities keep you from getting too sedentary, and the private beach is ideal for swimming. Rooms are bright and cheerful. Rates are low in this category. ✉ *Via V. Cavallaro 13, 90015 Contrada Caldura,* ☎ *0921/421354,* FAX *0921/423122. 65 rooms. Restaurant, bar, pool, tennis court, beach. AE, DC, MC, V.*

Santo Stefano di Camastra

16 *33 km (20 mi) east of Cefalù, 152 km (95 mi) west of Messina.*

When the original village of Santo Stefano di Camastra was destroyed in a landslide in 1682, the local duke, Giuseppe Lanza, rebuilt it on the coast according to strict military principles—a geometric street-grid, and artery roads connecting the center with the periphery. His innovations led directly to the duke being entrusted with the rebuilding of Catania and Noto following the destruction of those cities by a catastrophic earthquake 10 years later. Today, Santo Stefano looks like any of the other resorts along the coast, but for the abundance of ceramics shops lining every street, bulging with the vividly colored pottery products for which the town has established an international reputation. Quality, of course, is variable, and you will need a discriminating eye to pick out the best items. And then, haggle like mad. If you want an overview of some of the possibilities of pottery, the range of uses to which it can be put and the heights of mastery in the genre, drop in on the **Museo della Ceramica,** housed in the 18th-century Palazzo Trabia in the center of town. Plates, figurines, extravagant sculptures, and diverse exhibitions are arranged in a well-lit environment, along with explanations of the processes and techniques involved. ✉ *Via Palazzo,* ☎ *0921/331110.* 🎟 *Free.* ⏲ *May–Sept., weekdays 9–1 and 4–8; Oct.–Apr., weekdays 9–1 and 3:30–7:30.*

Shopping

CERAMICS

The Franco family has a long tradition of creating ceramic *objets* by borrowing styles from past eras. Thus, Renaissance Madonnas rub shoulders with florid Baroque vases, all richly colored and skillfully finished. View them at the two outlets of **Ceramiche Franco** (✉ Via Nazionale 8 and Via Nazionale 40) on Santo Stefano's main street.

WESTERN COAST TO AGRIGENTO

Land of Temples

Western Sicily has a remote air, less developed than the eastern coast, and bearing traces of the North African culture that for centuries exerted a strong influence on this end of the island. Influences are most tangible in the coastal towns of Trapani and Marsala, and the outlying island of Pantelleria, nearer to the Tunisian coast than the Sicilian. In contrast, the cobbled streets of the hilltop town of Erice, outside Trapani, retain a strong medieval complexion, giving the town the air of a last outpost gazing out over the Mediterranean. The Greek presence is still strong, however, in the splendidly isolated site of Segesta, and the cluster of ruined temples at Selinunte. But the crowning glory of this tour is the concentration of Greek temples at Agrigento, occupying a fabulous position on a height between the modern city and the sea.

Segesta

17 *30 km (19 mi) east of Trapani, 85 km (53 mi) southwest of Palermo.*

Segesta is the site of one of the most impressive **Greek temples,** constructed on the side of a windswept barren hill overlooking a valley of wild fennel. Virtually intact today, the temple is considered by some to be finer, in its proportions and setting, than any other Doric temple left standing. The Greeks started the temple in the 5th century BC but never finished it. The walls and roof never materialized, and the columns were never fluted. Just over 1 km (½ mi) away, near the top of the hill, are the remains of a fine **Greek theater,** with impressive views, especially at sunset, of nearby Monte Erice and the sea. ☎ *0924/46277.* *4,000 lire.* *Daily 9–1 hr before sunset.*

OFF THE BEATEN PATH

GIBELLINA AND SALAPARUTA – On the night of January 14, 1968, a fierce earthquake devastated the wine-producing district of the Valle del Belice, causing 400 deaths and more than 50,000 mostly poor inhabitants of the area to lose their homes. Two of the towns most affected were Gibellina and Salaparuta, and while most other damaged centers were (eventually) rebuilt, these were left as a memorial to the catastrophe. It's a disturbing, rather grim, though deeply peaceful landscape to visit today, a tangle of destruction in which broken walls protrude from mountains of rubble. In Gibellina, part of one hillside has been covered with a mantle of white concrete in which the lanes of the old town have been symbolically cut through, which you can wander among. Elsewhere, an amphitheater of scaffolding has been improvised where dramatic performances are enacted each summer, mainly of classical plays and concerts. Contact the tourist office (✉ Piazza XV Gennaio 1968, ☎ 0924/67877) at Gibellina Nuova for details. Gibellina Nuova itself, a new town built to accommodate the former inhabitants, 18 km (12 mi) west, is also worthy of a passing visit to see the collection of huge and diverse modern sculptures displayed here—a giant star built over the main S188, white spheres, a plough, a snail, and much more.

Erice

18 *35 km (22 mi) west of Segesta, 112 km (70 mi) west of Palermo.*

Erice perches 2,450 ft above sea level, an enchanting medieval mountaintop aerie of castles and palaces, fountains, and cobblestone streets. Erice was the ancient Eryx and was dedicated to a fertility goddess, whom the Phoenicians called Astarte; the Greeks, Aphrodite; and the Romans, Venus. According to Virgil, Aeneas built a temple to the goddess here, but it was destroyed when the Arabs took over and renamed the place Mohammed's Mountain. When the Normans arrived, they built a castle where today you'll find a public park with benches and belvederes, from which there are striking views of Trapani, the Egadi Islands, and, on a *very* clear day, Cape Bon and the Tunisian coast.

NEED A BREAK?

Fans of Sicilian sweets will make a beeline for **Pasticceria Grammatico** (✉ Via Vittorio Emanuele 14 and Via Guarnotte 1, ☎ 0923/869390), run by Maria Grammatico, a former nun who hit international fame with *Bitter Almonds,* her life story co-written with Mary Taylor Simeti. She learned how to make her sweet confections in the convent where she was brought up. Molded into a variety of shapes, including dolls and animals, her almond-paste creations are works of art. The balcony from the tea room upstairs has wonderful views. Maria's sister runs the show at the **Pasticceria del Convento** (✉ Via Guarnotte 1), selling the same delectable treats.

Dining and Lodging

$$ ✕ **Monte San Giuliano.** Buried within the labyrinth of lanes that make up this ancient citadel, this restaurant has a satisfyingly traditional feel. Sit out on the stone patio and sample such house specialties as the spicy Arab-influenced seafood couscous, or one of the startlingly good pasta dishes. ✉ *Vicolo San Rocco 7,* ☎ *0923/869595. AE, DC, MC, V. Closed Mon. and 2 wks in Jan. and Nov.*

$$ **Ermione.** Spectacular views and cool breezes are the rewards of a visit to Erice, and this 1960s hotel overlooking the Tyrrhenian Sea is in a position to offer both. Nearly every room has a good view, although some would say that the terrace bar has the most panoramic vista. The hotel restaurant is popular locally, with fish couscous a standout. Breakfast is included. ✉ *Via Pineta Comunale 43, 91016,* ☎ *0923/869138,* FAX *0923/869587. 46 rooms. Restaurant, bar, pool. AE, DC, MC, V.*

$$ ★ **Moderno.** Local craft work and some antiques decorate the gracious rooms of this intimate and well-run hotel on the cobblestone streets of the medieval town. Some rooms are in the modern annex. The main building has a fire blazing in the lounge in winter. The restaurant serves seafood pasta and homemade desserts. ✉ *Via Vittorio Emanuele 63, 91016,* ☎ *0923/869300,* FAX *0923/869139. 40 rooms. Restaurant, bar. AE, DC, MC, V.*

Trapani

⓳ *30 km (18 mi) west of Segesta, 107 km (67 mi) west of Palermo.*

The modern town of Trapani, below Erice, is the departure point for ferries to the Egadi Islands and the island of Pantelleria, near the African coast. The lanes near Corso Italia hold a handful of churches worth wandering into. **Santa Maria di Gesù,** on Via San Pietro, has Renaissance and Gothic doors and a Madonna by Andrea della Robbia (1435–1525), and **Sant'Agostino,** on Piazzetta Saturno, behind the town hall, with a 14th-century rose window. This rugged western end of Sicily is reminiscent of the terrain in American westerns—as it well should be, for many "spaghetti westerns" were filmed here. If you fancy North African couscous, Trapani is the place to try the Sicilian version, made with fish instead of meat. The result is a kind of fish stew with semolina, laced with cinnamon, saffron, and black pepper.

Dining

$$ ★ ✕ **P&G.** Couscous is a specialty of this small, popular restaurant on a quiet street between the train station and the Villa Margherita public gardens. The couscous features fish in summer (Friday only) and meat in winter. A mixed grill of meats in a zesty orange sauce will revive any appetite suffering from fish fatigue. Wash it all down with a bottle of Donnafugata, a good white from the Rallo vineyards at Marsala. ✉ *Via Spalti 1,* ☎ *0923/547701. Reservations essential. AE, DC, MC, V. Closed Sun. and Aug.*

Pantelleria

⓴ *100 km (62 mi) southwest of Sicily, 6 hrs by ferry from Trapani.*

Pantelleria, near the Tunisian coast, is one of Sicily's most evocative islands, although many find its starkness unappealing. Its volcanic formations, scant patches of forest, prehistoric tombs, and dramatic seascapes constitute an otherworldly landscape. From its grapes—the *zibibbo*—the locals make an amber-color dessert wine and a strong, sweet wine called Tanit. Daily ferries and hydrofoils connect the island with Trapani.

Marsala

21 *30 km (18 mi) south of Trapani, 140 km (87 mi) southwest of Palermo.*

The quiet seaside town of Marsala was once the main Carthaginian base in Sicily, from which Carthage fought for supremacy of the island against Greece and Rome. Some of the flavor of those times is recaptured by the well-preserved Punic warship displayed in the town's **Museo Archeologico Baglio Anselmi,** along with some of the amphoras and other artifacts recovered from the wreck. The vessel, which was probably sunk during the great sea battle that ended the First Punic War in 241 BC, was dredged up from the mud near the Egadi Islands in the 1970s, and is now installed under a climate-controlled plastic tent. ✉ *Via Boeo 30,* ☎ *0923/952535.* 🎫 *4,000 lire.* ⏲ *May–Sept., Mon.–Tues. and Thurs.–Fri. 9–2, Wed. and weekends 9–2 and 4–7; Oct.–Apr., Sun.–Tues. and Thurs.–Fri. 9–1, Wed. and Sat. 9–1 and 4–6.*

Nowadays, Marsala is more readily associated with the world-famous, rich-color, sweet-tasting wine named after the town. In 1773 a British merchant named John Woodhouse happened upon Marsala and discovered that the wine there was as good as the port the British had long imported from Portugal. Two other wine merchants, Whitaker and Ingram, rushed in, and by 1800 Marsala was exporting its wine all over the British Empire.

Selinunte

22 *88 km (55 mi) southeast of Marsala, 114 km (71 mi) south of Palermo.*

Near the town of Castelvetrano, an overwhelming array of ruined **Greek temples** is perched on a plateau overlooking the Mediterranean at Selinunte. The city was one of the most superb colonies of ancient Greece. The original complex held seven temples scattered over two sites separated by a harbor. Of the seven, only one—reconstructed in 1958—stands. Founded in the 7th century BC, Selinunte became the rich and prosperous rival of Segesta, which in 409 BC turned to the Carthaginians for help. The Carthaginians sent an army commanded by Hannibal to destroy the city. The temples were demolished, the city was razed, and 16,000 of Selinunte's inhabitants were slaughtered. The beautiful metopes preserved in Palermo's Museo Archeologico Regionale (☞ *above*) come from the frieze of Temple E here. A small **museum** on the site contains other excavated pieces. Selinunte is named after a local variety of wild celery that in spring still grows in profusion among the ruined columns and overturned capitals. ☎ *0924/46251.* 🎫 *4,000 lire.* ⏲ *Daily 9–1 hr before sunset.*

Agrigento

100 km (60 mi) southeast of Selinunte, 126 km (79 mi) south of Palermo.

The natural defenses of Akragas, the Greek city today called Agrigento, depended on its secure, and quite lovely, position between two rivers on a flood plain a short distance from the sea. Agrakas was settled by the Greeks in 582 BC and grew wealthy through trade with Carthage, just across the Mediterranean. Despite attacks from the Carthaginians at the end of the 5th century BC, the city survived through the Roman era, the Middle Ages (when it came under Arab and Norman rule), and into the modern age. Famous sons include the ancient Greek philosopher Empedocles (circa 490–430 BC) and the Italian playwright Luigi Pirandello.

You will be treated to what is considered by many experts to be the best-preserved collection of buildings from classical Greece in existence ★ today. Whether you first come upon the **Valle di Templi** (Valley of the Temples) in the early morning light, by their golden floodlights at night, or at very their best in February, when the valley is awash in the fragrant blossoms of thousands of almond trees during the Festa delle Mandorle, it is easy to see why Agrigento was celebrated by Pindar as "the most beautiful city built by mortal men." Exit from the highway, walk down from the parking lot on Via dei Templi, and turn left. The ridge on which the temples of Hercules, Concord, and Juno is in front of you.

23 The eight pillars of the **Tempio di Ercole** (Temple of Hercules) make up Agrigento's oldest temple complex, dating from the 6th century BC. Partially reconstructed in 1922, it reveals the remains of a large Doric temple that originally had 38 columns. Like all the area temples, it faces east. The Museo Archeologico Nazionale (☞ *below*) contains some of the marble warrior figures that once decorated its pediment.

24 Up the hill from the Temple of Hercules is the beautiful **Tempio di Concordia** (Concord), which owes its exceptional state of preservation to the fact that it was converted to an early Christian church in the 6th century and was extensively restored in the 18th. The structure dates from about 430 BC, and, like most of the temples here, was constructed of the local soft oolitic limestone that was originally coated in white stucco and brightly painted. The name of the temple, based on a Latin inscription found nearby, is in fact an error. It is now accepted that the inscription bears no relation to the building. To this day, however, it remains a well-established tradition in Agrigento for couples to visit the temple on their wedding day. On the left of the temple is a Paleochristian **necropolis.** Early Christian tombs were both cut into the rock and dug into underground catacombs.

25 Following along the Via Sacra, the next monument is the **Tempio di Giunone** (Juno), commanding an exquisite view of the valley, especially at sunset. It is similar but smaller than the Concordia and dates from about 450 BC. Traces of a fire that probably occurred during the Carthaginian attack in 406 BC, which destroyed the ancient town, can be seen on the walls of the cellar. Thirty of the original 34 columns still stand, of which 16 still retain their capitals. From the parking lot in the Piazzale dei Templi, where a bar sells drinks and ice cream, cross to the opposite side of the road.

26 Though never completed, the **Tempio di Giove** (Jupiter) was considered the eighth wonder of the world. The temple was probably built in gratitude for victory over Carthage and was constructed by prisoners captured in that war. Basically Doric in style, it did not have the usual colonnade of freestanding columns, but a series of half-columns attached to a solid wall. Inside the excavation you can see one of the 38 colossal figures, or telamones, of Atlas that supported the massive roof of the temple. This design is unique among known Doric temples, and, with a length of over 110 m, the building is the largest known classical temple. Note that the temple usually closes at 5.

- Hellenistic and Roman Quarter, **29**
- Museo Archeologico Nazionale, **28**
- Tempio di Castore e Polluce, **27**
- Tempio di Concordia, **24**
- Tempio di Ercole, **23**
- Tempio di Giove, **26**
- Tempio di Giunone, **25**

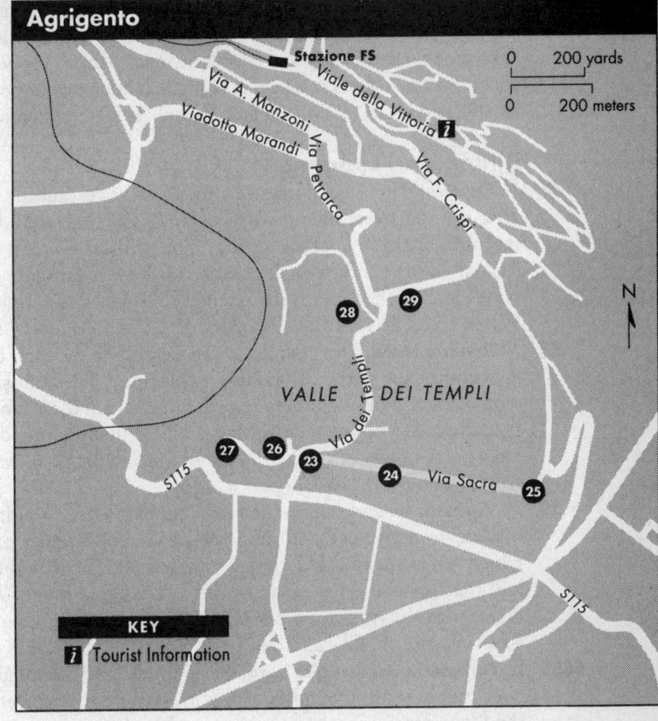

27 The four columns supporting part of an entablature of the **Tempio di Castore e Polluce** (Castor and Pollux) have become emblematic of Agrigento, but, in fact, the reconstruction of 1836 haphazardly put together elements from diverse buildings. Farther north is the **Sanctuario delle Divinita Ctonie** (Sanctuary of the Chthonic Divinities), where cultic altars and eight small temples dedicated to Demeter, Persephone, and other Underworld deities have been found. In the same vicinity are two columns, part of a temple dedicated to Hephaestus (Vulcan).

At the end of Via dei Templi, where it turns left and becomes Via Pe-
28 trarca, stands the **Museo Archeologico Nazionale.** An impressive collection of antiquities includes vases, votives, everyday objects, weapons, statues, and models of the temples as they once stood. ✉ *Contrada San Nicola,* ☎ *0922/401565.* 🎫 *8,000 lire.* ⏲ *Sun.–Tues. 9–1, Wed.–Sat. 9–1 and 2:30–5:30.*

On the opposite side of the road from the archaeological museum is
29 the **Hellenistic and Roman Quarter,** which consists of four parallel streets, running north and south, that have been uncovered, along with the foundations of some houses from the Roman settlement (2nd century BC). Some of these streets still have their original mosaic pavements.

There is little reason to go up the hill to the rather dreary modern city of Agrigento, where industrial speculation threatens to encroach upon the Valley of the Temples below—except to ring the doorbell at the **Convento di Santo Spirito** on the Salita di Santo Spirito off Via Porcello and try the almond cakes and the *kus-kus* (sweet cake) made of pistachio nuts and chocolate, that the nuns there prepare.

OFF THE BEATEN PATH

CASA PIRANDELLO – One of Agrigento's native sons was the distinguished dramatist Luigi Pirandello (1867–1936), whose plays, such as *Six Characters in Search of an Author,* express the fundamental ambiguity of life. Pirandello's ashes lie under a pine tree behind the house where he was born, in Piazzale Caos, a few kilometers west of town. His house has been made into a museum of Pirandello memorabilia. Every year, a festival of Pirandello's plays is held in Agrigento from late July to early August. ☎ *0922/511102.* ✉ *4,000 lire.* ⏲ *Daily 8:30–1 hr before sunset.*

Dining and Lodging

$$ ✕ **Caprice.** The high points of this popular restaurant in the temple area are the overflowing trays of antipasti and abundant plates of seafood, including pesce spada. The waiters—when they are not rushed—are proud to explain some of the less-familiar entries on the wine list, which is relatively extensive. ✉ *Via Panoramica dei Templi 51,* ☎ *0922/26469. AE, DC, MC, V. Closed Fri. and July 1–15.*

$$ ✕ **Taverna Mosè.** This restaurant can get busy in the early evening, when it becomes too dark for temple exploring. The atmosphere bustles with waiters shouting orders at each other and at the kitchen. The house specialties are homemade sausages and grilled fish, and the wine list has a good variety of choices. ✉ *Contrada San Biagio 6,* ☎ *0922/26778. AE. Closed Mon. and Aug.*

$$ ✕ **Vigneto.** Unless you make reservations at this popular restaurant, it's best to arrive early to snag one of the good tables on the terrace, which has a memorable view of the temples. Seasonal daily specials and the fish market's freshest top the changing menu. *Arrosti* (roast meats) are always a good bet. ✉ *Via Cavaleri Magazzeni 11,* ☎ *0922/414319. MC, V. Closed Tues.*

$$$$ 🏨 **Foresteria Baglio della Luna.** Fiery sunsets and moonlight cast a glow over this hotel in the valley below the temples. A tower dating from the 8th century is central to the stone farmhouse complex, set around a peaceful geranium- and ivy-filled courtyard and a garden beyond. Standard rooms are cozy, but nothing fancy, with mellow walls, bright flowered prints, and wooden furniture. The suites, one situated in the tower, are sumptuous and clubby, with fine wooden floors and ceilings, bold fabrics, and some antiques. The cozy, rustic restaurant serves Sicilian and Italian specialties, among them superb pasta dishes. Breakfast is included in the rate. ✉ *Contrada Maddalusa, Valle dei Templi, 92100,* ☎ *0922/511061,* FAX *0922/598802. 21 rooms, 3 suites. Restaurant, bar, air-conditioning, minibars. AE, MC, V.*

$$$ ★ 🏨 **Villa Athena.** There is much demand for this well-furnished former villa right in the midst of the archaeological zone, so make reservations as early as possible. Many rooms—they're all different—have terraces looking out on the large gardens and the swimming pool. The temples are an easy walk from the hotel, and there is a convivial atmosphere in the bar, where a multinational crowd swaps stories. ✉ *Via dei Templi 33, 92100,* ☎ *0922/596288,* FAX *0922/402180. 40 rooms. Restaurant, bar, pool. AE, DC, MC, V.*

$$–$$$ 🏨 **Jolly dei Templi.** Guests travel 8 km (5 mi) southeast of town to Villaggio Mosè to stay in this Jolly hotel. Rooms are large, bright, and airy, and if there's a sense of having seen it all before, you probably have—in one of the other Jolly hotels or in any well-equipped U.S. motel. That is the price to pay for what are always comfortable, hassle-free accommodations. The Pirandello restaurant here is excellent. ✉ *Parco Angeli, 92100 Villagio Mosè,* ☎ *0922/606144,* FAX *0922/606685. 146 rooms. Restaurant, bar, pool. AE, DC, MC, V.*

Nightlife and the Arts

On the first weekend in February, Agrigento hosts a **Festa delle Mandorle,** or Almond Blossom Festival, with international folk dances, a costumed parade, and the sale of marzipan and other sweets made from almonds.

SIRACUSA

Greek Sicily began along the Ionian coast, and some of the finest examples of Baroque art and architecture were also created here, particularly in Siracusa. The city was founded in 734 BC by Greek colonists from Corinth and soon grew to rival, and even surpass, Athens in splendor and power. Siracusa became the largest, wealthiest city-state in Magna Graecia and the bulwark of Greek civilization. Although it suffered from tyrannical rule, kings such as Dionysius filled their courts in the 5th century BC with Greeks of the highest artistic stature—among them, Pindar, Aeschylus, and Archimedes. The Athenians did not welcome the rise of Siracusa and sent a fleet to destroy the rival city, but the natives outsmarted them in what was one of the greatest naval battles of ancient history (413 BC). Siracusa continued to prosper until it was conquered two centuries later by the Romans.

There are essentially two areas to explore in Siracusa—the Parco Archeologico, on the mainland, and the island of Ortygia, the ancient city first inhabited by the Greeks, which juts out into the Ionian sea and is connected to the mainland by two small bridges.

Exploring Siracusa

Siracusa's old nucleus of Ortygia is a compact area, a pleasure to amble around without getting unduly tired. In contrast, mainland Siracusa is predominantly a grid of right-angled streets through which the main roads Corso Gelone and Viale Cadorna channel most of the traffic. At the northern end of Corso Gelone, above Viale Paolo Orsi, the orderly grid gives way to the ancient quarter of Neapolis, where the sprawling Parco Archeologico is accessible from Viale Teracati (an extension of Corso Gelone). East of Viale Teracati, about a 10-minute walk from the Parco Archeologico, the district of Tyche holds the archaeological museum and the church and catacombs of San Giovanni, both off Viale Teocrito. You *could* walk to these far-flung sites from Ortygia, but it's not a greatly inspiring hike, and you'd do better to take either a taxi or a city bus. Coming from the train station, it's a 15-minute trudge to Ortygia along Via Francesco Crispi and Corso Umberto.

A Good Tour: Parco Archeologico and Museo Archeologico

Start your tour of mainland Siracusa at the Parco Archeologico (entrance from Largo Anfiteatro). Before reaching the ticket booth, pause briefly at the meager remains of the **Ara di Ierone** ㉚. Beyond the ticket office, the extensive **Latomia del Paradiso** ㉛ stretches out on the right, while the archaeological park's *pièce de résistance* lies to the left: the awesome expanse of the **Teatro Greco** ㉜. Leave by the same way you entered, making a diversion before the park's exit (you'll need to show your entry ticket) to view the elliptical **Anfiteatro Romano** ㉝. From Largo Anfiteatro, head east along the busy Viale Teocrito, where, after a few minutes, you'll pass the **Museo Archeologico** ㉞. A few steps beyond is the much smaller but still intriguing **Museo del Papiro** ㉟. From here, retrace your steps along Viale Teocrito before turning right up Via San Giovanni to visit the church of San Giovanni and the **Catacombe di San Giovanni** ㊱ beneath. From here, drive or take one of the frequent city buses down Corso Gelone and Corso Umberto for the old city.

TIMING

Allow at least a full day for this tour, which can be quite taxing. In view of the fact that the Parco Archeologico has little or no shade, early morning or late afternoon would be the best times to visit on a hot day. You'll probably want to spend three or four hours here, with perhaps an hour afterwards to recuperate over lunch or a birra (beer). The archaeological museum might easily take another two or three hours, though the tour of the refreshingly cool catacombs lasts less than half an hour, and you will probably spend a similar amount of time in the Museo del Papiro.

Sights to See

33 **Anfiteatro Romano** (Roman Amphitheater). A comparison of this and the Teatro Greco (☞ *below*) reveals much about the differences between the Greek and Roman personalities. In the Roman amphitheater, the emphasis was on the spectacle of combative sports and the circus. The arena is one of the largest of its kind and was built around the 2nd century AD. The corridor where gladiators and beasts entered the ring is still intact, and the seats, some of which still bear the occupants' names, were hauled in and constructed on the site from huge slabs of limestone. A crowd-pleasing show, and not the elevation of men's minds, was the intention here. If the Parco Archeologico (Archaeological Park) is closed, go up Viale G. Rizzo from Viale Teracati, to the belvedere overlooking the ruins, which are floodlit at night. ✉ Parco Archeologico: *Viale Augusto,* ☎ *0931/66206.* 🎫 *4,000 lire.* ⏲ *Daily 9–1 hr before sunset (last tickets sold 2 hrs before sunset).*

30 **Ara di Ierone** (Altar of Hieron). Near the entrance to the Archaeological Park is the gigantic Altar of Hieron, which was once used by the Greeks for spectacular sacrifices involving hundreds of animals. ☞ *Anfiteatro Romano, above.*

36 **Catacombe di San Giovanni.** Not far from the Archaeological Park, off Viale Teocrito, the catacombs below the church of San Giovanni are one of the earliest-known Christian sites in the city. Inside the crypt of San Marciano is an altar where St. Paul preached on his way through Sicily to Rome. The frescoes in this small chapel are still bright and fresh, though some dating from the 4th century AD show their age. ✉ *Piazza San Giovanni.* 🎫 *4,000 lire.* ⏲ *Mid-Mar.–mid-Nov., Wed–Mon. 9–noon and 2–5:30; mid-Nov.–mid-Mar., Wed.–Mon. 9–1 and 3–5 (hrs subject to change).*

31 **Latomia del Paradiso.** Just beyond the ticket office of the Archaeological Park, you will come upon a lush tropical garden full of palm and citrus trees. This series of quarries served as prisons for the defeated Athenians, who were enslaved; the quarries once rang with the sound of their chisels and hammers. At one end is the Orecchio di Dionisio, with an ear-shape entrance and unusual acoustics inside, as you'll discover if you clap your hands. The legend is that Dionysius used to listen in at the top of the quarry to hear what the slaves were plotting below. ☞ *Anfiteatro Romano, above.*

34 **Museo Archeologico.** The impressive collection contained in Siracusa's splendid archaeological museum is arranged by region around a central atrium and ranges from neolithic pottery to fine Greek statues and vases. You will want to compare the Landolina Venus—a headless, stout goddess of love who rises out of the sea in measured modesty (she is a 1st-century-AD Roman copy of the Greek original)—with the much earlier (300 BC) elegant Greek statue of Hercules in Section C. Of a completely different style is a marvelous fanged Gorgon, its tongue sticking out, that once adorned the cornice of the temple of Athena to ward off evildoers. One exhibit depicts the Temple of Apollo, the oldest Doric temple in Sicily, on the island of Ortygia. ✉ *Viale Teocrito,* ☎ *0931/464022.* 🎫 *8,000 lire.* ⏲ *Tues.–Sat. 9–1 and 3:30–6:30, Mon. 3:30–6:30; 1st, 3rd, 5th Sun. of the month 9–12:30.*

Anfiteatro Romano, **33**
Ara di Ierone, **30**
Castello Maniace, **45**
Catacombe di San Giovanni, **36**
Duomo, **40**
Fonte Aretusa, **44**
Latomia del Paradiso, **31**
Museo Archeologico, **34**
Museo del Papiro, **35**
Museo Regionale, **43**
Palazzo Beneventano del Bosco, **41**
Piazza Archimede, **38**
Piazza del Duomo, **39**
Santa Lucia alla Badia, **42**
Teatro Greco, **32**
Tempio di Apollo, **37**

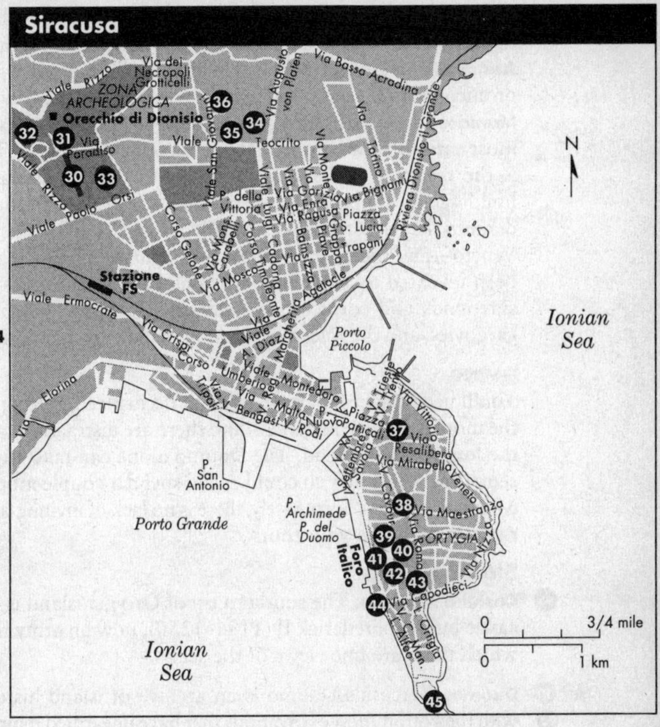

35 **Museo del Papiro.** Close to Siracusa's Museo Archeologico, the Papyrus Museum demonstrates how papyruses are prepared from reeds and then painted—an ancient tradition in the city. Siracusa, it seems, has the only climate outside the Nile Valley in which the papyrus plant—from which we get our word "paper"—thrives. ✉ *Viale Teocrito 66,* ☎ *0931/61616.* *Free.* *Tues.–Sun. 9–1.*

32 **Teatro Greco** (Greek Theater). The chief monument in the Archaeological Park—and indeed one of Sicily's greatest classical sites—is this most complete Greek theater existing from antiquity. Climb to the top of the seating area for a fine view: all the seats converge upon a single point—the stage—which has the natural scenery and the sky as its background. Hewn out of the hillside rock in the 5th century BC, the theater, which could accommodate 15,000, saw the premieres of the plays of Aeschylus, and in May and June of even-numbered years, Greek tragedies are still performed here. Drama as a kind of religious ritual was the intention when the theater was built. ☞ *Anfiteatro Romano, above.*

A Good Walk: Ortytia Island

The central part of Siracusa is a modern city, with Corso Gelone its main shopping street. At its southern end, Corso Umberto leads to the Ortygia Island bridge, which crosses a harbor lined with fish restaurants. Begin at Piazza Pancali, the square where you arrive after crossing the bridge that connects Ortygia to the mainland. Behind the piazza stand the scanty remains of the **Tempio di Apollo** ㊲. Proceed from here to **Piazza Archimede** ㊳, from which it's a short hop to **Piazza del Duomo** ㊴, the main square of the old town and site of Siracusa's ancient and splendid **Duomo** ㊵. Other impressive buildings to see in the piazza include **Palazzo Beneventano del Bosco** ㊶ and the church of **Santa Lucia alla Badia** ㊷; the Palazzo Bellomo, housing the **Museo Regionale** ㊸, is just round the corner. After you've had your fill of this, stroll onto the waterfront where a choice of bars cluster around the lovely **Fonte Aretusa** ㊹, a perfect spot for a break. Walking along the seafront promenade to the southern tip of Ortygia will bring you to the **Castello Maniace** ㊺. Apart from the Temple of Apollo, Ortygia is composed almost entirely of warm, restrained Baroque buildings. This uniformity is the result of an earthquake in 1693 that necessitated major rebuilding at a time when the Baroque was de rigueur. Be sure to wander into the backstreets—especially along Via della Maestranza or Via Veneto—and notice the bulbous wrought-iron balconies (said to have been invented to accommodate ladies' billowing skirts), the window surrounds and cornices of buildings decorated with mermaids and gargoyles, and the stucco decoration on Palazzo Lantieri on Via Roma.

TIMING

You'll need the best part of a day to do justice to Ortygia. Obviously, the more detours you make—and there are distractions aplenty here—the longer you'll spend. The Duomo alone can take an hour or so to see properly, while you could easily spend a couple more hours in the Museo Regionale. Fortunately, there is no lack of inviting bars and restaurants to break up your tour.

Sights to See

45 **Castello Maniace.** The southern tip of Ortygia island is occupied by a castle built by Frederick II (1194–1250), now an army barracks, from which there are fine views of the sea.

★ 40 **Duomo.** Siracusa's Duomo is an archive of island history, beginning with the bottommost excavations that have unearthed remnants of Sicily's distant past, when the Siculi inhabitants worshiped their deities here. During the 5th century BC, the Greeks built a temple to Athena over it, and in the 7th century, Siracusa's first Christian cathedral was built on top of the Greek structure. The elegant columns of the original temple were incorporated into the present structure and are clearly visible, embedded in the exterior wall along Via Minerva. The Greek columns were also used to dramatic advantage inside, where on one side they form chapels connected by elegant wrought-iron gates. The Baroque facade, added in 1700, displays a harmonious rhythm of concaves and convexes. In front, the piazza is encircled by pink and white oleanders and elegant buildings ornamented with filigree grillwork. ✉ *Piazza del Duomo.* ☎ *0931/65328.* ⏲ *Daily 8–noon and 4–7:30.*

44 **Fonte Aretusa.** Just off the promenade along the harbor, you'll find the Fountain of Arethusa, a freshwater spring next to the sea. This anomaly is explained by a Greek legend that tells how the nymph Arethusa was changed into a fountain by the goddess Artemis (Diana) when she tried to escape the advances of the river god Alpheus. She fled from Greece, into the sea, with Alpheus in close pursuit, and emerged in Sicily at this spring. Supposedly even today, if you throw a cup into the Alpheus River in Greece, it will emerge here at this fountain, which at present is home to a few tired ducks and some dull-color carp—but no cups. Steps lead to the tree-lined promenade along the harbor front.

43 **Museo Regionale.** Siracusa's principal museum of art is housed inside Palazzo Bellomo, a lovely Catalan-Gothic building with mullioned windows and an elegant exterior staircase. Among the select group of paintings and sculptures inside is a Santa Lucia by Caravaggio (1573–1610) and a damaged, but still brilliant, *Annunciation* by Antonello da Messina. ✉ *Via Capodieci 14,* ☎ *0931/69617.* 🎟 *8,000 lire.* ⏲ *Mon.–Sat. 9–1, Sun. 9–noon.*

41 **Palazzo Beneventano del Bosco.** In the right corner of Piazza del Duomo, this elegant palazzo has an impressive interior courtyard ending in a grand winding staircase. ✉ *Piazza del Duomo.*

38 **Piazza Archimede.** One of Ortygia's two main piazzas has at its center a Baroque fountain festooned with fainting sea nymphs and dancing jets of water.

39 **Piazza del Duomo.** In the heart of Ortygia, this ranks as one of Italy's most beautiful piazzas, its elongated space lined with Sicilian Baroque gems.

42 **Santa Lucia alla Badia.** This Baroque church stands at one end of Piazza del Duomo, featuring an engaging wrought-iron balcony and pleasant facade. ✉ *Piazza del Duomo. Closed for restoration.*

37 **Tempio di Apollo.** In the piazza on the other side of the bridge, you'll find the ruins of a temple dedicated to Apollo, a model of which you may have seen in the Museo Archeologico. In fact, little of this noble Doric temple still remains today, except for some crumbled walls and shattered columns; the window in the south wall belongs to a Norman church that was built much later on the same spot. ✉ *Piazza Pancali.*

OFF THE BEATEN PATH

CASTELLO EURIALO – West of the city, on the highlands that overlook the sea, the Euryalus Castle was created by Dionysius, with the help of Archimedes, for protection against the Carthaginians. This astonishing boat-shape structure once covered 15,000 square yards. The intricate maze of tunnels is fascinating, and the view from the heights is superb. ✉ *Belvedere, 8 km (5 mi) northwest of Siracusa.* 🎫 *Free.* ⏲ *Daily 9–1 hr before sunset.*

Dining and Lodging

$$–$$$ ★ ✕ **Ionico.** Enjoy seaside dining in the coastal Santa Lucia district. The Ionico boasts a terrace and veranda for alfresco meals, and the interior is plastered with diverse historical relics and has a cheerful open hearth for the winter. Chef-proprietor Roberto Giudice cooks meals to order or will suggest a specialty from a selection of market-fresh ingredients. Try the pasta *con acciughe e il pan grattato* (in an anchovy sauce). ✉ *Riviera Dionisio il Grande 194,* ☎ *0931/65540. AE, DC, MC, V. Closed Tues.*

$$ ✕ **Archimede.** The *antipasto misto* (mixed antipasto) should whet your appetite for the predominantly seafood menu of this small establishment in the *città vecchia* (old town), Ortygia. Risotto di mare and pesce spada are specialties, but the menu veers away from seafood when game is in season. Otherwise, sample the *involtini all'Archimede* (roulades stuffed with cheese and ham with bread crumbs). ✉ *Via Gemmellaro 8,* ☎ *0931/69701. AE, DC, MC, V. No dinner Sun.*

$$ ✕ **Arlecchino.** A bustling bohemian atmosphere pervades this restaurant, found midway between the archaeological zone and the old town. It's popular with artists and students, always a sign of good value. The Palermo-born proprietor serves specialties from his hometown, such as risotto *ai ricci* (with sea urchins) and homemade cassata for dessert. ✉ *Via dei Tolomei 5,* ☎ *0931/66386. AE, DC, MC, V. Closed Mon. (May–Sept.) and Sun. (Oct.–Apr.)*

$$ ✕ **Minosse.** You'll find this small, old-fashioned restaurant in the heart of Siracusa's old town. Fish is the specialty, and it comes broiled, baked, stuffed, and skewered. For an introduction to the local seafood, try the antipasto misto di frutti di mare. Ask for the daily special as your main course, or try the pesce spada alla brace. The *zuppa di pesce* (fish soup) is a local favorite. ✉ *Via Mirabella 6,* ☎ *0931/66366. AE, MC, V. No dinner Mon. Oct.–Mar.*

$$$$ 🏨 **Grand Hotel.** An elegant, fantasy-inspired design that would feel at home in Gotham prevails at this venerable institution, enjoying a prime position overlooking the Porto Grande as it has done since 1898 (except during recent 5-year restoration). A modern seascape sets a dreamy tone in the lobby, which is decked out in periwinkle leather club chairs, period antiques, gilt mirrors, and marble inlay floors lined with lights. Beyond the bolted-leather doors, rooms don fine wood floors, modern fixtures, batik-print curtains, and stained-glass windows. The Piccolo Museo (Little Museum) downstairs displays columns from the original structure. This is by far Siracusa's best offering. ✉ *Viale Mazzini 12, 96100,* ☎ *0931/464600,* FAX *0931/464611. 39 rooms, 19 suites. Restaurant, bar, minibars, meeting rooms, free parking. AE, DC, MC, V.*

$$$ 🏨 **Domus Mariae.** You can see the sea at the end of the corridor as you enter this hotel on Ortygia's eastern shore. Unusually, it is run by nuns of the Ursuline order, who help to create a placid and peaceful ambience. Don't expect monastic conditions, however: rugs and refined decor distinguish the public rooms, and guest rooms—half with seaviews—are spacious and comfortable. Availability is limited, so it's essential to reserve ahead. ✉ *Via Vittorio Veneto 76, 96100,* ☎ *0931/24854,* FAX *0931/24858. 12 rooms. Restaurant, bar. AE, DC, MC, V.*

$$$ 🏨 **Jolly Hotel.** The rooms are uniformly comfortable in this member of the Jolly hotel chain, Italy's answer to Holiday Inns. The big advantage, apart from knowing that the plugs work and the rooms are soundproofed, is the location. The hotel is ½ km (¼ mi) from the train station and within easy walking distance of the archaeological zone. ✉ *Corso Gelone 45, 96100,* ☎ *0931/461111,* FAX *0931/461126. 100 rooms. Restaurant, bar. AE, DC, MC, V.*

Nightlife and the Arts

The feast of the city's patroness, Santa Lucia (St. Lucy), is held on December 13 at **Santa Lucia alla Badia** (✉ Piazza del Duomo). A splendid silver statue of the saint is carried from the cathedral to the church on the site of her martyrdom, near the Catacombs of San Giovanni. A torchlight procession and band music accompany the bearers. In May and June of even-numbered years only (next 2000), Siracusa's impressive **Teatro Greco** (✉ Parco Archeologico, ☎ 0931/67710) is the setting for performances of classical drama and comedy.

EASTERN SICILY

On the Road to Taormina

Sicily's interior is for the most part underpopulated and untrammeled, though the Imperial Roman Villa at Casale, outside Piazza Armerina, gives precious evidence from an epoch gone by. Don't miss Caltagirone, a ceramics center of renown. On the coast, Siracusa (☞ *above*) offers a fascinating mix of ancient Greek, Renaissance, and Baroque architecture with some excellent museums. To the north, Catania packs the vivacity of Palermo, if not the artistic wealth; the city makes a good base for exploring lofty Mt. Etna, as does Taormina. Messina's scant attractions include its unparalleled position opposite the mountains of Calabria, and one of the island's best museum collections.

Enna

46 *105 km (63 mi) northeast of Agrigento, 136 km (85 mi) southeast of Palermo.*

Deep in Sicily's interior, the fortress city of Enna commands exceptional views of the surrounding rolling plains, and, in the distance, Mt. Etna. The narrow winding streets are dominated at one end by the impressive castle built by Frederick II, easily visible as you approach the town.

Lodging

$$ **Grande Albergo Sicilia.** Sicily's interior has a dearth of decent accommodations, so it's a relief to find Enna's only hotel a reliable and comfortable choice. In the heart of town (don't be put off by the unsightly facade), the Sicilia has bright, clean rooms, some with excellent views, and all equipped with TV and telephone. ✉ *Piazza Colaianni 5, 94100,* ☎ *0935/500850,* FAX *0935/500488. 76 rooms. Bar, parking (fee). AE, DC, MC, V.*

Piazza Armerina

47 *40 km (25 mi) south of Enna, 110 km (69 mi) west of Catania.*

Reached through pine and eucalyptus woods and low farmland, Piazza Armerina is a tiny Baroque town noted mainly for the sumptuous emperor's Imperial Roman Villa country house in nearby Casale (☞ *below*).

Dining

$$ ✕ **Centrale da Totò.** At this reliable trattoria, the emphasis is on a family clientele, rather than intimate or expense-account dining, and the portions reflect this *mangia, mangia* outlook. Try the *pappardelle alla Centrale* (wide pasta with a rich tomato sauce and fresh vegetables), or the *bocca di lupo* (literally "wolf's mouth," veal stuffed with eggplant, ham, and Parmesan). ✉ *Via Mazzini 29,* ☎ *0935/680153. AE, DC, MC, V. Closed Mon. Oct.–Mar.*

Nightlife and the Arts

The **Palio dei Normanni,** a medieval tournament with participants dressed in 14th-century fashion, takes place on August 13.

Casale

48 *6 km (4 mi) southwest of Piazza Armerina, 120 km (75 mi) west of Catania.*

The exceptionally well-preserved **Imperial Roman Villa** here is thought to have been a hunting lodge of the Emperor Maximianus Heraclius (4th century AD). The excavations were not begun until 1950, and the wall decorations and vaulting have been lost. However, some of the best mosaics of the Roman world cover more than 12,000 square ft under a shelter that hints at the layout of the original buildings. The mosaics were probably made by Carthaginian artisans, because they are similar to those in the Tunis Bardo Museum. The entrance was through a triumphal arch that led into an atrium surrounded by a portico of columns. Through this, the *thermae,* or bathhouse, is reached. It is colorfully decorated with mosaic nymphs, a Neptune, and slaves massaging bathers. The peristyle leads to the main villa, where in the Salone del Circo you look down on mosaics that illustrate Roman circus sports. Another apartment shows hunting scenes of tigers, elephants, and ostriches; the gym shows girls exercising; the private apartments are covered with scenes from Greek and Roman mythology; and Room 38 even reveals a touch of eroticism. ✉ *Imperial Roman Villa, Casale,* ☎ *0935/680036.* 🎫 *4,000 lire.* ⏲ *Daily 9–1 and 3–1 hr before sunset.*

Caltagirone

49 *30 km (18 mi) southeast of Piazza Armerina, 60 km (37 mi) southwest of Catania.*

Built over three hills, the charming Baroque town of Caltagirone is a leader in the Sicilian ceramics industry. Here you will find majolica balustrades, tile-decorated windowsills, and a monumental tile staircase of 142 steps—each decorated with a different pattern—leading up to the neglected **Santa Maria del Monte.** On the feast of San Giacomo (July 24), the staircase is illuminated with candles that form a tapestry design over the steps. It is the result of months of work preparing the 4,000 *coppi,* or cylinders of colored paper that hold oil lamps. At 9:30 PM on July 24, a squad of hundreds of boys springs into action to light the lamps, so that the staircase flares up all at once. ⏲ *Daily 7–noon and 4–7.*

There is an interesting **Museo della Ceramica** (Ceramics Museum) in the public gardens, which were designed by Ernesto Basile (1857–1932), the master of Sicilian art nouveau. The exhibits in the museum trace the history of the craft from specimens excavated from the earliest settlements, through the influential Arab period, to the present. ✉ *Museo della Ceramica, Giardino Pubblico,* ☎ *0933/21680.* 🎫 *8,000 lire.* ⏲ *Daily 9–6.*

Shopping

CERAMICS

The ceramic creations of De Simone, whose Picasso-like faces on plates and pitchers are popular abroad, can be seen at the shop, **Akatos** (✉ Via Romeo 14).

Palazzolo Acreide

50 *60 km (40 mi) southeast of Caltagirone, 40 km (25 mi) west of Siracusa.*

This small inland town is best known for its archaeological zone, the old Greek *Akrai,* containing the foundations of a temple dedicated to Aphrodite, and a well-preserved theater.

Dining

$ ✕ **Da Alfredo.** This one-man show (Alfredo is the owner-chef) is on one of the most attractive streets of this Baroque town between Caltagirone and Siracusa. Specialties depend on the season and the whims of Alfredo himself. Homemade pasta, such as penne and cheese-filled ravioli, are specialties, and the sauces are hearty and spicy. ✉ *Via Duca d'Aosta 27,* ☎ *0931/883266. No credit cards. Closed Wed.*

Noto

51 *34 km (21 mi) southeast of Palazzolo Acreide, 32 km (19 mi) southwest of Siracusa.*

Modeled on a hierarchical plan following the destruction of the old town during the great earthquake of 1693, Noto presents a pleasing ensemble of honey-color Baroque architecture, strikingly uniform in style, but never dull. Disaster struck again in March 1996, when the dome of the majestic cathedral, Noto's centerpiece (completed in 1776), collapsed during a thunderstorm, probably due to a previous botched restoration. Restoration is currently underway, but may take several years to repair the damage, adding to the rebuilding that has blighted this otherwise delightful town center.

Dining

$ ✕ **Il Giglio.** Seafood dishes with a Spanish touch are the specialty at this pleasant trattoria in the center of town run by Maria Luz Corruchaga and her husband, Corrado. Particularly recommended are pasta *al nero di seppia* (with cuttlefish), ravioli *di ricotta* (stuffed with ricotta) and served with fresh tomato and basil, and *zuppa di vongole e cozze* (clam and mussel soup). ✉ *Piazza Municipio,* ☎ *0931/838640. MC, V. No lunch Sat.*

Catania

52 *60 km (37 mi) north of Siracusa, 94 km (59 mi) south of Messina.*

The chief wonder of Catania, Sicily's second city, is that it is there at all. Its successive populations were deported by one Greek tyrant, sold into slavery by another, and driven out by the Carthaginians. Every time the city got back on its feet, it was struck by a new calamity: plague decimated the population in the Middle Ages, a mile-wide stream of lava from Mt. Etna swallowed most of the city in 1669, and 25 years later a disastrous earthquake forced the Catanese to begin again. Today the city needs considerable renovation. Traffic flows in ever-increasing volume and adds to the smog from the industrial zone between Catania and Siracusa, but the views of Mt. Etna from Catania are superb. To Mt. Etna, Catania also owes a fertile surrounding plain and its site on nine successive layers of lava. Many of Catania's buildings are constructed from solidified lava, and the black lava stone has given the city a singular appearance. As a result, Catania is known as the city of lava and oranges. Catania's greatest native son is the composer Vincenzo Bellini (1801–35), whose operas have thrilled audiences since their premieres about 170 years ago. His home, now the **Museo Bellini,** in Piazza San Francesco, preserves memorabilia of the man and his work. ✉ *Piazza San Francesco 3,* ☎ *095/7150535.* *Free.* *Mon.–Sat. 9–1:30, Sun. 9–12:30.*

The **Villa Bellini** (✉ To the north, just off Via Etnea), Catania's public gardens, on clear days has lovely views of snowcapped Mt. Etna. The **Duomo** is a fine work by Vaccarini (1736), as is the obelisk-balancing elephant carved out of lava stone in the piazza in front. Bellini is buried inside the cathedral. Also inside is the sumptuous Cappella di Sant'Agata, Catania's patron saint, who is credited with having held off, more than once, the fiery flows of lava that threatened the city. During her feast (February 3–5), huge 16-ft-tall, highly ornate carved wooden *cannelore* (large bundles of candles) are paraded through the streets at night. ✉ *Bottom end of Via Etnea,* ☎ *095/320044.* *Daily 8–noon and 4–7.*

OFF THE BEATEN PATH

ACIREALE – Sixteen kilometers (10 mi) up the coast from Catania, Acireale sits amid a clutter of rocky pinnacles and lush lemon groves. The craggy coast is known as the Riviera dei Ciclopi, after the legend narrated in the *Odyssey,* in which the blinded cyclops, Polyphemus, hurled boulders at the retreating Ulysses, creating the spires of rock, or *faraglioni.* The richly Baroque town comes into its own during its Carnival celebrations, when the streets are jammed with thousands of fancy-dressed revelers and floats dripping with flowers and gaudy papier-mâché models. Acireale is also known for its puppet theater, a Sicilian tradition that has all but died out in other parts.

Dining and Lodging

If you haven't had cannoli in Sicily yet, the pastry shops along Via Etnea are good places to try one of these wafer tubes filled with silky smooth ricotta cheese. If you're in need of something more substantial, duck into one of the trattorias along this street and order a dish of pasta *alla Norma.* It's named after one of Bellini's most famous operas and consists of short pasta with a rich eggplant-and-tomato sauce, garnished with basil leaves and grated ricotta cheese, really a typical Sicilian pasta dish.

$$ ★ ✕ **Costa Azzurra.** At this seafood restaurant in the Ognina district, reserve a table on the veranda by the edge of the sea with good views of the harbor. The fritto misto can be ordered as an antipasto or a main course, and the pesce spada steak is a simple classic, served grilled with a large slice of lemon. ✉ *Via De Cristofaro 4, Ognina, just north of the center, on the way to the Taormina road,* ☎ *095/494920. Jacket and tie. AE, DC, MC, V. Closed Mon.*

$$ ✕ **Pagano.** This restaurant, behind the Hotel Excelsior, has been around since the 1950s and remains a favorite with locals for genuine Catanese cooking. Seafood is the specialty, but it's the unpretentious kind that won't send the check orbiting into the stratosphere. Try *insalata di polipo* (octopus salad) as a starter and then sarde or *acciughe* (anchovies) in a variety of sauces. Like the sober, rather dated decor, the service is formal. ✉ *Via De Roberto 37,* ☎ *095/537045. AE, DC, MC, V. Closed 1 wk in mid-Aug. No lunch Sat.*

$$$ **Excelsior.** Ask for a room facing Piazza Verga, a neat tree-lined square in this quiet but central district of Catania. The Excelsior has air-conditioning and sound-insulated windows in all rooms. The rooftop garden is one of Catania's most chic meeting places, and the American Bar should provide solace to anyone waxing nostalgic for a Manhattan. ✉ *Piazza Verga 39, 95129,* ☎ *095/537071,* FAX *095/537015. 166 rooms. Restaurant, bar, air-conditioning, parking (fee). AE, DC, MC, V.*

$–$$ **Savona.** The Savona is an efficiently run and well-maintained hotel a shot put's throw from Piazza del Duomo. The rooms are spacious and comfortable, solidly furnished, and equipped with TV and telephones. Prices include Continental breakfast. Reception can help with parking suggestions. ✉ *Via Vittorio Emanuele 210, 95124,* ☎ *095/326982,* FAX *095/7158169. 25 rooms, 20 with bath. Bar. No credit cards.*

Nightlife and the Arts

The opera season at **Teatro Bellini** (✉ Piazza Bellini, Catania, ☎ 095/7306111), October to mid-June, attracts top singers and productions to the birthplace of the great operatic composer Vincenzo Bellini.

Mt. Etna

★ 53 *30 km (19 mi) north of Catania, 60 km (37 mi) south of Messina.*

Mt. Etna is one of the world's major active volcanoes and is the largest and highest in Europe—the cone of the crater rising to 10,958 ft above sea level. It has erupted 10 times in the past three decades, most spectacularly in 1971 and 1983, when rivers of molten lava destroyed the two highest stations of the cable car that rises from the town of Sapienza. Travel in the proximity of the crater depends on Mt. Etna's temperament, but you can walk up and down the enormous lava dunes and wander over its moonlike surface of dead craters. The rings of vegetation change markedly as you rise, with vineyards and pine trees gradually giving way to growths of broom and lichen. Catania is the departure point for excursions around—but not always to the top of—Mt. Etna. Buses leave from Catania's train station in the early morning, or you can take the **Circumetnea railroad** (Via Caronda 352, Catania, ☎ 095/541243) around the volcano's base. The private railway runs 114 km (71 mi) between Giarre-Riposto and Catania—30 km (19 mi) apart on the coast—almost circling Mt. Etna. The line is small, slow, and single track, but gives some dramatic vistas of the volcano and goes through lava fields. The round-trip takes about 5 hours, there are about 10 departures a day, and tickets cost 6,000 one way.

Taormina

★ 54 *43 km (27 mi) southwest of Messina, 50 km (31 mi) north of Catania.*

The natural beauty of the medieval mountaintop town of Taormina is so great that even the considerable overdevelopment that it has suffered in the past 50 years has not spoiled its grandeur. The view of the sea and Mt. Etna from its jagged cactus-covered cliffs is as close to perfection as a panorama can get, especially on clear days when the snow-capped volcano's white puffs of smoke are etched against the blue sky. Writers have extolled Taormina's beauty almost since its founding in the 6th century BC by Greeks from Naples. Goethe and D. H. Lawrence were among its enthusiasts. The Greeks put a lofty premium on finding impressive locations to stage their dramas, and Taormina's **Teatro Greco** occupies one of the finest sites of any such theater. It was built during the 3rd century BC and rebuilt by the Romans during the 2nd century AD. Its acoustics are exceptional: even today a stage whisper can be heard in the last rows. In summer, Taormina hosts an arts festival of music, film, and dance events, many of which are held in the Teatro Greco (☞ Nightlife and the Arts, *below*). ✉ *Via Teatro Greco.* 🎫 *4,000 lire.* ⏱ *Daily 9–1 hr before sunset.*

Taormina's many 14th- and 15th-century palaces have been carefully preserved. Especially beautiful is the **Palazzo Corvaja** (✉ Palazzo Corvaja, Largo Santa Caterina, ☎ 0942/23243), with characteristic black-lava and white-limestone inlays. Today it houses the tourist office. The medieval **Castello Saraceno** (✉ Monte Tauro), enticingly perched on an adjoining cliff above the town, can be reached by footpath or car.

NEED A BREAK? If a marzipan devotee, you should not leave Taormina without trying one of the gooey sweets—maybe in the guise of the ubiquitous *fico d'India* (prickly pear)—at **Bar Mocambo** (✉ Piazza 9 Aprile).

Dining and Lodging

$$ ✕ **Granduca.** There's an antiques shop in the entrance, and the antiques theme continues within this tastefully decorated restaurant, where cane chairs and luxurious plants jostle for space among the objets d'art. Your attention, however, will be principally occupied with the riveting views from the glassed-in terrace, when it's not focused on such well-executed dishes as *pappardelle al Granduca* (wide-ribbon pasta with a creamy nut sauce) or *polpettine alla Siciliana* (grilled meatballs wrapped in lemon leaves). There's also a wood-fired oven for pizzas. ✉ *Corso Umberto 172,* ☎ *0942/24983. AE, DC, MC, V. Closed Tues.*

$$ ✕ **Luraleo.** You can dine indoors by candlelight or in the vine-covered garden in summer. It's touristy, but the food is of a high standard, with the accent on fish—delight in the different risotto with salmon and pistachios, a house specialty. There is a rich selection of antipasti. Service can be slow. ✉ *Via Bagnoli Croce 27,* ☎ *0942/24279. AE, DC, MC, V. Closed Wed. Oct.–June.*

$$$$ ★ 🏨 **San Domenico Palace.** Sweeping views from this converted 15th-century convent will linger in your mind long after you're gone. Luxury and comfort are bywords in this deluxe hotel, which has managed

to sneak in a number of unobtrusive 20th-century comforts (such as wheelchair access and climate control). The essential Renaissance flavor is preserved, however, with the cloisters and the chapel, now a bar. Rooms are brimming with antiques and fresh flowers. ✉ *Piazza San Domenico 5, 98039,* ☎ *0942/23701,* FAX *0942/625506. 101 rooms. 2 restaurants, 2 bars, pool. AE, DC, MC, V.*

$$$$ **Grand Hotel Timeo.** Even though it reopened in 1998 after a 14-year hiatus, the deluxe Timeo wears a handsome confidence and graceful patina that suggests it's been here—in a princely perch overlooking the town and just below the Teatro Greco—untouched since the dolce vita days. A splash of Morocco mixes with an old-world Mediterranean flavor in the lobby, with wooden floors, tile- and brickwork, and vaulting. Wrought-iron, wicker chairs, and tropical plants gather around marble tables in the bar and adjoining palatial patio. The rooms further indulge with fine earth-toned linens and drapes, oriental rugs, gilded prints, and exquisite molding on butter-colored walls. A 3-day minimum stay applies. ✉ *Via Teatro Greco 59, 98030,* ☎ *0942/23801,* FAX *0942/628501. 46 rooms, 10 suites. Restaurant, bar, air-conditioning, in-room safes, minibars, room service, pool, convention center. AE, DC, MC, V. Closed mid-Nov.–mid-Mar. MAP, FAP.*

$$$–$$$$ **Romantik Villa Ducale.** Formerly the summer residence of a local aristocrat, this stupendously sited villa has been converted into a comfortable hotel by his great-grandson and his wife. Individually styled rooms furnished with antiques and an intimate wood-paneled library create an atmosphere at once homely and palatial, while the vast roof-terrace takes full advantage of the wide panorama embracing Etna and the bay below. There is no restaurant but snacks are always available, and breakfast is on the terrace. In the summer months, a free shuttle bus connects the hotel with the area's best beaches. ✉ *Via Leonardo da Vinci 60, 98039,* ☎ *0942/28153,* FAX *0942/28710. 14 rooms, 1 suite. Bar. Closed Jan. 15–Mar. 1. AE, MC, V.*

$$–$$$$ **Villa Diodoro.** High on a cliff near the Greek amphitheater, this hotel commands superlative views. One of its most attractive features is the relaxing, sprightly garden, where you can have a drink and watch the play of light over the sea. ✉ *Via Bagnoli Croci 75, 98039,* ☎ *0942/23312,* FAX *0942/23391. 103 rooms. Restaurant, bar, pool. AE, DC, MC, V.*

$$ **Aratena Rocks Hotel.** Here's a good choice if you want to stay near the sea, escaping the worst of Taormina's scrum. In fact, Giardini-Naxos—the resort at the foot of Taormina—makes a great base, in summer just as lively as Taormina, and the broad sandy beach is a bonus. The hotel stands at one end of the bay, right on the cape where Greek settlers first landed in Sicily. If you don't fancy swimming off the rocks here, there's a splendid pool, around which Sicilian singers and musicians entertain you every other night in summer. A twice-daily free bus service links the hotel to Taormina. ✉ *Via Calcide Eubea 55, 98035 Giardini-Naxos,* ☎ *0942/51348,* FAX *0942/51690. 49 rooms. Restaurant, bar, pool, free parking. Closed Nov.–Mar. AE, DC, MC, V.*

$$ **Villa Fiorita.** This converted private home near the Greek amphitheater has excellent northerly coastal views from nearly every room. Rooms vary in size and furnishings, but most are bright, breezy, and colorful, with large windows and balconies (do ask). Prices are reasonable considering the compact swimming pool and garden. The elevator is at the top of 65 steps. ✉ *Via Pirandello 39, 98039,* ☎ *0942/24122,* FAX *0942/625967. 24 rooms. Pool, sauna. AE, MC, V.*

Nightlife and the Arts

FESTIVALS

The Greek Theater and the Palazzo dei Congressi, near the entrance to the theater, are the main venues for the summer festival dubbed

Taormina Arte, held each year from May to September and embracing classical music, ballet, theater performances, and also the famous **film festival** in July and August. For information, call ☎ 0942/21142, or check with the tourist office.

MUSIC

Free classical music concerts take place in the Duomo and some of Taormina's other churches during December and January, in **Natale a Taormina** (Christmas in Taormina), an initiative sponsored by the tourist office. Performances usually start at around 7 PM and last about an hour.

Outdoor Activities and Sports

GOLF

Twenty-five kilometers (15 mi) west of Taormina, on the slopes of Mt. Etna, the 18-hole **Picciolo Golf Club** (✉ Via Picciolo 1, 95012 Castiglione di Sicilia, ☎ 0942/986171) is both scenic and cool. The clubhouse has a restaurant and some guest rooms.

Shopping

Ceramics shops abound, but **G. di Blasi** (✉ 103 Corso Umberto, ☎ 0942/24671) is a standout in both quantity and quality. A small stock of the rustic white country pottery in traditional shapes from Caltagirone are very special. Via Teatro Greco, which winds up to the ancient Amphitheater, is lined with tiny shops and stalls selling the ubiquitous cameos, glass beads, lava items, and coral necklaces. You can bargain. The **linen shops** here have nice cotton damask napkins bordered in grosgrain and pastel jacquard linen tablecloths that are worth investigating.

Castelmola

5 km (3 mi) west of Taormina, 65 km (40 mi) south of Messina.

If your passion for heights hasn't been quelled, visit Castelmola, the tiny town above Taormina, where local bars make their own refreshing almond wine—the perfect complement to the spectacular 360-degree panorama.

En Route The 50-km (30-mi) stretch of road between Taormina and Messina is flanked by lush vegetation and seascapes. Inlets punctuated by gigantic oddly shaped rocks distract from the road. It was along this coast, legend says, that the giant one-eyed cyclops hurled their boulders down on Ulysses and his terrified men as they fled to the sea and on to their next adventure in Homer's *Odyssey.*

Messina

55 *43 km (27 mi) northeast of Taormina, 94 km (59 mi) northeast of Catania.*

Messina's ancient history tells of series of disasters, but the city nevertheless managed to develop a fine university and a thriving cultural environment. But at 5 o'clock in the morning on December 28, 1908, Messina changed from a flourishing metropolis of 120,000 to a heap of rubble, shaken to pieces by an earthquake that turned into a tidal wave and left 80,000 dead and the city almost completely leveled. As you approach the sickle-shape bay, through which ferries connect Sicily to the mainland, you see nothing of relatively recent disaster, except for the modern countenance of a 3,000-year-old city. The somewhat flat look is a precaution of seismic planning: tall buildings are not permitted.

The reconstruction of Messina's Norman and Romanesque **Duomo,** originally constructed by the Norman King Roger II in 1197, has retained much of the original plan, including a handsome crown of Norman battlements, an enormous apse, and a splendid wood-beam ceiling. The adjoining **bell tower**—of a much later date—is one of the city's principal attractions. It contains one of the largest and most complex mechanical clocks in the world, constructed in 1933 with a host of gilded automatons—a roaring lion, a crowing rooster, and numerous biblical figures—that spring into action every day at the stroke of noon. ✉ *Piazza del Duomo,* ☎ *090/675175.* ⏲ *Daily 8–12:30 and 4–7.*

NEED A BREAK? **Billé** (✉ Corner of Piazza Cairoli and Via Cannizzaro) proffers good lunchtime snacks, if you don't mind standing up. You can sample (or take away) such typical Sicilian snacks as *arancini* (deep-fried, breaded rice balls stuffed with cheese or meat sauce), mozzarella in *carrozza* (deep-fried bread pockets), and *piddoni* (savory parcels of mozzarella or vegetables).

Messina is the birthplace of the great Renaissance painter Antonello da Messina, whose *Polyptych of the Rosary* (1473) can be viewed along with two large Caravaggios in the **Museo Regionale,** along the sea in the northern outskirts of the city. ✉ *Viale della Libertà,* ☎ *090/361292.* *8,000 lire.* ⏲ *Mon., Wed., Fri. 9–1:30; Tues., Thurs., Sat. 9–1:30 and 4–6:30 (Oct.–May, 3–5:30); July–Sept., also Tues., Thurs., and Sat. 8 PM–10:30 PM, Sun. 9 AM–12:30 PM.*

Dining and Lodging

$$$ ★ ✕ **Alberto Sporting.** Transferred from the center of town to Mortelle, Messina's seaside satellite 10 km (6 mi) up the coast, this deluxe restaurant still brings in plenty of business. If you're adventurous and feeling flush, have the waiter order for you: you'll get a succession of seafood courses. À la carte items are delicious, particularly the spaghetti con frutti di mare *al cartoccio* (cooked in silver foil) and the involtini di pesce spada. Vintage Marsala sipped with one of the rich homemade desserts makes for a grand finale. ✉ *Via Nazionale, Mortelle,* ☎ *090/321009. AE, DC, MC, V. Closed Mon., Nov., and Jan.*

$$$ **Royal Palace.** Amid a surprising lack of quality accommodation in downtown Messina, the Royal Palace stands out like a beacon. Occupying a modern six-story block just steps away from the station and Piazza Cairoli, the hotel offers a welcome hush from the bustle of the surrounding streets. Public rooms are grand and the bedrooms comfortably equipped, though the overall impression leans towards the anonymous (don't expect much character). ✉ *Via T. Cannizzaro 224, 98123,* ☎ *090/6503,* FAX *090/2921075. 106 rooms. Restaurant, bar. AE, DC, MC, V.*

Nightlife and the Arts

Messina stages a folklore parade of huge traditional effigies, called **Giganti,** each year on August 13 and 14.

THE AEOLIAN ISLANDS

Just off Sicily's northeast coast lies an archipelago of seven spectacular islands of volcanic origin. The Isole Eolie (Aeolian Islands), also known as the Isole Lipari (Lipari Islands), were named after Aeolus, the Greek god of the winds, who is said to keep all the Earth's winds stuffed in a bag in his cave here. The Aeolians are a fascinating world of grottoes and clear-water caves carved by waves through the centuries. Superb snorkeling and scuba diving abounds in the clearest and cleanest of Italy's waters. Of course, the beautiful people of high society discovered the archipelago years ago—since Roberto Rossellini courted his star Ingrid Bergman, prior to marrying her, in 1950—and you should not expect complete isolation, at least on the main islands. August, in particular, can get unpleasantly overcrowded, and lodging and travel should always be booked as early as possible.

Lipari provides the best range of accommodations and is a good jumping-off point for day trips to the other islands. Most exclusive are Vulcano and Panarea, the former noted for its black sands and stupendous sunsets (and prices), as well as the acrid smell of its sulphur emissions, while the latter is, according to some, the prettiest. Most spectacular is Stromboli (pronounced with the accent on the first syllable) with its constant eruptions, and remotest are Filicudi and Alicudi, where electricity has only recently been introduced. Access to the islands is gained via ferry and hydrofoil from Sicily or Naples (☞ Arriving and Departing *in* Sicily A to Z, *below*). The bars in the Aeolian Islands, and especially those on Lipari, are known for their granite of fresh strawberries, melon, peaches, and other fruits. Many Sicilians, especially Aeolians and in Messina, Taormina, and Catania, begin the hot summer days with a *granita di caffè* (a coffee ice topped with whipped cream), into which they dunk their breakfast rolls. You can get one any time of day.

Lipari

56 *37 km (23 mi) north of Milazzo (2 hrs 10 mins by ferry, 1 hr by hydrofoil); Milazzo 41 km (25 mi) west of Messina.*

The largest and most developed of the Aeolians, Lipari welcomes you with distinctive pastel-color houses. Fields of spiky agaves dot the northernmost tip of the island, **Acquacalda,** indented with pumice and obsidian quarries. In the west is **San Calogero,** where you can explore hot springs and mud baths. From the red lava base of the island rises a plateau crowned with a 16th-century castle and a 17th-century **Cathedral.** Next door is the **Museo Eoliano,** one of the best archaeological museums in Europe, with an intelligently arranged collection of prehistoric finds—some dating as far back as 4000 BC—from various sites in the archipelago. ✉ *Via Castello,* ☎ *090/9880174.* *Free.* *May–Sept., daily 9–2 and 4–7; Oct.–Apr., daily 3–6.*

Dining and Lodging

$$$ ✕ **Il Filippino.** The views from the flower-strewn outdoor terrace of this restaurant in the upper town are a fitting complement to the superb fare on offer. Founded in 1910, the restaurant is rated one of the archipelago's best, and on the whole lives up to expectations. Top choice is seafood, especially the zuppa di pesce, and the smoked pesce spada is a must, in season. Just leave some room for the local version of cassata, accompanied by sweet Malvasia wine from Salina. ✉ *Piazza Muncipio,* ☎ *090/9811002. AE, DC, MC, V. Closed Nov. 10–Dec. 20 and Mon. Oct.–May.*

$$–$$$ ★ **Gattopardo Park Hotel.** Bright bougainvillea and fiery hibiscus set the tone in this grand villa, whose restaurant enjoys sweeping views out to sea. Guest quarters are in the 19th-century main building, or in whitewashed bungalows in the surrounding tranquil parkland. Public rooms have wood-beamed ceilings and rustic-style furnishings. A minibus shuttles between the hotel and Spiagge Bianche. There are also trips round the island, boat excursions, and folk evenings. Half board is required in summer. ✉ *Via Diana, 98055,* ☎ *090/9811035,* FAX *090/9880207. 53 rooms. Restaurant, bar. AE, DC, MC, V. MAP.*

$$ **Villa Augustus.** Tucked away off a side street in the center of Lipari's old town, this is a peaceful enclave, where a simple homey spirit prevails, with friendly service and a discreet attention to detail. In ad-

dition to a palm-shaded garden, there is a roof-garden offering good views. The rooms are bright and spacious, and fully equipped. ✉ *Vico Ausonia 16, 98055,* ☎ *090/9811232,* FAX *090/9812233. 35 rooms. Piano bar, free parking. AE, DC, MC, V. Closed Nov.–Easter.*

Vulcano

57 *18 km (11 mi) northwest of Lipari (25 mins by ferry, 10 mins by hydrofoil), 55 km (34 mi) northwest of Milazzo.*

True to its name, Vulcano has a profusion of fumaroles sending up jets of hot vapor, but the volcano here has long been dormant. Many come to soak in the strong-smelling sulfur baths, whose odors will greet you, with the wind in the right direction, long before you disembark. The island has some of the archipelago's best beaches, though the volcanic black sand can be offputting at first. You can ascend to the crater (1,266 ft above sea level) on muleback for a wonderful view, or take boat rides into the grottoes around the base. From Capo Grillo there is a view of all the Aeolians.

Lodging

$$$–$$$$ ★ **Les Sables Noires.** Named for the black sands of the beach in front, this luxury hotel is superbly sited on the beautiful Porto di Ponente. The cool, modern decor, wicker furniture, and inviting pool (for those unwilling to lounge on the private beach) induce a sybaritic mood, while the white-walled guest rooms are also tasteful and spacious. The restaurant, naturally, looks out over the bay: sunsets, framed by the towering faraglioni (pillars of rock rising dramatically out of the sea), are sublime. ✉ *Porto di Ponente, 98050,* ☎ *090/9850,* FAX *090/9852454. 48 rooms. Restaurant, bar, pool, private beach. AE, DC, MC, V.*

Salina

58 *15 km (9 mi) north of Lipari (50 mins by ferry, 20 mins by hydrofoil), 52 km (38 mi) northwest of Milazzo.*

The second-largest island, Salina is also the most fertile—which accounts for its good wine, the golden Malvasia. Excursions go up Mt. Fossa delle Felci, which rises to over 3,000 ft. It is also the highest of the islands, and the vineyards and fishing villages along its slopes add to its allure. Malvasia wine here is locally produced, unlike that found on other islands. Salina has a good range of reasonably priced accommodations and restaurants—and fewer crowds.

Lodging

$$–$$$ **Bellavista.** This is a quiet hotel in a quiet location, even though it's right next to the port. Rooms are simply furnished and cheerfully decorated with bright materials and ceramic tiles. Almost all have sea views, which can be enjoyed from the balconies. The management provides you with a list of things to do while on Salina, and can organize boat excursions and transport round the island, though you may well opt for the dolce far niente. ✉ *Via Risorgimento, Santa Marina Salina, 98050,* ☎ FAX *090/9843009. 12 rooms. Restaurant. No credit cards.*

Panarea

59 *18 km (11 mi) north of Lipari (2 hrs by ferry, 25–50 mins by hydrofoil), 55 km (33 mi) north of Milazzo.*

Panarea has some of the most dramatic scenery of the islands: wild caves carved out of the rock and dazzling flora. The exceptionally clear water and the richness of life on the seabed make Panarea especially suitable for underwater exploration, though there is little in the way of beaches. The outlying rocks and islets make a gorgeous sight, and you can enjoy the panorama on an easy excursion to the small Bronze Age village at Capo Milazzese.

Lodging

$$$$ **La Raya.** This discreetly expensive hotel is perfectly in keeping with the elite style of Panarea, most exclusive of the Aeolian islands. Public rooms, including bars, a broad terrace and an open-air restaurant, are right on the portside; the residential area is a 10-minute walk inland, though the rooms still enjoy the serene prospect of sea and Stromboli from their balconies. The decor is elegant and understated, with Moorish-type hangings and low divans helping to create a tone of serene luxury. Families with young children are asked to book elsewhere. ✉ *San Pietro, 98050,* ☎ *090/983013,* FAX *090/983103. 29 rooms. Restaurant, bar, nightclub. AE, DC, MC, V. Closed mid-Oct.–mid-Apr.*

Stromboli

60 *40 km (25 mi) north of Lipari (3 hrs 45 mins by ferry, 65–90 mins by hydrofoil), 63 km (40 mi) north of Milazzo.*

This northernmost Aeolian (also accessible from Naples) consists entirely of the cone of an active volcano. The view from the sea—especially at night, as an endless stream of glowing red-hot lava flows into the water—is unforgettable. Stromboli is in a constant state of mild dissatisfaction, and every now and then its anger flares up, so authorities insist that you climb to the top (about 3,031 ft above sea level) only with a guide. The return climb, pause, and descent, usually starting at around 6 PM, take about four hours. You will find a small selection of reasonably priced hotels and restaurants in the main town, and a choice of lively clubs and cafés for the younger set. In addition to the round-island tour, excursions include boat trips around the naturally battlemented isle of Strombolicchio.

Alicudi

61 *65 km (40 mi) west of Lipari (3 hrs 25 mins–3 hrs 50 mins by ferry, 60–95 mins by hydrofoil), 102 km (68 mi) northwest of Milazzo.*

The farthest outpost of the Aeolians remains sparsely inhabited, wild, and at peace. Here and on Filicudi there is a tiny selection of accommodations, but you can rent rooms cheaply. Only the coming and going of hydrofoils disturbs the rhythm of life here, and the only noise is the occasional braying of donkeys.

Filicudi

62 *30 km (16 mi) west of Salina (3 hrs 25 mins–3 hrs 50 mins by ferry, 90 mins–2 hrs by hydrofoil), 82 km (54 mi) northwest of Milazzo.*

Just a dot in the sea, Filicudi is famous for its unusual volcanic rock formations and the enchanting **Grotta del Bue Marino** (Grotto of the Sea Ox). At Capo Graziano is a prehistoric village. The island has a handful of hotels and pensions, and some local families put up guests.

Lodging

$$ **La Canna.** Set on a height above the tiny port, this *pensione* commands fabulous views of sky and sea from its flower-strewn terrace. It's a wonderful prospect to wake up to, and a fit setting for the utter tranquility that characterizes any sojourn on this island. Rooms are small but adequate, kept clean and tidy by the friendly staff, and the cooking is exquisite (half- or full-board required in peak season—and

recommended at any time). Arrange to be collected at the port. ✉ *Via Rosa 43, 98050,* ☎ *090/9889956,* FAX *090/9889966. 8 rooms. Restaurant. MC, V. MAP, FAP.*

SICILY A TO Z

Arriving and Departing

By Boat

Frequent car ferries cross the strait between Villa San Giovanni in Calabria and Messina on the island. The crossing usually takes about a half hour, but during the summer months there can be considerable delays. From Naples, overnight car ferries (**Tirrenia,** ☎ 081/7201111) operate daily to Palermo. Passenger-only *aliscafi* (hydrofoils) also cross the strait from Reggio di Calabria in about 15 minutes.

By Plane

Sicily can be reached from all major cities via Rome, Milan, or Naples. Planes land at **Aeroporto Falcone-Borsellino** (✉ 32 km/19 mi west of Palermo, ☎ 091/591690) at Punta Raisi. Catania's **Aeroporto Fontanarossa** (✉ 5 km/3 mi south of city center, ☎ 095/7306266) also services flights. During the high season, there are also direct charter flights to Sicily from New York, London, and Paris.

BETWEEN THE AIRPORT AND DOWNTOWN

Hourly **Prestia & Comandè** (☎ 091/580457) buses ply between Palermo's Falcone-Borsellino airport and the city center (Piazza Castelnuovo and the central station); tickets cost 6,500 lire. Taxis charge around 70,000 lire for the same 45-minute trip. Catania's Fontanarossa airport is served by **Alibus** (☎ 095/7360450) which leaves about every half hour from the airport and the central train station, with a stop at Piazza Stesicoro, on Via Etnea. The journey takes around 25 minutes; tickets cost 1,300 lire. Taxis cost around 50,000 lire.

By Train

There are direct express trains from Milan and Rome to Palermo, Catania, and Siracusa. The Rome–Palermo and Rome–Siracusa trips take at least 11 hours. After Naples, the run is mostly along the coast, so try to book a window seat on the right if you're not on an overnight train. At Villa San Giovanni, in Calabria, the train is separated and loaded onto a ferryboat to cross the strait to Messina.

Getting Around

Renting a car is definitely the best way to get around Sicily. The trains are unreliable and slow, and the buses, though faster and air-conditioned in summer, can be subject to delays and strikes.

By Boat

The Aeolian Islands are reachable by hydrofoil from Naples, Messina, Palermo, and Milazzo. From Messina you can get ferry service to the islands. Call **Siremar** (☎ 081/5800340) and **SNAV** (☎ 081/7612348).

By Bus and Train

Air-conditioned coaches connect major and minor cities and are often faster and more convenient than local trains but slightly more expensive. Call 147/888088 for toll-free train information.

By Car

This is the ideal mode of Sicilian exploration. Modern highways circle and bisect the island, making all main cities easily reachable. A20 (supplemented by S113 at points) connects Messina and Palermo;

Messina and Catania are linked by A18; running through the interior, from Catania to west of Cefalù, is A19; threading west from Palermo, A29 runs to Trapani and the airport, with a leg stretching down to Mazara del Vallo. The supertstrada S115 runs along the southern coast, and connecting superstrade lace the island. Cars can be rented at airports and downtown locations in every major city (☞ Car Rentals, *below*).

By Train

Main lines connect Messina, Taormina, Siracusa, and Palermo. Secondary lines are generally very slow and unreliable. The Messina–Palermo run, along the northern coast, is especially scenic. Call 147/888088 for toll-free information.

Contacts and Resources

Car Rentals

Cars can be rented at airports and downtown locations in every major city.

CATANIA

Avis (✉ Aeroporto Fontanarossa, ☎ 095/340500; ✉ Via Federico De Roberto 10, ☎ 095/536470). **Hertz** (✉ Aeroporto Fontanarossa, ☎ 095/341595; ✉ Via Toselli 16/c, ☎ 095/322560). **Maggiore** (✉ Aeroporto Fontanarossa, ☎ 095/340594; ✉ Piazza Verga 48, ☎ 095/536927).

PALERMO

Avis (✉ Aeroporto Falcone Borsellino, ☎ 091/591684; ✉ Via Principe Scordia 28, ☎ 091/586940). **Hertz** (✉ Aeroporto Falcone Borsellino, ☎ 091/591682; ✉ Via Messina 7/e, ☎ 091/331668). **Maggiore** (✉ Falcone Borsellino airport, ☎ 091/591681; ✉ Via De Gasperi 179, ☎ 091/517305).

Emergencies

Police, Ambulance, Fire (☎ 113). **Hospital** (☎ 091/288141 Palermo; 095/7591111 Catania).

Guided Tours

Saturday-morning tours of Palermo and Monreale are provided by the Italian tour operator **CST** (✉ Via E. Amari 124, Palermo, ☎ 091/582294; ✉ Corso Umberto 101, Taormina, ☎ 0942/23301), leaving at 9 AM from outside the Politeama Hotel. CST also arranges complete seven-day tours of Sicily's major sights in a comfortable air-conditioned coach with an English-speaking guide. Departures are once a week from either Palermo and Catania, and the cost includes all meals and accommodations in three- or four-star hotels.

Visitor Information

Tourist offices (✉ Corso Umberto 177, 95024 Acireale, ☎ 095/604521; ✉ Viale della Vittoria 255, 92100 Agrigento, ☎ 0922/401352; ✉ Via Cesare Battisti 15, 92100 Agrigento, ☎ 0922/20454; ✉ Palazzo Libertini, 95041 Caltagirone, ☎ 0933/53809; ✉ Corso Vittorio Emanuele 109, 93100 Caltanisetta, ☎ 0934/530411; ✉ Via Cimarosa 10, 95124 Catania, ☎ 095/7306233; ✉ Stazione Centrale, 95129 Catania, ☎ 095/7306255; ✉ Aeroporto Fontanarossa, 95121 Catania, ☎ 095/7306266; ✉ Corso Ruggero 77, 90015 Cefalù, ☎ 0921/21050 or 0921/21458; ✉ Via Roma 413, 94100 Enna, ☎ 0935/528228; ✉ Piazza Napoleone Colajanni 6, 94100 Enna, ☎ 0935/500875; ✉ Via Conte Pepoli 11, 91016 Erice, ☎ 0923/869388; ✉ Corso Vittorio Emanuele 202, 98055 Lipari, ☎ 090/9880095; ✉ Via XI Maggio 100, 91025 Marsala, ☎ 0923/714097; ✉ Piazza della Repubblica, 98122 Messina,

☎ 090/672944; ✉ Via Calabria 301/b, 98123 Messina, ☎ 090/674236; ✉ Piazza Cairoli 45, 98123 Messina, ☎ 090/2936294; ✉ Piazza Duomo, 90046 Monreale, ☎ 091/6564570; ✉ Piazza Castelnuovo 35, 90141 Palermo, ☎ 091/583847; ✉ Aeroporto Falcone-Borsellino, 90045 Palermo, ☎ 091/591698; ✉ Via Cavour 1, 94015 Piazza Armerina, ☎ 0935/680201; ✉ Via San Sebastiano 43, 96100 Siracusa, ☎ 0931/67710; ✉ Via Maestranza 33, 96100 Siracusa, ☎ 0931/464255; ✉ Palazzo Corvaja, Largo Santa Caterina, 98039 Taormina, ☎ 0942/23243; ✉ Piazza Saturno, 91100 Trapani, ☎ 0923/29000; ✉ Via Francesco d'Assisi 25, 91100 Trapani, ☎ 0923/545511).

16 SARDINIA

An uncut jewel of an island, Sardinia remains unique and enigmatic. Too distant from Rome to be influenced by the character of the mainland, this island is as fascinating as its prehistoric stone structures, the *nuraghi*. Modern luxury can also be found here: just follow the jet-setters who sail their yachts to the Costa Smeralda. Beautiful in its severity, Sardinia is a prime destination if you're seeking a getaway.

Updated by Robert Andrews

THE SECOND-LARGEST ISLAND in the Mediterranean—just smaller than Sicily—Sardinia is about 180 km (112 mi) from mainland Italy and very much off the beaten track. A Phoenician stronghold in ancient times and later a Spanish dominion, Sardinia doesn't seem typically "Italian" in its color and flavor. It lies just a bit too far from the mainland—from imperial and papal Rome and from the palaces of the Savoy dynasty—to have been transformed by the events that forged a national character. Yet Giuseppe Garibaldi, the charismatic national hero who led his troops in fervid campaigns to unify Italy in the mid-19th century, chose to spend his last years in relative isolation on the small island of Caprera, just off the coast of Sardinia.

Although Sardinia (Sardegna in Italian) is less than an hour by air and only several hours by boat from mainland Italy, it is removed from the mainstream of tourism except for July and August, when Italians take its beautiful coasts and clean waters by storm. The interior is *never* crowded; Italian tourists in Sardinia come for the sea, less for the rugged and deserted mountain scenery.

Sardinia closely resembles Corsica, the French island across the 16-km-wide (10-mi-wide) windswept Strait of Bonifacio to the north. A dense bush, or *macchia,* barely penetrable in some districts, covers large areas. The terrain is rough, like the short, sturdy shepherds you see in the highlands—impassive figures engaged in one of the few gainful occupations that the stony land allows. Shaggy flocks of sheep and goats are familiar features in the Sardinian landscape, just as their meat and cheese are staples of the island's cuisine. The main highway linking Cagliari with Sassari was begun in 1820 by the Savoy ruler Carlo Felice; designated S131, but still referred to as the Strada Carlo Felice by the islanders, it heads northwest through the fertile Campidano Plain for 216 km (134 mi) to Sassari.

Aside from the chic opulence of the Costa Smeralda, there's little sophistication in Sardinia, but the cost of living on the island is typically higher than on the mainland. The sprawling cities of Cagliari and Sassari have a distinctly provincial air. Newer hotels may seem a little old-fashioned, and hotels—of any vintage—are hard to find inland. There's little traffic on the roads, and trains, buses, and people in general move at a gentle pace. In hamlets, women swathed in black shawls and long, full skirts look with suspicion upon strangers passing through. Sardinians are courteous but remote, perhaps because of their innate dignity.

Like mainland Italians, the Sardinians are of varied origin. On the northwest coast, fine traceries of ironwork around a balcony underscore the Spanish influence. In the northeast, the inhabitants boast Genoese or Pisan ancestry, and the headlands display the ruined fortresses of the ancient Pisan duchy of Malaspina on the Italian mainland. As you explore the southern coast, you'll come upon the physiognomies, customs, dialects, place-names, and holy buildings of the Turks, Moors, Phoenicians, Austrians, and the mainland Italians. If there are any pure Sardinians—or Sards—left, perhaps they can be found in the south-central mountains, south of Nuoro, under the 6,000-ft crests of the Gennargentu Massif, in the rugged country still ironically called Barbagia, "Land of Strangers."

Pleasures and Pastimes

Beaches

For their fine sand and lack of crowds, Sardinia's beaches are among the best in the Mediterranean; its waters are among the cleanest, with the exception of those in the immediate vicinity of Cagliari, Arbatax, and Porto Torres. The beach resorts of the Costa Smeralda are exclusive and expensive, but elsewhere on the island you can find a wide range of beaches.

Many agree that the most beautiful beaches on the island are those of Cala di Luna and Cala Sisine, hidden among the rocky cliffs between Baunei and Dorgali, on the eastern coast; these remote strands can be reached only by boat from Cala Gonone or Arbatax. For more accessible beaches with more amenities, go to Santa Margherita di Pula, near Cagliari, where you'll find several hotels; to Villasimius and the Costa Rei, on the southeastern coast; or to the sandy coves sheltered by wind-carved granite boulders on the northern coast in the Gallura district and the archipelago of La Maddalena. There are also beaches around Olbia, Alghero, and on the Costa Paradiso, near Castelsardo.

Dining

In the island's restaurants you'll find that Sardinian regional cuisine is basically Italian, with interesting local variations. Meat dishes are usually veal, lamb, or *porcheddu* (roast suckling pig). On the coast, seafood is king and is served in great variety. Langouste or *aragosta* (lobster) is a specialty of the northern coast and can get pricey. Foreign conquerors left legacies of bouillabaisse (known here as *zimino*), couscous, and paella, but there are native pastas: *malloreddus* (small shells of bran pasta sometimes flavored with saffron) and *culingiones* (the Sardinian version of ravioli). Sharp pecorino cheese made from sheep's milk and thin, crispy bread called *carta di musica* are typical island fare. Try the *sebadas* (fried cheese-filled ravioli doused with honey) for dessert. The local red wines are sturdy and strong, the whites tend toward a light and delicate quality. Amber-color Vernaccia is dry and heady.

Festivals

As one of Italy's most—perhaps *the* most—remote regions, Sardinia is not really a prime spot for sophisticated visual or performing arts. This same remoteness, however, can prove fruitful for sampling some of the culture here, sometimes natively inspired, sometimes drawing on the influences of the traders and invaders who have left their mark on the islands over the millennia. Sardinia's own brand of Catholicism—occasionally bordering on the grotesque—can be witnessed in the local *feste,* or festivals. Ostensibly, the festivals celebrate a saintly or religious occasion, but often they are imbued with an almost pagan feel.

The main festivals are at Cagliari (Festa di Sant'Efisio, May 1), Sassari (Ascension Day, the 40th day after Easter, and August 14), and Nuoro (penultimate Sunday in August). Some of the best are the smaller festivals in the scattered mountain villages of the interior; in Fonni, in the heart of the Barbagio, locals celebrate the Festa di San Giovanni, held June 24, in traditional costume. These festivities are not just expressions of religious devotion but also an explicit statement of community identity.

Fishing

Check locally for regulations on deep-sea fishing. Underwater fishing is restricted to the daylight hours, and no more than 5 kilos (11 pounds) of fish and shellfish may be taken. No oxygen tanks or nets may be used for underwater fishing. Freshwater fishing is good along the Flumendosa, Tirso, Rio Mannu, and other rivers rising in the mountainous interior and in the artificial basins of Flumendosa and Omodeo.

Golf

Sardinia has two world-class golf courses, including the Pevero Golf Club on the Costa Smeralda, which was designed by Robert Trent Jones;

and the Is Molas 18-hole course at Santa Margherita di Pula. Four more courses are planned for the Costa Smeralda.

Horseback Riding

Spaghetti westerns were once filmed in Sardinia, and it's easy to imagine why: the rugged, mountainous terrain of the inland is the perfect frontier setting for an adventure on horseback. On the barren hilltops of the Barbagio you may even catch a glimpse of the wild dwarf horse that is native to these parts, though numbers have dwindled over the years. If you prefer a more sedate way of seeing the island on horseback, you can stick to the coast, where the riding is easier but the scenery is still magnificent. Group itineraries and horse rentals can be arranged (☞ Contacts and Resources *in* Sardinia A to Z, *below*).

Kids' Stuff

Sardinia is a vast playground where children can explore and swim in season. There's nothing like a long hike along deserted beaches or through herb-perfumed hills to send them to bed early. Let them clamber over the nuraghi and poke into the countless *domus de janas* (witches' houses) and *tombe di giganti* (giants' tombs), fancifully named grottoes hewn in the rock by the island's prehistoric inhabitants. Near Alghero, at Anghelu Ruiu, and near the Costa Smeralda, at Arzachena, they served as burial places, but with a little imagination you can make up some fanciful fairy tales.

Lodging

The island's most luxurious hotels are on the Costa Smeralda. They have magnificent facilities but close from fall to spring; many are too out of the way to be good touring bases. Other, equally attractive coastal areas have seen a spate of resort hotels and villa colonies sprouting up; they, too, close from October through April, which narrows the choice of hotels considerably during the other months. In the cities suggested as touring bases, you can expect to find standards of comfort slightly below those on the mainland. The best accommodations may be available at commercial hotels, which can mean little atmosphere. In smaller towns throughout the island, you'll find modest hotels offering basic accommodations, restrained but genuine hospitality, and low rates.

Nightlife

Be prepared to part with a cool sum if you stay on the Costa Smeralda, and if that doesn't deter you, go to the complex at Porto Cervo for a selection of high-class bars, restaurants, and discos. Nightlife elsewhere on Sardinia means a quiet drink before turning in early, tired out from the day's outdoor activity. But as if to make up for the sleepy atmosphere of most of the island, the Costa Smeralda sparkles most nights in the summer.

Sailing

Sailing enthusiasts tack for Sardinia in droves by virtue of its craggy coast, full of wildly beautiful inlets only accessible by sea. You can witness the very rich engage in one of their favorite sports—yachting—at the posh resorts of Costa Smeralda each August, when a number of regattas are held.

Shopping

Sardinia is crafts heaven. Locally produced goods include bright woolen shawls and rugs, hand-carved wooden objects, gold filigree jewelry in traditional designs, coral jewelry, and, above all, handwoven baskets in all shapes and sizes. The best places to go for crafts are the various government-sponsored ISOLA centers in Cagliari, Sassari, Castelsardo, and Sant'Antioco.

Exploring Sardinia

The entire island is about 260 km (162 mi) from north to south, and roughly 120 km (75 mi) across. Driving is the best way to see the island's most interesting sights. Sardinia's mountainous terrain can make driving rigorous and slow. Local transportation is not geared to the needs of visitors, so you can cover more ground in less time if you have a car. If you are not traveling with a car, establish yourself in one of the larger towns and make excursions to as many attractions as time and schedules allow. There are bus and train connections to most places, except some areas of the Costa Smeralda and Su Nuraxi nuraghe.

Numbers in the text correspond to numbers in the margin and on the Sardinia and Cagliari maps.

Great Itineraries

Three days in Sardinia will only give you enough time to see one corner of the island. In five days, you will be able to venture out to some of the attractions in the north of the island. A fairly comprehensive tour taking in the coastline and interior can be accomplished in seven days.

IF YOU HAVE 3 DAYS

You would do well to confine your visit to 🏨 **Cagliari** ①–⑥ and its environs. In Sardinia's capital, you'll find Italianate architecture, churches of all styles, and the Museo Archeologico, with the island's best antiquity collection. If you do not have your own transport, you can make use of taxis or buses to make easy day trips from Cagliari. Your priority should be **Su Nuraxi** ⑫, the island's most imposing nuraghic monument. On your second or third day, head out to the small coastal village of 🏨 **Pula** ⑧; great beaches rim the coast and just outside is **Nora** ⑨, a Carthaginian and Roman archaeological site.

IF YOU HAVE 5 DAYS

Stay in 🏨 **Cagliari** ①–⑥ two days, still leaving enough time for a visit to 🏨 **Pula** ⑧. Spend your third night in 🏨 **Alghero** ⑱, an appealing walled town on the northwest coast with a distinctly Spanish flavor, perhaps stopping for lunch en route at ✉ **Oristano** ⑭. For your last two nights, you have a choice: you could spend them in the lap of luxury in one of the hotels in and outside 🏨 **Porto Cervo** ㉓; if you are on a limited budget and/or prefer adventure, make 🏨 **Nuoro** ⑯ your base from which to explore the rugged interior of the island; spend as little time as possible exploring the provincial capital before veering south into the mountainous Barbagia region, the island's most primitive district.

IF YOU HAVE 7 DAYS

Spend your first two days exploring 🏨 **Cagliari** ①–⑥. On the third day, you could hit the beaches at **Villasimius** ⑦ on the southeastern tip of the island. Alternatively, go southwest from Cagliari, taking in the remains of antiquity outside of 🏨 **Pula** ⑧, and moving up along the western coast on the Strada Carlo Felice as far as the sleepy village of **Sant' Antioco** ⑩. Here, you can catch a ferry over to the small island of 🏨 **San Pietro** ⑪ for the night, a favorite weekend retreat of wealthy Cagliarans, with delightful picnic and swimming spots. Continue up toward Oristano, making an inland detour to the fascinating nuraghe of **Su Nuraxi** ⑫, off the main road outside the quiet town of Barumini. Wildlife enthusiasts may want to take another jaunt north of Barumini to the **Giara di Gesturi** ⑬, a basalt plateau with the island's more exotic wildlife. On your fourth night, stay in 🏨 **Oristano** ⑭, which saw its heyday in the Middle Ages, but it now merits a cursory walk through town and glimpse of the Carthaginian ruins at **Tharros** ⑮, just outside the city. Head northeast for 🏨 **Nuoro** ⑯, a town of little interest, and

Sardinia

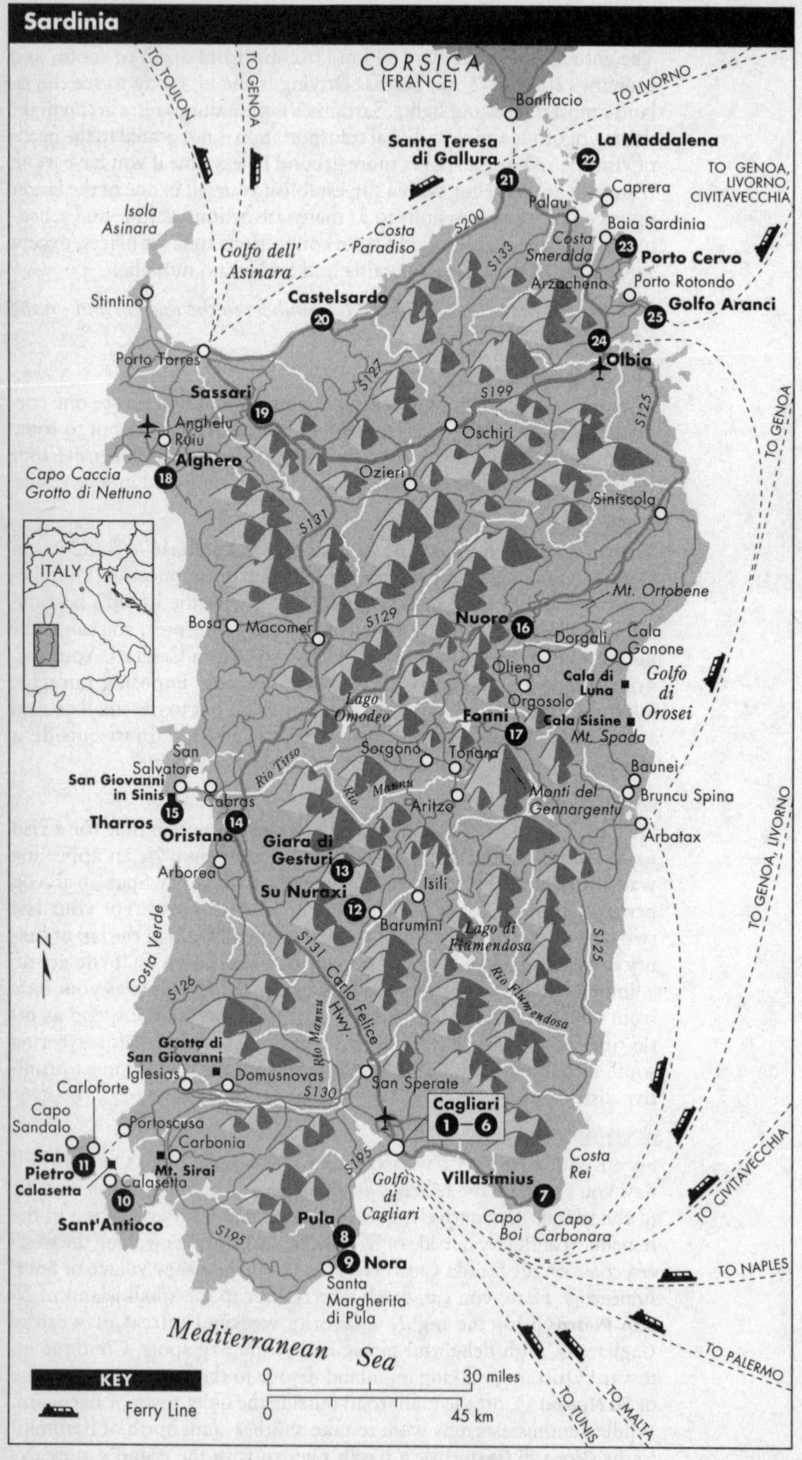
CORSICA
(FRANCE)
TO TOULON
TO GENOA
TO LIVORNO
Bonifacio
Santa Teresa di Gallura
La Maddalena
TO GENOA, LIVORNO, CIVITAVECCHIA
Caprera
Palau
Baia Sardinia
Costa Smeralda
Porto Cervo
Arzachena
Porto Rotondo
Golfo Aranci
Isola Asinara
Golfo dell' Asinara
Costa Paradiso
Stintino
Castelsardo
Porto Torres
Olbia
Sassari
Oschiri
Anghelu Ruiu
Alghero
Capo Caccia Grotto di Nettuno
Ozieri
Siniscola
TO GENOA
ITALY
Mt. Ortobene
Bosa
Macomer
Nuoro
Dorgali
Cala Gonone
Oliena
Cala di Luna
Golfo di Orosei
Lago Omodeo
Orgosolo
Fonni
Cala Sisine
Mt. Spada
San Salvatore
Sorgono
Tonara
Baunei
San Giovanni in Sinis
Cabras
Rio Tirso
Rio Mannu
Aritzo
Monti del Gennargentu
Bruncu Spina
Tharros
Oristano
Arbatax
Giara di Gesturi
Arborea
Isili
Su Nuraxi
Barumini
Lago di Flumendosa
TO GENOA, LIVORNO
Costa Verde
Carlo Felice Hwy.
Rio Flumendosa
Grotta di San Giovanni
Iglesias
Domusnovas
San Sperate
Carloforte
Capo Sandalo
Portoscusa
Cagliari
Carbonia
San Pietro
Calasetta
Mt. Sirai
Costa Rei
Villasimius
TO CIVITAVECCHIA
Sant'Antioco
Golfo di Cagliari
Pula
Capo Boi
Capo Carbonara
Nora
TO NAPLES
Santa Margherita di Pula
Mediterranean Sea
TO PALERMO
KEY
Ferry Line
0
30 miles
45 km
TO TUNIS
TO MALTA

strike south into the Barbagia region: tortuous roads wind and loop their way over a wild and primitive terrain that seems impervious to the 20th century. If you prefer coastal attractions to the inland ones, spend no more than half a day exploring the region and then head west from Nuoro on road 129 to Bosa, where you turn right into hilly and arid scrub country that eventually brings you to **Alghero** ⑱, on the northwest coast, where you should consider spending your fifth night. While heading northeast across an area fringed with low cliffs, inlets, and small bays, don't be distracted by **Sassari** ⑲, but stop to appreciate the exquisite nature of the seaside resorts, including **Castelsardo** ⑳, a walled citadel that is a delight for basket lovers, and to the relaxed fishing village of **Santa Teresa di Gallura** ㉑. If you have a night or two left and love the resort life, plan to pamper yourself on the sun-kissed beaches of one of Europe's premier summer holiday meccas, the Costa Smeralda, its most exclusive address being **Porto Cervo** ㉓.

When to Tour Sardinia

If you can help it, avoid Sardinia in steamy August, when not only is the island swamped with tourists from the mainland, but the Sards, too, take their annual break. A combination of unbearable heat, crowded beaches, accommodation shortage, and shuttered shops and offices can make for a less-than-idyllic vacation. May and September, on the other hand, are much quieter and still temperate. Sudden storms can be a hazard, but these quickly blow over. The sea remains warm enough for swimming well into October. The mountainous interior is probably at its best in the spring, when the woods and valleys are alive with color and burgeoning growth. For the gradations of color, the fall is also a good time. In winter, rain and clouds are common over high ground—and most of Sardinia is mountainous—and it snows most years in the Barbagia region. In the south, the weather rarely turns cold, but winter is not beach weather. Try to coincide your visit to Sardinia with one of the famous annual festivals (☞ Festivals *in* Pleasures and Pastimes, *above*). They are mega affairs, with accommodation and restaurant space at a premium, so plan well ahead.

CAGLIARI AND THE SOUTHERN COAST

Cagliari

268 km (166 mi) south of Olbia.

The island's capital reveals impressive Italianate architecture and churches in a variety of styles. Medieval Spanish conquerors from Aragon, as well as Pisans and Piemontese, all left their marks. Sardinia's largest city, Cagliari—the stress is on the first syllable—is characterized by its busy commercial center and waterfront with broad avenues, as well as by the typically narrow streets of the old hilltop citadel. Explorations from town can include the ancient site of Nora and the popular picnic islands of Sant'Antioco and San Pietro (☞ *below*).

❶ Begin your visit at the **Museo Archeologico,** within the walls of the castle that the Pisans erected in the early 1300s to ward off attacks by the Aragonese and Catalans, from what is now Spain. Among the intriguing artifacts from Nuraghic, Carthaginian, and Roman times are bronze statuettes from the tombs and dwellings of Sardinia's earliest inhabitants, who remain a prehistorical enigma. These aboriginal people left scant clues to their origins. Ancient writers called them the nuraghic people, from the name of their stone dwellings, the nuraghi. The structures' features are unique to Sardinia, just as the Aztec pyramids' are to Mexico. Archaeologists date the nuraghi from about

1300–1200 BC, a time when the ancient Israelites were establishing themselves in Canaan; when the Greeks were besieging Troy; when the Minoan civilization collapsed in Crete; when the Ramses pharaohs reigned in Egypt; and when many migrations were taking place along the shores and water routes of the Mediterranean. During the next 1,000 years, the nuraghic people gradually withdrew to the island's highland fastnesses to avoid more disciplined and better-armed invaders. (Their only weapons, say the chroniclers, were stones and boulders hurled down from the hilltops.) They eventually succumbed when the Romans, following on the heels of Carthaginian invaders, conquered the island in the 3rd century BC. ⊠ *Cittadella dei Musei, Piazza Arsenale,* ☎ *070/655911.* ⊡ *4,000 lire.* ⊙ *May–Sept., Tues., Wed., and Fri.–Sun. 9–2 and 3:30–8; Oct.–Apr., Tues.–Sun. 9–7.*

❷ The medieval **Torre di San Pancrazio** (Tower of San Pancrazio), part of the imposing Pisan defenses, is just outside the archaeological museum. If you're here on the weekend, you can climb up the tower for a fabulous panorama. ⊠ *Piazza Indipendenza,* ☎ *070/652130.* ⊡ *Free.* ⊙ *Apr.–Sept., Tues.–Sun. 9–1 and 3–7; Oct.–Mar., Tues.–Sun. 9–4:30.*

❸ The **Torre dell'Elefante** (Tower of the Elephant), twin to that of San Pancrazio, is at the seaward end of the bastions. *Via Università,* ☎ *070/652130.* ⊡ *Free.*

Piazza Palazzo, at the top of Via Martini, is where you'll find the
❹ **Duomo,** which has been extensively rebuilt and restored. The tiers of columns on the facade echo those of medieval Romanesque Pisan churches, but only the central portal is an authentic relic of that era. ⊠ *Piazza Palazzo,* ☎ *070/663837.* ⊙ *Daily 8–12:30 and 4–8.*

All around the church are the narrow streets of the **Spanish quarter,** where humble dwellings still open directly onto the sidewalk and the wash is hung out to dry on elaborate wrought-iron balconies.

❺ The Bastion of St. Remy, better known as the **Terrazza Umberto I,** is a monumental neoclassic staircase and arcade. It was added in the 19th century to the bastion built by the Spaniards 400 years earlier. ⊠ *Piazza Costituzione.*

❻ Below the Museo Archeologico are the **Anfiteatro Romano,** some very old churches, and a few good restaurants near the waterfront. The amphitheater, which dates from the 2nd century AD, is a well-preserved arena complete with underground passages and a beasts' pit, evidence of the importance of this Roman outpost. ⊠ *Viale Fra Ignazio,* ☎ *070/652130.* ⊡ *Free.* ⊙ *Apr.–Sept., Mon.–Sat. 9–1 and 4–8, Sun. 9–1 and 2:30–5; Oct.–Mar., daily 9–5.*

Dining and Lodging

$$$ ✕ **Dal Corsaro.** This formal restaurant near the port is one of the island's most commended eating places, so make reservations. The decor is refined, the welcome cordial. The menu features seafood and meat specialties, such as seafood antipasto and porcheddu. ⊠ *Viale Regina Margherita 28,* ☎ *070/664318. Reservations essential. AE, DC, MC, V. Closed Sun., Aug., and 1 wk at Christmas.*

$$ ✕ **Il Gatto.** "The Cat," near the train station and the central Piazza del Carmine, is popular with locals. Follow their lead and make sure you have reservations because the restaurant can fill up quickly. It serves some of the best Sardinian seafood, such as the risotto with shellfish, but for a change of pace try the zesty *insalata di funghi, rucola, e grana padano* (salad of mushrooms, arugula, and a young Parmesan cheese). ⊠ *Viale Trieste 15,* ☎ *070/663596. Reservations essential weekends. AE, DC, MC, V. No lunch weekends.*

Anfiteatro Romano, **6**
Duomo, **4**
Museo Archeologico, **1**
Terrazza Umberto I, **5**
Torre dell' Elefante, **3**
Torre di San Pancrazio, **2**

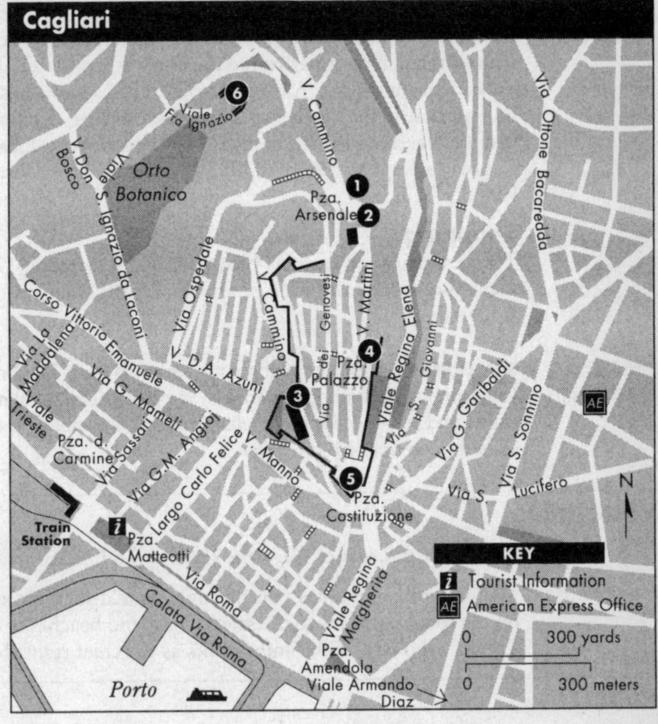

$$$ **Panorama.** With its unprepossessing exterior, this hotel in downtown Cagliari is geared toward the business class. Rooms are functional, spacious, and comfortable. Try to reserve one on the upper of the nine floors and enjoy the view over the harbor and bay. Rates are low in the category. ✉ *Viale Armando Diaz 231, 09100,* ☎ *070/307691,* FAX *070/305413. 97 rooms. Restaurant, bar, pool, meeting rooms. AE, DC, MC, V.*

$ **AeR Bundes Jack.** Despite the unprepossessing entrance under the arcades of Via Roma, this central third-floor pensione (there's an elevator) guarantees simple, solidly furnished rooms, sheltered from the hubbub of traffic and is impeccably clean. You can also expect polite service and reams of information from the kind family that runs it. The port is directly opposite (though rooms are all inward-facing), the bus and train stations steps away, and Via Roma itself presents an entertaining parade of shops and sit-down bars. ✉ *Via Roma 75, 09100,* ☎ FAX *070/657970. 14 rooms. No credit cards.*

Nightlife and the Arts

Sardinia's greatest annual festival, the **Festa di Sant'Efisio,** May 1–4, involves thousands of costumed villagers, many of them on horseback, parading through town, and a four-day procession between Cagliari and Pula (☞ *below*). It's a good chance to take part in the centuries-old folklore. Cagliari's **university** (✉ Via Università) holds concerts throughout the academic year.

Outdoor Activities and Sports

FISHING

For information on obtaining a fishing license, contact the **Assessorato Regionale alla Difesa dell'Ambiente** (✉ Via Biasi 7/9, Cagliari, 09100, ☎ 070/6066620).

SAILING

Berthing and provisions facilities are available on all coasts, though concentrated in the area around the Costa Smeralda and La Maddalena areas in the northeast. Altogether, there are 15 nautical schools, nearly half of these in the northeast. The harbor master, or *capitano di porto,* can issue permits for anchorage. The **Lega Navale Italiana** at Marina Piccola in Cagliari (☎ 070/303794) will furnish information on the island's facilities.

Shopping

The best place for crafts is **ISOLA** (✉ Via Bacaredda 176), a government-sponsored exhibition of artisanal crafts where most of the work is for sale.

OFF THE BEATEN PATH **SAN SPERATE** – Walls throughout this town 20 km (12 mi) north of Cagliari have been brightened with *murales* (mural paintings) by local artists and some well-known Italian painters, transforming the entire town into an open-air art gallery.

Villasimius

7 *50 km (31 mi) east of Cagliari, 296 km (184 mi) south of Olbia.*

The eastern route takes you through some dismal industrial suburbs on the road that leads to the scenic coast and beaches of Capo Boi and Capo Carbonara. Villasimius ranks as the chief resort here.

Pula

8 *29 km (18 mi) southwest of Cagliari, 314 km (195 mi) southwest of Olbia.*

The area southwest of the capital has its share of fine scenery and good beaches—resort villages sprawl along the coast, and the **Is Molas** championship golf course near Pula has won tributes from Tom Watson, Jack Nicklaus, and other professionals of the sport. On the marshy shoreline between Cagliari's Aeroporto di Elmas and Pula, huge flocks of flamingos are a common sight.

Visit the small **Museo Archeologico Comunale** (archaeological museum), with finds from the Nora site, including amphoras, anchors, and inscribed stones, mostly dredged up from the sea. ✉ *Corso Vittorio Emanuele 67,* ☎ *070/9209610.* *4,000 lire, or 7,000 lire including Nora (☞ below).* *Apr.–Oct., daily 9–8; Nov.–Mar., daily 9–6.*

★ 9 For the real thing, head to the narrow promontory less than 3 km (2 mi) outside the town of Pula called **Nora,** the site of a Phoenician, then Carthaginian, and later a Roman settlement. Extensive excavations have shed light on life in this ancient city from the 8th century BC onward. Many of the exhibits in Cagliari's archaeological museum were found here. An old Roman road passes the moss-covered ruins of temples, an amphitheater, and a small Roman theater. You can make out the channels through which hot air rose to warm the Roman baths; watch for the difference between the simple mosaic pavements laid by the Carthaginians and the more elaborate designs of the Romans. Taking in the views from Nora, you can see why the Phoenicians chose the site for settlement. They always scouted for locations with good harbors, cliffs to shelter their craft from the wind, and a position such as a promontory, from which they could defend themselves from attack. If the sea is calm, look under the clear waters along the shore for more **ruins** of the ancient city, submerged by earthquakes, rough seas, and erosion. ☎ *070/9209138.* *5,000 lire, or 7,000 including Museo Arche-*

ologico Comunale (☞ above). ⏲ Excavations: Apr.–Sept., daily 9–8; Oct.–Mar., daily 9–6; guided tours hourly.

Sant'Efisio, the little Romanesque church at the base of the Nora promontory, plays a part in one of the island's most colorful annual events. Efisio, the patron saint of Sardinia, was a 3rd-century Roman soldier who converted to Christianity. A procession in early May accompanies a statue of the saint all the way from Cagliari and back again. The processional round-trip takes four days, with festive stops along the way, and culminates in a huge parade down Cagliari's main avenue. If you're in Sardinia from May 1 to May 4, don't miss it. ✉ *Nora,* ☎ *070/9208473.* ⏲ *Sat. 3–6, Sun. 9:30–1 and 3–6:30; other times by appointment.*

Lodging

The hotels and beaches that cater to the summer hotel trade around Pula and Nora are concentrated a couple of kilometers south, in a conglomeration of hotels that is the town of Santa Margherita di Pula.

$$$–$$$$ ★ 🏨 **Is Morus.** A luxurious enclave, the Is Morus is on a sandy cove and offers all the amenities of a fine beach resort, with low, attractive buildings shaded by pinewoods, plus the option (for guests taking half or full board) of golfing at the fine Is Molas course, about 11 km (7 mi) away. ✉ *Santa Margherita di Pula, 09010,* ☎ *070/921171,* FAX *070/921596. 85 rooms. Restaurant, bar, pool, golf privileges, miniature golf, tennis court, beach. AE, DC, MC, V. Closed Jan.–mid-Apr. FAP, MAP.*

$$$ 🏨 **Flamingo.** Also directly on the beach and in a shady setting, this resort hotel features a main building and several two-story cottages nestled among eucalyptus trees. ✉ *Santa Margherita di Pula, 09010,* ☎ *070/9208361,* FAX *070/9208359. 134 rooms. Restaurant, piano bar, pool, miniature golf, tennis court, dance club. AE, DC, MC, V. Closed mid-Oct.–Apr.*

Outdoor Activities and Sports

GOLF

Guests at any of the hotels in Santa Margherita di Pula can avail of the international-standard 18-hole **Is Molas** course (☎ 070/9209165); the adjacent **Is Molas Golf Hotel** (✉ Località Is Molas, Santa Margherita di Pula, ☎ 070/9241006) offers special golfing vacations.

Sant'Antioco

⑩ *75 km (47 mi) west of Pula, 100 km (62 mi) west of Cagliari.*

Off the southwest coast is Sant'Antioco, one of two islands that is a popular holiday spot with good beaches. You drive over a causeway to get on the island, where the most hectic activity seems to be the silent repairing of nets by local fishermen who have already pulled in their daily catch. Before leaving the main town, also called Sant'Antioco, take some time to visit the **zona archeologica** at the top of the old city, affording terrific views over to the Sardinian mainland. Here you can see a Punic necropolis, and a tophet, or burial site dedicated to the Carthaginian goddess Tanit, scattered with urns that contained the cremated remains of stillborn children. 🎫 *8,000 lire, including guided tour of site, and ethnographic and archaeological museums.* ⏲ *Apr.–Sept., daily 9–1 and 3:30–7; Oct.–Mar., daily 9–1 and 3:30–6.*

OFF THE BEATEN PATH

CARBONIA AND IGLESIAS – If your curiosity prods you to explore more esoteric places, you could go just inland of Sant'Antioco to explore the rugged, once-booming mining country around Carbonia (14 km/9 mi northeast of Sant'Antioco), a town built by Mussolini in 1938 to serve as an administrative center for the coal miners and their families. With its time-frozen fascist architecture—ordered rows of houses around a core of monumental public buildings on the broad main piazza—it has been called an urban UFO set down in the Sardinian landscape. Nearby **Monte Sirai**, open daily 9–1 hour before sunset, holds the remains of Sardinia's most important Carthaginian military stronghold, impregnably sited atop a hill that dominates the outlook inland and far out to sea; admission is 5,000 lire. Iglesias (20 km/12 mi north of Carbonia) is an authentic Sardinian town, with a medieval cathedral; traveling east past Domusnovas on the Cagliari–Iglesias highway, you can detour and drive right through an immense cave, the Grotta di San Giovanni.

San Pietro

11 *5 km (3 mi) northwest of Sant'Antioco.*

A ferry at the small northern port of Calasetta connects Sant'Antioco with the smaller island of San Pietro at the main town of Carloforte. This is a favorite of wealthy Cagliaritans, many of whom have built weekend cottages here. The best views are from Capo Sandalo, on San Pietro's rugged western coast, but head to the island's southern tip for the beaches.

Lodging

$$ **Hieracon.** This ornate, Art Nouveau three-star lodging sits on the harborside in Carloforte. Rooms are modern, with whitewashed walls, TVs, telephones, and air-conditioning. A small internal garden is home to a few palms. Try to get a front-facing room, though there may be some traffic noise; the ones at top have low ceilings and no view. The central location means that you're a short walk from some good restaurants if you don't want to eat in. ✉ *Corso Cavour 63, 09014,* ☎ *0781/854028,* FAX *0781/854893. 17 rooms. Restaurant, bar, air-conditioning, minibars. AE, MC, V.*

BARUMINI TO THE COSTA SMERALDA

The Bare and the Beautiful

A more traditional—and wild—Sardinia awaits the traveler who ventures into the mountainous inland of the island. The Italian film directors, the Taviani brothers, made the hinterland of the Barbagia region, where traditional Sardinian customs are carried out in remote hilltop villages, the subject of an extraordinary portrait of rural life among the sheepherders of the area, *Padre Padrone* (1977). Inland Sardinians are hardy souls, used to living in a climate that is as unforgiving in winter as it is intolerable in summer. Old traditions, including the vendetta, are firmly rooted in the social fabric of this mountainous land that is both barren and beautiful. Here, rare species of wildlife share the rocky uplands with sturdy medieval churches and mysterious nuraghi, ancient stone citadels left by prehistoric people. You may want to make your base Oristano, on the west coast and the medieval center of Sardinian nationalism.

As you move northward the timeless beauty of the landscape begins to show greater sign of 20th-century development. The sunny resort of Alghero, the Spanish-influenced port on the west coast, is one of the island's premier holiday spots. In the 1960s and '70s, the Costa Smeralda, the luxury resort complex developed by the Aga Khan on the northeast corner of Sardinia, was *the* place to summer, along with the Côte d'Azur.

Su Nuraxi

★ 12 *60 km (37 mi) north of Cagliari.*

It is worth making a detour to the fascinating **nuraghe** of Su Nuraxi, off the main road outside the quiet little town of Barumini. You could spend hours clambering over this extraordinary structure of concentric rings of stone walls, chambers, passages, wells, and beehive tower. The main nuraghe is probably about half its original height, and some of the smaller towers around it have been reduced by pillaging and erosion to mere circles of stones on the ground.

The nuraghi were fortified villages, prehistoric versions of medieval walled towns and the forts of the American West. Though this particular type of construction is unique to Sardinia, similar buildings dating from the same era are found in other parts of the Mediterranean, such as Cyprus and the Balearic islands off Spain. Of the 7,000 nuraghi on Sardinia, Su Nuraxi is the most impressive, with those of Sant'Antine and Losa, both near Macomer, close runners-up. It's a good idea to take a flashlight along. *1 km (½ mi) west of Barumini.* ☎ *0337/ 813087.* 🎫 *7,000 lire.* ⏲ *Apr.–Sept., daily 8:30–7:30, Oct.–Mar., daily 8:30–5:30.*

Giara di Gesturi

13 *8 km (5 mi) north of Barumini, 68 km (42 mi) north of Cagliari.*

On the basalt plateau of Giara di Gesturi roam some of the island's more exotic wildlife, including a species of wild dwarf horse. Another rare species in the Giara is the mouflon, a wild sheep distinguishable from its domesticated counterpart by its long curving horns and skittishness. Long hunted for their decorative horns, the mouflon are now an endangered species, with only a few surviving on Sardinia and Corsica.

Oristano

14 *25 km (16 mi) north of Giara di Gesturi, 93 km (58 mi) northwest of Cagliari.*

Oristano, on the west coast, shone in the Middle Ages when it was capital of the Giudicato of Arborea, an independent duchy led by Sardinia's own Joan-of-Arc-type heroine, Eleanora di Arborea (circa 1340–1402). In the 14th century, Eleanora inherited the difficult task of defending the duchy's freedom, constantly undermined by the superior military might of the Spanish troops from Aragon. Although the duchy eventually reverted to Aragonese rule, Eleanora made a lasting contribution to Sardinia by implementing a code of law that was adopted throughout the island and remained in effect until Sardinia's unification with Italy in 1847. Now an important but slow-paced agricultural center, Oristano is the scene of livestock fairs and a rousing series of horse races, called Sa Sartiglia, marking the end of the February's Carnival.

OFF THE BEATEN PATH — **CABRAS** – Ten kilometers (6 mi) northwest of Oristano, you can see the extensive marshlands where fishermen pole round-bottomed rush boats through shallow ponds teeming with eel and crayfish.

Dining and Lodging

$$$ ★ ✕ **Il Faro.** Locals and visiting foodies consider this elegant seafood restaurant to be one of the best in the area, as it offers authentic and well-prepared seasonal dishes. The service is impeccable, the decor simple. There's *capretto allo spiedo* (spit-roasted goat) in the winter and an aromatic *zuppa di fave* (fava bean soup) with bacon and fennel in the

spring. ✉ *Via Bellini 25,* ☎ *0783/70002. AE, DC, MC, V. Closed Jan. 1–15 and July 1–15. No dinner Sun.*

$$ ✕ **Da Gino.** Extremely central (off Piazza Roma), this simple trattoria has authentic local dishes including seafood. Try the delicious spaghetti *alla bottarga* (with smoked fish roe). The service is friendly and attentive, making this a popular spot for locals and an ideal lunch stop. ✉ *Via Tirso 13,* ☎ *0783/71428. MC, V. Closed Sun.*

$$ ✕ **Salvatore.** This seafood restaurant near the church of Sacra Cuore pulls no punches or surprises, but the food is cooked to perfection. Seafood from the lagoons of Cabras and Santa Giusta is impeccably fresh. Specialties include grilled *anguillara* (eel). ✉ *Via Carbonia 1,* ☎ *0783/357134. DC, MC, V. Closed Sun.*

$ **Cama.** Near the train station, this hotel is also within walking distance of Oristano's old town center. Rooms are air-conditioned, but otherwise undistinguished. A parking lot and garage make it convenient for drivers. ✉ *Via Vittorio Veneto 119, 09170,* ☎ *0783/74374,* FAX *0783/74375. 54 rooms. Restaurant, bar, parking (fee). AE, DC, MC, V. Closed Dec. 20–Jan. 10.*

Nightlife and the Arts

The **Sartiglia** festival, on the last Sunday of Carnival season, includes rich costumes and a ritual joust. Each summer, the town holds an **arts and crafts exhibition,** with local foods and wines given prominence. Contact the tourist office (☞ Visitor Information *in* Sardinia A to Z, *below*) for information.

Tharros

15 *20 km (12 mi) west of Oristano, 113 km (70 mi) northwest of Cagliari.*

The ruins of the Carthaginian and Roman city of Tharros are along the road marked San Giovanni di Sinis; its position afforded it a strategic view over scenic Sinis peninsula. Like Nora to the south, the site was chosen because it commanded the best views of the harbor and could provide an easy escape route if inland tribes threatened. Four Corinthian columns still stand, and there are baths and fragments of mosaics from the Roman city. Like at Nora, there is much more submerged under water. *20 km (*mi) west of Oristano. 8,000 lire. ⏲ Daily 9–1 hr before sunset.

On your way to Tharros, you'll pass the ghost town of **San Salvatore,** revived briefly in the 1960s as a locale for spaghetti westerns and since abandoned. The saloon of the movie set still stands. Farther along, among the dunes, are large **rush huts** formerly used by fishermen and now much in demand as back-to-nature vacation homes. The 5th-century church of **San Giovanni di Sinis,** also on the peninsula, is the oldest Christian church in Sardinia.

Nuoro

16 *89 km (56 mi) northeast of Oristano, 181 km (113 mi) north of Cagliari.*

The somewhat shabby provincial capital of Nuoro is on the edge of a gorge in the harsh mountainous area that culminates in **Gennargentu,** the island's highest massif (6,000 ft). The only things likely to interest you in Nuoro are the views from the park on Sant'Onofrio hill and the exhibits in the **Museo della Vita e delle Tradizioni Popolari Sarde** (Museum of Sardinian Life and Folklore), where you can see a fabulous array of local costumes, domestic and agricultural implements, and traditional jewelry. ✉ *Via Mereu 56,* ☎ *0784/31426. 3,000* *lire.* ⏲ *Mid–late June and Sept., daily 9–1 and 3–7; July and Aug., daily 9–7; Oct.–mid-June, Mon.–Sat. 9–1 and 3–6, Sun. 9–1.*

Make an excursion about 3 km (2 mi) east to **Monte Ortobene** (2,900 ft) for some lofty views over the gulch below Nuoro. Here you can also see up close the imposing statue of Christ the Redeemer overlooking the city. Picnic tables make this a handy spot for an alfresco lunch stop.

OFF THE BEATEN PATH

ORGOSOLO – This old center of banditry halfway between Nuoro and Fonni is still a poor and undeveloped village, but the houses have been daubed with *murales* (mural paintings) vividly depicting political and cultural issues. The effect is startling and lively. The forest and grassy plane above the village make fine walking country.

Dining and Lodging

$$$ ★ ✕🏨 **Su Gologone.** Despite attracting tourists in droves, this bustling country inn (20 km/12 mi southeast of Nuoro) still manages a friendly atmosphere. The restaurant alone is worth a detour for an authentic Sardinian meal. Island specialties include *maccarones de busa* (thick homemade pasta), culingiones, porcheddu, and sebadas. Wash it all down with the local Vernaccia. The hotel organizes riding and trekking expeditions. ✉ *Località Su Gologone, 08025,* ☎ *0784/287512,* FAX *0784/287668. 65 rooms. Restaurant, bar, pool, miniature golf, 3 tennis courts. AE, DC, MC, V. Closed Nov.–Mar.*

Nightlife and the Arts

Nuoro's **Festa del Redentore** (Feast of the Redeemer) is held on the next-to-last Sunday in August. It's the best time to view the various traditional costumes of Sardinia's interior all together.

Shopping

Crafted for local festivals, wooden masks are available at local shops and make unusual and festive souvenirs. The local **ISOLA** shop (✉ Via Monsignor Bua 10) is in the heart of the old town.

Fonni

17 *30 km (19 mi) south of Nuoro, 137 km (85 mi) south of Olbia.*

In the heart of the Barbagia region, Fonni is the highest town on the island and a good base for excursions by car to all sights of interest in this mountainous district that is Sardinia's most primitive, not least Monte Spada and the Bruncu Spina refuge on the Gennargentu Massif. Life in some villages seems not to have changed much since the Middle Ages. Here a rigidly patriarchal society perpetuates the unrelenting practice of vendetta, and strangers are advised to mind their own business. High mountain roads wind and loop their way through the landscape; towns are small and undistinguished, their social fabric seemingly untouched by the 20th century. On feast days elaborate regional costumes are taken out of mothballs and worn as an explicit statement of community identity.

OFF THE BEATEN PATH

ARBATAX – If you have the stamina, take the rickety old train on a leg of the journey that runs on a single-gauge track between Cagliari and Arbatax, midway up the east coast. If all goes well, it takes about nine hours to cover the approximately 250 km (155 mi) of track, guaranteeing you a look at a Sardinia few tourists ever see. With daily, early-morning departures, the train rattles up into the Barbagia district through some breathtaking mountain scenery, then eases down into the desert landscape inland of Arbatax, where the trip ends on the dock next to the fishing boats. The train is run by the **Ferrovie Complementari** (☎

070/491304), and the ticket costs less than 15,000 lire. In Tortoli, just outside Arbatax, Dolce Casa (✉ Via Sarcidano 3, ☎ 0782/624235, FAX 0782/623484) is a modest, one-star hotel, scrupulously clean, run by an English-speaking couple. It's open June–September only.

Nightlife and the Arts

You can see one of the most characteristic of the Barbagia's celebrations in local costume in Fonni during the **Festa di San Giovanni,** held June 24.

Shopping

Special candies are made from honey and nougat and sold in hilltop Tonara, southwest of Fonni. In the mountain village of Aritzo, about 45 km (28 mi) south of Fonni, high up in the Barbagia, you'll find handcrafted wooden utensils and furniture.

En Route From Nuoro, take 129 west about 65 km (40 mi) to coastal Bosa, where you turn right into hilly and arid scrub country, with its abundance of cactus and juniper. Pines and olive trees shelter low buildings from the steady winds that make these parts ideal for sailing. About the only cash crop here is cork from the cork trees dotting the landscape. Yet in the low valleys and along the riverbeds, masses of oleander bloom in the summer, creating avenues of color.

Alghero

18 *40 km (25 mi) north of Bosa, 137 km (85 mi) southwest of Olbia.*

Among the larger centers on the northwest coast is Alghero, an appealing walled resort town with a distinctly Spanish flavor. It was built and inhabited in the 14th century by the Aragonese and Catalans, who constructed seaside ramparts and sturdy towers encompassing an inviting nucleus of narrow, winding streets. Rich, wrought-iron scrollwork decorates balconies and screened windows; Spanish motifs appear in stone portals and in bell towers. The dialect spoken here is a version of Catalan, not Italian: attend one of the masses conducted in Algherese to hear it.

Nearby are broad sandy beaches and the spectacular heights of **Capo Caccia,** an imposing limestone headland to the west. At the base of the sheer cliff, the pounding sea has carved an entrance to the vast **Grotta di Nettuno,** a fantastic cavern, which you must visit with a guide. By land, you reach the entrance at the base of the cliff by descending the more than 600 steps of the aptly named *escala del cabirol* (mountain goat's stairway), a dizzying enterprise—and the ascent is just as daunting. The excursion by sea is much less fatiguing, but is not possible in winter or when seas are rough. Boats leave the port of Alghero four times daily, or every hour or so in peak season, and the trip takes 2½ hours. *Boat tour:* ✉ *Navisarda,* ☎ *079/975599.* *Grotto 13,000 lire (includes mandatory tour); Boat tour 16,000 lire (excluding ticket for grotto).* ⊙ *Grotto: Apr.–Sept., daily 9–7; Oct., daily 10–5; Nov.–Mar., daily 9–2; tours on the hr. Boat tours: Apr., May, and Oct., daily 9, 10, 3, and 4; June–Sept., daily 9–5 on the hour.*

Dining and Lodging

$$–$$$ ✕ **Al Tuguri.** The name is dialect for "old abandoned house," though in fact the building has been sensitively renovated, retaining a rustic but smart ambience. Space is limited to one small upstairs room, and an even smaller attic, but this only enhances the feeling of friendly intimacy, fostered by the charming host, Benito Carbonella. He will explain the finer points of Catalan cookery, whose traditional recipes he has adapted, or "revisited." Ask for the sampling menu to see what he means. Seafood is the main ingredient, artfully prepared and presented in a variety of ways, for example mousse *de ricci* (with sea urchins). The desserts too are exceptional. ✉ *Via Maiorca 113,* ☎ *079/976772. MC, V. Closed Sun. and 4 wks Dec.–Jan.*

$$ ✕ **Da Pietro.** On a narrow street in the picturesque old town near Largo San Francesco, this seafood restaurant has vaulted ceilings and a bustling atmosphere. The menu features *bucatini all'algherese* (pasta with a sauce of clams, capers, tomatoes, and olives) and baked fish with a white-wine sauce. ✉ *Via Ambrogio Machin 18,* ☎ *079/979645. AE, DC, MC, V. Closed Wed. Oct.–May and 2 wks at Christmas.*

$$ ✕ **La Lepanto.** A covered veranda by the seafront marks out Alghero's top seafood restaurant, usually thronged with locals. The specialty is aragosta cooked in a variety of ways, including *alla catalana* (with tomato and onions). For starters, try risotto *nero di seppia* (with cuttlefish ink). ✉ *Via Carlo Alberto 133,* ☎ *079/979116. AE, DC, MC, V. Closed Mon. Oct.–May.*

$$$–$$$$ ★ **Villa Las Tronas.** The villa is a former royal mansion on a rocky bluff above the sea but still near the center of town. The gardens sheltering the hotel from the road impart a regal sense of seclusion, and there are great views across the water to the old town. Inside, the belle-epoque atmosphere is complemented by modern comforts and good en-suite facilities. The restaurant is open in summer only. ✉ *Lungomare Valencia 1, 07041,* ☎ *079/981818,* FAX *079/981044. 29 rooms. Restaurant, pool, exercise room, beach. AE, DC, MC, V.*

$$–$$$ **Carlos V.** Right opposite the Villa Las Tronas on the shore boulevard, about 1 km (½ mi) from the center of town, this modern hotel (pronounced Carlos Quinto) has gardens, porticoes, and terraces, one of which has a good-size swimming pool. All rooms—airy, modern, light affairs rather lacking in character—have a balcony, but don't settle for the slightly cheaper ones facing the back; the pleasure here is all in the magnificent sea view. Low season rates are a bargain, and there are discounts for longer stays. ✉ *Lungomare Valencia 24, 07041,* ☎ *079/979501,* FAX *079/980298. 110 rooms. Restaurant, pool, 2 tennis courts, meeting rooms. AE, MC, V.*

$–$$ **San Francesco.** Centrally located in Alghero's Spanish quarter, this hotel occupies the convent that was once attached to the church of San Francesco. The rooms are grouped around the 14th-century cloister and, though somewhat cramped, are modern and quiet. Breakfast is included in the price. ✉ *Via Machin 2, 07041,* ☎ FAX *079/980330. 21 rooms. Bar, meeting rooms. MC, V. Closed Nov.*

Shopping

Coral, still harvested in the bay, and gold jewelry are displayed in many specialist shops as well as more touristy outlets throughout Alghero's old quarter. For other handicrafts, try the local branch of **ISOLA** (✉ Via Catalogna 54).

Sassari

19 *34 km (21 mi) northeast of Alghero, 212 km (132 mi) north of Cagliari.*

Inland Sassari is an important university town and administrative center, notable for its historic, ornate cathedral and a good archaeological museum. Sassari is the hub of several highways and secondary roads leading to various scenic coastal resorts, among them Stintino and Castelsardo (☞ *below*).

Shopping

Sassari has Sardinia's main **ISOLA** outlet (✉ Giardini Pubblici), a purpose-built exhibition center in the public gardens next to Viale Mancini; it's a great place for gifts and souvenirs.

Castelsardo

20 *32 km (20 mi) northeast of Sassari, 100 km (62 mi) west of Olbia.*

The walled seaside citadel of Castelsardo is a delight for basket lovers. Roadside stands and shops in the old town sell tons of island crafts: rugs, wrought iron, and baskets—in myriad shapes and colors. Take the children to see the **Elephant Rock** on the road into Castelsardo; hollowed out by primitive man to become a *domus de janas* (literally, "fairy house," in fact a neolithic burial chamber) it resembles an elephant, trunk and all.

Shopping

There is an **ISOLA** workshop on Lungomare Colombo, where local handicrafts can be bought. The local specialty is a brightly colored basket made of dwarf palms.

Santa Teresa di Gallura

21 *68 km (42 mi) northeast of Castelsardo, 65 km (41 mi) northwest of Olbia.*

At the northern tip of Sardinia, Santa Teresa di Gallura retains the relaxed, carefree air of an authentic fishing village turned resort.

Lodging

$$$–$$$$ **Grand Hotel Corallaro.** This hotel offers luxury accommodations in a panoramic spot right by the beach, a brief walk from the town center. Rooms are functional and some have balconies. Public rooms are much grander, furnished with wicker chairs, and there are terraces and lawns to sip pre-prandial drinks. Half or full board is required in peak season. ✉ *Località Rena Bianca, 07028,* ☎ *0789/755475,* FAX *0789/755431. 81 rooms. Restaurant, pool, Turkish bath, exercise room. MC, V. Closed mid-Oct.–Easter. MAP, FAP.*

$–$$ ★ **Canne al Vento.** This cheerful, family-run hotel and restaurant on the main road into town is a quiet, tasteful haven. The restaurant specializes in authentic island cuisine, for example *zuppa cuata* (bread, cheese, and tomato soup), porcheddu, or seafood. ✉ *Via Nazionale 23, 07028,* ☎ *0789/754219,* FAX *0789/754948. 22 rooms. Restaurant. MC, V. Closed Mon. and Oct.–Easter.*

La Maddalena

22 *30 km (19 mi) east of Santa Teresa di Gallura, 45 km (20 mi) northwest of Olbia.*

From the port of Palau you can visit the archipelago of La Maddalena, seven granite islands embellished with lush green scrub and wind-bent pines. Pilgrims pay homage to **Garibaldi's tomb** (1807–82) on the grounds of his hideaway on Isola Caprera, the island to the east of Isola Maddalena ☎ *0789/727162.* *4,000 lire.* *Daily 9–1:30.*

Porto Cervo

★ 23 *30 km (19 mi) north of Olbia.*

Sardinia's northeastern coast is fringed with low cliffs, inlets, and small bays. This has become an upscale vacationland, with glossy resorts, such as Baia Sardinia and Porto Rotondo, just outside the confines of the famed Costa Smeralda, developed by the Aga Khan (born 1936), who accidentally discovered its charms—and potential—in 1965, when his yacht took shelter here from a storm. The Costa Smeralda is still dominated by his personality; its attractions remain geared to those who can measure themselves by the yardstick of his fabled riches.

Sardinia's most expensive hotels are here, and the world's most magnificent yachts anchor in the waters of Porto Cervo. The trend has been to keep this enclave of the really rich an exclusive haven by encouraging more multimillionaires to build discreetly luxurious villas, and planning four more golf courses for their leisure.

All along the coast, carefully tended lush vegetation surrounds vacation villages and elaborate villa colonies that have sprung up over the past decade in a range of spurious architectural styles best described as bogus Mediterranean.

Lodging

$$$$ **Cala di Volpe.** Long a magnet for the beautiful people, this luxury five-star establishment, now part of ITT Sheraton, was built to resemble an ancient Sardinian village. The hotel's decor is rustic-elegant, with beamed ceilings, Sardinian arts and crafts, and porticoes overlooking the sea. The presidential suite in the highest tower has a private pool. ✉ *Cala di Volpe, 07020,* ☎ *0789/976111,* FAX *0789/976617. 121 rooms, 12 suites. Restaurant, bar, air-conditioning, pool, 3 tennis courts, beach. AE, DC, MC, V. Closed mid-Oct.–Mar.*

$$$$ **Cervo.** Low Mediterranean buildings surround a large pool and garden in the heart of the Costa Smeralda's Porto Cervo. This complex is next to the marina and *piazzetta* (small piazza), a popular spot to see and be seen. The rooms are large and most have a terrace. Guests have access to five good tennis courts in summer. ✉ *Porto Cervo, 07020,* ☎ *0789/931111,* FAX *0789/931613. 111 rooms. Restaurant, piano bar, pool, 5 tennis courts, exercise room, squash, beach. AE, DC, MC, V.*

$$$ **Nibaru.** Pinkish-red brick buildings with tiled roofs stand in a secluded inlet set in lush gardens—not bad for a hotel that enjoys all the best features of the Costa Smeralda at comparatively low rates. Guest rooms are just a few yards from the sea and some superb swimming spots and also within easy access to the Pevero Golf Club and the tennis courts of Porto Cervo. ✉ *Località Cala di Volpe, 07020,* ☎ *0789/96038,* FAX *0789/96474. 45 rooms. Restaurant, bar, pool. AE, DC, MC, V. Closed Oct.–Apr.*

Outdoor Activities and Sports

GOLF

An 18-hole, world-class **Pevero Golf Course** (☎ 0789/96210), designed by Robert Trent Jones, is on the Bay of Pevero, near Porto Cervo.

SAILING

The **Yacht Club Costa Smeralda** (☎ 0789/91332) at Porto Cervo offers temporary memberships.

Shopping

Contemporary pottery displaying traditional motifs is a hot item, snatched up at whim along the Costa Smeralda. Porto Cervo's Sottopiazza has some big-name boutiques, and there's an **ISOLA** outlet here too.

Olbia

24 *30 km (19 mi) south of Porto Cervo, 106 km (66 mi) north of Nuoro.*

Set amid the resorts of Sardinia's northeastern coast, Olbia is a lively little seaport, not heavily industrialized, at the head of a long, wide bay. If you have any time to spare here, search out the little basilica of **San Simplicio,** a short walk behind the main Corso Umberto. The simple granite structure dates from the 11th century, part of the great Pisan church-building program, using pillars and columns recycled from Roman constructions. *Via San Simplicio.* ⏲ *Daily 6:30–12:30 and 4–7.*

Lodging

$$–$$$ **De Plam.** Though aesthetically unimpressive, this seafront hotel a walk from town can at least claim the best views in Olbia. The rooms are furnished in a motel style that is functional if not particularly memorable. It's convenient to the port (though still a taxi ride away). ✉ *Via de Filippi 33, 07026, ☎ 0789/25777, FAX 0789/22648. 60 rooms. Restaurant, bar, air-conditioning, meeting rooms. AE, DC, MC, V.*

Golfo Aranci

25 *19 km (12 mi) northeast of Olbia.*

At the mouth of the Gulf of Olbia, Golfo Aranci is a blossoming resort and debarkation point for FS ferries from the mainland. The craggy headland west of town has been left undeveloped as a nature reserve, and there are some inviting beaches within an easy drive.

SARDINIA A TO Z

Arriving and Departing

By Boat

Large modern ferries run by Tirrenia Lines, Navarma Lines, and the FS (Italian State Railways) connect the island (ports at Porto Torres, Olbia, Arbatax, and Cagliari) with the mainland. **Tirrenia** (☎ 167/824079 toll-free; 06/4742041 and 06/4742242 in Rome; 010/2758041 in Genoa; 081/7201111 in Naples) sails to several ports in Sardinia from Genoa, La Spezia, Civitavecchia, Fiumicino, Naples, Palermo, and Trapani. **Navarma** (☎ 0565/9361) transports passengers and cars between Livorno and Olbia. **FS** ferries (☎ 147/888088) carry trains as well as passengers and cars; they sail from Civitavecchia to Golfo Aranci, near Olbia. The Civitavecchia–Olbia/Golfo Aranci run takes about eight hours and there are overnight sailings. Depending on the season, the service is scheduled two or three times a week; reservations are essential in the summer.

By Plane

Alitalia and Meridiana connect Rome, Milan, Pisa, and other cities on the mainland and in southern Europe with Sardinia. Flying is by far the fastest and easiest way to get to the island. The Rome–Cagliari flight takes about an hour. Sardinia's major airports are at Cagliari and Alghero, with another, smaller one, at Olbia, providing access to the Costa Smeralda.

Cagliari's **Aeroporto di Elmas** (☎ 070/240119) at Elmas is about 6 km (4 mi) west of town center, and there is a regular bus service from the airport to Piazza Matteotti, in front of the train station. Alghero's **Aeroporto Fertilia** (☎ 079/935282) is 13 km (8 mi) from the city. A bus links the airport with the main bus station in the center of town. **Aeroporto Costa Smeralda** (☎ 0789/52600) is 4 km (2½ mi) southeast of Olbia, linked by local bus to Olbia.

Getting Around

By Bus

Cagliari is linked with the other towns of Sardinia by a network of buses. Local destinations are served by **ARST** (☎ 070/4098324). Major cities, excluding Olbia, are served by **PANI** (☎ 070/652326). The heart of the Sardinian bus system is the **Stazione Autolinee** (✉ Piazza Matteotti, across the square from the main tourist office) in Cagliari. City buses in Cagliari and Sassari operate on the same system as those on the mainland: buy your ticket first, at a tobacco shop or machine, and cancel it by punching it in the machine on the bus. Fares are 1,300 lire per ride.

By Car

The best way to get around Sardinia is to drive. The roads are generally in good condition, but bear in mind that such roadside conveniences as gas stations and refreshment stands are infrequent on some routes, especially in the east. Try and avoid driving at night, when mountain roads are particularly hazardous and slow. Cars may be taken on board most of the ferry lines connecting Sardinia with the mainland. The north–south S131 (Strada Carlo Felice) connects Cagliari, Oristano, Sassari, and Porto Torres. The S131 Dir and S129 connects the Carlo Felice Highway with Nuoro and the Barbagia. The S597 connects Sassari and Olbia.

By Train

The **Stazione Centrale** (☎ 147/888088 toll free) in Cagliari is next to the bus station on Piazza Matteotti. There are fairly good connections between Olbia, Cagliari, Sassari, and Oristano. You can reach Nuoro via Macomer; Alghero is reached via Sassari. Service on the few other local lines is infrequent and slow. The fastest train between Olbia and Cagliari takes more than four hours. Local trains connect Golfo Aranci, the FS port for the train ferry, with Olbia (20 min) and Sassari with Alghero (35 minutes).

Contacts and Resources

Car Rentals

ALGHERO

Maggiore-Budget (✉ Via Sassari 87, ☎ 079/979375; ✉ Aeroporto di Fertilia, ☎ 079/935045).

CAGLIARI

Avis (✉ Via Sonnino 87, ☎ 070/668128; ✉ Aeroporto di Elmas, ☎ 070/240081). **Hertz** (✉ Piazza Matteotti 8, ☎ 070/668105; ✉ Aeroporto di Elmas, ☎ 070/240037). **Maggiore** (✉ Viale Monastir 116, ☎ 070/273692).

OLBIA

Avis (✉ Via Genova 67, ☎ 0789/22420; ✉ Aeroporto Costa Smeralda). **Hertz** (✉ Via Regina Elena 34, ☎ 0789/21733; ✉ Aeroporto Costa Smeralda, ☎ 0789/66024).

SASSARI

Avis (✉ Via Mazzini 2, ☎ 079/235547). **Hertz** (✉ Corso Francesco Vico, ☎ 079/232184). **Maggiore** (✉ Piazza Santa Maria 6, ☎ 079/235507).

Emergencies

Police (☎ 112 or 113). **Hospital** (✉ Via Peretti, Cagliari, ☎ 070/543266). **Ambulance** (✉ Cagliari, ☎ 070/4092901).

Guided Tours

HORSEBACK RIDING

The **Associazione Nazionale di Turismo Equestre** (✉ Via Carso 35/a, Sassari, ☎ 079/299889) can provide information on renting mounts and joining riding parties with itineraries along the coast or into the heart of the island. The **Centro Vacanze Alabirdi** (✉ Arborea, near Oristano, ☎ 0783/800512) organizes horseback riding vacations. The **Centro Vacanze Su Gologone** (✉ Oliena, ☎ 0784/287512) also offers riding vacations.

ORIENTATION

Guided tours are good introductions to Sardinia. Travel from the Italian mainland is included, as are travel and accommodations on Sardinia. They should be booked through a travel agent.

To book a tour, contact a travel agent such as **Viaggi Orru** (✉ Via Roma 95, ☎ 070/659858). **Chiariva** offers two group tours of Sardinia by bus with guide. A nine-day tour leaves from Genoa; an eight-day tour departs from Rome. Both operate April–September. **Aviatour** has a similar eight-day tour leaving from either Milan or Rome. The tour also runs from April to September only. **Appian Line** can arrange a fly-drive package on the Costa Smeralda; transportation is by air, the rental car is picked up at the airport at Olbia. Accommodations are in good, but not outlandishly expensive, hotels on this famous coastline for the rich.

Late-Night Pharmacies

Late-night pharmacies are open on a rotating basis; information on current schedules is pinned up on any pharmacy door or can be obtained by calling (☎ 192).

Travel Agency

Cagliari (Viaggi Orru, ✉ Via Roma 95, ☎ 070/659858).

Visitor Information

Tourist offices (✉ Piazza Porta Terra 9, 07041 Alghero, ☎ 079/979054; ✉ Piazza Matteotti, 09100 Cagliari, ☎ 070/669255; ✉ Piazza Deffenu 9, 09100, ☎ 070/654811; 167/013153 toll-free; ✉ Aeroporto di Elmas, Cagliari, ☎ 070/240200; ✉ City Hall, 07026 Golfo Aranci, ☎ 0789/21672 June–Aug. only; ✉ Piazza Italia 19, 08025 Nuoro, ☎ 0784/30083; ✉ Via Catello Piro, 07026 Olbia, ☎ 0789/21453; ✉ Aeroporto Costa Smeralda, ☎ 0789/21453; ✉ Via Cagliari 278, 09170 Oristano, ☎ 0783/74191; ✉ Viale Umberto 72, 07100 Sassari, ☎ 079/231331; ✉ Via Roma 62, 07100 Sassari, ☎ 079/231777).

17 BACKGROUND AND ESSENTIALS

Portraits of Italy

Books and Videos

Chronology

Smart Travel Tips A to Z

Italian Vocabulary

THE ARTLESS ART OF ITALIAN COOKING

You are staying with friends in their villa in a windswept olive orchard above Florence. After a day in town—a morning at the Palazzo Pitti, afternoon in the Brancacci Chapel—you have returned to rest. In the garden, you find your hostess lifting heavy tomatoes into a basket, the acrid smell of their skins wafting up in the gentle September heat. You pick basil and tug figs from a tree that warms its back against the 14th-century kitchen wall. Inside, you watch while your hostess rinses the greens in the quarried stone sink. The tomatoes are still sun-warm when she scoops them, chopped, into a blender with the basil and a stream of olive oil; she pours the mixture into a faience bowl over steaming pasta. You eat at the kitchen table, pour wine from a crockery pitcher, and wipe your bowl with torn chunks of flour-flecked bread. Over the greens your hostess drizzles more olive oil and a bit of rock salt pinched from an open bowl. The figs melt in your mouth like chocolate. A scalding syrup of Arabic coffee streams from the *macchinetta,* and you're ready for a midnight survey of the olive groves.

Simple, earthy, at once wholesome and sensual, as sophisticated in its purity as the most complex cuisine, as inspired in its aesthetics as the art and architecture of its culture, Italian cooking strikes a chord that resonates today as it did in the Medici courts. Its enduring appeal can be traced to an ancient principle: respect for the essence of the thing itself—nothing more, nothing less. Like Michelangelo freeing the prisoners that dwelt within the stone—innate, organic—an Italian chef seems intuitively to seek out the crux of the thing he is about to cook and flatter it, subtly, with the purest of complements. To lay a translucent sheet of prosciutto—earthy, gamey, faintly redolent of brine—across the juicy pulchritude of a melon wedge is a stroke of insight into the nature of two ingredients as profound as the imaginings of Galileo.

Considering the pizzas, lasagnas, and red-drenched spaghetti that still pass for Italian food abroad (despite a wave of enlightenment that revived "Northern" techniques in the 1980s), it's no surprise that visitors to Italy are often struck by the austerity of the true Italian dishes put before them. The pasta is only lightly accented, not drowning in an industrial ladle-full of strong, soupy sauce. And while there may have been a parade of vegetable *antipasti,* the salad itself bears no resemblance to the smorgasbord of Anglo-American salad bars—it's a simple mix of greens, a drizzle of oil, a spritz, perhaps, of red-wine vinegar. If you've just come from Germanic countries, you'll notice a lack of Maggi, the bottled brown "flavor enhancer" that singes the tongue with monosodium glutamate, on the table. If you've come from Belgium, you'll miss the sauceboat of Hollandaise. And if you've come from France, you may shrug dismissively at the isolated ingredients you're served, saying as other Frenchmen before you, "But this is not really a true *cuisine* . . ."

Ah, but it is. Shunning the complexities of heavy French sauces and avoiding the elaborate farce, Italian cuisine—having unloaded the aspirations of *alta cucina* onto its northern neighbors when Catherine de' Medici moved (chefs and all) to Paris—stands alone, proud, purist, unaffected.

The Italians' pride comes in part from a confidence in their raw ingredients, an earthiness that informs the appreciation of every citizen-connoisseur, from the roughest peasant in workers' blue to the vintner in shoulder-tied cashmere: They are in touch with land and sea. In the country, your host can tell you the source of every ingredient on the table, from the neighbor's potted goose to the porcini gathered in the beech grove yesterday. In the city, the market replaces the country network, and aggressive shopping will trace the genealogy of every mushroom, every artichoke, every wooden scoop of olives. And in balconies overhanging the seashore, the squid floating in their rich, blue-black ink were bought from a fisherman on the beach at dawn.

The spectrum of Italian regional cooking is as broadly varied as Italy's terrain, and cuisine and countryside are intimately allied. Emerging into sunlight from the Great St. Bernard pass into the Valle d'Aosta, the Piedmont, the hills of Lombardy, you'll find wood-lined alpine trattorias offering rib-sticking gnocchi and air-dried beef, bubbling pots of *bagna cauda* (hot dipping sauce of olive oil and garlic), slabs of polenta, hearty walnut *torta* (cake). The pearl-spotted rice of Arborio, in the Po Valley, fuels an extraordinary array of risottos in Milan, where chefs shun olive oil in favor of the region's rich butter. Descend to Alba and savor the earthy perfume of truffles, the muscular Barolo wines. Cross over into Liguria and the cuisine changes as abruptly as the landscape: Wild herbs, greens, and ground nuts flavor a panoply of sauces (consider the famous pesto, flavored with a "riviera" basil rarely found elsewhere), served as condiments to meat as often as over pasta. The succulent pink pork of a Parma ham, the golden butterfat in a Reggiano cheese were nurtured on the same fertile soil of Emilia-Romagna, both the culinary and agricultural heart of Italy, while the *bistecca* of Tuscany comes from Chianina beef, pampered on local prairie grass and slaughtered at a tender age. Head south for sun-plumped eggplant, and quasi-tropical artichokes—in Rome, fried in delicate batter; in Calabria, stuffed with meat and sharp Pecorino from its hillside sheep herds. The chickpeas in Sicilian dishes remind you you're nearly in North Africa. And, of course, on this slender leg of land you are never far from the sea, and the harvest of its *frutti di mare* graces nearly every region—but none more than the islands and tide-washed shores of the south.

Careening in your rental car down the western coast, clinging to the waterfront through sea-shanty villages that cantilever over the roaring surf, you feel a morning lag: Your breakfast of *latte macchiato* and sugary *cornetto* has worn away. A real espresso would hit the spot; you hurtle down a web of switchbacks and pull into a seaside inn. You sip aromatic coffee and watch the waves. An hour passes in reverie—an aperitif, perhaps? Another hour over the Martini rosso, and you give in to the impulse, adjourning to the dining room. The odor of wood smoke drifts from the kitchen. A nutty risotto with a blush of tomato precedes a vast platter—austere, unembellished—of smoke-grilled fish, still sizzling, lightly brushed with oil, and glittering with rock salt. At the table beside yours, when the platter arrives, the woman rises and fillets the fish dexterously, serving her husband and sons.

There's a wholesomeness in the way Italians eat that is charming and contagious. If American foodies pick and kvetch and French gastronomes worship, Italians plunge into their meal with frank joy, earnest appreciation, and ebullient conversation. Yet they do not overindulge: portions are light, the drinking gentle, late suppers spartan with concern for digestion uppermost. It's as if the voice of Mamma still whispers moderation in their ear. They may, on the other hand, take disproportionate pleasure in watching guests eat, in surrounding them with congenial company, in pouncing on the bill. (This wholesome spirit even carries into the very bars: Unlike the dark, louche atmosphere of Anglo lounges and pubs, in Italy you'll drink your amaro in a fluorescent-lit coffee bar without a whiff of sin in the air.)

Yet for all their straightforwardness, Italians are utterly at ease with their heritage, steeped from birth in the art and architecture that surrounds them. Without a hint of the grandiose, they'll construct a still life of figs and Bosc pears worthy of Caravaggio; a butcher will drape iridescent pheasants and quail, heads dangling, with the panache of a couturier. Consider the artless beauty of ruby-raw beef on an emerald bed of arugula, named for the preferred colors of the Venetian painter Carpaccio; pure white porcelain on damask; a mosaic of olives and pimientos in blown glass; a flash of folkloric pottery on a polished plank of oak.

In fact, it must be said: A large part of the pleasure of Italian dining is dining in Italy. We have all eaten in Italian restaurants elsewhere. The food can be superb, the ingredients authentic, the pottery and linens imported by hand. Yet who can conjure the blood-red ocher crumbling to gold on a Roman wall, the indigo and pastel hues of fishing boats rocking in a marina, the snow flurry of sugar papers on a café floor? These impart the essence that—as much as the basil on your *bruschetta*—flavors your Italian dining experience.

Inside the great walls of Lucca, you are lunching—slowly, copiously, and at length—in the shade of a vaulted portico. Strips of roasted eggplant and pepper steeped in garlic and oil; tortelloni stuffed with squab in a pool of butter and sage; roasted veal laced with green peppercorns; blackberries in thick cream. The bottle of Brunello di Montalcino, alas, is drained. It has been a perfect morning, walking the ramparts, and you have found the perfect restaurant: a Raphaelesque perspective of arcades and archways, pillars, porches, and loges spreads before you. The shadows and lines are strong in the afternoon sun; you admire from your seat in the cross breeze. It's only slowly that you realize that this Merchant/Ivory moment has a sound track, so organic to the scene you hadn't noticed—but now you feel goose bumps rising on your neck. It is Puccini: A young woman is singing, beautifully, from a groined arcade across the square, accompanied by a portable tape player.

". . . Ma quando vien lo sgelo . . . il primo sole è mio . . ."

Your coffee goes cold, untouched until the song, the moment, are over—and, in all its multifaceted magnificence, your Italian meal as well.

— Nancy Coons

THE PASSIONATE EYE: ITALIAN ART THROUGH THE AGES

Italian art flows as naturally as its wine, its sunshine, and its amore, and it has been springing from the Italian spirit for nearly as long. Perhaps nowhere in the world has such a vital creative impulse flourished so bountifully within the noble sweep of the classical tradition. Perhaps no other country's cultural life has been so inextricably interwoven with its history.

And yet, Italy lives comfortably in the midst of all her accumulated treasures. She accepts them casually and affectionately, as she does her children and her flowers. True, some of her precious store has been gathered into world-famous museums, but Italians know best and love most intimately the art that surrounds their daily activity. They go to church among thousand-year-old mosaics, buy their groceries in a shop open since the time of Columbus, picnic on the steps of a temple that was old when Christ was born, and attend the opera in the same theaters where Rossini and Verdi saw their works premiered. Italy wears the raiment of her heritage with a light and touching grace. She must: It is the very fabric of her life. For travelers from other countries, however, Italian art remains unique, extraordinary, worthy of worship. Here we offer a short history, focusing on Italy's greatest artistic achievement, the Renaissance—often called the nursery of Western art. The discoveries of 14th- and 15th-century Italian artists making it possible to render a realistic image of a person or an object determined the course of Western art right up until the late 19th century. Following the essay is a glossary of art and architectural terms that will prove useful in understanding the artistic treasures of Italy.

Art in the Middle Ages

The eastern half of the Roman Empire, based in Constantinople (Byzantium) was powerful long after the fall of Rome in AD 476: Italy remained influenced—and at times ruled—by the Byzantines. The artistic revolution began when artists started to rebel against the Byzantine ethic, which dictated that art be exclusively Christian and that its aim be to arouse a sensation of mystical awe and reverence in the onlooker. This ethic forbade frivolous pagan portraits, bacchanalian orgy scenes, or delicate landscapes with maidens gathering flowers, as painted and sculpted by the Romans. Instead, biblical stories were depicted in richly colored mosaics—rows of figures against a gold background. (You can see some of the finest examples of this art at Ravenna, once the Western capital of the Empire, on the Adriatic coast.) Even altarpieces, painted on wood, followed the same model—stiff figures surrounded by gold, with no attempt made at an illusion of reality.

In the 13th century, the era of St. Francis and of a new humanitarian approach to Christianity, artists in Tuscany began to portray real people in real settings. Cimabue was the first to feel his way in this direction, but it was Giotto who broke decisively with the Byzantine style. Even if his sense of perspective is nowhere near correct and his figures still had typically Byzantine slanting eyes, he painted palpably solid people who, presumably, experienced real emotions.

By the end of the 14th century, the International Gothic Style (which had arrived in Italy from France) had made further progress toward realism, but more with depictions of plants, animals, and clothes than with the human figure. And, as you can see from Gentile da Fabriano's *Adoration of the Magi,* housed in the Galleria degli Uffizi in Florence, it was mainly a decorative art, still very much like a Byzantine mosaic.

Italian architecture during the Middle Ages followed a number of different trends. In the south, the solid Norman Romanesque style was dominant; towns such as Siena and Pisa in central Italy had their own Romanesque style, more graceful than its northern European counterparts. Like northern Romanesque, it was dominated by simple geometric forms, but buildings were covered with decorative toylike patterns done in multicolored marble. In northern Italy, building was in a more solemn red brick.

In Tuscany, the region around Florence, the 13th century was a time of great political and economic growth, and there was a desire to celebrate the new wealth and power in the region's buildings. This is why such civic centers as the Palazzo Vecchio in Florence are so big and fortresslike. Florence's cathedral, the Duomo, was built on a colossal scale mainly in order to outdo the Pisans and the Sienese, Florence's rivals. All these Tuscan cathedrals are in the Italian version of Gothic, a style that originated in France and found its expression there in tall, soaring, light-and-airy verticality, intended to elevate the soul. The spiritual aspect of Gothic never really caught on in Italy, where the top priority for a church (as representative of a city) was to be grander and more imposing than the neighboring cities' churches.

Art in the Renaissance

The Renaissance, or "rebirth," did not evolve simply from a set of newfound artistic skills; the movement represented a revolution in attitudes whereby each individual was thought to play a specific role in the divine scheme of things. By fulfilling this role, it was believed the individual gained a new dignity. It was no coincidence that this revolution took place in Florence, which in the 15th century was an influential, wealthy, highly evolved city-state. Artists here had the leisure, prestige, and self-confidence to develop their talent and produce works that would reflect this new dignity and strength as well as their own prowess.

The sculptor Donatello, for example, wanted to astound, rather than please, the spectator with his defiant warts-and-all likenesses and their intense, heroic gazes. In painting, Masaccio's figures have a similarly assured air.

Art had changed gears in the early Renaissance: The Classical Age was now the model for a noble, moving, and realistic art. Artists studied ancient Roman ruins for what they could learn about proportion and balance. They evolved the new science of perspective and took it to its limits with sometimes bizarre results, as in Uccello's dizzily receding *Deluge* (in Florence's church Santa Maria Novella) or his carousel-like *Battle of San Romano* (in the Uffizi in Florence). One of the most frequently used perspective techniques was that of foreshortening, or making an object seem smaller and more contracted, to create the illusion of distance. From this technique emerged the *sotto in su* effect—literally, "from below upwards," meaning that the action in the picture takes place above you, with figures, buildings, and landscapes correspondingly foreshortened. It's a clever visual trick that must have delighted visitors who walked into, for example, Mantegna's Camera degli Sposi in Mantua and saw what appeared to be people curiously looking down at them through a gap in the ceiling.

The concept of the universal man was epitomized by the artist who was at home with an array of disciplines, including the science of perspective, Greek, Latin, anatomy, sculpture, poetry, architecture, philosophy—even engineering, as in the case of Leonardo da Vinci, the universal man par excellence. Not surprisingly, there was a change in attitude toward artists: Whereas previously they had been considered merely anonymous workmen trained to carry out commissions, now they were seen as giant personalities, immensely skillful and with highly individual styles.

The new skills and realistic effects of Florentine painting rapidly found a sympathetic response among Venetian painters. Gentile Bellini and Antonio Carpaccio, just two of the many whose work fills the Accademia, took to covering their canvases with crowd scenes, buildings, canals, processions, dogs, ships, parrots, and chimneys. These were generally narrative paintings, telling the story of a saint's life or simply depicting everyday scenes.

It was the emphasis on color, though, that made Venetian art Venetian, and it was the 15th-century masters of color, preeminently Giovanni Bellini and Giorgione, who began to use it no longer as decoration but as a means to create a particular atmosphere. How different the effect of Giorgione's *Tempest* (in the Accademia) would be with a sunny blue sky instead of the ominous grays and dark greens that fill the background! For the first time, the atmosphere not the figures became the central focus of painting.

In architecture the Gothic excesses of the 13th century were toned down in the 14th, while the 15th ushered in a completely new approach. The humanist ideal was expressed through classical Roman design. In Florence, Brunelleschi used Roman columns for the basilica of San Lorenzo; Roman-style rustication (massive exterior blocks) for the Pitti Palace; and Roman round arches—as opposed to pointed Gothic ones—for his Ospedale degli Innocenti (Foundling Hospital), which is generally considered the first truly classical building of the Renaissance. Leon Battista Alberti's treatise on ideal proportion was even more influential as a manifesto of the Renaissance movement. Suddenly, architects had become erudite scholars and architecture far more earnest.

High Renaissance and Mannerism

Florence in the late 15th century and Rome in the early 16th (following its sacking in 1527) underwent a traumatic political and religious upheaval that naturally came to be reflected in art. Classical proportion and realism no longer seemed enough. The heroic style suddenly looked hollow and outdated. Tuscan artists such as Pontormo and Rosso Fiorentino found expression for their unease in discordant colors, elongated forms, tortured looks in staring eyes. Giambologna carved his *Hercules and the Centaur* (in Florence's Museo del Bargello) at the most agonizing moment of their battle, when Hercules bends the Centaur's back to the point where it is about to snap. This is Mannerism, a style in which optimism and self-confidence are gone. What remains is a self-conscious, stylized show of virtuosity, the effect of which is neither to please (like Gothic) nor to impress (like Renaissance art), but to disquiet. Even Bronzino's portraits are cold, unsmiling, and far removed from the relaxed mood of the Renaissance portrait. By the 1530s an artistic exodus from Florence had taken place; Michelangelo had left for Rome, and Florence's golden age was over.

Venice, meanwhile, was following its own path. Titian's painting was a more virtuoso version of Bellini's and Giorgione's poetic style, but Titian later shifted the emphasis back to figures, rather than atmosphere, as the central focus of his paintings. Titian's younger contemporaries in Venice—Veronese, Tintoretto, and Bassano—wanted to make names for themselves. They started working on huge canvases—which gave them more freedom of movement—playing all sorts of visual games: juggling with viewpoints and perspective and using dazzlingly bright colors. This visual trickery suggests a natural parallel with the self-conscious artifice of Florentine painting of the same period, but the exuberance of these Venetian painters, and the increasingly emotional quality of their work remained significantly more vital than the arid and ever more sterile works of central Italy toward the end of the 16th century.

Mannerism found a fairly precise equivalent in architecture. In Florence the rebellious younger generation (Michelangelo, Ammanati, Vasari) used the same architectural vocabulary as the Renaissance architects, but distorted it deliberately and bizarrely in a way that would have made Alberti's hair stand on end. Michelangelo's staircase at the Biblioteca Laurenziana in Florence, for example, spills down like a gush of stone water, filling almost the entire floor space of the vestibule. Likewise, the inside walls are treated as if they were facades, though with columns and niches disproportionately large for the size of the room.

Andrea del Palladio, whose theories and elegant palaces were to be immensely influential on architecture elsewhere in Europe and as far north as England, was one of the greatest architects of the period.

The 17th and 18th Centuries

In the second half of the 16th century, Italy was caught up in the Counter-Reformation. This movement was a reaction against the Protestant Reformation of the Christian church that was sweeping through Europe. The Counter-Reformation enlisted art as a weapon, an instrument for the diffusion of the Catholic faith. Artists were discouraged from expressing themselves as freely as they had been before and from creating anything that was not of a religious nature. But within this religious framework they were able to evolve a style that appealed to the senses.

The Baroque—an emotional and heroic style that lasted through most of the 17th century—was propaganda art, designed to overwhelm the masses through its visual illusion, dramatic lighting, strong colors, and violent movement. There was an element of seduction in this propaganda: The repressive religiosity of the Counter-

Reformation went hand in hand with a barely disguised eroticism. The best-known example of this ambiguity is Bernini's sculpture of the *Ecstasy of Santa Teresa* in Rome, in which the saint sinks back in what could be a swoon of either pain or pleasure, while a smiling angel stands over her holding an arrow. Both the painting and architecture of this period make extensive use of sensuous curves.

The cradle of the Baroque was Rome, where Pietro da Cortona and Bernini channeled their genius into spectacular theatrical frescoes, sculptures, palaces, and churches. Rome had become the artistic center of Italy. Florence was politically and artistically dead by this time, and Venice was producing only hack imitations of Titian's and Tintoretto's paintings.

In the 18th century, Venice came back into its own and Rome was practically finished as an artistic center. Venetian artists adopted the soft, overripe version of Baroque—known as Rococo—that had originated in France. Free from the spiritual ideals that motivated the Baroque style, Rococo celebrated sensuousness (and sensuality) for its own sake. Although Venice was nearing the last stages of its political decline, there was still immense wealth in the city, mostly in the hands of families who wished to make the world know about it—and what better way than through vast, dazzling Rococo canvases, reassuringly stylized and removed from reality? The revival began with Sebastiano Ricci and was expertly elaborated on by Tiepolo. But it could never have taken place had there not been a return to the city's great artistic traditions. Late-16th-century color technique and expertise were drawn on and fused with what had been learned from the Baroque to create the breathtaking, magical, decadent world of the Venetian Rococo.

This was the final flowering of Venetian painting. The death of Francesco Guardi in 1793, compounded by the fall of the Republic of Venice in 1797, marked the effective end of the city's artistic life. Neoclassicism found no champion here, except for the sculptor Canova, who, in any case, did his finest work after he left Venice.

Today, the great tradition of Italian art is widely diffused, perhaps diluted, but it is certainly too early to write its obituary. That has been done periodically over the past 20 centuries, inevitably to the chagrin of the mistaken commentator. In the midst of the burgeoning vitality, which charms and occasionally maddens the visitor, the arts are not long to be neglected. Italians live the tradition too deeply.

— Sheila Brownlee

ARTISTICALLY SPEAKING: A GLOSSARY

The eloquence of the world's greatest masterpieces can be deafening, and Italy's treasures—their message made manifest in marble, pigment, and precious metals—instill a spirit of awe. The privilege of enjoying this bounty of the ages can be greatly deepened and enhanced by a familiarity with the language and terms of art-speak. Here is a limited glossary for the interested layman. Many of these Italian words are now part of the basic art history vocabulary.

Acanthus: Sculptural ornamentation from antiquity; it's based on the foliage of the acanthus plant.

Apse: A semicircular terminus found behind the altar in a church.

Atrium: The courtyard in front of the entrance to an ancient Roman villa or an early church.

Badia: Abbey.

Baldacchino: A canopy—often made of stone—above a church altar, supported by columns.

Baptistery: A separate structure or area in a church where rites of baptism are held.

Baroque: A 17th-century European art movement in which dramatic, elaborate ornamentation was used to stir viewers' emotions. The most famous Italian Baroque artists were Carracci and Bernini.

Basilica: A rectangular Roman public building divided into aisles by rows of columns. Many early churches were built on the basilican plan, but the term is also applied to some churches without specific reference to architecture.

Belvedere: Usually a lookout point for vistas; the word means "beautiful view."

Campanile: A bell tower of a church.

Capital: The crowning section of a column, usually decorated with Doric, Ionic, or Corinthian ornament.

Chiaroscuro: Meaning "light/dark;" refers to the distribution of light and shade in a painting, either with a marked contrast or a muted tonal gradation.

Cinquecento: Literally "five-hundred," used in Italian to refer to the 16th century.

Contrapposto: A dramatic pose of a sculpted figure in which the upper portion of the body is placed in opposition to the lower portion.

Cortile: Courtyard.

Cupola: Dome.

Duomo: Cathedral.

Fresco: A wall-painting technique, used in Roman times and again in the early Renaissance, in which pigment was applied to wet plaster.

Gothic: Medieval architectural and ornamental style featuring pointed arches, high interior vaulting, and flying buttresses to emphasize height and via symbolism, an ascension to heaven. The term is also used to describe the painting style made famous by Giotto and Simone Martini.

Grotesques: Decorations of fanciful human and animal forms, embellished with flowers; first used in Nero's Golden House and rediscovered during the Renaissance.

Loggia: Roofed balcony or gallery.

Maestà: Majestic image of the Virgin Mary enthroned and surrounded by angels.

Mannerism: Style of the mid-16th century, in which artists—such as Bronzino and Il Rosso—sought to replace the warm, humanizing ideals of Leonardo and Raphael with super-elegant, coldly emotional forms. Portraits in the Mannerist style feature florid colors, high-fashion anatomies, and frosty demeanors.

Nave: The central aisle of a church.

Palazzo: A palace, or more generally, any large building.

Perspective: The illusion of three-dimensional space that was obtained in the early 15th century with the discovery that all parallel lines running in one direction meet at a single point on the horizon known as the vanishing point. Leonardo da Vinci later perfected aerial perspective, in which gradations of *sfumato* (haze) and color can be used to create the illusion of distance.

Piano nobile: The main floor of a palace (the first floor above ground level).

Pietà: Literally "piety," refers to an image of the Virgin Mary holding the crucified body of Christ on her lap.

Polyptych: A painting—often an altarpiece—on multiple wooden panels that are joined.

Predella: A series of small paintings found below the main section of an altarpiece.

Putti: Cherubs, cupids or other images of infant boys in painting.

Quattrocento: Literally "four-hundred;" refers to the 15th century.

Renaissance: Major school of Italian art, literature, and philosophy (14th century–16th century) that fused innovations in realism with the rediscovery of the great heritage of classical antiquity. After Giotto introduced a new naturalism into painting in the 14th century, Florentine artists of the 1430s, such as Masaccio and Fra Filippo Lippi, paved the way for the later 15th-century realism of Botticelli and Signorelli. While reaching first flower in Florence, the movement culminated in Rome with the High Renaissance (circa 1490–1520) and the masterpieces of Leonardo, Raphael, and Michelangelo.

Rococo: Light, dainty 18th-century art and architectural style created in reaction to heavy Baroque. Tiepolo is the leading painter of the Rococo style.

Romanesque: Architectural style of the 11th and 12th centuries that reworked ancient Roman forms, particularly barrel and groin vaults. Stark, severe, and magisterial, Romanesque basilicas are among Italy's most awe-inspiring churches.

Sacra conversazione: The motif of the "holy conversation," showing the Madonna and Child in the midst of and/or interacting with saints.

Tondo: Circular painting or sculpture.

Trompe l'oeil: An artistic technique employed to "fool the eye" into believing that the object or scene depicted is actually real.

Tryptych: A 3-paneled painting executed on wood.

Veduta: A painting of a city or landscape as viewed from afar, popular in the 18th century.

WHAT TO READ & WATCH BEFORE YOU GO

Books

The Italians, by Luigi Barzini, is a comprehensive, lively analysis of the Italian national character, still worthy reading although published in 1964 (Atheneum). More recent musings on Italian life include *Italian Days,* by Barbara Grizzuti Harrison (Ticknor & Fields), and *That Fine Italian Hand,* by Paul Hofmann (Henry Holt), for many years *New York Times* bureau chief in Rome.

Novels and historical fiction often impart a greater sense of a place than straight history books: Irving Stone's best-selling *The Agony and the Ecstasy* (NAL) romanticizes the life of Michelangelo, but paints an enduring picture of Renaissance Florence; Umberto Eco's *The Name of the Rose* (Harcourt Brace) is a gripping murder mystery that will leave you with tremendous insight into monastic life in Italy. On the lighter side, Florence is the setting for two of Magdalen Nabb's entertaining thrillers: *Death in Autumn* and *Death of a Dutchman* (HarperCollins).

Classics of the travel essay genre include James Morris's *World of Venice* (Harcourt Brace Jovanovich), Mary McCarthy's *Venice Observed* and *The Stones of Florence* (both HBJ also), Lawrence Durrell's *Sicilian Carousel* (out of print), Elizabeth Bowen's *A Time in Rome* (Penguin), and James Lees-Milne's *Roman Mornings* and *Venetian Mornings* (New Amsterdam). Historic musings about Italy are offered in Henry James's perceptive *Italian Hours* (offered in many editions, including *Traveling in Italy with Henry James: Essays,* William Morrow), Edith Wharton's *Italian Backgrounds* and *Italian Villas and their Gardens* (Ecco Press), and Axel Munthe's *Story of San Michele* (Carroll and Graf) about his celebrated villa on Capri.

If you are looking for a general historical and art history framework, Harry Hearder's *Italy, A Short History* (Cambridge) cuts right to the chase, with two thousand years covered in less than 300 pages, and Michael Levey's clear and concise treatment of the Renaissance (*Early Renaissance* and *High Renaissance,* Penguin) are good places to begin. A comprehensive introduction to Italian art is Frederick Hartt's *History of Italian Renaissance Art* (Abrams). The history of the Renaissance, the great artists and political figures and turbulent power struggles throughout the region make great reading when told by Christopher Hibbert (*The House of Medici: Its Rise and Fall,* William Morrow).

For more historical background, Edward Gibbon's *Decline and Fall of the Roman Empire* is available in three volumes (Modern Library). Consult Giorgio Vasari's *Lives of the Artists* and *The Autobiography of Benvenuto Cellini,* and Machiavelli's *The Prince* (all available in Penguin Classics) for eyewitness accounts of the 16th century. Otherwise, *The Civilization of the Renaissance in Italy,* by 19th-century Swiss historian Jacob Burckhardt (Modern Library), offers a classic foundation. Christopher Hibbert's *House of Medici* (Quill/William Morrow) details the family's rise and fall.

For aficionados of Rome's artistic treasures, Georgina Masson's *Companion Guide to Rome* (Penguin) is a must. Eloquent writing as well as important scholarship is found in the works of such celebrated art historians as Richard Krautheimer, John Pope-Hennessy, John Shearman, Irving Lavin, Charles de Tolnay, and André Chastel. *Inside Rome* (Phaidon Press) is a picture book that gives you a tantalizing peek into the sumptuous palaces, galleries, private homes, athletic clubs, and even historic coffeehouses of the eternal city. Fodor's *Holy Rome: A Millennium Guide to the Christian Sights* traces Christianity in Rome, as it can be seen today, through gorgeous photography, thematic essays, easy-to-follow itineraries, and biographical sketches. Palladio's architecture is beautifully distilled in James Ackerman's *Palladio* (Penguin). To some observers, the most beautiful book about the most beautiful city in the world is Richard de Combray's *Venice, Frail Barrier* (Doubleday).

Susan Sontag's *Volcano Lover* (Farrar Straus Giroux), set in 18th-century Naples, is about Sir William Hamilton, his wife Emma, and Lord Nelson. *The Leopard,* by Giuseppe di Lampedusa (Pantheon), is a compelling portrait of Sicily during the political upheavals of the 1860s. Historical fiction set in World War II includes *History: A Novel,* by Elsa Morante (Vintage Aventura), about the fate of inhabitants of wartime Rome, and *Bread and Wine* by Ignazio Silone (Signet Classics), about Italian peasants under the control of the Fascists. Anne Cornelison's nonfiction *Women of the Shadows* portrays the life of peasant women in early post–World War I southern Italy (Vintage). More recently, mysteries set in Italy have found great popularity, including the Urbino Macintyre series of Edward Sklepowich and the Lovejoy series of Jonathan Gash.

English and American expatriates have preferred everything Tuscan (and more recently, Umbrian) for decades now, and many writers have chronicled their experiences restoring a farmhouse and making sense of the local culture and color. Among the better examples of what is becoming a genre unto itself are Matthew Spender's *Within Tuscany: Reflections on a Time and Place* (Viking), *Under the Tuscan Sun: At Home in Italy* by Frances Mayes (Broadway Books), and Lisa St. Aubin de Terán's *A Valley in Italy: The Many Seasons of a Villa in Umbria* (HarperCollins). Tim Parks's *Italian Neighbors* (Grove) gives accounts of life in rural Tuscany and Verona by British expatriates. Fodor's Escape Guides showcases hundreds of fabulous photos and brilliant prose to illuminate superlative experiences in two of Italy's special regions. In the pages of Fodor's *Escape to Tuscany,* stay at the convent where *The English Patient* was filmed and go balooning over Chianti's vineyards. The Amalfi Coast is captured in an impossible array of blues in *Escape to the Amalfi Coast.*

To catch glimpses of the Tuscan landscape, pick up Harold Acton's *Great Houses of Tuscany: The Tuscan Villas* (Viking) or Carey More's *Views from a Tuscan Vineyard* (Pavillion). For a recent look at Umbrian life, try Lisa St. Aubin de Terán's *A Valley in Italy: The Many Seasons of a Villa in Umbria* (HarperCollins). The glories of historic Italian gardens are caught in the ravishing photographs of three recent volumes: Judith Chatfield's *Gardens of the Italian Lakes* (Rizzoli), Ethne Clark's *Gardens of Tuscany* (Weidenfeld & Nicolson), and Nicolas Saphiena's *Gardens of Naples* (Scala Books).

Although every year there are more and more cookbooks on Tuscan food, Waverley Root's *Food of Italy* (Vintage), published in 1977, is still a handy (if not infallible) reference. Take Faith Heller Wilinger's newly revised *Eating in Italy* (Morrow) to guide you to the good food and restaurants, and Burton Anderson's *Pocket Guide to Italian Wines* (Little Brown) to sort your way through the wine lists.

Videos

You'll recognize the idyllic scenery of central Italy in numerous films, recent among them Miramax's *The English Patient* (1996), Kenneth Branagh's *Much Ado About Nothing* (1993), Bernardo Bertolucci's *Stealing Beauty* (1996), and the sights of Florence in Merchant/Ivory's *A Room with a View* (1986). In *La Vita è Bella* (Life is Beautiful, 1997), Roberto Benigni, the director and actor in the lead role, reveals unstoppable verve, tenderness, and humility in a story about a family destroyed by the brutality of the Holocaust in fascist Italy. The film scooped up Oscars for best foreign film, actor, and dramatic score at the Academy Awards in 1999.

ITALY AT A GLANCE

ca. 1000 BC Etruscans arrive in central Italy.

ca. 800 Rise of Etruscan city-states.

753 Traditional date for the founding of Rome.

750 Greek city-states begin to colonize Sicily and southern Italy.

600 Latin language becomes dominant in Etruscan League; Rome becomes established urban center.

510 Foundation of the Roman republic; expulsion of Etruscans from Roman territory.

410 Rome adopts the 12 Tables of Law, based on Greek models.

343 Roman conquest of Greek colonies in Campania.

312 Completion of Via Appia (Appian Way) to the south of Rome; an extensive Roman road system begins to develop.

264–241 First Punic War (with Carthage): increased naval power helps Rome gain control of southern Italy and then Sicily.

218–200 Second Punic War: Hannibal's attempted conquest of Italy, using elephants, is eventually crushed.

176 Roman Forum begins to take shape as the principal civic center in Italy.

146 Third Punic War: Rome razes city of Carthage and emerges as the dominant Mediterranean force.

133 Rome rules entire Mediterranean Basin except Egypt.

49 Julius Caesar conquers Gaul.

45 Civil War leaves Julius Caesar as sole ruler; Caesar's Forum is established.

44 Julius Caesar is assassinated.

31 The Battle of Actium resolves the power struggle that continued after Caesar's death; Octavian becomes sole ruler.

27 Rome's Imperial Age begins; Octavian (now named Augustus) becomes the first emperor and is later deified. The Augustan Age is celebrated in the works of Virgil (70 BC–AD 19), Ovid (43 BC–AD 17), Livy (59 BC–AD 17), and Horace (65–8 BC).

14 AD Augustus dies.

29 Jesus is crucified in the Roman colony of Judea.

43 Rome invades Britain.

50 Rome is the largest city in the world, with a population of a million.

65 Emperor Nero begins the persecution of Christians in the empire; Saints Peter and Paul are executed.

70–80 Vespasian builds the Colosseum.

98–117 Trajan's military successes are celebrated with his Baths (98), Forum (110), and Column (113); the Roman Empire reaches its apogee.

165 A smallpox epidemic ravages the Empire.

ca. 150–200 Christianity gains a foothold within the Empire, with the theological writings of Clement, Tertullian, and Origen.

212 Roman citizenship is conferred on all nonslaves in the Empire.

238 The first wave of Germanic invasions penetrates Italy.

293 Diocletian reorganizes the Empire into West and East.

313 The Edict of Milan grants toleration of Christianity within the Empire.

330 Constantine founds a new Imperial capital (Constantinople) in the East.

410 Rome is sacked by Visigoths.

476 The last Roman Emperor, Romulus Augustus, is deposed. The Empire of Rome falls.

552 Eastern Emperor Justinian (527–565) recovers control of Italy.

570 Lombards gain control of much of Italy, including Rome.

590 Papal power expands under Gregory the Great.

610 Heraldius revives the Eastern Empire, thereafter known as the Byzantine Empire.

774 Frankish ruler Charlemagne (742–814) invades Italy under papal authority and is crowned Holy Roman Emperor by Pope Leo III (800).

ca. 800–900 The breakup of Charlemagne's (Carolingian) realm leads to the rise of Italian city-states.

811 Venice is founded by mainlanders escaping Barbarian invasions.

1054 The Schism develops between Greek (Orthodox) and Latin churches.

ca. 1060 Europe's first university is founded in Bologna.

1077 Pope Gregory VII leads the Holy See into conflict with the Germanic Holy Roman Empire.

1152–90 Frederick I (Barbarossa) is crowned Holy Roman Emperor (1155); punitive expeditions by his forces (Ghibellines) are countered by the Guelphs, creators of the powerful Papal States in central Italy. Guelph–Ghibelline conflict becomes a feature of medieval life.

1204 Crusaders, led by Venetian doge Dandolo, capture Constantinople.

1257 The first of four wars is declared between Genoa and Venice; at stake is the maritime control of the eastern Mediterranean.

1262 Florentine bankers issue Europe's first bills of exchange.

1264 Charles I of Anjou invades Italy, intervening in the continuing Guelph–Ghibelline conflict.

1275 Marco Polo (1254–1324) reaches the Orient.

1290–1375 Tuscan literary giants Dante Alighieri (1265–1321), Francesco Petrarch (1304–74), and Giovanni Boccaccio (1313–75) give written imprimatur to modern Italian language.

1309 The pope moves to Avignon in France, under the protection of French kings.

1355 Venetian doge Marino Falier is executed for treason.

1376 The pope returns to Rome, but rival Avignonese popes stand in opposition, creating the Great Schism until 1417.

1380 Venice finally disposes of the Genovese threat in the Battle of Chioggia.

1402 The last German intervention into Italy is repulsed by the Lombards.

1443 Brunelleschi's (1377–1446) cupola is completed on Florence's Duomo.

1447 Nicholas V founds the Vatican Library. This begins an era of nepotistic popes who devalue the status of the papacy but greatly enrich the artistic and architectural patronage of the Holy City.

1469–92 Lorenzo "Il Magnifico" (1449–92), the Medici patron of the arts, rules in Florence.

1498 Girolamo Savonarola (1452–98), the austere Dominican friar, is executed for heresy after leading Florence into a drive for moral purification, typified by his burning of books and decorations in the "Bonfire of Vanities."

1499 Leonardo da Vinci's (1452–1519) *Last Supper* is completed in Milan.

1508 Michelangelo (1475–1564) begins work on the Cappella Sistina.

1509 Raphael (1483–1520) begins work on his *Stanze* in the Vatican.

1513 Machiavelli's (1469–1527) *The Prince* is published.

1521 The Pope excommunicates Martin Luther (1483–1546) of Germany, precipitating the Protestant Reformation.

1545–63 The Council of Trent formulates the Catholic response to the Reformation.

1546 Andrea Palladio (1508–80), architectural genius, wins his first commission in Vicenza.

1571 The combined navies of Venice, Spain, and the Papacy defeat the Turks in the Battle of Lepanto.

1626 The Basilica di San Pietro is completed in Rome.

1633 Galileo Galilei (1564–1642) faces the Inquisition.

1652 Sant'Agnese in Agone church, Borromini's (1599–1667) Baroque masterpiece, is completed in Rome.

1667 The Piazza di San Pietro, designed by Bernini (1598–1680), is completed.

ca. 1700 Opera develops as an art form in Italy.

1720–90 The Great Age of the Grand Tour: Northern Europeans visit Italy and start the vogue for classical studies. Among the famous visitors are Edward Gibbon (1758), Jacques-Louis David (1775), and Johann Wolfgang von Goethe (1786).

1778 Teatro alla Scala is completed in Milan.

1796 Napoléon begins his Italian campaigns, annexing Rome and imprisoning Pope Pius VI four years later.

1815 Austria controls much of Italy after Napoléon's downfall.

1848 Revolutionary troops under Risorgimento (Unification) leaders Giuseppe Mazzini (1805–72) and Giuseppe Garibaldi (1807–82) establish a republic in Rome.

1849 French troops crush rebellion and restore Pope Pius IX.

1860 Garibaldi and his "Thousand" defeat the Bourbon rulers in Sicily and Naples.

1870 Rome is finally captured by Risorgimento troops and is declared capital of Italy by King Vittorio Emanuele II.

1900 King Umberto I is assassinated by an anarchist; he is succeeded by King Vittorio Emanuele III.

1915 Italy enters World War I on the side of the Allies.

1922 Fascist "black shirts" under Benito Mussolini (1883–1945) march on Rome; Mussolini becomes prime minister and later "Il Duce" (head of Italy).

1929 The Lateran Treaty: Mussolini recognizes Vatican City as a sovereign state, and the Church recognizes Rome as the capital of Italy.

1940–44 In World War II, Italy fights with the Axis powers until its capitulation (1943), when Mussolini flees Rome. Italian partisans and Allied troops from the landings at Anzio (January 1944) win victory at Cassino (March 1944) and force the eventual withdrawal of German troops from Italy.

1957 The Treaty of Rome is signed, and Italy becomes a founding member of the European Economic Community.

1966 November flood damages many of Florence's artistic treasures.

1968–79 The growth of left-wing activities leads to the formation of the Red Brigades and provokes right-wing reactions. Bombings and kidnappings culminate in the abduction and murder of Prime Minister Aldo Moro (1916–1978).

1980 Southern Italy is hit by a severe earthquake.

1991 Waves of refugees from neighboring Albania flood southern ports on the Adriatic. Mt. Etna erupts, spewing forth a lava stream that threatens the Sicilian town of Zafferana.

1992 The Christian Democrat Party, in power throughout the postwar period, loses its hold on a relative majority in Parliament.

1993 Italians vote for sweeping reforms after the Tangentopoli (Bribe City) scandal exposes widespread political corruption, including politicians' collusion with organized crime. A bomb outside the Galleria degli Uffizi in Florence kills five, but spares the museum's most precious artwork; authorities blame the Cosa Nostra, flexing its muscles in the face of a crackdown.

1994 A center-right coalition wins in spring elections, and media magnate Silvio Berlusconi becomes premier—only to be deposed within a year. Italian politics seem to be evolving into the equivalent of a two-party system.

1995 Newly appointed Lamberto Dini takes hold of the government's rudder and, as president of the Council of Ministers, institutes major reforms and replaces old-line politicians.

1996 A league of center-left parties wins national elections and puts together a government coalition that sees the Democratic Party of the Left (PDS), the former Communist party, into power for the first time ever in Italy. Thousands of Romans gathered in Piazza del Campidoglio to bid farewell to the late beloved actor Marcello Mastroianni, revered for his portraits of the consummate Italian charmer in films such as *La Dolce Vita, 8½*—both Federico Fellini films—and *Divorce Italian Style.*

1997 Political stability and an austerity program put Italy on track toward the European Monetary Union and adoption of the single Euro currency. Though only a copy, the statue of Roman emperor Marcus Aurelius is returned to its pedestal on the Campidoglio as a symbol of Rome's historic grandeur. A series of earthquakes hit the mountainous interior of central Italy, severely damaging villages and some historic towns. In Assisi, portions of the vault of the Basilica di San Francesco crumble, destroying frescoes by Cimabue.

1998 In February a U.S. Navy jet fighter on a low-flying training mission through the Italian Alps cuts a ski gondola cable, killing 20 people. Romano Prodi's center-left government, widely praised for its economic policies and lack of scandals, is brought down by a no confidence vote in October, when the Reformed-Communist Party (PCI) withdrew its support for Prodi. The center-left regroups and forms a new government under Massimo D'Alema, leader of the former Communist Party, who in large part continues Prodi's policies. The Pope visits Cuba, and over a million people see the Shroud of Turin, on display for a just a few months.

1999 Italy serves as a pricipal base for NATO air raids against Serbia. Rome continues preparations for the Giubileo (Holy Year) celebrations in 2000 with an array of public works projects (☞ Chapter 1). The International Olympic Committee chooses Turin to host the 2006 Winter Olympics.

Italy
SWITZERLAND
AUSTRIA
HUNGARY
SLOVENIA
CROATIA
BOSNIA AND HERZEGOVINA
MONTENEGRO
FRANCE
MONACO
ALPI
APPENNINO
TRENTINO-ALTO ADIGE
FRIULI-VENEZIA GIULIA
THE DOLOMITES
VENETO
LOMBARDY
VALLE D'AOSTA
PIEDMONT
LIGURIA
EMILIA-ROMAGNA
TUSCANY
THE MARCHES
UMBRIA
Cortina d'Ampezzo
Bolzano
Trento
Belluno
Udine
Trieste
Treviso
Venice
Vicenza
Padua
Verona
Brescia
Bergamo
Como
Lugano
Milan
Novara
Pavia
Aosta
Mt. Blanc
Turin
Asti
Genoa
Rapallo
La Spezia
San Remo
Mantua
Parma
Modena
Bologna
Ferrara
Ravenna
Rimini
SAN MARINO
Ancona
Macerata
Pescara
Lucca
Pisa
Livorno
Pistoia
Florence
Arezzo
Siena
Perugia
Assisi
Orvieto
Terni
Viterbo
Grosseto
Elba
Corsica
Lago Maggiore
Lago di Como
Lago di Garda
Po
Adige
Arno
Tiber
Golfo di Venezia
Adriatic Sea
Ligurian Sea
N

Rome
Tivoli
Anzio
Gaeta
Cassino
Isernia
Termoli
MOLISE
Gargano Peninsula
Foggia
APULIA
Bari
Brindisi
Lecce
Taranto
Golfo di Taranto
BASILICATA
Potenza
CAMPANIA
Naples
Vesuvius
Salerno
Paestum
Capri
SARDINIA
Olbia
Sassari
Cagliari
Tyrrhenian Sea
Cosenza
Crotone
Catanzaro
CALABRIA
Aeolian Islands
Messina
Reggio
Ionian Sea
Palermo
SICILY
Etna
Catania
Siracusa
Agrigento
Mediterranean Sea
ALGERIA
TUNISIA
Tunis
0 100 miles
0 150 km

ESSENTIAL INFORMATION

AIR TRAVEL

BOOKING YOUR FLIGHT

When you book **look for nonstop flights** and **remember that "direct" flights stop at least once.** Try to avoid connecting flights, which require a change of plane.

CARRIERS

When flying internationally, you must usually choose between a domestic carrier, the national flag carrier of the country you are visiting, and a foreign carrier from a third country. You may, for example, choose to fly Alitalia to Italy. National flag carriers have the greatest number of nonstops. Domestic carriers may have better connections to your hometown and serve a greater number of gateway cities. Third-party carriers may have a price advantage.

Alitalia—in addition to other major European airlines and smaller, privately run companies such as Meridiana and Air One—completes an extensive network of internal flights in Italy. Ask your domestic or Italian travel agent about discounts.

On international flights, Alitalia serves Rome, Milan, and Venice. The major international hubs in Italy are Milan and Rome, served by Continental Airlines, Delta Air Lines, and TWA. American Airlines, United Airlines, and Northwest Airlines fly into Milan. US Airways serves Rome.

Direct service from Heathrow is provided by Alitalia and British Airways. From Manchester there are one or two direct flights daily to Milan, and at least three weekly to Rome. Privately run Meridiana has direct flights between London and Olbia on Sardinia on Tuesday and Saturday in summer, and daily flights to Cagliari via Florence throughout the year. Lower-priced charter flights to a range of Italian destinations are available throughout the year.

➤ TO AND FROM ITALY: **Alitalia** (☎ 800/223–5730; 020/7602–7111 or 0990/448–259 in Britain). **American Airlines** (☎ 800/433–7300). **British Airways** (☎ 0345/222–111). **Continental Airlines** (☎ 800/231–0856). **Delta Air Lines** (☎ 800/241–4141). **Meridiana** (☎ 020/7839–2222). **Northwest Airlines** (☎ 800/225–2525). **TWA** (☎ 800/892–4141). **United Airlines** (☎ 800/538–2929). **US Airways** (☎ 800/428–4322).

➤ AROUND ITALY: **Air One** (☎ 06/488800). **Alitalia** (☎ 06/65621 or 06/65643 in Rome; 02/24991 in Milan; 1475/65640 within in Italy). **Meridiana** (☎ 06/478041).

CHECK-IN & BOARDING

Assuming that not everyone with a ticket will show up, airlines routinely overbook planes. When that happens, airlines ask for volunteers to give up their seats. In return these volunteers usually get a certificate for a free flight and are rebooked on the next flight out. If there are not enough volunteers, the airline must choose who will be denied boarding. The first to get bumped are passengers who checked in late and those flying on discounted tickets, so **get to the gate and check in as early as possible,** especially during peak periods.

Always **bring a government-issued photo ID to the airport.** You may be asked to show it before you are allowed to check in.

CUTTING COSTS

The least-expensive airfares to Italy must usually be purchased in advance and are nonrefundable. It's smart to **call a number of airlines, and when you are quoted a good price, book it on the spot**—the same fare may not be available the next day. Always **check different routings** and look into using different airports. Travel agents, especially low-fare specialists (☞ Discounts & Deals, *below*), are helpful.

Consolidators are another good source. They buy tickets for scheduled international flights at reduced rates from the airlines, then sell them at prices that beat the best fare available directly from the airlines, usually without restrictions. Sometimes you can even get your money back if you need to return the ticket. Carefully read the fine print detailing penalties for changes and cancellations, and **confirm your consolidator reservation with the airline.**

When you **fly as a courier** you trade your checked-luggage space for a ticket deeply subsidized by a courier service. There are restrictions on when you can book and how long you can stay.

➤ CONSOLIDATORS: **Cheap Tickets** (☎ 800/377–1000). **Discount Airline Ticket Service** (☎ 800/576–1600). **Unitravel** (☎ 800/325–2222). **Up & Away Travel** (☎ 212/889–2345). **World Travel Network** (☎ 800/409–6753).

ENJOYING THE FLIGHT

All flights within Italy are smoke free. However, smoking is allowed on a limited number of international flights; **contact your carrier about its smoking policy.** For more legroom **request an emergency-aisle seat.** Don't sit in the row in front of the emergency aisle or in front of a bulkhead, where seats may not recline. If you have dietary concerns, **ask for special meals when booking.** These can be vegetarian, low-cholesterol, or kosher, for example. On long flights, try to maintain a normal routine to help fight jet lag. At night **get some sleep.** By day **eat light meals, drink water** (not alcohol), and **move around the cabin** to stretch your legs.

FLYING TIMES

Flying time is 8½ hours from New York, 10–11 hours from Chicago, 11½ hours from Dallas (via New York), 11½ hours from Los Angeles, 2 hours from London (to Milan), and 12½ hours from Sydney.

HOW TO COMPLAIN

If your baggage goes astray or your flight goes awry, complain right away. Most carriers require that you **file a claim immediately.**

➤ AIRLINE COMPLAINTS: U.S. Department of Transportation **Aviation Consumer Protection Division** (✉ C-75, Room 4107, Washington, DC 20590, ☎ 202/366–2220). **Federal Aviation Administration Consumer Hotline** (☎ 800/322–7873).

AIRPORTS

The major gateways to Italy include Rome's **Aeroporto Leonardo da Vinci,** better known as **Fiumicino,** and Milan's **Aeroporto Malpensa 2000** (MXP). If you are going directly to Florence and landing at Rome's Fiumicino, you can make connections at the airport for a flight to Florence; you can also take the FS airport train to Rome's Termini Station, where fast trains for Florence are frequent during the day. Smaller, minor gateways are served by domestic and some international flights.

➤ AIRPORT INFORMATION: **Aeroporto Leonardo da Vinci** or **Fiumicino** (✉ 35 km/20 mi southeast of Rome, ☎ 06/65953640). **Aeroporto Malpensa 2000** (✉ 45 km/28 mi north of Milan, ☎ 02/74852200). **Bologna: Aeroporto Guglielmo Marconi** (✉ Borgo Panigale, 7 km/4½ mi from Bologna, ☎ 051/6479615). **Florence: Aeroporto A. Vespucci,** called Perétola (✉ 6 km/4 mi northwest of Florence, ☎ 055/333498) and **Aeroporto Galileo Galilei** (✉ Pisa, 80 km/50 mi west of Florence, ☎ 050/500707). **Milan: Aeroporto Linate** (✉ 10 km/6 mi east of Milan, ☎ 02/74852200). **Naples: Aeroporto Capodichino** (✉ 8 km/5 mi north of Naples, ☎ 081/7896111). **Palermo: Aeroporto Punta Raisi** (✉ 32 km/20 mi west of Palermo, ☎ 091/591698). **Venice: Aeroporto Marco Polo** (✉ Tessera, about 10 km/6 mi north of Venice, ☎ 041/2609260).

DUTY-FREE SHOPPING

As of July 1999 duty-free shopping in airports was eliminated in Italy (and Europe); you can still make in-flight duty-free purchases however.

BIKE TRAVEL

BIKES IN FLIGHT

Most airlines accommodate bikes as luggage, provided the bikes are dismantled and boxed. For bike boxes, often free at bike shops, you'll pay about $5 (at least $100 for bike bags) at airlines. International travelers can sometimes substitute a bike for a piece of checked luggage at no charge; otherwise, the cost is about $100. Domestic and Canadian airlines charge $25–$50.

BOAT & FERRY TRAVEL

Ferries connect the mainland with all major islands. To many of the destinations there is also hydrofoil (*alsicafo*) service, which is generally twice as fast as ferries and double the price. Service is considerably more frequent during the summer months. Car ferries operate to Sicily and Sardinia and many islands, including Elba, Ponza, Capri, Ischia, the Lido near Venice, and other islands.

Tirrenia operates ferries to Sicily and Sardinia. SNAV operates high-speed ferries between Naples and Palermo. Lauro has hydrofoils and car ferries to Ischia from Naples, and Capri is reached by Caremar. Adriatica connects Italy with Greece. FS ferries sail from Civitavecchia to Golfo Aranci, near Olbia. Navarma, Elba Ferries, and Toremar serve Elba from Piombino. For the Lake District contact Navigazione Laghi.

➤ BOAT & FERRY INFORMATION: **Adriatica** (☎ 06/4818341). **Caremar** (☎ 081/5513882). **Elba Ferries** (✉ Calata Carrara, Nuova Stazione Marittima, Livorno, ☎ 0586/898979). **FS** (☎ 0766/23273). **Lauro** (☎ 081/5522838). **Navarma** (✉ Viale Regina Margherita, Piombino, ☎ 0565/225211). **Navigazione Laghi** (✉ ☎ 167/551801 toll-free or 0322/233200). **SNAV** (☎ 081/7612348). **Tirrenia** (☎ 06/4742242 in Rome; 010/2758041 in Genoa; 091/333300 in Palermo). **Toremar** (✉ Piazzale Premuda 13, Piombino, ☎ 0565/31100).

BUS TRAVEL

Italy's bus network is extensive, although not as attractive an option as those in other European countries, partly because of the low cost and convenience of train travel. However, in some areas buses can be faster and more direct than local trains, so it's a good idea to **compare bus and train schedules.** Bus service outside cities is organized on a regional level, and often by private companies.

If you're traveling by bus from the United Kingdom, **bring a few French francs to spend en route.** And be sure to consider the train (☞ Train Travel, *below*), as bus fares are quite high, especially when you take the long and tiring overnight journey into account. Eurolines runs a weekly bus service to Rome that increases to three times a week between June and September.

➤ BUS INFORMATION: **Eurolines** (✉ 52 Grosvenor Gardens, London SW1W 0AU, ☎ 020/7730–8235 or 020/7730–3499; or contact any National Express agent).

TICKETS & SCHEDULES

Unlike city buses, for which you must buy your ticket from a machine, newsstand, or tobacconist and stamp it after you board, private bus lines usually have a ticket office in town or allow you to pay when you board.

BUSINESS HOURS

BANKS & OFFICES

Banks are open weekdays 8:30 to 1:30 and 2:45 to 3:45. Most churches are open from early morning until noon or 12:30, when they close for two hours or more; they open again in the afternoon, closing about 7 PM or later.

Post offices are open Monday–Saturday 9–2; central and main district post offices stay open until 6 PM weekdays, 9–2 on Saturday.

MUSEUMS & SIGHTS

A few major churches, such as St. Peter's in Rome and San Marco in Venice, are open all day. Note that sightseeing in churches during religious rites is discouraged. Museum hours vary and often change with the seasons. Many museums are closed one day a week, often on Monday. Always check locally. Most shops are open from 9 to 1 and from 3:30 or 4 to 7:30, Monday–Saturday.

SHOPS

In addition, clothing shops are generally closed on Monday mornings. Barbers and hairdressers, with some exceptions, are closed Sunday and Monday. Some tourist-oriented shops in places such as Rome and Venice are open all day, also on Sunday, as are some department stores and supermarkets.

CAMERAS & PHOTOGRAPHY

The *Kodak Guide to Shooting Great Travel Pictures* is an excellent tool and is available in bookstores or from Fodor's Travel Publications.

➤ PHOTO HELP: **Kodak Information Center** (☎ 800/242–2424). ***Kodak Guide to Shooting Great Travel Pictures*** ($16.50 plus $4 shipping); contact Fodor's Travel Publications (☎ 800/533–6478).

EQUIPMENT PRECAUTIONS

Always **keep your film, tape, or computer disks out of the sun.** Carry an extra supply of batteries, and **be prepared to turn on your camera, camcorder, or laptop** to prove to security personnel that the device is real. Always **ask for hand inspection of film,** which becomes clouded after successive exposure to airport X-ray machines, and **keep videotapes and computer disks away from metal detectors.**

CAR RENTAL

Renting a car in Italy is essential for exploring the countryside, but not if you plan to stick to city travel. Signage on country roads is usually pretty good, but be prepared for fast and impatient fellow drivers. Major car-rental companies have boxy Ford-type cars (such as Astras) and FIATs in various sizes that are always in good condition.

➤ MAJOR AGENCIES: **Alamo** (☎ 800/522–9696; 020/8759–6200 in the U.K.). **Avis** (☎ 800/331–1084; 800/879–2847 in Canada; 02/9353–9000 in Australia; 09/525–1982 in New Zealand). **Budget** (☎ 800/527–0700; 0144/227–6266 in the U.K.). **Dollar** (☎ 800/800–6000; 020/8897–0811 in the U.K., where it is known as Eurodollar; 02/9223–1444 in Australia). **Hertz** (☎ 800/654–3001; 800/263–0600 in Canada; 020/8897–2072 in the U.K.; 02/9669–2444 in Australia; 03/358–6777 in New Zealand). **National InterRent** (☎ 800/227–3876; 0345/222525 in the U.K., where it is known as Europcar InterRent).

CUTTING COSTS

Most major American car-rental companies have offices or affiliates in Italy, but the rates are generally better if you make a reservation from abroad rather than from within Italy. To get the best deal **book through a travel agent who will shop around.**

Do **look into wholesalers,** companies that do not own fleets but rent in bulk from those that do and often offer better rates than traditional car-rental operations. Payment must be made before you leave home. Note that in Italy no matter what your credit cards might refund you, Italian car-rental companies usually make it mandatory to purchase the collision-damage waiver (and do not allow your credit card to waive the fees).

➤ WHOLESALERS: **Auto Europe** (☎ 207/842–2000 or 800/223–5555, FAX 800–235–6321). **DER Travel Services** (✉ 9501 W. Devon Ave., Rosemont, IL 60018, ☎ 800/782–2424; FAX 800/282–7474 for information; 800/860–9944 for brochures). **Europe by Car** (☎ 212/581–3040 or 800/223–1516, FAX 212/246–1458). **Kemwel Holiday Autos** (☎ 914/835–3000 or 800/678–0678, FAX 914/835–5126).

INSURANCE

When driving a rented car you are generally responsible for any damage to or loss of the vehicle. Many companies impose mandatory theft insurance on all rentals; coverage costs $12–$18 a day or 25%.

Collision policies that car-rental companies sell for European rentals usually do not include stolen-vehicle coverage. Before you buy it, check your existing policies—you may already be covered. Note that in Italy, all car-rental companies make you buy theft-protection and collision-damage policies.

REQUIREMENTS & RESTRICTIONS

In Italy your own driver's license is acceptable. An International Driver's Permit is a good idea; it's available from the American or Canadian automobile association, and, in the United Kingdom, from the Automobile Association or Royal Automobile Club. These international permits are universally recognized, and having one in your wallet may save you a problem with the local authorities. In Italy you must be 21 years of age to rent an economy or sub-compact car and at least 25 years of age to rent a bigger car.

SURCHARGES

Before you pick up a car in one city and leave it in another **ask about drop-off charges or one-way service fees,** which can be substantial. Note, too, that some rental agencies charge extra if you return the car before the time specified in your contract. To avoid a hefty refueling fee **fill the tank just before you turn in the car,** but be aware that gas stations near the rental outlet may overcharge.

CAR TRAVEL

There is an extensive network of *autostrade* (toll highways), complemented by equally well-maintained but free *superstrade* (expressways). The ticket you are issued upon entering an autostrada must be returned when you exit and pay the toll; on some shorter autostrade, mainly connecting highways, the toll is paid upon entering. Viacard cards, on sale at many autostrada locations, make paying tolls easier and faster. A *raccordo* is a ring road surrounding a city. *Strade statali* (state highways, denoted by *S* or *SS* numbers) may be single-lane roads, as are all secondary roads; directions and turnoffs are not always clearly marked.

AUTO CLUBS

➤ IN AUSTRALIA: **Australian Automobile Association** (☎ 02/6247–7311).

➤ IN CANADA: **Canadian Automobile Association** (CAA, ☎ 613/247–0117).

➤ IN NEW ZEALAND: **New Zealand Automobile Association** (☎ 09/377–4660).

➤ IN THE U.K.: **Automobile Association** (AA, ☎ 0990/500–600). **Royal Automobile Club** (RAC, ☎ 0990/722–722 for membership; 0345/121–345 for insurance).

➤ IN THE U.S.: **American Automobile Association** (☎ 800/564–6222).

EMERGENCIES

ACI Emergency Service offers 24-hour road service. Dial 116 from any phone, 24 hours a day, to reach the ACI dispatch operator.

GASOLINE

Gas stations are generally open Monday–Saturday 7–7 with a break at lunchtime. Many stations have automatic self-service pumps which only accept bills of 10,000 lire and 50,000 lire. Gas stations on autostrade are open 24 hours. Gas costs about 1,900 lire per liter.

PARKING

Parking space is at a premium in most towns, but especially in the *centri storici* (historic centers), which are filled with narrow streets and restricted circulation zones. It is often a good idea (if not the only option) to park your car in a designated (preferably attended) lot. Parking in an area signposted ZONA DISCO (disk zone) is allowed for limited periods (from 30 minutes to two hours or more—the limit is posted); if you don't have the cardboard disk (inquire at the local tourist office) to show what time you parked, you can use a piece of paper. The *parcometro,* the Italian version of metered parking in which you put coins into a machine for a stamped ticket that you leave on the dashboard, has been introduced in some cities. It's advisable to **leave your car only in guarded parking areas.**

ROAD CONDITIONS

Autostrade are well maintained, as are most interregional highways. The condition of provincial (county) roads varies, but road maintenance at this level is generally good in Italy. Street and road signs are often challenging—a good map and patience are essential.

Italians drive fast and are impatient with those who don't. Tailgaiting is the norm here—the only way to avoid it is to get out of the way.

RULES OF THE ROAD

Driving is on the right. Regulations are largely as in Britain and the United States, except that the police have the power to levy on-the-spot fines. In most Italian towns the use of the horn is forbidden in certain, if not all, areas; a large sign, ZONA DI SILENZIO, indicates where. Speed limits are 130 kph (80 mph) on autostrade and 110 kph (70 mph) on state and provincial roads, unless otherwise marked. Fines for driving after drinking are heavy, including the suspension of license and the additional possibility of six months' imprisonment.

THE CHANNEL TUNNEL

Short of flying, the "Chunnel" is the fastest way to cross the English Channel: 35 minutes from Folkestone to Calais, 60 minutes from motorway to motorway, or 3 hours from London's Waterloo Station to Paris's Gare du Nord.

➤ CAR TRANSPORT: **Le Shuttle** (☎ 0990/353–535 in the U.K.).

➤ PASSENGER SERVICE: In the United Kingdom: **Eurostar** (☎ 0990/186–186), **InterCity Europe** (✉ Victoria Station, London, ☎ 0990/848–848 for credit-card bookings). In the United States: **BritRail Travel** (☎ 800/677–8585), **Rail Europe** (☎ 800/942–4866).

CHILDREN IN ITALY

Although Italians love children and are generally very tolerant and patient with them, they provide few amenities for them. In restaurants and trattorias you may find a high chair or a cushion for the child to sit on, but rarely do they offer a children's menu. Order a *mezza porzione* (half-portion) of any dish, or ask the waiter for a *porzione da bambino* (child's portion).

Discounts do exist. Always ask about a *sconto bambino* (child's discount) before purchasing tickets. Children under a certain height ride free on municipal buses and trams. Children under 18 who are EU citizens are admitted free to state-run museums and galleries, and there are similar privileges in many municipal or private museums.

If you are renting a car don't forget to **arrange for a car seat** when you reserve.

FLYING

If your children are two or older **ask about children's airfares.** As a general rule, infants under two not occupying a seat fly at greatly reduced fares or even for free. When booking **confirm carry-on allowances** if you're traveling with infants. In general, for babies charged 10% of the adult fare, you are allowed one carry-on bag and a collapsible stroller; if the flight is full the stroller may have to be checked or you may be limited to less.

Experts agree that it's a good idea to use safety seats aloft for children weighing less than 40 pounds. Airlines set their own policies: U.S. carriers usually require that the child be ticketed, even if he or she is young enough to ride free, since the seats must be strapped into regular seats. Do **check your airline's policy about using safety seats during takeoff and landing.** And since safety seats are not allowed everywhere in the plane, get your seat assignments early.

When reserving, **request children's meals or a freestanding bassinet** if you need them. But note that bulkhead seats, where you must sit to use the bassinet, may lack an overhead bin or storage space on the floor.

LODGING

Most hotels in Italy allow children under a certain age to stay in their parents' room at no extra charge, but others charge for them as extra adults; be sure to **find out the cutoff age for children's discounts.** The Luxury Collection of Sheraton Hotels has more than 20 properties in Italy, all of which welcome families. Notable are the two on the Lido in Venice, which are right on the beach and have a parklike area for children to enjoy. Club Med has a "Mini Club" (for ages 4–9) and a "Kids Club" (for ages 10 and 11) at its ski village in Sestriere. There are also kids' programs at summer resort villages in Metaponto (Basilicata) and on the islands of Sicily and Sardinia, marketed mainly to Europeans. Some of the Valtur vacation villages also have special facilities and activities for children.

➤ CONTACTS: **Sheraton Hotels** (☎ 800/221–2340). **Club Med** (✉ 40 W. 57th St., New York, NY 10019, ☎ 800/258–2633). **Valtur** (✉ Piazza della Repubblica 59, Roma, ☎ 06/4821000, FAX 06/4870981).

SIGHTS & ATTRACTIONS

Places that are especially good for children are indicated by a rubber duckie icon in the margin.

CONSULATES

➤ AUSTRALIA: **Australia Consulate** (✉ Via Borgogna 2, Milan, ☎ 02/777041).

➤ CANADA: **Canadian Consulate** (✉ Via Zara 30, Rome, ☎ 06/445981).

➤ NEW ZEALAND: **New Zealand Consulate** (✉ Via Zara 28, Rome, ☎ 06/4417171).

➤ U.K.: **U.K. Consulate** (✉ Via Venti Settembre 80A, Rome, ☎ 06/4825441).

➤ U.S.: **U.S. Consulate** (✉ Via Veneto 121, Rome, ☎ 06/46741).

CONSUMER PROTECTION

Whenever shopping or buying travel services in Italy, **pay with a major credit card** so you can cancel payment or get reimbursed if there's a problem. If you're doing business with a particular company for the first time, **contact your local Better Business Bureau and the attorney general's offices** in your state and the company's home state, as well. Have any complaints been filed? Finally, if you're buying a package or tour, always **consider travel insurance** that includes default coverage (☞ Insurance, *below*).

➤ LOCAL BBBs: **Council of Better Business Bureaus** (✉ 4200 Wilson Blvd., Suite 800, Arlington, VA 22203, ☎ 703/276–0100, FAX 703/525–8277).

CUSTOMS & DUTIES

When shopping, **keep receipts** for all purchases. Upon reentering the country, **be ready to show customs officials what you've bought.** If you feel a duty is incorrect or object to the way your clearance was handled, note the inspector's badge number and ask to see a supervisor. If the problem isn't resolved, write to the appropriate authorities, beginning with the port director at your point of entry.

IN AUSTRALIA

Australian residents who are 18 or older may bring home $A400 worth of souvenirs and gifts (including jewelry), 250 cigarettes or 250 grams of tobacco, and 1,125 ml of alcohol (including wine, beer, and spirits). Residents under 18 may bring back $A200 worth of goods. Prohibited items include meat products. Seeds, plants, and fruits need to be declared upon arrival.

➤ INFORMATION: **Australian Customs Service** (Regional Director, ✉ Box 8, Sydney, NSW 2001, ☎ 02/9213–2000, FAX 02/9213–4000).

IN CANADA

Canadian residents who have been out of Canada for at least 7 days may bring home C$500 worth of goods duty-free. If you've been away less than 7 days but more than 48 hours, the duty-free allowance drops to C$200; if your trip lasts 24–48 hours, the allowance is C$50. You may not pool allowances with family members. Goods claimed under the C$500 exemption may follow you by mail; those claimed under the lesser exemptions must accompany you. Alcohol and tobacco products may be included in the 7-day and 48-hour exemptions but not in the 24-hour exemption. If you meet the age requirements of the province or territory through which you reenter Canada, you may bring in, duty-free, 1.14 liters (40 imperial ounces) of wine or liquor *or* 24 12-ounce cans or bottles of beer or ale. If you are 16 or older you may bring in, duty-free, 200 cigarettes and 50 cigars. Check ahead of time with Revenue Canada or the Department of Agriculture for policies regarding meat products, seeds, plants, and fruits.

You may send an unlimited number of gifts worth up to C$60 each duty-free to Canada. Label the package UNSOLICITED GIFT—VALUE UNDER $60. Alcohol and tobacco are excluded.

➤ INFORMATION: **Revenue Canada** (✉ 2265 St. Laurent Blvd. S, Ottawa, Ontario K1G 4K3, ☎ 613/ 993–0534; 800/461–9999 in Canada).

IN ITALY

Of goods obtained anywhere outside the EU or goods purchased in a duty-free shop within an EU country, the allowances are: (1) 200 cigarettes or 100 cigarillos or 50 cigars or 250 grams of tobacco; (2) 2 liters of still table wine or 1 liter of spirits over 22% volume or 2 liters of spirits under 22% volume or 2 liters of fortified and sparkling wines; and (3) 50 milliliters of perfume and 250 milliliters of toilet water.

Of goods obtained (duty and tax paid) within another EU country, the allowances are: (1) 800 cigarettes or 400 cigarillos or 400 cigars or 1 kilogram of tobacco; (2) 90 liters of still table wine plus (3) 10 liters of spirits over 22% volume plus 20 liters of spirits under 22% volume plus 60 liters of sparkling wines plus 110 liters of beer.

IN NEW ZEALAND

Homeward-bound residents 17 or older may bring back $700 worth of souvenirs and gifts. Your duty-free allowance also includes 4.5 liters of wine or beer; one 1,125-ml bottle of spirits; and either 200 cigarettes, 250 grams of tobacco, 50 cigars, or a combination of the three up to 250 grams. Prohibited items include meat products, seeds, plants, and fruits.

➤ INFORMATION: **New Zealand Customs** (Custom House, ✉ 50 Anzac Ave., Box 29, Auckland, ☎ 09/359–6655, FAX 09/359–6732).

IN THE U.K.

If you are a U.K. resident and your journey was wholly within the European Union (EU), you won't have to pass through customs when you return to the United Kingdom. If you plan to bring back large quantities of alcohol or tobacco, check EU limits beforehand. From countries outside the EU, including Italy, you may bring home, duty-free, 200 cigarettes or 50 cigars; 1 liter of spirits or 2 liters of fortified or sparkling wine or liqueurs; 2 liters of still table wine; 60 ml of perfume; 250 ml of toilet water; plus £136 worth of other goods, including gifts and souvenirs. If returning from outside the EU, prohibited items include meat products, seeds, plants, and fruits.

➤ INFORMATION: **HM Customs and Excise** (✉ Dorset House, Stamford St., Bromley Kent BR1 1XX, ☎ 020/ 7202–4227).

IN THE U.S.

U.S. residents who have been out of the country for at least 48 hours (and who have not used the $400 allowance or any part of it in the past 30 days) may bring home $400 worth of foreign goods duty-free.

U.S. residents 21 and older may bring back 1 liter of alcohol duty-free. In addition, regardless of your age, you are allowed 200 cigarettes and 100 non-Cuban cigars. Antiques, which the U.S. Customs Service defines as objects more than 100 years old, enter duty-free, as do original works of art done entirely by hand, including paintings, drawings, and sculptures.

You may also send packages home duty-free: up to $200 worth of goods for personal use, with a limit of one parcel per addressee per day (and no alcohol or tobacco products or perfume worth more than $5); label the package PERSONAL USE and attach a list of its contents and their retail value. Do not label the package UNSOLICITED GIFT or your duty-free exemption will drop to $100. Mailed items do not affect your duty-free allowance on your return.

➤ INFORMATION: **U.S. Customs Service** (inquiries, ✉ 1300 Pennsylvania Ave. NW, Washington, DC 20229, ☎ 202/ 927–6724; complaints, ✉ Office of Regulations and Rulings, 1300 Pennsylvania Ave. NW, Washington, DC 20229; registration of equipment, ✉ Resource Management, 1300 Pennsylvania Ave. NW, Washington, DC 20229, ☎ 202/927–0540).

DINING

The restaurants we list are the cream of the crop in each price category. Properties indicated by an ✕🏨 are lodging establishments whose restaurant warrants a special trip.

CATEGORY	ROME, FLORENCE, VENICE, AND MILAN*	ELSEWHERE IN ITALY*
$$$$	over 120,000 lire	over 100,000 lire
$$$	80,000–120,000 lire	65,000–100,000 lire
$$	45,000–80,000 lire	30,000–65,000 lire
$	under 45,000 lire	under 30,000 lire

**Prices are per person for a three-course meal including service and tax.*

RESERVATIONS & DRESS

Reservations are always a good idea: we mention them only when they're essential or are not accepted. Book as far ahead as you can, and reconfirm as soon as you arrive. We mention dress only when men are required to wear a jacket or a jacket and tie.

DISABILITIES & ACCESSIBILITY

Italy has only recently begun to provide facilities such as ramps, telephones, and rest rooms for people with disabilities; such things are still the exception, not the rule. Travelers' wheelchairs must be transported free of charge, according to Italian law, but the logistics of getting a wheelchair on and off trains and buses can make this requirement irrelevant. Seats are reserved for people with disabilities on public transportation, but few buses have lifts for wheelchairs. High, narrow steps for boarding trains create additional problems. In many monuments and museums, even in some hotels and restaurants, architectural barriers make it difficult, if not impossible, for those with disabilities to gain access.

Contact the nearest Italian consulate about bringing a Seeing Eye dog into Italy. This requires an import license, a current certificate detailing the dog's inoculations, and a letter from your veterinarian certifying the dog's health.

➤ LOCAL RESOURCES: The **Italian Government Travel Office** (ENIT; ☞ Visitor Information, *below*) can give you a list of hotels that provide access and addresses of Italian associations for travelers with disabilities.

LODGING

When discussing accessibility with an operator or reservations agent **ask hard questions.** Are there any stairs, inside *or* out? Are there grab bars next to the toilet *and* in the shower/tub? How wide is the doorway to the room? To the bathroom? For the most extensive facilities meeting the latest legal specifications **opt for newer accommodations.**

SIGHTS & ATTRACTIONS

In Rome, St. Peter's, the Sistine Chapel, and the Vatican Museums are all accessible by wheelchair, as is the Uffizi Gallery in Florence.

➤ COMPLAINTS: **Disability Rights Section** (✉ U.S. Department of Justice, Civil Rights Division, Box 66738, Washington, DC 20035-6738, ☎ 202/514–0301; 800/514–0301; 202/514–0301 TTY; 800/514–0301 TTY, FAX 202/307–1198) for general complaints. **Aviation Consumer Protection Division** (☞ Air Travel, *above*) for airline-related problems. **Civil Rights Office** (✉ U.S. Department of Transportation, Departmental Office of Civil Rights, S-30, 400 7th St. SW, Room 10215, Washington, DC 20590, ☎ 202/366–4648, FAX 202/366–9371) for problems with surface transportation.

TRAVEL AGENCIES

In the United States, although the Americans with Disabilities Act requires that travel firms serve the needs of all travelers, some agencies specialize in working with people with disabilities.

➤ TRAVELERS WITH MOBILITY PROBLEMS: **Access Adventures** (✉ 206 Chestnut Ridge Rd., Rochester, NY 14624, ☎ 716/889–9096), run by a former physical-rehabilitation counselor. **Accessible Vans of Hawaii, Activity and Travel Agency** (✉ 186 Mehani Circle, Kihei, HI 96753, ☎ 808/879–5521 or 800/303–3750). **Accessible Vans of the Rockies, Activ-**

ity and Travel Agency (✉ 2040 W. Hamilton Pl., Sheridan, CO 80110, ☎ 303/806–5047 or 888/837–0065, FAX 303/781–2329). **CareVacations** (✉ 5-5110 50th Ave., Leduc, Alberta T9E 6V4, ☎ 780/986–6404 or 780/986–8332) has group tours and is especially helpful with cruise vacations. **Flying Wheels Travel** (✉ 143 W. Bridge St., Box 382, Owatonna, MN 55060, ☎ 507/451–5005 or 800/535–6790, FAX 507/451–1685). **Hinsdale Travel Service** (✉ 201 E. Ogden Ave., Suite 100, Hinsdale, IL 60521, ☎ 630/325–1335).

➤ TRAVELERS WITH DEVELOPMENTAL DISABILITIES: **Sprout** (✉ 893 Amsterdam Ave., New York, NY 10025, ☎ 212/222–9575 or 888/222–9575, FAX 212/222–9768).

DISCOUNTS & DEALS

Be a smart shopper and **compare all your options** before making decisions. A plane ticket bought with a promotional coupon from travel clubs, coupon books, and direct-mail offers may not be cheaper than the least expensive fare from a discount ticket agency. And always keep in mind that what you get is just as important as what you save.

DISCOUNT RESERVATIONS

To save money **look into discount-reservations services** with toll-free numbers, which use their buying power to get a better price on hotels, airline tickets, even car rentals. When booking a room, always **call the hotel's local toll-free number** (if one is available) rather than the central reservations number—you'll often get a better price. Always ask about special packages or corporate rates.

When shopping for the best deal on hotels and car rentals **look for guaranteed exchange rates,** which protect you against a falling dollar. With your rate locked in, you won't pay more, even if the price goes up in the local currency.

➤ AIRLINE TICKETS: ☎ **800/FLY–4–LESS.** ☎ **800/FLY–ASAP.**

➤ HOTEL ROOMS: **Hotel Reservations Network** (☎ 800/964–6835). **International Marketing & Travel Concepts** (☎ 800/790–4682). **Steigenberger Reservation Service** (☎ 800/223–5652). **Travel Interlink** (☎ 800/888–5898).

PACKAGE DEALS

Don't confuse packages and guided tours. When you buy a package, you travel on your own, just as though you had planned the trip yourself. Fly/drive packages, which combine airfare and car rental, are often a good deal. If you **buy a rail/drive pass** you may save on train tickets and car rentals. All Eurail- and Europass holders get a discount on Eurostar fares through the Channel Tunnel. A German Rail Pass is also good for travel aboard some KD River Steamers and some Deutsche Touring/Europabus routes. Greek Flexipass options may include sightseeing, hotels, and plane tickets.

ELECTRICITY

To use your U.S.-purchased electric-powered equipment **bring a converter and adapter.** The electrical current in Italy is 220 volts, 50 cycles alternating current (AC); wall outlets take Continental-type plugs, with two round prongs.

If your appliances are dual-voltage you'll need only an adapter. Don't use 110-volt outlets, marked FOR SHAVERS ONLY, for high-wattage appliances such as blow-dryers. Most laptops operate equally well on 110 and 220 volts and so require only an adapter.

GAY & LESBIAN TRAVEL

➤ LOCAL CONTACT: **Circolo di Cultura Omosessuale Mario Mieli** (✉ Via Corinto 5, Rome, ☎ 06/5413985). **Arci Gay** (✉ Via Torricelli 19, Milan, ☎ 02/58100399).

➤ GAY- AND LESBIAN-FRIENDLY TRAVEL AGENCIES: **Different Roads Travel** (✉ 8383 Wilshire Blvd., Suite 902, Beverly Hills, CA 90211, ☎ 323/651–5557 or 800/429–8747, FAX 323/651–3678). **Kennedy Travel** (✉ 314 Jericho Turnpike, Floral Park, NY 11001, ☎ 516/352–4888 or 800/237–7433, FAX 516/354–8849). **Now Voyager** (✉ 4406 18th St., San Francisco, CA 94114, ☎ 415/626–1169 or 800/255–6951,

FAX 415/626–8626). **Yellowbrick Road** (✉ 1500 W. Balmoral Ave., Chicago, IL 60640, ☎ 773/561–1800 or 800/642–2488, FAX 773/561–4497). **Skylink Travel and Tour** (✉ 1006 Mendocino Ave., Santa Rosa, CA 95401, ☎ 707/546–9888 or 800/225–5759, FAX 707/546–9891), serving lesbian travelers.

HEALTH

The Centers for Disease Control and Prevention (CDC) in Atlanta caution that most of Southern Europe is in the "intermediate" range for risk of contacting traveler's diarrhea. Part of this risk may be attributed to an increased consumption of olive oil and wine, which can have a laxative effect on stomachs used to a different diet. The CDC also advises all international travelers to swim only in chlorinated swimming pools, unless they are absolutely certain the local beaches and freshwater lakes are not contaminated.

➤ MEDICAL-ASSISTANCE COMPANIES: **International SOS Assistance** (✉ 8 Neshaminy Interplex, Suite 207, Trevose, PA 19053, ☎ 215/245–4707 or 800/523–6586, FAX 215/244–9617; ✉ 12 Chemin Riantbosson, 1217 Meyrin 1, Geneva, Switzerland, ☎ 4122/785–6464, FAX 4122/785–6424; ✉ 331 N. Bridge Rd., 17-00, Odeon Towers, Singapore 188720, ☎ 65/338–7800, FAX 65/338–7611).

HOLIDAYS

National holidays include January 1 (New Year's Day); January 6 (Epiphany); April 23 and 24 (Easter Sunday and Monday); April 25 (Liberation Day); May 1 (Labor Day or May Day); August 15 (Assumption of Mary, also known as Ferragosto); November 1 (All Saints' Day); December 8 (Immaculate Conception); December 25 and 26 (Christmas Day and Boxing Day).

The feast days of patron saints are observed locally. Many businesses and shops may be closed in Florence, Genoa, and Turin on June 24 (St. John the Baptist); in Rome on June 29 (Sts. Peter and Paul); in Palermo on July 15 (Santa Rosalia); in Naples on September 19 (San Gennaro); in Bologna on October 4 (San Petronio); in Trieste on November 3 (San Giusto); and in Milan on December 7 (St. Ambrose). Venice's feast of St. Mark is April 25, the same as Liberation Day. (Also ☞ Festivals and Seasonal Events *below.*)

INSURANCE

The most useful travel insurance plan is a comprehensive policy that includes coverage for trip cancellation and interruption, default, trip delay, and medical expenses (with a waiver for preexisting conditions).

Without insurance you will lose all or most of your money if you cancel your trip, regardless of the reason. Default insurance covers you if your tour operator, airline, or cruise line goes out of business. Trip-delay covers expenses that arise because of bad weather or mechanical delays. Study the fine print when comparing policies.

If you're traveling internationally, a key component of travel insurance is coverage for medical bills incurred if you get sick on the road. Such expenses are not generally covered by Medicare or private policies. U.K. residents can buy a travel-insurance policy valid for most vacations taken during the year in which it's purchased (but check preexisting-condition coverage). British and Australian citizens need extra medical coverage when traveling overseas.

Always **buy travel policies directly from the insurance company**; if you buy it from a cruise line, airline, or tour operator that goes out of business you probably will not be covered for the agency or operator's default, a major risk. Before you make any purchase **review your existing health and home-owner's policies** to find what they cover away from home.

➤ TRAVEL INSURERS: In the United States: **Access America** (✉ 6600 W. Broad St., Richmond, VA 23230, ☎ 804/285–3300 or 800/284–8300) and **Travel Guard International** (✉ 1145 Clark St., Stevens Point, WI 54481, ☎ 715/345–0505 or 800/826–1300). In Canada: **Voyager Insurance** (✉ 44 Peel Center Dr., Brampton, Ontario

L6T 4M8, ☎ 905/791–8700; 800/668–4342 in Canada).

➤ INSURANCE INFORMATION: In the United Kingdom: the **Association of British Insurers** (✉ 51–55 Gresham St., London EC2V 7HQ, ☎ 020/7600–3333, FAX 020/7696–8999). In Australia: the **Insurance Council of Australia** (☎ 03/9614–1077, FAX 03/9614–7924).

LANGUAGE

In the main tourist cities, language is not a big problem. Most hotels have English speakers at their reception desks, and you can always find someone who speaks at least a little English otherwise. Remember that the Italian language is pronounced exactly as it is written (many Italians try to speak English by enunciating every syllable, with disconcerting results). You may run into a language barrier in the countryside, but a phrase book and close attention to the Italians' astonishing use of pantomime and expressive gestures will go a long way. Try to **master a few phrases for daily use** and familiarize yourself with the terms you'll need for deciphering signs and museum labels.

LANGUAGES FOR TRAVELERS

A phrase book and language-tape set can help get you started.

➤ CONTACT: ***Fodor's Italian for Travelers*** (☎ 800/733–3000 in the U.S.; 800/668–4247 in Canada; $7 for phrasebook, $16.95 for audio set).

LODGING

Options are numerous, from hotels to camping grounds to short-term rentals in the city or country.

The lodgings we list are the cream of the crop in each price category. We always list the facilities that are available—but we don't specify whether they cost extra: When pricing accommodations, always ask what's included and what costs extra. Properties indicated by an ✕☖ are lodging establishments whose restaurants warrant a special trip.

CATEGORY	ROME, FLORENCE, VENICE, AND MILAN*	ELSEWHERE IN ITALY*
$$$$	over 500,000 lire	over 300,000 lire
$$$	350,000–500,000 lire	200,000–300,000 lire
$$	350,000–500,000 lire	100,000–200,000 lire
$	under 200,000 lire	under 100,000 lire

**Prices are for a standard double room for two including tax and service.*

Assume that hotels operate on the Continental Plan (CP, with a Continental breakfast daily), unless we specify that they use the Modified American Plan (MAP, with breakfast and dinner daily), or the Full American Plan (FAP, with all meals).

APARTMENT & VILLA RENTALS

If you want a home base that's roomy enough for a family and comes with cooking facilities **consider a furnished rental.** These can save you money, especially if you're traveling with a group. Home-exchange directories list rentals (often second homes owned by prospective house swappers), and some services search for a house or apartment for you and handle the paperwork. Some send an illustrated catalog; others send photographs only of specific properties. Registration fees may apply.

➤ INTERNATIONAL AGENTS: **At Home Abroad** (✉ 405 E. 56th St., Suite 6H, New York, NY 10022, ☎ 212/421–9165, FAX 212/752–1591). **Drawbridge to Europe** (✉ 5456 Adams Rd., Talent, OR 97540, ☎ 541/512–8927 or 888/268–1148, FAX 541/512–0978). **El Sol Vacation Homes** (✉ Box 329, Wayne, PA 19087, ☎ 610/353–2335, FAX 610/353–7756). **Europa-Let/Tropical Inn-Let** (✉ 92 N. Main St., Ashland, OR 97520, ☎ 541/482–5806 or 800/462–4486, FAX 541/482–0660). **Hideaways International** (✉ 767 Islington St., Portsmouth, NH 03801, ☎ 603/430–4433 or 800/843–4433, FAX 603/430–4444; membership $99). **Hometours International** (✉ Box 11503, Knoxville, TN 37939, ☎ 423/690–8484 or 800/367–4668). **Interhome** (✉ 1990 N.E.

163rd St., Suite 110, Miami Beach, FL 33162, ☎ 305/940–2299 or 800/882–6864, FAX 305/940–2911). **Rental Directories International** (✉ 2044 Rittenhouse Sq., Philadelphia, PA 19103, ☎ 215/985–4001, FAX 215/985–0323). **Rent-a-Home International** (✉ 7200 34th Ave. NW, Seattle, WA 98117, ☎ 206/789–9377, FAX 206/789–9379). **Vacation Home Rentals Worldwide** (✉ 235 Kensington Ave., Norwood, NJ 07648, ☎ 201/767–9393 or 800/633–3284, FAX 201/767–5510). **Villas and Apartments Abroad** (✉ 420 Madison Ave., Suite 1003, New York, NY 10017, ☎ 212/759–1025 or 800/433–3020, FAX 212/755–8316). **Villas International** (✉ 950 Northgate Dr., Suite 206, San Rafael, CA 94903, ☎ 415/499–9490 or 800/221–2260, FAX 415/499–9491).

➤ ITALY-ONLY AGENTS: **Cuendet USA** (✉ 165 Chestnut St., Allendale, NJ 07041, ☎ 201/327–2333; ✉ Suzanne T. Pidduck, c/o Rentals in Italy, 1742 Calle Corva, Camarillo, CA 93010, ☎ 800/726–6702). **Vacanze in Italia** (✉ 22 Railroad St., Great Barrington, MA 01230, ☎ 413/528–6610 or 800/533–5405).

➤ IN THE U.K.: **CV Travel** (✉ 43 Cadogan St., London SW3 2PR, ☎ 020/7581–0851). **Magic of Italy** (✉ 227 Shepherds Bush Rd., London W6 7AS, ☎ 020/8748–7575).

CAMPING

Camping is a good way to find accommodations in otherwise overcrowded resorts, and camper rental agencies operate throughout Italy; contact your travel agent for details. Make sure you **stay only on authorized campsites** (camping on private land is frowned upon), and get an international camping *carnet* (permit) from your local camping association before you leave home. The Touring Club Italiano publishes a multilingual *Guida Camping d'Italia* (Guide to the Camping in Italy), available in bookstores in Italy for about 30,000 lire, with more detailed information on sites. Camp rates for two people, with car and tent, average about 50,000 lire a day.

➤ DIRECTORY OF CAMPGROUNDS: Write to the **Federazione Italiana del Campeggio e del Caravanning** (✉ Federcampeggio, Casella Postale 23, 50041 Calenzano, Firenze, FAX 055/8825918) and request *Campeggiare in Italia;* send three international reply coupons to cover mailing. It's also available through the ENIT office in the United States and at tourist information offices in Italy (☞ Visitor Information, *below* and *in* individual chapters).

FARM HOLIDAYS & AGRITOURISM

Rural accommodations in the *agriturismo* (agritourism) category are increasingly popular with both Italians and visitors to Italy. You stay on a working farm or vineyard, often in stone farmhouses that accommodate a number of guests.

➤ AGENCIES: **Agriturist** (✉ Corso Vittorio 101, 00186 Roma, ☎ 06/6852342). **Essentially Tuscany** (✉ 30 York St., Nantucket, MA 02554, ☎ FAX 508/2282514). **Italy Farm Holidays** (✉ 547 Martling Ave., Tarrytown, NY 10591, ☎ 914/631–7880, FAX 914/631–8831). **Terra Nostra** (✉ Via XXIV Maggio 43, 00187 Roma, ☎ 06/46821). **Turismo Verde** (✉ Via Flaminia 56, 00196 Roma, ☎ 06/3611051).

HOME EXCHANGES

If you would like to exchange your home for someone else's **join a home-exchange organization,** which will send you its updated listings of available exchanges for a year and will include your own listing in at least one of them. It's up to you to make specific arrangements.

➤ EXCHANGE CLUBS: **HomeLink International** (✉ Box 650, Key West, FL 33041, ☎ 305/294–7766 or 800/638–3841, FAX 305/294–1448; $88 per year). **Intervac U.S.** (✉ Box 590504, San Francisco, CA 94159, ☎ 800/756–4663, FAX 415/435–7440; $83 per year).

HOSTELS

No matter what your age you can **save on lodging costs by staying at hostels.** In some 5,000 locations in more than 70 countries around the world, Hostelling International (HI), the umbrella group for a number of national youth-hostel associations, offers single-sex, dorm-style beds and, at many hostels, couples rooms and family accommodations. Membership in any HI national hostel association, open to travelers of all ages, allows you to stay in HI-affiliated hostels at member rates (one-year membership is about $25 for adults; hostels run about $10–$25 per night). Members also have priority if the hostel is full; they're eligible for discounts around the world, even on rail and bus travel in some countries.

➤ ORGANIZATIONS: **Australian Youth Hostel Association** (✉ 10 Mallett St., Camperdown, NSW 2050, ☎ 02/9565–1699, FAX 02/9565–1325). **Hostelling International—American Youth Hostels** (✉ 733 15th St. NW, Suite 840, Washington, DC 20005, ☎ 202/783–6161, FAX 202/783–6171). **Hostelling International—Canada** (✉ 400–205 Catherine St., Ottawa, Ontario K2P 1C3, ☎ 613/237–7884, FAX 613/237–7868). **Youth Hostel Association of England and Wales** (✉ Trevelyan House, 8 St. Stephen's Hill, St. Albans, Hertfordshire AL1 2DY, ☎ 01727/855215 or 01727/845047, FAX 01727/844126). **Youth Hostels Association of New Zealand** (✉ Box 436, Christchurch, ☎ 03/379–9970, FAX 03/365–4476). Membership in the United States $25, in Canada C$26.75, in the United Kingdom £9.30, in Australia $44, in New Zealand $24.

HOTELS

Italian hotels are awarded stars (one to five) based on their facilities and services. Keep in mind, however, that these are general indications, and that a charming three-star might make for a better stay than a more expensive four-star. In the major cities, room rates are on a par with other European capitals: deluxe and four-star rates can be downright extravagant. In those categories, **ask for one of the better rooms,** since less desirable rooms—and there usually are some—don't give you what you're paying for. Except in deluxe and some four-star hotels, rooms may be very small compared to U.S standards and bathrooms usually have showers rather than bathtubs. Hotels with three or more stars always have bathrooms in all rooms.

In all hotels there is a rate card inside the door of your room or inside the closet door; it tells you exactly what you will pay for that particular room (rates in the same hotel may vary according to the location and type of room). On this card, breakfast and any other optionals must be listed separately. Any discrepancy between the basic room rate and that charged on your bill is cause for complaint to the manager and to the police.

Although, by law, breakfast is supposed to be optional, most hotels quote room rates including breakfast. When you book a room, specifically **ask whether the rate includes breakfast** (*colazione*). You are under no obligation to take breakfast at your hotel, but in practice most hotels expect you to do so. It is encouraging to note that many of the hotels we recommend provide generous buffet breakfasts instead of simple, even skimpy "continental breakfasts." Remember, if the latter is the case, you can **eat for less at the nearest coffee bar.**

Hotels that we list as ($$) and ($)—moderate to inexpensively priced accommodations—may charge extra for optional air-conditioning. In older hotels the quality of the rooms may be very uneven; if you don't like the room you're given, request another. This applies to noise, too. Front rooms may be larger or have a view, but they also may have a lot of street noise. If you're a light sleeper, **request a quiet room when making reservations.** Rooms in lodgings listed in this guide have a shower and/or bath, unless noted otherwise. Remember to **specify whether you care to have a bath or shower** since not all rooms, especially lodgings outside major cities, have both. It is always a good idea to have your reservation, dates, and rate confirmed by fax.

During low season and whenever a hotel is not full, it is often possible to negotiate a discounted rate. Major cities, such as Rome and Milan, have no official off-season as far as hotel rates go, though some hotels do offer substantial discounts during the slower parts of the year. Always **inquire about special rates.** Major cities have hotel-reservation service booths in train stations.

The **Sheraton/The Luxury Collection** has more than 20 Italian properties, almost all five-star deluxe. **Jolly** has 32 four-star hotels in Italy. **Atahotels** has 20 mostly four- and five-star hotels. **Starhotels** has 14 mainly four-star hotels. **Space Hotels** has 80 independently owned four- and three-star hotels. **Prima Hotels** has about 20 independently owned four- and five-star hotels. **AGIP Motels** is a chain of about 50, mostly four-star motels on main highways; the motels are commercial, functional accommodations for business travelers and tourists needing 40 winks, but they—and the Jolly hotels—can be the best choice in many out-of-the-way places. The **Forte** group has taken over some top-of-the-line AGIP properties throughout Italy.

Best Western, an international association of independently owned hotels, has some 75 mainly three- and four-star hotels in Italy; call to request the *Europe and Middle East Atlas* that lists them. **Family Hotels,** which groups about 80 small (maximum 35 rooms) family-run, one-, two-, and three-star hotels, offers good value. A spin-off of this group, the **Sun Rays Pool** comprises four- and five-star hotels, as well as several *agriturismi* with horseback riding.

➤ TOLL-FREE NUMBERS: **Atahotels** (☎ 02/895261, FAX 02/89503643; E&M Associates, ☎ 212/599–8280 or 800/223–9832). **Best Western** (☎ 800/528–1234). **Family Hotels** (✉ Via Trieste 5, 50139 Florence, ☎ 055/4620080, FAX 055/482288). **Four Seasons** (☎ 800/332–3442). **Hilton** (☎ 800/445–8667). **Inter-Continental** (☎ 800/327–0200). **Jolly** (☎ 800/247–1277 in New York; 800/221–2626 elsewhere in U.S.; 800/237–0319 in Canada; 1670/17703 toll-free in Italy). **Marriott** (☎ 800/228–9290). **Omni** (☎ 800/843–6664). **Prima Hotels** (☎ 1670/14327 toll-free in Italy). **Renaissance Hotels & Resorts** (☎ 800/468–3571). **Ritz-Carlton** (☎ 800/341–3333). **Sheraton** (☎ 800/325–3535). **Sheraton/The Luxury Collection** (☎ 800/221–2340; 1678/835035 toll-free in Italy, FAX 212/421–5929). **Space Hotels** (☎ 1678/13013 toll-free in Italy). **Starhotels** (☎ 055/36921; 1678/60200 toll-free in Italy; 800/448–8355 for bookings, FAX 055/36924). **Supranational** (☎ 416/927–1133 or 800/843–3311). **Westin Hotels & Resorts** (☎ 800/228–3000).

MAIL & SHIPPING

The Italian mail system is notoriously slow. Allow up to 15 days for mail to and from the United States and Canada, about a week to and from the United Kingdom.

POSTAL RATES

Airmail letters and postcards (lightweight stationery) to the United States and Canada cost 1,300 lire for the first 20 grams; 2,700 lire up to 40 grams, and 3,100 lire up to 50 grams. Always stick the blue airmail tag on your mail, or write "Airmail" in big, clear characters to the side of the address. Postcards and letters (for the first 20 grams) to the United Kingdom, as well as to any other EU country, including Italy, cost 800 lire. You can buy stamps at tobacconists.

RECEIVING MAIL

Correspondence can be addressed to you in care of the Italian post office. Letters should be addressed to your name, "c/o Ufficio Postale Centrale," followed by "Fermo Posta" on the next line, and the name of the city (preceded by its postal code) on the next. You can **collect it at the central post office** by showing your passport or photo-bearing ID and paying a small fee. American Express also has a general-delivery service. There's no charge for cardholders, holders of American Express Traveler's checks, or anyone who booked a vacation with American Express.

MONEY MATTERS

The days when the country's high-quality attractions came with a comparatively low Mediterranean price tag are long gone. Italy's prices are in line with those in the rest of Europe, with costs in its main cities comparable to those in other major capitals, such as Paris and Madrid.

As in most countries, prices vary from region to region and are a bit lower in the countryside than in the cities. Good value for the money can be had in the scenic Trentino–Alto Adige region and the Dolomites, in Umbria and the Marches, and on the Amalfi Coast. With a few exceptions, southern Italy, Sicily, and Sardinia also offer good values, but hotels are not always up to par. Of Italy's major cities, Venice and Milan are the most expensive. Resorts such as the Costa Smeralda, Portofino, and Cortina d'Ampezzo cater to the rich and famous and charge top prices.

Admission to the Vatican Museums is 15,000 lire; to the Galleria degli Uffizi, 12,000 lire. The cheapest seat at Rome's Teatro dell'Opera runs 32,000 lire. A movie ticket is 12,000 lire. Getting into a Milan nightclub will set you back about 35,000 lire. A daily English-language newspaper is 2,500 lire. A Rome taxi ride (1⅓ km, or 1 mi) costs 10,000 lire. An inexpensive hotel room for two, including breakfast, in Rome is about 190,000 lire; an inexpensive Rome dinner is 40,000 lire, and a ½ liter carafe of house wine, 6,000 lire. A simple pasta item runs about 13,000 lire, a cup of coffee 1,200–1,400 lire, and a rosticceria lunch, about 15,000 lire. A Coca-Cola (standing) at a café is 2,200 lire and a pint of beer is 7,000 lire.

Prices throughout this guide are given for adults. Substantially reduced fees are almost always available for children, students, and senior citizens. For information on taxes, *see* Taxes, *below.*

CREDIT CARDS

Discover is generally not accepted in Italy. Throughout this guide, the following abbreviations are used: **AE**, American Express; **DC**, Diner's Club; **MC**, MasterCard; and **V**, Visa.

➤ REPORTING LOST CARDS: **American Express** (☎ 336/668–5110 international collect). **Diner's Club** (☎ 702/797–5532 collect). **MasterCard** (☎ 1678/70866 toll-free). **Visa** (☎ 1678/177232).

CURRENCY

The unit of currency in Italy is the lira. There are bills of 500,000 (practically impossible to change outside of banks), 100,000, 50,000, 10,000, 5,000, 2,000, and 1,000 lire. Coins are 500, 200, 100 and 50 lire.

CURRENCY EXCHANGE

For the most favorable rates, **change money through banks.** Although fees charged for ATM transactions may be higher abroad than at home, Cirrus and Plus exchange rates are excellent, because they are based on wholesale rates offered only by major banks. You won't do as well at exchange booths in airports or rail and bus stations, hotels, restaurants, or stores, although you may find the hours more convenient. To avoid lines at airport exchange booths, **get a bit of local currency before you leave home.**

At press time, the exchange rate was about 1,864 lire to the U.S. dollar; 1,271 lire to the Canadian dollar; 2,972 lire to the pound sterling; 1,233 to the Australian dollar; and 990 lire to the New Zealand dollar. Although prices are increasingly quoted in the Euro (European common currency), everyday business is still conducted in lire.

➤ EXCHANGE SERVICES: **International Currency Express** (☎ 888/842–0880 on East Coast; 888/278–6628 on West Coast). **Thomas Cook Currency Services** (☎ 800/287–7362 for telephone orders and retail locations).

TRAVELER'S CHECKS

Do you need traveler's checks? It depends on where you're headed. If you're going to rural areas and small towns, go with cash; traveler's checks are best used in cities. Lost or stolen checks can usually be replaced within 24 hours. To ensure a speedy refund, buy your own traveler's checks—don't let someone else pay for them: irregularities like this can cause delays. The person who bought the checks should make the call to request a refund.

ON-LINE ON THE ROAD

➤ INTERNET CAFÉS: **Internet Café** (✉ Via Marruccini 12, ☎ 06/4454953). **Internet Centre** (✉ Via delle Fosse di Castello 8, ☎ 06/ 6861464).

OUTDOORS & SPORTS

Italians are sports lovers, and several daily newspapers are devoted solely to sports. *Calcio* (soccer) is fiercely popular in Italy, and if you make the effort to get tickets to a match, you won't be denied fancy footwork and raving fans. The climate makes it almost impossible to resist the temptation to try a cannonball serve on the red-clay tennis courts, sink a birdie putt on a scenic green, or just hike up a hill to savor the fresh air and views. Come winter, skiers take to the resorts and slopes of the Apennines and the Alps for world-class conditions.

PACKING

The weather is considerably milder, in the winter at least, in Italy than in the north and central United States or Great Britain. In summer, stick with clothing that is as light as possible, as things can get steamy in the height of summer; a sweater may be necessary for cool evenings, especially in the mountains even during the hot months. Sunglasses, a hat, and sunblock are essential. Brief summer afternoon thunderstorms are common in Rome and inland cities, so an umbrella will come in handy. In winter bring a medium-weight coat and a raincoat for Rome and farther south. Northern Italy calls for heavier clothes, gloves, hats, and boots. Even in Rome and other milder areas, central heating may not be up to your standards, and interiors can be cold and damp; take wools or flannel rather than sheer fabrics. Bring sturdy shoes for winter and comfortable walking shoes in any season.

Italians dress exceptionally well. They do not usually wear shorts. Men aren't required to wear ties or jackets anywhere, except in some of the grander hotel dining rooms and top-level restaurants, but are expected to look reasonably sharp—and they do. Formal wear is the exception rather than the rule at the opera nowadays, though people in expensive seats usually do get dressed up.

A certain modesty of dress (no bare shoulders or knees) is expected in churches, and strictly enforced in many, especially in Rome at St. Peter's and the Vatican Museums and at the Basilica di San Marco in Venice.

For sightseeing, **pack a pair of binoculars**; they will help you get a good look at painted ceilings and domes. If you stay in budget hotels, **take your own soap.** Many such hotels do not provide it or give guests only one tiny bar per room.

In your carry-on luggage **bring an extra pair of eyeglasses or contact lenses** and **enough of any medication you take** to last the entire trip. You may also want your doctor to write a spare prescription using the drug's generic name, since brand names may vary from country to country. In luggage to be checked, **never pack prescription drugs or valuables.** To avoid customs delays, carry medications in their original packaging. And don't forget to copy down and carry addresses of offices that handle refunds of lost traveler's checks.

CHECKING LUGGAGE

How many carry-on bags you can bring with you is up to the airline. Most allow two, but not always, so make sure that everything you carry aboard will fit under your seat, and get to the gate early. Note that if you have a seat at the back of the plane, you'll probably board first, while the overhead bins are still empty.

If you are flying internationally, note that baggage allowances may be determined not by piece but by weight—generally 88 pounds (40 kilograms) in first class, 66 pounds (30 kilograms) in business class, and 44 pounds (20 kilograms) in economy.

Airline liability for baggage is limited to $1,250 per person on flights within the United States. On international flights it amounts to $9.07 per pound or $20 per kilogram for checked baggage (roughly $640 per 70-pound bag) and $400 per passenger for unchecked baggage. You can buy additional coverage at check-in for about $10 per $1,000 of coverage, but it excludes a rather extensive list of items, shown on your airline ticket.

Before departure **itemize your bags' contents** and their worth, and label the bags with your name, address, and phone number. (If you use your home address, cover it so that potential thieves can't see it readily.) Inside each bag **pack a copy of your itinerary.** At check-in **make sure that each bag is correctly tagged** with the destination airport's three-letter code. If your bags arrive damaged or fail to arrive at all, file a written report with the airline before leaving the airport.

PASSPORTS & VISAS

When traveling internationally **your passport** is essential even after you arrive in the country; without it no Italian hotel will let you have a room. It is a good idea to make **two photocopies of the data page** (one for someone at home and another for you, carried separately from your passport). If you lose your passport, promptly call the nearest embassy or consulate and the local police (☞ Consulates, *above*).

ENTERING ITALY

➤ AUSTRALIAN CITIZENS: Citizens of Australia need only a valid passport to enter Italy for stays of up to 90 days.

➤ CANADIAN CITIZENS: You need only a valid passport to enter Italy for stays of up to 90 days.

➤ NEW ZEALAND CITIZENS: Citizens of New Zealand need only a valid passport to enter Italy for stays of up to 90 days.

➤ U.K. CITIZENS: Citizens of the United Kingdom need only a valid passport to enter Italy for stays of up to 90 days.

➤ U.S. CITIZENS: All U.S. citizens, even infants, need only a valid passport to enter Italy for stays of up to 90 days.

PASSPORT OFFICES

The best time to apply for a passport or to renew is during the fall and winter. Before any trip, check your passport's expiration date, and, if necessary, renew it as soon as possible.

➤ AUSTRALIAN CITIZENS: **Australian Passport Office** (☎ 131–232).

➤ CANADIAN CITIZENS: **Passport Office** (☎ 819/994–3500 or 800/567–6868).

➤ NEW ZEALAND CITIZENS: **New Zealand Passport Office** (☎ 04/494–0700 for information on how to apply; 04/474–8000 or 0800/225–050 in New Zealand for information on applications already submitted).

➤ U.K. CITIZENS: **London Passport Office** (☎ 0990/210–410) for fees and documentation requirements and to request an emergency passport.

➤ U.S. CITIZENS: **National Passport Information Center** (☎ 900/225–5674; calls are 35¢ per minute for automated service, $1.05 per minute for operator service).

SAFETY

The best way to **protect yourself against purse snatchers and pickpockets** is to wear a money belt or a pouch on a string around your neck, both concealed. If you carry a bag or camera, be absolutely sure it has straps; you should sling it across your body bandolier-style. Always be astutely aware of stealthy pickpockets, especially when in jam-packed city buses and metros, when making your way through train corridors, and in busy piazzas.

LOCAL SCAMS

A word of caution: "gypsy" children are rife in Rome, especially around the Colosseum, and are adept pickpockets. One tactic is to approach a tourist and proffer a piece of cardboard with writing on it. While you attempt to read the message *on* it, the children's hands are busy *under* it, trying to make off with purses or valuables. If you see such a group (recognizable by their unkempt appearance), do not even let them near you—they are quick and know more tricks than you do.

SENIOR-CITIZEN TRAVEL

To qualify for age-related discounts **mention your senior-citizen status up front** when booking hotel reservations (not when checking out) and before you're seated in restaurants (not when paying the bill). When renting a car ask about promotional car-rental discounts, which can be cheaper than senior-citizen rates.

➤ EDUCATIONAL PROGRAMS: **Elderhostel** (✉ 75 Federal St., 3rd fl., Boston, MA 02110, ☎ 877/426–8056, FAX 877/426–2166). **Interhostel** (✉ University of New Hampshire, 6 Garrison Ave., Durham, NH 03824, ☎ 603/862–1147 or 800/733–9753, FAX 603/862–1113). **Folkways Institute** (✉ 14600 Southeast Aldridge Rd., Portland, OR 97236-6518, ☎ 503/658–6600 or 800/225–4666, FAX 503/658–8672).

SHOPPING

The notice PREZZI FISSI (fixed prices) means just that; in shops displaying this sign it's a waste of time to bargain unless you're buying a sizable quantity of goods or a particularly costly object. Always try to bargain, however, at outdoor markets (except food markets) and when buying from street vendors. For information on VAT refunds, *see* Taxes, *below.*

STUDENTS IN ITALY

Italy is a popular student destination, and in the major art cities there are plenty of facilities in the way of information and lodging geared to students' needs. Students with identification cards may obtain discounts at museums, galleries, exhibitions, and entertainment venues, and on some transportation.

LOCAL RESOURCES

The Centro Turistico Studentesco is a student and youth travel agency with offices in major Italian cities. CTS helps its clients find low-cost accommodations and bargain fares for travel in Italy and elsewhere. CTS is also the Rome representative for EuroTrain International.

TRAVEL AGENCIES

To save money, **look into deals available through student-oriented travel agencies.** To qualify you'll need a student ID card. Members of international student groups are also eligible.

➤ STUDENT IDS & SERVICES: **Council on International Educational Exchange** (CIEE, ✉ 205 E. 42nd St., 14th fl., New York, NY 10017, ☎ 212/822–2600 or 888/268–6245, FAX 212/822–2699) for mail orders only, in the United States. **Travel Cuts** (✉ 187 College St., Toronto, Ontario M5T 1P7, ☎ 416/979–2406 or 800/667–2887) in Canada.

TAXES

HOTEL

The service charge and the 9% IVA, or VAT tax, are included in the rate except in five-star deluxe hotels, where the IVA (12% on luxury hotels) may be a separate item added to the bill upon departure.

RESTAURANT

A service charge of approximately 15% is added to all restaurant bills; in some cases the menu may state that the service charge is already included in the menu prices.

VALUE-ADDED TAX (VAT)

Value-added tax (IVA or VAT) is 19% on clothing and luxury goods. On most consumer goods, it is already included in the amount shown on the price tag, whereas on services, it may not be.

To **get an IVA refund,** when you are leaving Italy take the goods and the invoice to the customs office at the airport or other point of departure and have the invoice stamped. (If you return to the United States or Canada directly from Italy, go through the procedure at Italian customs; if your return is, say, via Britain, take the Italian goods and invoice to British customs.) Under Italy's IVA-refund system, a non-EU resident can obtain a refund of tax paid after spending a total of 300,000 lire in one store (before tax—and note that price tags and prices quoted, unless otherwise stated, include IVA). Shop with your passport and ask the store for an invoice itemizing the article(s), price(s), and the amount of tax. Once back home—and within 90 days of the date of purchase—mail the stamped invoice to the store, which will send the IVA rebate to you.

A growing number of stores in Italy (and Europe—90,000 affiliated stores at last count) are members of the Tax-Free Shopping System, which expedites things by providing an invoice that is actually a Tax-Free Cheque in the amount of the refund—**ask for the E.T.S. refund form** (called a Shopping Cheque). Once stamped, it can be cashed at the Tax-Free Cash refund window at major airports and border crossings, you can also opt to have the refund credited to your credit card or bank account, or sent directly home. To save a step at the airport or border, you can send the Cheque to a Tax-Free Shopping address.

➤ VAT REFUNDS: **Europe Tax-Free Shopping** (✉ 233 S. Wacker Dr., Suite 9700, Chicago, IL 60606-6502, ☎ 312/382–1101).

TELEPHONES

COUNTRY & AREA CODES

The country code for Italy is 39. Here are area codes for major cities: Bologna, 051; Brindisi, 0831; Florence, 055; Genoa, 010; Milan, 02; Naples, 081; Palermo, 091; Perugia, 075; Pisa, 050; Rome, 06; Siena, 0577; Turin, 011; Venice, 041; Verona, 045. For example, a call from New York City to Rome would be dialed as 011 + 39 + 06 + phone number.

When dialing an Italian number from abroad, you no longer drop the initial 0 from the local area code. The country code is 1 for the United States and Canada, 61 for Australia, 64 for New Zealand, and 44 for the United Kingdom.

DIRECTORY & OPERATOR INFORMATION

For general information in English, dial 176. To place international telephone calls via operator-assisted service, dial 170 or long-distance access numbers (☞ International Calls *below*).

INTERNATIONAL CALLS

Since hotels tend to overcharge, sometimes exorbitantly, for long-distance and international calls, it is best to make such calls from public phones, using telephone cards. At Telefoni offices, operators sell international telephone cards and will help you place your call. There are Telefoni offices, designated TELECOM, in all cities and towns, usually in major train stations and in the center business districts. You can **make collect calls from any phone by dialing 172-1011,** which will get you an English-speaking operator. Rates to the United States are lowest 'round the clock on Sunday and 10 PM–8 AM (Italian time) on weekdays.

From major Italian cities, you can place a direct call to the United States by reversing the charges or using your phone credit card number. When calling from pay telephones, insert a 200-lire coin that will be returned upon completion of your call. You automatically reach an operator in the country of destination and thereby avoid all language difficulties.

LOCAL CALLS

For all calls within Italy—local and long distance—you must dial the regional area code (*prefisso*), which begins with a 0, as 06 for Rome, 041 for Venice. If you are calling from a public phone you must deposit a coin or use a calling card to get a dial tone.

LONG-DISTANCE SERVICES

AT&T, MCI, and Sprint access codes make calling long distance relatively convenient, but you may find the local access number blocked in many hotel rooms. First ask the hotel operator to connect you. If the hotel operator balks ask for an international operator, or dial the international operator yourself. One way to improve your odds of getting connected to your long-distance carrier is to travel with more than one company's calling card (a hotel may block Sprint, for example, but not MCI). If all else fails call from a pay phone.

➤ ACCESS CODES: **AT&T USADirect** (☎ 172–1011). **MCI Call USA** (☎ 172–1022). **Sprint Express** (☎ 172–1877).

PHONE CARDS

Prepaid *carte telefonice* (calling cards) are prevalent throughout Italy and more convenient than coins. You buy the card (values vary—5,000 lire, 10,000 lire, etc.) at Telefoni offices, post offices, and tobacconists. Tear off the corner of the card and insert it in the slot. When you dial, its value appears in the window. After you hang up, the card is returned so you can use it until its value runs out.

PUBLIC PHONES

Pay phones accept a 200-lire coin, two 100-lire coins, or a 500-lire coin, but consider buying a *carta telefonica* (☞ Phone Cards, *above*).

TIPPING

The following guidelines apply in major cities, but Italians tip smaller amounts in smaller cities and towns. In restaurants a service charge of about 15% usually appears as a separate item on your check. Some restaurants state on the menu that cover and service charge are included. Either way, it's customary to leave an additional 5%–10% tip for the waiter, depending on the service. Tip checkroom attendants 500 lire per person and rest room attendants 200 lire (more in expensive hotels and restaurants). Tip 100 lire for whatever you drink standing up at a coffee bar, 500 lire or more for table service in cafés. At a hotel bar tip 1,000 lire and up for a round or two of cocktails.

From Rome south, tip taxi drivers 5%–10% of the meter amount. Railway and airport porters charge a fixed rate per bag. Tip an additional 500 lire per person, and more if the porter is very helpful. Theater ushers expect 500 lire per person, and more for very expensive seats. Give a barber 2,000–3,000 lire and a hairdresser's assistant 3,000–8,000 lire for a shampoo or cut, depending on the type of establishment.

On sightseeing tours, tip guides about 2,000 lire per person for a half-day group tour, more if they are very good. In museums and other sights where admission is free, a contribution (500–1,000 lire) is expected. Service station attendants are tipped only for special services, for example, 1,000 lire for checking your tires.

In hotels, give the *portiere* (concierge) about 15% of his bill for services, or 5,000–10,000 lire if he has been generally helpful. For two people in a double room, leave the chambermaid about 1,000 lire per day, or about 4,000–5,000 a week, in a moderately priced hotel; tip a minimum of 1,000 lire for valet or room service. Double amounts in a very expensive hotel. In very expensive hotels, tip doormen 1,000 lire for calling a cab and 2,000 lire for carrying bags to the check-in desk, bellhops 3,000–5,000 lire for carrying your bags to the room, and 3,000–5,000 lire for room service.

TOURS & PACKAGES

On a prepackaged tour or independent vacation everything is prearranged so you'll spend less time planning—and often get it all at a good price.

BOOKING WITH AN AGENT

Travel agents are excellent resources. But it's a good idea to collect brochures from several agencies because some agents' suggestions may be influenced by relationships with tour and package firms that reward them for volume sales. If you have a special interest **find an agent with expertise in that area**; ASTA (☞ Travel Agencies, *below*) has a database of specialists worldwide.

Make sure your travel agent knows the accommodations and other services of the place they're recommending. Ask about the hotel's location, room size, beds, and whether it has a pool, room service, or programs for children, if you care about these. Has your agent been there in person or sent others whom you can contact?

Do some homework on your own, too: Local tourism boards can provide information about lesser-known and small-niche operators, some of which may sell only direct.

BUYER BEWARE

Each year consumers are stranded or lose their money when tour operators—even large ones with excellent reputations—go out of business. So **check out the operator.** Ask several travel agents about its reputation, and try to **book with a company that has a consumer-protection program.** (Look for information in the company's brochure.) In the United States, members of the National Tour Association and United States Tour Operators Association are required to set aside funds to cover your payments and travel arrangements in case the company defaults. It's also a good idea to choose a company that participates in the American Society of Travel Agent's Tour Operator Program (TOP); ASTA will act as mediator in any disputes between you and your tour operator.

Remember that the more your package or tour includes the better you can predict the ultimate cost of your vacation. Make sure you know exactly what is covered, and **beware of hidden costs.** Are taxes, tips, and transfers included? Entertainment and excursions? These can add up.

➤ TOUR-OPERATOR RECOMMENDATIONS: **American Society of Travel Agents** (☞ Travel Agencies, *below*). **National Tour Association** (NTA, ✉ 546 E. Main St., Lexington, KY 40508, ☎ 606/226–4444 or 800/682–8886). **United States Tour Operators Association** (USTOA, ✉ 342 Madison Ave., Suite 1522, New York, NY 10173, ☎ 212/599–6599 or 800/468–7862, FAX 212/599–6744).

GROUP TOURS

Among companies that sell tours to Italy, the following have a proven reputation and offer plenty of options. The classifications used below represent different price categories, and you'll probably encounter these terms when talking to a travel agent or tour operator. The key difference is usually in accommodations, which run from budget to better, and better-yet to best.

➤ SUPER-DELUXE: **Abercrombie & Kent** (✉ 1520 Kensington Rd., Suite 212, Oak Brook, IL 60521-2141, ☎ 630/954–2944 or 800/323–7308, FAX 630/954–3324). **Travcoa** (✉ 2350 S.E. Bristol St., Newport Beach, CA 92660, ☎ 949/476–2800 or 800/992–2003, FAX 949/476–2538).

➤ DELUXE: **Central Holidays** (✉ 120 Sylvan Ave., Englewood Cliffs, NJ 07632, ☎ 201/798–5777 or 800/935–5000, FAX 201/228–5355, 800/329–4248). **Donna Franca Tours** (✉ 470 Commonwealth Ave., Boston, MA 02215, ☎ 617/375–9400 or 800/225–6290, FAX 617/266–1062). **Globus** (✉ 5301 S. Federal Circle, Littleton, CO 80123-2980, ☎ 303/797–2800 or 800/221–0090, FAX 303/347–2080). **Maupintour** (✉ 1421 Research Park Dr., Suite 300, Lawrence, KS 66049-3858, ☎ 785/843–1211 or 800/255–4266, FAX 785/331–1057). **Perillo Tours** (✉ 577 Chestnut Ridge Rd., Woodcliff Lake, NJ 07675, ☎ 201/307–1234 or 800/431–1515, FAX 201/307–1808). **Tauck Tours** (✉ Box 5027, 276 Post Rd. W, Westport, CT 06881-5027, ☎ 203/226–6911 or 800/468–2825, FAX 203/222–7702).

➤ FIRST-CLASS: **Brendan Tours** (✉ 15137 Califa St., Van Nuys, CA 91411, ☎ 818/785–9696 or 800/421–8446, FAX 818/902–9876). **Caravan Tours** (✉ 401 N. Michigan Ave., Chicago, IL 60611, ☎ 312/321–9800 or 800/227–2826, FAX 312/321–9845). **Collette Tours** (✉ 162 Middle St., Pawtucket, RI 02860, ☎ 401/728–3805 or 800/832–4656, FAX 401/728–1380). **DER Tours** (✉ 9501 W. Devon St., Rosemont, IL 60018, ☎ 874/430–0000 or 800/937–1235, FAX 847/692–4141 or 800/282–7474; 800/860–9944 for brochures). **Insight International Tours** (✉ 745 Atlantic Ave., No. 720, Boston, MA 02111, ☎ 617/482–2000 or 800/582–8380, FAX 617/482–2425 or 800/622–5015). **Trafalgar Tours** (✉ 11 E. 26th St., Suite 1300, New York, NY 10010, ☎ 212/689–8977 or 800/854–0103, FAX 800/457–6644). **TWA Getaway Vacations** (☎ 800/438–2929).

➤ BUDGET: **Cosmos** (☞ Globus, *above*). **Trafalgar** (☞ *above*).

PACKAGES

Like group tours, independent vacation packages are available from major tour operators and airlines. The companies listed below offer vacation packages in a broad price range.

➤ AIR/HOTEL: **Continental Vacations** (☎ 800/634–5555). **DER Tours** (☞ Group Tours, *above*). **4th Dimension Tours** (✉ 7101 S.W. 99th Ave., Suite 106, Miami, FL 33173, ☎ 305/279–0014 or 800/644–0438, FAX 305/273–9777). **US Airways Vacations** (☎ 800/455–0123).

➤ FROM THE U.K.: **British Airways Holidays** (✉ Astral Towers, Betts Way, London Rd., Crawley, West Sussex RH10 2XA, ☎ 01293/722–727, FAX 01293/722–624). **Carefree Italy** (✉ Allied Dunbar House, East Park, Crawley, West Sussex RH10

6AJ, ☎ 01293/552277) offers accommodations in apartments, castles, and farmhouses. **Italian Escapades** (✉ 227 Shepherds Bush Rd., London W6 7AS, ☎ 020/8748–2661). **Page and Moy Holidays** (✉ 136–140 London Rd., Leicester LE2 1EN, ☎ 0116/250–7676, FAX 0116/254–9949).

THEME TRIPS

Travel Contacts (✉ Box 173, Camberley GU15 1YE, England, ☎ 01276/677217, FAX 01276/63477) represents over 150 tour operators in Europe.

➤ ADVENTURE: **Adventure Center** (✉ 1311 63rd St., Suite 200, Emeryville, CA 94608, ☎ 510/654–1879 or 800/227–8747, FAX 510/654–4200). **Mountain Travel-Sobek** (✉ 6420 Fairmount Ave., El Cerrito, CA 94530, ☎ 510/527–8100 or 888/687–6235, FAX 510/525–7710).

➤ ARCHAEOLOGY: **Archeological Tours** (✉ 271 Madison Ave., Suite 904, New York, NY 10016, ☎ 212/986–3054, FAX 212/370–1561).

➤ ART & ARCHITECTURE: **Amelia Tours International** (✉ 28 E. Old Country Rd., Hicksville, NY 11801, ☎ 516/433–0696 or 800/742–4591, FAX 516/822–6220). **IST Cultural Tours** (✉ 225 W. 34th St., Suite 1020, New York, NY 10122-0913, ☎ 212/563–1202 or 800/833–2111, FAX 212/594–6953).

➤ BALLOONING: **Bombard Society/The Very Private Europe of Buddy Bombard** (✉ 333 Pershing Way, West Palm Beach, FL 33401, ☎ 561/837–6610 or 800/862–8537, FAX 561/837–6623).

➤ BICYCLING: **Backroads** (✉ 801 Cedar St., Berkeley, CA 94710, ☎ 510/527–1555 or 800/462–2848, FAX 510/527–1444). **Bike Riders** (✉ Box 130254, Boston, MA 02113, ☎ 617/723–2354 or 800/473–7040, FAX 617/723–2355). **Butterfield & Robinson** (✉ 70 Bond St., Suite 300, Toronto, Ontario, Canada M5B 1X3, ☎ 416/864–1354 or 800/678–1147, FAX 416/864–0541). **Ciclismo Classico** (✉ 30 Marathon St., Arlington, MA 02474, ☎ 781/646–3377 or 800/866–7314, FAX 781/641–1512). **Classic Adventures** (✉ Box 143, Hamlin, NY 14464-0143, ☎ 716/964–8488 or 800/777–8090, FAX 716/964–7297). **Euro-Bike Tours** (✉ Box 990, De Kalb, IL 60115, ☎ 800/321–6060, FAX 815/758–8851). **Europeds** (✉ 761 Lighthouse Ave., Monterey, CA 93940, ☎ 831/646–4920 or 800/321–9552, FAX 831/655–4501). **Himalayan Travel** (✉ 110 Prospect St., Stamford, CT 06901, ☎ 203/359–3711 or 800/225–2380, FAX 203/359–3669). **Naturequest** (✉ 30872 South Coast Hwy., Suite 185, Laguna Beach, CA 92651-8162, ☎ 949/499–9561 or 800/369–3033, FAX 949/499–0812). **Progressive Travels** (✉ 224 W. Galer Ave., Suite C, Seattle, WA 98119, ☎ 206/285–1987 or 800/245–2229, FAX 206/285–1988). **Uniquely Europe/Europe Express** (✉ 19805 North Creek Pkwy., Suite 100, Bothell, WA 98011, ☎ 425/487–6711 or 800/426–3615, FAX 425/487–3750 or 800/270–0509).

➤ CRUISING: **Annemarie Victory Organization** (✉ 136 E. 64th St., New York, NY 10021, ☎ 212/486–0353, FAX 212/751–3149). **EuroCruises** (✉ 303 W. 13th St., New York, NY 10014-1207, ☎ 212/691–2099 or 800/688–3876, FAX 212/366–4747).

➤ FOOD & WINE: **Amelia Tours** (☞ Art and Architecture, *above*). **Annemarie Victory Organization** (☞ Cruising, *above*). **Cuisine International** (✉ Box 25228, Dallas, TX 75225, ☎ 214/373–1161, FAX 214/373–1162). **Donna Franca Tours** (☞ Group Tours, *above*). **Esperienze Italiane** (✉ Lidia Bastianich, c/o Felidia Ristorante, 242 E. 58th St., New York, NY 10022, ☎ 800/480–2426, FAX 212/935–7687). **International Cooking School of Italian Food and Wine** (✉ 201 E. 28th St., Suite 15B, New York, NY 10016-8538, ☎ 212/779–1921, FAX 212/779–3248). **The International Kitchen** (✉ 1209 N. Astor 11-N, Chicago IL 60610, ☎ 800/945–8606, FAX 847/295–0945).

➤ HOMES & GARDENS: **Coopersmith's England** (✉ Box 900, Inverness, CA 94937, ☎ 415/669–1914, FAX 415/669–1942). **Expo Garden Tours** (✉ 33 Fox Crossing, Litchfield, CT 06759, ☎ 860/567–0322 or 800/448–2685, FAX 860/567–0381).

➤ HORSEBACK RIDING: **Cross Country International Equestrian Vacations**

(✉ Box 1170, Millbrook, NY 12545, ☎ 914/677–6000 or 800/828–8768, FAX 914/677–6077). **Equitour** (✉ Box 807, Dubois, WY 82513, ☎ 307/455–3363 or 800/545–0019, FAX 307/455–2354).

➤ LEARNING: **Earthwatch** (✉ Box 9104, 680 Mount Auburn St., Watertown, MA 02472, ☎ 617/926–8200 or 800/776–0188, FAX 617/926–8532) organizes research expeditions. **Smithsonian Study Tours and Seminars** (✉ 1100 Jefferson Dr. SW, Room 3045, Washington, DC 20560-0702, ☎ 202/357–4700, FAX 202/633–9250).

➤ MOTORCYCLE: **Beach's Motorcycle Adventures** (✉ 2763 W. River Pkwy., Grand Island, NY 14072-2053, ☎ 716/773–4960, FAX 716/773–5227).

➤ MUSIC: **Dailey-Thorp Travel** (✉ 330 W. 58th St., Suite 610, New York, NY 10019-1817, ☎ 212/307–1555 or 800/998–4677, FAX 212/974–1420).

➤ PILGRIMAGES: **Pilgrimage Tours and Travel** (✉ 154 Village Rd., Manhasset, NY 11030, ☎ 516/627–2636 or 800/669–0757, FAX 516/365–1667).

➤ SPAS: **Spa Finders** (✉ 91 5th Ave., Suite 600, New York, NY 10003-3039, ☎ 212/924–6800 or 800/255–7727, FAX 212/924–7240). **Spa Trek Travel** (✉ 475 Park Ave. S., New York, NY 10016, ☎ 212/779–3480 or 800/272–3480, FAX 212/779–3471).

➤ TENNIS: **Championship Tennis Tours** (✉ 8040 E. Morgan Trail, Suite 12, Scottsdale, AZ 85258, ☎ 602/443–9449 or 800/468–3664, FAX 602/443–8982). **Steve Furgal's International Tennis Tours** (✉ 11808 Rancho Bernardo Rd., Suite 123-418, San Diego, CA 92128, ☎ 858/675–3555 or 800/258–3664, FAX 858/487–0518).

➤ VILLA RENTALS: **Eurovillas** (✉ 3212 Jefferson St., Suite 298, Napa, CA 94558, ☎ 800/767–0275, ☎ FAX 707/648–2066). **Rentvillas.com** (✉ 1742 Calle Corva, Camarillo, CA 93010-8428, ☎ 805/987–5278 or 800/726–6702, FAX 805/482–7976). (Also ☞ Lodging, *above*).

➤ WALKING/HIKING: **Abercrombie & Kent** (☞ Group Tours, Super-Deluxe, *above*). **Above the Clouds Trekking** (✉ Box 398, Worcester, MA 01602-0398, ☎ 508/799–4499 or 800/233–4499, FAX 508/797–4779). **Backroads** (☞ Bicycling, *above*). **Butterfield & Robinson** (☞ Bicycling, *above*). **Ciclismo Classico** (☞ Bicycling, *above*). **Country Walkers** (✉ Box 180, Waterbury, VT 05676-0180, ☎ 802/244–1387 or 800/464–9255, FAX 802/244–5661). **Euro-Bike Tours** (☞ Bicycling, *above*). **Mountain Travel-Sobek** (☞ Adventure, *above*). **Progressive Travels** (☞ Bicycling, *above*). **Uniquely Europe/Europe Express** (☞ Bicycling, *above*). **Wilderness Travel** (✉ 1102 Ninth St., Berkeley, CA 94710, ☎ 510/558–2488 or 800/368–2794, FAX 510/558–2489).

➤ YACHT CHARTERS: **Huntley Yacht Vacations** (✉ 210 Preston Rd., Wernersville, PA 19565, ☎ 610/678–2628 or 800/322–9224, FAX 610/670–1767). **Lynn Jachney Charters** (✉ Box 302, Marblehead, MA 01945, ☎ 781/639–0787 or 800/223–2050, FAX 781/639–0216). **Ocean Voyages** (✉ 1709 Bridgeway, Sausalito, CA 94965, ☎ 415/332–4681 or 800/299–4444, FAX 415/332–7460).

TRAIN TRAVEL

The fastest trains on the Ferrovie dello Stato (FS), the Italian State Railways, are the Eurostar trains, operating on several main lines, including Rome–Milan via Florence and Bologna. Seat reservations and supplement are included in the fare. Some of these (the ETR 460 trains) have little aisle and luggage space (though there is a space near the door where you can put large bags). To avoid having to squeeze through narrow aisles, board only at your car (look for the number on the reservation ticket). Car numbers are displayed on their exterior. Next-fastest trains are the Intercity (IC) trains, for which you pay a supplement and for which seat reservations may be required and **are always advisable.** *Interregionale* trains usually make more stops and are a little slower. *Regionale* and *locale* trains are the slowest; many serve commuters.

Note that in some Italian cities—Milan, Turin, Genoa, Naples, and Rome included—there are two or more main-line stations, although one is usually the principal terminal or through-station. Be sure of the name of the station at which your train will arrive, or from which it will depart.

There is refreshment service on all long-distance trains, with mobile carts and a cafeteria or dining car. Tap water on trains is not drinkable.

To save money, **look into rail passes.** But be aware that if you don't plan to cover many miles, you may come out ahead by buying individual tickets.

➤ FROM THE U.K.: **British Rail** (☎ 020/7834–2345). **French Railways** (☎ 0891/515–477); calls charged at 49p a minute peak rate, 39p all other times.

CLASSES

All Italian trains have first and second classes. On local trains the higher first-class fare gets you little more than a clean doily on the headrest of your seat, but on long-distance trains you get wider seats and more legroom and better ventilation and lighting. At peak travel times, first-class train travel is worth the difference. Remember to **always make seat reservations in advance,** for either class.

DISCOUNTS & PASSES

To save money **look into rail passes.** But be aware that if you don't plan to cover many miles, you may come out ahead by buying individual tickets.

If Italy is your only destination in Europe, **consider purchasing an Italian Railpass,** which allows unlimited travel on the entire Italian Rail network. The Italy Flexi Rail Card allows a limited number of travel days within one month: for 4 days of travel ($216 first class, $144 second class); 8 days of travel ($312 first class, $202 second class); and 12 days of travel ($389 first class, $259 second class). Passes for travel on consecutive days are also available: 8 days ($273 first class, $182 second class); 15 days ($341 first class, $228 second class); 21 days ($396 first class, $264 second class); and 30 days ($478 first class, $318 second class).

The Italian Kilometric Ticket is valid for two months and can be used by as many as five people to travel a total of 3,000 km (1,800 mi). The price is $289 for first class and $181 second class.

Once in Italy, **inquire about the Carta Verde (Green Card) if you're under 26** (40,000 lire for one year), which entitles the holder to a 20% discount on all first- and second-class tickets. Those under 26 should also inquire about discount travel fares under the Billet International Jeune (BIJ) and Euro Domino Junior schemes. Also in Italy, you can **purchase the Carta d'Argento (Silver Card) if you're over 60** (40,000 lire for one year), which allows a 40% discount on first-class rail travel and a 20% discount on second-class travel. For further information, check out the Ferrovie dello Stato (FS) Web site (www.fs-on-line.com).

Italy is one of 17 countries in which you can **use Eurailpasses,** which provide unlimited first-class travel in all of the participating countries. If you plan to rack up the miles, get a standard pass. Train travel is available for 15 days ($554), 21 days ($718), one month ($890), two months ($1,260), and three months ($1,558). You can also receive free or discounted fares on some ferry lines.

If your plans call for only limited train travel, **look into the Europass,** which costs less than a Eurailpass and allows train travel in France, Germany, Italy, Spain, and Switzerland within a two-month period ($348 for 5 days of travel; $368 for 6 days; $448 for 8 days; $528 for 10 days; and $728 for 15 days). Rail travel to Austria/Hungary, Portugal, Greece, and Benelux can be added for additional fees ($60 one country, $100 two countries). You can receive discounts for two or more people.

Please note that these fares are subject to change in 2000.

In addition to standard Eurailpasses, **ask about special rail-pass plans.** Among these are the Eurail Youthpass (for those under age 26), Eurail Saverpass and Eurail Saver Flexipass (which give a discount for two or more people traveling together), Eurail Flexipass (which allows a certain number of travel days within a set period), and the EurailDrive Pass (which combines travel by train and rental car).

Whichever pass you choose, remember that you must **purchase your Eurailpass or Europass before you leave** for Europe. You can get further information and order tickets at the Rail Europe Web site (www.raileurope.com).

Many travelers assume that rail passes guarantee them seats on the trains they wish to ride. Not so. You need to **book seats ahead even if you are using a rail pass.** Seat reservations are required on some European trains, particularly high-speed trains, and are a good idea on trains that may be crowded—particularly in summer on popular routes. You will also need a reservation if you purchase sleeping accommodations.

➤ INFORMATION AND PASSES: **Rail Europe** (✉ 226-230 Westchester Ave., White Plains, NY 10604, ☎ 914/682–5172 or 800/438–7245, www.raileurope.com; ✉ 2087 Dundas E., Suite 105, Mississauga, Ontario L4X 1M2, ☎ 416/602–4195). **DER Tours** (✉ Box 1606, Des Plaines, IL 60017, ☎ 800/782–2424, FAX 800/282–7474). **CIT Rail** (✉ 9501 W. Devon Ave., Suite 502, Rosemont, IL 60018, ☎ 800/248–7245).

➤ UNIQUE GUIDEBOOK: ***Italy by Train*** by Tim Jepson (Fodor's Travel Publications, ☎ 800/533–6478 or from bookstores); $16.

➤ TRAIN INFORMATION: **Ferrovie dello Stato** (FS, ☎ 147/888088 toll-free in Italy, www.fs-on-line.com).

TICKETS & SCHEDULES

Trains can be very crowded; it is always a good idea to make a reservation. To avoid long lines at station windows, **buy tickets and make seat reservations up to two months in advance** at travel agencies displaying the FS emblem. Tickets can be purchased at the last minute, but seat reservations can be made at agencies (or the train station) up until about five hours before the train departs from its city of origin. For trains that require a reservation (all Eurostar and some Intercity), you may be able to get a seat assignment just before boarding the train; look for the conductor on the platform.

All **tickets must be date-stamped in the small yellow or red machines near the tracks before you board.** Once stamped, your ticket is valid for six hours if your destination is within 200 km (124 mi), for 24 hours for destinations beyond that. You can get on and off at will at stops in between for the duration of the ticket's validity. If you forget to stamp your ticket in the machine, or you didn't make in time to buy the ticket, you must actively seek out a conductor and pay a 10,000-lire fine. Don't wait for the conductor to find out that you are without a valid ticket (unless the train is overcrowded and walking becomes impossible), as he might charge you a much heavier fine. You can buy train tickets for nearby destinations (within a 200-km/124-mi range) at tobacconists and at ticket machines in stations.

TRANSPORTATION

Public transportation is the fastest mode of travel among Italy's cities. It is also relatively inexpensive in comparison to the costs of renting a car and paying for gas and tolls. Italy's cities are served by an extensive state railway system (FS, ☞ Train Travel, *above*), with fast service on main lines (Milan–Venice–Florence–Rome–Naples) that in some cases beats plane travel in time and cost. A complete schedule of all trains in the country and fares can be bought from most newsstands for about $8.

Buses (☞ Bus Travel, *above*), less roomy but slightly less expensive than trains, offer more frequent service to certain smaller cities and towns that are served only by secondary train lines. Buses are also better relied upon in more rugged areas where train service is spotty: the Dolomites, Liguria, Tuscany, and the Amalfi Coast, for instance. Ferries and hydrofoils (☞ Boat & Ferry Travel, *above*) ply among the islands; some islands, such as Capri and Ischia, have helicopter service, a more expensive alternative.

Getting around in Italy by plane (☞ Air Travel, *above*) is an expensive but viable option, and it is the fastest means of traveling long distances, as in to Sicily and Sardinia. Look for special bargain rates that can defray costs. Train and bus connections between airports and city centers are usually smooth.

Italy has an intricate network of autostrade routes, good highways, and secondary roads, making renting a car (☞ Car Rental, *above*) for travel among most cities a doable but more-expensive alternative to public transportation (due to high gas prices). A car can be a good investment if you are interested in carefree countryside rambles, offering time to explore more remote towns. Having a car in major cities, however, often leads to parking and traffic headaches, plus additional expense in the form of garage and parking fees.

TRAVEL AGENCIES

A good travel agent puts your needs first. Look for an agency that has been in business at least five years, emphasizes customer service, and has someone on staff who specializes in your destination. In addition **make sure the agency belongs to a professional trade organization.** The American Society of Travel Agents (ASTA), with 27,000 agents in some 170 countries, is the largest and most influential in the field. Operating under the motto "Integrity in Travel," it maintains and enforces a strict code of ethics and will step in to help mediate any agent-client disputes if necessary. ASTA also maintains a Web site that includes a directory of agents. (If a travel agency is also acting as your tour operator, ☞ Buyer Beware *in* Tours & Packages *above.*)

➤ Local Agent Referrals: **American Society of Travel Agents** (ASTA, ☎ 800/965–2782 24-hr hot line, FAX 703/684–8319, www.astanet.com). **Association of British Travel Agents** (✉ 55–57 Newman St., London W1P 4AH, ☎ 020/7637–2444, FAX 020/7637–0713). **Association of Canadian Travel Agents** (✉ 1729 Bank St., Suite 201, Ottawa, Ontario K1V 7Z5, ☎ 613/521–0474, FAX 613/521–0805). **Australian Federation of Travel Agents** (✉ Level 3, 309 Pitt St., Sydney 2000, ☎ 02/9264–3299, FAX 02/9264–1085). **Travel Agents' Association of New Zealand** (✉ Box 1888, Wellington 10033, ☎ 04/499–0104, FAX 04/499–0786).

VISITOR INFORMATION

TOURIST INFORMATION

➤ At Home: **Italian Government Tourist Board** (ENIT; ✉ 630 5th Ave., New York, NY 10111, ☎ 212/245–4822, FAX 212/586–9249; ✉ 401 N. Michigan Ave., Chicago, IL 60611, ☎ 312/644–0990, FAX 312/644–3019; ✉ 12400 Wilshire Blvd., Suite 550, Los Angeles, CA 90025, ☎ 310/820–0098, FAX 310/820–6357; ✉ 1 Pl. Ville Marie, Suite 1914, Montréal, Québec H3B 3M9, ☎ 514/866–7667, FAX 514/392–1429; ✉ 1 Princes St., London W1R 8AY, ☎ 020/7408–1254, FAX 020/7493–6695).

➤ Tourist Offices in Italy: **Rome** (✉ Via Parigi 5, 00185, ☎ 06/48899255). **Florence** (✉ Via Cavour 1/r, next to Palazzo Medici–Riccardi, 50129, ☎ 055/290832). **Venice** (✉ San Marco 71/f, near the Museo Correr, 30124, ☎ 041/5298740). **Milan** (✉ Via Marconi 1, 20121, ☎ 02/72524300). **Naples** (✉ Piazza dei Martiri 58, 80121, ☎ 081/405311). **Palermo** (✉ Piazza Castelnuovo 35, 90141, ☎ 091/583847).

➤ U.S. Government Advisories: **U.S. Department of State** (✉ Overseas Citizens Services Office, Room 4811 N.S., 2201 C St. NW, Washington, DC 20520; ☎ 202/647–5225 for interactive hot line; 301/946–4400 for computer bulletin board; FAX 202/647–3000 for interactive hot line); enclose a self-addressed, stamped, business-size envelope.

WEB SITES

Do check out the World Wide Web when you're planning. You'll find everything from up-to-date weather forecasts to virtual tours of famous cities. Fodor's Web site, www.fodors.com, is a great place to start your online travels.

➤ SUGGESTED WEB SITES: For more information specifically on Italy, visit www.initaly.com and www.wel.it. The site for Ferrovie dello Stato, www.fs-on-line.com, is a good source for train information. The official site for the Italian Government Tourist Board is located at www.italiantourism.com. Check out (www.Jubil2000.org) for up-to-date information on the Jubilee in Rome.

WHEN TO GO

The main tourist season runs from April to mid-October. For serious sightseers the best months are from fall to early spring. The so-called low season may be cooler and inevitably rainier, but it has its rewards: less time waiting on lines and closer-up, unhurried views of what you want to see.

Tourists crowd the major art cities at Easter, when Italians flock to resorts and to the country. From March through May, busloads of eager schoolchildren on excursions take cities of artistic and historical interest by storm.

CLIMATE

Weatherwise, the best months for sightseeing are April, May, June, September, and October—generally pleasant and not too hot. The hottest months are July and August, when humidity can make things pretty unpleasant. Winters are relatively mild in most places on the main tourist circuit but always include some rainy spells. In general, the northern half of the peninsula and the entire Adriatic Coast, with the exception of Apulia, are rainier than the rest of Italy.

If you can avoid it, don't travel at all in Italy in August, when much of the population is on the move, especially around Ferragosto, the August 15 national holiday, when cities such as Rome and Milan are deserted and many restaurants and shops are closed. (Of course, with residents away on vacation, this makes crowds less of a bother for tourists.) Except for a few year-round resorts, such as Taormina and some towns on the Italian Riviera, coastal resorts usually close up tight from October or November to April; they're at their best in June and September, when everything is open but uncrowded.

➤ FORECASTS: **Weather Channel Connection** (☎ 900/932–8437), 95¢ per minute from a Touch-Tone phone.

MILAN

Jan.	40F	5C	May	74F	23C	Sept.	75F	24C
	32	0		57	14		61	16
Feb.	46F	8C	June	80F	27C	Oct.	63F	17C
	35	2		63	17		52	11
Mar.	56F	13C	July	84F	29C	Nov.	51F	10C
	43	6		67	20		43	6
Apr.	65F	18C	Aug.	82F	28C	Dec.	43F	6C
	49	10		66	19		35	2

ROME

Jan.	52F	11C	May	74F	23C	Sept.	79F	26C
	40	5		56	13		62	17
Feb.	55F	13C	June	82F	28C	Oct.	71F	22C
	42	6		63	17		55	13
Mar.	59F	15C	July	87F	30C	Nov.	61F	16C
	45	7		67	20		49	10
Apr.	66F	19C	Aug.	86F	30C	Dec.	55F	13C
	50	10		67	20		44	6

VENICE

Jan.	42F	6C	May	70F	21C	Sept.	75F	24C
	33	1		56	13		61	16
Feb.	46F	8C	June	76F	25C	Oct.	65F	19C
	35	2		63	17		53	12
Mar.	53F	12C	July	81F	27C	Nov.	53F	12C
	41	5		66	19		44	7
Apr.	62F	17C	Aug.	80F	27C	Dec.	46F	8C
	49	10		65	19		37	3

FESTIVALS AND SEASONAL EVENTS

Italy's top seasonal events are listed below, and any one of them could provide the stuff of lasting memories. It is revealing that the Italian "festa" can be translated either as "festival" or "holiday" or "feast"—food is usually the most fundamental aspect of Italian celebrations. Contact the **Italian Government Travel Office** (☞ Visitor Information *in* the Smart Travel Tips A to Z) for exact dates and further information.

➤ EARLY DEC.: The **Feast of St. Ambrose** (Festa di Sant'Ambrosio), in Milan, officially opens La Scala's opera season.

➤ DEC.–JUNE: The **Opera Season** is in full swing at La Scala in Milan and elsewhere, notably in Turin, Rome, Naples, Parma, Venice, and Genoa.

➤ DEC. 31: Rome stages a rousing **New Year's Eve** celebration, dubbed the Festa di San Silvestro, with fireworks in Piazza del Popolo.

➤ JAN. 5–6: Roman Catholic **Epiphany (Epifania) Celebrations** and decorations are evident throughout Italy. Notable is the Epiphany Fair at Piazza Navona in Rome.

➤ EARLY FEB.: The **Almond Blossom Festival** (Festa del Fiore di Mandorlo) in Agrigento is a week of folk music and dancing, with groups from many countries, in the Valley of the Temples.

➤ FEB. 29–MAR. 7: A big do in the 18th century, revived in the last half of the 20th century, **Carnival (Carnevale) in Venice** includes concerts, plays, masked balls, fireworks, and indoor and outdoor happenings of every sort. It is probably Italy's most famous festival, bringing in hundreds of thousands. During **Carnival in Viareggio,** masked pageants, fireworks, a flower show, and parades are among the festivities on the Tuscan Riviera.

➤ FEB. 29–MAR. 7: The **Carnival in Ivrea,** near Turin, includes three days of folklore, costumes, parades, and cooking in the streets. The party culminates with the Battle of the Oranges, on Quinquagesima Sunday (Mar. 5) and Shrove Monday (Mar. 6), which features real fruit flying through the air.

➤ APR. 17–23: **Settimana Santa** (Holy Week) features parades and outdoor events at every major city and most small towns in Italy, but Rome, Naples, Assisi, and Florence have particularly notable festivities.

➤ APR. 21: In Rome, a torchlit nighttime **Good Friday Procession** (Venerdì Santo) led by the pope winds from the Colosseum past the Roman Forum and up the Palatine Hill.

➤ APR. 23: The Easter Sunday **Scoppio del Carro,** or Explosion of the Cart, in Florence, is the eruption of a cartful of fireworks in the Piazza del Duomo, set off by a mechanical dove released from the altar during High Mass. Needless to say, **Easter Mass at the Vatican** in Rome is long, intense, and packed, with many people attending in elaborate holiday costumes.

➤ LATE APR.–EARLY JULY: The **Florence May Music Festival** is the oldest and most prestigious Italian festival of the performing arts.

➤ MAY 1: The **Feast of Sant'Efisio** in Cagliari sees a procession of marchers and others in splendid Sardinian costume.

➤ MID-MAY: During the **Race of the Candles** (Corsa dei Ceri), the procession of bearers, in local costume, carrying towering wooden pillars, leads to the top of Mt. Ingino in Gubbio.

➤ MAY 20–21: The **Sardinian Cavalcade** (Cavalcata Sarda) is a traditional procession of more than 3,000 people in Sardinian costume that makes its way through Sassari.

➤ MAY 28: The **Palio of the Archers** (Palio della Balestra) is a medieval crossbow contest in Gubbio, dating back to 1461, held the last Sunday in May.

➤ EARLY JUNE: The **Battle of the Bridge,** in Pisa, is a medieval parade and contest. The **Flower Festival** (Festa dei Fiori), in Genzano (Rome), is a religious procession along streets carpeted with flowers in splendid designs. The **Regatta of the Great Maritime Republics** sees keen competition among the four former maritime republics—Amalfi, Genoa, Pisa, and Venice.

➤ LATE JUNE: **Soccer Games in 16th-Century Costume,** in Florence, commemorate a match played in 1530. Festivities include fireworks displays.

➤ LATE JUNE–MID-JULY: The **Festival of Two Worlds** (Festa dei Due Mondi), in Spoleto, is perhaps Italy's most famous performing-arts festival, bringing in a worldwide audience for concerts, operas, ballets, film screenings, and crafts fairs. Plan well in advance.

➤ JUNE–EARLY AUG.: The **Summer Operetta Festival** (Festival Internazionale dell'Operetta) is held in Trieste.

➤ EARLY JULY AND MID-AUG.: The world-famous **Palio Horse Race,** in Siena, is a colorful bareback horse race with ancient Sienese factions showing their colors and participants competing for the *palio* (banner).

➤ EARLY JULY–LATE AUG.: The **Arena of Verona Outdoor Opera Season** heralds spectacular productions in the 22,000-seat Roman amphitheater of Verona.

➤ MID-JULY: The **Umbria Jazz Festival,** in Perugia (www.umbriajazz.com), brings in many of the biggest names in jazz each summer.

➤ MID-JULY: The **Feast of the Redeemer** (Festa del Redentore) is a procession of gondolas and other craft commemorating the end of the epidemic of 1575 in Venice. The fireworks over the lagoon are spectacular.

➤ LATE AUG.–EARLY SEPT.: The **Venice Film Festival,** oldest of the international film festivals, takes place mostly on the Lido.

➤ LATE AUG.–MID-SEPT.: The **Stresa Musical Weeks** comprise a series of concerts and recitals in Stresa.

➤ EARLY SEPT.: The **Historic Regatta** (Regata Storica) includes a traditional competition between two-oar gondolas in Venice. The **Joust of the Saracen** is a tilting contest with knights in 13th-century armor in Arezzo.

➤ MID-SEPT.: The **Joust of the Quintana** is a 17th-century-style joust and historical procession in Foligno.

➤ EARLY OCT.: Alba's **100 Towers Tournament** features costumes and races and is held simultaneously with the **Truffle Fair,** a food fair centered around the white truffle.

➤ OCT. 4: The **Feast of St. Francis** (Festa di San Francesco) is celebrated in Assisi, his birthplace.

WORDS AND PHRASES

English	Italian	Pronunciation
Basics		
Yes/no	Sí/No	see/no
Please	Per favore	pear fa-**vo**-ray
Yes, please	Sí grazie	see **grah**-tsee-ay
Thank you	Grazie	**grah**-tsee-ay
You're welcome	Prego	**pray**-go
Excuse me, sorry	Scusi	**skoo**-zee
Sorry!	Mi dispiace!	mee dis-spee-**ah**-chay
Good morning/afternoon	Buon giorno	bwohn **jor**-no
Good evening	Buona sera	**bwoh**-na **say**-ra
Good bye	Arrivederci	a-ree-vah-**dare**-chee
Mr. (Sir)	Signore	see-**nyo**-ray
Mrs. (Ma'am)	Signora	see-**nyo**-ra
Miss	Signorina	see-nyo-**ree**-na
Pleased to meet you	Piacere	pee-ah-**chair**-ray
How are you?	Come sta?	**ko**-may **stah**
Very well, thanks	Bene, grazie	**ben**-ay **grah**-tsee-ay
And you?	E lei?	ay **lay**-ee
Hello (phone)	Pronto?	**proan**-to
Numbers		
one	uno	**oo**-no
two	due	**doo**-ay
three	tre	tray
four	quattro	**kwah**-tro
five	cinque	**cheen**-kway
six	sei	say
seven	sette	**set**-ay
eight	otto	**oh**-to
nine	nove	**no**-vay
ten	dieci	dee-**eh**-chee
eleven	undici	**oon**-dee-chee
twelve	dodici	**doe**-dee-chee
thirteen	tredici	**tray**-dee-chee
fourteen	quattordici	kwa-**tore**-dee-chee
fifteen	quindici	**kwin**-dee-chee
sixteen	sedici	**say**-dee-chee
seventeen	diciassette	dee-cha-**set**-ay
eighteen	diciotto	dee-**cho**-to

nineteen	diciannove	dee-cha-**no**-vay
twenty	venti	**vain**-tee
twenty-one	ventuno	vain-**too**-no
twenty-two	ventidue	vayn-tee-**doo**-ay
thirty	trenta	**train**-ta
forty	quaranta	kwa-**rahn**-ta
fifty	cinquanta	cheen-**kwahn**-ta
sixty	sessanta	seh-**sahn**-ta
seventy	settanta	seh-**tahn**-ta
eighty	ottanta	o-**tahn**-ta
ninety	novanta	no-**vahn**-ta
one hundred	cento	**chen**-to
ten thousand	diecimila	dee-eh-chee-**mee**-la
one hundred thousand	centomila	chen-to-**mee**-la

Useful Phrases

Do you speak English?	Parla inglese?	**par**-la een-**glay**-zay
I don't speak Italian	Non parlo italiano	non **par**-lo ee-tal-**yah**-no
I don't understand	Non capisco	non ka-**peess**-ko
Can you please repeat?	Può ripetere?	pwo ree-**pet**-ay-ray
Slowly!	Lentamente!	**len**-ta-men-tay
I don't know	Non lo so	noan lo **so**
I'm American/	Sono americano(a)	**so**-no a-may-ree-**kah**-no(a)
	Sono inglese	**so**-no een-**glay**-zay
What's your name?	Come si chiama?	**ko**-may see kee-**ah**-ma
My name is . . .	Mi chiamo . . .	mee kee-**ah**-mo
What time is it?	Che ore sono?	kay **o**-ray **so**-no
How?	Come?	**ko**-may
When?	Quando?	**kwan**-doe
Yesterday/today/ tomorrow	Ieri/oggi/domani	**yer**-ee/**o**-jee/ do-**mah**-nee
This morning/ afternoon	Stamattina/Oggi pomeriggio	sta-ma-**tee**-na/**o**-jee po-mer-**ee**-jo
Tonight	Stasera	sta-**ser**-a
What?	Che cosa?	kay **ko**-za
What is it?	Che cos'è?	kay ko-**zay**
Why?	Perché?	pear-**kay**
Who?	Chi?	kee
Where is . . .	Dov'è . . .	doe-**veh**
the bus stop?	la fermata dell'autobus?	la fer-**mah**-ta del ow-toe-**booss**
the train station?	la stazione?	la sta-tsee-**oh**-nay
the subway station?	la metropolitana?	la may-tro-po-lee-**tah**-na
the terminal?	il terminal?	eel ter-mee-**nahl**
the post office?	l'ufficio postale?	loo-**fee**-cho po-**stah**-lay

the bank?	la banca?	la **bahn**-ka
the . . . hotel?	l'hotel . . .?	lo-**tel**
the store?	il negozio?	ell nay-**go**-tsee-o
the cashier?	la cassa?	la **kah**-sa
the . . . museum?	il museo . . .?	eel moo-**zay**-o
the hospital?	l'ospedale?	lo-spay-**dah**-lay
the first aid station?	il pronto soccorso?	eel **pron**-to so-**kor**-so
the elevator?	l'ascensore?	la-shen-**so**-ray
a telephone?	un telefono?	oon tay-**lay**-fo-no
Where are the restrooms?	Dov'è il bagno?	doe-**vay** eel **bahn**-yo
Here/there	Qui/là	kwee/la
Left/right	A sinistra/a destra	a see-**neess**-tra/a **des**-tra
Straight ahead	Avanti dritto	a-**vahn**-tee **dree**-to
Is it near/far?	È vicino/lontano?	ay vee-**chee**-no/ lon-**tah**-no
I'd like . . .	Vorrei . . .	vo-**ray**
a room	una camera	**oo**-na **kah**-may-ra
the key	la chiave	la kee-**ah**-vay
a newspaper	un giornale	oon jor-**nah**-lay
a stamp	un francobollo	oon frahn-ko-**bo**-lo
I'd like to buy . . .	Vorrei comprare . . .	vo-**ray** kom-**prah**-ray
a cigar	un sigaro	oon see-**gah**-ro
cigarettes	delle sigarette	day-lay see-ga-**ret**-ay
some matches	dei fiammiferi	day-ee fee-ah-**mee**-fer-ee
some soap	una saponetta	**oo**-na sa-po-**net**-a
a city plan	una pianta della città	**oo**-na **pyahn**-ta day-la chee-**tah**
a road map of . . .	una carta stradaledi . . .	**oo**-na **cart**-a stra-**dah**-lay dee
a country map	una carta geografica	**oo**-na **cart**-a jay-o-**grah**-fee-ka
a magazine	una rivista	**oo**-na ree-**veess**-ta
envelopes	delle buste	**day**-lay **booss**-tay
writing paper	della carta da lettere	**day**-la **cart**-a da **let**-air-ay
a postcard	una cartolina	**oo**-na car-toe-**lee**-na
a guidebook	una guida turistica	**oo**-na **gwee**-da too-**reess**-tee-ka
How much is it?	Quanto costa?	**kwahn**-toe **coast**-a
It's expensive/ cheap	È caro/economico	ay **car**-o/ay-ko-**no**-mee-ko
A little/a lot	Poco/tanto	**po**-ko/**tahn**-to
More/less	Più/meno	pee-**oo**/**may**-no
Enough/too (much)	Abbastanza/troppo	a-bas-**tahn**-sa/**tro**-po
I am sick	Sto male	sto **mah**-lay
Please call a doctor	Chiami un dottore	kee-**ah**-mee oon doe-**toe**-ray

Help!	Aiuto!	a-**yoo**-toe
Stop!	Alt!	ahlt
Fire!	Al fuoco!	ahl **fwo**-ko
Caution/Look out!	Attenzione!	a-ten-**syon**-ay

Dining Out

A bottle of . . .	Una bottiglia di . . .	**oo**-na bo-**tee**-lee-ah dee
A cup of . . .	Una tazza di . . .	**oo**-na **tah**-tsa dee
A glass of . . .	Un bicchiere di . . .	oon bee-key-**air**-ay dee
Bill/check	Il conto	eel **cone**-toe
Bread	Il pane	eel **pah**-nay
Breakfast	La prima colazione	la **pree**-ma ko-la-**tsee**-oh-nay
Cocktail/aperitif	L'aperitivo	la-pay-ree-**tee**-vo
Dinner	La cena	la **chen**-a
Fixed-price menu	Menù a prezzo fisso	may-**noo** a **pret**-so **fee**-so
Fork	La forchetta	la for-**ket**-a
I am diabetic	Ho il diabete	o eel dee-a-**bay**-tay
I am vegetarian	Sono vegetariano/a	**so**-no vay-jay-ta-ree-**ah**-no/a
I'd like . . .	Vorrei . . .	vo-**ray**
I'd like to order	Vorrei ordinare	vo-**ray** or-dee-**nah**-ray
Is service included?	Il servizio è incluso?	eel ser-**vee**-tzee-o ay een-**kloo**-zo
It's good/bad	È buono/cattivo	ay **bwo**-no/ka-tee-vo
It's hot/cold	È caldo/freddo	ay **kahl**-doe/**fred**-o
Knife	Il coltello	eel kol-**tel**-o
Lunch	Il pranzo	eel **prahnt**-so
Menu	Il menù	eel may-**noo**
Napkin	Il tovagliolo	eel toe-va-lee-**oh**-lo
Please give me . . .	Mi dia . . .	mee **dee**-a
Salt	Il sale	eel **sah**-lay
Spoon	Il cucchiaio	eel koo-kee-**ah**-yo
Sugar	Lo zucchero	lo **tsoo**-ker-o
Waiter/Waitress	Cameriere/ cameriera	ka-mare-**yer**-ay/ ka-mare-**yer**-a
Wine list	La lista dei vini	la **lee**-sta **day**-ee **vee**-nee

INDEX

Icons and Symbols

★ Our special recommendations
✕ Restaurant
Lodging establishment
✕ Lodging establishment whose restaurant warrants a special trip
Good for kids (rubber duck)
☞ Sends you to another section of the guide for more information
✉ Address
☎ Telephone number
⏲ Opening and closing times
Admission prices

Numbers in white and black circles ③❸ that appear on the maps, in the margins, and within the tours correspond to one another.

A

B

FODOR'S ITALY

EDITOR: Caragh Matthews Rockwood

Editorial Contributors: Stephanie Adler, Robert Andrews, Barbara Walsh Angelillo, Sheila Brownlee, Nancy Coons, Fionn Davenport, Jon Eldan, Robert I. C. Fisher, Robin S. Goldstein, Valerie Hamilton, Carla Lionello, Elise Meyer, Patricia Rucidlo, Helayne Schiff

Editorial Production: Stacey Kulig

Maps: David Lindroth, Inc., Mapping Specialists, cartographers; Steven K. Amsterdam and Bob Blake, map editors

Design: Fabrizio La Rocca, creative director; Guido Caroti, art director; Jolie Novak, picture editor; Melanie Marin, *photo researcher*

Cover Design: Pentagram

Production/Manufacturing: Robert B. Shields

COPYRIGHT

ISBN 0–679–00332–0

ISSN 0361–977X

SPECIAL SALES

Fodor's Travel Publications are available at special discounts for bulk purchases for sales promotions or premiums. Special editions, including personalized covers, excerpts of existing guides, and corporate imprints, can be created in large quantities for special needs. For more information, contact your local bookseller or write to Special Markets, Fodor's Travel Publications, 201 East 50th Street, New York, NY 10022. Inquiries from Canada should be directed to your local Canadian bookseller or sent to Random House of Canada, Ltd., Marketing Department, 2775 Matheson Boulevard East, Mississauga, Ontario L4W 4P7. Inquiries from the United Kingdom should be sent to Fodor's Travel Publications, 20 Vauxhall Bridge Road, London SW1V 2SA, England.

PRINTED IN THE UNITED STATES OF AMERICA

10 9 8 7 6 5 4 3 2 1

IMPORTANT TIP

Although all prices, opening times, and other details are based on information supplied to us at press time, changes occur all the time in the travel world, and Fodor's cannot accepts responsibility for facts that become outdated or for inadvertent errors or omissions. So **always confirm information when it matters,** especially if you're making a detour to visit a specific place.

PHOTOGRAPHY

Angelo Lomeo, cover (Santa Croce Church, Florence).

Art Resource: *Nimatallah*, 29 bottom.

Buca di Sant'Antonio, 30J.

G. Carfagna & Associati: *Giuseppe Carfagna*, 8B, 13A, 22B, 23A, 23B, 30C, 30E. *Marina Di Marco,* 19 bottom right.

Ente Nazionale Italiano per Il Turismo: *Fotocolor E.N.I.T.*, 2 bottom left, 2 bottom center, 3 top right, 3 bottom left, 3 bottom right, 6B, 18B, 19B.

Robert I.C. Fisher, 2 top, 4-5, 21 top left, 21C, 26, 30A.

Hotel Accademia, 30G.

The Image Bank: *Gio Barto,* 16 center left. *Antonio Bignami,* 17B. *Bullaty & Lomeo,* 1, 9D, 10A, 11D, 11 bottom left, 12B, 12C, 13C. *Stuart Dee,* 28 top. *Giuliano Cappelli,* 15A, 16C. *M.J. Cardenas,* 19A. *Kay Chernush,* 2 bottom right. *Giuliano Colliva,* 6A, 22A, 24C. *Paolo Curto,* 25 top. *Grant V. Faint,* 12A. *Froomer Pictures,* 25A. *David W. Hamilton,* 18A, 20B. *R. Johnson,* 10B, 14B, 15 top left, 15B, 32. *Paul Loven,* 8A. *Mahaux Photography,* 24B. *Aris Mihich,* 10C. *Giuseppe Molteni,* 22 bottom left. *Alberto Nardi,* 25B. *Carlos Navajas,* 7D. *Marvin E. Newman,* 30I. *Photo H.B.*, 16B. *Andrea Pistolesi,* 7 bottom left, 8C, 14A, 16A, 18C, 22C, 24A, 27. *F. Reginato,* 30D. *Antonio Rosario,* 30H. *Francesco Ruggeri,* 29 top. *Stefano Scatá,* 13B, 23C. *Bernard van Berg,* 6C. *R. Vignoli,* 20A. *Hans Wolf,* 3 top left, 17A.

Gualtiero Marchesi, 30F.

Osteria du Madon, 30B.

Antonio Sferlazzo, 7E, 11 top, 28 bottom.

ABOUT OUR WRITERS

Every Y2K trip is a significant trip. So if there was ever a time you needed excellent travel information, it's now. Acutely aware of that fact, we've pulled out all stops in preparing *Fodor's Italy.* To help you zero in on what to see in Italy, we've gathered some great color photos of the key sights in every region. To show you how to put it all together, we've created great itineraries and neighborhood walks. And to direct you to the places that are truly worth your time and money in this important year, we've rallied the team of endearingly picky know-it-alls we're pleased to call our writers. Having seen all corners of the regions they cover for us, they're real experts. If you knew them, you'd poll them for tips yourself.

After living and working in Italy for six years, **Rob Andrews**—who covers Italy's *mezzogiorno* (south) for Fodor's—decided he was getting too comfortable and retreated to the rougher pastures of England. But he's convinced his quarter-Italian blood is concentrated in his stomach, as he can't help extolling the Mediterranean diet, returning every year to get his fill. Robert is currently writing a guide to Sardinia.

Irish-born freelance writer and editor **Fionn Davenport** has spent most of his summers enjoying the delights of the Italian peninsula, a luxury of having an Italian mother. A former editor of *Fodor's Italy,* he now resides in Dublin and returns to explore the nooks and crannies of his beloved Milan, the Lake District, and the Dolomites whenever he can.

Jon Eldan studied European history in Berkeley, California, before packing his bags in 1994 to see the real thing. He now lives and bakes bread in Rome, and goes back to visit the old country from time to time. **Carla Lionello** grew up in Venice. Seven years ago she traded Piazza San Marco for the Spanish Steps and moved to Rome. Although she still hasn't learned to drive, it doesn't stop her from traveling all over Italy in search of endangered pastry. The duo reported on Rome and Venice for *Fodor's Italy 2000,* in addition to Umbria and the Marches and the Venetian Arc.

Fresh pesto, fishing villages, and Sampdoria soccer lured **Robin Goldstein** from his grandmotherly roots in Calabria and Apulia to the more seasonal shores of the Italian Riviera. Though his previous travel writing stints include Spain, Mexico, and Ecuador, Robin now resides in Genoa, where he teaches middle school science in between covering the Italian Riviera, Piedmont/Valle d'Aosta, and Emilia-Romagna beats for Fodor's.

Patricia Rucidlo lives in Florence with her dog, Tillie, who occasionally accompanies her on the Tuscan art history and food circuit. Though she has master's degrees in Italian Renaissance history and art history, Patti's true love is Italian food (as is Tillie's). Patti has also taught Italian cooking classes and ran her own catering business in the United States.

The editor would like to thank The International Kitchen for a sensational odyssey through Sicily, as well as Alitalia for its ever-superb service and generosity in making the trip happen.

Don't Forget to Write

We love feedback—positive and negative—and follow up on all suggestions. So contact the Italy editor at editors@fodors.com or c/o Fodor's, 201 East 50th Street, New York, NY 10022. Have a wonderful trip!

Karen Cure
Editorial Director